FORMS OF LITERATURE

A WRITER'S COLLECTION

FORMS OF LITERATURE

A WRITER'S COLLECTION

Jacqueline Costello   Amy Tucker

both of Queens College of the City University of New York

RANDOM HOUSE   •   NEW YORK

First Edition

987654321

Library of Congress Cataloging-in-Publication Data

Forms of literature.

  Includes indexes.
    1. Literature—Collections. 2. College readers.
I. Costello, Jacqueline. II. Tucker, Amy.
PN6014.F67   1988   808.8   87–28456
ISBN 0-394-34496-0

Manufactured in the United States of America

Cover Photo: Pierre Bonnard, *The Breakfast Room* (c. 1930–31). Oil on canvas, 62⅞ × 44⅞". Collection, The Museum of Modern Art, New York. Given anonymously. Photograph © 1988 The Museum of Modern Art, New York.

Book Design: Glen M. Edelstein

Text acknowledgments appear on pages 1027–1036.

To Ken and Steve

PREFACE

Forms of Literature, as the title suggests, explores the multiplicity of shapes and structures a literary work can take. Our selections were guided by the desire to balance the classic and the innovative—to include works commonly included in literary anthologies as well as to give utterance to voices that have not yet found their way into collections of this kind. Here you will encounter chapters on private writing—diaries, notebooks, journals—and on autobiographies and biographies, as well as chapters on short fiction, drama, film, poetry, and essays. We have tried to select works from a range of cultures and nationalities, and from a variety of fields: anthropology, biology, sociology, psychology, history. At the same time, we have included more selections by women writers, whose work has been underrepresented in "traditional" anthologies.

The subtitle of this book is *A Writer's Collection.* Our text is based on the belief that reading and writing are intertwined activities that comment on and enrich each other. And so we invite you to explore the reading process through the act of writing in response to a work of literature. In our introductions to each genre, in the discussion questions and writing exercises you will see in each chapter, you are encouraged to become active readers who participate in the construction of texts and their meaning. Accordingly, in each chapter, including our Appendix on Writing About Literature, we have reprinted writings by students that demonstrate the kind of critical and creative engagement with literature our assignments are designed to foster.

To guide you further in reading and writing about literature, we have worked to make our anthology intertextual: Many of the selections work well when read alongside selections from other chapters. To take one example of how intertextuality works, an essay reprinted in Chapter 7 entitled "Emotional Prodigality," written by the 19th-century physician Charles Fayette Taylor, sheds light on the narrator in Charlotte Perkins Gilman's short story "The Yellow Wallpaper" (in Chapter 4). In addition, reading excerpts from Alice James's diary reprinted in Chapter 2 will doubtless help you to understand the experience of the protagonist in Gilman's story. Throughout this anthology, you will find many such examples of literary works that comment on each other and enhance your reading of a given text.

ACKNOWLEDGMENTS

We would like to thank our students, who have influenced our choices in compiling this anthology, who have let us publish their writing, and who have helped us immeasurably with our own reading of literature. We are especially grateful to the people at Random House for seeing us through this project: Steve Pensinger and Lauren Shafer for their excellent suggestions and supervision, and Cynthia Ward for her judgment, perseverance, and good humor. Our thanks to our copy editor, Jeannine Ciliotta, as well as to our reviewers: Carl Brucker, Arkansas Tech University; Arlene Kuhner, Anchorage Community College; Rae Rosenthal, University of Maryland, College Park; Mike Vivion, University of Missouri.

Special thanks must go to our colleague and friend David Richter for making suggestions in each chapter of the manuscript, and for sharing so generously his ideas about poetry—without him the notes for Chapter 6 could not have been written. Other colleagues at Queens College have made contributions to this anthology: Nancy Comley, Robert Lyons, Edmund Epstein, Sue and Sid Shanker, and Moira Maynard—whose writing suggestions and students' responses are found at the conclusion of Chapter 6.

We want to thank our families for their encouragement, and most of all Ken and Steve, to whom we dedicate this book, for all the help and support they have given us over the years.

CONTENTS

Preface   vii

———— CHAPTER   1 ————

How Should One Read
a Book?   1

———— CHAPTER   2 ————

Notebooks, Journals,
Diaries   24

Sei Shonagon from *The Pillow Book*   30

Samuel Pepys from *The Diary of Samuel Pepys*   35

Charles Darwin from *Journal of Researches*   43

Alice James from *The Diary*   47

Sigmund Freud from *The Interpretation of Dreams*   52

Franz Kafka from *Diaries*   57

Martha Graham from *Notebooks*   62

Joan Didion *Los Angeles Notebook*   66

Reading/Writing   71

———— CHAPTER   3 ————

Auto/Biography   75

Charles Darwin from *The Autobiography of Charles Darwin*   80

Vincent Van Gogh from *The Complete Letters of Vincent Van Gogh*   86

Sherwood Anderson *Unforgotten*   95

M. F. K. Fisher *P Is for Peas*   103

Maxine Hong Kingston *No Name Woman*   107

Theresa A. Finegan *Interview with Patrick McMahon, an Irish Immigrant*
117
Natalie Zemon Davis *The Honor of Bertrande de Rols*   121

Reading/Writing   126

CHAPTER 4

Short Fiction   132

The *Walam Olum* of the Delaware Indians from *The Creation Song*   150
Five Teaching Tales

Aesop *The Wolf and the Mastiff*   154

Luke *The Prodigal Son*   154

Buddhist Parable *The Lost Son*   155

Ekai *Joshu Washes the Bowl*   157

Kate Chopin *Emancipation: A Fable*   158
Italo Calvino *Catherine the Wise*   167
Anton Chekhov *Heartache*   173
Charlotte Perkins Gilman *The Yellow Wallpaper*   179
James Joyce *Araby*   194
Franz Kafka *The Metamorphosis*   200
Ryunosuke Akutagawa *In a Grove*   236
Flannery O'Connor *A Good Man Is Hard to Find*   244
Bernard Malamud *The Magic Barrel*   258
Tillie Olsen *I Stand Here Ironing*   272
Donald Barthelme *The Glass Mountain*   279
Gabriel García Márquez *A Very Old Man with Enormous Wings*   284
James Alan McPherson *Why I Like Country Music*   290
Grace Paley *A Conversation With My Father*   303
Ursula Le Guin *The Ones Who Walk Away from Omelas*   308
Angela Carter *The Snow Child*   314
Jamaica Kincaid *The Circling Hand*   316

Reading/Writing   326

CHAPTER 5

Theater and Film   334

William Shakespeare *Othello*   353
Henrik Ibsen *A Doll House* (Translated by Rolf Fjelde)   454

Tina Howe *Painting Churches*   514

Akira Kurosawa *Rashomon* (Translated by Donald Richie)   564

Reading/Writing   609

CHAPTER 6

Poetry 612

James Joyce *Alone*   612

William Carlos Williams *Between Walls*   613

Francis Ponge *The Oyster*   618

Seamus Heaney *Oysters*   620

William Shakespeare *That time of year thou may'st in me behold*   623

Anne Bradstreet *Here Follows Some Verses Upon the Burning of Our House*   625

W. S. Merwin *The Last One*   628

e. e. cummings *somewhere i have never travelled*   631

Robert Frost *The Secret Sits*   633

William Carlos Williams *The Dance*   637

The Wedding Dance in the Open Air   637

Richard Wilbur *Digging for China*   640

Sappho *Seizure*   642

Li Ch'ing Chao *Autumn Evening Beside the Lake*   643

Alone in the Night   643

Sa'dī of Shīrāz *Precious are these heart-burning sighs*   644

Dear to me this lamentation   644

Anonymous *The Demon Lover*   645

Thomas Wyatt *They Flee from Me*   647

Edmund Spenser *One day I wrote her name upon the strand*   648

Sir Walter Raleigh *The Nymph's Reply to the Shepherd*   648

Christopher Marlowe *The Passionate Shepherd to His Love*   649

William Shakespeare *When to the sessions of sweet silent thought*   650

When I have seen by time's fell hand defaced   651

Since brass, nor stone, nor earth, nor boundless sea   651

When in disgrace with fortune and men's eyes   651

Not marble, nor the gilded monuments   652

Let me not to the marriage of true minds   652

Th'expense of spirit in a waste of shame   653

Contents

William Shakespeare *My mistress' eyes are nothing like the sun*   653

                    from *Twelfth Night*   654

Thomas Nashe *Adieu, Farewell, Earth's Bliss*   654

John Donne *Song*   656

         The Canonization   657

         Hymn to God My God, in My Sickness   658

         A Valediction: Forbidding Mourning   659

         The Flea   660

         Death, be not proud   661

         Batter my heart, three-personed God   662

Ben Jonson *On My First Daughter*   662

         On My First Son   663

         Still to be neat, still to be dressed   663

         Come, my Celia   664

Robert Herrick *Upon Julia's Clothes*   664

         Delight in Disorder   665

         His Prayer to Ben Jonson   665

George Herbert *Easter Wings*   666

         Jordan (I)   666

         The Collar   667

         The Pulley   668

John Milton *When I consider how my light is spent*   669

         Sonnet XXIII   669

Anne Bradstreet *Before the Birth of One of Her Children*   670

         A Letter to Her Husband, Absent Upon Public Employment   671

         In Memory of My Dear Grand-Child Elizabeth Bradstreet, Who Deceased August, 1665, Being a Year And a Half Old   671

         The Author to Her Book   672

Andrew Marvell *To His Coy Mistress*   673

         The Garden   674

John Dryden *To the Memory of Mr. Oldham*   676

Aphra Behn *The Willing Mistress*   677

Anne Finch *The Introduction*   678

Jonathan Swift *A Satirical Elegy on the Death of a Late Famous General*   680

Alexander Pope from Part II of *An Essay on Criticism*   681

Thomas Gray *Elegy Written in a Country Churchyard*   688

Christopher Smart from *Jubilate Agno*   692

Phillis Wheatley *On Being Brought from Africa to America*   694

To the Right Honorable William, Earl of Dartmouth, His Majesty's Principal Secretary of State for North America, Etc. 695

William Blake *The Clod & the Pebble*   696

The Lamb   697

The Tyger   697

Ah Sun-flower   698

The Sick Rose   698

London   699

Robert Burns *A Red, Red Rose*   699

To a Mouse   700

William Wordsworth *Sonnet: The world is too much with us*   701

The Solitary Reaper   702

Lines Composed a Few Miles above Tintern Abbey   703

Samuel Taylor Coleridge *Kubla Khan*   707

George Gordon, Lord Byron *She Walks in Beauty*   708

Percy Bysshe Shelley *Ozymandias*   709

Ode to the West Wind   710

John Keats *La Belle Dame sans Merci*   712

Ode to a Nightingale   714

Ode on a Grecian Urn   716

Elizabeth Barrett Browning *To George Sand*   718

Alfred, Lord Tennyson *Ulysses*   719

Robert Browning *My Last Duchess*   721

Emily Brontë *Alone I Sat; the Summer Day*   722

Riches I Hold in Light Esteem   722

Walt Whitman *Out of the Cradle Endlessly Rocking*   723

Crossing Brooklyn Ferry   729

Matthew Arnold *Dover Beach*   734

Emily Dickinson *A narrow Fellow in the Grass*   735

Tell all the Truth but tell it slant   736

I heard a Fly buzz—when I died   736

I never lost as much but twice   736

Success is counted sweetest   737

I taste a liquor never brewed   737

Contents

Emily Dickinson *A Bird came down the Walk*   738

There's a certain Slant of light   738

The Soul selects her own Society   739

Much Madness is divinest Sense   739

This is my letter to the World   740

I never saw a Moor   740

Because I could not stop for Death   740

Thomas Hardy *The Darkling Thrush*   741

Transformations   742

Gerard Manley Hopkins *God's Grandeur*   743

The Windhover   744

Spring And Fall   744

A. E. Housman *When I Was One-And-Twenty*   745

To an Athlete Dying Young   745

William Butler Yeats *The Scholars*   746

The Magi   747

Easter 1916   747

The Second Coming   749

The Wild Swans at Coole   750

Leda and the Swan   751

Sailing to Byzantium   751

The Song of Wandering Aengus   752

Among School Children   753

Amy Lowell *Patterns*   755

Robert Frost *Mending Wall*   758

Fire And Ice   759

After Apple-Picking   759

Desert Places   760

Acquainted with the Night   761

Rainer Maria Rilke *The Song the Beggar Sings*   762

Portrait of My Father as a Young Man   762

Spanish Dancer   763

Wallace Stevens *The Snow Man*   763

Thirteen Ways of Looking at a Blackbird   764

Anecdote of the Jar   766

Of Modern Poetry   767

William Carlos Williams *The Red Wheelbarrow*   767

Contents

William Carlos Williams *The Widow's Lament in Springtime*   768

        Spring and All   768

        A Sort of a Song   769

        To a Poor Old Woman   770

        The Young Housewife   770

        Raleigh Was Right   771

        Landscape with the Fall of Icarus   771

D. H. Lawrence *Snake*   772

Ezra Pound *In a Station of the Metro*   775

    Fan-Piece, for Her Imperial Lord   775

    The River-Merchant's Wife: A Letter   775

    The Jewel Stairs' Grievance   776

    Epitaphs   776

    The Garden   777

H. D. (Hilda Doolittle) *Heat*   777

Marianne Moore *Poetry*   778

T. S. Eliot *Journey of the Magi*   779

    The Love Song of J. Alfred Prufrock   780

John Crowe Ransom *Bells for John Whiteside's Daughter*   784

Anna Akhmatova *Requiem*   785

Claude McKay *The Tropics in New York*   792

Archibald MacLeish *Ars Poetica*   793

e. e. cummings *pity this busy monster*   794

    my father moved through dooms of love   794

Jean Toomer *Reapers*   796

    Face   797

Federico Garcia Lorca *Rider's Song*   797

    Sleepwalking Ballad   798

Jorge Luis Borges *The Blind Man*   800

Francis Ponge *The Cigarette*   801

    Les Mûres/blackberries   801

Arna Bontemps *A Black Man Talks of Reaping*   802

Countee Cullen *Incident*   803

Langston Hughes *The Negro Speaks of Rivers*   803

    Harlem   804

    Theme for English B   804

Pablo Neruda *The United Fruit Co.*   805

Contents

Pablo Neruda *Ode to My Socks* 807
W. H. Auden *Musée des Beaux Arts* 809
　　　　In Memory of W. B. Yeats 810
Buddhadeva Bose *Frogs* 812
Theodore Roethke *The Premonition* 813
　　　　Old Florist 813
　　　　I Knew a Woman 813
　　　　Dolor 814
　　　　The Waking 815
　　　　The Pike 815
　　　　My Papa's Waltz 816
Elizabeth Bishop *The Fish* 817
Robert Hayden *Those Winter Sundays* 819
　　　　Frederick Douglass 819
　　　　Runagate Runagate 820
Henry Reed *Naming of Parts* 822
John Berryman from *Homage to Mistress Bradstreet* 823
Dylan Thomas *A Refusal to Mourn the Death, by Fire, of a Child in London*
　　829
　　　　Fern Hill 829
　　　　The Force That Through the Green Fuse Drives the Flower 831
　　　　Do not go gentle into that good night 832
Robert Lowell *For the Union Dead* 832
Gwendolyn Brooks *the mother* 835
　　　　We Real Cool 836
Richard Wilbur *The Death of a Toad* 836
　　　　First Snow in Alsace 837
Denise Levertov *The Victors* 838
　　　　What Were They Like? 838
Maya Angelou *Africa* 839
Nissim Ezekiel *Night of the Scorpion* 840
Maxine W. Kumin *Making the Jam without You* 842
Allen Ginsberg *A Supermarket in California* 843
W. S. Merwin *When You Go Away* 844
　　　　Elegy 845
Philip Levine *Ricky* 845
Anne Sexton *Snow White and the Seven Dwarfs* 848

Adrienne Rich *A Valediction Forbidding Mourning*   852

        Planetarium   853

        Diving into the Wreck   854

Ted Hughes *Wodwo*   857

Sylvia Plath *Ariel*   858

        Daddy   859

        Tulips   861

Michael S. Harper *Reuben, Reuben*   863

Seamus Heaney *Digging*   863

        Death of a Naturalist   864

Margaret Atwood *This Is a Photograph of Me*   865

Modern American Indian Poems

    Love Poem, I   866

    Love Poem, II   867

    Love Poem, III   867

    Spring Poem, I   867

    Dream Poem, I   867

    Dream Poem, II   867

    War Poem, I   868

    War Poem, II   868

    War Poem, III   868

Joseph Concha *Snow, the Last*   868

        Grandfather and I   868

Tall Kia ahni *War God's Horse Song I*   869

Andrei Codrescu *Alberta*   870

Leslie Marmon Silko *Indian Song: Survival*   871

        Deer Song   875

        Reading/Writing   876

CHAPTER 7

Essays   883

Ken Haas *The Expatriates*   897

Michel de Montaigne *Of Liars*   898

Frederick Douglass *What to the Slave Is the Fourth of July?*   903

Charles Fayette Taylor *Emotional Prodigality*   920

Virginia Woolf *The Death of the Moth*   929

Bruno Bettelheim *"Snow White"*   933

George Orwell *Shooting an Elephant*   948

Flannery O'Connor *A Reasonable Use of the Unreasonable*   955

Alison Lurie *Male and Female*   960

Ted Hughes *Capturing Animals*   973

Nora Ephron *The Boston Photographs*   980

Stephen Jay Gould *The Panda's Thumb*   985

Sandra Blakeslee *Folklore Mirrors Life's Key Themes*   992

Alice Walker *In Search of Our Mothers' Gardens*   996

Reading/Writing   1004

APPENDIX

Writing About Literature   1011

Acknowledgments   1027

Author and Title Index   1037

Subject Index   1047

How Should One Read a Book?

Think back for a moment: Do you remember the first time you were able to look at a word on a page and translate that group of letters into a mental picture of something you knew? We recently asked a group of students to free-associate on paper about their earliest memories of learning to read. Here are a few of their responses:

Reading books dogs people Hamlet Scarlet Letter toys fables I read book little Daddy bedtime nice stories, playing furry books animals—wild lions. What do I like about books—horror stories, romances gothic novels *The Shining*. Shining TV soap operas, bedroom floor quiet peaceful, school late dark by the closet, TV in the living room, books on my desk, Daddy friends card games, school, boring, grades little fun, X-rated books why?

Hayley Greenberg

When I was very young I wanted to be like my parents and older brothers and sisters. Before I started school I began to open up books and pretend I was reading, though really I was just explaining the pictures. After my parents read a book to me several times, I became familiar with a few words. When I entered school, I learned the alphabet and each letter's appropriate sound. We were taught how to put the sounds together to form words; usually the teacher showed us a picture with the word to reinforce the idea of the word. But how did I internalize these words?

Rosann Costa

I don't remember when I first learned to read Spanish—it seems as if I was born reading. I do remember learning to read in English. I had this bumper sticker hanging up in my room which said, "POWs never have a nice day." When I was younger, I read the first word as "pow" (rhymes with "now"). Suddenly one day I understood what the letters stood for: Prisoners of War. After that, I would laugh, remembering how I had pronounced the word.

Zully Cano

We seem to begin reading with a sudden flash of recognition, when the printed sign becomes inseparable from a sound and an object or idea. Somehow, we progress from the tentative word-by-word decoding of the beginner to an understanding of how individual words combine to deliver a message, paint an impression, create a meaning. But most of us would be hard-pressed to describe exactly how this process came about, or even how we read as adults, much less how one *should* read. Perhaps we take the process for granted; perhaps it's simply too complex—or magical—for us to capture. Whatever the reason, reading is an elusive activity—solitary, personal, mysterious.

What all good readers seem to have in common, though, is that they have never *stopped* learning to read. Here, for example, author William Gass contrasts the way he read in his youth, *for speed*, with the way he reads now, *recursively*, going back over words and sentences he's just read to linger over sound and meaning:

Yes, in those early word-drunk years, I would down a book or two a day as though they were gins. I read for adventure, excitement, to sample the exotic and the strange, for climax and resolution, to participate in otherwise forbidden passions. I forgot what it was to be under my own power, under my own steam. I was, like so many adolescents, as eager to leap from my ordinary life as the salmon is to get upstream. I sought a replacement for the world. With a surreptitious lamp lit, I stayed awake to dream. I grew reckless. I read for speed.

When you read for speed you do not read recursively, looping along the line like a sewing machine, stitching something together—say the panel of a bodice to a sleeve—linking a pair of terms, the contents of a clause, closing a seam by following the internal directions of the sentence so that the word *you* is first fastened to the word *read,* and then the phrase *for speed* is attached to both in order that the entire expression can be finally fronted by a grandly capitalized *When* . . . while all of that, in turn, is gathered up to await the completion of the later segment that begins *you do not read recursively.* You can hear how long it seems to take—this patient process—and how confusing it can become. Nor do you linger over language, repeating some especially pleasant little passage, in the enjoyment, perhaps, of a modest rhyme (for example, the small clause, *when you read for speed*), or a particularly apt turn of phrase. . . .

Readers like William Gass have learned to go beyond reading as passive consumers and have become instead eager participants in a dialogue with the text. Good readers are apt to find themselves pausing for reflection, rereading phrases and paragraphs, arguing with the text, reading parts aloud. Reading *recursively* is this backward-forward movement of the mind whereby we revise earlier impressions of a text to accommodate new information and, at the same time, speculate about what is to come. It is this lively interaction with the text that another student focuses on in her free associations about reading:

> Take the book into your hands. Open your eyes and see the words. What you cannot see, you can read. Where you cannot go, you can read about. Take your wisdom and make it work. Take time to get the thoughts. Clear you mind & fill again. For people write to read again.
>   And children shall read instead of watch. And they shall think instead of being told.
>
> *Laura Burchell*

"People write to read again," Laura says. Many good readers would agree that *writing* is the activity that most enriches their reading. For writer Eudora Welty, the two acts are inseparable; here she writes about how one process influences the other:

> Since being read to and after, when I began reading to myself, there has never been a line read that I didn't *hear*. As my eyes followed the sentence, a voice was saying it silently to me. It isn't my mother's voice, or the voice of any person I can identify, certainly not my own. It is human, but inward, and it is inwardly that I listen to it. It is to me the voice of the story or the poem itself. The cadence, whatever it is that asks you to believe, the feeling that resides in the printed word, reaches me through the reader-voice.
>   I have supposed, but never found out, that this is the case with all readers—to read as listeners—and with all writers, to write as listeners. It may be part of the desire to write. The sound of what falls on the page begins the process of testing it for truth, for me. Whether I am right to trust so far I don't know. By now I don't know whether I could do either one, reading or writing, without the other.
>   My own words, when I am at work on a story, I hear too as they go, in the same voice that I hear when I read in books. When I write and the sound of it comes back to my ears, then I act to make my changes. I have always trusted this voice.

So, to borrow the title of an essay by Virginia Woolf (as we've done in naming this introduction), how should one read a book? Woolf's answer to the question is simply that no one can tell you how to read, they can only tell you how they themselves approach a work of literature. In reading, you must follow your own instincts. As the French writer Marguerite Duras cautions in her own essay on reading:

> One shouldn't interfere or meddle in the problems everyone has with reading, or pity children who don't read, or be impatient. What is at stake is a fabulous discovery—the discovery of the continent of reading. No one should urge or press anyone else to go and see what it is all about. There is enough information about culture, probably too much. You have to set out by yourself. Be born again by yourself. You have to be the first to discover the splendor of Baudelaire. And so you are. And if you don't feel that, you will never be a reader, it's too late.

The desire to read, the sense of adventure, must be yours alone; it can't be forced on you—else why should our student Hayley Greenberg, quoted earlier, have noted: "school, boring, grades   little fun"? That said, however, both Woolf and Duras agree that there are ways to *train* your instincts, to focus your perceptions, so that you can discover for yourself the pleasures of the poems, plays, stories, and essays you will encounter in this anthology and throughout your life. Vladimir Nabokov, a novelist who taught for a time at Cornell University, reminded the students in his "Masters of European Fiction," "My course, among other things, is a kind of detective investigation of the mystery of literary structures." Nabokov used to ask his students to select four items from the following list in answer to the question "What does it take to be a good reader?"

1. The reader should belong to a book club.
2. The reader should identify himself or herself with the hero or heroine.
3. The reader should concentrate on the socioeconomic angle.
4. The reader should prefer a story with action and dialogue to one with none.
5. The reader should have seen the book in a movie.
6. The reader should be a budding author.
7. The reader should have an imagination.
8. The reader should have memory.
9. The reader should have a dictionary.
10. The reader should have some artistic sense.

Some of these items, of course, are meant facetiously. As you have no doubt guessed, a good reader need not belong to the Book-of-the-Month club or have seen the film version of *Great Expectations*. Nor need one prefer action stories, or identify with a particular character. Instead, Nabokov urged that good readers bring with them the last four items on the list: imagination, memory, a dictionary, and some artistic sense—that is, some receptiveness to, and delight in, what is special about a work of literature.

The fact is that just about everyone possesses these four tools for reading, though one or two might get mislaid in the rush to complete assigned readings for school or in the heat of skimming to find out how a story ends. Indeed, a few of these items might at first appear to be excess baggage: Why, for instance, do readers need imagination, when the author has already imagined the story for them?

The answer is that no author can ever imagine the *whole* story for the reader. To do so—to tell, for example, every thought or memory you had and each impression you received in the course of a single day—would be impossible, even if it were worth the effort. Writers must be selective, and so it is up to *readers* to supply some of the details missing from a particular text. It is, in fact, the "unwritten" part of a text that invites our participation by prompting us to fill in the gaps and provide the missing connections. As we read, most of us unconsciously anticipate what lies ahead, just as we draw on our knowledge and experience to interpret characters and incidents. So reading is a creative process, and because we are contributing to the text it becomes a living event.

Consider the mental processes readers unconsciously perform when they read about actual events that occurred centuries ago. Take the example of a historical study excerpted in Chapter 3 of this anthology. In *The Return of Martin Guerre*, Natalie Zemon Davis retells the story of Martin Guerre, a French peasant who, in the 1540s, abandoned wife, child, and property. Years later, a man claiming to be Martin returned and resumed his old life in the village, but after three or four years of agreeable marriage the wife said she had been tricked by an impostor and brought him to trial. The man almost persuaded the court that he was Martin Guerre, but at the last moment the real Martin appeared, and the impostor was hanged.

Now these are the stripped-down elements of an oft-told tale handed down through the centuries. Even in this bare version, though, the story holds great dramatic possibilities, so much so that it was made into a film in 1983. But remember that the principal actors in this real-life tragedy were sixteenth-century peasants, few of whom could read or write down their family stories. It is therefore the author's job as an historian—and a storyteller—to animate the characters of the story and to track down the truth at a distance of three hundred years, given the scant documents at her disposal. Village records and testimonies from the trial of the "Martin Guerre" impostor tell us little about the motivations and emotions of the persons concerned, much less about their private thoughts and conversations. Yet these are precisely the elements we are curious to hear about. Let's isolate one brief moment in the story, that of the 'reunion' of the man who claimed to be Martin Guerre (later revealed as the impostor Pansette) and Bertrande, Martin's wife. Natalie Zemon Davis asks:

What of Bertrande de Rols? Did she know that the new Martin was not the man who had abandoned her eight years before? Perhaps not at the very first, when he arrived with all his "signs" and proofs. But the obstinate and honorable Bertrande does not seem a woman so easily fooled, not even by a charmer like Pansette.

We may pose the question, but history does not readily give up an answer. As readers, we must piece together what have we learned about the headstrong Bertrande, about the unhappy nine or ten years of her marriage before her husband disappeared without a trace, about the lonely position of an abandoned wife in a sixteenth-century French village, and so on—and picture for ourselves the moment of Bertrande's meeting with the man she was to accept as her husband for some years afterward. We know only that her four sisters-in-law brought Bertrande the news of their brother's return, and that after initial hesitation Bertrande embraced the man they called Martin. We might imagine Bertrande, on this day, arguing with a neighbor at the village mill, or perhaps sitting alone in her father's house, mending a shirt for her son, Sanxi. Her sisters-in-law, breathless from running, tell her of "Martin's" arrival at a nearby inn; Bertrande rises in confusion, one hand on the doorpost, the other twisting her apron. "Martin" strides purposefully up to the door, led to Bertrande by several shouting village children, and then stands very still, staring wonderingly. He tells her she is more beautiful than he remembered. To Bertrande, this man seems shorter and stockier than the husband who had left her years ago; but he speaks so familiarly to her, joking and whispering a secret the two of them had once shared, and he smiles so winningly, that at last she unclasps her apron, walks slowly toward him, and kisses his bearded cheek.

In our imaginations, then, though we still cannot be certain of what Bertrande actually knew or suspected, we can infuse the story with our own experience of human relationships, and impart some of our own life to these long-buried men and women. We instinctively participate in the text, working with the author, within the parameters of the facts and inferences she has provided. We *make use* of what she has given us.

And so it is with works of fiction. If we are to unravel the "mystery of literary structures," we must store away the clues each author provides from the outset of a work of literature, lest we miss their significance later on. Here is where the reader's memory is tested. In the drama section of this anthology, for example, we have included the screenplay of Akira Kurosawa's film *Rashomon. Rashomon* is recognized as one of the great achievements in cinematic history, in large measure because of the daring formal problem it poses: In the film, the story of a murder is repeated four times, told by four different characters whose testimonies conflict. To make sense of the screenplay, readers, like jurors in a courtroom case, must juggle the four overlapping testimonies, keeping in mind the character and motives of each witness. Needless to say, *Rashomon* is an extreme example of the way a reader's memory may be taxed; nevertheless, the willingness to search out revealing details is crucial to understanding any work of literature.

Still, how can we know, in our first encounter with a particular work of fiction, which elements are significant? Very often we cannot. Just as good writers revise their work, so good readers are *rereaders:* even if they do not reread the entire story or novel, they will almost certainly return, as William Gass points out, to earlier passages in the text before they proceed. The first reading introduces us to plot, character, setting, and so on. The second time around we read not to find out what happens, but to discover how the author makes it happen. These subsequent readings often lead us to a revision of previous impressions and interpretations, even as they raise new questions in our minds. One student, Vincent Suarez, writes about the difference between first and second readings:

> My favorite book is *2001: A Space Odyssey.* The first time I read it I couldn't put it down. It was the first book I read non-stop, and although I didn't understand a lot of it, I enjoyed reading it all the same. *2001* is also the only book I have read twice. The second time I read it I found myself able to put it down because I wanted to take my time and stop to think about it. It's not a very deep book, but it allowed my imagination to wander.

The first reading acquaints us with the general territory covered by a work of literature. And as Nabokov suggests, a good dictionary, like a good memory, is a compass by which to get our bearings. Let's investigate the meaning of a single word from Theodore Roethke's celebrated poem, "Elegy for Jane," a death lament for a student in a class he had taught. The word in question, *pickerel,* appears in the first stanza of the poem.

Elegy for Jane
My Student, Thrown by a Horse

I remember the neckcurls, limp and damp as tendrils;
And her quick look, a sidelong pickerel smile;
And how, once startled into talk, the light syllables leaped for her,
And she balanced in the delight of her thought,
A wren, happy, tail into the wind,
Her song trembling the twigs and small branches.
The shade sang with her;
The leaves, their whispers turned to kissing;
And the mold sang in the bleached valleys under the rose.

Oh, when she was sad, she cast herself down into such a pure depth,
Even a father could not find her:
Scraping her cheek against straw;
Stirring the clearest water.

My sparrow, you are not here,
Waiting like a fern, making a spiny shadow.
The sides of wet stones cannot console me,
Nor the moss, wound with the last light.

If only I could nudge you from this sleep,
My maimed darling, my skittery pigeon.
Over this damp grave I speak the words of my love:
I, with no rights in this matter,
Neither father nor lover.

So far in this introduction, we've briefly considered two literary forms, the journal and the historical biography; as this example shows, with poetry we are on very different ground. The sentences and paragraphs of the prose forms are replaced by the shorter lines and stanzas characteristic of poetry, and this compression of form makes the subtle shades of word definitions all the more crucial to the meaning of the poem.

Roethke, the son of a florist, wrote poems suffused with nature imagery, and nowhere is this aspect of his artistry more apparent than in this elegy for his student. In the four remaining stanzas of the poem, he describes the girl by turns as a wren, a sparrow, a "skittery pigeon"—delicate, homely comparisons (these are hardly exotic creatures) that evoke the girl's birdlike grace, vulnerability, and elusiveness. In this opening stanza, though, the poet compares her smile to that of a pickerel, which any pocket dictionary will tell you is a type of fish. This is rather a comical-sounding adjective, unexpected and incongruous; why does the author choose it?

If we are satisfied with that first simple and generalized definition of the word, the meaning of the stanza will be lost to us. A more comprehensive dictionary's definition of *pickerel* brings Jane into sharper focus: "1. any of a number of relatively small, American freshwater fishes. . . . 2. [British] a young pike." With this word, Roethke perhaps means to suggest Jane's relatively small stature and, more likely, her youth. The choice of a freshwater rather than an ocean fish implies the purity of the element the innocent young girl once inhabited, an image that becomes clearer in stanza 2—

Oh, when she was sad, she cast herself down into such a pure depth,
Even a father could not find her:
Scraping her cheek against straw;
Stirring the clearest water.

But the word is used as an adjective, remember. Why "pickerel smile"? The dictionary yields further meaning in its definition for *pike,* a word to which the earlier definition has directed us: "a slender, voracious, freshwater game fish *(Esox lucius)* with a narrow, pointed head and conspicuous, sharp teeth. . . ." The quicksilver glint of Jane's sidelong, sly, half-knowing smile now surfaces, startlingly, in the poet's recollection of his student, and swims subtly into our own consciousness. Young and slender, poised between reticence and voracity—hungrily eager to know, to speak her own thoughts— Jane lives for a moment in these lines. In the very word itself, *pickerel,* with its short and puckered syllables, we sense the tentative rapidity of the young woman's speech and movement.

Perhaps here, to Nabokov's list of reader's tools (imagination, memory, an openness and sensitivity to word meanings) we should write an addendum: Good readers often read with a pencil or pen. You make a book or story your own by annotation, jogging your memory and recording your reactions in the margin, defining words and underlining the sentences and paragraphs that seize you. Consider for a moment what you look like when you read, as we have asked these readers to do:

Usually, I read lying down on my bed. I prop two pillows behind me. The light in my room is too strong for my eyes, so when I read I usually turn on a small goose-neck lamp behind my bed. I have a brass headboard on the bed which is actually quite an annoyance. If I move at all the headboard bashes against the wall. The noise disturbs me immeasurably (I really should get rid of that old thing). Speaking of noise, I find it impossible to read in its presence. If a moth sneezes it distracts me.

Before I start reading I make sure there is quiet enveloping me. I wait till my roommates have finished chattering or watching TV and then I start reading. I purposely made my schedule so that I could stay up late at night and sleep late in the morning, just to allow myself that precious commodity called quiet. When I'm reading I usually concentrate very intently on the material. I try to absorb as much as I can (unless I'm reading my physics text).

Patrick Casey

The bedroom door is locked and the window shades are pulled down. A big comforter is over most of me, except for my head and my left arm. There are four pillows on the bed, behind my head, so that I can read without the light—which is directly above me—glaring off the pages. The other two pillows are the ones with little deer embroidered on them, and they're on either side of me. My right hand is always coming out from under the blanket to turn the pages. Sometimes I stop when I'm reading and stare at the venetian blinds. They are the screen for all my daydreams.

My mouth is always closed when I read and I periodically smile. I don't hear too many things when I read; my whole family could be trying to break down the door, and I won't hear a thing. Occasionally I've tried to listen to music while I read, but I always end up ignoring it, so I've stopped trying to be one of those people who listen to the radio at the same time.

Bibi Azweem

I start reading in an upright position, then I'm lying flat on my back, then I am on my stomach, which usually leads me to sitting once again. I always find myself counting to see how many pages I have left to read. After I have practically worn myself out, I become oh so tired. I try to stay awake by brightening the lights. That is something my mother tells me to do. She says, "When you get old and grey your eyes will remember these dull lights and get you for it." Then I usually turn on the radio, which I really must stop doing. I hear a song that I like and the book becomes history. I always give myself a good reason for putting down the book. Most of the time I say it's time to start dinner.

Cheryl Chesterfield

You have doubtless discovered how differences in the physical act of reading—in bed late at night, in front of the TV, at a table under the fluorescent lights in the school library—affect your experience of a book. If you find yourself distracted by noise or lulled into passive semi-consciousness by the to and fro movement of your eyes on the page, you may discover that reading with a pen or pencil stimulates you to respond, to read actively. Good readers, like good listeners, *attend,* conceiving ideas about what they read; asking questions; reacting to the story, poem, play, or essay, as well as to the way the author is telling it. From these scattered impressions we form inferences and generalizations, in literature as in life.

This is where the final requirement listed by Nabokov, *artistic sense,* comes in. Reading and writing are reciprocal acts, each commenting on and enriching the other, so that one of the most useful practices for good readers—and one of the suggestions we will make throughout this book—is to keep a notebook or journal. In this "reader's notebook," you are encouraged to record your impressions and comments about what you read. In the writing suggestions listed in the chapters of this anthology, for example, you may be asked to compare two stories, or to write a character sketch, or to supply your own version of what happens during a gap in the narrative, or to supply an alternative ending for a story. You are invited to get *into* the text, quite literally, so that you can see more clearly what the author is trying to do. Virginia Woolf put it this way:

> Do not dictate to your author; try to become him. Be his fellow-worker and accomplice. . . . Perhaps the quickest way to understand the elements of what a novelist is doing is not to read, but to write; to make your own experiment with the dangers and difficulties of words.

At Woolf's suggestion, we've devised the following experiment in reading and writing with a brief story by Ernest Hemingway called "Cat in the Rain." Below is the first paragraph of the story. Begin by reading this paragraph; then take five minutes or so to list whatever observations, comments, and questions you have concerning the paragraph.

There were only two Americans stopping at the hotel. They did not know any of the people they passed on the stairs on their way to and from their room. Their room was on the second floor facing the sea. It also faced the public garden and the war monument. There were big palms and green benches in the public garden. In the good weather there was always an artist with his easel. Artists liked the way the palms grew and the bright colors of the hotels facing the gardens and the sea. Italians came from a long way off to look up at the war monument. It was made of bronze and glistened in the rain. It was raining. The rain dripped from the palm trees. Water stood in pools on the gravel paths. The sea broke in a long line in the rain and slipped back down the beach to come up and break again in a long line in the rain. The motor cars were gone from the square by the war monument. Across the square in the doorway of the café a waiter stood looking out at the empty square.

Compare your own initial impressions with these two very different responses to the same paragraph, written by students we heard from earlier in this chapter:

It's raining.

War monument—What war?

Two Americans—Who are they? Where are they? What are they doing there?

The day is described negatively—"only 2 Americans," "motor cars were gone from the square," "the empty square." The only positive images—the bright colors of the palms that the artists liked so much—are remnants of days when the weather is fine.

Vincent Suarez

I get a feeling of gloom and boredom. I sense a sort of musty smell that may linger in a small town.

The sentences seem to be cut. There's a lot of repetition. I felt like I was reading sentences and not a story. I'm used to stories that have sentences that flow from one to the other. In this story, I feel cut off. I keep telling myself that there is no law that says how a story should be written.

I am confused. Where is this leading? I want to hear the rest of the story—maybe by then I'll understand what it all means.

Zully Cano

The first reader focuses on the questions Hemingway raises in this paragraph; the second listens to the sound of the story's flat, abbreviated sentences. Both readers seem to acknowledge that these omissions and stylistic habits are not oversights, any more than the repeated mention of the rain is the result of careless editing on the author's part. And chances are, having attended very closely to this paragraph, these readers will be more receptive to the sound and sense of the story as a whole.

Now with your initial observations in mind, complete the story, continuing as you read to jot down in your notebook or in the margin any observations or questions that come to mind:

> The American wife stood at the window looking out. Outside right under their window a cat was crouched under one of the dripping green tables. The cat was trying to make herself so compact that she would not be dripped on.
>
> "I'm going down and get that kitty," the American wife said.
>
> "I'll do it," her husband offered from the bed.
>
> "No, I'll get it. The poor kitty out trying to keep dry under a table."
>
> The husband went on reading, lying propped up with the two pillows at the foot of the bed.
>
> "Don't get wet," he said.
>
> The wife went downstairs and the hotel owner stood up and bowed to her as she passed the office. His desk was at the far end of the office. He was an old man and very tall.
>
> "Il piove," the wife said. She liked the hotel-keeper.
>
> "Si, si, Signora, brutto tempo. It's very bad weather."
>
> He stood behind his desk in the far end of the dim room. The wife liked him. She liked the deadly serious way he received any complaints. She liked his dignity. She liked the way he wanted to serve her. She liked the way he felt about being a hotel-keeper. She liked his old, heavy face and big hands.
>
> Liking him she opened the door and looked out. It was raining harder. A man in a rubber cape was crossing the empty square to the café. The cat would be around to the right. Perhaps she could go along under the eaves. As she stood in the doorway an umbrella opened behind her. It was the maid who looked after their room.
>
> "You must not get wet," she smiled, speaking Italian. Of course, the hotel-keeper had sent her.
>
> With the maid holding the umbrella over her, she walked along the gravel path until she was under their window. The table was there, washed bright green in the rain, but the cat was gone. She was suddenly disappointed. The maid looked up at her.
>
> "Ha perduto qualque cosa, Signora?"
>
> "There was a cat," said the American girl.
>
> "A cat?"
>
> "Si, il gatto."

"A cat?" the maid laughed. "A cat in the rain?"

"Yes," she said, "under the table." Then, "Oh, I wanted it so much. I wanted a kitty."

When she talked English the maid's face tightened.

"Come, Signora," she said. "We must get back inside. You will be wet."

"I suppose so," said the American girl.

They went back along the gravel path and passed in the door. The maid stayed outside to close the umbrella. As the American girl passed the office, the padrone bowed from his desk. Something felt very small and tight inside the girl. The padrone made her feel very small and at the same time really important. She had a momentary feeling of being of supreme importance. She went on up the stairs. She opened the door of the room. George was on the bed, reading.

"Did you get the cat?" he asked, putting the book down.

"It was gone."

"Wonder where it went to," he said, resting his eyes from reading.

She sat down on the bed.

"I wanted it so much," she said. "I don't know why I wanted it so much. I wanted that poor kitty. It isn't any fun to be a poor kitty out in the rain."

George was reading again.

She went over and sat in front of the mirror of the dressing table looking at herself with the hand glass. She studied her profile, first one side and then the other. Then she studied the back of her head and her neck.

"Don't you think it would be a good idea if I let my hair grow out?" she asked, looking at her profile again.

George looked up and saw the back of her neck, clipped close like a boy's.

"I like it the way it is."

"I get so tired of it," she said. "I get so tired of looking like a boy."

George shifted his position in the bed. He hadn't looked away from her since she started to speak.

"You look pretty darn nice," he said.

She laid the mirror down on the dresser and went over to the window and looked out. It was getting dark.

"I want to pull my hair back tight and smooth and make a big knot at the back that I can feel," she said. "I want to have a kitty to sit on my lap and purr when I stroke her."

"Yeah?" George said from the bed.

"And I want to eat at a table with my own silver and I want candles. And I want it to be spring and I want to brush my hair out in front of a mirror and I want a kitty and I want some new clothes."

"Oh, shut up and get something to read," George said. He was reading again.

His wife was looking out of the window. It was quite dark now and still raining in the palm trees.

"Anyway, I want a cat," she said, "I want a cat. I want a cat now. If I can't have long hair or any fun, I can have a cat."

George was not listening. He was reading his book. His wife looked out of the window where the light had come on in the square.

Someone knocked at the door.

"Avanti," George said. He looked up from his book.

In the doorway stood the maid. She held a big tortoise-shell cat pressed tight against her and swung down against her body.

"Excuse me," she said, "the padrone asked me to bring this for the Signora."

The questions and comments you have noted in the course of reading this story bring us back to the question of *how* we read. Pause for a moment and try to reconstruct the movements of your mind while you were reading this story. Here is part of Vincent Suarez's reconstruction of the process:

I began reading "Cat in the Rain" by trying to recall what the story was about, because I read it last semester in English 110. I got to the middle of the second page and realized that I hadn't been paying attention to what I was reading, so I started over. As I read the first paragraph I paid close attention to the details—because the teacher had asked us to. In my mind I could see the empty square with the bronze war monument "glistening in the rain" and a small café off to the side with a waiter lounging in the doorway. The scene seemed so quiet and peaceful that I wanted to stay in the first paragraph rather than continue on to the story of the unhappy American couple. Again, my mind must have roamed because the next picture that was forming in my mind was that of the wife and the maid standing under an umbrella and talking about the cat. As I read the discussion between the couple, I thought about my parents and what they might have been like when they were first married. Did my mother ever rattle on about what she wanted but didn't have? Did my father ever read a book while my mother was trying to talk to him?

. . . . Toward the end of the story, I began to wonder which, if any, of the characters were showing their true selves. Is this the way the couple's marriage really is or is the reader catching them on a bad day? . . . I wish I knew more about these people and their motivations.

In thinking back over the way you approached this story, you will probably discover how extensively, unavoidably, you have participated in the text. As a final experiment in active reading, we ask you to enter the text, as a co-writer of "Cat in the Rain." Indeed, Hemingway's story implicitly encourages you to do so. At the end of the story, the maid stands holding the cat in the doorway of the couple's room. That is the extent of what we are told:

Hemingway purposely leaves the story open-ended. This open-endedness gives rise to the third part of our experiment in reading and writing: Before you discuss the story further, write down in your notebook, as if you were the author continuing the story, what you think happens during the next few minutes or so after the maid has spoken.

When you have finished, you might want to compare your own coda to the story with those of your classmates, or with these two readers' responses:

> The girl took the cat and dried its fur and warmed its body with her warm hands. She set out a saucer of milk and scrutinized the way the kitty lapped the milk with its tongue. When she saw the cat was satisfied, she carried it with her to the window facing the sea. She sat herself on the rocking chair and looked out, all the while caressing the soft fur of the kitty with an expression as sullen as the rain.
>
> *Cecelia Awong*

> The wife looked at the cat. It wasn't the one she had seen, but it would have to do.
>
> "Thank you," she said, "and please thank the padrone for me."
>
> The maid handed her the cat. It struggled to free itself but the woman held it tightly. She sat down in the chair, snuggling the cat in her lap. The cat didn't want to snuggle. It jumped from her lap and ran under the bed.
>
> "Help me get that cat, George."
>
> George went on reading. Defeated, she got out of her chair and went over to the bed. She reached under the bed. The cat hissed and the wife started back with a cry. "It bit me."
>
> "You wanted to have a cat," her husband said.
>
> "I don't want that cat. I want a kitty that I can sit with and stroke. I want that cat that was out in the rain. I'm going to tell the padrone that he sent me a defective cat."
>
> "You do that," he said.
>
> She opened the door. The cat darted from under the bed and through the open door.
>
> She went over to the window and looked out. It was still raining, and had grown very dark.
>
> "I wonder what happened to my kitty. My kitty is a good kitty. Not like that nasty creature the maid brought up. That little cat in the rain would love me. Don't you think so?"
>
> "Sure," said George, immersed in his book.
>
> "I'm going out to look for my kitty," she said.
>
> "It's too dark. And it's almost time for dinner."
>
> "I'm not hungry. I'm going to talk to the padrone."
>
> Out in the hallway, crouched in the corner and purring softly, was the tortoise-shell cat. She looked at it. It looked back at her, not moving. She bent down and put out her hand.

"Here kitty, kitty. Here, kitty," she said. The cat didn't move. She inched closer to it, until she was about a foot away. The cat sat there purring.

"You are a good little kitty, aren't you," she said.

She reached out to pick up the cat. It jumped up and ran down the hall, out of sight.

Daniel Dubinsky

This is how, as a reader, you exercise your own imagination, both as a participant in the text and as an author of your own written responses. Notice how the student writers above have elaborated on the idea of the wife's dissatisfaction, and taken up the flat, unemotional tone of Hemingway's sentences as well as his extensive use of dialogue. Writing *as though* you were the author of a story you've been reading, in addition to writing *about* a work of literature, allows you to understand more profoundly what an author is striving for, as well as to appreciate the significance—and the 'rightness'—of the choices the author has made.

As you discuss your reactions to "Cat in the Rain" and some of the other selections in this anthology, you'll observe that no two readers notice all of the same things, raise identical questions, or echo exactly each other's interpretation. The variety of responses to a given work is precisely what makes literature, and the literature classroom, so special. Each reader brings to a given text his or her own repertoire of experiences with literature, life, and culture. The more we read, the better we are able to compare texts and make critical judgments. To read is always to read in relation to other texts, as well as to encounter the traditions and values of the culture that produced the text. Naturally, this encounter will differ for each individual, and the personal and cultural background of the reader will greatly influence his or her particular experience of the text.

As you have seen, *writing* is a way to deepen your reading or rereading of a text. Our experiment in reading "Cat in the Rain" points the way to an approach to reading all the texts in this anthology. Think of your notebook as a storehouse for any responses, associations, pleasures, and difficulties you have when reading a particular selection. Reading your reactions in class and hearing those of others will help you to confront your own preconceptions, consider different possibilities, and see how much you have, in fact, understood—even when, perhaps, you feel you have understood very little.

In addition, as in your reading of "Cat in the Rain," you may want to record questions in your notebook about a reading selection, for this kind of inquiry can open up a text for you and your classmates. A second reading of the work, provoking new questions or answers and revised interpretations, should help you to recognize how each reading is a new experience, a different reading, however subtle that difference may be.

The goal of these activities is not some privileged knowledge of the 'only true meaning' of a particular work, for that would reduce both the work and the reading to a single standard and purpose. Rather, we hope you will become active readers engaged in a recursive process: readers who are discovering the relationships between reading and writing, and who are beginning to see literary structures as elegant examples of common patterns of organizing experience. As one critic has pointed out, a work of literature should not be regarded as an object whose properties the reader tries to define with certainty, but rather as an *experience* of the reader, so that false starts, hesitations, errors, and changes of mind are not the predictable failings of ill-equipped 'beginners,' but part of the experience, and thus part of the meaning, of the literary work.

This is not to say, of course, that all literary interpretations are valid. Some interpretations simply do not make sense in terms of the information imparted by the story or poem. The *text* must be the basis for the reader's inferences. And here too, keeping a notebook will help you to collect your thoughts about a work of literature, and to find patterns of structure and meaning that you might not have noticed had you not written in response to the text.

Finally, many of the additional writing assignments we include at the end of each chapter in this book are designed to help you *use* what you have read by incorporating some of the ideas and structures suggested by other authors in your own writing. In this way, your "reader's journal" can serve as a sourcebook for the stories and essays you would like to write. A sentence read, a scene imagined by another author: these elements may fuel your own powers of creation. Here, for example, are two writing assignments—one an informal exercise, the other a fleshed-out essay—that were suggested by "Cat in the Rain," though in fact the students' responses bear very little relationship in tone or content to Hemingway's story. The first assignment, sparked by the nature of the dialogue in the story, asked students to record in their notebooks a conversation in which two people are talking but not listening to each other. This is Jeffrey Woo's humorous approach to the exercise:

"Excuse me, Professor, can you tell me what would happen if I added 7ml of glucose oxidase rather than 6ml?"

"You know, I remember once, back in Michigan, a grad student asked a similar question. He was working on the effects of enzyme inhibitors. . . ."

"Yes. But what I'd like to know is. . . ."

"He was a bright boy. I think he went on to California or someplace like that. He used mostly electrospectroscopy but he also used calorimetry. He really didn't find any difference between the two methods."

"That's very interesting. I'm thinking of applying to grad school myself. Can you give me any recommendations?"

"Oh yes, um, well, if you added a little more enzyme into the assay, the rate would be slightly affected. But the overall rate should be determined by the substrate you have in there. You know that the enzyme is rarely used up if it is used in very small quantities."

"Thank you."

"On the other hand, if you were to . . . "

"Thanks, Professor. I'll keep that in mind."

In the second assignment suggested by the theme of Hemingway's story, students were asked to write a brief autobiographical essay in answer to this question: "Did you ever think you wanted something, but when you got it, you realized it wasn't what you really wanted?" Here is Elena Perugachi's response:

Everyone has illusions, dreams, and expectations that someday these dreams will come true. I too am one of the crowd: I too wanted something with all my heart. When I got what I wanted, however, I realized that I still needed something else.

A couple of years ago, when I was still living in Ecuador, I used to think, "My God, how beautiful is the United States; I wish I could live there." I thought everything about the U.S. was new, clean, and fashionable. Perhaps I received this image from the American T.V. shows I used to watch, or perhaps from the wonderful things visitors used to say about this country. Oh, I had visited Peru and Colombia, both beautiful countries, but never wanted to live there. The United States was my first and only choice.

Such was my obsession to emigrate to this country that I realized I no longer wanted to live at home. I spoke to my father and luckily he understood. Both of us decided that New York was the best place for me. I applied to the college I wanted to attend and was accepted.

At last I left my family and came to New York. I had got what I wanted. I was the happiest person in the world. After a while, though, a terrible emptiness evolved in my heart. I realized how important my family and friends were to me. Here I had no friends.

After three or four weeks, I called my father, and when he answered the phone I started to cry bitterly. I asked him if I could come back home. He said, "I did everything that I could to send you to the United States, and now you tell me that you want to come home. I don't understand you. Let me ask you: who was it that wanted so desperately to leave? Who decided to live in a foreign country?" I admitted I had. He told me, "It was your own decision and now you have to struggle to become independent." I understood his words clearly.

A few months later, I had become accustomed to living here. I had made some friends and a small ray of light shone in my heart.

Now I realize how unstable we people are. Sometimes we get what we want, but we still look for more. We are never totally satisfied: we always need something or someone special. We are insatiable.

A story like "Cat in the Rain," then, can trigger a personal recollection, encouraging you to rediscover—indeed, revise—some aspect of your own past. And, in turn, the process of recalling and writing about your own personal associations may help you to discover new meaning in the story you have read.

We have discussed several kinds of writing exercises inspired by the reading selections in this anthology: notebook observations, imaginative 'continuations' or imitations of the text, and personal essays on themes suggested by those texts. Another type of writing exercise, one that often grows out of the assignments just mentioned, is the interpretive, or analytic, essay. This kind of essay considers *how* and *why* a story works. For example, the writers of the preliminary notebook entries on page 11 are already—unavoidably—remarking on some of the features of Hemingway's style and technique in "Cat in the Rain." They comment, as well, on the effect the story has had on them as readers. How does the author of the story achieve these effects? In the following essay, a student analyzes how different elements of "Cat in the Rain" contribute to our central impression of an unhappy woman trapped in a troubled marriage.

Woman in the Rain

"Cat in the Rain" by Ernest Hemingway presents a few brief but revealing glimpses into the lives of an American couple confined to their hotel room in Italy on a rainy day. In this story, a combination of gloomy weather, ordinary conversation, and seemingly insignificant events creates a strong impression of a troubled marriage.

From the beginning of this story, there is an atmosphere of boredom, isolation, and emptiness. The couple are the "only two Americans" at the hotel and they do not know any of the other people staying there. Their room faces the sea, a public garden with benches and big palms, and a war monument. "In the good weather there was always an artist with his easel. Artists liked the way the palms grew and the bright colors of the hotels facing the gardens and the sea." Now, however, the bad weather has left the square deserted and gray. The motor cars are gone, and in the doorway of the café a waiter stands looking out at the empty square.

The desolate mood created by this scene is reinforced by short simple sentences that sound much alike and by frequent repetitions of certain words and phrases. In the following passage, for example, repeated references to the rain add to the feeling of monotony and gloom:

It [the war monument] glistened in the rain. It was raining. The rain dripped from the palm trees. Water stood in pools on the gravel paths. The sea broke in a long line in the rain and slipped back down the beach to come up and break again in a long line in the rain.

Inside their hotel room, the conversation between the American couple sounds as empty as the deserted square. From her window, the wife notices a cat seeking shelter from the rain. Her husband, George, is too engrossed in his book to pay attention to his wife. His replies to her comments are empty words and phrases that indicate his indifference:

"I'm going down and get that kitty," the American wife said.
"I'll do it," her husband offered from the bed.
"No, I'll get it. The poor kitty out trying to keep dry under a table."
The husband went on reading, lying propped up with the two pillows at the foot of the bed.
"Don't get wet," he said.

Throughout the story, George is reading, and we are told that "George was not listening." The only time he reacts to his wife is to say, "Oh, shut up and get something to read." Like the empty square in the rain, this couple is isolated, not only in their hotel but also from each other.

It is not surprising that the American wife is lonely and frustrated. In contrast to her husband, the hotel-keeper makes her feel "very small and at the same time really important" because he pays attention to her and sends the maid to coax her out of the rain as she is looking for the cat. At the end of the story, it is the hotel-keeper, not George, who provides her with a cat. Her wish to have the cat also suggests her longing for affection and attention. She says, "I want to have a kitty to sit on my lap and purr when I stroke her," and then clumsily vents her frustration with a litany of other "wants": "And I want to eat at a table with my own silver and I want candles. And I want it to be spring and I want to brush my hair out in front of a mirror and I want a kitty and I want some new clothes."

This list of demands indicates that the wife doesn't really know what she wants or needs, but each of these items may signify something missing from her life and her marriage. "My own silver" may mean the security of a settled and comfortable life, and candles often imply romance. Spring is a traditional symbol of birth and renewal, perhaps reflecting her unconscious desire for a child, and the cat may be a child substitute. She also wants to brush her hair out and have some new clothes—to feel feminine, attractive, and renewed.

The American wife may not recognize her real needs because she is immature. For example, her appreciation of the padrone's fatherly gestures suggests that she is more like a child than a woman, and she is sometimes called "the American girl." She says that she is "tired of looking like a boy," and her manner of speaking and her outbursts are childish: "I want that poor kitty," and "I want a cat. I want a cat now. If I can't have long hair or any fun, I can have a cat."

Related to the wife's immaturity is her lack of identity in the story, which adds to our sense of her discontent. She is not even given a name, but referred to only as "the American wife" or "the American girl." She even identifies with the cat, saying "It isn't any fun being a poor kitty out in the rain." Like the cat trapped under the table by the rain, she is trapped by her own unnamed needs and by a marriage that offers no fulfillment. She looks in the mirror and studies her profile, "first one side and then the other," as if her reflection can tell her who she is.

The American wife may be immature and confused, but she does show signs of energy and emotion. On the other hand, George barely moves from the bed. At the end of the story, he is still reading as the maid arrives with a cat sent by the padrone. Based on these scenes from a marriage, the future of this relationship seems no brighter than this gloomy day in Italy.

Virgilio Romano

As all these different writing exercises demonstrate, our ways of reading and writing change, evolve, enrich one another, thus reflecting different stages in our development. Time and again in this anthology you will see professional writers, and the student writers whose work we have included at the end of each chapter, creating through this same recursive process. So although this book is organized into sections according to different literary structures—journals, autobiographies, short stories, dramas, poems, and essays—you will find that for many writers, one kind of writing activity spills into the next. Most authors, for example, keep journals in which strands of autobiography mingle with ideas that grow into poems or stories; later on, these writers may even compose essays about what they have discovered in the process of writing, or in the process of reading the work of other authors. Through experimentation, writers discover what they can and cannot do within the constraints of a particular literary form, and so they are prompted to turn to another form. For example, Natalie Zemon Davis explains why writing a screenplay led her to a book-length historical study:

Paradoxically, the more I savored the creation of the film, the more my appetite was whetted for something beyond it. I was prompted to dig deeper into the case, to make historical sense of it. Writing for actors rather than readers raised new questions about the motivations of people in the sixteenth century—about, say, whether they cared as much about truth as about property. Watching [the actor] Gérard Depardieu feel his way into the role of the false Martin Guerre gave me new ways to think about the accomplishment of the real impostor, Arnaud du Tilh [alias Pansette]. I felt I had my own historical laboratory, generating not proofs, but historical possibilities.

Similarly, filmmaker Akira Kurosawa took up the literary form of the autobiography to say what he could not express through the medium of film.

Kurosawa explains in *Something Like an Autobiography* that for many years he resisted writing his life story because he was convinced that it would turn out to be "nothing but talk about the movies." Yet he was finally persuaded to write his book, in part because he wanted to piece together the pattern of persons and events that shaped him as an artist. The painter Vincent Van Gogh wrote hundreds of letters to his brother Theo, confiding to him all the hopes and frustrations that had gone into each canvas he painted. Ted Hughes turned from capturing live animals when he was a boy to 'capturing' them on paper in the poetry he wrote years later; eventually he wrote an essay entitled "Capturing Animals" to shed light on these origins of his poetry.

The creative processes of reading and writing, as you have observed, are cyclical. An emphatic illustration of this recursive growth and melding of literary forms can be found in the creations of Francis Ponge, a French writer whose work is included in the poetry section of this anthology but might just as easily have been placed in any other chapter of this book. Ponge steadfastly resists categorizing, preferring to call his work "proems," combinations of prose and poetry. In fact, in a little book entitled *Soap,* Ponge managed to cover every conceivable literary option during the twenty-three years he spent intermittently working on the project.

Having written the introduction to the book called *Soap* in the form of a dramatic monologue, Ponge proceeds to show us an early poem entitled "Soap," then moves on to paragraphs interspersed with autobiographical notes about his circumstances at the time of writing, then to letters from readers of the original poem and essays Ponge wrote in reply, and finally to notes and a short prose piece called "The Theme of Soap," which comments on much of what has gone before. In all these forms Ponge explores the character of a commonplace and seemingly simple object: its feel, smell, function, significance. The multiform shape of the book suggests the foaming inexhaustibility of soap—and, for that matter, of any other subject.

Another of Ponge's collections has been translated into English as "The Voice of Things," and this title might apply equally to all of Ponge's work. The voice of things, Ponge makes clear, is *meant* to be heard by the reader-listener. Indeed, the literary work is called into existence not only by the writer, but by the reader. In turn, the work of art calls into existence both the speaker and the audience. Ponge puts it this way:

Puisque tu me lis, cher lecteur,	As you read me, dear reader,
donc je suis; puisque tu nous lis	then I am; as you read us
(mon livre et moi), cher lecteur,	(my book and I), dear reader,
donc nous sommes (Toi, lui et	then we are (You, it and I).
moi).	

As another twentieth-century poet, W. H. Auden, once observed, "A poem does not come to life until a reader makes his response to the words written by the poet." The same might be said of all forms of literature: They depend for their life on the dialogue between writer and reader. "Do not dictate to your author," Virginia Woolf advises. "Be his fellow-worker and accomplice." And so her question, "How Should One Read a Book?" really implies another: "How Should One Write a Book (or a poem or a play or an essay)?" These are the questions the reader of this anthology is invited to explore.

CHAPTER
2

Notebooks, Journals, Diaries

On October 20, 1913, Franz Kafka writes in his diary, "I am now reading *The Metamorphosis* at home and find it bad." The next day he complains, "I keep thinking of the black beetle, but will not write." This is how Kafka wrestles with a story which was to become one of the most celebrated of all time, a work he was not to publish until two years later: by confiding in the diary that covered the last thirteen years of his life and eventually filled more than thirteen notebooks. Where else should a bachelor, living in his parents' home, working in a government insurance office, pour out the minutest details of an inner life that began after dark and ended in the early hours of the morning? In fact, so many stories, poems, and essays begin this way, as informal notes jotted down in a journal or diary, that it seems logical for a reading anthology to begin here, with the workbooks in which writers speak to an audience of *one*.

Peering into a writer's notebook, we find a patchwork of failures and successes: false starts, discarded scraps, and some of the unfinished material that may eventually be stitched into the cloth of a story, essay, or poem. As you will see later on in this chapter, Kafka's diary overflows not only with incidents, scenery, and acquaintances, but with reflections on his own writing and the writing of others whose work he disliked or admired. It is this last use for your journal that we have already discussed briefly in the introduction to this book: In the chapters that follow, you will be encouraged to use your notebook as a forum for your responses to what you read.

For instance, students in a literature class were recently asked to record their thoughts about a selection included in this chapter. The selection is from *The Pillow Book* by Sei Shonagon, who kept a journal of court life in tenth-century Japan, where she served as lady-in-waiting to Empress Sadako. Here are remarks from the notebook of one student, Sandra Dennis; observe how her imagination fixes not only on what Shonagon writes, but on the personality of the author herself:

> After reading these excerpts from *The Pillow Book,* I can infer that Sei Shonagon is observant of detail, and a sensualist. In passages such as "One Has Carefully Scented a Robe" and "I Remember a Clear Morning," the reader is aware of the distinct pleasure the author derives from using and writing about the five senses. The latter passage tells me, too, that Shonagon, although extremely sensitive, is a woman of little tolerance or patience—particularly with people who are not as sensitive as she. In her list of "Embarrassing Things," again, she includes a man whom she loves but who gets drunk and keeps repeating himself. It seems to me that "embarrassment" is just another word for her impatience—I think if she really loved the man, patience would make the situation tolerable.

Besides keeping a journal to mull over what others say or write, professional and amateur authors use their notebooks to experiment—with uncommon or forbidden subjects, ideas, and styles. Just as artists use their sketchbooks to practice figures that may ultimately appear in their paintings, so writers use their notebooks for verbal improvisation. Let's return to our student writer, who takes Sei Shonagon's habit of capturing a scene in a brief word picture and makes it her own:

> I remember that lazy afternoon in Negril, Jamaica, when I spotted an industrious hummingbird sipping the nectar of a lone red blossom.

In her notebook, this student uses Shonagon's method of appealing to several senses at once—sight, taste, sound, smell—to retrieve an image that might otherwise have been lost to memory. Her notes summon and preserve a thought, a sensation, a moment in time. The process of keeping a journal has enriched her writing as well as her reading.

Of all the forms of writing represented in this anthology, notebooks, journals, and diaries are the most personal, for in them authors write *primarily* for themselves rather than for an audience of anonymous readers. Indeed, Samuel Pepys, the seventeenth-century English diarist, went so far as to safeguard his voluminous nine-year diary from prying eyes by writing in a system of shorthand that was not entirely deciphered until the nineteenth century. And for the risqué parts of his diary, Pepys employed a sort of double code, describing his amorous adventures in a bastardized hybrid of English, French, Italian, and Latin. Literature cannot get much more private than this.

Yet we emphasize here that diarists write *"primarily* for themselves," because it is naturally difficult for diarists to rid themselves of the notion that someone, sometime, will read what they have written. Thomas Mallon, whose *A Book of One's Own* examines journal-keeping through the ages, argues that whether they admit it or not, all diarists have a "you" in mind when they write, even if that "you" is hidden in their unconscious. "After reading hundreds of diaries in the last several years," Mallon writes, "I've come to feel sure of three things. One is that writing books is too good an idea to be left to authors; another is that almost no one has had an easy life; and the third is that no one ever kept a diary for just himself."

Even so, a journal seems to convey a more honest picture of its author than, say, an autobiography, for it is the least "composed" form of written expression. "Tell me what a person says when no one is listening," the saying goes, "and I will tell you who he is." Sei Shonagon says: "I wrote these notes at home, when I had a good deal of time to myself and thought no one would notice what I was doing. Everything that I have seen and felt is included. Since much of it might appear malicious and even harmful to other people, I was careful to keep my book hidden." It is this "hidden" side of Shonagon that our student, quoted earlier, focuses on in her own notebook entry.

One writer who dramatically illustrates this difference between writing for the public and writing for oneself is William Byrd, a wealthy landowner and tireless journal-keeper who lived in Virginia during the eighteenth century. In 1728, Byrd and some twenty other men set out to survey the disputed boundary line between Virginia and North Carolina. Out of this expedition, Byrd produced *two* "Histories of the Dividing Line Betwixt Virginia and North Carolina," one a formal document tidied up for publication, the other a secret, 'unbuttoned' version of the same events. In the "secret history," Byrd whispered impressions to himself that he could not speak aloud. Here are the conclusions of two entries Byrd wrote for the same day:

. . . We took up our Quarters on the Plantation of John Hill, where we pitch our Tent, with design to tarry till such time as the Surveyors cou'd work their way to us.	We took up our Quarters at the Plantation of John Hill, where we pitch't our Tent with design to rest there 'til Monday. This Man's House was so poorly furnish't, that Firebrand & his Carolina Train [Byrd's nicknames for his companions] cou'd not find in their Hearts to lodge in it, so we had the Pleasure of their Company in the Camp. They perfumed the Tent with their Rum Punch, & hunted the poor Parson with their unseemly Jokes, which turn'd my Stomach as much as their fragrant Liquor. I was grave & speechless the whole Evening, & retired early, by all which, I gave them to

> understand, I was not fond of the
> Conversation of those whose Wit,
> like the Commons at the
> University & Inns of Court is
> eternally the same.

Byrd's *History*—both versions—shows another common type of journal at work: the travel diary. Even people who do not usually keep diaries may occasionally carry notebooks with them on trips or vacations so that they can, on returning home, recall the pleasures of wandering through a great cathedral or lazing away an afternoon in some sleepy café. In the travel diary he kept on a journey to Italy, Franz Kafka remarks: "Inexcusable to travel— or even live—without taking notes." Notice how Kafka associates both *travel* and *life* with the activity of note-taking. In doing so, Kafka unconsciously recognizes that we write in notebooks to explore what is unusual or "foreign" in ourselves—to keep in touch with that distinctive self as much as with the outside world. It is not uncommon to hear writers say, "I don't know what I think until I see what I say." So we might say that in a sense all journals are travel diaries, though the writer may have ventured no farther than her sitting-room.

Take the case of another diarist, Alice James, who spent most of her life as an invalid. In the latter part of her life, increasingly housebound because of nervous ailments and, finally, cancer, she started to keep a notebook. She began by simply copying quotations from famous writers into a little leather-bound volume called a "commonplace book." James evidently derived strength and comfort from what these writers had to say on such subjects as love, moral courage, and death, for she continued this practice over several years. Then, on May 31, 1889, an abrupt change occurs in her notebook. While convalescing in a spa in the north of England, the writer decides to set down her *own* thoughts and feelings, rather than simply recording the words of others. The commonplace book all at once becomes a diary:

> I think that if I get into the habit of writing a bit about what happens, or rather doesn't happen, I may lose a little of the sense of loneliness and desolation which abides with me. My circumstances allowing of nothing but the ejaculation of one-syllabled reflections, a written monologue by that most interesting being, *myself,* may have its yet to be discovered consolations. I shall at least have it all my own way and it may bring relief as an outlet to that geyser of emotions, sensations, speculations and reflections which ferments perpetually within my poor old carcass for its sins; so here goes, my first Journal!

So, at the age of forty, Alice James finds a way to speak for herself, whether sketching witty portraits of her neighbors or venting passionate objections to the social oppression of women and servants. Her two brothers,

Henry and William, won fame through writing novels and psychological studies; Alice's art was private and more modest in scope, but in its way a literary triumph.

As Alice James and a number of others in this chapter demonstrate, the impulse to keep a journal is by no means confined to people who make their living by writing. It is the one literary form that draws alike on the talents of youngsters and elder statesmen, scientists, and athletes—as this news item bears witness:

Islanders Compile Postgame Journal

By KEVIN DUPONT

Special to The New York Times

LOS ANGELES, Jan. 20—Simply "to give them something else to think about," the Islander coach, Al Arbour, has asked all his players, veterans and rookies alike, to write their postgame thoughts on paper.

The coach's idea, which he implemented less than 10 days ago before a game against Philadelphia, is aimed at helping the Islanders improve their individual performances and at benefiting the team as a whole when Arbour asks them to exchange their thoughts in team meetings or on a one-on-one basis. . . .

Keeping It Brief

Denis Potvin, the team captain, generally keeps his offerings short.

"I try to be as concise as I can," he said. "Sometimes it's just three or four words, nothing major. Maybe something like, 'feeling stronger.' That's all, simple.

"But you can write anything you want. You can comment on how you feel after a game. Maybe it's a game where you really felt prepared. Well, after you've won or lost, maybe you dwell on what made you prepared. I think everyone is willing to do it. I think everyone wants to take the time to reflect on doing it."

After Saturday night's 6–5 loss to the Los Angeles Kings, on a goal scored with 92 seconds left in overtime, Potvin had his latest entry ready: "Just ran out of luck, that's all," he said. "We plain ran out of luck.". . .

To react, to experiment, to store information and work out ideas, to express private hopes and frustrations, "to give them something else to think about"—the uses and forms of diaries and notebooks are as various as the people who keep them. Sei Shonagon draws up strange and beautiful lists of things she finds annoying, or elegant, or embarrassing. Samuel Pepys reports with equally lavish detail events as public as the London Fire of 1666 and as private as an extramarital indiscretion. Charles Darwin wonders about the significance of similar bird species found throughout the Galapagos Islands; Sigmund Freud delves into his dreams and those of his patients. In these "travel notes" of their outward and inward journeys, both Darwin and Freud map the terrain they would later cover in great treatises that changed the course of modern science. Alice James chronicles her own illness, as well as the life that eddies around her, with supreme intelligence and humor. Franz Kafka, even as he fusses over the distractions of a family squabble, finds that his daily notations provide an outlet for despair—and occasionally the germ of a story. Martha Graham compiles a set of "working notebooks" brimming with quotations from her vast reading of psychology and ancient myth, and in doing so gives us a glimpse into the choreographer's working methods. In these "scripts" for Graham's dances we see the ideas that inspire her, and in turn descriptions of the dance movements through which Graham explores the human psyche and passions. Joan Didion splices vignettes, overheard conversations, and weather reports to create a "Los Angeles Notebook," an acid-etched portrait of the city.

Martha Graham announces in her notebook, "I am a thief—and I glory in it—I steal from the present and from the glorious past. . . ." Every author represented here snatches a little from the life that passes through the pages of his or her journal and assembles from these "found objects" something meaningful and new. As you read, observe not only the drift of each author's thought, but the distinctive appearance of each journal entry on the page. The entry may take the shape of a list of sentence fragments, a terse paragraph, a collection of phrases connected by dashes and running at angles up and down the page, a lengthy essay, or—in the case of the Didion piece—a series of observations carefully molded into a cohesive grouping. Sei Shonagon describes the kind of variety one inevitably discovers in these journals:

> . . . I set about filling the notebooks with odd facts, stories from the past, and all sorts of other things, often including the most trivial material. On the whole I concentrated on things and people that I found charming and splendid; my notes are also full of poems and observations on trees and plants, birds and insects.

Shonagon concludes, "Whatever people may think of my book, I still regret that it ever came to light." Whether we take Shonagon at her word or suspect that she wrote with others in mind, most readers will rejoice that this and other "secret histories" have come to light. As you write in your own journal, feel free to draw on—to "steal" inspiration from—the extraordinary range of this most private form of literary expression.

Sei Shonagon (965?–?)

For centuries before diary-keeping became a tradition in the West, educated Japanese were in the habit of keeping "pillow books"—diaries to be kept near one's pillow for the purpose of recording random impressions. Perhaps the most celebrated pillow book of all time is that of Sei Shonagon, the daughter of a scholarly provincial official, who at the age of twenty-seven began to serve the fifteen-year-old Empress Sadako in the Heian court during the last decade of the tenth century. Soon after joining the court, Shonagon began her diary. She continued this record of reflections, poems, and reminiscences for ten years, until her beloved empress died in childbirth. Shonagon's pillow book provides us with our most detailed picture of Japanese court life of the period.

We know little more than these bare facts about the writer of this extraordinary diary, aside from what we can infer about her from her writing. Lady Murasaki Shikibu, a contemporary of Shonagon's and the author of *The Tale of Genji,* wrote in her own pillow book:

> Sei Shonagon has the most extraordinary air of self-satisfaction. . . . Someone who makes such an effort to be different from others is bound to fall in people's esteem, and I can only think that her future will be a hard one.

Tradition has it that Sei Shonagon, the celebrated wit, beauty, and literary stylist, ended her days as a broken wretch living in poverty. But as one scholar has pointed out, this legend may have been the invention of moralists who, shocked by her independent spirit and worldliness, bestowed upon her the retribution they thought she deserved.

From *The Pillow Book* of Sei Shonagon

Translated by Ivan Morris

———— Elegant Things ————

A white coat worn over a violet waistcoat.
Duck eggs.
Shaved ice mixed with liana syrup and put in a new silver bowl.
A rosary of rock crystal.
Wistaria blossoms. Plum blossoms covered with snow.
A pretty child eating strawberries.

———— Things That Cannot Be Compared ————

Summer and winter. Night and day. Rain and sunshine. Youth and age. A person's laughter and his anger. Black and white. Love and hatred. The little indigo plant and the great philodendron. Rain and mist.

When one has stopped loving somebody, one feels that he has become someone else, even though he is still the same person.

In a garden full of evergreens the crows are all asleep. Then, towards the middle of the night, the crows in one of the trees suddenly wake up in a great flurry and start flapping about. Their unrest spreads to the other trees, and soon all the birds have been startled from their sleep and are cawing in alarm. How different from the same crows in daytime!

———— One of Her Majesty's Wet-Nurses ————

One of Her Majesty's wet-nurses who held the Fifth Rank left today for the province of Hyūga. Among the fans given her by the Empress as a parting gift was one with a painting of a travelers' lodging, not unlike the Captain of Ide's residence. On the other side was a picture of the capital in a heavy rainstorm with someone gazing at the scene. In her own hand the Empress had written the following sentence as if it were an ordinary piece of prose: "When you have gone away and face the sun that shines so crimson in the East, be mindful of the friends you left behind, who in this city gaze upon the endless rains." It was a very moving message, and I realized that I myself could not possibly leave such a mistress and go away to some distant place.

———— Embarrassing Things ————

While entertaining a visitor, one hears some servants chatting without any restraint in one of the back rooms. It is embarrassing to know that one's visitor can overhear. But how to stop them?

A man whom one loves gets drunk and keeps repeating himself.

To have spoken about someone not knowing that he could overhear. This is embarrassing even if it be a servant or some other completely insignificant person.

To hear one's servants making merry. This is equally annoying if one is on a journey and staying in cramped quarters or at home and hears the servants in a neighbouring room.

Parents, convinced that their ugly child is adorable, pet him and repeat the things he has said, imitating his voice.

An ignoramus who in the presence of some learned person puts on a knowing air and converses about men of old.

A man recites his own poems (not especially good ones) and tells one about the praise they have received—most embarrassing.

Lying awake at night, one says something to one's companion, who simply goes on sleeping.

In the presence of a skilled musician, someone plays a zither just for his own pleasure and without tuning it.

A son-in-law who has long since stopped visiting his wife runs into his father-in-law in a public place.

Things That Have Lost Their Power

A large boat which is high and dry in a creek at ebb-tide.

A woman who has taken off her false locks to comb the short hair that remains.

A large tree that has been blown down in a gale and lies on its side with its roots in the air.

The retreating figure of a *sumō* wrestler who has been defeated in a match.

A man of no importance reprimanding an attendant.

An old man who removes his hat, uncovering his scanty topknot.

A woman, who is angry with her husband about some trifling matter, leaves home and goes somewhere to hide. She is certain that he will rush about looking for her; but he does nothing of the kind and shows the most infuriating indifference. Since she cannot stay away for ever, she swallows her pride and returns.

I Remember a Clear Morning

I remember a clear morning in the Ninth Month when it had been raining all night. Despite the bright sun, dew was still dripping from the chrysanthemums in the garden. On the bamboo fences and criss-cross hedges I saw tatters of spider webs; and where the threads were broken the raindrops hung on them like strings of white pearls. I was greatly moved and delighted.

As it became sunnier, the dew gradually vanished from the clover and the other plants where it had lain so heavily; the branches began to stir, then suddenly sprang up of their own accord. Later I described to people how beautiful it all was. What most impressed me was that they were not at all impressed.

One Has Carefully Scented a Robe

One has carefully scented a robe and then forgotten about it for several days. When finally one comes to wear it, the aroma is even more delicious than on freshly scented clothes.

——— When Crossing a River ———

When crossing a river in bright moonlight, I love to see the water scatter in showers of crystal under the oxen's feet.

——— Things That Should Be Large ———

Priests. Fruit. Houses. Provision bags. Inksticks for inkstones.

Men's eyes: when they are too narrow, they look feminine. On the other hand, if they were as large as metal bowls, I should find them rather frightening.

Round braziers. Winter cherries. Pine trees. The petals of yellow roses.

Horses as well as oxen should be large.

——— Things That Should Be Short ———

A piece of thread when one wants to sew something in a hurry.

A lamp stand.

The hair of a woman of the lower classes should be neat and short.

The speech of a young girl.

——— It Is Getting So Dark ———

It is getting so dark that I can scarcely go on writing; and my brush is all worn out. Yet I should like to add a few things before I end.

I wrote these notes at home, when I had a good deal of time to myself and thought no one would notice what I was doing. Everything that I have seen and felt is included. Since much of it might appear malicious and even harmful to other people, I was careful to keep my book hidden. But now it has become public, which is the last thing I expected.

One day Lord Korechika, the Minister of the Centre, brought the Empress a bundle of notebooks. "What shall we do with them?" Her Majesty asked me. "The Emperor has already made arrangements for copying the 'Records of the Historian.'"

"Let me make them into a pillow," I said.

"Very well," said Her Majesty. "You may have them."

I now had a vast quantity of paper at my disposal, and I set about filling the notebooks with odd facts, stories from the past, and all sorts of other things, often including the most trivial material. On the whole I concentrated on things and people that I found charming and splendid; my notes are also full of poems and observations on trees and plants, birds and insects. I was sure that when people saw my book they would say, "It's even worse than I expected. Now one can really tell what she is like." After all, it is written entirely for my own amusement and I put things down exactly as they came to me. How could my casual jottings possibly bear comparison with the many impressive books that exist in our time? Readers have declared, however, that I can be proud of my work. This has surprised me greatly; yet I suppose it is not so strange that people should like it, for, as will be gathered from these notes of mine, I am the sort of person who approves of what others abhor and detests the things they like.

Whatever people may think of my book, I still regret that it ever came to light.

Questions for *The Pillow Book* of Sei Shonagon

1.   Many readers have noted Shonagon's scorn for the lower classes. Can you find evidence of this in the text? How would you explain Shonagon's social views?

2.   Shonagon is often praised for the evocative power of her language— even in translation, where much of this beauty, of course, is lost. Pick out several memorable sentences or images in the passages excerpted here, and describe why you find them effective.

3.   From Shonagon's record, what can you deduce about male and female roles and relationships at the Heian court?

4.   In the biographical note on Sei Shonagon, we point out that little is known about her, aside from what we can infer from her diary. What inferences can you make about her based on the selections you've read?

Samuel Pepys (1633–1703)

Perhaps the most famous diarist of all time, Samuel Pepys was reared in London, the fifth of eleven children born to a tailor and his wife. After graduating from Cambridge University, Pepys married Elizabeth St. Michel and embarked upon a career of civil service; he was soon delighted to find himself "a very rising man," serving as secretary of the Admiralty and a member of Parliament. In 1679, however, during the fanatical period of the Popish Plot (a supposed plot to burn London and kill the king), Pepys was briefly and wrongly imprisoned. He was eventually reinstated as secretary of the Navy and among other official appointments held the position of president of the Royal Society.

Whatever his political accomplishments, it is for the *Diary* that Pepys is justifiably celebrated. Begun on January 1, 1660, kept for a period of nine years, suddenly abandoned when Pepys feared he was going blind, the *Diary* is a million-word masterpiece of reporting. An assiduous recorder of newsworthy events and daily trivia alike, as well as an intuitive scholar of human psychology, Pepys wrote in secret, unbeknownst even to his closest friends, with breathtaking candor and gusto. As you will find in the following selections, he was above all passionate about life, whether pursuing an ill-starred affair with "Deb"—Deborah Willet, his wife's maid—or lamenting the destruction of his beloved London during the Great Fire.

From *The Diary* of Samuel Pepys

During the night of 2 September 1666, the Great Fire of London broke out. It was to rage for four days and nights. Few lives were lost, but some four-fifths of the total area of the city was laid waste. The fire began accidentally in a bakehouse in Pudding Lane, but was commonly believed to have been the work of papists and the foreign enemy.

2 September. Lords Day. Some of our maids sitting up late last night to get things ready against our feast today, Jane called us up, about 3 in the morning, to tell us of a great fire they saw in the City. So I rose, and slipped on my nightgown and went to her window, and thought it to be on the back side of Markelane at the furthest; but being unused to such fires as fallowed, I thought it far enough off, and so went to bed again and to sleep. About 7 rose again to dress myself, and there looked out at the window and saw the fire not so much as it was, and further off. So to my closet to set things to rights after yesterday's cleaning. By and by Jane comes and tells me that she hears that above 300 houses have been burned down tonight by the fire we saw, and that it was now burning down all Fishstreet by London Bridge. So I made myself ready presently, and walked to the Tower and there got up upon one of the high places, Sir J. Robinsons little son going up with me; and there I did see the houses at that end of the bridge all on fire, and an infinite great fire on this and the other side the end of the bridge—which, among other people, did trouble me for poor little Michell and our Sarah on the Bridge. So down, with my heart full of trouble, to the Lieutenant of the Tower, who tells me that it begun this morning in the King's bakers house in Pudding Lane, and that it hath burned down St Magnes Church and most part of Fishstreete already. So I down to the waterside and there got a boat and through bridge, and there saw a lamentable fire. Poor Michells house, as far as the Old Swan, already burned that way and the fire running further, that in a very little time it got as far as the Stillyard while I was there. Everybody endeavouring to remove their goods, and flinging into the river or bringing them into lighters that lay off. Poor people staying in their houses as long as till the very fire touched them, and then running into boats or clambering from one pair of stair by the waterside to another. And among other things, the poor pigeons I perceive were loath to leave their houses, but hovered about the windows and balconies till they were some of them burned, their wings, and fell down.

Having stayed, and in an hour's time seen the fire rage every way, and nobody to my sight endeavouring to quench it, but to remove their goods and leave all to the fire; and having seen it get as far as the Steeleyard, and the wind mighty high and driving it into the city, and everything, after so long a drought, proving combustible, even the very stones of churches. I to Whitehall with a gentleman with me who desired to go off from the Tower to see the fire in my boat—to Whitehall, and there up to the King's closet in the chapel, where people came about me and I did give them an account dismayed them all; and word was carried in to the King, so I was called for and did tell the King and Duke of York what I saw, and that unless his Majesty did command houses to be pulled down, nothing could stop the fire. They seemed much troubled, and the King commanded me to go to my Lord Mayor from him and command him to spare no houses but to pull down before the fire every way. The Duke of York bid me tell him that if he would have any more soldiers, he shall. Here meeting with Captain Cocke, I in his coach, which he lent me, and Creed with me, to Pauls; and there walked along Watling Street as well as I could, every creature coming away loaden with goods to save—and here and there sick people carried away in beds. Extraordinary good goods carried in carts and on backs. At last met my Lord Mayor in Canning Streete, like a man spent, with a hankercher about his neck. To the King's message, he cried like a fainting woman, "Lord, what can I do? I am spent! People will not obey me. I have been pull[ing] down houses. But the fire overtakes us faster then we can do it." That he needed no more soldiers; and that for himself, he must go and refresh himself, having been up all night. So he left me, and I him, and walked home—seeing people all almost distracted and no manner of means used to quench the fire. The houses too, so very thick thereabouts, and full of matter for burning, as pitch and tar, in Thames Street—and warehouses of oyle and wines and brandy and other things. Here I saw Mr Isaccke Houblon, that handsome man—prettily dressed and dirty at his door at Dowgate, receiving some of his brothers things whose houses were on fire; and as he says, have been removed twice already, and he doubts (as it soon proved) that they must be in a little time removed from his house also—which was a sad consideration. And to see the churches all filling with goods, by people who themselfs should have been quietly there at this time.

As soon as dined, I and Moone away and walked through the City, the streets full of nothing but people and horses and carts loaden with goods, ready to run over one another, and removing goods from one burned house to another—they now removing out of Canning Street (which received goods in the morning) into Lumbard Streete and further. We parted at Pauls, he home and I to Pauls Wharf, where I had appointed a boat to attend me; and took in Mr. Carcasse and his brother, whom I met in the street, and carried them below and above bridge, to and again, to see the fire, which was now got further, both below and above, and no likelihood of stopping it. Met with the King and Duke of York in their barge, and with them to Queen Hith and there called Sir Rd. Browne to them. Their order was only to pull down houses apace, and so below bridge at the waterside; but little was or could be done, the fire coming upon them so fast. Good hopes there was of stopping it at the Three Cranes above, and at Buttolphs Wharf below bridge, if care be used; but the wind carries it into the City, so as we know not by the waterside what it doth there. River full of lighter[s] and boats taking in goods, and good goods swimming in the water; and only, I observed that hardly one lighter or boat in three that had the goods of a house in, but there was a pair of virginalls in it. Having seen as much as I could now, I away to Whitehall by appointment, and there walked to St James's Park, and there met my wife and Creed and Wood and his wife and walked to my boat, and there upon the water again, and to the fire up and down, it still increasing and the wind great. So near the fire as we could for smoke; and all over the Thames, with one's face in the wind you were almost burned with a shower of firedrops—this is very true—so as houses were burned by these drops and flakes of fire, three or four, nay five or six houses, one from another. When we could endure no more upon the water, we to a little alehouse on the Bankside over against the Three Cranes, and there stayed till it was dark almost and saw the fire grow; and as it grow darker, appeared more and more, and in corners and upon steeples and between churches and houses, as far as we could see up the hill of the City, in a most horrid malicious bloody flame, not like the fine flame of an ordinary fire. We stayed till, it being darkish, we saw the fire as only one entire arch of fire from this to the other side the bridge, and in a bow up the hill, for an arch of above a mile long. It made me weep to see it. The churches, houses, and all on fire and flaming at once, and a horrid noise the flames made, and the cracking of houses at their ruine. So home with a sad heart, and there to find everybody discoursing and lamenting the fire; and poor Tom Hater came with some few of his goods saved out of his house, which is burned upon Fish Street Hill. I invited him to lie at my house, and did receive his goods; but was deceived in his lying there, the noise coming every moment of the growth of the fire, so as we were forced to begin to pack up our own goods and prepare for their removal. And did by mooneshine (it being brave, dry, and moonshine and warm weather) carry much of my goods into the garden, and Mr Hater and I did remove my money and iron chests into my cellar— as thinking that the safest place. And got my bags of gold into my office ready to carry away, and my chief papers of accounts also there, and my tallies into a box by themselfs. So great was our fear, as Sir W. Batten had carts come out of the country to fetch away his goods this night. We did put Mr Hater, poor man, to bed a little; but he got but very little rest, so much noise being in my house, taking down of goods. . . .

• • •

[1668] *25 October. Lords Day.* At night W. Batelier comes and sups with us; and after supper, to have my head combed by Deb, which occasioned the greatest sorrow to me that ever I knew in this world; for my wife, coming up suddenly, did find me imbracing the girl . . . I was at a wonderful loss upon it, and the girl also; and I endeavoured to put it off, but my wife was struck mute and grew angry, and as her voice came to her, grew quite out of order; and I do say little, but to bed; and my wife said little also, but could not sleep all night; but about 2 in the morning waked me and cried, and fell to tell me as a great secret that she was a Roman Catholique and had received the Holy Sacrament; which troubled me but I took no notice of it, but she went on from one thing to another, till at last it appeared plainly her trouble was at what she saw; but yet I did not know how much she saw and therefore said nothing to her. But after her much crying and reproaching me with inconstancy and preferring a sorry girl before her, I did give her no provocations but did promise all fair usage to her, and love, and foreswore any hurt that I did with her—till at last she seemed to be at ease again.

26 October. And so toward morning, a little sleep; and so I, with some little repose and rest, rose, and up and by water to Whitehall, but with my mind mightily troubled for the poor girl, whom I fear I have undone by this, my [wife] telling me that she would turn her out of door. However, I was obliged to attend the Duke of York, thinking to have had a meeting of Tanger today, but had not; but he did take me and Mr Wren into his closet and there did press me to prepare what I had to say upon the answers of my fellow officers to his great letter; which I promised to do against his coming to town again the next week. Thence by coach home and to dinner, finding my wife mightily discontented and the girl sad, and no words from my wife to her. So after dinner, they out with me about two or three things; and so home again, I all the evening busy and my wife full of trouble in her looks; and anon to bed—where about midnight, she wakes me and there falls foul on me again, affirming that she saw me hug and kiss the girl; the latter I denied, and truly; the other I confessed and no more. And upon her pressing me, did offer to give her under my hand that I would never see Mrs Pierce more, nor Knepp,[1] but did promise her perticular demonstrations of my true love to her, owning some indiscretion in what I did, but that there was no harm in it. She at last on these promises was quiet, and very kind we were, and so to sleep. . . .

9 November. Up, and I did by a little note which I flung to Deb, advise her that I did continue to deny that ever I kissed her, and so she might govern herself. The truth [is], that I did adventure upon God's pardoning me this lie, knowing how heavy a thing it would be for me to be the ruin of the poor girl; and next, knowing that if my wife should know all, it were impossible ever for her to be at peace with me again—and so our whole lives would be uncomfortable.

10 November. Up, and my wife still every day as ill as she is all night; will rise to see me outdoors, telling me plainly that she dares not let me see the girl; and so I out to the office where all the morning; and so home to dinner, where I find my wife mightily troubled again, more then ever, and she tells me that it is from her examining the girl and getting a confession now from her of all . . . —which doth mightily trouble me, as not being able to foresee the consequences of it as to our future peace together. So my wife would not go down to dinner, reproaching me with my unkindness and perjury, I having denied my ever kissing her—as also with all her old kindnesses to me, and my ill-using of her from the beginning, and the many temptations she hath refused out of faithfulness to me; whereof several she was perticular in, and especially from my Lord Sandwich by the sollicitation of Captain Ferrer; and then afterward, the courtship of my Lord Hinchingbrooke, even to the trouble of his Lady. All which I did acknowledge and was troubled for, and wept; and at last pretty good friends again, and so I to my office and there late, and so home to supper with her; and so to bed, where after half-an-hour's slumber, she wakes me and cries out that she should never sleep more, and so kept raving till past midnight, that made me cry and weep heartily all the while for her, and troubled for what she reproached me with as before; and at last, with new vows, and perticularly that I would myself bid the girl be gone and show my dislike to her—which I shall endeavour to perform, but with much trouble. . . .

12 November. I to my wife and to sit with her a little; and then called her and Willet to my chamber, and there did with tears in my eyes, which I could

---

[1] two other women friends of Pepys, Knepp being the object of his amorous attentions.

not help, discharge her and advise her to be gone as soon as she could, and never to see me or let me see her more while she was in the house; which she took with tears too, but I believe understands me to be her friend . . . With Mr. Gibson late at my chamber, making an end of my draft of a letter for the Duke of York, in answer to the answers of this office; which I have now done to my mind, so as, if the Duke of York likes it, will I think put an end to a great deal of the faults of this office, as well as my trouble for them. So to bed, and did lie now a little better then formerly, with but little and yet with some trouble.

14 November. Up, and had a mighty mind to have seen or given a note to Deb or to have given her a little money; to which purpose I wrapped up 40*s* in a paper, thinking to give her; but my wife rose presently, and would not let me be out of her sight; and went down before me into the kitchen, and came up and told me that she was in the kitchen and therefore would have me go round the other way; which she repeating, and I vexed at it, answered her a little angrily; upon which she instantly flew out into a rage, calling me dog and rogue, and that I had a rotten heart; all which, knowing that I deserved it, I bore with; and word being brought presently up that she was gone away by coach with her things, my wife was friends; and so all quiet, and I to the office with my heart sad, and find that I cannot forget the girl, and vexed I know not where to look for her. It will be I fear a little time before I shall be able to wear Deb out of my mind. . . .

18 November. Lay long in bed, talking with my wife, she being unwilling to have me go abroad, being and declaring herself jealous of my going out, for fear of my going to Deb; which I do deny—for which God forgive me, for I was no sooner out about noon but I did go by coach directly to Somerset House and there enquired among the porters there for Dr Allbun; and the first I spoke with told me he knew him, and that he was newly gone into Lincoln's Inn Fields, but whither he could not tell me, but that one of his fellows, not then in the way, did carry a chest of drawers thither with him, and that when he comes he would ask him. This put me in some hopes; and I to Whitehall and thence to Mr Povy's, but he at dinner; and therefore I away and walked up and down the Strand between the two turnstiles, hoping to see her out of a window; and then imployed a porter, one Osbeston, to find out this Doctors lodgings thereabouts; who by appointment comes to me to Hercules Pillars, where I dined alone, but tells me that he cannot find out any such but will enquire further. Thence back to Whitehall to the Treasury a while, and then to the Strand; and towards night did meet with the porter that carried the chest of drawers with this Doctor, but he would not tell me where he lived, being his good maister he told me; but if I would have a message to him, he would deliver it. At last, I told him my business was not with him, but a little gent[le]woman, one Mrs Willet, that is with him; and sent him to see how she did, from her friend in London, and no other token. He goes while I walk in Somerset House; at last he comes back and tells me she is well, and that I may see her if I will—but no more. So I could not be commanded by my reason, but I must go this very night; and so by coach, it being now dark, I to her, close by my tailor's; and there she came into the coach to me . . . And so home, and there told my wife a fair tale, God knows, how I spent the whole day; with which the poor wretch was satisfied, or at least seemed so; and so to supper and to bed, she having been mighty busy all day in getting of her house in order against tomorrow, to hang up our new hangings and furnishing our best chamber.

19 November. Up, and at the office all the morning, with my heart full of joy to think in what a safe condition all my matters now stand between my wife and Deb and me; and at noon, running upstairs to see the upholsters, who are at work upon hanging my best room and setting up my new bed, I find my wife sitting sad in the dining room; which inquiring into the reason of, she begun to call me all the false, rotten-hearted rogues in the world, letting me understand that I was with Deb yesterday; which, thinking impossible for her ever to understand, I did a while deny; but at last did, for the ease of my mind and hers, and for ever to discharge my heart of this wicked business, I did confess all; and above stairs in our bedchamber there I did endure the sorrow of her threats and vows and curses all the afternoon. And which was worst, she swore by all that was good that she would slit the nose of this girl, and be gone herself this very night from me; and did there demand 3 or 400*l* of me to buy my peace, that she might be gone without making any noise, or else protested that she would make all the world know of it. So, with most perfect confusion of face and heart, and sorrow and shame, in the greatest agony in the world, I did pass this afternoon, fearing that it will never have an end; but at last I did call for W. Hewers, who I was forced to make privy now to all; and the poor fellow did cry like a child [and] obtained what I could not, that she would be pacified, upon condition that I would give it under my hand never to see or speak with Deb while I live, as I did before of Pierce and Knepp; and which I did also, God knows, promise for Deb too, but I have the confidence to deny it, to the perjuring of myself. So before it was late, there was, beyond my hopes as well as desert, a tolerable peace; and so to supper, and pretty kind words . . . and so with some rest spent the night in bed, being most absolutely resolved, if ever I can maister this bout, never to give her occasion while I live of more trouble of this or any other kind, there being no curse in the world so great as this of the difference between myself and her; and therefore I do by the grace of God promise never to offend her more, and did this night begin to pray to God upon my knees alone in my chamber; which God knows I cannot yet do heartily, but I hope God will give me the grace more and more every day to fear Him, and to be true to my poor wife. This night the upholsters did finish the hanging of my best chamber, but my sorrow and trouble is so great about this business, that put me out of all joy. . . .

Questions for *The Diary* of Samuel Pepys

1.   We know Pepys lies to his wife and to Deb. As a diarist, does Pepys seem to be a reliable observer? Explain.

2.   What details of Pepys's account of the "Deb affair" strike you as particularly true-to-life? What does Pepys's conduct throughout the affair suggest to you about the man and his relationship with his wife? Describe Elizabeth Pepys's behavior.

3.   Which items in Pepys's record of the London Fire would appear in a newspaper account, and which would more likely be confined to a diary? What scenes or vignettes did you find most memorable or moving?

Charles Darwin (1809–1882)

The son of an affluent physician, Darwin grew up in Shrewsbury, England. By his own admission in his autobiography (part of which is reprinted in the next chapter), Darwin displayed as a schoolboy little of the brilliance that was to place him at the center of the scientific revolution in the nineteenth century. He studied medicine for two years at Edinburgh University, but had little interest in becoming a doctor. With the encouragement of his father, he went to Cambridge to study for the clergy, a profession toward which he again showed no inclination.

Darwin left Cambridge to sign up as a naturalist aboard the *Beagle*, which was bound for a voyage around the world. He kept detailed diaries of the five-year voyage, recording with equally keen interest his impressions of the gauchos of Argentina, the giant tortoises of the Galapagos Islands, and the terrain of the Falklands. Upon his return to England, he rewrote and edited the notebooks into a published *Journal of Researches* (1839), which in turn provided the foundation for the great work of Darwin's life, the *Origin of Species* (1859). During the twenty years it took him to write this treatise on evolution, his scientific notebooks continued to serve as the laboratory for his observations and data: Of his notebooks, Darwin wrote, "I worked on true Baconian principles, and without any theory collected facts on a wholesale scale. . . ."

From *Journal of Researches*

Bahia, or San Salvador. Brazil, Feb. 29th. [1832]

The day has past delightfully. Delight itself, however, is a weak term to express the feelings of a naturalist who, for the first time, has been wandering by himself in a Brazilian forest. Among the multitude of striking objects, the general luxuriance of the vegetation bears away the victory. The elegance of the grasses, the novelty of the parasitical plants, the beauty of the flowers, the glossy green of the foliage, all tend to this end. A most paradoxical mixture of sound and silence pervades the shady parts of the wood. The noise from the insects is so loud, that it may be heard even in a vessel anchored several hundred yards from the shore; yet within the recesses of the forest a universal silence appears to reign. To a person fond of natural history, such a day as this, brings with it a deeper pleasure than he ever can hope again to experience. After wandering about for some hours, I returned to the landing-place; but, before reaching it, I was overtaken by a tropical storm. I tried to find shelter under a tree which was so thick, that it would never have been penetrated by common English rain; but here, in a couple of minutes, a little torrent flowed down the trunk. It is to this violence of the rain we must attribute the verdure at the bottom of the thickest woods: if the showers were like those of a colder clime, the greater part would be absorbed or evaporated before it reached the ground. I will not at present attempt to describe the gaudy scenery of this noble bay, because, in our homeward voyage, we called here a second time, and I shall then have occasion to remark on it.

The geology of the surrounding country possesses little interest. Throughout the coast of Brazil, and certainly for a considerable space inland, from the Rio Plata to Cape St. Roque, lat. 5° S., a distance of more than 2000 geographical miles, wherever solid rock occurs, it belongs to a granitic formation. The circumstance of this enormous area being thus constituted of materials, which almost every geologist believes have been crystallized by the action of heat under pressure, gives rise to many curious reflections. Was this effect produced beneath the depths of a profound ocean? or did a covering of strata formerly extend over it, which has since been removed? Can we believe that any power, acting for a time short of infinity, could have denuded the granite over so many thousand square leagues?

[Argentina, March 1835]

We crossed the Luxan, which is a river of considerable size, though its course towards the sea-coast is very imperfectly known. It is even doubtful whether, in passing over the plains, it is evaporated, or whether it forms a tributary of the Sauce or Colorado. We slept in the village, which is a small place surrounded by gardens, and forms the most southern part, that is cultivated, of the province of Mendoza; it is five leagues south of the capital. At night I experienced an attack (for it deserves no less a name) of the *Benchuca* (a species of Reduvius) the great black bug of the Pampas. It is most disgusting to feel soft wingless insects, about an inch long, crawling over one's body. Before sucking they are quite thin, but afterwards become round and bloated with blood, and in this state they are easily crushed. They are also found in the northern parts of Chile and in Peru. One which I caught at Iquique was very empty. When placed on the table, and though surrounded by people, if a finger was presented, the bold insect would immediately draw its sucker, make a charge, and if allowed, draw blood. No pain was caused by the wound. It was curious to watch its body during the act of sucking, as it changed in less than ten minutes, from being as flat as a wafer to a globular form. This one feast, for which the benchuca was indebted to one of the officers, kept it fat during four whole months; but, after the first fortnight, the insect was quite ready to have another suck.

We rode on to Mendoza. The country was beautifully cultivated, and resembled Chile. This neighbourhood is celebrated for its fruit; and certainly nothing could appear more flourishing than the vineyards and the orchards of figs, peaches, and olives. We bought watermelons nearly twice as large as a man's head, most deliciously cool and well-flavoured, for a halfpenny apiece; and for the value of threepence, half a wheelbarrowful of peaches. The cultivated and enclosed part of this province is very small; there is little more than that which we passed through between Luxan and the capital. The land, as in Chile, entirely owes its fertility to artificial irrigation; and it is really wonderful to observe how abundantly productive a barren traversia is rendered by this simple process.

[Galapagos Islands, September 1835]

I will not here attempt to come to any definite conclusions, as the species have not been accurately examined; but we may infer, that, with the exception of a few wanderers, the organic beings found on this archipelago are peculiar to it; and yet that their general form strongly partakes of an American character. It would be impossible for any one accustomed to the birds of Chile and La Plata to be placed on these islands, and not to feel convinced that he was, as far as the organic world was concerned, on American ground. This similarity in type, between distant islands and continents, while the species are distinct, has scarcely been sufficiently noticed. The circumstance would be explained, according to the views of some authors, by saying that the creative power had acted according to the same law over a wide area.

It has been mentioned, that the inhabitants can distinguish the tortoises, according to the islands whence they are brought. I was also informed that many of the islands possess trees and plants which do not occur on others. For instance the berry-bearing tree, called Guyavita, which is common on James Island, certainly is not found on Charles Island, though appearing equally well fitted for it. Unfortunately, I was not aware of these facts till my collection was nearly completed: it never occurred to me, that the productions of islands only a few miles apart, and placed under the same physical conditions, would be dissimilar. I therefore did not attempt to make a series of specimens from the separate islands. It is the fate of every voyager, when he has just discovered what object in any place is more particularly worthy of his attention, to be hurried from it. In the case of the mocking-bird, I ascertained (and have brought home the specimens) that one species (*Orpheus trifasciatus*, Gould) is exclusively found in Charles Island; a second (*O. parvulus*) on Albermarle Island; and a third (*O. melanotus*) common to James and Chatham Islands. The two last species are closely allied, but the first would be considered by every naturalist as quite distinct. I examined many specimens in the different islands, and in each the respective kind was *alone* present. These birds agree in general plumage, structure, and habits; so that the different species replace each other in the economy of the different islands. These species are not characterized by the markings on the plumage alone, but likewise by the size and form of the bill, and other differences. I have stated, that in the thirteen species of ground-finches, a nearly perfect gradation may be traced, from a beak extraordinarily thick, to one so fine, that it may be compared to that of a warbler. I very much suspect, that certain members of the series are confined to different islands; therefore, if the collection had been made on any *one* island, it would not have presented so perfect a gradation. It is clear, that if several islands have each their peculiar species of the same genera, when these are placed together, they will have a wide range of character. But there is not space in this work, to enter on this curious subject.

Questions for Darwin's *Journal of Researches*

1.   Darwin's all-too-vivid description of the *Benchuca* insect depends on the observations of others, Darwin's own observations, and the inferences he is able to make on the basis of these observations. In this passage, can you point to one example of each of these scientific methods?

2.   The birds known as "Darwin's finches," found on the Galapagos Islands, have become a prime example of the process of evolution. In *Origin of Species,* Darwin comments further that the Galapagos Islands were inhabited by distinct species that were nevertheless much closer to one another than to the inhabitants of any other part of the world. What do his observations suggest about the evolution of any species?

Alice James (1848–1892)

It was Alice James's good fortune or curse to be born into an extraordinarily talented and successful family. Her brother William would become the most eminent American philosopher of his day, and her brother Henry the greatest novelist of the age. The youngest of five children and the only daughter of Mary James and Henry Sr., a writer and lecturer, Alice grew up in a comfortable middle-class household in New York City and later in Cambridge, Massachusetts. She eventually settled in England, and there in 1889 began the diary she would keep until her death three years later. As was typical of women in the mid-nineteenth century, James's education was casual and her activities limited. It is generally believed that the frustration bred by these circumstances led to her chronic invalidism. As Henry James wrote, "Alice's tragic health was, in a manner, the only solution for her of the practical problem of life."

From *The Diary* of Alice James

Dec. 12th [1889]

. . . One day when my shawls were falling off to the left my cushions falling out to the right and the duvet off my knees, one of those crises of misery in short which are all in the day's work for an invalid Kath.[1] exclaimed, "What an awful pity it is that you can't say *damn*." I agreed with her from my heart. It is an immense loss to have all robust and sustaining expletives refined away from one! at such moments of trial refinement is a feeble reed to lean upon. I wonder, whether, if I had had any education I should have been more, or less, of a fool than I am. It would have deprived me surely of those exquisite moments of mental flatulence which every now and then inflate the cerebral vacuum with a delicious sense of latent possibilities—of stretching oneself to cosmic limits, and who would ever give up the reality of dreams for relative knowledge?

---

[1]Kath.: Katharine P. Loring, Alice James's friend and companion.

July 28th [1890]

I lay in a meadow until the unwrinkled serenity entered into my bones and made me one with the browsing kine, the still greenery, the drifting clouds, and the swooping birds.

October 26th [1890]

William uses an excellent expression when he says in his paper on the "Hidden Self" that the nervous victim "abandons" certain portions of his consciousness. It may be the word commonly used by his kind. It is just the right one at any rate, altho' I have never unfortunately been able to abandon my consciousness and get five minutes' rest. I have passed thro' an infinite succession of conscious abandonments and in looking back now I see how it began in my childhood, altho' I wasn't conscious of the necessity until '67 or '68 when I broke down first, acutely, and had violent turns of hysteria. As I lay prostrate after the storm with my mind luminous and active and susceptible of the clearest, strongest impressions, I saw so distinctly that it was a fight simply between my body and my will, a battle in which the former was to be triumphant to the end. Owing to some physical weakness, excess of nervous susceptibility, the moral power *pauses,* as it were for a moment, and refuses to maintain muscular sanity, worn out with the strain of its constabulary functions. As I used to sit immovable reading in the library with waves of violent inclination suddenly invading my muscles taking some one of their myriad forms such as throwing myself out of the window, or knocking off the head of the benignant pater as he sat with his silver locks, writing at his table, it used to seem to me that the only difference between me and the insane was that I had not only all the horrors and suffering of insanity but the duties of doctor, nurse, and strait-jacket imposed upon me, too. Conceive of never being without the sense that if you let yourself go for a moment your mechanism will fall into pie and that at some given moment you must abandon it all, let the dykes break and the flood sweep in, acknowledging yourself abjectly impotent before the immutable laws. When all one's moral and natural stock in trade is a temperament forbidding the abandonment of an inch or the relaxation of a muscle, 'tis a never-ending fight. When the fancy took me of a morning at school to *study* my lessons by way of variety instead of shirking or wiggling thro' the most impossible sensations of upheaval, violent revolt in my head overtook me so that I had to "abandon" my brain, as it were. So it has always been, anything that sticks of itself is free to do so, but conscious and continuous cerebration is an impossible exercise and from just behind the eyes my head feels like a dense jungle into which no ray of light has ever penetrated. So, with the rest, you abandon the pit of your stomach, the palms of your hands, the soles of your feet, and refuse to keep them sane when you find in turn one moral impression after another producing despair in the one, terror in the other, anxiety in the third and so on until life becomes one long flight from remote suggestion and complicated eluding of the multifold traps set for your undoing.

May 31st [1891]

"happy" to discover her cancer

To him who waits, all things come! My aspirations may have been eccentric, but I cannot complain now, that they have not been brilliantly fulfilled. Ever since I have been ill, I have longed and longed for some palpable disease, no matter how conventionally dreadful a label it might have, but I was always driven back to stagger alone under the monstrous mass of subjective sensations, which that sympathetic being "the medical man" had no higher inspiration than to assure me I was personally responsible for, washing his hands of me with a graceful complacency under my very nose. Dr. Torry was the only man who ever treated me like a rational being, who did not assume, because I was victim to many pains, that I was, of necessity, an arrested mental development too.

Notwithstanding all the happiness and comfort here, I have been going downhill at a steady trot; so they sent for Sir Andrew Clark four days ago, and the blessed being has endowed me not only with cardiac complications, but says that a lump that I have had in one of my breasts for three months, which has given me a great deal of pain, is a tumour, that nothing can be done for me but to alleviate pain, that it is only a question of time, etc. This with a delicate embroidery of "the most distressing case of nervous hyperaesthesia" added to a spinal neurosis that has taken me off my legs for seven years; with attacks of rheumatic gout in my stomach for the last twenty, ought to satisfy the most inflated pathologic vanity. It is decidedly indecent to catalogue oneself in this way, but I put it down in a scientific spirit, to show that though I have no productive worth, I have a certain value as an indestructible quantity.

February 2nd [1892]

This long slow dying is no doubt instructive, but it is disappointingly free from excitements: "naturalness" being carried to its supreme expression. One sloughs off the activities one by one, and never knows that they're gone, until one suddenly finds that the months have slipped away and the sofa will never more be laid upon, the morning paper read, or the loss of the new book regretted; one revolves with equal content within the narrowing circle until the vanishing point is reached, I suppose.

Vanity, however, maintains its undisputed sway, and I take satisfaction in feeling as much myself as ever, perhaps simply a more concentrated essence in this curtailment. If I could concern myself about the fate of my soul, it would give doubtless a savor of uncertainty to the fleeting moments, but I never felt so absolutely uninterested in the poor, shabby, old thing. The fact is, I have been dead so long and it has been simply such a grim shoving of the hours behind me as I faced a ceaseless possible horror, since that hideous summer of '78, when I went down to the deep sea, its dark waters closed over me and I knew neither hope nor peace; that now it's only the shrivelling of an empty pea pod that has to be completed.

A little while ago we had rather an amusing episode with the kind and usually understanding Tuckey,[2] who was led away into assuring me that I should live a good bit still—I was terribly shocked and when he saw the havoc that he wrought, he reassuringly said: "but you'll be comfortable, too," at which I exclaimed: "Oh I don't care about that, but boo-hoo, it's so *inconvenient!*" and the poor man burst into a roar of laughter. I was glad afterwards that it happened, as I was taken quite by surprise, and was able to test the sincerity of my mortuary inclinations. I have always *thought* that I wanted to die, but I felt quite uncertain as to what my muscular demonstrations might be at the moment of transition, for I occasionally have a quiver as of an expected dentistical wrench when I fancy the actual moment. But my substance seemed equally outraged with my mind at Tuckey's dictum, so mayhap I shall be able to maintain a calm befitting so sublimated a spirit!— at any rate there is no humbuggy "strength of mind" about it, 'tis simply physical debility, 'twould be such a bore to be perturbed.

March 4th [1892]

I am being ground slowly on the grim grindstone of physical pain, and on two nights I had almost asked for K.'s lethal dose, but one steps hesitantly along such unaccustomed ways and endures from second to second; and I feel sure that it can't be possible but what the bewildered little hammer that keeps me going will very shortly see the decency of ending his distracted career; however this may be, physical pain however great ends in itself and falls away like dry husks from the mind, whilst moral discords and nervous horrors sear the soul. These last, Katharine has completely under the control of her rhythmic hand, so I go no longer in dread. Oh the wonderful moment when I felt myself floated for the first time into the deep sea of divine *cessation,* and saw all the dear old mysteries and miracles vanish into vapour! That first experience doesn't repeat itself, fortunately, for it might become a seduction.

Katharine can't help it, she's made that way, a simple embodiment of Health, as Baldwin called her, "the New England Professor of doing things."

---

[2]Dr. C. Lloyd Tuckey, a British pioneer of hypnosis therapy.

Final Entry by Katharine P. Loring

All through Saturday the 5th and even in the night, Alice was making sentences. One of the last things she said to me was to make a correction in the sentence of March 4th "moral discords and nervous horrors."

This dictation of March 4th was rushing about in her brain all day, and although she was very weak and it tired her much to dictate, she could not get her head quiet until she had had it written: then she was relieved and I finished Miss Woolson's story of "Dorothy" to her.

K. P. L.

Questions for *The Diary* of Alice James

1.   In a journal entry (not reprinted here), Alice James writes, after reading George Eliot's[3] *Letters and Journals,* that she is disgusted by Eliot's "moaning" about her physical ailments; instead, she suggests, Eliot might have told "what armour she had forged against them." What armor—what defenses— does James forge against her own lifelong physical pain?

2.   On October 26, 1890, James describes the first nervous breakdown she suffered more than twenty years before. In what ways does she make the experience vivid again, after so many years? (You might want to compare her experience to that of the narrator in the short story "The Yellow Wallpaper," on pages 179–191)

---

[3]The British novelist George Eliot, born Mary Ann Evans (1819–1880).

Sigmund Freud (1856–1939)

Sigmund Freud was born in Moravia, Czechoslovakia, and lived most of his life in Vienna, Austria. He received his medical degree from the University of Vienna in 1881 and began specializing in the treatment of nervous diseases. In collaboration with Dr. Joseph Breuer, a well-known Viennese physician, Freud started experimenting with hypnosis for the treatment of hysteria. In 1895, he and Breuer published *Studies on Hysteria,* which marks the beginning of psychoanalysis with the theory that the symptoms of hysterical patients are directly linked to earlier emotional traumas and represent pent-up emotional energy. Freud later replaced hypnosis with a technique called free association, and went on to revise and refine his revolutionary theories on the human mind in numerous books and papers that have been collected into the 23 volumes that comprise *The Complete Psychological Works of Sigmund Freud.* Freudian theory has greatly influenced not only psychology, but literature, anthropology, education, and art as well.

A heavy cigar smoker, Freud developed cancer of the jaw in 1923, and he underwent untold suffering and thirty-three operations before the disease killed him some sixteen years later. When the Nazis occupied Austria in 1938, Freud was forced to flee to London, where he died the following year.

Although Freud's private notebooks have not been published, we can see how those notebooks provided material for his published work, as in this excerpt—along with the footnotes Freud added later—from *The Interpretation of Dreams* (1900).

From *The Interpretation of Dreams*

. . . . Many people, therefore, who love their brothers and sisters and would feel bereaved if they were to die, harbour evil wishes against them in their unconscious, dating from earlier times; and these are capable of being realized in dreams.

It is of quite particular interest, however, to observe the behaviour of small children up to the age of two or three or a little older towards their younger brothers and sisters. Here, for instance, was a child who had so far been the only one; and now he was told that the stork had brought a new baby. He looked the new arrival up and down and then declared decisively: "The stork can take him away again!"[1] I am quite seriously of the opinion that a child can form a just estimate of the set-back he has to expect at the hands of the little stranger. A lady of my acquaintance, who is on very good terms to-day with a sister four years her junior, tells me that she greeted the news of her first arrival with this qualification: "But all the same I shan't give her my red cap." Even if a child only comes to realize the situation later on, his hostility will date from that moment. I know of a case in which a little girl of less than three tried to strangle an infant in its cradle because she felt that its continued presence boded her no good. Children at that time of life are capable of jealousy of any degree of intensity and obviousness. Again, if it should happen that the baby sister does in fact disappear after a short while, the elder child will find the whole affection of the household once more concentrated upon himself. If after that the stork should bring yet another baby, it seems only logical that the little favourite should nourish a wish that his new competitor may meet with the same fate as the earlier one, so that he himself may be as happy as he was originally and during the interval.[2] Normally, of course, this attitude of a child towards a younger brother or sister is a simple function of the difference between their ages. Where the gap in time is sufficiently long, an elder girl will already begin to feel the stirring of her maternal instincts toward the helpless newborn baby.

Hostile feelings towards brothers and sisters must be far more frequent in childhood than the unseeing eye of the adult observer can perceive.[3]

In the case of my own children, who followed each other in rapid succession, I neglected the opportunity of carrying out observations of this kind; but I am now making up for this neglect by observing a small nephew, whose autocratic rule was upset, after lasting for fifteen months, by the appearance of a female rival. I am told, it is true, that the young man behaves in the most chivalrous manner to his little sister, that he kisses her hand and

---

[1] [*Footnote added* 1909:] The three-and-a-half-year-old Hans (whose phobia was the subject of . . . analysis) exclaimed shortly after the birth of a sister, while he was suffering from a feverish sore throat: "I don't *want* a baby sister!" [Freud, 1909*b*, Section I.] During his neurosis eighteen months later he frankly confessed to a wish that his mother might drop the baby into the bath so that she would die. [Ibid., Section II (April 11).] At the same time, Hans was a good-natured and affectionate child, who soon grew fond of this same sister and particularly enjoyed taking her under his wing.

[2] [*Footnote added* 1914:] Deaths that are experienced in this way in childhood may quickly be forgotten in the family; but psycho-analytic research shows that they have a very important influence on subsequent neuroses.

[3] [*Footnote added* 1914:] Since this was written, a large number of observations have been made and recorded in the literature of psycho-analysis upon the originally hostile attitude of children towards their brothers and sisters and one of their parents. The [Swiss] author and poet Spitteler has given us a particularly genuine and naïve account of this childish attitude, derived from his own childhood [1914, 40]: "Moreover there was a second Adolf there: a little creature who they alleged was my brother, though I could not see what use he was and still less why they made as much fuss of him as of me myself. I was sufficient so far as I was concerned; why should I want a brother? And he was not merely useless, he was positively in the way. When I pestered my grandmother, he wanted to pester her too. When I was taken out in the perambulator, he sat opposite to me and took up half the space, so that we were bound to kick each other with our feet."

strokes her; but I have been able to convince myself that even before the end of his second year he made use of his powers of speech for the purpose of criticizing someone whom he could not fail to regard as superfluous. Whenever the conversation touched upon her he used to intervene in it and exclaim petulantly: "Too 'ickle! too 'ickle!" During the last few months the baby's growth has made enough progress to place her beyond this particular ground for contempt, and the little boy has found a different basis for his assertion that she does not deserve so much attention: at every suitable opportunity he draws attention to the fact that she has no teeth.[4] We all of us recollect how the eldest girl of another of my sisters, who was then a child of six, spent half an hour in insisting upon each of her aunts in succession agreeing with her: "Lucie can't understand that yet, can she?" she kept asking. Lucie was her rival—two and a half years her junior.

In none of my women patients, to take an example, have I failed to come upon this dream of the death of a brother or sister, which tallies with an increase in hostility. I have only found a single exception; and it was easy to interpret this as a confirmation of the rule. On one occasion during an analytic session I was explaining this subject to a lady, since in view of her symptom its discussion seemed to me relevant. To my astonishment she replied that she had never had such a dream. Another dream, however, occurred to her, which ostensibly had no connection with the topic—a dream which she had first dreamt when she was four years old and at that time the youngest of the family, and which she had dreamt repeatedly since: *A whole crowd of children—all her brothers, sisters and cousins of both sexes—were romping in a field. Suddenly they all grew wings, flew away and disappeared.* She had no idea what this dream meant; but it is not hard to recognize that in its original form it had been a dream of the death of all her brothers and sisters, and had been only slightly influenced by the censorship. I may venture to suggest the following analysis. On the occasion of the death of one of this crowd of children (in this instance the children of two brothers had been brought up together as a single family) the dreamer, not yet four years old at the time, must have asked some wise grown-up person what became of children when they were dead. The reply must have been: "They grow wings and turn into little angels." In the dream which followed upon this piece of information all the dreamer's brothers and sisters had wings like angels and—which is the main point—flew away. Our little baby-killer was left alone, strange to say: the only survivor of the whole crowd! We can hardly be wrong in supposing that the fact of the children romping in a *field* before flying away points to butterflies. It is as though the child was led by the same chain of thought as the peoples of antiquity to picture the soul as having a butterfly's wings.

At this point someone will perhaps interrupt: "Granted that children have hostile impulses towards their brothers and sisters, how can a child's mind

_____

[4][*Footnote added* 1909:] Little Hans, when he was three and a half, gave vent to a crushing criticism of his sister in the same words. It was because of her lack of teeth, he supposed, that she was unable to talk. [Freud, 1909*b*, Section I.]

reach such a pitch of depravity as to wish for the *death* of his rivals or of playmates stronger than himself, as though the death penalty were the only punishment for every crime?" Anyone who talks like this has failed to bear in mind that a child's idea of being "dead" has nothing much in common with ours apart from the word. Children know nothing of the horrors of corruption, of freezing in the ice-cold grave, of the terrors of eternal noth-ingness—ideas which grown-up people find it so hard to tolerate, as is proved by all the myths of a future life. The fear of death has no meaning to a child; hence it is that he will play with the dreadful word and use it as a threat against a playmate: "If you do that again, you'll die, like Franz!" Meanwhile the poor mother gives a shudder and remembers, perhaps, that the greater half of the human race fail to survive their childhood years. It was actually possible for a child, who was over eight years old at the time, coming home from a visit to the Natural History Museum, to say to his mother: "I'm so fond of you, Mummy: when you die I'll have you stuffed and I'll keep you in this room, so that I can see you *all* the time." So little resemblance is there between a child's idea of being dead and our own![5]

To children, who, moreover, are spared the sight of the scenes of suffering which precede death, being "dead" means approximately the same as being "gone"—not troubling the survivors any longer. A child makes no distinc-tion as to how this absence is brought about: whether it is due to a journey, to a dismissal, to an estrangement, or to death.[6] If, during a child's prehis-toric epoch, his nurse has been dismissed, and if soon afterwards his mother has died, the two events are superimposed on each other in a single series in his memory as revealed in analysis. When people are absent, children do not miss them with any great intensity; many mothers have learnt this to their sorrow when, after being away from home for some weeks on a summer holiday, they are met on their return by the news that the children have not once asked after their mummy. If their mother does actually make the jour-ney to that "undiscover'd country, from whose bourn no traveller returns," children seem at first to have forgotten her, and it is only later on that they begin to call their dead mother to mind.

Thus if a child has reasons for wishing the absence of another, there is

---

[5][*Footnote added* 1909:] I was astonished to hear a highly intelligent boy of ten remark after the sudden death of his father: "I know father's dead, but what I can't understand is why he doesn't come home to supper."—[*Added* 1919:] Further material on this subject will be found in the first [seven] volumes of the periodical *Imago* [1912–21], under the standing rubric of *Vom wahren Wesen der Kinderseele* [The True Nature of the Child Mind], edited by Frau Dr. H. von Hug-Hellmuth.

[6][*Footnote added* 1919:] An observation made by a parent who had a knowledge of psycho-analysis caught the actual moment at which his highly intelligent four-year-old daughter perceived the distinction between being "gone" and being "dead." The little girl had been troublesome at meal-time and noticed that one of the maids at the pension where they were staying was looking at her askance. "I wish Josefine was dead," was the child's comment to her father. "Why dead?" enquired her father soothingly; "wouldn't it do if she went away?" "No," replied the child; "then she'd come back again." The unbounded self-love (the narcissism) of children regards any interference as an act of *lèse majesté*; and their feelings demand (like the Draconian code) that any such crime shall receive the one form of punishment which admits of no degrees.

nothing to restrain him from giving his wish the form of the other child being dead. And the psychical reaction to dreams containing death-wishes proves that, in spite of the different content of these wishes in the case of children, they are nevertheless in some way or other the same as wishes expressed in the same terms by adults . . .

Questions for *The Interpretation of Dreams*

1.   Can you recall a dream or an incident from your childhood that illustrates Freud's observations about occasional feelings of hostility among young siblings?

2.   How does each of the footnotes he added to this portion of *The Interpretation of Dreams* lend additional support to Freud's interpretations?

Franz Kafka (1883–1924)

Born in Prague, Bohemia (now Czechoslovakia), Franz Kafka suffered from a profound feeling of inferiority to his extrovert father, and this self-doubt and anxiety dominated his life as well as his writing. His long and tormented love affair with Felice Bauer never led to marriage; he was often preoccupied with suicide; and his poor health culminated in the tuberculosis that killed him.

As the introduction to this chapter points out, Kafka worked as a civil servant by day and filled his evenings writing in his journal and composing stories about alienation, exile, fear, and failure, of which "The Metamorphosis" (1915), the exquisite and moving novella reprinted in Chapter 4, is representative. In fact, Kafka's sense of inadequacy was so intense that he never completed or published his three novels, *Amerika* (1927), *The Trial* (1925), and *The Castle* (1930). Although Kafka left instructions that his manuscripts were to be burned after his death, most of his books were published posthumously by his friend and literary executor, Max Brod.

Despite the unhappy details of Kafka's life, there were also occasions that gave him joy—traveling, attending the theater, talking with friends. These pleasurable moments, though largely missing from Kafka's fiction, can be found intermittently in his diaries, alongside the more frequent irritations and oppressions to which most diarists give vent in their private writing.

From *The Diaries* of Franz Kafka

Translated by Joseph Kresh

——— From *Travel Diaries*, Aug.–Sept. 1911 ———

It is always pleasant to remember walks in parks: one's joy that the day was still so light, watching out that it didn't get dark suddenly—this and fatigue governed one's manner of walking and looking about. The automobiles pursuing their rigid course along the wide, smooth streets. In the little garden restaurant, the red-uniformed band, unheard amidst the noise of the automobiles, laboring at its instruments for the entertainment of those in its immediate vicinity only. Parisians never previously seen walking hand in hand. Men in shirt sleeves, with their families, in the semidarkness under the trees amid the flower beds, notwithstanding the "keep off" signs. There the absence of Jews was most noticeable. Looking back at the tiny train, which seemed to have rolled off a merry-go-round and puffed away. The path to the lake of the Bois de Boulogne. My most vivid recollection of the first sight of the lake is the bent back of a man stooping down to us under the canopy of our boat to give us tickets. Probably because of my anxiety about the tickets and my inability to make the man explain whether the boat went around the lake or across to the island, and whether it stopped off anywhere. And for this reason I was so taken by him that I often see him, with equal vividness, bent all by himself over the lake without there being any boat. A lot of people in summer clothes on the dock. Boats with unskilful rowers in them. The low bank of the lake, it had no railing. A slow trip, reminding me of walks I used to take alone every Sunday several years ago. Lifting our feet out of the water in the bottom of the boat. The other passengers' astonishment, when they heard our Czech, at finding themselves in the same boat with foreigners such as we were. A lot of people on the slopes of the western bank, canes planted in the ground, outspread newspapers, a man and his daughters flat in the grass, some laughter, the low eastern bank; the paths bounded by a low fence of curving sticks linked together, to keep the lap dogs off the lawns, something we did away with long ago back home; a stray dog was running across the meadow; rowers toiling solemnly at their oars, a girl in their heavy boat. I left Max[1] over his grenadine, looking particularly lonely in the shadow at the edge of the half-empty garden café past which went a street that was intersected as if by chance by another street unknown to me. Automobiles and carriages drove out from the shadowy crossing into even more desolate-looking regions. Saw a large iron fence that was probably a part of the food tax bureau; it was open, however, and everyone could go through. Nearby you saw the glaring light of Luna Park, which only added to the twilight confusion. So much light and so empty. I stumbled perhaps five times on the way to Luna Park and back to Max.

[December 3, 1911]

. . . The unhappiness of the bachelor, whether seeming or actual, is so easily guessed at by the world around him that he will curse his decision, at least if he has remained a bachelor because of the delight he takes in secrecy. He walks around with his coat buttoned, his hands in the upper pockets of his jacket, his arms akimbo, his hat pulled down over his eyes, a false smile that has become natural to him is supposed to shield his mouth as his glasses do his eyes, his trousers are tighter than seem proper for his thin legs. But everyone knows his condition, can detail his sufferings. A cold breeze breathes upon him from within and he gazes inward with the even sadder half of his

---

[1] Max Brod.

double face. He moves incessantly, but with predictable regularity, from one apartment to another. The farther he moves away from the living, for whom he must still—and this is the worst mockery—work like a conscious slave who dare not express his consciousness, so much the smaller a space is considered sufficient for him. While it is death that must still strike down the others, though they may have spent all their lives in a sickbed—for even though they would have gone down by themselves long ago from their own weakness, they nevertheless hold fast to their loving, very healthy relatives by blood and marriage—he, this bachelor, still in the midst of life, apparently of his own free will resigns himself to an ever smaller space, and when he dies the coffin is exactly right for him.

[December 26, 1911]

It is unpleasant to listen to Father talk with incessant insinuations about the good fortune of people today and especially of his children, about the sufferings he had to endure in his youth. No one denies that for years, as a result of insufficient winter clothing, he had open sores on his legs, that he often went hungry, that when he was only ten he had to push a cart through the villages, even in winter and very early in the morning—but, and this is something he will not understand, these facts, taken together with the further fact that I have not gone through all this, by no means lead to the conclusion that I have been happier than he, that he may pride himself on these sores on his legs, which is something he assumes and asserts from the very beginning, that I cannot appreciate his past sufferings, and that, finally, just because I have not gone through the same sufferings I must be endlessly grateful to him. How gladly I would listen if he would talk on about his youth and parents, but to hear all this in a boastful and quarrelsome tone is torment. Over and over again he claps his hands together: "Who can understand that today! What do the children know! No one has gone through that! Does a child understand that today!" He spoke again in the same way today to Aunt Julie, who was visiting us. She too has the huge face of all Father's relatives. There is something wrong and somewhat disturbing about the set or color of her eyes. At the age of ten she was hired out as a cook. In a skimpy wet skirt, in the severe cold, she had to run out for something, the skin on her legs cracked, the skimpy skirt froze and it was only that evening, in bed, that it dried.

[January 19, 1914]

Anxiety alternating with self-assurance at the office. Otherwise more confident. Great antipathy to "Metamorphosis." Unreadable ending. Imperfect almost to its very marrow. It would have turned out much better if I had not been interrupted at the time by the business trip.

[*March 9, 1914*]

I shall never forget F.[2] in this place, therefore shan't marry. Is that definite?

Yes, that much I can judge of: I am almost thirty-one years old, have known F. for almost two years, must therefore have some perspective by now. Besides, my way of life here is such that I can't forget, even if F. didn't have such significance for me. The uniformity, regularity, comfort and dependence of my way of life keep me unresistingly fixed wherever I happen to be. Moreover, I have a more than ordinary inclination toward a comfortable and dependent life, and so even strengthen everything that is pernicious to me. Finally, I am getting older, any change becomes more and more difficult. But in all this I foresee a great misfortune for myself, one without end and without hope; I should be dragging through the years up the ladder of my job, growing ever sadder and more alone as long as I could endure it at all.

But you wanted that sort of life for yourself, didn't you?

An official's life could benefit me if I were married. It would in every way be a support to me against society, against my wife, against writing, without demanding too many sacrifices, and without on the other hand degenerating into indolence and dependence, for as a married man I should not have to fear that. But I cannot live out such a life as a bachelor.

But you could have married, couldn't you?

I couldn't marry then; everything in me revolted against it, much as I always loved F. It was chiefly concern over my literary work that prevented me, for I thought marriage would jeopardize it. I may have been right, but in any case it is destroyed by my present bachelor's life. I have written nothing for a year, nor shall I be able to write anything in the future; in my head there is and remains the one single thought, and I am devoured by it. I wasn't able to consider it all at the time. Moreover, as a result of my dependence, which is at least encouraged by this way of life, I approach everything hesitantly and complete nothing at the first stroke. That was what happened here too. . . .

[*May 4, 1915*]

In a better state because I read Strindberg[3] *(Separated)*. I don't read him to read him, but rather to lie on his breast. He holds me on his left arm like a child. I sit there like a man on a statue. Ten times I almost slip off, but at the eleventh attempt I sit there firmly, feel secure, and have a wide view.

---

[2]F.: Felice Bauer, a career woman from Berlin to whom Kafka twice became engaged. During the five years of their courtship, Kafka wrote to Felice almost daily, sometimes several times a day.
[3]August Strindberg (1849–1912): Swedish playwright and novelist.

Questions for *The Diaries* of Franz Kafka

1.   What point or points is Kafka arguing in his dialogue with himself about Felice?

2.   Based on these excerpts, discuss Kafka's ambivalence toward marriage: What themes run through his portrayals of the life of a son, a bachelor, and a husband?

3.   In October 1914 Kafka writes, "Leafed through the diary a little. Got a kind of inkling of the way a life like this is constituted." On the basis of the excerpts printed here, what observations can you make about the writer and his life?

Martha Graham (1894–   )

One of three daughters of a Philadelphia physician, Martha Graham was first inspired to dance when she was taken to see the Ruth St. Denis dance troupe. In 1916, at twenty-two—a ripe old age to embark on such a career—she entered the dance school run by St. Denis and her husband, Ted Shawn, in California. Despite her age and lack of training, Graham soon was invited to dance professionally with the Denishawn company. In 1929 she started her own company, which continues to this day to perform her choreography. Graham's works are characteristically dramatic narratives that explore the psychic quests of the great heroines of myth and history.

Graham might justifiably be called the most powerful creative force in the history of modern dance. From the pages of her notebooks—those hurried and often cryptic notes for the dances she created—one sees questions, meditations, and stage directions taking shape and animation before our eyes.

From *The Notebooks* of Martha Graham

From *The Bronzeless Net*

It seems to me that the only point of writing even a so-called autobiography—& I believe any/every autobiography can only be "so-called"—is to point a way to others who follow—

Purgation is something other than that—

Laughing—making fun of mistakes—is also something other—

The only justification for the pain & embarrassment of self-revealment is to point a way—perhaps to point a way from—rather than a way toward—

Too often it is a glorification of the incident surrounding the personal self & as such a personal appeasement of the Furies—

There is a degree of comfort—complacent—in an identification with another's predicament—

The result is negative—as all such comfort is—its tendency is to lull—rather than stimulate—to justify rather than face—to accept as reality—as causation—

Satan
    Azazel
    adversary
    Satanial
    accuser
    destroyer
    Prince of the power of the air
    Great Tempter

"God created man to be immortal, and made him to be an image of his
own eternity. Nevertheless thru envy of the devil came death into the
world: and they that do hold of his side do find it"
    Wisdom of Solomon—Man & his Gods—Homer Smith—
    Little Brown

"Movement never lies—"
                                       person   or 5
That was rather strong doctrine for a small (one) of four—

"She carries her head & moves her hands in a strange way"

The small person of 4 or 5 was not listening—
But she was—

The next time the grownup young lady who "carries her head in a strange
way" came to call, (the house) the small person of 4 or 5 circled around
her, looking, wondering, <u>pondering</u>—imitating—experimenting—
grotesquely, lavishly, intensively—
The result in the small assembly was mystification, amusement,
gradually discomfort—& ultimately it all ended in being lured to
"Lilywhite's Party"—which it took time to fathom meant—"bed"—
nothing more—

"Movement never lies—" at 4 or 5 that was an admonition—"Lie" in
a Presbyterian household was and still is a clanging word which sets
whispering all the little fluttering guilts which seek to become consumed
in the flame of one's conscience—

From *Center of the Hurricane*

People say—
How did you begin?
Well—that is the question
And who knows—
Not I—

How does it all begin?
I suppose it never begins, it just continues—
Life—
generations
Dancing—

One takes it up when one arrives with all the richness of blood as one
takes up one's ancestral physical heritage—
Of course, there must be strength of bone & muscle & heart & faith—
but one takes up at the time the necessity of one's heritage & in time it
may become one's "calling," one's "destiny," one's "fame"—
one's "immortality"—

I am a thief—and I am not ashamed. I steal from the best wherever
it happens to me—Plato—Picasso—Bertram Ross—the members
of my company never show me anything—except you expect me to
steal it—

I am a thief—
and I glory in it—
I steal from the present and from the glorious past—and I stand in the
dark of the future as a glorying & joyous thief—There are so many
wonderful things of the imagination to pilfer—so I stand accused—
I am a thief—but with this reservation—I think I know the value of
that I steal & treasure it for all time—not as a possession but as a
heritage & as legacy—

From *Voyage*

The Traveler's journey to god is complete when he retains knowledge of
Him—"Illumination," in the language of European mystics. The point at
which this is reached is called The Tavern, the resting place along
the road . . .

Image—   *Voyage*
  woman seated—   *Bob?*
    wide skirt making cavern of legs—
    man kneeling between her wide knees—
    Her feet clasp about him & he falls backward—down steps as
    she rises—

                Voyage
Image—   *Stuart*
  man & woman with crossed daggers—

Image—
    white silk curtain—as at window—
    lights of sunset thrown on it—
    occasionally it blows out as in a breeze—
    perhaps at the end when it is apparent sun has set—color gone—
       woman in silhouette as watching—waiting—
—   or
    pieces of curtain come in slowly as in Picasso painting—to fit
    into design behind woman during muezzin—
    Then she dances dramatically tragically, beautifully to end of Day—
    colors fly out & night begins—
    (people could walk colors in—especially if it is carnival time)

Image—
    Woman   & man   seated
     ↑   hands joined   ↑
    carries a dagger   sword between legs
                          rapier
    Valley of the Sphinx—
each section a vision of the race memory—

a participation in a state of "blessed madness" in the ritual of
anonymity, the race memory of ritualistic things.
    The Young Moon—

The drama is in the strangeness of meetings in the midst of the
rituals—the "shock of recognition—"

How one arrives at the dominion ruled by the "White Goddess"—
    she of inspiration—
    she the exciter of the Muse—
    She the Muse herself,
      who rules all expression—

The passage of sunset into night—with its moon-rise, moon high,
moon set, deep dark, dawn,—as the souls rite of passage from the
death of color into birth of new color—as self-examination—

Questions for *The Notebooks* of Martha Graham

1.   What, in Graham's opinion, is the point of writing an autobiography?
What other reasons can you give for writing one's autobiography?

2.   Can you describe Graham's working methods? How does she begin
creating her dances?

Joan Didion (1934–   )

A native of Sacramento, California, Joan Didion received her B.A. from the University of California and spent ten years with *Vogue* magazine, where she started as a copywriter and worked her way up to associate feature editor. Since 1963, Didion has published four novels (*Run River*, 1963; *Play It as It Lays*, 1970; *A Book of Common Prayer*, 1977; and *Democracy*, 1984), two collections of essays (*Slouching Towards Bethlehem*, 1968; *The White Album*, 1979), a work of nonfiction (*Salvador*, 1983), as well as short stories, articles, reviews, and screenplays.

Known for her precise, elegant, controlled prose, Didion revises her writing relentlessly. Central to her work—whether set in California or the troubled countries of Central America and Southeast Asia—is the theme of social disorder and disintegration. Like the poet W. B. Yeats, whom she quotes in *Slouching Towards Bethlehem*, Didion seems to believe that "things fall apart; the center cannot hold; / Mere anarchy is loosed upon the world."

Los Angeles Notebook

There is something uneasy in the Los Angeles air this afternoon, some unnatural stillness, some tension. What it means is that tonight a Santa Ana will begin to blow, a hot wind from the northeast whining down through the Cajon and San Gorgonio Passes, blowing up sandstorms out along Route 66, drying the hills and the nerves to the flash point. For a few days now we will see smoke back in the canyons, and hear sirens in the night. I have neither heard nor read that a Santa Ana is due, but I know it, and almost everyone I have seen today knows it too. We know it because we feel it. The baby frets. The maid sulks. I rekindle a waning argument with the telephone company, then cut my losses and lie down, given over to whatever it is in the air. To live with the Santa Ana is to accept, consciously or unconsciously, a deeply mechanistic view of human behavior.

I recall being told, when I first moved to Los Angeles and was living on an isolated beach, that the Indians would throw themselves into the sea when the bad wind blew. I could see why. The Pacific turned ominously glossy during a Santa Ana period, and one woke in the night troubled not only by the peacocks screaming in the olive trees but by the eerie absence of surf. The heat was surreal. The sky had a yellow cast, the kind of light sometimes called "earthquake weather." My only neighbor would not come out of her house for days, and there were no lights at night, and her husband roamed the place with a machete. One day he would tell me that he had heard a trespasser, the next a rattlesnake.

"On nights like that," Raymond Chandler once wrote about the Santa Ana, "every booze party ends in a fight. Meek little wives feel the edge of the carving knife and study their husbands' necks. Anything can happen." That was the kind of wind it was. I did not know then that there was any basis for the effect it had on all of us, but it turns out to be another of those cases in which science bears out folk wisdom. The Santa Ana, which is named for one of the canyons it rushes through, is a *foehn* wind, like the *foehn* of Austria and Switzerland and the *hamsin* of Israel. There are a number of persistent malevolent winds, perhaps the best known of which are the mistral of France and the Mediterranean sirocco, but a *foehn* wind has distinct characteristics: it occurs on the leeward slope of a mountain range and, although the air begins as a cold mass, it is warmed as it comes down the mountain and appears finally as a hot dry wind. Whenever and wherever a *foehn* blows, doctors hear about headaches and nausea and allergies, about "nervousness," about "depression." In Los Angeles some teachers do not attempt to conduct formal classes during a Santa Ana, because the children become unmanageable. In Switzerland the suicide rate goes up during the *foehn*, and in the courts of some Swiss cantons the wind is considered a mitigating circumstance for crime. Surgeons are said to watch the wind, because blood does not clot normally during a *foehn*. A few years ago an Israeli physicist discovered that not only during such winds, but for the ten or twelve hours which precede them, the air carries an unusually high ratio of positive to negative ions. No one seems to know exactly why that should be; some talk about friction and others suggest solar disturbances. In any case the positive ions are there, and what an excess of positive ions does, in the simplest terms, is make people unhappy. One cannot get much more mechanistic than that.

Easterners commonly complain that there is no "weather" at all in Southern California, that the days and the seasons slip by relentlessly, numbingly bland. That is quite misleading. In fact the climate is characterized by infrequent but violent extremes: two periods of torrential subtropical rains which continue for weeks and wash out the hills and send subdivisions sliding toward the sea; about twenty scattered days a year of the Santa Ana, which, with its incendiary dryness, invariably means fire. At the first prediction of a Santa Ana, the Forest Service flies men and equipment from northern California into the southern forests, and the Los Angeles Fire Department cancels its ordinary non-firefighting routines. The Santa Ana caused Malibu to burn the way it did in 1956, and Bel Air in 1961, and Santa Barbara in 1964. In the winter of 1966–67 eleven men were killed fighting a Santa Ana fire that spread through the San Gabriel Mountains.

Just to watch the front-page news out of Los Angeles during a Santa Ana is to get very close to what it is about the place. The longest Santa Ana period in recent years was in 1957, and it lasted not the usual three or four days but fourteen days, from November 21 until December 4. On the first day 25,000 acres of the San Gabriel Mountains were burning, with gusts reaching 100 miles an hour. In town, the wind reached Force 12, or hurricane force, on the Beaufort Scale; oil derricks were toppled and people ordered off the downtown streets to avoid injury from flying objects. On November 22 the fire in the San Gabriels was out of control. On November 24 six people were killed in automobile accidents, and by the end of the week the Los Angeles *Times* was keeping a box score of traffic deaths. On November 26 a prominent Pasadena attorney, depressed about money, shot and killed his wife, their two sons, and himself. On November 27 a South Gate divorcee, twenty-two, was murdered and thrown from a moving car. On November 30 the San Gabriel fire was still out of control, and the wind in town was blowing eighty miles an hour. On the first day of December four people died violently, and on the third the wind began to break.

It is hard for people who have not lived in Los Angeles to realize how radically the Santa Ana figures in the local imagination. The city burning is Los Angeles's deepest image of itself: Nathanael West perceived that, in *The Day of the Locust*; and at the time of the 1965 Watts riot what struck the imagination most indelibly were the fires. For days one could drive the Harbor Freeway and see the city on fire, just as we had always known it would be in the end. Los Angeles weather is the weather of catastrophe, of apocalypse, and, just as the reliably long and bitter winters of New England determine the way life is lived there, so the violence and the unpredictability of the Santa Ana affect the entire quality of life in Los Angeles, accentuate its impermanence, its unreliability. The wind shows us how close to the edge we are.

2

"Here's why I'm on the beeper, Ron," said the telephone voice on the all-night radio show. "I just want to say that this *Sex for the Secretary* creature—whatever her name is—certainly isn't contributing anything to the morals in this country. It's pathetic. Statistics *show*."

"It's *Sex and the Office*, honey," the disc jockey said. "That's the title. By Helen Gurley Brown. Statistics show what?"

"I haven't got them right here at my fingertips, naturally. But they *show*."

"I'd be interested in hearing them. Be constructive, you Night Owls."

"All right, let's take *one* statistic," the voice said, truculent now. "Maybe I haven't read the book, but what's this business she recommends about *going out with married men for lunch?*"

So it went, from midnight until 5 a.m., interrupted by records and by occasional calls debating whether or not a rattlesnake can swim. Misinformation about rattlesnakes is a leitmotiv of the insomniac imagination in Los Angeles. Toward 2 a.m. a man from "out Tarzana way" called to protest. "The Night Owls who called earlier must have been thinking about, uh, *The Man in the Gray Flannel Suit* or some other book," he said, "because Helen's one of the few authors trying to tell us what's really going *on*. Hefner's another, and he's also controversial, working in, uh, another area."

An old man, after testifying that he "personally" had seen a swimming rattlesnake, in the Delta-Mendota Canal, urged "moderation" on the Helen Gurley Brown question. "We shouldn't get on the beeper to call things pornographic before we've read them," he complained, pronouncing it porn-ee-oh-graphic. "I say, get the book. Give it a chance." The original *provocateur* called back to agree that she would get the book. "And then I'll burn it," she added.

"Book burner, eh?" laughed the disc jockey good-naturedly.

"I wish they still burned witches," she hissed.

$$\overline{3}$$

It is three o'clock on a Sunday afternoon and 105° and the air so thick with smog that the dusty palm trees loom up with a sudden and rather attractive mystery. I have been playing in the sprinklers with the baby and I get in the car and go to Ralph's Market on the corner of Sunset and Fuller wearing an old bikini bathing suit. That is not a very good thing to wear to the market but neither is it, at Ralph's on the corner of Sunset and Fuller, an unusual costume. Nonetheless a large woman in a cotton muumuu jams her cart into mine at the butcher counter. *"What a thing to wear to the market,"* she says in a loud but strangled voice. Everyone looks the other way and I study a plastic package of rib lamb chops and she repeats it. She follows me all over the store, to the Junior Food, to the Dairy Products, to the Mexican Delicacies, jamming my cart whenever she can. Her husband plucks at her sleeve. As I leave the checkout counter she raises her voice one last time: *"What a thing to wear to Ralph's,"* she says.

$$\overline{4}$$

A party at someone's house in Beverly Hills: a pink tent, two orchestras, a couple of French Communist directors in Cardin evening jackets, chili and hamburgers from Chasen's. The wife of an English actor sits at a table alone; she visits California rarely although her husband works here a good deal. An American who knows her slightly comes over to the table.

"Marvelous to see you here," he says.

"Is it," she says.

"How long have you been here?"

"Too long."

She takes a fresh drink from a passing waiter and smiles at her husband, who is dancing.

The American tries again. He mentions her husband.

"I hear he's marvelous in this picture."

She looks at the American for the first time. When she finally speaks she enunciates every word very clearly. "He . . . is . . . also . . . a . . . fag," she says pleasantly.

<u>5</u>

The oral history of Los Angeles is written in piano bars. "Moon River," the piano player always plays, and "Mountain Greenery." "There's a Small Hotel" and "This Is Not the First Time." People talk to each other, tell each other about their first wives and last husbands. "Stay funny," they tell each other, and "This is to die over." A construction man talks to an unemployed screenwriter who is celebrating, alone, his tenth wedding anniversary. The construction man is on a job in Montecito: "Up in Montecito," he says, "they got one square mile with 135 millionaires."

"Putrescence," the writer says.

"That's all you got to say about it?"

"Don't read me wrong, I think Santa Barbara's one of the most—Christ, *the* most—beautiful places in the world, but it's a beautiful place that contains a . . . *putrescence.* They just live on their putrescent millions."

"So give me putrescent."

"No, no," the writer says. "I just happen to think millionaires have some sort of lacking in their . . . in their elasticity."

A drunk requests "The Sweetheart of Sigma Chi." The piano player says he doesn't know it. "Where'd you learn to play the piano?" the drunk asks. "I got two degrees," the piano player says. "One in musical education." I go to a coin telephone and call a friend in New York. "Where are you?" he says. "In a piano bar in Encino," I say. "Why?" he says. "Why not," I say.

Questions for "Los Angeles Notebook"

1.   Elaborate on Didion's comment that "To live with the Santa Ana is to accept . . . a deeply mechanistic view of human behavior."

2.   Didion never states the thesis or main idea that connects the sections of "Los Angeles Notebook." What theme or themes run through the five vignettes? What does each vignette contribute to this composite portrait of the city?

3.   The final section of Didion's "Notebook" is perhaps the most elliptical in its relationship to the thesis of this selection. What do you think Didion wants to illustrate here, and what feeling or mood is she trying to capture?

READING/WRITING

In addition to using your notebook for responses to what you read, you may want to experiment with some of the subjects and structures found in the journals excerpted in this chapter. The following suggestions for writing have been prompted by these reading selections.

1. Begin compiling a "pillow book" of random impressions, like Sei Shonagon's, containing such items as observations of scenes in nature, character sketches, and lists of things that are "annoying" or "elegant" or "have lost their power." For example, take a look at the following student's list of "embarrassing things"; observe how he illustrates the abstract concept of "embarrassment" by citing concrete examples of times when he experienced this emotion:

Embarrassing Things

Cleaning up after your dog.

Getting caught staring at a cute girl.

Burping in class.

Locking yourself out of the house.

One who has just finished eating and walks around with crumbs on his face.

   I was hurrying across campus to get to my math class. It had rained heavily all that morning, so I was hopscotching my way around puddles in the pathway.
   I called to several friends ahead to wait for me, and right before I caught up to them, I came to a large puddle covering the entire path. I had to make a quick choice of either stepping into the water or jumping over it. So I jumped, wanting to seem cool because my friends were watching, but I didn't clear the puddle. Water and mud splashed everywhere, wetting my shoes, socks, and jeans, and spraying the pants of my friends as well. "Well done, Mr. Long," they said. I felt the more embarrassed because I had tried to look so casual.

                                                                          Vu Long

2. Experiment with keeping a book of daily events, as Alice James does, including, for instance, descriptions of incidents or acquaintances, social engagements, school activities—whatever occupies your day. In addition, in the manner of Pepys, record and comment on several news events of some importance.

3. Describe a dream you've had recently, including as many specific details as you can recall. Why do you think you had this dream? Try to analyze what the dream means to you.

4. Taking a leaf from Darwin's travel diary, carry your notebook outdoors and record your close observations of the animal or plant life beyond your window. Keep in mind that you needn't travel as far as South America to see exotic flora and fauna.

5. Kafka's notebooks suggest a number of journal entries: To begin with, Kafka often complains in his journal about not being able to work at home; describe what happens in your own home when you sit down to work. Or talk about how you feel when you read the work of a particular author. Or draw a portrait of "The life of a student," modeled on Kafka's description of "The life of a bachelor." Or conduct an imaginary argument with yourself, as Kafka does concerning his relationship with Felice.

6. Keep a "commonplace book." When you read a book or article that fires your imagination, jot down in your notebook whatever quotations you find useful or provocative, as Martha Graham does. Use your journal to brainstorm, or to "choreograph" an essay you'd like to write, or to experiment with ideas for poems or stories.

7. Compose a "City Notebook" of vignettes that illustrate some characteristic quality of your city or town, in the manner of Joan Didion's "Los Angeles Notebook." Do not explicitly state your thesis about your hometown, but rather dramatize your unspoken thesis in four or five brief segments, as Didion does—perhaps through dialogue, description of a scene, or narration of an incident.

   The following "New York Notebook" is an experiment with various points of view. We gave the assignment to the students in a writing class, and the results were so successful we decided to reprint as many examples as we had room for. So the "Notebook" below is actually a composite of five students' impressions of the city, with one section taken from each student's paper. Although the voices and textures of the sections are quite different, the pieces seem to fit together into a cohesive portrait.

(1)

During one of this summer's hot spells, I had the honor of riding in an unairconditioned "E" train to Manhattan. By the time the train had pulled into the Queens Plaza station, it had become jammed with people. A man dressed in Army fatigues entered the train through the center doors, and evidently noticed that there was more room in the back of the car. I followed his movements with my eyes as he made his way between the two rows of straphangers. As he brushed against the passengers, I noticed that the men instinctively checked for their wallets in the back pockets of their pants while the women drew their pocketbooks closer to themselves.

Frank Osterwald

(2)

On my way to a job interview I observed a long-legged, slim blonde strutting down Spring Street. That was no ordinary walk; that was a strut. Maybe that's why I couldn't take my eyes off her.

As she came upon the intersection and stood waiting for the light to change, a very unusual thing happened. Making her way across the street, she slipped and fell on her buns. Instead of getting up and completing her journey from one side of the street to the other, she got up and went back to where she was originally standing and started the whole evolution over again. In doing so, I guess, she erased the fall completely out of her life by retracking. I wonder how she handles bad love affairs.

Tyrone Simmons

(3)

I was walking around in my neighborhood on the Lower East Side the other day when I spotted a squirrel in a tree. I stopped a while and watched him. The little guy was munching on a nut, looking all around and stuffing it in as quick as he could.

The tree the squirrel was standing in was in the center of a small patch of grass that was still pretty green. It was one of those trees they stick in the middle of the concrete, you know, those trees you look at and say, "That's a tough tree, living in the city and all." Then you throw trash on it.

They used to have a lot of those trees in my neighborhood; then they took them all out. Now they only have them on the little lawn-type areas between the buildings in the Projects.

Soon the squirrel ran away. He had no choice, some kid had thrown a rock at him. I walked up to the kid and said, "Hey, why'd you do that? He was just eating, not bothering anyone."

The kid looked a little scared and confused. He didn't answer; he just stared at me. "Listen," I said, "I tell you what, you should be friends with these animals, you know why? Because if you're nice to them now, when they become mutants after the nuclear bomb you'll be on their side. I wouldn't want to be an enemy of no fifty-foot squirrel. Boy, they can kick your ass for sure." The kid smiled at me and walked away.

Looking back, even though I was angry with the kid for throwing the rock at the squirrel, there was one good thing that came out of the incident. I got him to smile, and he had a beautiful smile, the kind you remember.

Juan Melendez

(4)

One Saturday afternoon, while my cousin and I were cleaning out his garage, his Japanese neighbor asked if he could take a few pictures of us. We agreed and continued with the back-breaking work. After a while, curiosity made us ask him why we were such interesting subjects. The Japanese gentleman replied quietly, "My brother is thinking of moving to New York City, so we are taking pictures to send him of New Yorkers relaxing on a weekend."

Andrew Swierczewski

(5)

It's Sunday. We're gearing up for an exhausting week, and no one in my family is in the mood to cook. We decide to order Chinese food from the take-out place around the corner. By the looks of the place it seems that the whole neighborhood has had the same idea. The place is packed with familiar faces. Yet there is no conversation. One by one each person orders and waits alone in the crowd. When the order is ready each leaves without a word. Everyone is a familiar stranger.

Carol Chmulsewski

CHAPTER
3

Auto/Biography

"I cannot *write myself*," the French critic Roland Barthes insisted. "What, after all, is this 'I' who would write himself?" And yet—despite the questions all of us have about our true identities—in diverse ways and at different times in our lives, most of us *do* try to "write ourselves," in journals, letters, essays, or stories. Who has not felt the need at one time or another to consign a piece of his or her life to paper? We may like to think that we have the freedom to be the 'authors' of our own lives, but the fact is that we only have this kind of control over the events of our existence when we collect and arrange them in conversation or on paper. When the author John Cheever said, "I write to make sense of my life," he could have been speaking for many of us. Writing about our experiences makes a life teeming with events and emotions seem more manageable, less chaotic.

Writing autobiographically allows us not only to order personal experiences, but to discover their meaning. How can we comprehend all the implications of an event, an emotion, or a conversation at the same time as it is unfolding before us? The answer, Sigmund Freud argues, is that we cannot. In a number of his papers on psychoanalysis, Freud maintains that we make sense of an experience not in the heat of living it, but in the calm of *recollecting* it. His term for this psychological process is *nachträglichkeit,* a German word translated as "belatedness," "deferred action," or "deferred revision." By this term Freud suggests the way in which an individual "revises" experiences, impressions, and memories at later dates to accommodate subsequent experiences or new stages of development. Emotional shocks or traumas are especially susceptible to such repeated revisions. Consider, for instance, the young child who cannot understand the death of a parent and believes instead that this parent has simply gone away—perhaps because the child behaved badly. This early interpretation of the disturbing event will be revised as the child grows older and is able to replace the original explanation for the parent's absence with more mature understanding.

One example of the process of deferred revision can be seen in Sherwood Anderson's "Unforgotten," included in this chapter. In this autobiographical tale, the narrator presents a portrait of his father that will change quite powerfully by the end of the essay. The altered impression of the father is occasioned by a single significant event, an event that *rewrites* much of what has preceded it. Suddenly, the narrator sees his father from a new perspective, one that enables him to make sense of his father's irresponsible behavior—and to accept it. In the same way, our assessment of the significance of an event in our lives often changes as we grow older. So the person who is writing a personal narrative is never quite the same individual as the one who actually lived through the experience.

Taken together, the observations of Barthes, Cheever, and Freud point to the central problem confronting the autobiographer—namely, the varied, mysterious, and often conflicting selves that each of us calls "I." Vincent Van Gogh, painting canvas after canvas in the French countryside at Arles, wrote to his brother Theo, "If only I can manage to do a coherent whole. That is what I am trying to do." The same task presents itself when we set out to write autobiographically: we must somehow pull together the disconnected and seemingly random elements of our personalities and our lives into a "coherent whole." Unfortunately, people usually behave more erratically in life than in works of fiction; they are apt to change their minds and their opinions abruptly, often contradicting themselves both in word and deed.

What then do we mean when we speak of a person's "character" and "personality"? Our family and friends expect us to behave predictably, to act as we have in the past in similar situations. When someone breaks out of his usual pattern of behavior—the quiet, studious "type" who gets drunk at a party and capers around the room, or the normally good-natured bank teller who snaps at a customer—we say that this person is behaving "out of character." "You're acting strangely," a friend says; "you're not yourself today."

Yet to that bank teller, the fit of anger probably seems quite normal. The fact is that we present different aspects of our character to different people. Character is often a matter of what you *choose* to show the world—the stories that you elect to tell, and that vary according to the audience you are addressing at a given moment. Your parents, your husband or wife, your neighbors, your teachers, have slightly differing views of what you are "really like." The bantering tone you adopt with your closest friends, the things you choose to discuss with them, would be inappropriate in a discussion with your employer. It should come as no surprise to you that when Vincent Van Gogh (whose letters appear in this chapter) writes to his mother and sister, his literary style differs markedly from the 'sound' of his letters to his brother Theo.

How, finally, do people define themselves when composing their life stories? What do they choose to include and what do they leave out? We come into contact with so many people and situations in the course of a single day that the process of selection in autobiography may seem an impossible task. In writing or telling an autobiographical story, we attempt to find the connecting threads in the variety of experience, as well as to create a cohesive self despite inconsistencies of behavior and character. But once we have found the 'essential self' we want to write about, how do we give it shape and accent? That is, how do we weave the threads of our lives into a fabric—a framework of relationships between fibers, ideas, human beings? The autobiographer must imbue a group of experiences not only with significance but with emphasis and structure. In this sense, the autobiographical process, no less than the process of fiction-making, is one of *fabrication*. The verb "to fabricate," from the Latin *fabrica*, meaning workshop, is defined in the dictionary as both "to construct by putting together finished parts" and "to devise a deception." The autobiographer is an artisan, and the product of selection and construction, though the cloth be woven from real-life experience, is inevitably a kind of artifice.

As you will see in this chapter, people typically organize their lives on paper by focusing on what is important to them—a job, an avocation, an obsession. Charles Darwin, whose journal we looked at in the previous chapter, structures his autobiography in terms of the people and events that determined his development as a scientist, just as Sherwood Anderson concentrates on his growth as a writer. In her memoirs, entitled *The Woman Warrior*, the Chinese-American author Maxine Hong Kingston links her youthful experiences to those of the warrior-heroines she recalls from Chinese legend and from her own family history.

By the same token, as two other writers represented in this chapter demonstrate, a person need not set out to write an autobiography to produce one. In a collection of letters or essays written over an extended period of time, writers frequently return to subjects that occupy them throughout their lives. Vincent Van Gogh did not intend to write a formal autobiography, but in the last years of his life, each night after painting for some fourteen hours, he poured the story of his days into his correspondence with his beloved brother Theo. Vincent's ardent and beautifully written letters constitute a portrait of an artist driven to create despite crippling poverty and illness, a picture no less riveting and revealing than the numerous self-portraits he painted throughout his life. Indeed, Vincent's paintings and prose are all of a piece. Frequently in his letters we see Vincent describing a painting he has been working on; then pausing in the letter to sketch a facsimile of that painting; and finally speaking in the following letter of how, upon reflection, he returned to *rework* the original painting. Inescapably, whether on paper or canvas, Vincent comes back to the matter of his art, and, as in any creative activity, the recursive process of working and rethinking and revising gives richness to his letters, sketches, and oils. Similarly, M. F. K. Fisher, one of America's greatest gastronomes and finest essayists, presents something like an autobiography in her many collections of essays on food, by repeatedly showing how her subject fits into the whole of her experience. Food—its preparation and enjoyment, one's attitude toward it, the ritual of sharing meals with family and friends—becomes the instrument through which the author reveals the most important moments in her life, as well as the prevailing metaphor for the way she believes life should be savored.

It is common, too, for autobiographers to begin their life stories with *biography*, often with the story of a family member. Both Sherwood Anderson

and Maxine Hong Kingston, in the selections included here, narrate the stories of their forebears—a father who is a storyteller, an aunt who is a "no-
name woman"—as a way of introducing their autobiographies. In biographies, we write to make sense of other people's lives, and in the process we
are likely to uncover something about ourselves. Here is how Susan Cheever
describes the beginnings of her "biographical memoir" of her father after
his death from cancer in 1982:

> At first I thought it would be a slim volume of anecdote and remem-
> brance. I wanted to keep my father alive. I wanted to tell the story of
> a man who fought to adhere to some transcendent moral standard until
> the end of his life. I wanted to tell a writer's story. But each memory
> had layers of reality and fantasy, and unraveling them became a way
> of discovering who my father really was. I don't think I would have
> started this book if I had known where it was going to end, but having
> written it I know my father better than I ever did while he was alive.

Recording the story of someone close to us may provide a release for memories that are troubling or that teach important lessons. Recently, for example, the members of a writing class were asked to invent short stories. One
student, Wianyang Ju, chose instead to narrate an actual incident involving
a friend who was persecuted in China during the Cultural Revolution. In his
introduction to his story, entitled "The Last Supper," Wianyang explains that
he *had* to write a "real-life" rather than a "made-up" tale:

> This is not a made-up story, or an article on the famous painting by
> Leonardo da Vinci. I am not interested in art; my mother always says
> I have no art genetic factor in my body. This is a real story in my life.
> Time flies so fast that it has been fifteen years since the tragedy hit my
> heart. Sometimes I say to myself that the past has gone, and that too
> much recalling might hurt me. So I have tried to force myself to forget
> the nightmare. Unfortunately, I can't forget. I still feel the sore, which
> is like a snake, biting me all the time. If I had never had such a fearful
> experience, I would perhaps be happy and face life bravely. During the
> 1960s and 1970s in China, there were so many tragedies like Hsiao's
> in my story. How can I forget them? It is true that matters are improv-
> ing in China; however, we must not forget the lessons.
>
> I don't know what Hsiao is doing now. My best friend, where are
> you? Living in this free country, I still miss everyone in my mother-
> land. I hope the sun will light the dark shadow in my country and in
> the corner of my heart.

"We must not forget the lessons." This is the impulse that drives all historians, whether they are autobiographers or biographers. Theresa Finegan,
an Irish-American student, says she embarked on her "oral biography" of
her friend Patrick McMahon because she wanted to learn more about the

history of her family as Irish immigrants in America. Naturally, questions of accuracy multiply when the biographer is far removed in time and space from the subject he or she is writing about. Writing *historical biographies* is frequently a matter of sleuthing across centuries to reconstruct a life story, often with very few clues to go on. Moreover, conflicting reports and rumors may have been handed down over the years, so that the historian must decide which reports are most probable and important, and then make sense of what the philosopher Montaigne called the "naked unshaped" stuff of the past. For instance, when Natalie Zemon Davis decided to retell the well-known history of a sixteenth-century French peasant in *The Return of Martin Guerre,* she knew her book would have to include a biographical chapter on Guerre's wife, Bertrande de Rols. Yet about Bertrande relatively little is known. So, in the chapter of her book devoted to Bertrande (and excerpted here), Davis uses the sparse documents and contradictory accounts at her disposal to infer what she can about the life of an ordinary French peasant woman made famous by a quirk of circumstance. "What I offer you here," Davis says, "is in part my invention, but held tightly in check by the voices of the past."

Davis's description might be applied equally to biographies and autobiographies: Part fact, part invention, they are presided over by the voices of the past. The narratives of our lives and of those around us are, from childhood, the first and most important tales we tell. The selections here give ample illustration of the ways in which we order and reorder, interpret and reinterpret, personal experience.

Charles Darwin (1809–1882)

For a brief survey of Darwin's career, see the biographical note on page 43. The celebrated naturalist wrote most of the autobiography excerpted below in 1876, when he was sixty-seven years old, working on it intermittently until he was seventy-three, chiefly, as he says, for his children's interest and his own amusement. "I have taken no pains about my style of writing," Darwin insists, yet generations of readers have been won over by the clarity of his thought and the modesty and sincerity of his recollections. The following excerpt comes from the first chapter of the autobiography, which takes us up to Darwin's years at Cambridge University.

From *The Autobiography of Charles Darwin*

May 31st, 1876

Recollections of the Development of ——— My Mind and Character ———

A German editor having written to me to ask for an account of the development of my mind and character with some sketch of my autobiography, I have thought that the attempt would amuse me, and might possibly interest my children or their children. I know that it would have interested me greatly to have read even so short and dull a sketch of the mind of my grandfather written by himself, and what he thought and did and how he worked. I have attempted to write the following account of myself, as if I were a dead man in another world looking back at my own life. Nor have I found this difficult, for life is nearly over with me. I have taken no pains about my style of writing.

I was born at Shrewsbury on February 12th, 1809. I have heard my Father say that he believed that persons with powerful minds generally had memories extending far back to a very early period of life. This is not my case for my earliest recollection goes back only to when I was a few months over four years old, when we went to near Abergele for sea-bathing, and I recollect some events and places there with some little distinctness.

My mother died in July 1817, when I was a little over eight years old, and it is odd that I can remember hardly anything about her except her deathbed, her black velvet gown, and her curiously constructed work-table. I believe that my forgetfulness is partly due to my sisters, owing to their great grief, never being able to speak about her or mention her name; and partly to her previous invalid state. In the spring of this same year I was sent to a day-school in Shrewsbury,[1] where I staid a year. Before going to school I was educated by my sister Caroline, but I doubt whether this plan answered. I have been told that I was much slower in learning than my younger sister Catherine, and I believe that I was in many ways a naughty boy. Caroline was extremely kind, clever and zealous; but she was too zealous in trying to improve me; for I clearly remember after this long interval of years, saying to myself when about to enter a room where she was—"What will she blame me for now?" and I made myself dogged so as not to care what she might say.

By the time I went to this day-school my taste for natural history, and more especially for collecting, was well developed. I tried to make out the names of plants, and collected all sorts of things, shells, seals, franks, coins, and minerals. The passion for collecting, which leads a man to be a systematic naturalist, a virtuoso or a miser, was very strong in me, and was clearly innate, as none of my sisters or brother ever had this taste.

One little event during this year has fixed itself very firmly in my mind, and I hope that it has done so from my conscience having been afterwards sorely troubled by it; it is curious as showing that apparently I was interested at this early age in the variability of plants! I told another little boy (I believe it was Leighton,[2] who afterwards become a well-known Lichenologist and botanist) that I could produce variously coloured Polyanthuses and Primroses by watering them with certain coloured fluids, which was of course a monstrous fable, and had never been tried by me. I may here also confess that as a little boy I was much given to inventing deliberate falsehoods, and this was always done for the sake of causing excitement. For instance, I once gathered much valuable fruit from my Father's trees and hid them in the shrubbery, and then ran in breathless haste to spread the news that I had discovered a hoard of stolen fruit.[3] . . .

---

[1]Kept by Rev. G. Case, minister of the Unitarian Chapel in the High Street. Mrs. Darwin was a Unitarian and attended Mr. Case's chapel, and my father as a little boy went there with his elder sisters. But both he and his brother were christened and intended to belong to the Church of England; and after his early boyhood he seems usually to have gone to church and not to Mr. Case's. It appears (*St. James's Gazette*, December 15, 1883) that a mural tablet has been erected to his memory in the chapel, which is now known as the "Free Christian Church."—F.D. [Francis Darwin, a son of the naturalist]

[2]Rev. W. A. Leighton, who was a schoolfellow of my father's at Mr. Case's school, remembers his bringing a flower to school and saying that his mother had taught him how by looking at the inside of the blossom the name of the plant could be discovered. Mr. Leighton goes on, "This greatly roused my attention and curiosity, and I inquired of him repeatedly how this could be done?"—but his lesson was naturally enough not transmissible.—F.D. William Allport Leighton (1805–1899), botanist, educated at St. John's College, Cambridge; published *Flora of Shropshire, Lichen Flora of Great Britain,* and other works.—N.B. [Nora Barlow, Darwin's granddaughter]

[3]His Father wisely treated this tendency not by making crimes of the fibs, but by making light of the discoveries.—F.D.

I can say in my own favour that I was a boy humane, but I owed this entirely to the instruction and example of my sisters. I doubt indeed whether humanity is a natural or innate quality. I was very fond of collecting eggs, but I never took more than a single egg out of a bird's nest, except on one single occasion, when I took all, not for their value, but from a sort of bravado.

I had a strong taste for angling, and would sit for any number of hours on the bank of a river or pond watching the float; when at Maer[4] I was told that I could kill the worms with salt and water, and from that day I never spitted a living worm, though at the expense, probably, of some loss of success.

Once as a very little boy, whilst at the day-school, or before that time, I acted cruelly, for I beat a puppy I believe, simply from enjoying the sense of power; but the beating could not have been severe, for the puppy did not howl, of which I feel sure as the spot was near to the house. This act lay heavily on my conscience, as is shown by my remembering the exact spot where the crime was committed. It probably lay all the heavier from my love of dogs being then, and for a long time afterwards, a passion. Dogs seemed to know this, for I was an adept in robbing their love from their masters.

Nothing could have been worse for the development of my mind than Dr. Butler's school, as it was strictly classical, nothing else being taught except a little ancient geography and history. The school as a means of education to me was simply a blank. During my whole life I have been singularly incapable of mastering any language. Especial attention was paid to verse-making, and this I could never do well. I had many friends, and got together a grand collection of old verses, which by patching together, sometimes aided by other boys, I could work into any subject. Much attention was paid to learning by heart the lessons of the previous day; this I could effect with great facility learning forty or fifty lines of Virgil or Homer, whilst I was in morning chapel; but this exercise was utterly useless, for every verse was forgotten in forty-eight hours. I was not idle, and with the exception of versification, generally worked conscientiously at my classics, not using cribs. The sole pleasure I ever received from such studies, was from some of the odes of Horace, which I admired greatly. When I left the school I was for my age neither high nor low in it; and I believed that I was considered by all my masters and by my Father as a very ordinary boy, rather below the common standard in intellect. To my deep mortification my father once said to me, "You care for nothing but shooting, dogs, and rat-catching, and you will be a disgrace to yourself and all your family." But my father, who was the kindest man I ever knew, and whose memory I love with all my heart, must have been angry and somewhat unjust when he used such words. . . .

---

[4]The house of his uncle, Josiah Wedgwood, the younger.—F.D. Here lived a family of Wedgwood cousins, the youngest of whom became Charles's wife. Maer lay in the heart of the Shropshire country, only a 20 mile's ride from Shrewsbury.—N.B.

I had many friends amongst the schoolboys, whom I loved dearly, and I think that my disposition was then very affectionate. Some of these boys were rather clever, but I may add on the principle of "noscitur a socio" that not one of them ever became in the least distinguished.

With respect to science, I continued collecting minerals with much zeal, but quite unscientifically—all that I cared for was a new *named* mineral, and I hardly attempted to classify them. I must have observed insects with some little care, for when ten years old (1819) I went for three weeks to Plas Edwards on the sea-coast in Wales, I was very much interested and surprised at seeing a large black and scarlet Hemipterous insect, many moths (Zygæna) and a Cicindela, which are not found in Shropshire. I almost made up my mind to begin collecting all the insects which I could find dead, for on consulting my sister, I concluded that it was not right to kill insects for the sake of making a collection. From reading White's *Selborne* I took much pleasure in watching the habits of birds, and even made notes on the subject. In my simplicity I remember wondering why every gentleman did not become an ornithologist.

Towards the close of my school life, my brother worked hard at chemistry and made a fair laboratory with proper apparatus in the tool-house in the garden, and I was allowed to aid him as a servant in most of his experiments. He made all the gases and many compounds, and I read with care several books on chemistry, such as Henry and Parkes' *Chemical Catechism*. The subject interested me greatly, and we often used to go on working till rather late at night. This was the best part of my education at school, for it showed me practically the meaning of experimental science. The fact that we worked at chemistry somehow got known at school, and as it was an unprecedented fact, I was nicknamed "Gas." I was also once publicly rebuked by the headmaster, Dr. Butler, for thus wasting my time over such useless subjects; and he called me very unjustly a "poco curante,"[5] and as I did not understand what he meant it seemed to me a fearful reproach.

As I was doing no good at school, my father wisely took me away at a rather earlier age than usual, and sent me (October 1825) to Edinburgh University[6] with my brother, where I stayed for two years or sessions. My brother was completing his medical studies, though I do not believe he ever really intended to practise, and I was sent there to commence them. But soon after this period I became convinced from various small circumstances that my father would leave me property enough to subsist on with some comfort, though I never imagined that I should be so rich a man as I am; but my belief was sufficient to check any strenuous effort to learn medicine.

---

[5]*Poco curante* is an Italian expression meaning "not very attentive."
[6]He lodged at Mrs. Mackay's, 11 Lothian Street. What little the records of Edinburgh University can reveal has been published in the *Edinburgh Weekly Dispatch,* May 22, 1888; and in the *St. James's Gazette,* February 16, 1888. From the latter journal it appears that he and his brother Erasmus made more use of the library than was usual among the students of their time.—F.D.

The instruction at Edinburgh was altogether by Lectures, and these were intolerably dull, with the exception of those on chemistry by Hope;[7] but to my mind there are no advantages and many disadvantages in lectures compared with reading. Dr. Duncan's lectures on Materia Medica at 8 o'clock on a winter's morning are something fearful to remember. Dr. Munro made his lectures on human anatomy as dull, as he was himself, and the subject disgusted me. It has proved one of the greatest evils in my life that I was not urged to practise dissection, for I should soon have got over my disgust; and the practice would have been invaluable for all my future work. This has been an irremediable evil, as well as my incapacity to draw. I also attended regularly the clinical wards in the Hospital. Some of the cases distressed me a good deal, and I still have vivid pictures before me of some of them; but I was not so foolish as to allow this to lessen my attendance. I cannot understand why this part of my medical course did not interest me in a greater degree; for during the summer before coming to Edinburgh I began attending some of the poor people, chiefly children and women in Shrewsbury: I wrote down as full an account as I could of the cases with all the symptoms, and read them aloud to my father, who suggested further enquiries, and advised me what medicines to give, which I made up myself. At one time I had at least a dozen patients, and I felt a keen interest in the work.[8] My father, who was by far the best judge of character whom I ever knew, declared that I should make a successful physician,—meaning by this, one who got many patients. He maintained that the chief element of success was exciting confidence; but what he saw in me which convinced him that I should create confidence I know not. I also attended on two occasions the operating theatre in the hospital at Edinburgh, and saw two very bad operations, one on a child, but I rushed away before they were completed. Nor did I ever attend again, for hardly any inducement would have been strong enough to make me do so; this being long before the blessed days of chloroform. The two cases fairly haunted me for many a long year.

Questions for *The Autobiography of Charles Darwin*

1.   With what memories and observations does Darwin begin his autobiography, and why do you think he selected these, among all the events he might have narrated in the opening pages of his life story?

2.   From the brief glimpse you get of Darwin's early life, what personality traits and circumstances do you think molded Darwin's career?

---

[7]Thomas Charles Hope, 1766–1844, Professor of Chemistry at Edinburgh, 1799–1843.—N.B.

[8]I have heard him call to mind the pride he felt at the results of the successful treatment of a whole family with tartar emetic.—F.D.

3.   Darwin's father said his son would make a successful physician. Why do you think Darwin became a naturalist instead?

4.   Compare this selection with the excerpts from Darwin's journal in Chapter 2 of this anthology. How has Darwin's personality (as a writer, at least) changed in the forty years since the journals were written? What aspects of his character seem to have remained constant?

Vincent Van Gogh (1853–1890)

The son of a Dutch pastor, Van Gogh worked as an apprentice in an art gallery and a bookshop, and finally as a preacher, until, in 1880, after a series of emotional and religious crises, he became aware of his true vocation as an artist. At the beginning of his artistic career in Holland, Van Gogh worked on his mastery of drawing technique, and consciously set out to portray the humble life of working people—the same workers to whom he had tried to bring consolation in the Belgian coal-mining district where he had worked as a preacher. But it was in Paris, where he lived from 1886 to 1888, that his vision was transformed, as he came into contact with some of the great artists of the day—among them Toulouse-Lautrec, Pissarro, and Gauguin—as well as with the experiments with color and design of the Impressionists and the Japanese printmakers.

With the belief that he should abandon Impressionism, Van Gogh left Paris in February of 1888 for Arles, in the South of France, in search of more brilliant light and color. At Van Gogh's invitation, Gauguin joined him in Arles in October, but this experience of communal artistic life ended disastrously about two months later when Van Gogh—for reasons that are unclear—first tried to attack Gauguin, and then mutilated his own left ear. During the eighteen months that were left to him before he finally ended his life with a revolver shot, Van Gogh worked furiously—despite the fits of insanity (brought on, it appears, by epileptic attacks) that intermittently plagued him—on the color-soaked landscapes, still lifes, and portraits that were to earn him a place among the greatest artists in the history of Western painting. Van Gogh's intense though often thwarted need for communication with others was expressed in the hundreds of letters he wrote to his younger brother Theo, an art dealer, who gave him emotional sustenance and financial support throughout his life. In his letters to Theo (as well as those to Gauguin included here), Van Gogh tells of his sources of inspiration, his views on contemporary art and literature, and his hopes, fears, and dreams.

During his fifteen-month stay in Arles, before he moved on to St. Remy, Van Gogh managed to produce some 200 paintings, 100 drawings and watercolors, and 200 letters. The following excerpts from this extraordinary outpouring focus on Van Gogh's rift with Gauguin and subsequent breakdown.

From *The Complete Letters of Vincent Van Gogh*

[Sent by Gauguin to his friend and colleague Emile Schuffenecker on October 8, 1888, with the observation: "I am sending you a letter from Vincent, from which you will see where I stand with him, and all that is planned at present."]

My dear Gauguin,

This morning I received your excellent letter, which I sent on to my brother; your concept of impressionism in general, of which your portrait is a symbol, is striking. I can't tell you how curious I am to see it—but this much I know in advance: this work is too important to allow me to make an exchange. But if you will keep it for us, my brother will take it at the first opportunity—which I asked him directly—if you agree, and let's hope that it will be soon.

For, once again, we are trying to hasten the possibility of your coming here. I must tell you that even while working I keep thinking incessantly of that plan to found a studio, which will have you and myself as permanent residents, but which the two of us would turn into a refuge and place of shelter for comrades at moments when they are encountering a setback in their struggle.

After you left Paris, my brother and I stayed together for a time, which will forever remain unforgettable to me! The discussions covered a wider field—with Guillaumin, with the Pissarros, father and son, with Seurat, whose acquaintance I had not made (I visited his studio only a few hours before my departure).

Often these discussions had to do with the problems that are so very near my brother's heart and mine, *i.e.* the measures to be taken to safeguard the material existence of painters and to safeguard the means of production (paints, canvases) and to safeguard, in their direct interest, their share in the price which, under the present circumstances, pictures only bring a long time after they leave the artists' possession.

When you are here, we are going to go over all these discussions.

However this may be, when I left Paris, seriously sick at heart and in body, and nearly an alcoholic because of my rising fury at my strength failing me—then I shut myself up within myself, without having the courage to hope!

Now, however, hope is breaking for me vaguely on the horizon; that hope in intermittent flashes, like a lighthouse, which has sometimes comforted me during my solitary life.

And now I am longing so much to give you a large share in that faith, namely that to a certain extent we shall succeed in laying the foundations of something that will endure.

When we are talking over those strange days of discussions in the poverty-stricken studios and the cafés of the "little boulevard," you will get a clear insight into that idea of my brother's and mine, which until now has not been realized at all, at least as far as starting a company is concerned. Nevertheless, you will see that this idea is such that all that will have to be done to end the terrible situation of the last few years is precisely what we said, or something along parallel lines. When you hear the whole explanation, you will see that we have put things on an unshakable basis. And you will admit that we have gone a long way beyond the plan we communicated to you. That we have gone beyond it is no more than our duty as picture dealers, for perhaps you know that in the past I was in the art-dealing business for years, and I do not despise the profession in which I once earned my bread.

Suffice it to say that, although apparently you have isolated yourself from Paris, yet you will not stop feeling in fairly direct contact with Paris.

These days I have an extraordinary feverish energy; at the moment I am struggling with a landscape that has a blue sky over an immense vine, green, purple, yellow, with black and orange branches. Little figures of ladies with red sunshades and of vintagers with their cart enliven it even more. In the foreground, gray sand. Yet another square size 30 canvas for the adornment of the house.

I have a portrait of myself, all ash-colored. The ashen-gray color that is the result of mixing malachite green with an orange hue, on pale malachite ground, all in harmony with the reddish-brown clothes. But as I also exaggerate my personality, I have in the first place aimed at the character of a simple bonze worshiping the Eternal Buddha. It has cost me a lot of trouble, yet I shall have to do it all over again if I want to succeed in expressing what I mean. It will even be necessary for me to recover somewhat more from the stultifying influence of our so-called state of civilization in order to have a better model for a better picture. . . .

Ever yours, Vincent

[23 December]

My dear Theo,

Thank you very much for your letter, for the 100-fr. note enclosed and also for the 50-fr. money order.

I think myself that Gauguin was a little out of sorts with the good town of Arles, the little yellow house where we work, and especially with me.[1]

As a matter of fact, there are bound to be grave difficulties to overcome here too, for him as well as for me.

But these difficulties are more within ourselves than outside.

Altogether I think that either he will definitely go, or else definitely stay.

I told him to think it over and make his calculations all over again before doing anything.

---

[1] Gauguin had written to Theo that Vincent and he could not go on living together "because of incompatibility of temper." The quarrel was made up, and Gauguin wrote another letter, speaking of the first as a bad dream.

Gauguin is very powerful, strongly creative, but just because of that he must have peace.

Will he find it anywhere if he does not find it here?

I am waiting for him to make a decision with absolute serenity.

A good handshake.

Vincent

[*On the following day, December 24, a telegram arrived from Gauguin that called Theo to Arles. Vincent, in a state of terrible excitement and in a high fever, had cut off a piece of his own ear and taken it as a present to a woman in a brothel. There had been a violent scene; Roulin the postman managed to get him home, but the police intervened, found Vincent bleeding and unconscious in bed, and sent him to the hospital. Theo found him there, "poor fighter and poor, poor sufferer," and stayed over Christmas. Gauguin went back with Theo to Paris. By December 31 the news was better, and on January 1 Vincent wrote this letter in pencil.*]

[1 January]

My dear boy,

I hope that Gauguin will reassure you completely, and also a little about the painting business.

I expect to start work again soon.

The charwoman and my friend Roulin have taken care of the house, and have put everything in order.

When I get out, I shall be able to go my own little way here again, and soon the fine weather will be coming and I shall again start on the orchards in bloom.

My dear boy, I am so terribly distressed over your journey. I should have wished you had been spared that, for after all no harm came to me, and there was no reason why you should be so upset.

I cannot tell you how glad I am that you have made peace, and even more than that, with the Bongers.[2]

Tell this to André for me, and give him my cordial regards.

What would I not have given for you to have seen Arles when it was fine; now you have seen it in mourning.

However, be of good heart, address letters direct to me at Place Lamartine 2. I will send off Gauguin's pictures that are still at the house as soon as he wishes. We owe him the money that he spent on the furniture.

A handshake, I must go back to the hospital, but shall soon be out for good.

Ever yours, Vincent

Write a line to Mother for me too, so that no one will be worried.

---

[2]Theo was engaged to Johanna Bonger.

[On the back of the page was written, also in pencil, the following letter.]

My dear friend Gauguin,

I take this opportunity of my first absence from the hospital to write you a few words of very deep and sincere friendship. I often thought of you in the hospital, even at the height of fever and comparative weakness.

Look here—was my brother Theo's journey really necessary, old man?

Now at least do reassure him completely, and I entreat you, be confident yourself that after all no evil exists in this best of worlds in which everything is for the best.

Then I should like you to give my kind regards to good old Schuffenecker, to refrain, until after more mature reflection on both our parts, from speaking ill of our poor little yellow house, and to remember me to the painters whom I saw in Paris. I wish you prosperity in Paris, with a good handshake.

Yours sincerely, Vincent

Roulin has been truly kind to me, it was he who had the presence of mind to make me come out of that place before the others were convinced.

Please answer me.

Arles, 7 January 1889

Dear Mother and Sister,

For several weeks already I have firmly intended to write you a word or two to wish you a truly prosperous and happy New Year. Well, I am pretty late in doing this.

I think you may feel inclined to excuse me if I tell you that in December I was indisposed.

But at the same time I can inform you that I have completely recovered, and am at work again, and everything is normal.

Although it is winter here too, and, what is worse, part of the country is flooded, at times we have a good deal milder weather than you in Holland. Be so kind as to take good note of the fact that I am writing you these few words, in case Theo has told you about my having been indisposed for a while. However, I hope he understood of his own accord that it was not worth troubling to inform you of it.

But so that there may be no worrying on your part, nor even any question of it, I am writing you myself.

For this very reason I have postponed answering Jet Mauve's letter, which, however, I hope to do shortly; and at the same time I thank Wil kindly for her last letter.

My having been unwell has provided the opportunity for getting acquainted with quite a number of people, and I think it probable that I shall have to do a number of portraits.

I so much hope everything is all right with you all, especially your health. As for myself, my having been indisposed for a few days has in fact refreshed me considerably, and I think there is a chance that there will be nothing the matter with me for a long time to come.

Meanwhile I shall be very pleased to get a letter from you one of these days. Although it is still rather a thing of the future, I suppose you are often thinking of Theo's intended visit to you. I should not be greatly surprised if he went a little earlier than usual this year, that is *before* the exhibition instead of after.

But all the same he will have to act according to circumstances.

I could not help thinking of you rather often these days, be assured of that, and believe me,

Yours lovingly, Vincent

[19 March]

My dear brother,[3]

I seemed to see so much brotherly anxiety in your kind letter that I think it my duty to break my silence. I write to you in the full possession of my faculties and not as a madman, but as the brother you know. This is the truth. A certain number of people here (there were more than 80 signatures) addressed a petition to the Mayor (I think his name is M. Tardieu), describing me as a man not fit to be at liberty, or something like that.

The commissioner of police or the chief commissioner then gave the order to shut me up again.

Anyhow, here I am, shut up in a cell all the livelong day, under lock and key and with keepers, without my guilt being proved or even open to proof.

Needless to say, in the secret tribunal of my soul I have much to reply to all that. Needless to say, I cannot be angry, and it seems to me a case of qui s'excuse s'accuse.[4]

Only to let you know that as for setting me free—mind, I do not ask it, being persuaded that the whole accusation will be reduced to nothing—but I do say that as for getting me freed, you would find it difficult. If I did not restrain my indignation, I should at once be thought a dangerous lunatic. Let us hope and have patience. Besides, strong emotion can only aggravate my case. That is why I beg you for the present to let things be without meddling.

Take it as a warning from me that it might only complicate and confuse things.

All the more because you will understand that, while I am absolutely calm at the present moment, I may easily relapse into a state of overexcitement on account of fresh mental emotion.

So you understand what a staggering blow between the eyes it was to find so many people here cowardly enough to join together against one man, and that man ill.

---

[3]On Feb. 27 Theo wrote to his fiancée that Vincent had been taken to the hospital again.
[4]"He who excuses himself accuses himself." (French)

Very good—so much for your better guidance; as far as my mental state is concerned, I am greatly shaken, but I am recovering a sort of calm in spite of everything, so as not to get angry.

Besides, humility becomes me after the experience of the repeated attacks. So I am being patient.

The main thing, I cannot tell you this too often, is that you should keep calm too, and let nothing upset you in your business. After your marriage we can set ourselves to clearing all this up, and meanwhile I beg you to leave me quietly here. I am convinced that the Mayor as well as the commissioner is really rather friendly, and that they will do what they can to settle all this. Here, except for liberty, and except for many things that I could wish otherwise, I am not too badly off.

Besides, I told them that we were in no position to bear the expense. I cannot move without expense, and here are three months that I haven't been working, and mind, I could have worked if they had not vexed and worried me.

How are our mother and sister?

As I have nothing else to distract me—they even forbid me to smoke—though the other patients are allowed to—I think about all the people I know all day and all night long.

It is a shame—and all, so to speak, for nothing.

I will not deny that I would rather have died than have caused and suffered such trouble.

Well, well, to suffer without complaining is the one lesson that has to be learned in this life.

Now with all this, if I am to take up my task of painting again, I naturally need my studio, and some furniture, and we certainly have nothing to replace them with in case of loss. You know my work would not permit being reduced to living in hotels again. I must have my own fixed niche.

If these fellows here protest against me, I protest against them, and all they have to do is to give me damages and interest by friendly arrangement, in short, only to pay me back what I have lost through their blunders and ignorance.

If—say—I should become definitely insane—I certainly don't say that this is impossible—in any case I must be treated differently, and given fresh air, and my work, etc.

Then—honestly—I will submit.

But we have not got to that, and if I had had peace I should have recovered long ago.

They pester me because of my smoking and eating, but what's the use? After all, with all their sobriety, they only cause me fresh misery. My dear boy, the best we can do perhaps is to make fun of our petty griefs and, in a way, of the great griefs of human life too. Take it like a man, go straight to your goal. In present-day society we artists are only the broken pitchers. I so wish I could send you my canvases, but all of them are under lock and key, guarded by police and keepers. Don't try to release me, that will settle itself, but warn Signac[5] not to meddle in it, for he would be putting his hand into a hornets' nest—not until I write again. I shake your hand in thought. Give my kind regards to your fiancée, and to our mother and sister.

Ever yours, Vincent

─────── St. Rémy (May 1889)[6] ───────

My dear Theo,

Thanks for your letter. You are quite right to say that M. Salles has been splendid all through. I am under a great obligation to him.

I wanted to tell you that I think I have done well to come here; first of all, by seeing the *reality* of the life of the various madmen and lunatics in this menagerie, I am losing the vague dread, the fear of the thing. And little by little I can come to look upon madness as a disease like any other. Then the change of surroundings does me good, I think.

As far as I can make out, the doctor here is inclined to consider what I have had some sort of epileptic attack. But I did not ask him about it.

Have you received the case of pictures? I am anxious to know whether or not they have suffered.

I am working on two others—some violet irises and a lilac bush, two subjects taken from the garden.

The idea of work as a duty is coming back to me very strongly, and I think that all my faculties for work will come back to me fairly quickly. Only work often absorbs me so much that I think I shall always remain absent-minded and awkward in shifting for myself for the rest of my life too.

I shall not write you a long letter—I will try to reply to my new sister's letter, which touched me very much, but I do not know if I shall manage to do it.

A handshake.

Ever yours, Vincent

Questions for the Letters of Vincent Van Gogh

1.   In his letter to Gauguin, Van Gogh describes the self-portrait in which, he says, "I exaggerate my personality." What observations can you make about the man from the "self-portraits" he created in his *writing?* What do the *painted* portraits tell you about the artist?

---

[5]Theo had heard from Paul Signac, a Neo-Impressionist painter, that he was going to the South, and had asked him to visit Vincent.
[6]On May 8, Van Gogh left Arles, accompanied by the Reverend Salles, for a mental asylum in St. Rémy.

2.   What can you gather about Van Gogh's artistic methods and aspirations?

3.   As both the biographical note and the letters reveal, Van Gogh suffered from bouts of mental illness. Based on what you have read, what external forces do you think might have exacerbated his distress?

4.   What differences can you detect in the "voices" Van Gogh uses when writing to Theo, his mother and sister, and Gauguin?

Vincent van Gogh, *Self-Portrait with Straw Hat* (Paris).
The Metropolitan Museum of Art, New York. Bequest of Miss Adelaide Milton de Groot
(1876–1967), 1967.

Vincent van Gogh, *Self-Portrait Dedicated to Paul Gauguin,* September 1888.
Courtesy of the Harvard University Art Museums (Fogg Art Museums). Bequest—Collection of Maurice Wertheim, Class of 1906.

Vincent van Gogh, *Self-Portrait with Bandaged Ear.*
Oil on canvas
Courtauld Institute Galleries, London.

Sherwood Anderson (1876–1941)

Born in Camden, Ohio, Sherwood Anderson frequently had to leave school
and take odd jobs to help his family. His mother died when he was
fourteen, and his formal education ended. His father, as you will see in the
following selection from Anderson's memoirs, was a roving, easygoing,
somewhat irresponsible man, and a great teller of tall tales.

After serving briefly in the Spanish-American War, Anderson eventually
became the manager of a paint factory. But he walked out on his job
and his family, deliberately creating the impression that he'd lost his mind,
and went to Chicago to become a writer. Among his novels are *Windy
McPherson's Son* (1916), *Marching Men* (1917), and *Winesburg, Ohio* (1919).
Anderson's special talent is nowhere more evident than in his
short stories, many of which are collected in *The Triumph of the Egg* (1921),
Horses and Men (1923), and *Death in the Woods* (1933). It has been said that
Anderson's autobiography is half fiction, and his fiction nearly all
autobiography.

Unforgotten[1]

One of the strangest relationships in the world is that between father and
son. I know it now from having sons of my own. I am hoping they do not
turn out to be writers.

It is something dreadful to have a writer for a son. How unscrupulous we
writers are. I am thinking, as I write these words, of my own father, surely,
as I think of him, now that he is dead, now that I am myself a father of sons,
an unforgettable man.

I am thinking of the dangers of having a writer as a son. We writers use
everyone. We are after stories. We jerk people out of the lives in which they
live, or think they live, and put them into a world we invent. We use our
own lives so. Once I did an unfair mean thing to a certain man in Ohio. He
was my friend and I rather sold him out. He was angry. My name began to
get a little up in the world and he threatened me. He said he was going to
write telling just what kind of man I was.

"Please do," I said. "Rough it up. Send the whole story to me. I've half
forgotten." I pointed out that I could do the job better than he could. I meant
it, too. I was a story teller and I knew I could beat him telling the story.

---

[1]Published (revised) as "Discovery of a Father," *Reader's Digest*, XXXV (November, 1939), 21–
25.

There are certain men who are what I call "feeders." The story teller loves such men. They go about telling little things that have happened to them. They cannot write the stories but they can tell them. Put pens into their hands and away fly the stories.

There was an Irishman I knew in Chicago who was like that. I fed on him for years and in the end I ruined him. I had got so many good stories from him, had written and sold them, that I grew ashamed. I spoke to him. "Why don't you write the stories yourself?" I said. He began trying, has been at it ever since. He can't do it. He might well have been a success in life if I hadn't got into his head the notion that he could be a writer.

A man who worked for me on my farm was such a story teller. What tales he told! There is a certain naïveté in such men. They are really innocent. They look out upon life with clear innocent eyes. They tell you the most wonderful tales of things they feel, things they have done, things that have been done to them. They tell everything very clearly, with amazing innocence. The man worked for me one summer and I cleaned up on him. I got several beautiful stories, heard them from his lips, while we worked together, rushed at once into the house, put down the stories just as he had told them. Then I was a fool. At the end of the summer I told him what I had been doing and he grew afraid of me.

Or he thought I was getting too much for nothing. I should have kept my mouth shut. I lost a good feeder. Now the wonderful stories he might tell to many people through me are lost.

A boy wants something very special from his father. You are always hearing it said that fathers want their sons to be what they feel they cannot themselves be but I tell you it also works the other way. I know that, as a small boy, I wanted my father to be a certain thing he was not, could not be. I wanted him to be a proud silent dignified one. When I was with other small boys and he passed along the street, I wanted to feel in my breast the glow of pride.

"There he is. That is my father."

But he wasn't such a one. He couldn't be. It seemed to me then that he was always showing off. Let's say someone in our town had got up a show. They were always doing it. At that time it would have been the G.A.R., the Grand Army of the Republic. They did it to raise some money to help pay the rent of their hall.

So they had a show, the druggist in it, the fellow who clerked in the shoe store. A certain horse doctor was always in such shows in our town and, to be sure, a lot of women and girls. They got as many in it as they could so that all of the relatives of the actors would come. It was to be, of course, a comedy.

And there was my father. He had managed to get the chief comedy part. It was, let's say, a Civil War play and he was a comic Irish soldier. He had to do the most absurd things. They thought he was funny, but I didn't think so.

I thought he was terrible. I didn't see how mother could stand it. She even laughed with the others. It may be that I also would have laughed if it hadn't been my father.

Or there was a parade, say on the Fourth of July or on Decoration Day. He'd be in that too. He'd be right at the front of it. He had got himself appointed Grand Marshall or some such office, had got, to ride in the parade, a white horse hired from a livery stable.

He couldn't ride for shucks. He fell off the horse and everyone hooted with laughter but he did not care. He even seemed to like it. I remember one such occasion when he had done something ridiculous, and right out on the main street too, when I couldn't stand it. I was with some other boys and they were laughing and shouting at him and he was shouting back to them and having as good a time as they were. I ran away. There was an alleyway back of the stores on main street and I ran down that. There were some sheds, back of the Presbyterian church, where country people stabled horses during church on Sundays and I went in there. I had a good long cry.

Or I was in bed at night and father had come home a little lit up and had brought some men with him. He was a man who was never alone. There were always men hanging around him. Before he went broke, running a harness shop, when he had the shop, there were always a lot of men loafing in there. He went broke of course because he gave too much credit. He couldn't refuse it and I thought he hadn't any sense. I thought he was a fool. I had got to hating him. I'd be upstairs in bed in the front room of the little house we lived in and he'd bring his crowd of men friends and sit with them on the front porch of our house.

There'd be men I didn't think would want to be fooling around with him but they did. There might even be the superintendent of our schools and a quiet man who ran a hardware store in our town. Once I remember there was a white haired man who was cashier of the bank. It was a wonder to me they'd want to be seen with such a wind bag. That's what I thought he was. I know now what it was that attracted them but I didn't know then. Now I think it was because life in our town, as in all small towns, was at times pretty dull and he livened it up. He made them laugh. He could tell stories. He'd even get them to singing. If they didn't come to our house he'd get such a crowd and they'd go off, say at night, to where there was a grassy place by a creek. They'd cook food there and they'd drink beer. They'd sit about listening to him while he told his stories. I knew that most of the stories he told were lies.

He was always telling stories about himself. He'd say this or that wonderful thing had happened to him. It might be something that made him look like a fool. He didn't care. If it was a story, he'd tell it.

He was like this, let's say an Irishman came to our house. Right away father would say he was Irish. He'd tell what county in Ireland he was born in. He'd tell things that happened to him in Ireland when he was a boy. He'd make it seem so real, telling little details of his life as a boy in Ireland, that, if I hadn't known where he was born, in a county down in southern Ohio, I'd have believed him myself.

If it was a Scotchman the same thing happened. He became a Scotchman. He'd get a burr into his speech. Or he was a German or a Swede. He'd be anything the other man was.

I think now they all knew he was lying but they seemed to like him just the same. As a boy that was what I couldn't understand.

And there was mother. How could she stand it? I wanted to ask but never did. I was afraid. She was the kind you didn't ask such questions.

I'd be upstairs in my bed, in my room above the porch, and father would be telling some of his tales. There were a lot of stories about the Civil War. To hear him tell it he'd been in about every battle of the war. He'd known Grant, Sherman, McPherson, Sheridan and I don't know how many others. He'd been particularly intimate with General Grant so that when Grant went east, to take charge of all the armies, he took father along.

"I was an orderly, up at headquarters, and Sam Grant said to me, 'Irve,' he said, 'I'm going to take you along with me.'"

It seems he and Grant used to slip off together sometimes and have a quiet little drink together. That's what my father said. He'd tell about the day Lee surrendered and how, when the great moment came, they couldn't find Grant.

"You know," my father said, "about General Grant's book, his *Memoirs.* You've read it, eh? You've read of how he said he had a headache and how, when he got word that Lee was ready to call it quits, he was suddenly and miraculously cured?

"Huh," said father.

"He was in the woods with me," my father declared.

"I was in there, in the woods with my back against a tree. I was pretty well corned. I had got hold of a bottle of pretty good stuff. I found it in a house.

"So I was in the woods and they were looking for Grant. He was riding along a road and had got off his horse and had come into the woods. He found me in there. He had come . . . well, nature you know. He was covered with mud.

"I had the bottle in my hand. I was sitting there with my back to a tree. What'd I care? The war was over. I knew we had them licked."

My father said that he was the one who told Grant that Lee was ready to surrender. He said he was walking along a road with the bottle hidden under a coat and that an orderly riding along the road had told him. He said the orderly knew how thick he was with Sam Grant.

And then, there in the woods, he told Grant and Grant was embarrassed.

"But, Irve, look at me. I'm all covered with mud," he said to father.

And then, my father said, he and Grant decided to have a drink together. He said they took a couple of shots and then, because he didn't want Grant to show up potted before the immaculate Lee, he got to his feet and smashed the bottle against the tree.

"Sam Grant's dead now and I wouldn't want it to get out on him," my father said.

That's just one of the kind of things he'd tell and of course the men, sitting and listening, knew he was lying but they seemed to like it just the same. They laughed at him but he didn't seem to care. Once some of them counted up on him. He'd been sitting with them in the evening in front of the stores or on the porch of our house, telling how many years he'd been here, how many there. To hear him tell it there wasn't a state, not a city in the whole country he hadn't been in. "I was working three years there," he'd say. He was five years in another place, ten in another. They counted up on him. Everyone called him "Major" although he wasn't a major at all.

"Major," they said, "we been figuring you up. We make it out you're a hundred and eighty years old." Do you think he cared? Not he. He laughed the same as everyone else.

We had gone broke, down and out, and do you think he ever brought anything home? Not he. If there wasn't anything to eat in the house, off visiting he'd go. He'd go visiting around at farm houses near our town. They all wanted him. Sometimes he'd stay away for weeks, mother working to keep us fed, and then home he'd come bringing, let's say, a ham. He'd got it from some farmer friend. He'd slap it on the table in the kitchen. "You bet I'm going to see that my kids have something to eat," he'd say and mother would just stand there looking at him and smiling at him. She'd never say a word about all the weeks and months he'd been away, not leaving us a cent for food. Once I heard her speaking to a woman in our street. It may be that woman had dared to sympathize with her. "Oh," she said, "it's all right. Don't you worry. He isn't ever dull like most of the men in this street. Life is never dull when my man is about."

I'd be up in my room and father'd be down on the porch with some of his crowd. This would be on a summer night. He'd be spinning some of his tales. Then I didn't understand but now I know he never told any lies that hurt anyone. I know now that he just wanted to give people a show, make them laugh. He knew how bitter tasting life gets to almost everyone that lives. He had I think some notion of putting a kind of color on life, touching it here and there with a bit of color. I think he wanted to wash it over with color and I think mother knew.

I was up there in my room and I was awake. I was filled often with bitterness, hearing my father go on and on with his tales, and often I wished he wasn't my father. I'd even invent another man as my father.

To be sure I wanted to protect my mother. I'd make up stories of a secret marriage, that for some strange reason never got known, as though some man, say the president of a railroad company or maybe a congressman, had got married to my mother, thinking his wife was dead and that then it turned out she wasn't.

So they had to hush it up but I got born just the same. I wasn't really the son of my father. There was a mysterious man somewhere in the world, a very dignified quite wonderful man who was really my father. You get the point. I even made myself half believe some of these fancies.

And then there came a certain night. Mother was away from home when father came in and he was alone. He'd been off somewhere for two or three weeks. He found me alone in the house.

He came silently into the house and it was raining outside. It may be there was church that night and that mother had gone. I was alone and was sitting in the kitchen. I had a book before me and was sitting and reading by the kitchen table.

So in came my father. He had been walking in the rain and was very wet. He sat and looked at me and I was startled for, on that night, there was on his face the saddest look I had ever seen on a human face. For a long time he sat looking at me, not saying a word.

And then something happened to me.

There are times when a boy is so sad, he doesn't quite know why, that he thinks he can hardly bear to go on living. He thinks he'd rather die. The sadness comes mostly when it has been raining or it comes in the fall when the leaves fall off the trees. It isn't anything special. It is just sadness.

So there was father on the rainy summer night. He was sad and looking at him made me sad. He sat for a time, saying nothing, his clothes dripping. He must have been walking a long time in the rain. He got up out of his chair.

"You come on, you come with me," he said.

I got up and went with him out of the house. I was filled with wonder but, although he had suddenly become like a stranger to me, I wasn't afraid. We went along a street. At that time we lived in a little yellow frame house, quite far out at the edge of our town. It was a house we hadn't lived in very long. We had moved a lot. Once I heard my mother say to my father, "Well, I guess we'll have to be moving," she said. She said we were back three months on our rent and that there wasn't any money to pay it with. She didn't scold. She even laughed. She just took it as a fact that when the rent got far behind we had to move.

I was walking with my father and we went out of the town. We were on a dirt road. It was a road that led up a little hill, past fields and strips of woodland, and went on over the hill and down into a little valley, about a mile out of town, to where there was a pond. We walked in silence. The man who was always talking had stopped talking.

I didn't know what was up and had the queer feeling that I was with a stranger. I don't know now whether or not my father intended it so. I don't think he did.

The pond at the edge of the town was quite large. It was a place where a creek had been dammed and was owned by a man who sold ice in our town. We were there at the edge of the pond. We had come in silence. It was still raining hard and there were flashes of lightning followed by thunder. We were on a grassy bank at the pond's edge, when my father spoke, and in the darkness and rain his voice sounded strange. It was the only time during the evening that he did speak to me.

"Take off your clothes," he said and, still filled with wonder, I began to undress. There was a flash of lightning and I saw that he was already naked.

And so naked we went into the pond. He did not speak or explain. Taking my hand he led me down to the pond's edge and pulled me in. It may be that I was too frightened, too full of a feeling of strangeness to speak. Before that night my father had never seemed to pay any attention to me.

"And what is he up to now?" I kept asking myself that question. It was as though the man, my father I had not wanted as father, had got suddenly some kind of power over me.

I was afraid and then, right away, I wasn't afraid. We were in the pond in darkness. It was a large pond and I did not swim very well but he had put my hand on his shoulder. Still he did not speak but struck out at once into the darkness.

He was a man with very big shoulders and was a powerful swimmer. In the darkness I could feel the movement of his muscles. The rain poured down on us and the wind blew and there were the flashes of lightning followed by the peals of thunder.

And so we swam, I will never know for how long. It seemed hours to me. We swam thus in the darkness to the far edge of the pond and then back to where we had left our clothes. There was the rain on our faces. Sometimes my father turned and swam on his back and when he did he took my hand in his large powerful one and moved it over so that it rested always on his shoulder and sometimes as we swam thus I could look into his face. There would be a flash of lightning and I could see his face clearly.

It was as it was when he had come earlier into the kitchen where I sat reading the book. It was a face filled with sadness. There would be the momentary glimpse of his face and then again the darkness, the wind and the rain. In me there was a feeling I had never known before that night.

It was a feeling of closeness. It was something strange. It was as though there were only we two in the world. It was as though I had been jerked suddenly out of myself, out of a world of the school boy, out of a world in which I was ashamed of my father, out of a place where I had been judging my father.

He had become blood of my blood. I think I felt it. He the stronger swimmer and I the boy clinging to him in the darkness. We swam in silence and in silence we dressed, in our wet clothes, and went back along the road to the town and our house.

It had become a strange house to me. There was the little porch at the front where on so many nights my father had sat with the men. There was the tree by the spring and the shed at the back. There was a lamp lighted in the kitchen and when we came in, the water dripping from us, there was my mother. She was as she had always been. She smiled at us. I remember that she called us "boys." "What have you boys been up to?" she asked, but my father did not answer. As he had begun the evening's experience with me in silence so he ended it. He turned and looked at me and then he went, I thought with a new and strange dignity, out of the room.

He went to his room to get out of his wet clothes and I climbed the stairs to my own room. I undressed in darkness and got into bed. I was still in the grip of the feeling of strangeness that had taken possession of me in the darkness in the pond. I couldn't sleep and did not want to sleep. For the first time I had come to know that I was the son of my father. He was a story teller as I was to be. It may be that on the night of my childhood I even laughed a little softly there in the darkness in my bed in the room. If I did, I laughed knowing that, no matter how much as a story teller I might be using him, I would never again be wanting another father.

Questions for "Unforgotten"

1.   What did the young Anderson resent about his father, and what kind of father did he "invent" for himself?

2.   Describe the mother in this story.

3.   Why does Anderson move from a series of actions that seem to have been repeated many times to a specific event that occurred only once? Why was the swimming incident so important to Anderson?

4.   What did the narrator discover about his father? About himself?

5.   Anderson's autobiographical tale poses a question about the relationship between fact and fiction in any autobiographical story. In this selection, where do you think the author might be adding or making up details, or otherwise altering the 'facts'—as his father did—for the sake of a wonderful tale?

M. F. K. Fisher (1908–   )

After attending UCLA, Fisher spent three years in France at the University of Dijon. Her first book, *Serve It Forth* (1937), established her as a gastronome and writer of note. Subsequent books, such as *How to Cook a Wolf* (1942), *The Gastronomical Me* (1943), a celebrated translation of Brillat-Savarin's *The Physiology of Taste* (1949), *An Alphabet for Gourmets* (1949)—from which the following selection is taken—and *The Cooking of Provincial France* (1968), have established her as one of America's premier writers on food, and one of its great essayists. Indeed, W. H. Auden once said of Fisher, "I do not know of anyone in the United States today who writes better prose."

P Is for Peas

. . . NATURALLY! and for a few reasons why the best peas I ever ate in my life were, in truth, the best peas I ever ate in my life.

Every good cook, from Fanny Farmer to Escoffier, agrees on three things about these delicate messengers to our palates from the kind earth-mother: they must be very green, they must be freshly gathered, and they must be shelled at the very last second of the very last minute.

My peas, that is, the ones that reached an almost unbelievable summit of perfection, an occasion that most probably never would happen again, met these three gastronomical requirements to a point of near-ridiculous exactitude. It is possible, however, that even this technical impeccability would not have been enough without the mysterious blending, that one time, of weather, place, other hungers than my own. After all, I can compare bliss with near bliss, for I have often, blessèd me, eaten superlative green peas.

Once, for instance, my grandmother ran out into her garden, filled her apron with the fattest pods, sat rocking jerkily with a kind of nervous merriment for a very few minutes as she shelled them—and before we knew it she had put down upon the white-covered table a round dish of peas in cream. We ate them with our spoons, something we never could have done at home! Perhaps that added to their fragile, poignant flavor, but not much: they were truly *good.*

And then once in Paris, in June (what a hackneyed but wonderful combination of the somewhat overrated time-and-place motif!), I lunched at Foyot's, and in the dim room where hot-house roses stood on all the tables the very month roses climbed crazily outside on every trellis, I watched the headwaiter, as skilled as a magician, dry peas over a flame in a generous pan, add what looked like an equal weight of butter, which almost visibly sent out a cloud of sweet-smelling hay and meadow air, and then swirl the whole.

At the end he did a showy trick, more to amuse himself than me, but I sat open-mouthed, and I can still see the arc of little green vegetables flow up into the air and then fall, with a satisfying shush, back into the pan some three or four feet below and at least a yard from where they took off. I gasped, the headwaiter bowed faintly but with pride, and then we went about the comparatively mundane procedure of serving, tasting, and eating.

Those petits pois au beurre were, like my grandmother's, à la crème mode d'Iowa, good—*very* good. They made me think of paraphrasing Sidney Smith's remark about strawberries and saying, "Doubtless God could have made a better green pea, but doubtless He never did."

That was, however, before the year I started out, on a spring date set by strict local custom, to grow peas in a steep terraced garden among the vineyards between Montreux and Lausanne, on the Lake of Geneva.

The weather seemed perfect for planting by May Day, and I had the earth ready, the dry peas ready, the poles ready to set up. But Otto and Jules, my mentors, said no so sternly that I promised to wait until May 15, which could easily be labeled Pea-Planting Day in Swiss almanacs. They were right, of course: we had a cold snap that would have blackened any sprout about May 10. As I remember, the moon, its rising, and a dash of hailstones came into the picture too.

And then on May 15, a balmy sweet day if ever I saw one, my seeds went into the warm, welcoming earth, and I could agree with an old gardening manual which said understandingly, "Perhaps no vegetable is set out in greater expectancy . . . for the early planting fever is impatient."

A week later I put in another row, and so on for a month, and they did as they were meant to, which is one of the most satisfying things that can possibly happen to a gardener, whether greenhorn and eager or professional and weatherworn.

Then came the day with stars on it: time for what my grandmother would have called "the first mess of peas."

The house at Le Pâquis was still a-building, shapes of rooms but no roof, no windows, trestles everywhere on the wide terrace high above the lake, the ancient apple tree heavily laden with button-sized green fruit, plums coloring on the branches at the far end near the little meadow, set so surprisingly among the vineyards that gave Le Pâquis its name.

We put a clean cloth, red and white, over one of the carpenters' tables, and we kicked wood curls aside to make room for our feet under the chairs brought up from the apartment in Vevey. I set out tumblers, plates, silver, smooth, unironed napkins sweet from the meadow grass where they had dried.

While some of us bent over the dwarf-pea bushes and tossed the crisp pods into baskets, others built a hearth from stones and a couple of roof tiles lying about and made a lively little fire. I had a big kettle with spring water in the bottom of it, just off simmering, and salt and pepper and a pat of fine butter to hand. Then I put the bottles of Dézelay in the fountain, under the timeless spurt of icy mountain water, and ran down to be the liaison between the harvesters and my mother, who sat shelling peas from the basket on her lap into the pot between her feet, her fingers as intent and nimble as a lacemaker's.

I dashed up and down the steep terraces with the baskets, and my mother would groan and then hum happily when another one appeared, and below I could hear my father and our friends cursing just as happily at their wry backs and their aching thighs, while the peas came off their stems and into the baskets with a small sound audible in that still high air, so many hundred feet above the distant and completely silent Léman. It was suddenly almost twilight. The last sunlight on the Dents du Midi was fire-rosy, with immeasurable coldness in it.

"Time, gentlemen, time," my mother called in an unrehearsed and astonishing imitation of a Cornish barmaid.

They came in grateful hurry up the steep paths, almost nothing now in their baskets, and looks of smug success upon their faces. We raced through the rest of the shelling, and then while we ate rolled prosciutto and drank Swiss bitters or brandy and soda or sherry, according to our various habits, I dashed like an eighteenth-century courier on a secret mission of utmost military importance, the pot cautiously braced in front of me, to the little hearth.

I stirred up the fire. When the scant half-inch of water boiled, I tossed in the peas, a good six quarts or more, and slapped on the heavy lid as if a devil might get out. The minute steam showed I shook the whole like mad. Someone brought me a curl of thin pink ham and a glass of wine cold from the fountain. Revivified, if that were any more possible, I shook the pot again.

I looked up at the terrace, a shambles of sawed beams, cement mixers, and empty sardine tins left from the workmen's lunches. There sat most of the people in the world I loved, in a thin light that was pink with Alpen glow, blue with a veil of pine smoke from the hearth. Their voices sang with a certain remoteness into the clear air, and suddenly from across the curve of the Lower Corniche a cow in Monsieur Rogivue's orchard moved her head among the meadow flowers and shook her bell in a slow, melodious rhythm, a kind of hymn. My father lifted up his face at the sweet sound and, his fists all stained with green-pea juice, said passionately, "God, but I feel good!" I felt near to tears.

The peas were now done. After one more shake I whipped off the lid and threw in the big pat of butter, which had a bas-relief of William Tell upon it. I shook in salt, ground in pepper, and then swirled the pot over the low flames until Tell had disappeared. Then I ran like hell, up the path lined with candytuft and pinks, past the fountain where bottles shone promisingly through the crystal water, to the table.

Small brown roasted chickens lay on every plate, the best ones I have ever eaten, done for me that afternoon by Madame Doellenbach of the Vieux

Vevey and not chilled since but cooled in their own intangibly delicate juices. There was a salad of mountain lettuces. There was honest bread. There was plenty of limpid wine, the kind Brillat-Savarin said was like rock-water, tempting enough to make a hydrophobic drink. Later there was cheese, an Emmenthaler and a smuggled Reblochon . . .

. . . And later still we walked dreamily away, along the Upper Corniche to a café terrace, where we sat watching fireworks far across the lake at Evian, and drinking café noir and a very fine *fine*.

But what really mattered, what piped the high unforgettable tune of perfection, were the peas, which came from their hot pot onto our thick china plates in a cloud, a kind of miasma, of everything that anyone could ever want from them, even in a dream. I recalled the three basic requisites, according to Fanny Farmer and Escoffier . . . and again I recalled Sidney Smith, who once said that his idea of Heaven (and he was a cleric!) was pâté de foie gras to the sound of trumpets. Mine, that night and this night too, is fresh green garden peas, picked and shelled by my friends, to the sound of a cowbell.

Questions for "P Is for Peas"

1.   Embedded in Fisher's essay is her recipe for cooking peas. How many steps in the recipe can you recall?

2.   In another essay, Fisher speaks of the "magic chord" sounded by "the right blending of time, space, and the physical sensation of eating." How is that chord sounded in this essay—what elements make this particular family outing magical and memorable for her?

Maxine Hong Kingston (1940–   )

Although Maxine Hong Kingston was raised in Stockton, California, she grew up in a world more Chinese than American. Negotiating the very different demands and expectations of the two cultures and the two languages provided Kingston with much of the material for her writing. She was graduated from the University of California at Berkeley, and taught English in Hawaiian high schools for a number of years. Since 1977, Kingston has been visiting associate professor of English at the University of Hawaii.

The Woman Warrior: Memoirs of a Girlhood Among Ghosts (1976) received the general nonfiction award from the National Book Critics Circle, and was named one of the top ten nonfiction books of the decade by *Time* magazine in 1979. "No Name Woman," the following selection, is the first chapter of Kingston's highly unconventional autobiography, which merges legend, myth, fantasy, and fact into a genre very much the author's own. According to Kingston, her second book, *China Men* (1980), is a companion to *The Woman Warrior:* She wrote the two books almost simultaneously, and thinks of them as "one big book."

No Name Woman

"You must not tell anyone," my mother said, "what I am about to tell you. In China your father had a sister who killed herself. She jumped into the family well. We say that your father has all brothers because it is as if she had never been born.

"In 1924 just a few days after our village celebrated seventeen hurry-up weddings—to make sure that every young man who went 'out on the road' would responsibly come home—your father and his brothers and your grandfather and his brothers and your aunt's new husband sailed for America, the Gold Mountain. It was your grandfather's last trip. Those lucky enough to get contracts waved good-bye from the decks. They fed and guarded the stowaways and helped them off in Cuba, New York, Bali, Hawaii. 'We'll meet in California next year,' they said. All of them sent money home.

"I remember looking at your aunt one day when she and I were dressing; I had not noticed before that she had such a protruding melon of a stomach. But I did not think, 'She's pregnant,' until she began to look like other pregnant women, her shirt pulling and the white tops of her black pants showing.

She could not have been pregnant, you see, because her husband had been gone for years. No one said anything. We did not discuss it. In early summer she was ready to have the child, long after the time when it could have been possible.

"The village had also been counting. On the night the baby was to be born the villagers raided our house. Some were crying. Like a great saw, teeth strung with lights, files of people walked zigzag across our land, tearing the rice. Their lanterns doubled in the disturbed black water, which drained away through the broken bunds. As the villagers closed in, we could see that some of them, probably men and women we knew well, wore white masks. The people with long hair hung it over their faces. Women with short hair made it stand up on end. Some had tied white bands around their foreheads, arms, and legs.

"At first they threw mud and rocks at the house. Then they threw eggs and began slaughtering our stock. We could hear the animals scream their deaths—the roosters, the pigs, a last great roar from the ox. Familiar wild heads flared in our night windows; the villagers encircled us. Some of the faces stopped to peer at us, their eyes rushing like searchlights. The hands flattened against the panes, framed heads, and left red prints.

"The villagers broke in the front and the back doors at the same time, even though we had not locked the doors against them. Their knives dripped with the blood of our animals. They smeared blood on the doors and walls. One woman swung a chicken, whose throat she had slit, splattering blood in red arcs about her. We stood together in the middle of our house, in the family hall with the pictures and tables of the ancestors around us, and looked straight ahead.

"At that time the house had only two wings. When the men came back, we would build two more to enclose our courtyard and a third one to begin a second courtyard. The villagers pushed through both wings, even your grandparents' rooms, to find your aunt's, which was also mine until the men returned. From this room a new wing for one of the younger families would grow. They ripped up her clothes and shoes and broke her combs, grinding them underfoot. They tore her work from the loom. They scattered the cooking fire and rolled the new weaving in it. We could hear them in the kitchen breaking our bowls and banging the pots. They overturned the great waist-high earthenware jugs; duck eggs, pickled fruits, vegetables burst out and mixed in acrid torrents. The old woman from the next field swept a broom through the air and loosed the spirits-of-the-broom over our heads. 'Pig.' 'Ghost.' 'Pig,' they sobbed and scolded while they ruined our house.

"When they left, they took sugar and oranges to bless themselves. They cut pieces from the dead animals. Some of them took bowls that were not broken and clothes that were not torn. Afterward we swept up the rice and sewed it back up into sacks. But the smells from the spilled preserves lasted. Your aunt gave birth in the pigsty that night. The next morning when I went for the water, I found her and the baby plugging up the family well.

"Don't let your father know that I told you. He denies her. Now that you have started to menstruate, what happened to her could happen to you. Don't humiliate us. You wouldn't like to be forgotten as if you had never been born. The villagers are watchful."

Whenever she had to warn us about life, my mother told stories that ran like this one, a story to grow up on. She tested our strength to establish realities. Those in the emigrant generations who could not reassert brute survival died young and far from home. Those of us in the first American generations have had to figure out how the invisible world the emigrants built around our childhoods fits in solid America.

The emigrants confused the gods by diverting their curses, misleading them with crooked streets and false names. They must try to confuse their offspring as well, who, I suppose, threaten them in similar ways—always trying to get things straight, always trying to name the unspeakable. The Chinese I know hide their names; sojourners take new names when their lives change and guard their real names with silence.

Chinese-Americans, when you try to understand what things in you are Chinese, how do you separate what is peculiar to childhood, to poverty, insanities, one family, your mother who marked your growing with stories, from what is Chinese? What is Chinese tradition and what is the movies?

If I want to learn what clothes my aunt wore, whether flashy or ordinary, I would have to begin, "Remember Father's drowned-in-the-well sister?" I cannot ask that. My mother has told me once and for all the useful parts. She will add nothing unless powered by Necessity, a riverbank that guides her life. She plants vegetable gardens rather than lawns; she carries the odd-shaped tomatoes home from the fields and eats food left for the gods.

Whenever we did frivolous things, we used up energy; we flew high kites. We children came up off the ground over the melting cones our parents brought home from work and the American movie on New Year's Day—*Oh, You Beautiful Doll* with Betty Grable one year, and *She Wore a Yellow Ribbon* with John Wayne another year. After the one carnival ride each, we paid in guilt; our tired father counted his change on the dark walk home.

Adultery is extravagance. Could people who hatch their own chicks and eat the embryos and the heads for delicacies and boil the feet in vinegar for party food, leaving only the gravel, eating even the gizzard lining—could such people engender a prodigal aunt? To be a woman, to have a daughter in starvation time was a waste enough. My aunt could not have been the lone romantic who gave up everything for sex. Women in the old China did not choose. Some man had commanded her to lie with him and be his secret evil. I wonder whether he masked himself when he joined the raid on her family.

Perhaps she had encountered him in the fields or on the mountain where the daughters-in-law collected fuel. Or perhaps he first noticed her in the marketplace. He was not a stranger because the village housed no strangers. She had to have dealings with him other than sex. Perhaps he worked an adjoining field, or he sold her the cloth for the dress she sewed and wore. His demand must have surprised, then terrified her. She obeyed him; she always did as she was told.

When the family found a young man in the next village to be her husband, she had stood tractably beside the best rooster, his proxy, and promised before they met that she would be his forever. She was lucky that he was her age and she would be the first wife, an advantage secure now. The night she first saw him, he had sex with her. Then he left for America. She had almost forgotten what he looked like. When she tried to envision him, she only saw the black and white face in the group photograph the men had had taken before leaving.

The other man was not, after all, much different from her husband. They both gave orders: she followed. "If you tell your family, I'll beat you. I'll kill you. Be here again next week." No one talked sex, ever. And she might have separated the rapes from the rest of living if only she did not have to buy her oil from him or gather wood in the same forest. I want her fear to have lasted just as long as rape lasted so that the fear could have been contained. No drawn-out fear. But women at sex hazarded birth and hence lifetimes. The fear did not stop but permeated everywhere. She told the man, "I think I'm pregnant." He organized the raid against her.

On nights when my mother and father talked about their life back home, sometimes they mentioned an "outcast table" whose business they still seemed to be settling, their voices tight. In a commensal tradition, where food is precious, the powerful older people made wrongdoers eat alone. Instead of letting them start separate new lives like the Japanese, who could become samurais and geishas, the Chinese family, faces averted but eyes glowering sideways, hung on to the offenders and fed them leftovers. My aunt must have lived in the same house as my parents and eaten at an outcast table. My mother spoke about the raid as if she had seen it, when she and my aunt, a daughter-in-law to a different household, should not have been living together at all. Daughters-in-law lived with their husbands' parents, not their own; a synonym for marriage in Chinese is "taking a daughter-in-law." Her husband's parents could have sold her, mortgaged her, stoned her. But they had sent her back to her own mother and father, a mysterious act hinting at disgraces not told me. Perhaps they had thrown her out to deflect the avengers.

She was the only daughter; her four brothers went with her father, husband, and uncles "out on the road" and for some years became western men. When the goods were divided among the family, three of the brothers took land, and the youngest, my father, chose an education. After my grandparents gave their daughter away to her husband's family, they had dispensed all the adventure and all the property. They expected her alone to keep the traditional ways, which her brothers, now among the barbarians, could fumble without detection. The heavy, deep-rooted women were to maintain the past against the flood, safe for returning. But the rare urge west had fixed upon our family, and so my aunt crossed boundaries not delineated in space.

The work of preservation demands that the feelings playing about in one's guts not be turned into action. Just watch their passing like cherry blossoms. But perhaps my aunt, my forerunner, caught in a slow life, let dreams grow and fade and after some months or years went toward what persisted. Fear at the enormities of the forbidden kept her desires delicate, wire and bone. She looked at a man because she liked the way the hair was tucked behind his ears, or she liked the question-mark line of a long torso curving at the shoulder and straight at the hip. For warm eyes or a soft voice or a slow walk—that's all—a few hairs, a line, a brightness, a sound, a pace, she gave up family. She offered us up for a charm that vanished with tiredness, a pigtail that didn't toss when the wind died. Why, the wrong lighting could erase the dearest thing about him.

It could very well have been, however, that my aunt did not take subtle enjoyment of her friend, but, a wild woman, kept rollicking company. Imagining her free with sex doesn't fit, though. I don't know any women like that, or men either. Unless I see her life branching into mine, she gives me no ancestral help.

To sustain her being in love, she often worked at herself in the mirror, guessing at the colors and shapes that would interest him, changing them frequently in order to hit on the right combination. She wanted him to look back.

On a farm near the sea, a woman who tended her appearance reaped a reputation for eccentricity. All the married women blunt-cut their hair in flaps about their ears or pulled it back in tight buns. No nonsense. Neither style blew easily into heart-catching tangles. And at their weddings they displayed themselves in their long hair for the last time. "It brushed the backs of my knees," my mother tells me. "It was braided, and even so, it brushed the backs of my knees."

At the mirror my aunt combed individuality into her bob. A bun could have been contrived to escape into black streamers blowing in the wind or in quiet wisps about her face, but only the older women in our picture album wear buns. She brushed her hair back from her forehead, tucking the flaps behind her ears. She looped a piece of thread, knotted into a circle between her index fingers and thumbs, and ran the double strand across her forehead. When she closed her fingers as if she were making a pair of shadow geese bite, the string twisted together catching the little hairs. Then she pulled the thread away from her skin, ripping the hairs out neatly, her eyes watering from the needles of pain. Opening her fingers, she cleaned the thread, then rolled it along her hairline and the tops of her eyebrows. My mother did the same to me and my sisters and herself. I used to believe that the expression "caught by the short hairs" meant a captive held with a depilatory string. It especially hurt at the temples, but my mother said we were lucky we didn't have to have our feet bound when we were seven. Sisters used to sit on their beds and cry together, she said, as their mothers or their slave removed the bandages for a few minutes each night and let the blood gush back into their veins. I hope that the man my aunt loved appreciated a smooth brow, that he wasn't just a tits-and-ass man.

Once my aunt found a freckle on her chin, at a spot that the almanac said predestined her for unhappiness. She dug it out with a hot needle and washed her wound with peroxide.

More attention to her looks than these pullings of hairs and pickings at spots would have caused gossip among the villagers. They owned work clothes and good clothes, and they wore good clothes for feasting the new seasons. But since a woman combing her hair hexes beginnings, my aunt rarely found an occasion to look her best. Women looked like great sea snails—the corded wood, babies, and laundry they carried were the whorls on their backs. The Chinese did not admire a bent back; goddesses and warriors stood straight. Still there must have been a marvelous freeing of beauty when a worker laid down her burden and stretched and arched.

Such commonplace loveliness, however, was not enough for my aunt. She dreamed of a lover for the fifteen days of New Year's, the time for families to exchange visits, money, and food. She plied her secret comb. And sure enough she cursed the year, the family, the village, and herself.

Even as her hair lured her imminent lover, many other men looked at her. Uncles, cousins, nephews, brothers would have looked, too, had they been home between journeys. Perhaps they had already been restraining their curiosity, and they left, fearful that their glances, like a field of nesting birds, might be startled and caught. Poverty hurt, and that was their first reason for leaving. But another, final reason for leaving the crowded house was the never-said.

She may have been unusually beloved, the precious only daughter, spoiled and mirror gazing because of the affection the family lavished on her. When her husband left, they welcomed the chance to take her back from the in-laws; she could live like the little daughter for just a while longer. There are stories that my grandfather was different from other people, "crazy ever since the little Jap bayoneted him in the head." He used to put his naked penis on the dinner table, laughing. And one day he brought home a baby girl, wrapped up inside his brown western-style greatcoat. He had traded one of his sons, probably my father, the youngest, for her. My grandmother made him trade back. When he finally got a daughter of his own, he doted on her. They must have all loved her, except perhaps my father, the only brother who never went back to China, having once been traded for a girl.

Brothers and sisters, newly men and women, had to efface their sexual color and present plain miens. Disturbing hair and eyes, a smile like no other, threatened the ideal of five generations living under one roof. To focus blurs, people shouted face to face and yelled from room to room. The immigrants I know have loud voices, unmodulated to American tones even after years away from the village where they called their friendships out across the fields. I have not been able to stop my mother's screams in public libraries or over telephones. Walking erect (knees straight, toes pointed forward, not pigeon-toed, which is Chinese-feminine) and speaking in an inaudible voice, I have tried to turn myself American-feminine. Chinese communication was loud, public. Only sick people had to whisper. But at the dinner table, where the family members came nearest one another, no one could talk, not the outcasts nor any eaters. Every word that falls from the mouth is a coin lost. Silently they gave and accepted food with both hands. A preoccupied child who took his bowl with one hand got a sideways glare. A complete moment of total attention is due everyone alike. Children and lovers have no singularity here, but my aunt used a secret voice, a separate attentiveness.

She kept the man's name to herself throughout her labor and dying; she did not accuse him that he be punished with her. To save her inseminator's name she gave silent birth.

He may have been somebody in her own household, but intercourse with a man outside the family would have been no less abhorrent. All the village were kinsmen, and the titles shouted in loud country voices never let kinship be forgotten. Any man within visiting distance would have been neutralized as a lover—"brother," "younger brother," "older brother"—one hundred and fifteen relationship titles. Parents researched birth charts probably not so much to assure good fortune as to circumvent incest in a population that has but one hundred surnames. Everybody has eight million relatives. How useless then sexual mannerisms, how dangerous.

As if it came from an atavism deeper than fear, I used to add "brother" silently to boys' names. It hexed the boys, who would or would not ask me to dance, and made them less scary and as familiar and deserving of benevolence as girls.

But, of course, I hexed myself also—no dates. I should have stood up, both arms waving, and shouted out across libraries, "Hey, you! Love me back." I had no idea, though, how to make attraction selective, how to control its direction and magnitude. If I made myself American-pretty so that the five or six Chinese boys in the class fell in love with me, everyone else—the Caucasian, Negro, and Japanese boys—would too. Sisterliness, dignified and honorable, made much more sense.

Attraction eludes control so stubbornly that whole societies designed to organize relationships among people cannot keep order, not even when they bind people to one another from childhood and raise them together. Among the very poor and the wealthy, brothers married their adopted sisters, like doves. Our family allowed some romance, paying adult brides' prices and providing dowries so that their sons and daughters could marry strangers. Marriage promises to turn strangers into friendly relatives—a nation of siblings.

In the village structure, spirits shimmered among the live creatures, balanced and held in equilibrium by time and land. But one human being flaring up into violence could open up a black hole, a maelstrom that pulled in the sky. The frightened villagers, who depended on one another to maintain the real, went to my aunt to show her a personal, physical representation of the break she had made in the "roundness." Misallying couples snapped off the future, which was to be embodied in true offspring. The villagers punished her for acting as if she could have a private life, secret and apart from them.

If my aunt had betrayed the family at a time of large grain yields and peace, when many boys were born, and wings were being built on many houses, perhaps she might have escaped such severe punishment. But the men—hungry, greedy, tired of planting in dry soil—and had been forced to leave the village in order to send food-money home. There were ghost plagues, bandit plagues, wars with the Japanese, floods. My Chinese brother and sister had died of an unknown sickness. Adultery, perhaps only a mistake during good times, became a crime when the village needed food.

The round moon cakes and round doorways, the round tables of graduated size that fit one roundness inside another, round windows and rice bowls—these talismans had lost their power to warn this family of the law: a family must be whole, faithfully keeping the descent line by having sons to feed the old and the dead, who in turn look after the family. The villagers came to show my aunt and her lover-in-hiding a broken house. The villagers were speeding up the circling of events because she was too shortsighted to see that her infidelity had already harmed the village, that waves of consequences would return unpredictably, sometimes in disguise, as now, to hurt her. This roundness had to be made coin-sized so that she would see its circumference: punish her at the birth of her baby. Awaken her to the inexorable. People who refused fatalism because they could invent small resources insisted on culpability. Deny accidents and wrest fault from the stars.

After the villagers left, their lanterns now scattering in various directions toward home, the family broke their silence and cursed her. "Aiaa, we're going to die. Death is coming. Death is coming. Look what you've done. You've killed us. Ghost! Dead ghost! Ghost! You've never been born." She ran out into the fields, far enough from the house so that she could no longer hear their voices, and pressed herself against the earth, her own land no more. When she felt the birth coming, she thought that she had been hurt. Her body seized together. "They've hurt me too much," she thought. "This is gall, and it will kill me." With forehead and knees against the earth, her body convulsed and then relaxed. She turned on her back, lay on the ground. The black well of sky and stars went out and out and out forever; her body and her complexity seemed to disappear. She was one of the stars, a bright dot in blackness, without home, without a companion, in eternal cold and silence. An agoraphobia rose in her, speeding higher and higher, bigger and bigger; she would not be able to contain it; there would be no end to fear.

Flayed, unprotected against space, she felt pain return, focusing her body. This pain chilled her—a cold, steady kind of surface pain. Inside, spasmodically, the other pain, the pain of the child, heated her. For hours she lay on the ground, alternately body and space. Sometimes a vision of normal comfort obliterated reality: she saw the family in the evening gambling at the dinner table, the young people massaging their elders' backs. She saw them congratulating one another, high joy on the mornings the rice shoots came up. When these pictures burst, the stars drew yet further apart. Black space opened.

She got to her feet to fight better and remembered that old-fashioned women gave birth in their pigsties to fool the jealous, pain-dealing gods, who do not snatch piglets. Before the next spasms could stop her, she ran to the pigsty, each step a rushing out into emptiness. She climbed over the fence and knelt in the dirt. It was good to have a fence enclosing her, a tribal person alone.

Laboring, this woman who had carried her child as a foreign growth that sickened her every day, expelled it at last. She reached down to touch the hot, wet, moving mass, surely smaller than anything human, and could feel that it was human after all—fingers, toes, nails, nose. She pulled it up on to her belly, and it lay curled there, butt in the air, feet precisely tucked one under the other. She opened her loose shirt and buttoned the child inside. After resting, it squirmed and thrashed and she pushed it up to her breast. It turned its head this way and that until it found her nipple. There, it made little snuffling noises. She clenched her teeth at its preciousness, lovely as a young calf, a piglet, a little dog.

She may have gone to the pigsty as a last act of responsibility: she would protect this child as she had protected its father. It would look after her soul, leaving supplies on her grave. But how would this tiny child without family find her grave when there would be no marker for her anywhere, neither in the earth nor the family hall? No one would give her a family hall name. She had taken the child with her into the wastes. At its birth the two of them had felt the same raw pain of separation, a wound that only the family pressing tight could close. A child with no descent line would not soften her life but only trail after her, ghostlike, begging her to give it purpose. At dawn the villagers on their way to the fields would stand around the fence and look.

Full of milk, the little ghost slept. When it awoke, she hardened her breasts against the milk that crying loosens. Toward morning she picked up the baby and walked to the well.

Carrying the baby to the well shows loving. Otherwise abandon it. Turn its face into the mud. Mothers who love their children take them along. It was probably a girl; there is some hope of forgiveness for boys.

"Don't tell anyone you had an aunt. Your father does not want to hear her name. She has never been born." I have believed that sex was unspeakable and words so strong and fathers so frail that "aunt" would do my father mysterious harm. I have thought that my family, having settled among immigrants who had also been their neighbors in the ancestral land, needed to clean their name, and a wrong word would incite the kinspeople even here. But there is more to this silence: they want me to participate in her punishment. And I have.

In the twenty years since I heard this story I have not asked for details nor said my aunt's name; I do not know it. People who can comfort the dead can also chase after them to hurt them further—a reverse ancestor worship. The real punishment was not the raid swiftly inflicted by the villagers, but the family's deliberately forgetting her. Her betrayal so maddened them, they saw to it that she would suffer forever, even after death. Always hungry, always needing, she would have to beg food from other ghosts, snatch and steal it from those whose living descendants give them gifts. She would have to fight the ghosts massed at crossroads for the buns a few thoughtful citizens leave to decoy her away from village and home so that the ancestral spirits could feast unharassed. At peace, they could act like gods, not ghosts, their descent lines providing them with paper suits and dresses, spirit money, paper houses, paper automobiles, chicken, meat, and rice into eternity— essences delivered up in smoke and flames, steam and incense rising from each rice bowl. In an attempt to make the Chinese care for people outside the family, Chairman Mao encourages us now to give our paper replicas to the spirits of outstanding soldiers and workers, no matter whose ancestors they may be. My aunt remains forever hungry. Goods are not distributed evenly among the dead.

My aunt haunts me—her ghost drawn to me because now, after fifty years of neglect, I alone devote pages of paper to her, though not origamied into houses and clothes. I do not think she always means me well. I am telling on her, and she was a spite suicide, drowning herself in the drinking water. The Chinese are always very frightened of the drowned one, whose weeping ghost, wet hair hanging and skin bloated, waits silently by the water to pull down a substitute.

Questions for "No Name Woman"

1. In what ways is the aunt a "no name woman"?

2. Why does this woman "haunt" the author?

3. Like *The Return of Martin Guerre* (see pages 121–125), this is in a sense a detective story. The author has many questions about the aunt which her mother cannot or will not answer. What are some of the questions and how does Kingston answer them for herself?

4. The author claims that her family wanted her to participate in her aunt's punishment, "And I have," she writes. How has she done so? Why then has she written her aunt's story? What does the story reveal about the author?

5. What is this story about?

A native of New York, Theresa Finegan worked as a secretary before entering Queens College, where she majored in psychology. Here she explains how the interview reprinted in this chapter came about:

> As an Irish-American, I was interested in the Irish immigrant experience in America. I decided to interview a friend's granduncle, Patrick McMahon, about his earliest experiences after sailing from Ireland to the United States in 1926.
>
> In December of 1985, when I interviewed Pat McMahon, he was 83 years young, with a wiry 5'9" frame, snow white hair, and a ruddy complexion. The various job experiences he described are filled with the humor and candor of a lively storyteller who still has many tales to tell.
>
> Today, he makes frequent trips to the "old country" and is active in an Irish-American club in Middle Village, New York. Mr. McMahon has by no means forgotten his roots.
>
> The interview was conducted in two sessions, with family members sitting together in the living room of McMahon's house. The participants noted in the transcript are:

PM:	Patrick McMahon
BM:	Betty McMahon, Patrick's second wife
EG:	Betty's daughter
AM:	Andrew McCabe, Patrick's grandnephew
TAF:	Theresa A. Finegan

Special thanks are given to Andrew McCabe for his diligent assistance in the transcription of this interview.

Interview with Patrick McMahon, an Irish Immigrant

PM: My name is Pat McMahon and I came from County Monahan in 1926—on the *Baltic,* that was the name of the ship. Well, we had a nice trip: it was rough, but . . . any liquor we had with us, we had to dump before we got off.

Well I came here and got off all right. There was no Ellis Isle at that time—it was all finished. I went to my sister's house and that's where I stayed.

TAF: When you first came here, what do you remember about getting here—the stories you had heard about what people said it would be like? Were you disappointed?

PM: Oh, I was very disappointed.

TAF: Really?

EG: No gold lining the streets?

PM: It wasn't too easy getting a job other than on the trolley cars.

EG: Well, wasn't that better than Ireland, where there were no jobs?

PM: Well, it was . . . there was nothing in Ireland at that time.

EG: But you could come and get a job?

PM: You could come and get a job—Yeh . . . Oh and then the Depression came along and there was no such thing as getting a job.

EG: Were you working all through the Depression?

PM: No. Not at all. Here and there you'd get a little job. That's when I got the job painting the ceiling.

TAF: What job was that? [The job was part of the government's New Deal projects.]

PM: . . . I would paint on the ceiling, you know. I had never heard of calcimite in my life—that's the white stuff that they used to put on ceilings and you could wash it off with water. I never heard of that stuff. I went and put the paint on top of that and every time you put the brush down. . . . It was a horrid looking job!

EG: Did you get fired? Did you get paid?

PM: I didn't go back.

EG: Anything that goes wrong, Poppy leaves.

PM: I had a look and I thought that was bad enough. I went home and didn't go back the next day. That was all.

EG: How did you think the buildings were when you landed here? Did the place look big to you?

PM: Oh, yes. The places looked big. I didn't see much of them when I came off of the boat because Hughie and Benny and the rest of the men met me at the boat and took me to 1572 2nd Avenue.

EG: They were big enough . . . big change from home . . . big change from the farm?

PM: There was another fellow—he said he saw bigger ones in Dublin.

EG: Were you lonesome?

PM: Me? Not at all.

TAF: So, where did you hang out?

PM: There was no hanging out then.

BM: Didn't you go to the dances . . . on weekends . . . for entertainment?

PM: The Tuxedo [Mr. McMahon listed some of the New York dance halls] . . . Celtic Park . . . the first Sunday I was here, they had a big fight down there in Long Island—the Irish had a football field there. It was my first Sunday in the country and the fight started on the field where they were playing [Irish football] and then you seen all the fences cave in and everyone in the park was fighting.

We got creeping out—we left—we had nothing to fight about; that fight started in Ireland. That was the end of the park: it was closed after that.

I was great for football on the other side, but not here—it was too rough here. My God, it was rough. . . .

TAF: What was your first meal here like?

PM: The meals were good.

TAF: Was it like home?

PM: You never get any meals here like home.

. . . I got a job in a hospital: in the laundry, at Pelham [the Bronx], and in the evening, I used to see a bunch of doctors go into a room downstairs. I was told not to go in there. I was curious, and when they left one night, I went in there. I opened the door and looked in—and—there was a dead man on the table, and there was one man instructing the doctors. The doctor had the dead man's hair up like this. [Mr. McMahon indicated that the corpse's scalp was lifted]—You know—and he was pointing with a pencil at his brain. That was all I seen that day.

The next night, I opened the door again and looked in—and the dead man had a beard. Oh! His beard grew overnight! It was terrific! They used to buy them bodies from Bellevue [Hospital]. They were picked up from the Bowery and they'd sell them to them for five dollars. I think they put them in the incinerator after they finished. The body'd come in with a label on its leg—like a dead pig.

. . . Next I got a job on the Second Avenue Trolley—they were very old.

I was one night going up Second Avenue at about 96th Street and I seen a man's leg—and a shoe on it—on the street. I couldn't stop. I don't know what it was—I never seen it in the paper or anything else. Someone lost their leg under a trolley or something.

In the mornings, all [the trolley operators] had to have three dollars change, and if you didn't have it, you had to let the people on anyway. You couldn't keep them off. After a while, they all got wise to that.

You were only supposed to have three dollars change starting. . . .

AM: Did the company give it to you?

PM: You had to have your own.

AM: When you ran the trolley . . . when you took money from the people—did you keep that and give some of it to the company?

PM: I gave it all to the company. You had to put it in a box and ring up. Every one . . . you had to ring a bell.

TAF: How much was it to ride?

PM: One nickel.

TAF: Where did the line run?

PM: Second Avenue. All the way down to South Ferry and the 125th Street.

I was working the night that Al Smith was defeated. Al Smith ran for president one time and I was working the night shift at that time. I heard down at South Ferry that he was defeated—I got on my trolley car and I never stopped for nobody. I came up and put the trolley in and quit—because he lost. He was the first Catholic to run for President.

Questions for "Interview with Patrick McMahon"

1.   What can you infer about McMahon from his job experiences? From the way he addresses (and evades) the questions of the interviewers?

2.   By comparing this interview with one of the other selections in this chapter, what generalizations can you venture about the differences between spoken and written reminiscence?

Natalie Zemon Davis (1928–   )

Natalie Zemon Davis is a professor of history at Princeton University. She is the author of a number of articles on French history, as well as of *Society and Culture in Early Modern France* (1975). Davis collaborated on the screenplay for *Le Retour de Martin Guerre,* a film project that prompted her to write *The Return of Martin Guerre* (1983), from which the following chapter was taken. Here is the background of that story:

> In 1538 in Artigat, France, Martin Guerre and Bertrande de Rols were married. Both were from wealthy peasant families and both were, even by the standards of that time, very young—Martin around 14 and Bertrande perhaps a few years younger. For more than eight years, Martin was unable to consummate the marriage, and in the eyes of the village the couple appeared to be cast under a spell. Finally, the spell of impotence was lifted and Bertrande bore a son, Sanxi.
>
> In 1548, when Sanxi was several months old and Martin in his 24th year, Martin disappeared. Eight years later, he returned, or so everyone thought, but after three or four years of peaceful marriage Bertrande claimed she had been tricked by an impostor and brought him to trial. The man almost persuaded the court that he was Martin Guerre, but at the last moment the true Martin Guerre appeared, and the impostor— revealed as Arnaud du Tilh, alias Pansette—was sentenced to death.

In Chapter 3 of her book, reprinted here, Davis tries to define Bertrande's role in the community, as well as to reconstruct her life during the years of Martin's absence.

The Honor of Bertrande de Rols

When Martin Guerre left on his adventures, his wife was no more than twenty-two years old. The "beautiful young woman" may also have looked at her past with some regrets.

As best we can see, Bertrande had spent her childhood with at least one brother and close to her mother's side, learning to spin and do other woman's work. Girls in Artigat and nearby villages were sometimes sent out to service in another household—we find a merchant's wife in Le Fossat leaving dresses to her servant, for example—but in families like Bertrande's they more often helped at home until they married.

And then before Bertrande had time to dance to the violins with a village lad at the Assumption Day feast in Artigat or go through some other courtship ritual, she was wed to Martin Guerre. That she had started her "flowers," as the female menstrual flow was called, is probable, else the families would not have allowed the fertility drink the night of the wedding, intended to facilitate her pregnancy. But young as she was and in a strange house, she had the same sexual malaise as did Martin; she too was "bewitched," as she said to the court of Rieux years later. Now witches ordinarily dealt only with the male organ when trying to prevent intercourse between husband and wife.[1] But it could happen to a woman: as explained by the inquisitors in the *Malleus Maleficarum,* "the devil can so darken the wife's understanding that she considers her husband so loathsome that not for all the world would she allow him to lie with her."

Bertrande might not have put it in these words, but it seems clear that for a while she was relieved that they could not have intercourse. Yet, when urged by her relatives to separate from Martin, she firmly refused. Here we come to certain character traits of Bertrande de Rols, which she was already displaying in her sixteenth year: a concern for her reputation as a woman, a stubborn independence, and a shrewd realism about how she could maneuver within the constraints placed upon one of her sex. Her refusal to have her marriage dissolved, which might well have been followed by another marriage at her parents' behest, freed her temporarily from certain wifely duties. It gave her a chance to have a girlhood with Martin's younger sisters, with whom she got on well. And she could get credit for her virtue. As Coras was to say of her refusal to separate from Martin, "that act, like a touchstone, offered great proof of the *honnesteté* of the said de Rols." Some of the Artigat goodwives may have well uttered the same sentiments.

Then when Bertrande was ready for it, the old woman "appeared suddenly as if from heaven" and helped to lift the spell. She finally gave birth to a child, an event that meant for her (as it did for village women whose marriages began more smoothly) the first real step into adulthood. Bertrande had learned of that adult women's world from her own mother, from her Basque mother-in-law, and her godmothers. What did it hold in store for her? First, a world where organizational structure and public identity were associated exclusively with males. The particle "de," so often found in women's names in and around Artigat, did not come from the peasants trying to ape the nobility, but was a way of showing the classification system of village society. Bertrande was "de Rols," her father was Rols; Jeanne was "de Ban-

---

[1] Indeed, while reporting Bertrande's words, Coras's annotation [Coras was a judge at the trial of "Martin Guerre"] assumed that it was Martin who was under a spell and described only the forms of enchanting the male. Female "impotence" was due, he said, to natural causes, such as the woman's being "so narrow and closed in her secret parts that she could not endure carnal intercourse with a man" (pp. 40–44). But this was not the case with Bertrande. The canonists also paid little attention to the occult causes of female impotence. Pierre Darmon, *Le Tribunal de l'impuissance* (Paris, 1979), pp. 48–52.

quels," her father was Banquels; Arnaude was "de Tor," her father was Tor. The heirs along the Lèze River were always the male children, as we have seen, unless the family was unfortunate enough to have only girls. The village consuls summoned male villagers to their deliberations, convoking wives and widows only when there was an order to be given.

In the everyday life of the fields and the households, however, the women were always important. They performed the characteristically female tasks of hoeing, trimming the vines, and cutting the grapes. Jointly with their husbands, they rented and worked the land, sheared sheep, and took cows and calves in contracts of *gasailhe*. A certain Maragille Cortalle, widow from Saint-Ybars, even acquired eighteen lambs by herself *en gasailhe*, promising to maintain them "as a good father of the family" for four years. They spun thread for the weavers of Le Fossat and made loaves of bread to sell to other villagers. Women like Marguerite alias La Brugarsse of Le Carla lent out small sums of money, while the wives and widows of rural merchants, such as Bertrande de Gouthelas and Suzanne de Robert of Le Fossat, made substantial sales in grain, millet, and wine. They were, of course, midwives, and with few surgeons resident in the area they did much of the curing.

The women were most dependent on the good will of their husbands and sons when they were left as widows. In principle, the customs of the Languedoc guaranteed the widow the return of everything she had brought to the marriage as her dowry plus an "increase" of one third of the value of that dowry. In fact, in Artigat and surrounding burgs and villages, the marriage contracts do not say this. They spell out the wife's rights to the husband's estate only in the special case where her parents or widowed mother plan to live jointly with the couple. Most decisions are made in the husband's will. At best he provides that his wife can have the usufruct of all his goods so long as she lives "in widowhood" (some wills add "and in virtue"). If he really trusts her or wants to reward her "for her agreeable services," he specifies that she can enjoy his goods "without having to turn over accounts to anyone in the world." If she can not get along with his heirs, then he makes detailed provision for her: seven quarters of grain and one barrel of good wine each year, a dress and a pair of shoes and stockings every two years, wood for her heating, and the like. If she remarries, then he gives her a lump sum, which may be equivalent to her dowry or to her dowry and the increase.

The realities of this peasant world encouraged not only the skills of a good farm wife, but the woman's ability to get her way with the men and to calculate her advantages, say, in remaining a widow. A wife of Artigat could never hope to have the position of the noble Rose d'Espaigne, Lady of Durfort, an heiress who was buying up lands and harassing her sharecroppers just to the east of the village. But she could hope to enjoy the respect of other village women and informal power as a widow, being addressed by the worthy title of Na, able to bestow a vineyard on a newly married son and hosen on all her godchildren. And the women seem to have gone along with the system, passing it on through the deep tie and hidden complicity of mother and daughter. As wives, they selected their husbands as their universal heirs; as widows, they usually preferred their sons as heirs over their daughters. They were deeply offended and sought redress when insulted as a "bagasse," a prostitute. Indeed, one goodwife of Le Fossat sued a neighbor woman, not only for hitting her in a quarrel over poultry but also for calling her a "hen."

These were the values that Bertrande de Rols grew up with. In all her later adventures, Bertrande never showed herself as wanting to be outside this village society, to be rejected by it or to leave it. But she did seek to make her own way. It may have helped to have had the example close at hand of her mother-in-law, one of those self-assured Basque females. The women of the Labourd, often heirs and mistresses in their own right, were known for their "effrontery" and would later be notorious as witches.

Just as Bertrande, now mother to a son, was establishing herself on a new footing with her mother-in-law, Martin Guerre disappeared without a trace. This was a catastrophe. Even for peasants who enjoyed a good gossip, the unexpected disappearance of an important villager was troubling, leaving an anomalous gap among the young married couples. For the Guerres from the Basque country, here was yet another scandal to live down. Martin's parents died without news of their son. The elder Sanxi finally forgave him, leaving a testament naming Martin as heir both to the property in Hendaye and the lands in Artigat. The local notaries knew what to do when the universal heir was absent: "if he is dead or does not return," the formulas went, others are substituted in his place. For the time being, Pierre Guerre would be the administrator of the considerable properties of his late brother and the guardian of Martin's unmarried sisters.

At some point in those years—most likely in the early 1550's in the wake of the elder Sanxi's death—Pierre Guerre made an effort to salvage the relationship between the Guerres and the Rols and to help Martin's abandoned wife. Now a widower with daughters of his own, he married Bertrande's widowed mother.[2] Their marriage contract would have been of the elaborate kind, drawn up at the establishment of a joint household. Bertrande's mother would have brought whatever money or goods her husband had left her in the event that she remarried; Pierre would have made promises to support Bertrande and her son Sanxi; and they would have decided how to share any newly acquired goods. The neighboring house in which the old landlord and the young landlord had lived was presumably leased for short terms—no one would have trusted the young Bertrande to maintain it under the circumstances—and Pierre Guerre took over the headship of a household of mostly females on his own land.

---

[2]Coras does not give the date of the marriage of Pierre Guerre and Bertrande's mother, but this seems the most probable time. Pierre's daughters are never referred to as sisters or half-sisters of Bertrande, and he must have had them by a first marriage. Whatever economic arrangements her husband had made for her in his will, Bertrande's mother would have been induced by her daughter's predicament to remarry.

Bertrande's status was much reduced by all these events. Neither wife nor widow, she was under the same roof with her mother again. Neither wife nor widow, she had to face the other village women at the mill, the well, the tileworks, and at the harvest. And there was no easy remedy for her in the law. Since the laxer days of Pope Alexander III in the twelfth century, the doctors had insisted that a wife was not free to remarry in the absence of her husband, no matter how many years had elapsed, unless she had certain proof of his death. Of the alternate traditions in the civil law, it was the harsher one of Justinian that had prevailed. The Parlement of Toulouse cited it in judging a marriage case in 1557: "During the absence of the husband, the wife cannot remarry unless she has proof of his death . . . not even when he has been absent twenty years or more . . . And the death must be proven by witnesses, who give sure depositions, or by great and manifest presumptions."

Of course peasants might try to get around the law—it would hardly be the first time—and fabricate news of a drowning or a bullet, or simply ignore the law if there were a cooperative priest in the village. But Bertrande chose not to do so. Her practical interest kept her close to her son and what would some day be his inheritance. There was also her stiff-necked sense of herself and her reputation. Whatever glances or invitations came her way, the beautiful young woman lived (so everyone would later attest) "virtuously and honorably."

Meanwhile she worked, she raised her son Sanxi, and she waited. She may have been helped through her solitude by her four sisters-in-law and by the wise woman who had counseled her during her bewitchment. The rectors who had succeeded Messire Jacques Boëri in the church of Artigat were neither of them from local families and may not have always resided in the parish; Bertrande may have elaborated on her troubles only to Saint Catherine, whose chapel was in the cemetery. But she surely reflected on her life, dividing it into thirds as she did later when presenting herself to the judge of Rieux; the nine or ten years of her childhood, the nine or ten years of her marriage, the years of her waiting, which lengthened into eight or more. Beyond a young womanhood with only a brief period of sexuality, beyond a marriage in which her husband understood her little, may have feared her, and surely abandoned her, Bertrande dreamed of a husband and lover who would come back, and be different. Then in the summer of 1556, a man presented himself to her as the long-lost Martin Guerre. Previously he had been known as Arnaud du Tilh, alias Pansette.

Questions for "The Honor of Bertrande de Rols"

1.   In the introduction to her book, Davis says that historians find out about people who lived long ago by looking at letters, diaries, family histories, plays, stories, court documents, and the like. Return for a moment to

the selection and try to determine the kinds of sources Davis might have used for some of her inferences in this particular chapter.

2.   Why do you think Bertrande accepted Pansette as her husband Martin? What reasons would she have for rejecting him four years later?

READING/WRITING

The selections in this chapter present a number of approaches to writing autobiography and biography:

1. Over a period of one or two weeks, try writing a series of letters—to a friend, family member, classmate, or historical figure you would like to have known—in which you narrate the events of a particularly tumultuous period in your life. You might discuss, as Van Gogh does, a conflict in your personal life, or some of the successes and frustrations you have experienced in creative or professional aspirations. The events might have taken place some time ago, or are perhaps taking place as you write. In any case, try to describe the events clearly, and to capture in detail your reactions toward them.

2. After you have read the selection from Darwin's autobiography, compose an autobiographical essay in which you describe two or three people or events that influenced your choice of a prospective career, avocation, college major, or any other consuming interest you have.

3. Write an essay that combines narration and analysis on the subject of "The Discovery of a Father (or Mother)." Taking your cue from Sherwood Anderson's piece, narrate an incident involving you and your father or mother, and show how this occurrence changed the way you look at your parent and your relationship to him or her.

4. As an alternative to assignment 3, we offer this next writing suggestion, based on the structure of Maxine Hong Kingston's memoirs, *The Woman Warrior.* Each of the sections outlined below is modeled on a chapter from Kingston's book. You are invited to put together an autobiography that is really a kind of "family album," showing, as Kingston does, how your life has been intertwined with, and influenced by, the lives of members of your family. Your memoirs may consist of several or all of the following sections. There should, of course, be some common theme or thread that connects these sections, just as Kingston's concept of "the woman warrior" is carried throughout the chapters of her autobiography.

   a. A "secret story" about yourself or someone in your family, such as the one (reprinted in this section) Kingston tells about her aunt, the "no name woman."

b. A description of, or story about, a legendary hero or heroine whom you fantasized about or who influenced you when you were a child.

c. A story from the early life of one of your parents—the parent to whom you feel closer. Because the events you will narrate occurred before you were born, you will have to depend on your parents or other family members for "the facts."

d. A story about another relative, such as an aunt or grandfather.

e. A story about you as a child—a key incident in your youth, that might help the reader to understand the adult you have become.

In selecting your stories, remember to consider what significance these tales have for you. Why did you choose these particular events to narrate, out of all the stories your family has told you? How did these stories shape your childhood? In the following excerpt, for example, our student Mi-Young Cho responds to part (b) by suggesting how the story of a Korean heroine affected her own development as a youngster:

The Chant of Yoo, Kwarn Soon

I learned the chant of Yoo, Kwarn Soon, who was the heroine of Korean history, when I was around ten years old. When my friend and I played a game of clapping hands, we joyfully sang the chant of Yoo, Kwarn Soon.

When I was a junior high school student, I read the book of her heroic story. She fought bravely against Japanese rule with her bare hands. She was not strong physically, but her mind and spirit were filled with justice and love for her people.

No heroine is better known or loved than she. When Japan invaded Korea and ruled it for thirty-six years as a colony, Koreans suffered. The Japanese obliterated the Korean culture, language, and nationality. In that dark and terrible time, Yoo, Kwarn Soon was a fire which never died out. She did not give up hope for her country and shouted independence wherever she went. Even while she was in jail, she never submitted to the political power of the Japanese.

At the age of twenty, she was killed by them. Her body was cut into several pieces. But the spirit of freedom still lived in people's hearts; she had enlightened their consciousness of once again being independent.

I was very timid and introverted, especially in my early childhood until my high school years. I was never outgoing before others but was afraid even to talk in class. My teachers had a difficult time whenever I had to answer their questions because I would whisper in response. I felt that I could never be a courageous girl. Yet I loved Yoo, Kwarn Soon very much and respected her bravery and tenacity. I was impressed by her strong desire to be an independent person in her family and to be worthy of her country.

I wanted to be loved by others but did not even try to love others. I was afraid to open up before people. But when I thought about Yoo, Kwarn Soon,

I wished that I could somehow be like her. I dreamed about living such a dynamic, noble, and precious life, bravely offering myself for the sake of others.

5. For many of us, some of life's illuminating moments occur at the dinner table. Describe a memorable meal in your life—a pleasant or unpleasant event that stands out in your mind for reasons other than the food. Try to summon up all the sensory impressions you associate with the occasion, as M. F. K. Fisher does in her essay.

6. In a number of selections in this chapter, the authors discover something about themselves through interaction with family members. Pick one of these authors—Darwin, Van Gogh, Anderson, Fisher, Kingston—and analyze what the author discovers about himself or herself in the course of the selection you've read.

7. Write an "oral history": Interview an older family member, acquaintance, or stranger from the neighborhood about the jobs they've had, or their early memories of your neighborhood and the changes it has undergone over the years, or (if they're immigrants) their first impressions of this country.

8. Research and write a brief biography of a historical figure who fascinates you; perhaps rescue from oblivion some minor character in history by using contemporary historical documents, as Natalie Zemon Davis does, to infer what you can about this character's life.

9. Tell the story of a close friend who has captured your imagination. In the following excerpt from Wianyang Ju's story "The Last Supper" (the opening of which is quoted in the introduction to this chapter), the author dramatizes the horror he lived through during China's Cultural Revolution by focusing on the fate of his friend Hsiao. At this point in the story, which is unfortunately too long to be quoted here in its entirety, Ju has just received a letter from Hsiao after years of silence:

"Oh, it is from Hsiao!" I was surprised. Hsiao had been put in jail five years earlier because of a political "crime." I did not expect he would send me a letter. In the letter, he told me of his recent situation. His case had been reinvestigated, and he hoped his unredressed injustice might be clarified. Hsiao hoped I could send a violin to him since I was the only one he could ask for this. His father had committed suicide and his mother had become schizophrenic. He said he believed that I would satisfy his wishes because our lasting friendship was very intimate. He had a strong feeling that we would meet soon. Reading this unusual letter, I was immersed in recollection.

Hsiao was one of my oldest and best friends. The friendship between us could be traced back to our childhood. We were in the same class all through school. He always looked thin and refined. His parents both were music teachers. By the influence of his family, Hsiao had been playing violin since he was five. Before we entered high school, he had become a brilliant violinist. Some musicians predicted he could be a great violinist some day.

Although I knew little about music, I enjoyed hearing him practicing. Meanwhile, he also admired my wide scientific knowledge when I was explaining why a thick and short string could produce a lower tone. Because our parents were intellectuals, we were thrown out of school during the Cultural Revolution. At the age of 16, we were sent to a small village and began to take the test of life.[1] Only two years later, the tragedy happened. . . .

That was a dark and chilly night. Because of the rain, the leader of our team of farm workers allowed us to come home earlier. Despite the fact that we were so tired after work, Hsiao and I went out. He went to buy some food from the peasants and I went to invite a few of our friends to our small house because that day was the first anniversary of our being at this little village. We planned to ''celebrate'' it although it was not a happy day.

When I returned home with three of our friends, Hsiao had prepared everything for the dinner. He was a good cook; his intelligence could be reflected in any field.

We sat around the table. The flame of the candle twinkled in the dark. At the dinner, we talked a lot since we hadn't seen each other for a long time. All of us were glad because our friendship was still strong in such an unhappy situation. We spoke on so many topics. We seemed to forget that we were in this little village. We spoke about the news of the day and analysed the speech of some country leaders. We also touched upon where and how old we would be when Halley's Comet returned. We seemed interested in everything. However, we avoided discussing our future. Reality had broken our ideals, and our future was like the darkness that surrounded us. Who could understand it?

After we had drunk a couple of glasses of wine, I noticed that Hsiao hadn't opened his mouth.

''Hsiao, cheer up. Let's toast to our friendship!'' I stood up.

''Thanks, Wianyang. You know I have drunk three glasses already.'' Hsiao didn't raise his head. His eyes were focusing on his fingers so that I knew he was thinking of his violin again.

''C'mon, I am sure that the rate of alcohol in your blood is still below 0.005 percent. Your face has not turned red yet.'' I did not want to think about our future at this moment. Wine could help us to forget everything. I moved the cup over to Hsiao.

One friend followed me, ''Yes, let's drink, let us be drunk. Sometimes being drunk is better than facing reality.''

The flame of the candle was still twinkling and jumping, and the candle was becoming shorter and shorter. The shadows of our bodies were growing taller on the wall. It was so dark outside that we felt safe in this crude house.

''Talking, talking, when will these empty days end?'' Hsiao suddenly shouted out. ''Lincoln, Washington, and Lenin, who can save us?''

He took a breath. ''Newton, Einstein, they mean nothing to us!''

As we looked at his pale face, we remained quiet. Yes, we were young, but where were our hopes?

---

[1]In 1966, Mao closed all schools in China. He forced all students to settle down in the countryside in order to acquire ''education'' from the poor peasants. [author's note]

"Look at, look at my fingers. They have become thick and stiff. So many years of practice, so many years of study. What have I got? Only blame. They say that I am the descendant of the capitalist class, and I must remold my ideological form. Isn't this ridiculous?"

Hsiao didn't want to stop. He stood up. "Where is my goal in life? What are we living for in this world? Getting educated by the poor peasants in the countryside? What have we learnt from them? Selfish and shortsighted! Look at my fingers. They have destroyed me!"

The wine was burning in our bodies. I felt as if the fire in my heart was looking for a hole through which to escape. I wanted to cry. We had lost hope in our future.

One of our friends reminded us that we had to be careful about what we were saying. But at that moment, we couldn't control ourselves.

"I just don't understand why we aren't treated nicely. We love the country and we did nothing against the Communist Party and Chairman Mao. Why? Why?

"They are not human beings. They don't have hearts. Why doesn't God punish them?" Hsiao punched the table. "Let those communists come here. Let them experience such a life without hope. If they could live here more than one month, I, Hsiao, would seriously announce to the world that I support Mao's decision and his theory."

We looked at each other. Although we knew that talking about Mao was dangerous, nobody stopped him because we were all on friendly terms. Hsiao shouted out what he wanted to say.

"It is a fact that Mao and his comrades established the People's Republic of China, a socialist country in the East. Theoretically, the people in such a country would have the most freedom in the world and the country would have a democratic system. But where are these things here? Cheating! All of the politicians are swindlers."

Nobody disagreed with Hsiao's views. Freedom and democracy were decorations in this communist country.

"I have spoken with many people. What do they think of Mao? A king! The king of our country! History has been turned back, and our country has been back to the feudal period. Under his depotic and autocratic ruling, Chinese people are suffering. Look, look at his crafty face!" Hsiao turned to Mao's picture on the wall, "I hate you, I hate you!"

At that time, everyone had to put Mao's picture in every room. He wanted his country to become a great prison.

Mao, in the picture, had a sinister smile which gave us high disdain.

"Someday, it will be certain that history will try you!" Hsiao walked toward the picture and tore it.

We were shocked by his crazy action. If others knew that, the result would be serious. I ran over to the fragments of the picture and put them into a bag. Hsiao stood there like a dumb chicken. The air was frozen and everyone was scared. I felt how powerful and strong Mao was at that moment. What a devil he was!

Apparently, it was impossible to continue the dinner, so our friends went back with heavy hearts, Hsiao and I too.

I didn't sleep that night. The things that happened in the past, the dream of the future, and our recent situation, all of these were stirring in my mind.

Hsiao's words echoed in the darkness. Yes, the anger in the people's hearts would explode someday like a volcanic eruption, I believed that.

On the next morning, a group of policemen surrounded the village. Hsiao was taken away and he didn't come back. At the same time, I was interrogated many times. A few months later, it was said that Hsiao had been put in jail and sentenced to ten-year imprisonment. I didn't know, even now I don't know, how they knew what we did at that dinner. During that period, anything could happen. Nobody could be trusted, except myself.

"Son, what did he say? How is he?" My mother interrupted my recalling. She liked Hsiao very much and had been worried about his situation all the time.

I told my mother that he was all right and it was possible that he could come home earlier. As his best friend, I decided that I would go to see him if possible and bring him his violin.

That last supper, I call it "The last supper" because I haven't had a party with friends since then, had taken place five years before, but it made a deep impression on me. The supper, it could be said, ended my puerile youth. I became more mature and more soberminded after that time. That last supper was a turning point in my life.

CHAPTER
4
Short Fiction

From earliest times, when humans first lit fires to sit by, stories were told for the same reasons they are told today—to entertain, to instruct, to make sense out of a mysterious and often frightening world. Folklore—the tales, legends, and beliefs of a culture that are passed on orally—lies at the heart of every society, whether ancient or modern. As an article on folklore (included in Chapter 7 of this book) shows, so-called modern cultures perpetuate their own stories and superstitions in both traditional and innovative ways. Americans living in the 1980s, for example, pass on rumors of alligators living in urban sewer systems, report UFO sightings, consult their horoscopes, and flock to movies that feature vampires and haunted houses. Why this enduring fascination with the extraordinary and the occult? It seems to grow out of our anxiety about the forces of nature and our doubts about the ability of science and reason to combat these forces. At the same time, we clearly have a need to seek out the very things that frighten us.

Storytelling, then, is common to all cultures and all times. Although written literature has traveled a long way from the firelit chants of the distant past, we can easily see how myths, fables, parables, and tales paved the way for the literary forms of today.

Early Forms of Fiction

Set in the prehistoric past, *myths* embody the most profound beliefs of a people, and thus serve as both science and religion. These ancient stories relate extraordinary episodes and the exploits of superhuman beings to account for natural phenomena like flash floods and famines as well as for the nature of divinity and the mysteries of the human condition. The mythologist Joseph Campbell suggests that myth-making began with the first awareness of death, with the sudden realization that a being could exist and then exist no more—a shock that launched humankind on an endless quest to explain the seemingly senseless fact of our own mortality. Myths make it possible to deny the finality of death by portraying it as a journey and a transformation: Departing spirits move on to become stars in the skies or nymphs in the winds and the waters—in other words, eternal inhabitants of some perfect celestial world.

Interestingly enough, the mythologies of very different cultures all take shape around certain shared themes. For example, every mythology contains a creation story, which explains how the world came to be. One such story, told by the Delaware Indians of the northeastern United States, appears in this chapter. This myth comes from the *Walam Olum* (Painted Record), a poetic rendering of the origin and history of the tribe. Actually, what you will find reprinted on pages 150–153 are three versions of this genesis tale. The first is a series of pictographs, which illustrate the narrative with symbols based on the sign language used by the Delawares. Next is an attempt to reproduce the sounds of the original text, which was meant to be sung. Finally, we have an English translation of the Delaware song. Of course, much of the essence has been lost in this process, for the power of poetry, even more than that of prose, comes from sound and rhythm as well as sense.

Opening in a timeless, spaceless universe, the *Walam Olum* reveals how "At first, forever, lost in space, everywhere, the great Manito was. He made the extended land and the sky. He made the sun, the moon, the stars." Like other creation stories, including Genesis in the Bible, this tale goes on to explain how a Supreme Being created life and how evil transformed Paradise. As you can see, myth is both majestic and spiritual: Here gods and superhuman heroes reign and intervene in the affairs of mortals.

Two other ancient forms of fiction, *fables* and *parables,* are tales that point to a moral. Commonly featuring animals as characters, fables tell brief, witty stories that illustrate the consequences of human foibles like greed or laziness. Among the most famous fables in the West are those attributed to Aesop, a Greek slave who lived around 600 B.C. As you will see when you read "The Wolf and the Mastiff" on page 154, the moral or lesson of a traditional fable is usually stated at the end. Kate Chopin's nineteenth-century "fable," however, breaks the conventional mold—it is closer to parable.

Like fables, parables are teaching tales, but typically the characters are human, the content is more serious, and the moral is implied rather than stated outright. Parables answer ethical questions and teach spiritual or religious lessons. At the opening of this chapter, you'll find two Buddhist parables and one Christian parable, and further along in the section you may note a resemblance between these traditional parables and contemporary tales such as Bernard Malamud's "The Magic Barrel," a story that may bring to mind more than one moral.

Of all the traditional forms of narrative, though, the *folktale,* often called the *fairy tale,* seems closest to our modern stories, for it is apt to involve ordinary people and ordinary concerns such as love, money, and social status. At the same time, such stories almost always focus on marvelous and fantastic twists of plot. For centuries folktales were transmitted orally, with each teller adding his or her own touches. Incredible events (such as a girl who melts away and a rose that bites in Angela Carter's "The Snow Child") are presented as unremarkable incidents that could befall any one of us during an ordinary walk through the woods. The enormous appeal of such stories, even to the contemporary reader, may come from this special combination of realism and fantasy. As you read Italo Calvino's retelling of the Italian folktale "Catherine the Wise," the story of a shopkeeper's daughter who transforms herself through talent and wit, look for the characteristics that make this story lifelike, despite its freewheeling exaggerations and improbabilities.

Folktales carry messages as well as magic, as psychologist Bruno Bettelheim argues in *The Uses of Enchantment: The Meaning and Importance of Fairy Tales.* In this book, Bettelheim analyzes the appeal of these enchanted stories: how they help young children to make sense of their feelings and fears, while also suggesting the rewards of moral behavior. In this chapter, we reprint the popular fairy tale "Little Snow-White," as told by the Brothers Grimm. And in the Essays chapter (Chapter 7) of this anthology, we've included Bettelheim's analysis of this tale.

THE MODERN SHORT STORY

We recently asked a group of students to write in their journals for five minutes on a single word: *fiction.* From their notebooks we culled these reactions:

Although fiction is writing that isn't true, it comes from truth, from the experiences of the writer, so there is a fine line between fiction and non-fiction. Whenever I read fiction, I imagine that it is true, that the writer is talking about people who really exist and things that really happened.

Dalia Ehassian

Fiction is a story spewn from the imagination. In fiction, new and vivid worlds are created. While reading fiction, one travels through time and space and the minds of others and learns to view the world through new eyes.

Diane Rischer

Reconstructing reality to fit a perspective. Communicating that perspective to an audience. Creating a story that reveals a personal or universal truth.

Lorraine Baum

Fiction is a world unto itself. Fiction cuts across different genres, can be a novel, a short story, a narrative poem, a play. The magic of fiction is its relation to the real world, the way it can give us insight into our own lives and problems and those of others. The characters in fiction often seem real and alive, and the fiction writer uses different techniques to engross the reader in a story.

Jerry Meskup

Each of these writers has captured some of the special capabilities of fiction, a term that calls up a jumble of associations and meanings. "Does fiction equal imagination?" Soraya Chang, one of our students, asks. "Imagination—images, dreams, memories, pictures dancing in the mind." Fiction reinvents reality, and through the imaginative powers of the fiction-maker, we are encouraged to explore other possibilities, other lives, other selves.

Most ancient stories are straightforward and easily described. But as the students we quote suggest, the modern short story has evolved into a sophisticated and diversified genre that borrows from various literary modes and reflects any number of intellectual, moral, and social concerns. Like all forms of artistic expression, the short story is enriched by traditions and transformations, the product both of its own era and of the esthetic sensibilities and philosophical ideas of preceding generations. Below, we'll examine some of the characteristics that distinguish the fiction of our time.

The Realistic Story

The modern short story was not consciously formulated into a distinct literary genre until the nineteenth century. Modern stories differ from the early narrative forms we have discussed in a number of ways. First of all, most modern stories seem true to life. *Realism* attempts to portray the empirical world as faithfully as possible, and most often finds its subjects in everyday life and conduct. Hemingway's "Cat in the Rain," discussed in the introduction to this anthology, is credible at least partly because it portrays ordinary people in an ordinary situation—two Americans stuck in a hotel room on a rainy day, conversing but not really listening to each other. Similarly, the tragic elements of Anton Chekhov's "Heartache" are all the more moving to modern readers because the hero is recognizable to us: a poor cab driver, shabby and a little foolish, who has lost his son. As you read "Heartache," you will doubtless notice how the story is made more persuasive and poignant through the seemingly inconsequential details of daily life and through dialogue that rings true:

"What is it?" asks the officer.
Iona twists his mouth into a smile, strains his throat and croaks hoarsely: "My son, sir . . . er, my son died this week."
"H'm, what did he die of?"

Iona turns his whole body around to his fare and says, ''Who can tell? It must have been a fever. He lay in the hospital only three days and then he died. . . . It is God's will.''

''Get over, you devil!'' comes out of the dark. ''Have you gone blind, you old dog? Keep your eyes peeled!''

''Go on, go on,'' says the officer. ''We shan't get there until tomorrow at this rate. Give her the whip!''

The way the father, Iona, deals with the tragedy of his son's death is the subject of this story. As you may have gathered, myths, fables, and fairy tales usually do not consider the character's inner life and *point of view,* or personal way of perceiving events. On the other hand, the dynamics of a character's personality, and the social, economic, and psychological forces that act on that personality are frequently the central concerns of modern fiction. *Psychological realism,* which analyzes in detail the perceptions, emotions, and motivations of characters, dominates the fiction of our time.

These stories often present a crisis or a conflict in the life of a *protagonist* (the central figure in a narrative) and the changes this conflict brings about. An event might alter a character's course, reveal a facet of that character, lead to an understanding, give rise to a decision, illuminate some aspect of the human condition. In any case, the reader is convinced that both the characters and the events could well be real. Even stories that are *not* realistic typically incorporate some of the attributes of realism, for most readers need to feel that the fictional world they have entered, however different from their own, is at least possible, even if not probable.

Another difference between stories past and present is the ratio between *summary,* or what is told, and *scene,* or what is shown. Traditional narratives such as folktales and fables tend to summarize much of the action and tell us exactly what to think of a character. In ''Little Snow-white,'' for example, we are told that the stepmother ''was a beautiful woman, but proud and haughty, and she could not bear that anyone else should surpass her in beauty.'' Modern authors are less inclined to make explicit judgments about characters: Like playwrights, they prefer to present the revealing scene and to allow the characters to ''speak for themselves.'' In this sense, at least, the modern short story is close to drama.

Partly because they rely more on scene than on summary, modern stories make greater demands on their readers, who are often left to make up their own minds about the significance of images, characters, events, and dialogue. Gone are the myth's definite answers to eternal questions, the fable's neat moral, the fairy tale's promise of justice done and virtue rewarded. Instead, most serious modern fiction is marked by ambiguity, or multiple levels of meaning that allow for more than one interpretation. For example, you may recall from the introductory chapter the variety of responses ''Cat in the Rain'' elicited from our students. One reason for this story's ambiguity and resonance is that its *symbols*—objects or actions that represent something beyond themselves—carry multiple meanings. As several of our students observe, the cat in the story, the rain, the wife's desire for the cat, and the husband's uninterrupted reading all come to suggest a number of concepts that contribute to our perception of the characters and their relationship. It is important to remember, though, that not all interpretations of a story are valid: Readers must be able to support their theories and conclusions with evidence from the text, as do the students quoted in our introduction.

Departures from Realism

Not all modern stories are realistic, however, and what we call modernism in literature is not easily defined. What we can say is that modernism is marked by reaction against tradition, and by experimentation with literary forms. Unlike the heroes of most early fiction, for example, modern protagonists are less heroes than anti-heroes, not courageous kings but unexceptional, even unlikable, human beings. They may be innocent victims of an absurd and hostile universe, like the salesman Gregor Samsa in Franz Kafka's "The Metamorphosis"; frustrated parents, like the narrator of Tillie Olsen's "I Stand Here Ironing"; confused young people, like Leo Finkle in Bernard Malamud's "The Magic Barrel"; or a thoroughly despicable family, as in Flannery O'Connor's "A Good Man Is Hard to Find."

Similarly, our notion of *plot*, the sequence of narrative events in a work of fiction, may be upended by the modern short story. Instead of the traditional beginnings, middles, and endings that structure most fiction, action may seem minimal, even insignificant, as in Hemingway's "Cat in the Rain"; the normal chronology of events may be disrupted, as in "I Stand Here Ironing," a narrative that moves back and forth in time; the comfort of a resolution may be absent, leaving the reader of a story like "The Ones Who Walk Away from Omelas" with more questions than answers.

Many contemporary authors have also challenged the conventions of realism itself and harkened back to the ancient forms of fiction. Nonrealistic stories juxtapose the ordinary and the incredible, blending realism, illusion, and myth to create worlds at once familiar and foreign. The South American writer Gabriel García Márquez might well have had two famous myths in mind while composing "A Very Old Man with Enormous Wings," a story included in this chapter. The title character of García Márquez's tale appears to be an angel who has somehow fallen to earth, although this wizened and bedraggled man is hardly the splendid creature we associate with biblical tales. In addition, García Márquez might have been thinking of the Greek myth of Daedalus and his son, Icarus.

In that myth, Daedalus constructs an ingenious labyrinth to imprison the monstrous Minotaur, half-bull and half-man. Later, Daedalus and Icarus are imprisoned there themselves by King Minos of Crete. To escape, Daedalus makes wings for himself and his son, and warns Icarus not to fly too high, for the sun will melt his wings. As the two fly away, the boy becomes enraptured with his wonderful new power; ignoring his father's anguished commands, Icarus soars higher and higher until his wings fall away and he plunges into the sea. Reading García Márquez's story, you might consider the ways in which a contemporary writer transforms aspects of these myths for his own purposes while also enriching his work with *allusions,* references to figures or events in art or history.

The modern short story may also take *itself*—that is, the fiction-making process and the actual conventions of storytelling—as its subject. The effect of such stories is to remind us that we are in the act of reading fiction, much as viewers are startled by the incongruity of seeing Groucho Marx step out of a movie scene to address the audience directly and comment on the action of the film. *Metafiction* (from the Greek prefix *meta,* meaning changed in form, or going beyond, transcending)—fiction *about* fiction—explores the multifaceted nature of narrative itself. It calls our attention not only to its own technique, but to the process of fiction-making in general, and to our assumptions about stories and storytelling.

In Grace Paley's story, "A Conversation with My Father," for instance, the narrator appears to be Grace Paley herself, having a conversation *about* fiction with her real-life father. In fact, in the opening pages to *Enormous Changes at the Last Minute,* the collection of stories in which this selection appears, Paley writes, "Everyone in this book is imagined into life except the father. No matter what story he has to live in, he's my father, I. Goodside, M.D., artist, and storyteller." The writer of metafiction reminds us that we do not just *read* fiction, we all *live* in fictions—in the form of the individual and collective stories we tell about ourselves, others, and the world we inhabit—and that these fictions structure our lives and our cultures as well as our art forms.

As you read Paley's story, consider the meaning of the father's request: "I would like you to write a simple story just once more," he says, "the kind de Maupassant wrote, or Chekhov, the kind you used to write. Just recognizable people and then write down what happened to them next." The kind of story the narrator's father describes is just the sort most readers are likely to welcome. But the narrator repeatedly fails in her attempts to write an "old-fashioned" story that will satisfy her father, perhaps because she cannot—or will not—write a story that doesn't satisfy *her.* So the story is really about the fiction-making process, as well as about the growth of a story called "A Conversation with My Father."

Paley's "story about a story" should help prepare us for some of the metafictive games that Ursula Le Guin plays in "The Ones Who Walk Away from Omelas." The narrative begins in the world of fairy tale romance, but Le Guin won't let us relax in that world for long. As you read her story, observe how, in the course of the tale, the narrator questions the conventions of both the traditional romance and contemporary "realistic" fiction. Note too the changes wrought in the personality of the reliable, all-knowing narrator as the story veers off in an unexpected direction.

Another selection included in this chapter, ''The Glass Mountain'' by Donald Barthelme, stretches the shape of fiction still further. Composed of 100 numbered sentences and fragments, this brief story is characteristic of Barthelme's work, which often seems a collage of random bits and pieces of contemporary culture. Here you will find street slang, obscenities, and clichés alongside scholarly quotations, knights in armor, and an enchanted princess. Barthelme juxtaposes the symbols of romance and the detritus of city life to satirize both the traditions of literature and the facts of urban existence in the twentieth century.

THE ELEMENTS OF FICTION

What follows is a discussion of certain technical terms we have avoided until now. These terms are included here, for to understand how a story achieves its effect, we need a shared vocabulary to help us appreciate the different ways in which, in the words of one of our students, ''Fiction can teach, give pleasure.'' This vocabulary will be equally useful in the following chapter on drama, a literary form that is also built around setting, plot, characters, dialogue, and theme. Let's consider the components of fiction and the ways in which these basic elements interact and are transformed through the alchemy of a work of literature.

Setting

Setting, where and when a story takes place, is usually established at the outset. Occasionally, the setting is merely a vague backdrop, but modern stories most often occur in specific times and places that make the fictional terrain seem like the world inhabited by the reader. In many stories, the setting conveys the prevailing atmosphere or *mood* of the piece, as in the opening paragraph of Chekhov's ''Heartache,'' which summons up the time of day, the weather, and the utterly still figures of Iona Potapov and his horse in the center of a swirling white landscape:

> Evening twilight. Large flakes of snow are circling lazily about the street lamps which have just been lighted, settling in a thin soft layer on roofs, horses' backs, people's shoulders, caps. Iona Potapov, the cabby, is all white like a ghost. As hunched as a living body can be, he sits on the box without stirring. If a whole snowdrift were to fall on him, even then, perhaps he would not find it necessary to shake it off. His nag, too, is white and motionless.

In response to this opening paragraph, one student made these observations in her notebook:

> There is no movement here. The only motion is the falling snow, and even this is "circling lazily about the street." There is no desire for movement either, among the inhabitants of the scene. Iona is, at first, described as "white as a ghost," and then "as hunched as a living body can be." The horse is also white and motionless. The whole scene is frozen, without life.
>
> *Sally Shore*

This student's attentiveness to detail and nuance alerts her to the parallels between Iona and the frozen, lifeless scene in which he appears, thus enriching her appreciation of the ways in which the various elements of fiction can comment on and illuminate one another. Here the setting is inseparable from the characters who people it, the plot that unfolds in it, and the theme that emerges in Chekhov's moving exploration of grief.

Plot and Structure

Simply put, *plot* is what happens to the character or characters in a story—a series of causally related events that leads to some sort of change, however subtle, in a character's situation, knowledge, or understanding. More often than not, a plot begins with *exposition*, which establishes the setting, introduces major characters, and provides essential information. Next come *complications* that escalate into a *climax*, the moment of greatest tension and the turning point in the narrative. Finally, there is the *resolution* or *dénouement*: The crisis is resolved and the action subsides.

Whereas the plot in a novel can unfold in a leisurely manner and include extensive information about its characters, the short story demands compression, and its action and characters must be drawn quickly. The short story writer frequently focuses on a significant moment, a single *conflict* in a character's life, rather than on a series of dilemmas. In "A Conversation with My Father," the conflict—and all that follows—grows out of the father's wish for a traditional story and the narrator's resistance to "plot, the absolute line between two points which I've always despised. Not for literary reasons, but because it takes all the hope away. Everyone, real or invented, deserves the open destiny of life." *Conflict*, then, whether it is the clash between characters, ideas, ways of life, or choices, is essential to plot, for it is the springboard for movement, development, and change.

The conflicts of serious fiction are rarely problems that can readily be solved: They dramatize universal truths about human experience and the human condition—love and death, loss and loneliness, frustration and guilt.

Jamaica Kincaid's "The Circling Hand," for example, focuses on the tension between a mother and daughter as each contends with the girl's emerging adolescence. This conflict reveals as much about the complexities of family relationships as it does about a girl who is no longer a child but not yet a woman.

Plot, of course, does not spring full-blown from an author's pen, but results from careful ordering and design of scene and incident. The *structure* or *form* of a work points to its central concern and so provides a valuable key to its meaning. To determine the structure of a short story, we look for the ways in which its incidents and scenes are arranged into patterns. For example, Ryunosuke Akutagawa's "In a Grove" consists exclusively of the testimonies of seven characters being interrogated about a murder. We hear only their words, not even the questions asked of them, and there is neither comment on nor transition between the testimonies, as if the statements had been recorded verbatim by a court stenographer. We are confronted with seven stories, seven points of view, and given no help in deciding which to believe. Yet the way in which Akutagawa orders the testimonies strongly influences our response, for whichever version appears last will *seem* final, somehow more compelling than the others. At the same time, the multiple narration here points directly to the meaning of the work—namely, the relativity of truth and the subjectivity of viewpoint itself.

As you read the selections ahead, you will see that although some stories recount events that are tragic or horrifying, you may find yourself reacting less to the plight of the characters caught up in these events than to some philosophical idea provoked by the story. Traditional stories like "Catherine the Wise" and "Little Snow-white," as we have seen, tend to emphasize plot rather than any alteration in character. In modern fiction, though, the story typically pivots on a change in the protagonist's character, like the transformation Leo Finkle undergoes in "The Magic Barrel," or a change in the way the protagonist views something, like the gradual difference in Annie John's perception of her mother in "The Circling Hand." In each case, the structure of the work strongly affects our response to its ideas, events, and characters.

Plot and structure are, of course, inseparable from the characters they unveil: Through the interplay of character and action, we come to understand something about an individual, in literature and in life. After reading "I Stand Here Ironing," for instance, one of our students, Nasreen Khan, wrote: "Once you read this story, you get so involved in it that you read it again. It wakes you up by troubling you." A classmate, Lia Christoulopolous, explained her reaction in more detail:

> What drew me in was the way the author brings the past into the present. The author uses flashbacks to show scenes from the past and these scenes lead the mother to reveal her thoughts about her relationship with her daughter throughout Emily's unhappy childhood.

Character

As the reader we quote above observes, characters who are revealed to us through their own thoughts, words, and actions assume a vitality and fullness of dimension that no statement about them can convey. But not everything we need to know about a character can be acted out, so writers also draw on exposition to quicken the narrative and to focus on the principal action. Exposition provides information: "A certain man had two sons"; summarizes action: "The younger son gathered all together, and took his journey into a far country"; and combines summary with judgment: "and there wasted his substance with riotous living."

Additionally, descriptions of characters may include facts and comments, as well as details of their appearance that suggest an aspect of their personalities. For instance, the following portrait of the matchmaker in "The Magic Barrel" hints at the mysterious and contradictory nature of a character most readers find hard to forget:

> . . . Salzman, who had been long in the business, was of slight but dignified build, wearing an old hat, and an overcoat too short and tight for him. He smelled frankly of fish, which he loved to eat, and although he was missing a few teeth, his presence was not displeasing, because of an amiable manner curiously contrasted with mournful eyes. His voice, his lips, his wisp of beard, his bony fingers were animated, but give him a moment of repose and his mild blue eyes revealed a depth of sadness . . .

Unlike the one-dimensional heroes, heroines, and villains we associate with fairy tales and melodramas—the valiant prince, the innocent princess, the wicked stepmother—the individuals who come alive in a work of fiction reflect the complexity and quirkiness of human nature. Such characters are often people we can easily recognize; but bizarre, even fantastic characters can also be made perfectly believable through the narrative context in which they appear. You will encounter some strange types in the stories ahead: the matchmaker who seems to materialize out of thin air, the beleaguered old angel, the salesman who finds himself transformed into a giant insect. And still, we accept these characters because their behavior and milieu seem credible.

Narrator, Point of View, and Irony

Stories are written by authors, but told by narrators. The narrator is not the writer, but a *persona* (from the Latin word for "mask"), a character with a distinct voice created by that writer to tell the story. Because the narrator is, in effect, the prism through which the narrative is filtered, it is important that the teller suit the tale. For example, in the introduction to *Italian Folk-*

tales, Calvino describes the typical Sicilian storyteller whose personality he sought to capture in "Catherine the Wise":

> [She] fills her narrative with color, nature, objects; she conjures up magic, but frequently bases it on realism; hence her imaginative language, but a language firmly rooted in commonsensical speech and sayings. She is always ready to bring to life feminine characters who are active, enterprising, and courageous, in contrast to the traditional concept of the Sicilian woman as a passive and withdrawn creature.

The *point of view* of a story depends on who is telling it and where that teller is situated. Point of view colors our perception of a story's characters and incidents. A narrator can, for example, give us intimate and sympathetic contact with the protagonist, as in "Heartache"; at the other extreme, a narrator may hold the characters at arm's length, as in "A Good Man Is Hard to Find." Thus *who* tells the story and the *distance* between the narrator and the other characters are both intrinsic to what that story is about.

The casting of a narrator is one of the most important decisions an author must make, and there are several possibilities for this role. The most common device is the *third-person narrator,* one who is not a participant in the events, and who may be *omniscient, partly omniscient,* or *objective. Omniscient narrators* are godlike in knowledge and power, able to reveal any or all of the characters' inner thoughts and feelings. The narrator of "Catherine the Wise," for instance, can even tell us that one character's cheek "still smarts" from a blow Catherine deals him.

Far more frequently in twentieth-century fiction, one finds a narrator of *limited omniscience,* who cannot read all minds, but focuses—as if through the lens of a telescope—on one character, who knows and understands the character better than the character could ever understand himself or herself, and who is therefore able to present that character's point of view with great conviction. Even when fiction is presented from this viewpoint of limited omniscience, it is not uncommon for the narrator to shift subtly toward unlimited omniscience when such a turn suits the needs of the story. "The Magic Barrel," for instance, is told from the viewpoint of Leo Finkle, a young rabbinical student, but on occasion the viewpoint moves almost imperceptibly to that of Pinye Salzman, the marriage broker. After Leo explains why he wants Salzman to find him a wife, for example, we are told that "Salzman listened in embarrassed surprise, sensing a sort of apology. Later, however, he experienced a glow of pride in his work, an emotion that had left him years ago, and he heartily approved of Finkle."

An *objective narrator,* as in "Cat in the Rain," does not presume to know any more about the characters than what can be gathered from observation, so that their thoughts and feelings can only be suggested through dialogue, descriptions of actions, gestures, and the like, leaving inferences and judgments to the reader. In its most extreme form, objective narration may sound like a newspaper report, conveying no sense of a narrator or point of view at all. Such objectivity might be maddening to some readers, who may feel that the author has gone off and left them to do all the work.

A story told by one of the characters, either a central character or a peripheral observer, employs a *first-person narrator*. This *I* narrating the story may be the protagonist, as in "The Yellow Wallpaper" and "Araby," or the *I* may function not as the main actor but as a witness to events, like the narrator of "I Stand Here Ironing." The first-person narrator conveys a strong sense of immediacy and authenticity, but limits the knowledge of the reader, for this narrator can only describe characters and events from his or her own very limited perspective. The narrator of "I Stand Here Ironing," for example, is a mother whose daughter Emily is a mystery to her. Unlike an omniscient or partially omniscient third-person narrator, she can only speculate about Emily's thoughts and emotions. Nor is a first-person narrator necessarily reliable, for the speaker may misinterpret events—or, as is true of the narrator in "The Ones Who Walk Away from Omelas," may deliberately mislead the reader.

Whether they are narrated in the first person or the third, short stories generally confine themselves to a single point of view. One reason for doing so is undoubtedly the form's demand for brevity. More important, a single viewpoint corresponds to the way each of us must interpret the world, and at the same time lends unity and coherence to a story. Even so, writers sometimes experiment with *multiple narrators*, as we have noted in Akutagawa's "In a Grove."

Point of view may also create *irony* in a work of literature. Irony is the incongruity or contrast between word and meaning, appearance and reality, expectation and outcome, action and result. *Verbal irony* occurs when there is a discrepancy between the literal meaning and the actual intent of a statement. Verbal irony commonly results from overstatement, understatement, or sarcasm—using words of praise, for example, to convey disgust. The title "A Good Man Is Hard to Find" becomes archly ironic because it so grossly understates what we find in O'Connor's story. In addition, this story is riddled with a series of *dramatic ironies*, such as the dreadful consequence of the grandmother's seemingly insignificant decision to sneak her cat along on a family trip and of a little white lie she tells along the way.

Style, Tone, and Mood

The special language of a particular work of literature, the distinctive way in which a writer expresses himself or herself, is what we mean when we speak of the writer's *style*. An author's style depends on diction, syntax, rhythm, and imagery, as well as experiments with literary form. All these elements help to create the individual voices we hear in a work of prose or poetry.

Diction is the word choice, the vocabulary, that characterizes a speaker.

Compare, for example, the speech patterns of the main characters in "The Magic Barrel." In the following exchange, listen to the contrast between the colorful, idiomatic, Yiddish-inflected voice of the matchmaker and the educated, precise, rather formal response of the young rabbinical student—and consider what these few lines contribute to our impression of each character:

> "I knew her personally," said Salzman. "I wish you could see this girl. She is a doll. Also very intelligent. All day you could talk to her about books and theater and what not. She also knows current events."
> "I don't believe you mentioned her age?"

Syntax—grammar and sentence structure—is closely related to diction; short, simple words are often connected to short, simple sentence patterns, pared-down prose such as we have seen in Hemingway's "Cat in the Rain." At the other end of the spectrum are the rich, metaphorical language and frequently complex sentences of Tillie Olsen's narrator:

> She was a beautiful baby. She blew shining bubbles of sound. She loved motion, loved light, loved color and music and textures. She would lie on the floor in her blue overalls patting the surface so hard in ecstasy her hands and feet would blur. She was a miracle to me, but when she was eight months old I had to leave her daytimes with the woman downstairs to whom she was no miracle at all, for I worked or looked for work and for Emily's father, who "could no longer endure" (he wrote in his good-bye note) "sharing want with us."

Imagery, the original, evocative, and nonliteral use of language, is part of an author's repertoire. Images convey feelings, ideas, or sensory impressions with concrete pictures. In the passage quoted above, for example, think of the luminous metaphor of "shining bubbles of sound" and the image of baby hands and feet blurring in ecstasy. These impressions clash powerfully with the harsh disappointment relayed in the long, tortured, convoluted sentence that follows. It is the style of an individual work that establishes its *tone*, reflecting the narrator's attitude toward characters and events. You might, for example, describe the tone, or tones, in the foregoing excerpt as sincere, wistful, and deeply sad. Tone in writing, like the tone of someone's voice, can range from sympathetic to sardonic, amused to enraged, concerned to indifferent. Effective writing most often communicates tone through language that illustrates rather than insists. Whereas a less experienced writer might tell us that a character "was angry and determined not to give in," Flannery O'Connor deftly conveys the same information with revealing gestures and metaphors: "Bailey was looking straight ahead. His jaw was as rigid as a horseshoe. 'No,' he said."

The language of short stories shows great diversity: You will notice a wide range of voices in the selections here, a spectrum indicated by the three first-person narrators quoted below. Start with the earthy, conversational brusqueness of the narrator of the Italian folktale "Catherine the Wise":

Here in Palermo they tell, ladies and gentlemen, that once upon a time there was a very important shopkeeper in the city. He had a daughter who, from the time she was weaned, proved so wise that she was given her say on every single matter in the household. Recognizing the talent of his daughter, her father called her Catherine the Wise. When it came to studying all sorts of languages and reading every kind of book, no one could hold a candle to her.

Now listen to the lyrical nostalgia of a paragraph from James Alan McPherson's "Why I Like Country Music":

She was a pretty, chocolate brown little girl with dark brown eyes and two long black braids. After all these years, the image of these two braids evokes in me all there is to remember about Gweneth Lawson. They were plaited across the top of her head and hung to a point just above the back of her Peter Pan collar. Sometimes she wore two bows, one red and one blue, and these tended to sway lazily near the place on her neck where the smooth brown of her skin and the white of her collar met the ink-bottle black of her hair. Even when I cannot remember her face, I remember the rainbow of deep, rich colors in which she lived.

And contrast these passages with the intense, deliberately melodramatic prose of "Araby," with its incantations and metaphors (as in "needles of water" and senses that seem "to desire to veil themselves"):

It was a dark rainy evening and there was no sound in the house. Through one of the broken panes I heard the rain impinge upon the earth, the fine incessant needles of water playing in the sodden beds. Some distant lamp or lighted window gleamed below me. I was thankful that I could see so little. All my senses seemed to desire to veil themselves and, feeling that I was about to slip from them, I pressed the palms of my hands together until they trembled, murmuring: *"O love! O love!"* many times.

As even this brief third excerpt suggests, the *mood* of this protagonist, a schoolboy in the throes of his first love, is overheated and wildly romantic. To one student, Daniel Dubinsky, "The boy's words are very flowery and descriptive. Maybe the descriptions are too effusive. They make the boy seem a bit silly." This reader is reacting to the contrast between the mood of the story and the ironic, distanced tone of the narration, a calculated voice that undercuts the heightened emotions pervading the piece and leads the reader to view the boy's infatuation with a certain detachment. Mood, then, refers to the feelings that dominate a story's characters and incidents, which may differ considerably from the narrator's attitude toward these characters and events.

Most often, style and tone are consistent throughout a story, but occasionally it may suit a writer's purpose to change voices, even drastically. Ursula Le Guin's "The Ones Who Walk Away from Omelas" begins in the manner of a traditional romance. Notice, in this rhapsodic opening passage of the story, how the narrator uses stilted phrases and *alliteration* (the repetition of initial consonants in phrases such as "red roofs" and "set the swallows soaring") to paint a highly ornamental picture of an imaginary village:

> With a clamor of bells that set the swallows soaring, the Festival of Summer came to the city Omelas, bright-towered by the sea. The rigging of the boats in harbor sparkled with flags. In the streets between houses with red roofs and painted walls, between old moss-grown gardens and under avenues of trees, past great parks and public buildings, processions moved. Some were decorous: old people in long stiff robes of mauve and grey, grave master workmen, quiet, merry women carrying their babies, and chatting as they walked. In other streets the music beat faster, a shimmering of gong and tambourine, and the people went dancing, the procession was a dance.

Later on in the same story, however, the narrator switches from the voice of the romancer to that of a modern realist: With the introduction of a simple, searing image, that of a child confined to a small basement room, the story is stripped of its illusion. Gone are the lush adjectives, the rolling sentences, the sounds of ecstasy. The "real world" has intruded, in tone, style, and content:

> . . . In the room a child is sitting. It could be a boy or a girl. It looks about six, but actually is nearly ten. It is feeble-minded. Perhaps it was born defective, or perhaps it has become infantile through fear, malnutrition, and neglect. It picks its nose and occasionally fumbles with its toes or genitals, as it sits hunched in the corner farthest from the buckets and mops. It is afraid of the mops. It finds them horrible. It shuts its eyes, but it knows the mops are still standing there; and the door is locked; and nobody will come.

As you read the stories in this chapter, look for the ways in which the author's style and tone combine to give meaning and purpose to a work of fiction. Without the individual touches that transform puppets into characters and plots into stories, we would be left with sketches and summaries awaiting the life bestowed on them by an author's invention.

Theme

In a well-wrought story, all the elements of fiction work together to create the *theme*. The theme is the point of the story, something like the thesis or controlling idea of an essay—the abstraction or generalization that grows out of the cumulative effect of the narrative. Theme, of course, goes beyond the topic or subject matter of a story; theme provides insight. Whereas topics can be expressed in a word or phrase, themes require complete sentences. On the simplest level, a theme is like the moral of a fable or a parable: If, for example, the story involves a character who sacrifices everything for money only to wind up rich and miserable, the *subject* is the pursuit of money, and the *theme* is that money cannot buy happiness.

Of course, to affix a single "moral" to a story is to reduce literature to pulp, so it is important to distinguish between moral and theme. A story with a moral has a didactic purpose: It teaches a lesson and that lesson, not the story, is paramount. Most modern stories, even those that borrow from the teaching tales of the past, are not written solely to deliver a message; instead, they seek to alter our perspective by broadening our awareness of the human condition. Unlike morals, themes are an integral part of the work that cannot be neatly tacked on to story's end; they emerge gradually from plot, structure, characters, narrator, and so on.

Determining the theme of a sophisticated story is often difficult, but certain aspects of a work of literature may help us in the process. We have seen how the structure of a work contributes to its meaning and effect. Titles sometimes provide clues by directing our attention to a particular idea, though on occasion they can intentionally mislead us. The title of O'Connor's "A Good Man Is Hard to Find" sounds like a cliché but should resonate in a special way once you have read the piece. Settings too may foreshadow events—as does the forbidding description of the woods, "tall, dark, and deep," in the same O'Connor story—or give us clues to aspects of the characters, as in the opening paragraph of "Araby" describing the "blind," or dead-end, street with its rows of houses complacently turned in on themselves:

> North Richmond Street, being blind, was a quiet street except at the hour when the Christian Brothers' School set the boys free. An uninhabited house of two storeys stood at the blind end, detached from its neighbors in a square ground. The other houses of the street, conscious of decent lives within them, gazed at one another with brown imperturbable faces.

Occasionally, an author will include an analysis of characters or events within the text itself, and such commentary—as in the final paragraph of "I Stand Here Ironing"—can point directly to the theme. Any *change* in a character, situation, setting, and so on can be an important element in the theme.

If the story involves a discovery through which a character learns something about himself, like the narrator of "Araby," or the reader comes to understand something about a character, as we do in "Cat in the Rain," that discovery is apt to suggest the story's theme. Other clues to meaning may lie in the discrepancy between the tone and content of the narrative, as in "Araby" and "A Good Man Is Hard to Find," or in odd juxtapositions, like that of the real and the fantastic in "A Very Old Man with Enormous Wings." Peculiarities such as repeated phrases, ideas, or images can also point to theme: Of Gregor Samsa in "The Metamorphosis," one student, Patrick Casey, noticed:

> Gregor was, above all, tired. The text often refers to sleep: Gregor "awoke from uneasy dreams," thinks "about sleeping a little longer and forgetting all this nonsense," and has "an exhausting job." "A man needs his sleep," he thinks. He feels "a drowsiness that was utterly superfluous after such a long sleep," and later awakes out of "a deep sleep, more like a swoon."

In each of the stories ahead, you will want to pay attention not only to such patterns, but also to individual notes that seem unrelated or discordant. For you can be sure that skilled writers, like skilled composers and musicians, measure tone, rhythm, and theme with precision and purpose. It is equally important to recognize that although we have given you the vocabulary for approaching the stories, no simple analysis of components can capture the *experience* of a work of fiction—the meeting of artist and reader in the imaginative act that is literature.

The Walam Olum *of the Delaware Indians*

The Delaware Indians, an Algonquian tribe closely related to the Chippewas and the Shawnees, occupied much of eastern North America in the eighteenth century. They were among the first tribes encountered by white settlers, and were eventually forced westward by the colonists. Today the Delawares live mainly in Kansas and Oklahoma.

The *Walam Olum* (meaning "painted record") is the poetic record of the Delawares' creation and their history. The text consists of pictographs, which were usually engraved on wood or birch bark, and the narrative, which was passed on orally and meant to be sung. Below, we have reprinted the pictographs alongside the transcribed song, followed by the English translation.

From the Creation Song

I

1. Sayewi talli wemiguma wokgetaki,

   At first, in that place, at all times, above the earth,

2. Hackung kwelik owanaku wak yutali Kitanitowit-essop.

   On the earth, [was] an extended fog, and there the great Manito was.

3. Sayewis hallemiwis nolemiwi elemamik Kitanitowit-essop.

   At first, forever, lost in space, everywhere, the great Manito was.

4. Sohawalawak kwelik hakik owak[1] awasagamak.

He made the extended land and the sky.

5. Sohalawak gishuk nipahum alankwak.

He made the sun, the moon, the stars.

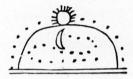

6. Wemi-sohalawak yuliky uchaan.

He made them all to move evenly.

7. Wich-owagan kshakan moshakwat[2] kwelik kshipehelep.

Then the wind blew violently, and it cleared, and the water flowed off far and strong.

8. Opeleken mani-menak delsin-epit.

And groups of islands grew newly, and there remained.

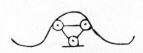

9. Lappinup Kitanitowit manito manitoak.

Anew spoke the great Manito, a manito to manitos,

10. Owiniwak angelatawiwak chichankwak wemiwak.

To beings, mortals, souls and all,

[1]Read, *woak.*
[2]Var. *moshskguat.*

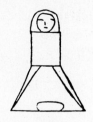

11. Wtenk manito jinwis lennowak
    mukom.

    And ever after he was a manito to men, and their grandfather.

12. Milap netami gaho owini gaho.

    He gave the first mother, the mother of beings.

13. Namesik milap, tulpewik milap,
    swesik milap, cholensak milap.

    He gave the fish, he gave the turtles, he gave the beasts, he gave the birds.

14. Makimani shak sohalawak makowini
    nakowak amangamek.

    But an evil Manito made evil beings only, monsters,

15. Sohalawak uchewak, sohalawak pun-
    gusak.

    He made the flies, he made the gnats.

16. Nitisak wemi owini w'delisinewuap.

    All beings were then friendly.

17. Kiwis, wunand wishimanitoak es-
    sopak.

    Truly the manitos were active and kindly.

18. Nijini netami lennowak, nigoha
    netarhi okwewi, nantinéwak.

    *To those very first men, and to those first mothers,
    fetched them wives,*

19. Gattamin netami mitzi nijini nantiné.

    And fetched them food, when first they desired it.

20. Wemi wingi-namenep, wemi ksin-
    elendamep, wemi wullatemanuwi.

    *All had cheerful knowledge, all had leisure, all
    thought in gladness.*

21. Shukand eli-kimi mekenikink wakon
    powako init'ako.

    *But very secretly an evil being, a mighty magician,
    came on earth,*

22. Mattalogas pallalogas maktaton owa-
    gan payat-chik yutali.

    *And with him brought badness, quarreling,
    unhappiness,*

23. Maktapan payat, wihillan payat,
    mboagan payat.

    *Brought bad weather, brought sickness, brought
    death.*

24. Won wemi wiwunch kamik atak
    kitahikan netamaki epit.

    *All this took place of old on the earth, beyond the
    great tidewater, at the first.*

Questions for "Creation Song"

1.   What characteristics does this myth share with the Old Testament story of Genesis, or with other creation stories you know?

2.   Based on part I of the *Walam Olum,* what might you expect in part II?

3.   There is more than one "Manito" in this section of the story. How would you translate this word into English? Who do the different Manitos seem to be?

Five Teaching Tales

Below are five teaching tales from different times and cultures. The first tale, "The Wolf and the Mastiff," is one of the hundreds of fables attributed to Aesop (620–560 B.C.?). Little is known about Aesop, but he is thought to have spent much of his life as a slave on the Greek island of Samos. Legends, unverifiable, link him with wild adventures and famous people of his time.

Next is one of the parables of Christ, "The Prodigal Son," which was recorded by the evangelist Luke, during the latter part of the first century A.D., in the New Testament of the Bible.

The third selection, "The Lost Son," comes from *Saddharmapundarīka (The Lotus of the Good Law),* which presents all the major doctrines of Mahayana Buddhism, a school of Buddhism that arose in India in the first or second century A.D.

"Joshu Washes the Bowl" is a short illustrative tale from *The Gateless Gate* by Ekai, also called Mu-mon, a Chinese Zen master who lived from 1183–1260. Zen Buddhism came from India to China in the sixth century and eventually spread to Japan. Through meditation, the Zen Buddhist seeks enlightenment, the discovery of one's true nature.

Finally, we have included a brief story written in the 1890s by the American author Kate Chopin, entitled "Emancipation: A Life Fable." Chopin is perhaps best known for her novel *The Awakening*, which, like a number of her short stories, deals with women's struggle for greater freedom and self-fulfillment.

The Wolf and the Mastiff

A Wolf, who was almost skin and bone, met a sleek, fat Mastiff. Greeting the Dog, the Wolf praised his good looks. "It would be easy for you," replied the

Mastiff, "to get as fat as I am." "What must I do?" asked the Wolf. "Almost nothing," said the Dog. As they trotted along, the Wolf noticed a bare spot on the Dog's neck. "What's that mark?" he inquired. "Oh, a trifle," answered the Dog; "the collar I wear when I am tied up is the cause." "Tied up!" exclaimed the Wolf. "Can you not always run where you please?" "Well, not always," said the Mastiff; "but what can that matter?" "It matters much to me," rejoined the Wolf, and, leaping away, he ran back to his native forest.

Moral: Better starve free, than be a fat slave.

The Prodigal Son

Jesus said to them: "A man had two sons. The younger of them said to his father, 'Father, give me the share of the estate that is coming to me.' So the father divided up the property. Some days later this younger son collected all his belongings and went off to a distant land, where he squandered his money on dissolute living. After he had spent everything, a great famine broke out in the country and he was in dire need. So he attached himself to one of the propertied class of the place, who sent him to his farm to take care of the pigs.

"He longed to fill his belly with the husks that were fodder for the pigs, but no one made a move to give him anything. Coming to his senses at last, he said: 'How many hired hands at my father's place have more than enough to eat, while here I am starving! I will break away and return to my father, and say to him, Father, I have sinned against God and against you; I no longer deserve to be called your son. Treat me like one of your hired hands.' With that he set off for his father's house. While he was still a long way off, his father caught sight of him and was deeply moved. He ran out to meet him, threw his arms around his neck, and kissed him. The son said to him, 'Father, I have sinned against God and against you; I no longer deserve to be called your son.' The father said to his servants: 'Quick! bring out the finest robe and put it on him; put a ring on his finger and shoes on his feet. Take the fatted calf and kill it. Let us eat and celebrate because this son of mine was dead and has come back to life. He was lost and is found.' Then the celebration began.

"Meanwhile the elder son was out on the land. As he neared the house on his way home, he heard the sound of music and dancing. He called one of the servants and asked him the reason for the dancing and the music. The servant answered, 'Your brother is home, and your father has killed the fatted calf because he has him back in good health.' The son grew angry at this and would not go in; but his father came out and began to plead with him.

"He said to his father in reply: 'For years now I have slaved for you. I never disobeyed one of your orders, yet you never gave me so much as a kid goat to celebrate with my friends. Then, when this son of yours returns after having gone through your property with loose women, you kill the fatted calf for him.'

"'My son,' replied the father, 'you are with me always, and everything I have is yours. But we had to celebrate and rejoice! This brother of yours was dead, and has come back to life. He was lost, and is found.'"

The Lost Son

A man parted from his father and went to another city; and he dwelt there many years. . . . The father grew rich and the son poor. While the son wandered in all directions [begging] in order to get food and clothes, the father moved to another land, where he lived in great luxury . . . wealthy from business, money-lending, and trade. In course of time the son, wandering in search of his living through town and country, came to the city in which his father dwelled. Now the poor man's father . . . forever thought of the son whom he had lost . . . years ago, but he told no one of this, though he grieved inwardly, and thought: "I am old, and well advanced in years, and though I have great possessions I have no son. Alas that time should do its work upon me, and that all this wealth should perish unused! . . . It would be bliss indeed if my son might enjoy all my wealth!"

Then the poor man, in search of food and clothing, came to the rich man's home. And the rich man was sitting in great pomp at the gate of his house, surrounded by a large throng of attendants . . . on a splendid throne, with a footstool inlaid with gold and silver, under a wide awning decked with pearls and flowers and adorned with hanging garlands of jewels; and he transacted business to the value of millions of gold pieces, all the while fanned by a fly-whisk. . . . When he saw him the poor man was terrified . . . and the hair of his body stood on end, for he thought that he had happened on a king or on some high officer of the state, and had no business there. "I must go," he thought, "to the poor quarter of the town, where I'll get food and clothing without trouble. If I stop here they'll seize me and set me to do forced labor, or some other disaster will befall me!" So he quickly ran away. . . .

But the rich man . . . recognized his son as soon as he saw him; and he was full of joy . . . and thought: "This is wonderful! I have found him who shall enjoy my riches. He of whom I thought constantly has come back, now that I am old and full of years!" Then, longing for his son, he sent swift messengers, telling them to go and fetch him quickly. They ran at full speed and overtook him; the poor man trembled with fear, the hair of his body stood on end . . . and he uttered a cry of distress and exclaimed, "I've done you no wrong!" But they dragged him along by force . . . until . . . fearful that he would be killed or beaten, he fainted and fell on the ground. His father in dismay said to the men, "Don't drag him along in that way!" and, without saying more, he sprinkled his face with cold water—for though he knew that the poor man was his son, he realized that his estate was very humble, while his own was very high.

So the householder told no one that the poor man was his son. He ordered one of his servants to tell the poor man that he was free to go where he chose . . . And the poor man was amazed [that he was allowed to go free], and he went off to the poor quarter of the town in search of food and clothing. Now in order to attract him back the rich man made use of the virtue of "skill in means." He called two men of low caste and of no great dignity and told them: "Go to that poor man . . . and hire him in your own names to do work in my house at double the normal daily wage; and if he asks what work he has to do tell him that he has to help clear away the refuse-dump." So these two men and the poor man cleared the refuse every day . . . in the house of the rich man, and lived in a straw hut nearby. . . . And the rich man saw through a window his son clearing refuse, and was again filled with compassion. So he came down, took off his wreath and jewels and rich clothes, put on dirty garments, covered his body with dust, and, taking a basket in his hand, went up to his son. And he greeted him at a distance and said, "Take this basket and clear away the dust at once!" By this means he managed to speak to his son. [And as time went on he spoke more often to him, and thus he gradually encouraged him. First he urged him to] remain in his service and not take another job, offering him double wages, together with any small extras that he might require, such as the price of a cooking-pot . . . or food and clothes. Then he offered him his own cloak, if he should want it. . . . And at last he said: "You must be cheerful, my good fellow, and think of me as a father . . . for I'm older than you and you've done me good service in clearing away my refuse. As long as you've worked for me you've shown no roguery or guile. . . . I've not noticed one of the vices in you that I've noticed in my other servants! From now on you are like my own son to me!"

Thenceforward the householder called the poor man "son," and the latter felt towards the householder as a son feels towards his father. So the householder, full of longing and love for his son, employed him in clearing away refuse for twenty years. By the end of that time the poor man felt quite at home in the house, and came and went as he chose, though he still lived in the straw hut.

Then the householder fell ill, and felt that the hour of his death was near. So he said to the poor man: "Come, my dear man! I have great riches . . . and am very sick. I need someone upon whom I can bestow my wealth as a deposit, and you must accept it. From now on you are just as much its owner as I am, but you must not squander it." And the poor man accepted the rich man's wealth . . . but personally he cared nothing for it, and asked for no share of it, not even the price of a measure of flour. He still lived in the straw hut, and thought of himself as just as poor as before.

Thus the householder proved that his son was frugal, mature, and mentally developed, and that though he knew that he was now wealthy he still remembered his past poverty, and was still . . . humble and meek. . . . So he sent for the poor man again, presented him before a gathering of his relatives, and in the presence of the king, his officers, and the people of town and country, he said: "Listen, gentlemen! This is my son, whom I begot . . . To him I leave all my family revenues, and my private wealth he shall have as his own."

Joshu Washes the Bowl

A monk told Joshu: "I have just entered the monastery. Please teach me."
Joshu asked: "Have you eaten your rice porridge?"
The monk replied: "I have eaten."
Joshu said: "Then you had better wash your bowl."
At that moment the monk was enlightened.

Emancipation: A Life Fable

There was once an animal born into this world, and opening his eyes upon Life, he saw above and about him confining walls, and before him were bars of iron through which came air and light from without; this animal was born in a cage.

Here he grew, and throve in strength and beauty under care of an invisible protecting hand. Hungering, food was ever at hand. When he thirsted water was brought, and when he felt the need of rest, there was provided a bed of straw upon which to lie; and here he found it good, licking his handsome flanks, to bask in the sun beam that he thought existed but to lighten his home.

Awaking one day from his slothful rest, lo! the door of his cage stood open: accident had opened it. In the corner he crouched, wondering and fearingly. Then slowly did he approach the door, dreading the unaccustomed, and would have closed it, but for such a task his limbs were purposeless. So out the opening he thrust his head, to see the canopy of the sky grow broader, and the world waxing wider.

Back to his corner but not to rest, for the spell of the Unknown was over him, and again and again he goes to the open door, seeing each time more Light.

Then one time standing in the flood of it; a deep in-drawn breath—a bracing of strong limbs, and with a bound he was gone.

On he rushes, in his mad flight, heedless that he is wounding and tearing his sleek sides—seeing, smelling, touching of all things; even stopping to put his lips to the noxious pool, thinking it may be sweet.

Hungering there is no food but such as he must seek and ofttimes fight for; and his limbs are weighted before he reaches the water that is good to his thirsting throat.

So does he live, seeking, finding, joying and suffering. The door which accident had opened is open still, but the cage remains forever empty!

Questions for Five Teaching Tales

1.   What similarities and differences do you notice between the Buddhist tale of the lost son and the Christian story of the prodigal son? What lesson does each parable teach?

2.   In what way might the monk have been enlightened in "Joshu Washes the Bowl"? What has Joshu taught the monk?

3.   How does the kind of lesson taught by "The Wolf and the Mastiff" differ from the lessons of the parables?

4.   Aesop's and Chopin's fables deal with a similar theme. In what ways are the two fables different? How does Chopin's fable allow for several interpretations? Why do you think the author built in this ambiguity of interpretation?

Jacob and Wilhelm Grimm
(1785–1863, 1786–1859)

The Brothers Grimm, as they are commonly called, were born in Hesse-Kassel, Germany. As children, Jacob and Wilhelm slept in the same bed and studied at the same work table; as law students, they roomed together, and when Wilhelm married, Jacob shared his brother's house in Kassel, where the brothers worked as librarians. In 1841 both became professors at the University of Berlin and members of the Academy of Science.

The Grimms' special contribution to the annals of folklore comes from their scholarly respect for the material they collected. Unlike earlier collectors who had freely manipulated the stories they had gathered, the Grimms chose fidelity to the voices of the tellers of these tales, most of whom were simple people from the farms and villages around Kassel. All together the Grimms gathered and transcribed 210 tales; the result of their efforts is known as *Grimm's Fairy Tales,* first published in 1823.

Little Snow-White

Translated by Margaret Hunt and James Stern

Once upon a time in the middle of winter, when the flakes of snow were falling like feathers from the sky, a Queen sat at a window sewing, and the frame of the window was made of black ebony. And whilst she was sewing and looking out of the window at the snow, she pricked her finger with the needle, and three drops of blood fell upon the snow. And the red looked pretty upon the white snow, and she thought to herself: "Would that I had a child as white as snow, as red as blood, and as black as the wood of the window-frame."

Soon after that she had a little daughter, who was as white as snow, and as red as blood, and her hair was as black as ebony; and she was therefore called Little Snow-white. And when the child was born, the Queen died.

After a year had passed the King took to himself another wife. She was a beautiful woman, but proud and haughty, and she could not bear that anyone else should surpass her in beauty. She had a wonderful looking-glass, and when she stood in front of it and looked at herself in it, and said:

"Looking-glass, Looking-glass, on the wall,
Who in this land is the fairest of all?"

the looking-glass answered:

"Thou, O Queen, art the fairest of all!"

Then she was satisfied, for she knew that the looking-glass spoke the truth.

But Snow-white was growing up, and grew more and more beautiful; and when she was seven years old she was as beautiful as the day, and more beautiful than the Queen herself. And once when the Queen asked her looking-glass:

"Looking-glass, Looking-glass, on the wall,
Who in this land is the fairest of all?"

it answered:

"Thou art fairer than all who are here, Lady Queen.
But more beautiful still is Snow-white, as I ween."

Then the Queen was shocked, and turned yellow and green with envy. From that hour, whenever she looked at Snow-white, her heart heaved in her breast, she hated the girl so much.

And envy and pride grew higher and higher in her heart like a weed, so that she had no peace day or night. She called a huntsman, and said: "Take the child away into the forest; I will no longer have her in my sight. Kill her, and bring me back her lung and liver as a token." The huntsman obeyed, and took her away; but when he had drawn his knife, and was about to pierce Snow-white's innocent heart, she began to weep, and said: "Ah, dear huntsman, leave me my life! I will run away into the wild forest, and never come home again."

And as she was so beautiful the huntsman had pity on her and said: "Run away, then, you poor child." "The wild beasts will soon have devoured you," thought he, and yet it seemed as if a stone had been rolled from his heart since it was no longer needful for him to kill her. And as a young boar just then came running by he stabbed it, and cut out its lung and liver and took them to the Queen as proof that the child was dead. The cook had to salt them, and the wicked Queen ate them, and thought she had eaten the lung and liver of Snow-white.

But now the poor child was all alone in the great forest, and so terrified that she looked at all the leaves on the trees, and did not know what to do. Then she began to run, and ran over sharp stones and through thorns, and the wild beasts ran past her, but did her no harm.

She ran as long as her feet would go until it was almost evening; then she saw a little cottage and went into it to rest herself. Everything in the cottage was small, but neater and cleaner than can be told. There was a table on which was a white cover, and seven little plates, and on each plate a little spoon; moreover, there were seven little knives and forks, and seven little mugs. Against the wall stood seven little beds side by side, and covered with snow-white counterpanes.

Little Snow-white was so hungry and thirsty that she ate some vegetables and bread from each plate and drank a drop of wine out of each mug, for she did not wish to take all from one only. Then, as she was so tired, she laid herself down on one of the little beds, but none of them suited her; one was too long, another too short, but at last she found that the seventh one was right, and so she remained in it, said a prayer and went to sleep.

When it was quite dark the owners of the cottage came back; they were seven dwarfs who dug and delved in the mountains for ore. They lit their seven candles, and as it was now light within the cottage they saw that some-one had been there, for everything was not in the same order in which they had left it.

The first said: "Who has been sitting on my chair?"

The second: "Who has been eating off my plate?"

The third: "Who has been taking some of my bread?"

The fourth: "Who has been eating my vegetables?"

The fifth: "Who has been using my fork?"

The sixth: "Who has been cutting with my knife?"

The seventh: "Who has been drinking out of my mug?"

Then the first looked round and saw that there was a little hollow on his bed, and he said: "Who has been getting into my bed?" The others came up and each called out: "Somebody has been lying in my bed too." But the seventh when he looked at his bed saw little Snow-white, who was lying asleep therein. And he called the others, who came running up, and they cried out with astonishment, and brought their seven little candles and let the light fall on little Snow-white. "Oh, heavens! oh, heavens!" cried they, "what a lovely child!" and they were so glad that they did not wake her up, but let her sleep on in the bed. And the seventh dwarf slept with his companions, one hour with each, and so passed the night.

When it was morning little Snow-white awoke, and was frightened when she saw the seven dwarfs. But they were friendly and asked her what her name was. "My name is Snow-white," she answered. "How have you come to our house?" said the dwarfs. Then she told them that her step-mother had wished to have her killed, but that the huntsman had spared her life, and that she had run for the whole day, until at last she had found their dwelling. The dwarfs said: "If you will take care of our house, cook, make the beds, wash, sew, and knit, and if you will keep everything neat and clean, you can stay with us and you shall want for nothing." "Yes," said Snow-white, "with all my heart," and she stayed with them. She kept the house in order for them; in the mornings they went to the mountains and looked for copper and gold, in the evenings they came back, and then their supper had to be ready. The girl was alone the whole day, so the good dwarfs warned her and said: "Beware of your step-mother, she will soon know that you are here; be sure to let no one come in."

But the Queen, believing that she had eaten Snow-white's lung and liver, could not but think that she was again the first and most beautiful of all; and she went to her looking-glass and said:

"Looking-glass, Looking-glass, on the wall,
Who in this land is the fairest of all?"

and the glass answered:

"Oh Queen, thou art fairest of all I see,
But over the hills, where the seven dwarfs dwell,
Snow-white is still alive and well,
And none is so fair as she."

Then she was astounded, for she knew that the looking-glass never spoke falsely, and she knew that the huntsman had betrayed her, and that little Snow-white was still alive.

And so she thought and thought again how she might kill her, for so long as she was not the fairest in the whole land, envy let her have no rest. And when she had at last thought of something to do, she painted her face, and dressed herself like an old pedlar-woman, and no one could have known her. In this disguise she went over the seven mountains to the seven dwarfs, and knocked at the door and cried: "Pretty things to sell, very cheap, very cheap." Little Snow-white looked out of the window and called out: "Good-day, my good woman, what have you to sell?" "Good things, pretty things," she answered; "stay-laces of all colors," and she pulled out one which was woven of bright-colored silk. "I may let the worthy old woman in," thought Snow-white, and she unbolted the door and bought the pretty laces. "Child," said the old woman, "what a fright you look; come, I will lace you properly for once." Snow-white had no suspicion, but stood before her, and let herself be laced with the new laces. But the old woman laced so quickly and laced so tightly that Snow-white lost her breath and fell down as if dead. "Now I am the most beautiful," said the Queen to herself, and ran away.

Not long afterwards, in the evening, the seven dwarfs came home, but how shocked they were when they saw their dear little Snow-white lying on the ground, and that she neither stirred nor moved, and seemed to be dead. They lifted her up, and, as they saw that she was laced too tightly, they cut the laces; then she began to breathe a little, and after a while came to life again. When the dwarfs heard what had happened they said: "The old pedlar-woman was no one else than the wicked Queen; take care and let no one come in when we are not with you."

But the wicked woman when she had reached home went in front of the glass and asked:

"Looking-glass, Looking-glass, on the wall,
Who in this land is the fairest of all?"

and it answered as before:

"Oh, Queen, thou art fairest of all I see,
But over the hills, where the seven dwarfs dwell,
Snow-white is still alive and well,
And none is so fair as she."

When she heard that, all her blood rushed to her heart with fear, for she saw plainly that little Snow-white was again alive. "But now," she said, "I will think of something that shall really put an end to you," and by the help of witchcraft, which she understood, she made a poisonous comb. Then she disguised herself and took the shape of another old woman. So she went over the seven mountains to the seven dwarfs, knocked at the door, and cried: "Good things to sell, cheap, cheap!" Little Snow-white looked out and said: "Go away; I cannot let anyone come in." "I suppose you can look," said the old woman, and pulled the poisonous comb out and held it up. It pleased the girl so well that she let herself be beguiled, and opened the door. When they had made a bargain the old woman said: "Now I will comb you properly for once." Poor little Snow-white had no suspicion, and let the old woman do as she pleased, but hardly had she put the comb in her hair than the poison in it took effect, and the girl fell down senseless. "You paragon of beauty," said the wicked woman, "you are done for now," and she went away.

But fortunately it was almost evening, when the seven dwarfs came home. When they saw Snow-white lying as if dead upon the ground they at once suspected the step-mother, and they looked and found the poisoned comb. Scarcely had they taken it out when Snow-white came to herself, and told them what had happened. Then they warned her once more to be upon her guard and to open the door to no one.

The Queen, at home, went in front of the glass and said:

"Looking-glass, Looking-glass, on the wall,
Who in this land is the fairest of all?"

then it answered as before:

"Oh, Queen, thou art fairest of all I see,
But over the hills, where the seven dwarfs dwell,
Snow-white is still alive and well,
And none is so fair as she."

When she heard the glass speak thus she trembled and shook with rage. "Snow-white shall die," she cried, "even if it costs me my life!"

Thereupon she went into a quite secret, lonely room, where no one ever came, and there she made a very poisonous apple. Outside it looked pretty, white with a red cheek, so that everyone who saw it longed for it; but whoever ate a piece of it must surely die.

When the apple was ready she painted her face, and dressed herself up as a farmer's wife, and so she went over the seven mountains to the seven dwarfs. She knocked at the door. Snow-white put her head out of the window and said: "I cannot let anyone in; the seven dwarfs have forbidden me." "It is all the same to me," answered the woman, "I shall soon get rid of my apples. There, I will give you one."

"No," said Snow-white, "I dare not take anything." "Are you afraid of poison?'' said the old woman; "look, I will cut the apple in two pieces; you eat the red cheek, and I will eat the white.'' The apple was so cunningly made that only the red cheek was poisoned. Snow-white longed for the fine apple, and when she saw the woman ate part of it she could resist no longer, and stretched out her hand and took the poisonous half. But hardly had she a bit of it in her mouth than she fell down dead. Then the Queen looked at her with a dreadful look, and laughed aloud and said: "White as snow, red as blood, black as ebony-wood! this time the dwarfs cannot wake you up again.''

And when she asked of the looking-glass at home:

> "Looking-glass, Looking-glass, on the wall,
> Who in this land is the fairest of all?''

it answered at last:

> "Oh, Queen, in this land thou art fairest of all.''

Then her envious heart had rest, so far as an envious heart can have rest.

The dwarfs, when they came home in the evening, found Snow-white lying upon the ground; she breathed no longer and was dead. They lifted her up, looked to see whether they could find anything poisonous, unlaced her, combed her hair, washed her with water and wine, but it was all of no use; the poor child was dead, and remained dead. They laid her upon a bier, and all seven of them sat round it and wept for her, and wept three days long.

Then they were going to bury her, but she still looked as if she were living, and still had her pretty red cheeks. They said: "We could not bury her in the dark ground,'' and they had a transparent coffin of glass made, so that she could be seen from all sides, and they laid her in it, and wrote her name upon it in golden letters, and that she was a king's daughter. Then they put the coffin out upon the mountain, and one of them always stayed by it and watched it. And birds came too, and wept for Snow-white; first an owl, then a raven, and last a dove.

And now Snow-white lay a long, long time in the coffin, and she did not change, but looked as if she were asleep; for she was as white as snow, as red as blood, and her hair was as black as ebony.

It happened, however, that a king's son came into the forest, and went to the dwarfs' house to spend the night. He saw the coffin on the mountain, and the beautiful Snow-white within it, and read what was written upon it in golden letters. Then he said to the dwarfs: "Let me have the coffin, I will give you whatever you want for it.'' But the dwarfs answered: "We will not part with it for all the gold in the world.'' Then he said: "Let me have it as a gift, for I cannot live without seeing Snow-white. I will honor and prize her as my dearest possession.'' As he spoke in this way the good dwarfs took pity upon him, and gave him the coffin.

And now the King's son had it carried away by his servants on their shoulders. And it happened that they stumbled over a tree-stump, and with the shock the poisonous piece of apple which Snow-white had bitten off came out of her throat. And before long she opened her eyes, lifted up the lid of the coffin, sat up, and was once more alive. "Oh, heavens, where am I?" she cried. The King's son, full of joy, said: "You are with me," and told her what had happened, and said: "I love you more than everything in the world; come with me to my father's palace, you shall be my wife."

And Snow-white was willing, and went with him, and their wedding was held with great show and splendor. But Snow-white's wicked step-mother was also bidden to the feast. When she had arrayed herself in beautiful clothes she went before the Looking-glass, and said:

"Looking-glass, Looking-glass, on the wall,
Who in this land is the fairest of all?"

the glass answered:

"Oh, Queen, of all here the fairest art thou,
But the young Queen is fairer by far as I trow."

Then the wicked woman uttered a curse, and was so wretched, so utterly wretched that she knew not what to do. At first she would not go to the wedding at all, but she had no peace, and had to go to see the young Queen. And when she went in she recognized Snow-white; and she stood still with rage and fear, and could not stir. But iron slippers had already been put upon the fire, and they were brought in with tongs, and set before her. Then she was forced to put on the red-hot shoes, and dance until she dropped down dead.

Questions for "Little Snow-White"

1. Why does the Queen wish to eat Snow-white's lungs and liver?

2. What purpose in the story do the seven dwarfs and Snow-white's sojourn with them serve?

3. What mistakes does Snow-white make? What do these errors in judgment reveal about her?

4. We know that Snow-white is seven years old when her stepmother sends her off to be killed, but we are not told how long she stays with the dwarfs. What details in the story indicate that she has grown up?

5. What message or messages does this story carry along with its magic?

6. "Good fairy tales are not for sissies," one critic writes. What might he mean by this comment? How does "Little Snow-white" support this observation?

Italo Calvino (1923–1986)

Born in Cuba and educated at the University of Turin, Italo Calvino was considered Italy's leading contemporary novelist at the time of his death. He began his career by writing realistic stories, but soon gave free rein to his inventiveness. Among his later works, most of which have been translated into numerous languages, are *Cosmicomics* (1965), *Invisible Cities* (1972), *The Castle of Crossed Destinies* (1973), *If on a Winter's Night a Traveler* (1979), *Italian Folktales* (1980), and *Mr. Palomar* (1986).

The American writer John Updike has observed that Calvino "took fiction into new places where it had never been before, and back into the fabulous and ancient sources of narrative." Speaking of *Italian Folktales*, novelist Ursula Le Guin called "its mixture of the deeply familiar with the totally unexpected" one of "its innumerable delights."

Catherine the Wise

Translated by George Martin

Here in Palermo they tell, ladies and gentlemen, that once upon a time there was a very important shopkeeper in the city. He had a daughter who, from the time she was weaned, proved so wise that she was given her say on every single matter in the household. Recognizing the talent of his daughter, her father called her Catherine the Wise. When it came to studying all sorts of languages and reading every kind of book, no one could hold a candle to her.

When the girl was sixteen, her mother died. Catherine was so grief-stricken that she shut herself up in her room and refused to come out. There she ate and slept, shunning all thoughts of strolls, theaters, and entertainment of any kind.

Her father, whose life centered on this only child of his, thought it advisable to hold a council on the matter. He called together all the lords (for, even though a shopkeeper, he was on familiar terms with the best people) and said, "Gentlemen, you are aware I have a daughter who is the apple of my eye. But ever since her mother's death, she's been keeping to the house like a cat and won't for the life of her stick her head outside."

The council replied, "Your daughter is known the world over for her vast wisdom. Open up a big school for her, so that she directs others in their studies, she will get this grief out of her system."

"That's a splendid idea," said the father, and called his daughter. "Listen, my daughter, since you refuse every diversion, I have decided to open a school and put you in charge of it. How does that suit you?"

Catherine was instantly charmed. She took charge of the teachers herself, and they got the school all ready. Outside they put up a sign: WHOEVER WISHES TO STUDY AT CATHERINE THE WISE'S IS WELCOME, FREE OF CHARGE.

Numbers of children, both boys and girls, flocked in at once, and she seated them at the desks, side by side, without distinction. Someone piped up, "But that boy there is the son of a coal merchant!" "That makes no difference: the coal merchant's son must sit beside the prince's daughter. First come, first served." And school began. Catherine had a cat-o'-nine-tails. She taught everyone alike, but woe to those that didn't do their lessons! The reputation of this school even reached the palace, and the prince himself decided to attend. He dressed up in his regal clothes, came in, found an empty place, and Catherine invited him to sit down. When it was his turn, Catherine asked him a question. The prince didn't know the answer. She dealt him a back-handed blow, from which his cheek still smarts.

Crimson with rage, the prince rose, ran back to the palace, and sought out his father. "A favor I beg, Majesty: I wish to get married! For a wife, I want Catherine the Wise."

The king sent for Catherine's father, who went at once, saying, "Your humble servant, Majesty!"

"Rise! My son has taken a fancy to your daughter. What are we to do but join them in matrimony?"

"As you will, Majesty. But I am a shopkeeper, whereas your son is of royal blood."

"That makes no difference. My son himself wants her."

The shopkeeper returned home. "Catherine, the prince wants to wed you. What do you have to say about that?"

"I accept."

The wool for the mattresses was not wanting, no more than the chests of drawers; in a week's time everything needed had been prepared. The prince assembled a retinue of twelve bridesmaids. The royal chapel was opened, and the couple got married.

Following the ceremony the queen told the bridesmaids to go and undress the princess for bed. But the prince said, "There's no need of people to undress or dress her, or of guards at the door." Once he was alone with his bride, he said, "Catherine, do you remember the slap you gave me? Are you sorry for it?"

"Sorry for it? If you ask for it, I'll do it again!"

"What! You're not sorry?"

"Not in the least."

"And you don't intend to be?"

"Who would?"

"So that's your attitude? Well, I'll now teach *you* a thing or two." He started unwinding a rope with which to lower her through a trapdoor into a pit. "Catherine," he said when the rope was ready, "either you repent, or I'll let you down into the pit!"

"I'll be cooler there," replied Catherine.

So the prince tied the rope around her and lowered her into the pit where all she found was a little table, a chair, a pitcher of water, and a piece of bread.

The next morning, according to custom, the father and mother came to greet the new wife.

"You can't come in," said the prince. "Catherine isn't feeling well."

Then he went and opened the trapdoor. "What kind of night did you spend?"

"Pleasant and refreshing," replied Catherine.

"Are you considering the slap you gave me?"

"I'm thinking of the one I owe you now."

Two days went by, and hunger began to gnaw at her stomach. Not knowing what else to do, she pulled a stay out of her corset and started making a hole in the wall. She dug and dug, and twenty-four hours later saw a tiny ray of daylight, at which she took heart. She made the hole bigger and peered through it. Who should be passing at that moment but her father's clerk. "Don Tommaso! Don Tommaso!" Don Tommaso couldn't imagine what this voice was, coming out of the wall like that. "It's me, Catherine the Wise. Tell my father I have to talk to him right away."

Don Tommaso returned with Catherine's father, showing him the tiny opening in the wall. "Father, as luck would have it, I'm at the bottom of a pit. You must have a passageway dug underground from our palace all the way here, with an arch and a light every twenty feet. Leave everything else to me."

The shopkeeper agreed to that and in the meantime he brought her food regularly—roast chicken and other nourishing dishes—and passed it through the opening in the wall.

Three times a day the prince peered through the trapdoor. "Are you sorry yet, Catherine, for the slap you gave me?"

"Sorry for what? Just imagine the slap you are going to get from me now!"

The workers finally got the underground passage dug, with an arch and a lantern every twenty feet. Catherine would pass through it to her father's house after the prince had looked in on her and reclosed the trapdoor.

It wasn't long before the prince was fed up with trying to get Catherine to apologize. He opened the trapdoor. "Catherine, I'm going to Naples. Have you nothing to tell me?"

"Have a good time, enjoy yourself, and write me upon your arrival in Naples."

"So I should go?"

"What? Are you still there?"

So the prince departed.

As soon as he shut the trapdoor, Catherine ran off to her father. "Papa, now is the time to help me. Get me a brigantine ready to sail, with housekeeper, servants, festive gowns—all to go to Naples. There let them rent me a palace across from the royal palace and await my arrival."

The shopkeeper sent the brigantine off. Meanwhile the prince had a frigate readied, and he too set sail. She stood on her father's balcony and watched him leave, then she went aboard another brigantine and was in Naples ahead of him. Little vessels, you know, make better time than big ones.

In Naples Catherine would come out on the balcony of her palace each day in a lovelier gown than the day before. The prince saw her and exclaimed, "How much like Catherine the Wise she is!" He fell in love with her and sent a messenger to her palace. "My lady, the prince would like very much to pay you a visit, if that won't inconvenience you."

"By all means!" she replied.

The king came regally dressed, made a big fuss over her, then sat down to talk. "Tell me, my lady, are you married?"

"Not yet. Are you?"

"Neither am I, isn't it obvious? You resemble a maiden, my lady, who captured my fancy in Palermo. I should like you to be my wife."

"With pleasure, Prince." And a week later they got married.

At the end of nine months Catherine gave birth to a baby boy that was a marvel to behold. "Princess," asked the prince, "what shall we call him?"

"Naples," said Catherine. So they named him Naples.

Two years went by, and the prince decided to leave town. The princess didn't like it, but he had made up his mind and couldn't be swayed. He drafted a document for Catherine saying the baby was his firstborn and in time would be king. Then he left for Genoa.

As soon as the prince had gone, Catherine wrote her father to send a brigantine to Genoa immediately with furniture, housekeeper, servants, and all the rest, and have them rent her a palace opposite the royal palace of Genoa and await her arrival. The shopkeeper loaded a ship and sent it off to Genoa.

Catherine also took a brigantine and reached Genoa before the prince. She settled down in her new palace, and when the prince saw this beautiful young lady with her royal coiffure, jewels, and wealth, he exclaimed, "How much like Catherine the Wise she is, and also my wife in Naples!" He dispatched a messenger to her, and she sent back word she would be happy to receive the prince.

They began talking. "Are you single?" asked the prince.

"A widow," answered Catherine. "And you?"

"I'm a widower, with one son. By the way, you look just like a lady I used to know in Palermo, not to mention one I knew in Naples."

"Really? We all have seven doubles in the world, so they say."

Thus, to make a long story short, they became man and wife in one week's time.

Nine months later, Catherine gave birth to another boy, even handsomer than the first. The prince was happy. "Princess, what shall we call him?"

"Genoa!" And so they named him Genoa.

Two years went by, and the king grew restless once more.

"You're going off like that and leaving me with a child on my hands?" asked the princess.

"I am drawing up a document for you," the prince reassured her, "stating that this is my son and little prince." While he made preparations to leave for Venice, Catherine wrote her father in Palermo for another brigantine with servants, housekeeper, furniture, new clothes and all. The brigantine sailed off to Venice. The prince departed on the frigate. The princess left on another brigantine and arrived before he did.

"Heavens!" exclaimed the prince when he beheld the beautiful lady at her casement. "She too looks exactly like my wife in Genoa, who looked exactly like my wife in Naples, who looked exactly like Catherine the Wise! But how can this be? Catherine is in Palermo shut up in the pit, the Neapolitan is in Naples, the Genoese in Genoa, while this one is in Venice!" He sent a messenger to her and then went to meet her.

"Would you believe, my lady, that you look like several other ladies I know—one in Palermo, one in Naples, one in Genoa—"

"Indeed! We are supposed to have seven doubles in this life."

And thus they continued their customary talk. "Are you married?"

"No, I'm a widow. And you?" "I am a widower, with two sons." In a week's time they were married.

This time Catherine had a little girl, radiant like the sun and moon. "What shall we call her?" asked the prince.

"Venice." So they baptized her Venice.

Two more years went by. "Listen, princess, I have to go back to Palermo. But first, I'm drawing up a document that spells out that this is my daughter and royal princess."

He departed, but Catherine reached Palermo first. She went to her father's house, walked through the underground passage and back into the pit. As soon as the prince arrived, he ran and pulled up the trapdoor. "Catherine, how are you?"

"Me? I'm fine!"

"Are you sorry for that slap you gave me?"

"Have you thought about the slap I owe you?"

"Come, Catherine, say you're sorry! Otherwise I'll take another wife."

"Go right ahead! No one is stopping you!"

"But if you say you're sorry, I'll take you back."

"No."

The prince then formally declared that his wife was dead and that he intended to remarry. He wrote all the kings for portraits of their daughters. The portraits arrived, and the most striking was of the king of England's daughter. The prince summoned mother and daughter to conclude the marriage.

The entire royal family of England arrived in Palermo, and the wedding was set for the morrow. What did Catherine do in the meantime but have three fine royal outfits readied for her three children—Naples, Genoa, and Venice. She dressed up like the queen she actually was, took the hand of

Naples, clothed as crown prince, climbed into a ceremonial carriage, followed by Prince Genoa and Princess Venice, and they drove off to the palace.

The wedding procession with the prince and the daughter of the king of England was approaching, and Catherine said to her children, "Naples, Genoa, Venice, go and kiss your father's hand!" And the children ran up to kiss the prince's hand.

At the sight of them, the prince could only admit defeat. "This is the slap you were to give me!" he exclaimed, and embraced the children. The princess of England was dumbfounded; she turned her back on everybody and stalked off.

Catherine explained all the mystery to her husband about the ladies who looked so much alike, and the prince couldn't apologize enough for what he had done.

They lived happily ever after,
While here we sit grinding our teeth.

Questions for "Catherine the Wise"

1.   In the introduction to this chapter, we quoted Calvino's description of the narrator he tried to capture in this Sicilian folktale. Go back to the story to find specific examples of the characteristics he cites. What else have you discovered about the personality of this narrator?

2.   What elements of the fairy tale appear in this story? What similarities and differences do you observe between this story and "Little Snow-White"?

3.   Although "Catherine the Wise" is a rendering of an ancient tale, it has a distinctly contemporary ring. What aspects of the story seem modern?

Anton Chekhov (1860–1904)

Born in Taganrog, Russia, Anton Chekhov was the son of an unsuccessful grocer who beat his children daily, in the belief that he was carrying out God's will. Despite a childhood dominated by hardship and fear, Chekhov developed into a major writer who was also a sensible, conscientious, even-tempered man.

Educated as a physician at Moscow University, Chekhov practiced medicine only occasionally, but attributed his powers of observation to his scientific training. By the time he was thirty, Chekhov was considered a major writer, and his fame grew rapidly over the years.

Chekhov's hundreds of short stories and numerous plays—several of which, like *Uncle Vanya* (1899), *The Three Sisters* (1901), and *The Cherry Orchard* (1904), are among the finest theatrical works in literature—reveal a keen sensitivity to the underlying social and psychological forces of life, while also providing a vivid picture of the Russia of his time. In most of his stories and plays, Chekhov portrays characters who must endure the essential isolation of the human condition. His work typically emphasizes mood rather than plot, as the story here illustrates.

In 1901, at the peak of his literary powers and his fame, Chekhov married Olga Knipper, a young actress who performed in a number of his plays. Only four years later, at the age of forty-four, he died of tuberculosis, a disease whose ravages he had endured for most of his adult life.

Heartache

Translated by Avraham Yarmolonsky

"To whom shall I tell my sorrow?"[1]

Evening twilight. Large flakes of wet snow are circling lazily about the street lamps which have just been lighted, settling in a thin soft layer on roofs, horses' backs, people's shoulders, caps. Iona Potapov, the cabby, is all white like a ghost. As hunched as a living body can be, he sits on the box without

---

[1]From an old Russian song.

stirring. If a whole snowdrift were to fall on him, even then, perhaps he would not find it necessary to shake it off. His nag, too, is white and motionless. Her immobility, the angularity of her shape, and the sticklike straightness of her legs make her look like a penny gingerbread horse. She is probably lost in thought. Anyone who has been torn away from the plow, from the familiar gray scenes, and cast into this whirlpool full of monstrous lights, of ceaseless uproar and hurrying people, cannot help thinking.

Iona and his nag have not budged for a long time. They had driven out of the yard before dinnertime and haven't had a single fare yet. But now evening dusk is descending upon the city. The pale light of the street lamps changes to a vivid color and the bustle of the street grows louder.

"Sleigh to the Vyborg District!" Iona hears. "Sleigh!"

Iona starts, and through his snow-plastered eyelashes sees an officer in a military overcoat with a hood.

"To the Vyborg District!" repeats the officer. "Are you asleep, eh? To the Vyborg District!"

As a sign of assent Iona gives a tug at the reins, which sends layers of snow flying from the horse's back and from his own shoulders. The officer gets into the sleigh. The driver clucks to the horse, cranes his neck like a swan, rises in his seat and, more from habit than necessity, flourishes his whip. The nag, too, stretches her neck, crooks her sticklike legs and irresolutely sets off.

"Where are you barging in, damn you?" Iona is promptly assailed by shouts from the massive dark wavering to and fro before him. "Where the devil are you going? Keep to the right!"

"Don't you know how to drive? Keep to the right," says the officer with vexation.

A coachman driving a private carriage swears at him; a pedestrian who was crossing the street and brushed against the nag's nose with his shoulder, looks at him angrily and shakes the snow off his sleeve. Iona fidgets on the box as if sitting on needles and pins, thrusts out his elbows and rolls his eyes like a madman, as though he did not know where he was or why he was there.

"What rascals they all are," the officer jokes. "They are doing their best to knock into you or be trampled by the horse. It's a conspiracy."

Iona looks at his fare and moves his lips. He wants to say something, but the only sound that comes out is a wheeze.

"What is it?" asks the officer.

Iona twists his mouth into a smile, strains his throat and croaks hoarsely: "My son, sir . . . er, my son died this week."

"H'm, what did he die of?"

Iona turns his whole body around to his fare and says, "Who can tell? It must have been a fever. He lay in the hospital only three days and then he died. . . . It is God's will."

"Get over, you devil!" comes out of the dark. "Have you gone blind, you old dog? Keep your eyes peeled!"

"Go on, go on," says the officer. "We shan't get there until tomorrow at this rate. Give her the whip!"

The driver cranes his neck again, rises in his seat, and with heavy grace swings his whip. Then he looks around at the officer several times, but the latter keeps his eyes closed and is apparently indisposed to listen. Letting his fare off in the Vyborg District, Iona stops by a teahouse and again sits motionless and hunched on the box. Again the wet snow paints him and his nag white. One hour passes, another. . . .

Three young men, two tall and lanky, one short and hunchbacked, come along swearing at each other and loudly pound the pavement with their galoshes.

"Cabby, to the Police Bridge!" the hunchback shouts in a cracked voice. "The three of us . . . twenty kopecks!"

Iona tugs at the reins and clucks to his horse. Twenty kopecks is not fair, but his mind is not on that. Whether it is a ruble or five kopecks, it is all one to him now, so long as he has a fare. . . . The three young men, jostling each other and using foul language, go up to the sleigh and all three try to sit down at once. They start arguing about which two are to sit and who shall be the one to stand. After a long ill-tempered and abusive altercation, they decide that the hunchback must stand up because he is the shortest.

"Well, get going," says the hunchback in his cracked voice, taking up his station and breathing down Iona's neck. "On your way! What a cap you've got, brother! You won't find a worse one in all Petersburg—"

"Hee, hee . . . hee, hee . . ." Iona giggles, "as you say—"

"Well, then, 'as you say,' drive on. Are you going to crawl like this all the way, eh? D'you want to get it in the neck?"

"My head is splitting," says one of the tall ones. "At the Dukmasovs' yesterday, Vaska and I killed four bottles of cognac between us."

"I don't get it, why lie?" says the other tall one angrily. "He is lying like a trouper."

"Strike me dead, it's the truth!"

"It is about as true as that a louse sneezes."

"Hee, hee," giggles Iona. "The gentlemen are feeling good!"

"Faugh, the devil take you!" cries the hunchback indignantly. "Will you get a move on, you old pest, or won't you? Is that the way to drive? Give her a crack of the whip! Giddap, devil! Giddap! Let her feel it!"

Iona feels the hunchback's wriggling body and quivering voice behind his back. He hears abuse addressed to him, sees people, and the feeling of loneliness begins little by little to lift from his heart. The hunchback swears till he chokes on an elaborate three-decker oath and is overcome by cough. The tall youths begin discussing a certain Nadezhda Petrovna. Iona looks round at them. When at last there is a lull in the conversation for which he has been waiting, he turns around and says: "This week . . . er . . . my son died."

"We shall all die," says the hunchback, with a sigh wiping his lips after his coughing fit. "Come, drive on, drive on. Gentlemen, I simply cannot stand this pace! When will he get us there?"

"Well, you give him a little encouragement. Biff him in the neck!"

"Do you hear, you old pest? I'll give it to you in the neck. If one stands on ceremony with fellows like you, one may as well walk. Do you hear, you old serpent? Or don't you give a damn what we say?"

And Iona hears rather than feels the thud of a blow on his neck.

"Hee, hee," he laughs. "The gentlemen are feeling good. God give you health!"

"Cabby, are you married?" asks one of the tall ones.

"Me? Hee, hee! The gentlemen are feeling good. The only wife for me now is the damp earth . . . Hee, haw, haw! The grave, that is! . . . Here my son is dead and me alive . . . It is a queer thing, death comes in at the wrong door . . . It don't come for me, it comes for my son. . . ."

And Iona turns round to tell them how his son died, but at that point the hunchback gives a sigh of relief and announces that, thank God, they have arrived at last. Having received his twenty kopecks, for a long while Iona stares after the revelers, who disappear into a dark entrance. Again he is alone and once more silence envelops him. The grief which has been allayed for a brief space comes back again and wrenches his heart more cruelly than ever. There is a look of anxiety and torment in Iona's eyes as they wander restlessly over the crowds moving to and fro on both sides of the street. Isn't there someone among those thousands who will listen to him? But the crowds hurry past, heedless of him and his grief. His grief is immense, boundless. If his heart were to burst and his grief to pour out, it seems that it would flood the whole world, and yet no one sees it. It has found a place for itself in such an insignificant shell that no one can see it in broad daylight.

Iona notices a doorkeeper with a bag and makes up his mind to speak to him.

"What time will it be, friend?" he asks.

"Past nine. What have you stopped here for? On your way!"

Iona drives a few steps away, hunches up and surrenders himself to his grief. He feels it is useless to turn to people. But before five minutes are over, he draws himself up, shakes his head as though stabbed by a sharp pain and tugs at the reins . . . He can bear it no longer.

"Back to the yard!" he thinks. "To the yard!"

And his nag, as though she knew his thoughts, starts out at a trot. An hour and a half later, Iona is sitting beside a large dirty stove. On the stove, on the floor, on benches are men snoring. The air is stuffy and foul. Iona looks at the sleeping figures, scratches himself and regrets that he has come home so early.

"I haven't earned enough to pay for the oats," he reflects. "That's what's wrong with me. A man that knows his job . . . who has enough to eat and has enough for his horse don't need to fret."

In one of the corners a young driver gets up, hawks sleepily and reaches for the water bucket.

"Thirsty?" Iona asks him.

"Guess so."

"H'm, may it do you good, but my son is dead, brother . . . did you hear? This week in the hospital. . . . What a business!"

Iona looks to see the effect of his words, but he notices none. The young man has drawn his cover over his head and is already asleep. The old man sighs and scratches himself. Just as the young man was thirsty for water so he thirsts for talk. It will soon be a week since his son died and he hasn't talked to anybody about him properly. He ought to be able to talk about it, taking his time, sensibly. He ought to tell how his son was taken ill, how he suffered, what he said before he died, how he died. . . . He ought to describe the funeral, and how he went to the hospital to fetch his son's clothes. His daughter Anisya is still in the country. . . . And he would like to talk about her, too. Yes, he has plenty to talk about now. And his listener should gasp and moan and keen. . . . It would be even better to talk to women. Though they are foolish, two words will make them blubber.

"I must go out and have a look at the horse," Iona thinks. "There will be time enough for sleep. You will have enough sleep, no fear. . . ."

He gets dressed and goes into the stable where his horse is standing. He thinks about oats, hay, the weather. When he is alone, he dares not think of his son. It is possible to talk about him with someone, but to think of him when one is alone, to evoke his image is unbearably painful.

"You chewing?" Iona asks his mare seeing her shining eyes. "There, chew away, chew away. . . . If we haven't earned enough for oats, we'll eat hay. . . . Yes. . . . I've grown too old to drive. My son had ought to be driving, not me. . . . He was a real cabby. . . . He had ought to have lived. . . ."

Iona is silent for a space and then goes on: "That's how it is, old girl. . . . Kuzma Ionych is gone. . . . Departed this life. . . . He went and died to no purpose. . . . Now let's say you had a little colt, and you were that little colt's own mother. And suddenly, let's say, that same little colt departed this life. . . . You'd be sorry, wouldn't you?"

The nag chews, listens and breathes on her master's hands. Iona is carried away and tells her everything.

Questions for "Heartache"

1.   Look closely at the first paragraph. What mood is created by the weather, the time of day, and the descriptions of Iona Potapov and his nag? How does this paragraph, combined with the epigraph (the prefatory quote) prepare you for the theme and the content of the piece?

2.   Describe each of the people to whom Iona tries to tell his sorrow. What conclusions can you draw about Chekhov's view of humankind based on Iona's brief interactions with them?

3.   Iona is sometimes referred to by his name; at other times he is called "the driver." Can you locate where this happens in the story and explain why?

4.   At one point we learn that Iona "hears abuse addressed to him, sees people, and the feeling of loneliness begins little by little to lift from his heart." How can you account for this apparent contradiction?

5.   Why do you think Chekhov decided to cast this story in the present tense? Rewrite a paragraph or two, changing present tense to past, and read both versions aloud. Now try to explain any differences you note in the effects of the present and past tense versions.

6.   Iona and his nag are described as "hunched," "motionless," and "white" more than once in this short piece. What purpose do these repetitions serve?

Charlotte Perkins Gilman (1860–1935)

Shortly after Charlotte Perkins Gilman was born, her father left his wife and two children. Raised by her mother in Hartford, Connecticut, Gilman studied art at the Rhode Island School of Design. From the beginning of her marriage to Charles Walter Stetson, a local artist, she suffered from depression, a condition that became serious after the birth of her daughter. A well-known specialist in women's nervous disorders placed her on a regimen of extended bed rest that called for almost total inactivity and isolation. This treatment came close to driving her completely mad, and she fled to California, far from her husband and her physician.

In California, Gilman supported her mother and daughter by running a boarding house, and during this time she began publishing her writing. She became a prominent lecturer and writer on feminism and the labor movement. In 1900 she embarked on a long and happy marriage to George Houghton Gilman, her first cousin. Debilitated by cancer in her last years, Gilman decided to end her life, explaining in the note she left behind that she preferred "chloroform to cancer."

"The Yellow Wallpaper," which first appeared in 1892, was followed by a number of other publications, including a volume of verse, several books on social and economic problems, three utopian novels, and an autobiography that was published posthumously.

The Yellow Wallpaper

It is very seldom that mere ordinary people like John and myself secure ancestral halls for the summer.

A colonial mansion, a hereditary estate, I would say a haunted house and reach the height of romantic felicity—but that would be asking too much of fate!

Still I will proudly declare that there is something queer about it.

Else, why should it be let so cheaply? And why have stood so long untenanted?

John laughs at me, of course, but one expects that.

John is practical in the extreme. He has no patience with faith, an intense horror of superstition, and he scoffs openly at any talk of things not to be felt and seen and put down in figures.

John is a physician, and *perhaps*—(I would not say it to a living soul, of course, but this is dead paper and a great relief to my mind)—*perhaps* that is one reason I do not get well faster.

You see, he does not believe I am sick! And what can one do?

If a physician of high standing, and one's own husband, assures friends and relatives that there is really nothing the matter with one but temporary nervous depression—a slight hysterical tendency—what is one to do?

My brother is also a physician, and also of high standing, and he says the same thing.

So I take phosphates or phosphites—whichever it is—and tonics, and air and exercise, and journeys, and am absolutely forbidden to "work" until I am well again.

Personally, I disagree with their ideas.

Personally, I believe that congenial work, with excitement and change, would do me good.

But what is one to do?

I did write for a while in spite of them; but it *does* exhaust me a good deal—having to be so sly about it, or else meet with heavy opposition.

I sometimes fancy that in my condition, if I had less opposition and more society and stimulus—but John says the very worst thing I can do is to think about my condition, and I confess it always makes me feel bad.

So I will let it alone and talk about the house.

The most beautiful place! It is quite alone, standing well back from the road, quite three miles from the village. It makes me think of English places that you read about, for there are hedges and walls and gates that lock, and lots of separate little houses for the gardeners and people.

There is a *delicious* garden! I never saw such a garden—large and shady, full of box-bordered paths, and lined with long grape-covered arbors with seats under them.

There were greenhouses, but they are all broken now.

There was some legal trouble, I believe, something about the heirs and co-heirs; anyhow, the place has been empty for years.

That spoils my ghostliness, I am afraid, but I don't care—there is something strange about the house—I can feel it.

I even said so to John one moonlight evening, but he said what I felt was a draught, and shut the window.

I get unreasonably angry with John sometimes. I'm sure I never used to be so sensitive. I think it is due to this nervous condition.

But John says if I feel so I shall neglect proper self-control; so I take pains to control myself—before him, at least, and that makes me very tired.

I don't like our room a bit. I wanted one downstairs that opened onto the piazza and had roses all over the window, and such pretty old-fashioned chintz hangings! But John would not hear of it.

He said there was only one window and not room for two beds, and no near room for him if he took another.

He is very careful and loving, and hardly lets me stir without special direction.

I have a schedule prescription for each hour in the day; he takes all care from me, and so I feel basely ungrateful not to value it more.

He said he came here solely on my account, that I was to have perfect rest and all the air I could get. "Your exercise depends on your strength, my dear," said he, "and your food somewhat on your appetite; but air you can absorb all the time." So we took the nursery at the top of the house.

It is a big, airy room, the whole floor nearly, with windows that look all ways, and air and sunshine galore. It was a nursery first, and then playroom and gymnasium, I should judge, for the windows are barred for little children, and there are rings and things in the walls.

The paint and paper look as if a boys' school had used it. It is stripped off—the paper—in great patches all around the head of my bed, about as far as I can reach, and in a great place on the other side of the room low down. I never saw a worse paper in my life. One of those sprawling, flamboyant patterns committing every artistic sin.

It is dull enough to confuse the eye in following, pronounced enough constantly to irritate and provoke study, and when you follow the lame uncertain curves for a little distance they suddenly commit suicide—plunge off at outrageous angles, destroy themselves in unheard-of contradictions.

The color is repellent, almost revolting: a smouldering unclean yellow, strangely faded by the slow-turning sunlight. It is a dull yet lurid orange in some places, a sickly sulphur tint in others.

No wonder the children hated it! I should hate it myself if I had to live in this room long.

There comes John, and I must put this away—he hates to have me write a word.

We have been here two weeks, and I haven't felt like writing before, since that first day.

I am sitting by the window now, up in this atrocious nursery, and there is nothing to hinder my writing as much as I please, save lack of strength.

John is away all day, and even some nights when his cases are serious.

I'm glad my case is not serious!

But these nervous troubles are dreadfully depressing.

John does not know how much I really suffer. He knows there is no reason to suffer, and that satisfies him.

Of course it is only nervousness. It does weigh on me so not to do my duty in any way!

I meant to be such a help to John, such a real rest and comfort, and here I am a comparative burden already!

Nobody would believe what an effort it is to do what little I am able—to dress and entertain, and order things.

It is fortunate Mary is so good with the baby. Such a dear baby!

And yet I *cannot* be with him, it makes me so nervous.

I suppose John never was nervous in his life. He laughs at me so about this wallpaper!

At first he meant to repaper the room, but afterward he said that I was letting it get the better of me, and that nothing was worse for a nervous patient than to give way to such fancies.

He said that after the wallpaper was changed it would be the heavy bedstead, and then the barred windows, and then that gate at the head of the stairs, and so on.

"You know the place is doing you good," he said, "and really, dear, I don't care to renovate the house just for a three months' rental."

"Then do let us go downstairs," I said. "There are such pretty rooms there."

Then he took me in his arms and called me a blessed little goose, and said he would go down to the cellar, if I wished, and have it whitewashed into the bargain.

But he is right enough about the beds and windows and things.

It is as airy and comfortable a room as anyone need wish, and, of course, I would not be so silly as to make him uncomfortable just for a whim.

I'm really getting quite fond of the big room, all but that horrid paper.

Out of one window I can see the garden—those mysterious deep-shaded arbors, the riotous old-fashioned flowers, and bushes and gnarly trees.

Out of another I get a lovely view of the bay and a little private wharf belonging to the estate. There is a beautiful shaded lane that runs down there from the house. I always fancy I see people walking in these numerous paths and arbors, but John has cautioned me not to give way to fancy in the least. He says that with my imaginative power and habit of story-making, a nervous weakness like mine is sure to lead to all manner of excited fancies, and that I ought to use my will and good sense to check the tendency. So I try.

I think sometimes that if I were only well enough to write a little it would relieve the press of ideas and rest me.

But I find I get pretty tired when I try.

It is so discouraging not to have any advice and companionship about my work. When I get really well, John says we will ask Cousin Henry and Julia down for a long visit; but he says he would as soon put fireworks in my pillow-case as to let me have those stimulating people about now.

I wish I could get well faster.

But I must not think about that. This paper looks to me as if it *knew* what a vicious influence it had!

There is a recurrent spot where the pattern lolls like a broken neck and two bulbous eyes stare at you upside down.

I get positively angry with the impertinence of it and the everlastingness. Up and down and sideways they crawl, and those absurd unblinking eyes are everywhere. There is one place where two breadths didn't match, and the eyes go all up and down the line, one a little higher than the other.

I never saw so much expression in an inanimate thing before, and we all know how much expression they have! I used to lie awake as a child and get more entertainment and terror out of blank walls and plain furniture than most children could find in a toy-store.

Imaginative even as child

I remember what a kindly wink the knobs of our big old bureau used to have, and there was one chair that always seemed like a strong friend.

I used to feel that if any of the other things looked too fierce I could always hop into that chair and be safe.

The furniture in this room is no worse than inharmonious, however, for we had to bring it all from downstairs. I suppose when this was used as a playroom they had to take the nursery things out, and no wonder! I never saw such ravages as the children have made here.

The wallpaper, as I said before, is torn off in spots, and it sticketh closer than a brother—they must have had perseverance as well as hatred. *repeats self*

Then the floor is scratched and gouged and splintered, the plaster itself is dug out here and there, and this great heavy bed, which is all we found in the room, looks as if it had been through the wars. *reminds her of herself*

But I don't mind it a bit—only the paper. *protests too much*

There comes John's sister. Such a dear girl as she is, and so careful of me! I must not let her find me writing. *pressure of secrecy*

She is a perfect and enthusiastic housekeeper, and hopes for no better profession. I verily believe she thinks it is the writing which made me sick! *common*

But I can write when she is out, and see her a long way off from these windows.

There is one that commands the road, a lovely shaded winding road, and one that just looks off over the country. A lovely country, too, full of great elms and velvet meadows.

This wallpaper has a kind of sub-pattern in a different shade, a particularly irritating one, for you can only see it in certain lights, and not clearly then.

But in the places where it isn't faded and where the sun is just so—I can see a strange, provoking, formless sort of figure that seems to skulk about behind that silly and conspicuous front design.

There's sister on the stairs!

Well, the Fourth of July is over! The people are all gone, and I am tired out. John thought it might do me good to see a little company, so we just had Mother and Nellie and the children down for a week.

Of course I didn't do a thing. Jennie sees to everything now.

But it tired me all the same.

John says if I don't pick up faster he shall send me to Weir Mitchell in the fall.

But I don't want to go there at all. I had a friend who was in his hands once, and she says he is just like John and my brother, only more so!

Besides, it is such an undertaking to go so far.

I don't feel as if it was worthwhile to turn my hand over for anything, and I'm getting dreadfully fretful and querulous.

I cry at nothing, and cry most of the time.

Of course I don't when John is here, or anybody else, but when I am alone.

serious cases, and Jennie is good and lets me alone when I want her to.

So I walk a little in the garden or down that lovely lane, sit on the porch under the roses, and lie down up here a good deal.

I'm getting really fond of the room in spite of the wallpaper. Perhaps *because* of the wallpaper.

It dwells in my mind so!

I lie here on this great immovable bed—it is nailed down, I believe—and follow that pattern about by the hour. It is as good as gymnastics, I assure you. I start, we'll say, at the bottom, down in the corner over there where it has not been touched, and I determine for the thousandth time that I *will* follow that pointless pattern to some sort of a conclusion.

I know a little of the principle of design, and I know this thing was not arranged on any laws of radiation, or alternation, or repetition, or symmetry, or anything else that I ever heard of.

It is repeated, of course, by the breadths, but not otherwise.

Looked at in one way, each breadth stands alone; the bloated curves and flourishes—a kind of "debased Romanesque" with delirium tremens—go waddling up and down in isolated columns of fatuity.

But, on the other hand, they connect diagonally, and the sprawling outlines run off in great slanting waves of optic horror, like a lot of wallowing sea-weeds in full chase.

The whole thing goes horizontally, too, at least it seems so, and I exhaust myself trying to distinguish the order of its going in that direction.

They have used a horizontal breadth for a frieze, and that adds wonderfully to the confusion.

There is one end of the room where it is almost intact, and there, when the crosslights fade and the low sun shines directly upon it, I can almost fancy radiation after all—the interminable grotesque seems to form around a common center and rush off in headlong plunges of equal distraction.

It makes me tired to follow it. I will take a nap, I guess.

I don't know why I should write this.

I don't want to.

I don't feel able.

And I know John would think it absurd. But I *must* say what I feel and think in some way—it is such a relief!

But the effort is getting to be greater than the relief.

Half the time now I am awfully lazy, and lie down ever so much. John says I mustn't lose my strength, and has me take cod liver oil and lots of tonics and things, to say nothing of ale and wine and rare meat.

Dear John! He loves me very dearly, and hates to have me sick. I tried to have a real earnest reasonable talk with him the other day, and tell him how I wish he would let me go and make a visit to Cousin Henry and Julia.

But he said I wasn't able to go, nor able to stand it after I got there; and I did not make out a very good case for myself, for I was crying before I had finished.

It is getting to be a great effort for me to think straight. Just this nervous weakness, I suppose.

And dear John gathered me up in his arms, and just carried me upstairs and laid me on the bed, and sat by me and read to me till it tired my head.

He said I was his darling and his comfort and all he had, and that I must take care of myself for his sake, and keep well.

He says no one but myself can help me out of it, that I must use my will and self-control and not let any silly fancies run away with me.

There's one comfort—the baby is well and happy, and does not have to occupy this nursery with the horrid wallpaper.

If we had not used it, that blessed child would have! What a fortunate escape! Why, I wouldn't have a child of mine, an impressionable little thing, live in such a room for worlds.

I never thought of it before, but it is lucky that John kept me here after all; I can stand it so much easier than a baby, you see.

Of course I never mention it to them any more—I am too wise—but I keep watch for it all the same.

There are things in that wallpaper that nobody knows about but me, or ever will.

Behind that outside pattern the dim shapes get clearer every day.

It is always the same shape, only very numerous.

And it is like a woman stooping down and creeping about behind that pattern. I don't like it a bit. I wonder—I begin to think—I wish John would take me away from here!

It is so hard to talk with John about my case, because he is so wise, and because he loves me so.

But I tried it last night.

It was moonlight. The moon shines in all around just as the sun does.

I hate to see it sometimes, it creeps so slowly, and always comes in by one window or another.

John was asleep and I hated to waken him, so I kept still and watched the moonlight on that undulating wallpaper till I felt creepy.

The faint figure behind seemed to shake the pattern, just as if she wanted to get out.

I got up softly and went to feel and see if the paper *did* move, and when I came back John was awake.

"What is it, little girl?" he said. "Don't go walking about like that—you'll get cold."

I thought it was a good time to talk, so I told him that I really was not gaining here, and that I wished he would take me away.

"Why, darling!" said he. "Our lease will be up in three weeks, and I can't see how to leave before.

"The repairs are not done at home, and I cannot possibly leave town just now. Of course, if you were in any danger, I could and would, but you really are better, dear, whether you can see it or not. I am a doctor, dear, and I know. You are gaining flesh and color, your appetite is better, I feel really much easier about you.''

"I don't weigh a bit more," said I, "nor as much; and my appetite may be better in the evening when you are here but it is worse in the morning when you are away!''

"Bless her little heart!" said he with a big hug. "She shall be as sick as she pleases! But now let's improve the shining hours by going to sleep, and talk about it in the morning!''

"And you won't go away?" I asked gloomily.

"Why, how can I, dear? It is only three weeks more and then we will take a nice little trip of a few days while Jennie is getting the house ready. Really, dear, you are better!''

"Better in body perhaps—" I began, and stoppped short, for he sat up straight and looked at me with such a stern, reproachful look that I could not say another word.

"My darling," said he, "I beg of you, for my sake and for our child's sake, as well as for your own, that you will never for one instant let that idea enter your mind! There is nothing so dangerous, so fascinating, to a temperament like yours. It is a false and foolish fancy. Can you not trust me as a physician when I tell you so?''

So of course I said no more on that score, and we went to sleep before long. He thought I was asleep first, but I wasn't, and lay there for hours trying to decide whether that front pattern and the back pattern really did move together or separately.

On a pattern like this, by daylight, there is a lack of sequence, a defiance of law, that is a constant irritant to a normal mind.

The color is hideous enough, and unreliable enough, and infuriating enough, but the pattern is torturing.

You think you have mastered it, but just as you get well under way in following, it turns a back-somersault and there you are. It slaps you in the face, knocks you down, and tramples upon you. It is like a bad dream.

The outside pattern is a florid arabesque, reminding one of a fungus. If you can imagine a toadstool in joints, an interminable string of toadstools, budding and sprouting in endless convolutions—why, that is something like it.

That is, sometimes!

There is one marked peculiarity about this paper, a thing nobody seems to notice but myself, and that is that it changes as the light changes.

When the sun shoots in through the east window—I always watch for that first long, straight ray—it changes so quickly that I never can quite believe it.

That is why I watch it always.

By moonlight—the moon shines in all night when there is a moon—I wouldn't know it was the same paper.

At night in any kind of light, in twilight, candlelight, lamplight, and worst of all by moonlight, it becomes bars! The outside pattern, I mean, and the woman behind it is as plain as can be.

I didn't realize for a long time what the thing was that showed behind, that dim sub-pattern, but now I am quite sure it is a woman.

By daylight she is subdued, quiet. I fancy it is the pattern that keeps her so still. It is so puzzling. It keeps me quiet by the hour.

I lie down ever so much now. John says it is good for me, and to sleep all I can.

Indeed he started the habit by making me lie down for an hour after each meal.

It is a very bad habit, I am convinced, for you see, I don't sleep.

And that cultivates deceit, for I don't tell them I'm awake—oh, no!

The fact is I am getting a little afraid of John.

He seems very queer sometimes, and even Jennie has an inexplicable look.

It strikes me occasionally, just as a scientific hypothesis, that perhaps it is the paper!

I have watched John when he did not know I was looking, and come into the room suddenly on the most innocent excuses, and I've caught him several times *looking at the paper!* And Jennie too. I caught Jennie with her hand on it once.

She didn't know I was in the room, and when I asked her in a quiet, a very quiet voice, with the most restrained manner possible, what she was doing with the paper, she turned around as if she had been caught stealing, and looked quite angry—asked me why I should frighten her so!

Then she said that the paper stained everything it touched, that she had found yellow smooches on all my clothes and John's and she wished we would be more careful!

Did not that sound innocent? But I know she was studying that pattern, and I am determined that nobody shall find it out but myself!

Life is very much more exciting now than it used to be. You see, I have something more to expect, to look forward to, to watch. I really do eat better, and am more quiet than I was.

John is so pleased to see me improve! He laughed a little the other day, and said I seemed to be flourishing in spite of my wallpaper.

I turned it off with a laugh. I had no intention of telling him it was *because* of the wallpaper—he would make fun of me. He might even want to take me away.

I don't want to leave now until I have found it out. There is a week more, and I think that will be enough.

I'm feeling so much better!

I don't sleep much at night, for it is so interesting to watch developments; but I sleep a good deal during the daytime.

In the daytime it is tiresome and perplexing.

There are always new shoots on the fungus, and new shades of yellow all over it. I cannot keep count of them, though I have tried conscientiously.

It is the strangest yellow, that wallpaper! It makes me think of all the yellow things I ever saw—not beautiful like buttercups, but old, foul, bad yellow things.

But there is something else about that paper—the smell! I noticed it the moment we came into the room, but with so much air and sun it was not bad. Now we have had a week of fog and rain, and whether the windows are open or not, the smell is here.

It creeps all over the house.

I find it hovering in the dining-room, skulking in the parlor, hiding in the hall, lying in wait for me on the stairs.

It gets into my hair.

Even when I go to ride, if I turn my head suddenly and surprise it—there is that smell!

Such a peculiar odor, too! I have spent hours in trying to analyze it, to find what it smelled like.

It is not bad—at first—and very gentle, but quite the subtlest, most enduring odor I ever met.

In this damp weather it is awful. I wake up in the night and find it hanging over me.

It used to disturb me at first. I thought seriously of burning the house— to reach the smell.

But now I am used to it. The only thing I can think of that it is like is the *color* of the paper! A yellow smell.

There is a very funny mark on this wall, low down, near the mopboard. A streak that runs round the room. It goes behind every piece of furniture, except the bed, a long, straight, even *smooch,* as if it had been rubbed over and over.

I wonder how it was done and who did it, and what they did it for. Round and round and round—round and round and round—it makes me dizzy!

I really have discovered something at last.

Through watching so much at night, when it changes so, I have finally found out.

The front pattern *does* move—and no wonder! The woman behind shakes it!

Sometimes I think there are a great many women behind, and sometimes only one, and she crawls around fast, and her crawling shakes it all over.

Then in the very bright spots she keeps still, and in the very shady spots she just takes hold of the bars and shakes them hard.

And she is all the time trying to climb through. But nobody could climb through that pattern—it strangles so; I think that is why it has so many heads.

They get through, and then the pattern strangles them off and turns them upside down, and makes their eyes white!

If those heads were covered or taken off it would not be half so bad.

I think that woman gets out in the daytime!

And I'll tell you why—privately—I've seen her!

I can see her out of every one of my windows!

It is the same woman, I know, for she is always creeping, and most women do not creep by daylight.

I see her in that long shaded lane, creeping up and down. I see her in those dark grape arbors, creeping all around the garden.

I see her on that long road under the trees, creeping along, and when a carriage comes she hides under the blackberry vines.

I don't blame her a bit. It must be very humiliating to be caught creeping by daylight!

I always lock the door when I creep by daylight. I can't do it at night, for I know John would suspect something at once.

And John is so queer now that I don't want to irritate him. I wish he would take another room! Besides, I don't want anybody to get that woman out at night but myself.

I often wonder if I could see her out of all the windows at once.

But, turn as fast as I can, I can only see out of one at one time.

And though I always see her, she *may* be able to creep faster than I can turn! I have watched her sometimes away off in the open country, creeping as fast as a cloud shadow in a high wind.

If only that top pattern could be gotten off from the under one! I mean to try it, little by little.

I have found out another funny thing, but I shan't tell it this time! It does not do to trust people too much.

There are only two more days to get this paper off, and I believe John is beginning to notice. I don't like the look in his eyes.

And I hear him ask Jennie a lot of professional questions about me. She had a very good report to give.

She said I slept a good deal in the daytime.

John knows I don't sleep very well at night, for all I'm so quiet!

He asked me all sorts of questions, too, and pretended to be very loving and kind.

As if I couldn't see through him!

Still, I don't wonder he acts so, sleeping under this paper for three months.

It only interests me, but I feel sure John and Jennie are affected by it.

Hurrah! This is the last day, but it is enough. John is to stay in town over night, and won't be out until this evening.

Jennie wanted to sleep with me—the sly thing; but I told her I should undoubtedly rest better for a night all alone.

That was clever, for really I wasn't alone a bit! As soon as it was moonlight and that poor thing began to crawl and shake the pattern, I got up and ran to help her.

I pulled and she shook. I shook and she pulled, and before morning we had peeled off yards of that paper.

A strip about as high as my head and half around the room.

And then when the sun came and that awful pattern began to laugh at me, I declared I would finish it today!

We go away tomorrow, and they are moving all my furniture down again to leave things as they were before.

Jennie looked at the wall in amazement, but I told her merrily that I did it out of pure spite at the vicious thing.

She laughed and said she wouldn't mind doing it herself, but I must not get tired.

How she betrayed herself that time!

But I am here, and no person touches this paper but Me—not *alive!*

She tried to get me out of the room—it was too patent! But I said it was so quiet and empty and clean now that I believed I would lie down again and sleep all I could, and not to wake me even for dinner—I would call when I woke.

So now she is gone, and the servants are gone, and the things are gone, and there is nothing left but that great bedstead nailed down, with the canvas mattress we found on it.

We shall sleep downstairs tonight, and take the boat home tomorrow.

I quite enjoy the room, now it is bare again.

How those children did tear about here!

This bedstead is fairly gnawed!

But I must get to work.

I have locked the door and thrown the key down into the front path.

I don't want to go out, and I don't want to have anybody come in, till John comes.

I want to astonish him.

I've got a rope up here that even Jennie did not find. If that woman does get out, and tries to get away, I can tie her!

But I forgot I could not reach far without anything to stand on!

This bed will *not* move!

I tried to lift and push it until I was lame, and then I got so angry I bit off a little piece at one corner—but it hurt my teeth.

Then I peeled off all the paper I could reach standing on the floor. It sticks horribly and the pattern just enjoys it! All those strangled heads and bulbous eyes and waddling fungus growths just shriek with derision!

I am getting angry enough to do something desperate. To jump out of the window would be admirable exercise, but the bars are too strong even to try.

Besides I wouldn't do it. Of course not. I know well enough that a step like that is improper and might be misconstrued.

I don't like to *look* out of the windows even—there are so many of those creeping women, and they creep so fast.

I wonder if they all come out of that wallpaper as I did?

But I am securely fastened now by my well-hidden rope—you don't get *me* out in the road there!

I suppose I shall have to get back behind the pattern when it comes night, and that is hard!

It is so pleasant to be out in this great room and creep around as I please!

I don't want to go outside. I won't, even if Jennie asks me to.

For outside you have to creep on the ground, and everything is green instead of yellow.

But here I can creep smoothly on the floor, and my shoulder just fits in that long smooch around the wall, so I cannot lose my way.

Why, there's John at the door!

It is no use, young man, you can't open it!

How he does call and pound!

Now he's crying to Jennie for an axe.

It would be a shame to break down that beautiful door!

"John, dear!" said I in the gentlest voice. "The key is down by the front steps, under a plantain leaf!"

That silenced him for a few moments.

Then he said, very quietly indeed, "Open the door, my darling!"

"I can't," said I. "The key is down by the front door under a plantain leaf!" And then I said it again, several times, very gently and slowly, and said it so often that he had to go and see, and he got it of course, and came in. He stopped short by the door.

"What is the matter?" he cried. "For God's sake, what are you doing!"

I kept on creeping just the same, but I looked at him over my shoulder.

"I've got out at last," said I, "in spite of you and Jane. And I've pulled off most of the paper, so you can't put me back!"

Now why should that man have fainted? But he did, and right across my path by the wall, so that I had to creep over him every time!

Questions for "The Yellow Wallpaper"

1. Describe the narrator of the story. What reasons can you suggest for her decline?

2. Give a brief character sketch of the narrator's husband.

3. What room of the house does the narrator occupy? How is this significant?

4.   Why do you think the narrator becomes obsessed by the yellow wallpaper?

5.   "The Yellow Wallpaper" has often been classified as a horror story. What elements of the horror story can you find in this tale?

6.   This story can also be read as a dramatic portrait of a descent into madness. How do tone, style, and content make this a convincing psychological drama? And how do you account for the fact that the narrative can be categorized as both psychological and horror fiction? Can you think of other stories that might also be read in these two ways?

7.   Here, from her autobiography, is Gilman's explanation of her reasons for writing "The Yellow Wallpaper":

WHY I WROTE "THE YELLOW WALLPAPER"

Many and many a reader has asked that. When the story first came out, in the *New England Magazine* about 1891, a Boston physician made protest in *The Transcript.* Such a story ought not to be written, he said; it was enough to drive anyone mad to read it.

Another physician, in Kansas I think, wrote to say that it was the best description of incipient insanity he had ever seen, and—begging my pardon—had I been there?

Now the story of the story is this:

For many years I suffered from a severe and continuous nervous breakdown tending to melancholia—and beyond. During about the third year of this trouble I went, in devout faith and some faint stir of hope, to a noted specialist in nervous diseases, the best known in the country.[1] This wise man put me to bed and applied the rest cure, to which a still-good physique responded so promptly that he concluded there was nothing much the matter with me, and sent me home with solemn advice to "live as domestic a life as far as possible," to "have but two hours' intellectual life a day," and "never to touch pen, brush, or pencil again" as long as I lived. This was in 1887.

I went home and obeyed those directions for some three months, and came so near the borderline of utter mental ruin that I could see over.

Then, using the remnants of intelligence that remained, and helped by a wise friend, I cast the noted specialist's advice to the winds and went to work again—work, the normal life of every human being; work, in which is joy and growth and service, without which one is a pauper and a parasite—ultimately recovering some measure of power.

Being naturally moved to rejoicing by this narrow escape, I wrote "The Yellow Wallpaper," with its embellishments and additions, to carry out the ideal (I never had hallucinations or objections to my mural decorations) and sent a copy to the physician who so nearly drove me mad. He never acknowledged it.

The little book is valued by alienists[2] and as a good specimen of one kind of

---

[1] Dr. S. Weir Mitchell of Philadelphia, the preeminent "nerve specialist" of the time. Mitchell is actually mentioned by the narrator of "The Yellow Wallpaper."
[2] alienist: obsolete word for psychiatrist.

literature. It has, to my knowledge, saved one woman from a similar fate—so terrifying her family that they let her out into normal activity and she recovered.

But the best result is this. Many years later I was told that the great specialist had admitted to friends of his that he had altered his treatment of neurasthenia since reading "The Yellow Wallpaper."

It was not intended to drive people crazy, but to save people from being driven crazy, and it worked.

How does "Why I Wrote 'The Yellow Wallpaper'" encourage readers to see the story in still another way? To shed further light on the informed opinions of the times in which "The Yellow Wallpaper" was written, we've included an article entitled "Emotional Prodigality" in Chapter 7 of this book. How do that author's attitudes toward women and his recommendations for treating their nervous disorders correspond to Gilman's story, and to her reasons for writing it?

James Joyce (1882–1941)

James Joyce was born in Dublin, Ireland. He was educated at Jesuit schools and graduated from University College in Dublin. Disillusioned with his Catholic upbringing and the chaotic state of politics in Ireland, Joyce left his country in 1904 for Italy with a young woman named Nora Barnacle, who later became his wife. Over the years, the Joyce family lived in Trieste, Paris, and Zurich. While Joyce worked on his stories and novels, he supported his family by teaching languages and borrowing money from friends and relatives. Throughout his life, Joyce suffered from weak eyes, a condition that led to numerous operations and periods of total blindness. He died of a perforated ulcer in Zurich, Switzerland.

The following selection is from *Dubliners* (1915), Joyce's first published fiction. Like all his major works, the fifteen stories in this collection are set in Dublin: Although Joyce would remain an expatriate all of his adult life, his writing continued to reflect the Ireland of his youth and his imagination. *Dubliners* was followed by the autobiographical *A Portrait of the Artist as a Young Man* (1916), *Exiles* (a play in the style of Ibsen, 1918), *Ulysses* (1922), and *Finnegan's Wake* (1939). Joyce's revolutionary experiments with language, structure, and technique have made him one of the most influential writers of our century.

Araby

North Richmond Street, being blind, was a quiet street except at the hour when the Christian Brothers' School set the boys free. An uninhabited house of two storeys stood at the blind end, detached from its neighbours in a square ground. The other houses of the street, conscious of decent lives within them, gazed at one another with brown imperturbable faces.

The former tenant of our house, a priest, had died in the back drawing-room. Air, musty from having been long enclosed, hung in all the rooms, and the waste room behind the kitchen was littered with old useless papers. Among these I found a few paper-covered books, the pages of which were curled and damp: *The Abbot*, by Walter Scott, *The Devout Communicant* and *The Memoirs of Vidocq*.[1] I liked the last best because its leaves were yellow. The

---

[1] *The Abbot* (1820): a popular historical romance.

The Devout Communicant: a book of religious meditations by an eighteenth-century English priest, Pacificus Baker.

The Memoirs of Vidocq: the memoirs of François-Eugene Vidocq (1775–1857), a famous French criminal who later changed his ways and became the head of a government criminal-investigation brigade.

wild garden behind the house contained a central apple-tree and a few strag-gling bushes under one of which I found the late tenant's rusty bicycle-pump. He had been a very charitable priest; in his will he had left all his money to institutions and the furniture of his house to his sister.

When the short days of winter came dusk fell before we had well eaten our dinners. When we met in the street the houses had grown sombre. The space of sky above us was the colour of ever-changing violet and towards it the lamps of the street lifted their feeble lanterns. The cold air stung us and we played till our bodies glowed. Our shouts echoed in the silent street. The career of our play brought us through the dark muddy lanes behind the houses where we ran the gauntlet of the rough tribes from the cottages, to the back doors of the dark dripping gardens where odours arose from the ashpits, to the dark odorous stables where a coachman smoothed and combed the horse or shook music from the buckled harness. When we returned to the street light from the kitchen windows had filled the areas. If my uncle was seen turning the corner we hid in the shadow until we had seen him safely housed. Or if Mangan's sister came out on the doorstep to call her brother in to his tea we watched her from our shadow peer up and down the street. We waited to see whether she would remain or go in and, if she remained, we left our shadow and walked up to Mangan's steps resignedly. She was waiting for us, her figure defined by the light from the half-opened door. Her brother always teased her before he obeyed and I stood by the railings looking at her. Her dress swung as she moved her body and the soft rope of her hair tossed from side to side.

Every morning I lay on the floor in the front parlour watching her door. The blind was pulled down to within an inch of the sash so that I could not be seen. When she came out on the doorstep my heart leaped. I ran to the hall, seized my books and followed her. I kept her brown figure always in my eye and, when we came near the point at which our ways diverged, I quickened my pace and passed her. This happened morning after morning. I had never spoken to her, except for a few casual words, and yet her name was like a summons to all my foolish blood.

Her image accompanied me even in places the most hostile to romance. On Saturday evenings when my aunt went marketing I had to go to carry some of the parcels. We walked through the flaring streets, jostled by drunken men and bargaining women, amid the curse of labourers, the shrill litanies of shop-boys who stood guard by the barrels of pigs' cheeks, the nasal chanting of street-singers, who sang a *come-all-you* about O'Donovan Rossa,[2] or a ballad about the troubles in our native land. These noises converged in a single sensation of life for me: I imagined that I bore my chalice safely through a throng of foes. Her name sprang to my lips at moments in strange prayers and praises which I myself did not understand. My eyes were often

---

[2]*come-all-you* . . . Rossa: Irish street singers made their living by singing songs that often began, "Come all you gallant Irishmen/And listen to my song." In this case, the singers' subject was O'Donovan Rossa, a popular hero jailed by the British for promoting violent rebellion.

full of tears (I could not tell why) and at times a flood from my heart seemed to pour itself out into my bosom. I thought little of the future. I did not know whether I would ever speak to her or not or, if I spoke to her, how I could tell her of my confused adoration. But my body was like a harp and her words and gestures were like fingers running upon the wires.

One evening I went into the back drawing-room in which the priest had died. It was a dark rainy evening and there was no sound in the house. Through one of the broken panes I heard the rain impinge upon the earth, the fine incessant needles of water playing in the sodden beds. Some distant lamp or lighted window gleamed below me. I was thankful that I could see so little. All my senses seemed to desire to veil themselves and, feeling that I was about to slip from them, I pressed the palms of my hands together until they trembled, murmuring: "O *love!* O *love!*" many times.

At last she spoke to me. When she addressed the first words to me I was so confused that I did not know what to answer. She asked me was I going to *Araby*. I forgot whether I answered yes or no. It would be a splendid bazaar, she said she would love to go.

"And why can't you?" I asked.

While she spoke she turned a silver bracelet round and round her wrist. She could not go, she said, because there would be a retreat[3] that week in her convent. Her brother and two other boys were fighting for their caps and I was alone at the railings. She held one of the spikes, bowing her head towards me. The light from the lamp opposite our door caught the white curve of her neck, lit up her hair that rested there and, falling, lit up the hand upon the railing. It fell over one side of her dress and caught the white border of a petticoat just visible as she stood at ease.

"It's well for you," she said.

"If I go," I said, "I will bring you something."

What innumerable follies laid waste my waking and sleeping thoughts after that evening! I wished to annihilate the tedious intervening days. I chafed against the work of school. At night in my bedroom and by day in the classroom her image came between me and the page I strove to read. The syllables of the word *Araby* were called to me through the silence in which my soul luxuriated and cast an Eastern enchantment over me. I asked for leave to go to the bazaar on Saturday night. My aunt was surprised and hoped it was not some Freemason[4] affair. I answered few questions in class. I watched my master's face pass from amiability to sternness; he hoped I was not beginning to idle. I could not call my wandering thoughts together. I had hardly any patience with the serious work of life which, now that it stood between me and my desire, seemed to me child's play, ugly monotonous child's play.

---

[3]A religious exercise that involves withdrawing from ordinary activities to concentrate on one's spiritual growth for a period of time.

[4]Freemason: a secret society that Irish Catholics believed to be a Protestant conspiracy against them.

On Saturday morning I reminded my uncle that I wished to go to the bazaar in the evening. He was fussing at the hallstand, looking for the hat-brush, and answered me curtly:

"Yes, boy, I know."

As he was in the hall I could not go into the front parlour and lie at the window. I left the house in bad humour and walked slowly towards the school. The air was pitilessly raw and already my heart misgave me.

When I came home to dinner my uncle had not yet been home. Still it was early. I sat staring at the clock for some time and, when its ticking began to irritate me, I left the room. I mounted the staircase and gained the upper part of the house. The high cold empty gloomy rooms liberated me and I went from room to room singing. From the front window I saw my companions playing below in the street. Their cries reached me weakened and indistinct and, leaning my forehead against the cool glass, I looked over at the dark house where she lived. I may have stood there for an hour, seeing nothing but the brown-clad figure cast by my imagination, touched discreetly by the lamplight at the curved neck, at the hand upon the railings and at the border below the dress.

When I came downstairs again I found Mrs. Mercer sitting at the fire. She was an old garrulous woman, a pawnbroker's widow, who collected used stamps for some pious purpose. I had to endure the gossip of the tea-table. The meal was prolonged beyond an hour and still my uncle did not come. Mrs. Mercer stood up to go: she was very sorry she couldn't wait any longer, but it was after eight o'clock and she did not like to be out late, as the night air was bad for her. When she had gone I began to walk up and down the room, clenching my fists. My aunt said:

"I'm afraid you may put off your bazaar for this night of Our Lord."

At nine o'clock I heard my uncle's latchkey in the halldoor. I heard him talking to himself and heard the hallstand rocking when it had received the weight of his overcoat. I could interpret these signs. When he was midway through his dinner I asked him to give me the money to go to the bazaar. He had forgotten.

"The people are in bed and after their first sleep now," he said.

I did not smile. My aunt said to him energetically:

"Can't you give him the money and let him go? You've kept him late enough as it is."

My uncle said he was very sorry he had forgotten. He said he believed in the old saying: "All work and no play makes Jack a dull boy." He asked me where I was going and, when I had told him a second time he asked me did I know *The Arab's Farewell to his Steed.*[5] When I left the kitchen he was about to recite the opening lines of the piece to my aunt.

---

[5]*The Arab's Farewell to his Steed:* a sentimental ballad about a desert nomad who succumbs to greed and sells his cherished horse. Then, deeply sorry, he flings away the gold he has received. This ballad was written by a popular poet, Caroline Norton (1808–1877).

I held a florin tightly in my hand as I strode down Buckingham Street towards the station. The sight of the streets thronged with buyers and glaring with gas recalled to me the purpose of my journey. I took my seat in a third-class carriage of a deserted train. After an intolerable delay the train moved out of the station slowly. It crept onward among ruinous houses and over the twinkling river. At Westland Row Station a crowd of people pressed to the carriage doors; but the porters moved them back, saying that it was a special train for the bazaar. I remained alone in the bare carriage. In a few minutes the train drew up beside an improvised wooden platform. I passed out on to the road and saw by the lighted dial of a clock that it was ten minutes to ten. In front of me was a large building which displayed the magical name.

I could not find any sixpenny entrance and, fearing that the bazaar would be closed, I passed quickly through a turnstile, handing a shilling to a weary-looking man. I found myself in a big hall girdled at half its height by a gallery. Nearly all the stalls were closed and the greater part of the hall was in darkness. I recognised a silence like that which pervades a church after a service. I walked into the centre of the bazaar timidly. A few people were gathered about the stalls which were still open. Before a curtain, over which the words *Café Chantant*[6] were written in coloured lamps, two men were counting money on a salver. I listened to the fall of the coins.

Remembering with difficulty why I had come I went over to one of the stalls and examined porcelain vases and flowered tea-sets. At the door of the stall a young lady was talking and laughing with two young gentlemen. I remarked their English accents and listened vaguely to their conversation.

"O, I never said such a thing!"

"O, but you did!"

"O, but I didn't!"

"Didn't she say that?"

"Yes. I heard her."

"O, there's a . . . fib!"

Observing me the young lady came over and asked me did I wish to buy anything. The tone of her voice was not encouraging; she seemed to have spoken to me out of a sense of duty. I looked humbly at the great jars that stood like eastern guards at either side of the dark entrance to the stall and murmured:

"No, thank you."

The young lady changed the position of one of the vases and went back to the two young men. They began to talk of the same subject. Once or twice the young lady glanced at me over her shoulder.

I lingered before her stall, though I knew my stay was useless, to make my interest in her wares seem the more real. Then I turned away slowly and

---

[6]*Café Chantant:* French name for a restaurant that features performers singing popular songs.

walked down the middle of the bazaar. I allowed the two pennies to fall against the six-pence in my pocket. I heard a voice call from one end of the gallery that the light was out. The upper part of the hall was now completely dark.

Gazing up into the darkness I saw myself as a creature driven and derided by vanity; and my eyes burned with anguish and anger.

Questions for "Araby"

1.   How does the opening description of North Richmond Street reflect an aspect of the narrator's character and foreshadow his experience in the story?

2.   Describe this narrator. Is the voice we hear that of the youngster, or is an older self speaking? Give reasons for your impressions.

3.   Like so many of Joyce's works, "Araby" centers on a moment of sudden revelation or insight, which he called the "epiphany." Where does the moment of epiphany occur in this tale?

4.   How do you explain the final line of this story?

Franz Kafka (1883–1924)

Details of this Czech writer's life are furnished in the biographical note on page 57 of this anthology. "The Metamorphosis" (1915) is the story of a traveling salesman who, for no apparent reason, undergoes a bizarre transformation that isolates him utterly. "The Metamorphosis" juxtaposes surreal, nightmarish events with macabre humor and realistic details of ordinary life, all rendered in a sober, matter-of-fact manner. Here is a hostile universe whose victims are estranged by the absurd misfortunes that inexplicably come their way, a world in which pointless suffering and gratuitous pain seem to characterize the human condition.

The Metamorphosis

Translated by Edwin and Willa Muir

I

As Gregor Samsa awoke one morning from uneasy dreams he found himself transformed in his bed into a gigantic insect. He was lying on his hard, as it were armor-plated, back and when he lifted his head a little he could see his dome-like brown belly divided into stiff arched segments on top of which the bed quilt could hardly keep in position and was about to slide off completely. His numerous legs, which were pitifully thin compared to the rest of his bulk, waved helplessly before his eyes.

What has happened to me? he thought. It was no dream. His room, a regular human bedroom, only rather too small, lay quiet between the four familiar walls. Above the table on which a collection of cloth samples was unpacked and spread out—Samsa was a commercial traveler—hung the picture which he had recently cut out of an illustrated magazine and put into a pretty gilt frame. It showed a lady, with a fur cap on and a fur stole, sitting upright and holding out to the spectator a huge fur muff into which the whole of her forearm had vanished!

Gregor's eyes turned next to the window, and the overcast sky—one could hear rain drops beating on the window gutter—made him quite melancholy. What about sleeping a little longer and forgetting all this nonsense, he thought, but it could not be done, for he was accustomed to sleep on his right side and in his present condition he could not turn himself over. However violently he forced himself towards his right side he always rolled on to his back again. He tried it at least a hundred times, shutting his eyes to keep from seeing his struggling legs, and only desisted when he began to feel in his side a faint dull ache he had never experienced before.

Oh God, he thought, what an exhausting job I've picked on! Traveling about day in, day out. It's much more irritating work than doing the actual business in the office, and on top of that there's the trouble of constant traveling, of worrying about train connections, the bed and irregular meals, casual acquaintances that are always new and never become intimate friends. The devil take it all! He felt a slight itching up on his belly; slowly pushed himself on his back nearer to the top of the bed so that he could lift his head more easily; identified the itching place which was surrounded by many small white spots the nature of which he could not understand and made to touch it with a leg, but drew the leg back immediately, for the contact made a cold shiver run through him.

He slid down again into his former position. This getting up early, he thought, makes one quite stupid. A man needs his sleep. Other commercials live like harem women. For instance, when I come back to the hotel of a morning to write up the orders I've got, these others are only sitting down to breakfast. Let me just try that with my chief; I'd be sacked on the spot. Anyhow, that might be quite a good thing for me, who can tell? If I didn't have to hold my hand because of my parents I'd have given notice long ago, I'd have gone to the chief and told him exactly what I think of him. That would knock him endways from his desk! It's a queer way of doing, too, this sitting high at a desk and talking down to employees, especially when they have to come quite near because the chief is hard of hearing. Well, there's still hope; once I've saved enough money to pay back my parents' debts to him—that should take another five or six years—I'll do it without fail. I'll cut myself completely loose then. For the moment, though, I'd better get up, since my train goes at five.

He looked at the alarm clock ticking on the chest. Heavenly Father! he thought. It was half-past six o'clock and the hands were quietly moving on, it was even past the half-hour, it was getting on toward a quarter to seven. Had the alarm clock not gone off? From the bed one could see that it had been properly set for four o'clock; of course it must have gone off. Yes, but was it possible to sleep quietly through that ear-splitting noise? Well, he had not slept quietly, yet apparently all the more soundly for that. But what was he to do now? The next train went at seven o'clock; to catch that he would need to hurry like mad and his samples weren't even packed up, and he himself wasn't feeling particularly fresh and active. And even if he did catch the train he wouldn't avoid a row with the chief, since the firm's porter would have been waiting for the five o'clock train and would have long since reported his failure to turn up. The porter was a creature of the chief's, spineless and stupid. Well, supposing he were to say he was sick? But that would be most unpleasant and would look suspicious, since during his five years' employment he had not been ill once. The chief himself would be sure to come with the sick-insurance doctor, would reproach his parents with their son's laziness and would cut all excuses short by referring to the insurance doctor, who of course regarded all mankind as perfectly healthy malingerers. And would he be so far wrong on this occasion? Gregor really felt quite well, apart from a drowsiness that was utterly superfluous after such a long sleep, and he was even unusually hungry.

As all this was running through his mind at top speed without his being able to decide to leave his bed—the alarm clock had just struck a quarter to seven—there came a cautious tap at the door behind the head of his bed. "Gregor," said a voice—it was his mother's—"it's a quarter to seven. Hadn't you a train to catch?" That gentle voice! Gregor had a shock as he heard his own voice answering hers, unmistakably his own voice, it was true, but with a persistent horrible twittering squeak behind it like an undertone, that left the words in their clear shape only for the first moment and then rose up reverberating round them to destroy their sense, so that one could not be sure one had heard them rightly. Gregor wanted to answer at length and explain everything, but in the circumstances he confined himself to saying: "Yes, yes, thank you, Mother, I'm getting up now." The wooden door between them must have kept the change in his voice from being noticeable outside, for his mother contented herself with this statement and shuffled away. Yet this brief exchange of words had made the other members of the family aware that Gregor was still in the house, as they had not expected, and at one of the side doors his father was already knocking, gently, yet with his fist. "Gregor, Gregor," he called, "what's the matter with you?" And after a little while he called again in a deeper voice: "Gregor, Gregor!" At the other side door his sister was saying in a low, plaintive tone: "Gregor? Aren't you well? Are you needing anything?" He answered them both at once: "I'm just ready," and did his best to make his voice sound as normal as possible by enunciating the words very clearly and leaving long pauses between them. So his father went back to his breakfast, but his sister whispered: "Gregor, open the door, do." However, he was not thinking of opening the door, and felt thankful for the prudent habit he had acquired in traveling of locking all doors during the night, even at home.

His immediate intention was to get up quietly without being disturbed, to put on his clothes and above all eat his breakfast, and only then to consider what else was to be done, since in bed, he was well aware, his meditations would come to no sensible conclusion. He remembered that often enough in bed he had felt small aches and pains, probably caused by awkward postures, which had proved purely imaginary once he got up, and he looked forward eagerly to seeing this morning's delusions gradually fall away. That the change in his voice was nothing but the precursor of a severe chill, a standing ailment of commercial travelers, he had not the least possible doubt.

To get rid of the quilt was quite easy; he had only to inflate himself a little and it fell off by itself. But the next move was difficult, especially because he was so uncommonly broad. He would have needed arms and hands to hoist himself up; instead he had only the numerous little legs which never stopped waving in all directions and which he could not control in the least. When he tried to bend one of them it was the first to stretch itself straight; and did he succeed at last in making it do what he wanted, all the other legs meanwhile waved the more wildly in a high degree of unpleasant agitation. "But what's the use of lying idle in bed," said Gregor to himself.

He thought that he might get out of bed with the lower part of his body first, but this lower part, which he had not yet seen and of which he could form no clear conception, proved too difficult to move; it shifted so slowly; and when finally, almost wild with annoyance, he gathered his forces together and thrust out recklessly, he had miscalculated the direction and bumped heavily against the lower end of the bed, and the stinging pain he felt informed him that precisely this lower part of his body was at the moment probably the most sensitive.

So he tried to get the top part of himself out first, and cautiously moved his head towards the edge of the bed. That proved easy enough, and despite its breadth and mass the bulk of his body at last slowly followed the movement of his head. Still, when he finally got his head free over the edge of the bed he felt too scared to go on advancing, for after all if he let himself fall in this way it would take a miracle to keep his head from being injured. And at all costs he must not lose consciousness now, precisely now; he would rather stay in bed.

But when after a repetition of the same efforts he lay in his former position again, sighing, and watched his little legs struggling against each other more wildly than ever, if that were possible, and saw no way of bringing any order into this arbitrary confusion, he told himself again that it was impossible to stay in bed and that the most sensible course was to risk everything for the smallest hope of getting away from it. At the same time he did not forget meanwhile to remind himself that cool reflection, the coolest possible, was much better than desperate resolves. In such moments he focused his eyes as sharply as possible on the window, but, unfortunately, the prospect of the morning fog, which muffled even the other side of the narrow street, brought him little encouragement and comfort. "Seven o'clock already," he said to himself when the alarm clock chimed again, "seven o'clock already and still such a thick fog." And for a little while he lay quiet, breathing lightly, as if perhaps expecting such complete repose to restore all things to their real and normal condition.

But then he said to himself: "Before it strikes a quarter past seven I must be quite out of this bed, without fail. Anyhow, by that time someone will have come from the office to ask for me, since it opens before seven." And he set himself to rocking his whole body at once in a regular rhythm, with the idea of swinging it out of the bed. If he tipped himself out in that way he could keep his head from injury by lifting it at an acute angle when he fell. His back seemed to be hard and was not likely to suffer from a fall on the carpet. His biggest worry was the loud crash he would not be able to help making, which would probably cause anxiety, if not terror, behind all the doors. Still, he must take the risk.

When he was already half out of the bed—the new method was more a game than an effort, for he needed only to hitch himself across by rocking to and fro—it struck him how simple it would be if he could get help. Two strong people—he thought of his father and the servant girl—would be amply sufficient; they would only have to thrust their arms under his convex back, lever him out of the bed, bend down with their burden and then be patient enough to let him turn himself right over on to the floor, where it was to be hoped his legs would then find their proper function. Well, ignoring the fact that the doors were all locked, ought he really to call for help? In spite of his misery he could not suppress a smile at the very idea of it.

He had got so far that he could barely keep his equilibrium when he rocked himself strongly, and he would have to nerve himself very soon for the final decision since in five minutes' time it would be a quarter past seven—when the front door bell rang. "That's someone from the office," he said to himself, and grew almost rigid, while his little legs only jigged about all the faster. For a moment everything stayed quiet. "They're not going to open the door," said Gregor to himself, catching at some kind of irrational hope. But then of course the servant girl went as usual to the door with her heavy tread and opened it. Gregor needed only to hear the first good morning of the visitor to know immediately who it was—the chief clerk himself. What a fate, to be condemned to work for a firm where the smallest omission at once gave rise to the gravest suspicion! Were all employees in a body nothing but scoundrels, was there not among them one single loyal devoted man who, had he wasted only an hour or so of the firm's time in a morning, was so tormented by conscience as to be driven out of his mind and actually incapable of leaving his bed? Wouldn't it really have been sufficient to send an apprentice to inquire—if any inquiry were necessary at all—did the chief clerk himself have to come and thus indicate to the entire family, an innocent family, that this suspicious circumstance could be investigated by no one less versed in affairs than himself? And more through the agitation caused by these reflections than through any act of will Gregor swung himself out of bed with all his strength. There was a loud thump, but it was not really a crash. His fall was broken to some extent by the carpet, his back, too, was less stiff than he thought, and so there was merely a dull thud, not so very startling. Only he had not lifted his head carefully enough and had hit it; he turned it and rubbed it on the carpet in pain and irritation.

"That was something falling down in there," said the chief clerk in the next room to the left. Gregor tried to suppose to himself that something like what had happened to him today might some day happen to the chief clerk; one really could not deny that it was possible. But as if in brusque reply to this supposition the chief clerk took a couple of firm steps in the next-door room and his patent leather boots creaked. From the right-hand room his sister was whispering to inform him of the situation: "Gregor, the chief clerk's here." "I know," muttered Gregor to himself; but he didn't dare to make his voice loud enough for his sister to hear it.

"Gregor," said his father now from the left-hand room, "the chief clerk has come and wants to know why you didn't catch the early train. We don't know what to say to him. Besides, he wants to talk to you in person. So open the door, please. He will be good enough to excuse the untidiness of your room." "Good morning, Mr. Samsa," the chief clerk was calling amiably meanwhile. "He's not well," said his mother to the visitor, while his father was still speaking through the door, "he's not well, sir, believe me. What else would make him miss a train! The boy thinks about nothing but his work. It makes me almost cross the way he never goes out in the evenings; he's been here the last eight days and has stayed at home every single evening. He just sits there quietly at the table reading a newspaper or looking through railway timetables. The only amusement he gets is doing fretwork. For instance, he spent two or three evenings cutting out a little picture frame; you would be surprised to see how pretty it is; it's hanging in his room; you'll see it in a minute when Gregor opens the door. I must say I'm glad you've come, sir; we should never have got him to unlock the door by ourselves; he's so obstinate; and I'm sure he's unwell, though he wouldn't have it to be so this morning." "I'm just coming," said Gregor slowly and carefully, not moving an inch for fear of losing one word of the conversation. "I can't think of any other explanation, madam," said the chief clerk, "I hope it's nothing serious. Although on the other hand I must say that we men of business—fortunately or unfortunately—very often simply have to ignore any slight indisposition, since business must be attended to." "Well, can the chief clerk come in now?" asked Gregor's father impatiently, again knocking on the door. "No," said Gregor. In the left-hand room a painful silence followed this refusal, in the right-hand room his sister began to sob.

Why didn't his sister join the others? She was probably newly out of bed and hadn't even begun to put on her clothes yet. Well, why was she crying? Because he wouldn't get up and let the chief clerk in, because he was in danger of losing his job, and because the chief would begin dunning his parents again for the old debts? Surely these were things one didn't need to worry about for the present. Gregor was still at home and not in the least thinking of deserting the family. At the moment, true, he was lying on the carpet and no one who knew the condition he was in could seriously expect him to admit the chief clerk. But for such a small discourtesy, which could plausibly be explained away somehow later on, Gregor could hardly be dismissed on the spot. And it seemed to Gregor that it would be much more sensible to leave him in peace for the present than to trouble him with tears and entreaties. Still, of course, their uncertainty bewildered them all and excused their behavior.

"Mr. Samsa," the chief clerk called now in a louder voice, "what's the matter with you? Here you are, barricading yourself in your room, giving only 'yes' and 'no' for answers, causing your parents a lot of unnecessary trouble and neglecting—I mention this only in passing—neglecting your business duties in an incredible fashion. I am speaking here in the name of your parents and of your chief, and I beg you quite seriously to give me an immediate and precise explanation. You amaze me, you amaze me. I thought you were a quiet, dependable person, and now all at once you seem bent on making a disgraceful exhibition of yourself. The chief did hint to me early this morning a possible explanation for your disappearance—with reference to the cash payments that were entrusted to you recently—but I almost pledged my solemn word of honor that this could not be so. But now that I see how incredibly obstinate you are, I no longer have the slightest desire to take your part at all. And your position in the firm is not so unassailable. I came with the intention of telling you all this in private, but since you are wasting my time so needlessly I don't see why your parents shouldn't hear it too. For some time past your work has been most unsatisfactory; this is not the season of the year for a business boom, of course, we admit that, but a season of the year for doing no business at all, that does not exist, Mr. Samsa, must not exist."

"But, sir," cried Gregor, beside himself and in his agitation forgetting everything else, "I'm just going to open the door this very minute. A slight illness, an attack of giddiness, has kept me from getting up. I'm still lying in bed. But I feel all right again. I'm getting out of bed now. Just give me a moment or two longer! I'm not quite so well as I thought. But I'm all right, really. How a thing like that can suddenly strike one down! Only last night I was quite well, my parents can tell you, or rather I did have a slight presentiment. I must have showed some sign of it. Why didn't I report it at the office! But one always thinks that an indisposition can be got over without staying in the house. Oh sir, do spare my parents! All that you're reproaching me with now has no foundation; no one has ever said a word to me about it. Perhaps you haven't looked at the last orders I sent in. Anyhow, I can still catch the eight o'clock train, I'm much the better for my few hours' rest. Don't let me detain you here sir; I'll be attending to business very soon, and do be good enough to tell the chief so and to make my excuses to him!"

And while all this was tumbling out pell-mell and Gregor hardly knew what he was saying, he had reached the chest quite easily, perhaps because of the practice he had had in bed, and was now trying to lever himself upright by means of it. He meant actually to open the door, actually to show himself and speak to the chief clerk; he was eager to find out what the others, after all their insistence, would say at the sight of him. If they were horrified then the responsibility was no longer his and he could stay quiet. But if they took it calmly, then he had no reason either to be upset, and could really get to the station for the eight o'clock train if he hurried. At first he slipped down a few times from the polished surface of the chest, but at length with a last heave he stood upright; he paid no more attention to the pains in the lower part of his body, however they smarted. Then he let himself fall against the back of a near-by chair, and clung with his little legs to the edges of it. That brought him into control of himself again and he stopped speaking, for now he could listen to what the chief clerk was saying.

"Did you understand a word of it?" the chief clerk was asking "surely he can't be trying to make fools of us?" "Oh dear," cried his mother, in tears, "perhaps he's terribly ill and we're tormenting him. Grete! Grete!" she called out then. "Yes, Mother?" called his sister from the other side. They were calling to each other across Gregor's room. "You must go this minute for the doctor. Gregor is ill. Go for the doctor, quick. Did you hear how he was speaking?" "That was no human voice," said the chief clerk in a voice noticeably low beside the shrillness of the mother's. "Anna! Anna!" his father was calling through the hall to the kitchen, clapping his hands, "get a locksmith at once!" And the two girls were already running through the hall with a swish of skirts—how could his sister have got dressed so quickly?—and were tearing the front door open. There was no sound of its closing again; they had evidently left it open, as one does in houses where some great misfortune has happened.

But Gregor was now much calmer. The words he uttered were no longer understandable, apparently, although they seemed clear enough to him, even clearer than before, perhaps because his ear had grown accustomed to the sound of them. Yet at any rate people now believed that something was wrong with him, and were ready to help him. The positive certainty with which these first measures had been taken comforted him. He felt himself drawn once more into the human circle and hoped for great and remarkable results from both the doctor and the locksmith, without really distinguishing precisely between them. To make his voice as clear as possible for the decisive conversation that was now imminent he coughed a little, as quietly as he could, of course, since this noise too might not sound like a human cough for all he was able to judge. In the next room meanwhile there was complete silence. Perhaps his parents were sitting at the table with the chief clerk, whispering, perhaps they were all leaning against the door and listening.

Slowly Gregor pushed the chair towards the door, then let go of it, caught hold of the door for support—the soles at the end of his little legs were somewhat sticky—and rested against it for a moment after his efforts. Then he set himself to turning the key in the lock with his mouth. It seemed, unhappily, that he hadn't really any teeth—what could he grip the key with?—but on the other hand his jaws were certainly very strong; with their help he did manage to set the key in motion, heedless of the fact that he was undoubtedly damaging them somewhere, since a brown fluid issued from his mouth, flowed over the key and dripped on the floor. "Just listen to that," said the chief clerk next door; "he's turning the key." That was a great encouragement to Gregor; but they should all have shouted encouragement to him, his father and mother too: "Go on, Gregor," they should have called out, "keep going, hold on to that key!" And in the belief that they were all following his efforts intently, he clenched his jaws recklessly on the key with all the force at his command. As the turning of the key progressed he circled round the lock, holding on now only with his mouth, pushing on the key, as required, or pulling it down again with all the weight of his body. The louder click of the finally yielding lock literally quickened Gregor. With a deep breath of relief he said to himself: "So I didn't need the locksmith," and laid his head on the handle to open the door wide.

Since he had to pull the door towards him, he was still invisible when it was really wide open. He had to edge himself slowly round the near half of the double door, and to do it very carefully if he was not to fall plump upon his back just on the threshold. He was still carrying out this difficult man-oeuvre, with no time to observe anything else, when he heard the chief clerk utter a loud "Oh!"—it sounded like a gust of wind—and now he could see the man, standing as he was nearest to the door, clapping one hand before his open mouth and slowly backing away as if driven by some invisible steady pressure. His mother—in spite of the chief clerk's being there her hair was still undone and sticking up in all directions—first clasped her hands and looked at his father, then took two steps towards Gregor and fell on the floor among her outspread skirts, her face quite hidden on her breast. His father knotted his fist with a fierce expression on his face as if he meant to knock Gregor back into the room, then looked uncertainly round the living room, covered his eyes with his hands and wept till his great chest heaved.

Gregor did not go now into the living room, but leaned against the inside of the firmly shut wing of the door, so that only half his body was visible and his head above it bending sideways to look at the others. The light had meanwhile strengthened; on the other side of the street one could see clearly a section of the endlessly long, dark gray building opposite—it was a hos-pital—abruptly punctuated by its row of regular windows; the rain was still falling, but only in large singly discernible and literally singly splashing drops. The breakfast dishes were set out on the table lavishly, for breakfast was the most important meal of the day to Gregor's father, who lingered it out for hours over various newspapers. Right opposite Gregor on the wall hung a photograph of himself on military service, as a lieutenant, hand on sword, a carefree smile on his face, inviting one to respect his uniform and military bearing. The door leading to the hall was open, and one could see that the front door stood open too, showing the landing beyond and the beginning of the stairs going down.

"Well," said Gregor, knowing perfectly that he was the only one who had retained any composure, "I'll put my clothes on at once, pack up my samples and start off. Will you only let me go? You see, sir, I'm not obstinate, and I'm willing to work; traveling is a hard life, but I couldn't live without it. Where are you going, sir? To the office? Yes? Will you give a true account of all this? One can be temporarily incapacitated, but that's just the moment for remembering former services and bearing in mind that later on, when the incapacity has been got over, one will certainly work with all the more industry and concentration. I'm loyally bound to serve the chief, you know that very well. Besides, I have to provide for my parents and my sister. I'm in great difficulties, but I'll get out of them again. Don't make things any worse for me than they are. Stand up for me in the firm. Travelers are not popular there, I know. People think they earn sacks of money and just have a good time. A prejudice there's no particular reason for revising. But you, sir, have a more comprehensive view of affairs than the rest of the staff, yes, let me tell you in confidence, a more comprehensive view than the chief himself, who, being the owner, lets his judgment easily be swayed against one of his employees. And you know very well that the traveler, who is never seen in the office almost the whole year round, can so easily fall a victim to gossip and ill luck and unfounded complaints, which he mostly knows nothing about, except when he comes back exhausted from his rounds, and only then suffers in person from their evil consequences, which he can no longer trace back to the original causes. Sir, sir, don't go away without a word to me to show that you think me in the right at least to some extent!''

But at Gregor's very first words the chief clerk had already backed away and only stared at him with parted lips over one twitching shoulder. And while Gregor was speaking he did not stand still one moment but stole away towards the door, without taking his eyes off Gregor, yet only an inch at a time, as if obeying some secret injunction to leave the room. He was already at the hall, and the suddenness with which he took his last step out of the living room would have made one believe he had burned the sole of his foot. Once in the hall he stretched his right arm before him towards the staircase, as if some supernatural power were waiting there to deliver him.

Gregor perceived that the chief clerk must on no account be allowed to go away in this frame of mind if his position in the firm were not to be endangered to the utmost. His parents did not understand this so well; they had convinced themselves in the course of years that Gregor was settled for life in this firm, and besides they were so occupied with their immediate troubles that all foresight had forsaken them. Yet Gregor had this foresight. The chief clerk must be detained, soothed, persuaded and finally won over; the whole future of Gregor and his family depended on it! If only his sister had been there! She was intelligent; she had begun to cry while Gregor was still lying quietly on his back. And no doubt the chief clerk, so partial to ladies, would have been guided by her; she would have shut the door of the flat and in the hall talked him out of his horror. But she was not there, and Gregor would have to handle the situation himself. And without remembering that he was still unaware what powers of movement he possessed, without even remembering that his words in all possibility, indeed in all likelihood, would again be unintelligible, he let go the wing of the door, pushed himself through the opening, started to walk towards the chief clerk, who was already ridiculously clinging with both hands to the railing on the landing; but immediately, as he was feeling for a support, he fell down with a little cry upon all his numerous legs. Hardly was he down when he experienced for the first time this morning a sense of physical comfort; his legs had firm ground under them; they were completely obedient, as he noted with joy; they even strove to carry him forward in whatever direction he chose; and he was inclined to believe that a final relief from all his sufferings was at hand. But in the same moment as he found himself on the floor, rocking with suppressed eagerness to move, not far from his mother, indeed just in front of her, she, who had seemed so crushed, sprang all at once to her feet, her arms and fingers outspread, cried: "Help, for God's sake, help!" bent her head down as if to see Gregor better, yet on the contrary kept backing senselessly away; had quite forgotten that the laden table stood behind her; sat upon it hastily, as if in absence of mind, when she bumped into it; and seemed altogether unaware that the big coffee pot beside her was upset and pouring coffee in a flood over the carpet.

"Mother, Mother," said Grègor in a low voice, and looked up at her. The chief clerk, for the moment, had quite slipped from his mind; instead, he could not resist snapping his jaws together at the sight of the streaming coffee. That made his mother scream again, she fled from the table and fell into the arms of his father, who hastened to catch her. But Gregor had now no time to spare for his parents; the chief clerk was already on the stairs; with his chin on the banisters he was taking one last backward look. Gregor made a spring, to be as sure as possible of overtaking him; the chief clerk must have divined his intention, for he leaped down several steps and vanished; he was still yelling "Ugh!" and it echoed through the whole staircase.

Unfortunately, the flight of the chief clerk seemed completely to upset Gregor's father, who had remained relatively calm until now, for instead of running after the man himself, or at least not hindering Gregor in his pursuit, he seized in his right hand the walking stick which the chief clerk had left behind on a chair, together with a hat and greatcoat, snatched in his left hand a large newspaper from the table and began stamping his feet and flourishing the stick and the newspaper to drive Gregor back into his room. No entreaty of Gregor's availed, indeed no entreaty was even understood, however humbly he bent his head his father only stamped on the floor the more loudly. Behind his father his mother had torn open a window, despite the cold weather, and was leaning far out of it with her face in her hands. A strong draught set in from the street to the staircase, the window curtains blew in, the newspapers on the table fluttered, stray pages whisked over the floor. Pitilessly Gregor's father drove him back, hissing and crying "Shoo!" like a savage. But Gregor was quite unpracticed in walking backwards, it really was a slow business. If he only had a chance to turn round he could get back to his room at once, but he was afraid of exasperating his father by the slowness of such a rotation and at any moment the stick in his father's hand might hit him a fatal blow on the back or on the head. In the end, however, nothing else was left for him to do since to his horror he observed that in moving backwards he could not even control the direction he took; and so, keeping an anxious eye on his father all the time over his shoulder, he began to turn round as quickly as he could, which was in reality very slowly. Perhaps his father noted his good intentions, for he did not interfere except every now and then to help him in the manoeuvre from a distance with the point of the stick. If only he would have stopped making that unbearable hissing noise! It made Gregor quite lose his head. He had turned almost completely round when the hissing noise so distracted him that he even turned a little the wrong way again. But when at last his head was fortunately right in front of the doorway, it appeared that his body was too broad simply to get through the opening. His father, of course, in his present mood was far from thinking of such a thing as opening the other half of the door, to let Gregor have enough space. He had merely the fixed idea of driving Gregor back into his room as quickly as possible. He would never have suffered Gregor to make the circumstantial preparations for standing up on end and perhaps slipping his way through the door. Maybe he was now making more noise than ever to urge Gregor forward, as if no obstacle impeded him; to Gregor, anyhow, the noise in his rear sounded no longer like the voice of one single father; this was really no joke, and Gregor thrust himself—come what might—into the doorway. One side of his body rose up, he was tilted at an angle in the doorway, his flank was quite bruised, horrid blotches stained the white door, soon he was stuck fast and, left to himself, could not have moved at all, his legs on one side fluttered trembling to the air, those on the other were crushed painfully to the floor—when from behind his father gave him a strong push which was literally a deliverance and he flew far into the room, bleeding freely. The door was slammed behind him with the stick, and then at last there was silence.

II

Not until it was twilight did Gregor awake out of a deep sleep, more like a swoon than a sleep. He would certainly have waked up of his own accord not much later, for he felt himself sufficiently rested and well-slept, but it seemed to him as if a fleeting step and a cautious shutting of the door leading into the hall had aroused him. The electric lights in the street cast a pale sheen here and there on the ceiling and the upper surfaces of the furniture, but down below, where he lay, it was dark. Slowly, awkwardly trying out his feelers, which he now first learned to appreciate, he pushed his way to the door to see what had been happening there. His left side felt like one single long, unpleasantly tense scar, and he had actually to limp on his two rows of legs. One little leg, moreover, had been severely damaged in the course of that morning's events—it was almost a miracle that only one had been damaged—and trailed uselessly behind him.

He had reached the door before he discovered what had really drawn him to it: the smell of food. For there stood a basin filled with fresh milk in which floated little sops of white bread. He could almost have laughed with joy, since he was now still hungrier than in the morning, and he dipped his head almost over the eyes straight into the milk. But soon in disappointment he withdrew it again; not only did he find it difficult to feed because of his tender left side—and he could only feed with the palpitating collaboration of his whole body—he did not like the milk either, although milk had been his favorite drink and that was certainly why his sister had set it there for him, indeed it was almost with repulsion that he turned away from the basin and crawled back to the middle of the room.

He could see through the crack of the door that the gas was turned on in the living room, but while usually at this time his father made a habit of reading the afternoon newspaper in a loud voice to his mother and occasionally to his sister as well, not a sound was now to be heard. Well, perhaps his father had recently given up this habit of reading aloud, which his sister had mentioned so often in conversation and in her letters. But there was the same silence all around, although the flat was certainly not empty of occupants. "What a quiet life our family has been leading," said Gregor to himself, and as he sat there motionless staring into the darkness he felt great pride in the fact that he had been able to provide such a life for his parents and sister in such a fine flat. But what if all the quiet, the comfort, the contentment were now to end in horror? To keep himself from being lost in such thoughts Gregor took refuge in movement and crawled up and down the room.

Once during the long evening one of the side doors was opened a little and quickly shut again, later the other side door too; someone had apparently wanted to come in and then thought better of it. Gregor now stationed himself immediately before the living room door, determined to persuade any hesitating visitor to come in or at least to discover who it might be; but the door was not opened again and he waited in vain. In the early morning, when the doors were locked, they had all wanted to come in, now that he had opened one door and the other had apparently been opened during the day, no one came in and even the keys were on the other side of the doors.

It was late at night before the gas went out in the living room, and Gregor could easily tell that his parents and his sister had all stayed awake until then, for he could clearly hear the three of them stealing away on tiptoe. No one was likely to visit him, not until the morning, that was certain; so he had plenty of time to meditate at his leisure on how he was to arrange his life afresh. But the lofty, empty room in which he had to lie flat on the floor filled him with an apprehension he could not account for, since it had been his very own room for the past five years—and with a half-unconscious action, not without a slight feeling of shame, he scuttled under the sofa, where he felt comfortable at once, although his back was a little cramped and he could not lift his head up, and his only regret was that his body was too broad to get the whole of it under the sofa.

He stayed there all night, spending the time partly in a light slumber, from which his hunger kept waking him up with a start, and partly in worrying and sketching vague hopes, which all led to the same conclusion, that he must lie low for the present and, by exercising patience and the utmost consideration, help the family to bear the inconvenience he was bound to cause them in his present condition.

Very early in the morning, it was still almost night, Gregor had the chance to test the strength of his new resolutions, for his sister, nearly fully dressed, opened the door from the hall and peered in. She did not see him at once, yet when she caught sight of him under the sofa—well, he had to be somewhere, he couldn't have flown away, could he?—she was so startled that without being able to help it she slammed the door shut again. But as if regretting her behavior she opened the door again immediately and came in on tiptoe, as if she were visiting an invalid or even a stranger. Gregor had pushed his head forward to the very edge of the sofa and watched her. Would she notice that he had left the milk standing, and not for lack of hunger, and would she bring in some other kind of food more to his taste? If she did not do it of her own accord, he would rather starve than draw her attention to the fact, although he felt a wild impulse to dart out from under the sofa, throw himself at her feet and beg her for something to eat. But his sister at once noticed, with surprise, that the basin was still full, except for a little milk that had been spilt all around it, she lifted it immediately, not with her bare hands, true, but with a cloth and carried it away. Gregor was wildly curious to know what she would bring instead, and made various speculations about it. Yet what she actually did next, in the goodness of her heart, he could never have guessed at. To find out what he liked she brought him a whole selection of food, all set out on an old newspaper. There were old, half-decayed vegetables, bones from last night's supper covered with a white sauce that had thickened; some raisins and almonds; a piece of cheese that Gregor would have called uneatable two days ago; a dry roll of bread, a buttered roll, and a roll both buttered and salted. Besides all that, she set down again the same basin, into which she had poured some water, and which was apparently to be reserved for his exclusive use. And with fine tact, knowing that Gregor would not eat in her presence, she withdrew quickly and even turned the key, to let him understand that he could take his ease as much as he liked. Gregor's legs all whizzed towards the food. His wounds must have healed completely, moreover, for he felt no disability, which amazed him and made him reflect how more than a month ago he had cut one finger a little with a knife and still suffered pain from the wound only the day before yesterday. Am I less sensitive now? he thought, and sucked greedily at the cheese, which above all the other edibles attracted him at once and strongly. One after another and with tears of satisfaction in his eyes he quickly devoured the cheese, the vegetables and the sauce; the fresh food, on the other hand, had no charms for him, he could not even stand the smell of it and actually dragged away to some little distance the things he could eat. He had long finished his meal and was only lying lazily on the same spot when his sister turned the key slowly as a sign for him to retreat. That roused him at once, although he was nearly asleep, and he hurried under the sofa again. But it took considerable self-control for him to stay under the sofa, even for the short time his sister was in the room, since the large meal had swollen his body somewhat and he was so cramped he could hardly breathe. Slight attacks of breathlessness afflicted him and his eyes were starting a little out of his head as he watched his unsuspecting sister sweeping together with a broom not only the remains of what he had eaten but even the things he had not touched, as if these were now of no use to anyone, and hastily shoveling it all into a bucket, which she covered with a wooden lid and carried away. Hardly had she turned her back when Gregor came from under the sofa and stretched and puffed himself out.

In this manner Gregor was fed, once in the early morning while his parents and the servant girl were still asleep, and a second time after they had all had their midday dinner, for then his parents took a short nap and the servant girl could be sent out on some errand or other by his sister. Not that they would have wanted him to starve, of course, but perhaps they could not have borne to know more about his feeding than from hearsay, perhaps too his sister wanted to spare them such little anxieties wherever possible, since they had quite enough to bear as it was.

Under what pretext the doctor and the locksmith had been got rid of on that first morning Gregor could not discover, for since what he said was not understood by the others it never struck any of them, not even his sister, that he could understand what they said, and so whenever his sister came into his room he had to content himself with hearing her utter only a sigh now and then and an occasional appeal to the saints. Later on, when she had got a little used to the situation—of course she could never get completely used to it—she sometimes threw out a remark which was kindly meant or could be so interpeted. "Well, he liked his dinner today," she would say when Gregor had made a good clearance of his food; and when he had not eaten, which gradually happened more and more often, she would say almost sadly: "Everything's been left standing again."

But although Gregor could get no news directly, he overheard a lot from the neighboring rooms, and as soon as voices were audible, he would run to the door of the room concerned and press his whole body against it. In the first few days especially there was no conversation that did not refer to him somehow, even if only indirectly. For two whole days there were family consultations at every mealtime about what should be done; but also between meals the same subject was discussed, for there were always at least two members of the family at home, since no one wanted to be alone in the flat and to leave it quite empty was unthinkable. And on the very first of these days the household cook—it was not quite clear what and how much she knew of the situation—went down on her knees to his mother and begged leave to go, and when she departed, a quarter of an hour later, gave thanks for her dismissal with tears in her eyes as if for the greatest benefit that could have been conferred on her, and without any prompting swore a solemn oath that she would never say a single word to anyone about what had happened.

Now Gregor's sister had to cook too, helping her mother; true, the cooking did not amount to much, for they ate scarcely anything. Gregor was always hearing one of the family vainly urging another to eat and getting no answer but: "Thanks, I've had all I want," or something similar. Perhaps they drank nothing either. Time and again his sister kept asking his father if he wouldn't like some beer and offered kindly to go and fetch it herself, and when he made no answer suggested that she could ask the concierge to fetch it, so that he need feel no sense of obligation, but then a round "No" came from his father and no more was said about it.

In the course of that very first day Gregor's father explained the family's financial position and prospects to both his mother and his sister. Now and then he rose from the table to get some voucher or memorandum out of the small safe he had rescued from the collapse of his business five years earlier.

One could hear him opening the complicated lock and rustling papers out and shutting it again. This statement made by his father was the first cheerful information Gregor had heard since his imprisonment. He had been of the opinion that nothing at all was left over from his father's business, at least his father had never said anything to the contrary, and of course he had not asked him directly. At that time Gregor's sole desire was to do his utmost to help the family to forget as soon as possible the catastrophe which had overwhelmed the business and thrown them all into a state of complete despair. And so he had set to work with unusual ardor and almost overnight had become a commercial traveler instead of a little clerk, with of course much greater chances of earning money, and his success was immediately translated into good round coin which he could lay on the table for his amazed and happy family. These had been fine times, and they had never recurred, at least not with the same sense of glory, although later on Gregor had earned so much money that he was able to meet the expenses of the whole household and did so. They had simply got used to it, both the family and Gregor; the money was gratefully accepted and gladly given, but there was no special uprush of warm feeling. With his sister alone had he remained intimate, and it was a secret plan of his that she, who loved music, unlike himself, and could play movingly on the violin, should be sent next year to study at the Conservatorium, despite the great expense that would entail, which must be made up in some other way. During his brief visits home the Conservatorium was often mentioned in the talks he had with his sister, but always merely as a beautiful dream which could never come true, and his parents discouraged even these innocent references to it; yet Gregor had made up his mind firmly about it and meant to announce the fact with due solemnity on Christmas Day.

Such were the thoughts, completely futile in his present condition, that went through his head as he stood clinging upright to the door and listening. Sometimes out of sheer weariness he had to give up listening and let his head fall negligently against the door, but he always had to pull himself together again at once, for even the slight sound his head made was audible next door and brought all conversation to a stop. "What can he be doing now?" his father would say after a while, obviously turning towards the door, and only then would the interrupted conversation gradually be set going again.

Gregor was now informed as amply as he could wish—for his father tended to repeat himself in his explanations, partly because it was a long time since he had handled such matters and partly because his mother could not always grasp things at once—that a certain amount of investments, a very small amount it was true, had survived the wreck of their fortunes and had even increased a little because the dividends had not been touched meanwhile. And besides that, the money Gregor brought home every month—he had kept only a few dollars for himself—had never been quite used up and now amounted to a small capital sum. Behind the door Gregor nodded his head eagerly, rejoiced at this evidence of unexpected thrift and foresight. True, he could really have paid off some more of this father's debts

he's like insect slaving

to the chief with his extra money, and so brought much nearer the day on which he could quit his job, but doubtless it was better the way his father had arranged it.

Yet this capital was by no means sufficient to let the family live on the interest of it; for one year, perhaps, or at the most two, they could live on the principal, that was all. It was simply a sum that ought not to be touched and should be kept for a rainy day; money for living expenses would have to be earned. Now his father was still hale enough but an old man, and he had done no work for the past five years and could not be expected to do much; during these five years, the first years of leisure in his laborious though unsuccessful life, he had grown rather fat and become sluggish. And Gregor's old mother, how was she to earn a living with her asthma, which troubled her even when she walked through the flat and kept her lying on a sofa every other day panting for breath beside an open window? And was his sister to earn her bread, she who was still a child of seventeen and whose life hitherto had been so pleasant, consisting as it did in dressing herself nicely, sleeping long, helping in the housekeeping, going out to a few mod-est entertainments and above all playing the violin? At first whenever the need for earning money was mentioned Gregor let go his hold on the door and threw himself down on the cool leather sofa beside it, he felt so hot with shame and grief.

Often he just lay there the long nights through without sleeping at all, scrabbling for hours on the leather. Or he nerved himself to the great effort of pushing an armchair to the window, then crawled up over the window sill and, braced against the chair, leaned against the window panes, obvi-ously in some recollection of the sense of freedom that looking out a window always used to give him. For in reality day by day things that were even a little way off were growing dimmer to his sight; the hospital across the street, which he used to execrate for being all too often before his eyes, was now quite beyond his range of vision, and if he had not known that he lived in Charlotte Street, a quiet street but still a city street, he might have believed that his window gave on a desert waste where gray sky and gray land blended indistinguishably into each other. His quick-witted sister only needed to observe twice that the armchair stood by the window; after that whenever she had tidied the room she always pushed the chair back to the same place at the window and even left the inner casements open.

If he could have spoken to her and thanked her for all she had to do for him, he could have borne her ministrations better; as it was, they oppressed him. She certainly tried to make as light as possible of whatever was dis-agreeable in her task, and as time went on she succeeded, of course, more and more, but time brought more enlightenment to Gregor too. The very way she came in distressed him. Hardly was she in the room when she rushed to the window, without even taking time to shut the door, careful as she was usually to shield the sight of Gregor's room from the others, and as if she were almost suffocating tore the casements open with hasty fingers, standing then in the open draught for a while even in the bitterest cold and drawing deep breaths. This noisy scurry of hers upset Gregor twice a day; he would crouch trembling under the sofa all the time, knowing quite well that she would certainly have spared him such a disturbance had she found it at all possible to stay in his presence without opening a window.

On one occasion, about a month after Gregor's metamorphosis, when there was surely no reason for her to be still startled at his appearance, she came a little earlier than usual and found him gazing out of the window, quite motionless, and thus well placed to look like a bogey. Gregor would not have been surprised had she not come in at all, for she could not immediately open the window while he was there, but not only did she retreat, she jumped back as if in alarm and banged the door shut; a stranger might well have thought that he had been lying in wait for her there meaning to bite her. Of course he hid himself under the sofa at once, but he had to wait until midday before she came again, and she seemed more ill at ease than usual. This made him realize how repulsive the sight of him still was to her, and that it was bound to go on being repulsive, and what an effort it must cost her not to run away even from the sight of the small portion of his body that stuck out from under the sofa. In order to spare her that, therefore, one day he carried a sheet on his back to the sofa—it cost him four hours' labor—and arranged it there in such as way as to hide him completely, so that even if she were to bend down she could not see him. Had she considered the sheet unnecessary, she would certainly have stripped it off the sofa again, for it was clear enough that this curtaining and confining of himself was not likely to conduce Gregor's comfort, but she left it where it was, and Gregor even fancied that he caught a thankful glance from her eye when he lifted the sheet carefully a very little with his head to see how she was taking the new arrangement.

For the first fortnight his parents could not bring themselves to the point of entering his room, and he often heard them expressing their appreciation of his sister's activities, whereas formerly they had frequently scolded her for being as they thought a somewhat useless daughter. But now, both of them waited outside the door, his father and his mother, while his sister tidied his room, and as soon as she came out she had to tell them exactly how things were in the room, what Gregor had eaten, how he had conducted himself this time and whether there was not perhaps some slight improvement in his condition. His mother, moreover, began relatively soon to want to visit him, but his father and sister dissuaded her at first with arguments which Gregor listened to very attentively and altogether approved. Later, however, she had to be held back by main force, and when she cried out: "Do let me in to Gregor, he is my unfortunate son! Can't you understand that I must go to him?" Gregor thought that it might be well to have her come in, not every day, of course, but perhaps once a week; she understood things, after all, much better than his sister, who was only a child despite the efforts she was making and had perhaps taken on so difficult a task merely out of childish thoughtlessness.

Gregor's desire to see his mother was soon fulfilled. During the daytime he did not want to show himself at the window, out of consideration for his parents, but he could not crawl very far around the few square yards of floor space he had, nor could he bear lying quietly at rest all during the night, while he was fast losing any interest he had ever taken in food, so that for mere recreation he had formed the habit of crawling crisscross over the walls and ceiling. He especially enjoyed hanging suspended from the ceiling; it was much better than lying on the floor; one could breathe more freely; one's body swung and rocked lightly; and in the almost blissful absorption induced by this suspension it could happen to his own suprise that he let go and fell plump on the floor. Yet he now had his body much better under control than formerly, and even such a big fall did him no harm. His sister at once remarked the new distraction Gregor had found for himself—he left traces behind him of the sticky stuff on his soles whenever he crawled—and she got the idea in her head of giving him as wide a field as possible to crawl in and of removing the pieces of furniture that hindered him, above all the chest of drawers and the writing desk. But that was more than she could manage all by herself; she did not dare ask her father to help her; and as for the servant girl, a young creature of sixteen who had had the courage to stay on after the cook's departure, she could not be asked to help, for she had begged as an especial favor that she might keep the kitchen door locked and open it only on a definite summons; so there was nothing left but to apply to her mother at an hour when her father was out. And the old lady did come, with exclamation of joyful eagerness, which, however, died away at the door of Gregor's room. Gregor's sister, of course, went in first, to see that everything was in order before letting his mother enter. In great haste Gregor pulled the sheet lower and tucked it more in folds so that it really looked as if it had been thrown accidentally over the sofa. And this time he did not peer out from under it; he renounced the pleasure of seeing his mother on this occasion and was only glad that she had come at all. "Come in, he's out of sight," said his sister, obviously leading her mother in by the hand. Gregor could now hear two two women struggling to shift the heavy old chest from its place, and his sister claiming the greater part of the labor for herself, without listening to the admonitions of her mother who feared she might overstrain herself. It took a long time. After at least a quarter of an hour's tugging his mother objected that the chest had better be left where it was, for in the first place it was too heavy and could never be got out before his father came home, and standing in the middle of the room like that it would only hamper Gregor's movements, while in the second place it was not all certain that removing the furniture would be doing a service to Gregor. She was inclined to think to the contrary; the sight of the naked walls made her own heart heavy, and why shouldn't Gregor have the same feeling, considering that he had been used to his furniture for so long and might feel forlorn without it. "And doesn't it look," she concluded in a low voice—in fact she had been almost whispering all the time as if to avoid letting Gregor, whose exact whereabouts she did not know, hear even the tones of her voice, for she was convinced that he could not understand her words—"doesn't it look as if we were showing him, by taking away his furniture, that we have given up hope of his ever getting better and are just leaving him coldly to himself? I think it would be best to keep his room exactly as it has always been, so that when he comes back to us he will find everything unchanged and be able all the more easily to forget what has happened in between.''

On hearing these words from his mother Gregor realized that the lack of all direct human speech for the past two months together with the monotony of family life must have confused his mind, otherwise he could not account for the fact that he had quite earnestly looked forward to having his room emptied of furnishing. Did he really want his warm room, so comfortably fitted with old family furniture, to be turned into a naked den in which he would certainly be able to crawl unhampered in all directions but at the price of shedding simultaneously all recollection of his human background? He had indeed been so near the brink of forgetfulness that only the voice of his mother, which he had not heard for so long, had drawn him back from it. Nothing should be taken out of his room; everything must stay as it was; he could not dispense with the good influence of the furniture on his state of mind; and even if the furniture did hamper him in his senseless crawling round and round, that was no drawback but a great advantage.

Unfortunately his sister was of the contrary opinion; she had grown accustomed, and not without reason, to consider herself an expert in Gregor's affairs as against her parents, and so her mother's advice was now enough to make her determined on the removal not only of the chest and the writing desk, which had been her first intention, but of all the furniture except the indispensable sofa. This determination was not, of course, merely the outcome of childish recalcitrance and of the self-confidence she had recently developed so unexpectedly and at such cost; she had in fact perceived that Gregor needed a lot of space to crawl about in, while on the other hand he never used the furniture at all, so far as could be seen. Another factor might have been also the enthusiastic temperament of an adolescent girl, which seeks to indulge itself on every opportunity and which now tempted Grete to exaggerate the horror of her brother's circumstances in order that she might do all the more for him. In a room where Gregor lorded it all alone over empty walls no one save herself was likely ever to set foot.

And so she was not to be moved from her resolve by her mother who seemed moreover to be ill at ease in Gregor's room and therefore unsure of herself, was soon reduced to silence and helped her daughter as best she could to push the chest outside. Now, Gregor could do without the chest, if need be, but the writing desk he must retain. As soon as the two women had got the chest out of his room, groaning as they pushed it, Gregor stuck his head out from under the sofa to see how he might intervene as kindly and cautiously as possible. But as bad luck would have it, his mother was the first to return, leaving Grete clasping the chest in the room next door where she was trying to shift it all by herself, without of course moving it from the spot. His mother however was not accustomed to the sight of him, it might sicken her and so in alarm Gregor backed quickly to the other end of the sofa, yet could not prevent the sheet from swaying a little in front. That was enough to put her on the alert. She paused, stood still for a moment and then went back to Grete.

Although Gregor kept reassuring himself that nothing out of the way was happening, but only a few bits of furniture were being changed round, he soon had to admit that all this trotting to and fro of the two women, their little ejaculations and the scraping of furniture along the floor affected him like a vast disturbance coming from all sides at once, and however much he tucked in his head and legs and cowered to the very floor he was bound to confess that he would not be able to stand it for long. They were clearing his room out; taking away everything he loved; the chest in which he kept his fret saw and other tools was already dragged off; they were now loosening the writing desk which had almost sunk into the floor, the desk at which he had done all his homework when he was at the commercial academy, at the grammar school before that, and, yes, even at the primary school—he had no more time to waste in weighing the good intentions of the two women, whose existence he had by now almost forgotten, for they were so exhausted that they were laboring in silence and nothing could be heard but the heavy scuffling of their feet.

And so he rushed out—the women were just leaning against the writing desk in the next room to give themselves a breather—and four times changed his direction, since he really did not know what to rescue first, then on the wall opposite, which was already otherwise cleared, he was struck by the picture of the lady muffled in so much fur and quickly crawled up to it and pressed himself to the glass, which was a good surface to hold on to and comforted his hot belly. This picture at least, which was entirely hidden beneath him, was going to be removed by nobody. He turned his head towards the door of the living room so as to observe the women when they came back.

They had not allowed themselves much of a rest and were already coming; Grete had twined her arm round her mother and was almost supporting her. "Well, what shall we take now?" said Grete, looking round. Her eyes met Gregor's from the wall. She kept her composure, presumably because of her mother, bent her head down to her mother, to keep her from looking up, and said, although in a fluttering, unpremeditated voice: "Come, hadn't we better go back to the living room for a moment?" Her intentions were clear enough to Gregor, she wanted to bestow her mother in safety and then chase him down from the wall. Well, just let her try it! He clung to his picture and would not give it up. He would rather fly in Grete's face.

But Grete's words had succeeded in disquieting her mother, who took a step to one side, caught sight of the huge brown mass on the flowered wallpaper, and before she was really conscious that what she saw was Gregor screamed in a loud, hoarse voice: "Oh God, oh God!" fell with outspread arms over the sofa as if giving up and did not move. "Gregor!" cried his sister, shaking her fist and glaring at him. This was the first time she had directly addressed him since his metamorphosis. She ran into the next room for some aromatic essence with which to rouse her mother from her fainting fit. Gregor wanted to help too—there was still time to rescue the picture—but he was stuck fast to the glass and had to tear himself loose; he then ran after his sister into the next room as if he could advise her, as he used to do; but then had to stand helplessly behind her; she meanwhile searched among various small bottles and when she turned round started in alarm at the sight of him; one bottle fell on the floor and broke; a splinter of glass cut Gregor's face and some kind of corrosive medicine splashed him; without pausing a moment longer Grete gathered up all the bottles she could carry and ran to her mother with them; she banged the door shut with her foot. Gregor was now cut off from his mother, who was perhaps nearly dying because of him; he dared not open the door for fear of frightening away his sister, who had to stay with her mother; there was nothing he could do but wait; and harassed by self-reproach and worry he began now to crawl to and fro, over everything, walls, furniture and ceiling, and finally in his despair, when the whole room seemed to be reeling round him, fell down on to the middle of the big table.

A little while elapsed, Gregor was still lying there feebly and all around was quiet, perhaps that was a good omen. Then the doorbell rang. The servant girl was of course locked in her kitchen, and Grete would have to open the door. It was his father. "What's been happening?" were his first words; Grete's face must have told him everything. Grete answered in a muffled voice, apparently hiding her head on his breast: "Mother has been fainting, but she's better now. Gregor's broken loose." "Just what I expected," said his father, "just what I've been telling you, but you women would never listen." It was clear to Gregor that his father had taken the worst interpretation of Grete's all too brief statement and was assuming that Gregor had been guilty of some violent act. Therefore Gregor must now try to propitiate his father, since he had neither time nor means for an explanation. And so he fled to the door of his own room and crouched against it, to let his father see as soon as he came in from the hall that his son had the good intention of getting back into his room immediately and that it was not necessary to drive him there, but that if only the door were opened he would disappear at once.

Yet his father was not in the mood to perceive such fine distinctions. "Ah!" he cried as soon as he appeared, in a tone which sounded at once angry and exultant. Gregor drew his head back from the door and lifted it to look at his father. Truly, this was not the father he had imagined to himself; admittedly he had been too absorbed of late in his new recreation of crawling over the ceiling to take the same interest as before in what was happening elsewhere in the flat, and he ought really to be prepared for some changes. And yet, and yet, could that be his father? The man who used to lie wearily sunk in bed whenever Gregor set out on a business journey; who welcomed him back of an evening lying in a long chair in a dressing gown; who could not really rise to his feet but only lifted his arms in greeting, and on the rare occasions when he did go out with his family, on one or two Sundays a year and on high holidays, walked between Gregor and his mother, who were slow walkers anyhow, even more slowly than they did, muffled in his old greatcoat, shuffling laboriously forward with the help of his crook-handled stick which he set down most cautiously at every step and, whenever he wanted to say anything, nearly always came to a full stop and gathered his escort around him? Now he was standing there in fine shape; dressed in a smart blue uniform with gold buttons, such as bank messengers wear; his strong double chin bulged over the stiff high collar of his jacket; from under his bushy eyebrows his black eyes darted fresh and penetrating glances; his onetime tangled white hair had been combed flat on either side of a shining and carefully exact parting. He pitched his cap, which bore a gold monogram, probably the badge of some bank, in a wide sweep across the whole room on to a sofa and with the tail-ends of his jacket thrown back, his hands in his trouser pockets, advanced with a grim visage towards Gregor. Likely enough he did not himself know what he meant to do; at any rate he lifted his feet uncommonly high, and Gregor was dumbfounded at the enormous size of his shoe soles. But Gregor could not risk standing up to him, aware as he had been from the very first day of his new life that his father believed only the severest measures suitable for dealing with him. And so he ran before his father, stopping when he stopped and scuttling forward again when his father made any kind of move. In this way they circled the room several times without anything decisive happening; indeed the whole operation did not even look like a pursuit because it was carried out so slowly. And so Gregor did not leave the floor, for he feared that his father might take as a piece of peculiar wickedness any excursion of his over the walls or the ceiling. All the same, he could not stay this course much longer, for while his father took one step he had to carry out a whole series of movements. He was already beginning to feel breathless, just as in his former life his lungs had not been very dependable. As he was staggering along, trying to concentrate his energy on running, hardly keeping his eyes open, in his dazed state never even thinking of any other escape than simply going forward; and having almost forgotten that the walls were free to him, which in this room were well provided with finely carved pieces of furniture full of knobs and crevices—suddenly something lightly flung landed close behind and rolled before him. It was an apple; a second apple followed immediately; Gregor came to a stop in alarm; there was no point in running on, for his father was determined to bombard him. He had filled his pockets with fruit from the dish on the sideboard and was now shying apple after apple, without taking particularly good aim for the moment. The small red apples rolled about the floor as if magnetized and cannoned into each other. An apple thrown without much force grazed Gregor's back and glanced off harmlessly. But another following immediately landed right on his back and sank in; Gregor wanted to drag himself forward, as if this startling, incredible pain could be left behind him: but he felt as if nailed to the spot and flattened himself out in a complete derangement of all his senses. With his last conscious look he saw the door of his room being torn open and his mother rushing out ahead of his screaming sister, in her underbodice, for her daughter had loosened her clothing to let her breathe more freely and recover from her swoon, he saw his mother rushing towards his father, leaving one after another behind her on the floor her loosened petticoats, stumbling over her petticoats straight to his father and embracing him, in complete union with him—but here Gregor's sight began to fail—with her hands clasped round his father's neck as she begged for her son's life.

III

The serious injury done to Gregor, which disabled him for more than a month—the apple went on sticking in his body as a visible reminder, since no one ventured to remove it—seemed to have made even his father recollect that Gregor was a member of the family, despite his present unfortunate and repulsive shape, and ought not to be treated as an enemy, that, on the contrary, family duty required the suppression of disgust and the exercise of patience, nothing but patience.

And although his injury had impaired, probably for ever, his power of movement, and for the time being it took him long, long minutes to creep across his room like an old invalid—there was no question now of crawling up the wall—yet in his own opinion he was sufficiently compensated for this worsening of his condition by the fact that towards evening the living-room door, which he used to watch intently for an hour or two beforehand, was always thrown open, so that lying in the darkness of his room, invisible to the family, he could see them all at the lamp-lit table and listen to their talk, by general consent as it were, very different from his earlier eavesdropping.

True, their intercourse lacked the lively character of former times, which he had always called to mind with a certain wistfulness in the small hotel bedrooms where he had been wont to throw himself down, tired out, on damp bedding. They were now mostly very silent. Soon after supper his father would fall asleep in his armchair; his mother and sister would admonish each other to be silent; his mother, bending low over the lamp, stitched at fine sewing for an underwear firm; his sister, who had taken a job as a salesgirl, was learning shorthand and French in the evenings on the chance of bettering herself. Sometimes his father woke up, and as if quite unaware that he had been sleeping said to his mother: "What a lot of sewing you're doing today!" and at once fell asleep again while the two women exchanged a tired smile.

With a kind of mulishness his father persisted in keeping his uniform on even in the house; his dressing gown hung uselessly on its peg and he slept fully dressed where he sat, as if he were ready for service at any moment and even here only at the beck and call of his superior. As a result, his uniform, which was not brand-new to start with, began to look dirty, despite all the loving care of the mother and sister to keep it clean, and Gregor often spent whole evenings gazing at the many greasy spots on the garment, gleaming with gold buttons always in a high state of polish, in which the old man sat sleeping in extreme discomfort and yet quite peacefully.

As soon as the clock struck ten his mother tried to rouse his father with gentle words and to persuade him after that to get into bed, for sitting there he could not have a proper sleep and that was what he needed most, since he had to go to duty at six. But with the mulishness that had obsessed him since he became a bank messenger he always insisted on staying longer at the table, although he regularly fell asleep again and in the end only with the greatest trouble could be got out of his armchair and into his bed. However insistently Gregor's mother and sister kept urging him with gentle reminders, he would go on slowly shaking his head for a quarter of an hour, keeping his eyes shut, and refuse to get to his feet. The mother plucked at his sleeve, whispering endearments in his ear, the sister left her lessons to come to her mother's help, but Gregor's father was not to be caught. He would only sink down deeper in his chair. Not until the two women hoisted him up by the armpits did he open his eyes and look at them both, one after the other, usually with the remark: "This is a life. This is the peace and quiet of my old age." And leaning on the two of them he would heave himself up, with difficulty, as if he were a great burden to himself, suffer them to lead him as far as the door and then wave them off and go on alone, while the mother abandoned her needlework and the sister her pen in order to run after him and help him farther.

Who could find time, in this overworked and tired-out family, to bother about Gregor more than was absolutely needful? The household was reduced more and more; the servant girl was turned off; a gigantic bony charwoman with white hair flying round her head came in morning and evening to do the rough work; everything else was done by Gregor's mother, as well as great piles of sewing. Even various family ornaments, which his mother and sister used to wear with pride at parties and celebrations, had to be sold, as Gregor discovered of an evening from hearing them all discuss the prices obtained. But what they lamented most was the fact that they could not leave the flat which was much too big for their present circumstances, because they could not think of any way to shift Gregor. Yet Gregor saw well enough that consideration for him was not the main difficulty preventing the removal, for they could have easily shifted him in some suitable box with a few air holes in it; what really kept them from moving into another flat was rather their own complete hopelessness and the belief that they had been singled out for a misfortune such as had never happened to any of their relations or acquaintances. They fulfilled to the uttermost all that the world demands of poor people, the father fetched breakfast for the small clerks in the bank, the mother devoted her energy to making underwear for strangers, the sister trotted to and fro behind the counter at the behest of customers, but more than this they had not the strength to do. And the wound in Gregor's back began to nag at him afresh when his mother and sister, after getting his father into bed, came back again, left their work lying, drew close to each other and sat cheek to cheek; when his mother, pointing towards his room, said: "Shut that door now, Grete," and he was left again in darkness, while next door the women mingled their tears or perhaps sat dry-eyed staring at the table.

Gregor hardly slept at all by night or by day. He was often haunted by the idea that the next time the door opened he would take the family's affairs in hand again just as he used to do; once more, after this long interval, there appeared in his thoughts the figures of the chief and the chief clerk, the commercial travelers and the apprentices, the porter who was so dull-witted, two or three friends in other firms, a chambermaid in one of the rural hotels, a sweet and fleeting memory, a cashier in a milliner's shop, whom he had wooed earnestly but too slowly—they all appeared, together with strangers or people he had quite forgotten, but instead of helping him and his family they were one and all unapproachable and he was glad when they vanished. At other times he would not be in the mood to bother about his family, he was only filled with rage at the way they were neglecting him, and although he had no clear idea of what he might care to eat he would make plans for getting into the larder to take the food that was after all his due, even if he were not hungry. His sister no longer took thought to bring him what might especially please him, but in the morning and at noon before she went to business hurriedly pushed into his room with her foot any food that was available, and in the evening cleared it out again with one sweep of the broom, heedless of whether it had been merely tasted, or—as most frequently happened—left untouched. The cleaning of his room, which she now did always in the evenings, could not have been more hastily done. Streaks of dirt stretched along the walls, here and there lay balls of dust and filth. At first Gregor used to station himself in some particularly filthy corner when his sister arrived, in order to reproach her with it, so to speak. But he could have sat there for weeks without getting her to make any improvements; she could see the dirt as well as he did, but she had simply made up her mind to leave it alone. And yet, with a touchiness that was new to her, which seemed anyhow to have infected the whole family, she jealously guarded her claim to be the sole caretaker of Gregor's room. His mother once subjected his room to a thorough cleaning, which was achieved only by means of several buckets of water—all this dampness of course upset Gregor too and he lay widespread, sulky and motionless on the sofa—but she was well punished for it. Hardly had his sister noticed the changed aspect of his room that evening than she rushed in high dudgeon into the living room and, despite the imploringly raised hands of her mother, burst into a storm of weeping, while her parents—her father had of course been startled out of his chair—looked on at first in helpless amazement; then they too began to go into action; the father reproached the mother on his right for not having left the cleaning of Gregor's room to his sister; shrieked at the sister on his left that never again was she to be allowed to clean Gregor's room; while the mother tried to pull the father into his bedroom, since he was beyond himself with agitation; the sister, shaken with sobs, then beat upon the table with her small fists; and Gregor hissed loudly with rage because not one of them thought of shutting the door to spare him such a spectacle and so much noise.

Still, even if the sister, exhausted by her daily work, had grown tired of looking after Gregor as she did formerly, there was no need for his mother's intervention or for Gregor's being neglected at all. The charwoman was there. This old widow, whose strong bony frame had enabled her to survive the worst a long life could offer, by no means recoiled from Gregor. Without being in the least curious she had once by chance opened the door of his room and at the sight of Gregor, who, taken by surprise, began to rush to and fro although no one was chasing him, merely stood there with her arms folded. From that time she never failed to open his door a little for a moment, morning and evening, to have a look at him. At first she even used to call him to her, with words which apparently she took to be friendly, such as: "Come along, then, you old dung beetle!" or "Look at the old dung beetle, then!" To such allocutions Gregor made no answer, but stayed motionless where he was, as if the door had never been opened. Instead of being allowed to disturb him so senselessly whenever the whim took her, she should rather have been ordered to clean out his room daily, that charwoman! Once, early in the morning—heavy rain was lashing on the windowpanes, perhaps a sign that spring was on the way—Gregor was so exasperated when she began addressing him again that he ran at her, as if to attack her, although slowly and feebly enough. But the charwoman instead of showing fright merely lifted high a chair that happened to be beside the door, and as she stood there with her mouth open wide it was clear that she meant to shut it only when she brought the chair down on Gregor's back. "So you're not coming any nearer?" she asked, as Gregor turned away again, and quietly put the chair back into the corner.

Gregor was now eating hardly anything. Only when he happened to pass the food laid out for him did he take a bit of something in his mouth as a pastime, kept it there for an hour at a time and usually spat it out again. At first he thought it was chagrin over the state of his room that prevented him from eating, yet he soon got used to the various changes in his room. It had become a habit in the family to push into his room things there was no room for elsewhere, and there were plenty of these now, since one of the rooms had been let to three lodgers. These serious gentlemen—all three of them with full beards, as Gregor once observed through a crack in the door—had a passion for order, not only in their own room but, since they were now members of the household, in all its arrangements, especially in the kitchen. Superfluous, not to say dirty, objects they could not bear. Besides, they had brought with them most of the furnishings they needed. For this reason many things could be dispensed with that it was no use trying to sell but that should not be thrown away either. All of them found their way into Gregor's room. The ash can likewise and the kitchen garbage can. Anything that was not needed for the moment was simply flung into Gregor's room by the charwoman, who did everything in a hurry; fortunately Gregor usually saw only the object, whatever it was, and the hand that held it. Perhaps she intended to take the things away again as time and opportunity offered, or to collect them until she could throw them all out in a heap, but in fact they just lay wherever she happened to throw them, except when Gregor pushed his way through the junk heap and shifted it somewhat, at first out of necessity, because he had not room enough to crawl, but later with increasing enjoyment, although after such excursions, being sad and weary to death, he would lie motionless for hours. And since the lodgers often ate their supper at home in the common living room, the living-room door stayed shut many an evening, yet Gregor reconciled himself quite easily to the shutting of the door, for often enough on evenings when it was opened he had disregarded it entirely and lain in the darkest corner of his room, quite unnoticed by the family. But on one occasion the charwoman left the door open a little and it stayed ajar even when the lodgers came in for supper and the lamp was lit. They set themselves at the top end of the table where formerly Gregor and his father and mother had eaten their meals, unfolded their napkins and took knife and fork in hand. At once his mother appeared in the other doorway with a dish of meat and close behind her his sister with a dish of potatoes piled high. The food steamed with a thick vapor. The lodgers bent over the food set before them as if to scrutinize it before eating, in fact the man in the middle, who seemed to pass for an authority with the other two, cut a piece of meat as it lay on the dish, obviously to discover if it were tender or should be sent back to the kitchen. He showed satisfaction, and Gregor's mother and sister, who had been watching anxiously, breathed freely and began to smile.

The family itself took its meals in the kitchen. Nonetheless, Gregor's father came into the living room before going into the kitchen and with one prolonged bow, cap in hand, made a round of the table. The lodgers all stood up and murmured something in their beards. When they were alone again they ate their food in almost complete silence. It seemed remarkable to Gregor that among the various noises coming from the table he could always distinguish the sound of their masticating teeth, as if this were a sign to Gregor that one needed teeth in order to eat, and that with toothless jaws even of the finest make one could do nothing. "I'm hungry enough," said Gregor sadly to himself, "But not for that kind of food. How these lodgers are stuffing themselves, and here am I dying of starvation!"

On that very evening—during the whole of his time there Gregor could not remember ever having heard the violin—the sound of violin-playing came from the kitchen. The lodgers had already finished their supper, the one in the middle had brought out a newspaper and given the other two a page apiece, and now they were leaning back at ease reading and smoking. When the violin began to play they pricked up their ears, got to their feet, and went on tiptoe to the hall door where they stood huddled together. Their movements must have been heard in the kitchen, for Gregor's father called out: "Is the violin-playing disturbing you, gentlemen? It can be stopped at once." "On the contrary," said the middle lodger, "could not Fräulein Samsa come and play in this room, beside us, where it is much more convenient and comfortable?'' ''Oh certainly,'' cried Gregor's father, as if he were the violin-player. The lodgers came back into the living room and waited. Presently Gregor's father arrived with the music stand, his mother carrying the music and his sister the violin. His sister quietly made everything ready to start playing; his parents, who had never let rooms before and so had an exaggerated idea of the courtesy due to lodgers, did not venture to sit down on their own chairs; his father leaned against the door, the right hand thrust between two buttons of his livery coat, which was formally buttoned up; but his mother was offered a chair by one of the lodgers and, since she left the chair just where he happened to put it, sat down in a corner to one side.

Gregor's sister began to play; the father and mother, from either side, intently watched the movements of her hands. Gregor, attracted by the playing, ventured to move forward a little until his head was actually inside the living room. He felt hardly any surprise at his growing lack of consideration for the others; there had been a time when he prided himself on being considerate. And yet just on this occasion he had more reason than ever to hide himself, since owing to the amount of dust which lay thick in his room and rose into the air at the slightest movement, he too was covered with dust; fluff and hair and remnants of food trailed with him, caught on his back and along his sides; his indifference to everything was much too great for him to turn on his back and scrape himself clean on the carpet, as once he had done several times a day. And in spite of his condition, no shame deterred him from advancing a little over the spotless floor of the living room.

To be sure, no one was aware of him. The family was entirely absorbed in the violin-playing; the lodgers, however, who first of all had stationed themselves, hands in pockets, much too close behind the music stand so that they could all have read the music, which must have bothered his sister, had soon retreated to the window, half-whispering with downbent heads, and stayed there while his father turned an anxious eye on them. Indeed, they were making it more than obvious that they had been disappointed in their expectation of hearing good or enjoyable violin-playing, that they had had more than enough of the performance and only out of courtesy suffered a continued disturbance of their peace. From the way they all kept blowing the smoke of their cigars high in the air through nose and mouth one could divine their irritation. And yet Gregor's sister was playing so beautifully. Her face leaned sideways, intently and sadly her eyes followed the notes of music. Gregor crawled a little farther forward and lowered his head to the ground so that it might be possible for his eyes to meet hers. Was he an animal, that music had such an effect upon him? He felt as if the way were opening before him to the unknown nourishment he craved. He was determined to push forward till he reached his sister, to pull at her skirt and so let her know that she was to come into his room with her violin, for no one here appreciated her playing as he would appreciate it. He would never let her out of his room, at least, not so long as she lived; his frightful appearance would become, for the first time, useful to him; he would watch all the doors of his room at once and spit at intruders; but his sister should need no constraint, she should stay with him of her own free will; she should sit beside him on the sofa, bend down her ear to him and hear him confide that he had had the firm intention of sending her to the Conservatorium, and that, but for his mishap, last Christmas—surely Christmas was long past?—he would have announced it to everybody without allowing a single objection. After this confession his sister would be so touched that she would burst into tears, and Gregor would then raise himself to her shoulder and kiss her on the neck, which, now that she went to business, she kept free of any ribbon or collar.

"Mr. Samsa!" cried the middle lodger, to Gregor's father, and pointed, without wasting any more words, at Gregor, now working himself slowly forwards. The violin fell silent, the middle lodger first smiled to his friends with a shake of the head and then looked at Gregor again. Instead of driving Gregor out, his father seemed to think it more needful to begin by soothing down the lodgers, although they were not at all agitated and apparently found Gregor more entertaining than the violin-playing. He hurried toward them and, spreading out his arms, tried to urge them back into their own room and at the same time to block their view of Gregor. They now began to be really a little angry, one could not tell whether because of the old man's behavior or because it had just dawned on them that all unwittingly they had such a neighbor as Gregor next door. They demanded explanations of his father, they waved their arms like him, tugged uneasily at their beards, and only with reluctance backed towards their room. Meanwhile Gregor's sister, who stood there as if lost when her playing was so abruptly broken off, came to life again, pulled herself together all at once after standing for a while holding violin and bow in nervelessly hanging hands and staring at her music, pushed her violin into the lap of her mother, who was still sitting in her chair fighting asthmatically for breath, and ran into the lodgers' room to which they were now being shepherded by her father rather more quickly than before. One could see the pillows and blankets on the beds flying under the accustomed fingers and being laid in order. Before the lodgers had actually reached their room she had finished making the beds and slipped out.

The old man seemed once more to be so possessed by his mulish self-asser-tiveness that he was forgetting all the respect he should show to his lodgers. He kept driving them on and driving them on until in the very door of the bedroom the middle lodger stamped his foot loudly on the floor and so brought him to a halt. "I beg to announce," said the lodger, lifting one hand and looking also at Gregor's mother and sister, "'that because of the dis-gusting conditions prevailing in this household and family"—here he spat on the floor with emphatic brevity—"I give you notice on the spot. Naturally I won't pay you a penny for the days I have lived here, on the contrary I shall consider bringing an action for damages against you, based on claims—believe me—that will be easily susceptible of proof." He ceased and stared straight in front of him, as if he expected something. In fact his two friends at once rushed into the breach with these words: "And we too give notice on the spot.'' On that he seized the door-handle and shut the door with a slam.

Gregor's father, groping with his hands, staggered forward and fell into his chair; it looked as if he were stretching himself there for his ordinary evening nap, but the marked jerking of his head, which was as if uncontrollable, showed that he was far from asleep. Gregor had simply stayed quietly all the time on the spot where the lodgers had espied him. Disappointment at the failure of his plan, perhaps also the weakness arising from extreme hunger, made it impossible for him to move. He feared, with a fair degree of certainty, that at any moment the general tension would discharge itself in a combined attack upon him, and he lay waiting. He did not react even to the noise made by the violin as it fell off his mother's lap from under her trembling fingers and gave out a resonant note.

''My dear parents,'' said his sister, slapping her hand on the table by way of introduction, ''things can't go on like this. Perhaps you don't realize that, but I do. I won't utter my brother's name in the presence of this creature, and so all I say is: we must try to get rid of it. We've tried to look after it and to put up with it as far as is humanly possible, and I don't think anyone could reproach us in the slightest.''

''She is more than right,'' said Gregor's father to himself. His mother, who was still choking for lack of breath, began to cough hollowly into her hand with a wild look in her eyes.

His sister rushed over to her and held her forehead. His father's thoughts seemed to have lost their vagueness at Grete's words, he sat more upright, fingering his service cap that lay among the plates still lying on the table from the lodgers' supper, and from time to time looked at the still form of Gregor.

''We must try to get rid of it,'' his sister now said explicitly to her father, since her mother was coughing too much to hear a word, ''it will be the death of both of you, I can see that coming. When one has to work as hard as we do, all of us, one can't stand this continual torment at home on top of it. At least I can't stand it any longer.'' And she burst into such a passion of sobbing that her tears dropped on her mother's face, where she wiped them off mechanically.

''My dear,'' said the old man sympathetically, and with evident understanding, ''but what can we do?''

Gregor's sister merely shrugged her shoulders to indicate the feeling of helplessness that had now overmastered her during her weeping fit, in contrast to her former confidence.

''If he could understand us,'' said her father, half questioningly; Grete, still sobbing, vehemently waved a hand to show how unthinkable that was.

''If he could understand us,'' repeated the old man, shutting his eyes to consider his daughter's conviction that understanding was impossible, ''then perhaps we might come to some agreement with him. But as it is—''

''He must go,'' cried Gregor's sister, ''That's the only solution, Father. You must just try to get rid of the idea that this is Gregor. The fact that we've believed it for so long is the root of all our trouble. But how can it be Gregor? If this were Gregor, he would have realized long ago that human beings can't live with such a creature, and he'd have gone away on his own accord. Then we wouldn't have any brother, but we'd be able to go on living and keep his memory in honor. As it is, this creature persecutes us, drives away our lodgers, obviously wants the whole apartment to himself and would have us all sleep in the gutter. Just look, Father," she shrieked all at once, "he's at it again!" And in an access of panic that was quite incomprehensible to Gregor she even quitted her mother, literally thrusting the chair from her as if she would rather sacrifice her mother than stay so near to Gregor, and rushed behind her father, who also rose up, being simply upset by the agitation, and half-spread his arms out as if to protect her.

Yet Gregor had not the slightest intention of frightening anyone, far less his sister. He had only begun to turn round in order to crawl back to his room, but it was certainly a startling operation to watch, since because of his disabled condition he could not execute the difficult turning movements except by lifting his head and then bracing it against the floor over and over again. He paused and looked round. His good intentions seemed to have been recognized; the alarm had only been momentary. Now they were all watching him in melancholy silence. His mother lay in her chair, her legs stiffly outstretched and pressed together, her eyes almost closing for sheer weariness; his father and his sister were sitting beside each other, his sister's arm around the old man's neck.

Perhaps I can go on turning round now, thought Gregor, and began his labors again. He could not stop himself from panting with the effort, and had to pause now and then to take breath. Nor did anyone harass him, he was left entirely to himself. When he had completed the turn-round he began at once to crawl straight back. He was amazed at the distance separating him from his room and could not understand how in his weak state he had managed to accomplish the same journey so recently, almost without remarking it. Intent on crawling as fast as possible, he barely noticed that not a single word, not an ejaculation from his family, interfered with his progress. Only when he was already in the doorway did he turn his head round, not completely, for his neck muscles were getting stiff, but enough to see that nothing had changed behind him except that his sister had risen to her feet. His last glance fell on his mother, who was not quite overcome by sleep.

Hardly was he well inside his room when the door was hastily pushed shut, bolted and locked. The sudden noise in his rear startled him so much that his little legs gave beneath him. It was his sister who had shown such haste. She had been standing ready waiting and had made a light spring forward, Gregor had not even heard her coming, and she cried "At last!" to her parents as she turned the key in the lock.

"And what now?" said Gregor to himself, looking round in the darkness. Soon he made the discovery that he was now unable to stir a limb. This did not surprise him, rather it seemed unnatural that he should ever actually have been able to move on these feeble little legs. Otherwise he felt relatively comfortable. True, his whole body was aching, but it seemed that the pain was gradually growing less and would finally pass away. The rotting apple in his back and the inflamed area around it, all covered with soft dust, already hardly troubled him. He thought of his family with tenderness and love. The decision that he must disappear was one that he held to even more strongly than his sister, if that were possible. In this state of vacant and peaceful meditation he remained until the tower clock struck three in the morning. The first broadening of light in the world outside the window entered his consciousness once more. Then his head sank to the floor of its own accord and from his nostrils came the last faint flicker of his breath.

When the charwoman arrived early in the morning—what between her strength and her impatience she slammed all the doors so loudly, never mind how often she had been begged not to do so, that no one in the whole apartment could enjoy any quiet sleep after her arrival—she noticed nothing unusual as she took her customary peep into Gregor's room. She thought he was lying motionless on purpose, pretending to be in the sulks; she credited him with every kind of intelligence. Since she happened to have the long-handled broom in her hand she tried to tickle him up with it from the doorway. When that too produced no reaction she felt provoked and poked at him a little harder, and only when she had pushed him along the floor without meeting any resistance was her attention aroused. It did not take her long to establish the truth of the matter, and her eyes widened, she let out a whistle, yet did not waste much time over it but tore open the door of the Samsas' bedroom and yelled into the darkness at the top of her voice: "Just look at this, it's dead; it's lying here dead and done for!"

Mr. and Mrs. Samsa started up in their double bed and before they realized the nature of the charwoman's announcement had some difficulty in overcoming the shock of it. But then they got out of bed quickly, one on either side, Mr. Samsa throwing a blanket over his shoulders, Mrs. Samsa in nothing but her nightgown; in this array they entered Gregor's room. Meanwhile the door of the living room opened, too, where Grete had been sleeping since the advent of the lodgers; she was completely dressed as if she had not been to bed, which seemed to be confirmed also by the paleness of her face. "Dead?" said Mrs. Samsa, looking questioningly at the charwoman, although she could have investigated for herself, and the fact was obvious enough without investigation. "I should say so," said the charwoman, proving her words by pushing Gregor's corpse a long way to one side with her broomstick. Mrs. Samsa made a movement as if to stop her, but checked it. "Well," said Mr. Samsa, "now thanks be to God." He crossed himself, and the three women followed his example. Grete, whose eyes never left the corpse, said: "Just see how thin he was. It's such a long time since he's eaten anything. The food came out again just as it went in." Indeed, Gregor's body was completely flat and dry, as could only now be seen when it was no longer supported by the legs and nothing prevented one from looking closely at it.

"Come in beside us, Grete, for a little while," said Mrs. Samsa with a tremulous smile, and Grete, not without looking back at the corpse, followed her parents into their bedroom. The charwoman shut the door and opened the window wide. Although it was so early in the morning a certain softness was perceptible in the fresh air. After all, it was already the end of March.

The three lodgers emerged from their room and were surprised to see no breakfast; they had been forgotten. "Where's our breakfast?" said the middle lodger peevishly to the charwoman. But she put her finger to her lips and hastily, without a word, indicated by gestures that they should go into Gregor's room. They did so and stood, their hands in the pockets of their somewhat shabby coats, around Gregor's corpse in the room where it was now fully light.

At that the door of the Samsas' bedroom opened and Mr. Samsa appeared in his uniform, his wife on one arm, his daughter on the other. They all looked a little as if they had been crying; from time to time Grete hid her face on her father's arm.

"Leave my house at once!" said Mr. Samsa, and pointed to the door without disengaging himself from the women. "What do you mean by that?" said the middle lodger, taken somewhat aback, with a feeble smile. The two others put their hands behind them and kept rubbing them together, as if in gleeful expectation of a fine set-to in which they were bound to come off the winners. "I mean just what I say," answered Mr. Samsa, and advanced in a straight line with his two companions towards the lodger. He stood his ground at first quietly, looking at the floor as if his thoughts were taking a new pattern in his head. "Then let us go, by all means," he said, and looked up at Mr. Samsa as if in a sudden access of humility he were expecting some renewed sanction for this decision. Mr. Samsa merely nodded briefly once or twice with meaning eyes. Upon that the lodger really did go with long strides into the hall, his two friends had been listening and had quite stopped rubbing their hands for some moments and now went scuttling after him as if afraid that Mr. Samsa might get into the hall before them and cut them off from their leader. In the hall they all three took their hats from the rack, their sticks from the umbrella stand, bowed in silence and quitted the apartment. With a suspiciousness which proved quite unfounded Mr. Samsa and the two women followed them out to the landing; leaning over the banister they watched the three figures slowly but surely going down the long stairs, vanishing from sight at a certain turn of the staircase on every floor and coming into view again after a moment or so; the more they dwindled, the more the Samsa family's interest in them dwindled, and when a butcher's boy met them and passed them on the stairs coming up proudly with a tray on his head, Mr. Samsa and the two women soon left the landing and as if a burden had been lifted from them went back into their apartment.

They decided to spend this day in resting and going for a stroll; they had not only deserved such a respite from work, but absolutely needed it. And so they sat down at the table and wrote three notes of excuse, Mr. Samsa to his board of management, Mrs. Samsa to her employer and Grete to the head of her firm. While they were writing, the charwoman came in to say that she was going now, since her morning's work was finished. At first they only nodded without looking up, but as she kept hovering there they eyed her irritably. "Well?" said Mr. Samsa. The charwoman stood grinning in the doorway as if she had good news to impart to the family but meant not to say a word unless properly questioned. The small ostrich feather standing upright on her hat, which had annoyed Mr. Samsa ever since she was engaged, was waving gaily in all directions. "Well, what is it then?" asked Mrs. Samsa, who obtained more respect from the charwoman than the others. "Oh," said the charwoman, giggling so amiably that she could not at once continue, "just this, you don't need to bother about how to get rid of the thing next door. It's been seen to already." Mrs. Samsa and Grete bent over their letters again, as if preoccupied; Mr. Samsa, who perceived that she was eager to begin describing it all in detail, stopped her with a decisive hand. But since she was not allowed to tell her story, she remembered the great hurry she was in, being obviously deeply huffed: "Bye, everybody," she said, whirling off violently, and departed with a frightful slamming of doors.

"She'll be given notice tonight," said Mr. Samsa, but neither from his wife nor his daughter did he get any answer, for the charwoman seemed to have shattered again the composure they had barely achieved. They rose, went to the window and stayed there, clasping each other tight. Mr. Samsa turned to his chair to look at them and quietly observed them for a little. Then he called out: "Come along, now, do. Let bygones be bygones. And you might have some consideration for me." The two of them complied at once, hastened to him, caressed him and quickly finished their letters.

Then they all three left the apartment together, which was more than they had done for months, and went by tram into the open country outside the town. The tram, in which they were the only passengers, was filled with warm sunshine. Leaning comfortably back in their seats they canvassed their prospects for the future, and it appeared on closer inspection that they were not at all bad, for the jobs they had got, which so far they had never really discussed with each other, were all three admirable and likely to lead to better things later on. The greatest immediate improvement in their condition would of course arise from moving to another house; they wanted to take a smaller and cheaper but also better situated and more easily run apartment than the one they had, which Gregor had selected. While they were thus conversing, it struck both Mr. and Mrs. Samsa, almost at the same moment, as they became aware of their daughter's increasing vivacity, that in spite of all the sorrow of recent times, which had made her cheeks pale, she had bloomed into a pretty girl with a good figure. They grew quieter and half unconsciously exchanged glances of complete agreement, having come to the conclusion that it would soon be time to find a good husband for her. And it was like a confirmation of their new dreams and excellent intentions that at the end of their journey their daughter sprang to her feet first and stretched her young body.

Questions for "The Metamorphosis"

1.   Describe Gregor Samsa's character as completely as you can, supporting your impressions with evidence from the text. Pay attention to seemingly minor details, such as the picture in Gregor's room of the lady in fur.

2.   From whose point of view is most of the story told? How would you describe the tone of the narrative? What does this tone help to convey about the characters and the content of the story?

3.   Discuss the attitudes of Gregor's family members, especially that of his sister, toward Gregor. How do these attitudes change as the story unfolds? How might you account for such changes?

4.   What do you think is the climax, or moment of greatest interest and significance, of "The Metamorphosis"? What, then, does the rest of the story accomplish?

5.   What connections can you make between this story and the excerpts from the author's diary that appear in Chapter 2?

6.   In his notebook, one of our students observes that Gregor feels he has to work to save enough money to pay back his parents' debts even though "This debt has nothing to do with Gregor. Maybe this debt is like original sin—it's not our fault but we have it anyway." Is there anything else in the story that might be a veiled allusion to the biblical story of Adam and Eve? And if so, of what relevance is the biblical story to Kafka's novella?

Ryunosuke Akutagawa (1892–1927)

Raised in Tokyo and adopted as a child by his uncle, Ryunosuke
Akutagawa specialized in English literature at Tokyo Imperial University.
As undergraduates, he and two of his classmates launched a literary
magazine called *New Thought,* and it was in student journals of this kind
that Akutagawa published his first two stories, both of which won
immediate attention for this innovative, often renegade, stylist.

Akutagawa refused offers of teaching positions at the universities of
Tokyo and Kyoto, dedicating himself instead to writing. He wrote
prolifically and revised assiduously. Sensitive, often depressed, and frail in
health, Akutagawa committed suicide at the age of thirty-five. The
screenplay for *Rashomon,* reprinted in the drama chapter of this anthology,
is based on the following story—one of the hundred-odd stories
Akutagawa wrote in his brief career.

In a Grove

Translated by Takashi Kojima

The Testimony of a Woodcutter Questioned
——— by a High Police Commissioner ———

Yes, sir. Certainly, it was I who found the body. This morning, as usual, I
went to cut my daily quota of cedars, when I found the body in a grove in a
hollow in the mountains.

The exact location? About 150 yards off the Yamashina stage road. It's an
out-of-the-way grove of bamboo and cedars.

The body was lying flat on its back dressed in a bluish silk kimono and a
wrinkled headdress of the Kyoto style. A single sword stroke had pierced the
breast. The fallen bamboo blades around it were stained with bloody
blossoms.

No, the blood was no longer flowing. The wound had dried up, I believe.
And also, a gadfly was stuck fast there, hardly noticing my footsteps.

You ask me if I saw a sword or any such thing? No, nothing, sir. I found
only a rope at the root of a cedar nearby. And . . . well, in addition to a rope,
I found a comb. That was all. Apparently he must have made a battle of it
before he was murdered, because the grass and fallen bamboo blades had
been trampled down all around.

A horse was nearby? No, sir. It's hard enough for a man to enter, let alone
a horse.

The Testimony of a Traveling Buddhist Priest
—— Questioned by a High Police Commissioner ——

The time? Certainly, it was about noon yesterday, sir. The unfortunate man was on the road from Sekiyama to Yamashina. He was walking toward Sekiyama with a woman accompanying him on horseback, who I have since learned was his wife. A scarf hanging from her head hid her face from view. All I saw was the color of her clothes, a lilac-colored suit. Her horse was a sorrel with a fine mane.

The lady's height? Oh, about four feet five inches. Since I am a Buddhist priest, I took little notice about her details. Well, the man was armed with a sword as well as a bow and arrows. And I remember that he carried some twenty-odd arrows in his quiver.

Little did I expect that he would meet such a fate. Truly, human life is as evanescent as the morning dew or a flash of lightning. My words are inadequate to express my sympathy for him.

The Testimony of a Policeman Questioned
—— by a High Police Commissioner ——

The man that I arrested? He is a notorious brigand called Tajomaru. When I arrested him, he had fallen off his horse. He was groaning on the bridge at Awataguchi.

The time? It was in the early hours of last night. For the record, I might say that the other day I tried to arrest him, but unfortunately he escaped. He was wearing a dark-blue silk kimono and a large plain sword. And, as you see, he got a bow and arrows somewhere.

You say that this bow and these arrows look like the ones owned by the dead man? Then Tajomaru must be the murderer. The bow wound with leather strips, the black lacquered quiver, the seventeen arrows with hawk feathers—these were all in his possession, I believe.

Yes, sir, the horse is, as you say, a sorrel with a fine mane. A little beyond the stone bridge I found the horse grazing by the roadside, with his long rein dangling. Surely there is some providence in his having been thrown by the horse.

Of all the robbers prowling around Kyoto, this Tajomaru has brought the most grief to the women in town. Last autumn a wife who came to the mountain behind the Pindora of the Toribe Temple, presumably to pay a visit, was murdered, along with a girl. It has been suspected that it was his doing. If this criminal murdered the man, you cannot tell what he may have done with the man's wife. May it please your honor to look into this problem as well.

The Testimony of an Old Woman Questioned
—— by a High Police Commissioner ——

Yes, sir, that corpse is the man who married my daughter. He does not come from Kyoto. He was a samurai in the town of Kokufu in the province of Wakasa. His name was Kanazawa no Takehiro, and his age was twenty-six. He was of a gentle disposition, so I am sure he did nothing to provoke the anger of others.

My daughter? Her name is Masago, and her age is nineteen. She is a spirited, fun-loving girl, but I am sure she has never known any man except Takehiro. She has a small, oval, dark-complexioned face with a mole at the corner of her left eye.

Yesterday Takehiro left for Wakasa with my daughter. What a misfortune that things should have come to such a sad end! What has become of my daughter? I am resigned to giving up my son-in-law as lost, but the fate of my daughter worries me sick. For heaven's sake, leave no stone unturned to find her. I hate that robber Tajomaru, or whatever his name is. Not only my son-in-law, but my daughter . . . (Her later words were drowned in tears.)

—— Tajomaru's Confession ——

I killed him, but not her.

Where's she gone? I can't tell. Oh, wait a minute. No torture can make me confess what I don't know. Now things have come to such a head, I won't keep anything from you.

Yesterday a little past noon I met that couple. Just then a puff of wind blew, and raised her hanging scarf, so that I caught a glimpse of her face. Instantly it was again covered from my view. That may have been one reason; she looked like a Bodhisattva.[1] At that moment I had made up my mind to capture her even if I had to kill her man.

Why? To me killing isn't a matter of such great consequence as you might think. When a woman is captured, her man has to be killed anyway. In killing, I use the sword I wear at my side. Am I the only one who kills people? You, you don't use your swords. You kill people with your power, with your money. Sometimes you kill them on the pretext of working for their good. It's true they don't bleed. They are in the best of health, but all the same you've killed them. It's hard to say who is a greater sinner, you or me. (An ironical smile.)

But it would be good if I could capture a woman without killing her man. So I made up my mind to capture her, and do my best not to kill him. But it's out of the question on the Yamashina stage road, so I managed to lure the couple into the mountains.

---

[1]In Buddhism, a Bodhisattva is one who, out of compassion, forgoes a state of spiritual bliss in order to save others.

It was quite easy. I became their traveling companion, and I told them there was an old mound in the mountain over there, and that I had dug it open and found many mirrors and swords. I went on to tell them I'd buried the things in a grove behind the mountain, and that I'd like to sell them at a low price to anyone who would care to have them. Then . . . you see, isn't greed terrible? He was beginning to be moved by my talk before he knew it. In less than half an hour they were driving their horse toward the mountain with me.

When he reached the grove, I told them that the treasures were buried in it, and I asked them to come and see. The man had no objection—he was blinded by greed. The woman said she would wait on horseback. It was natural for her to say so, at the sight of a thick grove. To tell you the truth, my plan worked just as I wished. So I went into the grove with him, leaving her behind alone.

The grove is only bamboo for some distance. About fifty yards ahead there's a rather open clump of cedars. It was a convenient spot for my purpose. Pushing my way through the grove, I told him a plausible lie that the treasures were buried under the cedars. When I told him this, he laboriously pushed his way toward the slender cedars visible through the grove. After a while the bamboo thinned out, and we came to where a number of cedars grew in a row. As soon as we got there, I seized him from behind. Because he was a trained, sword-bearing warrior, he was quite strong, but he was taken by surprise, so there was no help for him. I soon tied him up to the root of a cedar.

Where did I get a rope? Thank heaven, being a robber, I had rope with me, since I might have to scale a wall at any moment. Of course it was easy to stop him from calling out by gagging his mouth with fallen bamboo leaves.

When I disposed of him, I went to his woman and asked her to come and see him, because he seemed to have been suddenly taken sick. It's needless to say that this plan also worked well. The woman, her sedge hat off, came into the depths of the grove, where I led her by the hand. The instant she caught sight of her husband, she drew a small sword. I've never seen a woman of such violent temper. If I'd been off guard, I'd have got a thrust in my side. I dodged, but she kept on slashing at me. She might have wounded me deeply or killed me. But I'm Tajomaru. I managed to strike down her small sword without drawing my own. The most spirited woman is defenseless without a weapon. At last I could satisfy my desire for her without taking her husband's life.

Yes . . . without taking his life. I didn't want to kill him. I was about to run away from the grove, leaving the woman behind in tears, when she frantically clung to my arm. In broken fragments of words, she asked that either her husband or I die. She said it was more trying than death to have her shame known to two men. She gasped out that she wanted to be the wife of whichever survived. Then a furious desire to kill him seized me.

Telling you in this way, no doubt I seem a crueler man than you. But that's because you didn't see her face. Especially her burning eyes at that moment. As I saw her eye to eye, I wanted to make her my wife even if I were to be struck by lightning. I wanted to make her my wife . . . this single desire filled my mind. This was not simply lust, as you might think. At that time if I'd had no other desire than lust, I surely wouldn't have minded knocking her down and running away. Then I wouldn't have stained my sword with his blood. But the moment I gazed at her face in the dark grove, I decided not to leave without killing him.

But I didn't like to resort to unfair means to kill him. I untied him and told him to cross swords with me. The rope that was found at the root of the cedar is the rope I dropped at the time. Furious with anger, he drew his thick sword. And quick as a wink, he sprang at me ferociously, without speaking a word. I needn't tell you how our fight turned out. The twenty-third stroke . . . please remember this. I'm impressed with this fact still. Nobody under the sun has ever clashed swords with me twenty strokes. (A cheerful smile.)

When he fell, I turned toward her, lowering my bloodstained sword. But to my great astonishment she was gone. I wondered where she had run to. I looked for her in the clump of cedars. I listened, but heard only a groaning sound from the throat of the dying man.

As soon as we crossed swords, she may have run away through the grove to call for help. When I thought of that, I decided it was a matter of life and death to me. So, robbing him of his sword, and bow and arrows, I ran out to the mountain road. There I found her horse still grazing quietly. It would be a waste of words to tell you the later details, but before I entered town I had already parted with the sword. That's my confession. I know that my head will be hung in chains anyway, so give me the maximum penalty. (A defiant attitude.)

The Confession of a Woman Who Has —— Come to the Shimizu Temple ——

That man in the blue silk kimono, after forcing me to yield to him, laughed mockingly as he looked at my bound husband. How horrified my husband must have been! But no matter how hard he struggled in agony, the rope cut into him all the more tightly. In spite of myself I ran stumblingly toward his side. Or rather I tried to run toward him, but the man knocked me down. Just at that moment I saw an indescribable light in my husband's eyes. Something beyond expression . . . his eyes make me shudder even now. That instantaneous look of my husband, who couldn't speak a word, told me all his heart. The flash in his eyes was neither anger nor sorrow . . . only a cold light, a look of loathing. More struck by the look in his eyes than by the blow of the thief, I called out in spite of myself and fell unconscious.

In the course of time I came to, and found that the man in blue silk was gone. I saw only my husband still bound to the root of the cedar. I raised myself from the bamboo blades with difficulty, and looked into his face; but the expression in his eyes was just the same as before.

Beneath the cold contempt in his eyes, there was hatred. Shame, grief, and anger . . . I don't know how to express my heart at that time. Reeling to my feet, I went up to my husband.

"Takehiro," I said to him, "since things have come to this pass, I cannot live with you. I'm determined to die . . . but you must die, too. You saw my shame. I can't leave you alive as you are."

This was all I could say. Still he went on gazing at me with loathing and contempt. My heart breaking, I looked for his sword. It must have been taken by the robber. Neither his sword nor his bow and arrow were to be seen in the grove. But fortunately my small sword was lying at my feet. Raising it overhead, once more I said, "Now give me your life. I'll follow you right away."

When he heard these words, he moved his lips with difficulty. Since his mouth was stuffed with leaves, of course his voice could not be heard. But at a glance I understood his words. Despising me, his look said only, "Kill me." Neither conscious nor unconscious, I stabbed the small sword through the lilac-colored kimono into his breast.

Again at this time I must have fainted. By the time I managed to look up, he had already breathed his last—still in bonds. A streak of sinking sunlight streamed through the clump of cedars and bamboos, and shone on his pale face. Gulping down my sobs, I untied the rope from his dead body. And . . . and what has become of me since, I have no more strength to tell you. Anyway, I hadn't the strength to die. I stabbed my own throat with the small sword, I threw myself into a pond at the foot of the mountain, and I tried to kill myself in many ways. Unable to end my life, I am still living in dishonor. (A lonely smile.) Worthless as I am, I must have been forsaken even by the most merciful Kwannon.[2] I killed my own husband. I was violated by the robber. Whatever can I do? Whatever can I . . . I . . . (Gradually, violent sobbing.)

The Story of the Murdered Man, as Told
——— Through a Medium ———

After violating my wife, the robber, sitting there, began to speak comforting words to her. Of course I couldn't speak. My whole body was tied fast to the root of a cedar. But meanwhile I winked at her many times, as much as to say, "Don't believe the robber." I wanted to convey some such meaning to her. But my wife, sitting dejectedly on the bamboo leaves, was staring at her lap. To all appearances, she was listening to his words. I was racked with

---

[2]Kwannon: Japanese goddess of mercy.

jealousy. In the meantime the robber went on with his clever talk, from one subject to another. The robber finally made his brazen proposal. "Once your virtue is stained, you won't get along well with your husband, so won't you be my wife instead? It's my love for you that made me violent toward you."

While the criminal talked, my wife raised her face as if in a trance. She had never looked so beautiful as at that moment. What did my beautiful wife say in answer to him while I was sitting bound there? I am lost in space, but I have never thought of her answer without burning with anger and jealousy. Truly she said, "Then take me away with you wherever you go."

This is not the whole of her sin. If that were all, I would not be tormented so much in the dark. When she was leaving the grove as if in a dream, her hand in the robber's, she suddenly turned pale, and pointed at me tied to the root of the cedar, and said, "Kill him! I cannot marry you as long as he lives." "Kill him!" she cried many times, as if she had gone crazy. Even now these words threaten to blow me headlong into the bottomless abyss of darkness. Has such a hateful thing come out of a human mouth ever before? Have such cursed words ever struck a human ear, even once? Even once such a . . . (A sudden cry of scorn.) At these words the robber himself turned pale. "Kill him!" she cried, clinging to his arms. Looking hard at her, he answered neither yes nor no. . . . But hardly had I thought about his answer before she had been knocked down into the bamboo leaves. (Again a cry of scorn.) Quietly folding his arm, he looked at me and said, "What would you like done with her? Kill her or save her? You have only to nod. Kill her?" For these words alone I would like to pardon his crime.

While I hesitated, she shrieked and ran into the depths of the grove. The robber instantly snatched at her, but he failed even to grasp her sleeve.

After she ran away, he took up my sword, and my bow and arrows. With a single stroke he cut one of my bonds. I remember his mumbling, "My fate is next." Then he disappeared from the grove. All was silent after that. No, I heard someone crying. Untying the rest of my bonds, I listened carefully, and noticed that it was my own crying. (Long silence.)

I raised my exhausted body from the root of the cedar. In front of me there was shining the small sword which my wife had dropped. I took it up and stabbed it into my breast. A bloody lump rose to my mouth, but I felt no pain. When my breast grew cold, everything was as silent as the dead in their graves. What profound silence! Not a single bird note was heard in the sky over this grave in the hollow of the mountains. Only a lonely light lingered on the cedars and the mountain. The light gradually grew fainter, till the cedars and bamboo were lost to view. Lying there, I was enveloped in deep silence.

Then someone crept up to me. I tried to see who it was. But darkness had already been gathering round me. Someone . . . that someone drew the small sword softly out of my breast in its invisible hand. At the same time blood again flowed into my mouth. And once and for all I sank down into the darkness of space.

Questions for "In a Grove"

1.   This story is presented simply as a series of testimonies with no authorial intrusion. Why do you think Akutagawa chose to tell the story in this way?

2.   What details in the first four testimonies would seem to implicate Tajomaru? Make a list, separating facts, inferences, and opinions, in each of these witnesses' statements.

3.   What discrepancies do you observe among the testimonies?

4.   Which of the three confessions do you find most credible? Carefully consider the question of motivation in each case—what reasons does each confessor present for the killing? What in each of the various narrators may distort his or her account of the crime? What do these narrators unwittingly reveal about themselves?

5.   Review the order in which the seven testimonies are presented. How would the meaning and impact of the story change if these testimonies were rearranged? Pay particular attention to the order of the three confessions. Why do you think Akutagawa placed the story of the murdered man last?

6.   What happens at the end of the last account, when the knife is drawn out? Who withdraws it, and why?

Flannery O'Connor (1925–1964)

A native of Savannah, Georgia, Flannery O'Connor was educated at the Women's College of Georgia, and won a fellowship to the Writer's Workshop of the State University of Iowa, where she earned a master's degree. Among her works are two novels, *Wise Blood* (1952) and *The Violent Bear It Away* (1960), and two collections of short stories, *A Good Man Is Hard to Find* (1955) and *Everything That Rises Must Converge* (1965).

After receiving her degree, O'Connor came to New York to pursue her writing career, but the onset of systemic lupus, a progressive disorder of the auto-immune system, brought her back to her mother's farm in Georgia two years later. She died at the age of thirty-nine, but her extraordinary talent earned her critical recognition and awards, including three O'Henry prizes and, posthumously, the National Book Award for *The Complete Stories* in 1980.

O'Connor was a fiercely religious Catholic who created violent and grotesque characters because, she said, "man has in his soul a powerful destructive element, which often makes him behave in a violent and grotesque manner." As one critic observes, O'Connor "wrote about what she knew best: what it means to be a living contradiction. For her it meant an eternal cheeriness and loathing for life; graciousness and fear of human contact; acquiescence and enduring fury."

A Good Man Is Hard to Find

The grandmother didn't want to go to Florida. She wanted to visit some of her connections in east Tennessee and she was seizing at every chance to change Bailey's mind. Bailey was the son she lived with, her only boy. He was sitting on the edge of his chair at the table, bent over the orange sports section of the *Journal*. "Now look here, Bailey," she said, "see here, read this," and she stood with one hand on her thin hip and the other rattling the newspaper at his bald head. "Here this fellow that calls himself The Misfit is aloose from the Federal Pen and headed toward Florida and you read here what it says he did to these people. Just you read it. I wouldn't take my children in any direction with a criminal like that aloose in it. I couldn't answer to my conscience if I did."

Bailey didn't look up from his reading so she wheeled around then and faced the children's mother, a young woman in slacks, whose face was as broad and innocent as a cabbage and was tied round with a green head-kerchief that had two points on the top like rabbit's ears. She was sitting on the sofa, feeding the baby his apricots out of a jar. "The children have been to Florida before," the old lady said. "You all ought to take them somewhere else for a change so they would see different parts of the world and be broad. They never have been to east Tennessee."

The children's mother didn't seem to hear her but the eight-year-old boy, John Wesley, a stocky child with glasses, said, "If you don't want to go to Florida, why dontcha stay at home?" He and the little girl, June Star, were reading the funny papers on the floor.

"She wouldn't stay at home to be queen for a day," June Star said without raising her yellow head.

"Yes, and what would you do if this fellow, The Misfit, caught you?" the grandmother asked.

"I'd smack his face," John Wesley said.

"She wouldn't stay at home for a million bucks," June Star said. "Afraid she'd miss something. She has to go everywhere we go."

"All right, Miss," the grandmother said. "Just remember that the next time you want me to curl your hair."

June Star said her hair was naturally curly.

The next morning the grandmother was the first one in the car, ready to go. She had her big black valise that looked like the head of a hippopotamus in one corner, and underneath it she was hiding a basket with Pitty Sing, the cat, in it. She didn't intend for the cat to be left alone in the house for three days because he would miss her too much and she was afraid he might brush against one of the gas burners and accidentally asphyxiate himself. Her son, Bailey, didn't like to arrive at a motel with a cat.

She sat in the middle of the back seat with John Wesley and June Star on either side of her. Bailey and the children's mother and the baby sat in front and they left Atlanta at eight forty-five with the mileage on the car at 55890. The grandmother wrote this down because she thought it would be interesting to say how many miles they had been when they got back. It took them twenty minutes to reach the outskirts of the city.

The old lady settled herself comfortably, removing her white cotton gloves and putting them up with her purse on the shelf in front of the back window. The children's mother still had on slacks and still had her head tied up in a green kerchief, but the grandmother had on a navy blue straw sailor hat with a bunch of white violets on the brim and a navy blue dress with a small white dot in the print. Her collars and cuffs were white organdy trimmed with lace and at her neckline she had pinned a purple spray of cloth violets containing a sachet. In case of an accident, anyone seeing her dead on the highway would know at once that she was a lady.

She said she thought it was going to be a good day for driving, neither too hot nor too cold, and she cautioned Bailey that the speed limit was fifty-five miles an hour and that the patrolmen hid themselves behind billboards and small clumps of trees and sped out after you before you had a chance to slow down. She pointed out interesting details of the scenery: Stone Mountain; the blue granite that in some places came up to both sides of the highway; the brilliant red clay banks slightly streaked with purple; and the various crops that made rows of green lacework on the ground. The trees were full of silver-white sunlight and the meanest of them sparkled. The children were reading comic magazines and their mother had gone back to sleep.

"Let's go through Georgia fast so we won't have to look at it much," John Wesley said.

"If I were a little boy," said the grandmother, "I wouldn't talk about my native state that way. Tennessee has the mountains and Georgia has the hills."

"Tennessee is just a hillbilly dumping ground," John Wesley said, "and Georgia is a lousy state too."

"You said it," June Star said.

"In my time," said the grandmother, folding her thin veined fingers, "children were more respectful of their native states and their parents and everything else. People did right then. Oh look at the cute little pickaninny!" she said and pointed to a Negro child standing in the door of a shack. "Wouldn't that make a picture, now?" she asked and they all turned and looked at the little Negro out of the back window. He waved.

"He didn't have any britches on," June Star said.

"He probably didn't have any," the grandmother explained. "Little niggers in the country don't have things like we do. If I could paint, I'd paint that picture," she said.

The children exchanged comic books.

The grandmother offered to hold the baby and the children's mother passed him over the front seat to her. She set him on her knee and bounced him and told him about the things they were passing. She rolled her eyes and screwed up her mouth and stuck her leathery thin face into his smooth bland one. Occasionally he gave her a faraway smile. They passed a large cotton field with five or six graves fenced in the middle of it, like a small island. "Look at the graveyard!" the grandmother said, pointing it out. "That was the old family burying ground. That belonged to the plantation."

"Where's the plantation?" John Wesley asked.

"Gone With the Wind," said the grandmother. "Ha. Ha."

When the children finished all the comic books they had brought, they opened the lunch and ate it. The grandmother ate a peanut butter sandwich and an olive and would not let the children throw the box and the paper napkins out the window. When there was nothing else to do they played a game by choosing a cloud and making the other two guess what shape it suggested. John Wesley took one the shape of a cow and June Star guessed a cow and John Wesley said, no, an automobile, and June Star said he didn't play fair, and they began to slap each other over the grandmother.

The grandmother said she would tell them a story if they would keep quiet. When she told a story, she rolled her eyes and waved her head and was very dramatic. She said once when she was a maiden lady she had been courted by a Mr. Edgar Atkins Teagarden from Jasper, Georgia. She said he was a very good-looking man and a gentleman and that he brought her a watermelon every Saturday afternoon with his initials cut in it, E.A.T. Well, one Saturday, she said, Mr. Teagarden brought the watermelon and there was nobody at home and he left it on the front porch and returned to his buggy to Jasper, but she never got the watermelon, she said, because a nigger boy ate it when he saw the initials, E.A.T.! This story tickled John Wesley's funny bone and he giggled and giggled but June Star didn't think it was any good. She said she wouldn't marry a man that just brought her a watermelon on Saturday. The grandmother said she would have done well to marry Mr. Teagarden because he was a gentleman and had bought Coca-Cola stock when it first came out and that he had died only a few years ago, a very wealthy man.

They stopped at The Tower for barbecued sandwiches. The Tower was a part stucco and part wood filling station and dance hall set in a clearing outside of Timothy. A fat man named Red Sammy Butts ran it and there were signs stuck here and there on the building and for miles up and down the highway saying, TRY RED SAMMY'S FAMOUS BARBEQUE. NONE LIKE FAMOUS RED SAMMY'S! RED SAM! THE FAT BOY WITH THE HAPPY LAUGH. A VETERAN! RED SAMMY'S YOUR MAN!

Red Sammy was lying on the bare ground outside The Tower with his head under a truck while a gray monkey about a foot high, chained to a small chinaberry tree, chattered nearby. The monkey sprang back into the tree and got on the highest limb as soon as he saw the children jump out of the car and run toward him.

Inside, The Tower was a long dark room with a counter at one end and tables at the other and dancing space in the middle. They all sat down at a board table next to the nickelodeon and Red Sam's wife, a tall burnt-brown woman with hair and eyes lighter than her skin, came and took their order. The children's mother put a dime in the machine and played "The Tennessee Waltz," and the grandmother said that tune always made her want to dance. She asked Bailey if he would like to dance but he only glared at her. He didn't have a naturally sunny disposition like she did and trips made him nervous. The grandmother's brown eyes were very bright. She swayed her head from side to side and pretended she was dancing in her chair. June Star said play something she could tap to so the children's mother put in another dime and played a fast number and June Star stepped out onto the dance floor and did her tap routine.

"Ain't she cute?" Red Sam's wife said, leaning over the counter. "Would you like to come be my little girl?"

"No I certainly wouldn't," June Star said. "I wouldn't live in a broken-down place like this for a million bucks!" and she ran back to the table.

"Ain't she cute?" the woman repeated, stretching her mouth politely.

"Aren't you ashamed?" hissed the grandmother.

Red Sam came in and told his wife to quit lounging on the counter and hurry with these people's order. His khaki trousers reached just to his hip bones and his stomach hung over them like a sack of meal swaying under his shirt. He came over and sat down at a table nearby and let out a combination sigh and yodel. "You can't win," he said. "You can't win," and he wiped his sweating red face off with a gray handkerchief. "These days you don't know who to trust," he said. "Ain't that the truth?"

"People are certainly not nice like they used to be," said the grandmother.

"Two fellers come in here last week," Red Sammy said, "driving a Chrysler. It was a old beat-up car but it was a good one and these boys looked all right to me. Said they worked at the mill and you know I let them fellers charge the gas they bought? Now why did I do that?"

"Because you're a good man!" the grandmother said at once.

"Yes'm, I suppose so," Red Sam said as if he were struck with the answer.

His wife brought the orders, carrying the five plates all at once without a tray, two in each hand and one balanced on her arm. "It isn't a soul in this green world of God's that you can trust," she said. "And I don't count nobody out of that, not nobody," she repeated, looking at Red Sammy.

"Did you read about that criminal, The Misfit, that's escaped?" asked the grandmother.

"I wouldn't be a bit surprised if he didn't attack this place right here," said the woman. "If he hears about it being here, I wouldn't be none surprised to see him. If he hears it's two cent in the cash register, I wouldn't be a tall surprised if he . . . "

"That'll do," Red Sam said. "Go bring these people their Co'Colas," and the woman went off to get the rest of the order.

"A good man is hard to find," Red Sammy said. "Everything is getting terrible. I remember the day you could go off and leave your screen door unlatched. Not no more."

He and the grandmother discussed better times. The old lady said that in her opinion Europe was entirely to blame for the way things were now. She said the way Europe acted you would think we were made of money and Red Sam said it was no use talking about it, she was exactly right. The children ran outside into the white sunlight and looked at the monkey in the lacy chinaberry tree. He was busy catching fleas on himself and biting each one carefully between his teeth as if it were a delicacy.

They drove off again into the hot afternoon. The grandmother took cat naps and woke up every few minutes with her own snoring. Outside of Toomsboro she woke up and recalled an old plantation that she had visited in this neighborhood once when she was a young lady. She said the house had six white columns across the front and that there was an avenue of oaks leading up to it and two little wooden trellis arbors on either side in front where you sat down with your suitor after a stroll in the garden. She recalled exactly which road to turn off to get to it. She knew that Bailey would not be willing to lose any time looking at an old house, but the more she talked about it, the more she wanted to see it once again and find out if the little twin arbors were still standing. "There was a secret panel in this house," she said craftily, not telling the truth but wishing that she were, "and the story went that all the family silver was hidden in it when Sherman came through but it was never found . . . "

"Hey!" John Wesley said. "Let's go see it! We'll find it! We'll poke all the woodwork and find it! Who lives there? Where do you turn off at? Hey Pop, can't we turn off there?"

"We never have seen a house with a secret panel!" June Star shrieked. "Let's go to the house with the secret panel! Hey Pop, can't we go see the house with the secret panel!"

"It's not far from here, I know," the grandmother said. "It wouldn't take over twenty minutes."

Bailey was looking straight ahead. His jaw was as rigid as a horseshoe. "No," he said.

The children began to yell and scream that they wanted to see the house with the secret panel. John Wesley kicked the back of the front seat and June Star hung over her mother's shoulder and whined desperately into her ear that they never had any fun even on their vacation, that they could never do what THEY wanted to do. The baby began to scream and John Wesley kicked the back of the seat so hard that his father could feel the blows in his kidney.

"All right!" he shouted and drew the car to a stop at the side of the road. "Will you all shut up? Will you all just shut up for one second? If you don't shut up, we won't go anywhere."

"It would be very educational for them," the grandmother murmured.

"All right," Bailey said, "but get this: this is the only time we're going to stop for anything like this. This is the one and only time."

"The dirt road that you have to turn down is about a mile back," the grandmother directed. "I marked it when we passed."

"A dirt road," Bailey groaned.

After they had turned around and were headed toward the dirt road, the grandmother recalled other points about the house, the beautiful glass over the front doorway and the candle-lamp in the hall. John Wesley said that the secret panel was probably in the fireplace.

"You can't go inside this house," Bailey said. "You don't know who lives there."

"While you all talk to the people in front, I'll run around behind and get in a window," John Wesley suggested.

"We'll all stay in the car," his mother said.

They turned onto the dirt road and the car raced roughly along in a swirl of pink dust. The grandmother recalled the times when there were no paved roads and thirty miles was a day's journey. The dirt road was hilly and there were sudden washes in it and sharp curves on dangerous embankments. All at once they would be on a hill, looking down over the blue tops of trees for miles around, then the next minute, they would be in a red depression with the dust-coated trees looking down on them.

"This place had better turn up in a minute," Bailey said, "or I'm going to turn around."

The road looked as if no one had traveled on it in months.

"It's not much farther," the grandmother said and just as she said it, a horrible thought came to her. The thought was so embarrassing that she turned red in the face and her eyes dilated and her feet jumped up, upsetting her valise in the corner. The instant the valise moved, the newspaper top she had over the basket under it rose with a snarl and Pitty Sing, the cat, sprang onto Bailey's shoulder.

The children were thrown to the floor and their mother, clutching the baby, was thrown out the door onto the ground; the old lady was thrown into the front seat. The car turned over once and landed right-side-up in a gulch on the side of the road. Bailey remained in the driver's seat with the cat—gray-striped with a broad white face and an orange nose—clinging to his neck like a caterpillar.

As soon as the children saw they could move their arms and legs, they scrambled out of the car, shouting, "We've had an ACCIDENT!" The grandmother was curled up under the dashboard, hoping she was injured so that Bailey's wrath would not come down on her all at once. The horrible thought she had had before the accident was that the house she had remembered so vividly was not in Georgia but in Tennessee.

Bailey removed the cat from his neck with both hands and flung it out the window against the side of a pine tree. Then he got out of the car and started looking for the children's mother. She was sitting against the side of the red gutted ditch, holding the screaming baby, but she only had a cut down her face and a broken shoulder. "We've had an ACCIDENT!" the children screamed in a frenzy of delight.

"But nobody's killed," June Star said with disappointment as the grandmother limped out of the car, her hat still pinned to her head but the broken front brim standing up at a jaunty angle and the violet spray hanging off the side. They all sat down in the ditch, except the children, to recover from the shock. They were all shaking.

"Maybe a car will come along," said the children's mother hoarsely.

"I believe I have an injured organ," said the grandmother, pressing her side, but no one answered her. Bailey's teeth were clattering. He had on a yellow sport shirt with bright blue parrots designed on it and his face was as yellow as the shirt. The grandmother decided that she would not mention that the house was in Tennessee.

The road was about ten feet above and they could see only the tops of the trees on the other side of it. Behind the ditch they were sitting in there were more woods, tall and dark and deep. In a few minutes they saw a car some distance away on top of a hill, coming slowly as if the occupants were watching them. The grandmother stood up and waved both arms dramatically to attract their attention. The car continued to come on slowly, disappeared around a bend and appeared again, moving even slower, on top of the hill they had gone over. It was a big black battered hearse-like automobile. There were three men in it.

It came to a stop just over them and for some minutes, the driver looked down with a steady expressionless gaze to where they were sitting, and didn't speak. Then he turned his head and muttered something to the other two and they got out. One was a fat boy in black trousers and a red sweat shirt with a silver stallion embossed on the front of it. He moved around on the right side of them and stood staring, his mouth partly open in a kind of loose grin. The other had on khaki pants and a blue striped coat and a gray hat pulled down very low, hiding most of his face. He came around slowly on the left side. Neither spoke.

The driver got out of the car and stood by the side of it, looking down at them. He was an older man than the other two. His hair was just beginning to gray and he wore silver-rimmed spectacles that gave him a scholarly look. He had a long creased face and didn't have on any shirt or undershirt. He had on blue jeans that were too tight for him and was holding a black hat and a gun. The two boys also had guns.

"We've had an ACCIDENT!" the children screamed.

The grandmother had the peculiar feeling that the bespectacled man was someone she knew. His face was as familiar to her as if she had known him all her life but she could not recall who he was. He moved away from the car and began to come down the embankment, placing his feet carefully so that he wouldn't slip. He had on tan and white shoes and no socks, and his ankles were red and thin. "Good afternoon," he said. "I see you all had you a little spill."

"We turned over twice!" said the grandmother.

"Oncet," he corrected. "We seen it happen. Try their car and see will it run, Hiram," he said quietly to the boy with the gray hat.

"What you got that gun for?" John Wesley asked. "Whatcha gonna do with that gun?"

"Lady," the man said to the children's mother, "would you mind calling them children to sit down by you? Children make me nervous. I want all you to sit down right together there where you're at."

"What are you telling US what to do for?" June Star asked.

Behind them the line of woods gaped like a dark open mouth. "Come here," said their mother. *swallows them*

"Look here now," Bailey began suddenly, "we're in a predicament! We're in . . ."

her big mouth — knows too much

The grandmother shrieked. She scrambled to her feet and stood staring. "You're The Misfit!" she said. "I recognized you at once!"

"Yes'm," the man said, smiling slightly as if he were pleased in spite of himself to be known, "but it would have been better for all of you, lady, if you hadn't of reckernized me."

Bailey turned his head sharply and said something to his mother that shocked even the children. The old lady began to cry and The Misfit reddened.

"Lady," he said, "don't you get upset. Sometimes a man says things he don't mean. I don't reckon he meant to talk to you thataway."

"You wouldn't shoot a lady, would you?" the grandmother said and removed a clean handkerchief from her cuff and began to slap at her eyes with it.

The Misfit pointed the toe of his shoe into the ground and made a little hole and then covered it up again. "I would hate to have to," he said.

"Listen," the grandmother almost screamed, "I know you're a good man. You don't look a bit like you have common blood. I know you must come from nice people!"

"Yes mam," he said, "finest people in the world." When he smiled he showed a row of strong white teeth. "God never made a finer woman than my mother and my daddy's heart was pure gold," he said. The boy with the red sweat shirt had come around behind them and was standing with his gun at his hip. The Misfit squatted down on the ground. "Watch them children, Bobby Lee," he said. "You know they make me nervous." He looked at the six of them huddled together in front of him and he seemed to be embarrassed as if he couldn't think of anything to say. "Ain't a cloud in the sky," he remarked, looking up at it. "Don't see no sun but don't see no cloud neither."

"Yes, it's a beautiful day," said the grandmother. "Listen," she said, "you shouldn't call yourself The Misfit because I know you're a good man at heart. I can just look at you and tell."

"Hush!" Bailey yelled. "Hush! Everybody shut up and let me handle this!" He was squatting in the position of a runner about to sprint forward but he didn't move.

"I pre-chate that, lady," The Misfit said and drew a little circle in the ground with the butt of his gun.

"It'll take a half a hour to fix this here car," Hiram called, looking over the raised hood of it.

"Well, first you and Bobby Lee get him and that little boy to step over yonder with you," The Misfit said, pointing to Bailey and John Wesley. "The boys want to ask you something," he said to Bailey. "Would you mind stepping back in them woods there with them?"

"Listen," Bailey began, "we're in a terrible predicament! Nobody realizes what this is," and his voice cracked. His eyes were as blue and intense as the parrots on his shirt and he remained perfectly still.

The grandmother reached up to adjust her hat brim as if she were going to the woods with him but it came off in her hand. She stood staring at it and after a second she let it fall on the ground. Hiram pulled Bailey up by the arm as if he were assisting an old man. John Wesley caught hold of his father's hand and Bobby Lee followed. They went off toward the woods and just as they reached the dark edge, Bailey turned and supporting himself against a gray naked pine trunk, he shouted, "I'll be back in a minute, Mamma, wait on me!"

"Come back this instant!" his mother shrilled but they all disappeared into the woods.

"Bailey Boy!" the grandmother called in a tragic voice but she found she was looking at The Misfit squatting on the ground in front of her. "I just know you're a good man," she said desperately. "You're not a bit common!"

"Nome, I ain't a good man," The Misfit said after a second as if he had considered her statement carefully, "but I ain't the worst in the world neither. My daddy said I was different breed of dog from my brothers and sisters. 'You know,' Daddy said, 'it's some that can live their whole life out without asking about it and it's others has to know why it is, and this boy is one of the latters. He's going to be into everything!' " He put on his black hat and looked up suddenly and then away deep into the woods as if he were embarrassed again. "I'm sorry I don't have on a shirt before you ladies," he said, hunching his shoulders slightly. "We buried our clothes that we had on when we escaped and we're just making do until we can get better. We borrowed these from some folks we met," he explained.

"That's perfectly all right," the grandmother said. "Maybe Bailey has an extra shirt in his suitcase."

"I'll look and see terrectly," The Misfit said.

"Where are they taking him?" the children's mother screamed.

"Daddy was a card himself," The Misfit said. "You couldn't put anything over on him. He never got in trouble with the Authorities though. Just had the knack of handling them."

"You could be honest too if you'd only try," said the grandmother. "Think how wonderful it would be to settle down and live a comfortable life and not have to think about somebody chasing you all the time."

The Misfit kept scratching in the ground with the butt of his gun as if he were thinking about it. "Yes'm, somebody is always after you," he murmured.

The grandmother noticed how thin his shoulder blades were just behind his hat because she was standing up looking down on him. "Do you ever pray?" she asked.

He shook his head. All she saw was the black hat wiggle between his shoulder blades. "Nome," he said.

There was a pistol shot from the woods, followed closely by another. Then silence. The old lady's head jerked around. She could hear the wind move through the tree tops like a long satisfied insuck of breath. "Bailey Boy!" she called.

"I was a gospel singer for a while," The Misfit said. "I been most everything. Been in the arm service, both land and sea, at home and abroad, been twict married, been an undertaker, been with the railroads, plowed Mother Earth, been in a tornado, seen a man burnt alive oncet," and he looked up at the children's mother and the little girl who were sitting close together, their faces white and their eyes glassy; "I even seen a woman flogged," he said.

"Pray, pray," the grandmother began, "pray, pray . . . "

"I never was a bad boy that I remember of," The Misfit said in an almost dreamy voice, "but somewheres along the line I done something wrong and got sent to the penitentiary. I was buried alive," and he looked up and held her attention to him by a steady stare.

"That's when you should have started to pray," she said. "What did you do to get sent to the penitentiary that first time?"

"Turn to the right, it was a wall," The Misfit said, looking up again at the cloudless sky. "Turn to the left, it was a wall. Look up it was a ceiling, look down it was a floor. I forgot what I done, lady. I set there and set there, trying to remember what it was I done and I ain't recalled it to this day. Oncet in a while, I would think it was coming to me, but it never come."

"Maybe they put you in by mistake," the old lady said vaguely.

"Nome," he said. "It wasn't no mistake. They had the papers on me."

"You must have stolen something," she said.

The Misfit sneered slightly. "Nobody had nothing I wanted," he said. "It was a head-doctor at the penitentiary said what I had done was kill my daddy but I known that for a lie. My daddy died in nineteen ought nineteen of the epidemic flu and I never had a thing to do with it. He was buried in the Mount Hopewell Baptist churchyard and you can go there and see for yourself."

"If you would pray," the old lady said, "Jesus would help you."

"That's right," The Misfit said.

"Well then, why don't you pray?" she asked trembling with delight suddenly.

"I don't want no help," he said. "I'm doing all right by myself."

Bobby Lee and Hiram came ambling back from the woods. Bobby Lee was dragging a yellow shirt with bright blue parrots in it.

"Throw me that shirt, Bobby Lee," The Misfit said. The shirt came flying at him and landed on his shoulder and he put it on. The grandmother couldn't name what the shirt reminded her of. "No, lady," The Misfit said while he was buttoning it up, "I found out the crime don't matter. You can do one thing or you can do another, kill a man or take a tire off his car, because sooner or later you're going to forget what it was you done and just be punished for it."

The children's mother had begun to making heaving noises as if she couldn't get her breath. "Lady," he asked, "would you and that little girl like to step off yonder with Bobby Lee and Hiram and join your husband?"

"Yes, thank you," the mother said faintly. Her left arm dangled helplessly and she was holding the baby, who had gone to sleep, in the other. "Hep that lady up, Hiram," The Misfit said as she struggled to climb out of the ditch, "and Bobby Lee, you hold onto that little girl's hand."

"I don't want to hold hands with him," June Star said. "He reminds me of a pig."

The fat boy blushed and laughed and caught her by the arm and pulled her off into the woods after Hiram and her mother.

Alone with The Misfit, the grandmother found that she had lost her voice. There was not a cloud in the sky nor any sun. There was nothing around her but woods. She wanted to tell him that he must pray. She opened and closed her mouth several times before anything came out. Finally she found herself saying, "Jesus, Jesus," meaning Jesus will help you, but the way she was saying it, it sounded as if she might be cursing.

"Yes'm," The Misfit said as if he agreed. "Jesus thown everything off balance. It was the same case with Him as with me except He hadn't committed any crime and they could prove I had committed one because they had the papers on me. Of course," he said, "they never shown me my papers. That's why I sign myself now. I said long ago, you get you a signature and sign everything you do and keep a copy of it. Then you'll know what you done and you can hold up the crime to the punishment and see do they match and in the end you'll have something to prove you ain't been treated right. I call myself The Misfit," he said, "because I can't make what all I done wrong fit what all I gone through in punishment."

There was a piercing scream from the woods, followed closely by a pistol report. "Does it seem right to you, lady, that one is punished a heap and another ain't punished at all?"

"Jesus!" the old lady cried. "You've got good blood! I know you wouldn't shoot a lady! I know you come from nice people! Pray! Jesus, you ought not to shoot a lady. I'll give you all the money I've got!"

"Lady," The Misfit said, looking beyond her far into the woods, "there never was a body that give the undertaker a tip."

There were two more pistol reports and the grandmother raised her head like a parched old turkey hen crying for water and called, "Bailey Boy, Bailey Boy!" as if her heart would break.

"Jesus was the only One that ever raised the dead," The Misfit continued, "and He shouldn't have done it. He thown everything off balance. If He did what He said, then it's nothing for you to do but throw away everything and follow Him, and if He didn't, then it's nothing for you to do but enjoy the few minutes you got left the best way you can—by killing somebody or burning down his house or doing some other meanness to him. No pleasure but meanness," he said and his voice had become almost a snarl.

"Maybe He didn't raise the dead," the old lady mumbled, not knowing what she was saying and feeling so dizzy that she sank down in the ditch with her legs twisted under her.

"I wasn't there so I can't say He didn't," The Misfit said. "I wisht I had of been there," he said, hitting the ground with his fist. "It ain't right I wasn't there because if I had of been there I would of known. Listen lady," he said in a high voice, "if I had of been there I would of known and I wouldn't be like I am now." His voice seemed about to crack and the grandmother's head cleared for an instant. She saw the man's face twisted close to her own as if he were going to cry and she murmured, "Why you're one of my babies. You're one of my own children!" She reached out and touched him on the shoulder. The Misfit sprang back as if a snake had bitten him and shot her three times through the chest. Then he put his gun down on the ground and took off his glasses and began to clean them.

Hiram and Bobby Lee returned from the woods and stood over the ditch, looking down at the grandmother who half sat and half lay in a puddle of blood with her legs crossed under her like a child's and her face smiling up at the cloudless sky.

Without his glasses, The Misfit's eyes were red-rimmed and pale and defenseless-looking. "Take her off and thow her where you thown the others," he said, picking up the cat that was rubbing itself against his leg.

"She was a talker, wasn't she?" Bobby Lee said, sliding down the ditch with a yodel.

"She would of been a good woman," The Misfit said, "if it had been somebody there to shoot her every minute of her life."

"Some fun!" Bobby Lee said.

"Shut up, Bobby Lee," The Misfit said. "It's no real pleasure in life."

Questions for "A Good Man Is Hard to Find"

1.   What similarities can you point to in the conversations that the grandmother has with Red Sammy and with The Misfit?

2.   As we pointed out in the introduction to this chapter, this story reverberates with ironies. What, for example, is ironic about the grandmother sneaking her cat along for the trip? About her reasons for doing so? How many other ironies do you notice?

3.   The climactic moments in O'Connor's fiction have been described as "those moments when her characters undergo a traumatic collapse of their illusions of righteousness and self-sufficiency." How can you apply this comment to the final pages of "A Good Man Is Hard to Find"?

4.   What is the prevailing mood of this story? How does that mood differ from the tone of the narration?

5.   Describe your reaction to the final events of this story. Can you explain why you felt this way?

6.   Look back at the paragraph on page 255 in which The Misfit says, "Jesus was the only one that ever raised the dead." What does he mean by the comments that follow? How does this paragraph shed light on his behavior?

Bernard Malamud (1914–1986)

Raised in Brooklyn and educated at City College of New York and Columbia University, Bernard Malamud taught English at Oregon State University, Bennington College, and Harvard University. Malamud's first novel, *The Natural*, appeared in 1952; *The Assistant* (1957) won the Rosenthal award in 1958, and both *The Magic Barrel* (a collection of stories, 1958) and *The Fixer* (1966) received National Book Awards and Pulitzer Prizes for literature.

In Malamud's work, which often deals with Jewish themes and characters, dreams and fantasies merge with the real world. Although Malamud's characters are outsiders—unhappy, unloved tenants in a grim universe—none is beyond redemption, and it is most often love that redeems them. Indeed, as one critic has remarked, "Love is the redemptive grace in Malamud's fiction, its highest good. The defeat of love is tragedy. Love rejected, love misplaced, love betrayed, loveless lust: these are the main evils. . . . " Malamud once described himself as a chronicler of "simple people struggling to make their lives better in a world of bad luck." According to Malamud, "Life is a tragedy full of joy."

The Magic Barrel

Not long ago there lived in uptown New York, in a small, almost meager room, though crowded with books, Leo Finkle, a rabbinical student in the Yeshivah University. Finkle, after six years of study, was to be ordained in June and had been advised by an acquaintance that he might find it easier to win himself a congregation if he were married. Since he had no present prospects of marriage, after two tormented days of turning it over in his mind, he called in Pinye Salzman, a marriage broker whose two-line advertisement he had read in the *Forward*.

The matchmaker appeared one night out of the dark fourth-floor hallway of the graystone rooming house where Finkle lived, grasping a black, strapped portfolio that had been worn thin with use. Salzman, who had been long in the business, was of slight but dignified build, wearing an old hat, and an overcoat too short and tight for him. He smelled frankly of fish, which he loved to eat, and although he was missing a few teeth, his presence was not displeasing, because of an amiable manner curiously contrasted with mournful eyes. His voice, his lips, his wisp of beard, his bony fingers were animated, but give him a moment of repose and his mild blue eyes revealed a depth of sadness, a characteristic that put Leo a little at ease although the situation, for him, was inherently tense.

He at once informed Salzman why he had asked him to come, explaining that his home was in Cleveland, and that but for his parents, who had married comparatively late in life, he was alone in the world. He had for six years devoted himself almost entirely to his studies, as a result of which, understandably, he had found himself without time for a social life and the company of young women. Therefore he thought it the better part of trial and error—of embarrassing fumbling—to call in an experienced person to advise him on these matters. He remarked in passing that the function of the marriage broker was ancient and honorable, highly approved in the Jewish community, because it made practical the necessary without hindering joy. Moreover, his own parents had been brought together by a matchmaker. They had made, if not a financially profitable marriage—since neither had possessed any worldly goods to speak of—at least a successful one in the sense of their everlasting devotion to each other. Salzman listened in embarrassed surprise, sensing a sort of apology. Later, however, he experienced a glow of pride in his work, an emotion that had left him years ago, and he heartily approved of Finkle.

The two went to their business. Leo had led Salzman to the only clear place in the room, a table near a window that overlooked the lamp-lit city. He seated himself at the matchmaker's side but facing him, attempting by an act of will to suppress the unpleasant tickle in his throat. Salzman eagerly unstrapped his portfolio and removed a loose rubber band from a thin packet of much-handled cards. As he flipped through them, a gesture and sound that physically hurt Leo, the student pretended not to see and gazed steadfastly out the window. Although it was still February, winter was on its last legs, signs of which he had for the first time in years begun to notice. He now observed the round white moon, moving high in the sky through a cloud menagerie, and watched with half-open mouth as it penetrated a huge hen, and dropped out of her like an egg laying itself. Salzman, though pretending through eyeglasses he had just slipped on, to be engaged in scanning the writing on the cards, stole occasional glances at the young man's distinguished face, noting with pleasure the long, severe scholar's nose, brown eyes heavy with learning, sensitive yet ascetic lips, and a certain, almost hollow quality of the dark cheeks. He gazed around at shelves upon shelves of books and let out a soft, contented sigh.

When Leo's eyes fell upon the cards, he counted six spread out in Salzman's hand.

"So few?" he asked in disappointment.

"You wouldn't believe me how much cards I got in my office," Salzman replied. "The drawers are already filled to the top, so I keep them now in a barrel, but is every girl good for a new rabbi?"

Leo blushed at this, regretting all he had revealed of himself in a curriculum vitae he had sent to Salzman. He had thought it best to acquaint him with his strict standards and specifications, but in having done so, felt he had told the marriage broker more than was absolutely necessary.

He hesitantly inquired, "Do you keep photographs of your clients on file?"

"First comes family, amount of dowry, also what kind promises," Salzman replied, unbuttoning his tight coat and settling himself in the chair. "After comes pictures, rabbi."

"Call me Mr. Finkle. I'm not yet a rabbi."

Salzman said he would, but instead called him doctor, which he changed to rabbi when Leo was not listening too attentively.

Salzman adjusted his horn-rimmed spectacles, gently cleared his throat and read in an eager voice the contents of the top card:

"Sophie P. Twenty four years. Widow one year. No children. Educated high school and two years college. Father promises eight thousand dollars. Has wonderful wholesale business. Also real estate. On the mother's side comes teachers, also one actor. Well known on Second Avenue."

Leo gazed up in surprise. "Did you say a widow?"

"A widow don't mean spoiled, rabbi. She lived with her husband maybe four months. He was a sick boy she made a mistake to marry him."

"Marrying a widow has never entered my mind."

"This is because you have no experience. A widow, especially if she is young and healthy like this girl, is a wonderful person to marry. She will be thankful to you the rest of her life. Believe me, if I was looking now for a bride, I would marry a widow."

Leo reflected, then shook his head.

Salzman hunched his shoulders in an almost imperceptible gesture of disappointment. He placed the card down on the wooden table and began to read another:

"Lily H. High school teacher. Regular. Not a substitute. Has savings and new Dodge car. Lived in Paris one year. Father is successful dentist thirty-five years. Interested in professional man. Well Americanized family. Wonderful opportunity."

"I knew her personally," said Salzman. "I wish you could see this girl. She is a doll. Also very intelligent. All day you could talk to her about books and theyater and what not. She also knows current events."

"I don't believe you mentioned her age?"

"Her age?" Salzman said, raising his brows. "Her age is thirty-two years."

Leo said after a while, "I'm afraid that seems a little too old."

Salzman let out a laugh. "So how old are you, rabbi?"

"Twenty-seven."

"So what is the difference, tell me, between twenty-seven and thirty-two? My own wife is seven years older than me. So what did I suffer?—Nothing. If Rothschild's daughter wants to marry you, would you say on account her age, no?"

"Yes," Leo said dryly.

Salzman shook off the no in the yes. "Five years don't mean a thing. I give you my word that when you will live with her for one week you will forget her age. What does it mean five years—that she lived more and knows more than somebody who is younger? On this girl, God bless her, years are not wasted. Each one that it comes makes better the bargain.''

"What subject does she teach in high school?"

"Languages. If you heard the way she speaks French, you will think it is music. I am in the business twenty-five years, and I recommend her with my whole heart. Believe me, I know what I'm talking, rabbi.''

"What's on the next card?" Leo said abruptly.

Salzman reluctantly turned up the third card:

"Ruth K. Nineteen years. Honor student. Father offers thirteen thousand cash to the right bridegroom. He is a medical doctor. Stomach specialist with marvelous practice. Brother-in-law owns own garment business. Particular people.''

Salzman looked as if he had read his trump card.

"Did you say nineteen?" Leo asked with interest.

"On the dot."

"Is she attractive?" He blushed. "Pretty?"

Salzman kissed his finger tips. "A little doll. On this I give you my word. Let me call the father tonight and you will see what means pretty.''

But Leo was troubled. "You're sure she's that young?"

"This I am positive. The father will show you the birth certificate.''

"Are you positive there isn't something wrong with her?" Leo insisted.

"Who says there is wrong?"

"I don't understand why an American girl her age should go to a marriage broker."

A smile spread over Salzman's face.

"So for the same reason you went, she comes.''

Leo flushed. "I am pressed for time.''

Salzman, realizing he had been tactless, quickly explained. "The father came, not her. He wants she should have the best, so he looks around himself. When we will locate the right boy he will introduce him and encourage. This makes a better marriage than if a young girl without experience takes for herself. I don't have to tell you this.''

"But don't you think this young girl believes in love?" Leo spoke uneasily.

Salzman was about to guffaw but caught himself and said soberly, "Love comes with the right person, not before.''

Leo parted dry lips but did not speak. Noticing that Salzman had snatched a glance at the next card, he cleverly asked, "How is her health?''

"Perfect," Salzman said, breathing with difficulty. "Of course, she is a little lame on her right foot from an auto accident that it happened to her when she was twelve years, but nobody notices on account she is so brilliant and also beautiful.''

Leo got up heavily and went to the window. He felt curiously bitter and upbraided himself for having called in the marriage broker. Finally, he shook his head.

"Why not?" Salzman persisted, the pitch of his voice rising.

"Because I detest stomach specialists."

"So what do you care what is his business? After you marry her do you need him? Who says he must come every Friday night in your house?"

Ashamed of the way the talk was going, Leo dismissed Salzman, who went home with heavy, melancholy eyes.

Though he had felt only relief at the marriage broker's departure, Leo was in low spirits the next day. He explained it as arising from Salzman's failure to produce a suitable bride for him. He did not care for his type of clientele. But when Leo found himself hesitating whether to seek out another matchmaker, one more polished than Pinye, he wondered if it could be—his protestations to the contrary, and although he honored his father and mother—that he did not, in essence, care for the matchmaking institution? This thought he quickly put out of mind yet found himself still upset. All day he ran around in the woods—missed an important appointment, forgot to give out his laundry, walked out of a Broadway cafeteria without paying and had to run back with the ticket in his hand; had even not recognized his landlady in the street when she passed with a friend and courteously called out, "A good evening to you, Doctor Finkle." By nightfall, however, he had regained sufficient calm to sink his nose into a book and there found peace from this thoughts.

Almost at once there came a knock on the door. Before Leo could say enter, Salzman, commercial cupid, was standing in the room. His face was gray and meager, his expression hungry, and he looked as if he would expire on his feet. Yet the marriage broker managed, by some trick of the muscles, to display a broad smile.

"So good evening. I am invited?"

Leo nodded, disturbed to see him again, yet unwilling to ask the man to leave.

Beaming still, Salzman laid his portfolio on the table. "Rabbi, I got for you tonight good news."

"I've asked you not to call me rabbi. I'm still a student."

"Your worries are finished. I have for you a first-class bride."

"Leave me in peace concerning this subject." Leo pretended lack of interest.

"The world will dance at your wedding."

"Please, Mr. Salzman, no more."

"But first must come back my strength," Salzman said weakly. He fumbled with the portfolio straps and took out of the leather case an oily paper bag, from which he extracted a hard, seeded roll and a small, smoked white fish. With a quick motion of his hand he stripped the fish out of its skin and began ravenously to chew. "All day in a rush," he muttered.

Leo watched him eat.

"A sliced tomato you have maybe?" Salzman hesitantly inquired.

"No."

The marriage broker shut his eyes and ate. When he had finished he carefully cleaned up the crumbs and rolled up the remains of the fish, in the paper bag. His spectacled eyes roamed the room until he discovered, amid some piles of books, a one-burner gas stove. Lifting his hat he humbly asked, "A glass tea you got, rabbi?"

Conscience-stricken, Leo rose and brewed the tea. He served it with a chunk of lemon and two cubes of lump sugar, delighting Salzman.

After he had drunk his tea, Salzman's strength and good spirits were restored.

"So tell me, rabbi," he said amiably, "you considered some more the three clients I mentioned yesterday?"

"There was no need to consider."

"Why not?"

"None of them suits me."

"What then suits you?"

Leo let it pass because he could give only a confused answer.

Without waiting for a reply, Salzman asked, "You remember this girl I talked to you—the high school teacher?"

"Age thirty-two?"

But, surprisingly, Salzman's face lit in a smile. "Age twenty-nine."

Leo shot him a look. "Reduced from thirty-two?"

"A mistake," Salzman avowed. "I talked today with the dentist. He took me to his safety deposit box and showed me the birth certificate. She was twenty-nine years last August. They made her a party in the mountains where she went for her vacation. When her father spoke to me the first time I forgot to write the age and I told you thirty-two, but now I remember this was a different client, a widow."

"The same one you told me about? I thought she was twenty-four?"

"A different. Am I responsible that the world is filled with widows?"

"No, but I'm not interested in them, nor for that matter, in school teachers."

Salzman pulled his clasped hands to his breast. Looking at the ceiling he devoutly exclaimed, "Yiddishe kinder, what can I say to somebody that he is not interested in high school teachers? So what then you are interested?"

Leo flushed but controlled himself.

"In what else will you be interested," Salzman went on, "if you not interested in this fine girl that she speaks four languages and has personally in the bank ten thousand dollars? Also her father guarantees further twelve thousand. Also she has a new car, wonderful clothes, talks on all subjects, and she will give you a first-class home and children. How near do we come in our life to paradise?"

"If she's so wonderful, why wasn't she married ten years ago?"

"Why?" said Salzman with a heavy laugh. "—Why? Because she is *partikiler*. That is why. She wants the *best*."

Leo was silent, amused at how he had entangled himself. But Salzman had aroused his interest in Lily H., and he began seriously to consider calling on her. When the marriage broker observed how intently Leo's mind was at work on the facts he had supplied, he felt certain they would soon come to an agreement.

Late Saturday afternoon, conscious of Salzman, Leo Finkle walked with Lily Hirschorn along Riverside Drive. He walked briskly and erectly, wearing with distinction the black fedora he had that morning taken with trepidation out of the dusty hat box on his closet shelf, and the heavy black Saturday coat he had thoroughly whisked clean. Leo also owned a walking stick, a present from a distant relative, but quickly put temptation aside and did not use it. Lily, petite and not unpretty, had on something signifying the approach of spring. She was au courant, animatedly, with all sorts of subjects, and he weighed her words and found her surprisingly sound—score another for Salzman, whom he uneasily sensed to be somewhere around, hiding perhaps high in a tree along the street, flashing the lady signals with a pocket mirror; or perhaps a cloven-hoofed Pan, piping nuptial ditties as he danced his invisible way before them, strewing wild buds on the walk and purple grapes in their path, symbolizing fruit of a union, though there was of course still none.

Lily startled Leo by remarking, "I was thinking of Mr. Salzman, a curious figure, wouldn't you say?"

Not certain what to answer, he nodded.

She bravely went on, blushing. "I for one am grateful for his introducing us. Aren't you?"

He courteously replied, "I am."

"I mean," she said with a little laugh—and it was all in good taste, or at least gave the effect of being not in bad—"do you mind that we came together so?"

He was not displeased with her honesty, recognizing that she meant to set the relationship aright, and understanding that it took a certain amount of experience in life, and courage, to want to do it quite that way. One had to have some sort of past to make that kind of beginning.

He said that he did not mind. Salzman's function was traditional and honorable—valuable for what it might achieve, which, he pointed out, was frequently nothing.

Lily agreed with a sigh. They walked on for a while and she said after a long silence, again with a nervous laugh, "Would you mind if I asked you something a little bit personal? Frankly, I find the subject fascinating." Although Leo shrugged, she went on half embarrassedly, "How was it that you came to your calling? I mean was it a sudden passionate inspiration?"

Leo after a time, slowly replied, "I was always interested in the Law."

"You saw revealed in it the presence of the Highest?"

He nodded and changed the subject. "I understand that you spent a little time in Paris, Miss Hirschorn?"

"Oh, did Mr. Salzman tell you, Rabbi Finkle?" Leo winced but she went on, "It was ages ago and almost forgotten. I remember I had to return for my sister's wedding."

And Lily would not be put off. "When," she asked in a trembly voice, "did you become enamored of God?"

He stared at her. Then it came to him that she was talking not about Leo Finkle, but of a total stranger, some mystical figure, perhaps even passionate prophet that Salzman had dreamed up for her—no relation to the living or dead. Leo trembled with rage and weakness. The trickster had obviously sold her a bill of goods, just as he had him, who'd expected to become acquainted with a young lady of twenty-nine, only to behold, the moment he laid eyes upon her strained and anxious face, a woman past thirty-five and aging rapidly. Only his self-control had kept him this long in her presence.

"I am not," he said gravely, "a talented religious person," and in seeking words to go on, found himself possessed by shame and fear. "I think," he said in a strained manner, "that I came to God not because I loved Him, but because I did not."

This confession he spoke harshly because its unexpectedness shook him.

Lily wilted. Leo saw a profusion of loaves of bread go flying like ducks high over his head, not unlike the winged loaves by which he had counted himself to sleep last night. Mercifully, then, it snowed, which he would not put past Salzman's machinations.

He was infuriated with the marriage broker and swore he would throw him out of the room the minute he reappeared. But Salzman did not come that night, and when Leo's anger had subsided, an unaccountable despair grew in its place. At first he thought this was caused by his disappointment in Lily, but before long it became evident that he had involved himself with Salzman without a true knowledge of his own intent. He gradually realized—with an emptiness that seized him with six hands—that he had called in the broker to find him a bride because he was incapable of doing it himself. This terrifying insight he had derived as a result of his meeting and conversation with Lily Hirschorn. Her probing questions had somehow irritated him into revealing—to himself more than her—the true nature of his relationship to God, and from that it had come upon him, with shocking force, that apart from his parents, he had never loved anyone. Or perhaps it went the other way, that he did not love God so well as he might, because he had not loved man. It seemed to Leo that his whole life stook starkly revealed and he saw himself for the first time as he truly was—unloved and loveless. This bitter but somehow not fully unexpected revelation brought him to a point of panic, controlled only by extraordinary effort. He covered his face with his hands and cried.

The week that followed was the worst of his life. He did not eat and lost weight. His beard darkened and grew ragged. He stopped attending seminars and almost never opened a book. He seriously considered leaving the Yeshivah, although he was deeply troubled at the thought of the loss of all his years of study—saw them like pages torn from a book, strewn over the city—and at the devastating effect of this decision upon his parents. But he had lived without knowledge of himself, and never in the Five Books and all the Commentaries—mea culpa—had the truth been revealed to him. He did not know where to turn, and in all this desolating loneliness there was no *to whom,* although he often thought of Lily but not once could bring himself to go downstairs and make the call. He became touchy and irritable, especially with his landlady, who asked him all manner of personal questions; on the other hand, sensing his own disagreeableness, he waylaid her on the stairs and apologized abjectly, until mortified, she ran from him. Out of this, how-ever, he drew the consolation that he was a Jew and that a Jew suffered. But gradually, as the long and terrible week drew to a close, he regained his composure and some idea of purpose in life: to go on as planned. Although he was imperfect, the ideal was not. As for his quest of a bride, the thought of continuing afflicted him with anxiety and heartburn, yet perhaps with this new knowledge of himself he would be more successful than in the past. Perhaps love would now come to him and a bride to that love. And for this sanctified seeking who needed a Salzman?

The marriage broker, a skeleton with haunted eyes, returned that very night. He looked, withal, the picture of frustrated expectancy—as if he had steadfastly waited the week at Miss Lily Hirschorn's side for a telephone call that never came.

Casually coughing, Salzman came immediately to the point: "So how did you like her?"

Leo's anger rose and he could not refrain from chiding the matchmaker: "Why did you lie to me, Salzman?"

Salzman's pale face went dead white, the world had snowed on him.

"Did you not state that she was twenty-nine?" Leo insisted.

"I give you my word—"

"She was thirty-five, if a day. *At least* thirty-five."

"Of this don't be too sure. Her father told me—"

"Never mind. The worst of it was that you lied to her."

"How did I lie to her, tell me?"

"You told her things about me that weren't true. You made me out to be more, consequently less than I am. She had in mind a totally different per-son, a sort of semi-mystical Wonder Rabbi."

"All I said, you was a religious man."

"I can imagine."

Salzman sighed. "This is my weakness that I have," he confessed. "My wife says to me I shouldn't be a salesman, but when I have two fine people that they would be wonderful to be married, I am so happy that I talk too much." He smiled wanly. "This is why Salzman is a poor man."

Leo's anger left him. "Well, Salzman, I'm afraid that's all."

The marriage broker fastened hungry eyes on him.

"You don't want any more a bride?"

"I do," said Leo, "but I have decided to seek her in a different way. I am no longer interested in an arranged marriage. To be frank, I now admit the necessity of premarital love. That is, I want to be in love with the one I marry."

"Love?" said Salzman, astounded. After a moment he remarked, "For us, our love is our life, not for the ladies. In the ghetto they—"

"I know, I know," said Leo. "I've thought of it often. Love, I have said to myself, should be a by-product of living and worship rather than its own end. Yet for myself I find it necessary to establish the level of my need and fulfill it."

Salzman shrugged but answered, "Listen, rabbi, if you want love, this I can find for you also. I have such beautiful clients that you will love them the minute your eyes will see them."

Leo smiled unhappily. "I'm afraid you don't understand."

But Salzman hastily unstrapped his portfolio and withdrew a manila packet from it.

"Pictures," he said, quickly laying the envelope on the table.

Leo called after him to take the pictures away, but as if on the wings of the wind, Salzman had disappeared.

March came. Leo had returned to his regular routine. Although he felt not quite himself yet—lacked energy—he was making plans for a more active social life. Of course it would cost something, but he was an expert in cutting corners; and when there were no corners left he would make circles rounder. All the while Salzman's pictures had lain on the table, gathering dust. Occasionally as Leo sat studying, or enjoying a cup of tea, his eyes fell on the manila envelope, but he never opened it.

The days went by and no social life to speak of developed with a member of the opposite sex—it was difficult, given the circumstances of his situation. One morning Leo toiled up the stairs to his room and stared out the window at the city. Although the day was bright his view of it was dark. For some time he watched the people in the street below hurrying along and then turned with a heavy heart to his little room. On the table was the packet. With a sudden relentless gesture he tore it open. For a half-hour he stood by the table in a state of excitement, examining the photographs of the ladies Salzman had included. Finally, with a deep sigh he put them down. There were six, of varying degrees of attractiveness, but look at them long enough and they all became Lily Hirschorn: all past their prime, all starved behind bright smiles, not a true personality in the lot. Life, despite their frantic yoo-hooings, had passed them by; they were pictures in a briefcase that stank of fish. After a while, however, as Leo attempted to return the photographs into the envelope, he found in it another, a snapshot of the type taken by a machine for a quarter. He gazed at it a moment and let out a cry.

Her face deeply moved him. Why, he could at first not say. It gave him the impression of youth—spring flowers, yet age—a sense of having been used to the bone, wasted; this came from the eyes, which were hauntingly familiar, yet absolutely strange. He had a vivid impression that he had met her before, but try as he might he could not place her although he could almost recall her name, as if he had read it in her own handwriting. No, this couldn't be; he would have remembered her. It was not, he affirmed, that she had an extraordinary beauty—no, though her face was attractive enough; it was that *something* about her moved him. Feature for feature, even some of the ladies of the photographs could do better; but she leaped forth to his heart—had *lived,* or wanted to—more than just wanted, perhaps regretted how she had lived—had somehow deeply suffered: it could be seen in the depths of those reluctant eyes, and from the way the light enclosed and shone from her, and within her, opening realms of possibility: this was her own. Her he desired. His head ached and eyes narrowed with the intensity of his gazing, then as if an obscure fog had blown up in the mind, he experienced fear of her and was aware that he had received an impression, somehow, of evil. He shuddered, saying softly, it is thus with us all. Leo brewed some tea in a small pot and sat sipping it without sugar, to calm himself. But before he had finished drinking, again with excitement he examined the face and found it good: good for Leo Finkle. Only such a one could understand him and help him seek whatever he was seeking. She might, perhaps, love him. How she had happened to be among the discards in Salzman's barrel he could never guess, but he knew he must urgently go find her.

Leo rushed downstairs, grabbed up the Bronx telephone book, and searched for Salzman's home address. He was not listed, nor was his office. Neither was he in the Manhattan book. But Leo remembered having written down the address on a slip of paper after he had read Salzman's advertisement in the "personals" column of the *Forward.* He ran up to this room and tore through his papers, without luck. It was exasperating. Just when he needed the matchmaker he was nowhere to be found. Fortunately Leo remembered to look in his wallet. There on a card he found his name written and a Bronx address. No phone number was listed, the reason—Leo now recalled—he had originally communicated with Salzman by letter. He got on his coat, put a hat on over his skull cap and hurried to the subway station. All the way to the far end of the Bronx he sat on the edge of his seat. He was more than once tempted to take out the picture and see if the girl's face was as he remembered it, but he refrained, allowing the snapshot to remain in his inside coat pocket, content to have her so close. When the train pulled into the station he was waiting at the door and bolted out. He quickly located the street Salzman had advertised.

The building he sought was less than a block from the subway, but it was not an office building, not even a loft, nor a store in which one could rent office space. It was a very old tenement house. Leo found Salzman's name in pencil on a soiled tag under the bell and climbed three dark flights to his apartment. When he knocked, the door was opened by a thin, asthmatic, gray-haired woman, in felt slippers.

"Yes?" she said, expecting nothing. She listened without listening. He could have sworn he had seen her, too, before but knew it was an illusion.

"Salzman—does he live here? Pinye Salzman," he said, "the matchmaker?"

She stared at him a long minute. "Of course."

He felt embarrassed. "Is he in?"

"No." Her mouth, though left open, offered nothing more.

"The matter is urgent. Can you tell me where his office is?"

"In the air." She pointed upward.

"You mean he has no office?" Leo asked.

"In his socks."

He peered into the apartment. It was sunless and dingy, one large room divided by a half-open curtain, beyond which he could see a sagging metal bed. The near side of a room was crowded with rickety chairs, old bureaus, a three-legged table, racks of cooking utensils, and all the apparatus of a kitchen. But there was no sign of Salzman or his magic barrel, probably also a figment of the imagination. An odor of frying fish made Leo weak to the knees.

"Where is he?" he insisted. "I've got to see your husband."

At length she answered, "So who knows where he is? Every time he thinks a new thought he runs to a different place. Go home, he will find you."

"Tell him Leo Finkle."

She gave no sign she had heard.

He walked downstairs, depressed.

But Salzman, breathless, stood waiting at his door.

Leo was astounded and overjoyed. "How did you get here before me?"

"I rushed."

"Come inside."

They entered. Leo fixed tea, and a sardine sandwich for Salzman. As they were drinking he reached behind him for the packet of pictures and handed them to the marriage broker.

Salzman put down his glass and said expectantly, "You found somebody you like?"

"Not among these."

The marriage broker turned away.

"Here is the one I want." Leo held forth the snapshot.

Salzman slipped on his glasses and took the picture into his trembling hand. He turned ghastly and let out a groan.

"What's the matter?" cried Leo.

"Excuse me. Was an accident this picture. She isn't for you."

Salzman frantically shoved the manila packet into his portfolio. He thrust the snapshot into his pocket and fled down the stairs.

Leo, after momentary paralysis, gave chase and cornered the marriage broker in the vestibule. The landlady made hysterical outcries but neither of them listened.

"Give me back the picture, Salzman."

"No." The pain in his eyes was terrible.

"Tell me who she is then."

"This I can't tell you. Excuse me."

He made to depart, but Leo, forgetting himself, seized the matchmaker by his tight coat and shook him frenziedly.

"Please," sighed Salzman. *"Please."*

Leo ashamedly let him go. "Tell me who she is," he begged. "It's very important for me to know."

"She is not for you. She is a wild one—wild, without shame. This is not a bride for a rabbi."

"What do you mean wild?"

"Like an animal. Like a dog. For her to be poor was a sin. This is why to me she is dead now."

"In God's name, what do you mean?"

"Her I can't introduce to you," Salzman cried.

"Why are you so excited?"

"Why, he asks," Salzman said, bursting into tears. "This is my baby, my Stella, she should burn in hell."

Leo hurried up to bed and hid under the covers. Under the covers he thought his life through. Although he soon fell asleep he could not sleep her out of his mind. He woke, beating his breast. Though he prayed to be rid of her, his prayers went unanswered. Through days of torment he endlessly struggled not to love her; fearing success, he escaped it. He then concluded to convert her to goodness, himself to God. The idea alternately nauseated and exalted him.

He perhaps did not know that he had come to a final decision until he encountered Salzman in a Broadway cafeteria. He was sitting alone at a rear table, sucking the bony remains of a fish. The marriage broker appeared haggard, and transparent to the point of vanishing.

Salzman looked up at first without recognizing him. Leo had grown a pointed beard and his eyes were weighted with wisdom.

"Salzman," he said, "love has at last come to my heart."

"Who can love from a picture?" mocked the marriage broker.

"It is not impossible."

"If you can love her, then you can love anybody. Let me show you some new clients that they just sent me their photographs. One is a little doll."

"Just her I want," Leo murmured.

"Don't be a fool, doctor. Don't bother with her."

"Put me in touch with her, Salzman," Leo said humbly. "Perhaps I can be of service."

Salzman had stopped eating and Leo understood with emotion that it was now arranged.

Leaving the cafeteria, he was, however, afflicted by a tormenting suspicion that Salzman had planned it all to happen this way.

Leo was informed by letter that she would meet him on a certain corner, and she was there one spring night, waiting under a street lamp. He appeared, carrying a small bouquet of violets and rosebuds. Stella stood by the lamp post, smoking. She wore white with red shoes, which fitted his expectations, although in a troubled moment he had imagined the dress red, and only the shoes white. She waited uneasily and shyly. From afar he saw that her eyes—clearly her father's—were filled with desperate innocence. He pictured, in her, his own redemption. Violins and lit candles revolved in the sky. Leo ran forward with flowers outthrust.

Around the corner, Salzman, leaning against a wall, chanted prayers for the dead.

Questions for "The Magic Barrel"

1.   What elements of the fairy tale and the fable do you find in this story? What moral—or morals—might be drawn from the story?

2.   Describe Pinye Salzman.

3.   What is the point of the episode with Lily Hirschorn?

4.   What is the turning point in Leo's quest for a wife? Why does he choose Stella? What is Salzman's role in this choice—how responsible is he for what happens?

5.   Read the last full paragraph aloud and discuss its effect. Why doesn't the story end here? How do you explain the last line of the story?

Tillie Olsen (1912–   )

Tillie Olsen was born in Omaha, Nebraska, and grew up in poverty. Her formal education ended in the eleventh grade, and she spent the following twenty-five years raising four children and working at various jobs in industry and as a typist-transcriber. Although she published short fiction in the 1930s, work and motherhood left her little time to write until 1955, when her youngest child began school. Four of her stories, including "I Stand Here Ironing," appeared in the collection *Tell Me a Riddle* in 1961. In addition to writing highly acclaimed short stories, Olsen has published an afterword for an important reprint of Rebecca Harding Davis's *Life in the Iron Mills*; a novel, *Yonnondio* (1974); and a collection of nonfiction, *Silences* (1978), which explores the relationships between circumstances and achievement for writers, particularly women. She has also edited a collection of readings, *Mother to Daughter; Daughter to Mother* (1984). In a lyrical and evocative style, Olsen most often writes about characters whose development is hindered by the vagaries of social class, gender, race, and what she calls "the unnatural thwarting of what struggles to come into being but cannot."

I Stand Here Ironing

I stand here ironing, and what you asked me moves tormented back and forth with the iron.

"I wish you would manage the time to come in and talk with me about your daughter. I'm sure you can help me understand her. She's a youngster who needs help and whom I'm deeply interested in helping."

"Who needs help." . . . Even if I came, what good would it do? You think because I am her mother I have a key, or that in some way you could use me as a key? She has lived for nineteen years. There is all that life that has happened outside of me, beyond me.

And when is there time to remember, to sift, to weigh, to estimate, to total? I will start and there will be an interruption and I will have to gather it all together again. Or I will become engulfed with all I did or did not do, with what should have been and what cannot be helped.

She was a beautiful baby. The first and only one of our five that was beautiful at birth. You do not guess how new and uneasy her tenancy in her now-loveliness. You did not know her all those years she was thought homely, or see her poring over her baby pictures, making me tell her over and over how beautiful she had been—and would be, I would tell her—and was now, to the seeing eye. But the seeing eyes were few or nonexistent. Including mine.

I nursed her. They feel that's important nowadays. I nursed all the children, but with her, with all the fierce rigidity of first motherhood, I did like the books then said. Though her cries battered me to trembling and my breasts ached with swollenness, I waited till the clock decreed.

Why do I put that first? I do not even know if it matters, or if it explains anything.

She was a beautiful baby. She blew shining bubbles of sound. She loved motion, loved light, loved color and music and textures. She would lie on the floor in her blue overalls patting the surface so hard in ecstasy her hands and feet would blur. She was a miracle to me, but when she was eight months old I had to leave her daytimes with the woman downstairs to whom she was no miracle at all, for I worked or looked for work and for Emily's father, who "could no longer endure" (he wrote in his good-bye note) "sharing want with us."

I was nineteen. It was the pre-relief, pre-WPA world of the depression. I would start running as soon as I got off the streetcar, running up the stairs, the place smelling sour, and awake or asleep to startle awake, when she saw me she would break into a clogged weeping that could not be comforted, a weeping I can hear yet.

After a while I found a job hashing at night so I could be with her days, and it was better. But it came to where I had to bring her to his family and leave her.

It took a long time to raise the money for her fare back. Then she got chicken pox and I had to wait longer. When she finally came, I hardly knew her, walking quick and nervous like her father, looking like her father, thin, and dressed in a shoddy red that yellowed her skin and glared at the pockmarks. All the baby loveliness gone.

She was two. Old enough for nursery school they said, and I did not know then what I know now—the fatigue of the long day, and the lacerations of group life in the kinds of nurseries that are only parking places for children.

Except that it would have made no difference if I had known. It was the only place there was. It was the only way we could be together, the only way I could hold a job.

And even without knowing, I knew. I knew the teacher that was evil because all these years it has curdled into my memory, the little boy hunched in the corner, her rasp, "why aren't you outside, because Alvin hits you? that's no reason, go out, scaredy." I know Emily hated it even if she did not clutch and implore "don't go Mommy" like the other children, mornings.

She always had a reason why we should stay home. Momma, you look sick. Momma, I feel sick. Momma, the teachers aren't there today, they're sick. Momma, we can't go, there was a fire there last night. Momma, it's a holiday today, no school, they told me.

But never a direct protest, never rebellion. I think of our others in their three-, four-year-oldness—the explosions, the tempers, the denunciations, the demands—and I feel suddenly ill. I put the iron down. What in me demanded that goodness in her? And what was the cost, the cost to her of such goodness?

The old man living in the back once said in his gentle way: "You should smile at Emily more when you look at her." What *was* in my face when I looked at her? I loved her. There were all the acts of love.

It was only with the others I remembered what he said, and it was the face of joy, and not of care or tightness or worry I turned to them—too late for Emily. She does not smile easily, let alone almost always as her brothers and sisters do. Her face is closed and sombre, but when she wants, how fluid. You must have seen it in her pantomimes, you spoke of her rare gift for comedy on the stage that rouses a laughter out of the audience so dear they applaud and applaud and do not want to let her go.

Where does it come from, that comedy? There was none of it in her when she came back to me that second time, after I had had to send her away again. She had a new daddy now to learn to love, and I think perhaps it was a better time.

Except when we left her alone nights, telling ourselves she was old enough.

"Can't you go some other time, Mommy, like tomorrow?" she would ask. "Will it be just a little while you'll be gone? Do you promise?"

The time we came back, the front door open, the clock on the floor in the hall. She rigid awake. "It wasn't just a little while. I didn't cry. Three times I called you, just three times, and then I ran downstairs to open the door so you could come faster. The clock talked loud. I threw it away, it scared me what it talked."

She said the clock talked loud again that night I went to the hospital to have Susan. She was delirious with the fever that comes before red measles, but she was fully conscious all the week I was gone and the week after we were home when she could not come near the new baby or me.

She did not get well. She stayed skeleton thin, not wanting to eat, and night after night she had nightmares. She would call for me, and I would rouse from exhaustion to sleepily call back: "You're all right, darling, go to sleep, it's just a dream," and if she still called, in a sterner voice, "now go to sleep, Emily, there's nothing to hurt you." Twice, only twice, when I had to get up for Susan anyhow, I went in to sit with her.

Now when it is too late (as if she would let me hold and comfort her like I do the others) I get up and go to her at once at her moan or restless stirring. "Are you awake, Emily? Can I get you something?" And the answer is always the same: "No, I'm all right, go back to sleep, Mother."

They persuaded me at the clinic to send her away to a convalescent home in the country where "she can have the kind of food and care you can't manage for her, and you'll be free to concentrate on the new baby." They still send children to that place. I see pictures on the society page of sleek young women planning affairs to raise money for it, or dancing at the affairs, or decorating Easter eggs or filling Christmas stockings for the children.

They never have a picture of the children so I do not know if the girls still wear those gigantic red bows and the ravaged looks on the every other Sunday when parents can come to visit "unless otherwise notified"—as we were notified the first six weeks.

Oh it is a handsome place, green lawns and tall trees and fluted flower beds. High up on the balconies of each cottage the children stand, the girls in their red bows and white dresses, the boys in white suits and giant red ties. The parents stand below shrieking up to be heard and the children shriek down to be heard, and between them the invisible wall "Not To Be Contaminated by Parental Germs or Physical Affection."

There was a tiny girl who always stood hand in hand with Emily. Her parents never came. One visit she was gone. "They moved her to Rose Cottage," Emily shouted in explanation. "They don't like you to love anybody here."

She wrote once a week, the labored writing of a seven-year-old. "I am fine. How is the baby. If I write my leter nicly I will have a star. Love." There never was a star. We wrote every other day, letters she could never hold or keep but only hear read—once. "We simply do not have room for children to keep any personal possessions," they patiently explained when we pieced one Sunday's shrieking together to plead how much it would mean to Emily, who loved so to keep things, to be allowed to keep her letters and cards.

Each visit she looked frailer. "She isn't eating," they told us.

(They had runny eggs for breakfast or mush with lumps, Emily said later, I'd hold it in my mouth and not swallow. Nothing ever tasted good, just when they had chicken.)

It took us eight months to get her released home, and only the fact that she gained back so little of her seven lost pounds convinced the social worker.

I used to try to hold and love her after she came back, but her body would stay stiff, and after a while she'd push away. She ate little. Food sickened her, and I think much of life too. Oh she had physical lightness and brightness, twinkling by on skates, bouncing like a ball up and down up and down over the jump rope, skimming over the hill; but these were momentary.

She fretted about her appearance, thin and dark and foreign-looking at a time when every little girl was supposed to look or thought she should look a chubby blonde replica of Shirley Temple. The doorbell sometimes rang for her, but no one seemed to come and play in the house or be a best friend. Maybe because we moved so much.

There was a boy she loved painfully through two school semesters. Months later she told me how she had taken pennies from my purse to buy him candy. "Licorice was his favorite and I brought him some every day, but he still liked Jennifer better'n me. Why, Mommy?" The kind of question for which there is no answer.

School was a worry to her. She was not glib or quick in a world where glibness and quickness were easily confused with ability to learn. To her overworked and exasperated teachers she was an overconscientious "slow learner" who kept trying to catch up and was absent entirely too often.

I let her be absent, though sometimes the illness was imaginary. How different from my now-strictness about attendance with the others. I wasn't working. We had a new baby, I was home anyhow. Sometimes, after Susan grew old enough, I would keep her home from school, too, to have them all together.

Mostly Emily had asthma, and her breathing, harsh and labored, would fill the house with a curiously tranquil sound. I would bring the two old dresser mirrors and her boxes of collections to her bed. She would select beads and single earrings, bottle tops and shells, dried flowers and pebbles, old postcards and scraps, all sorts of oddments; then she and Susan would play Kingdom, setting up landscapes and furniture, peopling them with action.

Those were the only times of peaceful companionship between her and Susan. I have edged away from it, that poisonous feeling between them, that terrible balancing of hurts and needs I had to do between the two, and did so badly, those earlier years.

Oh there are conflicts between the others too, each one human, needing, demanding, hurting, taking—but only between Emily and Susan, no, Emily toward Susan that corroding resentment. It seems so obvious on the surface, yet it is not obvious. Susan, the second child, Susan, golden- and curly-haired and chubby, quick and articulate and assured, everything in appearance and manner Emily was not; Susan, not able to resist Emily's precious things, losing or sometimes clumsily breaking them; Susan telling jokes and riddles to company for applause while Emily sat silent (to say to me later: that was *my* riddle, Mother, I told it to Susan); Susan, who for all the five years' difference in age was just a year behind Emily in developing physically.

I am glad for that slow physical development that widened the difference between her and her contemporaries, though she suffered over it. She was too vulnerable for that terrible world of youthful competition, of preening and parading, of constant measuring of yourself against every other, of envy, "If I had that copper hair," "If I had that skin. . . ." She tormented herself enough about not looking like the others, there was enough of the unsureness, the having to be conscious of words before you speak, the constant caring—what are they thinking of me? without having it all magnified by the merciless physical drives.

Ronnie is calling. He is wet and I change him. It is rare there is such a cry now. That time of motherhood is almost behind me when the ear is not one's own but must always be racked and listening for the child cry, the child call. We sit for a while and I hold him, looking out over the city spread in charcoal with its soft aisles of light. *"Shoogily,"* he breathes and curls closer. I carry him back to bed, asleep. *Shoogily.* A funny word, a family word, inherited from Emily, invented by her to say: *comfort.*

In this and other ways she leaves her seal, I say aloud. And startle at my saying it. What do I mean? What did I start to gather together, to try and make coherent? I was at the terrible, growing years. War years, I do not remember them well. I was working, there were four smaller ones now, there was not time for her. She had to help be a mother, and housekeeper, and shopper. She had to set her seal. Mornings of crisis and near hysteria trying to get lunches packed, hair combed, coats and shoes found, everyone to school or Child Care on time, the baby ready for transportation. And always the paper scribbled on by a smaller one, the book looked at by Susan then mislaid, the homework not done. Running out to that huge school where she was one, she was lost, she was a drop; suffering over the unpreparedness, stammering and unsure in her classes.

There was so little time left at night after the kids were bedded down. She would struggle over books, always eating (it was in those years she developed her enormous appetite that is legendary in our family) and I would be ironing, or preparing food for the next day, or writing V-mail to Bill, or tending the baby. Sometimes, to make me laugh, or out of her despair, she would imitate happenings or types at school.

I think I said once: "Why don't you do something like this in the school amateur show?" One morning she phoned me at work, hardly understandable through the weeping: "Mother, I did it. I won, I won; they gave me first prize; they clapped and clapped and wouldn't let me go."

Now suddenly she was Somebody, and as imprisoned in her difference as she had been in anonymity.

She began to be asked to perform at other high schools, even in colleges, then at city and statewide affairs. The first one we went to, I only recognized her that first moment when thin, shy, she almost drowned herself into the curtains. Then: Was this Emily? The control, the command, the convulsing and deadly clowning, the spell, then the roaring, stamping audience, unwilling to let this rare and precious laughter out of their lives.

Afterwards: You ought to do something about her with a gift like that— but without money or knowing how, what does one do? We have left it all to her, and the gift has as often eddied inside, clogged and clotted, as been used and growing.

She is coming. She runs up the stairs two at a time with her light graceful step, and I know she is happy tonight. Whatever it was that occasioned your call did not happen today.

"Aren't you ever going to finish the ironing, Mother? Whistler painted his mother in a rocker. I'd have to paint mine standing over an ironing board." This is one of her communicative nights and she tells me everything and nothing as she fixes herself a plate of food out of the icebox.

She is so lovely. Why did you want me to come in at all? Why were you concerned? She will find her way.

She starts up the stairs to bed. "Don't get me up with the rest in the morning." "But I thought you were having midterms." "Oh, those," she comes back in, kisses me, and says quite lightly, "in a couple of years when we'll all be atom-dead they won't matter a bit."

She has said it before. She *believes* it. But because I have been dredging the past, and all that compounds a human being is so heavy and meaningful in me, I cannot endure it tonight.

I will never total it all. I will never come in to say: She was a child seldom smiled at. Her father left me before she was a year old. I had to work her first six years when there was work, or I sent her home and to his relatives. There were years she had care she hated. She was dark and thin and foreign-looking in a world where the prestige went to blondeness and curly hair and dimples, she was slow where glibness was prized. She was a child of anxious, not proud, love. We were poor and could not afford for her the soil of easy growth. I was a young mother, I was a distracted mother. There were the other children pushing up, demanding. Her younger sister seemed all that she was not. There were years she did not want me to touch her. She kept too much in herself, her life was such she had to keep too much in herself. My wisdom came too late. She has much to her and probably little will come of it. She is a child of her age, of depression, of war, of fear.

Let her be. So all that is in her will not bloom—but in how many does it? There is still enough left to live by. Only help her to know—help make it so there is cause for her to know—that she is more than this dress on the ironing board, helpless before the iron.

Questions for "I Stand Here Ironing"

1. To whom is the narrator speaking?

2. Reconstruct, in chronological order, the events of Emily's life, and then list specific examples of the many ways in which the narrator thinks she has failed her daughter.

3. How might you explain Emily's gift for comedy?

4. What does the penultimate paragraph accomplish?

5. Describe the narrator. What does she know now that she didn't know—or couldn't acknowledge—in the past?

6. What is your reaction to the final paragraph? Why does the narrator compare her daughter to the dress on the ironing board? What might we infer about the narrator herself from this plea?

7. Describe the structure of this narrative. What is the cumulative effect of this pattern?

Donald Barthelme (1931–   )

Donald Barthelme was born in Philadelphia, grew up in Texas, where he worked as a reporter and editor for Texas newspapers, and now lives in New York City. Before becoming a full-time writer, Barthelme also served as a museum director, was managing editor of *Location,* an art and literature review, and taught English at City College in New York.

Known for his pictorial collages as well as his writing, Barthelme is a regular contributor to the *New Yorker.* Among his many books of fiction are *Come Back, Dr. Caligari* (1964), *Snow White* (1967), *Unspeakable Practices, Unnatural Acts* (1968), *City Life* (1970), *Sadness* (1972), *The Dead Father* (1975), *Great Days* (1979), *Sixty Stories* (1982), *Overnight to Many Distant Cities* (1983), and *Paradise* (1986).

The Glass Mountain

1. I was trying to climb the glass mountain.
2. The glass mountain stands at the corner of Thirteenth Street and Eighth Avenue.
3. I had attained the lower slope.
4. People were looking up at me.
5. I was new in the neighborhood.
6. Nevertheless I had acquaintances.
7. I had strapped climbing irons to my feet and each hand grasped a sturdy plumber's friend.[1]
8. I was 200 feet up.
9. The wind was bitter.
10. My acquaintances had gathered at the bottom of the mountain to offer encouragement.
11. "Shithead."
12. "Asshole."
13. Everyone in the city knows about the glass mountain.
14. People who live here tell stories about it.
15. It is pointed out to visitors.
16. Touching the side of the mountain, one feels coolness.

---

[1]Plumber's friend: a device with a large suction cup at the end of a handle, used to clear drains.

17. Peering into the mountain, one sees sparkling blue-white depths.
18. The mountain towers over that part of Eighth Avenue like some splendid, immense office building.
19. The top of the mountain vanishes into the clouds, or on cloudless days, into the sun.
20. I unstuck the righthand plumber's friend leaving the lefthand one in place.
21. Then I stretched out and reattached the righthand one a little higher up, after which I inched my legs into new positions.
22. The gain was minimal, not an arm's length.
23. My acquaintances continued to comment.
24. "Dumb motherfucker."
25. I was new in the neighborhood.
26. In the streets were many people with disturbed eyes.
27. Look for yourself.
28. In the streets were hundreds of young people shooting up in doorways, behind parked cars.
29. Older people walked dogs.
30. The sidewalks were full of dogshit in brilliant colors: ocher, umber, Mars yellow, sienna, viridian, ivory black, rose madder.
31. And someone had been apprehended cutting down trees, a row of elms broken-backed among the VWs and Valiants.
32. Done with a power saw, beyond a doubt.
33. I was new in the neighborhood yet I had accumulated acquaintances.
34. My acquaintances passed a brown bottle from hand to hand.
35. "Better than a kick in the crotch."
36. "Better than a poke in the eye with a sharp stick."
37. "Better than a slap in the belly with a wet fish."
38. "Better than a thump on the back with a stone."
39. "Won't he make a splash when he falls, now?"
40. "I hope to be here to see it. Dip my handkerchief in the blood."
41. "Fart-faced fool."
42. I unstuck the lefthand plumber's friend leaving the righthand one in place.
43. And reached out.
44. To climb the glass mountain, one first requires a good reason.
45. No one has ever climbed the mountain on behalf of science, or in search of celebrity, or because the mountain was a challenge.
46. Those are not good reasons.
47. But good reasons exist.
48. At the top of the mountain there is a castle of pure gold, and in a room in the castle tower sits . . .
49. My acquaintances were shouting at me.
50. "Ten bucks you bust your ass in the next four minutes!"
51. . . . a beautiful enchanted symbol.

52. I unstuck the righthand plumber's friend leaving the lefthand one in place.
53. And reached out.
54. It was cold there at 206 feet and when I looked down I was not encouraged.
55. A heap of corpses both of horses and riders ringed the bottom of the mountain, many dying men groaning there.
56. "A weakening of the libidinous interest in reality has recently come to a close." (Anton Ehrenzweig)[2]
57. A few questions thronged into my mind.
58. Does one climb a glass mountain, at considerable personal discomfort, simply to disenchant a symbol?
59. Do today's stronger egos still *need* symbols?
60. I decided that the answer to these questions was "yes."
61. Otherwise what was I doing there, 206 feet above the power-sawed elms, whose white meat I could see from my height?
62. The best way to fail to climb the mountain is to be a knight in full armor—one whose horse's hoofs strike fiery sparks from the sides of the mountain.
63. The following-named knights had failed to climb the mountain and were groaning in the heap: Sir Giles Guilford, Sir Henry Lovell, Sir Albert Denny, Sir Nicholas Vaux, Sir Patrick Grifford, Sir Gisbourne Gower, Sir Thomas Grey, Sir Peter Coleville, Sir John Blunt, Sir Richard Vernon, Sir Walter Willoughby, Sir Stephen Spear, Sir Roger Faulconbridge, Sir Clarence Vaughan, Sir Hubert Ratcliffe, Sir James Tyrrel, Sir Walter Herbert, Sir Robert Brakenbury, Sir Lionel Beaufort, and many others.[3]
64. My acquaintances moved among the fallen knights.
65. My acquaintances moved among the fallen knights, collecting rings, wallets, pocket watches, ladies' favors.
66. "Calm reigns in the country, thanks to the confident wisdom of everyone." (M. Pompidou)[4]
67. The golden castle is guarded by a lean-headed eagle with blazing rubies for eyes.
68. I unstuck the lefthand plumber's friend, wondering if—
69. My acquaintances were prising out the gold teeth of not-yet-dead knights.
70. In the streets were people concealing their calm behind a façade of vague dread.
71. "The conventional symbol (such as the nightingale, often associated with melancholy), even though it is recognized only through agreement, is not a sign (like the traffic light) because, again, it presumably arouses

---

[2]Art historian and critic (1908–1966).
[3]Names chosen or invented to portray English knighthood.
[4]Former President of France. The quotation is probably inauthentic.

deep feelings and is regarded as possessing properties beyond what the eye alone sees." (A *Dictionary of Literary Terms*)

72. A number of nightingales with traffic lights tied to their legs flew past me.
73. A knight in pale pink armor appeared above me.
74. He sank, his armor making tiny shrieking sounds against the glass.
75. He gave me a sideways glance as he passed me.
76. He uttered the word *"Muerte"*[5] as he passed me.
77. I unstuck the righthand plumber's friend.
78. My acquaintances were debating the question, which of them would get my apartment?
79. I reviewed the conventional means of attaining the castle.
80. The conventional means of attaining the castle are as follows: "The eagle dug its sharp claws into the tender flesh of the youth, but he bore the pain without a sound, and seized the bird's two feet with his hands. The creature in terror lifted him high up into the air and began to circle the castle. The youth held on bravely. He saw the glittering palace, which by the pale rays of the moon looked like a dim lamp; and he saw the windows and balconies of the castle tower. Drawing a small knife from his belt, he cut off both the eagle's feet. The bird rose up in the air with a yelp, and the youth dropped lightly onto a broad balcony. At the same moment a door opened, and he saw a courtyard filled with flowers and trees, and there, the beautiful enchanted princess." *(The Yellow Fairy Book)*[6]
81. I was afraid.
82. I had forgotten the Bandaids.
83. When the eagle dug its sharp claws into my tender flesh—
84. Should I go back for the Bandaids?
85. But if I went back for the Bandaids I would have to endure the contempt of my acquaintances.
86. I resolved to proceed without the Bandaids.
87. "In some centuries, his [man's] imagination has made life an intense practice of all the lovelier energies." (John Masefield)[7]
88. The eagle dug its sharp claws into my tender flesh.
89. But I bore the pain without a sound, and seized the bird's two feet with my hands.
90. The plumber's friends remained in place, standing at right angles to the side of the mountain.
91. The creature in terror lifted me high in the air and began to circle the castle.
92. I held on bravely.

---

[5]"Death." (Spanish)
[6]A collection of fairy tales edited by Andrew Lang.
[7]A traditional English poet (1878–1967); became Poet Laureate of England in 1930.

93. I saw the glittering palace, which by the pale rays of the moon looked like a dim lamp; and I saw the windows and balconies of the castle tower.

94. Drawing a small knife from my belt, I cut off both the eagle's feet.

95. The bird rose up in the air with a yelp, and I dropped lightly onto a broad balcony.

96. At the same moment a door opened, and I saw a courtyard filled with flowers and trees, and there, the beautiful enchanted symbol.

97. I approached the symbol, with its layers of meaning, but when I touched it, it changed into only a beautiful princess.

98. I threw the beautiful princess headfirst down the mountain to my acquaintances.

99. Who could be relied upon to deal with her.

100. Nor are eagles plausible, not at all, not for a moment.

Questions for "The Glass Mountain"

1.   What was your reaction to the numbered sentences and fragments? What significance might the numbering have?

2.   Describe the tone of this story. What effect does this tone create?

3.   How does Barthelme poke fun at the use of symbols in literature? What elements of the traditional fairy tale has he transposed, and what is the effect of these distortions?

4.   What other conventions of literature does this story satirize? What aspects of contemporary city life does Barthelme also satirize?

5.   What is your sense of this narrator? What does he reveal about himself?

Gabriel García Márquez (1928–   )

Winner of the Nobel Prize for Literature in 1982, Gabriel García Márquez was born in Aracataca, Colombia, and worked as a journalist in South America, Europe, and the United States for 18 years. Many of his publications have been translated from the Spanish, including his best-known novels, *One Hundred Years of Solitude* (1967), *The Autumn of the Patriarch* (1975), and *Chronicle of a Death Foretold* (1981).

García Márquez is one of a group of Latin American writers who have been credited with awakening international interest in Latin American literature. Many critics attribute his popularity to his juxtaposition of the real and the fantastic; as one critic observes: "García Márquez holds on to the journalistic details, the minutiae of the factual, that constitute the great novelistic inheritance of Western realism, and at the same time throws doubt on their reliability through his narrative technique and by means of subtle introduction of mythic elements."

According to García Márquez, his goal is "a perfect integration of journalism and literature. . . . journalism helps maintain contact with reality which is essential to literature. And vice-versa: literature teaches you how to write. . . . I learned how to be a journalist by reading good literature."

A Very Old Man with Enormous Wings

Translated by Gregory Rabassa

─────── A Tale for Children ───────

On the third day of rain they had killed so many crabs inside the house that Pelayo had to cross his drenched courtyard and throw them into the sea, because the newborn child had a temperature all night and they thought it was due to the stench. The world had been sad since Tuesday. Sea and sky were a single ash-gray thing and the sands of the beach, which on March nights glimmered like powdered light, had become a stew of mud and rotten shellfish. The light was so weak at noon that when Pelayo was coming back to the house after throwing away the crabs, it was hard for him to see what it was that was moving and groaning in the rear of the courtyard. He had to go very close to see that it was an old man, a very old man, lying face down in the mud, who, in spite of his tremendous efforts, couldn't get up, impeded by his enormous wings.

Frightened by that nightmare, Pelayo ran to get Elisenda, his wife, who was putting compresses on the sick child, and he took her to the rear of the courtyard. They both looked at the fallen body with mute stupor. He was dressed like a ragpicker. There were only a few faded hairs left on his bald skull and very few teeth in his mouth, and his pitiful condition of a drenched great-grandfather had taken away any sense of grandeur he might have had. His huge buzzard wings, dirty and half-plucked, were forever entangled in the mud. They looked at him so long and so closely that Pelayo and Elisenda very soon overcame their surprise and in the end found him familiar. Then they dared speak to him, and he answered in an incomprehensible dialect with a strong sailor's voice. That was how they skipped over the inconvenience of the wings and quite intelligently concluded that he was a lonely castaway from some foreign ship wrecked by the storm. And yet, they called in a neighbor woman who knew everything about life and death to see him, and all she needed was one look to show them their mistake.

"He's an angel," she told them. "He must have been coming for the child, but the poor fellow is so old that the rain knocked him down."

On the following day everyone knew that a flesh-and-blood angel was held captive in Pelayo's house. Against the judgment of the wise neighbor woman, for whom angels in those times were the fugitive survivors of a celestial conspiracy, they did not have the heart to club him to death. Pelayo watched over him all afternoon from the kitchen, armed with his bailiff's club, and before going to bed he dragged him out of the mud and locked him up with the hens in the wire chicken coop. In the middle of the night, when the rain stopped, Pelayo and Elisenda were still killing crabs. A short time afterward the child woke up without a fever and with a desire to eat. Then they felt magnanimous and decided to put the angel on a raft with fresh water and provisions for three days and leave him to his fate on the high seas. But when they went out into the courtyard with the first light of dawn, they found the whole neighborhood in front of the chicken coop having fun with the angel, without the slightest reverence, tossing him things to eat through the openings in the wire as if he weren't a supernatural creature but a circus animal.

Father Gonzaga arrived before seven o'clock, alarmed at the strange news. By that time onlookers less frivolous than those at dawn had already arrived and they were making all kinds of conjectures concerning the captive's future. The simplest among them thought that he should be named mayor of the world. Others of sterner mind felt that he should be promoted to the rank of five-star general in order to win all wars. Some visionaries hoped that he could be put to stud in order to implant on earth a race of winged wise men who could take charge of the universe. But Father Gonzaga, before becoming a priest, had been a robust woodcutter. Standing by the wire, he reviewed his catechism in an instant and asked them to open the door so that he could take a close look at that pitiful man who looked more like a huge decrepit hen among the fascinated chickens. He was lying in a corner drying his open wings in the sunlight among the fruit peels and breakfast leftovers that the early risers had thrown him. Alien to the impertinences of the world, he only lifted his antiquarian eyes and murmured something in his dialect when Father Gonzaga went into the chicken coop and said good morning to him in Latin. The parish priest had his first suspicion of an imposter when he saw that he did not understand the language of God or know how to greet His ministers. Then he noticed that seen close up he was much too human: he had an unbearable smell of the outdoors, the back side of his wings was strewn with parasites and his main feathers had been mistreated by terrestrial winds, and nothing about him measured up to the proud dignity of angels. Then he came out of the chicken coop and in a brief sermon warned the curious against the risks of being ingenuous. He reminded them that the devil had the bad habit of making use of carnival tricks in order to confuse the unwary. He argued that if wings were not the essential element in determining the difference between a hawk and an airplane, they were even less so in the recognition of angels. Nevertheless, he promised to write a letter to his bishop so that the latter would write to his primate so that the latter would write to the Supreme Pontiff in order to get the final verdict from the highest courts.

His prudence fell on sterile hearts. The news of the captive angel spread with such rapidity that after a few hours the courtyard had the bustle of a marketplace and they had to call in troops with fixed bayonets to disperse the mob that was about to knock the house down. Elisenda, her spine all twisted from sweeping up so much marketplace trash, then got the idea of fencing in the yard and charging five cents admission to see the angel.

The curious came from far away. A traveling carnival arrived with a flying acrobat who buzzed over the crowd several times, but no one paid any attention to him because his wings were not those of an angel but, rather, those of a sidereal bat. The most unfortunate invalids on earth came in search of health: a poor woman who since childhood had been counting her heartbeats and had run out of numbers; a Portuguese man who couldn't sleep because the noise of the stars disturbed him; a sleepwalker who got up at night to undo the things he had done while awake; and many others with less serious ailments. In the midst of that shipwreck disorder that made the earth tremble, Pelayo and Elisenda were happy with fatigue, for in less than a week they had crammed their rooms with money and the line of pilgrims waiting their turn to enter still reached beyond the horizon.

The angel was the only one who took no part in his own act. He spent his time trying to get comfortable in his borrowed nest, befuddled by the hellish heat of the oil lamps and sacramental candles that had been placed along the wire. At first they tried to make him eat some mothballs, which, according to the wisdom of the wise neighbor woman, were the food prescribed for angels. But he turned them down, just at he turned down the papal lunches that the penitents brought him, and they never found out whether it was because he was an angel or because he was an old man that in the end he ate nothing but eggplant mush. His only supernatural virtue seemed to be patience. Especially during the first days, when the hens pecked at him searching for the stellar parasites that proliferated in his wings, and the cripples pulled out feathers to touch their defective parts with, and even the most merciful threw stones at him, trying to get him to rise so they could see him standing. The only time they succeeded in arousing him was when they burned his side with an iron for branding steers, for he had been motionless for so many hours that they thought he was dead. He awoke with a start, ranting in his hermetic language and with tears in his eyes, and he flapped his wings a couple of times, which brought on a whirlwind of chicken dung and lunar dust and a gale of panic that did not seem to be of this world. Although many thought that his reaction had been one not of rage but of pain, from then on they were careful not to annoy him, because the majority understood that his passivity was not that of a hero taking his ease but that of a cataclysm in repose.

Father Gonzaga held back the crowd's frivolity with formulas of maidservant inspiration while awaiting the arrival of a final judgment on the nature of the captive. But the mail from Rome showed no sense of urgency. They spent their time finding out if the prisoner had a navel, if his dialect had any connection with Aramaic, how many times he could fit on the head of a pin, or whether he wasn't just a Norwegian with wings. Those meager letters might have come and gone until the end of time if a providential event had not put an end to the priest's tribulations.

It so happened that during those days, among so many other carnival attractions, there arrived in town the traveling show of the woman who had been changed into a spider for having disobeyed her parents. The admission to see her was not only less than the admission to see the angel, but people were permitted to ask her all manner of questions about her absurd state and to examine her up and down so that no one would ever doubt the truth of her horror. She was a frightful tarantula the size of a ram and with the head of a sad maiden. What was most heart-rending, however, was not her outlandish shape but the sincere affliction with which she recounted the details of her misfortune. While still practically a child she had sneaked out of her parents' house to go to a dance, and while she was coming back through the woods after having danced all night without permission, a fearful thunderclap rent the sky in two and through the crack came the lightning bolt of brimstone that changed her into a spider. Her only nourishment came from the meatballs that charitable souls chose to toss into her mouth. A spectacle like that, full of so much human truth and with such a fearful lesson, was bound to defeat without even trying that of a haughty angel who scarcely deigned to look at mortals. Besides, the few miracles attributed to the angel showed a certain mental disorder, like the blind man who didn't recover his sight but grew three new teeth, or the paralytic who didn't get to walk but almost won the lottery, and the leper whose sores sprouted sunflowers. Those consolation miracles, which were more like mocking fun, had already ruined the angel's reputation when the woman who had been changed into a spider finally crushed him completely. That was how Father Gonzaga was cured forever of his insomnia and Pelayo's courtyard went back to being as empty as during the time it had rained for three days and crabs walked through the bedrooms.

The owners of the house had no reason to lament. With the money they saved they built a two-story mansion with balconies and gardens and high netting so that crabs wouldn't get in during the winter, and with iron bars on the windows so that angels wouldn't get in. Pelayo also set up a rabbit warren close to town and gave up his job as bailiff for good, and Elisenda bought some satin pumps with high heels and many dresses of iridescent silk, the kind worn on Sunday by the most desirable women in those times. The chicken coop was the only thing that didn't receive any attention. If they washed it down with creolin and burned tears of myrrh inside it every so often, it was not in homage to the angel but to drive away the dungheap stench that still hung everywhere like a ghost and was turning the new house into an old one. At first, when the child learned to walk, they were careful that he not get too close to the chicken coop. But then they began to lose their fears and got used to the smell, and before the child got his second teeth he'd gone inside the chicken coop to play, where the wires were falling apart. The angel was no less standoffish with him than with other mortals, but he tolerated the most ingenious infamies with the patience of a dog who had no illusions. They both came down with chicken pox at the same time. The doctor who took care of the child couldn't resist the temptation to listen to the angel's heart, and he found so much whistling in the heart and so many sounds in his kidneys that it seemed impossible for him to be alive. What surprised him most, however, was the logic of his wings. They seemed so natural on that completely human organism that he couldn't understand why other men didn't have them too.

When the child began school it had been some time since the sun and rain had caused the collapse of the chicken coop. The angel went dragging himself about here and there like a stray dying man. They would drive him out of the bedroom with a broom and a moment later find him in the kitchen. He seemed to be in so many places at the same time that they grew to think that he'd been duplicated, that he was reproducing himself all through the house, and the exasperated and unhinged Elisenda shouted that it was awful living in that hell full of angels. He could scarcely eat and his antiquarian eyes had also become so foggy that he went about bumping into posts. All he had left were the bare cannulae of his last feathers. Pelayo threw a blanket over him and extended him the charity of letting him sleep in the shed, and only then did they notice that he had a temperature at night, and was delirious with the tongue twisters of an old Norwegian. That was one of the few times they became alarmed, for they thought he was going to die and not even the wise neighbor woman had been able to tell them what to do with dead angels.

And yet he not only survived his worst winter, but seemed improved with the first sunny days. He remained motionless for several days in the farthest corner of the courtyard, where no one would see him, and at the beginning of December some large, stiff feathers began to grow on his wings, the feathers of a scarecrow, which looked more like another misfortune of decrepitude. But he must have known the reason for those changes, for he was quite careful that no one should notice them, that no one should hear the sea chanteys that he sometimes sang under the stars. One morning Elisenda was cutting some bunches of onions for lunch when a wind that seemed to come from the high seas blew into the kitchen. Then she went to the window and caught the angel in his first attempts at flight. They were so clumsy that his fingernails opened a furrow in the vegetable patch and he was on the point of knocking the shed down with the ungainly flapping that slipped on the light and couldn't get a grip on the air. But he did manage to gain altitude. Elisenda let out a sigh of relief, for herself and for him, when she saw him pass over the last houses, holding himself up in some way with the risky flapping of a senile vulture. She kept watching him even when she was through cutting the onions and she kept on watching until it was no longer possible for her to see him, because then he was no longer an annoyance in her life but an imaginary dot on the horizon of the sea.

Questions for "A Very Old Man with Enormous Wings"

1.   Why do you think the author subtitled this story "A Tale for Children"? Does it seem to be a tale for children?

2.   Who—or what—do you think the old man really is?

3.   Despite its elements of the fantastic, this story—like all of this writer's fiction—is somehow rooted to the real world. How does García Márquez achieve these realistic moments?

4.   How does García Márquez's use of allusion, which we mention in the introduction to this chapter, enrich the story?

James Alan McPherson (1943–   )

As a youngster, James Alan McPherson delivered newspapers and worked in a supermarket in his native Georgia. He earned a law degree at Harvard University, and later worked as a reporter for a Massachusetts newspaper intended for the black community. McPherson has taught writing and Afro-American literature at the University of Iowa and the University of California. Since 1969, he has served as a contributing editor for *The Atlantic* magazine.

McPherson's first collection of short stories, *Hue and Cry,* appeared in 1969. Reviewers have remarked on his keen powers of observation, his ability to draw vivid characters, and his often brilliant dialogue. The selection that follows is from *Elbow Room* (1972), McPherson's second book of short stories.

Why I Like Country Music

No one will believe that I like country music. Even my wife scoffs when told such a possibility exists. "Go on!" Gloria tells me. "I can see blues, bebop, maybe even a little buckdancing. But not bluegrass." Gloria says, "Hillbilly stuff is not just music. It's like the New York Stock Exchange. The minute you see a sharp rise in it, you better watch out."

I tend to argue the point, but quietly, and mostly to myself. Gloria was born and raised in New York; she has come to believe in the stock exchange as the only index of economic health. My perceptions were shaped in South Carolina; and long ago I learned there, as a waiter in private clubs, to gauge economic flux by the tips people gave. We tend to disagree on other matters too, but the thing that gives me most frustration is trying to make her understand why I like country music. Perhaps it is because she hates the South and has capitulated emotionally to the horror stories told by refugees from down home. Perhaps it is because Gloria is third generation Northern-born. I do not know. What I do know is that, while the two of us are black, the distance between us is sometimes as great as that between Ibo and Yoruba.[1] And I do know that despite her protestations, I like country music.

"You are crazy," Gloria tells me.

I tend to argue the point, but quietly, and mostly to myself.

Of course I do not like all country stuff; just pieces that make the right

---

[1] Ibo and Yoruba: Nigerian tribes.

connections. I like banjo because sometimes I hear ancestors in the strumming. I like the fiddlelike refrain in "Dixie" for the very same reason. But most of all I like square dancing—the interplay between fiddle and caller, the stomping, the swishing of dresses, the strutting, the proud turnings, the laughter. Most of all I like the laughter. In recent months I have wondered why I like this music and this dance. I have drawn no general conclusions, but from time to time I suspect it is because the square dance is the only dance form I ever mastered.

"I wouldn't say that in public," Gloria warns me.

I agree with her, but still affirm the truth of it, although quietly, and mostly to myself.

Dear Gloria: This is the truth of how it was:

In my youth in that distant country, while others learned to strut, I grew stiff as a winter cornstalk. When my playmates harmonized their rhythms, I stood on the sidelines in atonic detachment. While they shimmied, I merely jerked in lackluster imitation. I relate these facts here, not in remorse or self-castigation, but as a true confession of my circumstances. In those days, down in our small corner of South Carolina, proficiency in dance was a form of storytelling. A boy could say, "I traveled here and there, saw this and fought that, conquered him and made love to her, lied to them, told a few others the truth, just so I could come back here and let you know what things out there are really like." He could communicate all this with smooth, graceful jiggles of his round bottom, synchronized with intricately coordinated sweeps of his arms and small, unexcited movements of his legs. Little girls could communicate much more.

But sadly, I could do none of it. Development of these skills depended on the ministrations of family and neighbors. My family did not dance; our closest neighbor was a true-believing Seventh Day Adventist. Moreover, most new dances came from up North, brought to town usually by people returning to riff on the good life said to exist in those far Northern places. They prowled our dirt streets in rented Cadillacs; paraded our brick sidewalks exhibiting styles abstracted from the fullness of life in Harlem, South Philadelphia, Roxbury, Baltimore and the South Side of Chicago. They confronted our provincial clothes merchants with the arrogant reminder, "But people ain't wearin' this in New Yo*kkk!*" Each of their movements, as well as their world-weary smoothness, told us locals meaningful tales of what was missing in our lives. Unfortunately, those of us under strict parental supervision, or those of us without Northern connections, could only stand at a distance and worship these envoys of culture. We stood on the sidelines—styleless, gestureless, danceless, doing nothing more than an improvised one-butt shuffle—hoping for one of them to touch our lives. It was my good fortune, during my tenth year on the sidelines, to have one of these Northerners introduce me to the square dance.

My dear, dear Gloria, her name was Gweneth Lawson:

She was a pretty, chocolate brown little girl with dark brown eyes and two long black braids. After all these years, the image of these two braids evokes in me all there is to remember about Gweneth Lawson. They were plaited across the top of her head and hung to a point just above the back of her Peter Pan collar. Sometimes she wore two bows, one red and one blue, and these tended to sway lazily near the place on her neck where the smooth brown of her skin and the white of her collar met the ink-bottle black of her hair. Even when I cannot remember her face, I remember the rainbow of deep, rich colors in which she lived. This is so because I watched them, every weekday, from my desk directly behind hers in our fourth-grade class. And she wore the most magical perfume, or lotion, smelling just slightly of fresh-cut lemons, that wafted back to me whenever she made the slightest move-ment at her desk. Now I must tell you this much more, dear Gloria: when-ever I smell fresh lemons, whether in the market or at home, I look around me—not for Gweneth Lawson, but for some quiet corner where I can revive in private certain memories of her. And in pursuing these memories across such lemony bridges, I rediscover that I loved her.

Gweneth was from the South Carolina section of Brooklyn. Her parents had sent her south to live with her uncle, Mr. Richard Lawson, the brick mason, for an unspecified period of time. Just why they did this I do not know, unless it was their plan to have her absorb more of South Carolina folkways than conditions in Brooklyn would allow. She was a gentle, soft-spoken girl; I recall no condescension in her manner. This was all the more admirable because our unrestrained awe of a Northern-born black person usually induced in him some grand sense of his own importance. You must know that in those days older folks would point to someone and say, ''He's from the North,'' and the statement would be sufficient in itself. Mothers made their children behave by advising that, if they led exemplary lives and attended church regularly, when they died they would go to New York. Only someone who understands what London meant to Dick Whittington, or how California and the suburbs function in the national mind, could appreciate the mythical dimensions of this Northlore.

But Gweneth Lawson was above regional idealization. Though I might have loved her partly because she was a Northerner, I loved her more because of the world of colors that seemed to be suspended about her head. I loved her glowing forehead and I loved her bright, dark brown eyes; I loved the black braids, the red and blue and sometimes yellow and pink ribbons; I loved the way the deep, rich brown of her neck melted into the pink or white cloth of her Peter Pan collar; I loved the lemony vapor on which she floated and from which, on occasion, she seemed to be inviting me to be buoyed up, up, up into her happy world; I loved the way she caused my heart to tumble whenever, during a restless moment, she seemed about to turn her head in my direction; I loved her more, though torturously, on the many occasions when she did not turn. Because I was a shy boy, I loved the way I could love her silently, at least six hours a day, without ever having to disclose my love.

My platonic state of mind might have stretched onward into a blissful infinity had not Mrs. Esther Clay Boswell, our teacher, made it her business to pry into the affair. Although she prided herself on being a strict disciplinarian, Mrs. Boswell was not without a sense of humor. A round, full-breasted woman in her early forties, she liked to amuse herself, and sometimes the class as well, by calling the attention of all eyes to whomever of us violated the structure she imposed on classroom activities. She was particularly hard on people like me who could not contain an impulse to daydream, or those who allowed their eyes to wander too far away from lessons printed on the blackboard. A black and white sign posted under the electric clock next to the door summed up her attitude toward this kind of truancy: NOTICE TO ALL CLOCKWATCHERS, it read, TIME PASSES. WILL YOU? Nor did she abide timidity in her students. Her voice booming, "Speak up, boy!" was more than enough to cause the more emotional among us, including me, to break into convenient flows of warm tears. But by doing this we violated yet another rule, one on which depended our very survival in Mrs. Esther Clay Boswell's class. She would spell out this rule for us as she paced before her desk, slapping a thick, homemade ruler against the flat of her brown palm. "There ain't no *ba*bies in here," she would recite. *Thaap!* "Anybody thinks he's still a *baby* . . ." *Thaap!* ". . . should crawl back home to his mama's *titty.*" *Thaap!* "You little bunnies shed your *last water . . .*" *Thaap!* " . . . the minute you left home to come in here." *Thaap!* "From now on, you g'on do all your *cryin' . . .*" *Thaap!* " . . . in *church!*" *Thaap!* Whenever one of us compelled her to make this speech it would seem to me that her eyes paused overlong on my face. She would seem to be daring me, as if suspicious that, in addition to my secret passion for Gweneth Lawson, which she might excuse, I was also in the habit of throwing fits of temper.

She had read me right. I was the product of too much attention from my father. He favored me, paraded me around on his shoulder, inflated my ego constantly with what, among us at least, was a high compliment: "You my nigger if you don't get no bigger." This statement, along with my father's generous attentions, made me selfish and used to having my own way. I *expected* to have my own way in most things, and when I could not, I tended to throw tantrums calculated to break through any barrier raised against me.

Mrs. Boswell was also perceptive in assessing the extent of my infatuation with Gweneth Lawson. Despite my stealth in telegraphing emissions of affection into the back part of Gweneth's brain, I could not help but observe, occasionally, Mrs. Boswell's cool glance pausing on the two of us. But she never said a word. Instead, she would settle her eyes momentarily on Gweneth's face and then pass quickly to mine. But in that instant she seemed to be saying, "Don't look back now, girl, but I *know* that bald-headed boy behind you has you on his mind." She seemed to watch me daily, with a combination of amusement and absolute detachment in her brown eyes. And when she stared, it was not at me but at the normal focus of my attention: the end of Gweneth Lawson's black braids. Whenever I sensed Mrs. Boswell watching I would look away quickly, either down at my brown desk top or across the room to the blackboard. But her eyes could not be eluded this easily. Without looking at anyone in particular, she could make a specific point to one person in a manner so general that only long afterward did the real object of her attention realize it had been intended for him.

"Now you little brown bunnies," she might say, "and you black buck rabbits and you few cottontails mixed in, some of you starting to smell yourselves under the arms without knowing what it's all about." And here, it sometimes seemed to me, she allowed her eyes to pause casually on me before resuming their sweep of the entire room. "Now I know your mamas already made you think life is a bed of roses, but in *my* classroom you got to know the footpaths through the *sticky* parts of the rosebed." It was her custom during this ritual to prod and goad those of us who were developing reputations for meekness and indecision; yet her method was Socratic in that she compelled us, indirectly, to supply our own answers by exploiting one person as the walking symbol of the error she intended to correct. Clarence Buford, for example, an oversized but good-natured boy from a very poor family, served often as the helpmeet in this exercise.

"Buford," she might begin, slapping the ruler against her palm, "how does a tongue-tied country boy like you expect to get a wife?"

"I don't want no wife," Buford might grumble softly.

Of course the class would laugh.

"Oh yes you do," Mrs. Boswell would respond. "All you buck rabbits want wives." *Thaap!* "So how do you let a girl know you not just a bump on a log?"

"I know! I know!" a high voice might call from a seat across from mine. This, of course, would be Leon Pugh. A peanut-brown boy with curly hair, he seemed to know everything. Moreover, he seemed to take pride in being the only one who knew answers to life questions and would wave his arms excitedly whenever our attentions were focused on such matters. It seemed to me his voice would be extra loud and his arms waved more strenuously whenever he was certain that Gweneth Lawson, seated across from him, was interested in an answer to Mrs. Esther Clay Boswell's question. His eager arms, it seemed to me, would be reaching out to grasp Gweneth instead of the question asked.

"Buford, you twisted-tongue, bunion-toed country boy," Mrs. Boswell might say, ignoring Leon Pugh's hysterical arm-waving, "you gonna let a cottontail like Leon get a girlfriend before you?"

"I don't want no girlfriend," Clarence Buford would almost sob. "I don't like no girls."

The class would laugh again while Leon Pugh manipulated his arms like a flight navigator under battle conditions. "I know! I know! I swear to *God* I know!"

When at last Mrs. Boswell could turn in his direction, I might sense that she was tempted momentarily to ask me for an answer. But as in most such exercises, it was the worldly-wise Leon Pugh who supplied this. "What do *you* think, Leon?" she would ask inevitably, but with a rather lifeless slap of the ruler against her palm.

"My daddy told me . . ." Leon would shout, turning slyly to beam at Gweneth, " . . . my daddy and my big brother from the Bronx New York told me that to git *anythin'* in this world you gotta learn how to blow your own horn."

"Why, Leon?" Mrs. Boswell might ask in a bored voice.

"Because," the little boy would recite, puffing out his chest, "because if you don't blow your own horn ain't nobody else g'on blow it for you. That's what my daddy said."

"What do you think about that, Buford?" Mrs. Boswell would ask.

"I don't want no girlfriend anyhow," the puzzled Clarence Buford might say.

And then the cryptic lesson would suddenly be dropped.

This was Mrs. Esther Clay Boswell's method of teaching. More than anything written on the blackboard, her questions were calculated to make us turn around in our chairs and inquire in guarded whispers of each other, and especially of the wise and confident Leon Pugh, "What does she mean?" But none of us, besides Pugh, seemed able to comprehend what it was we ought to know but did not know. And Mrs. Boswell, plump brown fox that she was, never volunteered any more in the way of confirmation than was necessary to keep us interested. Instead, she paraded around us, methodically slapping the homemade ruler against her palm, suggesting by her silence more depth to her question, indeed, more implications in Leon's answer, than we were then able to perceive. And during such moments, whether inspired by self-ishness or by the peculiar way Mrs. Boswell looked at me, I felt that finding answers to such questions was a task she had set for me, of all the members of the class.

Of course Leon Pugh, among other lesser lights, was my chief rival for the affections of Gweneth Lawson. All during the school year, from September through the winter rains, he bested me in my attempts to look directly into her eyes and say a simple, heartfelt "hey." This was my ambition, but I never seemed able to get close enough to her attention. At Thanksgiving I helped draw a bounteous yellow cornucopia on the blackboard, with fruits and flow-ers matching the colors that floated around Gweneth's head; Leon Pugh made one by himself, a masterwork of silver paper and multicolored crepe, which he hung on the door. Its silver tail curled upward to a point just below the face of Mrs. Boswell's clock. At Christmas, when we drew names out of a hat for the exchange of gifts, I drew the name of Queen Rose Phipps, a fairly unattractive squash-yellow girl of absolutely no interest to me. Pugh, whether through collusion with the boy who handled the lottery or through pure luck, pulled forth from the hat the magic name of Gweneth Lawson. He gave her a set of deep purple bows for her braids and a basket of pecans from his father's tree. Uninterested now in the spirit of the occasion, I delivered to Queen Rose Phipps a pair of white socks. Each time Gweneth wore the purple bows she would glance over at Leon and smile. Each time Queen Rose wore my white socks I would turn away in embarrassment, lest I should see them pulling down into her shoes and exposing her skinny ankles.

After class, on wet winter days, I would trail along behind Gweneth to the bus stop, pause near the steps while she entered, and follow her down the aisle until she chose a seat. Usually, however, in clear violation of the code of conduct to which all gentlemen were expected to adhere, Leon Pugh would already be on the bus and shouting to passersby, "Move off! Get away! This here seat by me is reserved for the girl from Brooklyn New York." Discouraged but not defeated, I would swing into the seat next nearest her and cast calf-eyed glances of wounded affection at the back of her head or at the brown, rainbow profile of her face. And at her stop, some eight or nine blocks from mine, I would disembark behind her along with the crowd of other love-struck boys. There would then follow a well-rehearsed scene in which all of us, save Leon Pugh, pretended to have gotten off the bus either too late or too soon to wend our proper paths homeward. And at slight cost to ourselves we enjoyed the advantage of being able to walk close by her as she glided toward her uncle's green-frame house. There, after pausing on the wooden steps and smiling radiantly around the crowd like a spring sun in that cold winter rain, she would sing, "Bye, y'all," and disappear into the structure with the mystery of a goddess. Afterward I would walk away, but slowly, much slower than the other boys, warmed by the music and light in her voice against the sharp, wet winds of the February afternoon.

I loved her, dear Gloria, and I danced with her and smelled the lemony youth of her and told her that I loved her, all this in a way you would never believe:

You would not know or remember, as I do, that in those days, in our area of the country, we enjoyed a pleasingly ironic mixture of Yankee and Confederate folkways. Our meals and manners, our speech, our attitudes toward certain ambiguous areas of history, even our acceptance of tragedy as the normal course of life—these things and more defined us as Southern. Yet the stern morality of our parents, their toughness and penny-pinching and attitudes toward work, their covert allegiance toward certain ideals, even the directions toward which they turned our faces, made us more Yankee than Cavalier. Moreover, some of our schools were named for Confederate men of distinction, but others were named for the stern-faced believers who had swept down from the North to save a people back, back long ago, in those long forgotten days of once upon a time. Still, our schoolbooks, our required classroom songs, our flags, our very relation to the statues and monuments in public parks, negated the story that these dreamers from the North had ever come. We sang the state song, memorized the verses of homegrown poets, honored in our books the names and dates of historical events both before and after that Historical Event which, in our region, supplanted even the division of the millennia introduced by the followers of Jesus Christ. Given the silent circumstances of our cultural environment, it was ironic, and perhaps just, that we maintained a synthesis of two traditions no longer supportive of each other. Thus it became traditional at our school to celebrate the arrival of spring on May first by both the ritual plaiting of the Maypole and square dancing.

On that day, as on a few others, the Superintendent of Schools and several officials were likely to visit our schoolyard and stand next to the rusty metal swings, watching the fourth, fifth, and sixth graders bob up and down and behind and before each other, around the gaily painted Maypoles. These happy children would pull and twist long runs of billowy crepe paper into wondrous, multicolored plaits. Afterward, on the edges of thunderous applause from teachers, parents and visiting dignitaries, a wave of elaborately costumed children would rush out onto the grounds in groups of eight and proceed with the square dance. "Dog*gone!*" the Superintendent of Schools was heard to exclaim on one occasion. "Y'all do it so good it just makes your *bones* set up and take notice."

Such was the schedule two weeks prior to May first, when Mrs. Boswell announced to our class that as fourth graders we were now eligible to participate in the festivities. The class was divided into two general sections of sixteen each, one group preparing to plait the pole and a second group, containing an equal number of boys and girls, practicing turns for our part in the square dance. I was chosen to square dance; so was Leon Pugh. Gweneth Lawson was placed with the pole plaiters. I was depressed until I remembered, happily, that I could not dance a lick. I reported this fact to Mrs. Boswell just after the drawing, during recess, saying that my lack of skill would only result in our class making a poor showing. I asked to be reassigned to the group of Maypole plaiters. Mrs. B. looked me over with considerable amusement tugging at the corners of her mouth. "Oh, you don't have to *dance* to do the square dance," she said. "That's a dance that was made up to mock folks that couldn't dance." She paused a second before adding thoughtfully: "The worse you are at dancing, the better you can square dance. It's just about the best dance in the world for a stiff little bunny like you."

"I want to plait the Maypole," I said.

"You'll square dance or I'll grease your little butt," Mrs. Esther Clay Boswell said.

"I ain't gonna do *nothin'!*" I muttered. But I said this quietly, and mostly to myself, while walking away from her desk. For the rest of the day she watched me closely, as if she knew what I was thinking.

The next morning I brought a note from my father. "Dear Mrs. Boswell:" I had watched him write earlier that morning, "My boy does not square dance. Please excuse him as I am afraid he will break down and cry and mess up the show. Yours truly . . ."

Mrs. Boswell said nothing after she had read the note. She merely waved me to my seat. But in the early afternoon, when she read aloud the lists of those assigned to dancing and Maypole plaiting, she paused as my name rolled off her tongue. "You don't have to stay on the square dance team," she called to me. "You go on out in the yard with the Maypole team."

I was ecstatic. I hurried to my place in line some three warm bodies behind Gweneth Lawson. We prepared to march out.

"Wait a minute," Mrs. Boswell called. "Now it looks like we got seventeen bunnies on the Maypole team and fifteen on the square dance. We have to even things up." She made a thorough examination of both lists, scratching her head. Then she looked carefully up and down the line of stomping Maypoleites. "Miss Gweneth Lawson, you cute little cottontail you, it looks like you gonna have to go over to the square dance team. That'll give us eight sets of partners for the square dance . . . but now we have another problem." She made a great display of counting the members of the two squads of square dancers. "Now there's sixteen square dancers all right, but when we pair them off we got a problem of higher mathematics. With nine girls and only seven *boys,* looks like we gotta switch a girl from square dancing to Maypole and a boy from Maypole to square dancing."

I waited hopefully for Gweneth Lawson to volunteer. But just at that moment the clever Leon Pugh grabbed her hand and began jitterbugging as though he could hardly wait for the record player to be turned on and the dancing to begin.

"What a cute couple," Mrs. Boswell observed absently. "Now which one of you other girls wants to join up with the Maypole team?"

Following Pugh's example, the seven remaining boys grabbed the girls they wanted as partners. Only skinny Queen Rose Phipps and shy Beverly Hankins remained unclaimed. Queen Rose giggled nervously.

"Queen Rose," Mrs. B. called, "I know you don't mind plaiting the Maypole." She waved her ruler in a gesture of casual dismissal. Queen Rose raced across the room and squeezed into line.

"Now," Mrs. Boswell said, "I need a boy to come across to the square dancers."

I was not unmindful of the free interchange of partners involved in square dancing, even though Leon Pugh had beat me in claiming the partner of my choice. All I really wanted was one moment swinging Gweneth Lawson in my arms. I raised my hand slowly.

"Oh, not *you,* little bunny," Mrs. Boswell said. "You and your daddy claim you don't like to square dance." She slapped her ruler against her palm. *Thaap! Thaap!* Then she said, "Clarence Buford, I *know* a big-footed country boy like you can square dance better than anybody. Come on over here and kiss cute little Miss Beverly Hankins."

"I don't like no girls *noway,"* Buford mumbled. But he went over and stood next to the giggling Beverly Hankins.

"Now!" said Mrs. B. "March on out in that yard and give that pole a good plaiting!"

We started to march out. Over my shoulder, as I reached the door, I glimpsed the overjoyed Leon Pugh whirling lightly on his toes. He sang in a confident tone:

"I saw the Lord give Moses a pocketful of roses.
I skid Ezekiel's wheel on a ripe banana peel.
I rowed the Nile, flew over a stile,

Saw Jack Johnson pick his teeth
With toenails from Jim Jeffries' feets . . ."

"Grab your partners!" Mrs. Esther Clay Boswell was saying as the oak door slammed behind us.

I had been undone. For almost two weeks I was obliged to stand on the sidelines and watch Leon Pugh allemande left and do-si-do my beloved Gweneth. Worse, she seemed to be enjoying it. But I must give Leon proper credit: he was a dancing fool. In a matter of days he had mastered, and then improved on, the various turns and bows and gestures of the square dance. He leaped while the others plodded, whirled each girl through his arms with lightness and finesse, chattered playfully at the other boys when they tumbled over their own feet. Mrs. Boswell stood by the record player calling, "Put some *strut* in it, Buford, you big potato sack. Watch Leon and see how *he* does it." I leaned against the classroom wall and watched the dancers, my own group having already exhausted the limited variations possible in matters of Maypole plaiting.

At home each night I begged my father to send another note to Mrs. Boswell, this time stating that I had no interest in the Maypole. But he resisted my entreaties and even threatened me with a whipping if I did not participate and make him proud of me. The real cause of his irritation was the considerable investment he had already made in purchasing an outfit for me. Mrs. Boswell had required all her students, square dancers and Maypole plaiters alike, to report on May first in outfits suitable for square dancing. My father had bought a new pair of dungarees, a blue shirt, a red and white polka-dot bandanna and a cowboy hat. He was in no mood to bend under the emotional weight of my new demands. As a matter of fact, early in the morning of May first he stood beside my bed with the bandanna in his left hand and his leather belt in his right hand, just in case I developed a sudden fever.

I dragged myself heavily through the warm, blue spring morning toward school, dressed like a carnival cowboy. When I entered the classroom I sulked against the wall, being content to watch the other children. And what happy buzzings and jumping and excitement they made as they compared costumes. Clarence Buford wore a Tom Mix hat and a brown vest over a green shirt with red six-shooter patterns embossed on its collar. Another boy, Paul Carter, was dressed entirely in black, with a fluffy white handkerchief puffing from his neck. But Leon Pugh caught the attention of all our eyes. He wore a red and white checkered shirt, a loose green bandanna clasped at his throat by a shining silver buffalo head, brown chaps sewed onto his dungarees, and shiny brown cowboy boots with silver spurs that clanked each time he moved. In his hand he carried a carefully creased brown cowboy hat. He announced his fear that it would lose its shape and planned to put it on only when the dancing started. He would allow no one to touch it. Instead, he stood around clanking his feet and smoothing the crease in his fabulous hat and saying loudly, "My daddy says it pays to look good no matter what you put on."

The girls seemed prettier and much older than their ages. Even Queen Rose Phipps wore rouge on her cheeks that complemented her pale color. Shy Beverly Hankins had come dressed in a blue and white checkered bonnet and a crisp blue apron; she looked like a frontier mother. But Gweneth Lawson, my Gweneth Lawson, dominated the group of girls. She wore a long red dress with sheaves and sheaves of sparkling white crinoline belling it outward so it seemed she was floating. On her honey-brown wrists golden bracelets sparkled. A deep blue bandanna enclosed her head with the wonder of a summer sky. Black patent leather shoes glistened like half-hidden stars beneath the red and white of her hemline. She stood smiling before us and we marveled. At that moment I would have given the world to have been able to lead her about on my arm.

Mrs. Boswell watched us approvingly from behind her desk. Finally, at noon, she called, "Let's go on out!" Thirty-two living rainbows cascaded toward the door. Pole plaiters formed one line. Square dancers formed another. Mrs. Boswell strolled officiously past us in review. It seemed to me she almost paused while passing the spot where I stood on line. But she brushed past me, straightening an apron here, applying spittle and a rub to a rouged cheek there, waving a wary finger at an overanxious boy. Then she whacked her ruler against her palm and led us out into the yard. The fifth and sixth graders had already assembled. On one end of the playground were a dozen or so tall painted poles with long, thin wisps of green and blue and yellow and rust-brown crepe floating lazily on the sweet spring breezes.

"Maypole teams *up!*" called Mr. Henry Lucas, our principal, from his platform by the swings. Beside him stood the white Superintendent of Schools (who said later of the square dance, it was reported to all the classes, "Lord, y'all square dance so *good* it makes me plumb *ashamed* us white folks ain't takin' better care of our art stuff."). "Maypole teams up!" Mr. Henry Lucas shouted again. Some fifty of us, screaming shrilly, rushed to grasp our favorite color crepe. Then, to the music of "Sing Praise for All the Brightness and the Joy of Spring," we pulled and plaited in teams of six or seven until every pole was twisted as tight and as colorfully as the braids on Gweneth Lawson's head. Then, to the applause of proud teachers and parents and the whistles of the Superintendent of Schools, we scattered happily back under the wings of our respective teachers. I stood next to Mrs. Boswell, winded and trembling but confident I had done my best. She glanced down at me and said in a quiet voice, "I do believe you are learning the rhythm of the thing."

I did not respond.

"Let's go!" Leon Pugh shouted to the other kids, grabbing Gweneth Lawson's arm and taking a few clanking steps forward.

"Wait a minute, Leon," Mrs. Boswell hissed. "Mr. Lucas has to change the record."

Leon sighed. "But if we don't git out there first, all them other teams will take the best spots."

"Wait!" Mrs. Boswell ordered.

Leon sulked. He inched closer to Gweneth. I watched him swing her hand impatiently. He stamped his feet and his silver spurs jangled.

Mrs. Boswell looked down at his feet. "Why, Leon," she said, "you can't go out there with razors on your shoes."

"These ain't razors," Leon muttered. "These here are spurs my brother in Bronx New York sent me just for this here dance."

"You have to take them off," Mrs. Boswell said.

Leon growled. But he reached down quickly and attempted to jerk the silver spurs from the heels of his boots. They did not come off. "No time!" he called, standing suddenly. "Mr. Lucas done put the record on."

"Leon, you might *cut* somebody with those things," Mrs. Boswell said. "Miss Gweneth Lawson's pretty red dress could get caught in those things and then she'll fall as surely as I'm standin' here."

"I'll just go out with my boots off," Leon replied.

But Mrs. Boswell shook her head firmly. "You just run on to the lunchroom and ask cook for some butter or mayo. That'll help 'em slip off." She paused, looking out over the black dirt playground, "And if you miss this first dance, why there'll be a second and maybe even a third. We'll get a Maypole plaiter to sub for you."

My heart leaped. Leon sensed it and stared at me. His hand tightened on Gweneth's as she stood radiant and smiling in the loving spring sunlight. Leon let her hand drop and bent quickly, pulling at the spurs with the fury of a Samson.

"Square dancers *up!*" Mr. Henry Lucas called.

"Sonofa*bitch!*" Leon grunted.

"Square dancers *up!*" called Mr. Lucas.

The fifth and sixth graders were screaming and rushing toward the center of the yard. Already the record was scratching out the high, slick voice of the caller. *"Sonofabitch!"* Leon moaned.

Mrs. Boswell looked directly at Gweneth, standing alone and abandoned next to Leon. "Miss Gweneth Lawson," Mrs. Boswell said in a cool voice, "it's a cryin' shame there ain't no prince to take you to that ball out there."

I do not remember moving, but I know I stood with Gweneth at the center of the yard. What I did there I do not know, but I remember watching the movements of others and doing what they did just after they had done it. Still, I cannot remember just when I looked into my partner's face or what I saw there. The scratchy voice of the caller bellowed directions and I obeyed:

*"Allemande left with your left hand
Right to your partner with a right and left grand . . ."*

Although I was told later that I made an allemande right instead of left, I have no memory of the mistake.

*"When you get to your partner pass her by
And pick up the next girl on the sly . . ."*

Nor can I remember picking up any other girl. I only remember that during many turns and do-si-dos I found myself looking into the warm brown eyes of Gweneth Lawson. I recall that she smiled at me. I recall that she laughed on another turn. I recall that I laughed with her an eternity later.

> " . . . *promenade that dear old thing*
> *Throw your head right back and sing* be-*cause, just*
> be-*cause . . ."*

I do remember quite well that during the final promenade before the record ended, Gweneth stood beside me and I said to her in a voice much louder than that of the caller, "When I get up to Brooklyn I hope I see you." But I do not remember what she said in response. I want to remember that she smiled.

I know I smiled, dear Gloria. I smiled with the lemonness of her and the loving of her pressed deep into those saving places of my private self. It was my plan to savor these, and I did savor them. But when I reached New York, many years later, I did not think of Brooklyn. I followed the old, beaten, steady paths into uptown Manhattan. By then I had learned to dance to many other kinds of music. And I had forgotten the savory smell of lemon. But I think sometimes of Gweneth now when I hear country music. And although it is difficult to explain to you, I still maintain that I am no mere arithmetician in the art of the square dance. I am into the calculus of it.

"Go on!" you will tell me, backing into your Northern mythology. "I can see the hustle, the hump, maybe even the Ibo highlife. But no hillbilly."

These days I am firm about arguing the point, but, as always, quietly, and mostly to myself.

Questions for "Why I Like Country Music"

1.   Why does the narrator like country music? Why, for example, doesn't the author call the story "Why I Like Square Dancing," or "How I Fell in Love with Gweneth Lawson"?

2.   How does McPherson create "real" characters like Gweneth Lawson, Mrs. Esther Clay Boswell, and Leon Pugh, that we can see and hear, and that stay in our minds?

3.   What can you tell about the narrator of this story? Describe the tone of his reminiscences and how this tone affects our understanding of the piece.

Grace Paley (1922–   )

The daughter of Russian immigrants, Grace Paley has lived in New York City for most of her life. Her parents spoke Russian and Yiddish at home, and Paley's experience with American, Russian, and Jewish cultures informs much of her work. She attended Hunter College but dropped out after a year, horrifying her parents.

Paley has taught at Columbia and Syracuse University, and now teaches at City College and Sarah Lawrence College. In addition to teaching and writing, she has been active in the antiwar and feminist movements. Although not a prolific writer, she has earned acclaim and many fans for her three collections of short stories, *The Little Disturbances of Man* (1959), *Enormous Changes at the Last Minute* (1974), from which the following selection is taken, and *Later the Same Day* (1985). In 1986, Paley was named New York's first state author.

A Conversation with My Father

My father is eighty-six years old and in bed. His heart, that bloody motor, is equally old and will not do certain jobs any more. It still floods his head with brainy light. But it won't let his legs carry the weight of his body around the house. Despite my metaphors, this muscle failure is not due to his old heart, he says, but to a potassium shortage. Sitting on one pillow, leaning on three, he offers last-minute advice and makes a request.

"I would like you to write a simple story just once more," he says, "the kind de Maupassant wrote, or Chekhov, the kind you used to write. Just recognizable people and then write down what happened to them next."

I say, "Yes, why not? That's possible." I want to please him, though I don't remember writing that way. I *would* like to try to tell such a story, if he means the kind that begins: "There was a woman . . ." followed by plot, the absolute line between two points which I've always despised. Not for literary reasons, but because it takes all hope away. Everyone, real or invented, deserves the open destiny of life.

Finally I thought of a story that had been happening for a couple of years right across the street. I wrote it down, then read it aloud. "Pa," I said, "how about this? Do you mean something like this?"

Once in my time there was a woman and she had a son. They lived nicely, in a small apartment in Manhattan. This boy at about fifteen became a junkie, which is not unusual in our neighborhood. In order to maintain her close friendship with him, she became a junkie too. She said it was part of the youth culture, with which she felt very much at home. After a while, for a number of reasons, the boy gave it all up and left the city and his mother in disgust. Hopeless and alone, she grieved. We all visit her.

"O.K., Pa, that's it," I said, "an unadorned and miserable tale."

"But that's not what I mean," my father said. "You misunderstood me on purpose. You know there's a lot more to it. You know that. You left everything out. Turgenev wouldn't do that. Chekhov wouldn't do that. There are in fact Russian writers you never heard of, you don't have an inkling of, as good as anyone, who can write a plain ordinary story, who would not leave out what you have left out. I object not to facts but to people sitting in trees talking senselessly, voices from who knows where . . ."

"Forget that one, Pa, what have I left out now? In this one?"

"Her looks, for instance."

"Oh, Quite handsome, I think. Yes."

"Her hair?"

"Dark, with heavy braids, as though she were a girl or a foreigner."

"What were her parents like, her stock? That she became such a person. It's interesting, you know."

"From out of town. Professional people. The first to be divorced in their county. How's that? Enough?" I asked.

"With you, it's all a joke," he said. "What about the boy's father? Why didn't you mention him? Who was he? Or was the boy born out of wedlock?"

"Yes," I said. "He was born out of wedlock."

"For Godsakes, doesn't anyone in your stories get married? Doesn't anyone have the time to run down to City Hall before they jump into bed?"

"No," I said. "In real life, yes. But in my stories, no."

"Why do you answer me like that?"

"Oh, Pa, this is a simple story about a smart woman who came to N.Y.C. full of interest love trust excitement very up to date, and about her son, what a hard time she had in this world. Married or not, it's of small consequence."

"It is of great consequence," he said.

"O.K.," I said.

"O.K. O.K. yourself," he said, "but listen. I believe you that she's good-looking, but I don't think she was so smart."

"That's true," I said. "Actually that's the trouble with stories. People start out fantastic. You think they're extraordinary, but it turns out as the work goes along, they're just average with a good education. Sometimes the other way around, the person's a kind of dumb innocent, but he outwits you and you can't even think of an ending good enough."

"What do you do then?" he asked. He had been a doctor for a couple of decades and then an artist for a couple of decades and he's still interested in details, craft, technique.

"Well, you just have to let the story lie around till some agreement can be reached between you and the stubborn hero."

"Aren't you talking silly, now?" he asked. "Start again," he said. "It so happens I'm not going out this evening. Tell the story again. See what you can do this time."

"O.K.," I said. "But it's not a five-minute job." Second attempt:

Once, across the street from us, there was a fine handsome woman, our neighbor. She had a son whom she loved because she'd known him since birth (in helpless chubby infancy, and in the wrestling, hugging ages, seven to ten, as well as earlier and later). This boy, when he fell into the fist of adolescence, became a junkie. He was not a hopeless one. He was in fact hopeful, an ideologue and successful converter. With his busy brilliance, he wrote persuasive articles for his high-school newspaper. Seeking a wider audience, using important connections, he drummed into Lower Manhattan newsstand distribution a periodical called *Oh! Golden Horse!*

In order to keep him from feeling guilty (because guilt is the stony heart of nine tenths of all clinically diagnosed cancers in America today, she said), and because she had always believed in giving bad habits room at home where one could keep an eye on them, she too became a junkie. Her kitchen was famous for a while—a center of intellectual addicts who knew what they were doing. A few felt artistic like Coleridge and others were scientific and revolutionary like Leary. Although she was often high herself, certain good mothering reflexes remained, and she saw to it that there was lots of orange juice around and honey and milk and vitamin pills. However, she never cooked anything but chili, and that no more than once a week. She explained, when we talked to her, seriously, with neighborly concern, that it was her part in the youth culture and she would rather be with the young, it was an honor, than with her own generation.

One week, while nodding through an Antonioni film, this boy was severely jabbed by the elbow of a stern and proselytizing girl, sitting beside him. She offered immediate apricots and nuts for his sugar level, spoke to him sharply, and took him home.

She had heard of him and his work and she herself published, edited, and wrote a competitive journal called *Man Does Live By Bread Alone.* In the organic heat of her continuous presence he could not help but become interested once more in his muscles, his arteries, and nerve connections. In fact he began to love them, treasure them, praise them with funny little songs in *Man Does Live . . .*

> the fingers of my flesh transcend
> my transcendental soul
> the tightness in my shoulders end
> my teeth have made me whole

To the mouth of his head (that glory of will and determination) he brought hard apples, nuts, wheat germ, and soybean oil. He said to his old friends, From now on, I guess I'll keep my wits about me. I'm going on the natch. He said he was about to begin a spiritual deep-breathing journey. How about you too, Mom? he asked kindly.

His conversion was so radiant, splendid, that neighborhood kids his age began to say that he had never been a real addict at all, only a journalist along for the smell of the story. The mother tried several times to give up what had become without her son and his friends a lonely habit. This effort only brought it to supportable levels. The boy and his girl took their electronic mimeograph and moved to the bushy edge of another borough. They were very strict. They said they would not see her again until she had been off drugs for sixty days.

At home alone in the evening, weeping, the mother read and reread the seven issues of *Oh! Golden Horse!* They seemed to her as truthful as ever. We often crossed the street to visit and console. But if we mentioned any of our children who were at college or in the hospital or dropouts at home, she would cry out, My baby! My baby! and burst into terrible, face-scarring, time-consuming tears. The End.

First my father was silent, then he said, "Number One: You have a nice sense of humor. Number Two: I see you can't tell a plain story. So don't waste time." Then he said sadly, "Number Three: I suppose that means she was alone, she was left like that, his mother. Alone. Probably sick?"

I said, "Yes."

"Poor woman. Poor girl, to be born in a time of fools, to live among fools. The end. The end. You were right to put that down. The end."

I didn't want to argue, but I had to say, "Well, it is not necessarily the end, Pa."

"Yes," he said, "what a tragedy. The end of a person."

"No, Pa," I begged him. "It doesn't have to be. She's only about forty. She could be a hundred different things in this world as time goes on. A teacher or a social worker. An ex-junkie! Sometimes it's better than having a master's in education."

"Jokes," he said. "As a writer that's your main trouble. You don't want to recognize it. Tragedy! Plain tragedy! Historical tragedy! No hope. The end."

"Oh, Pa," I said. "She could change."

"In your own life, too, you have to look it in the face." He took a couple of nitroglycerin. "Turn to five," he said, pointing to the dial on the oxygen tank. He inserted the tubes into his nostrils and breathed deep. He closed his eyes and said, "No."

I had promised the family to always let him have the last word when arguing, but in this case I had a different responsibility. That woman lives across the street. She's my knowledge and my invention. I'm sorry for her. I'm not going to leave her there in that house crying. (Actually neither would Life, which unlike me has no pity.)

Therefore: She did change. Of course her son never came home again. But right now, she's the receptionist in a storefront community clinic in the East Village. Most of the customers are young people, some old friends. The head doctor has said to her, "If we only had three people in this clinic with your experiences . . ."

"The doctor said that?" My father took the oxygen tubes out of his nostrils and said, "Jokes. Jokes again."

"No, Pa, it could really happen that way, it's a funny world nowadays."

"No," he said. "Truth first. She will slide back. A person must have character. She does not."

"No, Pa," I said. "That's it. She's got a job. Forget it. She's in the storefront working."

"How long will it be?" he asked. "Tragedy! You too. When will you look it in the face?"

Questions for "A Conversation with My Father"

1.   How do the narrator and her father differ in their ideas of a satisfying story? What is your idea of a good story?

2.   In what specific ways is this a story about the *process* of writing a story?

3.   At the conclusion of this story about stories, the narrator and her father are arguing about the ending of her latest attempt to tell "a plain story." How does this disagreement reflect two different cultures, two different generations, perhaps even two different genders?

4.   What ironies do you find in this story?

5.   What do you think the narrator's father is saying in the last lines of the story?

Ursula Le Guin (1929–   )

Born in Berkeley, California, Ursula Le Guin was educated at Radcliffe College and Columbia University, and spent a year in Paris on a Fulbright fellowship. Although her work is often classified as science fiction, Le Guin characteristically draws on a number of genres—including fantasy, metafiction, and realism—to create a highly individual medium for her inquiries into the ways we live, might live, should live. According to Le Guin, "It is above all by the imagination that we achieve perception, compassion, and hope."

"The Ones Who Walk Away from Omelas" appears in *The Wind's Twelve Quarters* (1975), a collection of some of Le Guin's shorter works. Le Guin has written more than twenty books, and is the only author to win three Nebulas and four Hugos (the most prestigious science fiction prizes), as well as the National Book Award.

The Ones Who Walk Away from Omelas

———— Variations on a Theme by William James ————

With a clamor of bells that set the swallows soaring, the Festival of Summer came to the city Omelas, bright-towered by the sea. The rigging of the boats in harbor sparkled with flags. In the streets between houses with red roofs and painted walls, between old moss-grown gardens and under avenues of trees, past great parks and public buildings, processions moved. Some were decorous: old people in long stiff robes of mauve and grey, grave master workmen, quiet, merry women carrying their babies and chatting as they walked. In other streets the music beat faster, a shimmering of gong and tambourine, and the people went dancing, the procession was a dance. Children dodged in and out, their high calls rising like the swallows' crossing flights over the music and the singing. All the processions wound towards the north side of the city, where on the great water-meadow called the Green Fields boys and girls, naked in the bright air, with mud-stained feet and ankles and long, lithe arms, exercised their restive horses before the race. The horses wore no gear at all but a halter without bit. Their manes were braided with streamers of silver, gold, and green. They flared their nostrils and pranced and boasted to one another; they were vastly excited, the horse being the only animal who has adopted our ceremonies as his own. Far off to the north and west the mountains stood up half encircling Omelas on her bay. The air of morning was so clear that the snow still crowning the Eighteen Peaks burned with white-gold fire across the miles of sunlit air, under the dark blue of the sky. There was just enough wind to make the banners that marked the racecourse snap and flutter now and then. In the silence of the broad green meadows one could hear the music winding through the city streets, farther and nearer and ever approaching, a cheerful faint sweetness of the air that from time to time trembled and gathered together and broke out into the great joyous clanging of the bells.

Joyous! How is one to tell about joy? How describe the citizens of Omelas?

They were not simple folk, you see, though they were happy. But we do not say the words of cheer much any more. All smiles have become archaic. Given a description such as this one tends to make certain assumptions. Given a description such as this one tends to look next for the King, mounted on a splendid stallion and surrounded by his noble knights, or perhaps in a golden litter borne by great-muscled slaves. But there was no king. They did not use swords, or keep slaves. They were not barbarians. I do not know the rules and laws of their society, but I suspect that they were singularly few. As they did without monarchy and slavery, so they also got on without the stock exchange, the advertisement, the secret police, and the bomb. Yet I repeat that these were not simple folk, not dulcet shepherds, noble savages, bland utopians. They were not less complex than us. The trouble is that we have a bad habit, encouraged by pedants and sophisticates, of considering happiness as something rather stupid. Only pain is intellectual, only evil interesting. This is the treason of the artist: a refusal to admit the banality of evil and the terrible boredom of pain. If you can't lick 'em, join 'em. If it hurts, repeat it. But to praise despair is to condemn delight, to embrace violence is to lose hold of everything else. We have almost lost hold; we can no longer describe a happy man, nor make any celebration of joy. How can I tell you about the people of Omelas? They were not naïve and happy children—though their children were, in fact, happy. They were mature, intelligent, passionate adults whose lives were not wretched. O miracle! but I wish I could describe it better. I wish I could convince you. Omelas sounds in my words like a city in a fairy tale, long ago and far away, once upon a time. Perhaps it would be best if you imagined it as your own fancy bids, assuming it will rise to the occasion, for certainly I cannot suit you all. For instance, how about technology? I think that there would be no cars or helicopters in and above the streets; this follows from the fact that the people of Omelas are happy people. Happiness is based on a just discrimination of what is necessary, what is neither necessary nor destructive, and what is destructive. In the middle category, however—that of the unnecessary but undestructive, that of comfort, luxury, exuberance, etc.—they could perfectly well have central heating, subway trains, washing machines, and all kinds of marvelous devices not yet invented here, floating light-sources, fuelless power, a cure for the common cold. Or they could have none of that: it doesn't matter. As you like it. I incline to think that people from towns up and down the coast have been coming in to Omelas during the last days before the Festival on very fast little trains and double-decked trams, and that the train station of Omelas is actually the handsomest building in town, though plainer than the magnificent Farmers' Market. But even granted trains, I fear that Omelas so far strikes some of you as goody-goody. Smiles, bells, parades, horses, bleh. If so, please add an orgy. If an orgy would help, don't hesitate. Let us not, however, have temples from which issue beautiful nude priests and priestesses already half in ecstasy and ready to copulate with any man or woman, lover or stranger, who desires union with the deep god-head of the blood, although that was my first idea. But really it would be better not to have any temples in Omelas—at least, not manned temples. Religion yes, clergy no. Surely the beautiful nudes can just wander about, offering themselves like divine soufflés to the hunger of the needy and the rapture of the flesh. Let them join the procession. Let tambourines be struck above the copulations, and the glory of desire be proclaimed upon the gongs, and (a not unimportant point) let the offspring of these delightful rituals be beloved and looked after by all. One thing I know there is none of in Omelas is guilt. But what else should there be? I thought at first there were no drugs, but that is puritanical. For those who like it, the faint insistent sweetness of *drooz* may perfume the ways of the city, *drooz* which first brings a great light-ness and brilliance to the mind and limbs, and then after some hours a dreamy languor, and wonderful visions at last of the very arcana and inmost secrets of the Universe, as well as exciting the pleasure of sex beyond all belief; and it is not habit-forming. For more modest tastes I think there ought to be beer. What else, what else belongs in the joyous city? The sense of victory, surely, the celebration of courage. But as we did without clergy, let us do without soldiers. The joy built upon successful slaughter is not the right kind of joy; it will not do; it is fearful and it is trivial. A boundless and gen-erous contentment, a magnanimous triumph felt not against some outer enemy but in communion with the finest and fairest in the souls of all men everywhere and the splendor of the world's summer: this is what swells the hearts of the people of Omelas, and the victory they celebrate is that of life. I really don't think many of them need to take *drooz*.

Most of the processions have reached the Green Fields by now. A marvel-ous smell of cooking goes forth from the red and blue tents of the provision-ers. The faces of small children are amiably sticky; in the benign grey beard of a man a couple of crumbs of rich pastry are entangled. The youths and girls have mounted their horses and are beginning to group around the start-ing line of the course. An old woman, small, fat, and laughing, is passing out flowers from a basket, and tall young men wear her flowers in their shining hair. A child of nine or ten sits at the edge of the crowd, alone, playing on a wooden flute. People pause to listen, and they smile, but they do not speak to him, for he never ceases playing and never sees them, his dark eyes wholly rapt in the sweet, thin magic of the tune.

He finishes, and slowly lowers his hands holding the wooden flute.

As if that little private silence were the signal, all at once a trumpet sounds from the pavilion near the starting line: imperious, melancholy, piercing.

The horses rear on their slender legs, and some of them neigh in answer. Sober-faced, the young riders stroke the horses' necks and soothe them, whispering, "Quiet, quiet, there my beauty, my hope. . . ." They begin to form in rank along the starting line. The crowds along the racecourse are like a field of grass and flowers in the wind. The Festival of Summer has begun.

Do you believe? Do you accept the festival, the city, the joy? No? Then let me describe one more thing.

In a basement under one of the beautiful public buildings of Omelas, or perhaps in the cellar of one of its spacious private homes, there is a room. It has one locked door, and no window. A little light seeps in dustily between cracks in the boards, secondhand from a cobwebbed window somewhere across the cellar. In one corner of the little room a couple of mops, with stiff, clotted, foul-smelling heads, stand near a rusty bucket. The floor is dirt, a little damp to the touch, as cellar dirt usually is. The room is about three paces long and two wide: a mere broom closet or disused tool room. In the room a child is sitting. It could be a boy or a girl. It looks about six, but actually is nearly ten. It is feeble-minded. Perhaps it was born defective, or perhaps it has become imbecile through fear, malnutrition, and neglect. It picks its nose and occasionally fumbles vaguely with its toes or genitals, as it sits hunched in the corner farthest from the bucket and the two mops. It is afraid of the mops. It finds them horrible. It shuts its eyes, but it knows the mops are still standing there; and the door is locked; and nobody will come. The door is always locked; and nobody ever comes, except that sometimes—the child has no understanding of time or interval—sometimes the door rattles terribly and opens, and a person, or several people, are there. One of them may come in and kick the child to make it stand up. The others never come close, but peer in at it with frightened, disgusted eyes. The food bowl and the water jug are hastily filled, the door is locked, the eyes disappear. The people at the door never say anything, but the child, who has not always lived in the tool room, and can remember sunlight and its mother's voice, sometimes speaks. "I will be good," it says. "Please let me out. I will be good!" They never answer. The child used to scream for help at night, and cry a good deal, but now it only makes a kind of whining, "eh-haa, eh-haa," and it speaks less and less often. It is so thin there are no calves to its legs; its belly protrudes; it lives on a half-bowl of corn meal and grease a day. It is naked. Its buttocks and thighs are a mass of festered sores, as it sits in its own excrement continually.

They all know it is there, all the people of Omelas. Some of them have come to see it, others are content merely to know it is there. They all know that it has to be there. Some of them understand why, and some do not, but they all understand that their happiness, the beauty of their city, the tenderness of their friendships, the health of their children, the wisdom of their scholars, the skill of their makers, even the abundance of their harvest and the kindly weathers of their skies, depends wholly on this child's abominable misery.

This is usually explained to children when they are between eight and twelve, whenever they seem capable of understanding; and most of those who come to see the child are young people, though often enough an adult comes, or comes back, to see the child. No matter how well the matter has been explained to them, these young spectators are always shocked and sickened at the sight. They feel disgust, which they had thought themselves superior to. They feel anger, outrage, impotence, despite all the explanations. They would like to do something for the child. But there is nothing they can do. If the child were brought up into the sunlight out of that vile place, if it were cleaned and fed and comforted, that would be a good thing, indeed; but if it were done, in that day and hour all the prosperity and beauty and delight of Omelas would wither and be destroyed. Those are the terms. To exchange all the goodness and grace of every life in Omelas for that single, small improvement: to throw away the happiness of thousands for the chance of the happiness of one: that would be to let guilt within the walls indeed.

The terms are strict and absolute; there may not even be a kind word spoken to the child.

Often the young people go home in tears, or in a tearless rage, when they have seen the child and faced this terrible paradox. They may brood over it for weeks or years. But as time goes on they begin to realize that even if the child could be released, it would not get much good of its freedom: a little vague pleasure of warmth and food, no doubt, but little more. It is too degraded and imbecile to know any real joy. It has been afraid too long even to be free of fear. Its habits are too uncouth for it to respond to humane treatment. Indeed, after so long it would probably be wretched without walls about it to protect it, and darkness for its eyes, and its own excrement to sit in. Their tears at the bitter injustice dry when they begin to perceive the terrible justice of reality, and to accept it. Yet it is their tears and anger, the trying of their generosity and the acceptance of their helplessness, which are perhaps the true source of the splendor of their lives. Theirs is no vapid, irresponsible happiness. They know that they, like the child, are not free. They know compassion. It is the existence of the child, and their knowledge of its existence, that makes possible the nobility of their architecture, and poignancy of their music, the profundity of their science. It is because of the child that they are so gentle with children. They know that if the wretched one were not there snivelling in the dark, the other one, the flute-player, could make no joyful music as the young riders line up in their beauty for the race in the sunlight of the first morning of summer.

Now do you believe in them? Are they not more credible? But there is one more thing to tell, and this is quite incredible.

At times one of the adolescent girls or boys who go to see the child does not go home to weep or rage, does not, in fact, go home at all. Sometimes also a man or woman much older falls silent for a day or two, and then leaves home. These people go out into the street, and walk down the street alone. They keep walking, and walk straight out of the city of Omelas, through the beautiful gates. They keep walking across the farmlands of Omelas. Each one goes alone, youth or girl, man or woman. Night falls; the traveler must pass down village streets, between the houses with yellow-lit windows, and on out into the darkness of the fields. Each alone, they go west or north, towards the mountains. They go on. They leave Omelas, they walk ahead into the darkness, and they do not come back. The place they go towards is a place even less imaginable to most of us than the city of happiness. I cannot describe it at all. It is possible that it does not exist. But they seem to know where they are going, the ones who walk away from Omelas.

Questions for "The Ones Who Walk Away from Omelas"

1.   When does the narrator begin to suggest that the tale is about to switch from the traditional fantasy we've been led to anticipate to a very different sort of story? Look for those passages that cause you to question the reliability of the narrator and the credibility of her story.

2.   Little more than halfway into the story, the narrator asks, "Do you believe? Do you accept the festival, the city, the joy?" Why does she assume that your answer is no?

3.   After the narrator asks us if we believe in Omelas, she proposes to "describe one more thing": How do tone and style change in the description that ensues? Afterward, we are challenged with "Now do you believe in them?" Do you? Why or why not?

4.   As the epigraph indicates, this story presents "Variations on a theme by William James." William James (1842–1910) was a noted American philosopher and psychologist, brother to the novelist Henry James and diarist Alice James. The inspiration for "The Ones Who Walk Away from Omelas" comes from the following passage in an essay called "The Moral Philosopher and the Moral Life." Describe the ways in which Le Guin has illustrated this theme from James and transformed it for her own purposes.

Or if the hypothesis were offered us to a world in which Messrs. Fourier's and Bellamy's and Morris's utopias should all be outdone, and millions kept permanently happy on the one simple condition that a certain lost soul on the far-off edge of things should lead a life of lonely torment, what except a specific and independent sort of emotion can it be which would make us immediately feel, even though an impulse arose within us to clutch at the happiness so offered, how hideous a thing would be its enjoyment when deliberately accepted as the fruit of such a bargain? . . . All the higher, more penetrating ideals are revolutionary. They present themselves far less in the guise of effects of past experience than in that of probable cause of future experience, factors to which the environment and the lessons it has so far taught us must learn to bend.

Angela Carter (1940–   )

Raised in South London, Angela Stalker began working at the age of eighteen as a journalist for suburban newspapers. By the time she was twenty she had already completed her first novel, *Shadow Dance,* which was published six years later. In 1960 she married Paul Carter, moved to Bristol, and began studying English literature at the University of Bristol.

Carter's fictional spectrum is broad, ranging from realism to fantasy and science fiction. She has also written children's books and a feminist study of the Marquis de Sade. The following selection is taken from *The Bloody Chamber* (1979), a collection of "adult tales" spun from well-known fairy tales for children.

The Snow Child

Midwinter—invincible, immaculate. The Count and his wife go riding, he on a grey mare and she on a black one, she wrapped in the glittering pelts of black foxes; and she wore high, black, shining boots with scarlet heels, and spurs. Fresh snow fell on snow already fallen; when it ceased, the whole world was white. "I wish I had a girl as white as snow," says the Count. They ride on. They come to a hole in the snow; this hole is filled with blood. He says: "I wish I had a girl as red as blood." So they ride on again; here is a raven, perched on a bare bough. "I wish I had a girl as black as that bird's feather."

As soon as he completed her description, there she stood, beside the road, white skin, red mouth, black hair and stark naked; she was the child of his desire and the Countess hated her. The Count lifted her up and sat her in front of him on his saddle but the Countess had only one thought: how shall I be rid of her?

The Countess dropped her glove in the snow and told the girl to get down to look for it; she meant to gallop off and leave her there but the Count said: "I'll buy you new gloves." At that, the furs sprang off the Countess's shoulders and twined round the naked girl. Then the Countess threw her diamond brooch through the ice of a frozen pond: "Dive in and fetch it for me," she said; she thought the girl would drown. But the Count said: "Is she a fish, to swim in such cold weather?" Then her boots leapt off the Countess's feet and on to the girl's legs. Now the Countess was bare as a bone and the girl furred and booted; the Count felt sorry for his wife. They came to a bush of roses, all in flower. "Pick me one," said the Countess to the girl. "I can't deny you that," said the Count.

So the girl picks a rose, pricks her finger on the thorn; bleeds; screams; falls.

Weeping, the Count got off his horse, unfastened his breeches and thrust his virile member into the dead girl. The Countess reined in her stamping mare and watched him narrowly; he was soon finished.

Then the girl began to melt. Soon there was nothing left of her but a feather a bird might have dropped; a bloodstain, like the trace of a fox's kill on the snow; and the rose she had pulled off the bush. Now the Countess had all her clothes on again. With her long hand, she stroked her furs. The Count picked up the rose, bowed and handed it to his wife; when she touched it, she dropped it.

"It bites!" she said.

Questions for "The Snow Child"

1.   What emotions—on the part of the Count, on the part of the Countess—dominate this story?

2.   Why is the girl described as "the child of his [the Count's] desire"? Why does she die? And why does she melt?

3.   What might the rose signify? Why does it kill the girl, but not the Countess?

4.   What similarities and differences do you observe between this version of a traditional fairy tale and that of "Little Snow-White" told by the Brothers Grimm? What elements of "The Snow Child" might lead one to call it an "adult fairy tale"?

5.   What morals can you offer for this tale?

Jamaica Kincaid (1950–   )

Jamaica Kincaid was raised in St. John's, Antigua, in the West Indies. She is a staff writer for the *New Yorker* magazine, and her stories have also appeared in *Rolling Stone* and *The Paris Review*. Kincaid lives with her husband and daughter in Vermont and New York City.

Kincaid's first book, a collection of short stories entitled *At the Bottom of the River*, was published in 1984. The story reprinted below, originally published in the *New Yorker*, subsequently appeared as a chapter in Kincaid's novel *Annie John* (1985), the story of a young girl coming of age in Antigua.

The Circling Hand

During my holidays from school, I was allowed to stay in bed until long after my father had gone to work. He left our house every weekday at the stroke of seven by the Anglican church bell. I would lie in bed awake, and I could hear all the sounds my parents made as they prepared for the day ahead. As my mother made my father his breakfast, my father would shave, using his shaving brush that had an ivory handle and a razor that matched; then he would step outside to the little shed he had built for us as a bathroom, to quickly bathe in water that he had instructed my mother to leave outside overnight in the dew. That way, the water would be very cold, and he believed that cold water strengthened his back. If I had been a boy, I would have gotten the same treatment, but since I was a girl, and on top of that went to school only with other girls, my mother would always add some hot water to my bathwater to take off the chill. On Sunday afternoons, while I was in Sunday school, my father took a hot bath; the tub was half filled with plain water, and then my mother would add a large caldronful of water in which she had just boiled some bark and leaves from a bay-leaf tree. The bark and leaves were there for no reason other than that he liked the smell. He would then spend hours lying in this bath, studying his pool coupons or drawing examples of pieces of furniture he planned to make. When I came home from Sunday school, we would sit down to our Sunday dinner.

My mother and I often took a bath together. Sometimes it was just a plain bath, which didn't take very long. Other times, it was a special bath in which the barks and flowers of many different trees, together with all sorts of oils, were boiled in the same large caldron. We would then sit in this bath in a

---
316
---

darkened room with a strange-smelling candle burning away. As we sat in this bath, my mother would bathe different parts of my body; then she would do the same to herself. We took these baths after my mother had consulted with her obeah woman, and with her mother and a trusted friend, and all three of them had confirmed that from the look of things around our house—the way a small scratch on my instep had turned into a small sore, then a large sore, and how long it had taken to heal; the way a dog she knew, and a friendly dog at that, suddenly turned and bit her; how a porcelain bowl she had carried from one eternity and hoped to carry into the next suddenly slipped out of her capable hands and broke into pieces the size of grains of sand; how words she spoke in jest to a friend had been completely misunderstood—one of the many women my father had loved, had never married, but with whom he had had children was trying to harm my mother and me by setting bad spirits on us.

When I got up, I placed my bedclothes and my nightie in the sun to air out, brushed my teeth, and washed and dressed myself. My mother would then give me my breakfast, but since, during my holidays, I was not going to school, I wasn't forced to eat an enormous breakfast of porridge, eggs, an orange or half a grapefruit, bread and butter, and cheese. I could get away with just some bread and butter and cheese and porridge and cocoa. I spent the day following my mother around and observing the way she did everything. When we went to the grocer's, she would point out to me the reason she bought each thing. I was shown a loaf of bread or a pound of butter from at least ten different angles. When we went to market, if that day she wanted to buy some crabs she would inquire from the person selling them if they came from near Parham, and if the person said yes my mother did not buy the crabs. In Parham was the leper colony, and my mother was convinced that the crabs ate nothing but the food from the lepers' own plates. If we were then to eat the crabs, it wouldn't be long before we were lepers ourselves and living unhappily in the leper colony.

How important I felt to be with my mother. For many people, their wares and provisions laid out in front of them, would brighten up when they saw her coming and would try hard to get her attention. They would dive underneath their stalls and bring out goods even better than what they had on display. They were disappointed when she held something up in the air, looked at it, turning it this way and that, and then, screwing up her face, said, "I don't think so," and turned and walked away—off to another stall to see if someone who only last week had sold her some delicious christophine had something that was just as good. They would call out after her turned back that next week they expected to have eddoes or dasheen or whatever, and my mother would say, "We'll see," in a very disbelieving tone of voice. If then we went to Mr. Kenneth, it would be only for a few minutes, for he knew exactly what my mother wanted and always had it ready for her. Mr. Kenneth had known me since I was a small child, and he would always remind me of little things I had done then as he fed me a piece of raw liver he had set aside for me. It was one of the few things I liked to eat, and, to boot, it pleased my mother to see me eat something that was so good for me, and she would tell me in great detail the effect the raw liver would have on my red blood corpuscles.

We walked home in the hot midmorning sun mostly without event. When I was much smaller, quite a few times while I was walking with my mother she would suddenly grab me and wrap me up in her skirt and drag me along with her as if in a great hurry. I would hear an angry voice saying angry things, and then, after we had passed the angry voice, my mother would release me. Neither my mother nor my father ever came straight out and told me anything, but I had put two and two together and I knew that it was one of the women that my father had loved and with whom he had had a child or children, and who never forgave him for marrying my mother and having me. It was one of those women who were always trying to harm my mother and me, and they must have loved my father very much, for not once did any of them ever try to hurt him, and whenever he passed them on the street it was as if he and these women had never met.

When we got home, my mother started to prepare our lunch (pumpkin soup with droppers, banana fritters with salt fish stewed in antroba and tomatoes, fungie with salt fish stewed in antroba and tomatoes, or pepper pot, all depending on what my mother had found at market that day). As my mother went about from pot to pot, stirring one, adding something to the other, I was ever in her wake. As she dipped into a pot of boiling something or other to taste for correct seasoning, she would give me a taste of it also, asking me what I thought. Not that she really wanted to know what I thought, for she had told me many times that my taste buds were not quite developed yet, but it was just to include me in everything. While she made our lunch, she would also keep an eye on her washing. If it was a Tuesday and the colored clothes had been starched, as she placed them on the line I would follow, carrying a basket of clothespins for her. While the starched colored clothes were being dried on the line, the white clothes were being whitened on the stone heap. It was a beautiful stone heap that my father had made for her; an enormous circle of stone, about six inches high, in the middle of our yard. On it the soapy white clothes were spread out; as the sun dried them, bleaching out all stains, they had to be made wet again by dousing them with buckets of water. On my holidays, I did this for my mother. As I watered the clothes, she would come up behind me, instructing me to get the clothes thoroughly wet, showing me a shirt that I should turn over so that the sleeves were exposed.

Over our lunch, my mother and father talked to each other about the houses my father had to build; how disgusted he had become with one of his apprentices, or with Mr. Oatie; what they thought of my schooling so far; what they thought of the noises Mr. Jarvis and his friends made for so many days when they locked themselves up inside Mr. Jarvis's house and drank rum and ate fish they had caught themselves and danced to the music of an accordion that they took turns playing. On and on they talked. As they talked, my head would move from side to side, looking at them. When my eyes rested on my father, I didn't think very much of the way he looked. But when my eyes rested on my mother, I found her beautiful. Her head looked as it if should be on a sixpence. What a beautiful long neck, and long plaited hair, which she pinned up around the crown of her head because when her hair hung down it made her too hot. Her nose was the shape of a flower on the brink of opening. Her mouth, moving up and down as she ate and talked at the same time, was such a beautiful mouth I could have looked at it forever if I had to and not mind. Her lips were wide and almost thin, and when she said certain words I could see small parts of big white teeth—so big, and pearly, like some nice buttons on one of my dresses. I didn't much care about what she said when she was in this mood with my father. She made him laugh so. She could hardly say a word before he would burst out laughing. We ate our food, I cleared the table, we said goodbye to my father as he went back to work, I helped my mother with the dishes, and then we settled into the afternoon.

When my mother, at sixteen, after quarreling with her father, left his house on Dominica and came to Antigua, she packed all her things in an enormous wooden trunk that she had bought in Roseau for almost six shillings. She painted the trunk yellow and green outside, and she lined the inside with wallpaper that had a cream background with pink roses printed all over it. Two days after she left her father's house, she boarded a boat and sailed for Antigua. It was a small boat, and the trip would have taken a day and a half ordinarily, but a hurricane blew up and the boat was lost at sea for almost five days. By the time it got to Antigua, the boat was practically in splinters, and though two or three of the passengers were lost overboard, along with some of the cargo, my mother and her trunk were safe. Now, twenty-four years later, this trunk was kept under my bed, and in it were things that had belonged to me, starting from just before I was born. There was the chemise, made of white cotton, with scallop edging around the sleeves, neck, and hem, and white flowers embroidered on the front—the first garment I wore after being born. My mother had made that herself, and once, when we were passing by, I was even shown the tree under which she sat as she made this garment. There were some of my diapers, with their handkerchief hemstitch that she had also done herself; there was a pair of white wool booties with matching jacket and hat; there was a blanket in white wool and a blanket in white flannel cotton; there was a plain white linen hat with lace trimming; there was my christening outfit; there were two of my baby bottles: one in the shape of a normal baby bottle, and the other shaped like a boat, with a nipple on either end; there was a thermos in which my mother had kept a tea that was supposed to have a soothing effect on me; there was the dress I wore on my first birthday: a yellow cotton with green smocking on the front; there was the dress I wore on my second birthday: pink cotton with green smocking on the front; there was also a photograph of me on my second birthday wearing my pink dress and my first pair of earrings, a chain around my neck, and a pair of bracelets, all specially made of gold from British Guiana; there was the first pair of shoes I grew out of after I knew how to walk; there was the dress I wore when I first went to school, and the first notebook in which I wrote; there were the sheets for my crib and the sheets for my first bed; there was my first straw hat, my first straw basket—decorated with flowers—my grandmother had sent me from Dominica; there were my report cards, my certificates of merit from school, and my certificates of merit from Sunday school.

From time to time, my mother would fix on a certain place in our house and give it a good cleaning. If I was at home when she happened to do this, I was at her side, as usual. When she did this with the trunk, it was a tremendous pleasure, for after she had removed all the things from the trunk, and aired them out, and changed the camphor balls, and then refolded the things and put them back in their places in the trunk, as she held each thing in her hand she would tell me a story about myself. Sometimes I knew the story first hand, for I could remember the incident quite well; sometimes what she told me had happened when I was too young to know anything; and sometimes it happened before I was even born. Whichever way, I knew exactly what she would say, for I had heard it so many times before, but I never got tired of it. For instance, the flowers on the chemise, the first garment I wore after being born, were not put on correctly, and that is because when my mother was embroidering them I kicked so much that her hand was unsteady. My mother said that usually when I kicked around in her stomach and she told me to stop I would, but on that day I paid no attention at all. When she told me this story, she would smile at me and say, "You see, even then you were hard to manage." It pleased me to think that, before she could see my face, my mother spoke to me in the same way she did now. On and on my mother would go. No small part of my life was so unimportant that she hadn't made a note of it, and now she would tell it to me over and over again. I would sit next to her and she would show me the very dress I wore on the day I bit another child my age with whom I was playing. "Your biting phase," she called it. Or the day she warned me not to play around the coal pot, because I liked to sing to myself and dance around the fire. Two seconds later, I fell into the hot coals, burning my elbows. My mother cried when she saw that it wasn't serious, and now, as she told me about it, she would kiss the little black patches of scars on my elbows.

As she told me the stories, I sometimes sat at her side, leaning against her, or I would crouch on my knees behind her back and lean over her shoulder. As I did this, I would occasionally sniff at her neck, or behind her ears, or at her hair. She smelled sometimes of lemons, sometimes of sage, sometimes of roses, sometimes of bay leaf. At times I would no longer hear what it was she was saying; I just liked to look at her mouth as it opened and closed over words, or as she laughed. How terrible it must be for all the people who had no one to love them so and no one whom they loved so, I thought. My father, for instance. When he was a little boy, his parents, after kissing him goodbye and leaving him with his grandmother, boarded a boat and sailed to South America. He never saw them again, though they wrote to him and sent him presents—packages of clothes on his birthday and at Christmas. He then grew to love his grandmother, and she loved him, for she took care of him and worked hard at keeping him well fed and clothed. From the beginning, they slept in the same bed, and as he became a young man they continued to do so. When he was no longer in school and had started working, every night, after he and his grandmother had eaten their dinner, my father would go off to visit his friends. He would then return home at around midnight and fall asleep next to his grandmother. In the morning, his grandmother would awake at half past five or so, a half hour before my father, and prepare his bath and breakfast and make everything proper and ready for him, so that at seven o'clock sharp he stepped out the door off to work. One morning, though, he overslept, because his grandmother didn't wake him up. When he awoke, she was still lying next to him. When he tried to wake her, he couldn't. She had died lying next to him sometime during the night. Even though he was overcome with grief, he built her coffin and made sure she had a nice funeral. He never slept in that bed again, and shortly afterward he moved out of that house. He was eighteen years old then.

When my father first told me this story, I threw myself at him at the end of it, and we both started to cry—he just a little, I quite a lot. It was a Sunday afternoon; he and my mother and I had gone for a walk in the botanical gardens. My mother had wandered off to look at some strange kind of thistle, and we could see her as she bent over the bushes to get a closer look and reach out to touch the leaves of the plant. When she returned to us and saw that we had both been crying, she started to get quite worked up, but my father quickly told her what had happened and she laughed at us and called us her little fools. But then she took me in her arms and kissed me, and she said that I needn't worry about such a thing as her sailing off or dying and leaving me all alone in the world. But if ever after that I saw my father sitting alone with a faraway look on his face, I was filled with pity for him. He had been alone in the world all that time, what with his mother sailing off on a boat with his father and his never seeing her again, and then his grandmother dying while lying next to him in the middle of the night. It was more than anyone should have to bear. I loved him so and wished that I had a mother to give him, for, no matter how much my own mother loved him, it could never be the same.

When my mother got through with the trunk, and I had heard again and again just what I had been like and who had said what to me at what point in my life, I was given my tea—a cup of cocoa and a buttered bun. My father by then would return home from work, and he was given his tea. As my mother went around preparing our supper, picking up clothes from the stone heap, or taking clothes off the clothesline, I would sit in a corner of our yard and watch her. She never stood still. Her powerful legs carried her from one part of the yard to the other, and in and out of the house. Sometimes she might call out to me to go and get some thyme or basil or some other herb for her, for she grew all her herbs in little pots that she kept in a corner of our little garden. Sometimes when I gave her the herbs, she might stoop down and kiss me on my lips and then on my neck. It was in such a paradise that I lived.

The summer of the year I turned twelve, I could see that I had grown taller; most of my clothes no longer fit. When I could get a dress over my head, the waist then came up to just below my chest. My legs had become more spindlelike, the hair on my head even more unruly than usual, small tufts of hair had appeared under my arms, and when I perspired the smell was strange, as if I had turned into a strange animal. I didn't say anything about it, and my mother and father didn't seem to notice, for they didn't say anything, either. Up to then, my mother and I had many dresses made out of the same cloth, though hers had a different, more grownup style, a boat neck or a sweetheart neckline, and a pleated or gored skirt, while my dresses had high necks with collars, a deep hemline, and, of course, a sash that tied in the back. One day, my mother and I had gone to get some material for new dresses to celebrate her birthday (the usual gift from my father), when I came upon a piece of cloth—a yellow background, with figures of men, dressed in a long-ago fashion, seated at pianos that they were playing, and all around them musical notes flying off into the air. I immediately said how much I loved this piece of cloth and how nice I thought it would look on us both, but my mother replied, "Oh, no. You are getting too old for that. It's time you had your own clothes. You just cannot go around the rest of your life looking like a little me." To say that I felt the earth swept away from under me would not be going too far. It wasn't just what she said, it was the way she said it. No accompanying little laugh. No bending over and kissing my little wet forehead (for suddenly I turned hot, then cold, and all my pores must have opened up, for fluids just flowed out of me). In the end, I got my dress with the men playing their pianos, and my mother got a dress with red and yellow overgrown hibiscus, but I was never able to wear my own dress or see my mother in hers without feeling bitterness and hatred, directed not so much toward my mother as toward, I suppose, life in general.

As if that were not enough, my mother informed me that I was on the verge of becoming a young lady, so there were quite a few things I would have to do differently. She didn't say exactly just what it was that made me on the verge of becoming a young lady, and I was so glad of that, because I didn't want to know. Behind a closed door, I stood naked in front of a mirror and looked at myself from head to toe. I was so long and bony that I more than filled up the mirror, and my small ribs pressed out against my skin. I tried to push my unruly hair down against my head so that it would lie flat, but as soon as I let it go it bounced up again. I could see the small tufts of hair under my arms. And then I got a good look at my nose. It had suddenly spread across my face, almost blotting out my cheeks, taking up my whole face, so that if I didn't know I was me standing there I would have wondered about that strange girl—and to think that only so recently my nose had been a small thing, the size of a rosebud. But what could I do? I thought of begging my mother to ask my father if he could build for me a set of clamps into which I could screw myself at night before I went to sleep and which would surely cut back on my growing. I was about to ask her this when I remembered that a few days earlier I had asked in my most pleasing, winning way for a look through the trunk. A person I did not recognize answered in a voice I did not recognize, "Absolutely not! You and I don't have time for that anymore." Again, did the ground wash out from under me? Again, the answer would have to be yes, and I wouldn't be going too far.

Because of this young-lady business, instead of days spent in perfect harmony with my mother, I trailing in her footsteps, she showering down on me her kisses and affection and attention, I was now sent off to learn one thing and another. I was sent to someone who knew all about manners and how to meet and greet important people in the world. This woman soon asked me not to come again, since I could not resist making farting-like noises each time I had to practice a curtsy, it made the other girls laugh so. I was sent for piano lessons. The piano teacher, a shriveled-up old spinster from Lancashire, England, soon asked me not to come back, since I seemed unable to resist eating from the bowl of plums she had placed on the piano purely for decoration. In the first case, I told my mother a lie—I told her that the manners teacher had found that my manners needed no improvement, so I needn't come anymore. This made her very pleased. In the second case, there was no getting around it—she had to find out. When the piano teacher told her of my misdeed, she turned and walked away from me, and I wasn't sure that if she had been asked who I was she wouldn't have said, "I don't know," right then and there. What a new thing this was for me: my mother's back turned on me in disgust. It was true that I didn't spend all my days at my mother's side before this, that I spent most of my days at school, but before this young-lady business I could sit and think of my mother, see her doing one thing or another, and always her face bore a smile for me. Now I often saw her with the corners of her mouth turned down in disapproval of me. And why was my mother carrying my new state so far? She took to pointing out that one day I would have my own house and I might want it to be a different house from the one she kept. Once, when showing me a way to store linen, she patted the folded sheets in place and said, "Of course, in your own house you might choose another way." That the day might actually come when we would live apart I had never believed. My throat hurt from the tears I held bottled up tight inside. Sometimes we would both forget the new order of things and would slip into our old ways. But that didn't last very long.

In the middle of all these new things, I had forgotten that I was to enter a new school that September. I had then a set of things to do, preparing for school. I had to go to the seamstress to be measured for new uniforms, since my body now made a mockery of the old measurements. I had to get shoes, a new school hat, and lots of new books. In my new school, I needed a different exercise book for each subject, and in addition to the usual—English, arithmetic, and so on—I now had to take Latin and French, and attend classes in a brand-new science building. I began to look forward to my new school. I hoped that everyone there would be new, that there would be no one I had ever met before. That way, I could put on a new set of airs; I could say I was something that I was not, and no one would ever know the difference.

On the Sunday before the Monday I started at my new school, my mother became cross over the way I had made my bed. In the center of my bedspread, my mother had embroidered a bowl overflowing with flowers and two lovebirds on either side of the bowl. I had placed the bedspread on my bed in a lopsided way so that the embroidery was not in the center of my bed, the way it should have been. My mother made a fuss about it, and I could see that she was right and I regretted very much not doing that one little thing that would have pleased her. I had lately become careless, she said, and I could only silently agree with her.

I came home from church, and my mother still seemed to hold the bedspread against me, so I kept out of her way. At half past two in the afternoon, I went off to Sunday school. At Sunday school, I was given a certificate for best student in my study-of-the-Bible group. It was a surprise that I would receive the certificate on that day, though we had known about the results of the test weeks before. I rushed home with my certificate in hand, feeling that with this prize I would reconquer my mother—a chance for her to smile on me again.

When I got to our house, I rushed into the yard and called out to her, but no answer came. I then walked into the house. At first, I didn't hear anything. Then I heard sounds coming from the direction of my parents' room. My mother must be in there, I thought. When I got to the door, I could see that my mother and father were lying in their bed. It didn't interest me what they were doing—only that my mother's hand was on the small of my father's back and that it was making a circular motion. But her hand! It was white and bony, as if it had long been dead and had been left out in the elements. It seemed not to be her hand, and yet it could only be her hand, so well did I know it. It went around and around in the same circular motion, and I looked at it as if I would never see anything else in my life again. If I were to forget everything else in the world, I could not forget her hand as it looked then. I could also make out that the sounds I had heard were her kissing my father's ears and his mouth and his face. I looked at them for I don't know how long.

When I next saw my mother, I was standing at the dinner table that I had just set, having made a tremendous commotion with knives and forks as I got them out of their drawer, letting my parents know that I was home. I had set the table and was now half standing near my chair, half draped over the table, staring at nothing in particular and trying to ignore my mother's presence. Though I couldn't remember our eyes having met, I was quite sure that she had seen me in the bedroom, and I didn't know what I would say if she mentioned it. Instead, she said in a voice that was sort of cross and sort of something else, "Are you going to just stand there doing nothing all day?"

The something else was new; I had never heard it in her voice before. I couldn't say exactly what it was, but I know that it caused me to reply, "And what if I do?" and at the same time to stare at her directly in the eyes. It must have been a shock to her, the way I spoke. I had never talked back to her before. She looked at me, and then, instead of saying some squelching thing that would put me back in my place, she dropped her eyes and walked away. From the back, she looked small and funny. She carried her hands limp at her sides. I was sure I could never let those hands touch me again; I was sure I could never let her kiss me again. All that was finished.

I was amazed that I could eat my food, for all of it reminded me of things that had taken place between my mother and me. A long time ago, when I wouldn't eat my beef, complaining that it involved too much chewing, my mother would first chew up pieces of meat in her own mouth and then feed it to me. When I had hated carrots so much that even the sight of them would send me into a fit of tears, my mother would try to find all sorts of ways to make them palatable for me. All that was finished now. I didn't think that I would ever think of any of it again with fondness. I looked at my parents. My father was just the same, eating his food in the same old way, his two rows of false teeth clop-clopping like a horse being driven off to market. He was regaling us with another one of his stories about when he was a young man and played cricket on one island or the other. What he said now must have been funny, for my mother couldn't stop laughing. He didn't seem to notice that I was not entertained.

My father and I then went for our customary Sunday-afternoon walk. My mother did not come with us. I don't know what she stayed home to do. On our walk, my father tried to hold my hand, but I pulled myself away from him, doing it in such a way that he would think I felt too big for that now.

That Monday, I went to my new school. I was placed in a class with girls I had never seen before. Some of them had heard about me, though, for I was the youngest among them and was said to be very bright. I liked a girl named Albertine, and I liked a girl named Gweneth. At the end of the day, Gwen and I were in love, and so we walked home arm in arm together.

When I got home, my mother greeted me with the customary kiss and inquiries. I told her about my day, going out of my way to provide pleasing details, leaving out, of course, any mention at all of Gwen and my overpowering feelings for her.

Questions for "The Circling Hand"

1.   How does the narrator feel about her mother in the first half of the story? Describe their relationship and the world Annie inhabits.

2.   What do the items stored in Annie's mother's trunk represent?

3.   At what point is Annie's idyllic existence first threatened? Discuss the different incidents that illustrate a change in the relationship between Annie and her mother.

4.   Why does Annie's mother suddenly refuse her request to look through the items in the trunk? What does she mean when she says, "You and I don't have time for that any more"?

5.   Describe Annie John. Why is she looking forward to her new school?

6.   Why does Annie pull her hand away from her father's as they are walking together at the end of the story?

7.   What connection can you make between Annie's infatuation with Gwen and her altered relationship with her mother? Why, at the story's end, does Annie tell her mother everything that had happened that day, "leaving out, of course, any mention at all of Gwen"?

READING/WRITING

The stories in this chapter have prompted the multitude of writing assignments listed below, and many more we do not have space to include. You may wish to delve into a few of these exercises in reading and writing—or to create your own assignment.

1. In the introduction to his anthology *Italian Folktales,* Italo Calvino notes that he was guided by a Tuscan proverb, "The tale is not beautiful if nothing is added to it." "In other words," explains Calvino, "its value consists in what is woven and rewoven into it." Choose a folktale from your own culture or a story that has been passed down by family members, and retell it in your own way. You may wish to alter elements of the story, and you'll surely want to add your own embellishments and elaborations.

2. Compare the story of "Little Snow-White" told by the Brothers Grimm to Angela Carter's "The Snow Child." What similarities and differences do you observe? How does each treat the subject of jealousy? How has Carter transformed the traditional fairy tale for her own purposes?

3. Early in the introduction to this section, we remark on certain shared themes in myths from diverse cultures. Striking similarities can also be found among other ancient forms of fiction from different times and places. For an exercise in comparison/contrast, select a few myths, legends, parables or other early tales that treat kindred themes, and analyze some of their shared or dissimilar elements, as one of our students does in the following essay. You may wish to supplement your own ideas with research, as this writer has done:

The Psychology of Creation Myths

The first scientists were mythmakers who drew on narrative to explain the world around them and how that world came to be. Central to the mythology of every culture is a creation story, in which an omnipotent being creates the world and watches over the creatures that inhabit it. Such stories offer reassurance, for they imply that things happen for divine reasons that may not be apparent to mortals. So creation stories provide a sense of order in a world that often appears chaotic.

But this idea of a divine plan can also pose a problem, for at times life may seem pointlessly cruel. People hurt each other, and people die, even the very young. There are wars and earthquakes and famines and floods. Without a way to explain such events, people might question a God who allows such suffering, and thus many creation myths also attempt to account for the existence of evil. In more than one such story, the cause of evil is a woman.

In the West, for example, probably the best known creation myth is the biblical tale of Adam and Eve. In this story, God creates the world and all its creatures with a simple command that they appear. He forms Adam, the first man, "in his own image" and makes him master of all the creatures on earth. To provide the man with a suitable companion, God removes one of Adam's ribs while he sleeps, and from this rib comes Eve, the first woman.

Adam and Eve live in the Garden of Eden, a paradise where they can have whatever they want except the fruit of a certain tree. God warns them that if they eat of this tree, they will suffer "the pain of death."

Adam and Eve enjoy perfect happiness until the serpent, "the most subtle of all the wild beasts," talks Eve into eating the forbidden fruit. She, in turn, convinces Adam to do the same. Because they have disobeyed, God banishes them from the Garden of Eden. He tells the woman that she will suffer pain in childbirth and that the man will be her lord. He tells the man that he will now suffer every day to earn his food and die "with sweat on his brow."

In Greek mythology mankind also enjoys a life "free of toils and ills" until a woman comes along. In this myth, Zeus, the mightiest of the Greek gods, creates a beautiful young maiden whom the gods shower with gifts—silvery raiments, an embroidered veil, garlands of bright flowers, and a crown of gold. She is called Pandora, "the gift of all." But she is also given a box in which each of the gods has placed something evil, and she is forbidden ever to open it.

Pandora is sent to earth and presented to Epimetheus, a young man who accepts her gladly. Pandora, however, cannot stop thinking about the box. One day she lifts the lid—and out fly plagues innumerable, all of the woes and sorrows that have tortured humanity ever since.

These two creation stories share striking similarities: In both cases, the first humans live in a paradise, where their every need is met, and one thing alone is forbidden. Most important, it is a woman's transgression that unleashes evil onto the world. But why do these stories blame woman for the tribulations that mark our lives?

Historically, most societies have been patriarchal, and one reason women have been cast as the culprits may be that the tellers of tales and the makers of myths were traditionally men. Why, then, would men blame evil on women?

The need to make woman the scapegoat may simply reflect human psychology. We all have violent and destructive impulses, a part of our makeup that Sigmund Freud called the *id.* We try to repress this aspect of our character because it would be too degrading and painful to admit to forbidden urges or wicked tendencies. Refusing to accept malevolent forces as a part of this world may reflect an unwillingness to acknowledge evil as a part of human nature. In some cases, then, it may have been convenient simply to point a finger at a woman, traditionally regarded in many cultures as a member of the "weaker sex."

Another explanation might come from the psychological theories of Carl Jung, who postulates that all men have a feminine side to their personalities, called the *anima,* and women a masculine side, the *animus.* Perhaps, just as these creation stories suggest a need to deny the dark side of human nature by attributing evil to some external source, so they also reflect man's need to reject his feminine component. At the same time, men may wish to deny their dependence on women, who give life to men and their children.

Interestingly, not all creation stories attempt to explain the origin of evil. The myths of the American Indians, for example, appear unconcerned with this age-old dilemma. In one story told by the Iroquois tribe, God creates the earth with the help of animals. There is no woman who brings catastrophe to the world, and, in fact, the first man comes from the rib of Mother Earth (Marriot 22–25).

Perhaps a myth such as this one ignores the issue of evil because some cultures, like those of the American Indians, emphasize the relationship between humans and nature. Here nature is embodied in the maternal figure of Mother Earth, who provides both life and nourishment. But Mother Earth also has a destructive side: She brings many gifts, but she also brings earthquakes, famines, and floods (Schecter 160–161). The Indian cultures seem able to accept these dual aspects of nature, which eliminates the need for a scapegoat such as woman.

Whether or not creation myths offer an explanation for evil, they still suggest that there are reasons for life and all of its burdens. In some ways, this idea is comforting, but it may also encourage blame, subjugation, and a dangerous acceptance of the way things are, even when things are clearly unfair. And although most people no longer take creation stories literally, many of us cling to another kind of myth—stereotypes about men and women, religious and racial groups that allow discrimination in the first place and shield us from the truth about ourselves.

Susan Mahon

Bibliography

Abrahams, Roger D. *Afro-American Folktales.* New York: Pantheon, 1985.

Brandon, S. G. F. *Creation Legends of the Ancient Near East.* London: Hodder and Stoughton, 1963.

The Jerusalem Bible. New York: Doubleday, 1968.

Marriot, Alice, and Carol K. Rachlin. *American Indian Mythology.* New York: Thomas Y. Crowell Company, 1968.

Schecter, Harold, and Jonna Gormely Semeiks, eds. *Patterns in Popular Culture.* New York: Harper & Row, 1980.

4. At the end of "Heartache" we are told that "Iona is carried away and tells her [his horse] everything." Using direct quotation, write what you imagine Iona says to the mare. Now consider, in a brief essay: Why *doesn't* Chekhov quote Iona in this instance?

5. Discuss the ways in which setting helps to establish both mood and theme in "Heartache" and "Cat in the Rain," reprinted in Chapter 1 of this anthology.

6. Keeping in mind that "The Yellow Wallpaper" was written nearly a hundred years ago, rewrite the story from the husband's point of view.

7. Taking your inspiration from "Araby," write about a time when you suffered a humiliation and, in the manner of Joyce's narrator, draw upon figurative language that will help to convey the intensity of your feelings at that time. Alternatively, you may wish to re-create an experience that led to an "epiphany"—a sudden, intuitive understanding of some aspect of the human condition brought about by a simple and striking vision, whether happy or sad.

8. Analyze the ways in which style, tone, and mood contribute to theme in "Araby."

9. Opening with "I stand here . . ." (or "I sit here . . ."), write a first-person dramatic monologue of your own in which you reflect on a period from your past. Imagine that you are speaking to a silent listener as you contrast what you once were, once thought, to what you now are, now think.

10. Write an analysis of the character of the narrator of "I Stand Here Ironing." In the course of her monologue about her daughter Emily, what does she reveal about herself?

11. Compare Ursula Le Guin's use of metafiction in "The Ones Who Walk Away from Omelas" to that of Grace Paley in "A Conversation with My Father" or to that of Donald Barthelme in "The Glass Mountain." How does each writer call into question the nature and conventions of fiction? Consider the relationship of the writer to his or her text; the relationship of that text to "real life"; and the concepts of plot, character, setting, narrator, and point of view in each work.

12. Write a fable in which you, like Le Guin, give life to an abstract

concept, such as the ideal of justice, the notion of altruism, or the pursuit of happiness.

13. Write "an unadorned and miserable tale" like the one the narrator first presents in "A Conversation with My Father," or choose a paragraph from a newspaper article with which you can work. Exchange tales with a classmate, and ask each other questions such as those the father asks. Then revise and improvise on your "unadorned" tale, fleshing it out with the kind of background information and specific details your partner requested. Finally, read your revision to your partner—is he or she now satisfied? Are you? If not, try rewriting once more. Afterward, write another story, one that recounts the composing process you went through in the previous exercise. Following Paley, you may wish to include in this story the exchanges between you and your reader.

14. In the introduction to this section, we note that "A Good Man Is Hard to Find" reverberates with irony. Write a detailed consideration of the different kinds of irony that appear in this story. You'll want to pay special attention to the grandmother, and the ways in which her actions serve both to move the plot and reinforce the theme. In addition to addressing the ironic implications of this character's words, deeds, and assumptions, consider other elements such as tone and point of view.

15. Compare the the ways in which Malamud and García Márquez combine realism and fantasy for their own purposes in "The Magic Barrel" and "A Very Old Man with Enormous Wings."

16. For an essay on the theme of "The Magic Barrel," use the following questions to guide your thinking:

    a. What, finally, does Leo Finkle want?
    b. How does he become aware of these deeper desires?
    c. What functions do the other characters in the story serve?
    d. What is the meaning of the last line of the story?

17. Both "Why I Like Country Music" and "Araby" center on a first love. Write a comparison/contrast paper in which you discuss similarities and differences in the first-person narrator's "voice" in two stories.

18. Narrate and analyze the course of your first love—a crush you had at an early age—on a classmate, a movie star, a piano teacher. . . . Perhaps structure your essay as McPherson structures "Why I Like Country Music," basing it on these elements:

1. *First meeting:* Describe in detail the moment you first became aware of this person. What did he or she look like, act like? In your description, summon up as many sensory impressions as you can.

2. *Conflict:* Did you have a rival for the affections of this person, as McPherson's narrator did? Or did the conflict arise from this person's lack of interest in you? Or from your own shyness and fear?

3. *Climax and resolution:* Describe the "big moment." Did you finally get to sit next to him or her on the school bus? Dance with him or her? Receive your first kiss? Get pushed down in the schoolyard?

Here is one student's response to this assignment. What elements has she borrowed from McPherson and made her own?

Why I Hate the Autoharp

The other day, while I was nestled in my chair, reading a book, my husband turned on the radio. Engrossed in the madcap escapades of Virginia Brandon, I paid no attention to the music until I heard the harsh twang of the autoharp accompanying an obscure folk song. I told Roger that the sound of the autoharp was irritating me and asked if I could change the station. He laughed and said, "I can't understand why the autoharp should bother you. But go on. Change it." As I randomly selected another station, I knew I'd never tell him why I hate the autoharp. He could never have guessed that I associate the autoharp with my first love, Edward D. Hamilton.

As a child, I felt as though I was a member of a band of roving gypsies; my family traveled from city to city in search of lucrative employment. I was thrilled when we finally settled in Queens, New York. I couldn't wait to go to school and make new friends.

On the morning of my first day of class, the principal brought me to my fourth-grade teacher, Mrs. Granahan. As Mrs. Granahan introduced me to the class, I scanned the faces of my classmates. In the last row of the room, I saw the finest-looking boy I'd seen in my ten years. He had wavy brown hair that fell over one eye, and the other eye was the color of a clear blue sky. He wore a crisp white shirt with a long thin tie neatly knotted at the base of his throat. He was cuter than Steve McQueen, Paul Newman, and James Dean put together. I was in love.

Mrs. Granahan nudged me out of my reverie when she told me to take my seat next to an amiable-looking girl. Mrs Granahan then smiled pleasantly and said, "Class, we will begin our day with Show and Tell. Ramona will play her autoharp and sing for us." The girl next to me introduced herself, and told me that Ramona performed on her autoharp and sang for the class once a week, every week.

"Quiet, please, Ramona is about to begin," the teacher announced.

Ramona tossed back her long black hair and said, "I will perform my favorite song. I hope you enjoy it." With a sweeping motion of her hand,

Ramona began to play her autoharp. Twang, twang, twang, she played. She twanged on her autoharp and then she began to sing, "If I had a hammer, I'd hammer in the morning, I'd hammer in the evening. . . ."

I was not paying attention to Ramona. I was staring at the cute boy with the wavy brown hair over one eye. He was staring at Ramona all gaga-eyed. Alina, the girl next to me, said, "Forget it. That's Edward D. Hamilton. He and Ramona are an item."

The days rolled in and out like the tide. Every day, I saw Ramona and Edward holding hands in the schoolyard. I saw them holding hands in the halls. I saw them swinging their clasped hands while they walked to the bus stop. And every week, I had to listen to Ramona play her autoharp and sing "If I Had a Hammer," while Edward stared at her all gaga-eyed. My life was lacking; it was lacking Edward D. Hamilton.

Christmas was almost here and our class was to celebrate by performing "Toyland." Mrs. Granahan assigned the parts according to our clothing size. Ramona was small. She played the part of the fairy princess. I was tall. I was given the part of a toy soldier who played the saxophone. I was very disappointed. But Mrs. Granahan said, "There are no small parts, only small actors." I decided that if I had to be a toy soldier, I would be the best toy soldier in the play. And then I found out that Edward was going to be a toy soldier, because he fit the costume.

My life was getting sunnier. On the day of the play, Edward told me that I was the prettiest toy soldier he had ever seen. Elated, I floated onto the stage and gave my best performance. When the fairy princess touched me with her wand, I moved to the center of the stage with Edward. We sang. We danced. And we drifted back into our sleeplike state when the enchantment was over.

When the Christmas season ended, we resumed our daily lessons. Ramona resumed her weekly performance on the autoharp. Edward resumed his unwavering attention to Ramona. And I . . . well, and I had had my moment of glory with Edward D. Hamilton.

Yes, dear Roger, I find the harsh twanging sound of the autoharp quite irritating. You may have thought I was unreasonable. Even slightly deranged. But you will never know about Ramona and her autoharp, nor will you ever know about Edward D. Hamilton.

Eugenia Calleo

19. Discuss the significance of the narrative structure of "In a Grove."

20. Taking your cue from "The Circling Hand," write a story that illustrates how a relationship between parent and child—or child and sibling—changes as that child enters adolescence. You may wish to draw on your own experience or on that of someone you've observed closely.

21. From one of the stories in this chapter, select a main character who interests you and compose a detailed analysis of that character. In your essay, consider the different facets of this personality, the ways in which these traits are conveyed in the story, and the relationship between these characteristics and the theme of the story.

22. Choose what you believe to be an especially rich passage from any of the stories in this section. Analyze those elements of fiction that play a role in this passage, and show how the excerpt you've chosen is representative of the narrative as a whole.

23. Select representative passages from two stories in this chapter for a thoughtful comparison of their individual styles and the ways that each style contributes to theme. In your essay, you'll want to consider such components of style as diction, syntax, imagery, and tone.

CHAPTER
5

Theater and Film

READERS AND SPECTATORS

In this chapter we have reprinted the scripts of three plays and a film. Yet to do so is an injustice to each work, for none of them was originally written to be read. Dramatic pieces are meant to be performed, to be seen and heard. What happens on the page is profoundly different from what occurs on the stage or the screen, and these two media, print and performance, engage us in opposite ways. Compare these two hypothetical situations:

> You are alone in your living room, reading a humorous short story. Outside your window, two neighbors are chatting noisily, momentarily distracting you from the story; you look up, lose your place on the page, and take a few moments to imagine the appearance of a character you've just read about, or to daydream about what you're going to have for dinner. When the noise of your neighbors (and your stomach) has died down, you return to your book, reread a paragraph or two, and pick up the action where you left off.

> You are in a darkened theater, watching a comedy—either a play or a film. There are hundreds of people around you laughing at the proceedings; their mirth is infectious and makes you laugh all the louder. At a certain point your mind wanders (hunger again?), so that when your attention returns to the stage or screen you realize to your confusion that you have lost the thread of the action. You have missed an important gesture or statement. But the moment has passed, and there is no way to recapture it.

In one of these scenarios you are a reader; in the other, a member of an audience—part of a group of listeners as well as viewers. Reading is a solitary activity, drama a communal one. To the reader, other people are a distraction; conversely, the group psychology of an audience *enhances* the viewer's experience of theater or film (as anyone who has had the misfortune of watching a movie on an airplane, listening to the soundtrack through a headset, will readily attest). Then too, many details of the setting of a short story are left to the reader's imagination, whereas the setting of the theatrical production is laid out before the audience. On the other hand, we may learn aspects of the plot or characters in a short story—through the intervention of a narrator—which can only be hinted at on the stage.

Most important, unlike the printed page, which will look the same each time you return to it, the play or film is evanescent: It is not about words but about actors moving around and saying those words. True, plays and films are made up of the same primary elements as novels and short stories—setting, character, and a plot typically developed by exposition, conflict, climax, and resolution. Yet although drama shares some of the components of fiction, the language it speaks is very different indeed.

FICTION VS. DRAMA

It is probably best to discuss the two dramatic forms, theater and film, separately, since they are in many ways as different from each other as they are from other forms of literature. To illustrate how theater works, we'll try an experiment in speculation, using the original notations Henrik Ibsen made in his journal when he conceived the idea for *A Doll House,* one of the plays reprinted here. Ibsen was inspired by the real-life story of a woman he knew who had forged a check to pay for her invalid husband's convalescence, and who was sent away by her husband to an asylum when he discovered her crime. In October 1878 the Norwegian playwright, living in Rome, jotted down the following notes for the play he would not begin writing until six months later:

Notes for a Modern Tragedy

. . . A woman cannot be herself in modern society. It is an exclusively male society, with laws made by men and with prosecutors and judges who assess feminine conduct from a masculine standpoint.

She has committed forgery, and is proud of it; for she has done it out of love for her husband, to save his life. But this husband of hers takes his standpoint, conventionally honourable, on the side of the law, and sees the situation with male eyes.

Consider for a moment what would have happened if Ibsen had decided to use these notes as the premise for a short story rather than a play. How might he have manipulated those elements shared by fiction and drama to transform an item of gossip and a series of generalizations into a work of fiction meant to be *read* rather than performed? To begin with, he would need a point of view from which to present the events of the story. He might choose to have the wife tell her own side of the tale, or the husband—or he might describe the unhappy marriage through the eyes of the couple's oldest child. Each of these possible narrators, of course, would have a limited and biased point of view; for a fuller and more objective version of the story, Ibsen might employ an omniscient narrator, one who is not a participant in the story, but who has full knowledge of the events and characters.

In any case, the writer would take pains to let the reader know the thoughts and motivations of some, if not all, of the characters, whether by telling us or by having us overhear their conversations—though this last element, dialogue, need not be included in the story. Having decided on a narrator, Ibsen would choose a setting, or more likely several settings, in which to unfold the events of the plot: perhaps the parlor in the house where the husband lies ill, or the veranda of the convalescent home, or a room in the asylum where the accused wife is confined, or each of these locations in turn. Description of each locale, and of the appearance, dress, and gestures of the characters, might be minutely detailed, or barely sketched and left to the reader's imagination.

Now let's examine how Ibsen actually cultivated this seed of a plot in *A Doll House,* working as he did to create a realistic play that broke away from many of the stilted conventions of the nineteenth-century dramas that preceded it. Like most plays written in the late nineteenth and even in the twentieth century, *A Doll House* was created for the proscenium stage—a boxlike playing area framed by an arch. The audience is placed "out front," separated from the stage at a fixed and distant vantage point, but privy to the thoughts and actions of the characters. There is no narrator to tell us the significance of an event, or to describe the characters or setting: We witness the events as they unfold and judge for ourselves. Moreover, between the words of the author and the eyes and ears of the audience, other creative forces intervene: the work of directors, setting and lighting designers, property and stage managers, actors. Their job is to turn written words into a three-dimensional world that bears some resemblance to the world out front, on the other side of the proscenium arch. How does this company dramatize a story to give the illusion of life within the spatial and temporal constraints of the stage?

Start with the set. Ibsen's play takes place in the living room of the home of Torvald Helmer and his wife Nora. Ibsen carefully spells out the appearance of the room in his stage directions:

> A comfortable room, tastefully but not expensively furnished. A door to the right in the back wall leads to the entryway, another to the left leads to HELMER'S study. Between these doors, a piano. Midway in the left-hand wall a door, and further back a window. Near the window a round table with an armchair and a small sofa. In the right-hand wall, toward the rear a door, and nearer the foreground a porcelain stove with two armchairs and a rocking chair beside it. Between the stove and the side door, a small table. Engravings on the walls. An *étagère* with china figures and other small art objects; a small bookcase with richly bound books; the floor carpeted; a fire burning in the stove. It is a winter day.

The tasteful but inexpensive furnishings, coupled with the etchings and the deluxe book editions, betoken the upper-middle-class pretensions of the inhabitants; and the glass display case with its porcelain figures will eventually tell us something about the wife's status in this marriage. This much of the description might well be found in a short story. But unlike many short stories, this play confines itself to a single set; and we must ask ourselves *why,* and why this particular room? Not all theater pieces are so confined, of course: Many have several stage sets. But it is precisely the spatial and temporal *limitations* imposed on all theatrical works that give this live art form its singular tension and its magic. You might notice, as well, the emphasis on the doors of the room, which will regulate the entrances and exits of the characters. Then too, the doors suggest the room's relation to the world outside this home and to the other rooms in the house, none of which we will ever see: Helmer's study, for instance, is off limits to us as it is to his wife. What is kept from sight—what happens offstage—is easily as significant as what lies in plain view.

Still, however specific he has tried to be, the playwright has left some leeway here for the director and designers of the production. What is a "comfortable" room, and is that couch cosily worn or stiff-backed and just for show? Perhaps, since Ibsen's story is as timely now as when it was first performed, the director of a particular production decides to update the play by setting it not in Norway of the 1870s but in Iowa in the 1980s. What would be the properties of a "comfortable" living room in such a vehicle? Would a theater-in-the-round production, in which the audience encircles the stage, dilute the claustrophobic sense we get from the single boxlike proscenium set? How would this alteration affect our response to the play? Consider the costumes of the women at the time the play was written (for a detailed analysis of such clothing, consult Alison Lurie's essay in Chapter 7 of this book): How do they reinforce the theme of the play, and how would the effect be altered if the women characters appeared in modern dress? These are all details for the director and the designers to work out. And unlike readers of a short story who exercise their powers of visualization, we in the audience have nothing to say in the matter. We simply take in the spectacle.

The stage has been set, and now must be peopled. In a short story version of *A Doll House,* as we have pointed out, Ibsen would have been free, had he wished, to tell the tale in straight narrative, without dialogue. But in play form, without the help of a narrator, how could Ibsen portray, for example, a marriage in which neither husband nor wife acknowledges that the relationship is troubled? Watch how Kate Chopin, an American contemporary of Ibsen's, portrays a similarly strained marriage in her short tale, "The Story of an Hour." At this point in the story the wife reacts to news of her husband's death:

> She knew that she would weep again when she saw the kind, tender hands folded in death; the face that had never looked save with love upon her, fixed and gray and dead. But she saw beyond that bitter

moment a long procession of years to come that would belong to her absolutely. And she opened and spread her arms out to them in welcome.

There would be no one to live for during those coming years; she would live for herself. There would be no powerful will bending hers in that blind persistence with which men and women believe they have a right to impose a private will upon a fellow-creature. A kind intention or a cruel intention made the act seem no less a crime as she looked upon it in that brief moment of illumination.

Here Chopin treats one of Ibsen's themes, that of the immorality of imposing one's private will upon another creature, even in marriage—a revolutionary view of matrimony that jolted the contemporary audience of both the story and the play out of their seats. But Chopin conveys the theme through the medium of the omniscient narrator, who can tell us even more about the wife's thoughts than the character herself would be able to do. In theater, on the other hand, it is chiefly the spoken interaction of characters that advances the plot. Without dialogue there can be no play, as the characters in Samuel Beckett's play *Endgame* (1957)—in a moment of self-conscious metafiction—themselves acknowledge:

> CLOV: I'll leave you.
> HAMM: No!
> CLOV: What is there to keep me here?
> HAMM: The dialogue.

Let's examine how Ibsen's play covers some of the same ground as the paragraphs just quoted from Chopin's story. As we've pointed out, although the shape of a play may be similar to that of a short story or novel—with its series of events leading to complication, climax, and resolution—the audience must be led through this progression almost exclusively by means of the actors' speech and gestures. Dialogue is used to supply exposition (providing the audience with important information), to reveal an individual's personality, to show relationships between characters, and even to sound the themes of the play. Sometimes an exchange between characters can accomplish all these missions simultaneously. This is the case with these stage directions and spoken lines from the opening of *A Doll House*, in which the Helmers' marriage is painted with a few swift strokes:

> *A bell rings in the entryway; shortly after we hear the door being unlocked.* NORA *comes into the room, humming happily to herself; she is wearing street clothes and carries an armload of packages, which she puts down on the table to the right. She has left the hall door open; and through it a* DELIVERY BOY *is seen, holding a Christmas tree and a basket which he gives to the* MAID *who let them in.*

NORA   Hide the tree well, Helene. The children mustn't get a glimpse of it till this evening, after it's trimmed. (*To the* DELIVERY BOY, *taking out her purse*) How much?

DELIVERY BOY   Fifty, ma'am.

NORA   There's a crown. No, keep the change. (*The* BOY *thanks her and leaves.* NORA *shuts the door. She laughs softly to herself while taking off her street things. Drawing a bag of macaroons from her pocket, she eats a couple, then steals over and listens at her husband's study door.*) Yes, he's home. (*Hums again as she moves to the table, right.*)

HELMER   (*from the study*) Is that my little lark twittering out there?

NORA   (*busy opening some packages*) Yes, it is.

HELMER   Is that my squirrel rummaging around?

NORA   Yes!

HELMER   When did my squirrel get in?

NORA   Just now. (*Putting the macaroon bag in her pocket and wiping her mouth*) Do come in, Torvald, and see what I've bought.

HELMER   Can't be disturbed. (*After a moment he opens the door and peers in, pen in hand.*) Bought, you say? All that there? Has the little spendthrift been out throwing money around again?

NORA   Oh, but Torvald, this year we really should let ourselves go a bit. It's the first Christmas we haven't had to economize.

HELMER   But you know we can't go squandering.

NORA   Oh yes, Torvald, we can squander a little now. Can't we? Just a tiny, wee bit. Now that you've got a big salary and are going to make piles and piles of money.

HELMER   Yes—starting New Year's. But then it's a full three months till the raise comes through.

NORA   Pooh! We can borrow that long.

From these brief interactions—between Nora and the delivery boy, and Nora and Torvald—we learn something of what has taken place before the events of Act I, and much that has bearing on the scenes to follow. Torvald's accusatory question about Nora's "throwing money around again" serves as exposition, providing the background of a recurrent problem in the couple's relationship—Nora's spending—and leading us to suspect that Nora's generous tip to the delivery boy, along with her armful of packages, indicates more than just an overflowing of Christmas spirit. But we must balance this impression with Torvald's preoccupied self-importance and tight-lipped disapproval of so much gift-giving; we mark the way he chides and teases his wife as though she were a child or a fool. Nora's own alternately clipped and cajoling responses to her husband's questions speak volumes as well: She seems to have heard these questions before, and has learned to hold her tongue and submit, or wheedle and play the "squirrel" her husband expects—forms of subterfuge mirrored in her squireling away of the bag of macaroons. Finally, this snatch of dialogue foreshadows the theme of the play, for the quiet struggle between the two characters reveals some truth about the relationship of men and women in marriage as well as in the world beyond this comfortable living room.

This much we have learned from reading the first page of Ibsen's play; but again, in doing so we should keep in mind how much more there is to the scene than what appears in print. How shall the director conduct, or *block*, the action of the scene? Which characters should be spotlighted, and which left in shadow? As we read, we must imagine the gestures, timing, and various intonations the actors might use in delivering their lines. For instance, in response to Torvald's greeting, the actress playing Nora might gaily sing out "Yes, it is"—like the "twittering lark" her husband wishes her to be— or instead answer curtly, resignedly, as though braced for the inevitable lecture on spending. What is absent from the page is not only the color and movement of this spectacle, but its special sound: Nora rustling through the door in her long cape, humming gaily, stealthily crumpling the package of sweets. Readers of the play must enter into the drama, calling up these elements from their own experience and imagination.

THE CHANGING MASK OF TRAGEDY

Up to now we have examined the features of drama in general, and of what Ibsen called "a modern tragedy" in particular. But what is "modern" about this tragedy? For one thing, as you've gathered from the foregoing discussion, *A Doll House* takes up the lives of ordinary individuals who are neither exceptionally noble nor elevated in social status. Moreover, the protagonist, a woman, is trapped as much by social constraints as by her own weaknesses of character: Her downfall, as Ibsen wrote in his notes, is engineered in part by "an exclusively male society, with laws made by men. . . ." Through his preoccupation with social issues and psychological realism, his criticism of outmoded laws and institutions, Ibsen articulated the concerns of the dramatists who revolutionized theater at the end of the nineteenth century.

By looking at the conventions of classical tragedy, as described by the Greek philosopher Aristotle in the fourth century B.C., we can better understand how modern tragedy both resembles and departs from its predecessors. Almost invariably, critical discussions of tragedy start with Aristotle, who defined tragedy for the ages in his *Poetics*. Aristotle described tragedy as "an imitation of an action that is serious, complete in itself, and of a certain magnitude." The protagonist of this drama enjoys great reputation and eminence in the community, making his downfall—his isolation and possible death— all the more striking and poignant.

Broadly speaking, tragedy is the consequence of some combination of circumstance and character. Often it is precipitated by a misjudgment or misguided action on the hero's part—perhaps resulting from a character flaw such as excessive ambition or pride. But for the hero to have erred and suffered does not in itself constitute tragedy; rather, the reversal of the hero's expectations and fortunes occurs at the moment of his *perception* or recognition of the error he has made. In the course of watching these events unfold, we as audience are engaged, caught up in the fate of the hero, so much so that we feel dread at the inexorable working of destiny and may be moved to tears at the misfortunes of the characters. Yet as Aristotle observed, we come away uplifted rather than depressed by the drama, having felt compassion for the characters and witnessed a portion of life's suffering and grandeur.

As we have seen in the case of Ibsen's play, tragedy has evolved over the course of the centuries, so that even in the seventeenth century, for example, Shakespeare did not feel compelled to obey the unities of time and place that Aristotle had observed in his definition of classical Greek drama. Whereas Greek tragedians strove to confine their action to one locale and to a 24-hour time span, Shakespeare, in a play such as *Othello* (included in this chapter), used settings as far removed as Venice and Cyprus, and stretched the action over an indefinite period of time. Still, in Shakespeare's play the important elements of classical tragedy are very much in evidence: Othello is a noble warrior, a heroic figure, whose death, along with the destruction of those closest to him, is brought about in part by the flaw he recognizes when he characterizes himself as "one that loved not wisely, but too well." Here lies Othello's tragic weakness, one which under other circumstances might be perceived as a strength. As Iago, one of the most hypnotic villains in all of Western literature, remarks, it is in Othello's free and open nature to think men honest, and so Iago can easily deceive Othello into believing his wife unfaithful.

Having noted the general features of tragedy as they figure in *Othello,* we may observe at close range the way Shakespeare galvanizes these elements into life. We will look at an isolated moment in the play, from Scene iii of Act III, to see how the disintegration of Othello's character is achieved. Briefly, here is the background of the scene: Othello, the Moorish leader of the Venetian army, has chosen Cassio to be his lieutenant, a position Iago covets. To displace Cassio, Iago tries to poison Othello's mind with the unfounded suspicion that Cassio is having an affair with Othello's wife, Desdemona. In the conversation we are about to overhear, Iago begins to set his plot in motion.

Remember we have said that spectators of a play, in the absence of a narrator, must gather for themselves the meaning of a scene from the characters' speech and actions, and that *readers* of a play are faced with an even greater challenge, for they have to imagine the gestures, intonations, and movements of the actors in performance. In other words, these readers must go one step further in their participation in drama than in their response to other forms of literature we have examined in this anthology—all the more so in the case of Shakespeare's plays, for which the playwright provided very little in the way of stage direction. To see how this leap of the imagination might be accomplished, we asked a group of students to respond in their notebooks to the following scene from *Othello*, before they had read the play. In discussing the excerpt, they were to consider two aspects of the experience of reading plays in general: the literary as well as the theatrical elements of the drama. We now invite you to do the same. As you read the passage for yourself, jot down in your notebook: (1) your impressions of the two characters in the scene, how they interact, and how Iago manages to work on Othello; and (2) your vision of how the actors playing these roles would gesticulate, say a particular line, or move about the stage. Here is the passage from Act III:

OTHELLO: Why? Why is this?
  Think'st thou I'd make a life of jealousy,
  To follow still° the changes of the moon
  With fresh suspicions? No! To be once in doubt
  Is to be resolved. Exchange me for a goat   180
  When I shall turn the business of my soul
  To such exsufflicate and blown° surmises,
  Matching thy inference. 'Tis not to make me jealous
  To say my wife is fair, feeds well, loves company,
  Is free of speech, sings, plays, and dances;   185
  Where virtue is, these are more virtuous.
  Nor from mine own weak merits will I draw
  The smallest fear or doubt of her revolt,
  For she had eyes, and chose me. No, Iago;
  I'll see before I doubt; when I doubt, prove;   190
  And on the proof there is no more but this:
  Away at once with love or jealousy!
IAGO: I am glad of this; for now I shall have reason
  To show the love and duty that I bear you
  With franker spirit. Therefore, as I am bound,   195
  Receive it from me. I speak not yet of proof.
  Look to your wife; observe her well with Cassio;
  Wear your eyes thus: not jealous nor secure.
  I would not have your free and noble nature
  Out of self-bounty° be abused. Look to't.   200
  I know our country disposition well:
  In Venice they do let heaven see the pranks
  They dare not show their husbands; their best conscience
  Is not to leave't undone, but kept unknown.°

---

[178]**to follow still** to change always (as the phases of the moon).
[182]**exsufflicate and blown** inflated and flyblown.
[200]**self-bounty** innate kindness (which attributes his own motives to others).
[203-4]**their . . . unknown** i.e., their morality does not forbid adultery, but it does forbid being found out.

OTHELLO: Dost thou say so? 205
IAGO: She did deceive her father, marrying you;
   And when she seemed to shake and fear your looks,
   She loved them most.
OTHELLO: And so she did.
IAGO: Why, go to then!
   She that so young could give out such a seeming
   To seel° her father's eyes up close as oak°— 210
   He thought 'twas witchcraft. But I am much to blame.
   I humbly do beseech you of your pardon
   For too much loving you.
OTHELLO: I am bound to thee forever.
IAGO: I see this hath a little dashed your spirits.
OTHELLO: Not a jot, not a jot.
IAGO: Trust me, I fear it has. 215
   I hope you will consider what is spoke
   Comes from my love. But I do see y' are moved.
   I am to pray you not to strain° my speech
   To grosser issues nor to larger reach°
   Than to suspicion. 220
OTHELLO: I will not.
IAGO: Should you do so, my lord,
   My speech should fall into such vile success
   Which my thoughts aimed not. Cassio's my worthy friend—
   My lord, I see y' are moved.
OTHELLO: No, not much moved.
   I do not think but Desdemona's honest. 225
IAGO: Long live she so. And long live you to think so.
OTHELLO: And yet, how nature erring from itself—
IAGO: Ay, there's the point, as (to be bold with you)
   Not to affect many proposèd matches
   Of her own clime, complexion, and degree°, 230
   Whereto we see in all things nature tends°—
   Foh! one may smell in such a will most rank,
   Foul disproportions, thoughts unnatural.
   But, pardon me, I do not in position°
   Distinctly° speak of her; though I may fear 235
   Her will, recoiling to her better judgment,

---

[210]**seel** hoodwink.
[210]**oak** (a close-grained wood).
[218]**strain** enlarge the meaning.
[219]**reach** meaning.
[230]**degree** social station.
[231]**in . . . tends** i.e., all things in nature seek out their own kind.
[234]**position** general argument.
[235]**Distinctly** specifically.

May fall to match° you with her country forms°
And happily° repent.

OTHELLO: Farewell, farewell!
If more thou dost perceive, let me know more.
Set on thy wife to observe. Leave me, Iago.   240

IAGO: My lord, I take my leave.   [*Going.*]

OTHELLO: Why did I marry? This honest creature doubtless
Sees and knows more, much more, than he unfolds. . . .

Below are the commentaries of two of our students, who were asked to imagine the scene without having read or seen the rest of the play. Note that although these readers have "blocked" the characters' movements differently, they have independently arrived at similar observations about Iago and Othello. Keep in mind that in 1604, when *Othello* was produced, dramatic staging was a very different matter from today. In London's Globe Theater, where much of Shakespeare's work was performed, dramas were staged without scenery, props, or special lighting. As it happens, our students' staging would have worked as well in Shakespeare's time as in our own:

The scene takes place somewhere outside the castle, or citadel. It is late at night. The surroundings are dark, with only a little light coming from the moon. (Othello compares the phases of the moon with his suspicions.) Iago does most of the talking and Othello listens; Iago moves around the setting while Othello is very still. I see Iago as a man small in stature but strong in character as he hovers near Othello. Iago's body looks almost awkward in Othello's presence. He is a lanky man with the greasy look of a fox in the wild. He looks at Othello out of the sides of his small, slanted eyes.

As Iago moves closer to Othello, he casts his shadow over him, and conveys his power through the series of questions he asks. He leads Othello to a conclusion which Othello would never have drawn on his own. Toward the end of the scene, Othello's face loses all expression as he begins to distrust his beloved Desdemona. Iago finally stares straight into Othello's eyes like a hungry animal moving in for the kill. The rich scent of deceit is burning in him. Othello backs off and hastily bids his confidant goodnight. Iago walks slowly away. Othello lowers his face into his trembling hands.

Juan Pauli

---

²³⁷**fall to match** happen to compare.
²³⁷**country forms** i.e., the familiar appearance of her countrymen.
²³⁸**happily** by chance.

At the beginning of the scene, Othello is stern in his disbelief. In line 192, Othello tries to dismiss the conversation; his hand brushes the air as if to brush away this idle chatter: "Away at once with love or jealousy!"

In the following speech, Iago realizes that his approach to madden Othello is not working, so he tries a different tactic. Moving quickly, sideways, to catch up to Othello, he inches closer in line 194, saying he feels compelled to speak because of his love for the Moor. Othello turns to touch Iago's shoulder reassuringly, guiding Iago as if he were a child. Iago looks into Othello's eyes guilelessly, and reaches out with an open gesture when he says, "Receive it from me." As Iago speaks of Desdemona's betrayal of her father, Othello raises his hand to rub his cheek in a thoughtful gesture and exclaims "And so she did," as if he had just heard something new. He turns toward Iago, yields to doubt of his former firm beliefs, and binds himself to Iago forever.

Iago gloats by observing "I see this hath a little dashed your spirits." Othello replies with hollow heartiness, "Not a jot." At this point Othello is nothing like the man we have seen at the beginning of this scene. He has been weakened by Iago's twisted logic. In line 224 we have a clear example of Othello's breakdown as he answers Iago with a "No, not much moved," instead of a firm No.

Helen Pappas

THE COMIC IMPULSE

You have undoubtedly noticed that even in the preceding excerpt from *Othello,* with all its tragic implications, there are comic moments arising from Iago's ironic comments and cocksure manipulation of his prey. Just as a tragedy like *Othello* may contain comic features, so comedies may contain elements of tragedy. And as you might imagine, *tragicomedy—A Doll House* is one notable example of this dramatic form—lies somewhere between the two modes. That is, Ibsen's play begins as a comedy, as we've observed in the opening scene of the drama, but ends in conflict, doubt, and pain.

What are the distinguishing marks of comedy? The most obvious is that it elicits laughter more often than tears. In contrast to classical tragedy, comedy usually concerns the lives of everyday people and revolves around their conflicting values and beliefs. These characters are seen as social beings with humorous foibles rather than as solitary figures isolated from the rest of the world by flawed character or fate. Comedy allows its audience to maintain a certain distance from the events it depicts. For in this dramatic mode we are comfortably assured of a happy ending; we can laugh at the mishaps and misunderstandings on the stage, since we know they are bound to be temporary.

But rarely are comedy and tragedy to be found in their unadulterated forms, in life or in art. Particularly in the twentieth century, as we noted in the preceding chapter, the boundaries between literary forms have broken down; now we see hybrids of form and genre. *Painting Churches,* a two-act play by Tina Howe included in this chapter, is primarily a comedy, but like most comedies contains the potential for tragedy. To be sure, the play is raucously funny and ends in reconciliation of the conflicting parties—in this case the embattled generations of parent and child. In fact, the play ends quite literally in the spirit of *komoidia,* the Greek word for revel-song from which the term *comedy* derives, as the daughter watches her parents join in a gentle waltz in the fading afternoon light. But the family has suffered a good deal along the way to this "happy" ending; the audience now recognizes, along with the daughter, that one parent is irretrievably on the way to senility, and that both are moving closer to death.

Painting Churches mixes genres in another significant way. It is written in prose, like Ibsen's play, rather than in the blank verse of Shakespeare's plays, and yet Howe makes frequent use of poetry, having her characters quote from a number of poems you will recognize when you come to the poetry section of this anthology. As you read the play, you may wish to refer to the quoted poems in their original state as they appear in Chapter 6, and to note how differently they function when they appear in the context of a drama. Again, this comparison will reveal significant differences between drama and other forms of literature.

Taken together, these elements of literature and performance, sound, light, and spectacle, constitute a work of the theater, an art form which, in the act of performing, becomes fundamentally different from, and greater than, the printed script. Another of Tina Howe's works, a one-act play entitled *Museum,* provides a comic analogue that goes to the heart of the live theatrical experience. In the play, a group of museum-goers meander through a gallery while endlessly discussing their reactions to the various exhibits. One woman, Tink, insists that her friend, an artist whose statues are on display, has told her that a secret is embedded in each of these sculptures. But the surprise of each piece, she explains, is invisible to the naked eye—"You can only find it through vibrations of sound or touch." Prodding each piece, ignoring the museum guard's exasperated "That's against museum regulations!", Tink at last releases the miracle buried in one of the sculptures. The statue, made of rags, bones, and feathers, unexpectedly comes to life; through sound and light the sculpture becomes a work of the theater, to the great joy—and amusingly varied commentary—of the crowd collected around it:

TINK: [*The lights dim. A floodlight pours down on the statue and Bach's*
  Dorian *Toccata and Fugue in D Minor, BWV 538 for organ swells from*
  a speaker concealed in the pedestal.] I FOUND IT! I FOUND IT! . . .
  EVERYONE: [*Is thunderstruck. They gaze at Tink and the statue, chills racing*

*up their backs. There's a hush and a slow realization that the music is
part of the statue]* . . .
JULIE JENKINS: It's a wave . . . cresting!
GIORGIO: It's a stunning Renaissance landscape. . . .
MICHAEL WALL: It's the urban vision of the futurist. . . .
FRED IZUMI: [*Recites some Haiku in Japanese*]
GILDA NORRIS: "And lo, the angel of the Lord came upon them, and
the glory of the Lord shone around about them. . . ."

Active and imaginative readers, in the privacy of their homes, become part
of the theatrical company, creating mental pictures of the stage and performers. Still, *reading* this dialogue, going through the play alone in our living
rooms, is not so rich and comic an experience as *witnessing* the way the lines
are interwoven by an awestruck chorus of actors, any more than reading
about the wonder of the artist's statue is as miraculous as seeing it awakened
and transformed by the sounds and lights and illusions that are the special
province of the theater.

THE LANGUAGE OF FILM

As we indicated at the outset of this discussion, we might best approach the
medium of film by first determining how it differs from the art form it is most
often compared with, theater. Theater and film are both dramatic arts, and
usually (although not always) share the use of spoken language. But it is
chiefly language and the actor's use of it that is the heart and engine of the
theater. Sets, costumes, props, lighting, the direction of the actors' placement
on the stage, are all meant to enhance the power of the words being projected across the footlights in a live performance. Consequently, it is possible
to conceive of a play with one actor, in one costume, standing in one spot
and holding our attention for an entire evening in the theater, if the playwright's script and actor's talent are exceptional. Indeed, as we've noted earlier, the tension and force of the theater springs from the very fact that the
drama takes place in confined quarters.

On the other hand, it is freedom of *movement,* movement that can take the
viewer in an instant from the Helmers' living room to a ruined temple in
twelfth-century Japan, that distinguishes film from other art forms. For this
reason, the word "film" seems a less appropriate description of this medium
than "moving pictures" or "cinema" (from the Greek *kinema,* motion). To
be sure, theater and dance depend on the movement of bodies through space;
but motion pictures are built on three kinds of movement, two of which are
unique to this art form. Movies may begin with the action of the actors or
objects up on the screen, yet two additional components of filmmaking are
perhaps even more critical to the medium: the movement of the *camera
itself*—tilting up or down, circling an actor, careering along a racetrack, and

so forth—and the dynamics created by the way the individual images are put together in the process of *film editing.* When we watch a film, it is the combined impression of these movements that our eye follows, that captures our imagination, even hypnotizes us.

This essential distinction between film and theater is usually demonstrated with unfortunate results when plays are 'translated' into film. Film directors frequently attempt to make the play more "cinematic" by including sequences that would not normally appear on stage—a process known as "opening up" the action of the play. Most often, however, these sequences only weaken the thrust of the drama. In *A Doll House,* for example, the Helmers attend a costume party at a neighbor's apartment upstairs. In the theatrical production of the play, we do not follow the couple to the party, but rather see their return, some hours later, to their own parlor, where Nora grows more frantic that Helmer will finally read the letter he has received revealing his wife's crime. The air is charged with her mounting desperation and our own anticipation of Helmer's reaction. If this scene were filmed, on the other hand, the camera might take us upstairs to the party, thereby dissipating some of the anxiety we are meant to live through with Nora as each moment for her becomes longer and heavier with dread.

Actually, when cinema was in its infancy at the beginning of this century, movies were seen as little more than a means of permanently recording stage versions of plays and novels. But this was before several generations of talented filmmakers, working with tools made available by advancing technology, capitalized on the special mode of organizing material that is peculiar to this art form. Let's examine the special properties of cinema more closely.

First, motion pictures have their own way of manipulating point of view, through the placement and movement of the camera. The motion picture camera roves. Thus the filmmaker, unlike the writer and director of a play, can present action from many points of view, whether from the vantage point of one actor or another, or of an onlooker watching those actors from across the street, or of a bird in the sky. In observing the development of the action, the spectator is transported from one place to another; in the space of a second we can jump from a panorama of a battlefield to a closeup of the tear running down a soldier's cheek.

We have only to look at a single sequence from Akira Kurosawa's film *Rashomon* (1950), the screenplay of which is reprinted in this chapter, to see the extraordinary range of impressions the camera is capable of creating through movement. (A film *sequence* consists of a series of *shots,* a shot being an uninterrupted run of film that may last anywhere from a fraction of a second to several minutes.) Let's examine the sequence in the film that consists simply of a woodcutter walking through a forest (see page 570). One of the most interesting features of this segment is that it is *wordless,* so that although natural sounds and musical themes play an important part in the scene, the story here is told almost exclusively through visual images.

The sequence begins with a *long shot*—a shot in which an object is viewed from a considerable distance—of the dense woods. This scene is photographed from a low angle, so that we are looking up at the sun through the branches of the trees overhead, much as the woodcutter might be glancing up as he walks. In the next moment the camera focuses on a *closeup* of a tiny fragment of the scene: the woodcutter's ax, glinting in the sunlight; then we are shown the woodcutter's face, and the ax over his shoulder. Afterward we have another long shot of the woodcutter, but this time from a "bird's-eye" view, high up in the trees. Thus the camera, guided by the director and camera operator, picks out fragments of the whole scene to be photographed.

Now that we have seen the objects at which Kurosawa chose to aim his camera, and where he placed the camera in order to get those images, we must go back through the sequence to find out how he moved the camera through the scenery. At the opening of the sequence, as we look up through the trees, the camera is *traveling* through the woods—that is, moving at a speed independent of the speed at which the subject (in this case, the woodcutter) is moving. The closeup of the woodcutter's face is taken with the camera *tracking* backward—in other words, moving at the same speed as the subject being filmed. As we follow the woodcutter from high above, the camera is *panning,* or turning from one side of the scene to the other while remaining fixed on its axis; in the following shot of a single tree, the camera *tilts,* again while fixed on its axis, from the top of the tree down to the woodcutter at the bottom. A few shots later, we again see a closeup of the woodcutter, but this time of his back rather than his face, and this shot is taken by the camera tracking *forward,* following in the man's footsteps.

So far we have discussed the specialized vocabulary of filmmaking. But what about the syntax of this language? How are its images put together? Unconsciously, in taking apart the film sequence described above, we have been talking not simply of a collection of shots, but of their relation to one another. Indeed, as viewers we are often so caught up in the characters or plot of a movie that we do not pay attention to the way the individual shots have been combined; yet if you were to turn off the sound while watching a film on television, you would immediately become aware of the "cutting" and splicing of the images. The structural unity and effectiveness of a motion picture depend upon the way separate pieces of light-sensitive celluloid are assembled. Only when this raw material is synthesized, through editing, is the film endowed with life.

In other words, film editing, or *montage,* is the syntax by which the separate shots—in the case of *Rashomon,* over 400 of them—become an organic whole, a motion picture. For instance, films have their own way of conveying a sense of time: Simply through the way images are spliced, the filmmaker can prolong a bit of action from one moment to the next or transport us through centuries in an instant. Cutting back and forth frequently between two events may indicate that those events are occurring simultaneously. On the other hand, a *slow dissolve,* in which one scene dissolves while a new scene appears to emerge from it, may be used to indicate that time has elapsed between two events. The same effect can be conveyed by a *fadeout,* in which the image on the screen fades to black. In *Rashomon,* Kurosawa indicates the passing of several hours by another method: He shows a character from a long shot, followed by a medium shot of the same man, and then by a closeup of the man. Elsewhere in the film, to show both the passage of time and a change in location, Kurosawa employs the rather old-fashioned device of the *wipe,* in which a line passes across the screen like a windshield wiper, eliminating the first shot and replacing it with the next shot.

Our interpretation of the scenes before us is powerfully influenced by the way the filmmakers manipulate us through editing. The activity of selection and arrangement for the purpose of implanting an emotion or idea is the secret of film construction, the juxtaposition of images making certain connections for us much as it does in a Chinese ideogram. An ideogram combines two pictographs, each corresponding to an object; but their combined meaning corresponds to a *concept.* For example, in Chinese,

tree   the sun   The sun seen in the trees; hence, east.

We might borrow a similar analogy from Japanese *haiku.* A haiku is a three-line poem that combines pictorial images to convey an impression or abstract concept—

    A lonely crow
    On a leafless bough,
    One autumn eve.

In film, similarly, two images may be juxtaposed to achieve a psychological effect that is different from, and more forceful than, the individual shots.

The way this method of composition works in cimena was dramatically demonstrated in a famous experiment conducted in the 1920s by two Russian filmmakers and theorists, Lev Kuleshov and V. I. Pudovkin. Here Pudovkin describes the experiment, contrived to illustrate how film art depends on the inspired combination of raw materials:

We took from some film or other several close-ups of the well-known Russian actor Mosjukhin. We chose close-ups which were static and which did not express any feeling at all—quiet close-ups. We joined these close-ups, which were all similar, with other bits of film in three different combinations. In the first combination the close-up of Mos-jukhin was immediately followed by a shot of a plate of soup standing on a table. It was obvious and certain that Mosjukhin was looking at this soup. In the second combination the face of Mosjukhin was joined to shots showing a coffin in which lay a dead woman. In the third the close-up was followed by a shot of a little girl playing with a funny toy bear. When we showed the three combinations to an audience which had not been let into the secret the result was terrific. The public raved about the acting of the artist. They pointed out the heavy pensiveness of his mood over the forgotten soup, were touched and moved by the deep sorrow with which he looked on the dead woman, and admired the light, happy smile with which he surveyed the girl at play. But we knew that in all three cases the face was exactly the same.

But the combination of various pieces in one or another order is not sufficient. It is necessary to be able to control and manipulate the length of these pieces, because the combination of pieces of varying length is effective in the same way as the combination of sounds of various length in music, by creating the rhythm of the film and by means of their varying effect on the audience. Quick, short pieces rouse excitement, while long pieces have a soothing effect.

In short, when two or more images are edited together in a motion picture, the result is greater than the simple sum of these images. Stated mathematically, $A + B$ in film does not equal AB; rather, $A + B$ equals C. In effect, a new super-image is created, and it is this overall impression that we are left with when we watch a film. Pudovkin's experiment shows how spectators are affected not only by the actor's performance or the separate shots, but by the synthesis of the editing process. This is the *gestalt* of cinema—the unified psychological configuration that is essentially different from its individual parts.

To see how this psychological principle is applied within the context of the sights and sounds of a motion picture, we'll return one last time to the wood-cutter sequence from *Rashomon,* this time picking up the action a bit farther along in the woodcutter's walk. Throughout the sequence, music has been playing—the "woodcutter's theme," which later becomes the underlying musical theme of the entire film. Suddenly the woodcutter halts, and an extreme closeup of his face fills the screen. The music stops. We cut to a closeup of a woman's hat, dangling on a tree branch; the shot is accompanied by the soft tinkle of bell-like music that will eventually be associated with the woman. The woodcutter slowly walks on, and the theme music resumes. He halts again—we see a closeup of a man's hat; walks on and again—a piece of rope; and again—an amulet case. The rhythm of this gradual discovery of 'clues,' a process in which we first see the woodcutter's mildly puzzled expression and then the object to which he is reacting, has thus been established. Suddenly the woodcutter stumbles, and jumps back with a look of horror: Before him are the stiffly raised hands of a corpse. A gong is sounded. The steady, leisurely pace of the sequence has been altered; the camera now moves rapidly alongside the woodcutter as he runs panic-stricken through the woods. A walk through the forest has turned into a detective story and finally into a murder mystery. Our shock and excitement are increased not only by what the camera sees, not only by the way the actor responds, but by the way the sequence's rhythm has been disturbed and its pace quickened. An emotional and esthetic effect has thus been achieved through the combination of cinematic movements—of actor, camera, and montage.

William Shakespeare (1564–1616)

William Shakespeare was born in Stratford-upon-Avon, the eldest son of a
prosperous glovemaker and official in local politics, and of Mary Arden,
whose family were well-to-do landowners. While Shakespeare was still in
grammar school, his family suffered declining fortunes, and he did not go
on to a university. At eighteen, he married Anne Hathaway, who was eight
years his senior and already pregnant with their first child, Susanna. Their
twins, Judith and Hamnet, were born two years later.

At some point in the decade after his marriage, Shakespeare left
Stratford, alone, for London, to pursue a career in the theater—though
acting was considered an unsuitable profession for a gentleman. By the
early 1590s he had become an actor of some note and had seen his first
plays produced; by 1600 he was acclaimed as the foremost playwright of
his day. As a result of his successes, he held a one-tenth interest in the
Globe Theater, and appears to have amassed considerable wealth. By the
time he retired to Stratford around 1611 he had written 37 plays, which
comprised historical dramas, comedies, romances, and tragedies, as well as
a group of the most extraordinary sonnets the world has seen.

Like most writers of his time, Shakespeare took the basic plots of his
plays from various sources—folk stories, early tales, historical incidents,
and the like. For *Othello*, one of his later tragedies, Shakespeare used a
loosely knit Italian short story by Giraldi Cinthio. He fashioned from this
relatively crude material one of his most impressively structured and highly
plotted dramas.

The Tragedy of Othello

THE MOOR OF VENICE

Edited by Alvin Kernan

CHARACTERS

OTHELLO, *the Moor*
BRABANTIO, *father to Desdemona*
CASSIO, *an honorable lieutenant*
IAGO, *a villain*

RODERIGO, *a gulled gentleman*

DUKE OF VENICE

SENATORS

MONTANO, *Governor of Cyprus*

GENTLEMEN OF CYPRUS

LODOVICO AND GRATIANO, *two noble Venetians*

SAILORS

CLOWN

DESDEMONA, *wife to Othello*

EMILIA, *wife to Iago*

BIANCA, *a courtesan*

(MESSENGER, HERALD, OFFICERS, GENTLEMEN, MUSICIANS, ATTENDANTS)

Scene. *Venice and Cyprus.*

ACT I

Scene I [*Venice. A street.*]

RODERIGO: Tush! Never tell me? I take it much unkindly
   That thou, Iago, who hast had my purse
   As if the strings were thine, shouldst know of this.
IAGO: 'Sblood°, but you'll not hear me! If ever I did dream
   Of such a matter, abhor me.
RODERIGO: Thou told'st me   5
   Thou didst hold him in thy hate.
IAGO: Despise me
   If I do not. Three great ones of the city,
   In personal suit to make me his lieutenant,
   Off-capped° to him; and, by the faith of man,
   I know my price; I am worth no worse a place.   10
   But he, as loving his own pride and purposes,
   Evades them with a bombast circumstance°,
   Horribly stuffed with epithets of war;
   Nonsuits° my mediators. For, "Certes," says he,
   "I have already chose my officer." And what was he?   15
   Forsooth, a great arithmetician°,

---

⁴**'Sblood** by God's blood.
⁹**Off-capped** doffed their caps—as a mark of respect.
¹²**bombast circumstance** stuffed, roundabout speech.
¹⁴**Nonsuits** rejects.
¹⁶**arithmetician** theorist (rather than practical).

One Michael Cassio, a Florentine,
(A fellow almost damned in a fair wife)°
That never set a squadron in the field,
Nor the division of a battle knows   20
More than a spinster; unless the bookish theoric,
Wherein the tonguèd° consuls can propose
As masterly as he. Mere prattle without practice
Is all his soldiership. But he, sir, had th' election;
And I, of whom his eyes had seen the proof   25
At Rhodes, at Cyprus, and on other grounds
Christian and heathen, must be belee'd and calmed
By debitor and creditor. This counter-caster°,
He, in good time, must his lieutenant be,
And I—God bless the mark!—his Moorship's ancient°.   30
RODERIGO: By heaven, I rather would have been his hangman.
IAGO: Why, there's no remedy. 'Tis the curse of service:
Preferment goes by letter and affection°,
And not by old gradation°, where each second
Stood heir to th' first. Now, sir, be judge yourself,   35
Whether I in any just term am affined°
To love the Moor.
RODERIGO: I would not follow him then.
IAGO: O, sir, content you.
I follow him to serve my turn upon him.
We cannot all be masters, nor all masters   40
Cannot be truly followed. You shall mark
Many a duteous and knee-crooking° knave
That, doting on his own obsequious bondage,
Wears out his time, much like his master's ass,
For naught but provender; and when he's old, cashiered.   45
Whip me such honest knaves! Others there are
Who, trimmed in forms and visages of duty,
Keep yet their hearts attending on themselves,
And, throwing but shows of service on their lords,
Do well thrive by them, and when they have lined their coats,   50

---

¹⁸**A . . . wife** (a much-disputed passage, probably best taken as a general sneer at Cassio as a dandy and a ladies' man. But in the story from which Shakespeare took his plot the counterpart of Cassio is married, and it may be that at the beginning of the play Shakespeare had decided to keep him married but later changed his mind).
²²**tonguèd** eloquent.
²⁸**counter-caster** i.e., a bookkeeper who casts *(reckons up)* figures on a counter *(abacus)*.
³⁰**ancient** standard-bearer; an under-officer.
³³**letter and affection** recommendations (from men of power) and personal preference.
³⁴**old gradation** seniority.
³⁶**affined** bound.
⁴²**knee-crooking** bowing.

Do themselves homage. These fellows have some soul;
And such a one do I profess myself. For, sir,
It is as sure as you are Roderigo,
Were I the Moor, I would not be Iago.
In following him, I follow but myself. 55
Heaven is my judge, not I for love and duty,
But seeming so, for my peculiar° end;
For when my outward action doth demonstrate
The native° act and figure of my heart
In complement extern°, 'tis not long after 60
But I will wear my heart upon my sleeve
For daws to peck at; I am not what I am.
RODERIGO: What a full fortune does the thick-lips owe°
If he can carry't thus!
IAGO: Call up her father,
Rouse him. Make after him, poison his delight, 65
Proclaim him in the streets, incense her kinsmen,
And though he in a fertile climate dwell,
Plague him with flies; though that his joy be joy,
Yet throw such chances of vexation on't
As it may lose some color. 70
RODERIGO: Here is her father's house. I'll call aloud.
IAGO: Do, with like timorous° accent and dire yell
As when, by night and negligence, the fire
Is spied in populous cities.
RODERIGO: What, ho, Brabantio! Signior Brabantio, ho! 75
IAGO: Awake! What, ho, Brabantio! Thieves! Thieves!
Look to your house, your daughter, and your bags!
Thieves! Thieves!

BRABANTIO *above*° [*at a window*].

BRABANTIO: What is the reason of this terrible summons?
What is the matter there? 80
RODERIGO: Signior, is all your family within?
IAGO: Are your doors locked?
BRABANTIO: Why, wherefore ask you this?
IAGO: Zounds, sir, y'are robbed! For shame. Put on your gown!

---

[57]**peculiar** personal.
[59]**native** natural, innate.
[60]**complement extern** outward appearance.
[63]**owe** own.
[72]**timorous** frightening.
[78]**s.d. above** (i.e., on the small upper stage above and to the rear of the main platform stage, which resembled the projecting upper story of an Elizabethan house).

Your heart is burst, you have lost half your soul.
Even now, now, very now, an old black ram 85
Is tupping your white ewe. Arise, arise!
Awake the snorting citizens with the bell,
Or else the devil will make a grandsire of you.
Arise I say!

BRABANTIO: What, have you lost your wits?

RODERIGO: Most reverend signior, do you know my voice? 90

BRABANTIO: Not I. What are you?

RODERIGO: My name is Roderigo.

BRABANTIO: The worser welcome!
I have charged thee not to haunt about my doors.
In honest plainness thou hast heard me say
My daughter is not for thee; and now, in madness, 95
Being full of supper and distemp'ring draughts°,
Upon malicious knavery dost thou come
To start° my quiet.

RODERIGO: Sir, sir, sir—

BRABANTIO: But thou must needs be sure
My spirits and my place° have in their power 100
To make this bitter to thee.

RODERIGO: Patience, good sir.

BRABANTIO: What tell'st thou me of robbing? This is Venice.
My house is not a grange°.

RODERIGO: Most grave Brabantio,
In simple and pure soul I come to you.

IAGO: Zounds, sir, you are one of those that will not serve God if 105
the devil bid you. Because we come to do you service and you
think we are ruffians, you'll have your daughter covered with a
Barbary° horse, you'll have your nephews° neigh to you, you'll
have coursers for cousins°, and gennets for germans°.

BRABANTIO: What profane wretch art thou? 110

IAGO: I am one, sir, that comes to tell you your daughter and the
Moor are making the beast with two backs.

BRABANTIO: Thou art a villain.

IAGO: You are—a senator.

BRABANTIO: This thou shalt answer. I know thee, Roderigo.

RODERIGO: Sir, I will answer anything. But I beseech you, 115

---

⁹⁶**distemp'ring draughts** unsettling drinks.
⁹⁸**start** disrupt.
¹⁰⁰**place** rank, i.e., of senator.
¹⁰³**grange** isolated house.
¹⁰⁸**Barbary** Arabian, i.e., Moorish.
¹⁰⁸**nephews** i.e., grandsons.
¹⁰⁹**cousins** relations.
¹⁰⁹**gennets for germans** Spanish horses for blood relatives.

If't be your pleasure and most wise consent,
As partly I find it is, that your fair daughter,
At this odd-even° and dull watch o' th' night,
Transported, with no worse nor better guard
But with a knave of common hire, a gondolier,   120
To the gross clasps of a lascivious Moor—
If this be known to you, and your allowance,
We then have done you bold and saucy wrongs;
But if you know not this, my manners tell me
We have your wrong rebuke. Do not believe   125
That from the sense of all civility°
I thus would play and trifle with your reverence.
Your daughter, if you have not given her leave,
I say again, hath made a gross revolt,
Tying her duty, beauty, wit, and fortunes   130
In an extravagant° and wheeling stranger
Of here and everywhere. Straight satisfy yourself.
If she be in her chamber, or your house,
Let loose on me the justice of the state
For thus deluding you.

BRABANTIO: Strike on the tinder, ho!   135
Give me a taper! Call up all my people!
This accident° is not unlike my dream.
Belief of it oppresses me already.
Light, I say! Light!   *Exit [above]*.

IAGO: Farewell, for I must leave you.
It seems not meet, nor wholesome to my place,   140
To be produced—as, if I stay, I shall—
Against the Moor. For I do know the State,
However this may gall him with some check°,
Cannot with safety cast° him; for he's embarked
With such loud reason to the Cyprus wars,   145
Which even now stands in act°, that for their souls
Another of his fathom° they have none
To lead their business; in which regard,
Though I do hate him as I do hell-pains,
Yet, for necessity of present life,   150
I must show out a flag and sign of love,

---

[118]**odd-even** between night and morning.
[126]**sense of all civility** feeling of what is proper.
[131]**extravagant** vagrant, wandering (Othello is not Venetian and thus may be considered a wandering soldier of fortune).
[137]**accident** happening.
[143]**check** restraint.
[144]**cast** dismiss.
[146]**stands in act** takes place.
[147]**fathom** ability.

Which is indeed but sign. That you shall surely find him,
Lead to the Sagittary° that raisèd search:
And there will I be with him. So farewell.   [*Exit.*]

Enter BRABANTIO [*in his nightgown*], *with* SERVANTS *and torches.*

BRABANTIO: It is too true an evil. Gone she is;   155
  And what's to come of my despisèd time
  Is naught but bitterness. Now, Roderigo,
  Where didst thou see her?—O unhappy girl!—
  With the Moor, say'st thou?—Who would be a father?—
  How didst thou know 'twas she?—O, she deceives me   160
  Past thought!—What said she to you? Get moe° tapers!
  Raise all my kindred!—Are they married, think you?
RODERIGO: Truly I think they are.
BRABANTIO: O Heaven! How got she out? O treason of the blood!
  Fathers, from hence trust not your daughters' minds   165
  By what you see them act°. Is there not charms
  By which the property° of youth and maidhood
  May be abused? Have you not read, Roderigo,
  Of some such thing?
RODERIGO: Yes, sir, I have indeed.
BRABANTIO: Call up my brother.—O, would you had had her!—   170
  Some one way, some another.—Do you know
  Where we may apprehend her and the Moor?
RODERIGO: I think I can discover him, if you please
  To get good guard and go along with me.
BRABANTIO: Pray you lead on. At every house I'll call;   175
  I may command at most.—Get weapons, ho!
  And raise some special officers of night.—
  On, good Roderigo; I will deserve your pains°.   [*Exeunt.*]

Scene II [*A street.*]

Enter OTHELLO, IAGO, ATTENDANTS *with torches.*

IAGO: Though in the trade of war I have slain men,
  Yet do I hold it very stuff° o' th' conscience
  To do no contrived murder. I lack iniquity

---

¹⁵³**Sagittary** (probably the name of an inn).
¹⁶¹**moe** more.
¹⁶⁶**act** do.
¹⁶⁷**property** true nature.
¹⁷⁸**deserve your pains** be worthy of (and reward) your efforts.
I.ii. ²**stuff** essence.

Sometime to do me service. Nine or ten times
I had thought t' have yerked° him here, under the ribs.   5
OTHELLO: 'Tis better as it is.
IAGO: Nay, but he prated,
And spoke such scurvy and provoking terms
Against your honor, that with the little godliness I have
I did full hard forbear him. But I pray you, sir,
Are you fast married? Be assured of this,   10
That the magnifico° is much beloved,
And hath in his effect a voice potential
As double as the Duke's°. He will divorce you,
Or put upon you what restraint or grievance
The law, with all his might to enforce it on,   15
Will give him cable°.
OTHELLO: Let him do his spite.
My services which I have done the Signiory°
Shall out-tongue his complaints. 'Tis yet to know°—
Which when I know that boasting is an honor
I shall promulgate—I fetch my life and being   20
From men of royal siege°, and my demerits°
May speak unbonneted to as proud a fortune
As this that I have reached°. For know, Iago,
But that I love the gentle Desdemona,
I would not my unhousèd° free condition   25
Put into circumscription and confine
For the seas' worth. But look, what lights come yond?

Enter CASSIO, *with* [OFFICERS *and*] *torches.*

IAGO: Those are the raisèd father and his friends.
You were best to go in.
OTHELLO: Not I. I must be found.
My parts, my title, and my perfect soul°   30
Shall manifest me rightly. Is it they?
IAGO: By Janus, I think no.

---

⁵**yerked** stabbed.
¹¹**magnifico** nobleman.
¹²⁻¹³**hath . . . Duke's** i.e., can be as effective as the Duke.
¹⁶**cable:** range, scope.
¹⁷**Signiory** the rulers of Venice.
¹⁸**yet to know** unknown as yet.
²¹**siege** rank.
²¹**demerits** deserts.
²²⁻²³**May . . . reached** i.e., are the equal of the family I have married into.
²⁵**unhousèd** unconfined.
³⁰**perfect soul** clear, unflawed conscience.

OTHELLO: The servants of the Duke? And my lieutenant?
　The goodness of the night upon you, friends.
　What is the news?
CASSIO:　　　　　　　The Duke does greet you, general;　　　　　35
　And he requires your haste-posthaste appearance
　Even on the instant.
OTHELLO:　　　　　　What is the matter, think you?
CASSIO: Something from Cyprus, as I may divine.
　It is a business of some heat. The galleys
　Have sent a dozen sequent° messengers　　　　　　　　　40
　This very night at one another's heels,
　And many of the consuls, raised and met,
　Are at the Duke's already. You have been hotly called for.
　When, being not at your lodging to be found,
　The Senate hath sent about three several° quests　　　　45
　To search you out.
OTHELLO:　　　　　　'Tis well I am found by you.
　I will but spend a word here in the house,
　And go with you.　　　　　　　　　　　[Exit.]
CASSIO:　　　　　Ancient, what makes he here?
IAGO: Faith, he tonight hath boarded a land carack°.
　If it prove lawful prize, he's made forever.　　　　　　50
CASSIO: I do not understand.
IAGO:　　　　　　　He's married.
CASSIO:　　　　　　　　　To who?

[Enter OTHELLO.]

IAGO: Marry°, to—Come captain, will you go?
OTHELLO:　　　　　　　　　Have with you.
CASSIO: Here comes another troop to seek for you.

Enter BRABANTIO, RODERIGO, with OFFICERS and torches.

IAGO: It is Brabantio. General, be advised.
　He comes to bad intent.
OTHELLO:　　　　Holla! Stand there!　　　　　55
RODERIGO: Signior, it is the Moor.
BRABANTIO:　　　　Down with him, thief!　[They draw swords.]
IAGO: You, Roderigo? Come, sir, I am for you.

---

[40]**sequent** successive.
[45]**several** separate.
[49]**carack** treasure ship.
[52]**Marry** By Mary (an interjection).

OTHELLO: Keep up your bright swords, for the dew will rust them.
  Good signior, you shall more command with years
  Than with your weapons.   60
BRABANTIO: O thou foul thief, where hast thou stowed my daughter?
  Damned as thou art, thou hast enchanted her!
  For I'll refer me to all things of sense°,
  If she in chains of magic were not bound,
  Whether a maid so tender, fair, and happy,   65
  So opposite to marriage that she shunned
  The wealthy, curlèd darlings of our nation,
  Would ever have, t'incur a general mock°,
  Run from her guardage to the sooty bosom
  Of such a thing as thou—to fear, not to delight.   70
  Judge me the world if 'tis not gross in sense°
  That thou hast practiced° on her with foul charms,
  Abused her delicate youth with drugs or minerals
  That weaken motion°. I'll have't disputed on;
  'Tis probable, and palpable to thinking.   75
  I therefore apprehend and do attach° thee
  For an abuser of the world, a practicer
  Of arts inhibited and out of warrant°.
  Lay hold upon him. If he do resist,
  Subdue him at his peril.
OTHELLO: Hold your hands,   80
  Both you of my inclining and the rest.
  Were it my cue to fight, I should have known it
  Without a prompter. Whither will you that I go
  To answer this your charge?
BRABANTIO: To prison, till fit time
  Of law and course of direct session   85
  Call thee to answer.
OTHELLO: What if I do obey?
  How may the Duke be therewith satisfied,
  Whose messengers are here about my side
  Upon some present° business of the state
  To bring me to him?

---

[63]**refer . . . sense** i.e., base (my argument) on all ordinary understanding of nature.
[68]**general mock** public shame.
[71]**gross in sense** obvious.
[72]**practiced** used tricks.
[74]**motion** thought, i.e., reason.
[76]**attach** arrest.
[78]**inhibited . . . warrant** prohibited and illegal (black magic).
[89]**present** immediate.

OFFICER: 'Tis true, most worthy signior.   90
  The Duke's in council, and your noble self
  I am sure is sent for.
BRABANTIO: How? The Duke in council?
  In this time of the night? Bring him away.
  Mine's not an idle cause. The Duke himself,
  Or any of my brothers° of the state,   95
  Cannot but feel this wrong as 'twere their own;
  For if such actions may have passage free,
  Bondslaves and pagans shall our statesmen be.   *Exeunt.*

Scene III [A council chamber.]

Enter DUKE, SENATORS, *and* OFFICERS *[set at a table, with lights and* ATTENDANTS*]*.

DUKE: There's no composition° in this news
  That gives them credit°.
FIRST SENATOR: Indeed, they are disproportioned.
  My letters say a hundred and seven galleys.
DUKE: And mine a hundred forty.
SECOND SENATOR: And mine two hundred.
  But though they jump° not on a just accompt°—   5
  As in these cases where the aim° reports
  'Tis oft with difference—yet do they all confirm
  A Turkish fleet, and bearing up to Cyprus.
DUKE: Nay, it is possible enough to judgment°.
  I do not so secure me in the error,   10
  But the main article I do approve
  In fearful sense°.
SAILOR *(Within):*   What, ho! What, ho! What, ho!

Enter SAILOR.

OFFICER: A messenger from the galleys.
DUKE: Now? What's the business?
SAILOR: The Turkish preparation makes for Rhodes.

---

⁹⁵**brothers** i.e., the other senators.
I.iii. ¹**composition** agreement.
²**gives them credit** makes them believable.
⁵**jump** agree.
⁵**just accompt** exact counting.
⁶**aim** approximation.
⁹**to judgment** when carefully considered.
¹⁰⁻¹²**I do . . . sense** i.e., just because the numbers disagree in the reports, I do not doubt
that the principal information (that the Turkish fleet is out) is fearfully true.

So was I bid report here to the State   15
  By Signior Angelo.
DUKE: How say you by this change?
FIRST SENATOR: This cannot be
  By no assay of reason. 'Tis a pageant°
  To keep us in false gaze°. When we consider
  Th' importancy of Cyprus to the Turk,   20
  And let ourselves again but understand
  That, as it more concerns the Turk than Rhodes,
  So may he with more facile question° bear it,
  For that it stands not in such warlike brace°,
  But altogether lacks th' abilities   25
  That Rhodes is dressed in. If we make thought of this,
  We must not think the Turk is so unskillful
  To leave that latest which concerns him first,
  Neglecting an attempt of ease and gain
  To wake and wage a danger profitless.   30
DUKE: Nay, in all confidence he's not for Rhodes.
OFFICER: Here is more news.

Enter a MESSENGER.

MESSENGER: The Ottomites, reverend and gracious,
  Steering with due course toward the isle of Rhodes,
  Have there injointed them with an after° fleet.   35
FIRST SENATOR: Ay, so I thought. How many, as you guess?
MESSENGER: Of thirty sail; and now they do restem
  Their backward course, bearing with frank appearance
  Their purposes toward Cyprus. Signior Montano,
  Your trusty and most valiant servitor,   40
  With his free duty° recommends° you thus,
  And prays you to believe him.
DUKE: 'Tis certain then for Cyprus.
  Marcus Luccicos, is not he in town?
FIRST SENATOR: He's now in Florence.   45
DUKE: Write from us to him; post-posthaste dispatch.
FIRST SENATOR: Here comes Brabantio and the valiant Moor.

---

[18]**pageant** show, pretense.
[19]**in false gaze** looking the wrong way.
[23]**facile question** easy struggle.
[24]**warlike brace** "military posture."
[35]**after** following.
[41]**free duty** unlimited respect.
[41]**recommends** informs.

Enter BRABANTIO, OTHELLO, CASSIO, IAGO, RODERIGO, *and* OFFICERS.

DUKE: Valiant Othello, we must straight° employ you
   Against the general° enemy Ottoman.
   [*To* BRABANTIO] I did not see you. Welcome, gentle signior.   50
   We lacked your counsel and your help tonight.
BRABANTIO: So did I yours. Good your grace, pardon me.
   Neither my place, nor aught I heard of business,
   Hath raised me from my bed; nor doth the general care
   Take hold on me; for my particular grief   55
   Is of so floodgate and o'erbearing nature
   That it engluts and swallows other sorrows,
   And it is still itself.
DUKE: Why, what's the matter?
BRABANTIO: My daughter! O, my daughter!
SENATORS: Dead?
BRABANTIO: Ay, to me.
   She is abused, stol'n from me, and corrupted   60
   By spells and medicines bought of mountebanks;
   For nature so prepost'rously to err,
   Being not deficient, blind, or lame of sense,
   Sans° witchcraft could not.
DUKE: Whoe'er he be that in this foul proceeding   65
   Hath thus beguiled your daughter of herself,
   And you of her, the bloody book of law
   You shall yourself read in the bitter letter
   After your own sense; yea, though our proper° son
   Stood in your action°.
BRABANTIO: Humbly I thank your Grace.   70
   Here is the man—this Moor, whom now, it seems,
   Your special mandate for the state affairs
   Hath hither brought.
ALL: We are very sorry for't.
DUKE [*To* OTHELLO]: What in your own part can you say to this?
BRABANTIO: Nothing, but this is so.   75
OTHELLO: Most potent, grave, and reverend signiors,
   My very noble and approved° good masters,
   That I have ta'en away this old man's daughter,

---

⁴⁸**straight** at once.
⁴⁹**general** universal.
⁶⁴**Sans** without.
⁶⁹**proper** own.
⁷⁰**Stood in your action** were the accused in your suit.
⁷⁷**approved** tested, proven by past performance,

         true I have married her.
        ind front° of my offending   80
       ent, no more. Rude am I in my speech,
       olessed with the soft phrase of peace.
      these arms of mine had seven years' pith°
Till now some nine moons wasted°, they have used
Their dearest° action in the tented field;   85
And little of this great world can I speak
More than pertains to feats of broils and battle;
And therefore little shall I grace my cause
In speaking for myself. Yet, by your gracious patience,
I will a round° unvarnished tale deliver   90
Of my whole course of love—what drugs, what charms,
What conjuration, and what mighty magic,
For such proceeding I am charged withal,
I won his daughter—
BRABANTIO: A maiden never bold,
Of spirit so still and quiet that her motion   95
Blushed at herself°, and she, in spite of nature,
Of years, of country, credit, everything,
To fall in love with what she feared to look on!
It is a judgment maimed and most imperfect
That will confess perfection so could err   100
Against all rules of nature, and must be driven
To find out practices of cunning hell
Why this should be. I therefore vouch again
That with some mixtures pow'rful o'er the blood,
Or with some dram, conjured to this effect,   105
He wrought upon her.
DUKE: To vouch this is no proof,
Without more wider and more overt test
Than these thin habits° and poor likelihoods
Of modern° seeming do prefer against him.
FIRST SENATOR: But, Othello, speak.   110
Did you by indirect and forcèd courses
Subdue and poison this young maid's affections?

---

⁸⁰**head and front** extreme form (front = *forehead*).
⁸³**pith** strength.
⁸⁴**wasted** past.
⁸⁵**dearest** most important.
⁹⁰**round** blunt.
⁹⁵⁻⁹⁶**her motion/Blushed at herself** i.e., she was so modest that she blushed at every thought (and movement).
¹⁰⁸**habits** clothing.
¹⁰⁹**modern** trivial.

Or came it by request, and such fair question°
As soul to soul affordeth?

OTHELLO: I do beseech you,
Send for the lady to the Sagittary   115
And let her speak of me before her father.
If you do find me foul in her report,
The trust, the office, I do hold of you
Not only take away, but let your sentence
Even fall upon my life.

DUKE: Fetch Desdemona hither.   120

OTHELLO: Ancient, conduct them; you best know the place.

[Exit IAGO, *with two or three* ATTENDANTS.]

And till she come, as truly as to heaven
I do confess the vices of my blood,
So justly to your grave ears I'll present
How I did thrive in this fair lady's love,   125
And she in mine.

DUKE: Say it, Othello.

OTHELLO: Her father loved me; oft invited me;
Still° questioned me the story of my life
From year to year, the battle, sieges, fortune
That I have passed.   130
I ran it through, even from my boyish days
To th' very moment that he bade me tell it.
Wherein I spoke of most disastrous chances,
Of moving accidents by flood and field,
Of hairbreadth scapes i' th' imminent° deadly breach,   135
Of being taken by the insolent foe
And sold to slavery, of my redemption thence
And portance° in my travel's history,
Wherein of anters° vast and deserts idle°,
Rough quarries, rocks, and hills whose heads touch heaven,   140
It was my hint to speak. Such was my process.
And of the Cannibals that each other eat,
The Anthropophagi°, and men whose heads

---

¹¹³**question** discussion.
¹²⁸**Still** regularly.
¹³⁵**imminent** threatening.
¹³⁸**portance** manner of acting.
¹³⁹**anters** caves.
¹³⁹**idle** empty, sterile.
¹⁴³**Anthropophagi** maneaters.

Grew beneath their shoulders. These things to hear
Would Desdemona seriously incline; 145
But still the house affairs would draw her thence;
Which ever as she could with haste dispatch,
She'd come again, and with a greedy ear
Devour up my discourse. Which I observing,
Took once a pliant hour, and found good means 150
To draw from her a prayer of earnest heart
That I would all my pilgrimage dilate°,
Whereof by parcels she had something heard,
But not intentively°. I did consent,
And often did beguile her of her tears 155
When I did speak of some distressful stroke
That my youth suffered. My story being done,
She gave me for my pains a world of kisses.
She swore in faith 'twas strange, 'twas passing° strange;
'Twas pitiful, 'twas wondrous pitiful. 160
She wished she had not heard it; yet she wished
That heaven had made her such a man. She thanked me,
And bade me, if I had a friend that loved her,
I should but teach him how to tell my story,
And that would woo her. Upon this hint I spake. 165
She loved me for the dangers I had passed,
And I loved her that she did pity them.
This only is the witchcraft I have used.
Here comes the lady. Let her witness it.

Enter DESDEMONA, IAGO, ATTENDANTS.

DUKE: I think this tale would win my daughter too. 170
　Good Brabantio, take up this mangled matter at the best°.
　Men do their broken weapons rather use
　Than their bare hands.
BRABANTIO: 　　　　　　　I pray you hear her speak.
　If she confess that she was half the wooer,
　Destruction on my head if my bad blame 175
　Light on the man. Come hither, gentle mistress.
　Do you perceive in all this noble company
　Where most you owe obedience?

152**dilate** relate in full.
154**intentively** at length and in sequence.
159**passing** surpassing.
171**take . . . best** i.e., make the best of this disaster.

DESDEMONA: My noble father,
   I do perceive here a divided duty.
   To you I am bound for life and education;   180
   My life and education both do learn me
   How to respect you. You are the lord of duty,
   I am hitherto your daughter. But here's my husband,
   And so much duty as my mother showed
   To you, preferring you before her father,   185
   So much I challenge° that I may profess
   Due to the Moor my lord.
BRABANTIO: God be with you. I have done.
   Please it your Grace, on to the state affairs.
   I had rather to adopt a child than get° it.
   Come hither, Moor.   190
   I here do give thee that with all my heart
   Which, but thou hast already, with all my heart
   I would keep from thee. For your sake°, jewel,
   I am glad at soul I have no other child,
   For thy escape would teach me tyranny,   195
   To hang clogs on them. I have done, my lord.
DUKE: Let me speak like yourself and lay a sentence°
   Which, as a grise° or step, may help these lovers.
   When remedies are past, the griefs are ended
   By seeing the worst, which late on hopes depended°.   200
   To mourn a mischief that is past and gone
   Is the next° way to draw new mischief on.
   What cannot be preserved when fortune takes,
   Patience her injury a mock'ry makes.
   The robbed that smiles, steals something from the thief;   205
   He robs himself that spends a bootless° grief.
BRABANTIO: So let the Turk of Cyprus us beguile:
   We lose it not so long as we can smile.
   He bears the sentence well that nothing bears
   But the free comfort which from thence he hears;   210
   But he bears both the sentence and the sorrow
   That to pay grief must of poor patience borrow.
   These sentences, to sugar, or to gall,

---

[186]**challenge** claim as right.
[189]**get** beget.
[193]**For your sake** because of you.
[197]**lay a sentence** provide a maxim.
[198]**grise** step.
[200]**late on hopes depended** was supported by hope (of a better outcome) until lately.
[202]**next** closest, surest.
[206]**bootless** valueless.

Being strong on both sides, are equivocal.
But words are words. I never yet did hear   215
That the bruisèd heart was piercèd° through the ear.
I humbly beseech you, proceed to th' affairs of state.
DUKE: The Turk with a most mighty preparation makes for Cyprus.
Othello, the fortitude° of the place is best known to you; and
though we have there a substitute° of most allowed sufficiency°,   220
yet opinion, a more sovereign mistress of effects, throws a more
safer voice on you°. You must therefore be content to slubber°
the gloss of your new fortunes with this more stubborn and
boisterous° expedition.
OTHELLO: The tyrant Custom, most grave senators,
Hath made the flinty and steel couch of war   225
My thrice-driven° bed of down. I do agnize°
A natural and prompt alacrity
I find in hardness and do undertake
These present wars against the Ottomites.
Most humbly, therefore, bending to your state,   230
I crave fit disposition for my wife,
Due reference of place, and exhibition°,
With such accommodation and besort
As levels with° her breeding.
DUKE: Why, at her father's.
BRABANTIO: I will not have it so.
OTHELLO: Nor I.   235
DESDEMONA: Nor would I there reside,
To put my father in impatient thoughts
By being in his eye. Most gracious Duke,
To my unfolding° lend your prosperous° ear,
And let me find a charter° in your voice,   240
T' assist my simpleness.

---

²¹⁶**piercèd** (some editors emend to *piecèd,* i.e., "healed." But *piercèd* makes good sense:
Brabantio is saying in effect that his heart cannot be further hurt [pierced] by the indignity of
the useless, conventional advice the Duke offers him. *Pierced* can also mean, however,
"lanced" in the medical sense, and would then mean "treated").
²¹⁹**fortitude** fortification.
²²⁰**substitute** viceroy.
²²⁰**most allowed sufficiency** generally acknowledged capability.
²²¹⁻²²²**opinion . . . you** i.e., the general opinion, which finally controls affairs, is that you
would be the best man in this situation.
²²²**slubber** besmear.
²²³⁻²²⁴**stubborn and boisterous** rough and violent.
²²⁶**thrice-driven** i.e., softest.
²²⁶**agnize** know in myself.
²³²**exhibition** grant of funds.
²³⁴**levels with** is suitable to.
²³⁹**unfolding** explanation.
²³⁹**prosperous** favoring.
²⁴⁰**charter** permission.

DUKE: What would you, Desdemona?

DESDEMONA: That I love the Moor to live with him,
   My downright violence, and storm of fortunes,
   May trumpet to the world. My heart's subdued
   Even to the very quality of my lord.°   245
   I saw Othello's visage in his mind,
   And to his honors and his valiant parts
   Did I my soul and fortunes consecrate.
   So that, dear lords, if I be left behind,
   A moth of peace, and he go to the war,   250
   The rites° for why I love him are bereft me,
   And I a heavy interim shall support
   By his dear absence. Let me go with him.

OTHELLO: Let her have your voice°.
   Vouch with me, heaven, I therefore beg it not   255
   To please the palate of my appetite,
   Nor to comply with heat°—the young affects°
   In me defunct—and proper satisfaction°;
   But to be free and bounteous to her mind;
   And heaven defend° your good souls that you think   260
   I will your serious and great business scant
   When she is with me. No, when light-winged toys
   Of feathered Cupid seel° with wanton° dullness
   My speculative and officed instrument°,
   That my disports corrupt and taint my business,   265
   Let housewives make a skillet of my helm,
   And all indign° and base adversities
   Make head° against my estimation°!—

DUKE: Be it as you shall privately determine,
   Either for her stay or going. Th' affair cries haste,   270
   And speed must answer it.

FIRST SENATOR: You must away tonight.

OTHELLO: With all my heart.

---

²⁴⁴⁻²⁴⁵**My . . . lord** i.e., I have become one in nature and being with the man I married
(therefore, I too would go to the wars like a soldier).
²⁵¹**rites** (may refer either to the marriage rites or to the rites, formalities, of war).
²⁵⁴**voice** consent.
²⁵⁷**heat** lust.
²⁵⁷**affects** passions.
²⁵⁸**proper satisfaction** i.e., consummation of the marriage.
²⁶⁰**defend** forbid.
²⁶³**seel** sew up.
²⁶³**wanton** lascivious.
²⁶⁴**speculative . . . instrument** i.e., sight (and, by extension, the mind).
²⁶⁷**indign** unworthy.
²⁶⁸**Make head** form an army, i.e., attack.
²⁶⁸**estimation** reputation.

DUKE: At nine i' th' morning here we'll meet again.
Othello, leave some officer behind,
And he shall our commission bring to you, 275
And such things else of quality and respect
As doth import you.
OTHELLO: So please your grace, my ancient;
A man he is of honesty and trust.
To his conveyance I assign my wife,
With what else needful your good grace shall think 280
To be sent after me.
DUKE: Let it be so.
Good night to every one. [*To* BRABANTIO] And, noble signior,
If virtue no delighted° beauty lack,
Your son-in-law is far more fair than black.
FIRST SENATOR: Adieu, brave Moor. Use Desdemona well. 285
BRABANTIO: Look to her, Moor, if thou hast eyes to see:
She has deceived her father, and may thee.

Exeunt DUKE, SENATORS, OFFICERS, &c.

OTHELLO: My life upon her faith! Honest Iago,
My Desdemona must I leave to thee.
I prithee let thy wife attend on her, 290
And bring them after in the best advantage°.
Come, Desdemona. I have but an hour
Of love, of worldly matter, and direction
To spend with thee. We must obey the time.

Exit [MOOR *with* DESDEMONA].

RODERIGO: Iago? 295
IAGO: What say'st thou, noble heart?
RODERIGO: What will I do, think'st thou?
IAGO: Why, go to bed and sleep.
RODERIGO: I will incontinently° drown myself.
IAGO: If thou dost, I shall never love thee after. Why, thou silly 300
gentleman?
RODERIGO: It is silliness to live when to live is torment; and then
have we a prescription to die when death is our physician.
IAGO: O villainous! I have looked upon the world for four times
seven years, and since I could distinguish betwixt a benefit and 305

---

²⁸³**delighted** delightful.
²⁹¹**advantage** opportunity.
²⁹⁹**incontinently** at once.

an injury, I never found man that knew how to love himself. Ere
I would say I would drown myself for the love of a guinea hen, I
would change my humanity with a baboon.

RODERIGO: What should I do? I confess it is my shame to be so fond,
but it is not in my virtue° to amend it.   310

IAGO: Virtue? A fig! 'Tis in ourselves that we are thus, or thus. Our
bodies are our gardens, to the which our wills are gardeners; so
that if we will plant nettles or sow lettuce, set hyssop and weed
up thyme, supply it with one gender of herbs or distract° it with
many—either to have it sterile with idleness or manured with   315
industry—why, the power and corrigible° authority of this lies
in our wills. If the balance of our lives had not one scale of
reason to poise another of sensuality, the blood and baseness of
our natures would conduct us to most prepost'rous conclusions°.
But we have reason to cool our raging motions, our carnal sting   320
or unbitted° lusts, whereof I take this that you call love to be a
sect or scion°.

RODERIGO: It cannot be.

IAGO: It is merely a lust of the blood and a permission of the will.
Come, be a man! Drown thyself? Drown cats and blind puppies! I   325
have professed me thy friend, and I confess me knit to thy
deserving with cables of perdurable toughness. I could never
better stead° thee than now. Put money in thy purse. Follow
thou the wars; defeat thy favor° with an usurped° beard. I say,
put money in thy purse. It cannot be long that Desdemona   330
should continue her love to the Moor. Put money in thy purse.
Nor he his to her. It was a violent commencement in her and
thou shalt see an answerable° sequestration—put but money in
thy purse. These Moors are changeable in their wills—fill thy
purse with money. The food that to him now is as luscious as   335
locusts° shall be to him shortly as bitter as coloquintida°. She
must change for youth; when she is sated with his body, she will
find the errors of her choice. Therefore, put money in thy purse.
If thou wilt needs damn thyself, do it a more delicate way than

---

310**virtue** strength (Roderigo is saying that his nature controls him).
314**distract** vary.
316**corrigible** corrective.
319**conclusions** ends.
321**unbitted** i.e., uncontrolled.
322**sect or scion** offshoot.
328**stead** serve.
329**defeat thy favor** disguise your face.
329**usurped** assumed.
333**answerable** similar.
336**locusts** (a sweet fruit).
336**coloquintida** a purgative derived from a bitter apple.

drowning. Make all the money thou canst. If sanctimony° and a   340
frail vow betwixt an erring° barbarian and supersubtle Venetian
be not too hard for my wits, and all the tribe of hell, thou shalt
enjoy her. Therefore, make money. A pox of drowning thyself, it
is clean out of the way. Seek thou rather to be hanged in
compassing° thy joy than to be drowned and go without her.   345

RODERIGO: Wilt thou be fast to my hopes, if I depend on the issue?

IAGO: Thou art sure of me. Go, make money. I have told thee often,
and I retell thee again and again, I hate the Moor. My cause is
hearted°; thine hath no less reason. Let us be conjunctive° in
our revenge against him. If thou canst cuckold him, thou dost   350
thyself a pleasure, me a sport. There are many events in the
womb of time, which will be delivered. Traverse, go, provide thy
money! We will have more of this tomorrow. Adieu.

RODERIGO: Where shall we meet i' th' morning?

IAGO: At my lodging.   355

RODERIGO: I'll be with thee betimes.

IAGO: Go to, farewell. Do you hear, Roderigo?

RODERIGO: I'll sell all my land.   *Exit.*

IAGO: Thus do I ever make my fool my purse;
For I mine own gained knowledge° should profane   360
If I would time expend with such snipe
But for my sport and profit. I hate the Moor,
And it is thought abroad that 'twixt my sheets
H'as done my office. I know not if't be true,
But I, for mere suspicion in that kind,   365
Will do, as if for surety°. He holds me well;
The better shall my purpose work on him.
Cassio's a proper° man. Let me see now:
To get his place, and to plume up my will°
In double knavery. How? How? Let's see.   370
After some time, to abuse Othello's ears
That he is too familiar with his wife.
He hath a person and a smooth dispose°

---

³⁴⁰**sanctimony** sacred bond (of marriage).
³⁴¹**erring** wandering.
³⁴⁵**compassing** encompassing, achieving.
³⁴⁹**hearted** deep-seated in the heart.
³⁴⁹**conjunctive** joined.
³⁶⁰**gained knowledge** i.e., practical, worldly wisdom.
³⁶⁶**surety** certainty.
³⁶⁸**proper** handsome.
³⁶⁹**plume up my will** (many explanations have been offered for this crucial line, which in
Q₁ reads "make up my will." The general sense is something like "to make more proud and
gratify my ego").
³⁷³**dispose** manner.

To be suspected—framed° to make women false.
The Moor is of a free and open nature   375
That thinks men honest that but seem to be so;
And will as tenderly be led by th' nose
As asses are.
I have't! It is engendered! Hell and night
Must bring this monstrous birth to the world's light.   [*Exit.*]   380

ACT II

Scene I [Cyprus.]

Enter MONTANO *and two* GENTLEMEN [*one above*].°

MONTANO: What from the cape can you discern at sea?
FIRST GENTLEMAN: Nothing at all, it is a high-wrought flood.
I cannot 'twixt the heaven and the main
Descry a sail.
MONTANO: Methinks the wind hath spoke aloud at land;   5
A fuller blast ne'er shook our battlements.
If it hath ruffianed so upon the sea,
What ribs of oak, when mountains melt on them,
Can hold the mortise? What shall we hear of this?
SECOND GENTLEMAN: A segregation° of the Turkish fleet.   10
For do but stand upon the foaming shore,
The chidden billow seems to pelt the clouds;
The wind-shaked surge, with high and monstrous main°,
Seems to cast water on the burning Bear
And quench the guards of th' ever-fixèd pole.°   15
I never did like molestation view
On the enchafèd flood.
MONTANO: If that the Turkish fleet
Be not ensheltered and embayed, they are drowned;
It is impossible to bear it out.

---

³⁷⁴**framed** designed.
  II.i. s.d. (the Folio arrangement of this scene requires that the First Gentleman stand above—on the upper stage—and act as a lookout reporting sights which cannot be seen by Montano standing below on the main stage).
  ¹⁰**segregation** separation.
  ¹³**main** (both "ocean" and "strength").
  ¹⁴⁻¹⁵**Seems . . . pole** (the constellation Ursa Minor contains two stars which are the *guards,* or companions, of the *pole,* or North Star.)

Enter a [third] GENTLEMAN.

THIRD GENTLEMAN: News, lads! Our wars are done.   20
  The desperate tempest hath so banged the Turks
  That their designment halts. A noble ship of Venice
  Hath seen a grievous wrack and sufferance°
  On most part of their fleet.
MONTANO: How? Is this true?
THIRD GENTLEMAN: The ship is here put in,   25
  A Veronesa; Michael Cassio,
  Lieutenant to the warlike Moor Othello,
  Is come on shore; the Moor himself at sea,
  And is in full commission here for Cyprus.
MONTANO: I am glad on't. 'Tis a worthy governor.   30
THIRD GENTLEMAN: But this same Cassio, though he speak of comfort
  Touching the Turkish loss, yet he looks sadly
  And prays the Moor be safe, for they were parted
  With foul and violent tempest.
MONTANO: Pray heavens he be;
  For I have served him, and the man commands   35
  Like a full soldier. Let's to the seaside, ho!
  As well to see the vessel that's come in
  As to throw out our eyes for brave Othello,
  Even till we make the main and th' aerial blue
  An indistinct regard°.
THIRD GENTLEMAN: Come, let's do so;   40
  For every minute is expectancy
  Of more arrivancie°.

Enter CASSIO.

CASSIO: Thanks, you the valiant of the warlike isle,
  That so approve° the Moor. O, let the heavens
  Give him defense against the elements,   45
  For I have lost him on a dangerous sea.
MONTANO: Is he well shipped?
CASSIO: His bark is stoutly timbered, and his pilot
  Of very expert and approved allowance°;
  Therefore my hopes, not surfeited to death°,   50

---

[23]**sufferance** damage.
[39-40]**the main . . . regard** i.e., the sea and sky become indistinguishable.
[42]**arrivancie** arrivals.
[44]**approve** ("honor" or, perhaps, "are as warlike and valiant as your governor").
[49]**approved allowance** known and tested.
[50]**not surfeited to death** i.e., not so great as to be in danger.

Stand in bold cure°. (*Within:* A sail, a sail, a sail!)
CASSIO: What noise?
FIRST GENTLEMAN: The town is empty; on the brow o' th' sea
  Stand ranks of people, and they cry, "A sail!"
CASSIO: My hopes do shape him for the governor.   [*A shot.*]   55
SECOND GENTLEMAN: They do discharge their shot of courtesy:
  Our friends at least.
CASSIO: I pray you, sir, go forth
  And give us truth who 'tis that is arrived.
SECOND GENTLEMAN: I shall.   [*Exit.*]
MONTANO: But, good lieutenant, is your general wived?   60
CASSIO: Most fortunately. He hath achieved a maid
  That paragons° description and wild fame°;
  One that excels the quirks of blazoning pens°,
  And in th' essential vesture of creation°
  Does tire the ingener°.

Enter [*Second*] GENTLEMAN.

               How now? Who has put in?   65
GENTLEMAN: 'Tis one Iago, ancient to the general.
CASSIO: H'as had most favorable and happy speed:
  Tempests themselves, high seas, and howling winds,
  The guttered° rocks and congregated° sands,
  Traitors ensteeped° to enclog the guiltless keel,   70
  As having sense° of beauty, do omit
  Their mortal° natures, letting go safely by
  The divine Desdemona.
MONTANO: What is she?
CASSIO: She that I spake of, our great captain's captain,
  Left in the conduct of the bold Iago,   75
  Whose footing° here anticipates our thoughts
  A se'nnight's° speed. Great Jove, Othello guard,
  And swell his sail with thine own pow'rful breath,

---

⁵¹**Stand in bold cure** i.e., are likely to be restored.
⁶²**paragons** exceeds.
⁶²**wild fame** extravagant report.
⁶³**quirks of blazoning pens** ingenuities of praising pens.
⁶⁴**essential vesture of creation** essential human nature as given by the Creator.
⁶⁵**tire the ingener** a difficult line that probably means something like "outdo the human ability to imagine and picture."
⁶⁹**guttered** jagged.
⁶⁹**congregated** gathered.
⁷⁰**ensteeped** submerged.
⁷¹**sense** awareness.
⁷²**mortal** deadly.
⁷⁶**footing** landing.
⁷⁷**se'nnight's** week's.

That he may bless this bay with his tall° ship,
Make love's quick pants in Desdemona's arms,   80
Give renewed fire to our extincted spirits.

Enter DESDEMONA, IAGO, RODERIGO, *and* EMILIA.

O, behold! The riches of the ship is come on shore!
You men of Cyprus, let her have your knees.   [*Kneeling.*]
Hail to thee, lady! and the grace of heaven,
Before, behind thee, and on every hand,   85
Enwheel thee round.
DESDEMONA: I thank you, valiant Cassio.
What tidings can you tell of my lord?
CASSIO: He is not yet arrived, nor know I aught
But that he's well and will be shortly here.
DESDEMONA: O but I fear. How lost you company?   90
CASSIO: The great contention of sea and skies
Parted our fellowship. (*Within:* A sail, a sail!)   [*A shot.*]
But hark. A sail!
SECOND GENTLEMAN: They give this greeting to the citadel;
This likewise is a friend.
CASSIO: See for the news.   [*Exit* GENTLEMAN.]   95
Good ancient, you are welcome. [*To* EMILIA] Welcome, mistress.
Let it not gall your patience, good Iago,
That I extend° my manners. 'Tis my breeding°
That gives me this bold show of courtesy.   [*Kisses* EMILIA.]
IAGO: Sir, would she give you so much of her lips   100
As of her tongue she oft bestows on me,
You would have enough.
DESDEMONA: Alas, she has no speech.
IAGO: In faith, too much.
I find it still when I have leave to sleep°.
Marry, before your ladyship°, I grant,   105
She puts her tongue a little in her heart
And chides with thinking.
EMILIA: You have little cause to say so.
IAGO: Come on, come on! You are pictures° out of door,
Bells in your parlors, wildcats in your kitchens,

---

⁷⁹**tall** brave.
⁹⁸**extend** stretch.
⁹⁸**breeding** careful training in manners (Cassio is considerably more the polished gentleman than Iago, and aware of it).
¹⁰⁴**still . . . sleep** i.e., even when she allows me to sleep she continues to scold.
¹⁰⁵**before your ladyship** in your presence.
¹⁰⁸**pictures** models (of virtue).

Saints in your injuries°, devils being offended,   110
  Players in your housewifery°, and housewives in your beds.
DESDEMONA: O, fie upon thee, slanderer!
IAGO: Nay, it is true, or else I am a Turk:
  You rise to play, and go to bed to work.
EMILIA: You shall not write my praise.
IAGO: No, let me not.   115
DESDEMONA: What wouldst write of me, if thou shouldst praise me?
IAGO: O gentle lady, do not put me to't.
  For I am nothing if not critical.
DESDEMONA: Come on, assay. There's one gone to the harbor?
IAGO: Ay, madam.
DESDEMONA [*Aside*]: I am not merry; but I do beguile   120
  The thing I am by seeming otherwise.—
  Come, how wouldst thou praise me?
IAGO: I am about it; but indeed my invention
  Comes from my pate as birdlime° does from frieze°—
  It plucks out brains and all. But my Muse labors,   125
  And thus she is delivered:
  If she be fair° and wise: fairness and wit,
  The one's for use, the other useth it.
DESDEMONA: Well praised. How if she be black° and witty?
IAGO: If she be black, and thereto have a wit,   130
  She'll find a white that shall her blackness fit.
DESDEMONA: Worse and worse!
EMILIA: How if fair and foolish?
IAGO: She never yet was foolish that was fair,
  For even her folly helped her to an heir.   135
DESDEMONA: Those are old fond° paradoxes to make fools laugh i'
  th' alehouse. What miserable praise hast thou for her that's foul
  and foolish?
IAGO: There's none so foul, and foolish thereunto,
  But does foul pranks which fair and wise ones do.   140
DESDEMONA: O heavy ignorance. Thou praisest the worst best. But
  what praise couldst thou bestow on a deserving woman

110**in your injuries** when you injure others.
111**housewifery** this word can mean "careful, economical household management," and Iago would then be accusing women of only pretending to be good housekeepers, while in bed they are either [1] economical of their favors, or more likely [2] serious and dedicated workers.
124**birdlime** a sticky substance put on branches to catch birds.
124**frieze** rough cloth.
127**fair** light-complexioned.
129**black** brunette.
136**fond** foolish.

indeed—one that in the authority of her merit did justly put on
the vouch of very malice itself°?

IAGO: She that was ever fair, and never proud;   145
　　Had tongue at will, and yet was never loud;
　　Never lacked gold, and yet went never gay;
　　Fled from her wish, and yet said "Now I may";
　　She that being angered, her revenge being nigh,
　　Bade her wrong stay, and her displeasure fly;   150
　　She that in wisdom never was so frail
　　To change the cod's head for the salmon's tail°;
　　She that could think, and nev'r disclose her mind;
　　See suitors following, and not look behind:
　　She was a wight° (if ever such wights were)—   155
DESDEMONA: To do what?
IAGO: To suckle fools and chronicle small beer°.
DESDEMONA: O most lame and impotent conclusion. Do not learn of
　　him, Emilia, though he be thy husband. How say you, Cassio? Is
　　he not a most profane and liberal° counselor?   160
CASSIO: He speaks home°, madam. You may relish him more in°
　　the soldier than in the scholar. [*Takes* DESDEMONA's *hand.*]
IAGO [*Aside*]: He takes her by the palm. Ay, well said, whisper! With
　　as little a web as this will I ensnare as great a fly as Cassio. Ay,
　　smile upon her, do! I will gyve° thee in thine own courtship.—   165
　　You say true; 'tis so, indeed!—If such tricks as these strip you
　　out of your lieutenantry, it had been better you had not kissed
　　your three fingers so oft—which now again you are most apt to
　　play the sir° in. Very good! Well kissed! An excellent curtsy°!
　　'Tis so, indeed. Yet again your fingers to your lips? Would they   170
　　were clyster pipes° for your sake! [*Trumpets within.*] The Moor! I
　　know his trumpet°.
CASSIO: 'Tis truly so.
DESDEMONA: Let's meet him and receive him.
CASSIO: Lo, where he comes.   175

　　[143-144]**one . . . itself** i.e., a woman so honest and deserving that even malice would be
forced to approve of her.
　　[152]**To . . . tail** i.e., to exchange something valuable for something useless.
　　[155]**wight** person.
　　[157]**chronicle small beer** i.e., keep household accounts (the most trivial of occupations in
Iago's opinion).
　　[160]**liberal** licentious.
　　[161]**speaks home** thrusts deeply with his speech.
　　[161]**relish him more in** enjoy him more as.
　　[165]**gyve** bind.
　　[169]**the sir** the fashionable gentleman.
　　[169]**curtsy** courtesy, i.e., bow.
　　[171]**clyster pipes** enema tubes.
　　[172]**his trumpet** (great men had their own distinctive calls).

Enter OTHELLO *and* ATTENDANTS.

OTHELLO: O my fair warrior!
DESDEMONA: My dear Othello.
OTHELLO: It gives me wonder great as my content   175
  To see you here before me. O my soul's joy!
  If after every tempest come such calms,
  May the winds blow till they have wakened death.   180
  And let the laboring bark climb hills of seas
  Olympus-high, and duck again as low
  As hell's from heaven. If it were now to die,
  'Twere now to be most happy; for I fear
  My soul hath her content so absolute   185
  That not another comfort like to this
  Succeeds in unknown fate.
DESDEMONA: The heavens forbid
  But that our loves and comforts should increase
  Even as our days do grow.
OTHELLO: Amen to that, sweet powers!
  I cannot speak enough of this content;   190
  It stops me here [*touches his heart*]; it is too much of joy.
  And this, and this, the greatest discords be   [*They kiss.*]
  That e'er our hearts shall make!
IAGO [*Aside*]:   O, you are well tuned now!
  But I'll set down the pegs° that make this music,
  As honest as I am.
OTHELLO: Come, let us to the castle.   195
  News, friends! Our wars are done; the Turks are drowned.
  How does my old acquaintance of this isle?
  Honey, you shall be well desired in Cyprus;
  I have found great love amongst them. O my sweet,
  I prattle out of fashion, and I dote   200
  In mine own comforts. I prithee, good Iago,
  Go to the bay and disembark my coffers.
  Bring thou the master to the citadel;
  He is a good one and his worthiness
  Does challenge° much respect. Come, Desdemona,   205
  Once more well met at Cyprus.

          Exit OTHELLO *and* DESDEMONA [*and all but* IAGO *and* RODERIGO].

IAGO [*To an* ATTENDANT]: Do thou meet me presently at the harbor.

---

¹⁹⁴**set down the pegs** loosen the strings (to produce discord).
²⁰⁵**challenge** require, exact.

[*To* RODERIGO] Come hither. If thou be'st valiant (as they say base
men being in love have then a nobility in their natures more
than is native to them), list me. The lieutenant tonight watches   210
on the court of guard°. First, I must tell thee this: Desdemona is
directly in love with him.

RODERIGO: With him? Why, 'tis not possible.

IAGO: Lay thy finger thus [*puts his finger to his lips*], and let thy soul
be instructed. Mark me with what violence she first loved the   215
Moor but for bragging and telling her fantastical lies. To love
him still for prating? Let not thy discreet heart think it. Her eye
must be fed. And what delight shall she have to look on the
devil? When the blood is made dull with the act of sport, there
should be a game° to inflame it and to give satiety a fresh   220
appetite, loveliness in favor°, sympathy in years°, manners, and
beauties; all which the Moor is defective in. Now for want of
these required conveniences°, her delicate tenderness will find
itself abused, begin to heave the gorge°, disrelish and abhor the
Moor. Very nature will instruct her in it and compel her to some   225
second choice. Now sir, this granted—as it is a most pregnant°
and unforced position—who stands so eminent in the degree of
this fortune as Cassio does? A knave very voluble; no further
conscionable° than in putting on the mere form of civil and
humane° seeming for the better compass of his salt° and most   230
hidden loose° affection. Why none! Why, none! A slipper° and
subtle knave, a finder of occasion, that has an eye can stamp and
counterfeit advantages, though true advantage never present
itself. A devilish knave. Besides, the knave is handsome, young,
and hath all those requisites in him that folly and green minds   235
look after. A pestilent complete knave, and the woman hath
found him already.

RODERIGO: I cannot believe that in her; she's full of most blessed
condition.

IAGO: Blessed fig's-end! The wine she drinks is made of grapes. If   240
she had been blessed, she would never have loved the Moor.

---

²¹¹**court of guard** guardhouse.
²²⁰**game** sport (with the added sense of "gamey," "rank").
²²¹**favor** countenance, appearance.
²²¹**sympathy in years** sameness of age.
²²³**conveniences** advantages.
²²⁴**heave the gorge** vomit.
²²⁶**pregnant** likely.
²²⁸⁻²⁹**no further conscionable** having no more conscience.
²³⁰**humane** polite.
²³⁰**salt** lecherous.
²³¹**loose** immoral.
²³¹**slipper** slippery.

Blessed pudding! Didst thou not see her paddle with the palm of
his hand? Didst not mark that?

RODERIGO: Yes, that I did; but that was but courtesy.

IAGO: Lechery, by this hand! [*Extends his index finger.*] An index° and   245
obscure prologue to the history of lust and foul thoughts. They
met so near with their lips that their breaths embraced together.
Villainous thoughts, Roderigo. When these mutualities so
marshal the way, hard at hand comes the master and main
exercise, th' incorporate° conclusion: Pish! But, sir, be you ruled   250
by me. I have brought you from Venice. Watch you tonight; for
the command, I'll lay't upon you. Cassio knows you not. I'll not
be far from you. Do you find some occasion to anger Cassio,
either by speaking too loud, or tainting° his discipline, or from
what other course you please which the time shall more   255
favorably minister.

RODERIGO: Well.

IAGO: Sir, he's rash and very sudden in choler°, and haply may
strike at you. Provoke him that he may; for even out of that will
I cause these of Cyprus to mutiny, whose qualification shall   260
come into no true taste° again but by the displanting of Cassio.
So shall you have a shorter journey to your desires by the means
I shall then have to prefer them; and the impediment most
profitably removed without which there were no expectation of
our prosperity.   265

RODERIGO: I will do this if you can bring it to any opportunity.

IAGO: I warrant thee. Meet me by and by at the citadel. I must fetch
his necessaries ashore. Farewell.

RODERIGO: Adieu.   *Exit.*

IAGO: That Cassio loves her, I do well believe't;   270
That she loves him, 'tis apt and of great credit.
The Moor, howbeit that I endure him not,
Is of a constant, loving, noble nature,
And I dare think he'll prove to Desdemona
A most dear° husband. Now I do love her too;   275
Not out of absolute° lust, though peradventure°
I stand accountant for as great a sin,

---

²⁴⁵**index** pointer.
²⁵⁰**incorporate** carnal.
²⁵⁴**tainting** discrediting.
²⁵⁸**choler** anger.
²⁶⁰⁻²⁶¹**qualification . . . taste** i.e., appeasement will not be brought about (wine was
"qualified" by adding water).
²⁷⁵**dear** expensive.
²⁷⁶**out of absolute** absolutely out of.
²⁷⁶**peradventure** perchance.

But partly led to diet° my revenge,
For that I do suspect the lusty Moor
Hath leaped into my seat; the thought whereof   280
Doth, like a poisonous mineral, gnaw my inwards;
And nothing can or shall content my soul
Till I am evened with him, wife for wife.
Or failing so, yet that I put the Moor
At least into a jealousy so strong   285
That judgment cannot cure. Which thing to do,
If this poor trash of Venice, whom I trace°
For his quick hunting, stand the putting on,
I'll have our Michael Cassio on the hip,
Abuse him to the Moor in the right garb°   290
(For I fear Cassio with my nightcap too),
Make the Moor thank me, love me, and reward me
For making him egregiously an ass
And practicing upon° his peace and quiet,
Even to madness. 'Tis here, but yet confused: 295
Knavery's plain face is never seen till used.   *Exit.*

Scene II [A street.]

Enter OTHELLO'S HERALD, *with a proclamation.*

HERALD: It is Othello's pleasure, our noble and valiant general, that
upon certain tidings now arrived importing the mere perdition°
of the Turkish fleet, every man put himself into triumph. Some
to dance, some to make bonfires, each man to what sport and
revels his addition° leads him. For, besides these beneficial news,   5
it is the celebration of his nuptial. So much was his pleasure
should be proclaimed. All offices° are open, and there is full
liberty of feasting from this present hour of five till the bell have
told eleven. Bless the isle of Cyprus and our noble general
Othello!   *Exit.*   10

---

²⁷⁸**diet** feed.
²⁸⁷**trace** (most editors emend to "trash," meaning to hang weights on a dog to slow his
hunting: but "trace" clearly means something like "put on the trace" or "set on the track").
²⁹⁰**right garb** i.e., "proper fashion."
²⁹⁴**practicing upon** scheming to destroy.
II.ii. ²**mere perdition** absolute destruction.
⁵**addition** rank.
⁷**offices** kitchens and storerooms of food.

Scene III [*The citadel of Cyprus.*]

Enter OTHELLO, DESDEMONA, CASSIO, *and* ATTENDANTS.

OTHELLO: Good Michael, look you to the guard tonight.
  Let's teach ourselves that honorable stop,
  Not to outsport direction.
CASSIO: Iago hath discretion what to do;
  But notwithstanding, with my personal eye   5
  Will I look to't.
OTHELLO: Iago is most honest.
  Michael, good night. Tomorrow with your earliest
  Let me have speech with you. [*To* DESDEMONA] Come, my dear
    love,
  The purchase made, the fruits are to ensue.   10
  That profit's yet to come 'tween me and you.
  Good night.   *Exit* [OTHELLO *with* DESDEMONA *and* ATTENDANTS].

Enter IAGO.

CASSIO: Welcome, Iago. We must to the watch.
IAGO: Not this hour, lieutenant; 'tis not yet ten o' th' clock. Our
  general cast° us thus early for the love of his Desdemona; who   15
  let us not therefore blame. He hath not yet made wanton the
  night with her, and she is sport for Jove.
CASSIO: She's a most exquisite lady.
IAGO: And, I'll warrant her, full of game.
CASSIO: Indeed, she's a most fresh and delicate creature.   20
IAGO: What an eye she has! Methinks it sounds a parley to
  provocation.
CASSIO: An inviting eye; and yet methinks right modest.
IAGO: And when she speaks, is it not an alarum° to love?
CASSIO: She is indeed perfection.   25
IAGO: Well, happiness to their sheets! Come, lieutenant, I have a
  stoup° of wine, and here without are a brace of Cyprus gallants
  that would fain have a measure to the health of black Othello.
CASSIO: Not tonight, good Iago. I have very poor and unhappy
  brains for drinking; I could well wish courtesy would invent   30
  some other custom of entertainment.

II.iii. ¹⁵**cast** dismissed.
²⁴**alarum** the call to action, "general quarters."
²⁷**stoup** two-quart tankard.

IAGO: O, they are our friends. But one cup! I'll drink for you.

CASSIO: I have drunk but one tonight, and that was craftily
    qualified° too; and behold what innovation it makes here. I am
    unfortunate in the infirmity and dare not task my weakness with   35
    any more.

IAGO: What, man! 'Tis a night of revels, the gallants desire it.

CASSIO: Where are they?

IAGO: Here, at the door. I pray you call them in.

CASSIO: I'll do't, but it dislikes me.   *Exit.*   40

IAGO: If I can fasten but one cup upon him
    With that which he hath drunk tonight already,
    He'll be as full of quarrel and offense
    As my young mistress' dog. Now, my sick fool Roderigo,
    Whom love hath turned almost the wrong side out,   45
    To Desdemona hath tonight caroused
    Potations pottle-deep°; and he's to watch.
    Three else° of Cyprus, noble swelling spirits,
    That hold their honors in a wary distance°,
    The very elements of this warlike isle,
    Have I tonight flustered with flowing cups,
    And they watch too. Now, 'mongst this flock of drunkards
    Am I to put our Cassio in some action
    That may offend the isle. But here they come.

Enter CASSIO, MONTANO, *and* GENTLEMEN.

    If consequence do but approve my dream,   55
    My boat sails freely, both with wind and stream.

CASSIO: 'Fore God, they have given me a rouse° already.

MONTANO: Good faith, a little one; not past a pint, as I am a soldier.

IAGO: Some wine, ho!
    [*Sings*] And let me the canakin clink, clink;   60
            And let me the canakin clink.
                A soldier's a man;
                O man's life's but a span.
                Why then, let a soldier drink.
    Some wine, boys!   65

CASSIO: 'Fore God, an excellent song!

IAGO: I learned it in England, where indeed they are most potent in

---

³⁴**qualified** diluted.
⁴⁷**pottle-deep** to the bottom of the cup.
⁴⁸**else** others.
⁴⁹**hold . . . distance** are scrupulous in maintaining their honor.
⁵⁷**rouse** drink.

potting. Your Dane, your German, and your swag-bellied°
Hollander—Drink, ho!—are nothing to your English.

CASSIO: Is your Englishman so exquisite° in his drinking? 70

IAGO: Why, he drinks you with facility your Dane dead drunk; he
sweats not to overthrow your Almain; he gives your Hollander a
vomit ere the next pottle can be filled.

CASSIO: To the health of our general!

MONTANO: I am for it, lieutenant, and I'll do you justice. 75

IAGO: O sweet England!

[*Sings*] King Stephen was and a worthy peer;
    His breeches cost him but a crown;
    He held them sixpence all too dear,
    With that he called the tailor lown°. 80
    He was a wight of high renown,
    And thou art but of low degree:
    'Tis pride that pulls the country down;
    And take thine auld cloak about thee.

Some wine, ho! 85

CASSIO: 'Fore God, this is a more exquisite song than the other.

IAGO: Will you hear't again?

CASSIO: No, for I hold him to be unworthy of his place that does
those things. Well, God's above all; and there be souls must be
saved, and there be souls must not be saved. 90

IAGO: It's true, good lieutenant.

CASSIO: For mine own part—no offense to the general, nor any man
of quality—I hope to be saved.

IAGO: And so do I too, lieutenant.

CASSIO: Ay, but, by your leave, not before me. The lieutenant is to 95
be saved before the ancient. Let's have no more of this; let's to
our affairs.—God forgive us our sins!—Gentlemen, let's look to
our business. Do not think, gentlemen, I am drunk. This is my
ancient; this is my right hand, and this is my left. I am not
drunk now. I can stand well enough, and I speak well enough. 100

GENTLEMEN: Excellent well!

CASSIO: Why, very well then. You must not think then that I am
drunk. *Exit.*

MONTANO: To th' platform, masters. Come, let's set the watch.

IAGO: You see this fellow that is gone before. 105
He's a soldier fit to stand by Caesar
And give direction; and do but see his vice.
'Tis to his virtue a just equinox°,

---

⁶⁸**swag-bellied** pendulous-bellied.
⁷⁰**exquisite** superb.
⁸⁰**lown** lout.
¹⁰⁸**just equinox** exact balance (of dark and light).

The one as long as th' other. 'Tis pity of him.
I fear the trust Othello puts him in,   110
On some odd time of his infirmity,
Will shake this island.
MONTANO: But is he often thus?
IAGO: 'Tis evermore his prologue to his sleep:
He'll watch the horologe a double set°
If drink rock not his cradle.
MONTANO: It were well   115
The general were put in mind of it.
Perhaps he sees it not, or his good nature
Prizes the virtue that appears in Cassio
And looks not on his evils. Is not this true?

Enter RODERIGO.

IAGO [*Aside*]: How now, Roderigo?   120
I pray you after the lieutenant, go!   [*Exit* RODERIGO.]
MONTANO: And 'tis great pity that the noble Moor
Should hazard such a place as his own second
With one of an ingraft° infirmity.
It were an honest action to say so   125
To the Moor.
IAGO: Not I, for this fair island!
I do love Cassio well and would do much
To cure him of this evil.   [Help! Help! *Within.*]
But hark? What noise?

Enter CASSIO, *pursuing* RODERIGO.

CASSIO: Zounds, you rogue! You rascal!   130
MONTANO: What's the matter, lieutenant?
CASSIO: A knave teach me my duty? I'll beat the knave into a
twiggen° bottle.
RODERIGO: Beat me?
CASSIO: Dost thou prate, rogue?   [*Strikes him.*]   135
MONTANO: Nay, good lieutenant! I pray you, sir, hold your hand.
[*Stays him.*]
CASSIO: Let me go, sir, or I'll knock you o'er the mazzard°.
MONTANO: Come, come, you're drunk!
CASSIO: Drunk?   [*They fight.*]

---

¹¹⁴**watch . . . set** stay awake twice around the clock.
¹²⁴**ingraft** ingrained.
¹³³**twiggen** wicker-covered.
¹³⁷**mazzard** head.

IAGO [*Aside to* RODERIGO]: Away, I say! Go out and cry a mutiny!

[*Exit* RODERIGO.]   140

Nay, good lieutenant. God's will, gentlemen!
Help, ho! Lieutenant. Sir. Montano.
Help, masters! Here's a goodly watch indeed!   [*A bell rung.*]
Who's that which rings the bell? Diablo, ho!
The town will rise. God's will, lieutenant,   145
You'll be ashamed forever.

Enter OTHELLO *and* ATTENDANTS.

OTHELLO: What is the matter here?
MONTANO: Zounds, I bleed still. I am hurt to the death.
He dies.   [*He and* CASSIO *fight again.*]
OTHELLO: Hold for your lives!
IAGO: Hold, ho! Lieutenant. Sir. Montano. Gentlemen!   150
Have you forgot all place of sense and duty?
Hold! The general speaks to you. Hold, for shame!
OTHELLO: Why, how now, ho? From whence ariseth this?
Are we turned Turks, and to ourselves do that
Which heaven hath forbid the Ottomites°?   155
For Christian shame put by this barbarous brawl!
He that stirs next to carve for his own rage
Holds his soul light°; he dies upon his motion.
Silence that dreadful bell! It frights the isle
From her propriety°. What is the matter, masters?   160
Honest Iago, that looks dead with grieving,
Speak. Who began this? On thy love, I charge thee.
IAGO: I do not know. Friends all, but now, even now,
In quarter° and in terms like bride and groom
Devesting them for bed; and then, but now—   165
As if some planet had unwitted men—
Swords out, and tilting one at other's breasts
In opposition bloody. I cannot speak
Any beginning to this peevish odds°,
And would in action glorious I had lost   170
Those legs that brought me to a part of it!
OTHELLO: How comes it, Michael, you are thus forgot?
CASSIO: I pray you pardon me; I cannot speak.

---

[155]**heaven . . . Ottomites** i.e., by sending the storm which dispersed the Turks.
[158]**Holds his soul light** values his soul lightly.
[160]**propriety** proper order.
[164]**In quarter** on duty.
[169]**odds** quarrel.

OTHELLO: Worthy Montano, you were wont to be civil;
 Thy gravity and stillness of your youth   175
 The world hath noted, and your name is great
 In mouths of wisest censure°. What's the matter
 That you unlace° your reputation thus
 And spend your rich opinion° for the name
 Of a night-brawler? Give me answer to it.   180
MONTANO: Worthy Othello, I am hurt to danger.
 Your officer, Iago, can inform you.
 While I spare speech, which something now offends° me,
 Of all that I do know; nor know I aught
 By me that's said or done amiss this night,   185
 Unless self-charity be sometimes a vice,
 And to defend ourselves it be a sin
 When violence assails us.
OTHELLO: Now, by heaven,
 My blood begins my safer guides to rule,
 And passion, having my best judgment collied°,   190
 Assays to lead the way. If I once stir
 Or do but lift this arm, the best of you
 Shall sink in my rebuke. Give me to know
 How this foul rout began, who set it on;
 And he that is approved in this offense,   195
 Though he had twinned with me, both at a birth,
 Shall lose me. What? In a town of war
 Yet wild, the people's hearts brimful of fear,
 To manage° private and domestic quarrel?
 In night, and on the court and guard of safety?   200
 'Tis monstrous. Iago, who began't?
MONTANO: If partially affined, or leagued in office°,
 Thou dost deliver more or less than truth,
 Thou art no soldier.
IAGO: Touch me not so near.
 I had rather have this tongue cut from my mouth   205
 Than it should do offense to Michael Cassio.
 Yet I persuade myself to speak the truth

---

 [177] **censure** judgment.
 [178] **unlace** undo (the term refers specifically to the dressing of a wild boar killed in the hunt).
 [179] **opinion** reputation.
 [183] **offends** harms, hurts.
 [190] **collied** darkened.
 [199] **manage** conduct.
 [202] **If . . . office** if you are partial because you are related ("affined") or the brother officer (of Cassio).

Shall nothing wrong him. This is it, general.
Montano and myself being in speech,
There comes a fellow crying out for help,   210
And Cassio following him with determined sword
To execute upon him. Sir, this gentleman
Steps in to Cassio and entreats his pause.
Myself the crying fellow did pursue,
Lest by his clamor—as it so fell out—   215
The town might fall in fright. He, swift of foot,
Outran my purpose; and I returned then rather
For that I heard the clink and fall of swords,
And Cassio high in oath; which till tonight
I ne'er might say before. When I came back—   220
For this was brief—I found them close together
At blow and thrust, even as again they were
When you yourself did part them.
More of this matter cannot I report;
But men are men; the best sometimes forget.   225
Though Cassio did some little wrong to him,
As men in rage strike those that wish them best,
Yet surely Cassio I believe received
From him that fled some strange indignity,
Which patience could not pass°.
OTHELLO: I know, Iago,   230
Thy honesty and love doth mince° this matter,
Making it light to Cassio. Cassio, I love thee;
But never more be officer of mine.

Enter DESDEMONA, *attended.*

Look if my gentle love be not raised up.
I'll make thee an example.
DESDEMONA: What is the matter, dear?   235
OTHELLO: All's well, sweeting; come away to bed.
[*To* MONTANO] Sir, for your hurts, myself will be your surgeon.
Lead him off.   [MONTANO *led off.*]
Iago, look with care about the town
And silence those whom this vile brawl distracted.   240
Come, Desdemona: 'tis the soldiers' life
To have their balmy slumbers waked with strife.

---

²²⁹**pass** allow to pass.
²³¹**mince** cut up (i.e., tell only part of).

Exit [with all but IAGO *and* CASSIO].

IAGO: What, are you hurt, lieutenant?

CASSIO: Ay, past all surgery.

IAGO: Marry, God forbid! 245

CASSIO: Reputation, reputation, reputation! O, I have lost my
reputation! I have lost the immortal part of myself, and what
remains is bestial. My reputation, Iago, my reputation.

IAGO: As I am an honest man, I had thought you had received some
bodily wound. There is more sense° in that than in reputation. 250
Reputation is an idle and most false imposition°, oft got without
merit and lost without deserving. You have lost no reputation at
all unless you repute yourself such a loser. What, man, there are
more ways to recover the general again. You are but now cast in
his mood°—a punishment more in policy° than in malice— 255
even so as one would beat his offenseless dog to affright an
imperious lion. Sue to him again, and he's yours.

CASSIO: I will rather sue to be despised than to deceive so good a
commander with so slight, so drunken, and so indiscreet an
officer. Drunk! And speak parrot°! And squabble! Swagger! 260
Swear! and discourse fustian° with one's own shadow! O thou
invisible spirit of wine, if thou hast no name to be known by, let
us call thee devil!

IAGO: What was he that you followed with your sword?
What had he done to you? 265

CASSIO: I know not.

IAGO: Is't possible?

CASSIO: I remember a mass of things, but nothing distinctly: a
quarrel, but nothing wherefore. O God, that men should put an
enemy in their mouths to steal away their brains! that we should 270
with joy, pleasance, revel, and applause transform ourselves into
beasts!

IAGO: Why, but you are now well enough. How came you thus
recovered?

CASSIO: It hath pleased the devil drunkenness to give place to the 275
devil wrath. One unperfectness shows me another, to make me
frankly despise myself.

IAGO: Come, you are too severe a moraler. As the time, the place,
and the condition of this country stands, I could heartily wish

---

²⁵⁰**sense** physical feeling.
²⁵¹**imposition** external thing.
²⁵⁴⁻⁵⁵**cast in his mood** dismissed because of his anger.
²⁵⁵**in policy** politically necessary.
²⁶⁰**speak parrot** gabble without sense.
²⁶¹**discourse fustian** speak nonsense ("fustian" was a coarse cotton cloth used for stuffing).

this had not befall'n, but since it is as it is, mend it for your own   280
good.

CASSIO: I will ask him for my place again: he shall tell me I am a
drunkard. Had I as many mouths as Hydra, such an answer
would stop them all. To be now a sensible man, by and by a
fool, and presently a beast! O strange! Every inordinate cup is   285
unblest, and the ingredient is a devil.

IAGO: Come, come, good wine is a good familiar creature if it be
well used. Exclaim no more against it. And, good lieutenant, I
think you think I love you.

CASSIO: I have well approved it, sir. I drunk?   290

IAGO: You or any man living may be drunk at a time, man. I tell
you what you shall do. Our general's wife is now the general. I
may say so in this respect, for all he hath devoted and given up
himself to the contemplation, mark, and devotement of her
parts° and graces. Confess yourself freely to her; importune her   295
help to put you in your place again. She is of so free, so kind, so
apt, so blessed a disposition she holds it a vice in her goodness
not to do more than she is requested. This broken joint between
you and her husband entreat her to splinter°; and my fortunes
against any lay° worth naming, this crack of your love shall   300
grow stronger than it was before.

CASSIO: You advise me well.

IAGO: I protest, in the sincerity of love and honest kindness.

CASSIO: I think it freely; and betimes in the morning I will beseech
the virtuous Desdemona to undertake for me. I am desperate of   305
my fortunes if they check° me.

IAGO: You are in the right. Good night, lieutenant; I must to the
watch.

CASSIO: Good night, honest Iago.   *Exit* CASSIO.

IAGO: And what's he then that says I play the villain,   310
When this advice is free° I give, and honest,
Probal to° thinking, and indeed the course
To win the Moor again? For 'tis most easy
Th' inclining° Desdemona to subdue
In any honest suit; she's framed as fruitful°   315
As the free elements°. And then for her

---

^{294–95}**devotement of her parts** devotion to her qualities.
²⁹⁹**splinter** splint.
³⁰⁰**lay** wager.
³⁰⁶**check** repulse.
³¹¹**free** generous and open.
³¹²**Probal to** provable by.
³¹⁴**inclining** inclined (to be helpful).
³¹⁵**framed as fruitful** made as generous.
³¹⁶**elements** i.e., basic nature.

To win the Moor—were't to renounce his baptism,
All seals and symbols of redeemèd sin—
His soul is so enfettered to her love
That she may make, unmake, do what she list,   320
Even as her appetite° shall play the god
With his weak function°. How am I then a villain
To counsel Cassio to this parallel course,
Directly to his good? Divinity of hell!
When devils will the blackest sins put on°,   325
They do suggest at first with heavenly shows°,
As I do now. For whiles this honest fool
Plies Desdemona to repair his fortune,
And she for him pleads strongly to the Moor,
I'll pour this pestilence into his ear: 330
That she repeals him° for her body's lust;
And by how much she strives to do him good,
She shall undo her credit with the Moor.
So will I turn her virtue into pitch,
And out of her own goodness make the net   335
That shall enmesh them all. How now, Roderigo?

Enter RODERIGO.

RODERIGO: I do follow here in the chase, not like a hound that
 hunts, but one that fills up the cry°. My money is almost spent; I
 have been tonight exceedingly well cudgeled; and I think the
 issue will be, I shall have so much experience for my pains; and 340
 so, with no money at all, and a little more wit, return again to
 Venice.
IAGO: How poor are they that have not patience!
 What wound did ever heal but by degrees?
 Thou know'st we work by wit, and not by witchcraft;   345
 And wit depends on dilatory time.
 Does't not go well? Cassio hath beaten thee,
 And thou by that small hurt hath cashiered Cassio.
 Though other things grow fair against the sun,
 Yet fruits that blossom first will first be ripe.   350
 Content thyself awhile. By the mass, 'tis morning!

---

[321]**appetite** liking.
[322]**function** thought.
[325]**put on** advance, further.
[326]**shows** appearances.
[331]**repeals him** asks for (Cassio's reinstatement).
[338]**fills up the cry** makes up one of the hunting pack, adding to the noise but not actually tracking.

Pleasure and action make the hours seem short.
Retire thee, go where thou art billeted.
Away, I say! Thou shalt know more hereafter.
Nay, get thee gone!   *Exit* RODERIGO.
           Two things are to be done: 355
My wife must move° for Cassio to her mistress;
I'll set her on;
Myself awhile° to draw the Moor apart
And bring him jump° when he may Cassio find
Soliciting his wife. Ay, that's the way!   360
Dull not device by coldness and delay.   *Exit.*

ACT III

Scene I [A street.]

Enter CASSIO *[and]* MUSICIANS.

CASSIO: Masters, play here. I will content your pains°.
  Something that's brief; and bid "Good morrow, general."

                        [They play.]

Enter CLOWN°.

CLOWN: Why, masters, have your instruments been in Naples° that
  they speak i' th' nose thus?
MUSICIAN: How, sir, how?   5
CLOWN: Are these, I pray you, wind instruments?
MUSICIAN: Ay, marry, are they, sir.
CLOWN: O, thereby hangs a tale.
MUSICIAN: Whereby hangs a tale, sir?
CLOWN: Marry, sir, by many a wind instrument that I know. But,   10
  masters, here's money for you; and the general so likes your
  music that he desires you, for love's sake, to make no more
  noise with it.
MUSICIAN: Well, sir, we will not.
CLOWN: If you have any music that may not be heard, to't again.   15
  But, as they say, to hear music the general does not greatly care.

---

³⁵⁶**move** petition.
³⁵⁸**awhile** at the same time.
³⁵⁹**jump** at the precise moment and place.
III.i. ¹**content your pains** reward your efforts.
s.d. Clown fool.
³**Naples** this may refer either to the Neopolitan nasal tone, or to syphilis—rife in Naples—
which breaks down the nose.

MUSICIAN: We have none such, sir.

CLOWN: Then put up your pipes in your bag, for I'll away. Go, vanish into air, away! *Exit* MUSICIANS.

CASSIO: Dost thou hear me, mine honest friend? 20

CLOWN: No. I hear not your honest friend. I hear you.

CASSIO: Prithee keep up thy quillets°. There's a poor piece of gold for thee. If the gentlewoman that attends the general's wife be stirring, tell her there's one Cassio entreats her a little favor of speech. Wilt thou do this? 25

CLOWN: She is stirring, sir. If she will stir hither, I shall seem to notify unto her°. *Exit* CLOWN.

Enter IAGO.

CASSIO: In happy time, Iago.

IAGO: You have not been abed then?

CASSIO: Why no, the day had broke before we parted.
I have made bold, Iago, to send in to your wife; 30
My suit to her is that she will to virtuous Desdemona
Procure me some access.

IAGO: I'll send her to you presently,
And I'll devise a mean to draw the Moor
Out of the way, that your converse and business
May be more free. 35

CASSIO: I humbly thank you for't. *Exit* [IAGO].
I never knew
A Florentine° more kind and honest.

Enter EMILIA.

EMILIA: Good morrow, good lieutenant. I am sorry
For your displeasure°; but all will sure be well.
The general and his wife are talking of it, 40
And she speaks for you stoutly. The Moor replies
That he you hurt is of great fame in Cyprus
And great affinity°, and that in wholesome wisdom
He might not but refuse you. But he protests he loves you,
And needs no other suitor but his likings 45
To bring you in again.

---

[22]**quillets** puns.
[26-27]**seem . . . her** (the Clown is mocking Cassio's overly elegant manner of speaking).
[37]**Florentine** i.e., Iago is as kind as if he were from Cassio's home town, Florence.
[39]**displeasure** discomforting.
[43]**affinity** family.

CASSIO: Yet I beseech you,
  If you think fit, or that it may be done,
  Give me advantage of some brief discourse
  With Desdemona alone.
EMILIA: Pray you come in.
  I will bestow you where you shall have time   50
  To speak your bosom° freely.
CASSIO: I am much bound to you.   [*Exeunt.*]

Scene II [*The citadel.*]

Enter OTHELLO, IAGO, *and* GENTLEMEN.

OTHELLO: These letters give, Iago, to the pilot
  And by him do my duties to the Senate.
  That done, I will be walking on the works;
  Repair° there to me.
IAGO: Well, my good lord, I'll do't.
OTHELLO: This fortification, gentlemen, shall we see't?   5
GENTLEMEN: We'll wait upon your lordship.   *Exeunt.*

Scene III [*The citadel.*]

Enter DESDEMONA, CASSIO, *and* EMILIA.

DESDEMONA: Be thou assured, good Cassio, I will do
  All my abilities in thy behalf.
EMILIA: Good madam, do. I warrant it grieves my husband
  As if the cause were his.
DESDEMONA: O, that's an honest fellow. Do not doubt, Cassio,   5
  But I will have my lord and you again
  As friendly as you were.
CASSIO: Bounteous madam,
  Whatever shall become of Michael Cassio,
  He's never anything but your true servant.
DESDEMONA: I know't; I thank you. You do love my lord.   10
  You have known him long, and be you well assured
  He shall in strangeness stand no farther off
  Than in a politic distance.°

---

⁵¹**bosom** inmost thoughts.
III.ii. ⁴**Repair** go.
III.iii. ¹²⁻¹³**He . . . distance** i.e., he shall act no more distant to you than is necessary for
political reasons.

CASSIO: Ay, but, lady,
  That policy may either last so long,
  Or feed upon such nice° and waterish diet,   15
  Or breed itself so out of circumstances°,
  That, I being absent, and my place supplied°,
  My general will forget my love and service.
DESDEMONA: Do not doubt° that; before Emilia here
  I give thee warrant of thy place. Assure thee,   20
  If I do vow a friendship, I'll perform it
  To the last article. My lord shall never rest;
  I'll watch him tame° and talk him out of patience;
  His bed shall seem a school, his board a shrift°;
  I'll intermingle everything he does   25
  With Cassio's suit. Therefore be merry, Cassio,
  For thy solicitor shall rather die
  Than give thy cause away.

Enter OTHELLO *and* IAGO [*at a distance*].

EMILIA: Madam, here comes my lord.
CASSIO: Madam, I'll take my leave.   30
DESDEMONA: Why, stay, and hear me speak.
CASSIO: Madam, not now. I am very ill at ease,
  Unfit for mine own purposes.
DESDEMONA: Well, do your discretion.   *Exit* CASSIO.
IAGO: Ha! I like not that.
OTHELLO: What dost thou say?   35
IAGO: Nothing, my lord; or if—I know not what.
OTHELLO: Was not that Cassio parted from my wife?
IAGO: Cassio, my lord? No, sure, I cannot think it
  That he would steal away so guilty-like,
  Seeing your coming.
OTHELLO: I do believe 'twas he.   40
DESDEMONA [*Coming to them*]: How now, my lord?
  I have been talking with a suitor here,
  A man that languishes in your displeasure.
OTHELLO: Who is't you mean?
DESDEMONA: Why, your lieutenant, Cassio. Good my lord,   45

---

  ¹⁵**nice** trivial.
  ¹⁶**Or . . . circumstances** i.e., or grow so on the basis of accidental happenings and political needs.
  ¹⁷**supplied** filled.
  ¹⁹**doubt** imagine.
  ²³**watch him tame** (animals were tamed by being kept awake).
  ²⁴**board a shrift** table (seem) a confessional.

If I have any grace or power to move you,
His present° reconciliation take.
For if he be not one that truly loves you,
That errs in ignorance, and not in cunning,
I have no judgment in an honest face.   50
I prithee call him back.

OTHELLO: Went he hence now?

DESDEMONA: I' sooth so humbled
That he hath left part of his grief with me
To suffer with him. Good love, call him back.

OTHELLO: Not now, sweet Desdemon; some other time.   55

DESDEMONA: But shall't be shortly?

OTHELLO: The sooner, sweet, for you.

DESDEMONA: Shall't be tonight at supper?

OTHELLO: No, not tonight.

DESDEMONA: Tomorrow dinner then?

OTHELLO: I shall not dine at home;
I meet the captains at the citadel.

DESDEMONA: Why then, tomorrow night, on Tuesday morn,   60
On Tuesday noon, or night, on Wednesday morn.
I prithee name the time, but let it not
Exceed three days. In faith, he's penitent;
And yet his trespass, in our common reason
(Save that, they say, the wars must make example   65
Out of her best), is not almost a fault
T' incur a private check.° When shall he come?
Tell me, Othello. I wonder in my soul
What you would ask me that I should deny
Or stand so mamm'ring° on. What? Michael Cassio,   70
That came awooing with you, and so many a time,
When I have spoke of you dispraisingly,
Hath ta'en your part—to have so much to do
To bring him in? By'r Lady, I could do much—

OTHELLO: Prithee no more. Let him come when he will!   75
I will deny thee nothing.

DESDEMONA: Why, this is not a boon;
'Tis as I should entreat you wear your gloves,
Or feed on nourishing dishes, or keep you warm,
Or sue to you to do a peculiar profit°
To your own person. Nay, when I have a suit   80

---

⁴⁷**present** immediate
^{66–67}**is . . . check** is almost not serious enough for a private rebuke (let alone a public disgrace).
⁷⁰**mamm'ring** hesitating.
⁷⁹**peculiar profit** particularly personal good.

Wherein I mean to touch your love indeed,
It shall be full of poise° and difficult weight,
And fearful to be granted.
OTHELLO: I will deny thee nothing!
Whereon I do beseech thee grant me this,
To leave me but a little to myself.   85
DESDEMONA: Shall I deny you? No. Farewell, my lord.
OTHELLO: Farewell, my Desdemona: I'll come to thee straight°.
DESDEMONA: Emilia, come. Be as your fancies teach you;
Whate'er you be, I am obedient.   *Exit [with* EMILIA].
OTHELLO: Excellent wretch! Perdition catch my soul   90
But I do love thee! And when I love thee not,
Chaos is come again.
IAGO: My noble lord—
OTHELLO: What dost thou say, Iago?
IAGO: Did Michael Cassio, when you wooed my lady,
Know of your love?   95
OTHELLO: He did, from first to last. Why dost thou ask?
IAGO: But for a satisfaction of my thought,
No further harm.
OTHELLO: Why of thy thought, Iago?
IAGO: I did not think he had been acquainted with her.
OTHELLO: O, yes, and went between us° very oft.   100
IAGO: Indeed?
OTHELLO: Indeed? Ay, indeed! Discern'st thou aught in that?
Is he not honest?
IAGO: Honest, my lord?
OTHELLO: Honest? Ay, honest.
IAGO: My lord, for aught I know.
OTHELLO: What dost thou think?
IAGO: Think, my lord?
OTHELLO: Think, my lord?   105
By heaven, thou echoest me,
As if there were some monster in thy thought
Too hideous to be shown. Thou dost mean something.
I heard thee say even now, thou lik'st not that,
When Cassio left my wife. What didst not like?   110
And when I told thee he was of my counsel°
Of my whole course of wooing, thou cried'st "Indeed?"
And didst contract and purse thy brow together,

---

⁸²**poise** weight.
⁸⁷**straight** at once.
¹⁰⁰**between us** i.e., as messenger.
¹¹¹**of my counsel** in my confidence.

As if thou then hadst shut up in thy brain
Some horrible conceit°. If thou dost love me,   115
Show me thy thought.
IAGO: My lord, you know I love you.
OTHELLO: I think thou dost;
And, for I know thou'rt full of love and honesty
And weigh'st thy words before thou giv'st them breath,
Therefore these stops° of thine fright me the more;   120
For such things in a false disloyal knave
Are tricks of custom°; but in a man that's just
They're close dilations°, working from the heart
That passion cannot rule.
IAGO: For Michael Cassio,
I dare be sworn, I think that he is honest.   125
OTHELLO: I think so too.
IAGO: Men should be what they seem;
Or those that be not, would they might seem none!
OTHELLO: Certain, men should be what they seem.
IAGO: Why then, I think Cassio's an honest man.
OTHELLO: Nay, yet there's more in this?   130
I prithee speak to me as to thy thinkings,
As thou dost ruminate, and give thy worst of thoughts
The worst of words.
IAGO: Good my lord, pardon me:
Though I am bound to every act of duty,
I am not bound to that all slaves are free to.   135
Utter my thoughts? Why, say they are vile and false,
As where's that palace whereinto foul things
Sometimes intrude not? Who has that breast so pure
But some uncleanly apprehensions
Keep leets and law days°, and in sessions sit   140
With meditations lawful?
OTHELLO: Thou dost conspire against thy friend, Iago,
If thou but think'st him wronged, and mak'st his ear
A stranger to thy thoughts.
IAGO: I do beseech you—
Though I perchance am vicious in my guess   145
(As I confess it is my nature's plague
To spy into abuses, and of my jealousy
Shape faults that are not), that your wisdom

---

[115]**conceit** thought.
[120]**stops** interruptions.
[122]**of custom** customary.
[123]**close dilations** expressions of hidden thoughts.
[140]**leets and law days** meetings of local courts.

From one that so imperfectly conceits
Would take no notice, nor build yourself a trouble   150
Out of his scattering and unsure observance.
It were not for your quiet nor your good,
Nor for my manhood, honesty, and wisdom,
To let you know my thoughts.
OTHELLO: What dost thou mean?
IAGO: Good name in man and woman, dear my lord,   155
  Is the immediate jewel of their souls.
  Who steals my purse steals trash; 'tis something, nothing;
  'Twas mine, 'tis his, and has been slave to thousands;
  But he that filches from me my good name
  Robs me of that which not enriches him   160
  And makes me poor indeed.
OTHELLO: By heaven, I'll know thy thoughts!
IAGO: You cannot, if my heart were in your hand;
  Nor shall not whilst 'tis in my custody.
OTHELLO: Ha!
IAGO: O, beware, my lord, of jealousy!   165
  It is the green-eyed monster, which doth mock
  The meat it feeds on. That cuckold lives in bliss
  Who, certain of his fate, loves not his wronger;
  But O, what damnèd minutes tells° he o'er
  Who dotes, yet doubts—suspects, yet fondly° loves!   170
OTHELLO: O misery.
IAGO: Poor and content is rich, and rich enough;
  But riches fineless° is as poor as winter
  To him that ever fears he shall be poor.
  Good God the souls of all my tribe defend   175
  From jealousy!
OTHELLO: Why? Why is this?
  Think'st thou I'd make a life of jealousy,
  To follow still° the changes of the moon
  With fresh suspicions? No! To be once in doubt
  Is to be resolved. Exchange me for a goat   180
  When I shall turn the business of my soul
  To such exsufflicate and blown° surmises,
  Matching thy inference. 'Tis not to make me jealous
  To say my wife is fair, feeds well, loves company,
  Is free of speech, sings, plays, and dances;   185
  Where virtue is, these are more virtuous.

___

[169]**tells** counts.
[170]**fondly** foolishly.
[173]**fineless** infinite.
[178]**To follow still** to change always (as the phases of the moon).
[182]**exsufflicate and blown** inflated and flyblown.

Nor from mine own weak merits will I draw
The smallest fear or doubt of her revolt,
For she had eyes, and chose me. No, Iago;
I'll see before I doubt; when I doubt, prove; 190
And on the proof there is no more but this:
Away at once with love or jealousy!
IAGO: I am glad of this; for now I shall have reason
To show the love and duty that I bear you
With franker spirit. Therefore, as I am bound, 195
Receive it from me. I speak not yet of proof.
Look to your wife; observe her well with Cassio;
Wear your eyes thus: not jealous nor secure.
I would not have your free and noble nature
Out of self-bounty° be abused. Look to't. 200
I know our country disposition well:
In Venice they do let heaven see the pranks
They dare not show their husbands; their best conscience
Is not to leave't undone, but kept unknown.°
OTHELLO: Dost thou say so? 205
IAGO: She did deceive her father, marrying you;
And when she seemed to shake and fear your looks,
She loved them most.
OTHELLO: And so she did.
IAGO: Why, go to then!
She that so young could give out such a seeming
To seel° her father's eyes up close as oak°— 210
He thought 'twas witchcraft. But I am much to blame.
I humbly do beseech you of your pardon
For too much loving you.
OTHELLO: I am bound to thee forever.
IAGO: I see this hath a little dashed your spirits.
OTHELLO: Not a jot, not a jot.
IAGO: Trust me, I fear it has. 215
I hope you will consider what is spoke
Comes from my love. But I do see y' are moved.
I am to pray you not to strain° my speech
To grosser issues nor to larger reach°
Than to suspicion. 220

---

²⁰⁰**self-bounty** innate kindness (which attributes his own motives to others).
²⁰³⁻⁴**their . . . unknown** i.e., their morality does not forbid adultery, but it does forbid
being found out.
²¹⁰**seel** hoodwink.
²¹⁰**oak** (a close-grained wood).
²¹⁸**strain** enlarge the meaning of.
²¹⁹**reach** meaning.

OTHELLO: I will not.

IAGO: Should you do so, my lord,
 My speech should fall into such vile success
 Which my thoughts aimed not. Cassio's my worthy friend—
 My lord, I see y' are moved.

OTHELLO: No, not much moved.
 I do not think but Desdemona's honest.   225

IAGO: Long live she so. And long live you to think so.

OTHELLO: And yet, how nature erring from itself—

IAGO: Ay, there's the point, as (to be bold with you)
 Not to affect many proposèd matches
 Of her own clime, complexion, and degree°,   230
 Whereto we see in all things nature tends°—
 Foh! one may smell in such a will most rank,
 Foul disproportions, thoughts unnatural.
 But, pardon me, I do not in position°
 Distinctly° speak of her; though I may fear   235
 Her will, recoiling to her better judgment,
 May fall to match° you with her country forms°,
 And happily° repent.

OTHELLO: Farewell, farewell!
 If more thou dost perceive, let me know more.
 Set on thy wife to observe. Leave me, Iago.   240

IAGO: My lord, I take my leave.   *[Going.]*

OTHELLO: Why did I marry? This honest creature doubtless
 Sees and knows more, much more, than he unfolds.

IAGO [*Returns*]: My lord, I would I might entreat your honor
 To scan this thing no farther. Leave it to time.   245
 Although 'tis fit that Cassio have his place,
 For sure he fills it up with great ability,
 Yet, if you please to hold him off awhile,
 You shall by that perceive him and his means,
 Note if your lady strain his entertainment°   250
 With any strong or vehement importunity;
 Much will be seen in that. In the meantime
 Let me be thought too busy in my fears
 (As worthy cause I have to fear I am)
 And hold her free, I do beseech your honor.   255

---

²³⁰**degree** social station.
²³¹**in . . . tends** i.e., all things in nature seek out their own kind.
²³⁴**position** general argument.
²³⁵**Distinctly** specifically.
²³⁷**fall to match** happen to compare.
²³⁷**country forms** i.e., the familiar appearances of her countrymen.
²³⁸**happily** by chance.
²⁵⁰**strains his entertainment** urge strongly that he be reinstated.

OTHELLO: Fear not my government°.
IAGO: I once more take my leave.   *Exit.*
OTHELLO: This fellow's of exceeding honesty,
   And knows all qualities°, with a learnèd spirit
   Of human dealings. If I do prove her haggard°,
   Though that her jesses° were my dear heartstrings,   260
   I'd whistle her off and let her down the wind°
   To prey at fortune. Haply for° I am black
   And have not those soft parts° of conversation
   That chamberers° have, or for I am declined
   Into the vale of years—yet that's not much—   265
   She's gone. I am abused, and my relief
   Must be to loathe her. O curse of marriage,
   That we can call these delicate creatures ours,
   And not their appetites! I had rather be a toad
   And live upon the vapor of a dungeon   270
   Than keep a corner in the thing I love
   For others' uses. Yet 'tis the plague to great ones;
   Prerogatived are they less than the base.
   'Tis destiny unshunnable, like death.
   Even then this forkèd° plague is fated to us   275
   When we do quicken°. Look where she comes.

Enter DESDEMONA *and* EMILIA.

   If she be false, heaven mocked itself!
   I'll not believe't.
DESDEMONA: How now, my dear Othello?
   Your dinner, and the generous islanders
   By you invited, do attend° your presence.   280
OTHELLO: I am to blame.
DESDEMONA: Why do you speak so faintly?
   Are you not well?
OTHELLO: I have a pain upon my forehead, here°.
DESDEMONA: Why, that's with watching; 'twill away again.

---

[256]**government** self-control.
[258]**qualities** natures, types of people.
[259]**haggard** a partly trained hawk which has gone wild again.
[260]**jesses** straps which held the hawk's legs to the trainer's wrist.
[261]**I'd . . . wind** I would release her (like an untamable hawk) and let her fly free.
[262]**Haply for** it may be because.
[263]**soft parts** gentle qualities and manners.
[264]**chamberers** courtiers—or, perhaps, accomplished seducers.
[275]**forkèd** horned (the sign of the cuckold was horns).
[276]**do quicken** are born.
[280]**attend** wait.
[283]**here** (he points to his imaginary horns).

Let me but bind it hard, within this hour   285
It will be well.
OTHELLO: Your napkin° is too little;

[*He pushes the handkerchief away, and it falls.*]

Let it° alone. Come, I'll go in with you.
DESDEMONA: I am very sorry that you are not well.
                                              Exit [*with* OTHELLO.].
EMILIA: I am glad I have found this napkin;
This was her first remembrance from the Moor.   290
My wayward husband hath a hundred times
Wooed me to steal it; but she so loves the token
(For he conjured her she should ever keep it)
That she reserves it evermore about her
To kiss and talk to. I'll have the work ta'en out°   295
And give't Iago. What he will do with it,
Heaven knows, not I; I nothing° but to please his fantasy°.

Enter IAGO.

IAGO: How now? What do you here alone?
EMILIA: Do not you chide; I have a thing for you.
IAGO: You have a thing for me? It is a common thing—   300
EMILIA: Ha?
IAGO: To have a foolish wife.
EMILIA: O, is that all? What will you give me now
For that same handkerchief?
IAGO: What handkerchief?
EMILIA: What handkerchief!   305
Why, that the Moor first gave to Desdemona,
That which so often you did bid me steal.
IAGO: Hast stol'n it from her?
EMILIA: No, but she let it drop by negligence,
And to th' advantage°, I, being here, took't up.   310
Look, here 't is.
IAGO: A good wench. Give it me.

---

²⁸⁶**napkin** elaborately worked handkerchief.
²⁸⁷**it** (it makes a considerable difference in the interpretation of later events whether this "it" refers to Othello's forehead or to the handkerchief; nothing in the text makes the reference clear).
²⁹⁵**work ta'en out** needlework copied.
²⁹⁷**I nothing** I wish nothing.
²⁹⁷**fantasy** fancy, whim.
³¹⁰**to th' advantage** being lucky.

EMILIA: What will you do with't, that you have been so earnest
    To have me filch it?

IAGO: Why, what is that to you?   [*Takes it.*]

EMILIA: If it be not for some purpose of import°,
    Give't me again. Poor lady, she'll run mad   315
    When she shall lack° it.

IAGO: Be not acknown on't°.
    I have use for it. Go, leave me.   *Exit* EMILIA.
    I will in Cassio's lodging lose this napkin
    And let him find it. Trifles light as air
    Are to the jealous confirmations strong
    As proofs of Holy Writ. This may do something.   320
    The Moor already changes with my poison:
    Dangerous conceits are in their natures poisons,
    Which at the first are scarce found to distaste°,
    But, with a little°, act upon the blood,   325
    Burn like the mines of sulfur. I did say so.

Enter OTHELLO.

    Look where he comes! Not poppy nor mandragora°,
    Nor all the drowsy syrups of the world,
    Shall ever medicine thee to that sweet sleep
    Which thou owedst° yesterday.

OTHELLO: Ha! ha! False to me?   330

IAGO: Why, how now, general? No more of that.

OTHELLO: Avaunt! be gone! Thou hast set me on the rack.
    I swear 'tis better to be much abused
    Than but to know't a little.

IAGO: How now, my lord?

OTHELLO: What sense had I of her stol'n hours of lust?   335
    I saw't not, thought it not, it harmed not me;
    I slept the next night well, fed well, was free and merry;
    I found not Cassio's kisses on her lips.
    He that is robbed, not wanting° what is stol'n,
    Let him not know't, and he's not robbed at all.   340

IAGO: I am sorry to hear this.

---

[314]**import** importance.
[316]**lack** miss.
[316]**Be not acknown on't** forget you ever saw it.
[324]**are scarce found to distaste** scarcely can be tasted.
[325]**with a little** in a short time.
[327]**poppy nor mandragora** soporifics.
[330]**owedst** possessed.
[339]**wanting** missing.

OTHELLO: I had been happy if the general camp,
   Pioners° and all, had tasted her sweet body,
   So I had nothing known. O now, forever
   Farewell the tranquil mind! Farewell content!   345
   Farewell the plumèd troops, and the big wars
   That makes ambition virtue! O, farewell!
   Farewell the neighing steed and the shrill trump,
   The spirit-stirring drum, th' ear-piercing fife,
   The royal banner, and all quality,   350
   Pride, pomp, and circumstance° of glorious war!
   And O you mortal engines° whose rude throats
   Th' immortal Jove's dread clamors° counterfeit,
   Farewell! Othello's occupation's gone!
IAGO: Is't possible, my lord?   355
OTHELLO: Villain, be sure thou prove my love a whore!
   Be sure of it; give me the ocular proof;
   Or, by the worth of mine eternal soul,
   Thou hadst been better have been born a dog
   Than answer my waked wrath!
IAGO: Is't come to this?   360
OTHELLO: Make me to see't; or at the least so prove it
   That the probation° bear no hinge nor loop
   To hang a doubt on—or woe upon thy life!
IAGO: My noble lord—
OTHELLO: If thou dost slander her and torture me,   365
   Never pray more; abandon all remorse;
   On horror's head horrors accumulate;
   Do deeds to make heaven weep, all earth amazed;
   For nothing canst thou to damnation add
   Greater than that.
IAGO: O grace! O heaven forgive me!   370
   Are you a man? Have you a soul or sense?
   God b' wi' you! Take mine office. O wretched fool,
   That lov'st to make thine honesty a vice!
   O monstrous world! Take note, take note, O world,
   To be direct and honest is not safe.   375
   I thank you for this profit, and from hence
   I'll love no friend, sith° love breeds such offense.
OTHELLO: Nay, stay. Thou shouldst be honest.

---

[343]**Pioners** (the basest manual laborers in the army, who dug trenches and mines.)
[351] **circumstance** pageantry.
[352]**mortal engines** lethal weapons, i.e., cannon.
[353]**clamors** i.e., thunder.
[362]**probation** proof.
[377]**sith** since.

IAGO: I should be wise; for honesty's a fool
    And loses that it works for.
OTHELLO: By the world,   380
    I think my wife be honest, and think she is not;
    I think that thou art just, and think thou art not.
    I'll have some proof. My name, that was as fresh
    As Dian's° visage, is now begrimed and black
    As mine own face. If there be cords, or knives,   385
    Poison, or fire, or suffocating streams,
    I'll not endure it. Would I were satisfied!
IAGO: I see you are eaten up with passion.
    I do repent me that I put it to you.
    You would be satisfied?
OTHELLO: Would? Nay, and I will.   390
IAGO: And may; but how? How satisfied, my lord?
    Would you, the supervisor°, grossly gape on?
    Behold her topped?
OTHELLO: Death and damnation! O!
IAGO: It were a tedious° difficulty, I think,
    To bring them to that prospect°. Damn them then,   395
    If ever mortal eyes do see them bolster°
    More than their own! What then? How then?
    What shall I say? Where's satisfaction?
    It is impossible you should see this,
    Were they as prime° as goats, as hot as monkeys,   400
    As salt as wolves in pride°, and fools as gross
    As ignorance made drunk. But yet, I say,
    If imputation and strong circumstances
    Which lead directly to the door of truth
    Will give you satisfaction, you might have't.   405
OTHELLO: Give me a living reason she's disloyal.
IAGO: I do not like the office°.
    But sith I am entered in this cause so far,
    Pricked° to't by foolish honesty and love,
    I will go on. I lay with Cassio lately,   410
    And being troubled with a raging tooth,

---

[384]**Dian's** Diana's (goddess of the moon and of chastity).
[392]**supervisor** onlooker.
[394]**tedious** hard to arrange.
[395]**prospect** sight (where they can be seen).
[396]**bolster** go to bed.
[400−01]**prime, salt** lustful.
[401]**pride** heat.
[407]**office** duty.
[409]**Pricked** spurred.

I could not sleep.
There are a kind of men so loose of soul
That in their sleeps will mutter their affairs.
One of this kind is Cassio.   415
In sleep I heard him say, "Sweet Desdemona,
Let us be wary, let us hide our loves!"
And then, sir, would he gripe° and wring my hand,
Cry "O sweet creature!" Then kiss me hard,
As if he plucked up kisses by the roots   420
That grew upon my lips; laid his leg o'er my thigh,
And sigh, and kiss, and then cry, "Cursèd fate
That gave thee to the Moor!"
OTHELLO: O monstrous! monstrous!
IAGO: Nay, this was but his dream.
OTHELLO: But this denoted a foregone conclusion°,   425
   'Tis a shrewd doubt°, though it be but a dream.
IAGO: And this may help to thicken other proofs
   That do demonstrate° thinly.
OTHELLO: I'll tear her all to pieces!
IAGO: Nay, yet be wise. Yet we see nothing done;
   She may be honest yet. Tell me but this: 430
   Have you not sometimes seen a handkerchief
   Spotted with strawberries in your wife's hand?
OTHELLO: I gave her such a one; 'twas my first gift.
IAGO: I know not that; but such a handkerchief—
   I am sure it was your wife's—did I today   435
   See Cassio wipe his beard with.
OTHELLO: If it be that—
IAGO: If it be that or any that was hers,
   It speaks against her with the other proofs.
OTHELLO: O, that the slave had forty thousand lives!
   One is too poor, too weak for my revenge.   440
   Now do I see 'tis true. Look here, Iago:
   All my fond love thus do I blow to heaven.
   'Tis gone.
   Arise, black vengeance, from the hollow hell!
   Yield up, O love, thy crown and hearted° throne   445

---

[418]**gripe** seize.
[425]**foregone conclusion** consummated fact.
[426]**shrewd doubt** penetrating guess.
[428]**demonstrate** show, appear.
[445]**hearted** seated in the heart.

To tyrannous hate! Swell, bosom, with thy fraught°,
For 'tis of aspics'° tongues.

IAGO: Yet be content°.

OTHELLO: O, blood, blood, blood!

IAGO: Patience, I say. Your mind may change.

OTHELLO: Never, Iago. Like to the Pontic Sea°,   450
Whose icy current and compulsive course
Nev'r keeps retiring ebb, but keeps due on
To the Propontic and the Hellespont,
Even so my bloody thoughts, with violent pace,
Shall nev'r look back, nev'r ebb to humble love,   455
Till that a capable and wide° revenge
Swallow them up. [*He kneels.*] Now, by yond marble heaven,
In the due reverence of a sacred vow
I here engage my words.

IAGO: Do not rise yet.   [IAGO *kneels.*]
Witness, you ever-burning lights above,   460
You elements that clip° us round about,
Witness that here Iago doth give up
The execution° of his wit, hands, heart
To wronged Othello's service! Let him command,
And to obey shall be in me remorse°,   465
What bloody business ever°.   [*They rise.*]

OTHELLO: I greet thy love,
Not with vain thanks but with acceptance bounteous°,
And will upon the instant put thee to't°
Within these three days let me hear thee say
That Cassio's not alive.   470

IAGO: My friend is dead. 'Tis done at your request.
But let her live.

OTHELLO: Damn her, lewd minx! O, damn her! Damn her!
Come, go with me apart. I will withdraw
To furnish me with some swift means of death

446**fraught** burden.
447**aspics'** asps'.
447**content** patient, quiet.
450**Pontic Sea** the Black Sea (famous for the strong and constant current with which it flows through the Bosporus into the Mediterranean, where the water level is lower).
456**capable and wide** sufficient and far-reaching.
461**clip** enfold.
463**execution** workings, action.
465**remorse** pity.
466**ever** soever.
467**bounteous** absolute.
468**to't** i.e., to the work you have said you are prepared to do.

For the fair devil. Now art thou my lieutenant.   475
IAGO: I am your own forever.   *Exeunt.*

Scene IV [A street.]

Enter DESDEMONA, EMILIA, *and* CLOWN.

DESDEMONA: Do you know, sirrah, where Lieutenant Cassio lies°?
CLOWN: I dare not say he lies anywhere.
DESDEMONA: Why, man?
CLOWN: He's a soldier, and for me to say a soldier lies, 'tis stabbing.
DESDEMONA: Go to. Where lodges he?   5
CLOWN: To tell you where he lodges is to tell you where I lie.
DESDEMONA: Can anything be made of this?
CLOWN: I know not where he lodges, and for me to devise a lodging,
    and say he lies here or he lies there, were to lie in mine own
    throat°.   10
DESDEMONA: Can you enquire him out, and be edified° by report?
CLOWN: I will catechize the world for him; that is, make questions,
    and by them answer.
DESDEMONA: Seek him, bid him one hither. Tell him I have moved°
    my lord on his behalf and hope all will be well.   15
CLOWN: To do this is within the compass° of man's wit, and
    therefore I will attempt the doing it.   *Exit* CLOWN.
DESDEMONA: Where should° I lose the handkerchief, Emilia?
EMILIA: I know not, madam.
DESDEMONA: Believe me, I had rather have lost my purse   20
    Full of crusadoes°. And but my noble Moor
    Is true of mind, and made of no such baseness
    As jealous creatures are, it were enough
    To put him to ill thinking.
EMILIA: Is he not jealous?
DESDEMONA: Who? He? I think the sun where he was born   25
    Drew all such humors° from him.
EMILIA: Look where he comes.

III.iv. ¹**lies** lodges.
⁹⁻¹⁰**lie in mine own throat** (to lie in the throat is to lie absolutely and completely).
¹¹**edified** enlightened (Desdemona mocks the Clown's overly elaborate diction).
¹⁴**moved** pleaded with.
¹⁶**compass** reach.
¹⁸**should** might.
²¹**crusadoes** Portuguese gold coins.
²⁶**humors** characteristics.

Enter OTHELLO.

DESDEMONA: I will not leave him now till Cassio
  Be called to him. How is't with you, my lord?
OTHELLO: Well, my good lady. [*Aside*] O, hardness to dissemble°!—
  How do you, Desdemona?
DESDEMONA: Well, my good lord.   30
OTHELLO: Give me your hand. This hand is moist°, my lady.
DESDEMONA: It hath felt no age nor known no sorrow.
OTHELLO: This argues° fruitfulness and liberal° heart.
  Hot, hot, and moist. This hand of yours requires
  A sequester° from liberty; fasting and prayer;   35
  Much castigation; exercise devout;
  For here's a young and sweating devil here
  That commonly rebels. 'Tis a good hand,
  A frank one.
DESDEMONA: You may, indeed, say so;
  For 'twas that hand that gave away my heart.   40
OTHELLO: A liberal hand! The hearts of old gave hands,
  But our new heraldry° is hands, not hearts.
DESDEMONA: I cannot speak of this. Come now, your promise!
OTHELLO: What promise, chuck?
DESDEMONA: I have sent to bid Cassio come speak with you.   45
OTHELLO: I have a salt and sorry rheum° offends me.
  Lend me thy handkerchief.
DESDEMONA: Here, my lord.
OTHELLO: That which I gave you.
DESDEMONA: I have it not about me.
OTHELLO: Not?
DESDEMONA: No, indeed, my lord.
OTHELLO: That's a fault.   50
  That handkerchief
  Did an Egyptian to my mother give.
  She was a charmer°, and could almost read

---

²⁹**hardness to dissemble** (Othello may refer here either to the difficulty he has in maintaining his appearance of composure, or to what he believes to be Desdemona's hardened hypocrisy).
³¹**moist** (a moist, hot hand was taken as a sign of a lustful nature).
³³**argues** suggests.
³³**liberal** free, open (but also with a suggestion of "licentious"; from here on in this scene Othello's words bear a double meaning, seeming to be normal but accusing Desdemona of being unfaithful).
³⁵**sequester** separation.
⁴²**heraldry** heraldic symbolism.
⁴⁶**a salt and sorry rheum** a heavy, running head cold.
⁵³**charmer** magician.

The thoughts of people. She told her, while she kept it
'Twould make her amiable° and subdue my father   55
Entirely to her love; but if she lost it
Or made a gift of it, my father's eye
Should hold her loathèd, and his spirits should hunt
After new fancies. She, dying, gave it me,
And bid me, when my fate would have me wived,   60
To give it her. I did so; and take heed on't;
Make it a darling like your precious eye.
To lose't or give't away were such perdition
As nothing else could match.
DESDEMONA: Is't possible?
OTHELLO: 'Tis true. There's magic in the web° of it.   65
   A sibyl that had numbered in the world
   The sun to course two hundred compasses,
   In her prophetic fury° sewed the work;
   The worms were hallowed that did breed the silk,
   And it was dyed in mummy° which the skillful   70
   Conserved of maidens' hearts.
DESDEMONA: Indeed? Is't true?
OTHELLO: Most veritable. Therefore look to't well.
DESDEMONA: Then would to God that I had never seen't!
OTHELLO: Ha! Wherefore?
DESDEMONA: Why do you speak so startingly and rash?   75
OTHELLO: Is't lost? Is't gone? Speak, is it out o' th' way?
DESDEMONA: Heaven bless us!
OTHELLO: Say you?
DESDEMONA: It is not lost. But what an if it were?
OTHELLO: How?   80
DESDEMONA: I say it is not lost.
OTHELLO: Fetch't, let me see't!
DESDEMONA: Why, so I can; but I will not now.
   This is a trick to put me from my suit:
   Pray you let Cassio be received again.   85
OTHELLO: Fetch me the handkerchief! My mind misgives.
DESDEMONA: Come, come!
   You'll never meet a more sufficient° man—
OTHELLO: The handkerchief!
DESDEMONA: A man that all his time

---

⁵⁵**amiable** desirable.
⁶⁵**web** weaving.
⁶⁸**prophetic fury** seized by the spirit and able to prophesy.
⁷⁰**mummy** liquid drained from embalmed bodies.
⁸⁸**sufficient** complete, with all proper qualities.

Hath founded his good fortunes on your love, 90
Shared dangers with you—
OTHELLO: The handkerchief!
DESDEMONA: I'faith, you are to blame.
OTHELLO: Away! *Exit* OTHELLO.
EMILIA: Is not this man jealous? 95
DESDEMONA: I nev'r saw this before.
Sure there's some wonder in this handkerchief;
I am most unhappy in the loss of it.
EMILIA: 'Tis not a year or two shows us a man.
They are all but stomachs, and we all but food; 100
They eat us hungerly, and when they are full,
They belch us.

Enter IAGO *and* CASSIO.

Look you, Cassio and my husband.
IAGO: There is no other way; 'tis she must do't.
And lo the happiness! Go and importune her.
DESDEMONA: How now, good Cassio? What's the news with you? 105
CASSIO: Madam, my former suit. I do beseech you
That by your virtuous means I may again
Exist, and be a member of his love
Whom I with all the office° of my heart
Entirely honor. I would not be delayed. 110
If my offense be of such mortal kind
That nor my service past, nor present sorrows,
Nor purposed merit in futurity,
Can ransom me into his love again,
But to know so must be my benefit°. 115
So shall I clothe me in a forced content,
And shut myself up in some other course
To fortune's alms.
DESDEMONA: Alas, thrice-gentle Cassio,
My advocation° is not now in tune.
My lord is not my lord; nor should I know him 120
Were he in favor° as in humor altered.
So help me every spirit sanctified
As I have spoken for you all my best

---

[109]**office** duty.
[115]**benefit** good.
[119]**advocation** advocacy.
[121]**favor** countenance.

And stood within the blank° of his displeasure
For my free speech. You must awhile be patient.   125
What I can do I will; and more I will
Than for myself I dare. Let this suffice you.

IAGO: Is my lord angry?

EMILIA: He went hence but now,
And certainly in strange unquietness.

IAGO: Can he be angry? I have seen the cannon   130
When it hath blown his ranks into the air
And, like the devil, from his very arm
Puffed his own brother. And is he angry?
Something of moment° then. I will go meet him.
There's matter in't indeed if he be angry.   135

DESDEMONA: I prithee do so.   *Exit* [IAGO.]
                        Something sure of state°,
Either from Venice or some unhatched practice°
Made demonstrable here in Cyprus to him,
Hath puddled° his clear spirit; and in such cases
Men's natures wrangle with inferior things,   140
Though great ones are their object. 'Tis even so.
For let our finger ache, and it endues°
Our other, healthful members even to a sense
Of pain. Nay, we must think men are not gods,
Nor of them look for such observancy   145
As fits the bridal. Beshrew me much, Emilia,
I was, unhandsome warrior as I am,
Arraigning his unkindness with my soul;
But now I find I had suborned the witness,
And he's indicted falsely.

EMILIA: Pray heaven it be   150
State matters, as you think, and no conception
Nor no jealous toy° concerning you.

DESDEMONA: Alas the day! I never gave him cause.

EMILIA: But jealous souls will not be answered so;
They are not ever jealous for the cause,   155
But jealous for they're jealous. It is a monster
Begot upon itself, born on itself.

---

¹²⁴**blank** bull's-eye of a target.
¹³⁴**moment** importance.
¹³⁶**of state** state affairs.
¹³⁷**unhatched practice** undisclosed plot.
¹³⁹**puddled** muddied.
¹⁴²**endues** leads.
¹⁵²**toy** trifle.

DESDEMONA: Heaven keep the monster from Othello's mind!
EMILIA: Lady, amen.
DESDEMONA: I will go seek him. Cassio, walk here about.   160
    If I do find him fit°, I'll move your suit
    And seek to effect it to my uttermost.
CASSIO: I humbly thank your ladyship.   *Exit* [DESDEMONA *with* EMILIA].

Enter BIANCA.

BIANCA: Save you, friend Cassio!
CASSIO: What make you from home?
    How is't with you, my most fair Bianca?   165
    I' faith, sweet love, I was coming to your house.
BIANCA: And I was going to your lodging, Cassio.
    What, keep a week away? Seven days and nights?
    Eightscore eight hours? And lovers' absent hours
    More tedious than the dial eightscore times?   170
    O weary reck'ning°.
CASSIO: Pardon me, Bianca.
    I have this while with leaden thoughts been pressed,
    But I shall in a more continuate° time
    Strike off this score° of absence. Sweet Bianca,

[Gives her DESDEMONA's *handkerchief.]*

    Take me this work out.
BIANCA: O Cassio, whence came this?   175
    This is some token from a newer friend.
    To the felt absence now I feel a cause.
    Is't come to this? Well, well.
CASSIO: Go to, woman!
    Throw your vile guesses in the devil's teeth,
    From whence you have them. You are jealous now   180
    That this is from some mistress, some remembrance.
    No, by my faith, Bianca.
BIANCA: Why, whose is it?
CASSIO: I know not neither; I found it in my chamber.
    I like the work well; ere it be demanded°,

---

¹⁶¹**fit** receptive.
¹⁷¹**reck'ning** addition.
¹⁷³**continuate** uninterrupted.
¹⁷⁴**Strike off this score** i.e., pay this bill (the score being the account of drinks kept in a tavern).
¹⁸⁴**demanded** asked for (by the person who lost it).

As like enough it will, I would have it copied.   185
Take it and do't, and leave me for this time.
BIANCA: Leave you? Wherefore?
CASSIO: I do attend here on the general
  And think it no addition, nor my wish,
  To have him see me womaned.
BIANCA: Why, I pray you?   190
CASSIO: Not that I love you not.
BIANCA: But that you do not love me!
  I pray you bring° me on the way a little,
  And say if I shall see you soon at night.
CASSIO: 'Tis but a little way that I can bring you,
  For I attend here; but I'll see you soon.   195
BIANCA: 'Tis very good. I must be circumstanced°.   *Exeunt omnes.*

ACT IV

Scene I [A street.]

Enter OTHELLO *and* IAGO.

IAGO: Will you think so?
OTHELLO: Think so, Iago?
IAGO: What,
  To kiss in private?
OTHELLO: An unauthorized° kiss?
IAGO: Or to be naked with her friend in bed
  An hour or more, not meaning any harm?
OTHELLO: Naked in bed, Iago, and not mean harm?   5
  It is hypocrisy against the devil.
  They that mean virtuously, and yet do so,
  The devil their virtue tempts, and they tempt heaven.
IAGO: If they do nothing, 'tis a venial slip.
  But if I give my wife a handkerchief—   10
OTHELLO: What then?
IAGO: Why, then 'tis hers, my lord; and being hers,
  She may, I think, bestow't on any man.
OTHELLO: She is protectress of her honor too.
  May she give that?   15

---

¹⁹²**bring** accompany.
¹⁹⁶**be circumstanced** accept things as they are.
IV.i. ²**unauthorized** illicit.

IAGO: Her honor is an essence that's not seen;
   They have it very oft that have it not.
   But for the handkerchief—
OTHELLO: By heaven, I would most gladly have forgot it!
   Thou said'st—O, it comes o'er my memory   20
   As doth the raven° o'er the infected house,
   Boding to all—he had my handkerchief.
IAGO: Ay, what of that?
OTHELLO: That's not so good now.
IAGO: What if I had said I had seen him do you wrong?
   Or heard him say—as knaves be such abroad°   25
   Who having, by their own importunate suit,
   Or voluntary dotage° of some mistress,
   Convincèd or supplied° them, cannot choose
   But they must blab—
OTHELLO: Hath he said anything?
IAGO: He hath, my lord; but be you well assured,   30
   No more than he'll unswear.
OTHELLO: What hath he said?
IAGO: Why, that he did—I know not what he did.
OTHELLO: What? what?
IAGO: Lie—
OTHELLO: With her?
IAGO: With her, on her; what you will.   35
OTHELLO: Lie with her? Lie on her?—We say lie on her when they
   belie her.—Lie with her! Zounds, that's fulsome°.—
   Handkerchief—confessions—handkerchief!—To confess, and be
   hanged for his labor—first to be hanged, and then to confess! I
   tremble at it. Nature would not invest herself in such shadowing   40
   passion without some instruction°. It is not words that shakes
   me thus.—Pish! Noses, ears, and lips? Is't possible—Confess?—
   Handkerchief?—O devil!   *Falls in a trance.*
IAGO: Work on.
   My med'cine works! Thus credulous fools are caught,
   And many worthy and chaste dames even thus,   45
   All guiltless, meet reproach°. What, ho! My lord!
   My lord, I say! Othello!

---

[21]**raven** (a harbinger of death).
[25]**abroad** i.e., in the world.
[27]**voluntary dotage** weakness of the will.
[28]**Convincèd or supplied** persuaded or gratified (the mistress).
[37]**fulsome** foul, repulsive.
[40–41]**Nature . . . instruction** i.e., my mind would not become so darkened (with anger) unless there were something in this (accusation); (it should be remembered that Othello believes in the workings of magic and supernatural forces).
[46]**reproach** shame.

Enter CASSIO.

How now, Cassio?

CASSIO: What's the matter?

IAGO: My lord is fall'n into an epilepsy.

This is his second fit; he had one yesterday.　　　　50

CASSIO: Rub him about the temples.

IAGO: The lethargy° must have his quiet course.

If not, he foams at mouth, and by and by

Breaks out to savage madness. Look, he stirs.

Do you withdraw yourself a little while.　　　　55

He will recover straight. When he is gone,

I would on great occasion° speak with you.　　　　[*Exit* CASSIO.]

How is it, general? Have you not hurt your head?

OTHELLO: Dost thou mock° me?

IAGO:　　　　　　　　　　I mock you not, by heaven.

Would you would bear your fortune like a man.　　　　60

OTHELLO: A hornèd man's a monster and a beast.

IAGO: There's many a beast then in a populous city,

And many a civil° monster.

OTHELLO: Did he confess it?

IAGO:　　　　　　　　　　Good, sir, be a man.

Think every bearded fellow that's but yoked　　　　65

May draw° with you. There's millions now alive

That nightly lie in those unproper° beds

Which they dare swear peculiar.° Your case is better.

O, 'tis the spite of hell, the fiend's arch-mock,

To lip a wanton in a secure couch,　　　　70

And to suppose her chaste. No, let me know;

And knowing what I am, I know what she shall be.

OTHELLO: O, thou art wise! 'Tis certain.

IAGO:　　　　　　　　　　　Stand you awhile apart;

Confine yourself but in a patient list.°

Whilst you were here, o'erwhelmèd with your grief—　　　　75

A passion most unsuiting such a man—

Cassio came hither. I shifted him away°

---

⁵²**lethargy** coma.

⁵⁷**great occasion** very important matter.

⁵⁹**mock** (Othello takes Iago's comment as a reference to his horns—which it is).

⁶³**civil** city-dwelling.

⁶⁶**draw** i.e., like the horned ox.

⁶⁷**unproper** i.e., not exclusively the husband's.

⁶⁸**peculiar** their own alone.

⁷⁴**a patient list** the bounds of patience.

⁷⁷**shifted him away** got rid of him by a strategem.

And laid good 'scuses upon your ecstasy°,
Bade him anon return, and here speak with me;
The which he promised. Do but encave° yourself   80
And mark the fleers°, the gibes, and notable° scorns
That dwell in every region of his face.
For I will make him tell the tale anew:
Where, how, how oft, how long ago, and when
He hath, and is again to cope your wife.   85
I say, but mark his gesture. Marry patience,
Or I shall say you're all in all in spleen°,
And nothing of a man.
OTHELLO: Dost thou hear, Iago?
I will be found most cunning in my patience;
But—dost thou hear?—most bloody.
IAGO: That's not amiss;   90
But yet keep time in all. Will you withdraw?

[OTHELLO *moves to one side, where his remarks are not audible to* CASSIO *and* IAGO.]

Now will I question Cassio of Bianca,
A huswife° that by selling her desires
Buys herself bread and cloth. It is a creature
That dotes on Cassio, as 'tis the strumpet's plague   95
To beguile many and be beguiled by one.
He, when he hears of her, cannot restrain
From the excess of laughter. Here he comes.

Enter CASSIO.

As he shall smile, Othello shall go mad:
And his unbookish° jealousy must conster°   100
Poor Cassio's smiles, gestures, and light behaviors
Quite in the wrong. How do you, lieutenant?
CASSIO: The worser that you give me the addition°
Whose want even kills me.

---

⁷⁸**ecstasy** trance (the literal meaning, "outside oneself," bears on the meaning of the change Othello is undergoing).
⁸⁰**encave** hide.
⁸¹**fleers** mocking looks or speeches.
⁸¹**notable** obvious.
⁸⁷**spleen** passion, particularly anger.
⁹³**huswife** housewife (but with the special meaning here of "prostitute").
¹⁰⁰**unbookish** ignorant.
¹⁰⁰**conster** construe.
¹⁰³**addition** title.

IAGO: Ply Desdemona well, and you are sure on't.   105
  Now, if this suit lay in Bianca's power,
  How quickly should you speed!

CASSIO: Alas, poor caitiff!°

OTHELLO: Look how he laughs already!

IAGO: I never knew woman love man so.

CASSIO: Alas, poor rogue! I think, i' faith, she loves me.   110

OTHELLO: Now he denies it faintly, and laughs it out.

IAGO: Do you hear, Cassio?

OTHELLO: Now he importunes him
  To tell it o'er. Go to! Well said, well said!

IAGO: She gives it out that you shall marry her.
  Do you intend it?   115

CASSIO: Ha, ha, ha!

OTHELLO: Do ye triumph, Roman? Do you triumph?

CASSIO: I marry? What, a customer°? Prithee bear some charity to
  my wit; do not think it so unwholesome. Ha, ha, ha!

OTHELLO: So, so, so, so. They laugh that win.   120

IAGO: Why, the cry goes that you marry her.

CASSIO: Prithee, say true.

IAGO: I am a very villain else.

OTHELLO: Have you scored° me? Well.

CASSIO: This is the monkey's own giving out. She is persuaded I will   125
  marry her out of her own love and flattery, not out of my
  promise.

OTHELLO: Iago beckons me; now he begins the story.

[OTHELLO *moves close enough to hear.*]

CASSIO: She was here even now; she haunts me in every place. I
  was the other day talking on the sea bank with certain
  Venetians, and thither comes the bauble°, and falls me thus
  about my neck—   130

OTHELLO: Crying "O dear Cassio!" as it were. His gesture imports it.

CASSIO: So hangs, and lolls, and weeps upon me; so shakes and pulls
  me! Ha, ha, ha!

OTHELLO: Now he tells how she plucked him to my chamber. O, I
  see that nose of yours, but not that dog I shall throw it to.   135

CASSIO: Well, I must leave her company.

IAGO: Before me!° Look where she comes.

---

[107]**caitiff** wretch.
[118]**customer** one who sells, a merchant (here, a prostitute).
[124]**scored** marked, defaced.
[130]**bauble** plaything.
[137]**Before me!** (an exclamation of surprise).

Enter BIANCA.

CASSIO: 'Tis such another fitchew!° Marry a perfumed one? What
do you mean by this haunting of me?

BIANCA: Let the devil and his dam haunt you! What did you mean   140
by that same handkerchief you gave me even now? I was a fine
fool to take it. I must take out the work? A likely piece of work
that you should find it in your chamber and know not who left
it there! This is some minx's token, and I must take out the
work? There! [*She throws down the handkerchief.*] Give it your   145
hobbyhorse°. Wheresoever you had it, I'll take out no work
on't.

CASSIO: How now, my sweet Bianca? How now? how now?

OTHELLO: By heaven, that should be my handkerchief!

BIANCA: If you'll come to supper tonight, you may; if you will not,   150
come when you are next prepared for°.   *Exit.*

IAGO: After her, after her!

CASSIO: Faith, I must; she'll rail in the streets else.

IAGO: Will you sup there?

CASSIO: Yes, I intend so.   155

IAGO: Well, I may chance to see you, for I would very fain speak
with you.

CASSIO: Prithee come. Will you?

IAGO: Go to, say no more.   [*Exit* CASSIO.]

OTHELLO [*Comes forward*]: How shall I murder him, Iago?   160

IAGO: Did you perceive how he laughed at his vice?

OTHELLO: O Iago!

IAGO: And did you see the handkerchief?

OTHELLO: Was that mine?

IAGO: Yours, by this hand! And to see how he prizes the foolish   165
woman your wife! She gave it him, and he hath giv'n it his
whore.

OTHELLO: I would have him nine years a-killing!—A fine woman, a
fair woman, a sweet woman?

IAGO: Nay, you must forget that.   170

OTHELLO: Ay, let her rot, and perish, and be damned tonight; for she
shall not live. No, my heart is turned to stone; I strike it, and it
hurts my hand. O the world hath not a sweeter creature! She
might lie by an emperor's side and command him tasks.

IAGO: Nay, that's not your way°.   175

OTHELLO: Hang her! I do but say what she is. So delicate with her

---

¹³⁸**fitchew** polecat, i.e., strong-smelling creature.
¹⁴⁶**hobbyhorse** prostitute.
¹⁵¹**next prepared for** next expected—i.e., never.
¹⁷⁵**way** proper course.

needle. An admirable musician. O, she will sing the savageness
out of a bear! Of so high and plenteous wit and invention° —
IAGO: She's the worse for all this.
OTHELLO: O, a thousand, a thousand times. And then, of so gentle a   180
condition°?
IAGO: Ay, too gentle.
OTHELLO: Nay, that's certain. But yet the pity of it, Iago. O Iago, the
pity of it, Iago.
IAGO: If you are so fond over her iniquity, give her patent to offend;   185
for if it touch° not you, it comes near nobody.
OTHELLO: I will chop her into messes°! Cuckold me!
IAGO: O, 'tis foul in her.
OTHELLO: With mine officer!
IAGO: That's fouler.   190
OTHELLO: Get me some poison, Iago, this night. I'll not expostulate
with her, lest her body and beauty unprovide my mind° again.
This night, Iago!
IAGO: Do it not with poison. Strangle her in her bed, even the bed
she hath contaminated.   195
OTHELLO: Good, good! The justice of it pleases. Very good!
IAGO: And for Cassio, let me be his undertaker°. You shall hear
more by midnight.
OTHELLO: Excellent good!   [*A trumpet.*]
              What trumpet is that same?
IAGO: I warrant something from Venice.

Enter LODOVICO, DESDEMONA, *and* ATTENDANTS.
                                    'Tis Lodovico.   200
This comes from the Duke. See, your wife's with him.
LODOVICO: God save you, worthy general.
OTHELLO: With° all my heart, sir.
LODOVICO: The Duke and the senators of Venice greet you.
                              [*Gives him a letter.*]
OTHELLO: I kiss the instrument of their pleasures.

                              [*Opens the letter and reads.*]

178**invention** imagination.
180-81**gentle a condition** (1) well born (2) of a gentle nature.
186**touch** affects.
187**messes** bits.
192**unprovide my mind** undo my resolution.
197**undertaker** (not "burier" but "one who undertakes to do something").
202**With** i.e., I greet you with.

DESDEMONA: And what's the news, good cousin Lodovico?   205
IAGO: I am very glad to see you, signior.
   Welcome to Cyprus.
LODOVICO: I thank you. How does Lieutenant Cassio?
IAGO: Lives, sir.
DESDEMONA: Cousin, there's fall'n between him and my lord
   An unkind° breach; but you shall make all well.   210
OTHELLO: Are you sure of that?
DESDEMONA: My lord?
OTHELLO [*Reads*]: "This fail you not to do, as you will—"
LODOVICO: He did not call; he's busy in the paper.
   Is there division 'twixt my lord and Cassio?   215
DESDEMONA: A most unhappy one. I would do much
   T' atone° them, for the love I bear to Cassio.
OTHELLO: Fire and brimstone!
DESDEMONA: My lord?
OTHELLO: Are you wise?
DESDEMONA: What, is he angry?
LODOVICO: May be th' letter moved him;
   For, as I think, they do command him home,   220
   Deputing Cassio in his government°.
DESDEMONA: Trust me, I am glad on't.
OTHELLO: Indeed?
DESDEMONA: My lord?
OTHELLO: I am glad to see you mad.
DESDEMONA: Why, sweet Othello—
OTHELLO: Devil!   [*Strikes her.*]
DESDEMONA: I have not deserved this.   225
LODOVICO: My lord, this would not be believed in Venice,
   Though I should swear I saw't. 'Tis very much.
   Make her amends; she weeps.
OTHELLO: O devil, devil!
   If that the earth could teem° with woman's tears,
   Each drop she falls° would prove a crocodile°.   230
   Out of my sight!
DESDEMONA: I will not stay to offend you.   [*Going.*]
LODOVICO: Truly, an obedient lady.
   I do beseech your lordship call her back.

---

²¹⁰**unkind** unnatural.
²¹⁷**atone** reconcile.
²²¹**government** office.
²²⁹**teem** conceive.
²³⁰**falls** drops.
²³⁰**crocodile** (the crocodile was supposed to shed false tears to lure its victims).

OTHELLO: Mistress!
DESDEMONA: My lord?
OTHELLO: What would you with her, sir?
LODOVICO: Who? I, my lord?   235
OTHELLO: Ay! You did wish that I would make her turn.
  Sir, she can turn, and turn, and yet go on
  And turn again; and she can weep, sir, weep;
  And she's obedient; as you say, obedient.
  Very obedient. Proceed you in your tears.   240
  Concerning this, sir—O well-painted passion!
  I am commanded home.—Get you away;
  I'll send for you anon.—Sir, I obey the mandate
  And will return to Venice.—Hence, avaunt!   [*Exit* DESDEMONA.]
  Cassio shall have my place. And, sir, tonight   245
  I do entreat that we may sup together.
  You are welcome, sir, to Cyprus.—Goats and monkeys!   *Exit.*
LODOVICO: Is this the noble Moor whom our full Senate
  Call all in all sufficient? Is this the nature
  Whom passion could not shake? whose solid virtue   250
  The shot of accident nor dart of chance
  Could neither graze nor pierce?
IAGO: He is much changed.
LODOVICO: Are his wits safe? Is he not light of brain?
IAGO: He's that he is; I may not breathe my censure.
  What he might be (if, what he might, he is not)   255
  I would to heaven he were!
LODOVICO: What, strike his wife?
IAGO: Faith, that was not so well; yet would I knew
  That stroke would prove the worst.
LODOVICO: Is it his use?°
  Or did the letters work upon his blood°
  And new-create his fault?
IAGO: Alas, alas!   260
  It is not honesty in me to speak
  What I have seen and known. You shall observe him,
  And his own courses° will denote him so
  That I may save my speech. Do but go after
  And mark how he continues.   265
LODOVICO: I am sorry that I am deceived in him.   *Exeunt.*

---

[258]**use** habit.
[259]**blood** passion.
[263]**courses** actions.

Scene II [*The citadel.*]

Enter OTHELLO *and* EMILIA.

OTHELLO: You have seen nothing then?
EMILIA: Nor ever heard, nor ever did suspect.
OTHELLO: Yes, you have seen Cassio and she together.
EMILIA: But then I saw no harm, and then I heard
   Each syllable that breath made up° between them.   5
OTHELLO: What, did they never whisper?
EMILIA: Never, my lord.
OTHELLO: Nor send you out o' th' way?
EMILIA: Never.
OTHELLO: To fetch her fan, her gloves, her mask, nor nothing?
EMILIA: Never, my lord.   10
OTHELLO: That's strange.
EMILIA: I durst, my lord, to wager she is honest,
   Lay down my soul at stake°. If you think other,
   Remove your thought. It doth abuse your bosom.
   If any wretch have put this in your head,   15
   Let heaven requite it with the serpent's curse°,
   For if she be not honest°, chaste, and true,
   There's no man happy. The purest of their wives
   Is foul as slander.
OTHELLO: Bid her come hither. Go.   *Exit* EMILIA.
   She says enough; yet she's a simple bawd°   20
   That cannot say as much. This is a subtle whore,
   A closet lock and key of villainous secrets,
   And yet she'll kneel and pray; I have seen her do't.

Enter DESDEMONA *and* EMILIA.

DESDEMONA: My lord, what is your will?
OTHELLO: Pray you, chuck, come hither.
DESDEMONA: What is your pleasure?
OTHELLO: Let me see your eyes.   25
   Look in my face.
DESDEMONA: What horrible fancy's this?

IV.ii. ⁵**that breath made up** spoken.
¹³**at stake** as the wager.
¹⁶**serpent's curse** (God's curse on the serpent after the fall in Eden).
¹⁷**honest** chaste.
²⁰**bawd** procuress.

OTHELLO [*To* EMILIA]: Some of your function°, mistress:
    Leave procreants alone and shut the door;
    Cough or cry hem if anybody come.
    Your mystery°, your mystery! Nay, dispatch!   *Exit* EMILIA.   30
DESDEMONA: Upon my knee, what doth your speech import?
    I understand a fury in your words°.
OTHELLO: Why, what art thou?
DESDEMONA: Your wife, my lord; your true
    And loyal wife.
OTHELLO: Come, swear it, damn thyself;
    Lest, being like one of heaven, the devils themselves   35
    Should fear to seize thee. Therefore be double-damned:
    Swear thou art honest.
DESDEMONA: Heaven doth truly know it.
OTHELLO: Heaven truly knows that thou art false as hell.
DESDEMONA: To whom, my lord? With whom? How am I false?
OTHELLO: Ah, Desdemon! Away! Away! Away!   40
DESDEMONA: Alas the heavy day! Why do you weep?
    Am I the motive° of these tears, my lord?
    If haply° you my father do suspect
    An instrument of this your calling back,
    Lay not your blame on me. If you have lost him,   45
    I have lost him too.
OTHELLO: Had it pleased heaven
    To try me with affliction, had they rained
    All kinds of sores and shames on my bare head,
    Steeped° me in poverty to the very lips,
    Given to captivity me and my utmost hopes,   50
    I should have found in some place of my soul
    A drop of patience. But alas, to make me
    The fixèd figure for the time of scorn°
    To point his slow and moving finger at.
    Yet could I bear that too, well, very well.   55
    But there where I have garnered up my heart,
    Where either I must live or bear no life,
    The fountain from the which my current runs
    Or else dries up—to be discarded thence,
    Or keep it as a cistern for foul toads   60

---

[27]**Some of your function** do your proper work (as the operator of a brothel).
[30]**mystery** trade.
[32]**words** (Q1 adds to this line, "But not the words").
[42]**motive** cause.
[43]**haply** by chance.
[49]**Steeped** submerged.
[53]**The . . . scorn** the very image of scorn in our time.

To knot and gender° in—turn thy complexion there,
Patience, thou young and rose-lipped cherubin!
I here look grim as hell!°
DESDEMONA: I hope my noble lord esteems me honest.
OTHELLO: O, ay, as summer flies are in the shambles°,   65
That quicken even with blowing°. O thou weed,
Who art so lovely fair, and smell'st so sweet,
That the sense aches at thee, would thou hadst never been born!
DESDEMONA: Alas, what ignorant° sin have I committed?
OTHELLO: Was this fair paper, this most goodly book,   70
Made to write "whore" upon? What committed?
Committed? O thou public commoner°,
I should make very forges of my cheeks
That would to cinders burn up modesty,
Did I but speak thy deeds. What committed?   75
Heaven stops the nose at it, and the moon winks°;
The bawdy wind that kisses all it meets
Is hushed within the hollow mine of earth
And will not hear't. What committed?
DESDEMONA: By heaven, you do me wrong!   80
OTHELLO: Are not you a strumpet?
DESDEMONA: No, as I am a Christian!
If to preserve this vessel for my lord
From any other foul unlawful touch
Be not to be a strumpet, I am none.
OTHELLO: What, not a whore?
DESDEMONA: No, as I shall be saved!   85
OTHELLO: Is't possible?
DESDEMONA: O, heaven forgive us!
OTHELLO: I cry you mercy° then.
I took you for that cunning whore of Venice
That married with Othello. [*Calling*] You, mistress,

Enter EMILIA.

That have the office opposite to Saint Peter   80
And keep the gate of hell! You, you, ay, you!
We have done our course; there's money for your pains.

---

⁶¹**knot and gender** twist in bunches and procreate.
⁶¹⁻⁶³**turn . . . hell** (the rough sense would seem to be, "even Patience would grow pale,
turn complexion, at Desdemona's perfidy, but that Othello looks grimly on").
⁶⁵**shambles** abattoirs.
⁶⁶**quicken even with blowing** become impregnated as soon as they lay their eggs.
⁶⁹**ignorant** unknowing.
⁷²**commoner** prostitute.
⁷⁶**winks** closes its eyes (the moon was the symbol of chastity).
⁸⁷**cry you mercy** ask your pardon.

[Throws her some coins.]

I pray you turn the key and keep our counsel.   *Exit.*
EMILIA: Alas, what does this gentleman conceive?
   How do you, madam? How do you, my good lady?   95
DESDEMONA: Faith, half asleep.
EMILIA: Good madam, what's the matter with my lord?
DESDEMONA: With who?
EMILIA: Why, with my lord, madam.
DESDEMONA: Who is thy lord?
EMILIA: He that is yours, sweet lady.   100
DESDEMONA: I have none. Do not talk to me, Emilia.
   I cannot weep, nor answers have I none
   But what should go by water°. Prithee tonight
   Lay on my bed my wedding sheets, remember;
   And call thy husband hither.
EMILIA: Here's a change indeed!   *Exit.*   105
DESDEMONA: 'Tis meet I should be used so, very meet.
   How have I been behaved, that he might stick
   The small'st opinion on my least misuse°?

Enter IAGO *and* EMILIA.

IAGO: What is your pleasure, madam? How is't with you?
DESDEMONA: I cannot tell. Those that do teach young babes   110
   Do it with gentle means and easy tasks.
   He might have chid me so; for, in good faith,
   I am a child to chiding.
IAGO: What is the matter, lady?
EMILIA: Alas, Iago, my lord hath so bewhored her,
   Thrown such despite° and heavy terms upon her   115
   That true hearts cannot bear it.
DESDEMONA: Am I that name, Iago?
IAGO: What name, fair lady?
DESDEMONA: Such as she said my lord did say I was.
EMILIA: He called her whore. A beggar in his drink
   Could not have laid such terms upon his callet°.   120
IAGO: Why did he so?
DESDEMONA: I do not know; I am sure I am none such.
IAGO: Do not weep, do not weep. Alas the day.
EMILIA: Hath she forsook so many noble matches,

---

[103]**water** tears.
[107-08]**stick . . . misuse** base any doubt on my smallest fault.
[115]**despite** abuse.
[120]**callet** slut.

Her father and her country, and her friends, 125
To be called whore? Would it not make one weep?
DESDEMONA: It is my wretched fortune.
IAGO: Beshrew° him for't!
How comes this trick upon him?
DESDEMONA: Nay, heaven doth know.
EMILIA: I will be hanged if some eternal villain,
Some busy and insinuating rogue, 130
Some cogging°, cozening slave, to get some office,
Have not devised this slander. I will be hanged else.
IAGO: Fie, there is no such man! It is impossible.
DESDEMONA: If any such there be, heaven pardon him.
EMILIA: A halter pardon him! And hell gnaw his bones! 135
Why should he call her whore? Who keeps her company?
What place? What time? What form? What likelihood?
The Moor's abused by some most villainous knave,
Some base notorious knave, some scurvy fellow.
O heavens, that such companions° thou'dst unfold°, 140
And put in every honest hand a whip
To lash the rascals naked through the world
Even from the east to th' west!
IAGO: Speak within door°.
EMILIA: O, fie upon them! Some such squire° he was
That turned your wit the seamy side without 145
And made you to suspect me with the Moor.
IAGO: You are a fool. Go to.
DESDEMONA: Alas, Iago,
What shall I do to win my lord again?
Good friend, go to him, for, by this light of heaven,
I know not how I lost him. Here I kneel: 150
If e'er my will did trespass 'gainst his love
Either in discourse of thought° or actual deed,
Or that mine eyes, mine ears, or any sense
Delighted them in any other form;
Or that I do not yet, and ever did, 155
And ever will (though he do shake me off
To beggarly divorcement) love him dearly,
Comfort forswear me. Unkindness may do much,
And his unkindness may defeat° my life,

---

[127]**Beshrew** curse.
[131]**cogging** cheating.
[140]**companions** fellows, rogues.
[140]**unfold** disclose.
[143]**within door** more quietly and moderately.
[144]**squire** (a term of contempt).
[152]**discourse of thought** thinking.
[159]**defeat** destroy.

But never taint my love. I cannot say "whore."   160
It does abhor me now I speak the word;
To do the act might the addition earn
Not the world's mass of vanity could make me.
IAGO: I pray you be content. 'Tis but his humor°.
The business of the state does him offense.   165
DESDEMONA: If 'twere no other.
IAGO: It is but so, I warrant.   [*Trumpets within.*]
Hark how these instruments summon to supper.
The messengers of Venice stay the meat°.
Go in, and weep not. All things shall be well.

[*Exeunt* DESDEMONA *and* EMILIA.]
Enter RODERIGO.

How now, Roderigo?   170
RODERIGO: I do not find that thou deal'st justly with me.
IAGO: What in the contrary?
RODERIGO: Every day thou daff'st° me with some device°, Iago, and
    rather, as it seems to me now, keep'st from me all conveniency°
    than suppliest me with the least advantage of hope. I will indeed   175
    no longer endure it; nor am I yet persuaded to put up° in peace
    what already I have foolishly suffered.
IAGO: Will you hear me, Roderigo?
RODERIGO: I have heard too much, and your words and
    performances are no kin together.   180
IAGO: You charge me most unjustly.
RODERIGO: With naught but truth. I have wasted myself out of my
    means. The jewels you have had from me to deliver Desdemona
    would half have corrupted a votarist°. You have told me she
    hath received them, and returned me expectations and comforts   185
    of sudden respect° and acquaintance; but I find none.
IAGO: Well, go to; very well.
RODERIGO: Very well? Go to? I cannot go to, man; nor 'tis not very
    well. Nay, I think it is scurvy, and begin to find myself fopped°
    in it.   190
IAGO: Very well.

---

[164]**humor** mood.
[168]**stay the meat** await the meal.
[173]**daff'st** put off.
[173]**device** scheme.
[174]**conveniency** what is needful.
[176]**put up** accept.
[184]**votarist** nun.
[186]**sudden respect** immediate consideration.
[189]**fopped** duped.

RODERIGO: I tell you 'tis not very well. I will make myself known to Desdemona. If she will return me my jewels, I will give over my suit and repent my unlawful solicitation. If not, assure yourself I will seek satisfaction of you. 195

IAGO: You have said now?

RODERIGO: Ay, and said nothing but what I protest° intendment of doing.

IAGO: Why, now I see there's mettle° in thee, and even from this instant do build on thee a better opinion than ever before. Give 200 me thy hand, Roderigo. Thou hast taken against me a most just exception°; but yet I protest I have dealt most directly° in thy affair.

RODERIGO: It hath not appeared.

IAGO: I grant indeed it hath not appeared, and your suspicion is not 205 without wit and judgment. But, Roderigo, if thou hast that in thee indeed which I have greater reason to believe now than ever—I mean purpose, courage and valor—this night show it. If thou the next night following enjoy not Desdemona, take me from this world with treachery and devise engines for° my life. 210

RODERIGO: Well, what is it? Is it within reason and compass°?

IAGO: Sir, there is especial commission come from Venice to depute Cassio in Othello's place.

RODERIGO: Is that true? Why, then Othello and Desdemona return again to Venice. 215

IAGO: O, no; he goes into Mauritania and taketh away with him the fair Desdemona, unless his abode be lingered here by some accident; wherein none can be so determinate° as the removing of Cassio.

RODERIGO: How do you mean, removing him? 220

IAGO: Why, by making him uncapable of Othello's place—knocking out his brains.

RODERIGO: And that you would have me to do?

IAGO: Ay, if you dare do yourself a profit and a right. He sups tonight with a harlotry°, and thither will I go to him. He knows 225 not yet of his honorable fortune. If you will watch his going thence, which I will fashion to fall out° between twelve and one, you may take him at your pleasure. I will be near to

---

[197]**protest** aver.
[199]**mettle** spirit.
[202]**exception** objection.
[202]**directly** straightforwardly.
[210]**engines for** schemes against.
[211]**compass** possibility.
[218]**determinate** effective.
[225]**harlotry** female.
[227]**fall out** occur.

second° your attempt, and he shall fall between us. Come, stand
not amazed at it, but go along with me. I will show you such a   230
necessity in his death that you shall think yourself bound to put
it on him. It is now high supper time, and the night grows to
waste. About it.

RODERIGO: I will hear further reason for this.

IAGO: And you shall be satisfied.   *Exeunt.*   235

Scene III [*The citadel.*]

    Enter OTHELLO, LODOVICO, DESDEMONA, EMILIA, *and* ATTENDANTS.

LODOVICO: I do beseech you, sir, trouble yourself no further.

OTHELLO: O, pardon me; 'twill do me good to walk.

LODOVICO: Madam, good night. I humbly thank your ladyship.

DESDEMONA: Your honor is most welcome.

OTHELLO: Will you walk, sir? O, Desdemona.   5

DESDEMONA: My lord?

OTHELLO: Get you to bed on th' instant; I will be returned forthwith.
   Dismiss your attendant there. Look't be done.

DESDEMONA: I will, my lord.
        Exit [OTHELLO, *with* LODOVICO *and* ATTENDANTS].

EMILIA: How goes it now? He looks gentler than he did.   10

DESDEMONA: He says he will return incontinent°,
   And hath commanded me to go to bed.
   And bade me to dismiss you.

EMILIA: Dismiss me?

DESDEMONA: It was his bidding; therefore, good Emilia,
   Give me my nightly wearing, and adieu.   15
   We must not now displease him.

EMILIA: I would you had never seen him!

DESDEMONA: So would not I. My love doth so approve him
   That even his stubbornness, his checks°, his frowns—
   Prithee unpin me—have grace and favor.   20

EMILIA: I have laid these sheets you bade me on the bed.

DESDEMONA: All's one°. Good Father, how foolish are our minds!
   If I do die before, prithee shroud me
   In one of these same sheets.

EMILIA: Come, come! You talk.

DESDEMONA: My mother had a maid called Barbary.   25
   She was in love; and he she loved proved mad

---

²²⁹**second** support.
IV.iii. ¹¹**incontinent** at once.
¹⁹**checks** rebukes.
²²**All's one** no matter.

And did forsake her. She had a song of "Willow";
An old thing 'twas, but it expressed her fortune,
And she died singing it. That song tonight
Will not go from my mind; I have much to do   30
But to go hang my head all at one side
And sing it like poor Barbary. Prithee dispatch.
EMILIA: Shall I go fetch your nightgown?
DESDEMONA: No, unpin me here.
This Lodovico is a proper man.   35
EMILIA: A very handsome man.
DESDEMONA: He speaks well.
EMILIA: I know a lady in Venice would have walked barefoot to
Palestine for a touch of his nether lip.
DESDEMONA [*Sings*]:
"The poor soul sat singing by a sycamore tree,   40
Sing all a green willow;
Her hand on her bosom, her head on her knee,
Sing willow, willow, willow.
The fresh streams ran by her and murmured her moans;
Sing willow, willow, willow;   45
Her salt tears fell from her, and soft'ned the stones—
Sing willow, willow, willow—"
Lay by these.   [*Gives* EMILIA *her clothes.*]
"Willow, Willow"—
Prithee hie° thee; he'll come anon°.   50
"Sing all a green willow must be my garland
Let nobody blame him; his scorn I approve"—
Nay, that's not next. Hark! Who is't that knocks?
EMILIA: It is the wind.
DESDEMONA [*Sings*]:
"I called my love false love; but what said he then?   55
Sing willow, willow, willow:
If I court moe° women, you'll couch with moe men."
So, get thee gone; good night. Mine eyes do itch.
Doth that bode weeping?
EMILIA: 'Tis neither here nor there.
DESDEMONA: I have heard it said so. O, these men, these men.   60
Dost thou in conscience think, tell me, Emilia,
That there be women do abuse their husbands
In such gross kind?
EMILIA: There be some such, no question.

---

⁵⁰**hie** hurry.
⁵⁰**anon** at once.
⁵⁷**moe** more.

DESDEMONA: Wouldst thou do such a deed for all the world?

EMILIA: Why, would not you?

DESDEMONA: No, by this heavenly light!   65

EMILIA: Nor I neither by this heavenly light.
  I might do't as well i' th' dark.

DESDEMONA: Wouldst thou do such a deed for all the world?

EMILIA: The world's a huge thing; it is a great price for a small vice.

DESDEMONA: In troth, I think thou wouldst not.   70

EMILIA: In troth, I think I should; and undo't when I had done.
  Marry, I would not do such a thing for a joint-ring°, nor for
  measures of lawn°, nor for gowns, petticoats, nor caps, nor any
  petty exhibition°, but for all the whole world? Why, who would
  not make her husband a cuckold to make him a monarch? I   75
  should venture purgatory for't.

DESDEMONA: Beshrew me if I would do such a wrong for the whole
  world.

EMILIA: Why, the wrong is but a wrong i' th' world; and having the
  world for your labor, 'tis a wrong in your own world, and you   80
  might quickly make it right.

DESDEMONA: I do not think there is any such woman.

EMILIA: Yes, a dozen; and as many to th' vantage as would store°
  the world they played for.
  But I do think it is their husbands' faults   85
  If wives do fall. Say that they slack their duties
  And pour our treasures into foreign° laps;
  Or else break out in peevish jealousies,
  Throwing restraint upon us; or say they strike us,
  Or scant our former having in despite° —   90
  Why, we have galls; and though we have some grace,
  Yet have we some revenge. Let husbands know
  Their wives have sense like them. They see, and smell,
  And have their palates both for sweet and sour,
  As husbands have. What is it that they do   95
  When they change° us for others? Is it sport?
  I think it is. And doth affection° breed it?
  I think it doth. Is't frailty that thus errs?
  It is so too. And have not we affections?

---

⁷²**joint-ring** (a ring with two interlocking halves).
⁷³**lawn** fine linen.
⁷⁴**exhibition** payment.
⁸³**to . . . store** in addition as would fill.
⁸⁷**foreign** alien, i.e., other than the wife.
⁹⁰**scant . . . despite** reduce, in spite, our household allowance (?).
⁹⁶**change** exchange.
⁹⁷**affection** strong feeling, desire.

Desires for sport? and frailty? as men have?   100
Then let them use us well; else let them know,
The ills we do, their ills instruct us so°.
DESDEMONA: Good night, good night. Heaven me such uses° send,
Not to pick bad from bad, but by bad mend.   *Exeunt.*

ACT V

Scene I [A street.]

Enter IAGO *and* RODERIGO.

IAGO: Here, stand behind this bulk°; straight will he come.
Wear thy good rapier bare, and put it home.
Quick, quick! Fear nothing; I'll be at thy elbow.
It makes us, or it mars us, think on that,
And fix most firm thy resolution.   5
RODERIGO: Be near at hand; I may miscarry in't.
IAGO: Here, at thy hand. Be bold, and take thy stand.   *[Moves to one*
                                                        side.]

RODERIGO: I have no great devotion to the deed,
And yet he hath given me satisfying reasons.
'Tis but a man gone. Forth my sword! He dies!   10
IAGO: I have rubbed this young quat° almost to the sense°,
And he grows angry. Now, whether he kill Cassio,
Or Cassio him, or each do kill the other,
Every way makes my gain. Live Roderigo,
He calls me to a restitution large   15
Of gold and jewels that I bobbed° from him
As gifts to Desdemona.
It must not be. If Cassio do remain,
He hath a daily beauty in his life
That makes me ugly; and besides, the Moor   20
May unfold me to him; there stand I in much peril.
No, he must die. But so, I hear him coming.

Enter CASSIO.

---

¹⁰²**instruct us so** teach us to do likewise.
¹⁰³**uses** practices.
V.i. ¹**bulk** projecting stall of a shop.
¹¹**quat** pimple.
¹¹**to the sense** raw.
¹⁶**bobbed** swindled.

RODERIGO: I know his gait. 'Tis he. Villain, thou diest!   [*Thrusts at*
                        CASSIO.]

CASSIO: That thrust had been mine enemy indeed
  But that my coat° is better than thou know'st.   25
  I will make proof of thine.   [*Fights with* RODERIGO.]
RODERIGO: O, I am slain!°
CASSIO: I am maimed forever. Help, ho! Murder! Murder!

              Enter OTHELLO [*to one side*].

OTHELLO: The voice of Cassio. Iago keeps his word.
RODERIGO: O, villain that I am!
OTHELLO: It is even so.
CASSIO: O help, ho! Light! A surgeon!   30
OTHELLO: 'Tis he. O brave Iago, honest and just,
  That hast such noble sense of thy friend's wrong!
  Thou teachest me. Minion°, your dear lies dead,
  And your unblest° fate hies°. Strumpet, I come.
  Forth of my heart those charms, thine eyes, are blotted.   35
  Thy bed, lust-stained, shall with lust's blood be spotted.

      Exit OTHELLO. *Enter* LODOVICO *and* GRATIANO.

CASSIO: What, ho? No watch? No passage°? Murder! Murder!
GRATIANO: 'Tis some mischance. The voice is very direful.
CASSIO: O, help!
LODOVICO: Hark!   40
RODERIGO: O wretched villain!
LODOVICO: Two or three groan. 'Tis heavy night.
  These may be counterfeits. Let's think't unsafe
  To come into the cry without more help.
RODERIGO: Nobody come? Then shall I bleed to death.   45
LODOVICO: Hark!

           Enter IAGO [*with a light*].

---

²⁵**coat** i.e., a mail shirt or bulletproof vest.
²⁶**slain** (most editors add here a stage direction that has Iago wounding Cassio in the leg from behind, but remaining unseen. However, nothing in the text requires this, and Cassio's wound can be given him in the fight with Roderigo, for presumably when Cassio attacks Roderigo the latter would not simply accept the thrust but would parry. Since Iago enters again at line 46, he must exit at some point after line 22.)
³³**Minion** hussy, i.e., Desdemona.
³⁴**unblest** unsanctified.
³⁴**hies** approaches swiftly.
³⁷**passage** passers-by.

GRATIANO: Here's one comes in his shirt, with light and weapons.
IAGO: Who's there? Whose noise is this that cries on murder?
LODOVICO: We do not know.
IAGO: Do not you hear a cry?
CASSIO: Here, here! For heaven's sake, help me!
IAGO: What's the matter?   50
GRATIANO: This is Othello's ancient, as I take it.
LODOVICO: The same indeed, a very valiant fellow.
IAGO: What are you here that cry so grievously?
CASSIO: Iago? O, I am spoiled, undone by villains.
  Give me some help.   55
IAGO: O me, lieutenant! What villains have done this?
CASSIO: I think that one of them is hereabout
  And cannot make away.
IAGO: O treacherous villains!
  [*To* LODOVICO *and* GRATIANO] What are you there?
  Come in, and give some help.   60
RODERIGO: O, help me here!
CASSIO: That's one of them.
IAGO: O murd'rous slave! O villain!   [*Stabs*
                                     RODERIGO.]
RODERIGO: O damned Iago! O inhuman dog!
IAGO: Kill men i' th' dark?—Where be these bloody thieves?—
  How silent is this town!—Ho! Murder! Murder!—   65
  What may you be? Are you of good or evil?
LODOVICO: As you shall prove us, praise us.
IAGO: Signior Lodovico?
LODOVICO: He, sir.
IAGO: I cry you mercy. Here's Cassio hurt by villains.   70
GRATIANO: Cassio?
IAGO: How is't, brother?
CASSIO: My leg is cut in two.
IAGO: Marry, heaven forbid!
  Light, gentlemen. I'll bind it with my shirt.

Enter BIANCA.

BIANCA: What is the matter, ho? Who is't that cried?   75
IAGO: Who is't that cried?
BIANCA: O my dear Cassio! My sweet Cassio!
  O Cassio, Cassio, Cassio!
IAGO: O notable strumpet!—Cassio, may you suspect
  Who they should be that have thus mangled you?   80
CASSIO: No.
GRATIANO: I am sorry to find you thus. I have been to seek you.

IAGO: Lend me a garter. So. O for a chair
To bear him easily hence.
BIANCA: Alas, he faints! O Cassio, Cassio, Cassio! 85
IAGO: Gentlemen all, I do suspect this trash
To be a party in this injury.—
Patience awhile, good Cassio.—Come, come.
Lend me a light. Know we this face or no?
Alas, my friend and my dear countryman 90
Roderigo? No.—Yes, sure.—Yes, 'tis Roderigo!
GRATIANO: What, of Venice?
IAGO: Even he, sir. Did you know him?
GRATIANO: Know him? Ay.
IAGO: Signior Gratiano? I cry your gentle pardon.
These bloody accidents must excuse my manners 95
That so neglected you.
GRATIANO: I am glad to see you.
IAGO: How do you, Cassio?—O, a chair, a chair!
GRATIANO: Roderigo?
IAGO: He, he, 'tis he! [*A chair brought in.*] O, that's well said°; the
chair.
Some good man bear him carefully from hence. 100
I'll fetch the general's surgeon. [*To* BIANCA] For you, mistress,
Save you your labor. [*To* CASSIO] He that lies slain here, Cassio,
Was my dear friend. What malice was between you?
CASSIO: None in the world; nor do I know the man.
IAGO: What, look you pale?—O, bear him out o' th' air. 105

[CASSIO *is carried off.*]

Stay you, good gentlemen.—Look you pale, mistress?
Do you perceive the gastness° of her eye?
Nay, if you stare, we shall hear more anon.
Behold her well; I pray you look upon her.
Do you see, gentlemen? Nay, guiltiness will speak, 110
Though tongues were out of use°.

[*Enter* EMILIA.]

EMILIA: Alas, what is the matter? What is the matter, husband?
IAGO: Cassio hath here been set on in the dark

---

⁹⁹**well said** well done.
¹⁰⁷**gastness** terror.
¹¹¹**tongues were out of use** men no longer spoke.

By Roderigo and fellows that are scaped.
He's almost slain, and Roderigo quite dead.   115
EMILIA: Alas, good gentleman! Alas, good Cassio!
IAGO: This is the fruits of whoring. Prithee, Emilia,
　　Go know of Cassio where he supped tonight.
　　[*To* BIANCA] What, do you shake at that?
BIANCA: He supped at my house; but I therefore shake not.   120
IAGO: O, did he so? I charge° you go with me.
EMILIA: Oh fie upon thee, strumpet!
BIANCA: I am no strumpet, but of life as honest
　　As you that thus abuse me.
EMILIA:　　　　　　　　　　　As I? Fie upon thee!
IAGO: Kind gentlemen, let's go see poor Cassio dressed°.   125
　　[*To* BIANCA] Come, mistress, you must tell's another tale.
　　Emilia, run you to the citadel
　　And tell my lord and lady what hath happed.   [*Exit* EMILIA.]
　　Will you go on afore?   *Exeunt* [*all but* IAGO.].
　　　　　　　　　This is the night
　　That either makes me or fordoes me quite°.   [*Exit*.]   130

Scene II. [DESDEMONA'S chamber.]

　　　　　Enter OTHELLO [*with a light*]; *and* DESDEMONA *in her bed.*

OTHELLO: It is the cause, it is the cause, my soul.
　　Let me not name it to you, you chaste stars.
　　It is the cause. Yet I'll not shed her blood,
　　Nor scar that whiter skin of hers than snow
　　And smooth as monumental alabaster.   5
　　Yet she must die, else she'll betray more men.
　　Put out the light, and then put out the light.
　　If I quench thee, thou flaming minister°,
　　I can again thy former light restore,
　　Should I repent me; but once put out thy light,   10
　　Thou cunning'st° pattern of excelling nature,
　　I know not where is that Promethean heat°
　　That can thy light relume°. When I have plucked the rose,

---

¹²¹**charge** command.
¹²⁵**dressed** bandaged.
¹³⁰**fordoes me quite** completely ruins me.
V.ii. ⁸**minister** worker, servant.
¹¹**cunning'st** most intricate and skillfully wrought (by nature excelling itself).
¹²**Promethean heat** divine fire (Prometheus is the Titan who stole fire from heaven and
gave it to man).
¹³**relume** relight.

I cannot give it vital° growth again;
It needs must wither. I'll smell thee on the tree.   [*He kisses her.*]   15
O balmy breath, that dost almost persuade
Justice to break her sword. One more, one more!
Be thus when thou art dead, and I will kill thee,
And love thee after. One more, and that's the last!
So sweet was ne'er so fatal. I must weep,   20
But they are cruel tears. This sorrow's heavenly;
It strikes where it doth love. She wakes.

DESDEMONA: Who's there? Othello?

OTHELLO: Ay, Desdemona.

DESDEMONA: Will you come to bed, my lord?

OTHELLO: Have you prayed tonight, Desdemon?

DESDEMONA: Ay, my lord.   25

OTHELLO: If you bethink yourself of any crime
     Unreconciled as yet to heaven and grace,
     Solicit for it straight.

DESDEMONA: Alack, my lord, what may you mean by that?

OTHELLO: Well, do it, and be brief; I will walk by°.   30
     I would not kill thy unpreparèd spirit.
     No, heavens forfend! I would not kill thy soul.

DESDEMONA: Talk you of killing?

OTHELLO: Ay, I do.

DESDEMONA: Then heaven
     Have mercy on me!

OTHELLO: Amen, with all my heart.

DESDEMONA: If you say so, I hope you will not kill me.   35

OTHELLO: Humh.

DESDEMONA: And yet I fear you; for you're fatal then
     When your eyes roll so. Why I should fear I know not,
     Since guiltiness I know not; but yet I feel I fear.

OTHELLO: Think on thy sins.

DESDEMONA: They are loves I bear to you.   40

OTHELLO: Ay, and for that thou diest.

DESDEMONA: That death's unnatural that kills for loving.
     Alas, why gnaw you so your nether lip?
     Some bloody passion shakes your very frame.
     These are portents; but yet I hope, I hope,   45
     They do not point on me.

OTHELLO: Peace and be still.

DESDEMONA: I will so. What's the matter?

---

¹⁴**vital** living.
³⁰**by** nearby.

OTHELLO: That handkerchief which I so loved and gave thee,
    Thou gav'st to Cassio.

DESDEMONA: No, by my life and soul!
    Send for the man and ask him.

OTHELLO: Sweet soul, take heed,   50
    Take heed of perjury; thou art on thy deathbed.

DESDEMONA: Ay, but not yet to die.

OTHELLO: Presently°.
    Therefore confess thee freely of thy sin,
    For to deny each article° with oath
    Cannot remove nor choke the strong conception   55
    That I do groan withal. Thou art to die.

DESDEMONA: Then Lord have mercy on me.

OTHELLO: I say, amen.

DESDEMONA: And have you mercy too. I never did
    Offend you in my life; never loved Cassio
    But with such general warranty° of heaven   60
    As I might love. I never gave him token.

OTHELLO: By heaven, I saw my handkerchief in's hand!
    O perjured woman! thou dost stone° my heart,
    And mak'st me call what I intend to do
    A murder, which I thought a sacrifice.   65
    I saw the handkerchief.

DESDEMONA: He found it then.
    I never gave it him. Send for him hither.
    Let him confess a truth.

OTHELLO: He hath confessed.

DESDEMONA: What, my lord?

OTHELLO: That he hath used thee.

DESDEMONA: How? Unlawfully?

OTHELLO: Ay.   70

DESDEMONA: He will not say so.

OTHELLO: No, his mouth is stopped.
    Honest Iago hath ta'en order for't°.

DESDEMONA: O, my fear interprets. What, is he dead?

OTHELLO: Had all his hairs been lives, my great revenge
    Had stomach° for them all.   75

---

⁵²**Presently** immediately.
⁵⁴**article** item (of the charge of adultery. Othello makes heavy use of legal terms in this scene).
⁶⁰**warranty** allowance.
⁶³**stone** turn to stone.
⁷²**ta'en order for't** made sure of it.
⁷⁵**stomach** appetite.

DESDEMONA: Alas, he is betrayed, and I undone!

OTHELLO: Out, strumpet! Weep'st thou for him to my face?

DESDEMONA: O, banish me, my lord, but kill me not!

OTHELLO: Down, strumpet!

DESDEMONA: Kill me tomorrow; let me live tonight! 80

OTHELLO: Nay, if you strive—

DESDEMONA: But half an hour!

OTHELLO: Being done, there is no pause.

DESDEMONA: But while I say one prayer!

OTHELLO: It is too late.   *Smothers her.*

EMILIA *at the door.*

EMILIA [*Calls within*]: My lord, my lord! What, ho, my lord, my lord!

OTHELLO: What noise is this? Not dead? Not yet quite dead? 85
   I that am cruel am yet merciful;
   I would not have thee linger in thy pain.
   So, so.

EMILIA [*Within*]: What, ho! My lord, my lord!

OTHELLO: Who's there?

EMILIA: [*Within*]: O, good my lord, I would speak a word with you.

OTHELLO: Yes, 'tis Emilia.—By and by.—She's dead.— 90
   'Tis like she comes to speak of Cassio's death.
   The noise was high°. Ha! No more moving?
   Still as the grave.—Shall she come in? Were't good?—
   I think she stirs again. No.—What's best to do?
   If she come in, she'll sure speak to my wife. 95
   My wife! My wife! What wife? I have no wife.
   O, insupportable! O heavy hour!
   Methinks it should be now a huge eclipse
   Of sun and moon, and that th' affrighted globe
   Should yawn° at alteration.°

EMILIA [*Within*]:   I do beseech you 100
   That I may speak with you, O good my lord!

OTHELLO: I had forgot thee. O, come in, Emilia.
   Soft, by and by.—Let me the curtains draw.—
      [*Draws the bed hangings and then opens the door.*]
   Where art thou?

Enter EMILIA.

What's the matter with thee now?

---

⁹²**high** loud (Q1 reads ''here'').
⁹⁸⁻¹⁰⁰**Methinks . . . alteration** (the Elizabethans believed that great changes in human affairs were reflected by disorders in nature).
¹⁰⁰**yawn** gape open (as in an earthquake).

EMILIA: O my good lord, yonder's foul murders done! 105
OTHELLO: What? Now?
EMILIA: But now, my lord.
OTHELLO: It is the very error° of the moon.
　She comes more nearer earth than she was wont
　And makes men mad. 110
EMILIA: Cassio, my lord, hath killed a young Venetian
　Called Roderigo.
OTHELLO:　　　　　　Roderigo killed?
　And Cassio killed?
EMILIA:　　　　　　No, Cassio is not killed.
OTHELLO: Not Cassio killed? Then murder's out of tune,
　And sweet revenge grows harsh. 115
DESDEMONA: O, falsely, falsely murdered!
EMILIA:　　　　　　　　　　O Lord! What cry is that?
OTHELLO: That? What?
EMILIA: Out and alas! that was my lady's voice.
　Help! Help, ho! Help! O lady, speak again!
　Sweet Desdemona! O sweet mistress, speak! 120
DESDEMONA: A guiltless death I die.
EMILIA: O, who hath done this deed?
DESDEMONA: Nobody—I myself. Farewell.
　Commend me to my kind lord. O, farewell! 　　　[*She dies.*]
OTHELLO: Why, how should she be murd'red?
EMILIA:　　　　　　　　　　Alas, who knows? 125
OTHELLO: You heard her say herself, it was not I.
EMILIA: She said so. I must needs report the truth.
OTHELLO: She's like a liar gone to burning hell!
　'Twas I that killed her.
EMILIA:　　　　　　O, the more angel she,
　And you the blacker devil! 130
OTHELLO: She turned to folly, and she was a whore.
EMILIA: Thou dost belie her, and thou art a devil.
OTHELLO: She was false as water.
EMILIA:　　　　　　　　Thou art rash as fire to say
　That she was false. O, she was heavenly true!
OTHELLO: Cassio did top her. Ask thy husband else. 135
　O, I were damned beneath all depth in hell
　But that I did proceed upon just grounds
　To this extremity. Thy husband knew it all.

---

[108]**error** wandering out of regular course (disorders in the heavens were believed by some to cause disorders on earth, as well as vice versa).

EMILIA: My husband?

OTHELLO: Thy husband.

EMILIA: That she was false to wedlock?

OTHELLO: Ay, with Cassio. Had she been true,   140
   If heaven would make me such another world
   Of one entire and perfect chrysolite°,
   I'd not have sold her for it.

EMILIA: My husband?

OTHELLO: Ay, 'twas he that told me on her first.
   An honest man he is, and hates the slime   145
   That sticks on filthy deeds.

EMILIA: My husband?

OTHELLO: What needs this iterance? Woman, I say thy husband.

EMILIA: O mistress, villainy hath made mocks with love!
   My husband say she was false?

OTHELLO: He, woman.
   I say, thy husband. Dost understand the word?   150
   My friend, thy husband; honest, honest Iago.

EMILIA: If he say so, may his pernicious soul
   Rot half a grain a day! He lies to th' heart.
   She was too fond of her most filthy bargain.

OTHELLO: Hah?   155

EMILIA: Do thy worst.
   This deed of thine is no more worthy heaven
   Than thou wast worthy her.

OTHELLO: Peace, you were best.°

EMILIA: Thou hast not half that pow'r to do me harm
   As I have to be hurt. O gull! O dolt!   160
   As ignorant as dirt! Thou hast done a deed—

[OTHELLO *moves to draw his sword.*]

   I care not for thy sword; I'll make thee known,
   Though I lost twenty lives. Help! Help! Ho! Help!
   The Moor hath killed my mistress! Murder! murder!

Enter MONTANO, GRATIANO, *and* IAGO [*and Others*].

MONTANO: What is the matter? How now, general?   165

EMILIA: O, are you come, Iago? You have done well,
   That men must lay their murders on your neck.

GRATIANO: What is the matter?

---

¹⁴²**chrysolite** topaz.
¹⁵⁸**Peace, you were best** i.e., you had better be silent.

EMILIA: Disprove this villain, if thou be'st a man.
He says thou told'st him that his wife was false.   170
I know thou didst not; thou'rt not such a villain.
Speak, for my heart is full.
IAGO: I told him what I thought, and told no more
Than what he found himself was apt and true.
EMILIA: But did you ever tell him she was false?   175
IAGO: I did.
EMILIA: You told a lie, an odious damnèd lie!
Upon my soul, a lie! A wicked lie!
She false with Cassio? Did you say with Cassio?
IAGO: With Cassio, mistress. Go to, charm° your tongue.   180
EMILIA: I will not charm my tongue; I am bound to speak:
My mistress here lies murdered in her bed.
ALL: O heavens forfend!
EMILIA: And your reports have set the murder on.
OTHELLO: Nay, stare not, masters. It is true indeed.   185
GRATIANO: 'Tis a strange truth.
MONTANO: O monstrous act!
EMILIA: Villainy, villainy, villainy!
I think upon't—I think I smell't!—O villainy!
I thought so then.—I'll kill myself for grief.—
O villainy, villainy!   190
IAGO: What, are you mad? I charge you get you home.
EMILIA: Good gentlemen, let me have leave to speak.
'Tis proper I obey him, but not now.
Perchance, Iago, I will ne'er go home.
OTHELLO: O! O! O!   [*Falls on the bed.*]
EMILIA: Nay, lay thee down and roar,   195
For thou hast killed the sweetest innocent
That e'er did lift up eye.
OTHELLO: O, she was foul!   [*Rises.*]
I scarce did know you, uncle. There lies your niece,
Whose breath, indeed, these hands have newly stopped.   200
I know this act shows horrible and grim.
GRATIANO: Poor Desdemon! I am glad thy father's dead.
Thy match was mortal to him, and pure grief
Shore his old thread in twain. Did he live now,
This sight would make him do a desperate turn;   205
Yea, curse his better angel from his side,
And fall to reprobation°.

180**charm** control.
207**reprobation** damnation.

OTHELLO: 'Tis pitiful; but yet Iago knows
  That she with Cassio hath the act of shame
  A thousand times committed. Cassio confessed it;   210
  And she did gratify his amorous works
  With that recognizance and pledge of love,
  Which I first gave her. I saw it in his hand.
  It was a handkerchief, an antique token
  My father gave my mother.   215
EMILIA: O God! O heavenly God!
IAGO: Zounds, hold your peace!
EMILIA: 'Twill out, 'twill out! I peace?
  No, I will speak as liberal as the north°.
  Let heaven and men and devils, let them all,
  All, all, cry shame against me, yet I'll speak.   220
IAGO: Be wise, and get you home.
EMILIA: I will not.

[IAGO *draws and threatens* EMILIA.]

GRATIANO: Fie! Your sword upon a woman?
EMILIA: O thou dull Moor, that handkerchief thou speak'st of
  I found by fortune, and did give my husband;
  For often with a solemn earnestness—   225
  More than indeed belonged to such a trifle—
  He begged of me to steal't.
IAGO: Villainous whore!
EMILIA: She give it Cassio? No, alas, I found it,
  And I did give't my husband.
IAGO: Filth, thou liest!
EMILIA: By heaven, I do not, I do not, gentlemen.   230
  O murd'rous coxcomb! What should such a fool
  Do with so good a wife?
OTHELLO: Are there no stones° in heaven
  But what serves for the thunder? Precious villain!

[*The* MOOR *runs at* IAGO, *but is disarmed by* MONTANO. IAGO *kills his wife.*]

GRATIANO: The woman falls. Sure he hath killed his wife.
EMILIA: Ay, ay. O, lay me by my mistress' side.   [*Exit* IAGO.]   235
GRATIANO: He's gone, but his wife's killed.
MONTANO: 'Tis a notorious° villain. Take you this weapon,

---

²¹⁸**liberal as the north** freely (and bitingly) as the north wind blows.
²³²**stones** thunderbolts.
²³⁷**notorious** out-and-out.

Which I have recovered from the Moor.
Come, guard the door without. Let him not pass,
But kill him rather. I'll after that same villain,   240
For 'tis a damnèd slave.   *Exit [with all but* OTHELLO *and* EMILIA].
OTHELLO: I am not valiant neither;
But every puny whipster° gets my sword.
But why should honor outlive honesty?
Let it go all.
EMILIA: What did thy song bode, lady?
Hark, canst thou hear me? I will play the swan,   245
And die in music. [*Sings*] "Willow, willow, willow."
Moor, she was chaste. She loved thee, cruel Moor,
So come my soul to bliss as I speak true.
So speaking as I think, alas, I die.   [*She dies.*]
OTHELLO: I have another weapon in this chamber;   250
It was a sword of Spain, the ice-brook's temper.
O, here it is.—Uncle, I must come forth.
GRATIANO [*Within*]: If thou attempt it, it will cost thee dear.
Thou hast no weapon, and perforce must suffer.
OTHELLO: Look in upon me then and speak with me,   255
Or, naked as I am, I will assault thee.

[*Enter* GRATIANO.]

GRATIANO: What is the matter?
OTHELLO: Behold, I have a weapon;
A better never did itself sustain
Upon a soldier's thigh. I have seen the day
That with this little arm and this good sword   260
I have made my way through more impediments
Than twenty times your stop. But O vain boast!
Who can control his fate? 'Tis not so now.
Be not afraid, though you do see me weaponed.
Here is my journey's end, here is my butt°,   265
And very seamark of my utmost sail°.
Do you go back dismayed? 'Tis a lost fear.
Man but a rush° against Othello's breast.
And he retires. Where should Othello go?
Now, how dost thou look now? O ill-starred wench!   270
Pale as thy smock! When we shall meet at compt°,

---

²⁴²**puny whipster** small top-whipping boy (?).
²⁶⁵**butt** target, stopping place.
²⁶⁶**seamark of my utmost sail** maker of my furthest journey.
²⁶⁸**Man but a rush** attack with only a reed.
²⁷¹**compt** Judgment Day.

This look of thine will hurl my soul from heaven,
And fiends will snatch at it. Cold, cold, my girl?
Even like thy chastity.
O cursèd, cursèd slave! Whip me, ye devils,   275
From the possession of° this heavenly sight!
Blow me about in winds! roast me in sulfur!
Wash me in steep-down gulfs of liquid fire!
O Desdemon! Dead Desdemon; dead. O! O!

     Enter LODOVICO, CASSIO, MONTANO, *and* IAGO *[as prisoner,] with Officers.*

LODOVICO: Where is this rash and most unfortunate man?   280
OTHELLO: That's he that was Othello? Here I am.
LODOVICO: Where is that viper? Bring the villain forth.
OTHELLO: I look down towards his feet°—but that's a fable.
  If that thou be'st a devil, I cannot kill thee.   *[Wounds* IAGO.]
LODOVICO: Wrench his sword from him.   [OTHELLO *is disarmed.]*
IAGO: I bleed, sir, but not killed.   285
OTHELLO: I am not sorry neither. I'd have thee live;
  For in my sense, 'tis happiness to die.
LODOVICO: O thou Othello that was once so good,
  Fall'n in the practice° of a cursèd slave,
  What shall be said to thee?
OTHELLO: Why, anything: 290
  An honorable murderer, if you will;
  For naught I did in hate, but all in honor.
LODOVICO: This wretch hath part confessed his villainy.
  Did you and he consent in Cassio's death?
OTHELLO: Ay.   295
CASSIO: Dear general, I never gave you cause.
OTHELLO: I do believe it, and I ask your pardon.
  Will you, I pray, demand that demi-devil
  Why he hath thus ensnared my soul and body?
IAGO: Demand me nothing. What you know, you know.   300
  From this time forth I never will speak word.
LODOVICO: What, not to pray?
GRATIANO: Torments will ope your lips.
OTHELLO: Well, thou dost best.
LODOVICO: Sir, you shall understand what hath befall'n,
  Which, as I think, you know not. Here is a letter   305
  Found in the pocket of the slain Roderigo;

---

²⁷⁶**the possession of** being possessed by.
²⁸³**towards his feet** i.e., for his cloven hoofs.
²⁸⁹**practice** plotting.

And here another. The one of them imports
The death of Cassio to be undertook
By Roderigo.

OTHELLO: O villain!

CASSIO: Most heathenish and most gross!   310

LODOVICO: Now here's another discontented paper
  Found in his pocket too; and this, it seems,
  Roderigo meant t' have sent this damnèd villain;
  But that, belike, Iago in the interim
  Came in and satisfied him.

OTHELLO: O thou pernicious caitiff!   315
  How came you, Cassio, by that handkerchief
  That was my wife's?

CASSIO: I found it in my chamber;
  And he himself confessed it but even now
  That there he dropped it for a special purpose
  Which wrought to his desire.

OTHELLO: O fool! Fool! Fool!   320

CASSIO: There is besides in Roderigo's letter,
  How he upbraids Iago that he made him
  Brave me upon the watch; whereon it came
  That I was cast; and even but now he spake,
  After long seeming dead—Iago hurt him,   325
  Iago set him on.

LODOVICO: You must forsake this room and go with us.
  Your power and your command is taken off,
  And Cassio rules in Cyprus. For this slave,
  If there be any cunning cruelty   330
  That can torment him much and hold him long,
  It shall be his. You shall close prisoner rest
  Till that the nature of your fault be known
  To the Venetian state. Come, bring away.

OTHELLO: Soft you, a word or two before you go.   335
  I have done the state some service and they know't.
  No more of that. I pray you, in your letters,
  When you shall these unlucky deeds relate,
  Speak of me as I am. Nothing extenuate,
  Nor set down aught in malice. Then must you speak   340
  Of one that loved not wisely, but too well;
  Of one not easily jealous, but, being wrought,
  Perplexed in the extreme; of one whose hand,
  Like the base Judean°, threw a pearl away

---

³⁴⁴**Judean** (most editors use the Q1 reading, "Indian," here, but F is clear: both readings point toward the infidel, the unbeliever.)

Richer than all his tribe; of one whose subdued eyes,   345
Albeit unusèd to the melting mood,
Drops tears as fast as the Arabian trees
Their med'cinable gum. Set you down this.
And say besides that in Aleppo once,
Where a malignant and a turbaned Turk   350
Beat a Venetian and traduced the state,
I took by th' throat the circumcisèd dog
And smote him—thus.   [*He stabs himself.*]
LODOVICO: O bloody period!°
GRATIANO: All that is spoke is marred.
OTHELLO: I kissed thee ere I killed thee. No way but this,   355
    Killing myself, to die upon a kiss.   [*He falls over* DESDEMONA *and dies.*]
CASSIO: This did I fear, but thought he had no weapon;
    For he was great of heart.
LODOVICO [*To* IAGO]:   O Spartan dog,
    More fell° than anguish, hunger, or the sea!
    Look on the tragic loading of this bed.   360
    This is thy work. The object poisons sight;
    Let it be hid.   [*Bed curtains drawn.*]
                Gratiano, keep° the house,
    And seize upon the fortunes of the Moor,
    For they succeed on you. To you, lord governor,
    Remains the censure of this hellish villain,   365
    The time, the place, the torture. O, enforce it!
    Myself will straight aboard, and to the state
    This heavy act with heavy heart relate.   *Exeunt.*

Questions for *Othello*

1.   Readers often note that in this play each character is balanced by a similar or contrasting character—for example, Desdemona/Emilia, Desdemona/Iago, Cassio/Iago, and so on. Find as many contrasting pairs as you can, and discuss one or two of them that particularly interest you. (You may also wish to use your analysis as the basis for a writing assignment.)

2.   Contrast the two settings, Venice and Cyprus. How does the change in locale reflect changes in the social and psychological behavior of the characters?

---

[354]**period** end.
[359]**fell** cruel.
[362]**keep** remain in.

3.   What purposes does Scene iii of Act IV serve in furthering the action of the play?

4.   Why does Iago say he wants to undermine Othello? What do *you* think are his motives?

5.   Iago is able to deceive, in turn, Roderigo, Brabantio, Cassio, and Othello. Describe in some detail what methods he uses to manipulate each character.

6.   Pick a speech you find especially revealing of the character of Iago, and analyze what its imagery and meaning tell us about the speaker. Do the same for the character of Desdemona.

7.   Discuss the various images of women presented in this play. Pick one of the female characters and analyze how she contributes to the action of this tragedy.

8.   Does racism figure as a theme in this play? How important is Othello's blackness to the outcome of the drama?

9.   Find several instances in which characters switch from poetry to prose in their speeches, and analyze the reasons for—and effects of—the shifts to prose.

10.   If you were the director of a production of *Othello,* which stage or screen actors would you choose to play the principal roles? Choose a scene from the play and explain how you would block out the action in your production. Perhaps consider how the production would look if set in modern times.

11.   Contrast the Othello of Act I with the Othello of Act IV: Pick out two speeches that illustrate the change in his character and analyze how Shakespeare reveals and dramatizes this change.

12.   Aristotle said that despite all the suffering chronicled in tragedies, despite the dread and compassion they arouse in us, tragedies are ultimately not depressing to the audience. Do you agree? If so, why do you think this is true?

Henrik Ibsen (1828–1906)

Norway's best-known author grew up in poverty as a result of the bankruptcy of his father's business. At sixteen, Ibsen was apprenticed to a druggist for three years. In 1850 he published his first play, *Cataline,* a tragedy in verse. His early plays received little attention, but he earned great success with *The Pretenders* (1863), and was awarded a government travel grant that enabled him to move to Italy, where he spent nearly thirty years. It was during this period that Ibsen achieved prominence as a dramatist, often shocking audiences with the intense realism and daring content of his social dramas. In works such as *The League of Youth* (1869), *Pillars of Society* (1877), *A Doll House* (1879), and *Ghosts* (1881), Ibsen dealt with controversial social problems such as political corruption, the status of women, and venereal disease—topics that departed dramatically from the traditional concerns of the Scandinavian and continental theater. No other playwright has had more influence on the theater of the twentieth century.

A Doll House

Translated by Rolf Fjelde

CHARACTERS

TORVALD HELMER, *a lawyer*
NORA, *his wife*
DR. RANK
MRS. LINDE
NILS KROGSTAD, *a bank clerk*
THE HELMERS' THREE SMALL CHILDREN
ANNE-MARIE, *their nurse*
HELENE, *a maid*
A DELIVERY BOY

The action takes place in HELMER'S *residence.*

ACT I

A comfortable room, tastefully but not expensively furnished. A door to the right in the back wall leads to the entryway, another to the left leads to HELMER'S *study. Between these doors, a piano. Midway in the left-hand wall a door, and further back a window. Near the window a round table with an armchair and a small sofa. In the right-hand wall, toward the rear a door, and nearer the foreground a porcelain stove with two armchairs and a rocking chair beside it. Between the stove and the side door, a small table. Engravings on the walls. An étagère with china figures and other small art objects; a small bookcase with richly bound books; the floor carpeted; a fire burning in the stove. It is a winter day.*

A bell rings in the entryway; shortly after we hear the door being unlocked. NORA *comes into the room, humming happily to herself; she is wearing street clothes and carries an armload of packages, which she puts down on the table to the right. She has left the hall door open; and through it a* DELIVERY BOY *is seen, holding a Christmas tree and a basket which he gives to the* MAID *who let them in.*

NORA   Hide the tree well, Helene. The children mustn't get a glimpse of it till this evening, after it's trimmed. (*To the* DELIVERY BOY, *taking out her purse*) How much?

DELIVERY BOY   Fifty, ma'am.

NORA   There's a crown. No, keep the change. (*The* BOY *thanks her and leaves.* NORA *shuts the door. She laughs softly to herself while taking off her street things. Drawing a bag of macaroons from her pocket, she eats a couple, then steals over and listens at her husband's study door.*) Yes, he's home. (*Hums again as she moves to the table, right.*)

HELMER   (*from the study*) Is that my little lark twittering out there?

NORA   (*busy opening some packages*) Yes, it is.

HELMER   Is that my squirrel rummaging around?

NORA   Yes!

HELMER   When did my squirrel get in?

NORA   Just now. (*Putting the macaroon bag in her pocket and wiping her mouth*) Do come in, Torvald, and see what I've bought.

HELMER   Can't be disturbed. (*After a moment he opens the door and peers in, pen in hand.*) Bought, you say? All that there? Has the little spendthrift been out throwing money around again?

NORA   Oh, but Torvald, this year we really should let ourselves go a bit. It's the first Christmas we haven't had to economize.

HELMER   But you know we can't go squandering.

NORA   Oh yes, Torvald, we can squander a little now. Can't we? Just a tiny, wee bit. Now that you've got a big salary and are going to make piles and piles of money.

HELMER   Yes—starting New Year's. But then it's a full three months till the raise comes through.

NORA   Pooh! We can borrow that long.

HELMER   Nora! (*Goes over and playfully takes her by the ear*) Are your scatterbrains off again? What if today I borrowed a thousand crowns, and you squandered them over Christmas week, and then on New Year's Eve a roof tile fell on my head, and I lay there—

NORA *(putting her hand on his mouth)* Oh! Don't say such things!

HELMER Yes, but what if it happened—then what?

NORA If anything so awful happened, then it just wouldn't matter if I had debts or not.

HELMER Well, but the people I'd borrowed from?

NORA Them? Who cares about them! They're strangers.

HELMER Nora, Nora, how like a woman! No, but seriously, Nora, you know what I think about that. No debts! Never borrow! Something of freedom's lost—and something of beauty, too—from a home that's founded on borrowing and debt. We've made a brave stand up to now, the two of us; and we'll go right on like that the little while we have to.

NORA *(going toward the stove)* Yes, whatever you say, Torvald.

HELMER *(following her)* Now, now, the little lark's wings mustn't droop. Come on, don't be a sulky squirrel. *(Taking out his wallet)* Nora, guess what I have here.

NORA *(turning quickly)* Money!

HELMER There, see. *(Hands her some notes)* Good grief, I know how costs go up in a house at Christmastime.

NORA Ten—twenty—thirty—forty. Oh, thank you, Torvald; I can manage no end on this.

HELMER You really will have to.

NORA Oh yes, I promise I will! But come here so I can show you everything I bought. And so cheap! Look, new clothes for Ivar here—and a sword. Here a horse and a trumpet for Bob. And a doll and a doll's bed here for Emmy; they're nothing much, but she'll tear them to bits in no time anyway. And here I have dress material and handkerchiefs for the maids. Old Anne-Marie really deserves something more.

HELMER And what's in that package there?

NORA *(with a cry)* Torvald, no! You can't see that till tonight!

HELMER I see. But tell me now, you little prodigal, what have you thought of for yourself?

NORA For myself? Oh, I don't want anything at all.

HELMER Of course you do. Tell me just what—within reason—you'd most like to have.

NORA I honestly don't know. Oh, listen, Torvald—

HELMER Well?

NORA *(fumbling at his coat buttons, without looking at him)* If you want to give me something, then maybe you could—you could—

HELMER Come on, out with it.

NORA   *(hurriedly)* You could give me money, Torvald. No more than you think you can spare, then one of these days I'll buy something with it.

HELMER   But Nora—

NORA   Oh, please, Torvald darling, do that! I beg you, please. Then I could hang the bills in pretty gilt paper on the Christmas tree. Wouldn't that be fun?

HELMER   What are those little birds called that always fly through their fortunes?

NORA   Oh yes, spendthrifts. I know all that. But let's do as I say, Torvald; then I'll have time to decide what I really need most. That's very sensible, isn't it?

HELMER   *(smiling)* Yes, very—that is, if you actually hung onto the money I give you, and you actually used it to buy yourself something. But it goes for the house and for all sorts of foolish things, and then I only have to lay out some more.

NORA   Oh, but Torvald—

HELMER   Don't deny it, my dear little Nora. *(Putting his arm around her waist)* Spendthrifts are sweet, but they use up a frightful amount of money. It's incredible what it costs a man to feed such birds.

NORA   Oh, how can you say that! Really, I save everything I can.

HELMER   *(laughing)* Yes, that's the truth. Everything you can. But that's nothing at all.

NORA   *(humming, with a smile of quiet satisfaction)* Hm, if you only knew what expenses we larks and squirrels have, Torvald.

HELMER   You're an odd little one. Exactly the way your father was. You're never at a loss for scaring up money; but the moment you have it, it runs right out through your fingers; you never know what you've done with it. Well, one takes you as you are. It's deep in your blood. Yes, these things are hereditary, Nora.

NORA   Ah, I could wish I'd inherited many of Papa's qualities.

HELMER   And I couldn't wish you anything but just what you are, my sweet little lark. But wait; it seems to me you have a very— what should I call it?—a very suspicious look today—

NORA   I do?

HELMER   You certainly do. Look me straight in the eye.

NORA   *(looking at him)* Well?

HELMER   *(shaking an admonitory finger)* Surely my sweet tooth hasn't been running riot in town today, has she?

NORA   No. Why do you imagine that?

HELMER   My sweet tooth really didn't make a little detour through the confectioner's?

NORA   No, I assure you, Torvald—

HELMER   Hasn't nibbled some pastry?

NORA   No, not at all.

HELMER   Nor even munched a macaroon or two?

NORA   No, Torvald, I assure you, really—

HELMER   There, there now. Of course I'm only joking.

NORA   *(going to the table, right)* You know I could never think of going against you.

HELMER   No, I understand that; and you *have* given me your word. *(Going over to her)* Well, you keep your little Christmas secrets to yourself, Nora darling. I expect they'll come to light this evening, when the tree is lit.

NORA   Did you remember to ask Dr. Rank?

HELMER   No. But there's no need for that; it's assumed he'll be dining with us. All the same, I'll ask him when he stops by here this morning. I've ordered some fine wine. Nora, you can't imagine how I'm looking forward to this evening.

NORA   So am I. And what fun for the children, Torvald!

HELMER   Ah, it's so gratifying to know that one's gotten a safe, secure job, and with a comfortable salary. It's a great satisfaction, isn't it?

NORA   Oh, it's wonderful!

HELMER   Remember last Christmas? Three whole weeks before, you shut yourself in every evening till long after midnight, making flowers for the Christmas tree, and all the other decorations to surprise us. Ugh, that was the dullest time I've ever lived through.

NORA   It wasn't at all dull for me.

HELMER   *(smiling)* But the outcome *was* pretty sorry, Nora.

NORA   Oh, don't tease me with that again. How could I help it that the cat came in and tore everything to shreds.

HELMER   No, poor thing, you certainly couldn't. You wanted so much to please us all, and that's what counts. But it's just as well that the hard times are past.

NORA   Yes, it's really wonderful.

HELMER   Now I don't have to sit here alone, boring myself, and you don't have to tire your precious eyes and your fair little delicate hands—

NORA   *(clapping her hands)* No, is it really true, Torvald, I don't have to? Oh, how wonderfully lovely to hear! *(Taking his arm.)* Now I'll tell you just how I've thought we should plan things. Right after Christmas—*(The doorbell rings)* Oh, the bell. *(Straightening the room up a bit)* Somebody would have to come. What a bore!

HELMER   I'm not at home to visitors, don't forget.

MAID   *(from the hall doorway)* Ma'am, a lady to see you—

NORA   All right, let her come in.

MAID   *(to Helmer)* And the doctor's just come too.

HELMER   Did he go right to my study?

MAID   Yes, he did.

HELMER *goes into his room. The* MAID *shows in* MRS. LINDE, *dressed in traveling clothes, and shuts the door after her.*

MRS. LINDE   *(in a dispirited and somewhat hesitant voice)* Hello, Nora.

NORA   *(uncertain)* Hello—

MRS. LINDE   You don't recognize me.

NORA   No, I don't know—but wait, I think—*(Exclaiming)* What! Kristine! Is it really you?

MRS. LINDE   Yes, it's me.

NORA   Kristine! To think I didn't recognize you. But then, how could I? *(More quietly)* How you've changed, Kristine!

MRS. LINDE   Yes, no doubt I have. In nine—ten long years.

NORA   Is it so long since we met! Yes, it's all of that. Oh, these last eight years have been a happy time, believe me. And so now you've come in to town, too. Made the long trip in the winter. That took courage.

MRS. LINDE   I just got here by ship this morning.

NORA   To enjoy yourself over Christmas, of course. Oh, how lovely! Yes, enjoy ourselves, we'll do that. But take your coat off. You're not still cold? *(Helping her)* There now, let's get cozy here by the stove. No, the easy chair there! I'll take the rocker here. *(Seizing her hands)* Yes, now you have your old look again; it was only in that first moment. You're a bit more pale, Kristine—and maybe a bit thinner.

MRS. LINDE   And much, much older, Nora.

NORA   Yes, perhaps, a bit older; a tiny, tiny bit; not much at all. *(Stopping short; suddenly serious)* Oh, but thoughtless me, to sit here, chattering away. Sweet, good Kristine, can you forgive me?

MRS. LINDE   What do you mean, Nora?

NORA   *(softly)* Poor Kristine, you've become a widow.

MRS. LINDE   Yes, three years ago.

NORA   Oh, I knew it, of course; I read it in the papers. Oh Kristine, you must believe me; I often thought of writing you then, but I kept postponing it, and something always interfered.

MRS. LINDE   Nora dear, I understand completely.

NORA   No, it was awful of me, Kristine. You poor thing, how much you must have gone through. And he left you nothing?

MRS. LINDE   No.

NORA   And no children?

MRS. LINDE   No.

NORA   Nothing at all, then?

MRS. LINDE   Not even a sense of loss to feed on.

NORA *(looking incredulously at her)* But Kristine, how could that be?

MRS. LINDE *(smiling wearily and smoothing her hair)* Oh, sometimes it happens, Nora.

NORA So completely alone. How terribly hard that must be for you. I have three lovely children. You can't see them now; they're out with the maid. But now you must tell me everything—

MRS. LINDE No, no, no, tell me about yourself.

NORA No, you begin. Today I don't want to be selfish. I want to think only of you today. But there *is* something I must tell you. Did you hear of the wonderful luck we had recently?

Mrs. LINDE No, what's that?

NORA My husband's been made manager in the bank, just think!

MRS. LINDE Your husband? How marvelous!

NORA Isn't it? Being a lawyer is such an uncertain living, you know, especially if one won't touch any cases that aren't clean and decent. And of course Torvald would never do that, and I'm with him completely there. Oh, we're simply delighted, believe me! He'll join the bank right after New Year's and start getting a huge salary and lots of commissions. From now on we can live quite differently—just as we want. Oh, Kristine, I feel so light and happy! Won't it be lovely to have stacks of money and not a care in the world?

MRS. LINDE Well, anyway, it would be lovely to have enough for necessities.

NORA No, not just for necessities, but stacks and stacks of money!

MRS. LINDE *(smiling)* Nora, Nora, aren't you sensible yet? Back in school you were such a free spender.

NORA *(with a quiet laugh)* Yes, that's what Torvald still says. *(Shaking her finger)* But "Nora, Nora" isn't as silly as you all think. Really, we've been in no position for me to go squandering. We've had to work, both of us.

MRS. LINDE You too?

NORA Yes, at odd jobs—needlework, crocheting, embroidery, and such—*(Casually)* and other things too. You remember that Torvald left the department when we were married? There was no chance of promotion in his office, and of course he needed to earn more money. But that first year he drove himself terribly. He took on all kinds of extra work that kept him going morning and night. It wore him down, and then he fell deathly ill. The doctors said it was essential for him to travel south.

MRS. LINDE Yes, didn't you spend a whole year in Italy?

NORA That's right. It wasn't easy to get away, you know. Ivar had just been born. But of course we had to go. Oh, that was a beautiful trip, and it saved Torvald's life. But it cost a frightful sum, Kristine.

MRS. LINDE   I can well imagine.

NORA   Four thousand, eight hundred crowns it cost. That's really a lot of money.

MRS. LINDE   But it's lucky you had it when you needed it.

NORA   Well, as it was, we got it from Papa.

MRS. LINDE   I see. It was just about the time your father died.

NORA   Yes, just about then. And, you know, I couldn't make the trip out to nurse him. I had to stay here, expecting Ivar any moment, and with my poor sick Torvald to care for. Dearest Papa, I never saw him again, Kristine. Oh, that was the worst time I've known in all my marriage.

MRS. LINDE   I know how you loved him. And then you went off to Italy?

NORA   Yes. We had the means now, and the doctors urged us. So we left a month after.

MRS. LINDE   And your husband came back completely cured?

NORA   Sound as a drum!

MRS. LINDE   But—the doctor?

NORA   Who?

MRS. LINDE   I thought the maid said he was a doctor, the man who came in with me.

NORA   Yes, that was Dr. Rank—but he's not making a sick call. He's our closest friend, and he stops by at least once a day. No, Torvald hasn't had a sick moment since, and the children are fit and strong, and I am, too. *(Jumping up and clapping her hands)* Oh, dear God, Kristine, what a lovely thing to live and be happy! But how disgusting of me—I'm talking of nothing but my own affairs. *(Sits on a stool close by* KRISTINE, *arms resting across her knees)* Oh, don't be angry with me! Tell me, is it really true that you weren't in love with your husband? Why did you marry him, then?

MRS. LINDE   My mother was still alive, but bedridden and helpless—and I had two younger brothers to look after. In all conscience, I didn't think I could turn him down.

NORA   No, you were right there. But was he rich at the time?

MRS. LINDE   He was very well off, I'd say. But the business was shaky, Nora. When he died, it all fell apart, and nothing was left.

NORA   And then—?

MRS. LINDE   Yes, so I had to scrape up a living with a little shop and a little teaching and whatever else I could find. The last three years have been like one endless workday without a rest for me. Now it's over, Nora. My poor mother doesn't need me, for she's passed on. Nor the boys, either; they're working now and can take care of themselves.

NORA   How free you must feel—

MRS. LINDE   No—only unspeakably empty. Nothing to live for now. *(Standing up anxiously)* That's why I couldn't take it any longer out in that desolate hole. Maybe here it'll be easier to find something to do and keep my mind occupied. If I could only be lucky enough to get a steady job, some office work—

NORA   Oh, but Kristine, that's so dreadfully tiring, and you already look so tired. It would be much better for you if you could go off to a bathing resort.

MRS. LINDE   *(going toward the window)* I have no father to give me travel money, Nora.

NORA   *(rising)* Oh, don't be angry with me.

MRS. LINDE   *(going to her)* Nora dear, don't you be angry with me. The worst of my kind of situation is all the bitterness that's stored away. No one to work for, and yet you're always having to snap up your opportunities. You have to live; and so you grow selfish. When you told me the happy change in your lot, do you know I was delighted less for your sakes than for mine?

NORA   How so? Oh, I see. You think maybe Torvald could do something for you.

MRS. LINDE   Yes, that's what I thought.

NORA   And he will, Kristine! Just leave it to me; I'll bring it up so delicately—find something attractive to humor him with. Oh, I'm so eager to help you.

MRS. LINDE   How very kind of you, Nora, to be so concerned over me—doubly kind, considering you really know so little of life's burdens yourself.

NORA   I—? I know so little—?

MRS. LINDE   *(smiling)* Well, my heavens—a little needlework and such—Nora, you're just a child.

NORA   *(tossing her head and pacing the floor)* You don't have to act so superior.

MRS. LINDE   Oh?

NORA   You're just like the others. You all think I'm incapable of anything serious—

MRS. LINDE   Come now—

NORA   That I've never had to face the raw world.

MRS. LINDE   Nora dear, you've just been telling me all your troubles.

NORA   Hm! Trivia! *(Quietly)* I haven't told you the big thing.

MRS. LINDE   Big thing? What do you mean?

NORA   You look down on me so, Kristine, but you shouldn't. You're proud that you worked so long and hard for your mother.

MRS. LINDE   I don't look down on a soul. But it is true; I'm proud—and happy, too—to think it was given to me to make my mother's last days almost free of care.

NORA \ And you're also proud thinking of what you've done for your brothers.

MRS. LINDE I feel I've a right to be.

NORA I agree. But listen to this, Kristine—I've also got something to be proud and happy for.

MRS. LINDE I don't doubt it. But whatever do you mean?

NORA Not so loud. What if Torvald heard! He mustn't, not for anything in the world. Nobody must know, Kristine. No one but you.

MRS. LINDE But what is it, then?

NORA Come here. *(Drawing her down beside her on the sofa)* It's true—I've also got something to be proud and happy for. I'm the one who saved Torvald's life.

MRS. LINDE Saved—? Saved how?

NORA I told you about the trip to Italy. Torvald never would have lived if he hadn't gone south—

MRS. LINDE Of course, your father gave you the means—

NORA *(smiling)* That's what Torvald and all the rest think, but—

MRS. LINDE But—?

NORA Papa didn't give us a pin. I was the one who raised the money.

MRS. LINDE You? The whole amount?

NORA Four thousand, eight hundred crowns. What do you say to that?

MRS. LINDE But Nora, how was it possible? Did you win the lottery?

NORA *(disdainfully)* The lottery? Pooh! No art to that.

MRS. LINDE But where did you get it from then?

NORA *(humming, with a mysterious smile)* Hmm, tra-la-la-la.

MRS. LINDE Because you couldn't have borrowed it.

NORA No? Why not?

MRS. LINDE A wife can't borrow without her husband's consent.

NORA *(tossing her head)* Oh, but a wife with a little business sense, a wife who knows how to manage—

MRS. LINDE Nora, I simply don't understand—

NORA You don't have to. Whoever said I *borrowed* the money? I could have gotten it other ways. *(Throwing herself back on the sofa)* I could have gotten it from some admirer or other. After all, a girl with my ravishing appeal—

MRS. LINDE You lunatic.

NORA I'll bet you're eaten up with curiosity, Kristine.

MRS. LINDE Now listen here, Nora—you haven't done something indiscreet?

NORA *(sitting up again)* Is it indiscreet to save your husband's life?

MRS. LINDE   I think it's indiscreet that without his knowledge
you—

NORA   But that's the point: he mustn't know! My Lord, can't you
understand? He mustn't ever know the close call he had. It was
to *me* the doctors came to say his life was in danger—that
nothing could save him but a stay in the south. Didn't I try
strategy then! I began talking about how lovely it would be for
me to travel abroad like other young wives; I begged and I cried;
I told him please to remember my condition, to be kind and
indulge me; and then I dropped a hint that he could easily take
out a loan. But at that, Kristine, he nearly exploded. He said I
was frivolous, and it was his duty as man of the house not to
indulge me in whims and fancies—as I think he called them.
Aha, I thought, now you'll just have to be saved—and that's
when I saw my chance.

MRS. LINDE   And your father never told Torvald the money wasn't
from him?

NORA   No, never. Papa died right about then. I'd considered
bringing him into my secret and begging him never to tell. But
he was too sick at the time—and then, sadly, it didn't matter.

MRS. LINDE   And you've never confided in your husband since?

NORA   For heaven's sake, no! Are you serious? He's so strict on
that subject. Besides—Torvald, with all his masculine pride—
how painfully humiliating for him if he ever found out he was
in debt to me. That would just ruin our relationship. Our
beautiful happy home would never be the same.

MRS. LINDE   Won't you ever tell him?

NORA   *(thoughtfully, half smiling)* Yes—maybe sometime, years
from now, when I'm no longer so attractive. Don't laugh! I only
mean when Torvald loves me less than now, when he stops
enjoying my dancing and dressing up and reciting for him. Then
it might be wise to have something in reserve—*(Breaking off)*
How ridiculous! That'll never happen—Well, Kristine, what do
you think of my big secret? I'm capable of something too, hm?
You can imagine, of course, how this thing hangs over me. It
really hasn't been easy meeting the payments on time. In the
business world there's what they call quarterly interest and what
they call amortization, and these are always so terribly hard to
manage. I've had to skimp a little here and there, wherever I
could, you know. I could hardly spare anything from my house
allowance, because Torvald has to live well. I couldn't let the
children go poorly dressed; whatever I got for them, I felt I had
to use up completely—the darlings!

MRS. LINDE   Poor Nora, so it had to come out of your own budget,
then?

NORA   Yes, of course. But I was the one most responsible, too.

Every time Torvald gave me money for new clothes and such, I never used more than half; always bought the simplest, cheapest outfits. It was a godsend that everything looks so well on me that Torvald never noticed. But it did weigh me down at times, Kristine. It *is* such a joy to wear fine things. You understand.

MRS. LINDE   Oh, of course.

NORA   And then I found other ways of making money. Last winter I was lucky enough to get a lot of copying to do. I locked myself in and sat writing every evening till late in the night. Ah, I was tired so often, dead tired. But still it was wonderful fun, sitting and working like that, earning money. It was almost like being a man.

MRS. LINDE   But how much have you paid off this way so far?

NORA   That's hard to say, exactly. These accounts, you know, aren't easy to figure. I only know that I've paid out all I could scrape together. Time and again I haven't known where to turn. *(Smiling)* Then I'd sit here dreaming of a rich old gentleman who had fallen in love with me—

MRS. LINDE   What! Who is he?

NORA   Oh, really! And that he'd died, and when his will was opened, there in big letters it said, "All my fortune shall be paid over in cash, immediately, to that enchanting Mrs. Nora Helmer."

MRS. LINDE   But Nora dear—who *was* this gentleman?

NORA   Good grief, can't you understand? The old man never existed; that was only something I'd dream up time and again whenever I was at my wits' end for money. But it makes no difference now; the old fossil can go where he pleases for all I care; I don't need him or his will—because now I'm free. *(Jumping up)* Oh, how lovely to think of that, Kristine! Carefree! To know you're carefree, utterly carefree, to be able to romp and play with the children, and to keep up a beautiful, charming home—everything just the way Torvald likes it! And think, spring is coming, with big blue skies. Maybe we can travel a little then. Maybe I'll see the ocean again. Oh yes, it *is* so marvelous to live and be happy!

(The front doorbell rings.)

MRS. LINDE   *(rising)* There's the bell. It's probably best that I go.

NORA   No, stay. No one's expected. It must be for Torvald.

MAID   *(from the hall doorway)* Excuse me, ma'am—there's a gentleman here to see Mr. Helmer, but I didn't know—since the doctor's with him—

NORA   Who is the gentleman?

KROGSTAD   *(from the doorway)* It's me, Mrs. Helmer.

(MRS. LINDE *starts and turns away toward the window.*)

NORA   *(stepping toward him, tense, her voice a whisper)* You? What is it? Why do you want to speak to my husband?

KROGSTAD   Bank business—after a fashion. I have a small job in the investment bank, and I hear now your husband is going to be our chief—

NORA   In other words, it's—

KROGSTAD   Just dry business, Mrs. Helmer. Nothing but that.

NORA   Yes, then please be good enough to step into the study. *(She nods indifferently, as she sees him out by the hall door, then returns and begins stirring up the stove.)*

MRS. LINDE   Nora—who was that man?

NORA   That was a Mr. Krogstad—a lawyer.

MRS. LINDE   Then it really was him.

NORA   Do you know that person?

MRS. LINDE   I did once—many years ago. For a time he was a law clerk in our town.

NORA   Yes, he's been that.

MRS. LINDE   How he's changed.

NORA   I understand he had a very unhappy marriage.

MRS. LINDE   He's a widower now.

NORA   With a number of children. There now, it's burning. *(She closes the stove door and moves the rocker a bit to one side.)*

MRS. LINDE   They say he has a hand in all kinds of business.

NORA   Oh? That may be true; I wouldn't know. But let's not think about business. It's so dull.

(DR. RANK *enters from* HELMER'S *study.*)

RANK   *(still in the doorway)* No, no, really—I don't want to intrude, I'd just as soon talk a little while with your wife. *(Shuts the door, then notices* MRS. LINDE*)* Oh, beg pardon, I'm intruding here too.

NORA   No, not at all. *(Introducing him)* Dr. Rank, Mrs. Linde.

RANK   Well now, that's a name much heard in this house. I believe I passed the lady on the stairs as I came.

MRS. LINDE   Yes, I take the stairs very slowly. They're rather hard on me.

RANK   Uh-hm, some touch of internal weakness?

MRS. LINDE   More overexertion, I'd say.

RANK   Nothing else? Then you're probably here in town to rest up in a round of parties?

MRS. LINDE   I'm here to look for work.

RANK   Is that the best cure for overexertion?

MRS. LINDE   One has to live, Doctor.

RANK   Yes, there's a common prejudice to that effect.

NORA   Oh, come on, Dr. Rank—you really do want to live yourself.

RANK   Yes, I really do. Wretched as I am, I'll gladly prolong my torment indefinitely. All my patients feel like that. And it's quite the same, too, with the morally sick. Right at this moment there's one of those moral invalids in there with Helmer—

MRS. LINDE   *(softly)* Ah!

NORA   Who do you mean?

RANK   Oh, it's a lawyer, Krogstad, a type you wouldn't know. His character is rotten to the root—but even he began chattering all-importantly about how he had to *live.*

NORA   Oh? What did he want to talk to Torvald about?

RANK   I really don't know. I only heard something about the bank.

NORA   I didn't know that Krog—that this man Krogstad had anything to do with the bank.

RANK   Yes, he's gotten some kind of berth down there. (*To* MRS. LINDE) I don't know if you also have, in your neck of the woods, a type of person who scuttles about breathlessly, sniffing out hints of moral corruption, and then maneuvers his victim into some sort of key position where he can keep an eye on him. It's the healthy these days that are out in the cold.

MRS. LINDE   All the same, it's the sick who most need to be taken in.

RANK   *(with a shrug)* Yes, there we have it. That's the concept that's turning society into a sanatorium.

(NORA, *lost in her thoughts, breaks out into quiet laughter and claps her hands.*)

RANK   Why do you laugh at that? Do you have any real idea of what society is?

NORA   What do I care about dreary old society? I was laughing at something quite different—something terribly funny. Tell me, Doctor—is everyone who works in the bank dependent now on Torvald?

RANK   Is that what you find so terribly funny?

NORA   *(smiling and humming)* Never mind, never mind! *(Pacing the floor)* Yes, that's really immensely amusing: that we—that Torvald has so much power now over all those people. *(Taking the bag out of her pocket)* Dr. Rank, a little macaroon on that?

RANK   See here, macaroons! I thought they were contraband here.

NORA   Yes, but these are some that Kristine gave me.

MRS. LINDE   What? I—?

NORA   Now, now, don't be afraid. You couldn't possibly know that Torvald had forbidden them. You see, he's worried they'll ruin my teeth. But hmp! Just this once! Isn't that so, Dr. Rank? Help yourself! *(Puts a macaroon in his mouth)* And you too, Kristine. And I'll also have one, only a little one—or two, at the most. *(Walking about again)* Now I'm really tremendously happy. Now there's just one last thing in the world that I have an enormous desire to do.

RANK   Well! And what's that?

NORA   It's something I have such a consuming desire to say so Torvald could hear.

RANK   And why can't you say it?

NORA   I don't dare. It's quite shocking.

MRS. LINDE   Shocking?

RANK   Well, then it isn't advisable. But in front of us you certainly can. What do you have such a desire to say so Torvald could hear?

NORA   I have such a huge desire to say—to hell and be damned!

RANK   Are you crazy?

MRS. LINDE   My goodness, Nora!

RANK   Go on, say it. Here he is.

NORA   *(hiding the macaroon bag)* Shh, shh, shh!

(HELMER *comes in from his study, hat in hand, overcoat over his arm.*)

NORA   *(going toward him)* Well, Torvald dear, are you through with him?

HELMER   Yes, he just left.

NORA   Let me introduce you—this is Kristine, who's arrived here in town.

HELMER   Kristine—? I'm sorry, but I don't know—

NORA   Mrs. Linde, Torvald dear. Mrs. Kristine Linde.

HELMER   Of course. A childhood friend of my wife's, no doubt?

MRS. LINDE   Yes, we knew each other in those days.

NORA   And just think, she made the long trip down here in order to talk with you.

HELMER   What's this?

MRS. LINDE   Well, not exactly—

NORA   You see, Kristine is remarkably clever in office work, and so she's terribly eager to come under a capable man's supervision and add more to what she already knows—

HELMER   Very wise, Mrs. Linde.

NORA   And then when she heard that you'd become a bank manager—the story was wired out to the papers—then she came in as fast as she could and—Really, Torvald, for my sake you can do a little something for Kristine, can't you?

HELMER   Yes, it's not at all impossible. Mrs. Linde, I suppose you're a widow?

MRS. LINDE   Yes.

HELMER   Any experience in office work?

MRS. LINDE   Yes, a good deal.

HELMER   Well, it's quite likely that I can make an opening for you—

NORA   *(clapping her hands)* You see, you see!

HELMER   You've come at a lucky moment, Mrs. Linde.

MRS. LINDE   Oh, how can I thank you?

HELMER   Not necessary. *(Putting his overcoat on)* But today you'll have to excuse me—

RANK   Wait, I'll go with you. *(He fetches his coat from the hall and warms it at the stove.)*

NORA   Don't stay out long, dear.

HELMER   An hour; no more.

NORA   Are you going too, Kristine?

MRS. LINDE   *(putting on her winter garments)* Yes, I have to see about a room now.

HELMER   Then perhaps we can all walk together.

NORA   *(helping her)* What a shame we're so cramped here, but it's quite impossible for us to—

MRS. LINDE   Oh, don't even think of it! Good-bye, Nora dear, and thanks for everything.

NORA   Good-bye for now. Of course you'll be back again this evening. And you too, Dr. Rank. What? If you're well enough? Oh, you've got to be! Wrap up tight now.

(In a ripple of small talk the company moves out into the hall; children's voices are heard outside on the steps.)

NORA   There they are! There they are! *(She runs to open the door. The children come in with their nurse,* ANNE-MARIE.*)* Come in, come in! *(Bends down and kisses them)* Oh, you darlings—! Look at them, Kristine. Aren't they lovely!

RANK   No loitering in the draft here.

HELMER   Come, Mrs. Linde—this place is unbearable now for anyone but mothers.

(DR. RANK, HELMER, and MRS. LINDE *go down the stairs.* ANNE-MARIE *goes into the living room with the children.* NORA *follows, after closing the hall door.)*

NORA   How fresh and strong you look. Oh, such red cheeks you have! Like apples and roses. *(The children interrupt her throughout the following.)* And it was so much fun? That's wonderful. Really? You pulled both Emmy and Bob on the sled? Imagine, all together! Yes, you're a clever boy, Ivar. Oh, let me hold her a bit, Anne-Marie. My sweet little doll baby! *(Takes the smallest from the nurse and dances with her)* Yes, yes, Mama will dance with Bob as well. What? Did you throw snowballs? Oh, if I'd only been there! No, don't bother, Anne-Marie—I'll undress them myself. Oh yes, let me. It's such fun. Go in and rest; you look half frozen. There's hot coffee waiting for you on the stove. *(The nurse goes into the room to the left. Nora takes the children's winter things off, throwing them about, while the children talk to her all at once.)*

Is that so? A big dog chased you? But it didn't bite? No, dogs never bite little, lovely doll babies. Don't peek in the packages, Ivar! What is it? Yes, wouldn't you like to know. No, no, it's an ugly something. Well? Shall we play? What shall we play? Hide-and-seek? Yes, let's play hide-and-seek. Bob must hide first. I must? Yes, let me hide first. *(Laughing and shouting, she and the children play in and out of the living room and the adjoining room to the right. At last NORA hides under the table. The children come storming in, search, but cannot find her, then hear her muffled laughter, dash over to the table, lift the cloth and find her. Wild shouting. She creeps forward as if to scare them. More shouts. Meanwhile, a knock at the hall door; no one has noticed it. Now the door half opens, and KROGSTAD appears. He waits a moment; the game goes on.)*

KROGSTAD   Beg pardon, Mrs. Helmer—

NORA   *(with a strangled cry, turning and scrambling to her knees)* Oh! what do you want?

KROGSTAD   Excuse me. The outer door was ajar; it must be someone forgot to shut it—

NORA   *(rising)* My husband isn't home, Mr. Krogstad.

KROGSTAD   I know that.

NORA   Yes—then what do you want here?

KROGSTAD   A word with you.

NORA   With—? *(To the children, quietly)* Go in to Anne-Marie. What? No, the strange man won't hurt Mama. When he's gone, we'll play some more. *(She leads the children into the room to the left and shuts the door after them. Then, tense and nervous)* You want to speak to me?

KROGSTAD   Yes, I want to.

NORA   Today? But it's not yet the first of the month—

KROGSTAD   No, it's Christmas Eve. It's going to be up to you how merry a Christmas you have.

NORA   What is it you want? Today I absolutely can't—

KROGSTAD   We won't talk about that till later. This is something else. You do have a moment to spare, I suppose?

NORA   Oh yes, of course—I do, except—

KROGSTAD   Good. I was sitting over at Olsen's Restaurant when I saw your husband go down the street—

NORA   Yes?

KROGSTAD   With a lady.

NORA   Yes. So?

KROGSTAD   If you'll pardon my asking: wasn't that lady a Mrs.
Linde?

NORA   Yes.

KROGSTAD   Just now come into town?

NORA   Yes, today.

KROGSTAD   She's a good friend of yours?

NORA   Yes, she is. But I don't see—

KROGSTAD   I also knew her once.

NORA   I'm aware of that.

KROGSTAD   Oh? You know all about it. I thought so, Well, then let
me ask you short and sweet: is Mrs. Linde getting a job at the
bank?

NORA   What makes you think you can cross-examine me, Mr.
Krogstad—you, one of my husband's employees? But since you
ask, you might as well know—yes, Mrs. Linde's going to be
taken on at the bank. And I'm the one who spoke for her, Mr.
Krogstad. Now you know.

KROGSTAD   So I guessed right.

NORA   *(pacing up and down)* Oh, one does have a tiny bit of
influence, I should hope. Just because I am a woman, don't
think it means that—When one has a subordinate position, Mr.
Krogstad, one really ought to be careful about pushing
somebody who—hm—

KROGSTAD   Who has influence?

NORA   That's right.

KROGSTAD   *(in a different tone)* Mrs. Helmer, would you be good
enough to use your influence on my behalf?

NORA   What? What do you mean?

KROGSTAD   Would you please make sure that I keep my
subordinate position in the bank?

NORA   What does that mean? Who's thinking of taking away
your position?

KROGSTAD   Oh, don't play the innocent with me. I'm quite aware
that your friend would hardly relish the chance of running into
me again; and I'm also aware now whom I can thank for being
turned out.

NORA   But I promise you—

KROGSTAD   Yes, yes, yes, to the point: there's still time, and I'm
advising you to use your influence to prevent it.

NORA   But Mr. Krogstad, I have absolutely no influence.

KROGSTAD   You haven't? I thought you were just saying—

NORA   You shouldn't take me so literally. I! How can you believe
that I have any such influence over my husband?

KROGSTAD   Oh, I've known your husband from our student days. I don't think the great bank manager's more steadfast than any other married man.

NORA   You speak insolently about my husband, and I'll show you the door.

KROGSTAD   The lady has spirit.

NORA   I'm not afraid of you any longer. After New Year's, I'll soon be done with the whole business.

KROGSTAD   *(restraining himself)* Now listen to me, Mrs. Helmer. If necessary, I'll fight for my little job in the bank as if it were life itself.

NORA   Yes, so it seems.

KROGSTAD   It's not just a matter of income; that's the least of it. It's something else—All right, out with it! Look, this is the thing. You know, just like all the others, of course, that once, a good many years ago, I did something rather rash.

NORA   I've heard rumors to that effect.

KROGSTAD   The case never got into court; but all the same, every door was closed in my face from then on. So I took up those various activities you know about. I had to grab hold somewhere; and I dare say I haven't been among the worst. But now I want to drop all that. My boys are growing up. For their sakes, I'll have to win back as much respect as possible here in town. That job in the bank was like the first rung in my ladder. And now your husband wants to kick me right back down in the mud again.

NORA   But for heaven's sake, Mr. Krogstad, it's simply not in my power to help you.

KROGSTAD   That's because you haven't the will to—but I have the means to make you.

NORA   You certainly won't tell my husband that I owe you money?

KROGSTAD   Hm—what if I told him that?

NORA   That would be shameful of you. *(Nearly in tears)* This secret—my joy and my pride—that he should learn it in such a crude and disgusting way—learn it from you. You'd expose me to the most horrible unpleasantness—

KROGSTAD   Only unpleasantness?

NORA   *(vehemently)* But go on and try. It'll turn out the worst for you, because then my husband will really see what a crook you are, and then you'll *never* be able to hold your job.

KROGSTAD   I asked if it was just domestic unpleasantness you were afraid of?

NORA   If my husband finds out, then of course he'll pay what I owe at once, and then we'd be through with you for good.

KROGSTAD   *(a step closer)* Listen, Mrs. Helmer—you've either got a very bad memory, or else no head at all for business. I'd better put you a little more in touch with the facts.

NORA   What do you mean?

KROGSTAD   When your husband was sick, you came to me for a loan of four thousand, eight hundred crowns.

NORA   Where else could I go?

KROGSTAD   I promised to get you that sum—

NORA   And you got it.

KROGSTAD   I promised to get you that sum, on certain conditions. You were so involved in your husband's illness, and so eager to finance your trip, that I guess you didn't think out all the details. It might just be a good idea to remind you. I promised you the money on the strength of a note I drew up.

NORA   Yes, and that I signed.

KROGSTAD   Right. But at the bottom I added some lines for your father to guarantee the loan. He was supposed to sign down there.

NORA   Supposed to? He did sign.

KROGSTAD   I left the date blank. In other words, your father would have dated his signature himself. Do you remember that?

NORA   Yes, I think—

KROGSTAD   Then I gave you the note for you to mail to your father. Isn't that so?

NORA   Yes.

KROGSTAD   And naturally you sent it at once—because only some five, six days later you brought me the note, properly signed. And with that, the money was yours.

NORA   Well, then; I've made my payments regularly, haven't I?

KROGSTAD   More or less. But—getting back to the point—those were hard times for you then, Mrs. Helmer.

NORA   Yes, they were.

KROGSTAD   Your father was very ill, I believe.

NORA   He was near the end.

KROGSTAD   He died soon after?

NORA   Yes.

KROGSTAD   Tell me, Mrs. Helmer, do you happen to recall the date of your father's death? The day of the month, I mean.

NORA   Papa died the twenty-ninth of September.

KROGSTAD   That's quite correct; I've already looked into that. And now we come to a curious thing—*(Taking out a paper)* which I simply cannot comprehend.

NORA   Curious thing? I don't know—

KROGSTAD   This is the curious thing: that your father co-signed the note for your loan three days after his death.

NORA   How—? I don't understand.

KROGSTAD   Your father died the twenty-ninth of September. But look. Here your father dated his signature October second. Isn't that curious, Mrs. Helmer? (NORA *is silent.*) Can you explain it to me? (NORA *remains silent.*) It's also remarkable that the words "October second" and the year aren't written in your father's hand, but rather in one that I think I know. Well, it's easy to understand. Your father forgot perhaps to date his signature, and then someone or other added it, a bit sloppily, before anyone knew of his death. There's nothing wrong in that. It all comes down to the signature. And there's no question about *that,* Mrs.Helmer. It really *was* your father who signed his own name here, wasn't it?

NORA   *(after a short silence, throwing her head back and looking squarely at him)* No, it wasn't. I signed Papa's name.

KROGSTAD   Wait, now—are you fully aware that this is a dangerous confession?

NORA   Why? You'll soon get your money.

KROGSTAD   Let me ask you a question—why didn't you send the paper to your father?

NORA   That was impossible. Papa was so sick. If I'd asked him for his signature, I also would have had to tell him what the money was for. But I couldn't tell him, sick as he was, that my husband's life was in danger. That was just impossible.

KROGSTAD   Then it would have been better if you'd given up the trip abroad.

NORA   I couldn't possibly. The trip was to save my husband's life. I couldn't give that up.

KROGSTAD   But didn't you ever consider that this was a fraud against me?

NORA   I couldn't let myself be bothered by that. You weren't any concern of mine. I couldn't stand you, with all those cold complications you made, even though you knew how badly off my husband was.

KROGSTAD   Mrs. Helmer, obviously you haven't the vaguest idea of what you've involved yourself in. But I can tell you this: it was nothing more and nothing worse than I once did—and it wrecked my whole reputation.

NORA   You? Do you expect me to believe that you ever acted bravely to save your wife's life?

KROGSTAD   Laws don't inquire into motives.

NORA   Then they must be very poor laws.

KROGSTAD   Poor or not—if I introduce this paper in court, you'll be judged according to law.

NORA   This I refuse to believe. A daughter hasn't a right to protect her dying father from anxiety and care? A wife hasn't a right to save her husband's life? I don't know much about laws, but I'm sure that somewhere in the books these things are allowed. And you don't know anything about it—you who practice the law? You must be an awful lawyer, Mr. Krogstad.

KROGSTAD   Could be. But business—the kind of business we two are mixed up in—don't you think I know about that? All right. Do what you want now. But I'm telling you *this:* if I get shoved down a second time, you're going to keep me company.

> *(He bows and goes out through the hall.)*

NORA   *(pensive for a moment, then tossing her head)* Oh, really! Trying to frighten me! I'm not so silly as all that. *(Begins gathering up the children's clothes, but soon stops)* But—? No, but that's impossible! I did it out of love.

THE CHILDREN   *(in the doorway, left)* Mama, that strange man's gone out the door.

NORA   Yes, yes, I know it. But don't tell anyone about the strange man. Do you hear. Not even Papa!

THE CHILDREN   No, Mama. But now will you play again?

NORA   No, not now.

THE CHILDREN   Oh, but Mama, you promised.

NORA   Yes, but I can't now. Go inside; I have too much to do. Go in, go in, my sweet darlings. *(She herds them gently back in the room and shuts the door after them. Settling on the sofa, she takes up a piece of embroidery and makes some stitches, but soon stops abruptly.)* No! *(Throws the work aside, rises, goes to the hall door and calls out)* Helene! Let me have the tree in here. *(Goes to the table, left, opens the table drawer, and stops again)* No, but that's utterly impossible!

MAID   *(with the Christmas tree)* Where should I put it, Ma'am?

NORA   There. The middle of the floor.

MAID   Should I bring anything else?

NORA   No, thanks. I have what I need.

> *(The MAID, who has set the tree down, goes out.)*

NORA   *(absorbed in trimming the tree)* Candles here—and flowers here. That terrible creature! Talk, talk, talk! There's nothing to it at all. The tree's going to be lovely. I'll do anything to please you, Torvald. I'll sing for you, dance for you—

(HELMER comes in from the hall, with a sheaf of papers under his arm.)

NORA   Oh! You're back so soon?

HELMER   Yes. Has anyone been here?

NORA   Here? No.

HELMER   That's odd. I saw Krogstad leaving the front door.

NORA   So? Oh yes, that's true. Krogstad was here a moment.

HELMER   Nora, I can see by your face that he's been here, begging you to put in a good word for him.

NORA   Yes.

HELMER   And it was supposed to seem like your own idea? You
were to hide it from me that he'd been here. He asked you that,
too, didn't he?

NORA   Yes, Torvald, but—

HELMER   Nora, Nora, and you could fall for that? Talk with that
sort of person and promise him anything? And then in the
bargain, tell me an untruth.

NORA   An untruth—?

HELMER   Didn't you say that no one had been here? *(Wagging his
finger)* My little songbird must never do that again. A songbird
needs a clean beak to warble with. No false notes. *(Putting his
arm about her waist)* That's the way it should be, isn't it? Yes, I'm
sure of it. *(Releasing her)* And so, enough of that. *(Sitting by the
stove)* Ah, how snug and cozy it is here. *(Leafing among his papers)*

NORA   *(busy with the tree, after a short pause)* Torvald!

HELMER   Yes.

NORA   I'm so much looking forward to the Stenborg's costume
party, day after tomorrow.

HELMER   And I can't wait to see what you'll surprise me with.

NORA   Oh, that stupid business.

HELMER   What?

NORA   I can't find anything that's right. Everything seems so
ridiculous, so inane.

HELMER   So my little Nora's come to *that* recognition?

NORA   *(going behind his chair, her arms resting on its back)* Are you
very busy, Torvald?

HELMER   Oh—

NORA   What papers are those?

HELMER   Bank matters.

NORA   Already?

HELMER   I've gotten full authority from the retiring management
to make all necessary changes in personnel and procedure. I'll
need Christmas week for that. I want to have everything in
order by New Year's.

NORA   So that was the reason this poor Krogstad—

HELMER   Hm.

NORA   *(still leaning on the chair and slowly stroking the nape of his
neck)* If you weren't so very busy, I would have asked you an
enormous favor, Torvald.

HELMER   Let's hear. What is it?

NORA   You know, there isn't anyone who has your good taste—
and I want so much to look well at the costume party. Torvald,
couldn't you take over and decide what I should be and plan my
costume?

HELMER   Ah, is my stubborn little creature calling for a lifeguard?

NORA   Yes, Torvald, I can't get anywhere without your help.

HELMER   All right—I'll think it over. We'll hit on something.

NORA   Oh, how sweet of you. *(Goes to the tree again. Pause.)* Aren't the red flowers pretty—? But tell me, was it really such a crime that this Krogstad committed?

HELMER   Forgery. Do you have any idea what that means?

NORA   Couldn't he have done it out of need?

HELMER   Yes, or thoughtlessness, like so many others. I'm not so heartless that I'd condemn a man categorically for just one mistake.

NORA   No, of course not, Torvald!

HELMER   Plenty of men have redeemed themselves by openly confessing their crimes and taking their punishments.

NORA   Punishment—?

HELMER   But now Krogstad didn't go that way. He got himself out by sharp practices, and that's the real cause of his moral breakdown.

NORA   Do you really think that would—?

HELMER   Just imagine how a man with that sort of guilt in him has to lie and cheat and deceive on all sides, has to wear a mask even with the nearest and dearest he has, even with his own wife and children. And with the children, Nora—that's where it's most horrible.

NORA   Why?

HELMER   Because that kind of atmosphere of lies infects the whole life of a home. Every breath the children take in is filled with the terms of something degenerate.

NORA   *(coming closer behind him)* Are you sure of that?

HELMER   Oh, I've seen it often enough as a lawyer. Almost everyone who goes bad early in life has a mother who's a chronic liar.

NORA   Why just—the mother?

HELMER   It's usually the mother's influence that's dominant, but the father's works in the same way, of course. Every lawyer is quite familiar with it. And still this Krogstad's been going home year in, year out, poisoning his own children with lies and pretense; that's why I call him morally lost. *(Reaching his hands out toward her)* So my sweet little Nora must promise me never to plead his cause. Your hand on it. Come, come, what's this? Give me your hand. There, now. All settled. I can tell you it'd be impossible for me to work alongside of him. I literally feel physically revolted when I'm anywhere near such a person.

NORA   *(withdraws her hand and goes to the other side of the Christmas tree)* How hot it is here! And I've got so much to do.

HELMER   *(getting up and gathering his papers)* Yes, and I have to think about getting some of these read through before dinner. I'll think about your costume, too. And something to hang on the tree in gilt paper, I may even see about that. *(Putting his hand on her head)* Oh you, my darling little songbird.

> *(He goes into his study and closes the door after him.)*

NORA   *(softly, after a silence)* Oh, really! it isn't so. It's impossible. It must be impossible.

ANNE-MARIE   *(in the doorway, left)* The children are begging so hard to come in to Mama.

NORA   No, no, no, don't let them in to me! You stay with them, Anne-Marie.

ANNE-MARIE   Of course, Ma'am. *(Closes the door)*

NORA   *(pale with terror)* Hurt my children—! Poison my home? *(A moment's pause; then she tosses her head.)* That's not true. Never. Never in all the world.

ACT II

Same room. Beside the piano the Christmas tree now stands stripped of ornament, burned-down candle stubs on its ragged branches. NORA'S *street clothes lie on the sofa.* NORA, *alone in the room, moves restlessly about; at last she stops at the sofa and picks up her coat.*

NORA   *(dropping the coat again)* Someone's coming! *(Goes toward the door, listens)* No—there's no one. Of course—nobody's coming today, Christmas Day—or tomorrow, either. But maybe—*(Opens the door and looks out)* No, nothing in the mailbox. Quite empty. *(Coming forward)* What nonsense! He won't do anything serious. Nothing terrible could happen. It's impossible. Why, I have three small children.

(ANNE-MARIE, *with a large carton, comes in from the room to the left.*)

ANNE-MARIE   Well, at last I found the box with the masquerade clothes.

NORA   Thanks. Put it on the table.

ANNE-MARIE   *(does so)* But they're all pretty much of a mess.

NORA   Ahh! I'd love to rip them in a million pieces!

ANNE-MARIE   Oh, mercy, they can be fixed right up. Just a little patience.

NORA   Yes, I'll go get Mrs. Linde to help me.

ANNE-MARIE   Out again now? In this nasty weather? Miss Nora will catch cold—get sick.

NORA   Oh, worse things could happen—How are the children?

ANNE-MARIE   The poor mites are playing with their Christmas presents, but—

NORA   Do they ask for me much?

ANNE-MARIE   They're so used to having Mama around, you know.

NORA   Yes, but Anne-Marie, I *can't* be together with them as much as I was.

ANNE-MARIE   Well, small children get used to anything.

NORA   You think so? Do you think they'd forget their mother if she was gone for good?

ANNE-MARIE   Oh, mercy—gone for good!

NORA   Wait, tell me, Anne-Marie—I've wondered so often—how could you ever have the heart to give your child over to strangers?

ANNE-MARIE   But I had to, you know, to become little Nora's nurse.

NORA   Yes, but how could you *do* it?

ANNE-MARIE   When I could get such a good place? A girl who's poor and who's gotten in trouble is glad enough for that. Because that slippery fish, he didn't do a thing for me, you know.

NORA   But your daughter's surely forgotten you.

ANNE-MARIE   Oh, she certainly has not. She's written to me, both when she was confirmed and when she was married.

NORA   *(clasping her about the neck)* You old Anne-Marie, you were a good mother for me when I was little.

ANNE-MARIE   Poor little Nora, with no other mother but me.

NORA   And if the babies didn't have one, then I know that you'd—What silly talk! *(Opening the carton)* Go in to them. Now I'll have to—Tomorrow you can see how lovely I'll look.

ANNE-MARIE   Oh, there won't be anyone at the party as lovely as Miss Nora.

(She goes off into the room, left.)

NORA   *(begins unpacking the box, but soon throws it aside)* Oh, if I dared to go out. If only nobody would come. If only nothing would happen here while I'm out. What craziness—nobody's coming. Just don't think. This muff—needs a brushing. Beautiful gloves, beautiful gloves. Let it go. Let it go! One, two, three, four, five, six—*(With a cry)* Oh, there they are! *(Poises to move toward the door, but remains irresolutely standing.* MRS. LINDE *enters from the hall, where she has removed her street clothes.)*

NORA   Oh, it's you, Kristine. There's no one else out there? How good that you've come.

MRS. LINDE   I hear you were up asking for me.

NORA   Yes, I just stopped by. There's something you really can help me with. Let's get settled on the sofa. Look, there's going to be a costume party tomorrow evening at the Stenborgs' right above us, and now Torvald wants me to go as a Neapolitan peasant girl and dance the tarantella that I learned in Capri.

MRS. LINDE   Really, you are giving a whole performance?

NORA   Torvald says yes, I should. See, here's the dress. Torvald had it made for me down there; but now it's all so tattered that I just don't know—

MRS. LINDE   Oh, we'll fix that up in no time. It's nothing more than the trimmings—they're a bit loose here and there. Needle and thread? Good, now we have what we need.

NORA   Oh, how sweet of you!

MRS. LINDE   *(sewing)* So you'll be in disguise tomorrow, Nora. You know what? I'll stop by then for a moment and have a look at you all dressed up. But listen, I've absolutely forgotten to thank you for that pleasant evening yesterday.

NORA   *(getting up and walking about)* I don't think it was as pleasant as usual yesterday. You should have come to town a bit sooner, Kristine—Yes, Torvald really knows how to give a home elegance and charm.

MRS. LINDE   And you do, too, if you ask me. You're not your father's daughter for nothing. But tell me, is Dr. Rank always so down in the mouth as yesterday?

NORA   No, that was quite an exception. But he goes around critically ill all the time—tuberculosis of the spine, poor man. You know, his father was a disgusting thing who kept mistresses and so on—and that's why the son's been sickly from birth.

MRS. LINDE   *(lets her sewing fall to her lap)* But my dearest Nora, how do you know about such things?

NORA   *(walking more jauntily)* Hmp! When you've had three children, then you've had a few visits from—women who know something of medicine, and they tell you this and that.

MRS. LINDE   *(resumes sewing; a short pause)* Does Dr. Rank come here every day?

NORA   Every blessed day. He's Torvald's best friend from childhood, and *my* good friend, too. Dr. Rank almost belongs to this house.

MRS. LINDE   But tell me—is he quite sincere? I mean, doesn't he rather enjoy flattering people?

NORA   Just the opposite. Why do you think that?

MRS. LINDE   When you introduced us yesterday, he was proclaiming that he'd often heard my name in this house; but later I noticed that your husband hadn't the slightest idea who I really was. So how could Dr. Rank—?

NORA   But it's all true, Kristine. You see, Torvald loves me beyond words, and, as he puts it, he'd like to keep me all to himself. For a long time he'd almost be jealous if I even mentioned any of my old friends back home. So of course I dropped that. But with Dr. Rank I talk a lot about such things, because he likes hearing about them.

MRS. LINDE   Now listen, Nora; in many ways you're still like a

child. I'm a good deal older than you, with a little more
experience. I'll tell you something; you ought to put an end to
all this with Dr. Rank.

NORA   What should I put an end to?

MRS. LINDE   Both parts of it, I think. Yesterday you said something
about a rich admirer who'd provide you with money—

NORA   Yes, one who doesn't exist—worse luck. So?

MRS. LINDE   Is Dr. Rank well off?

NORA   Yes, he is.

MRS. LINDE   With no dependents?

NORA   No, no one. But—

MRS. LINDE   And he's over here every day?

NORA   Yes, I told you that.

MRS. LINDE   How can a man of such refinement be so grasping?

NORA   I don't follow you at all.

MRS. LINDE   Now don't try to hide it, Nora. You think I can't guess
who loaned you the forty-eight hundred crowns?

NORA   Are you out of your mind? How could you think of such a
thing! A friend of ours, who comes here every single day. What
an intolerable situation that would have been!

MRS. LINDE   Then it really wasn't him.

NORA   No, absolutely not. It never even crossed my mind for a
moment—And he had nothing to lend in those days; his
inheritance came later.

MRS. LINDE   Well, I think that was a stroke of luck for you, Nora
dear.

NORA   No, it never would have occurred to me to ask Dr. Rank—
Still, I'm quite sure that if I had asked him—

MRS. LINDE   Which you won't, of course.

NORA   No, of course not. I can't see that I'd ever need to. But I'm
quite positive that if I talked to Dr. Rank—

MRS. LINDE   Behind your husband's back?

NORA   I've got to clear up this other thing; *that's* also behind his
back. I've *got* to clear it all up.

MRS. LINDE   Yes, I was saying that yesterday, but—

NORA   *(pacing up and down)* A man handles these problems so
much better than a woman—

MRS. LINDE   One's husband does, yes.

NORA   Nonsense. *(Stopping)* When you pay everything you owe,
then you get your note back, right?

MRS. LINDE   Yes, naturally.

NORA   And can rip it into a million pieces and burn it up—that
filthy scrap of paper!

MRS. LINDE   *(looking hard at her, laying her sewing aside, and rising
slowly)* Nora, you're hiding something from me.

NORA   You can see it in my face?

MRS. LINDE   Something's happened to you since yesterday morning. Nora, what is it?

NORA   *(hurring toward her)* Kristine! *(Listening)* Shh! Torvald's home. Look, go in with the children a while. Torvald can't bear all this snipping and stitching. Let Anne-Marie help you.

MRS. LINDE   *(gathering up some of the things)* All right, but I'm not leaving here until we've talked this out. *(She disappears into the room, left, as* TORVALD *enters from the hall.)*

NORA   Oh, how I've been waiting for you, Torvald dear.

HELMER   Was that the dressmaker?

NORA   No, that was Kristine. She's helping me fix up my costume. You know, it's going to be quite attractive.

HELMER   Yes, wasn't that a bright idea I had?

NORA   Brilliant! But then wasn't I good as well to give in to you?

HELMER   Good—because you give in to your husband's judgment? All right, you little goose, I know you didn't mean it like that. But I won't disturb you. You'll want to have a fitting, I suppose.

NORA   And you'll be working?

HELMER   Yes. *(Indicating a bundle of papers)* See. I've been down to the bank. *(Starts toward his study)*

NORA   Torvald.

HELMER   *(stops)* Yes.

NORA   If your little squirrel begged you, with all her heart and soul, for something—?

HELMER   What's that?

NORA   Then would you do it?

HELMER   First, naturally, I'd have to know what it was.

NORA   Your squirrel would scamper about and do tricks, if you'd only be sweet and give in.

HELMER   Out with it.

NORA   Your lark would be singing high and low in every room—

HELMER   Come on, she does that anyway.

NORA   I'd be a wood nymph and dance for you in the moonlight.

HELMER   Nora—don't tell me it's that same business from this morning?

NORA   *(coming closer)* Yes, Torvald, I beg you, please!

HELMER   And you actually have the nerve to drag that up again?

NORA   Yes, yes, you've got to give in to me; you have to let Krogstad keep his job in the bank.

HELMER   My dear Nora, I've slated his job for Mrs. Linde.

NORA   That's awfully kind of you. But you could just fire another clerk instead of Krogstad.

HELMER   This is the most incredible stubbornness! Because you go and give an impulsive promise to speak up for him, I'm expected to—

NORA   That's not the reason, Torvald. It's for your own sake. That man does writing for the worst papers; you said it yourself. He could do you any amount of harm. I'm scared to death of him—

HELMER   Ah, I understand. It's the old memories haunting you.

NORA   What do you mean by that?

HELMER   Of course, you're thinking about your father.

NORA   Yes, all right. Just remember how those nasty gossips wrote in the papers about Papa and slandered him so cruelly. I think they'd have had him dismissed if the department hadn't sent you up to investigate, and if you hadn't been so kind and open-minded toward him.

HELMER   My dear Nora, there's a notable difference between your father and me. Your father's official career was hardly above reproach. But mine is; and I hope it'll stay that way as long as I hold my position.

NORA   Oh, who can ever tell what vicious minds can invent? We could be so snug and happy now in our quiet, carefree home— you and I and the children, Torvald! That's why I'm pleading with you so—

HELMER   And just by pleading for him you make it impossible for me to keep him on. It's already known at the bank that I'm firing Krogstad. What if it's rumored around now that the new bank manager was vetoed by his wife—

NORA   Yes, what then—?

HELMER   Oh yes—as long as your little bundle of stubbornness gets her way—! I should go and make myself ridiculous in front of the whole office—give people the idea I can be swayed by all kinds of outside pressure. Oh, you can bet I'd feel the effects of that soon enough! Besides—there's something that rules Krogstad right out at the bank as long as I'm the manager.

NORA   What's that?

HELMER   His moral failings I could maybe overlook if I had to—

NORA   Yes, Torvald, why not?

HELMER   And I hear he's quite efficient on the job. But he was a crony of mine back in my teens—one of those rash friendships that crop up again and again to embarrass you later in life. Well, I might as well say it straight out: we're on a first-name basis. And that tactless fool makes no effort at all to hide it in front of others. Quite the contrary—he thinks that entitles him to take a familiar air around me, and so every other second he comes booming out with his "Yes, Torvald!" and "Sure thing, Torvald!" I tell you, it's been excruciating for me. He's out to make my place in the bank unbearable.

NORA   Torvald, you can't be serious about all this.

HELMER   Oh no? Why not?

NORA   Because these are such petty considerations.

HELMER   What are you saying? Petty? You think I'm petty!

NORA   No, just the opposite, Torvald dear. That's exactly why—

HELMER   Never mind. You call my motives petty; then I might as well be just that. Petty! All right! We'll put a stop to this for good. *(Goes to the hall door and calls)* Helene!

NORA   What do you want?

HELMER   *(searching among his papers)* A decision. *(The* MAID *comes in.)* Look here; take this letter, go out with it at once. Get hold of a messenger and have him deliver it. Quick now. It's already addressed. Wait, here's some money.

MAID   Yes, sir. *(She leaves with the letter.)*

HELMER   *(straightening his papers)* There, now, little Miss Willful.

NORA   *(breathlessly)* Torvald, what was that letter?

HELMER   Krogstad's notice.

NORA   Call it back, Torvald! There's still time. Oh Torvald, call it back! Do it for my sake—for your sake, for the children's sake! Do you hear, Torvald; do it! You don't know how this can harm us.

HELMER   Too late.

NORA   Yes, too late.

HELMER   Nora dear, I can forgive you this panic, even though basically you're insulting me. Yes, you are! Or isn't it an insult to think that I should be afraid of a courtroom hack's revenge? But I forgive you anyway, because this shows so beautifully how much you love me. *(Takes her in his arms)* This is the way it should be, my darling Nora. Whatever comes, you'll see: when it really counts, I have strength and courage enough as a man to take on the whole weight myself.

NORA   *(terrified)* What do you mean by that?

HELMER   The whole weight, I said.

NORA   *(resolutely)* No, never in all the world.

HELMER   Good. So we'll share it, Nora, as man and wife. That's as it should be. *(Fondling her)* Are you happy now? There, there, there—not these frightened dove's eyes. It's nothing at all but empty fantasies—Now you should run through your tarantella and practice your tambourine. I'll go to the inner office and shut both doors, so I won't hear a thing; you can make all the noise you like. *(Turning in the doorway)* And when Rank comes, just tell him where he can find me. *(He nods to her and goes with his papers into the study, closing the door.)*

NORA   *(standing as though rooted, dazed with fright, in a whisper)* He really could do it. He will do it. He'll do it in spite of everything. No, not that, never, never! Anything but that! Escape! A way out—*(The doorbell rings.)* Dr. Rank! Anything but that! Anything, whatever it is! *(Her hands pass over her face, smoothing it; she pulls herself together, goes over and opens the hall door.* DR. RANK *stands outside, hanging his fur coat up. During the following scene, it begins getting dark.)*

NORA   Hello, Dr. Rank. I recognized your ring. But you mustn't go in to Torvald yet; I believe he's working.

RANK   And you?

NORA   For you, I always have an hour to spare—you know that. *(He has entered, and she shuts the door after him.)*

RANK   Many thanks. I'll make use of these hours while I can.

NORA   What do you mean by that? While you can?

RANK   Does that disturb you?

NORA   Well, it's such an odd phrase. Is anything going to happen?

RANK   What's going to happen is what I've been expecting so long—but I honestly didn't think it would come so soon.

NORA   *(gripping his arm)* What is it you've found out? Dr. Rank, you have to tell me!

RANK   *(sitting by the stove)* It's all over with me. There's nothing to be done about it.

NORA   *(breathing easier)* Is it you—then—?

RANK   Who else? There's no point in lying to one's self. I'm the most miserable of all my patients, Mrs. Helmer. These past few days I've been auditing my internal accounts. Bankrupt! Within a month I'll probably be laid out and rotting in the churchyard.

NORA   Oh, what a horrible thing to say.

RANK   The thing itself is horrible. But the worst of it is all the other horror before it's over. There's only one final examination left; when I'm finished with that, I'll know about when my disintegration will begin. There's something I want to say. Helmer with his sensitivity has such a sharp distaste for anything ugly. I don't want him near my sickroom.

NORA   Oh, but Dr. Rank—

RANK   I won't have him in there. Under no condition. I'll lock my door to him—As soon as I'm completely sure of the worst, I'll send you my calling card marked with a black cross, and you'll know then the wreck has started to come apart.

NORA   No, today you're completely unreasonable. And I wanted you so much to be in a really good humor.

RANK   With death up my sleeve? And then to suffer this way for somebody else's sins. Is there any justice in that? And in every single family, in some way or another, this inevitable retribution of nature goes on—

NORA   *(her hands pressed over her ears)* Oh, stuff! Cheer up! Please— be gay!

RANK   Yes, I'd just as soon laugh at it all. My poor, innocent spine, serving time for my father's gay army days.

NORA   *(by the table, left)* He was so infatuated with asparagus tips and *pâté de foie gras,* wasn't that it?

RANK   Yes—and with truffles.

NORA   Truffles, yes. And then with oysters, I suppose?

RANK   Yes, tons of oysters, naturally.

NORA   And then the port and champagne to go with it. It's so sad that all these delectable things have to strike at our bones.

RANK   Especially when they strike at the unhappy bones that never shared in the fun.

NORA   Ah, that's the saddest of all.

RANK   *(looks searchingly at her)* Hm.

NORA   *(after a moment)* Why did you smile?

RANK   No, it was you who laughed.

NORA   No, it was you who smiled, Dr. Rank!

RANK   *(getting up)* You're even a bigger tease than I'd thought.

NORA   I'm full of wild ideas today.

RANK   That's obvious.

NORA   *(putting both hands on his shoulders)* Dear, dear Dr. Rank, you'll never die for Torvald and me.

RANK   Oh, that loss you'll easily get over. Those who go away are soon forgotten.

NORA   *(looks fearfully at him)* You believe that?

RANK   One makes new connections, and then—

NORA   Who makes new connections?

RANK   Both you and Torvald will when I'm gone. I'd say you're well under way already. What was that Mrs. Linde doing here last evening?

NORA   Oh, come—you can't be jealous of poor Kristine?

RANK   Oh yes, I am. She'll be my successor here in the house. When I'm down under, that woman will probably—

NORA   Shh! Not so loud. She's right in there.

RANK   Today as well. So you see.

NORA   Only to sew on my dress. Good gracious, how unreasonable you are. *(Sitting on the sofa)* Be nice now, Dr. Rank. Tomorrow you'll see how beautifully I'll dance, and you can imagine then that I'm dancing only for you—yes, and of course for Torvald, too—that's understood. *(Takes various items out of the carton)* Dr. Rank, sit over here and I'll show you something.

RANK   *(sitting)* What's that?

NORA   Look here. Look.

RANK   Silk stockings.

NORA   Flesh-colored. Aren't they lovely? Now it's so dark here, but tomorrow—No, no, no, just look at the feet. Oh well, you might as well look at the rest.

RANK   Hm—

NORA   Why do you look so critical? Don't you believe they'll fit?

RANK   I've never had any chance to form an opinion on that.

NORA   *(glancing at him a moment)* Shame on you. *(Hits him lightly on the ear with the stockings)* That's for you. *(Puts them away again)*

RANK   And what other splendors am I going to see now?

NORA   Not the least bit more, because you've been naughty. *(She hums a little and rummages among her things.)*

RANK   *(after a short silence)* When I sit here together with you like this, completely easy and open, then I don't know—I simply can't imagine—whatever would have become of me if I'd never come into this house.

NORA   *(smiling)* Yes, I really think you feel completely at ease with us.

RANK   *(more quietly, staring straight ahead)* And then to have to go away from it all—

NORA   Nonsense, you're not going away.

RANK   *(his voice unchanged)*—and not even be able to leave some poor show of gratitude behind, scarcely a fleeting regret—no more than a vacant place that anyone can fill.

NORA   And if I asked you now for—? No—

RANK   For what?

NORA   For a great proof of your friendship—

RANK   Yes, yes?

NORA   No, I mean—for an exceptionally big favor—

RANK   Would you really, for once, make me so happy?

NORA   Oh, you haven't the vaguest idea what it is.

RANK   All right, then tell me.

NORA   No, but I can't, Dr. Rank—it's all out of reason. It's advice and help, too—and a favor—

RANK   So much the better. I can't fathom what you're hinting at. Just speak out. Don't you trust me?

NORA   Of course. More than anyone else. You're my best and truest friend, I'm sure. That's why I want to talk to you. All right, then, Dr. Rank: there's something you can help me prevent. You know how deeply, how inexpressibly dearly Torvald loves me; he'd never hesitate a second to give up his life for me.

RANK   *(leaning close to her)* Nora—do you think he's the only one—

NORA   *(with a slight start)* Who—?

RANK   Who'd gladly give up his life for you.

NORA   *(heavily)* I see.

RANK   I swore to myself you should know this before I'm gone. I'll never find a better chance. Yes, Nora, now you know. And also you know now that you can trust me beyond anyone else.

NORA   *(rising, natural and calm)* Let me by.

RANK   *(making room for her, but still sitting)* Nora—

NORA   *(in the hall doorway)* Helene, bring the lamp in. *(Goes over to the stove)* Ah, dear Dr. Rank, that was really mean of you.

RANK   *(getting up)* That I've loved you just as deeply as somebody else? Was *that* mean?

NORA   No, but that you came out and told me. That was quite unnecessary—

RANK   What do you mean? Have you known—?

(The MAID *comes in with the lamp, sets it on the table, and goes out again.)*

RANK   Nora—Mrs. Helmer—I'm asking you: have you known about it?

NORA   Oh, how can I tell what I know or don't know? Really, I don't know what to say—Why did you have to be so clumsy, Dr. Rank! Everything was so good.

RANK   Well, in any case, you now have the knowledge that my body and soul are at your command. So won't you speak out?

NORA   *(Looking at him)* After that?

RANK   Please, just let me know what it is.

NORA   You can't know anything now.

RANK   I have to. You mustn't punish me like this. Give me the chance to do whatever is humanly possible for you.

NORA   Now there's nothing you can do for me. Besides, actually, I don't need any help. You'll see—it's only my fantasies. That's what it is. Of course! *(Sits in the rocker, looks at him, and smiles)* What a nice one you are, Dr. Rank. Aren't you a little bit ashamed, now that the lamp is here?

RANK   No, not exactly. But perhaps I'd better go—for good?

NORA   No, you certainly can't do that. You must come here just as you always have. You know Torvald can't do without you.

RANK   Yes, but *you?*

NORA   You know how much I enjoy it when you're here.

RANK   That's precisely what threw me off. You're a mystery to me. So many times I've felt you'd almost rather be with me than with Helmer.

NORA   Yes—you see, there are some people that one loves most and other people that one would almost prefer being with.

RANK   Yes, there's something to that.

NORA   When I was back home, of course I loved Papa most. But I always thought it was so much fun when I could sneak down to the maids' quarters, because they never tried to improve me, and it was always so amusing, the way they talked to each other.

RANK   Aha, so it's *their* place that I've filled.

NORA   *(jumping up and going to him)* Oh, dear sweet Dr. Rank, that's not what I meant at all. But you can understand that with Torvald it's just the same as with Papa—

(The MAID enters from the hall.)

MAID Ma'am—please! *(She whispers to NORA and hands her a calling card.)*

NORA *(glancing at the card)* Ah! *(Slips it into her pocket)*

RANK Anything wrong?

NORA No, no, not at all. It's only some—it's my new dress—

RANK Really? But—there's your dress.

NORA Oh, that. But this is another one—I ordered it—Torvald mustn't know—

RANK Ah, now we have the big secret.

NORA That's right. Just go in with him—he's back in the inner study. Keep him there as long as—

RANK Don't worry. He won't get away.   *(Goes into the study)*

NORA *(to the MAID)* And he's standing waiting in the kitchen.

MAID Yes, he came up by the back stairs.

NORA But didn't you tell him somebody was here?

MAID Yes, but that didn't do any good.

NORA He won't leave?

MAID No, he won't go till he's talked with you, ma'am.

NORA Let him come in, then—but quietly. Helene, don't breathe a word about this. It's a surprise for my husband.

MAID Yes, yes, I understand—   *(Goes out.)*

NORA This horror—it's going to happen. No, no, no, it can't happen, it mustn't. *(She goes and bolts HELMER's door. The MAID opens the hall door for KROGSTAD and shuts it behind him. He is dressed for travel in a fur coat, boots and a fur cap.)*

NORA *(going toward him)* Talk softly. My husband's home.

KROGSTAD Well, good for him.

NORA What do you want?

KROGSTAD Some information.

NORA Hurry up, then. What is it?

KROGSTAD You know, of course, that I got my notice.

NORA I couldn't prevent it, Mr. Krogstad. I fought for you to the bitter end, but nothing worked.

KROGSTAD Does your husband's love for you run so thin? He knows everything I can expose you to, and all the same he dares to—

NORA How can you imagine he knows anything about this?

KROGSTAD Ah, no—I can't imagine it either, now. It's not at all like my fine Torvald Helmer to have so much guts—

NORA Mr. Krogstad, I demand respect for my husband!

KROGSTAD Why, of course—all due respect. But since the lady's keeping it so carefully hidden, may I presume to ask if you're also a bit better informed than yesterday about what you've actually done?

NORA   More than you ever could teach me.

KROGSTAD   Yes, I *am* such an awful lawyer.

NORA   What is it you want from me?

KROGSTAD   Just a glimpse of how you are, Mrs. Helmer. I've been thinking about you all day long. A cashier, a night-court scribbler, a —well, a type like me also has a little of what they call a heart, you know.

NORA   Then show it. Think of my children.

KROGSTAD   Did you or your husband ever think of mine? But never mind. I simply wanted to tell you that you don't need to take this thing too seriously. For the present, I'm not proceeding with any action.

NORA   Oh no, really! Well—I knew that.

KROGSTAD   Everything can be settled in a friendly spirit. It doesn't have to get around town at all; it can stay just among us three.

NORA   My husband may never know anything of this.

KROGSTAD   How can you manage that? Perhaps you can pay me the balance?

NORA   No, not right now.

KROGSTAD   Or you know some way of raising the money in a day or two?

NORA   No way that I'm willing to use.

KROGSTAD   Well, it wouldn't have done you any good, anyway. If you stood in front of me with a fistful of bills, you still couldn't buy your signature back.

NORA   Then tell me what you're going to do with it.

KROGSTAD   I'll just hold onto it—keep it on file. There's no outsider who'll even get wind of it. So if you've been thinking of taking some desperate step—

NORA   I have!

KROGSTAD   Been thinking of running away from home—

NORA   I have!

KROGSTAD   Or even of something worse—

NORA   How could you guess that?

KROGSTAD   You can drop those thoughts.

NORA   How could you guess I was thinking of *that?*

KROGSTAD   Most of us think about *that* at first. I thought about it too, but I discovered I hadn't the courage—

NORA   *(lifelessly)* I don't either.

KROGSTAD   *(relieved)* That's true, you haven't the courage? You too?

NORA   I don't have it—I don't have it.

KROGSTAD   It would be terribly stupid, anyway. After that first storm at home blows out, why, then—I have here in my pocket a letter for your husband—

NORA   Telling everything?

KROGSTAD   As charitably as possible.

NORA   *(quickly)* He mustn't ever get that letter. Tear it up. I'll find some way to get money.

KROGSTAD   Beg pardon, Mrs. Helmer, but I think I just told you—

NORA   Oh, I don't mean the money I owe you. Let me know how much you want from my husband, and I'll manage it.

KROGSTAD   I don't want any money from your husband.

NORA   What do you want, then?

KROGSTAD   I'll tell you what. I want to recoup, Mrs. Helmer; I want to get on in the world—and there's where your husband can help me. For a year and a half I've kept myself clean of anything disreputable—all that time struggling with the worst conditions; but I was satisfied, working my way up step by step. Now I've been written right off, and I'm just not in the mood to come crawling back. I tell you, I want to move on. I want to get back in the bank—in a better position. Your husband can set up a job for me—

NORA   He'll never do that!

KROGSTAD   He'll do it. I know him. He won't dare breathe a word of protest. And once I'm in there together with him, you just wait and see! Inside of a year, I'll be the manager's right-hand man. It'll be Nils Krogstad, not Torvald Helmer, who runs the bank.

NORA   You'll never see the day!

KROGSTAD   Maybe you think you can—

NORA   I have the courage now—for *that.*

KROGSTAD   Oh, you don't scare me. A smart, spoiled lady like you—

NORA   You'll see; you'll see!

KROGSTAD   Under the ice, maybe? Down in the freezing, coal-black water? There, till you float up in the spring, ugly, unrecognizable, with your hair falling out—

NORA   You don't frighten me.

KROGSTAD   Nor do you frighten me. One doesn't do these things, Mrs. Helmer. Besides, what good would it be? I'd still have him safe in my pocket.

NORA   Afterwards? When I'm no longer—?

KROGSTAD   Are you forgetting that *I'll* be in control then over your final reputation? (NORA *stands speechless, staring at him.*) Good; now I've warned you. Don't do anything stupid. When Helmer's read my letter, I'll be waiting for his reply. And bear in mind that it's your husband himself who's forced me back to my old ways. I'll never forgive him for that. Good-bye, Mrs. Helmer.

> *(He goes out through the hall.)*

NORA   *(goes to the hall door, opens it a crack, and listens)* He's gone. Didn't leave the letter. Oh no, no, that's impossible too! *(Opening the door more and more)* What's that? He's standing outside—not going downstairs. He's thinking it over? Maybe he'll—? (*A letter falls in the mailbox; then* KROGSTAD's *footsteps are heard, dying away down a flight of stairs.* NORA *gives a muffled cry and runs over toward the sofa table. A short pause.*) In the mailbox. (*Slips warily over to the hall door*) It's lying there. Torvald, Torvald—now we're lost!

MRS. LINDE   (*entering with the costume from the room, left*) There now, I can't see anything else to mend. Perhaps you'd like to try—

NORA   (*in a hoarse whisper*) Kristine, come here.

MRS. LINDE   (*tossing the dress on the sofa*) What's wrong? You look upset.

NORA   Come here. See that letter? *There!* Look—through the glass in the mailbox.

MRS. LINDE   Yes, yes, I see it.

NORA   That letter's from Krogstad—

MRS. LINDE   Nora—it's Krogstad who loaned you the money!

NORA   Yes, and now Torvald will find out everything.

MRS. LINDE   Believe me, Nora, it's best for both of you.

NORA   There's more you don't know. I forged a name.

MRS. LINDE   But for heaven's sake—?

NORA   I only want to tell you that, Kristine, so that you can be my witness.

MRS. LINDE   Witness? Why should I—?

NORA   If I should go out of my mind—it could easily happen—

MRS. LINDE   Nora!

NORA   Or anything else occurred—so I couldn't be present here—

MRS. LINDE   Nora, Nora, you aren't yourself at all!

NORA   And someone should try to take on the whole weight, all of the guilt, you follow me—

MRS. LINDE   Yes, of course, but why do you think—?

NORA   Then you're the witness that it isn't true, Kristine. I'm very much myself; my mind right now is perfectly clear; and I'm telling you: nobody else has known about this; I alone did everything. Remember that.

MRS. LINDE   I will. But I don't understand all this.

NORA   Oh, how could you ever understand it? It's the miracle now that's going to take place.

MRS. LINDE   The miracle?

NORA   Yes, the miracle. But it's so awful, Kristine. It mustn't take place, not for anything in the world.

MRS. LINDE   I'm going right over and talk with Krogstad.

NORA   Don't go near him; he'll do you some terrible harm!

MRS. LINDE   There was a time once when he'd gladly have done anything for me.

NORA   He?

MRS. LINDE   Where does he live?

NORA   Oh, how do I know? Yes. *(Searches in her pocket)* Here's his card. But the letter, the letter—!

HELMER   *(from the study, knocking on the door)* Nora!

NORA   *(with a cry of fear)* Oh! What is it? What do you want?

HELMER   Now, now, don't be so frightened. We're not coming in. You locked the door—are you trying on the dress?

NORA   Yes, I'm trying it. I'll look just beautiful, Torvald.

MRS. LINDE   *(who has read the card)* He's living right around the corner.

NORA   Yes, but what's the use? We're lost. The letter's in the box.

MRS. LINDE   And your husband has the key?

NORA   Yes, always.

MRS. LINDE   Krogstad can ask for his letter back unread; he can find some excuse—

NORA   But it's just this time that Torvald usually—

MRS. LINDE   Stall him. Keep him in there. I'll be back as quick as I can. *(She hurries out through the hall entrance.)*

NORA   *(goes to* HELMER's *door, opens it, and peers in)* Torvald!

HELMER   *(from the inner study)* Well—does one dare set foot in one's own living room at last? Come on, Rank, now we'll get a look—*(In the doorway)* But what's this?

NORA   What, Torvald dear?

HELMER   Rank had me expecting some grand masquerade.

RANK   *(in the doorway)* That was my impression, but I must have been wrong.

NORA   No one can admire me in my splendor—not until tomorrow.

HELMER   But Nora dear, you look so exhausted. Have you practiced too hard?

NORA   No, I haven't practiced at all yet.

HELMER   You know, it's necessary—

NORA   Oh, it's absolutely necessary, Torvald. But I can't get anywhere without your help. I've forgotten the whole thing completely.

HELMER   Ah, we'll soon take care of that.

NORA   Yes, take care of me, Torvald, please! Promise me that? Oh, I'm so nervous. That big party—You must give up everything this evening for me. No business—don't even touch your pen. Yes? Dear Torvald, promise?

HELMER   It's a promise. Tonight I'm totally at your service—you little helpless thing. Hm—but first there's one thing I want to— *(Goes toward the hall door)*

NORA   What are you looking for?

HELMER   Just to see if there's any mail.

NORA   No, no, don't do that, Torvald!

HELMER   Now what?

NORA   Torvald, please. There isn't any.

HELMER   Let me look, though. (*Starts out.* NORA, *at the piano, strikes the first notes of the tarantella.* HELMER, *at the door, stops.*) Aha!

NORA   I can't dance tomorrow if I don't practice with you.

HELMER   *(going over to her)* Nora dear, are you really so frightened?

NORA   Yes, so terribly frightened. Let me practice right now; there's still time before dinner. Oh, sit down and play for me, Torvald. Direct me. Teach me, the way you always have.

HELMER   Gladly, if it's what you want. (*Sits at the piano*)

NORA   *(snatches the tambourine up from the box, then a long, varicolored shawl, which she throws around herself, whereupon she springs forward and cries out)* Play for me now! Now I'll dance!

(HELMER *plays and* NORA *dances.* RANK *stands behind* HELMER *at the piano and looks on.*)

HELMER   *(as he plays)* Slower. Slow down.

NORA   Can't change it.

HELMER   Not so violent, Nora!

NORA   Has to be just like this.

HELMER   *(stopping)* No, no, that won't do at all.

NORA   *(laughing and swinging her tambourine)* Isn't that what I told you?

RANK   Let me play for her.

HELMER   *(getting up)* Yes, go on, I can teach her more easily then.

(RANK *sits at the piano and plays;* NORA *dances more and more wildly.* HELMER *has stationed himself by the stove and repeatedly gives her directions; she seems not to hear them; her hair loosens and falls over her shoulders; she does not notice, but goes on dancing.* MRS. LINDE *enters.*)

MRS. LINDE   *(standing dumbfounded at the door)* Ah—!

NORA   *(still dancing)* See what fun, Kristine!

HELMER   But Nora darling, you dance as if your life were at stake.

NORA   And it is.

HELMER   Rank, stop! This is pure madness. Stop it, I say!

(RANK *breaks off playing, and* NORA *halts abruptly.*)

HELMER   *(going over to hear)* I never would have believed it. You've forgotten everything I taught you.

NORA   *(throwing away the tambourine)* You see for yourself.

HELMER   Well, there's certainly room for instruction here.

NORA   Yes, you see how important it is. You've got to teach me to the very last minute. Promise me that, Torvald?

HELMER   You can bet on it.

NORA You mustn't, either today or tomorrow, think about anything else but me; you mustn't open any letters—or the mailbox—

HELMER Ah, it's still the fear of that man—

NORA Oh yes, yes, that too.

HELMER Nora, it's written all over you—there's already a letter from him out there.

NORA I don't know. I guess so. But you mustn't read such things now; there mustn't be anything ugly between us before it's all over.

RANK *(quietly to* HELMER*)* You shouldn't deny her.

HELMER *(putting his arm around her)* The child can have her way. But tomorrow night, after you've danced—

NORA Then you'll be free.

MAID *(in the doorway, right)* Ma'am, dinner is served.

NORA We'll be wanting champagne, Helene.

MAID Very good, ma'am.   *(Goes out)*

HELMER So—a regular banquet, hm?

NORA Yes, a banquet—champagne till daybreak! *(Calling out)* And some macaroons, Helene. Heaps of them—just this once.

HELMER *(taking her hands)* Now, now, now—no hysterics. Be my own little lark again.

NORA Oh, I will soon enough. But go on in—and you, Dr. Rank. Kristine, help me put up my hair.

RANK *(whispering, as they go)* There's nothing wrong—really wrong, is there?

HELMER Oh, of course not. It's nothing more than this childish anxiety I was telling you about.   *(They go out, right.)*

NORA Well?

MRS. LINDE Left town.

NORA I could see by your face.

MRS. LINDE He'll be home tomorrow evening. I wrote him a note.

NORA You shouldn't have. Don't try to stop anything now. After all, it's a wonderful joy, this waiting here for the miracle.

MRS. LINDE What is it you're waiting for?

NORA Oh, you can't understand that. Go in to them, I'll be along in a moment.

(MRS. LINDE *goes into the dining room.* NORA *stands a short while as if composing herself; then she looks at her watch.*)

NORA Five. Seven hours to midnight. Twenty-four hours to the midnight after, and then the tarantella's done. Seven and twenty-four? Thirty-one hours to live.

HELMER *(in the doorway, right)* What's become of the little lark?

NORA *(going toward him with open arms)* Here's your lark!

ACT III

Same scene. The table, with chairs around it, has been moved to the center of the room. A lamp on the table is lit. The hall door stands open. Dance music drifts down from the floor above. MRS. LINDE *sits at the table, absently paging through a book, trying to read, but apparently unable to focus her thoughts. Once or twice she pauses, tensely listening for a sound at the outer entrance.*

MRS. LINDE *(glancing at her watch)* Not yet—and there's hardly any time left. If only he's not—*(Listening again)* Ah, there he is. *(She goes out in the hall and cautiously opens the outer door. Quiet footsteps are heard on the stairs. She whispers.)* Come in. Nobody's here.

KROGSTAD *(in the doorway)* I found a note from you at home. What's back of all this?

MRS. LINDE I just *had* to talk to you.

KROGSTAD Oh? And it just *had* to be here in this house?

MRS. LINDE At my place it was impossible; my room hasn't a private entrance. Come in; we're all alone. The maid's asleep, and the Helmers are at the dance upstairs.

KROGSTAD *(entering the room)* Well, well, the Helmers are dancing tonight? Really?

MRS. LINDE Yes, why not?

KROGSTAD How true—why not?

MRS. LINDE All right, Krogstad, let's talk.

KROGSTAD Do we two have anything more to talk about?

MRS. LINDE We have a great deal to talk about.

KROGSTAD I wouldn't have thought so.

MRS. LINDE No, because you've never understood me, really.

KROGSTAD Was there anything more to understand—except what's all too common in life? A calculating woman throws over a man the moment a better catch comes by.

MRS. LINDE You think I'm so thoroughly calculating? You think I broke it off lightly?

KROGSTAD Didn't you?

MRS. LINDE Nils—is that what you really thought?

KROGSTAD If you cared, then why did you write me the way you did?

MRS. LINDE What else could I do? If I had to break off with you, then it was my job as well to root out everything you felt for me.

KROGSTAD *(wringing his hands)* So that was it. And this—all this, simply for money!

MRS. LINDE Don't forget I had a helpless mother and two small brothers. We couldn't wait for you, Nils; you had such a long road ahead of you then.

KROGSTAD That may be; but you still hadn't the right to abandon me for somebody else's sake.

MRS. LINDE   Yes—I don't know. So many, many times I've asked
myself if I did have that right.

KROGSTAD   *(more softly)* When I lost you, it was as if all the solid
ground dissolved from under my feet. Look at me; I'm a half-
drowned man now, hanging onto a wreck.

MRS. LINDE   Help may be near.

KROGSTAD   It was near—but then you came and blocked it off.

MRS. LINDE   Without my knowing it, Nils. Today for the first time
I learned that it's you I'm replacing at the bank.

KROGSTAD   All right—I believe you. But now that you know, will
you step aside?

MRS. LINDE   No, because that wouldn't benefit you in the slightest.

KROGSTAD   Not "benefit" me, hm! I'd step aside anyway.

MRS. LINDE   I've learned to be realistic. Life and hard, bitter
necessity have taught me that.

KROGSTAD   And life's taught me never to trust fine phrases.

MRS. LINDE   Then life's taught you a very sound thing. But you do
have to trust in actions, don't you?

KROGSTAD   What does that mean?

MRS. LINDE   You said you were hanging on like a half-drowned
man to a wreck.

KROGSTAD   I've good reason to say that.

MRS. LINDE   I'm also like a half-drowned woman on a wreck. No
one to suffer with; no one to care for.

KROGSTAD   You made your choice.

MRS. LINDE   There wasn't any choice then.

KROGSTAD   So—what of it?

MRS. LINDE   Nils, if only we two shipwrecked people could reach
across to each other.

KROGSTAD   What are you saying?

MRS. LINDE   Two on one wreck are at least better off than each on
his own.

KROGSTAD   Kristine!

MRS. LINDE   Why do you think I came into town?

KROGSTAD   Did you really have some thought of me?

MRS. LINDE   I have to work to go on living. All my born days, as
long as I can remember, I've worked, and it's been my best and
my only joy. But now I'm completely alone in the world; it
frightens me to be so empty and lost. To work for yourself—
there's no joy in that. Nils, give me something—someone to
work for.

KROGSTAD   I don't believe all this. It's just some hysterical
feminine urge to go out and make a noble sacrifice.

MRS. LINDE   Have you ever found me to be hysterical?

KROGSTAD   Can you honestly mean this? Tell me—do you know
everything about my past?

MRS. LINDE   Yes.

KROGSTAD   And you know what they think I'm worth around here.

MRS. LINDE   From what you were saying before, it would seem that with me you could have been another person.

KROGSTAD   I'm positive of that.

MRS. LINDE   Couldn't it happen still?

KROGSTAD   Kristine—you're saying this in all seriousness? Yes, you are! I can see it in you. And do you really have the courage, then—?

MRS. LINDE   I need to have someone to care for; and your children need a mother. We both need each other. Nils, I have faith that you're good at heart—I'll risk everything together with you.

KROGSTAD   *(gripping her hands)* Kristine, thank you, thank you— Now I know I can win back a place in their eyes. Yes—but I forgot—

MRS. LINDE   *(listening)* Shh! The tarantella. Go now! Go on!

KROGSTAD   Why? What is it?

MRS. LINDE   Hear the dance up there? When that's over, they'll be coming down.

KROGSTAD   Oh, then I'll go. But—it's all pointless. Of course, you don't know the move I made against the Helmers.

MRS. LINDE   Yes, Nils, I know.

KROGSTAD   And all the same, you have the courage to—?

MRS. LINDE   I know how far despair can drive a man like you.

KROGSTAD   Oh, if I only could take it all back.

MRS. LINDE   You easily could—your letter's still lying in the mailbox.

KROGSTAD   Are you sure of that?

MRS. LINDE   Positive. But—

KROGSTAD   *(looks at her searchingly)* Is that the meaning of it, then? You'll have your friend at any price. Tell me straight out. Is that it?

MRS. LINDE   Nils—anyone who's sold herself for somebody else once isn't going to do it again.

KROGSTAD   I'll demand my letter back.

MRS. LINDE   No, no.

KROGSTAD   Yes, of course. I'll stay here till Helmer comes down; I'll tell him to give me my letter again—that it only involves my dismissal—that he shouldn't read it—

MRS. LINDE   No, Nils, don't call the letter back.

KROGSTAD   But wasn't that exactly why you wrote me to come here?

MRS. LINDE   Yes, in that first panic. But it's been a whole day and night since then, and in that time I've seen such incredible things in this house. Helmer's got to learn everything; this dreadful secret has to be aired; those two have to come to a full understanding; all these lies and evasions can't go on.

KROGSTAD   Well, then, if you want to chance it. But at least there's one thing I can do, and do right away—

MRS. LINDE   *(listening)* Go now, go quick! The dance is over. We're not safe another second.

KROGSTAD   I'll wait for you downstairs.

MRS. LINDE   Yes, please do; take me home.

KROGSTAD   I can't believe it; I've never been so happy. *(He leaves by way of the outer door; the door between the room and the hall stays open.)*

MRS. LINDE   *(straightening up a bit and getting together her street clothes)* How different now! How different! Someone to work for, to live for—a home to build. Well, it is worth the try! Oh, if they'd only come! *(Listening)* Ah, there they are. Bundle up. *(She picks up her hat and coat.* NORA'S *and* HELMER'S *voices can be heard outside; a key turns in the lock, and* HELMER *brings* NORA *into the hall almost by force. She is wearing the Italian costume with a large black shawl about her; he has on evening dress, with a black domino open over it.)*

NORA   *(struggling in the doorway)* No, no, no, not inside! I'm going up again. I don't want to leave so soon.

HELMER   But Nora dear—

NORA   Oh, I beg you, please, Torvald. From the bottom of my heart, *please*—only an hour more!

HELMER   Not a single minute, Nora darling. You know our agreement. Come on, in we go; you'll catch cold out here. *(In spite of her resistance, he gently draws her into the room.)*

MRS. LINDE   Good evening.

NORA   Kristine!

HELMER   Why, Mrs. Linde—are you here so late?

MRS. LINDE   Yes, I'm sorry, but I did want to see Nora in costume.

NORA   Have you been sitting here, waiting for me?

MRS. LINDE   Yes. I didn't come early enough; you were all upstairs; and then I thought I really couldn't leave without seeing you.

HELMER   *(removing* NORA'S *shawl)* Yes, take a good look. She's worth looking at, I can tell you that, Mrs. Linde. Isn't she lovely?

MRS. LINDE   Yes, I should say—

HELMER   A dream of loveliness, isn't she? That's what everyone thought at the party, too. But she's horribly stubborn—this sweet little thing. What's to be done with her? Can you imagine, I almost had to use force to pry her away.

NORA   Oh, Torvald, you're going to regret you didn't indulge me, even for just a half hour more.

HELMER   There, you see. She danced her tarantella and got a tumultuous hand—which was well earned, although the performance may have been a bit too naturalistic—I mean it rather overstepped the proprieties of art. But never mind— what's important is, she made a success, an overwhelming success. You think I could let her stay on after that and spoil the effect? Oh no; I took my lovely little Capri girl—my capricious little Capri girl, I should say—took her under my arm; one quick tour of the ballroom, a curtsy to every side, and then—as they say in novels—the beautiful vision disappeared. An exit should always be effective, Mrs. Linde, but that's what I can't get Nora to grasp. Phew, it's hot in here. *(Flings the domino on a chair and opens the door to his room)* Why's it dark in here? Oh yes, of course. Excuse me. *(He goes in and lights a couple of candles.)*

NORA   *(in a sharp, breathless whisper)* So?

MRS. LINDE   *(quietly)* I talked with him.

NORA   And—?

MRS. LINDE   Nora—you must tell your husband everything.

NORA   *(dully)* I knew it.

MRS. LINDE   You've got nothing to fear from Krogstad, but you have to speak out.

NORA   I won't tell.

MRS. LINDE   Then the letter will.

NORA   Thanks, Kristine. I know now what's to be done. Shh!

HELMER   *(reentering)* Well, then, Mrs. Linde—have you admired her?

MRS. LINDE   Yes, and now I'll say good night.

HELMER   Oh, come, so soon? Is this yours, this knitting?

MRS. LINDE   Yes, thanks. I nearly forgot it.

HELMER   Do you knit, then?

MRS. LINDE   Oh yes.

HELMER   You know what? You should embroider instead.

MRS. LINDE   Really? Why?

HELMER   Yes, because it's a lot prettier. See here, one holds the embroidery so, in the left hand, and then one guides the needle with the right—so—in an easy, sweeping curve—right?

MRS. LINDE   Yes, I guess that's—

HELMER   But, on the other hand, knitting—it can never be anything but ugly. Look, see here, the arms tucked in, the knitting needles going up and down—there's something Chinese about it. Ah, that was really a glorious champagne they served.

MRS. LINDE   Yes, good night, Nora, and don't be stubborn anymore.

HELMER   Well put, Mrs. Linde!

MRS. LINDE   Good night, Mr. Helmer.

HELMER   *(accompanying her to the door)* Good night, good night. I

hope you get home all right. I'd be very happy to—but you
don't have far to go. Good night, good night. *(She leaves. He shuts
the door after her and returns.)* There, now, at last we got her out
the door. She's a deadly bore, that creature.

NORA   Aren't you pretty tired, Torvald?

HELMER   No, not a bit.

NORA   You're not sleepy?

HELMER   Not at all. On the contrary, I'm feeling quite exhilarated.
But you? Yes, you really look tired and sleepy.

NORA   Yes, I'm very tired. Soon now I'll sleep.

HELMER   See! You see! I was right all along that we shouldn't stay
longer.

NORA   Whatever you do is always right.

HELMER   *(kissing her brow)* Now my little lark talks sense. Say, did
you notice what a time Rank was having tonight?

NORA   Oh, was he? I didn't get to speak with him.

HELMER   I scarcely did either, but it's a long time since I've seen
him in such high spirits. *(Gazes at her a moment, then comes nearer
her)* Hm—it's marvelous, though, to be back home again—to be
completely alone with you. Oh, you bewitchingly lovely young
woman!

NORA   Torvald, don't look at me like that!

HELMER   Can't I look at my richest treasure? At all that beauty
that's mine, mine alone—completely and utterly.

NORA   *(moving around to the other side of the table)* You mustn't talk
to me that way tonight.

HELMER   *(following her)* The tarantella is still in your blood, I can
see—and it makes you even more enticing. Listen. The guests
are beginning to go. *(Dropping his voice)* Nora—it'll soon be quiet
through this whole house.

NORA   Yes, I hope so.

HELMER   You do, don't you, my love? Do you realize—when I'm
out at a party like this with you—do you know why I talk to
you so little, and keep such a distance away; just send you a
stolen look now and then—you know why I do it? It's because
I'm imagining then that you're my secret darling, my secret
young bride-to-be, and that no one suspects there's anything
between us.

NORA   Yes, yes; oh, yes, I know you're always thinking of me.

HELMER   And then when we leave and I place the shawl over
those fine young rounded shoulders—over that wonderful
curving neck—then I pretend that you're my young bride, that
we're just coming from the wedding, that for the first time I'm
bringing you into my house—that for the first time I'm alone
with you—completely alone with you, your trembling young
beauty! All this evening I've longed for nothing but you. When I

saw you turn and sway in the tarantella—my blood was pounding till I couldn't stand it—that's why I brought you down here so early—

NORA   Go away, Torvald! Leave me alone. I don't want all this.

HELMER   What do you mean? Nora, you're teasing me. You will, won't you? Aren't I your husband—?

(A knock at the outside door)

NORA   *(startled)* What's that?

HELMER   *(going toward the hall)* Who is it?

RANK   *(outside)* It's me. May I come in a moment?

HELMER   *(with quiet irritation)* Oh, what does he want now? *(Aloud)* Hold on. *(Goes and opens the door)* Oh, how nice that you didn't just pass us by!

RANK   I thought I heard your voice, and then I wanted so badly to have a look in. *(Lightly glancing about)* Ah, me, these old familiar haunts. You have it snug and cozy in here, you two.

HELMER   You seemed to be having it pretty cozy upstairs, too.

RANK   Absolutely. Why shouldn't I? Why not take in everything in life? As much as you can, anyway, and as long as you can. The wine was superb—

HELMER   The champagne especially.

RANK   You noticed that too? It's amazing how much I could guzzle down.

NORA   Torvald also drank a lot of champagne this evening.

RANK   Oh?

NORA   Yes, and that always makes him so entertaining.

RANK   Well, why shouldn't one have a pleasant evening after a well-spent day?

HELMER   Well spent? I'm afraid I can't claim that.

RANK   *(slapping him on the back)* But I can, you see!

NORA   Dr. Rank, you must have done some scientific research today.

RANK   Quite so.

HELMER   Come now—little Nora talking about scientific research!

NORA   And can I congratulate you on the results?

RANK   Indeed you may.

NORA   Then they were good?

RANK   The best possible for both doctor and patient—certainty.

NORA   *(quickly and searchingly)* Certainty?

RANK   Complete certainty. So don't I owe myself a gay evening afterwards?

NORA   Yes, you're right, Dr. Rank.

HELMER   I'm with you—just so long as you don't have to suffer for it in the morning.

RANK Well, one never gets something for nothing in life.

NORA Dr. Rank—are you very fond of masquerade parties?

RANK Yes, if there's a good array of odd disguises—

NORA Tell me, what should we two go as at the next masquerade?

HELMER You little feather head—already thinking of the next!

RANK We two? I'll tell you what: you must go as Charmed Life—

HELMER Yes, but find a costume for *that!*

RANK Your wife can appear just as she looks every day.

HELMER That was nicely put. But don't you know what you're going to be?

RANK Yes, Helmer, I've made up my mind.

HELMER Well?

RANK At the next masquerade I'm going to be invisible.

HELMER That's a funny idea.

RANK They say there's a hat—black, huge—have you never heard of the hat that makes you invisible? You put it on, and then no one on earth can see you.

HELMER *(suppressing a smile)* Ah, of course.

RANK But I'm quite forgetting what I came for. Helmer, give me a cigar, one of the dark Havanas.

HELMER With the greatest pleasure. *(Hold out his case)*

RANK Thanks. *(Takes one and cuts off the tip)*

NORA *(striking a match)* Let me give you a light.

RANK Thank you. *(She holds the match for him; he lights the cigar.)* And now good-bye.

HELMER Good-bye, good-bye, old friend.

NORA Sleep well, Doctor.

RANK Thanks for that wish.

NORA Wish me the same.

RANK You? All right, if you like—Sleep well. And thanks for the light.

> *(He nods to them both and leaves.)*

HELMER *(his voice subdued)* He's been drinking heavily.

NORA *(absently)* Could be. (HELMER *takes his keys from his pocket and goes out in the hall.)* Torvald—what are you after?

HELMER Got to empty the mailbox; it's nearly full. There won't be room for the morning papers.

NORA Are you working tonight?

HELMER You know I'm not. Why—what's this? Someone's been at the lock.

NORA At the lock—?

HELMER Yes, I'm positive. What do you suppose—? I can't imagine one of the maids—? Here's a broken hairpin. Nora, it's yours—

NORA *(quickly)* Then it must be the children.

HELMER   You'd better break them of that. Hm, hm—well, opened
it after all. *(Takes the contents out and calls into the kitchen)* Helene!
Helene, would you put out the lamp in the hall. *(He returns to the
room, shutting the hall door, then displays the handful of mail.)* Look
how it's piled up. *(Sorting through them)* Now what's this?

NORA   *(at the window)* The letter! Oh, Torvald, no!

HELMER   Two calling cards—from Rank.

NORA   From Dr. Rank?

HELMER   *(examining them)* ''Dr. Rank, Consulting Physician.'' They
were on top. He must have dropped them as he left.

NORA   Is there anything on them?

HELMER   There's a black cross over the name. See? That's a
gruesome notion. He could almost be announcing his own
death.

NORA   That's just what he's doing.

HELMER   What! You've heard something? Something he's told
you?

NORA   Yes. That when those cards came, he'd be taking his leave
of us. He'll shut himself in now and die.

HELMER   Ah, my poor friend! Of course I knew he wouldn't be
here much longer. But so soon—And then to hide himself away
like a wounded animal.

NORA   If it has to happen, then it's best it happens in silence—
don't you think so, Torvald?

HELMER   *(pacing up and down)* He's grown right into our lives. I
simply can't imagine him gone. He with his suffering and
loneliness—like a dark cloud setting off our sunlit happiness.
Well, maybe it's best this way. For him, at least. *(Standing still)*
And maybe for us too, Nora. Now we're thrown back on each
other completely. *(Embracing her)* Oh you, my darling wife, how
can I hold you close enough? You know what, Nora—time and
again I've wished you were in some terrible danger, just so I
could stake my life and soul and everything, for your sake.

NORA   *(tearing herself away, her voice firm and decisive)* Now you
must read your mail, Torvald.

HELMER   No, no, not tonight. I want to stay with you, dearest.

NORA   With a dying friend on your mind?

HELMER   You're right. We've both had a shock. There's ugliness
between us—these thoughts of death and corruption. We'll have
to get free of them first. Until then—we'll stay apart.

NORA   *(clinging about his neck)* Torvald—good night! Good night!

HELMER   *(kissing her on the cheek)* Good night, little songbird. Sleep
well, Nora. I'll be reading my mail now.

(He takes the letters into his room and shuts the door after him.)

NORA   (*with bewildered glances, groping about, seizing* HELMER'S *domino, throwing it around her, and speaking in short, hoarse, broken whispers*) Never see him again. Never, never. (*Putting her shawl over her head*) Never see the children either—them, too. Never, never. Oh, the freezing black water! The depths—down—Oh, I wish it were over—He has it now; he's reading it—now. Oh no, no, not yet. Torvald, good-bye, you and the children—(*She starts for the hall; as she does,* HELMER *throws open his door and stands with an open letter in his hand.*)

HELMER   Nora!

NORA   (*screams*) Oh—!

HELMER   What is this? You know what's in this letter?

NORA   Yes, I know. Let me go! Let me out!

HELMER   (*holding her back*) Where are you going?

NORA   (*struggling to break loose*) You can't save me, Torvald!

HELMER   (*slumping back*) True! Then it's true what he writes? How horrible! No, no, it's impossible—it can't be true.

NORA   It *is* true. I've loved you more than all this world.

HELMER   Ah, none of your slippery tricks.

NORA   (*taking one step toward him*) Torvald—!

HELMER   What *is* this you've blundered into!

NORA   Just let me loose. You're not going to suffer for my sake. You're not going to take on my guilt.

HELMER   No more playacting. (*Locks the hall door*) You stay right here and give me a reckoning. You understand what you've done? Answer! You understand?

NORA   (*looking squarely at him, her face hardening*) Yes. I'm beginning to understand everything now.

HELMER   (*striding about*) Oh, what an awful awakening! In all these eight years—she who was my pride and joy—a hypocrite, a liar—worse, worse—a criminal! How infinitely disgusting it all is! The shame! (NORA *says nothing and goes on looking straight at him. He stops in front of her.*) I should have suspected something of the kind. I should have known. All your father's flimsy values—Be still! All your father's flimsy values have come out in you. No religion, no morals, no sense of duty—Oh, how I'm punished for letting him off! I did it for your sake, and you repay me like this.

NORA   Yes, like this.

HELMER   Now you've wrecked all my happiness—ruined my whole future. Oh, it's awful to think of. I'm in a cheap little grafter's hands; he can do anything he wants with me, ask for anything, play with me like a puppet—and I can't breathe a word. I'll be swept down miserably into the depths on account of a featherbrained woman.

NORA   When I'm gone from this world, you'll be free.

HELMER   Oh, quit posing. Your father had a mess of those
speeches too. What good would that ever do me if you were
gone from this world, as you say? Not the slightest. He can still
make the whole thing known; and if he does, I could be falsely
suspected as your accomplice. They might even think that I was
behind it—that I put you up to it. And all that I can thank you
for—you that I've coddled the whole of our marriage. Can you
see now what you've done to me?

NORA   *(icily calm)* Yes.

HELMER   It's so incredible, I just can't grasp it. But we'll have to
patch up whatever we can. Take off the shawl. I said, take if off!
I've got to appease him somehow or other. The thing has to be
hushed up at any cost. And as for you and me, it's got to seem
like everything between us is just as it was—to the outside
world, that is. You'll go right on living in this house, of course.
But you can't be allowed to bring up the children; I don't dare
trust you with them—Oh, to have to say this to someone I've
loved so much! Well, that's done with. From now on happiness
doesn't matter; all that matters is saving the bits and pieces, the
appearance—*(The doorbell rings.* HELMER *starts.)* What's that? And
so late. Maybe the worst—? You think he'd—? Hide, Nora! Say
you're sick. (NORA *remains standing motionless.* HELMER *goes and opens
the door.)*

MAID   *(half dressed, in the hall)* A letter for Mrs. Helmer.

HELMER   I'll take it. *(Snatches the letter and shuts the door)* Yes, it's
from him. You don't get it; I'm reading it myself.

NORA   Then read it.

HELMER   *(by the lamp)* I hardly dare. We may be ruined, you and I.
But—I've got to know. *(Rips open the letter, skims through a few
lines, glances at an enclosure, then cries out joyfully)* Nora! (NORA *looks
inquiringly at him.)* Nora! Wait—better check it again—Yes, yes,
it's true. I'm saved. Nora, I'm saved!

NORA   And I?

HELMER   You too, of course. We're both saved, both of us. Look.
He's sent back your note. He says he's sorry and ashamed—that
a happy development in his life—oh, who cares what he says!
Nora, we're saved! No one can hurt you. Oh, Nora, Nora—but
first, this ugliness all has to go. Let me see—*(Takes a look at the
note)* No, I don't want to see it; I want the whole thing to fade
like a dream. *(Tears the note and both letters to pieces, throws them
into the stove and watches them burn)* There—now there's nothing
left—He wrote that since Christmas Eve you—Oh, they must
have been three terrible days for you, Nora.

NORA   I fought a hard fight.

HELMER   And suffered pain and saw no escape but—No, we're not
going to dwell on anything unpleasant. We'll just be grateful and
keep on repeating, it's over now, it's over! You hear me, Nora?
You don't seem to realize—it's over. What's it mean—that
frozen look? Oh, poor little Nora, I understand. You can't believe
I've forgiven you. But I have, Nora; I swear I have. I know that
what you did, you did out of love for me.

NORA   That's true.

HELMER   You love me the way a wife ought to love her husband.
It's simply the means that you couldn't judge. But you think I
love you any the less for not knowing how to handle your
affairs? No, no—just lean on me: I'll guide you and teach you. I
wouldn't be a man if this feminine helplessness didn't make you
twice as attractive to me. You mustn't mind those sharp words I
said—that was all in the first confusion of thinking my world
had collapsed. I've forgiven you, Nora; I swear I've forgiven you.

NORA   My thanks for your forgiveness. *(She goes out through the
door, right.)*

HELMER   No, wait—*(Peers in)* What are you doing in there?

NORA   *(inside)* Getting out of my costume.

HELMER   *(by the open door)* Yes, do that. Try to calm yourself and
collect your thoughts again, my frightened little songbird. You
can rest easy now; I've got wide wings to shelter you with.
(Walking about close by the door) How snug and nice our home is,
Nora. You're safe here; I'll keep you like a hunted dove I've
rescued out of a hawk's claws. I'll bring peace to your poor,
shuddering heart. Gradually it'll happen, Nora; you 'll see.
Tomorrow all this will look different to you; then everything will
be as it was. I won't have to go on repeating I forgive you; you'll
feel it for yourself. How can you imagine I'd ever conceivably
want to disown you—or even blame you in any way? Ah, you
don't know a man's heart, Nora. For a man there's something
indescribably sweet and satisfying in knowing he's forgiven his
wife—and forgiven her out of a full and open heart. It's as if she
belongs to him in two ways now: in a sense he's given her fresh
into the world again, and she's become his wife and his child as
well. From now on that's what you'll be to me—you little
bewildered, helpless thing. Don't be afraid of anything, Nora;
just open your heart to me, and I'll be conscience and will to
you both—(NORA *enters in her regular clothes.)* What's this? Not in
bed? You've changed your dress?

NOREA   Yes, Torvald, I've changed my dress.

HELMER   But why now, so late?

NORA   Tonight I'm not sleeping.

HELMER   But Nora dear—

NORA   *(looking at her watch)* It's still not so very late. Sit down, Torvald; we have a lot to talk over. *(She sits at one side of the table.)*

HELMER   Nora—what is this? That hard expression—

NORA   Sit down. This'll take some time. I have a lot to say.

HELMER   *(sitting at the table directly opposite her)* You worry me, Nora. And I don't understand you.

NORA   No, that's exactly it. You don't understand me. And I've never understood you either—until tonight. No, don't interrupt. You can just listen to what I say. We're closing out accounts, Torvald.

HELMER   How do you mean that?

NORA   *(after a short pause)* Doesn't anything strike you about our sitting here like this?

HELMER   What's that?

NORA   We've been married now eight years. Doesn't it occur to you that this is the first time we two, you and I, man and wife, have ever talked seriously together?

HELMER   What do you mean—seriously?

NORA   In eight whole years—longer even—right from our first acquaintance, we've never exchanged a serious word on any serious thing.

HELMER   You mean I should constantly go and involve you in problems you couldn't possibly help me with?

NORA   I'm not talking of problems, I'm saying that we've never sat down seriously together and tried to get to the bottom of anything.

HELMER   But dearest, what good would that ever do you?

NORA   That's the point right there: you've never understood me. I've been wronged greatly, Torvald—first by Papa, and then by you.

HELMER   What! By us—the two people who've loved you more than anyone else?

NORA   *(shaking her head)* You never loved me. You've thought it fun to be in love with me, that's all.

HELMER   Nora, what a thing to say!

NORA   Yes, it's true now, Torvald. When I lived at home with Papa, he told me all his opinions, so I had the same ones too; or if they were different I hid them, since he wouldn't have cared for that. He used to call me his doll-child, and he played with me the way I played with my dolls. Then I came into your house—

HELMER   How can you speak of our marriage like that?

NORA   *(unperturbed)* I mean, then I went from Papa's hands into yours. You arranged everything to your own taste, and so I got the same taste as you—or I pretended to; I can't remember. I guess a little of both, first one, then the other. Now when I look back, it seems as if I'd lived here like a beggar—just from hand

to mouth. I've lived by doing tricks for you, Torvald. But that's
the way you wanted it. It's a great sin what you and Papa did to
me. You're to blame that nothing's become of me.

HELMER   Nora, how unfair and ungrateful you are! Haven't you
been happy here?

NORA   No, never. I thought so—but I never have.

HELMER   Not—not happy!

NORA   No, only lighthearted. And you've always been so kind to
me. But our home's been nothing but a playpen. I've been your
doll-wife here, just as at home I was Papa's doll-child. And in
turn the children have been my dolls. I thought it was fun when
you played with me, just as they thought it fun when I played
with them. That's been our marriage, Torvald.

HELMER   There's some truth in what you're saying—under all the
raving exaggeration. But it'll all be different after this. Playtime's
over; now for the schooling.

NORA   Whose schooling—mine or the children's?

HELMER   Both yours and the children's, dearest.

NORA   Oh, Torvald, you're not the man to teach me to be a good
wife to you.

HELMER   And you can say that?

NORA   And I—how am I equipped to bring up children?

HELMER   Nora!

NORA   Didn't you say a moment ago that that was no job to trust
me with?

HELMER   In a flare of temper! Why fasten on that?

NORA   Yes, but you were so very right. I'm not up to the job.
There's another job I have to do first. I have to try to educate
myself. You can't help me with that. I've got to do it alone. And
that's why I'm leaving you now.

HELMER   *(jumping up)* What's that?

NORA   I have to stand completely alone, if I'm ever going to
discover myself and the world out there. So I can't go on living
with you.

HELMER   Nora, Nora!

NORA   I want to leave right away. Kristine should put me up for
the night—

HELMER   You're insane! You've no right! I forbid you!

NORA   From here on, there's no use forbidding me anything. I'll
take with me whatever is mine. I don't want a thing from you,
either now or later.

HELMER   What kind of madness is this!

NORA   Tomorrow I'm going home—I mean, home where I came
from. It'll be easier up there to find something to do.

HELMER   Oh, you blind, incompetent child!

NORA   I must learn to be competent, Torvald.

HELMER   Abandon your home, your husband, your children! And you're not even thinking what people will say.

NORA   I can't be concerned about that. I only know how essential this is.

HELMER   Oh, it's outrageous. So you'll run out like this on your most sacred vows.

NORA   What do you think are my most sacred vows?

HELMER   And I have to tell you that! Aren't they your duties to your husband and children?

NORA   I have other duties equally sacred.

HELMER   That isn't true. What duties are they?

NORA   Duties to myself.

HELMER   Before all else, you're a wife and a mother.

NORA   I don't believe in that anymore. I believe that, before all else, I'm a human being, no less than you—or anyway, I ought to try to become one. I know the majority thinks you're right, Torvald, and plenty of books agree with you, too. But I can't go on believing what the majority says, or what's written in books. I have to think over these things myself and try to understand them.

HELMER   Why can't you understand your place in your own home? On a point like that, isn't there one everlasting guide you can turn to? Where's your religion?

NORA   Oh, Torvald, I'm really not sure what religion is.

HELMER   What—?

NORA   I only know what the minister said when I was confirmed. He told me religion was this thing and that. When I get clear and away by myself, I'll go into that problem too. I'll see if what the minister said was right, or, in any case, if it's right for me.

HELMER   A young woman your age shouldn't talk like that. If religion can't move you, I can try to rouse your conscience. You do have some moral feeling? Or, tell me—has that gone too?

NORA   It's not easy to answer that, Torvald. I simply don't know. I'm all confused about these things. I just know I see them so differently from you. I find out, for one thing, that the law's not at all what I'd thought—but I can't get it through my head that the law is fair. A woman hasn't a right to protect her dying father or save her husband's life! I can't believe that.

HELMER   You talk like a child. You don't know anything of the world you live in.

NORA   No, I don't. But now I'll begin to learn for myself. I'll try to discover who's right, the world or I.

HELMER   Nora, you're sick; you've got a fever. I almost think you're out of your head.

NORA   I've never felt more clearheaded and sure in my life.

HELMER   And—clearheaded and sure—you're leaving your
husband and children?

NORA   Yes.

HELMER   Then there's only one possible reason.

NORA   What?

HELMER   You no longer love me.

NORA   No. That's exactly it.

HELMER   Nora! You can't be serious!

NORA   Oh, this is so hard, Torvald—you've been so kind to me
always. But I can't help it. I don't love you anymore.

HELMER   *(struggling for composure)* Are you also clearheaded and
sure about that?

NORA   Yes, completely. That's why I can't go on staying here.

HELMER   Can you tell me what I did to lose your love?

NORA   Yes, I can tell you. It was this evening when the
miraculous thing didn't come—then I knew you weren't the
man I'd imagined.

HELMER   Be more explicit; I don't follow you.

NORA   I've waited now so patiently eight long years—for, my
Lord, I know miracles don't come every day. Then this crisis
broke over me, and such a certainty filled me: *now* the
miraculous event would occur. While Krogstad's letter was lying
out there, I never for an instant dreamed that you could give in
to his terms. I was so utterly sure you'd say to him: go on, tell
your tale to the whole wide world. And when he'd done that—

HELMER   Yes, what then? When I'd delivered my own wife into
shame and disgrace—!

NORA   When he'd done that, I was so utterly sure that you'd step
forward, take the blame on yourself and say: I am the guilty one.

HELMER   Nora—!

NORA   You're thinking I'd never accept such a sacrifice from you?
No, of course not. But what good would my protests be against
you? That was the miracle I was waiting for, in terror and hope.
And to stave that off, I would have taken my life.

HELMER   I'd gladly work for you day and night, Nora—and take
on pain and deprivation. But there's no one who gives up honor
for love.

NORA   Millions of women have done just that.

HELMER   Oh, you think and talk like a silly child.

NORA   Perhaps. But you neither think nor talk like the man I
could join myself to. When your big fright was over—and it
wasn't from any threat against me, only for what might damage
you—when all the danger was past, for you it was just as if
nothing had happened. I was exactly the same, your little lark,
your doll, that you'd have to handle with double care now that

I'd turned out so brittle and frail. *(Gets up)* Torvald—in that instant it dawned on me that for eight years I've been living here with a stranger, and that I'd even conceived three children—oh, I can't stand the thought of it! I could tear myself to bits.

HELMER   *(heavily)* I see. There's a gulf that's opened between us— that's clear. Oh, but Nora, can't we bridge it somehow?

NORA   The way I am now, I'm no wife for you.

HELMER   I have the strength to make myself over.

NORA   Maybe—if your doll gets taken away.

HELMER   But to part! To part from you! No, Nora, no—I can't imagine it.

NORA   *(going out, right)* All the more reason why it has to be. *(She reenters with her coat and a small overnight bag, which she puts on a chair by the table.)*

HELMER   Nora, Nora, not now! Wait till tomorrow.

NORA   I can't spend the night in a strange man's room.

HELMER   But couldn't we live here like brother and sister—

NORA   You know very well how long that would last. *(Throws her shawl about her)* Good-bye, Torvald. I won't look in on the children. I know they're in better hands than mine. The way I am now, I'm no use to them.

HELMER   But someday, Nora—someday—?

NORA   How can I tell? I haven't the least idea what'll become of me.

HELMER   But you're my wife, now and wherever you go.

NORA   Listen, Torvald—I've heard that when a wife deserts her husband's house just as I'm doing, then the law frees him from all responsibility. In any case, I'm freeing you from being responsible. Don't feel yourself bound, any more than I will. There has to be absolute freedom for us both. Here, take your ring back. Give me mine.

HELMER   That too?

NORA   That too.

HELMER   There it is.

NORA   Good. Well, now it's all over. I'm putting the keys here. The maids know all about keeping up the house—better than I do. Tomorrow, after I've left town, Kristine will stop by to pack up everything that's mine from home. I'd like those things shipped to me.

HELMER   Over! All over! Nora, won't you ever think about me?

NORA   I'm sure I'll think of you often, and about the children and the house here.

HELMER   May I write you?

NORA   No—never. You're not to do that.

HELMER   Oh, but let me send you—

NORA   Nothing. Nothing.

HELMER   Or help you if you need it.

NORA   No. I accept nothing from strangers.

HELMER   Nora—can I never be more than a stranger to you?

NORA   *(picking up the overnight bag)* Ah, Torvald—it would take the greatest miracle of all—

HELMER   Tell me the greatest miracle!

NORA   You and I both would have to transform ourselves to the point that—Oh, Torvald, I've stopped believing in miracles.

HELMER   But I'll believe. Tell me! Transform ourselves to the point that—?

NORA   That our living together could be a true marriage.

(She goes out down the hall.)

HELMER   *(sinks down on a chair by the door, face buried in his hands)* Nora! Nora! *(Looking about and rising)* Empty. She's gone. *(A sudden hope leaps in him)* The greatest miracle—?

(From below, the sound of a door slamming shut)

Questions for *A Doll House*

1.   In a famous statement about the play, Ibsen remarked that *A Doll House* is about human rights more than women's rights. What do you think he meant by this assertion? What aspects of the play can you point to that illustrate Ibsen's statement?

2.   Nora has obviously changed by the end of the play; has Torvald?

3.   In the context of the play, items in the Helmer household such as the glass étagère and the Christmas tree take on a symbolic significance. In the same way, the characters' actions—Nora's tarantella, for instance—tell us something of their emotional state. Choose two or three of these emblems and discuss the way Ibsen uses them in the play.

4.   What purpose does the character of Dr. Rank serve in the play?

5.   The drama of the Helmers' disintegrating marriage is of course the focus of the play, but there are several subplots as well. Describe these, and analyze their function in the drama.

6.   What are the comic elements of *A Doll House*? Where lies the tragedy of the play?

7.   Comment on some aspects of the structure of the play: How, for example, does Ibsen engineer the climax of each Act?

Tina Howe (1938–   )

Tina Howe was born in New York City. She received her B.A. from Sarah Lawrence College, and did graduate studies at the Sorbonne in Paris, Columbia Teachers College in New York, and Chicago Teachers College. Her plays include *Museum* (1976), *The Art of Dining* (1979), and *Coastal Disturbances* (1986). *Painting Churches,* reprinted here, won the 1983 Obie (Off-Broadway) Award for distinguished playwrighting.

Howe, who lives in Manhattan with her husband and two children, currently teaches playwrighting at New York University. She has commented that each of her plays "moves according to its own logic and design. I see terrible dangers in insisting on tidy parallels and meaningful departures. It drains away all the mystery."

Painting Churches concerns a young artist trying to come to terms with her aging parents; *Coastal Disturbances* focuses on the relationships between lovers. Yet, as a writer for *The New York Times* observed, ". . . both plays evoke similar issues: about different ways of loving, the compassion that results from a genuine acceptance of another's failings, the painful knowledge of real intimacy, the hard-won battle for forgiveness."

Painting Churches

PAINTING CHURCHES was initially produced by The Second Stage at the South Street Theatre in 1983; artistic directors, Robyn Goodman and Carole Rothman.

DIRECTOR: *Carole Rothman*
SETTING: *Heidi Landesman*
LIGHTING: *Frances Aronson*
COSTUMES: *Nan Cibula*
SOUND: *Gary Harris*

CAST

(in order of appearance)

FANNY CHURCH *Marian Seldes*

GARDNER CHURCH *Donald Moffat*
MARGARET CHURCH (MAGS) *Frances Conroy*

CHARACTERS

FANNY SEDGWICK CHURCH, *a Bostonian from a fine old family, in her sixties*
GARDNER CHURCH, *her husband, an eminent New England poet from a finer family, in his seventies*
MARGARET CHURCH (MAGS), *their daughter, a painter, in her early thirties*

During the scene changes, the opening measures of the following Chopin waltzes are played:

As the house lights dim, the Waltz in A Minor, opus posthumous

Setting up Act I, Scene 2, the Waltz in E Minor, opus posthumous

Setting up Act I, Scene 3, the Waltz in E Major, opus posthumous

To close Act I, the final notes of the Waltz in B Minor, opus 69, no. 2. As the house lights dim for Act II, the Waltz in A flat Major, opus 64, no. 3

Setting up Act II, Scene 2, repeat the Waltz in A Minor, opus posthumous

To accompany the final moments of GARDNER's and FANNY's dance, the Waltz in D flat Major, opus 70, no. 3

ACT I

Scene 1

TIME: *Several years ago.*
PLACE: *The living room of the Churches' townhouse on Beacon Hill one week before everything will be moved to Cape Cod. Empty packing cartons line the room and all the furniture has been tagged with brightly colored markers. At first glance it looks like any discreet Boston interior, but on closer scrutiny one notices a certain flamboyance. Oddities from secondhand stores are mixed in with the fine old furniture, and exotic handmade curios vie with tasteful family objets d'art. What makes the room remarkable, though, is the play of light that pours through three soaring arched windows. At one hour it's hard edged and brilliant; the next, it's dappled and yielding. It transforms whatever it touches, giving the room a distinct feeling of unreality. It's several years ago, a bright spring morning.*

FANNY *is sitting on the sofa, wrapping a valuable old silver coffee service. She's wearing a worn bathrobe and fashionable hat. As she works, she makes a list of everything on a yellow legal pad.* GARDNER *can be heard typing in his study down the hall.*

FANNY: [*She picks up a coffee pot.*] God, this is good-looking! I'd forgotten how handsome Mama's old silver was! It's probably worth a fortune. It certainly weighs enough! [*Calling out.*] GARRRRRRRRRRRRRRRRRRRDNERRRRRRRRRRRR? . . . Well, it should bring us a pretty penny, that's for sure. [*Wraps it, places it in a carton, and then picks up the tray that goes with it. She holds it up like a mirror and adjusts her hat. Louder in another register.*] OH, GARRRRRRRRRRRRRRRRRRDNERRRRR? . . .
[*He continues typing.*]
FANNY: [*She then reaches for a small box and opens it with reverence.*] Grandma's Paul Revere teaspoons! . . . [*She takes out several and fondles them.*] I don't care how desperate things get, these will never go! One has to maintain some standards! [*She writes on her list.*] "Grandma's Paul Revere teaspoons, Cotuit!" . . . WASN'T IT THE AMERICAN WING OF THE METROPOLITAN MUSEUM OF ART THAT WANTED GRANDMA'S PAUL REVERE TEASPOONS SO BADLY? . . . [*She looks at her reflection in the tray again.*] This is a very good-looking hat, if I do say so. I was awfully smart to grab it up.
[*Silence.*]
DON'T YOU REMEMBER A DISTINGUISHED-LOOKING MAN COMING TO THE HOUSE AND OFFERING US FIFTY THOUSAND DOLLARS FOR GRANDMA'S PAUL REVERE TEASPOONS? . . . HE HAD ON THESE MARVELOUS SHOES! THEY WERE SO POINTED AT THE ENDS WE COULDN'T IMAGINE HOW HE EVER GOT THEM ON AND THEY WERE SHINED TO WITHIN AN INCH OF THEIR LIVES AND I REMEMBER HIM SAYING HE CAME FROM THE . . . AMERICAN WING OF THE METROPOLITAN MUSEUM OF ART! . . . HELLO? . . . GARDNER? . . . ARE YOU THERE!
[*The typing stops.*]
FANNY: YOO-HOOOOOOO . . . [*Like a fog horn.*] GARRRRRRRRRRRDNERRRRRRR? . . .
GARDNER: [*Offstage; from his study.*] YES, DEAR . . . IS THAT YOU? . . .
FANNY: OF COURSE IT'S ME! WHO ELSE COULD IT POSSIBLY BE? . . . DARLING, PLEASE COME HERE FOR A MINUTE.
[*The typing resumes.*]
FANNY: FOR GOD'S SAKE, WILL YOU STOP THAT DREADFUL TYPING BEFORE YOU SEND ME STRAIGHT TO THE NUT HOUSE? . . . [*In a new register.*] GARRRRRRRRRRRRRDNERRRRRR? . . .
[*He stops.*]

GARDNER: [*Offstage.*]
WHAT'S THAT?
MAGS IS BACK
FROM THE NUT
HOUSE? . . .

FANNY: I SAID . . . Lord, I hate
this yelling. . . . PLEASE . . .
COME . . . HERE!

[*Brief silence.*]

GARDNER: [*Offstage.*] I'LL BE
WITH YOU IN A MOMENT, I
DIDN'T HEAR HER RING.
[*Starts singing.*] "Nothing
Could be Finer Than to Be in
Carolina."

FANNY: It's a wonder I'm not in
a strait jacket already.
Actually, it might be rather
nice for a change . . .
peaceful. DARLING . . . I
WANT TO SHOW YOU MY
NEW HAT!

[*Silence.* GARDNER *enters, still singing. He's wearing mismatched tweeds and is holding a stack of papers which keep drifting to the floor.*]

GARDNER: Oh, don't you look nice! Very attractive, very attractive!

FANNY: But I'm still in my bathrobe.

GARDNER: [*Looking around the room, leaking more papers.*] Well, where's Mags?

FANNY: Darling, you're dropping your papers all over the floor.

GARDNER: [*Spies the silver tray.*] I remember this! Aunt Alice gave it to us, didn't she? [*He picks it up.*] Good Lord, it's heavy. What's it made of? Lead?!

FANNY: No, Aunt Alice did *not* give it to us. It was Mama's.

GARDNER: Oh, yes . . .
[*He starts to exit with it.*]

FANNY: Could I have it back, please?

GARDNER: [*Hands it to her, dropping more papers.*] Oh, sure thing. . . . Where's Mags? I thought you said she was here.

FANNY: I didn't say Mags was here, I asked *you* to come here.

GARDNER: [*Papers spilling.*] Damned papers keep falling. . . .

FANNY: I wanted to show you my new hat. I bought it in honor of Mags' visit. Isn't it marvelous?

GARDNER: [*Picking up the papers as more drop.*] Yes, yes, very nice . . .

FANNY: Gardner, you're not even looking at it!

GARDNER: Very becoming . . .

FANNY: You don't think it's too bright, do you? I don't want to look like a traffic light. Guess how much it cost?

GARDNER: [*A whole sheaf of papers slides to the floor; he dives for them.*] OH, SHIT!

FANNY: [*Gets to them first.*] It's all right, I've got them, I've got them. [*She hands them to him.*]

GARDNER: You'd think they had wings on them. . . .

FANNY: Here you go . . . GARDNER: . . . damned things won't hold still!

FANNY: Gar? . . .

GARDNER: [*Has become engrossed in one of the pages.*] Mmmmm?

FANNY: HELLO?

GARDNER: [*Startled.*] What's that?

FANNY: [*In a whisper.*] My hat. Guess how much it cost.

GARDNER: Oh, yes. Let's see . . . ten dollars?

FANNY: Ten dollars . . . IS THAT ALL? . . .

GARDNER: Twenty?

FANNY: GARDNER, THIS HAPPENS TO BE A DESIGNER HAT! DESIGNER HATS START AT FIFTY DOLLARS . . . SEVENTY-FIVE!

GARDNER: [*Jumps.*] Was that the door bell?

FANNY: No, it wasn't the door bell. Though it's high time Mags were here. She was probably in a train wreck!

GARDNER: [*Looking through his papers.*] I'm beginning to get fond of Wallace Stevens again.

FANNY: This damned move is going to kill me! Send me straight to my grave!

GARDNER: [*Reading from a page.*]

"The mules that angels ride come slowly down
The blazing passes, from beyond the sun.
Descensions of their tinkling bells arrive.
These muleteers are dainty of their way . . ."

[*Pause.*] Don't you love that! "These muleteers are *dainty* of their way"!? . . .

FANNY: Gar, the hat. How much?

[GARDNER *sighs.*]

FANNY: Darling? . . .

GARDNER: Oh, yes. Let's see . . . fifty dollars? Seventy-five?

FANNY: It's French.

GARDNER: Three hundred!

FANNY: [*Triumphant.*] No, eighty-five cents.

GARDNER: Eighty-five cents! . . . I thought you said . . .

FANNY: That's right . . . eighty . . . five . . . *cents!*

GARDNER: Well, you sure had me fooled!

FANNY: I found it at the thrift shop.

GARDNER: I thought it cost at least fifty dollars or seventy-five. You know, designer hats are very expensive!

FANNY: It was on the mark-down table. [*She takes it off and shows him the label.*] See that! Lily Daché! When I saw that label, I nearly keeled over right into the fur coats!

GARDNER: [*Handling it.*] Well, what do you know, that's the same label that's in my bathrobe.

FANNY: Darling, Lily Daché designed hats, not men's bathrobes!

GARDNER: Yup . . . Lily Daché . . . same name . . .

FANNY: If you look again, I'm sure you'll see . . .

GARDNER: . . . same script, same color, same size. I'll show you. [*He exits.*]

FANNY: Poor lamb can't keep anything straight anymore. [*Looks at herself in the tray again.*] God, this is a good-looking hat!

GARDNER: [*Returns with a nondescript plaid bathrobe. He points to the label.*] See that? . . . What does it say?

FANNY: [*Refusing to look at it.*] Lily Daché was a *hat* designer! She designed ladies' *hats*!

GARDNER: What . . . does . . . it . . . say?

FANNY: Gardner, you're being ridiculous.

GARDNER: [*Forcing it on her.*] Read . . . the label!

FANNY: Lily Daché did *not* design this bathrobe, I don't care what the label says!

GARDNER: READ! [FANNY *reads it.*] ALL RIGHT, NOW WHAT DOES IT SAY? . . .

FANNY: [*Chagrined.*] Lily Daché.

GARDNER: I told you!

FANNY: Wait a minute, let me look at that again. [*She does; then throws the robe at him in disgust.*] Gar, Lily Daché never designed a bathrobe in her life! Someone obviously ripped the label off one of her hats and then sewed it into the robe.

GARDNER: [*Puts it on over his jacket.*] It's damned good-looking. I've always loved this robe. I think you gave it to me. . . . Well, I've got to get back to work.

[*He abruptly exits.*]

FANNY: Where did you get that robe anyway? . . . I didn't give it to you, did I? . . .

[*Silence.* GARDNER *resumes typing.*]

FANNY: [*Holding the tray up again and admiring herself.*] You know, I think I *did* give it to him. I remember how excited I was when I found it at the thrift shop . . . fifty cents and never worn! *I* couldn't have sewn that label in it to impress him, could I? . . . I can't be that far gone! . . . The poor lamb wouldn't even notice it, let alone understand its cachet. . . . Uuuuuuh, this damned tray is even heavier than the coffee pot. They must have been amazons in the old days! [*Writes on her pad.*] "Empire tray, Parke-Bernet Galleries," and good riddance! [*She wraps it and drops it into the carton with the coffee pot.*] Where *is* that wretched Mags? It would be just like her to get into a train wreck! She was supposed to be here hours ago. Well, if she doesn't show up soon, I'm going to drop dead of exhaustion. God, wouldn't that be wonderful? . . . Then they could just cart me off into storage with all the old chandeliers and china . . .

[*The doorbell rings.*]

FANNY: IT'S MAGS, IT'S MAGS!
[*A pause. Dashing out of the
room, colliding into* GARDNER.]
GOOD GOD, LOOK AT ME!
I'M STILL IN MY
BATHROBE!

GARDNER: [*Offstage.*] COMING,
COMING . . . I'VE GOT IT . . .
COMING! [*Dashing into the
room, colliding into* FANNY.] I'VE
GOT IT . . . HOLD ON . . .
COMING . . . COMING. . . .

FANNY: [*Offstage.*] MAGS IS HERE! IT'S MAGS. . . . SHE'S FINALLY
HERE!

[GARDNER *exits to open the front door.* MAGS *comes staggering in carrying a suitcase and an
enormous duffle bag. She wears wonderfully distinctive clothes and has very much her own look.
She's extremely out of breath and too wrought up to drop her heavy bags.*]

MAGS: I'm sorry . . . I'm sorry I'm so late. . . . Everything went
wrong! A passenger had a heart attack outside of New London
and we had to stop. . . . It was terrifying! All these medics and
policemen came swarming onto the train and the conductor kept
running up and down the aisles telling everyone not to leave
their seats under any circumstances. . . . Then the New London
fire department came screeching down to the tracks, sirens
blaring, lights whirling, and all these men in black rubber suits
starting pouring through the doors. . . . *That* took two hours. . . .
FANNY: DARLING . . . DARLING . . . WHERE ARE YOU? . . .
MAGS: *Then,* I couldn't get a cab at the station. There just weren't
any! I must have circled the block fifteen times. Finally I just
stepped out into the traffic with my thumb out, but no one
would pick me up . . . so I walked. . . .
FANNY: [*Offstage.*] Damned zipper's stuck. . . .
GARDNER: You walked all the way from the South Station?
MAGS: Well actually, I ran. . . .
GARDNER: You had poor Mum scared to death.
MAGS: [*Finally puts the bags down with a deep sigh.*] I'm sorry. . . . I'm
really sorry. It was a nightmare.
FANNY: [*Reenters the room, her dress over her head. The zipper's stuck; she
staggers around blindly.*] Damned zipper! Gar, will you please help
me with this?
MAGS: I sprinted all the way up Beacon Hill.
GARDNER: [*Opening his arms wide.*] Well, come here and let's get a
look at you. [*He hugs her.*] Mags! . . .
MAGS: [*Squeezing him tight.*] Oh, Daddy . . . Daddy!
GARDNER: My Mags!
MAGS: I never thought I'd get here! . . . Oh, you look wonderful!
GARDNER: Well, you don't look so bad yourself!
MAGS: I love your hair. It's gotten so . . . white!

FANNY: [*Still lost in her dress, struggling with the zipper.*] This is *so* typical . . . just as Mags arrives, my zipper has to break! [FANNY *grunts and struggles.*]

MAGS: [*Waves at her.*] Hi, Mum. . . .

FANNY: Just a minute, dear, my zipper's . . .

GARDNER: [*Picks up* MAGS' *bags.*] Well, sit down and take a load off your feet. . . .

MAGS: I was so afraid I'd never make it. . . .

GARDNER: [*Staggering under the weight of her bags.*] What have you got in here? Lead weights?

MAGS: I can't believe you're finally letting me do you.

FANNY: [*Flings her arms around* MAGS, *practically knocking her over.*] OH, DARLING . . . MY PRECIOUS MAGS, YOU'RE HERE AT LAST.

GARDNER: [*Lurching around in circles.*] Now let's see . . . where should I put these? . . .

FANNY: I was sure your train had derailed and you were lying dead in some ditch!

MAGS: [*Pulls away from* FANNY *to come to* GARDNER'S *rescue.*] Daddy, please, let me . . . these are much too heavy.

FANNY: [*Finally noticing* MAGS.] GOOD LORD, WHAT HAVE YOU DONE TO YOUR HAIR?!

MAGS: [*Struggling to take the bags from* GARDNER.] Come on, give them to me . . . please? [*She sets them down by the sofa.*]

FANNY: [*As her dress starts to slide off one shoulder.*] Oh, not again! . . . Gar, would you give me a hand and see what's wrong with this zipper. One minute it's stuck, the next it's falling to pieces. [GARDNER *goes to her and starts fussing with it.*]

MAGS: [*Pacing.*] I don't know, it's been crazy all week. Monday, I forgot to keep an appointment I'd made with a new model. . . . Tuesday, I overslept and stood up my advanced painting students. . . . Wednesday, the day of my meeting with Max Zoll, I forgot to put on my underpants. . . .

FANNY: GOD DAMNIT, GAR, CAN'T YOU DO ANYTHING ABOUT THIS ZIPPER?!

MAGS: I mean, there I was, racing down Broome Street in this gauzy Tibetan skirt when I tripped and fell right at his feet . . . SPLATTT! My skirt goes flying over my head and there I am . . . everything staring him in the face . . .

FANNY: COME ON, GAR, USE A LITTLE MUSCLE!

MAGS: [*Laughing.*] Oh, well, all that matters is that I finally got here. . . . I mean . . . there you are. . . .

GARDNER: [*Struggling with the zipper.*] I can't see it, it's too small!

FANNY: [*Whirls away from* GARDNER, *pulling her dress off altogether.*] OH, FORGET IT! JUST FORGET IT! . . . The trolley's probably missing half its teeth, just like someone else I know. [*To* MAGS.] I grind my teeth in my sleep now, I've worn them all down to stubs. Look at that! [*She flings open her mouth and points.*] Nothing left but the gums!

GARDNER: I never hear you grind your teeth. . . .

FANNY: That's because I'm snoring so loud. How could you hear anything through all that racket? It even wakes me up. It's no wonder poor Daddy has to sleep downstairs.

MAGS: [*Looking around.*] Jeez, look at the place! So, you're finally doing it . . . selling the house and moving to Cotuit year round. I don't believe it. I just don't believe it!

GARDNER: Well, how about a drink to celebrate Mags' arrival?

MAGS: You've been here so long. Why move now?

FANNY: Gardner, what are you wearing that bathrobe for? . . .

MAGS: You can't move. I won't let you!

FANNY: [*Softly to* GARDNER.] Really, darling, you ought to pay more attention to your appearance.

MAGS: You love this house. *I* love this house . . . this room . . . the light.

GARDNER: So, Mags, how about a little . . . [*He drinks from an imaginary glass.*] to wet your whistle?

FANNY: We can't start drinking now, it isn't even noon yet!

MAGS: I'm starving. I've got to get something to eat before I collapse!
[*She exits toward the kitchen.*]

FANNY: What *have* you done to your hair, dear? The color's so queer and all your nice curl is gone.

GARDNER: It looks to me as if she dyed it.

FANNY: Yes, that's it. You're absolutely right! It's a completely different color. She dyed it bright red!
[MAGS *can be heard thumping and thudding through the icebox.*]

FANNY: NOW, MAGS, I DON'T WANT YOU FILLING UP ON SNACKS. . . . I'VE MADE A PERFECTLY BEAUTIFUL LEG OF LAMB FOR LUNCH! . . . HELLO? . . . DO YOU HEAR ME? . . .
[*To* GARDNER.] No one in our family has *ever* had red hair, it's so common looking.

GARDNER: I like it. It brings out her eyes.

FANNY: WHY ON EARTH DID YOU DYE YOUR HAIR *RED,* OF ALL COLORS?! . . .

MAGS: [*Returns, eating Saltines out of the box.*] I didn't dye my hair, I just added some highlight.

FANNY: I suppose that's what your arty friends in New York do . . . dye their hair all the colors of the rainbow!

GARDNER: Well, it's damned attractive if you ask me . . . damned attractive!

[MAGS *unzips her duffle bag and rummages around in it while eating the Saltines.*]

FANNY: Darling, I told you not to bring a lot of stuff with you. We're trying to get rid of things.

MAGS: [*Pulls out a folding easel and starts setting it up.*] AAAAAHHHHHH, here it is. Isn't it a beauty? I bought it just for you!

FANNY: Please don't get crumbs all over the floor. Crystal was just here yesterday. It was her last time before we move.

MAGS: [*At her easel.*] God, I can hardly wait! I can't believe you're finally letting me do you.

FANNY: "*Do*" us? . . . What *are* you talking about?

GARDNER: [*Reaching for the Saltines.*] Hey, Mags, could I have a couple of those?

MAGS: [*Tosses him the box.*] Sure! [*To* FANNY.] Your portrait.

GARDNER: Thanks. [*He starts munching on a handful.*]

FANNY: You're planning to paint our portrait now? While we're trying to move? . . .

GARDNER: [*Sputtering Saltines.*] Mmmmm, I'd forgotten just how delicious Saltines are!

MAGS: It's a perfect opportunity. There'll be no distractions; you'll be completely at my mercy. Also, you promised.

FANNY: I did?

MAGS: Yes, you did.

FANNY: Well, I must have been off my rocker.

MAGS: No, you said, "You can paint us, you can dip us in concrete, you can do anything you want with us, just so long as you help us get out of here!"

GARDNER: [*Offering the box of Saltines to* FANNY.] You really ought to try some of these, Fan, they're absolutely delicious!

FANNY: [*Taking a few.*] Why, thank you.

MAGS: I figure we'll pack in the morning and you'll pose in the afternoons. It'll be a nice diversion.

FANNY: These *are* good!

GARDNER: Here, dig in . . . take some more.

MAGS: I have some wonderful news . . . amazing news! I wanted to wait 'til I got here to tell you.

[*They eat their Saltines, passing the box back and forth as* MAGS *speaks.*]

MAGS: You'll die! Just fall over into the packing cartons and die! Are you ready? . . . BRACE YOURSELVES. . . . OK, HERE GOES. . . . I'm being given a one woman show at one of the most important galleries in New York this fall. Me, Margaret Church, exhibited at Castelli's, 420 West Broadway. . . . Can you believe it?! . . . MY PORTRAITS HANGING IN THE SAME ROOMS THAT HAVE SHOWN RAUSCHENBERG, JOHNS,

WARHOL, KELLY, LICHTENSTEIN, STELLA, SERRA, ALL THE
HEAVIES. . . . It's incredible, beyond belief . . . I mean, at my
age. . . . Do you know how good you have to be to get in there?
It's a miracle . . . an honest-to-God, star-spangled miracle!

[*Pause.*]

FANNY: [*Mouth full.*] Oh, darling, that's wonderful. We're so happy for you!

GARDNER: [*His mouth full.*] No one deserves it more, no one deserves it more!

MAGS: Through some fluke, some of Castelli's people showed up at
our last faculty show at Pratt and were knocked out. . . .

FANNY: [*Reaching for the box of Saltines.*] More, more . . .

MAGS: They said they hadn't seen anyone handle light like me since
the French Impressionists. They said I was this weird blend of
Pierre Bonnard, Mary Cassatt and David Hockney. . . .

GARDNER: [*Swallowing his own mouthful.*] I told you they were good.

MAGS: Also, no one's doing portraits these days. They're considered
passé. I'm so out of it, I'm in.

GARDNER: Well, you're loaded with talent and always have been.

FANNY: She gets it all from Mama, you know. Her miniature of
Henry James is still one of the main attractions at the
Atheneum. Of course no woman of breeding could be a
professional artist in her day. It simply wasn't done. But talk
about talent . . . that woman had talent to burn!

MAGS: I want to do one of you for the show.

FANNY: Oh, do Daddy, he's the famous one.

MAGS: No, I want to do you both. I've always wanted to do you and
now I've finally got a good excuse.

FANNY: It's high time somebody painted Daddy again! I'm sick to
death of that dreadful portrait of him in the National Gallery
they keep reproducing. He looks like an undertaker!

GARDNER: Well, I think you should just do Mum. She's never looked
handsomer.

FANNY: Oh, come on, I'm a perfect fright and you know it.

MAGS: I want to do you both. Side by side. In this room. Something
really classy. You look so great. Mum with her crazy hats and
everything and you with that face. If I could just get you to hold
still long enough and actually pose.

GARDNER: [*Walking around, distracted.*] Where are those papers I just
had? God damnit, Fanny. . . .

MAGS: I have the feeling it's either now or never.

GARDNER: I can't hold on to anything around here. [*He exits to his
study.*]

MAGS: I've always wanted to do you. It would be such a challenge.

FANNY: [*Pulling MAGS next to her onto the sofa.*] I'm so glad you're
finally here, Mags. I'm very worried about Daddy.

MAGS: Mummy, please. I just got here.

FANNY: He's getting quite gaga.

MAGS: Mummy! . . .

FANNY: You haven't seen him in almost a year. Two weeks ago he walked through the front door of the Codmans' house, kissed Emily on the cheek and settled down in the maid's room, thinking he was home!

MAGS: Oh, come on, you're exaggerating.

FANNY: He's as mad as a hatter and getting worse every day! It's this damned new book of his. He works on it around the clock. I've read some of it, and it doesn't make one word of sense, it's all at sixes and sevens. . . .

GARDNER: [*Poking his head back in the room, spies some of his papers on a table and grabs them.*] Ahhh, here they are.
[*He exits.*]

FANNY: [*Voice lowered.*] Ever since this dry spell with his poetry, he's been frantic, absolutely . . . frantic!

MAGS: I hate it when you do this.

FANNY: I'm just trying to get you to face the facts around here.

MAGS: There's nothing wrong with him! He's just as sane as the next man. Even saner, if you ask me.

FANNY: You know what he's doing now? You couldn't guess in a million years! . . . He's writing criticism! Daddy! [*She laughs.*] Can you believe it? The man doesn't have one analytic bone in his body. His mind is a complete jumble and always has been!
[*There's a loud crash from* GARDNER'S *study.*]

GARDNER: [*Offstage.*] SHIT!

MAGS: He's abstracted. . . . That's the way he is.

FANNY: He doesn't spend any time with me anymore. He just holes up in that filthy study with Toots. God, I hate that bird! Though actually they're quite cunning together. Daddy's teaching him Gray's Elegy. You ought to see him in there, Toots perched on top of Daddy's head, spouting out verse after verse . . .
Daddy, tap-tap-tapping away on his typewriter. They're quite a pair.

GARDNER: [*Pokes his head back in.*] Have you seen that Stevens poem I was reading before?

FANNY: [*Long suffering.*] NO, I HAVEN'T SEEN THAT STEVENS POEM YOU WERE READING BEFORE! . . . Things are getting very tight around here, in case you haven't noticed. Daddy's last Pulitzer didn't even cover our real estate tax, and now that he's too doddery to give readings anymore, that income is gone. . . .
[*Suddenly handing* MAGS *the sugar bowl she'd been wrapping.*] Mags, *do* take this sugar bowl. You can use it to serve tea to your students at that wretched art school of yours. . . .

MAGS: It's called Pratt! The Pratt Institute.

FANNY: Pratt, Splatt, whatever . . .

MAGS: And I don't serve tea to my students, I teach them how to paint.

FANNY: Well, I'm sure none of them has ever seen a sugar bowl as handsome as this before.

GARDNER: [*Reappearing again.*] You're sure you haven't seen it? . . .

FANNY: [*Loud and angry.*] YES, I'M SURE I HAVEN'T SEEN IT! I JUST TOLD YOU I HAVEN'T SEEN IT!

GARDNER: [*Retreating.*] Right you are, right you are.

[*He exits.*]

FANNY: God!

[*Silence.*]

MAGS: What do you have to yell at him like that for?

FANNY: Because the poor thing's as deaf as an adder!

[MAGS *sighs deeply; silence.*]

FANNY: [*Suddenly exuberant, leads her over to a lamp.*] Come, I want to show you something.

MAGS: [*Looking at it.*] What is it?

FANNY: Something I made. [MAGS *is about to turn it on.*] WAIT, DON'T TURN IT ON YET! It's got to be dark to get the full effect. [*She rushes to the windows and pulls down the shades.*]

MAGS: What *are* you doing? . . .

FANNY: Hold your horses a minute. You'll see. . . . [*As the room gets darker and darker.*] Poor me, you wouldn't believe the lengths I go to to amuse myself these days. . . .

MAGS: [*Touching the lamp shade.*] What is this? It looks like a scene of some sort.

FANNY: It's an invention I made . . . a kind of magic lantern.

MAGS: Gee . . . it's amazing. . . .

FANNY: What I did was buy an old engraving of the Grand Canal. . . .

MAGS: You *made* this?

FANNY: . . . and then color it in with crayons. Next, I got out my sewing scissors and cut out all the street lamps and windows . . . anything that light would shine through. Then I pasted it over a plain lampshade, put the shade on this old horror of a lamp, turned on the switch and . . . [*She turns it on.*] VOILÀ . . . VENICE TWINKLING AT DUSK! It's quite effective, don't you think? . . .

MAGS: [*Walking around it.*] Jeeez . . .

FANNY: And see, I poked out all the little lights on the gondolas with a straight pin.

MAGS: Where on earth did you get the idea?

FANNY: Well you know, idle minds . . .

[FANNY *spins the shade, making the lights whirl.*]

MAGS: It's really amazing. I mean, you could sell this in a store!

FANNY: LOOK OUT, LOOK OUT!
MAGS: [*Rushes over to him.*] Oh, Daddy, are you all right?

GARDNER: [*Enters.*] HERE IT IS. IT WAS RIGHT ON TOP OF MY DESK THE WHOLE TIME. [*He crashes into a table.*] OOOOOWWWWW!

FANNY: WATCH WHERE YOU'RE GOING, WATCH WHERE YOU'RE GOING!

GARDNER: [*Hopping up and down on one leg.*] GOD DAMNIT! . . . I HIT MY SHIN.
FANNY: I was just showing Mags my lamp. . . .
GARDNER: [*Limping over to it.*] Oh, yes, isn't that something? Mum is awfully clever with that kind of thing. . . . It was all her idea. Buying the engraving, coloring it in, cutting out all those little dots.
FANNY: Not "dots" . . . lights and windows, lights and windows!
GARDNER: Right, right . . . lights and windows.
FANNY: Well, we'd better get some light back in here before someone breaks their neck. [*She zaps the shades back up.*]
GARDNER: [*Puts his arm around* MAGS.] Gee, it's good to have you back.
MAGS: It's good to be back.
GARDNER: And I like that new red hair of yours. It's very becoming.
MAGS: But I told you, I hardly touched it. . . .
GARDNER: Well, something's different. You've got a glow. So . . . how do you want us to pose for this grand portrait of yours? . . . [*He poses self-consciously.*]
MAGS: Oh, Daddy, setting up a portrait takes a lot of time and thought. You've got to figure out the background, the lighting, what to wear, the sort of mood you want to . . .
FANNY: OOOOH, LET'S DRESS UP, LET'S DRESS UP! [*She grabs a packing blanket, drapes it around herself and links arms with* GARDNER, *striking an elegant pose.*] This is going to be fun. She was absolutely right! Come on, Gar, look distinguished!
MAGS: Mummy, please, it's not a game!
FANNY: [*More and more excited.*] You still have your tuxedo, don't you? And I'll wear my marvelous long black dress that makes me look like the fascinating woman in the Sargent painting! [*She strikes the famous profile pose.*]
MAGS: MUMMY?! . . .
FANNY: I'm sorry, we'll behave, just tell us what to do.
[*They settle down next to each other.*]
GARDNER: That's right, you're the boss.
FANNY: Yes, you're the boss.

MAGS: But I'm not ready yet; I haven't set anything up.

FANNY: Relax, darling, we just want to get the hang of it. . . .

[*They stare straight ahead, trying to look like suitable subjects, but they can't hold still. They keep making faces, lifting an eyebrow, wriggling a nose, twitching a lip. Nothing big and grotesque, just flickering changes; a half-smile here, a self-important frown there. They steal glances at each other every so often.*]

GARDNER: How am I doing, Fan?

FANNY: Brilliantly, absolutely brilliantly!

MAGS: But you're making faces.

FANNY: *I'm* not making faces. [*Turning to* GARDNER *and making a face.*] Are *you* making faces, Gar?

GARDNER: [*Instantly making one.*] Certainly not! I'm the picture of restraint!
[*Without meaning to, they get sillier and sillier. They start giggling, then laughing.*]

MAGS: [*Can't help but join in.*] You two are impossible . . . completely impossible! I was crazy to think I could ever pull this off! [*Laughing away.*] Look at you . . . just . . . look at you!

BLACKOUT

Scene 2

Two days later, around five in the afternoon. Half of the Church household has been dragged into the living room for packing. Overflowing cartons are everywhere. They're filled with pots and pans, dishes and glasses, and the entire contents of two linen closets. MAGS has placed a stepladder under one of the windows. A pile of tablecloths and curtains is flung beneath it. Two side chairs are in readiness for the eventual pose.

MAGS: [*Has just pulled a large crimson tablecloth out of a carton. She unfurls it with one shimmering toss.*] PERFECT . . . PERFECT! . . .

FANNY: [*Seated on the sofa, clutches an old pair of galoshes to her chest.*] Look at these old horrors; half the rubber is rotted away and the fasteners are falling to pieces. . . . GARDNER? . . . OH, GARRRRRRRRRRRDNERRRRRR? . . .

MAGS: [*Rippling out the tablecloth with shorter snapping motions.*] Have you ever seen such a color?. . .

FANNY: I'VE FOUND YOUR OLD SLEDDING GALOSHES IN WITH THE POTS AND PANS. DO YOU STILL WANT THEM?

MAGS: It's like something out of a Rubens! . . . [*She slings it over a chair and then sits on a footstool to finish the Sara Lee banana cake she started. As she eats, she looks at the tablecloth making happy grunting sounds.*]

FANNY: [*Lovingly puts the galoshes on over her shoes and wiggles her feet.*] God, these bring back memories! There were real snowstorms in the old days. Not these pathetic little two-inch droppings we have now. After a particularly heavy one, Daddy and I used to go sledding on the Common. This was way before you were born. . . . God, it was a hundred years ago! . . . Daddy would stop writing early, put on these galoshes and come looking for me, jingling the fasteners like castanets. It was a kind of mating call, almost. . . . [*She jingles them.*] The Common was always deserted after a storm; we had the whole place to ourselves. It was so romantic. . . . We'd haul the sled up Beacon Street, stop under the State House, and aim it straight down to the Park Street Church, which was much further away in those days. . . . Then Daddy would lie down on the sled, I'd lower myself on top of him, we'd rock back and forth a few times to gain momentum and then . . . WHOOOOOOOOSSSSSSSHHHHH . . . down we'd plunge like a pair of eagles locked in a spasm of lovemaking. God, it was wonderful! . . . The city whizzing past us at ninety miles an hour . . . the cold . . . the darkness . . . Daddy's hair in my mouth . . . GAR . . . REMEMBER HOW WE USED TO GO SLEDDING IN THE OLD DAYS? . . . Sometimes he'd lie on top of me. That was fun. I liked that even more. [*In her foghorn voice.*] GARRRRRRRRRRRDNERRRRRR? . . .

MAGS: Didn't he say he was going out this afternoon?

FANNY: Why, so he did! I completely forgot. [*She takes off the galoshes.*] I'm getting just as bad as him. [*She drops them into a different carton—wistful.*] Gar's galoshes, Cotuit.
[*A pause.*]

MAGS: [*Picks up the tablecloth again; holds it high over her head.*] Isn't this fabulous? . . . [*She then wraps* FANNY *in it.*] It's the perfect backdrop. Look what it does to your skin.

FANNY: Mags, what *are* you doing?

MAGS: It makes you glow like a pomegranate. . . . [*She whips it off her.*] Now all I need is a hammer and nails. . . . [*She finds them.*] YES! [*She climbs up the stepladder and starts hammering a corner of the cloth into the moulding of one of the windows.*] This is going to look so great! . . . I've never seen such color!

FANNY: Darling, what is going on? . . .

MAGS: Rembrandt, eat your heart out! You seventeenth-century Dutch has-been, you. [*She hammers more furiously.*]

FANNY: MARGARET, THIS IS NOT A CONSTRUCTION SITE. . . . PLEASE . . . STOP IT. . . . YOOHOOOOO . . . DO YOU HEAR ME? . . .

[GARDNER *suddenly appears, dressed in a raincoat.*]

GARDNER: YES, DEAR, HERE I AM. I JUST STEPPED OUT FOR A WALK DOWN CHESTNUT STREET. BEAUTIFUL AFTERNOON, ABSOLUTELY BEAUTIFUL!

FANNY: [*To* MAGS.] YOU'RE GOING TO RUIN THE WALLS TO SAY NOTHING OF MAMA'S BEST TABLECLOTH. . . . MAGS, DO YOU HEAR ME? . . . YOOHOO! . . .

GARDNER: WHY, THAT LOOKS VERY NICE, MAGS, very nice indeed. . . .

FANNY: DARLING, I MUST INSIST you stop that dreadful . . .

MAGS: [*Steps down; stands back and looks at it.*] That's it. That's *IT!*

FANNY: [*To* GARDNER, *worried.*] Where have *you* been? [MAGS *kisses her fingers at the backdrop and settles back into her banana cake.*]

GARDNER: [*To* FANNY.] You'll never guess who I ran into on Chestnut Street . . . Pate Baldwin!

[*He takes his coat off and drops it on the floor. He then sits in one of the posing chairs.*]

MAGS: [*Mouth full of cake.*] Oh, Daddy, I'm nowhere near ready for you yet.

FANNY: [*Picks up his coat and hands it to him.*] Darling, coats do *not* go on the floor.

GARDNER: [*Rises, but forgets where he's supposed to go.*] He was in terrible shape. I hardly recognized him. Well, it's the Parkinson's disease. . . .

FANNY: You mean, Hodgkin's disease. . . .

GARDNER: Hodgkin's disease? . . .

MAGS: [*Leaves her cake and returns to the tablecloth.*] Now to figure out exactly how to use this gorgeous light. . . .

FANNY: Yes, Pate has Hodgkin's disease, not Parkinson's disease. Sammy Bishop has Parkinson's disease. In the closet . . . your coat goes . . . in the closet!

GARDNER: You're absolutely right! Pate has Hodgkin's disease. [*He stands motionless, the coat over his arm.*]

FANNY: . . . and Goat Davis has Addison's disease.

GARDNER: I always get them confused.

FANNY: [*Pointing towards the closet.*] That way. . . . [GARDNER *exits to the closet;* FANNY *calls after him.*] Grace Phelps has it too, I think. Or, it might be Hodgkin's, like Pate. I can't remember.

GARDNER: [*Returns with a hanger.*] Doesn't the Goat have Parkinson's disease?

FANNY: No, that's Sammy Bishop.

GARDNER: God, I haven't seen the Goat in ages! [*The coat still over his arm, he hands* FANNY *the hanger.*]

FANNY: He hasn't been well.

GARDNER: Didn't Heppy . . . *die?*!

FANNY: What are you giving me this for? . . . Oh, Heppy's been dead for years. She died on the same day as Luster Bright, don't you remember?

GARDNER: I always liked her.

FANNY: [*Gives him back the hanger.*] Here, I don't want this.

GARDNER: She was awfully attractive.

FANNY: Who?

GARDNER: Heppy!

FANNY: Oh, yes, Heppy had real charm.

MAGS: [*Keeps adjusting the tablecloth.*] Better . . . better . . .

GARDNER: . . . which is something the Goat is short on, if you ask me. He has Hodgkin's disease, doesn't he?
[*Puts his raincoat back on and sits down.*]

FANNY: Darling, what *are* you doing? I thought you wanted to hang up your coat!

GARDNER: [*After a pause.*] OH, YES, THAT'S RIGHT! [*He goes back to the closet; a pause.*]

FANNY: Where were we?

GARDNER: [*Returns with yet another hanger.*] Let's see. . . .

FANNY: [*Takes both hangers from him.*] FOR GOD'S SAKE, GAR, PAY ATTENTION!

GARDNER: It was something about the Goat. . . .

FANNY: [*Takes the coat from* GARDNER.] HERE, LET ME DO IT! . . . [*Under her breath to* MAGS.] See what I mean about him? You don't know the half of it! [*She hangs it up in the closet.*] . . . Not the half.

MAGS: [*Still tinkering with the backdrop.*] Almost . . . almost . . .

GARDNER: [*Sitting back down in one of the posing chairs.*] Oh, Fan, did I tell you, I ran into Pate Baldwin just now. I'm afraid he's not long for this world.

FANNY: [*Returning.*] Well, it's that Hodgkin's disease. . . . [*She sits on the posing chair next to him.*]

GARDNER: God, I hate to see him go. He's one of the great editors of our times. I couldn't have done it without him. He gave me everything, everything!

MAGS: [*Makes a final adjustment.*] Yes, that's it! [*She stands back and gazes at them.*] You look wonderful! . . .

FANNY: Isn't it getting to be . . . [*She taps at an imaginary watch on her wrist and drains an imaginary glass.*] cocktail time?!

GARDNER: [*Looks at his watch.*] On the button, on the button! [*He rises.*]

FANNY: I'll have the usual, please. Do join us, Mags! Daddy bought some Dubonnet especially for you!

MAGS: Hey. I was just getting some ideas.

GARDNER: [*To* MAGS, *as he exits for the bar.*] How about a little . . . *Dubonnet* to wet your whistle?

FANNY: Oh, Mags, it's like old times having you back with us like this!

GARDNER: [*Offstage.*] THE USUAL FOR YOU, FAN?

FANNY: I wish we saw more of you. . . . PLEASE! . . . Isn't he darling? Have you ever known anyone more darling than Daddy? . . .

GARDNER: [*Offstage. Hums Jolson's "You Made Me Love You."*] MAGS, HOW ABOUT YOU? . . . A LITTLE . . . DUBONNET? . . .

FANNY: Oh, *do* join us!   MAGS: [*To* GARDNER.] No, nothing, thanks.

FANNY: Well, what do you think of your aged parents picking up and moving to Cotuit year round? Pretty crazy, eh what? . . . Nothing but the gulls, oysters and us!

GARDNER: [*Returns with* FANNY's *drink.*] Here you go. . . .

FANNY: Why thank you, Gar. [*To* MAGS.] You sure you won't join us?

GARDNER: [*Lifts his glass towards* FANNY *and* MAGS.] Cheers!

[GARDNER *and* FANNY *take that first life-saving gulp.*]

FANNY: Aaaaahhhhh!   GARDNER: Hits the spot, hits the spot!

MAGS: Well, I certainly can't do you like that!

FANNY: Why not? I think we look very . . . *comme il faut!*

    [*She slouches into a rummy pose;* GARDNER *joins her.*]

    WAIT . . . I'VE GOT IT! I'VE GOT IT!

[*She whispers excitedly to* GARDNER.]

MAGS: Come on, let's not start this again!

GARDNER: What's that? . . . Oh, yes . . . yes, yes . . . I know the one you mean. Yes, right, right . . . of course.

    [*A pause.*]

FANNY: How's . . . *this?!* . . . [FANNY *grabs a large serving fork and they fly into an imitation of Grant Wood's* American Gothic.]

MAGS: . . . and I wonder why it's taken me all these years to get you to pose for me. You just don't take me seriously! Poor old Mags and her ridiculous portraits . . .

FANNY: Oh, darling, your portraits aren't *ridiculous!* They may not be all that one *hopes* for, but they're certainly not . . .

MAGS: Remember how you behaved at my first group show in Soho? . . . Oh, come on, you remember. It was a real circus! Think back. . . . It was about six years ago. . . . Daddy had just been awarded some presidential medal of achievement and you insisted he wear it around his neck on a bright red ribbon, and you wore this . . . *huge* feathered hat to match! I'll never forget it! It was the size of a giant pizza with twenty-inch red turkey feathers shooting straight up into the air. . . . Oh, come on, you remember, don't you? . . .

FANNY: [*Leaping to her feet.*] HOLD EVERYTHING! THIS IS IT! THIS IS

REALLY IT! Forgive me for interrupting, Mags darling, it'll just take a minute. [*She whispers excitedly to* GARDNER.]

MAGS: I had about eight portraits in the show, mostly of friends of mine, except for this old one I'd done of Mrs. Crowninshield.

GARDNER: All right, all right . . . let's give it a whirl.

[*A pause; then they mime Michelangelo's* Pietà *with* GARDNER *lying across* FANNY's *lap as the dead Christ.*]

MAGS: [*Depressed.*] The *Pietà*. Terrific!

FANNY: [*Jabbing* GARDNER *in the ribs.*] Hey, we're getting good at this.

GARDNER: Of course it would help if we didn't have all these modern clothes on.

MAGS: AS I WAS SAYING . . .

FANNY: Sorry, Mags . . . sorry . . .

[*Huffing and creaking with the physical exertion of it all, they return to their seats.*]

MAGS: . . . As soon as you stepped foot in the gallery you spotted it and cried out, "MY GOD, WHAT'S MILLICENT CROWNINSHIELD DOING HERE?" Everyone looked up what with Daddy's clanking medal and your amazing hat which I was sure would take off and start flying around the room. A crowd gathered. . . . Through some utter fluke, you latched on to *the* most important critic in the city, I mean . . . Mr. Modern Art himself, and you hauled him over to the painting, trumpeting out for all to hear, "THAT'S MILLICENT CROWNINSHIELD! I GREW UP WITH HER. SHE LIVES RIGHT DOWN THE STREET FROM US IN BOSTON. BUT IT'S A VERY POOR LIKENESS, IF YOU ASK ME! HER NOSE ISN'T NEARLY THAT LARGE AND SHE DOESN'T HAVE SOMETHING QUEER GROWING OUT OF HER CHIN! THE CROWNINSHIELDS ARE REALLY QUITE GOOD-LOOKING, STUFFY, BUT GOOD-LOOKING NONETHELESS!"

GARDNER: [*Suddenly jumps up, ablaze.*] WAIT, WAIT . . . IF IT'S MICHELANGELO YOU WANT . . . I'm sorry, Mags. . . . One more . . . just one more . . . please?

MAGS: Sure, why not? Be my guest.

GARDNER: *Fanny, prepare yourself!*

[*More whispering.*]

FANNY: But I think *you* should be God.

GARDNER: Me? . . . Really?

FANNY: Yes, it's much more appropriate.

GARDNER: Well, if you say so . . . [FANNY *and* GARDNER *ease down to the floor with some difficulty and lie on their sides,* FANNY *as Adam,* GARDNER *as God, their fingers inching closer and closer in the attitude of Michelangelo's* The Creation. *Finally they touch.*]

MAGS: [*Cheers, whistles, applauds.*] THREE CHEERS . . . VERY GOOD . . . NICELY DONE, NICELY DONE! [*They hold the pose a moment* more, *flushed with pleasure; then rise, dust themselves off and grope back to their chairs.*] So, there we were. . . .

FANNY: Yes, *do* go on! . . .

MAGS: . . . huddled around Millicent Crowninshield, when you whipped into your pocketbook and suddenly announced, "HOLD EVERYTHING! I'VE GOT A PHOTOGRAPH OF HER RIGHT HERE, THEN YOU CAN SEE WHAT SHE REALLY LOOKS LIKE!" . . . You then proceeded to crouch down to the floor and dump everything out of your bag, and I mean . . . *everything!* . . . leaking packets of sequins and gummed stars, sea shells, odd pieces of fur, crochet hooks, a monarch butterfly embedded in plastic, dental floss, antique glass buttons, small jingling bells, lace . . . I thought I'd die! Just sink to the floor and quietly die! . . . You couldn't find it, you see. I mean, you spent the rest of the afternoon on your hands and knees crawling through this ocean of junk, muttering, "It's *got* to be here somewhere; I know I had it with me!" . . . Then Daddy pulled me into the thick of it all and said, "By the way, have you met our daughter Mags yet? She's the one who did all these pictures . . . paintings . . . portraits . . . whatever you call them." [*She drops to her hands and knees and begins crawling out of the room.*] By this time, Mum had somehow crawled out of the gallery and was lost on another floor. She began calling for me . . . "YOO-HOO, MAGS . . . WHERE ARE YOU? . . . OH, MAGS, DARLING . . . HELLO? . . . ARE YOU THERE? . . ." [*She reenters and faces them.*] This was at my *first* show.

BLACKOUT

Scene 3

Twenty-four hours later. The impact of the impending move has struck with hurricane force. FANNY *has lugged all their clothing into the room and dumped it in various cartons. There are coats, jackets, shoes, skirts, suits, hats, sweaters, dresses, the works. She and* GARDNER *are seated on the sofa, going through it all.*

FANNY: [*Wearing a different hat and dress, holds up a ratty overcoat.*] What about this gruesome old thing?

GARDNER: [*Is wearing several sweaters and vests, a Hawaiian holiday shirt, and a variety of scarves and ties around his neck. He holds up a pair of shoes.*] God . . . remember these shoes? Pound gave them to me when he came back from Italy. I remember it vividly.

FANNY: *Do* let me give it to the thrift shop! [*She stuffs the coat into the appropriate carton.*]

GARDNER: He bought them for me in Rome. Said he couldn't resist; bought himself a pair too since we both wore the same size. God, I miss him! [*Pause.*] HEY, WHAT ARE YOU DOING WITH MY OVERCOAT?!

FANNY: Darling, it's threadbare!

GARDNER: But that's my overcoat! [*He grabs it out of the carton.*] I've been wearing it every day for the past thirty-five years!

FANNY: That's just my point: It's had it.

GARDNER: [*Puts it on over everything else.*] There's nothing wrong with this coat!

FANNY: I trust you remember that the cottage is an eighth the size of this place and you simply won't have room for half this stuff! [*She holds up a sports jacket.*] This dreary old jacket, for instance. You've had it since Hector was a pup!

GARDNER: [*Grabs it and puts it on over his coat.*] Oh, no, you don't. . . .

FANNY: . . . and this God-awful hat . . .

GARDNER: Let me see that.

[*He stands next to her and they fall into a lovely tableau.*]

MAGS: [*Suddenly pops out from behind a wardrobe carton with a flash camera and takes a picture of them.*] PERFECT!

FANNY: [*Hands flying to her face.*] GOOD GOD, WHAT WAS THAT? . . .

GARDNER: [*Hands flying to his heart.*] JESUS CHRIST, I'VE BEEN SHOT!

MAGS: [*Walks to the center of the room, advancing the film.*] That was terrific. See if you can do it again.

FANNY: What *are* you doing? . . .

GARDNER: [*Feeling his chest.*] Is there blood?

FANNY: I see lace everywhere. . . .

MAGS: It's all right, I was just taking a picture of you. I often use a Polaroid at this stage.

FANNY: [*Rubbing her eyes.*] Really, Mags, you might have given us some warning!

MAGS: But that's the whole point: to catch you unawares!

GARDNER: [*Rubbing his eyes.*] It's the damndest thing. . . . I see lace everywhere.

FANNY: Yes, so do I. . . .

GARDNER: It's rather nice, actually. It looks as if you're wearing a veil.

FANNY: I *am* wearing a veil!

[*The camera spits out the photograph.*]

MAGS: OH GOODY, HERE COMES THE PICTURE!

FANNY: [*Grabs the partially developed print out of her hands.*] Let me see, let me see. . . .

GARDNER: Yes, let's have a look.

[*They have another quiet moment together looking at the photograph.*]

MAGS: [*Tiptoes away from them and takes another picture.*] YES!

FANNY: NOT AGAIN! PLEASE,   GARDNER: WHAT WAS THAT?
DARLING!   . . . WHAT HAPPENED? . . .

[*They stagger towards each other.*]

MAGS: I'm sorry, I just couldn't resist. You looked so . . .

FANNY: WHAT ARE YOU TRYING TO DO . . . *BLIND* US?!

GARDNER: Really, Mags, enough is enough. . . .

[GARDNER *and* FANNY *keep stumbling about kiddingly.*]

FANNY: Are you still there, Gar?

GARDNER: Right as rain, right as rain!

MAGS: I'm sorry; I didn't mean to scare you. It's just a photograph
can show you things you weren't aware of. Here, have a look.
[*She gives them to* FANNY.] Well, I'm going out to the kitchen to get
something to eat. Anybody want anything?
[*She exits.*]

FANNY: [*Looking at the photos, half-amused, half-horrified.*] Oh, Gardner,
have you ever? . . .

GARDNER: [*Looks at them and laughs.*] Good grief . . .

MAGS: [*Offstage; from the kitchen.*] IS IT ALL RIGHT IF I TAKE THE
REST OF THIS TAPIOCA FROM LAST NIGHT?

FANNY: IT'S ALL RIGHT WITH ME. How about you, Gar?

GARDNER: Sure, go right ahead. I've never been that crazy about
tapioca.

FANNY: What are you talking about, tapioca is one of your favorites.

MAGS: [*Enters, slurping from a large bowl.*] Mmmmmmmm . . .

FANNY: Really, Mags, I've never seen anyone eat as much as you.

MAGS: [*Takes the photos back.*] It's strange. I only do this when I come
home.

FANNY: What's the matter, don't I feed you enough?

GARDNER: Gee, it's hot in here!
[*Starts taking off his coat.*]

FANNY: God knows, you didn't eat anything as a child! I've never
seen such a fussy eater. Gar, what *are* you doing?

GARDNER: Taking off some of these clothes. It's hotter than Tofit in
here!
[*Shedding clothes to the floor.*]

MAGS: [*Looking at her photos.*] Yes, I like you looking at each other
like that. . . .

FANNY: [*To* GARDNER.] Please watch where you're dropping things;
I'm trying to keep some order around here.

GARDNER: [*Picks up what he dropped, dropping even more in the process.*]
Right, right. . . .

MAGS: Now all I've got to do is figure out what you should wear.

FANNY: Well, I'm going to wear my long black dress, and you'd be a
fool not to do Daddy in his tuxedo. He looks so distinguished in
it, just like a banker!

MAGS: I haven't really decided yet.

FANNY: Just because you walk around looking like something the cat dragged in, doesn't mean Daddy and I want to, do we, Gar? [GARDNER *is making a worse and worse tangle of his clothes.*]

FANNY: HELLO? . . .

GARDNER: [*Looks up at* FANNY.] Oh, yes, awfully attractive, awfully attractive!

FANNY: [*To* MAGS.] If you don't mind me saying so, I've never seen you looking so forlorn. You'll never catch a husband looking that way. Those peculiar clothes, that God-awful hair . . . really, Mags, it's very distressing!

MAGS: I don't think my hair's so bad, not that it's terrific or anything . . .

FANNY: Well, I don't see other girls walking around like you. I mean, girls from your background. What would Lyman Wigglesworth think if he saw you in the street?

MAGS: Lyman Wigglesworth?! . . . Uuuuuuughhhhhhh!
[*She shudders.*]

FANNY: All right then, that brilliant Cabot boy . . . what *is* his name?

GARDNER: Sammy.

FANNY: No, not Sammy . . .

GARDNER: Stephen . . . Stanley . . . Stuart . . . Sheldon . . . Sherlock . . . Sherlock! It's *Sherlock!*

MAGS: Spence!

FANNY: SPENCE, THAT'S IT! HIS NAME IS SPENCE!   GARDNER: THAT'S IT . . . SPENCE! SPENCE CABOT!

FANNY: Spence Cabot was first in his class at Harvard.

MAGS: Mum, he has no facial hair.

FANNY: He has his own law firm on Arlington Street.

MAGS: Spence Cabot has six fingers on his right hand!

FANNY: So, he isn't the best-looking thing in the world. Looks isn't everything. He can't help it if he has extra fingers. Have a little sympathy!

MAGS: But the extra one has this weird nail on it that looks like a talon. . . . It's long and black and . . . [*She shudders.*]

FANNY: No one's perfect, darling. He has lovely handwriting and an absolutely saintly mother. Also, he's as rich as Croesus! He's a lot more promising than some of those creatures you've dragged home. What was the name of that dreadful Frenchman who smelled like sweaty socks? . . . Jean Duke of Scripto?

MAGS: [*Laughing.*] Jean-Luc Zichot!

FANNY: . . . and that peculiar little Oriental fellow with all the teeth! Really, Mags, he could have been put on display at the circus!

MAGS: Oh, yes, Tsu Chin. He was strange, but very sexy. . . .

FANNY: [*Shudders.*] He had such tiny . . . feet! Really, Mags, you've got to bear down. You're not getting any younger. Before you know it, all the nice young men will be taken and then where will you be? . . . All by yourself in that grim little apartment of yours with those peculiar clothes and that bright red hair . . .

MAGS: MY HAIR IS NOT BRIGHT RED!

FANNY: I only want what's best for you, you know that. You seem to go out of your way to look wanting. I don't understand it. . . . Gar, what *are* you putting your coat on for? . . . You look like some derelict out on the street. We don't wear coats in the house. [*She helps him out of it.*] That's the way. . . . I'll just put this in the carton along with everything else. . . . [*She drops it into the carton, then pauses.*] Isn't it about time for . . . *cocktails!*

GARDNER: What's that?

[FANNY *taps her wrist and mimes drinking.*]

GARDNER: [*Looks at his watch.*] Right you are, right you are! [*Exits to the bar.*] THE USUAL? . . .

FANNY: *Please!*

GARDNER: [*Offstage.*] HOW ABOUT SOMETHING FOR YOU, MAGS?

MAGS: SURE, WHY NOT? . . . LET 'ER RIP!

GARDNER: [*Offstage.*] WHAT'S THAT? . . .

FANNY: SHE SAID YES. SHE   MAGS: I'LL HAVE SOME
SAID YES!   DUBONNET!

GARDNER: [*Poking his head back in.*] How about a little Dubonnet?

FANNY: That's just what she said. . . . She'd like some . . . Dubonnet!

GARDNER: [*Goes back to the bar and hums another Jolson tune.*] GEE, IT'S GREAT HAVING YOU BACK LIKE THIS, MAGS. . . . IT'S JUST GREAT! [*More singing.*]

FANNY: [*Leaning closer to* MAGS.] You have such *potential*, darling! It breaks my heart to see how you've let yourself go. If Lyman Wigglesworth . . .

MAGS: Amazing as it may seem, I don't *care* about Lyman Wigglesworth!

FANNY: From what I've heard, he's quite a lady killer!

MAGS: But with whom? . . . Don't think I haven't heard about his fling with . . . Hopie Stonewall!

FANNY: [*Begins to laugh.*] Oh, God, let's not get started on Hopie Stonewall again . . . ten feet tall with spots on her neck. . . . [*To* GARDNER.] OH, DARLING, DO HURRY BACK! WE'RE TALKING ABOUT PATHETIC HOPIE STONEWALL!

MAGS: It's not so much her incredible height and spotted skin; it's those tiny pointed teeth and the size eleven shoes!

FANNY: I love it when you're like this!

[MAGS *starts clomping around the room making tiny pointed teeth nibbling sounds.*]

FANNY: GARDNER . . . YOU'RE MISSING EVERYTHING! [*Still laughing.*] Why is it Boston girls are always so . . . tall?

MAGS: Hopie Stonewall isn't a Boston girl; she's a giraffe. [*She prances around the room with an imaginary dwarf-sized Lyman.*] She's perfect for Lyman Wigglesworth!

GARDNER: [*Returns with* FANNY's *drink, which he hands her.*] Now, where were we? . . .

FANNY: [*Trying not to laugh.*] HOPIE STONEWALL! . . .

GARDNER: Oh, yes, she's the very tall one, isn't she?
 [FANNIE *and* MAGS *burst into gales.*]

MAGS: The only hope for us . . . "Boston girls" is to get as far away from our kind as possible.

FANNY: She always asks after you, darling. She's very fond of you, you know.

MAGS: Please, I don't want to hear!

FANNY: Your old friends are *always* asking after you.

MAGS: It's not so much how creepy they all are, as how much they remind me of myself!

FANNY: But you're not "creepy," darling . . . just . . . shabby!

MAGS: I mean, give me a few more inches and some brown splotches here and there, and Hopie and I could be sisters!

FANNY: [*In a whisper to* GARDNER.] Don't you love it when Mags is like this? I could listen to her forever!

MAGS: I mean . . . look at me!

FANNY: [*Gasping.*] Don't stop, don't stop!

MAGS: Awkward . . . plain . . . I don't know how to dress, I don't know how to talk. When people find out Daddy's my father, they're always amazed. . . . "Gardner Church is YOUR father?! Aw, come on, you're kidding?!"

FANNY: [*In a whisper.*] Isn't she divine? . . .

MAGS: Sometimes I don't even tell them. I pretend I grew up in the Midwest somewhere . . . farming people . . . we work with our hands.

GARDNER: [*To* MAGS.] Well, how about a little refill? . . .

MAGS: No, no more thanks.
 [*Pause.*]

FANNY: What did you have to go and interrupt her for? She was just getting up a head of steam. . . .

MAGS: [*Walking over to her easel.*] The great thing about being a portrait painter, you see, is it's the *other* guy that's exposed; you're safely hidden behind the canvas and easel. [*Standing behind it.*] You can be as plain as a pitchfork, as inarticulate as mud, but it doesn't matter because you're completely concealed: your body, your face, your intentions. Just as you make your most intimate move, throw open your soul . . . they stretch and yawn, remembering the dog has to be let out at five. . . . To be so invisible while so enthralled . . . it takes your breath away!

GARDNER: Well put, Mags. Awfully well put!

MAGS: That's why I've always wanted to paint you, to see if I'm up

to it. It's quite a risk. Remember what I went through as a child
with my great masterpiece? . . .

FANNY: You painted a masterpiece when you were a child? . . .

MAGS: Well, it was a masterpiece to me.

FANNY: I had no idea you were precocious as a child. Gardner, do
you remember Mags painting a masterpiece as a child?

MAGS: I didn't paint it. It was something I made!

FANNY: Well, this is all news to me! Gar, *do* get me another drink! I
haven't had this much fun in years! [*She hands him her glass and
reaches for* MAGS'.] Come on, darling, join me. . . .

MAGS: No, no more, thanks. I don't really like the taste.

FANNY: Oh, come on, kick up your heels for once!

MAGS: No, nothing . . . really.

FANNY: Please? Pretty please? . . . To keep me company?!

MAGS: [*Hands* GARDNER *her glass.*] Oh, all right, what the hell . . .

FANNY: That's a good girl!   GARDNER: [*Exiting.*] Coming right
up, coming right up!

FANNY: [*Yelling after him.*] DON'T GIVE ME TOO MUCH NOW. THE
LAST ONE WAS AWFULLY STRONG . . . AND HURRY BACK SO
YOU DON'T MISS ANYTHING! . . . Daddy's so cunning, I don't
know what I'd do without him. If anything should happen to
him, I'd just . . .

MAGS: Mummy, nothing's going to happen to him! . . .

FANNY: Well, wait 'til you're our age, it's no garden party. Now . . .
where were we? . . .

MAGS: My first masterpiece . . .

FANNY: Oh, yes, but *do* wait 'til Daddy gets back so he can hear it
too. . . . YOO-HOO . . . GARRRRRRDNERRRRRRR? . . . ARE YOU
COMING? . . . [*Silence.*] Go and check on him, will you?

GARDNER: [*Enters with both drinks. He's very shaken.*] I couldn't find the
ice.

FANNY: Well, *finally!*

GARDNER: It just up and disappeared. . . . [*Hands* FANNY *her drink.*]
There you go.

[FANNY *kisses her fingers and takes a hefty swig.*]

GARDNER: Mags.

[*He hands* MAGS *her drink.*]

MAGS: Thanks, Daddy.

GARDNER: Sorry about the ice.

MAGS: No problem, no problem.

[GARDNER *sits down; silence.*]

FANNY: [*To* MAGS.] Well, drink up, drink up! [MAGS *downs it in one
gulp.*] GOOD GIRL! . . . Now, what's all this about a masterpiece?
. . .

MAGS: I did it during that winter you sent me away from the dinner
table. I was about nine years old.

FANNY: We sent you from the dinner table?

MAGS: I was banished for six months.

FANNY: You *were?* . . . How extraordinary!

MAGS: Yes, it *was* rather extraordinary!

FANNY: But why?

MAGS: Because I played with my food.

FANNY: You did?

MAGS: I used to squirt it out between my front teeth.

FANNY: Oh, I remember that! God, it used to drive me crazy, absolutely . . . crazy! [*Pause.*] "MARGARET, STOP THAT OOZING RIGHT THIS MINUTE, YOU ARE *NOT* A TUBE OF TOOTHPASTE!"

GARDNER: Oh, yes . . .

FANNY: It was perfectly disgusting!

GARDNER: I remember. She used to lean over her plate and squirt it out in long runny ribbons. . . .

FANNY: That's enough, dear.

GARDNER: They were quite colorful, actually; decorative almost. She made the most intricate designs. They looked rather like small, moist Oriental rugs. . . .

FANNY: [*To* MAGS.] But why, darling? What on earth possessed you to do it?

MAGS: I couldn't swallow anything. My throat just closed up. I don't know, I must have been afraid of choking or something.

GARDNER: I remember one in particular. We'd had chicken fricassee and spinach. . . . She made the most extraordinary . . .

FANNY: [*To* GARDNER.] WILL YOU PLEASE SHUT UP?! [*Pause.*] Mags, what *are* you talking about? You never choked in your entire life! This is the most distressing conversation I've ever had. Don't you think it's distressing, Gar?

GARDNER: Well, that's not quite the word I'd use.

FANNY: What word *would* you use, then?

GARDNER: I don't know right off the bat, I'd have to think about it.

FANNY: THEN, THINK ABOUT IT!

[*Silence.*]

MAGS: I guess I was afraid of making a mess. I don't know; you were awfully strict about table manners. I was always afraid of losing control. What if I started to choke and began spitting up over everything? . . .

FANNY: All right, dear, that's enough.

MAGS: No, I was really terrified about making a mess; you always got so mad whenever I spilled. If I just got rid of everything in neat little curlicues beforehand, you see . . .

FANNY: I SAID: THAT'S ENOUGH!

[*Silence.*]

MAGS: *I* thought it was quite ingenious, but you didn't see it that

way. You finally sent me from the table with, "When you're
ready to eat like a human being, you can come back and join
us!" . . . So, it was off to my room with a tray. But I couldn't
seem to eat there either. I mean, it was so strange settling down
to dinner in my *bedroom*. . . . So I just flushed everything down
the toilet and sat on my bed listening to you: clinkity-clink,
clatter clatter, slurp, slurp . . . but that got pretty boring after a
while, so I looked around for something to do. It was
wintertime, because I noticed I'd left some crayons on top of my
radiator and they'd melted down into these beautiful
shimmering globs, like spilled jello, trembling and pulsating. . . .
[*Overlapping*]

GARDNER: [*Eyes closed.*] "This luscious and impeccable fruit of life
Falls, it appears, of its own weight to earth. . . ."

MAGS: Naturally, I wanted to try it myself, so I grabbed a red one
and pressed it down against the hissing lid. It oozed and bubbled
like raspberry jam!

GARDNER: "When you were Eve, its acrid juice was sweet,
Untasted, in its heavenly, orchard air. . . ."

MAGS: I mean, that radiator was really hot! It took incredible will
power not to let go, but I held on, whispering, "Mags, if you let
go of this crayon, you'll be run over by a truck on Newberry
Street, so help you God!" . . . So I pressed down harder, my
fingers steaming and blistering. . . .

FANNY: I had no idea about any of this, did you, Gar?

MAGS: Once I'd melted one, I was hooked! I finished off my entire
supply in one night, mixing color over color until my head
swam! . . . The heat, the smell, the brilliance that sank and rose
. . . I'd never felt such exhilaration! . . . Every week I spent my
allowance on crayons. I must have cleared out every box of
Crayolas in the city!

GARDNER: [*Gazing at* MAGS.] You know, I don't think I've ever seen
you looking prettier! You're awfully attractive when you get
going!

FANNY: Why, what a lovely thing to say.

MAGS: AFTER THREE MONTHS THAT RADIATOR WAS . . .
SPECTACULAR! I MEAN, IT LOOKED LIKE SOME COLOSSAL
FRUIT CAKE, FIVE FEET TALL! . . .

FANNY: It sounds perfectly hideous.

MAGS: It was a knockout; shimmering with pinks and blues,
lavenders and maroons, turquoise and golds, oranges and
creams. . . . For every color, I imagined a taste . . . YELLOW:
lemon curls dipped in sugar . . . RED: glazed cherries laced with
rum . . . GREEN: tiny peppermint leaves veined with chocolate
. . . PURPLE: . . .

FANNY: That's quite enough!

MAGS: And then the frosting . . . ahhh, the frosting! A satiny mix of white and silver . . . I kept it hidden under blankets during the day. . . . My huge . . . [*She starts laughing.*] looming . . . teetering sweet . . .

FANNY: I ASKED YOU TO STOP! GARDNER, WILL YOU PLEASE GET HER TO STOP!

GARDNER: See here, Mags, Mum asked you to . . .

MAGS: I was so . . . *hungry* . . . losing weight every week. I looked like a scarecrow what with the bags under my eyes and bits of crayon wrapper leaking out of my clothes. It's a wonder you didn't notice. But finally you came to my rescue . . . if you could call what happened a rescue. It was more like a rout!

FANNY: Darling . . . *Please!*   GARDNER: Now, look, young lady
                                                . . .

MAGS: The winter was almost over. . . . It was very late at night. . . . I must have been having a nightmare because suddenly you and Daddy were at my bed, shaking me. . . . I quickly glanced towards the radiator to see if it was covered. . . . *It wasn't!* It glittered and towered in the moonlight like some . . . gigantic Viennese pastry! You followed my gaze and saw it. Mummy screamed . . . "WHAT HAVE YOU GOT IN HERE? . . . MAGS, WHAT HAVE YOU BEEN DOING?" . . . She crept forward and touched it, and then jumped back. "IT'S FOOD!" she cried . . . "IT'S ALL THE FOOD SHE'S BEEN SPITTING OUT! OH, GARDNER, IT'S A MOUNTAIN OF ROTTING GARBAGE!"

FANNY: [*Softly.*] Yes . . . it's coming back . . . it's coming back. . . .

MAGS: Daddy exited as usual; left the premises. He fainted, just keeled over onto the floor. . . .

GARDNER: Gosh, I don't remember any of this. . . .

MAGS: My heart stopped! I mean, I knew it was all over. My lovely creation didn't have a chance. Sure enough . . . out came the blow torch. Well, it couldn't have *really* been a blow torch, I mean, where would you have ever gotten a blow torch? . . . I just have this very strong memory of you standing over my bed, your hair streaming around your face, aiming this . . . flame thrower at my confection . . . my cake . . . my tart . . . my strudel. . . . "IT'S GOT TO BE DESTROYED IMMEDIATELY! THE THING'S ALIVE WITH VERMIN! . . . JUST LOOK AT IT! . . . IT'S PRACTICALLY CRAWLING ACROSS THE ROOM!" . . . Of course in a sense you were right. It *was* a monument of my cast-off dinners, only I hadn't built it with food. . . . I found my own materials. I was languishing with hunger, but oh, dear Mother . . . I FOUND MY OWN MATERIALS! . . .

FANNY: Darling . . . *please*?!

MAGS: I tried to stop you, but you wouldn't listen. . . . OUT SHOT THE FLAME! . . . I remember these waves of wax rolling across

the room and Daddy coming to, wondering what on earth was going on. . . . Well, what did you know about my abilities? . . . You see, I had . . . I mean, I *have* abilities. . . . [*Struggling to say it.*] I have abilities. I have . . . strong abilities. I have . . . very strong abilities. They are very strong . . . very, very strong. . . .
[*She rises and runs out of the room overcome as* FANNY *and* GARDNER *watch, speechless.*]

THE CURTAIN FALLS

ACT II

Scene 1

Three days later. Miracles have been accomplished. Almost all of the Churches' furniture has been moved out, and the cartons of dishes and clothing are gone. All that remains are odds and ends. MAGS' *tableau looms, impregnable.* FANNY *and* GARDNER *are dressed in their formal evening clothes, frozen in their pose. They hold absolutely still.* MAGS *stands at her easel, her hands covering her eyes.*

FANNY: All right, you can look now.
MAGS: [*Removes her hands.*] Yes! . . . I told you you could trust me on the pose.
FANNY: Well, thank God you let us dress up. It makes all the difference. Now we really look like something.
MAGS: [*Starts to sketch them.*] I'll say. . . .
[*A silence as she sketches.*]
GARDNER: [*Recites Yeats's "The Song of Wandering Aengus" in a wonderfully resonant voice as they pose.*]
"I went out to the hazel wood,
Because a fire was in my head,
And cut and peeled a hazel wand,
And hooked a berry to a thread,
And when white moths were on the wing,
And moth-like stars were flickering out,
I dropped the berry in a stream
And caught a little silver trout.

When I had laid it on the floor
I went to blow the fire aflame,
But something rustled on the floor,
And someone called me by my name:

It had become a glimmering girl
With apple blossoms in her hair
Who called me by my name and ran
And faded through the brightening air.

Though I am old with wandering
Through hollow lands and hilly lands,
I will find out where she has gone,
And kiss her lips and take her hands;
And walk among long dappled grass,
And pluck till time and times are done,
The silver apples of the moon,
The golden apples of the sun.''

FANNY: That's lovely, dear. Just lovely. Is it one of yours?

GARDNER: No, no, it's Yeats. I'm using it in my book.

FANNY: Well, you recited it beautifully, but then you've always recited beautifully. That's how you wooed me, in case you've forgotten. . . . You must have memorized every love poem in the English language! There was no stopping you when you got going . . . your Shakespeare, Byron, and Shelley . . . you were shameless . . . *shameless!*

GARDNER: [*Eyes closed.*] ''I will find out where she has gone, And kiss her lips and take her hands . . . ''

FANNY: And then there was your own poetry to do battle with; your sonnets and quatrains. When you got going with them, there was nothing left of me! You could have had your pick of any girl in Boston! Why you chose me, I'll never understand. I had no looks to speak of and nothing much in the brains department. . . . Well, what did you know about women and the world? . . . What did any of us know? . . . [*Silence.*] GOD, MAGS, HOW LONG ARE WE SUPPOSED TO SIT LIKE THIS? . . . IT'S AGONY!

MAGS: [*Working away.*] You're doing fine . . . just fine. . . .

FANNY: [*Breaking her pose.*] It's so . . . boring!

MAGS: Come on, don't move. You can have a break soon.

FANNY: I had no idea it would be so boring!

GARDNER: Gee, I'm enjoying it.

FANNY: You would! . . .

[*A pause.*]

GARDNER: [*Begins reciting more Yeats, almost singing it.*]
''He stood among a crowd at Drumahair;
His heart hung all upon a silken dress,
And he had known at last some tenderness,
Before earth made of him her sleepy care;

—— 545 ——

But when a man poured fish into a pile,
It seemed they raised their little silver heads . . . ''

FANNY: Gar . . . PLEASE! [*She lurches out of her seat.*] God, I can't take this anymore!

MAGS: [*Keeps sketching* GARDNER.] I know it's tedious at first, but it gets easier. . . .

FANNY: It's like a Chinese water torture! . . . [*Crosses to* MAGS *and looks at* GARDNER *posing.*] Oh, darling, you look marvelous, absolutely marvelous! Why don't you just do Daddy!?

MAGS: Because you look marvelous too. I want to do you both!

FANNY: Please! . . . I have one foot in the grave and you know it! Also, we're way behind in our packing. There's still one room left which everyone seems to have forgotten about!

GARDNER: Which one is that?

FANNY: You know perfectly well which one it is!

GARDNER: I do? . . .

FANNY: Yes, you do!

GARDNER: Well, it's news to me.

FANNY: I'll give you a hint. It's in . . . *that* direction. [*She points.*]

GARDNER: The dining room?

FANNY: No.

GARDNER: The bedroom?

FANNY: No.

GARDNER: Mags' room?

FANNY: No.

GARDNER: The kitchen?

FANNY: *Gar*?! . . .

GARDNER: The guest room?

FANNY: Your God-awful study!

GARDNER: Oh, shit!

FANNY: That's right, ''Oh, shit!'' It's books and papers up to the ceiling! If you ask me, we should just forget it's there and quietly tiptoe away. . . .

GARDNER: My study! . . .

FANNY: Let the new owners dispose of everything. . . .

GARDNER: [*Gets out of his posing chair.*] Now, just one minute. . . .

FANNY: You never look at half the stuff in there!

GARDNER: I don't want you touching those books! They're mine!

FANNY: Darling, we're moving to a cottage the size of a handkerchief! Where, pray tell, is there room for all your books?

GARDNER: I don't know. We'll just have to make room!

MAGS: [*Sketching away.*] RATS!

FANNY: I don't know what we're doing fooling around with Mags like this when there's still so much to do. . . .

GARDNER: [*Sits back down, overwhelmed.*] My study! . . .

FANNY: You can stay with her if you'd like, but one of us has got to tackle those books!
[*She exits to his study.*]

GARDNER: I'm not up to this.

MAGS: Oh, good, you're staying!

GARDNER: There's a lifetime of work in there. . . .

MAGS: Don't worry, I'll help. Mum and I will be able to pack everything up in no time.

GARDNER: God. . . .

MAGS: It won't be so bad. . . .

GARDNER: I'm just not up to it.

MAGS: We'll all pitch in. . . .

[GARDNER *sighs, speechless. A silence as* FANNY *comes staggering in with an arm load of books which she drops to the floor with a crash.*]

GARDNER: WHAT WAS THAT?!   MAGS: GOOD GRIEF!
. . .

FANNY: [*Sheepish.*] Sorry, sorry. . . .
[*She exits for more.*]

GARDNER: I don't know if I can take this. . . .

MAGS: Moving is awful . . . I know. . . .

GARDNER: [*Settling back into his pose.*] Ever since Mum began tearing the house apart, I've been having these dreams. . . . I'm a child again back at Sixteen Louisberg Square . . . and this stream of moving men is carrying furniture into our house . . . van after van of tables and chairs, sofas and love seats, desks and bureaus . . . rugs, bathtubs, mirrors, chiming clocks, pianos, iceboxes, china cabinets . . . but what's amazing is that all of it is familiar. . . . [FANNY *comes in with another load which she drops on the floor. She exits for more.*] No matter how many items appear, I've seen every one of them before. Since my mother is standing in the midst of it directing traffic, I ask her where it's all coming from, but she doesn't hear me because of the racket . . . so finally I just scream out . . . "WHERE IS ALL THIS FURNITURE COMING FROM?" . . . Just as a moving man is carrying Toots into the room, she looks at me and says, "Why, from the land of Skye!" . . . The next thing I know, *people* are being carried along with it. . . . [FANNY *enters with her next load; drops it and exits.*] People I've never seen before are sitting around our dining-room table. A group of foreigners is going through my books, chattering in a language I've never heard before. A man is playing a Chopin polonaise on Aunt Alice's piano. Several children are taking baths in our tubs from Cotuit. . . .

MAGS: It sounds marvelous.

GARDNER: Well, it isn't marvelous at all because all of these perfect strangers have taken over our things. . . .

[FANNY *enters, hurls down another load and exits.*]

MAGS: How odd. . . .

GARDNER: Well, it *is* odd, but then something even odder happens. . . .

MAGS: [*Sketching away.*] Tell me, tell me!

GARDNER: Well, our beds are carried in. They're all made up with sheets and everything, but instead of all these strange people in them, *we're* in them! . . .

MAGS: What's so odd about that? . . .

GARDNER: Well, you and Mum are brought in, both sleeping like angels . . . Mum snoring away to beat the band. . . .

MAGS: Yes . . .

[FANNY *enters with another load; lets it fall.*]

GARDNER: But there's no one in mine. It's completely empty, never even been slept in! It's as if I were dead or had never even existed. . . . [FANNY *exits.*] "HEY . . . WAIT UP!" I yell to the moving men . . . "THAT'S MY BED YOU'VE GOT THERE!" But they don't stop; they don't even acknowledge me. . . . "HEY, COME BACK HERE . . . I WANT TO GET INTO MY BED!" I cry again and I start running after them . . . down the hall, through the dining room, past the library. . . . Finally I catch up to them and hurl myself right into the center of the pillow. Just as I'm about to land, the bed suddenly vanishes and I go crashing down to the floor like some insect that's been hit by a fly swatter!

FANNY: [*Staggers in with her final load; drops it with a crash and then collapses in her posing chair.*] THAT'S IT FOR ME! I'M DEAD! [*Silence.*] Come on, Mags, how about you doing a little work around here.

MAGS: That's all I've been doing! This is the first free moment you've given me!

FANNY: You should see all the books in there . . . and papers! There are enough loose papers to sink a ship!

GARDNER: Why is it we're moving, again? . . .

FANNY: Because life is getting too complicated here.

GARDNER: [*Remembering.*] Oh, yes . . .

FANNY: And we can't afford it anymore.

GARDNER: That's right, that's right. . . .

FANNY: We don't have the . . . *income* we used to!

GARDNER: Oh, yes . . . *income!*

FANNY: [*Assuming her pose again.*] Of course, we have our savings and various trust funds, but I wouldn't dream of touching those!

GARDNER: No, no, you must never dip into capital!

FANNY: I told Daddy I'd be perfectly happy to buy a gun and put a bullet through our heads so we could avoid all this, but he wouldn't hear of it!

MAGS: [*Sketching away.*] No, I shouldn't think so.
[*Pause.*]

FANNY: I've always admired people who kill themselves when they get to our stage of life. Well, no one can touch my Uncle Edmond in that department. . . .

MAGS: I know, I know. . . .

FANNY: The day before his seventieth birthday he climbed to the top of the Old North Church and hurled himself facedown into Salem Street! They had to scrape him up with a spatula! God, he was a remarkable man . . . state senator, president of Harvard. . . .

GARDNER: [*Rises and wanders over to his books.*] Well, I guess I'm going to have to do something about all of these. . . .

FANNY: Come on, Mags, help Daddy! Why don't you start bringing in his papers. . . .
[GARDNER *sits on the floor; picks up a book and soon is engrossed in it.* MAGS *keeps sketching, oblivious; silence.*]

FANNY: [*To* MAGS.] Darling?. . . . HELLO? . . . God, you two are impossible! Just look at you . . . heads in the clouds! No one would ever know we've got to be out of here in two days. If it weren't for me, nothing would get done around here. . . . [*She starts stacking* GARDNER'S *books into piles.*] There! That's all the maroon ones!

GARDNER: [*Looks up.*] What do you mean, *maroon* ones?! . . .

FANNY: All your books that are maroon are in *this* pile . . . and your books that are green in *that* pile! . . . I'm trying to bring some order into your life for once. This will make unpacking so much easier.

GARDNER: But, my dear Fanny, it's not the color of a book that distinguishes it, but what's *inside* it!

FANNY: This will be a great help, you'll see. Now what about this awful striped thing? [*She picks up a slim, aged volume.*] Can't it go?
. . .

GARDNER: No!

FANNY: But it's as queer as Dick's hat band! There are no others like it.

GARDNER: Open it and read. Go on . . . open it!

FANNY: We'll get nowhere at this rate.

GARDNER: I said . . . READ!

FANNY: Really, Gar, I . . .

GARDNER: Read the dedication!

FANNY: [*Opens and reads.*] "To Gardner Church, you led the way. With gratitude and affection, Robert Frost."
[*She closes it and hands it to him.*]

GARDNER: It was published the same year as my *Salem Gardens.*

FANNY: [*Picking up a very worn book.*] Well, what about this dreadful thing? It's filthy. [*She blows off a cloud of dust.*]

GARDNER: Please . . . *please*?!

FANNY: [*Looking through it.*] It's all in French.

GARDNER: [*Snatching it away from her.*] André Malraux gave me that! . . .

FANNY: I'm just trying to help.

GARDNER: It's a first edition of Baudelaire's *Fleurs du Mal.*

FANNY: [*Giving it back.*] Well, pardon me for living!

GARDNER: Why do you have to drag everything in here in the first place? . . .

FANNY: Because there's no room in your study. You ought to see the mess in there! . . . WAKE UP, MAGS, ARE YOU GOING TO PITCH IN OR NOT?! . . .

GARDNER: I'm not up to this.

FANNY: Well, you'd better be unless you want to be left behind!

MAGS: [*Stops her sketching.*] All right, all right . . . I just hope you'll give me some more time later this evening.

FANNY: [*To MAGS.*] Since you're young and in the best shape, why don't you bring in the books and I'll cope with the papers. [*She exits to the study.*]

GARDNER: Now just a minute. . . .

FANNY: [*Offstage.*] WE NEED A STEAM SHOVEL FOR THIS!

MAGS: OK, what do you want me to do?

GARDNER: Look, I don't want you messing around with my . . . [FANNY *enters with an armful of papers which she drops into an empty carton.*]

GARDNER: HEY, WHAT'S GOING ON HERE?! . . .

FANNY: I'm packing up your papers. COME ON, MAGS, LET'S GET CRACKING!
[*She exits for more papers.*]

GARDNER: [*Plucks several papers out of the carton.*] What is this? . . .

MAGS: [*Exits into his study.*] GOOD LORD, WHAT HAVE YOU DONE IN HERE?! . . .

GARDNER: [*Reading.*] This is my manuscript.
[FANNY *enters with another batch which she tosses on top of the others.*]

GARDNER: What *are* you doing?! . . .

FANNY: Packing, darling . . . PACKING!
[*She exits for more.*]

GARDNER: SEE HERE, YOU CAN'T MANHANDLE MY THINGS THIS WAY! [MAGS *enters, staggering under a load of books which she sets down on the floor.*] I PACK MY MANUSCRIPT! I KNOW WHERE EVERYTHING IS!

FANNY: [*Offstage.*] IF IT WERE UP TO YOU, WE'D NEVER GET OUT OF HERE! WE'RE UNDER A TIME LIMIT, GARDNER. KITTY'S PICKING US UP IN TWO DAYS . . . TWO . . . DAYS!

[*She enters with a larger batch of papers and heads for the carton.*]

GARDNER: [*Grabbing* FANNY'S *wrist.*] NOW, HOLD IT! . . . JUST . . .
HOLD IT RIGHT THERE! . . .
FANNY: OOOOOWWWWWWWW!
GARDNER: *I* PACK MY THINGS! . . .
FANNY: LET GO, YOU'RE HURTING ME!
GARDNER: THAT'S MY MANUSCRIPT! GIVE IT TO ME!
FANNY: [*Lifting the papers high over her head.*] I'M IN CHARGE OF
THIS MOVE, GARDNER! WE'VE GOT TO GET CRACKING!
GARDNER: I said . . . GIVE IT TO ME!
MAGS: Come on, Mum, let him have it.

[*They struggle.*]

GARDNER: [*Finally wrenches the pages from her.*] LET . . . ME . . . HAVE
IT! . . . THAT'S MORE LIKE IT! . . .
FANNY: [*Soft and weepy.*] You see what he's like? . . . I try and help
with his packing and what does he do? . . .
GARDNER: [*Rescues the rest of his papers from the carton.*] YOU DON'T
JUST THROW EVERYTHING INTO A BOX LIKE A PILE OF
GARBAGE! THIS IS A BOOK, FANNY. SOMETHING I'VE BEEN
WORKING ON FOR TWO YEARS! . . . [*Trying to assemble his
papers, but only making things worse, dropping them all over the place.*]
You show a little respect for my things. . . . You don't just throw
them around every which way. . . . It's tricky trying to make
sense of poetry; it's much easier to write the stuff . . . that is, if
you've still got it in you. . . .
MAGS: Here, let me help. . . . [*Taking some of the papers.*]
GARDNER: Criticism is tough sledding. You can't just dash off a few
images here, a few rhymes there. . . .
MAGS: Do you have these pages numbered in any way?
FANNY: [*Returning to her posing chair.*] HA!
GARDNER: This is just the introduction.
MAGS: I don't see any numbers on these.
GARDNER: [*Exiting to his study.*] The important stuff is in my study. . . .
FANNY: [*To* MAGS.] You don't know the half of it . . . *not the half!* . . .
GARDNER: [*Offstage; thumping around.*] HAVE YOU SEEN THOSE
YEATS POEMS I JUST HAD? . . .
MAGS: [*Reading over several pages.*] What is this? . . . It doesn't make
sense. It's just fragments . . . pieces of poems.
FANNY: That's it, honey! That's his book. His great critical study!
Now that he can't write his own poetry, he's trying to explain
other people's. The only problem is, he can't get beyond typing
them out. The poor lamb doesn't have the stamina to get beyond
the opening stanzas, let alone trying to make sense of them.

GARDNER: [*Thundering back with more papers which keep falling.*] GOD DAMNIT, FANNY, WHAT DID YOU DO IN THERE? I CAN'T FIND ANYTHING!

FANNY: I just took the papers that were on your desk.

GARDNER: Well, the entire beginning is gone.
[*He exits.*]

FANNY: I'M TRYING TO HELP YOU, DARLING!

GARDNER: [*Returns with another arm load.*] SEE THAT? . . . NO SIGN OF CHAPTER ONE OR TWO. . . . [*He flings it all down to the floor.*]

FANNY: Gardner . . . PLEASE?!

GARDNER: [*Kicking through the mess.*] I TURN MY BACK FOR ONE MINUTE AND WHAT HAPPENS? . . . MY ENTIRE STUDY IS TORN APART!
[*He exits.*]

MAGS: Oh, Daddy . . . don't . . . please . . . Daddy . . . *please*?!

GARDNER: [*Returns with a new batch of papers which he tosses up into the air.*] THROWN OUT! . . . THE BEST PART IS THROWN OUT! . . . LOST. . . .
[*He starts to exit again.*]

MAGS: [*Reads one of the fragments to steady herself.*]
"I have known the inexorable sadness of pencils,
Neat in their boxes, dolor of pad and paperweight,
All the misery of manilla folders and mucilage . . . "
They're beautiful . . . just beautiful.

GARDNER: [*Stops.*] Hey, what's that you've got there?

FANNY: It's your manuscript, darling. You see, it's right where you left it.

GARDNER: [*To* MAGS.] Read that again.

MAGS: "I have known the inexorable sadness of pencils,
Neat in their boxes, dolor of pad and paperweight,
All the misery of manilla folders and mucilage . . . "

GARDNER: Well, well, what do you know. . . .

FANNY: [*Hands him several random papers.*] You see . . . no one lost anything. Everything's here, still intact.

GARDNER: [*Reads.*] "I knew a woman, lovely in her bones,
When small birds sighed, she would sigh back at them;
Ah, when she moved, she moved more ways than one:
The shapes a bright container can contain! . . . "

FANNY: [*Hands him another.*] And . . .

GARDNER: [*Reads.*] Ahh . . . Frost . . .
"Some say the world will end in fire,
Some say ice.
From what I've tasted of desire
I hold with those who favor fire."

FANNY: [*Under her breath to* MAGS.] He can't give up the words. It's

the best he can do. [*Handing him another.*] Here you go, here's
more.

GARDNER:

"Farm boys wild to couple
With anything   with soft-wooded trees
With mounds of earth   mounds
Of pinestraw   will keep themselves off
Animals by legends of their own . . . "

MAGS: [*Eyes shut.*] Oh, Daddy, I can't bear it . . . I . . .

FANNY: Of course no one will ever publish this.

GARDNER: Oh, here's a marvelous one. Listen to this!

"There came a Wind like a Bugle—
It quivered through the Grass
And a Green Chill upon the Heat
So ominous did pass
We barred the Windows and the
   Doors
As from an Emerald Ghost—
The Doom's electric Moccasin . . . "

SHIT, WHERE DID THE REST OF IT GO? . . .

FANNY: Well, don't ask *me.*

GARDNER: It just stopped in mid-air!

FANNY: Then go look for the original.

GARDNER: Good idea, good idea!

[*He exits to his study.*]

FANNY: [*To* MAGS.] He's incontinent now, too. He wets his pants, in
case you haven't noticed. [*She starts laughing.*] You're not
laughing. Don't you think it's funny? Daddy needs diapers . . . I
don't know about you, but I could use a drink! GAR . . . WILL
YOU GET ME A SPLASH WHILE YOU'RE OUT THERE? . . .

MAGS: STOP IT!

FANNY: It means we can't go out anymore. I mean, what would
people say? . . .

MAGS: Stop it. Just stop it.

FANNY: My poet laureate can't hold it in! [*She laughs harder.*]

MAGS: That's enough . . . STOP IT . . . Mummy . . . I beg of you . . .
please stop it!

GARDNER: [*Enters with a book and indeed a large stain has blossomed on
his trousers. He plucks it away from his leg.*] Here we go . . . I found
it. . . .

FANNY: [*Pointing at it.*] See that? See? . . . He just did it again! [*Goes
off into a shower of laughter.*]

MAGS: [*Looks, turns away.*] SHUT . . . UP! . . . [*Building to a howl.*]
WILL YOU PLEASE JUST . . . SHUT . . . UP!

FANNY: [*To* GARDNER.] Hey, what about that drink?

GARDNER: Oh, yes . . . sorry, sorry . . .
[*He heads towards the bar.*]

FANNY: Never mind, I'll get it, I'll get it. [*She exits, convulsed; silence.*]

GARDNER: Well, where were we? . . .

MAGS: [*Near tears.*] Your poem.

GARDNER: Oh, yes . . . the Dickinson. [*He shuts his eyes, reciting from memory, holding the book against his chest.*]
"There came a Wind like a Bugle—
It quivered through the Grass
And a Green Chill upon the Heat
So ominous did pass
We barred the Windows and the Doors
As from an Emerald Ghost—"
[*Opens the book and starts riffling through it.*] Let's see now, where's the rest? . . . [*He finally finds it.*] Ahhh, here we go! . . .

FANNY: [*Reenters, drink in hand.*] I'm back! [*Takes one look at* GARDNER *and bursts out laughing again.*]

MAGS: I don't believe you! How you can laugh at him?! . . .

FANNY: I'm sorry, I wish I could stop, but there's really nothing else to do. Look at him . . . just . . . look at him . . . !
[*This is all simultaneous as* MAGS *gets angrier and angrier.*]

MAGS: It's so cruel. . . . You're so . . . incredibly cruel to him. . . . I mean, YOUR DISDAIN REALLY TAKES MY BREATH AWAY! YOU'RE IN A CLASS BY YOURSELF WHEN IT COMES TO HUMILIATION! . . .

GARDNER: [*Reading.*]
"The Doom's electric Moccasin
That very instant passed—
On a strange Mob of panting Trees
And Fences fled away
And Rivers where the Houses ran
Those looked that lived—that Day—
The Bell within the steeple wild
The flying tidings told—
How much can come
And much can go,
And yet abide the World!"
[*He shuts the book with a bang, pauses and looks around the room, confused.*] Now, where was I? . . .

FANNY: Safe and sound in the middle of the living room with Mags and me.

GARDNER: But I was looking for something, wasn't I? . . .

FANNY: Your manuscript.

GARDNER: THAT'S RIGHT! MY MANUSCRIPT! My manuscript!

FANNY: And here it is all over the floor. See, you're standing on it.

GARDNER: [*Picks up a few pages and looks at them.*] Why, so I am . . .

FANNY: Now all we have to do is get it up off the floor and packed neatly into these cartons!

GARDNER: Yes, yes, that's right. Into the cartons.

FANNY: [*Kicks a carton over to him.*] Here, you use this one and I'll start over here. . . . [*She starts dropping papers into a carton nearby.*] BOMBS AWAY! . . . Hey . . . this is fun! . . .

GARDNER: [*Picks up his own pile, lifts it high over his head and flings it down into the carton.*] BOMBS AWAY . . . This *is* fun! . . .

FANNY: I told you! The whole thing is to figure out a system!

GARDNER: I don't know what I'd do without you, Fan. I thought I'd lost everything.

FANNY: [*Makes dive-bomber noises and machine-gun explosions as she wheels more and more papers into the carton.*] TAKE THAT AND THAT AND THAT! . . .

GARDNER: [*Joins in the fun, outdoing her with dips, dives and blastings of his own.*] BLAM BLAM BLAM BLAM! . . . ZZZZZZZRAAAAAA FOOM! . . . BLATTY-DE-BLATTY-DE-BLATTY-DE-KABOOOOOOOOM! . . . WHAAAAAAA . . . DA-DAT-DAT-DAT-DAT . . . WHEEEEEEEE AAAAAAAAAAAA . . . FOOOOOO . . . [*THEY get louder and louder as papers fly every which way.*]

FANNY: [*Mimes getting hit with a bomb.*] AEEEEEEIIIIIIIIIIIII! YOU GOT ME RIGHT IN THE GIZZARD! [*She collapses on the floor and starts going through death throes, having an absolute ball.*]

GARDNER: TAKE THAT AND THAT AND THAT AND THAT . . . [*A series of explosions follow.*]

MAGS: [*Furious.*] This is how you help him? . . . THIS IS HOW YOU PACK HIS THINGS? . . .

FANNY: I keep him company. I get involved . . . which is a hell of a lot more than you do!

MAGS: [*Wild with rage.*] BUT YOU'RE MAKING A MOCKERY OF HIM . . . YOU TREAT HIM LIKE A CHILD OR SOME DIM-WITTED SERVING BOY. HE'S JUST AN AMUSEMENT TO YOU! . . .

FANNY: [*Fatigue has finally overtaken her. She's calm, almost serene.*] . . . And to you who see him once a year, if that . . . What is he to *you*? . . . I mean, what do you give him from yourself that costs you something? . . . Hmmmmmm? . . . [*Imitating her.*] "Oh, hi Daddy, it's great to see you again. How have you been? . . . Gee, I love your hair. It's gotten so . . . *white*!" . . . What color do you expect it to get when he's this age? . . . I mean, if you care so much how he looks, why don't you come and see him once in a while? . . . But oh, no . . . you have your paintings to do and your shows to put on. You just come and see us when the whim strikes. [*Imitating her.*] "Hey, you know what would be really great? . . . To do a portrait of you! I've always wanted to paint you, you're such great subjects!" . . . *Paint* us?! . . . What about opening your eyes and really *seeing* us? . . . Noticing what's going on around here for a change! It's all over for Daddy and me. This is it! "Finita la commedia!" . . . All I'm trying to do is exit with a little flourish; have some fun. . . . What's so terrible about that? . . . It can get pretty grim around here, in case you haven't noticed . . . Daddy, tap-tap-tapping out his nonsense all day; me traipsing around to the thrift shops trying to amuse myself . . . He never keeps me company anymore; never takes me out anywhere. . . . I'd put a bullet through my head in a minute, but then who'd look after him? . . . What do you think we're moving to the cottage for? . . . So I can watch him like a hawk and make sure he doesn't get lost. Do you think that's anything to look forward to? . . . Being Daddy's nursemaid out in the middle of nowhere? I'd much rather stay here in Boston with the few friends I have left, but you can't always do what you want in this world! "L'homme propose, Dieu dispose!" . . . If you want to paint us so badly, you ought to paint us as we really are. There's your picture! . . . [*She points to* GARDNER *who's quietly playing with a paper glide.*] Daddy spread out on the floor with all his toys and me hovering over him to make sure he doesn't hurt himself! [*She goes over to him.*] YOO-HOO . . . GAR? . . . HELLO? . . .

GARDNER: [*Looks up at her.*] Oh, hi there, Fan. What's up?

FANNY: How the packing coming? . . .

GARDNER: Packing? . . .

FANNY: Yes, you were packing your manuscript, remember? [*She lifts up a page and lets it fall into a carton.*]

GARDNER: Oh, yes. . . .

FANNY: Here's your picture, Mags. Face over this way . . . turn your easel over here. . . . [*She lets a few more papers fall.*] Up, up . . . and away. . . .

BLACKOUT

Scene 2

The last day. All the books and boxes are gone. The room is completely empty except for MAGS' *backdrop. Late afternoon light dapples the walls; it changes from pale peach to deeper violet. The finished portrait sits on the easel, covered with a cloth.* MAGS *is taking down the backdrop.*

FANNY: [*Offstage; to* GARDNER.] DON'T FORGET TOOTS!

GARDNER: [*Offstage; from another part of the house.*] WHAT'S THAT? . . .

FANNY: [*Offstage.*] I SAID: DON'T FORGET TOOTS! HIS CAGE IS SITTING IN THE MIDDLE OF YOUR STUDY! [*Silence.*]

FANNY: [*Offstage.*] HELLO? . . .   GARDNER: [*Offstage.*] I'LL BE
ARE YOU THERE? . . .   RIGHT WITH YOU; I'M
                                   GETTING TOOTS!

GARDNER: [*Offstage.*] WHAT'S THAT? I CAN'T HEAR YOU!

FANNY: [*Offstage.*] I'M GOING THROUGH THE ROOMS ONE MORE
TIME TO MAKE SURE WE DIDN'T FORGET ANYTHING. . . .
KITTY'S PICKING US UP IN FIFTEEN MINUTES, SO PLEASE BE
READY. . . . SHE'S DROPPING MAGS OFF AT THE STATION
AND THEN IT'S OUT TO ROUTE 3 AND THE CAPE
HIGHWAY. . . .

GARDNER: [*Enters, carrying* TOOTS *in his cage.*] Well, this is it. The big
moment has finally come, eh what, Toots? [*He sees* MAGS.] Oh, hi
there, Mags, I didn't see you. . . .

MAGS: Oh, hi, Daddy, I'm just taking this down. . . . [*She does and
walks over to* TOOTS.] Oh, Toots, I'll miss you. [*She makes little
chattering noises into his cage.*]

GARDNER: Come on, recite a little Gray's Elegy for Mags before we
go.

MAGS: Yes, Mum said he was really good at it now.

GARDNER: Well, the whole thing is to keep at it every day. [*Slowly to*
TOOTS.]
"The curfew tolls the knell of parting day,
The lowing herd wind slowly o'er the lea . . ."
Come on, show Mags your stuff!
[*Slower.*]
"The curfew tolls the knell of the parting day,
The lowing herd wind slowly o'er the lea . . . "
[*Silence;* GARDNER *makes little chattering sounds.*]
Come on, Toots, old boy. . . .

MAGS: How does it go?

GARDNER: [*To* MAGS.] "The curfew tolls the knell of parting day,
The lowing herd wind slowly o'er the lea . . ."

MAGS: [*Slowly to* TOOTS.] "The curfew tolls for you and me,
As quietly the herd winds down . . . "

GARDNER: No, no, it's, "The curfew tolls the knell of parting
day . . . "!

MAGS: [*Repeating after him.*] "The curfew tolls the knell of parting
day . . . "

GARDNER: "The lowing herd wind slowly o'er the lea . . . "

MAGS: [*With a deep breath.*] "The curfew tolls at parting day,
The herd low slowly down the lea . . . no, *knell!*
They come winding down the *knell!* . . . "

GARDNER: Listen, Mags . . . *listen!*
[*A pause.*]

TOOTS: [*Loud and clear with* GARDNER'S *inflection.*]

"The curfew tolls the knell of parting day,
The lowing herd wind slowly o'er the lea,
The ploughman homeward plods his weary way,
And leaves the world to darkness and to me."

MAGS: HE SAID IT. . . . HE SAID IT! . . . AND IN YOUR VOICE! . . .
OH, DADDY, THAT'S AMAZING!

GARDNER: Well, Toots is very smart, which is more than I can say
for a lot of people I know. . . .

MAGS: [*To* TOOTS.] Polly want a cracker? Polly want a cracker?

GARDNER: You can teach a parakeet to say anything; all you need is
patience. . . .

MAGS: But *poetry* . . . that's so hard. . . .

FANNY: [*Enters carrying a suitcase and* GARDNER'*s typewriter in its case.
She's dressed in her traveling suit, wearing a hat to match.*] WELL,
THERE YOU ARE! I THOUGHT YOU'D DIED!

MAGS: [*To* FANNY.] HE SAID IT! I FINALLY HEARD TOOTS RECITE
GRAY'S ELEGY. [*She makes silly clucking sounds into the cage.*]

FANNY: Isn't it uncanny how much he sounds like Daddy?
Sometimes when I'm alone here with him, I've actually thought
he *was* Daddy and started talking to him. Oh, yes, Toots and I
have had quite a few meaty conversations together!
[FANNY *wolf-whistles into the cage; then draws back.* GARDNER *covers the
cage with a traveling cloth. Silence.*]

FANNY: [*Looking around the room.*] God, the place looks so bare.

MAGS: I still can't believe it . . . Cotuit, year round. I wonder if
there'll be any phosphorus when you get there?

FANNY: What on earth are you talking about? [*She carries the discarded
backdrop out into the hall.*]

MAGS: Remember that summer when the ocean was full of
phosphorus?

GARDNER: [*Taking* TOOTS *out into the hall.*] Oh, yes. . . .

MAGS: It was a great mystery where it came from or why it settled
in Cotuit. But one evening when Daddy and I were taking a
swim, suddenly it was there!

GARDNER: [*Returns.*] I remember.

MAGS: I don't know where Mum was. . . .

FANNY: [*Reentering.*] Probably doing the dishes!

MAGS: [*To* GARDNER.] As you dove into the water, this shower of
silvery green sparks erupted all around you. It was incredible! I
thought you were turning into a saint or something; but then
you told me to jump in too and the same thing happened to
me. . . .

GARDNER: Oh, yes, I remember that . . . the water smelled all queer.

MAGS: What *is* phosphorus, anyway?

GARDNER: Chemicals, chemicals . . .

FANNY: No, it isn't. Phosphorus is a green liquid inside insects.

Fireflies have it. When you see sparks in the water it means
insects are swimming around. . . .

GARDNER: Where on earth did you get that idea?

FANNY: If you're bitten by one of them, it's fatal!

MAGS: . . . and the next morning it was still there. . . .

GARDNER: It was the damndest stuff to get off! We'd have to stay in
the shower a good ten minutes. It comes from chemical waste,
you see. . . .

MAGS: Our bodies looked like mercury as we swam around. . . .

GARDNER: It stained all the towels a strange yellow green.

MAGS: I was in heaven, and so were you for that matter. You'd
finished your day's poetry and would turn somersaults like some
happy dolphin. . . .

FANNY: Damned dishes . . . why didn't I see any of this?! . . .

MAGS: I remember one night in particular. . . . We sensed the
phosphorus was about to desert us; blow off to another town.
We were chasing each other under water. At one point I lost
you, the brilliance was so intense . . . but finally your foot
appeared . . . then your leg. I grabbed it! . . . I remember wishing
the moment would hold forever; that we could just be fixed
there, laughing and iridescent. . . . Then I began to get panicky
because I knew it would pass; it was passing already. You were
slipping from my grasp. The summer was almost over. I'd be
going back to art school; you'd be going back to Boston. . . .
Even as I was reaching for you, you were gone. We'd never be
like that again.

[*Silence.*]

FANNY: [*Spies* MAGS's *portrait covered on the easel.*] What's that over
there? Don't tell me we forgot something!

MAGS: It's your portrait. I finished it.

FANNY: You finished it? How on earth did you manage that?

MAGS: I stayed up all night.

FANNY: You did? . . . *I* didn't hear you, did you hear her, Gar? . . .

GARDNER: Not a peep, not a peep!

MAGS: Well, I wanted to get it done before you left. You know, see
what you thought. It's not bad, considering . . . I mean, I did it
almost completely from memory. The light was terrible and I
was trying to be quiet so I wouldn't wake you. It was hardly an
ideal situation. . . . I mean, you weren't the most cooperative
models. . . . [*She suddenly panics and snatches the painting off the
easel. She hugs it to her chest and starts dancing around the room with
it.*] Oh, God, you're going to hate it! You're going to hate it! How
did I ever get into this? . . . Listen, you don't really want to see it
. . . it's nothing . . . just a few dabs here and there. . . . It was
awfully late when I finished it. The light was really impossible
and my eyes were hurting like crazy. . . . Look, why don't we

just go out to the sidewalk and wait for Kitty so she doesn't have
to honk. . . .

GARDNER: [*Snatches the painting out from under her.*] WOULD YOU
JUST SHUT UP A MINUTE AND LET US SEE IT? . . .

MAGS: [*Laughing and crying.*] But it's nothing, Daddy . . . *really!* . . .
I've done better with my eyes closed! It was so late I could
hardly see anything and then I spilled a whole bottle of thinner
into my palette. . . .

GARDNER: [*Sets it down on the easel and stands back to look at it.*] THERE!

MAGS: [*Dancing around them in a panic.*] Listen, it's just a quick
sketch. . . . It's still wet. . . . I didn't have enough time. . . . It
takes at least forty hours to do a decent portrait. . . .
[*Suddenly it's very quiet as* FANNY *and* GARDNER *stand back to look at it.*]

MAGS: [*More and more beside herself, keeps leaping around the room
wrapping her arms around herself, making little whimpering sounds.*]
Please don't . . . no . . . don't . . . oh, please! . . . Come on, don't
look. . . . Oh, God, don't . . . please. . . .
[*An eternity passes as* FANNY *and* GARDNER *gaze at it.*]

GARDNER: Well . . .

FANNY: Well . . . [*More silence.*]

FANNY: I think it's perfectly   GARDNER: Awfully clever, awfully
dreadful!   clever!

FANNY: What on earth did you do to my face? . . .

GARDNER: I particularly like Mum!

FANNY: Since when do I have purple skin?! . . .

MAGS: I told you it was nothing, just a silly . . .

GARDNER: She looks like a million dollars!

FANNY: AND WILL YOU LOOK AT MY HAIR . . . IT'S BRIGHT
ORANGE!

GARDNER: [*Views it from another angle.*] It's really very good!

FANNY: [*Pointing*] That doesn't look anything like me!

GARDNER: . . . first rate!

FANNY: Since when do I have purple skin and bright orange hair?!
. . .

MAGS: [*Trying to snatch it off the easel.*] Listen, you don't have to
worry about my feelings . . . really . . . I . . .

GARDNER: [*Blocking her way.*] NOT SO FAST . . .

FANNY: . . . and look at how I'm sitting! I've never sat like that in
my life!

GARDNER: [*Moving closer to it.*] Yes, yes, it's awfully clever . . .

FANNY: I HAVE NO FEET!

GARDNER: The whole thing is quite remarkable!

FANNY: And what happened to my legs, pray tell? . . . They just
vanish below the knees! . . . At least my dress is presentable. I've
always loved that dress.

GARDNER: It sparkles somehow. . . .

FANNY: [*To* GARDNER.] Don't you think it's becoming?

GARDNER: Yes, very becoming, awfully becoming . . .

FANNY: [*Examining it at closer range.*] Yes, she got the dress very well, how it shows off what's left of my figure. . . . My smile is nice too.

GARDNER: Good and wide. . . .

FANNY: I love how the corners of my mouth turn up. . . .

GARDNER: It's very clever. . . .

FANNY: They're almost quivering. . . .

GARDNER: Good lighting effects!

FANNY: Actually, I look quite . . . *young,* don't you think?

GARDNER: [*To* MAGS.] You're awfully good with those highlights.

FANNY: [*Looking at it from different angles.*] And *you* look darling! . . .

GARDNER: Well, I don't know about that. . . .

FANNY: No, you look absolutely darling. Good enough to eat!

MAGS: [*In a whisper.*] They like it. . . . They like it!

[*A silence as* FANNY *and* GARDNER *keep gazing at it.*]

FANNY: You know what it is? The wispy brush strokes make us look like a couple in a French Impressionist painting.

GARDNER: Yes, I see what you mean. . . .

FANNY: . . . a Manet or Renoir . . .

GARDNER: It's very evocative.

FANNY: There's something about the light. . . . [*They back up to survey it from a distance.*]

FANNY: You know those Renoir café scenes? . . .

GARDNER: She doesn't lay on the paint with a trowel; it's just touches here and there. . . .

MAGS: They *like* it! . . .

FANNY: You know the one with the couple dancing? . . . Not that we're dancing. There's just something similar in the mood . . . a kind of gaiety, almost. . . . The man has his back to you and he's swinging the woman around. . . . OH, GAR, YOU'VE SEEN IT A MILLION TIMES! IT'S HANGING IN THE MUSEUM OF FINE ARTS! . . . They're dancing like this. . . .

[*She goes up to him and puts an arm on his shoulders.*]

MAGS: They like it. . . . They like it!

FANNY: She's got on this wonderful flowered dress with ruffles at the neck and he's holding her like this. . . . That's right . . . and she's got the most rhapsodic expression on her face. . . .

GARDNER: [*Getting into the spirit of it, takes* FANNY *in his arms and slowly begins to dance around the room.*] Oh, yes . . . I know the one you mean. . . . They're in a sort of haze . . . and isn't there a little band playing off to one side? . . .

FANNY: Yes, that's it!

[*Kitty's horn honks outside.*]

MAGS: [*Is the only one who hears it.*] There's Kitty! [*She's torn and keeps looking toward the door, but finally gives in to their stolen moment.*]

FANNY: . . . and there's a man in a dark suit playing the violin and someone's conducting, I think. . . . And aren't Japanese lanterns strung up? . . .

[*They pick up speed, dipping and whirling around the room. Strains of a far-away Chopin waltz are heard.*]

GARDNER: Oh, yes! There are all these little lights twinkling in the trees. . . .

FANNY: . . . and doesn't the woman have a hat on?. . . . A big red hat? . . .

GARDNER: . . . and lights all over the dancers, too. Everything shimmers with this marvelous glow. Yes, yes . . . I can see it perfectly! The whole thing is absolutely extraordinary!
[*The lights become dreamy and dappled as they dance around the room.* MAGS *watches them, moved to tears as . . .*]

SLOWLY THE CURTAIN FALLS

Questions for *Painting Churches*

1.   Reread the author's description of the stage setting at the beginning of the play. Howe remarks of the lighting, "It transforms whatever it touches, giving the room a distinct feeling of unreality." What purposes does this lighting serve?

2.   We're told that the Churches come from aristocratic old Boston families. Do you think their social status is important to the meaning of the play?

3.   Look at the scene (Act I, Scene iii) in which Mags says she's "Awkward . . . plain," and so on. Why is Fanny so pleased when Mags talks this way?

4.   Why does Mags eat so ravenously when she's at her parents' home?

5.   Mags discusses at length two memories from her childhood. In Act I she describes the "great masterpiece" she created in her youth; in Act II she remembers swimming with her father when the ocean was filled with phosphorus. How is each incident significant to the play?

6.   Discuss the structure of the two Acts in the play and their relation to each other.

7.   What does Fanny's invention, her "magic lantern" lampshade, tell you about her?

8.   Two major actions are going on in this drama: the moving of the Churches and the painting of their portrait. Are they related?

9.   Fanny tells Mags, "You ought to paint us as we really are." Does Mags paint her parents as they really are? Why is this portrait so important to Mags?

10.   *Painting Churches* is filled with references to music (particularly the Chopin waltzes played throughout the drama), painting, and literature. Pick out one or two of these references and discuss how they work symbolically in the play.

Akira Kurosawa (1910–   )

The youngest of seven children, Kurosawa was born in Tokyo to an old samurai family. Early in life he decided to become a painter, but the course of his life was changed when, in 1936, needing money, he responded on a whim to a newspaper ad recruiting assistant directors to work in a Japanese film studio. He began writing scripts in 1940 and has directed over 25 films since 1942. Kurosawa's first and only film teacher once remarked, "From the very beginning, Kurosawa was completely engrossed in separating what is real from what is false." This statement characterizes much of the director's greatest work. Kurosawa has received many awards for his films, including the Golden Lion at the 1950 Venice Film Festival for *Rashomon*, the Academy Award in 1976 for *Dersu Uzala*, and the 1980 Grand Prize at the Cannes film festival for *Kagemusha*.

In 1985, at the age of seventy-five, Kurosawa completed *Ran*, his retelling of Shakespeare's *King Lear*, and again received an Academy Award nomination. Among his best-known films are *Ikiru*, *Yojimbo*, and *The Seven Samurai*, which was remade in Hollywood as *The Magnificent Seven*.

Rashomon

Translated by Donald Richie

The title sequence consists of some ten shots of the half-ruined gate, Rashomon, in the rain. Superimposed over these are the title and credits, including, in the prints distributed in the United States, vignettes (oval-shaped insets) showing the major characters in action. Various details of the gate are seen, its steps, the base of a column, the eaves of the roof, puddles on the ground. Everywhere there is evidence of the downpour. Gagaku, traditional court music, is heard during the credits, then the sound of the torrential rain.

The final title reads: "Kyoto, in the twelfth century, when famines and civil wars had devastated the ancient capital."

Note: In our text, camera position is indicated by initials: LS for long shot; MS, medium shot; MCU, medium closeup; and CU, closeup. The stills keyed to the text should suggest the meaning of these terms. Camera movement is indicated by the following: *pan* (camera turning sideways while remaining fixed on its axis); *tilt* (camera moving up or down while fixed on its axis); *dolly* (camera moving toward or away from the fixed subject); *track* (camera moving at the same speed as the subject being filmed); and *travel* (camera moving at a speed independent of a moving subject). We have also noted at the end of each shot its duration in seconds. In two cases, shots last less than a second (shots 204 and 205), and these are listed in fractions.

Left to right: Tajomaru, the bandit; Masago, the wife; Takehiro, the samurai; the woodcutter; the priest; the commoner; the medium; the police agent.

The Rashomon Gate.

1   *Long shot. Two men, a priest and a woodcutter, are sitting motionless, taking shelter under the gate.*   *(4 seconds)*

2   *Medium shot from the side of the two, the woodcutter in the foreground, as they stare out at the rain with heads bowed. The woodcutter raises his head.*

WOODCUTTER: I can't understand it. I just can't understand it at all.   *(16)*

3   *Close-up of the priest; he looks at the woodcutter and back again at the rain.*
                                                                              (11)

4   *LS from directly in front. The two men continue to stare vacantly at the rain.*
                                                                              (5)

5   *A general view of the gate; a man enters from behind the camera and runs toward the gate, splashing through puddles. Thunder is heard.*   *(15)*

6   *LS from reverse angle. The man runs past a fallen column and disappears from the frame.*   *(2)*

7   *MS of the steps of the gate; he enters from behind the camera and runs up the steps to shelter.*   *(4)*

8   *MS. Out of the rain, he turns and looks back outside, then removes a rag covering his head and wrings it out. The woodcutter's voice is heard off-camera.*

WOODCUTTER *(off)*: I just can't understand it. *(11)*

9   *LS. The newcomer, in the background, turns toward the priest and woodcutter, who are sitting in the foreground.* *(3)*

10   *MS of the newcomer. He goes toward the others—the camera panning with him—and sits down behind the woodcutter.*

COMMONER: What's the matter? *(25)*

11   *MS of the woodcutter and commoner.*

COMMONER: What can't you understand?
WOODCUTTER: I've never heard of anything so strange.
COMMONER: Why don't you tell me about it? *(13)*

12   *MS of all three men, the priest in the foreground. The commoner looks toward the priest.*

COMMONER: Good thing we have a priest here—he looks smart too.

PRIEST: Oh, even Abbot Konin of the Kiyomizu Temple, though he's known for his learning, wouldn't be able to understand this.

COMMONER: Then you know something about this story?

PRIEST: I've heard it with my own ears, seen it with my own eyes. And only today.

COMMONER: Where?

PRIEST: In the prison courtyard.

COMMONER: The prison?

PRIEST: A man has been murdered.

COMMONER: What of it? One or two more . . . *(He stands up.)* (42)

13   *MS of the commoner standing over the others; he looks down.*

COMMONER: Only one? Why, if you go up to the top of this gate you'll always find five or six bodies. Nobody bothers about them. *(He begins to take off his shirt.)* (7)

14   *MS of the priest; he turns and looks up at the commoner.*

PRIEST: Oh, you're right. Wars, earthquakes, great winds, fires, famines, plague—each new year is full of disaster. *(He wipes his hand across his face.)* (19)

15 (=13)   *MS. The commoner wrings out his wet shirt.*

PRIEST *(off)*: And now every night the bandits descend upon us. (5)

16 (=14)   *MS of the priest.*

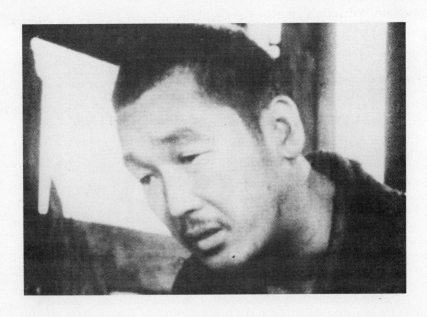

PRIEST: I, for one, have seen hundreds of men dying, killed like animals. *(Pause.)* Yet . . . even I have never heard anything as horrible as this before. (19)

17   *MS of the woodcutter, who has been listening; he turns to the priest.* (3)

18 (= 14)   *MS. The priest turns toward the woodcutter.* (3)

19   *MS of the woodcutter and priest.*

WOODCUTTER: Horrible—it's horrible.

The woodcutter looks away; dolly in to CU of the priest.

PRIEST: There was never anything as terrible as this. Never. It is more horrible than fires or wars or epidemics—or bandits. *(Camera stays on him.)*
COMMONER *(off)*: Look here now, priest—let's not have any sermons.

The priest looks up. (30)

20 (= 13)   *MS of the commoner.*

COMMONER: I only wanted to know about this strange story of yours because it might amuse me while I wait out the rain. But I'd just as soon sit quietly and listen to the rain than hear any sermons from you. *(His wet shirt over his shoulder, he moves toward the camera.)* (15)

21   *LS. The commoner moves away, leaving the priest and woodcutter sitting as before.*

22   *MS of the commoner at the other side of the gate; he peers at some loose boards, then rips two of them free.* (14)

23   *LS. He crosses back to squat in front of the woodcutter and priest, and begins to pull the boards to pieces. The woodcutter rises and runs over to him.*

WOODCUTTER: Maybe you can tell me what it all means. I don't understand it. *(He squats down.)* All three of them . . .
COMMONER: All three of whom?
WOODCUTTER: It's those three I wanted to tell you about.
COMMONER: All right, tell me then, but don't get so excited. This rain won't let up for some time. *(Both men look up.)* (33)

24   *CU of the great signboard of the gate, seen in the opening shot of the titles: the sign reads "Rashomon" in large Japanese characters. The camera tilts down from the signboard to the men far below. The woodcutter moves closer to the commoner.* (11)

25   *CU of the woodcutter.*

WOODCUTTER: It was three days ago. I'd gone into the mountains for
wood. . . .   *(15)*

26   *The dazzling light of the sun breaks through the branches of trees overhead as
the camera travels through a dense woods. Music begins, a steady rhythm supporting
a melody initially associated with the woodcutter but later becoming the underlying
musical theme of the entire film.*   *(5)*

27   *CU of the woodcutter's ax, seen in a traveling shot, glinting in the sunlight as
the woodcutter walks through the woods.*   *(7)*

28   *CU of the woodcutter's face as he walks, ax over his shoulder, the camera
tracking backward.*   *(5)*

29   *LS. Panning from high above, the camera follows him.*   *(9)*

30   *A tree; the camera tilts from top to bottom to discover the woodcutter in the
distance.*   *(7)*

31   *The camera pans with the woodcutter as he approaches a narrow bridge,
crosses it, and goes off.*   *(11)*

32   *A forward-traveling shot of the sky seen through the branches of the trees
passing overhead.*   *(6)*

33   *CU of the woodcutter's back as he walks, the camera tracking after him.*   *(5)*

34   *A traveling shot as he moves from LS closer to camera.*   *(9)*

35 (=32)   *The sky and the tree branches.*   *(6)*

36   *The camera travels toward the woodcutter, crosses in front of him, and pans
around to follow his back receding into the woods.*   *(15)*

37 (=26)   *The sun through the tree branches.*   *(5)*

38   *The woodcutter from above. The camera travels as the woodcutter approaches,
pans, and travels with him again, closer now, occasionally losing sight of him in the
underbrush.*   *(15)*

39   *Extreme closeup of the back of the woodcutter's head, the camera tracking after
him; again, leaves sometimes block the view.*   *(5)*

40   *ECU. A traveling shot alongside the woodcutter; the view is frequently blocked.*
                                                                              (4)

41   *ECU of the woodcutter's face as he walks, the camera tracking backward.
Suddenly he halts. Music ends.*   *(9)*

42   *CU of a woman's reed hat with veil, dangling on a branch near the ground.
The woodcutter, in the background, looks at it and comes forward to touch the veil.
Audible is a soft tinkle like the sound of wind chimes; it develops into a bell-like*

music which is later associated with the woman. The woodcutter slowly walks on, the camera panning to watch as he recedes farther into the woods. The main thematic music begins again. *(25)*

43   *MS. Traveling shot alongside the woodcutter; he looks about on either side as he walks cautiously on.* *(5)*

44   *He approaches the camera and (CU) looks down. He halts.*

45   *CU of a man's hat lying at his feet; he bends over to pick it up. The camera tilts up with him as he stands straight again. He comes forward and goes off.* *(11)*

46   *LS. He approaches, stops again (MS), and looks down; this time he picks up a piece of rope, and stares in front of him.* *(27)*

47   *LS of something lying in the leaves.* *(1)*

48   *CU. It is an amulet case.* *(2)*

49   *CU of the woodcutter as he moves forward (pan) but stumbles; he jumps back with a look of horror on his face.* *(11)*

50   *MS. The stiffly raised hands of a corpse are in front of him. A gong is sounded.* *(2)*

51   *CU of the woodcutter's face; he leaps back, turns around and, his back to the camera, runs into the woods, dropping his ax as he goes.* *(7)*

52   *MS. The camera moves rapidly alongside the woodcutter as he runs panic-stricken through the woods. His speech runs over this and the next two shots.*

WOODCUTTER *(off)*: I ran as fast as I could to tell the police. That was three days ago. Then the police called me to testify. *(3)*

53   *MS. The camera continues to move with the woodcutter.* *(3)*

54   *MS. The camera continues with him. (Wipe.)* *(3)*

55   *MS of the woodcutter kneeling on the sand of the prison courtyard.*

WOODCUTTER: Yes, sir. It was I who found the body first. *(Pause. He is obviously being questioned though we hear only his answers.)* Was there a sword or anything? No, sir. Nothing at all. Only a woman's hat, caught on a branch . . . and a man's hat that had been trampled on. And a piece of rope . . . and further off an amulet case of red brocade. *(Pause.)* Yes, sir. Yes, that was all I saw. I swear it. *(He bows.) (Wipe.)* *(52)*

56   *MS of the priest kneeling in the prison courtyard. Behind him is the woodcutter. The priest is testifying.*

PRIEST: Yes, sir, I saw the murdered man when he was still alive. Well, it was about three days ago. It was in the afternoon. Yes. It was on the road between Sekiyama and Yamashina. *(23)*

57 *The priest is walking along a road which winds through a bamboo grove. Music in. Pan as he approaches the camera and passes it. He stops. From the opposite direction a samurai approaches, leading a horse by the bridle. On the horse is a woman, sitting sidesaddle. The priest steps back and looks after them (pan) as they recede into the distance.*

PRIEST *(off)*: Her hat had a veil. I couldn't see her face. The man was
   armed. He had a sword, bow and arrows. *(A gong sounds.)*   *(35)*

58 (=56)   *MS of the priest in the prison courtyard.*

PRIEST: I never thought I would see him again; then, to see him
   dead like that. Oh, it is true—life is ephemeral, as fleeting as the
   morning dew. But the pity of it. What a pity that he should have
   died like that. *(He bows.) (Wipe.)*   *(29)*

59   *MS. The police agent is proudly testifying. Beside him, tied up, sits the bandit, Tajomaru. Behind them sit the woodcutter and the priest.*

POLICE AGENT: Yes, it was I who caught Tajomaru. Yes, indeed. That
   very same notorious bandit who has been so much talked about,
   even in the outskirts of the city.   *(10)*

60   *CU of the bandit gazing vacantly up at the sky, the voice of the agent continuing.*   *(2)*

61   *The sky, filled with huge summer clouds.*

POLICE AGENT *(continuing, off)*: Yes, this is the very same bandit,
   Tajomaru, your honor. When I finally caught him . . .   *(2)*

62 (=59)   *MS of the agent testifying.*

POLICE AGENT: . . . he was dressed like he is now, and carried that
   Korean sword. It was toward evening, day before yesterday, by
   the riverbank at Katsura. *(Dolly to CU of agent.)*   *(16)*

63   *The riverbank. Music in. The agent walks toward the camera, hears a horse neigh, and runs (pan) along the bank toward a man lying as though in agony (LS). He leans over to lift the man and loses his grip, stumbling back into the river.*   *(21)*

64   *MS. Tajomaru, in the foreground, groaning, apparently in agony, writhing in the sand. In the background, the agent in the river. The camera travels from them to reveal, farther down the bank, a bow, arrows, a horse.*

POLICE AGENT *(off)*: There was a black-lacquered quiver holding
   seventeen arrows in all—they all had hawk feathers. The bow
   was bound in leather . . . and there was a gray horse.   *(19)*

65   *CU of the agent in the prison courtyard; the camera backs away from CU of him to same position as shot 59.*

POLICE AGENT: And they all belonged to the murdered man. But just imagine a fierce bandit like Tajomaru here being thrown by the very animal that he himself had stolen. It was retribution.

The bandit wheels toward him threateningly, hisses through his teeth, then bursts into laughter.

TAJOMARU: Retribution? Don't be stupid. On that day. . . . (34)

66 *LS. A hill, low clouds. Triumphant music. Tajomaru, shouting, gallops across and off the screen.*

TAJOMARU *(continuing, off)*: . . . while I was riding that gray horse I suddenly got very thirsty. (9)

67 *MS of Tajomaru, continuing in the prison courtyard.*

TAJOMARU: So when I got near Osaka Pass I had a drink at a stream. (7)

68 *LS from above. Tajomaru, stretched on the ground, drinks from a small stream. His heavy panting is heard.* (13)

69 (=67) *MS of Tajomaru in the prison courtyard.*

TAJOMARU: There must have been a snake or something in the upper stream, because after a few hours I began to have this terrible colic. Toward evening it got so I couldn't bear it any longer and so I got off the horse and lay down. *(Dolly back to the two-shot [59] of Tajomaru and the police agent.)* And you thought I'd fallen off—hah! *(He hisses and kicks the quiver lying in front of the agent.)* It takes a pretty stupid person to have an idea that stupid. (29)

70 *CU of Tajomaru.*

TAJOMARU: No, I'm telling the truth. I know you're going to cut off my head sooner or later—I'm not hiding anything. It was me, Tajomaru, who killed that man. Yes, I did it. It was a hot afternoon, about three days ago, that I first saw them. And then all of a sudden there was this cool breeze. If it hadn't been for that breeze, maybe I wouldn't have killed him.

The bell-like music, like distant wind chimes, is heard as he concludes; the tinkling continues into the next shot. (32)

71 *In the woods; the camera tilts from the great crown of an enormous tree down to its roots to reveal the bandit sprawled out sleeping at the base of another huge tree nearby. Music denoting the traveling couple fades in over the tinkling bells.* (10)

72 *MS of Tajomaru asleep; the camera dollies in to CU of him and pans around to reveal the samurai leading the horse on which the woman is riding.* (20)

73   *Back-traveling shot of the pair coming down the road.*   *(3)*

74   *CU of the bandit; he looks sleepily in their direction.*   *(3)*

75   *CU of the woman on horseback, her face barely visible through the veil of her hat.*   *(3)*

76 (=74)   *CU. Tajomaru closes his eyes, scratches, appears to be falling asleep again, but suddenly glances in the direction of the couple.*   *(19)*

77   *LS. The pair approach the "sleeping" figure.*   *(6)*

78   *MS profile of the samurai as he sees Tajomaru and hesitates.*   *(2)*

79 (=74)   *CU. Tajomaru, his eyes half-open, staring back at the samurai.*   *(4)*

80   *MS. The samurai, now seen from in front, continues to assess Tajomaru.*   *(3)*

81 (=74)   *CU. Tajomaru staring back; he scratches his leg lazily, closing his eyes again.*   *(11)*

82   *CU. The samurai decides to move on, leading the horse toward the camera.*   *(5)*

83 (=74)   *CU of Tajomaru, his eyes shut. Then, to the sound of the bell-like music, a fresh breeze stirs his hair; he opens his eyes, looks in the couple's direction, and gives a start.*   *(13)*

84   *CU of the feet of the woman, gently swinging with the movements of the horse; the camera tilts up to show her face as the veil is blown aside.*   *(3)*

85   *ECU of Tajomaru, now wide-awake, looking.*   *(3)*

86   *CU of the woman on horseback (pan), her veil parting to reveal her face fully.*   *(3)*

87 (=85)   *ECU. Tajomaru raises himself up.*   *(4)*

88   *MS from behind Tajomaru, now in a sitting position. Pan as the horse and couple move past him in the background. Tajomaru turns and looks after them, then sinks back under the tree as they continue to move farther down the road.*   *(25)*

89   *MS of Tajomaru, from in front. His sword rests between his legs, and now he slowly pulls it closer to him.*   *(12)*

90 (=70)   *In the prison courtyard, Tajomaru continues his testimony.*

TAJOMARU: It was just a glimpse. First I saw her, then she was gone—I thought I had seen an angel. And right then I decided I would take her, that I'd have her even if I had to kill the man. . . . *(He laughs.)* But if I could do it without killing him, then that would be all the better. So I decided not to kill him but to somehow get the woman alone. The road to Yamashina was hardly the place to do it though.   *(35)*

91   *LS. Tajomaru runs through the woods toward the camera. Chase music in. (3)*

92   *LS from the side; the camera travels with him as he races along.*   *(2)*

93   *MS. He runs down a slope (pan).*   *(3)*

94   *MS. Pan to follow him as he leaps over a small brook and approaches the couple in the background. Music out.*   *(4)*

95   *MS of Tajomaru's back, the couple visible over his shoulder. The samurai stops and turns.*

SAMURAI: What do you want?   *(3)*

96   *CU of Tajomaru's face. He stares back at the samurai, absently slaps at a mosquito that has landed on his neck, then walks (pan) behind the horse (MS), glancing up at the woman.*   *(15)*

97   *CU as Tajomaru eyes the pair, then walks to the front of horse (MS) and crouches down.*

SAMURAI *(off)*: What is it?   *(11)*

98   *MS from behind the samurai as he approaches Tajomaru.*

SAMURAI *(threateningly)*: What do you want?

Tajomaru rises and crosses back behind the horse (pan), into a clearing. As the samurai crosses in front of the horse into the clearing, Tajomaru suddenly draws his sword and swings it smartly—the samurai at once reaches for his own sword, but the bandit laughs loudly, for he is merely displaying his.   *(26)*

99   *MS. Reverse angle from behind Tajomaru's back as he proudly raises his sword.*

TAJOMARU: Isn't that splendid? Just look!   *(5)*

100   *MS of Tajomaru as he steps up to the samurai and presents the sword, hilt first.*

TAJOMARU: Here, take it. Look at it. *(The samurai makes no move to accept it.)* Near here I found this old tomb *(points past camera)* with lots of things like this in it. I broke it open and inside found swords, daggers, mirrors. . . . I buried them all here in the woods and no one but me knows where. But if you're interested I might sell some of them to you cheap. *(Presents the sword again.)*   *(30)*

101   *CU from reverse angle as Tajomaru holds out the sword. The samurai abruptly takes it and examines it. Tajomaru glances in the woman's direction and scratches his cheek. (Wipe.)*   *(16)*

102   *The forest, enormous trees. Idyllic music. The camera tilts down to reveal the woman sitting on the ground alone, the horse grazing behind her.*   *(25)*

103   *CU of the bow and arrows, which have been left lying on the ground near
the woman.*   *(3)*

104   *LS. The bandit and the samurai are climbing a slope in the woods; a
traveling shot from above and behind them. Music with drums accompanies the trek
through the woods.*   *(13)*

105   *MS from above and in front of them as they continue up the slope (pan).* *(9)*

106   *LS. They push on through the woods (pan).*   *(9)*

107   *MS. Pan as they go on. Suddenly Tajomaru stops and draws his sword. The
man recoils, thinking the bandit is about to fight. Tajomaru laughs and with a
shout pokes his sword toward the samurai. Then he begins slashing at the
obstructing underbrush with the sword (pan).*   *(13)*

108   *CU. Pan as the bandit hacks his way forward. He pauses.*

TAJOMARU: It's over there in that grove.   *(11)*

109   *CU of the samurai, eyeing the bandit.*

SAMURAI: You walk ahead of me.   *(4)*

110   *MS. Tajomaru, in the background, waits, then turns from the camera and
starts out, leading the way for the samurai.*   *(10)*

111   *MS. Tajomaru, hacking through the underbrush, leads the way as the two
come toward the camera, which tracks backward.*   *(7)*

112   *MS. Now the camera tracks forward and follows their backs.*   *(6)*

113   *MS. They approach the camera; it pans as they go off.*   *(14)*

114   *MS. They approach from LS. Tajomaru stops and gestures.*

TAJOMARU: It's over there. *(He replaces his sword in its scabbard.)*

*The samurai moves past and in front of him (pan), and stands looking with his
back to Tajomaru.*   *(23)*

115   *CU of Tajomaru—pan as he attacks the other man, knocking him to the
ground. Fight music punctuates the action. They roll over each other, but Tajomaru
kicks the samurai away, then leaps through the air after him. The remainder of the
fight is never seen, for as Tajomaru leaps, a wipe leads into shot 116.*   *(18)*

116   *MS. A traveling shot of Tajomaru running through the woods. He pauses for
a moment to point back in the direction of the samurai, laughing and shouting.*   *(7)*

117   *CU. The camera continues to travel with him.*   *(4)*

118   *LS. Still running and laughing loudly, he starts down a hill.*   *(7)*

119   *LS from the bottom of the hill. Tajomaru descends, stops, and peers through
the bushes (CU).*   *(25)*

120   *Over his shoulder, far below, stands the woman, waiting by a small brook. She crouches to dangle her hand in the water.*   *(12)*

121   *MS. A closer view of the waiting woman.*   *(4)*

122 (=119)   *CU. Tajomaru looks down at her, his eyes wide.*   *(4)*

123   *CU of the woman, serenely passing the time.*   *(3)*

124 (=119)   *CU. Tajomaru peering down.*   *(2)*

125   *ECU of the woman's hand, playing with the water as it flows gently past. Suddenly her hand stops.*   *(5)*

126   *CU of the woman from the side as she turns abruptly to the camera, puzzled, and lifts her veil.*   *(3)*

127 (=119)   *CU. Tajomaru sees she has noticed something and leaps forward from his hiding place.*   *(3)*

128   *CU from reverse angle. Tajomaru's back as he bounds down toward her away from the camera.*   *(6)*

129   *MS. Reverse angle from over the woman's shoulder. Tajomaru runs swiftly up to her and stops, panting, in front of her.*

TAJOMARU: Something terrible has happened. Your husband's been
   bitten by a snake.   *(5)*

130   *MS. Reverse angle of the woman from behind Tajomaru. Shocked, she stands up, removing her hat.*   *(3)*

131   *CU of the bareheaded woman; she stares incredulously at the bandit.*   *(4)*

132   *CU of Tajomaru in the prison courtyard, continuing his testimony.*

TAJOMARU: She became very pale and stared at me as though her
   eyes were frozen. She looked like a child when it turns suddenly
   serious. The sight of her made me jealous of that man; I started
   to hate him. I wanted to show her what he looked like, all tied
   up like that. I hadn't even thought of a thing like that before,
   but now I did.   *(29)*

133   *MS. A traveling shot of Tajomaru running through the woods, pulling the woman after him. Travel music begins.*   *(5)*

134   *MS of the woman; a traveling shot as she is pulled along by the wrist.*   *(3)*

135   *CU. A traveling shot of her hat dragging behind her; it snags on a branch (camera stops) and is left behind.*   *(7)*

136   *They run from LS up to the camera, which pans to reveal the samurai, tightly bound up, sitting in the clearing where Tajomaru attacked him. The woman stops abruptly.*   *(5)*

137   *CU of the samurai, helpless.*   (1)

138   *CU. The woman stands transfixed by the sight of her husband, Tajomaru behind her; the bandit steps forward past her.*   (7)

139   *LS from behind the husband, the woman and Tajomaru in the background: Tajomaru steps back to look at both of them.*   (9)

140   *MS from behind the husband, the woman in the background.*   (4)

141   *MS from behind the bandit, the husband in the background.*   (3)

142   *MS from the side of the woman, the bandit in the background.*   (4)

143   *MS from the side of the bandit, the woman in the background.*   (5)

144   *MS from behind the husband, the bandit in the background. The samurai looks toward his wife.*   (6)

145   *MS from the side of the woman, her husband in the background. The camera moves swiftly toward her and pans around her (CU) as she suddenly turns to attack the bandit with her dagger. She races toward him, her weapon outstretched, but he dodges the thrust and springs around to look at her with admiring disbelief.*   (18)

146   *CU of her frenzied face as she regains her balance and whirls to charge again.*   (3)

147   *MS from behind her as she runs at him again (pan); he dodges, she turns and charges at him with the dagger held straight before her. Hysterical now, she misses and stumbles out of sight. The camera remains on Tajomaru's laughing face.*   (5)

148   *MS. Tajomaru in the foreground, the woman in the background; she dives forward and grabs his leg, but he pulls free.*   (4)

149   *CU of Tajomaru; he stares down at her, excited by her desperate spirit.*   (3)

150   *CU of the woman, stretched on the ground; she menaces him with the dagger held straight up at him, every muscle tense and ready.*   (3)

151 (=149)   *CU. Tajomaru's admiration is unbounded.*   (3)

152 (=150)   *CU. She won't relent.*

TAJOMARU *(off)*: She was fierce, determined . . .   (5)

153   *MS of the two of them; he continues to stand over her, silent, watchful.*

TAJOMARU *(off)*: She fought like a cat.

She rises, slashes at him.   (14)

154   *MS from reverse angle as he grabs her.*   (4)

155   *CU. He shouts in pain as she sinks her teeth into his forearm; he flings her away and (pan) she trips to the ground.*   (4)

156   CU of Tajomaru; he licks his wound and moves forward.   *(9)*

157   CU of the woman as she rises to attack again.   *(2)*

158   LS. She chases him, wildly slicing the air with her dagger (pan). He circles round a tree and continues in the opposite direction (pan).   *(6)*

159   MS from left. He reaches another tree, swings around it, and waits for her next move. She thrusts at him, sobbing, and they chase each other around the tree.

(16)

160   MS from right. He runs off (traveling shot); she follows, but collapses, exhausted; he stands jubilant over her.   *(12)*

161   LS. The woman in the foreground, helplessly sobbing; Tajomaru in the background. He stalks up to her, she lunges yet again, but now he grabs and holds her.   *(15)*

162   CU of the husband watching them; he bows his head.   *(5)*

163   CU. The woman claws Tajomaru's face; he wrests his head free and pushes her to the ground (camera tilts down). She struggles but he kisses her.   *(7)*

164   The sky seen through the branches of the trees (pan).   *(2)*

165   CU of the bandit kissing her; she stares straight up.   *(4)*

166 (=164)   The sky seen through the overhead branches (pan).   *(2)*

167   CU from reverse angle; Tajomaru holding her, kissing her.   *(1)*

168 (=164)   The sky and trees. The camera has stopped panning; now the sun is seen shining brilliantly through the branches. Bell-like music begins.   *(3)*

169   ECU from reverse angle; Tajomaru kissing the woman, as she stares blankly up at the sun.   *(3)*

170 (=168)   The sun through the branches; slowly the scene goes out of focus.   *(4)*

171 (=169)   ECU. The woman closes her eyes.   *(4)*

172   ECU of the dagger in her hand, Tajomaru tightly gripping her wrist. Her fingers loosen, the dagger drops to the ground.   *(3)*

173   ECU of the dagger sticking point first in the ground.   *(2)*

174   MS of Tajomaru's back, the woman in his arms. The camera slowly dollies toward them. Her hand encircles his back, her fingers move caressingly; she tightens her grip on him. She is giving herself.   *(11)*

175   MS. In the prison courtyard, Tajomaru is laughing and kicking his feet exultantly.

TAJOMARU: And so I had her—just as I'd planned, and without killing the husband. And that was how I did it. Besides, I hadn't intended to kill him. But then. . . .   *(21)*

176   *CU of Tajomaru's back as he walks away from the camera to go off into the woods; the woman rushes after him (LS).*   *(4)*

177   *MS from the reverse angle. She throws herself at his feet.*

WOMAN: Wait. Stop. One of you must die. Either you or my
    husband.   *(13)*

178   *CU of her husband. Bound up, he stares without expression.*   *(3)*

179   *CU of Tajomaru staring at the samurai; then he looks down at the woman.*
    (3)

180   *CU of the woman kneeling, seen from over Tajomaru's shoulder.*

WOMAN: Either you or he must die. To be doubly disgraced,
    disgraced before two men, is more than I can bear.   *(7)*

181   *CU of Tajomaru looking down at her.*   *(2)*

182 (= 180)   *CU. The woman continues to speak intensely.*

WOMAN: I want . . . I will belong to whoever kills the other.   *(10)*

183   *ECU of the woman; her honor at stake, she looks up expectantly at the
bandit.*   *(5)*

184   *ECU of Tajomaru. A fierce resolution comes over his face.*   *(5)*

185   *CU of the woman on the ground. Tajomaru walks away to the samurai in
the background (LS). The woman remains in the foreground with lowered eyes.
Tajomaru takes out his sword.*   *(11)*

186   *MS. Tajomaru cuts the ropes binding the samurai, and holds out the
unsheathed sword he has robbed from him. The samurai whips the sword from its
scabbard and slashes at Tajomaru. The samurai then springs to his feet and they
begin to fight (pan). They move away from the camera into the background.*   *(18)*

187   *MS. The two duel, slashing and parrying. Martial music.*   *(9)*

188   *CU. Tajomaru turns, thrusts at the samurai.*   *(1)*

189   *CU of Tajomaru's sword as the samurai dodges; Tajomaru pulls back and
they cross swords again.*   *(2)*

190   *MS. The two of them fighting, Tajomaru in the foreground; the bandit heads
away from the camera and scrambles up a slight incline.*   *(8)*

191   *MS. He slips and falls, but remains there in a sitting position, glaring
defiantly at his opponent.*   *(7)*

192   *MS from reverse angle. The bandit's back in the foreground, the samurai
visible below. Tajomaru scratches idly, then charges down the incline past the other
man. Now in the background, the bandit turns and starts to walk insouciantly
away, then whirls on his opponent.*   *(13)*

193 *Tajomaru lunges forward, the samurai backs out of the frame, Tajomaru follows. The samurai charges back into the frame, followed again by the bandit. They fight toward the background; the samurai stumbles.*   *(7)*

194 *CU. The samurai, stumbling, falls to a sitting position.*   *(1)*

195 *MS. Tajomaru, in the background, circles menacingly around the samurai in the foreground.*   *(11)*

196 (=194) *CU of the samurai on guard, ready to ward off Tajomaru's attack.*
(3)

197 *CU of the bandit jabbing at the fallen samurai.*   *(2)*

198 (=194) *CU of the samurai warding off the thrust.*   *(2)*

199 (=197) *CU of the bandit circling (pan), brandishing his sword, sometimes feinting a lunge.*   *(8)*

200 (=194) *The samurai, still in a sitting position, turns with Tajomaru.*   *(1)*

201 (=197) *CU of the bandit circling (pan) in the other direction.*   *(1)*

202 (=194) *CU of the samurai, still sitting, sword in a defensive position.*   *(4)*

203 (=197) *CU of the bandit (pan) taunting, feinting—finally he lunges.*   *(10)*

204 *ECU. The samurai, who has kept in his free hand the rope that had bound him, now whips the rope at Tajomaru.*   *(1/2)*

205 (=197) *CU. The bandit wards off the rope.*   *(1/2)*

206 *MS. The samurai is on his feet again, and the two cross swords, circling around so that the samurai's back is to the camera.*   *(4)*

207 *MS from reverse angle. The two men fight, running, struggling; they begin to duel around a tree, Tajomaru pursuing.*   *(5)*

208 *Camera dollies in to ECU of the two men fighting around the tree.*   *(7)*

209 *LS through the bushes of a thicket. The samurai is forced back into the thicket, his back to the camera; then he stumbles and falls on his back. Tajomaru moves in on him. The samurai's sword has become entangled in the undergrowth. Dolly in to MS of Tajomaru, who laughs, raises his sword to throw it, and spears the samurai with a mighty heave. Tajomaru stands looking down.*   *(27)*

210 *MS. In the prison courtyard, Tajomaru continues.*

TAJOMARU: I wanted to kill him honestly, since I had to kill him. And he fought really well. We crossed swords over twenty-three times. Think of that! No one had ever crossed over twenty with me before. Then I killed him. *(He laughs.)*

The camera has dollied back to reveal the police agent, as well as the priest and the woodcutter in the background.

TAJOMARU *(answering the unheard voice of the official questioner)*: What's that? The woman? Oh, she wasn't around anywhere. Probably got frightened and ran away. She must have been really upset. Anyway, when I came down the path again I found the horse grazing there. About that woman—it was her temper that interested me, but she turned out to be just like any other woman. I didn't even look for her. *(Pause.)* What? His sword? Oh, I sold that in town on the same day, then drank the money up. *(Pause.)* Her dagger? I remember, it looked valuable, had some kind of inlay in it. You know what I did? I forgot all about it. What a fool thing to do. Walked off and forgot it. That was the biggest mistake I ever made. *(Laughs uproariously, kicking his feet on the ground.)* (97)

211   CU *of the rain pouring off the eaves of the Rashomon; the sound of the great downpour. Tilt down to reveal the three men below.* (14)

212   MS *of the woodcutter, in the foreground, and the commoner, sitting by a fire; the commoner stretches and yawns.*

COMMONER: Oh, that Tajomaru, he's famous for that sort of thing. He's worse than all the other bandits in Kyoto. Why, last fall a young girl went off with her maid to worship at the Toribe Temple and they found them murdered there afterwards. He must have done it. *(He rises to fetch some wood.)* (31)

213   LS. *The priest in the foreground; the commoner, in the background, continues talking as he crosses behind the priest.*

COMMONER: They say the woman ran away and left her horse behind. I just bet he killed her.

He pulls some loose planks from the side of the gate. The priest rises to walk back to the commoner.

PRIEST: But the woman turned up in prison too, you know.

The commoner turns to listen. (19)

214   MS *from reverse angle, commoner in the foreground. The priest approaches the commoner.*

PRIEST: It seems she went to seek refuge at some temple and the police found her there.

The voice of the woodcutter cuts across this.

WOODCUTTER *(off)*: It's a lie! (8)

215   *CU of the woodcutter, the priest and commoner visible in the background.*

WOODCUTTER: It's a lie. They're all lies! Tajomaru's confession, the
woman's story—they're lies!

COMMONER: Well, men are only men. That's why they lie. *(He pulls a
board loose and turns to speak again.)* They can't tell the truth, not
even to themselves.

PRIEST: That may be true. But it's because men are so weak. That's
why they lie. That's why they must deceive themselves.

COMMONER: Not another sermon! *(He starts to move forward.)*   *(34)*

216   *MS of the commoner, leaning forward as he puts the wood on the fire.*

COMMONER: I don't mind a lie. Not if it's interesting. What kind of
story did she tell? *(He looks up.)*   *(11)*

217   *MS of the priest.*

PRIEST: Hers was a completely different story from the bandit's. *(He
comes up and kneels between the others, the camera panning with him.)*
Everything was different.   *(10)*

218   *CU of the priest.*

PRIEST: Tajomaru talked about her temper, her strength. I saw
nothing like that at all. I found her very pitiful. I felt great
compassion for her.   *(20)*

219   *LS of the woman in the prison courtyard, the woodcutter and priest in the
background. The main thematic music begins softly and continues, almost
uninterrupted, throughout the woman's version of the story. At times gentle, at other
times frenzied, it is the only musical theme through shot 254. The woman is bent
over weeping; she raises her head.*   *(13)*

220   *MS of the woman.*

WOMAN: And then, after having taken advantage of me, he told
me—oh, so proudly—that he was the famous bandit Tajomaru.
And then he sneered at my husband.   *(38)*

221   *CU as she continues, now more possessed.*

WOMAN: Oh, how terrible it must have been for him. But the more
he struggled, the tighter the ropes became. I couldn't stand it.
Not even realizing what I was doing, I ran toward him, or tried
to.   *(42)*

222   *LS. The woods. With her back to the camera, the woman runs toward her
husband; the bandit pushes past her, knocking her down, and goes up to the
husband bound by the tree. He takes the husband's sword and starts to leave.*   *(10)*

223   *MS of Tajomaru as he turns to sneer at the husband. The woman's sobs are
heard and Tajomaru begins to laugh and point at the husband, then turns away. (7)*

224 *LS as Tajomaru stops to laugh again, jumping up and down; then he runs off, disappearing into the woods.* *(11)*

225 *LS. The woman lies weeping on the ground by her husband.* *(7)*

226 *LS. The same, from nearer.* *(5)*

227 *MS. The same, nearer still.* *(7)*

228 *CU of the woman, sobbing; finally she raises her head to look brokenheartedly at her husband.* *(19)*

229 *CU of her husband, in profile. He stares at the ground.* *(3)*

230 (= 228) *CU. She looks at him, then begins to rise.* *(7)*

231 *LS from behind the woman as she rushes toward her husband in the background and throws herself on him.* *(5)*

232 *CU from over his shoulder. She sobs on his breast, looks up, and is shocked by what she sees.* *(21)*

233 *CU of the husband from over her shoulder. He looks at her coldly, cynically.* *(3)*

234 *MS. In the prison courtyard, the woman continues, the woodcutter and priest visible in the background.*

WOMAN: Even now I remember his eyes. . . . What I saw in them was not sorrow, not even anger. It was . . . a cold hatred of me. *(36)*

235 *MS in the woods, the woman seen over her husband's shoulder. She pulls herself away from him, staring at him. As she speaks, she moves from side to side before him, the camera moving with her.*

WOMAN: Don't look at me like that. Don't! Beat me, kill me if you must, but don't look at me like that. Please don't! *(43)*

236 *CU. She covers her face with her hands and starts to sink back to the ground.* *(16)*

237 *ECU of the top of her head as she lies shaking and sobbing.* *(32)*

238 *CU. Suddenly she looks up, glances around, starts to rise.* *(4)*

239 *LS. The pair in the background; in the foreground is the dagger, still sticking point first in the ground. She rises to her feet, comes forward and retrieves it, and rushes back to her husband, starting to cut his bonds.* *(13)*

240 *CU. The dagger cutting through the rope.* *(1)*

241 *MS over the husband's shoulder; she extends the dagger to him.*

WOMAN: Then kill me if you will. Kill me with one stroke— quickly!

The camera dollies toward her face, then pans around to show the husband still staring at her as before. (29)

242 *CU. She looks up imploringly, rises, and starts to back away.* (9)

243 *MS. The camera dollies with her as she backs away.*

WOMAN: Oh, don't! Please don't!

She raises her hands to her face, still clutching the dagger. (9)

244 *CU of the husband's hard, unmoved face.*

WOMAN: *(off)*: Don't —don't look at me like that! (1)

245 *CU. She comes forward again, dagger extended.*

WOMAN: Don't. (7)

246 (= 244) *CU of the husband staring; her sobs are heard.* (1)

247 (=245) *CU of the woman, backing off again, crying.* (3)

248 (=244) *CU of the husband, as before.* (1)

249 (=245) *CU. She continues to move, the camera seeming to weave with her painful approach and retreat before her husband. She holds the dagger almost absent-mindedly; her desperation grows.* (7)

250 (=244) *CU of the husband, staring implacably.* (1)

251   *CU of the woman as she moves steadily forward now; her world forever destroyed, she holds the dagger high, without seeming to be aware of it. The camera tracks with her in the direction of her husband until she suddenly lunges off screen.*

(21)

252 (=234)   *MS of the woman in the prison courtyard, continuing her testimony.*

WOMAN: And then I fainted. When I opened my eyes and looked around, I saw there, in my husband's chest, the dagger. *(She begins to weep again.)* I didn't know what to do. I ran through the forest—I must have, although I don't remember. Then I found myself standing by a pond. . . .   *(105)*

253   *Shot of a lake, illuminated by a low sun, a strong breeze moving over the surface.*

WOMAN *(continuing, off):* . . . at the foot of a hill.   *(5)*

254 (=234)   *MS of the woman in the prison courtyard.*

WOMAN: I threw myself into it. I tried to kill myself. But, I failed. *(She sobs.)* What should a poor helpless woman like me do? *(She sinks to the ground.)*   *(50)*

255   *CU of the steps of the Rashomon with the rain pouring down. The dreary, loud sound of the rain. Visible above the steps are the three men, seated. The camera*

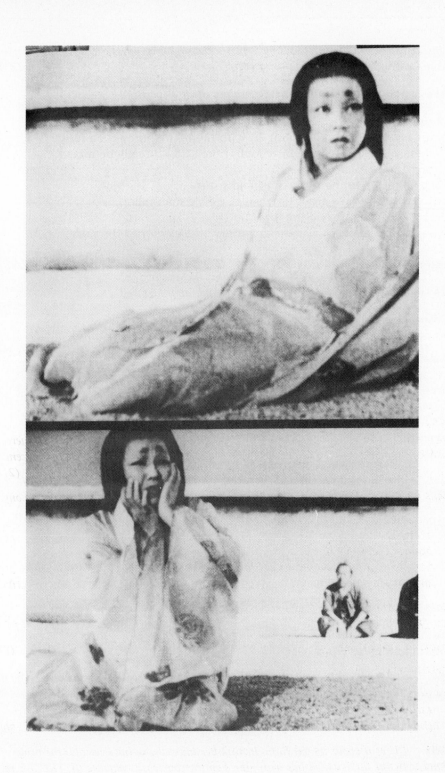

tilts up as the commoner stands; he comes forward, looks out at the sky, spits disgustedly, and turns back to the group.   *(23)*

256   *MS. He rejoins the other two around the fire (pan).*

COMMONER: I see. But the more I listen the more mixed up I get. *(He sits down.)* Women lead you on with their tears; they even fool themselves. Now if I believed what she said I'd really be mixed up.
PRIEST: But according to the husband's story . . .
COMMONER: But he's dead. How could a dead man talk?
PRIEST: He spoke throught a medium.
WOODCUTTER: Lies. *(He rises and comes toward the camera.)* His story was all lies.
PRIEST: Dead men tell no lies.   *(46)*

257   *CU of the commoner, in the foreground, and the priest.*

COMMONER: All right, priest—why is that?
PRIEST: They must not. I must not believe that men are so sinful.   *(7)*

258   *CU of the two from reverse angle.*

COMMONER: Oh, I don't object to that. After all, who's honest nowadays? Look, everyone wants to forget unpleasant things, so they make up stories. It's easier that way. *(Grinning, he bites into a piece of fruit. The priest looks distraught.)* But never mind. Let's hear this dead man's story.   *(31)*

259   *The ceiling and beams of the great gate illuminated by a tremendous flash of lightning.*   *(1)*

260   *LS from above the three men as they look up. A roll of thunder is heard.*   *(3)*

261   *MS of a fallen statue outside the gate. The rain falls even harder, flooding in rapid cascades past the statue.*   *(3)*

262   *CU of the statue.*   *(2)*

263   *CU of a hand bell being violently shaken in the air. The scene has abruptly shifted back to the prison courtyard.*   *(1)*

264   *MS of the medium, a woman, her hair and robes blowing in the wind. She is rattling the bell, dancing madly. The bell clatters, the wind howls, and a weird, unearthly voice drones on like a record player slowing down. A drum beats slowly. The wind, voice, and drum continue through shot 273.*   *(3)*

265   *LS from above the medium. Behind her kneel the woodcutter and the priest. She circles the altar which has been placed in the courtyard, shaking the bell.*   *(6)*

266 (=263)   *CU of the bell being shaken.*

267   *MS of the medium writhing about on her feet. She begins to turn dizzily in circles. Suddenly she stops completely still.*   *(11)*

268   *CU of the medium, now possessed by the other world.*   *(3)*

269   *CU of the bell dropping from her hand.*   *(1)*

270 (=268)   *CU. She turns abruptly to face the camera.*   *(1)*

271   *LS. She rushes toward the foregound and stands, mouth open, her eyes wild, as the camera dollies in. Her mouth begins to move and suddenly the voice of the dead man is heard.*

SAMURAI-MEDIUM *(as though at a great distance)*: I am in darkness now.
   I am suffering in the darkness. Cursed be those who cast me into
   this hell of darkness. *(The medium starts to fall.)*   *(27)*

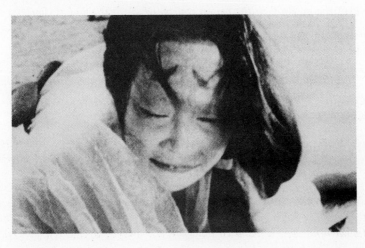

272 *MS of the medium falling behind the altar to the ground. She moves convulsively on the ground, the camera panning with her.* *(15)*

273 *MS. She sits upright as the camera dollies in to an ECU. Her mouth opens and over the sound of the wind the voice of the samurai is heard.*

SAMURAI-MEDIUM: The bandit, after attacking my wife, sat down beside her and tried to console her. *(The sound of the unearthly voice and drum stops abruptly.)* *(27)*

274 *LS. The woods. In the clearing where the rape took place, the bandit is sitting beside the woman, talking to her, touching her arm to get her attention. The samurai's story is accompanied by a somber musical theme which plays over most of the scenes through shot 305.*

SAMURAI-MEDIUM *(off)*: She sat there on the leaves, looking down, looking at nothing. The bandit was cunning.

Camera dollies back to reveal the husband bound in the foreground.

SAMURAI-MEDIUM *(off)*: He told her that after she had given herself, she would no longer be able to live with her husband—why didn't she go with him, the bandit, rather than remain behind to be unhappy with her husband? He said he had only attacked her because of his great love for her.

The husband turns his head toward them. *(28)*

275 *CU of the wife as she looks up as though she believes what Tajomaru is saying, her eyes dreamy.*

SAMURAI-MEDIUM *(off)*: My wife looked at him, her face soft, her eyes veiled. *(8)*

276 *CU of the medium in the prison courtyard, as at the end of shot 273.*

SAMURAI-MEDIUM: Never, in all of our life together, had I seen her more beautiful. *(6)*

277 *CU of the husband in the woods; he stares at the others, then closes his eyes.*

SAMURAI-MEDIUM *(off)*: And what did my beautiful wife reply to the bandit in front of her helpless husband? *(17)*

278 *MS. The woman looks up at Tajomaru, imploringly.*

WOMAN: Take me. Take me away with you. *(11)*

279 *CU of the medium in the prison courtyard; she rises, the wind whipping her hair. The unearthly voice fades in and out.*

SAMURAI-MEDIUM: That is what she said. *(The medium turns away, then abruptly faces the camera again.)* But that is not all she did, or else I would not now be in darkness. *(15)*

280 *MS, in the woods, from behind the husband's back. Tajomaru picks up the husband's sword and moves off screen. He returns, leading the woman off into the woods.* *(10)*

281 *CU of Tajomaru as he is jerked to a stop by the woman.* *(2)*

282 *MS of the woman holding Tajomaru by the hand. She points toward her husband.*

WOMAN: Kill him. As long as he is alive I cannot go with you. *(She moves behind Tajomaru, clutching him.)* Kill him! *(12)*

283 *MS of the medium in the prison courtyard, the wind howling about her.*

SAMURAI-MEDIUM: I still hear those words. *(The medium writhes in circles on her knees.)* They are like a wind blowing me to the bottom of this dark pit. Has anyone ever uttered more pitiless words? Even the bandit was shocked to hear them. *(25)*

284 *ECU of the woman in the woods, clinging to the bandit's shoulder, digging her nails into him.*

WOMAN: Kill him! *(7)*

285 *LS from behind the husband's back; the woman takes a step toward the husband, pointing at him.*

WOMAN: Kill him—kill him! *(10)*

286 *CU of Tajomaru, yanking the woman back to him. The look in his eyes makes her back off.* *(8)*

287 (=285) *LS. The bandit throws the woman from him.* *(2)*

288 *MS of the woman as she falls to the ground; the bandit places his foot on her back.* *(3)*

289 *CU of the medium in the prison courtyard. She throws her head back and then forward and the dead man's laughter pours from her unmoving lips.* *(5)*

290 (=285) *LS. Tajomaru, still standing over the woman, addresses the husband.*

TAJOMARU: What do you want me to do with this woman? Kill her? Spare her? Just nod if you agree.

The camera dollies around to show the husband in profile.

SAMURAI-MEDIUM *(off)*: For these words I almost forgave the bandit. *(27)*

291   *LS of the husband in the background; in the foreground (MS) Tajomaru
continues pressing the woman to the ground with his foot.*

TAJOMARU: What do you want me to do? Kill her? Let her go?

*Now Tajomaru walks toward the husband. As soon as he has gone a few steps, the
woman springs up and runs away. Tajomaru turns to chase her, the camera
panning to show them disappear among the trees. Her screams die away in the
stillness of the woods.*   *(18)*

292   *LS of the husband; still bound, he makes no effort to free himself.*   *(9)*

293   *MS of the husband.*   *(6)*

294   *CU of the husband.*   *(4)*

295   *Dead leaves on the ground in the late afternoon sun.*

SAMURAI-MEDIUM *(off)*: Hours later—I don't known how many.   *(5)*

296   *MS of the husband's back. Tajomaru appears in the background, on the far
side of the clearing, stomping along, slashing in disgust with some rope at the
bushes. He walks up to the husband and stands looking down.*   *(27)*

297   *MS from reverse angle. Tajomaru takes his sword and cuts the captive's
bonds.*

TAJOMARU: Well, she got away. Now I'll have to worry about her
   talking. *(He turns and goes.)*

The husband looks off after him, then up at the sky.   *(45)*

298   *Trees against the sky.*

SAMURAI-MEDIUM *(off)*: It was quiet.   *(4)*

299   *Dead leaves on the ground.*

SAMURAI-MEDIUM *(off)*: Then I heard someone crying. . . .

*The camera tilts up along the leaves to reveal the husband (MS). The bell-like tinkle
of wind chimes is heard.*   *(11)*

300   *CU of the husband crying. The camera dollies back and he rises to his feet.
He moves painfully (pan), rests his head against a tree. There is the soft sound of
grief, but it comes from the husband himself.*   *(39)*

301   *CU as he rests his head against the tree, sobbing. Finally he raises his head
and begins to wander off, but stops when he notices something on the ground.*   *(28)*

302   *MS from behind the husband, the dagger sticking up before him. Slowly he
goes to it, picks it up, and turns to walk back toward the camera, staring at the
dagger.*   *(32)*

303   *LS as he moves into the clearing; he stops, raises the dagger high above his head and brutally thrusts it into his chest. He begins to fall.*   *(16)*

304   *MS. His falling motion is completed by the medium in the prison courtyard (priest and woodcutter sit in the background). The medium sinks down as though dead, then slowly sits up.*   *(21)*

305   *CU of the medium.*

SAMURAI-MEDIUM: Everything was quiet—how quiet it was. It grew dark and a mist seemed to envelop me. I lay quietly in this stillness. Then someone seemed to approach me. Softly, gently. Who could it have been? Then someone's hand grasped the dagger and drew it out. *(The medium falls forward.)*

Music up and out.   *(59)*

306   *LS. In the shelter of the Rashomon, the priest and commoner are seated at the fire; the woodcutter is pacing up and down, the camera panning with him.*   *(18)*

307   *MS as the woodcutter stops in the background and turns to the others.*

WOODCUTTER: That's not true. There wasn't any dagger there—he was killed by a sword.

The commoner looks up from tending the fire. The woodcutter, very agitated, moves farther into the background and sits down; the commoner rises and goes back to sit beside him.   *(40)*

308   *MS from reverse angle. The commoner sits next to the woodcutter; the priest is in the background.*

COMMONER: Now it's getting interesting. You must have seen the whole thing. Why didn't you tell the police?
WOODCUTTER: I didn't want to get involved.
COMMONER: But now you want to talk about it? Well, come on and tell us then. Yours seems the most interesting of all these stories.   *(32)*

309   *MS from reverse angle, the priest in the foreground.*

PRIEST: I don't want to hear. I don't want to have to listen to any more horrible stories.

The commoner stands and comes forward to the priest.

COMMONER *(to the priest)*: Stories like this are ordinary enough now. I heard that demons used to live in the castle here by the gate, but they all ran away, because what men do now horrified them so. *(He goes back to the woodcutter.)*   *(17)*

310   *CU of the woodcutter and commoner.*

COMMONER: How much do you know about this story?

WOODCUTTER: I found a woman's hat. . . .

COMMONER: You already said that.

WOODCUTTER: Then, when I'd walked about twenty yards farther, I heard a woman crying. I looked out from behind a bush and saw a man tied up. There was a woman crying. And there was Tajomaru.

COMMONER: Wait a minute. Then it was a lie when you said that you found the body?

WOODCUTTER: I didn't want to get involved.

COMMONER: All right, then. Go on. What was Tajomaru doing?

WOODCUTTER: He was down on his knees in front of the woman and seemed to be begging her to forgive him. *(57)*

311   *MS. The woods. Tajomaru crouches by the woman, the samurai behind them. She is sobbing. From the beginning to the end of the woodcutter's story, there is a noticeable absence of music. The only sounds heard, aside from those made by the three people, are occasional noises natural to the woods.*

TAJOMARU: Until now, whenever I wanted to do anything bad, I always did it. It was for me and so it was good. But today is different. I've already taken you, but now I want you more and more—and I suffer. Go away with me. If you want, I'll marry you. Look. *(He bows his head low.)* I am Tajomaru, the famous bandit, known all over Miyako, and yet here I am on my knees in front of you. *(38)*

312   *MS from the side. Tajomaru puts his hand on her, trying to soothe her.*

TAJOMARU: If you want, I'll even stop being a bandit. I've got enough money hidden away. You can live comfortably. And if you don't want me to steal, then I'll work hard—I'll even sell things in the street. I'll make you happy. I'll do anything to please you if you'll only come away with me, marry me. *(She only sobs the harder.)* *(27)*

313   *CU from same angle as shot 311. Now the bandit tries to cajole her.*

TAJOMARU: Please say yes. If you don't, I'll have to kill you. *(13)*

314   *ECU of Tajomaru; he is becoming desperate.*

TAJOMARU: Don't cry. Answer. Tell me you'll be my wife. *(Unable to endure her silence, he suddenly pushes her.)* *(9)*

315   *ECU from over Tajomaru's shoulder. He bends over solicitously again.*

TAJOMARU: Tell me. *(8)*

316   *CU from reverse angle. She sits up, almost in possession of herself.*

WOMAN: But, how could I answer? How could I, a woman, answer a question like that? *(She rises on her knees, the camera panning as she crawls over to the dagger and yanks it out of the ground.)* *(19)*

317 *MS of the samurai, trussed up, in the foreground. Tajomaru leaps aside and trips to the ground as the woman spins around with the dagger in her hand. But she is going to her husband with it. She cuts his bonds, then backs away sobbing, stumbling, and falls to the ground between the two men.*

318 *MS of Tajomaru, crouching on the ready.*

TAJOMARU: I understand. You mean that we men must decide. *(He reaches for his sword.)* *(7)*

319 *LS from behind Tajomaru. The samurai is struggling to free himself of the bonds now that the rope has been cut.* *(2)*

320 *MS of the samurai as he jumps to his feet and nervously backs away.*

SAMURAI *(holding up his hand in front of him)*: Stop! I refuse to risk my life for such a woman. *(8)*

321 *CU. Tajomaru looks at him hesitantly.* *(12)*

322 *CU. The woman sits up and looks in disbelief at her husband.* *(9)*

323 *MS. The samurai, now haughty and self-possessed, walks up to his wife.*

SAMURAI: You shameless whore! Why don't you kill yourself? *(19)*

324 *MS from farther away, so that Tajomaru is visible in the foreground.*

SAMURAI *(to Tajomaru)*: If you want her, I'll give her to you. I regret the loss of my horse much more than I will regret the loss of this woman. *(He turns away.)* *(11)*

325 *CU of the woman; shocked, she turns from her husband to look at the bandit.* *(3)*

326 *MS. She stares up at Tajomaru, who looks from her to the samurai.* *(7)*

327 *MS, the samurai in the foreground, Tajomaru staring at him. The samurai looks from one to the other.* *(17)*

328 *ECU. Tajomaru looks at the woman distrustfully.* *(4)*

329 *CU. She, sweating visibly, looks at Tajomaru.* *(8)*

330 (=328) *CU. Tajomaru looks at her with distaste, wipes the sweat from his face.* *(8)*

331 *MS. She watches him cross behind her as if to go, then gets up and runs after him (pan), both of them passing the husband, who stands immobile.*

WOMAN: Wait!

Tajomaru turns and calls back.

TAJOMARU: And don't try to follow me.   *(13)*

332   *MS. Through Tajomaru's legs the woman is seen falling to the ground, her husband standing behind her. Then the husband steps forward.*   *(11)*

333   *MS of the husband.*

SAMURAI: Don't waste your time in crying. No matter how hard you cry no one is going to be taken in by it.   *(5)*

334   *MS of Tajomaru as he steps forward to contradict.*

TAJOMARU: Don't talk like that to her. It's unmanly of you. After all, women cannot help crying. They are naturally weak.   *(11)*

335   *CU of the woman on the ground. Her weeping has been heard behind Tajomaru's words; now the sobs change and she laughs. She rises, screeching with hysterical laughter.*

WOMAN: It's not me, not me—it's you two who are weak. *(Pan as she goes to her husband.)* If you are my husband then why don't you kill this man? Then you can tell me to kill myself. That is what a real man would do. But you aren't a real man. That is why I was crying. I'm tired, tired of this farce. *(Pan as she crosses to the bandit.)* I thought that Tajomaru might find some way out. I thought that if he would only save me I would do anything for him.   *(70)*

336   *CU of the woman and Tajomaru. She spits in his face, then backs off, laughing (pan).*

WOMAN: But he's not a man either. He's just like my husband!   *(11)*

337   *MS of Tajomaru, looking shamefaced.*

WOMAN *(off):* Just remember. . . .   *(5)*

338 (= 335)   *CU of the woman.*

WOMAN: . . . that a woman loves only a real man. *(She moves nearer the bandit—pan.)* And when she loves, she loves madly, forgetting everything else. But a woman can be won only by strength—by the strength *(she is now at Tajomaru's side)* of the swords you are wearing.   *(11)*

339   *MS of the husband. He looks at her abjectly, then reaches for his sword.*   *(5)*

340   *CU of the husband as he moves toward Tajomaru, now ready for a fight.*   *(1)*

341   *MS of all three; the woman and bandit, his sword already drawn, are in the foreground. From too far away, the samurai hurriedly swings his sword at Tajomaru, then backs quickly off. The woman smiles scornfully.*   *(3)*

342   *MS. The woman looks from one to the other, laughing and pointing gleefully.*   *(13)*

343   LS. The two men, from high above, through the branches of the trees. They stand facing each other from a safe distance, the woman between them.   *(7)*

344   CU of the woman. She seems to realize what is happening and a frightened look comes over her face. The sound of the combatants' nervous panting is heard now, and runs throughout the fight scene. It is a tense, gasping sound, unrelieved by music or any sound other than the occasional clash of swords.   *(10)*

345   MS of the bandit, circling, feinting, a concerned expression on his face.   *(9)*

346   MS of the samurai, advancing uncertainly.   *(13)*

347 (= 345)   MS of the bandit advancing.   *(3)*

348 (= 346)   MS of the samurai advancing.   *(2)*

349   CU of the woman, watching fearfully. The camera dollies back until the two raised swords are visible in the frame. Suddenly the tips of the swords touch.   *(16)*

350   LS. The men recoil from the touching of the swords, stumbling backward away from each other. The samurai trips to the ground. Tajomaru runs after the samurai, but falls down himself. Both men swing wildly and blindly as they get to their feet and run in opposite directions from each other.   *(7)*

351   LS. Tajomaru in the foreground. The men are separated now by a great distance.   *(5)*

352   CU of the woman as she peeks out from behind the stump of a tree.   *(14)*

353   MS of the samurai, who has fallen against the side of a slope. Finally he stands up and advances.   *(17)*

354   MS. Back-tracking shot of Tajomaru, advancing fearfully. His arm shaking violently, he seems almost unable to bear the weight of the sword. His breath comes in short gasps.   *(14)*

355 (= 353)   MS of the samurai advancing, terror written on his face.   *(2)*

356 (= 354)   MS of Tajomaru advancing.   *(2)*

357   CU of the woman, terrified; the camera dollies back as the men enter from either side of the frame. Each thrusts, frightening the other, but this time the samurai turns to run first, and Tajomaru pursues him over the slope (pan).   *(17)*

358   MS. They both slip and fall on the slope. Tajomaru thrusts at the samurai but misses, and his sword sticks in the ground. He can't extract it. Now the samurai swings, but the bandit rolls out of the way.   *(5)*

359   LS. Tajomaru continues to roll away (pan) to another part of the slope, which he tries to crawl up but fails to get a handhold.   *(6)*

360   CU as Tajomaru dodges another thrust.   *(1)*

361   MS. The samurai scampers after him but keeps stumbling and missing with his flailing swings.   *(10)*

362 MS. *The bandit gets back to his sword but still can't pull it out. The samurai keeps lunging and missing; Tajomaru keeps dodging.* (27)

363 LS. *The bandit runs and makes another attempt to mount the rise but falls (pan). Now he runs away from the slope (pan) and falls by a tree stump. The samurai aims another stroke wildly as Tajomaru falls behind the stump.* (16)

364 MS. *The samurai's sword lodges itself in the stump; Tajomaru seizes the opportunity by leaping up at his assailant and pushing him down.* (1)

365 MS. *Tajomaru tries to run past the fallen man but the samurai grabs him by the ankle and pulls him down. Dragging the samurai after him, Tajomaru begins to inch toward his own sword.* (9)

366 MS from reverse angle. *Slowly and with great effort, the bandit inches toward his sword, the samurai holding onto his foot. Then Tajomaru kicks him away and at last frees the sword from the ground.* (20)

367 MS. *The samurai, still on the ground, backs off in alarm.* (6)

368 MS. *Tajomaru, out of breath, rises shakily.* (9)

369 LS. *Pan as Tajomaru advances on the samurai, who pushes himself along on his hands farther and farther into a thicket. Dolly in on the trapped man, who screams.*

SAMURAI: I don't want to die! I don't want to die!

Pan to Tajomaru raising his sword and hurling it, out of frame, into the man lying in front of him. Then he whirls around triumphantly. (73)

370 LS. *Tajomaru in the foreground, the woman cowering in the background. He backs away from the body and stumbles to the ground in front of the woman.* (20)

371 MS of Tajomaru and the woman. *They stare over at the body. Tajomaru, an idiotic expression on his face, rises and takes her hands, but she pulls them away and begins to back off frantically (pan), ending near the tree stump in which her husband's sword is still lodged. She utters little inarticulate cries. Tajomaru has followed stupidly, and now, half-crazed, he pulls the dead man's sword free and swings it mightily at her as she flees.* (38)

372 LS. *She rushes off into the woods; he follows but trips. She disappears as he lies collapsed on the ground.* (22)

373 MS of Tajomaru's back. *He sits up slowly, breathing hard, dirty, sweaty, exhausted. Silence—then the sound of distant cicada.* (9)

374 LS as he sits stupefied. *After a long time, he gets to his feet and goes off, to where the body lies, reappearing a moment later with his own bloody sword as well as the samurai's.* (43)

375 MS. *Dragging the swords along, Tajomaru backs off and limps away into the woods.* (21)

376   *LS. The Rashomon. The three men sitting, framed overhead by a huge horizontal beam. The sound of the great downpour. The commoner laughs.*   *(5)*

377   *MS. The priest is in the foreground. The commoner stands.*

COMMONER: And I suppose that is supposed to be true.

WOODCUTTER *(getting to his feet)*: I don't tell lies. I saw it with my own eyes.

COMMONER: That I doubt.

WOODCUTTER: I don't tell lies.

COMMONER: Well, so far as that goes, no one tells lies after he has said that he's going to tell one.

PRIEST: But it's horrible. If men don't trust one another then the earth becomes a kind of hell.

COMMONER: You are right. The world we live in is a hell.

PRIEST: No. I trust men. *(He turns away from the commoner and rises.)*   *(23)*

378   *CU of the priest, standing by a column.*

PRIEST: But I don't want to believe that this world is a hell.

The commoner appears behind him, laughing.

COMMONER: No one will hear you, no matter how loud you shout. Just think now. Which one of these stories do you believe?

Before the priest can answer, the woodcutter begins to speak. As he does the camera pans past the column to a MS of him.

WOODCUTTER: I don't understand any of them. They don't make any sense.

The commoner steps forward from behind the column and goes up to the woodcutter.

COMMONER: Well, don't worry about it. It isn't as though men were reasonable. *(He turns to walk off.)*   *(23)*

379   *LS. The commoner walks to the fire he has built, squats, and throws several of the burning pieces of lumber out into the rain. Just then the cry of a baby is heard. All look around. The commoner stands up.*   *(23)*

380   *MS. The three men try to locate the source of the crying. Then the commoner runs to the back and heads behind a partition of the gate. The priest and the woodcutter look at each other, then run over to the broken panels of the partition (pan) and peer through to where the commoner has disappeared.*   *(19)*

381   *MS from the other side of the partition. The heads of the two men appear through openings in the panels; in the distance, the commoner is kneeling over the baby, stripping off its few clothes.*   *(4)*

382   *MS of the commoner as he finishes removing the clothes and examines them.*
(8)

383   *MS of the priest and woodcutter watching; they dash around the partition (pan), the priest picking up the infant and the woodcutter going up to the commoner and pushing him.*

WOODCUTTER: What are you doing?
COMMONER: What does it look like?   *(14)*

384   *CU of the priest holding the baby protectively.*   *(1)*

385   *MS of the three men, priest in the background, commoner partially hidden by some steps (shot from a low angle).*

WOODCUTTER: That's horrible.
COMMONER: What's so horrible about it? Somebody else would have
   taken those baby clothes if I hadn't. Why shouldn't it be me?
WOODCUTTER: You are evil.
COMMONER: Evil? Me? And if so, then what are the parents of that
   baby? *(Pan as he moves up close to the woodcutter.)* They had a good
   time making it—then they throw it away like this. That's real
   evil for you.
WOODCUTTER: No, you're wrong. Look! Look here at the amulet case
   it has on. It's something the parents left to guard over it. Think
   what they must have gone through to give this baby up.
COMMONER: Oh, well. If you're going to sympathize with other
   people. . . .
WOODCUTTER: Selfish. . . .
COMMONER: And what's wrong with that? That's the way we are,
   the way we live. Look, half of us envy the lives that dogs lead.
   You just can't live unless you're what you call "selfish."

The commoner turns and goes off. The woodcutter moves into CU.

WOODCUTTER: Brute! *(With gathering anger.)* All men are selfish and
   dishonest. They all have excuses. The bandit, the husband . . .
   you! *(His face distorted in anger, he leaps in the direction of the
   commoner.)*   *(77)*

386   *CU as the woodcutter grabs the commoner by the neck and shakes him; they struggle out into the rain, and continue to argue there.*

COMMONER: And you say you don't lie! That's just funny. Look, you
   may have fooled the police, but you don't fool me.   *(15)*

387   *CU from reverse angle, the woodcutter facing the camera now. The commoner's words have affected the woodcutter. Guiltily he lets go his hold on the commoner.*
(7)

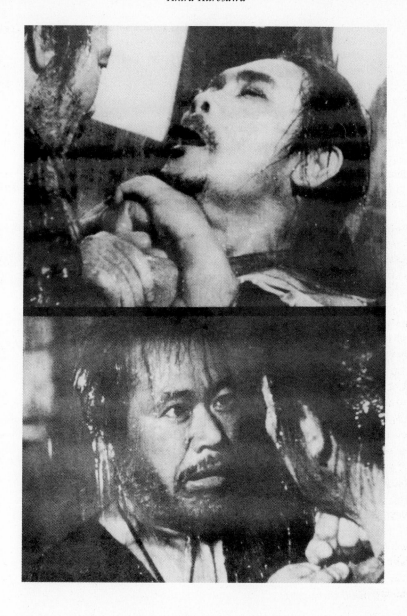

388 *CU from reverse angle. The commoner smiles, then shoves the woodcutter; he comes forward and shoves him again, this time out of frame. Smiling, the commoner follows him out.* *(9)*

389 *MS of the two men back under the roof, out of the rain. As the commoner speaks, he continues to shove the woodcutter back (pan), finally pushing him against the partition near the priest.*

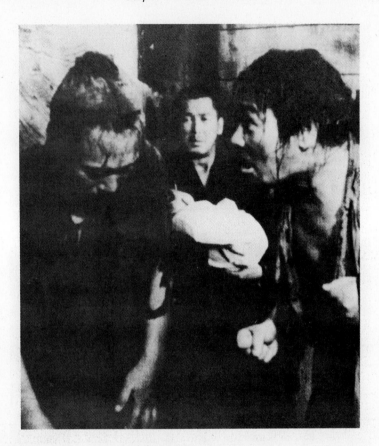

COMMONER: And so where is that dagger? That pearl-inlay handle that the bandit said was so valuable? Did the earth open up and swallow it? Or did someone steal it? Am I right? It would seem so. Now *there* is a really selfish action for you. *(He slaps the woodcutter and laughs harshly.)* (34)

390   *CU of the priest holding the baby.* (3)

391   *LS of all three men.*

COMMONER: Anything else you want to tell me? If not, I think I'll be going.

The baby starts to cry. The commoner glances at it; then, laughing, he turns to go.
(19)

392   *LS from outside the gate. The commoner comes out in the rain toward the camera and disappears off. The other two remain under the gate, seen in LS through the rain. (Dissolve.)* (19)

393   *MS. The two men, from closer; the sound of the rain diminishes. (Dissolve.)*

                                                                             (11)

394   *MS. The two men, closer yet; rain slowly stopping. (Dissolve.)*   *(9)*

395   *CU. The two men still standing as before; the sound of rain has stopped; the baby cries.*

                                                                                     (7)

396   *LS. The two men seen from outside the gate as in shot 392, but now the rain has stopped. Drops of water drip from the gate onto the steps. The priest steps forward.*

                                                                                   (11)

397   *MS. He walks past the woodcutter, patting the baby, and leaves the frame. The woodcutter stands for a moment, then follows.*   *(11)*

398   *MS. The woodcutter approaches the priest and moves to take the baby away from him; the priest violently resists.*

PRIEST: What are you trying to do? Take away what little it has left?   *(7)*

399   *MS. Priest in the foreground. The woodcutter, very humble now, shakes his head.*

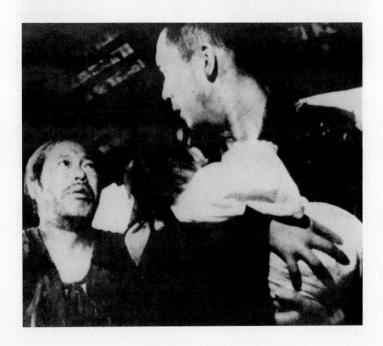

WOODCUTTER: I have six children of my own. One more wouldn't
make it any more difficult. *(29)*

400   *MS from reverse angle; woodcutter in the foreground.*

PRIEST: I'm sorry. I shouldn't have said that. *(10)*

401 (=399)   *MS. Priest in the foreground.*

WOODCUTTER: Oh, you can't afford not to be suspicious of people
these days. I'm the one who ought to be ashamed. *(23)*

402 (=400)   *MS. Woodcutter in the foreground.*

PRIEST: No, I'm grateful to you. Because, thanks to you, I think I
will be able to keep my faith in men. *(27)*

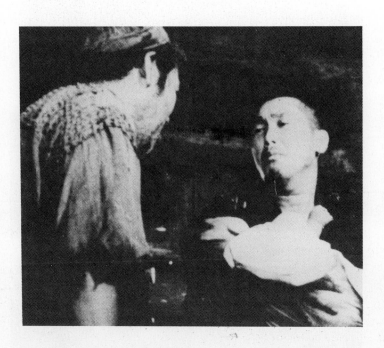

403 (=399)   *MS. Priest in the foreground. The woodcutter bows, and the baby,
who has been crying all during this dialogue, stops. The priest holds out the baby
and the woodcutter takes it. Finale music begins, a distinctly traditional Japanese
music.* *(7)*

404   *MS from farther back. The woodcutter accepts the baby and steps back. The men bow to each other and the woodcutter turns to go.*   *(27)*

405   *LS from behind the men as the woodcutter, holding the infant, leaves the gate; the sky is clear, the priest watches as he goes.*   *(11)*

406   *LS from reverse angle. The woodcutter moves toward the camera. He stops and bows again to the priest. Then he turns and continues on his way, the camera tracking backward with him. The whole gate and the sunny sky come into frame. The woodcutter walks past the camera; the tracking stops and the priest is seen, small, standing under the gate.*   *(49)*

407   *The great signboard of the gate. Music up and out.*   *(9)*

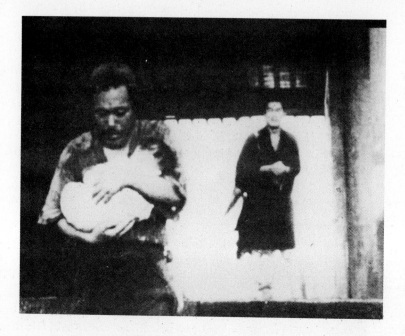

Questions for *Rashomon*

1.   What would you say is the theme of this film? Some critics fault Kurosawa for making it impossible to tell what events in the film actually took place. Why do you think he chose to emphasize this ambiguity?

2.   Describe, in as much detail as possible, the character of each individual in the film. What reason does each character have to lie?

3.   Consider the significance of some of the visual images through which Kurosawa tells his story. Why, for instance, does he cut to the dagger on p. 579 or the fallen statue on p. 588?

4.   Discuss the differences in the settings of the film. Why does he place the narrators of the story in the ruined temple? How does the intercutting between the woods and the police courtyard affect the story?

5.   What is the effect of having the prisoners in the police courtyard face the viewer when giving their testimony?

6.   How different would the film be if the character of the commoner had been omitted?

7.   Some Japanese critics, upon first seeing *Rashomon* in 1950, found the script too complicated. Do you agree with this objection? Why or why not?

READING/WRITING

You may want to write an analytic essay about one of the selections in this chapter, or compare some aspect of theater and film, or research a topic suggested by a selection, or experiment with writing your own dialogue or scene. Here are a few ideas to get you started:

1. *Othello, A Doll House,* and *Rashomon* all deal with aspects of marriage: descriptions of the various roles husbands and wives play, questions of infidelity, and the like. Analyze one of these themes as it appears in two of these works; compare how the theme is handled by the two authors.

2. Shakespeare took the idea for *Othello* from an Italian short story by Cinthio. Look up the story in your library (it is included, for example, in the Signet edition of *Othello*) and discuss how Shakespeare changed and adapted his source for his own purposes.

3. Ibsen's play is "open-ended": We hear the slamming of the door, but the fate of the characters is left unresolved at the end of Act III. How would you resolve the plot? Write your own Act IV, in which you dramatize your conclusions.

4. Choose one scene from *A Doll House* and describe as specifically as possible how you would stage it if you were the director. Consider matters of costume (for this you may want to consult the Alison Lurie essay in Chapter 7), scenery, and lighting, and explain how you would direct the actors' speech and movements around the stage. What changes would you make if you were to set the play in the 1980s?

5. Actors often create detailed biographies of the characters they play, the better to help them bring these figures to life on the stage. Devise a detailed biography and character study of Nils Krogstad, Dr. Rank, or Kristine Linde, in which you both flesh out and analyze one of these characters in greater depth than Ibsen has done. If you were an actor playing one of these roles, what key features of the character would motivate your performance?

6. Write a persuasive essay in which you either defend or condemn Nora's decision to leave her family.

7. Pick two or three of the poems quoted in *Painting Churches*—for example, Yeats's "Song of the Wandering Aengus," Roethke's "Dolor" and "I Knew a Woman," Frost's "Fire and Ice," and Gray's "Elegy Written in a Country Churchyard" (look up the complete poems in Chapter 6 of this anthology)—and analyze their significance in the play. Alternatively, analyze the significance—or humor, or

poignancy—of the paintings the Churches "act out" when they're posing for Mags.

8. Analyze the workings of one of the relationships presented in *Painting Churches:* father/daughter, mother/daughter, or husband/wife. What seem to be the "rules" and ideas governing the way the two members of the relationship treat each other?

9. Choose one of the tales you have read in the short fiction chapter of this book, and explain—or demonstrate—how you would turn it into a play or a film. You might want to take a single scene from one of these stories and "translate" it into dialogue.

10. *Rashomon* is, among other things, about the subjectivity of truth and the relativity of viewpoint. In your journal, try an experiment with different points of view. Select an event—say, an argument you had with a friend, or a brief news item that has caught your interest—and write two versions of the same story, as told from the different perspectives of two people involved in the event. In the following sketch from his notebook, for example, one student elaborates on a news report of a mugging; notice how, in these two interior monologues, he tries to slip inside the skin of both mugger and victim:

Night time. I hate the night time. It figures I'd pick a job that requires a little night work. I hope I score soon—it's getting pretty cold. Damn weather. The moon's blacked out by the clouds. I hope I don't get mugged while I'm waiting.

Footsteps. Looks like a well-dressed couple. That guy's pretty big; probably snap my neck in two if I try anything. And I'm probably the only stiff around these days who doesn't carry a weapon—but who wants to face a rap for armed robbery?

Slow night—I should know better than to work on Sundays. If I didn't need the money so bad I'd be home right now watching Sunday Night at the Movies.

Footsteps again. This guy don't seem too tough. Looks kind of like a weasel. Very expensive clothes—I think this is the one. No one in sight; now if he just comes a little closer to the alleyway he's mine. I hope he doesn't notice the crack in my old Toys'R'Us gun.

Now: "Stop you Mother —— and don't move or I'll blow your butt away." Always scares the crap out of them. "Give me the money and the family jewels will survive the night."

O.K. He's going for his wallet. Jesus, he's got a gun, and I think his is the real thing.

"Hey, man, just be cool, this ain't a real gun. Don't shoot, man, I was just. . . ."

This city has become an asylum, only the sane are locked up and the insane are out on the streets. They're scum, preying on innocent people. Well, I know what to do now that you've told me. It was a good idea to get a gun, it's time they got what was coming to them. If the police won't do their job we'll have to do it for them.

You picked a good night to go hunting. This place has all sorts of cracks for the scum of this city to ooze out of. Please, just let me have one tonight. I'm glad you are with me.

I think I see him, hiding in that alley. Why don't I walk a little closer, just to make it easy for him. He thinks he's frightened me with his vulgarity. How could I be afraid with you here? His confidence grows; he thinks I'm just another poor sucker to be plucked and thrown away with the rest.

Now, now is the time. He'll pay for what he and the others have done to this society, the murderers, the rapists, and muggers. Look how he pleads for his life. How pathetic they are. Just a little longer; soon he will die; now.

Michael Kaminis

11. Compare the screenplay of *Rashomon* with Akutagawa's short story "In a Grove" (pp. 236–243), on which the movie is based. What major differences do you perceive? What changes in plot or character has Kurosawa made—why, for instance, has Kurosawa added the character of the commoner, or the scene at the end of the film involving the abandoned infant? How has the director "opened up" the action of the story in adapting it for the screen?

12. Investigate the historical background of twelfth-century Japan, the time in which *Rashomon* is set: What can you discover about the roles of the clergy and the samurai class, or about the status of women? Alternatively, you may want to research the concept of "saving face." How does this concept compare with the Western notion of "guilt," and how does it influence the behavior of the characters in *Rashomon*?

13. *Rashomon*, like *A Doll House*, leaves us with an unresolved plot, for we never discover exactly what happened that day in the woods. Using the clues provided by the film, discuss what *you* think is a likely scenario for the events described in the film. (This will naturally involve close comparison of the four main characters and their testimonies.) Did the samurai's wife submit, as her husband and the bandit allege, to the bandit's advances? And who was responsible for the samurai's death? You may choose to defend the "truth" of one of the four testimonies, or you may fashion your own composite version of the events, given the "facts" at your disposal.

CHAPTER

6

Poetry

POETRY AND PROSE

In the introduction to Chapter 4, we looked at this excerpt from James Joyce's short story "Araby":

> Some distant lamp or lighted window gleamed below me. I was thankful that I could see so little. All my senses seemed to desire to veil themselves and, feeling that I was about to slip from them, I pressed the palms of my hands together until they trembled, murmuring: *"O love! O love!"* many times.

Now compare this poem, written by the same author:

Alone

> The moon's greygolden meshes make
> All night a veil,
> The shorelamps in the sleeping lake
> Laburnum tendrils trail.
>
> The sly reeds whisper to the night
> A name—her name—
> And all my soul is a delight,
> A swoon of shame.

The prose excerpt and the poem are rooted in the same experience: the adoring lover, solitary, gives himself over to the mixture of shame and delight that comes from summoning up the secret name of the beloved. The two passages even share the language of night, distant lamps, veils, and whispered incantations. And yet these two expressions of the same complex emotion are fundamentally different. What is it that James Joyce—or any writer, for that matter—can do in poetry that he cannot do in prose?

A likely starting place for such an investigation would be with a definition of poetry, if a precise definition of the term were easy to come by. The poet Ezra Pound once observed that distinguishing clearly between prose and poetry would be impossible unless one wrote "a complete treatise on the art of writing." Many people associate poetry with rhyme, but a poem need not have rhyme or even that recurrent "beat" called poetic meter. True, poetry concerns itself with the sounds and rhythms of words—but then, to a certain extent, so does good prose, as the quotation from "Araby" demonstrates.

What we can begin by saying, though, is that traditional *verse,* even the trite verse on greeting cards, is distinguishable from prose in that it is written in lines that attend to rhythm and frequently to rhyme. *Poetry,* memorable poetry, distills and compresses language and feeling to an even greater extent than prose or commonplace verse. This concentration of meaning and emotion is conveyed through the sound and look of the poem. Modern poetry, beginning around the middle of the nineteenth century with the work of the American poet Walt Whitman, frequently dispenses with predetermined meter and rhyme, but still concerns itself with the relationship between the sense and the sound of words, and with the way the words are arranged typographically on the page—in lines and occasionally in stanzas, rather than in the sentences and paragraphs we expect from prose. William Carlos Williams's brief poem "Between Walls," for instance, consists of one sentence; punctuated and copied out as prose, the sentence looks like this:

Between walls, the back wings of the hospital where nothing will grow, lie cinders in which shine the broken pieces of a green bottle.

But Williams wrote it this way:

——— **Between Walls** ———

the back wings
of the

hospital where
nothing

will grow lie
cinders

in which shine
the broken

pieces of a green
bottle

As you read these two renditions, you may notice that the same elements—when rearranged—can act on you, affect you, in different ways.
How is this so? In the poem, the arrangement of lines guides us in the way
we look at the words, hear them, speak them. This is not to say that the sense
stops abruptly at the end of each line. But by setting off words and images
on the page and letting space flow around them, Williams shows us how to
attend to a common object, the broken bottle on the ash heap, in an uncommon, unprosaic way. All at once we see the green glass shining in the cinders, much as "a certain slant of light," to borrow Emily Dickinson's phrase,
might suddenly call our attention to that old vase on the mantel we've lived
with but overlooked all these years. We might say, then, that while the prose
version of Williams's words is a statement of meaning, the poetic version
expresses an attitude toward what is said.

Poems characteristically work through images and implications rather
than outright statements. William Butler Yeats wrote, in a famous definition,
"Out of the argument with ourselves we make poetry, out of the argument
with others rhetoric." In the next chapter we'll be looking at "the argument
with others" in the form of the essay. For the present, though, we will investigate the poet's dialogue with the self. Here we'll consider the special ways
in which poems engage us as readers, inviting us to reread and to respond
imaginatively.

Perhaps we can better understand the way poets look at the world by comparing two definitions of a common object. Here is a definition of the word
seashell from *The American Heritage Dictionary:*

The calcareous shell of a marine mollusk or similar marine organism.

And below is a definition of the same word from the Aztec Indians of Mexico, along with several other Aztec definitions compiled by a Franciscan
monk in the sixteenth century. After you've read them, consider the differences you perceive between the two definitions. To get at the nature of these
differences, try composing two definitions, one like Webster's and one like
the Aztecs', of the same object—definitions of a familiar object such as *house*
or *oyster* (two words that will be cropping up a bit farther along in our dis-

cussion of poetry). Then describe any contrasts you notice between the "voices" you've used in composing these two definitions.

Seashell

It is white. One is large, one is small. It is spiraled, marvelous. It is that which can be blown, which resounds. I blow the seashell. I improve, I polish the seashell.

Ruby-throated Hummingbird

It is ashen, ash colored. At the top of its head and the throat, its feathers are flaming, like fire. They glisten, they glow.

Amoyotl (a water-strider)

It is like a fly, small and round. It has legs, it has wings; it is dry. It goes on the surface of the water; it is a flyer. It buzzes, it sings.

Bitumen (a shellfish)

It falls out on the ocean shore; it falls out like mud.

Little Blue Heron

It resembles the brown crane in color; it is ashen, grey. It smells like fish, rotten fish, stinking fish. It smells of fish, rotten fish.

A Mushroom

It is round, large, like a severed head.

A Mountain

High, pointed; pointed on top, pointed at the summit, towering; wide, cylindrical, round; a round mountain, low, low-ridged; rocky, with many rocks; craggy with many crags; rough with rocks; of earth, with trees; grassy; with herbs; with shrubs; with water; dry; white; jagged;

with a sloping plain, with gorges, with caves; precipitous, having gorges; canyon land, precipitous land with boulders.

I climb the mountain; I scale the mountain. I live on the mountain. I am born on the mountain. No one becomes a mountain—no one turns himself into a mountain. The mountain crumbles.

Another Mountain

It is wooded; it spreads green.

These Aztec definitions are not poems, but they seem to bear the same embryonic relation to poetry that, say, the "freewriting" you jot down in your notebook bears to your more formally composed prose. The elders who passed these definitions down from one generation to the next seem to approach such everyday objects as if for the first time. The Aztec glossary combines concrete observations with expressions of the observer's relationship to the object, so that the meaning of the word is inseparable from the thoughts and emotions of the observer. Unlike conventional dictionary citations, these definitions talk about the speaker's experience of the object as much as about the object itself. This subjectivity is part of the nature of poetry, but it is the *freshness* of viewpoint, the sense of discovery, that makes some poems appeal to us and live on in our thoughts. In these Aztec utterances, too, we begin to hear the sound and rhythmic movement of poetry; we might even imagine the seashell definition written like this:

> It is white.
> One is large, one is small.
> It is spiraled,
> marvelous.
> It is that
> which can be blown,
> which resounds.
> I blow the seashell.
> I improve,
> I polish
> the seashell.

Like the Aztec elders who composed these definitions, poets "polish" and "improve"—rediscover and redefine—what is marvelous in an 'ordinary' name or in the object it represents.

—— WORD CHOICE AND TRANSLATION ——

It is the poet's art, Percy Bysshe Shelley proclaims in his "Defense of Poetry," to make up fresh metaphors and word associations that express the "unapprehended relations of things." Very often poets lead us to recognition of an abstract idea or emotion by using everyday words in unexpected ways. Consider the following lines from poems you'll see later on in this discussion. What words or phrases strike you?

> The whiskey on your breath
> Could make a small boy dizzy;
> But I hung on like death:
> Such waltzing was not easy.
> *from "My Papa's Waltz" by*
> *Theodore Roethke*

> (i do not know what it is about you that closes
> and opens; only something in me understands
> the voice of your eyes is deeper than all roses)
> nobody, not even the rain, has such small hands
> *from "somewhere i have never travelled" by*
> *e. e. cummings*

> I, starting up, the light did spy,
> And to my God my heart did cry
> To strengthen me in my distress
> And not to leave me succorless.
> Then coming out beheld a space,
> The flame consume my dwelling place.
> *from "Here Follows Some Verses Upon the*
> *Burning of Our House" by Anne Bradstreet*

How does a little boy, waltzing with his tipsy father, hang on "like death"? What are the "hands" of the rain and the "voice of your eyes"? Why does Bradstreet say that flames consumed her "dwelling place" rather than her "house" or "home"? A poet's selection of words prompts such questions.

Let's examine word choice and its relationship to the meaning of the poem as a whole in a pair of works that focus on the same object. The first is a work by the French author Francis Ponge, whom we mentioned in the introduction to this anthology. Ponge's works are like playful, more developed versions of the Aztec definitions quoted earlier. In his "proems," which lie halfway between prose and poetry, Ponge 'defines' everyday objects—soap, an orange, an oyster, a pebble—and, from his special vantage point, these objects emerge virtually as fictional 'characters.' Below are two English translations of Ponge's proem "The Oyster." Each translation has its merits; as you read, think about which one you prefer, and why. Again, you might begin by listing any differences you notice between them in word choice and structure. Then consider the effect of such differences in connotation, sound, and meaning. (For an additional experiment in close reading, you may want to *write* an extended description of a commonplace object on the order of Ponge's "proems," additional examples of which appear on pages 801–802.)

The oyster, about as big as a fair-sized pebble, is rougher, less evenly colored, brightly whitish. It is a world stubbornly closed. Yet it can be opened: one must hold it in a cloth, use a dull jagged knife, and try more than once. Avid fingers get cut, nails get chipped: a rough job. The repeated pryings mark its cover with white rings, like haloes.

Inside one finds a whole world, to eat and drink; under a *firmament* (properly speaking) of nacre, the skies above collapse on the skies below, forming nothing but a puddle, a viscous greenish blob that ebbs and flows on sight and smell, fringed with blackish lace along the edge.

Once in a rare while a globule pearls in its nacre throat, with which one instantly seeks to adorn oneself.

Translated by Beth Archer

The oyster, the size of an average pebble, is of more rugged appearance, of a less solid color, brilliantly whitish. It's a stubbornly closed world. However it can be opened: it must then be held in the hollow of a rag, a jagged but not sharp knife used, and several cracks made at it. Finicky fingers get cut, break their nails at it: it's a rough job. The blows landed on it mark its casing with white rings, with sort of haloes.

In the interior is found a whole world, to eat and drink: under a *firmament* (appropriately) of nacre, heavens above settle upon heavens below, to form nothing more than a pool, a viscous and greenish sachet, which ebbs and flows to sight and smell, fringed with a blackish lace along the edges.

Sometimes very rare a formula pearls in their gullet of nacre, whereby is found at once an adornment.

Translated by Cid Corman

Like the Aztec elders, Ponge defines the object by observing its physical properties and by recording his responses to it, ultimately seeking to uncover what the object represents or signifies. The oyster is a world in itself, forbidding and difficult to pry open: a world that eventually discloses a self-contained little animal and, on rare occasions, a pearl. Here is what one student finds in her first encounter with the poem:

The idea of an oyster being a stubbornly closed world gives the connotation that it doesn't want to be opened. So do not enter. It can be opened, however, if one uses the right procedure. It could cost a few broken nails, though.

Its interior is described as a whole world to eat and drink, filled with heavenly sights and scents. The term "a formula pearls in their gullet of nacre" gives the picture of a throat holding onto something very precious and tasty.

Ellen Buckley

You can see by comparing the two versions of Ponge's work that the two translators have interpreted the original and rendered its sounds and meanings in subtly different ways. As Robert Frost once said, poetry is "what gets lost in translation." Another student remarked in her journal, after reading the efforts of Ponge's translators:

Here we have two people re-telling the ideas of a poet, so that other speakers intervene between the speaker of the original poem and the reader. The translations remind me of the "telephone game" we used to play as children. We sat in a circle, and one person began the game by whispering a sentence to the person next to her. As each child in the circle repeated the sentence to her neighbor, the original words were slightly and unconsciously changed and rearranged, so that when the last person said the sentence aloud, it was very different from the original.

Sara Blum

Still, we have included several translated poems in this chapter, because even in their 'second-hand' state, these works—like the translated stories and plays in this anthology—give great pleasure. Because sound and sense are altered or revised when a poem shifts from one language to another, a translation of a poem should be thought of as a separate poem, and it is noteworthy that the best translators are usually fine poets in their own right: See, for example, Kenneth Rexroth's translations of the Chinese poet Li Ch'ing Chao, a woman who lived during the eleventh century (pages 642–643) and Robert Bly's translations of Pablo Neruda (pages 805–809).

What we discover in both translations of Ponge's proem is that the properties of the oyster (object) and "The Oyster" (poem) are parallel. Descriptive poems such as this one have been called, in German, *Dinggedichte,* or "Thing-poems," in which the selection and arrangement of details hints at another interpretation of the object being described. Ponge's word choice allows us to see how the poem *is like* the oyster, so that the description actually becomes a parable of how one writes and reads a poem. Take a few moments now to write down some of your observations about "The Oyster." How might Ponge's description of the oyster suggest, at the same time, a description of how one writes or reads a poem? When you have finished writing, compare your observations with those of other readers of "The Oyster."

W. H. Auden once remarked, "Poetry is speech at its most personal, the most intimate of dialogues. A poem does not come to life until a reader makes his response to the words written by the poet." This two-fold creation, both the oyster and "The Oyster," "ebbs and flows to sight and smell"; that is, it springs to life when savored by the oyster eater and the reader/consumer of the poem. Prying open the shell to disclose the oyster/poem takes some trouble but repays the effort, since what the poet offers up is "a whole world to eat and drink"—in other words, as our reader Ellen Buckley has suggested, a precious world of tastes, sights, scents, and sounds.

IMAGES LITERAL AND FIGURATIVE

A poet conveys these sensory impressions and ideas through concrete representations called *images.* We have seen how Francis Ponge describes the oyster. Compare the images by which the Irish poet Seamus Heaney makes our senses alive to the experience of eating oysters:

Oysters

Our shells clacked on the plates.
My tongue was a filling estuary,
My palate hung with starlight:
As I tasted the salty Pleiades
Orion dipped his foot into the water.   5

Alive and violated
They lay on their beds of ice:
Bivalves: the split bulb
And philandering sigh of ocean.
Millions of them ripped and shucked and scattered.   10

We had driven to that coast
Through flowers and limestone
And there we were, toasting friendship,
Laying down a perfect memory
In the cool of thatch and crockery.   15

Over the Alps, packed deep in hay and snow,
The Romans hauled their oysters south to Rome:
I saw damp panniers disgorge
The frond-lipped, brine-stung
Glut of privilege   20

And was angry that my trust could not repose
In the clear light, like poetry or freedom
Leaning in from sea. I ate the day
Deliberately, that its tang
Might quicken me all into verb, pure verb.   25

We hear the clack of shells on the plates, taste the salt, see the "split bulb" of the bivalves on their beds of ice. These are the *literal* images that allow us to share this act, this meal, with the speaker[1] of the poem. But just as Ponge uses his oyster to suggest the act of poetic creation, so, as we shall see, Heaney has a larger theme in mind than simply "laying down a perfect memory" of a day among friends in the clear light of the seacoast.

---

[1]We use the word *speaker* because, as in the case of the short fiction discussed in Chapter 4, the writer of the work is not necessarily the same as the *I* who is speaking in the story or poem.

There are several different kinds of *point of view* a poet might adopt. A *dramatic monologue* is a poem written as a speech or the half-spoken thoughts of a speaker who is very different from the poet (as in Browning's "My Last Duchess," on pages 721–722); often this monologue is addressed to some other character who remains silent, though we may be able to infer that character's responses. In a *mask lyric*, like Tennyson's "Ulysses" (pages 719–720) or Eliot's "Prufrock" (pages 780–784), the speaker is a character other than the poet, but that character represents one aspect or *persona* of the poet, articulating an emotional problem or situation which seems to parallel that of the poet. In other poems, the "I" who speaks is virtually identical with the poet—which appears to be the case here in Heaney's poem. In this particular work, the poet reflects upon a past event which he begins to make sense of now, as he writes.

If we attend to the images more closely, we discover that they are used in this poem, as in Ponge's, *figuratively,* to express an abstract idea through concrete means. *Figures of speech* are images that mean something other than the literal denotation of the words. What does Heaney's diction, his word choice, tell us? The poet might have decided to continue the celestial imagery of the first stanza into the second stanza, by describing the oysters as, for instance, a glistening constellation arrayed on what Ponge calls a *"firmament* (appropriately) of nacre." But Heaney's oysters are "alive and violated" on their chilly beds, not merely shucked (removed from their shells), these few dozen oysters on the plate, but "Millions of them ripped and shucked and scattered." The language has taken a violent turn. Why?

"We had driven to that coast," the speaker tells us in stanza 3, presumably with no other purpose than to enjoy one another's company and the pleasures of the palate. But this perfect memory gives way, in stanza 4, to the image of the ancient Romans hauling home baskets of oysters for the dinner tables of the privileged. The juxtaposition of these two stanzas implies a comparison: Are we not, sitting at our laden tables, like those wealthy Romans, enjoying the "brine-stung/ Glut of privilege"? And is not such privilege gained at the expense of those who are conquered and violated, who have not the repose to enjoy such luxuries as poetry and freedom and a peaceful day among friends?

It is this suggested comparison that brings new shades of meaning to the event in the poem's final stanzas. The direct cause of the speaker's guilt and anger at his own complacency is left unspecified—here readers might think of any place, from Northern Ireland to South Africa, where people are starving or battling for their lives and their ideals. The speaker says he "ate the day/ Deliberately" as he has devoured the oysters, so that its lesson might "quicken" him into "pure verb," into commitment and action. Notice how, appropriately, the speaker's own verbs grow more active in this last stanza, as he becomes "angry that my trust could not repose/ In the clear light."

As you can see, through those implicit comparisons called *metaphors* ("My tongue was a filling estuary") and the explicit comparisons called *similes* ("My tongue was like a filling estuary"), poets use images for something more than sensual adornment of their themes. These figures of speech are part of the meaning of the poem. To cite several other typical examples of how figurative language works in poetry: Writers may use exaggeration, as when Heaney summons up starry images in his first stanza to underscore his sensual delirium; they may use understatement, as when Anne Bradstreet, in a poem you will see shortly, quietly describes the burning of her house and possessions: "My pleasant things in ashes lie"; they may personify inanimate objects, attributing human characteristics to them, as when Ponge and Heaney call the oysters "stubbornly closed" or "violated."

But as a footnote to the foregoing discussion, we should add that a poet may also use images to *undercut,* or work against, the sense of the poem. A fascinating example of this phenomenon can be found at the heart of this Shakespearean sonnet, which we will look at more closely later on in this introduction. Take some time to read through the poem. Then go back and underscore any words or images that stand out in your second reading. What, in your estimation, is the collective effect of these images? What picture of the speaker emerges from them?

That Time of Year Thou May'st in Me Behold

That time of year thou may'st in me behold
When yellow leaves, or none, or few, do hang
Upon those boughs which shake against the cold,
Bare ruined choirs where late the sweet birds sang.
In me thou see'st the twilight of such day   5
As after sunset fadeth in the west,
Which by and by black night doth take away,
Death's second self, that seals up all in rest.
In me thou see'st the glowing of such fire
That on the ashes of his youth doth lie,   10
As the deathbed whereon it must expire,
Consumed with that which it was nourished by.
This thou perceiv'st, which makes thy love more strong,
To love that well which thou must leave ere long.

This beautiful and moving poem is frequently anthologized, and understandably so. What readers most often comment on is the way Shakespeare carefully builds up the sequence of images—of autumn, twilight, a dying fire—to convey the sense of the speaker's growing older and closer to death. And here is where many readings of the poem's imagery end. But while the images of the poem pull forcefully in the direction of age, cold, darkness, and death, these same images also seem to tug in the opposite direction, away from the *sense* of what the speaker is saying. The metaphors of the sweet birds and the glowing embers, the hot colors of the yellow leaves and the fading sunset, actually work as *counter-images* in the poem, suggesting that although the speaker's powers may be waning, there is much life and song and passion in him yet: He is, like the fire, "Consumed with that which it was nourished by." Indeed, one student, Joanne Iglio, in writing about the poem put all these images in the sonnet together to form a picture of warmth and intimacy: The confluence of imagery, she said, gave her the impression of sitting by a fire at sunset looking out at an autumn day—a pastime that struck her as quintessentially romantic. This, then, is the wonderful paradox of the poem: All the while, through the force of his metaphors for his waning strength, the speaker has in fact used these same images to convince the listener and the reader of his extraordinary powers as a poet and lover.

SYMBOLS

Through metaphor, writers suggest the qualities of an abstraction, an emotion or idea, by comparing it to a specific image—a bare branch, a darkening sky, a glowing fire—which is familiar and readily grasped by the reader. A *symbol* is also an image that stands for something else, but its meaning may be somewhat more elusive, for a symbol is apt to call up a complex series of interrelated meanings.

In using devices such as symbols, writers are simply making use of the way our minds actually work. We think symbolically, and nowhere is this natural symbolic faculty more apparent than in our dreams. In Chapter 2, for instance, we include Sigmund Freud's analysis of a typical dream: A patient repeatedly dreams that her brothers and sisters sprout wings and fly away. While the patient unconsciously "censors" the meaning of the dream, Freud clearly sees its symbolic content. It is not uncommon for a child to wish for the disappearance—the symbolic 'death' —of rival siblings. By the same mental process, most of us intuitively understand the symbolic significance we impart to commonplace words—words such as *rose* or *shadow* or *home*.

As you might expect, however, many objects have symbolic meanings that vary from culture to culture. To take just one example: Westerners are likely to interpret the image of a serpent as a symbol of Satan or evil, harkening back to the biblical representation of the snake in the Garden of Eden. For Japanese and Chinese readers, however, the snake and dragon are good luck symbols. In speaking with others from different nationalities or cultures, you will no doubt discover a number of such culturally determined differences in interpretation. This cultural variation is one reason that discussions of literature, both in the classroom and among friends, are crucial to our understanding: Through dialogue, through our collective experience with a work of art, we come to a richer and more textured interpretation of the work.

To see how a symbol operates on several levels within the context of a poem, we'll take the example of a work composed by the seventeenth-century American poet Anne Bradstreet. "Here Follows Some Verses upon the Burning of Our House, July 10th, 1666" was inspired by an actual event in the poet's life. In 1630, Bradstreet had left behind a life of relative comfort in England to emigrate with her husband to the newly established Massachusetts Bay Colony. In the inhospitable environment of this primitive Puritan settlement, Bradstreet lived a devout life, bore and reared eight children, and somehow managed to write poetry—an unheard-of activity for an American woman of her era. In many of her poems, Bradstreet draws on images from her domestic life; the following poem, in particular, builds on the images of *dwelling place* and *house*, with all the rich meanings these words convey.

Here Follows Some Verses
——— upon the Burning of Our House ———

July 10th, 1666

Copied Out of a Loose Paper

In silent night when rest I took
For sorrow near I did not look
I wakened was with thund'ring noise
And piteous shrieks of dreadful voice.
That fearful sound of "Fire!" and "Fire!"   5
Let no man know is my desire.
I, starting up, the light did spy,
And to my God my heart did cry
To strengthen me in my distress
And not to leave me succorless.   10
Then, coming out, beheld a space
The flame consume my dwelling place.
And when I could no longer look,
I blest His name that gave and took,
That laid my goods now in the dust.   15
Yea, so it was, and so 'twas just.
It was His own, it was not mine,
Far be it that I should repine;
He might of all justly bereft
But yet sufficient for us left.   20
When by the ruins oft I past
My sorrowing eyes aside did cast,
And here and there the places spy
Where oft I sat and long did lie:
Here stood that trunk, and there that chest,   25
There lay that store I counted best.
My pleasant things in ashes lie,
And them behold no more shall I.
Under thy roof no guest shall sit,
Nor at thy table eat a bit.   30
No pleasant tale shall e'er be told,
Nor things recounted done of old.

HERE FOLLOWS SOME VERSES . . .: Copied by her son Simon, presumably from a
manuscript by Mrs. Bradstreet, this poem was first published in J. H. Ellis, *Works*, 1867.
   14. I blest . . . took: *Cf.* Job i: 21:"* * * The Lord gave, and the Lord hath taken away;
blessed be the name of the Lord."

No candle e'er shall shine in thee,
Nor bridegroom's voice e'er heard shall be.
In silence ever shall thou lie,   35
Adieu, Adieu, all's vanity.
Then straight I 'gin my heart to chide,
And did thy wealth on earth abide?
Didst fix thy hope on mold'ring dust?
The arm of flesh didst make thy trust?   40
Raise up thy thoughts above the sky
That dunghill mists away may fly.
Thou hast an house on high erect,
Framed by that mighty Architect,
With glory richly furnished,   45
Stands permanent though this be fled.
It's purchased and paid for too
By Him who hath enough to do.
A price so vast as is unknown
Yet by His gift is made thine own;   50
There's wealth enough, I need no more,
Farewell, my pelf, farewell my store.
The world no longer let me love,
My hope and treasure lies above.

Bradstreet begins with the autobiographical event: Awakened by shrieks in the night, she is forced to flee and witness the burning of her "dwelling place." A dwelling, we know, is a residence; but in these opening stanzas, Bradstreet has not said "residence" or "abode" or "house," and so her choice of words invites us to examine more closely the literal or dictionary meaning of "dwelling." We find in the dictionary that "to dwell" means not only "to live as a resident," but also "to linger" in a place or "to fasten one's attention" on an object or subject. Further, the dictionary reveals a meaning the modern reader might have missed: The word *dwell* comes from the Old English *dwellen*, which means "to delay, hinder, or deceive." Seen from this perspective, Bradstreet's choice encourages us to consider the dwelling in this poem as a *temporary* residence, a place where the speaker—misguidedly, it would seem—has hitherto fastened her attention. This subtle revelation

---

36. **All's vanity:** *Cf.* Ecclesiastes i: 2: "Vanity of vanities, saith the Preacher, vanity of vanities; all is vanity."
52. **Pelf:** Money or wealth regarded with contempt.
54. *Cf.* Luke xxii: 34: "For where your treasure is, there will your heart be also."

prepares us for her quiet acceptance, in lines 17–18, of the destruction of her home:

> It was His own, it was not mine,
> Far be it that I should repine;

The word *house* is mentioned only in the poem's title and in line 43. Yet most of us doubtless bring to the poem a cluster of associations or *connotations* that cling to the word *house* (associations you've already discovered if you tried the definition exercises in this introduction) in addition to its literal dictionary meaning or *denotation.* As the speaker ruefully points to the ashes where her "pleasant things"—trunk, chest, table—once stood, we understand the significance of the house as a place of rest, shelter, and hospitality, a repository of material possessions and sweet memories. In line 14 the speaker invokes "His name that gave and took," so that we see this earthly dwelling place as impermanent, subject to sudden destruction—much as our lives on this earth last until such time as our bodies, like our earthly goods, are turned to ashes and dust.

The implicit equation of the earthly house with its human inhabitants—and of the destruction of the house with the mortality of the flesh—becomes clearer towards the end of the poem. The "house on high erect" stands in direct contrast to the house described in the preceding stanzas. God is the "Architect" of this heavenly house which, unlike the earthly house, is permanent and far more precious than the worldly "treasures" by which the poet had set so much store.

To Bradstreet's Puritan contemporaries, as well as to modern readers familiar with the New Testament, the symbol of the house would reverberate even more powerfully. These readers would no doubt be aware of the biblical references that reinforce the poem's symbolic meaning—not only the explicit references to biblical verses cited in the footnotes, but the references implied by the house/body/heavenly abode metaphor of the poem. For example, Bradstreet seems to have had in mind this quotation from II Corinthians 5.1: "For we know that if our earthly house of *this* tabernacle were dissolved, we have a building of God, an house not made with hands, eternal in the heavens." Similarly in John 14.2, Jesus says, "In my father's house are many mansions: if it were not so, I would have told you. I go to prepare a place for you."

These indirect literary and historical references or allusions in the poem are not crucial to our understanding of it, because *house* is a symbol whose significance is easily grasped by most readers. Still, our awareness of the biblical symbolism of the house further enriches our sense of the layering of meaning in the work. What Bradstreet has constructed, finally, is a whole network of one-to-one correspondences—house/body, fire/death, and the like—to show how she deals with the destruction of her house in the context of her religious beliefs.

The house in Bradstreet's poem is a symbol that has a clear and objective form. Yet literature also presents us with symbols that are far less concrete. W. S. Merwin's eerie poem "The Last One" achieves much of its terrifying force through the use of such oblique symbolism. As you read the poem, try to name exactly what is meant by "The Last One." What is this "it," the shadow of "the last one," that "went on growing"? And when you have decided what "it" is, go back through the poem to answer this question: How do you know?

———— The Last One ————

Well they'd made up their minds to be everywhere because why not.
Everywhere was theirs because they thought so.
They with two leaves they whom the birds despise.
In the middle of stones they made up their minds.
They started to cut.   5

Well they cut everything because why not.
Everything was theirs because they thought so.
It fell into its shadows and they took both away.
Some to have some for burning.

Well cutting everything they came to the water.   10
They came to the end of the day there was one left standing.
They would cut it tomorrow they went away.
The night gathered in the last branches.
The shadow of the night gathered in the shadow on the water.
The night and the shadow put on the same head.   15
And it said Now.

Well in the morning they cut the last one.
Like the others the last one fell into its shadow.
It fell into its shadow on the water.
They took it away its shadow stayed on the water.   20

Well they shrugged they started trying to get the shadow away.
They cut right to the ground the shadow stayed whole.
They laid boards on it the shadow came out on top.
They shone lights on it the shadow got blacker and clearer.
They exploded the water the shadow rocked.   25
They built a huge fire on the roots.
They sent up black smoke between the shadow and the sun.

The new shadow flowed without changing the old one.
They shrugged they went away to get stones.

They came back the shadow was growing. 30
They started setting up stones it was growing.
They looked the other way it went on growing.
They decided they would make a stone out of it.
They took stones to the water they poured them into the shadow.
They poured them in they poured them in the stones vanished. 35
The shadow was not filled it went on growing.
That was one day.

The next day was just the same it went on growing.
They did all the same things it was just the same.
They decided to take its water from under it. 40
They took away water they took it away the water went down.
The shadow stayed where it was before.
It went on growing it grew onto the land.
They started to scrape the shadow with machines.
When it touched the machines it stayed on them. 45
They started to beat the shadow with sticks.

Where it touched the sticks it stayed on them.
They started to beat the shadow with hands.
Where it touched the hands it stayed on them.
That was another day. 50

Well the next day started about the same it went on growing.
They pushed lights into the shadow.
Where the shadow got onto them they went out.
They began to stomp on the edge it got their feet.
And when it got their feet they fell down. 55
It got into eyes the eyes went blind.
The ones that fell down it grew over and they vanished.
The ones that went blind and walked into it vanished.
The ones that could see and stood still
It swallowed their shadows. 60
Then it swallowed them too and they vanished.
Well the others ran.

The ones that were left went away to live if it would let them.
They went as far as they could.
The lucky ones with their shadows. 65

Trying to affix a precise name, a label, to the "it" in Merwin's poem is a little like trying to pin down jello. The symbol begins to slither away. Here are reactions to the poem recorded by two astute readers in their journals:

> I guess the "they" in "The Last One" is us, humankind. We are " . . . they whom the birds despise." We've destroyed the natural world, which was created for us. Line 7 states that they thought "everything was theirs." In reality, nothing is ours; everything belongs to nature. We didn't invent water and clean air and fresh grass and trees. All these things were here before us, and we take the liberty of destroying each one of them.
>
> *Paula Papachristos*

> "The Last One" shows the arrogance of man; nothing in the environment is sacred to him. Man cut down all the trees, but he forgot about the problems that would occur because of ecological imbalance. These problems are symbolized by the shadow. The shadow keeps on growing and can't be stopped by the means invented by man. Finally the shadow overcomes and kills man—all this because of human greed.
>
> *Frank Osterwald*

We might say with these readers that the shadow of The Last One stands for the problems caused by "encroaching technology," or the "technological arrogance" of "them," the protagonists of the poem, who hack mindlessly away at the environment. To a great extent, the poem supports this interpretation. But we would be doing a disservice to this particular work if we were to insist on an exact equation of symbol and referent: *it* = technology. The central, *transcendent* symbol of "The Last One" becomes something more than these phrases, an entity that gathers meaning to itself as the poem progresses and that resists our efforts to reduce its significance to a plain phrase. "It" becomes all the more menacing for its elusiveness; it can be hinted at, but it cannot be contained or neatly summed up in the way that readers expect in expository prose.

Obviously, not all poetic symbols are so amorphous, as we have seen in Bradstreet's symbolic use of the idea of "house." But the relationship between image and meaning in poetry is typically more complicated than in prose. The metaphor or symbol cannot be lifted out of the poem the way a metaphor in an essay can be extrapolated from the rest of a paragraph. By way of analogy, we might point out that relationships between poetic images and sensory impressions are equally complex. Poets very often make use of the intertwining of sense perceptions called *synesthesia* (from the Greek words for "blended feeling"), a device through which an impression normally provided by one of our five senses is perceived through another of those senses—as when a painter describes a "cool shade of green" or a musician speaks of a "blue note." Through the special medium of poetry, then, e. e.

cummings can describe "somewhere i have never travelled," a poem we quoted from a few pages ago, by creating fresh combinations of words and sensations—by writing, for instance, in the final stanza, about the "feel" or the "sound" of a look in his lover's eyes. Here is the poem:

———— somewhere i have never travelled ————

somewhere i have never travelled,gladly beyond
any experience,your eyes have their silence:
in your most frail gesture are things which enclose me,
or which i cannot touch because they are too near

your slightest look easily will unclose me
though i have closed myself as fingers,
you open always petal by petal myself as Spring opens
(touching skilfully,mysteriously)her first rose

or if your wish be to close me,i and
my life will shut very beautifully,suddenly,   10
as when the heart of this flower imagines
the snow carefully everywhere descending;

nothing which we are to perceive in this world equals
the power of your intense fragility:whose texture
compels me with the colour of its countries,
rendering death and forever with each breathing

(i do not know what it is about you that closes
and opens; only something in me understands
the voice of your eyes is deeper than all roses)
nobody,not even the rain,has such small hands   20

Notice how in the second stanza of the poem Cummings similarly manipulates sensory data and metaphor in surprising ways. The basic metaphor in this stanza is that the lover "opens" the speaker as Spring opens her first rose. But what do these lines mean? What happens in these lines, and how does the poet make it happen? To find some answers to these questions, we asked a group of students to rewrite the last two lines of the second stanza in prose, as the sentence might appear in a love letter. Here are several of their 'translations' of the two lines:

You always open me (myself) petal by petal, as Spring opens her first rose.

You take away my protective 'layers,' the way Spring opens her first rose petal by petal.

Just as in springtime a flower develops and grows gradually, so I blossom when my beloved touches me.

You peel away my doubts and make my happiness bloom just as Spring opens up rose buds.

I am revitalized, opened up, by your love.

It's clear that no matter how many attempts we make to capture the meaning of these lines, prose can never quite *get at* what the poetic lines communicate through their very form—through inversion and scrambling of standard word order; through the placement of "myself" (the speaker) between "you open" at the beginning of the line and "Spring opens" at the end of the line, as though equating the lover's power with the natural force of the seasons; through the phrase "petal by petal," which announces the flower metaphor *before* we get to the actual comparison "as Spring opens . . . her first rose"; through the poet's breaking the rules of punctuation, as when he omits the space after the comma in "skilfully, mysteriously," thereby connecting even more closely the skill and mystery of the actions Spring and the lover are able to perform.

In short, the poetic lines convey meaning through manipulation of metaphor, symbol, diction, syntax, and punctuation. In this way, the grammar and word order of a poem, in addition to the symbols it contains, operate as a metaphor for what the poet is saying. The meaning of the poetic metaphor or symbol cannot be considered apart from its context in the poem.

So when Robert Frost remarked that poetry is what gets lost in translation, he was speaking not only of translation from, say, French to English, but from poetry to paraphrase. In Frost's poem "Mending Wall," the speaker wants to tell his neighbor,

> 'Something there is that doesn't love a wall,
> That wants it down.' I could say 'Elves' to him,
> But it's not elves exactly. . . .

The speaker refuses to name just what it is that "doesn't love a wall" between neighbors—it is something *like* elves, but "not elves exactly." Poetry explores these complicated relationships between humans and their environment elliptically, in a way that would be unsuitable, for instance, in expository prose. Frost celebrates the elusiveness of meaning—the mystery of the relationship between the symbol and the thing it signifies—in a deceptively simple rhyme called "The Secret Sits." Here is the poem in its entirety:

The Secret Sits

We dance round in a ring and suppose,
But the Secret sits in the middle and knows.

THE MUSIC OF POETRY

By the same token, as we suggested at the beginning of this discussion, a good part of the meaning of a poem resides in its music. The repeated sounds and rhythms of poetry recall its origins in oral tradition, in song and dance and ceremony.

Poets use repeated combinations of sound and rhythm not only to create music and memorability but to amplify meaning. If you reread the poem "somewhere i have never travelled," for instance, you will become aware of the way cummings repeats the words "open" and "close" and variations of these words—"closes," "enclose," "unclose," and so on—to drive home the content of the lines. The repetition calls attention to the dilating and contracting movement, the systolic and diastolic action or heartbeat, that is the core of the poem. This pattern of sound, then, is yet another element of the poem that is likely to be lost in prose 'translations' of poetic lines such as those we invited our students to attempt.

Now if we go back to the question posed at the outset of this introduction—What is it that a writer like James Joyce can do in poetry that he cannot do in prose?—we may reread Joyce's poem "Alone" with melody in mind. Joyce's poem is a *lyric poem. Narrative poems*—ballads such as "The Demon Lover" (pages 645–647) and epics such as Homer's *Odyssey*—tell stories and describe heroic actions, whereas lyrics emphasize emotion and song. Lyric poems—which take forms as various as the ode, the sestina, and the sonnet—are usually brief and intense expressions of a speaker's mood. We'll return, then, to Joyce's poem on the first page of this introduction, this time listening to the music of the piece, and to the way sound makes meaning vivid.

Perhaps the most obvious musical repetitions in Joyce's poem are those of the rhyme scheme—the *end rhymes* of make/lake, veil/trail, night/delight, name/shame. When analyzing poems, we describe such sound patterns by giving each new rhyme a successive letter of the alphabet. In this poem, the rhyme scheme of each stanza is *abab.* Rhyme words may also occur within the line, as in Joyce's rhyming of *moon* and *swoon,* or *night* (in the middle of line 2) with *night* and *delight* (at the end of lines 5 and 7). There are, as well, a number of other lush tonal repetitions in this lyric: the liquid *l* sounds, for instance, of lines 3 and 4. Consonants may be repeated at the beginning of the word, as in *l*ake/*L*aburnum; this initial repetition is called *alliteration.* The repetition of consonants may also occur at the end of words, as in vei*l* and trai*l*—a pattern called *consonance*—or in the middle of words, as in shore*l*amps and *sl*eeping. A similar pattern of consonant repetition emerges in the persistent, whispery *s* sounds of Joyce's poem. Equally noteworthy in this lyric is the poet's emphasis on assonance—that is, on the repetition of vowel sounds. Here, Joyce's drawing out of vowels, the *o*s and *oo*s and *i*s of the poem, make the entire lyric a kind of protracted swoon or sigh, befitting the speaker's furtive homage to the whispered secret name of the beloved.

If poetry is song, it is in equal measure dance. As the French poet Paul

Valery once said, "Prose is walking and poetry is dancing." Poetry, far more than prose, is about physical motion—about the movement of words through the space of the page and through the time it takes to utter them. All poetry plays with tempo, with the pattern of stresses (syllables spoken with more force or volume) and pauses that link words and lines. English words and phrases, as you know, are made of up stressed and unstressed syllables. For instance, here is the stress pattern of the foregoing sentence as it would normally be uttered:

ENGlish WORDS and PHRAses, as you KNOW, are MADE up of STRESSED and UNstressed SYLlables.

Of couse, in speech or prose we pay far less attention to these patterns than in poetry, where sound and rhythm are crucial.

With these sound patterns in mind, let's return for a moment to the Shakespearean sonnet we looked at earlier, this time to examine the poem's structure, rhyme, and rhythm. A *sonnet*, a verse form containing 14 lines, may take one of two basic structures. The *Italian* or *Petrarchan* sonnet is divided into 8 lines (octet) and 6 lines (sestet); the *English* or *Shakespearean* sonnet is composed of three 4-line groupings (quatrains), each with its own rhyme scheme, and a concluding 2-line rhyme (couplet). Reread Shakespeare's sonnet, attending closely to the rhyme scheme and alternation of stressed and unstressed syllables, as we have highlighted them in the first four lines below. You might try to mark the rest of the poem according to the stressed and unstressed syllables you hear.

That time of year thou may'st in me behold	*a*
When yellow leaves, or none, or few, do hang	*b*
Upon those boughs which shake against the cold,	*a*
Bare ruined choirs, where late the sweet bird sang.	*b*
In me thou see'st the twilight of such day	*c*
As after sunset fadeth in the west,	*d*
Which by and by black night doth take away,	*c*
Death's second self, that seals up all in rest.	*d*
In me thou see'st the glowing of such fire	*e*
That on the ashes of his youth doth lie,	*f*
As the deathbed whereon it must expire,	*e*
Consumed with that which it was nourished by.	*f*
This thou perceiv'st, which makes thy love more strong,	*g*
To love that well which thou must leave ere long.	*g*

Like most sonnets, this poem is written in iambic pentameter, which is to say that most of the lines are made up of 5 (hence, *pent-*) *iambs*, which are metrical units, or "feet," having one unstressed and one stressed syllable (as in the word depend). As you can see, the poet is able to sustain this rhythmic pattern for the length of the poem. Yet to do so without variation would be to lull the reader into the monotony of sing-song; as a result, poets usually throw in changes in meter in the form of *spondees* (two stressed syllables: the last time), *trochees* (a stressed and an unstressed syllable: cosmic), and *pyrrhic* feet (two unstressed syllables: the light and the dark). Thus Shakespeare provides, at the beginning of line 11 of his sonnet, pyrrhic and spondaic feet:

As the DEATHBED whereON it MUST exPIRE

The effect of these two variations is to bring us up short, to make us halt and linger over the word *deathbed:* The significance of the word is all the more weighty for its emphasis in the poetic line.

Generally speaking, the highly regular stress pattern of iambic meter tends to establish a more formal tone. Indeed, the relatively long poetic line of iambic pentameter is by far the most common verse meter in English; along with even longer poetic lines, it is often used for serious meditative verse. Shorter poetic lines, on the other hand, frequently convey a lighter mood. The same is true of three-syllable meters, such as *anapest* (like a child) and *dactyl* (possible), which quicken our reading pace because of our natural tendency to race over unstressed syllables.[1]

The following poems should illustrate this point. As you might expect, poetic rhythm is nowhere more apparent than in poems *about* dance, which is the case in these next two examples. The first is Theodore Roethke's celebrated "My Papa's Waltz," the first stanza of which, quoted earlier, is here reprised (you will have to turn to page 816 to finish this dance). The poem is written in trimeter, each line having three feet:

> The WHISkey ON your BREATH
> Could MAKE a SMALL boy DIZzy;
> But I hung ON like DEATH:
> Such WALTZing WAS not EAsy.

Some commentators like to point out that the poem, with its three regularly stressed feet, imitates the waltz of the title. But a musical waltz is danced in 3/4 time, which means that there are three beats to a measure, the first beat in the measure being the strongest. (Think of any waltz you know: OOM pah pah, OOM pah pah). To make the poem a waltz, we'd have to change the two-beat iambic measure to a three-beat *dactyl*. To show you how the waltz might work, we'll change the meter (and ruin the poetry) by adding some empty unstressed syllables to the stanza:

---

[1]Here are the names of the line lengths in English verse:

monometer:	one foot	pentameter:	five feet
dimeter:	two feet	hexameter:	six feet
trimeter:	three feet	heptameter:	seven feet
tetrameter:	four feet	octameter:	eight feet

The WHISkey that WAS on your BREATH
Could MAKE any LITtle boy DIZzy;
But *I* hung on TO you like DEATH:
Such WALTZing you KNOW was not EAsy.

So what Roethke's version achieves is not the gliding rhythm of a real waltz, but an approximation of "my papa's waltz," an inebriated and comical late-night romp, full of missteps, a dance rough enough to shake every pan in the kitchen and make a young boy cling for dear life. The lumbering and at times awkward meter (conveyed by the sound and meaning of the line "You beat time on my head") is pounded home by the line breaks and rhyme scheme of the poem. Most of the lines are *end-stopped* or read as a unit, rather than *enjambed*, with the phrasing of one line running into the next. The *abab* rhyme scheme makes the line breaks even more pronounced, and the imperfect rhymes (sometimes called *slant rhymes*) of the first two stanzas (dizzy/easy; pans/countenance) underscore both the father's unbalanced dance and the mother's frowning unwillingness to participate.

Let's try another drunken dance, this one a bit harder to get the hang of because it is written not in *fixed* or *closed form*, but as is sometimes the case in modern poetry, in *free* or *open form*, without regular meter or rhyme. Before you read the poem, turn for a moment to page 638, and look at the picture that inspired it: "The Wedding Dance" by the sixteenth-century Flemish painter Pieter Brueghel the Elder.

William Carlos Williams's breathless poem "The Dance" takes Brueghel's work as its starting point. We have reprinted the poem below alongside another version of the poem which Williams composed some fifteen years after the first. (The later poem may have been based on another, similar painting by Brueghel.) Both poems are written in *free verse;* this does not mean that they are formless, but rather that they use poetic sound and rhythm more flexibly than traditional verse forms.

Although our comments here will be limited for the most part to the earlier version, the two poems provide insight into the very different ways an artist may choose to approach the same subject. Read both poems, and take a few moments to jot down some of the similarities and differences you observe between them. You might begin by thinking about any similarities you find between Brueghel's painting and the poems. How does each attempt to capture the spirit of Brueghel's work? Which poem do you prefer, and why?

——— The Dance ———	The Wedding Dance — in the Open Air —
In Breughel's[1] great picture, The Kermess,[2] the dancers go round, they go round and around, the squeal and the blare and the	Disciplined by the artist to go round & round

tweedle of bagpipes, a bugle and fiddles
tipping their bellies (round as the thick-
sided glasses whose wash they impound)
their hips and their bellies off balance
to turn them. Kicking and rolling about
the Fair Grounds, swinging their butts, those
shanks must be sound to bear up under such
rollicking measures, prance as they dance
in Breughel's great picture, The Kermess.

in holiday gear
a riotously gay rabble of
peasants and their

ample-bottomed doxies
fills
the market square

featured by the women in
their starched
white headgear

they prance or go openly
toward the wood's
edges

round and around in
rough shoes and
farm breeches

mouths agape
Oya!
kicking up their heels

[1]A variant spelling of *Brueghel*.
[2]A festival or dance in the Low Countries.

In both poems there is a rhyme scheme and metrical pattern, though in neither are these elements as obvious as in, for example, the Shakespearean sonnet. In the later poem, the repeated sounds are *-ound* and *-ear,* or approximations thereof: *round/ & round, round and around,* and *gear, their, square, headgear.* At the same time, an intricate metrical pattern emerges, a pattern thrown into relief when some of the lines are isolated and said aloud:

> Disciplined by the artist
>
> ample-bottomed doxies
>
> featured by the women in
>
> kicking up their heels

In the earlier poem, "The Dance," rhyme and meter are more pronounced. The music of the dance comes through to us in the *onomatopoeia* (that is, the use of words that imitate the sound they describe) of "the *squeal* and the *blare* and the *tweedle*" of the musical instruments, as well as in the pronounced repetition of words that sound like *round.* Follow the *-ound* words as they serpentine through the lines of the poem: Williams is leading us verbally through the swirl and din of the dancing couples in much the same way as Brueghel's composition guides us visually through the crowd. In the painting, we follow the linked arms of the dancers and the alternating of white and dark hats and costumes as they wind back among the trees and then

The Wedding Dance, c. 1566 by Pieter Bruegel the Elder. The Detroit Institute of Arts, City of Detroit Purchase.

snake around again to the foreground. Williams's poem is similarly compressed and circular in design; indeed, the repetition of the first and last lines announces that we have come full circle.

The rhythm of "The Dance" is trickier still, for it depends on our pausing at intervals *within* the lines. These internal pauses or caesurae in poetry are dictated by the natural rhythm of the language. In some cases the caesurae in "The Dance" are indicated by commas or line endings; in other cases these pauses need to be supplied by the reader, who must listen carefully to the beat of the dance—or else be tripped up and lose the rhythm altogether. We do not propose to analyze at length the metrics of this poem; we simply ask you to reread the poem aloud according to the stresses and pauses (//) indicated below:

> in BREUghel's great PICture the KERmess,
> the DANcers go ROUND//they go ROUND and
> aROUND//the SQUEAL and the BLARE and the
> TWEEDle of BAGpipes//a BUGle and FIDdles//
> TIPping their BELlies//ROUND as the THICK-
> sided GLASses whose WASH they imPOUND//
> their HIPS and their BELlies off BALance
> to TURN them//KICKing and ROLLing aBOUT
> the FAIR GROUNDS//SWINGing their BUTTS//those

SHANKS must be SOUND//to BEAR up UNder such
ROLlicking MEASures//PRANCE as they DANCE
in BREUghel's great PICture the KERmess

If you've followed this rhythmic pattern of emphasis, the whirlwind beat of the tipsy wedding celebration is likely to emerge in full force. Here we have a drunken dance that is even more challenging to keep up with than Roethke's waltz, but equally infectious in its merry sound, as this reader points out in her comparison of Williams's earlier and later poems about "The Dance":

> "The Wedding Dance in the Open Air" suggests control to me, more than Williams's earlier poem, "The Dance"—in fact, Williams begins the later work with the word "Disciplined." This second poem is
> > slowed down
> > not as jolly
> > less frenzied
> > more sedate
>
> It has stops, stanzas, unlike "The Dance," which is chock-full and absolutely dense with so much motion and frivolity and boisterous noise. "The Dance" has a concentration of sound and movement that almost makes you dizzy as you go round and around.
>
> Both poems, though, have a kind of rhyme scheme. Also, in both, it seems to me that what is essential is the idea of the *artist*, whether painter or poet.
>
> *Sandra Krol*

DIGGING

Like all lasting works of literature, a good poem invites you to reread—to delve beneath the surface for deeper awareness of music and meaning—and, very often, to respond in writing to what you have read. We have already shown you several students' responses to various poems. Now we offer one last poem for your consideration, along with brief writings by students who were asked by their teacher, Moira Maynard, to reinterpret the central metaphor of the piece in terms of their own lives. As you read the poem for the first time, try to answer these preliminary questions our colleague put to her students:

> Who is the "I" in the poem and how old is he when he is digging? Is he the same person as the "I" who narrates the story?
>
> What is he digging for?
>
> Why does he stop?
>
> Does he find what he is looking for?

Here is the poem, by Richard Wilbur, called "Digging for China":

———— Digging for China ————

"Far enough down is China," somebody said.
"Dig deep enough and you might see the sky
As clear as at the bottom of a well.
Except it would be real—a different sky.
Then you could burrow down until you came   5
To China! Oh, it's nothing like New Jersey.
There's people, trees, and houses, and all that,
But much, much different. Nothing looks the same."

I went and got the trowel out of the shed
And sweated like a coolie all that morning,   10
Digging a hole beside the lilac-bush,
Down on my hands and knees. It was a sort
Of praying, I suspect. I watched my hand
Dig deep and darker, and I tried and tried
To dream a place where nothing was the same.   15
The trowel never did break through to blue.

Before the dream could weary of itself
My eyes were tired of looking into darkness,
My sunbaked head of hanging down a hole.
I stood up in a place I had forgotten,   20
Blinking and staggering while the earth went round
And showed me silver barns, the fields dozing
In palls of brightness, patens, growing and gone
In the tides of leaves, and the whole sky china blue.
Until I got my balance back again   25
All that I saw was China, China, China.

After you have read the poem to get a sense of the incident described and the speaker's attitude toward it, reread the poem aloud, listening for the ways in which the poet plays with words, images, and sounds. It might be interesting to turn away from the poem for a moment and jot down in your notebook some of the words and phrases you recall most vividly—or perhaps to write for five minutes on your thoughts and questions about the poem.

As we have invited you to do in previous chapters, you may want to discuss your responses with other readers of the poem. Each of these exercises, of course, asks you to respond creatively to the poem, and these activities and questions should help you in your reading of the other poems you will encounter in this chapter. Before you turn to the poems collected in the fol-

---

23. **pall:** a cloth cover for a coffin; covering that obscures; (*ecclesiastical*) a cloth used to cover the chalice or altar. **paten:** a plate, esp. the plate that holds the Eucharistic bread in the Catholic mass.

lowing pages, we'll leave you with a freewriting activity our colleague asked her class to try: Write for five or ten minutes in any form you choose, describing yourself digging. In your paragraph or poem, make two things clear: (1) what you are digging for and (2) whether you find it or not. When you have finished, consider the responses written by the following students—all, as it happens, non-native speakers of English—for whom the poem became a way to sift through their own experiences and unearth their own insights:

Digging for My Country

I've heard of it, but never saw it—
It is close, but I can't reach it—
I was a child when it was gone.
The name of my country has vanished
Because for some people it does not exist anymore.
If I want to go back to my country
I've got to get permission from the government.
My country doesn't exist on the map
But it exists in my heart.

Nadia Husein

Many kids dig to look for their future, but as a kid I dug to find the past. I live in Israel in a city that has an ancient name. One summer I went with a group of archeologists to dig for the early remains of my city. It was very difficult digging, but we knew we were looking for our history, which was buried for over 2000 years. I found that I was digging into a family's kitchen. Amazing that after 2000 years people live in the same place, building their future out of their past.

Eli Cohen

I have been digging for myself for a long time. I think it is the most difficult thing in the world. I started to understand myself when I was twenty years old. I still feel I didn't dig for myself enough until now. Someday, I will find myself. Then the sky will clear for me, and I will be able to dig for others.

Tsu-Kang Wang

In Wilbur's poem, the speaker's world is turned around by the act of digging. Dizzied with the effort, his younger self rises to find the familiar world, "a place I had forgotten," suddenly transformed, now silvery and foreign. This is how poetry teaches us to burrow. This is how, in the space of a poem, we see what is new in the familiar, and familiar in the new, until we get our balance back again.

A SELECTION OF POEMS

Sappho

[*ca. 612 B.C.–?*]

Seizure

Translated by Willis Barnstone

To me he seems like a god
as he sits facing you and
hears you near as you speak
softly and laugh

in a sweet echo that jolts   5
the heart in my ribs. For now
as I look at you my voice
is empty and

can say nothing as my tongue
cracks and slender fire is quick   10
under my skin. My eyes are dead
to light, my ears

pound, and sweat pours over me.
I convulse, paler than grass,
and feel my mind slip as I   15
go close to death.

Li Ch'ing Chao

Sung Dynasty [A.D. 1081–1141]

Autumn Evening Beside the Lake

Translated by Kenneth Rexroth

Wind passes over the lake.
The swelling waves stretch away

Without limit. Autumn comes with the twilight,
And boats grow rare on the river.
Flickering waters and fading mountains   5
Always touch the heart of man.
I never grow tired of singing
Of their boundless beauty.
The lotus pods are already formed,
And the water lilies have grown old.   10
The dew has brightened the blossoms
Of the arrowroot along the riverbank.
The herons and seagulls sleep
On the sand with their
Heads tucked away, as though   15
They did not wish to see
The men who pass by on the river.

Alone in the Night

Translated by Kenneth Rexroth

The warm rain and pure wind
Have just freed the willows from
The ice. As I watch the peach trees,
Spring rises from my heart and blooms on
My cheeks. My mind is unsteady,   5
As if I were drunk. I try
To write a poem in which
My tears will flow together
With your tears. My rouge is stale.
My hairpins are too heavy.   10
I throw myself across my
Gold cushions, wrapped in my lonely
Doubled quilt, and crush the phoenixes
In my headdress. Alone, deep
In bitter loneliness, without   15
Even a good dream, I lie,
Trimming the lamp in the passing night.

Sa'dī of Shīrāz

[1184?–1292?]

Two Versions of a Classical Persian Lyric

Precious Are These Heart-Burning Sighs

Translated by E. G. Browne

Precious are these heart-burning sighs, for lo,
This way or that, they help the days to go.
All night I wait for one whose dawn-like face
Lendeth fresh radiance to the morning's grace.
My Friend's sweet face if I again might see   5
I'd thank my lucky star eternally.
Shall I then fear man's blame? The brave man's heart
Serves as his shield to counter slander's dart.
Who wins success hath many a failure tholed.°   endured
The New Year's Day is reached through Winter's cold.   10
For Laylá many a prudent lover yearns,
But Majnún wins her, who his harvest burns.
I am thy slave: pursue some wilder game:
No tether's needed for the bird that's tame.
A strength is his who casts both worlds aside   15
Which is to worldly anchorites denied.
Tomorrow is not: yesterday is spent:
To-day, O Sa'dí, take thy heart's content!

Dear to Me This Lamentation

Translated by R. A. Nicholson

Dear to me this lamentation, though it melt my soul with fire,
For it passes the day somehow: surely else I should expire.
Not so beautiful is Morning, setting earth and heaven alight,
As the face for which I waited, waited all this weary night.

PRECIOUS ARE. . .11–12. **Laylá** (or Lailà) and **Majnún**: legendary lovers who meet with a disastrous fate. After their deaths, they are reunited in celestial splendor.

Ah, if I may see again that love-enkindling face, now far,　　5
Thanks I'll say till Resurrection unto my victorious star.
If I shrink when blame is cast on me, I play the woman's part:
Howsoe'er the arrow pierce thee, meet it with a manly heart!
They that hunger after pleasure needs must know the taste of
　　pain:
He that hopes for New Year's springtide, let him freeze and not　　10
　　complain.
Prudent harvester of reason love's deep bliss did never learn:
'Tis Majnún reads Lailà's secret—he whose wits in frenzy burn.
Fling thy noose about another! Self-devoted here I stand:
Who would tie the foot of falcon long familiar with his hand?
Lovers gambling all the goods away of that world and of this　　15
Are endowed with something precious that our sleek ascetics
　　miss.
Yesterday is gone, To-morrow not yet come. Do thou waylay
Opportunity, O Sa'dí! Make the utmost of To-day!

Anonymous

The Demon Lover

"O where have you been, my long, long love,
　　This long seven years and more?"
"O I'm come to seek my former vows
　　Ye granted me before."

"O hold your tongue of your former vows,　　5
　　For they will breed sad strife;
O hold your tongue of your former vows
　　For I am become a wife."

He turn'd him right and round about,
　　And the tear blinded his ee;　　10
"I wad never hae trodden on Irish ground,
　　If it had not been for thee.

"I might have had a king's daughter,
　　Far, far beyond the sea;

I might have had a king's daughter,   15
    Had it not been for love o' thee.''

"If ye might have had a king's daughter,
    Yersell ye had to blame;
Ye might have taken the king's daughter,
    For ye kend that I was nane.   20

"If I was to leave my husband dear,
    And my two babes also,
O what have you to take me to,
    If with you I should go?"

"I hae seven ships upon the sea,   25
    The eighth brought me to land;
With four-and-twenty bold mariners,
    And music on every hand."

She has taken up her two little babes,
    Kiss'd them baith cheek and chin;   30
"O fair ye weel, my ain two babes,
    For I'll never see you again."

She set her foot upon the ship,
    No mariners could she behold;
But the sails were o' the taffetie,   35
    And the masts o' the beaten gold.

She had not sail'd a league, a league,
    A league but barely three,
When dismal grew his countenance,
    And drumlie grew his ee.   40

They had not sailed a league, a league,
    A league but barely three,
Until she espied his cloven foot,
    And she wept right bitterlie.

"O hold your tongue of your weeping," says he,   45
    "Of your weeping now let me be;
I will show you how the lilies grow
    On the banks of Italy."

"O what hills are yon, yon pleasant hills,
    That the sun shines sweetly on?"   50

"O yon are the hills of heaven," he said,
  "Where you will never win."

"O whaten a mountain is yon," she said,
  "All so dreary wi' frost and snow?"
"O yon is the mountain of hell," he cried,   55
  "Where you and I will go."

He struck the tapmast wi' his hand,
  The foremast wi' his knee;
And he brak that gallant ship in twain,
  And sank her in the sea.   60

Thomas Wyatt

[1503–1542]

They Flee from Me

They flee from me, that sometime did me seek,
With naked foot stalking in my chamber.
I have seen them, gentle, tame, and meek,
That now are wild, and do not remember
That sometime they put themselves in danger   5
To take bread at my hand; and now they range,
Busily seeking with a continual change.

Thanked be Fortune it hath been otherwise,
Twenty times better; but once in special,
In thin array, after a pleasant guise,   10
When her loose gown from her shoulders did fall,
And she me caught in her arms long and small,°   thin
And therewith all sweetly did me kiss
And softly said, "Dear heart, how like you this?"

It was no dream, I lay broad waking.   15
But all is turned, thorough° my gentleness,   through
Into a strange fashion of forsaking;
And I have leave to go, of her goodness,
And she also to use newfangleness.
But since that I so kindely am served,   20
I fain would know what she hath deserved.

Edmund Spenser

[1552–1599]

One Day I Wrote Her Name upon the Strand

One day I wrote her name upon the strand°,   beach
But came the waves and washéd it away:
Agayne I wrote it with a second hand,
But came the tyde, and made my paynes his pray.
"Vayne man," sayd she, "that doest in vaine assay,   5
A mortall thing so to immortalize,
For I my selve shall lyke to this decay,
And eek° my name bee wypéd out lykewize."   also
"Not so," quod° I, "let baser things devize°   said/devise
To dy in dust, but you shall live by fame: 10
My verse your vertues rare shall eternize,
And in the hevens wryte your glorious name.
Where whenas death shall all the world subdew,
Our love shall live, and later life renew."

Sir Walter Raleigh

[ca. 1552–1618]

The Nymph's Reply to the Shepherd

If all the world and love were young,
And truth in every shepherd's tongue,
These pretty pleasures might me move
To live with thee and be thy love.

Time drives the flocks from field to fold   5
When rivers rage and rocks grow cold,
And Philomel becometh dumb;
The rest complains of cares to come.

THE NYMPH'S REPLY TO THE SHEPHERD: An answer to Christopher Marlowe's "The Passionate Shepherd to His Love," p. 649.
7. **Philomel:** the nightingale. According to Ovid's *Metamorphoses,* Philomel's brother-in-law Tereus had her tongue cut out to prevent her from revealing that he had raped her.

The flowers do fade, and wanton fields
To wayward winter reckoning yields;   10
A honey tongue, a heart of gall,
Is fancy's spring, but sorrow's fall.

Thy gowns, thy shoes, thy beds of roses,
Thy cap, thy kirtle,° and thy posies   long dress
Soon break, soon wither, soon forgotten—   15
In folly ripe, in reason rotten.

Thy belt of straw and ivy buds,
Thy coral clasps and amber studs,
All these in me no means can move
To come to thee and be thy love.   20

But could youth last and love still breed,
Had joys no date° nor age no need,   end
Then these delights my mind might move
To live with thee and be thy love.

Christopher Marlowe

[1564–1593]

The Passionate Shepherd to His Love

Come live with me and be my love,
And we will all the pleasures prove°   try
That valleys, groves, hills, and fields,
Woods, or steepy mountain yields.

And we will sit upon the rocks,   5
Seeing the shepherds feed their flocks,
By shallow rivers to whose falls
Melodious birds sing madrigals.

And I will make thee beds of roses
And a thousand fragrant posies,   10
A cap of flowers, and a kirtle°   a long dress
Embroidered all with leaves of myrtle;

THE PASSIONATE SHEPHERD TO HIS LOVE: See Raleigh's "The Nymph's Reply to the
Shepherd."

A gown made of the finest wool
Which from our pretty lambs we pull;
Fair lined slippers for the cold,   15
With buckles of the purest gold;

A belt of straw and ivy buds,
With coral clasps and amber studs:
And if these pleasures may thee move,
Come live with me, and be my love.   20

The shepherds' swains shall dance and sing
For thy delight each May morning:
If these delights thy mind may move,
Then live with me and be my love.

William Shakespeare

(1564–1616)

From Sonnets

When to the Sessions of Sweet Silent Thought

When to the sessions of sweet silent thought
I summon up remembrance of things past
I sigh the lack of many a thing I sought,
And with old woes new wail my dear time's waste:
Then can I drown an eye, unused to flow,   5
For precious friends hid in death's dateless° night,   endless
And weep afresh love's long since canceled woe,
And moan the expense° of many a vanished sight: loss
Then can I grieve at grievances foregone,
And heavily from woe to woe tell o'er   10
The sad account of fore-bemoanéd moan,
Which I new pay as if not paid before.
But if the while I think on thee, dear friend,
All losses are restored and sorrows end.

WHEN TO THE SESSIONS. . .1. **sessions**: meetings of a judicial body.

When I Have Seen by Time's Fell Hand Defaced

When I have seen by time's fell° hand defaced   destructive
The rich-proud cost of outworn buried age;
When sometime° lofty towers I see down-razed,   formerly
And brass eternal slave to mortal rage;
When I have seen the hungry ocean gain   5
Advantage on the kingdom of the shore,
And the firm soil win of the watery main,
Increasing store with loss, and loss with store;
When I have seen such interchange of state,
Or state itself confounded to decay,   10
Ruin hath taught me thus to ruminate,
That time will come and take my love away.
This thought is as a death, which cannot choose
But weep to have that which it fears to lose.

Since Brass, nor Stone, nor Earth, nor Boundless Sea

Since brass, nor stone, nor earth, nor boundless sea
But sad mortality o'er-sways their power,
How with this rage shall beauty hold a plea,
Whose action is no stronger than a flower?
O, how shall summer's honey breath hold out   5
Against the wreckful siege of battering days,
When rocks impregnable are not so stout,
Nor gates of steel so strong, but Time decays?
O fearful meditation! where, alack,
Shall Time's best jewel from Time's chest lie hid?   10
Or what strong hand can hold his swift foot back?
Or who his spoil of beauty can forbid?
O, none, unless this miracle have might,
That in black ink my love may still shine bright.

When in Disgrace with Fortune and Men's Eyes

When, in disgrace with fortune and men's eyes,
I all alone beweep my outcast state,
And trouble deaf heaven with my bootless° cries,   useless

And look upon myself, and curse my fate,
Wishing me like to one more rich in hope, 5
Featured like him, like him with friends possessed,
Desiring this man's art and that man's scope,
With what I most enjoy contented least;
Yet in these thoughts myself almost despising,
Haply I think on thee—and then my state, 10
Like to the lark at break of day arising
From sullen earth, sings hymns at heaven's gate;
For thy sweet love remembered such wealth brings
That then I scorn to change my state with kings.

Not Marble, nor the Gilded Monuments

Not marble, nor the gilded monuments
Of princes, shall outlive this powerful rhyme;
But you shall shine more bright in these conténts
Than unswept stone, besmeared with sluttish time.
When wasteful war shall statues overturn, 5
And broils root out the work of masonry,
Nor Mars his sword nor war's quick fire shall burn
The living record of your memory.
'Gainst death and all-oblivious enmity
Shall you pace forth; your praise shall still find room. 10
Even in the eyes of all posterity
That wear this world out to the ending doom°.   judgment day
So, till the judgment that yourself arise,
You live in this, and dwell in lovers' eyes.

Let Me Not to the Marriage of True Minds

Let me not to the marriage of true minds
Admit impediments°. Love is not love   hindrances
Which alters when it alteration finds,
Or bends with the remover to remove:
Oh, no! it is an ever-fixéd mark, 5
That looks on tempests and is never shaken;
It is the star to every wandering bark,°   ship
Whose worth's unknown, although his height be taken.

LET ME NOT TO THE MARRIAGE OF TRUE MINDS 8. **height be taken**: its elevation be
measured.

Love's not Time's fool, though rosy lips and cheeks
Within his bending sickle's compass come;   10
Love alters not with his brief hours and weeks,
But bears° it out even to the edge of doom.°   lasts/judgment day
If this be error and upon me proved,
I never writ, nor no man ever loved.

Th' Expense of Spirit in a Waste of Shame

Th' expense of spirit in a waste of shame
Is lust in action; and till action, lust
Is perjured, murderous, bloody, full of blame,
Savage, extreme, rude, cruel, not to trust;
Enjoyed no sooner but despisèd straight: 5
Past reason hunted; and no sooner had,
Past reason hated, as a swallowed bait,
On purpose laid to make the taker mad:
Mad in pursuit, and in possession so;
Had, having, and in quest to have, extreme;   10
A bliss in proof,° and proved, a very woe;   in the experience
Before, a joy proposed; behind, a dream.
All this the world well knows; yet none knows well
To shun the heaven that leads men to this hell.

My Mistress' Eyes Are Nothing Like the Sun

My mistress' eyes are nothing like the sun;
Coral is far more red than her lips' red;
If snow be white, why then her breasts are dun;
If hairs be wires, black wires grow on her head.
I have seen roses damasked,° red and white,   variegated 5
But no such roses see I in her cheeks;
And in some perfumes is there more delight
Than in the breath that from my mistress reeks.
I love to hear her speak, yet well I know
That music hath a far more pleasing sound;   10
I grant I never saw a goddess go°;   walk
My mistress, when she walks, treads on the ground.
And yet, by heaven, I think my love as rare
As any she belied with false compare.

From *Twelfth Night*

When that I was and a little tiny boy,
   With hey, ho, the wind and the rain,
A foolish thing was but a toy,
   For the rain it raineth every day.

But when I came to man's estate,   5
   With hey, ho, the wind and the rain,
'Gainst knaves and thieves men shut their gate,
   For the rain it raineth every day.

But when I came, alas! to wive,
   With hey, ho, the wind and the rain,   10
By swaggering could I never thrive,
   For the rain it raineth every day.

But when I came unto my beds,
   With hey, ho, the wind and the rain,
With toss-pots still had drunken heads,   15
   For the rain it raineth every day.

A great while ago the world begun,
   With hey, ho, the wind and the rain,
But that's all one, our play is done,
   And we'll strive to please you every day.   20

Thomas Nashe

[1567–1601]

Adieu, Farewell, Earth's Bliss

Adieu, farewell, earth's bliss;
This world uncertain is;
Fond° are life's lustful joys;   foolish

ADIEU, FAREWELL, EARTH'S BLISS: Said to have been written during the plague that spread through London between 1592 and 1594.

Death proves them all but toys°;   trifles
None from his darts can fly;   5
I am sick, I must die.
   Lord, have mercy on us!

Rich men, trust not in wealth,
Gold cannot buy you health;
Physic himself must fade.   10
All things to end are made,
The plague full swift goes by;
I am sick, I must die.
   Lord, have mercy on us!

Beauty is but a flower   15
Which wrinkles will devour;
Brightness falls from the air;
Queens have died young and fair;
Dust hath closed Helen's eye.
I am sick, I must die.   20
   Lord, have mercy on us!

Strength stoops unto the grave,
Worms feed on Hector brave;
Swords may not fight with fate,
Earth still holds ope her gate.   25
"Come, come!" the bells do cry.
I am sick, I must die.
   Lord, have mercy on us.

Wit with his wantonness
Tasteth death's bitterness;   30
Hell's executioner
Hath no ears for to hear
What vain art can reply.
I am sick, I must die.
   Lord, have mercy on us.   35

Haste, therefore, each degree,
To welcome destiny;
Heaven is our heritage,
Earth but a player's stage;
Mount we unto the sky.   40
I am sick, I must die.
   Lord, have mercy on us.

John Donne

[1572–1631]

Song

Go, and catch a falling star,
   Get with child a mandrake root,
Tell me, where all past years are,
   Or who cleft the devil's foot,
Teach me to hear mermaids singing   5
Or to keep off envy's stinging,
      And find
      What wind
Serves to advance an honest mind.

If thou beest born to strange sights,   10
   Things invisible to see,
Ride ten thousand days and nights,
   Till age snow white hairs on thee;
Thou, when thou return'st, wilt tell me
All strange wonders that befell thee,   15
      And swear,
      No where
Lives a woman true, and fair.

If thou find'st one, let me know:
   Such a pilgrimage were sweet.   20
Yet do not, I would not go,
   Though at next door we might meet:
Though she were true when you met her,
And last till you write your letter,
      Yet she   25
      Will be
False, ere I come, to two, or three.

---

2. **mandrake root**: Resembling a human body, the forked root of the mandrake was used as a medicine to induce conception.

The Canonization

For God's sake hold your tongue, and let me love,
   Or chide my palsy, or my gout,
My five gray hairs, or ruined fortune, flout,
     With wealth your state, your mind with arts improve,
        Take you a course,° get you a place,°   direction/appointment 5
        Observe His Honor, or His Grace,
Or the King's real, or his stampéd face°   on a coin
     Contemplate; what you will, approve°,   try
     So you will let me love.

Alas, alas, who's injured by my love?   10
   What merchant's ships have my sighs drowned?
Who says my tears have overflowed his ground?
     When did my colds a forward spring remove?
       When did the heats which my veins fill
       Add one more to the plaguy bill?°   list of victims 15
Soldiers find wars, and lawyers find out still
     Litigious men, which quarrels move,
     Though she and I do love.

Call us what you will, we're made such by love;
   Call her one, me another fly,   20
We're tapers too, and at our own cost die,
     And we in us find th' eagle and the dove
       The phoenix riddle hath more wit°   sense
       By us: we two being one, are it.
So, to one neutral thing both sexes fit.   25
     We die and rise the same, and prove
     Mysterious by this love.

We can die by it, if not live by love,
   And if unfit for tombs and hearse
Our legend be, it will be fit for verse;   30
     And if no piece of chronicle we prove,
       We'll build in sonnets pretty rooms;
       As well a well-wrought urn becomes

---

   21. **at our own cost die**: Death was a metaphor for sexual intercourse; each act of sexual congress supposedly shortened one's life by a day.
   23. **the phoenix riddle**: a legendary, mythological bird, the only one of its kind. It is consumed in fire and then resurrected from the ashes to begin life anew.

The greatest ashes, as half-acre tombs;
  And by these hymns, all shall approve   35
  Us canonized for love:

And thus invoke us: You whom reverend love
  Made one another's hermitage;
You, to whom love was peace, that now is rage;
  Who did the whole world's soul contract, and drove   40
    Into the glasses of your eyes
    (So made such mirrors, and such spies,
That they did all to you epitomize)
  Countries, towns, courts: Beg from above
  A pattern of your love!

Hymn to God My God, in My Sickness

Since I am coming to that holy room
  Where, with Thy choir of saints for evermore,
I shall be made Thy music; as I come
  I tune the instrument here at the door,
  And what I must do then, think here before.   5

Whilst my physicians by their love are grown
  Cosmographers, and I their map, who lie
Flat on this bed, that by them may be shown
That this is my southwest discovery
Per fretum febris, by these straits to die,   10

I joy, that in these straits, I see my West;
  For, though their currents yield return to none,
What shall my West hurt me? As West and East
  In all flat maps (and I am one) are one,
  So death doth touch the resurrection.   15

Is the Pacific Sea my home? Or are
  The Eastern riches? Is Jerusalem?

HYMN TO GOD . . . 9–10. Magellan had discovered the straits which bear his name in 1520. They lie at the southern tip of South America and are hence southwest from England. *Per fretum febris:* through the straits of fever.
11. ". . . strait is the gate, and narrow is the way, which leadeth unto life. . ." (Matthew vii.14). **West:** i.e., death.

Anyan,° and Mágellan, and Gíbraltar,   Bering Straits
   All straits, and none but straits, are ways to them,
Whether where Japhet dwelt, or Cham, or Shem.   20

We think that Paradise and Calvary,
   Christ's cross, and Adam's tree, stood in one place;
Look, Lord, and find both Adams met in me;
   As the first Adam's sweat surrounds my face,
   May the last Adam's blood my soul embrace.   25

So, in his purple wrapped, receive me, Lord;
   By these his thorns give me his other crown;
And, as to others' souls I preached Thy word,
   Be this my text, my sermon to mine own:
   Therefore that he may raise the Lord throws down.   30

A Valediction: Forbidding Mourning

As virtuous men pass mildly away,
   And whisper to their souls to go,
Whilst some of their sad friends do say,
   "The breath goes now," and some say, "No,"

So let us melt, and make no noise,   5
   No tear-floods, nor sigh-tempests move;
'Twere profanation of our joys
   To tell the laity our love.

Moving of the earth° brings harms and fears,   earthquakes
   Men reckon what it did and meant;   10
But trepidation of the spheres,
   Though greater far, is innocent.

Dull sublunary° lovers' love   earthly
   (Whose soul is sense) cannot admit

---

20. The three sons of Noah, who settled in Europe, Africa, and Asia respectively after the Flood.
30. Adapted from Psalms cxlvi.8: ". . . the Lord raiseth them that are bowed down."
A VALEDICTION: FORBIDDING MOURNING 11. **trepidation of the spheres**: movement in the outermost of the heavenly spheres. In Ptolemy's astronomy these outer spheres caused others to vary from their orbits.

Absence, because it doth remove 15
    Those things which elemented° it. composed

But we, by a love so much refined
    That our selves know not what it is,
Inter-assured of the mind,
    Care less, eyes, lips, and hands to miss. 20

Our two souls therefore, which are one,
    Though I must go, endure not yet
A breach, but an expansion,
    Like gold to airy thinness beat.

If they be two, they are two so 25
    As stiff twin compasses are two:
Thy soul, the fixed foot, makes no show
    To move, but doth, if the other do;

And though it in the center sit,
    Yet when the other far doth roam, 30
It leans, and hearkens after it,
    And grows erect, as that comes home.

Such wilt thou be to me, who must,
    Like the other foot, obliquely run;
Thy firmness makes my circle just, 35
    And makes me end where I begun.

The Flea

Mark but this flea, and mark in this
How little that which thou deny'st me is;
It sucked me first, and now sucks thee,
And in this flea our two bloods mingled be;
Thou know'st that this cannot be said 5
A sin, nor shame, nor loss of maidenhead;
    Yet this enjoys before it woo,

---

26. **twin compasses**: the two feet of a mathematical compass used for drawing circles.

And pampered swells with one blood made of two,
And this, alas, is more than we would do.

Oh stay, three lives in one flea spare,   10
Where we almost, yea, more than married are.
This flea is you and I, and this
Our marriage bed and marriage temple is;
Though parents grudge, and you, we are met
And cloistered in these living walls of jet.   15
   Though use° make you apt to kill me,   custom
   Let not to that, self-murder added be,
   And sacrilege, three sins in killing three.

Cruel and sudden, hast thou since
Purpled thy nail in blood of innocence?   20
Wherein could this flea guilty be,
Except in that drop which it sucked from thee?
Yet thou triumph'st and say'st that thou
Find'st not thyself, nor me the weaker now.
   'Tis true. Then learn how false fears be: 25
   Just so much honor, when thou yield'st to me,
   Will waste, as this flea's death took life from thee.

Death, Be Not Proud

Death, be not proud, though some have callèd thee
Mighty and dreadful, for thou are not so;
For those whom thou think'st thou dost overthrow
Die not, poor Death, nor yet canst thou kill me.
From rest and sleep, which but thy pictures be,   5
Much pleasure; then from thee much more must flow,
And soonest our best men with thee do go,
Rest of their bones, and soul's delivery.
Thou art slave to fate, chance, kings, and desperate men,
And dost with poison, war, and sickness dwell,   10
And poppy or charms can make us sleep as well
And better than thy stroke; why swell'st thou then?
One short sleep past, we wake eternally
And death shall be no more; Death, thou shalt die.

DEATH, BE NOT PROUD and BATTER MY HEART . . .: from *Holy Sonnets.*

Batter My Heart, Three-Personed God

Batter my heart, three-personed God; for You
As yet but knock, breathe, shine, and seek to mend;
That I may rise and stand, o'erthrow me, and bend
Your force to break, blow, burn, and make me new.
I, like an usurped town, to another due,   5
Labor to admit You, but O, to no end;
Reason, Your viceroy in me, me should defend,
But is captived, and proves weak or untrue.
Yet dearly I love You, and would be lovéd fain°,   gladly
But am betrothed unto Your enemy.   10
Divorce me, untie or break that knot again;
Take me to You, imprison me, for I,
Except You enthrall me, never shall be free,
Nor ever chaste, except You ravish me.

Ben Jonson

[1573–1637]

On My First Daughter

Here lies, to each her parents' ruth°,   sorrow
Mary, the daughter of their youth;
Yet all heaven's gifts being heaven's due,
It makes the father less to rue.
At six months' end she parted hence   5
With safety of her innocence;
Whose soul heaven's queen, whose name she bears,
In comfort of her mother's tears,
Hath placed amongst her virgin-train:
Where, while that severed doth remain,   10
This grave partakes the fleshy birth;
Which cover lightly, gentle earth!

On My First Son

Farewell, thou child of my right hand, and joy;
My sin was too much hope of thee, loved boy:
Seven years thou wert lent to me, and I thee pay,
Exacted by thy fate, on the just day.
O could I lose all father now! for why   5
Will man lament the state he should envý,
To have so soon 'scaped world's and flesh's rage,
And, if no other misery, yet age?
Rest in soft peace, and asked, say, "Here doth lie
Ben Jonson his best piece of poetry."   10
For whose sake henceforth all his vows be such
As what he loves may never like too much.

Still to Be Neat, Still to Be Dressed

Still to be neat, still to be dressed,
As you were going to a feast;
Still to be powdered, still perfumed:
Lady, it is to be presumed,
Though art's hid causes are not found,   5
All is not sweet, all is not sound.

Give me a look, give me a face,
That makes simplicity a grace;
Robes loosely flowing, hair as free:
Such sweet neglect more taketh me   10
Than all the adulteries of art;
They strike mine eyes, but not my heart.

ON MY FIRST SON: 1. **child of my right hand**: the literal meaning, in Hebrew, of
Benjamin, the boy's name.
4. **the just day**: Jonson's son died on his seventh birthday.
STILL TO BE NEAT: Compare with Herrick's "Delight in Disorder," p. 665.

Come, My Celia

Come, my Celia, let us prove°,   experience
While we can, the sports of love;
Time will not be ours forever:
He at length our good will sever.
Spend not, then, his gifts in vain;   5
Suns that set may rise again,
But if once we lose this light,
'Tis with us perpetual night.
Why should we defer our joys?
Fame and rumor are but toys.   10
Cannot we delude the eyes
Of a few poor household spies?
Or his easier ears beguile,
Thus removéd by our wile?
'Tis no sin love's fruits to steal,   15
But the sweet thefts to reveal;
To be taken, to be seen,
These have crimes accounted been.

Robert Herrick

[1591–1664]

Upon Julia's Clothes

Whenas in silks my Julia goes,
Then, then, methinks, how sweetly flows
That liquefaction of her clothes.

Next, when I cast mine eyes and see
That brave vibration each way free,   5
O how that glittering taketh me!

COME, MY CELIA: Compare with Marvell's "To His Coy Mistress," pp. 673–674.

Delight in Disorder

A sweet disorder in the dress
Kindles in clothes a wantonness.
A lawn° about the shoulders thrown   fine, thin fabric
Into a fine distractiön;
An erring lace, which here and there   5
Enthralls the crimson stomacher,
A cuff neglectful, and thereby
Ribbons to flow confusedly;
A winning wave, deserving note,
In the tempestuous petticoat;   10
A careless shoestring, in whose tie
I see a wild civility;
Do more betwitch me than when art
Is too precise in every part.

His Prayer to Ben Jonson

When I a verse shall make,
    Know I have prayed thee,
For old religion's sake,
    Saint Ben, to aid me.

Make the way smooth for me,   5
    When I, thy Herrick,
Honoring thee, on my knee
    Offer my lyric.

Candles I'll give to thee,
    And a new altar;   10
And thou, Saint Ben, shalt be
    Writ in my psalter.

DELIGHT IN DISORDER 6. **stomacher**: ornamental covering worn under the lacing of the bodice.
HIS PRAYER TO BEN JONSON 12. **psalter**: a book containing the Psalms.

George Herbert

[1593–1633]

Easter Wings

Lord, who createdst man in wealth and store,°   abundance
Though foolishly he lost the same,
    Decaying more and more
      Till he became
        Most poor: 5
        With thee
      O let me rise
    As larks, harmoniously,
And sing this day thy victories:
Then shall the fall further the flight in me.   10

My   tender   age   in   sorrow   did   begin;
    And still with sicknesses and shame
      Thou didst so punish sin,
        That I became
        Most thin.   15
        With thee
      Let me combine,
    And feel this day thy victory:
For, if I imp my wing on thine,
Affliction   shall   advance   the   flight   in   me.   20

Jordan (I)

Who says that fictions only and false hair
Become a verse? Is there in truth no beauty?
Is all good structure in a winding stair?
May no lines pass, except they do their duty
    Not to a true, but painted chair?   5

EASTER WINGS 19. **imp**: a term from falconry: to graft new feathers onto the wing of a hawk to increase its flying capacity.
    JORDAN (I): The Jordan is the principal river in the Holy Land. (This is one of two "Jordan" poems by Herbert.)

Is it no verse, except enchanted groves
And sudden arbors shadow coarse-spun lines?
Must purling streams refresh a lover's loves?
Must all be veiled while he that reads, divines,
    Catching the sense at two removes?   10

Shepherds are honest people; let them sing:
Riddle who list, for me, and pull for prime:
I envy no man's nightingale or spring;
Nor let them punish me with loss of rhyme,
    Who plainly say, *My God, My King.*   15

The Collar

I struck the board° and cried, "No more;   table
    I will abroad!
What? shall I ever sigh and pine?
My lines and life are free, free as the road,
    Loose as the wind, as large as store.°   an abundance 5
        Shall I be still in suit?
    Have I no harvest but a thorn
    To let me blood, and not restore
What I have lost with cordial° fruit?   reviving, stimulating
        Sure there was wine   10
    Before my sighs did dry it; there was corn
    Before my tears did drown it.
Is the year only lost to me?
    Have I no bays to crown it,
No flowers, no garlands gay? All blasted?   15
        All wasted?
    No so, my heart; but there is fruit,
        And thou hast hands.
    Recover all thy sigh-blown age
On double pleasures: leave thy cold dispute   20
Of what is fit and not. Forsake thy cage,
        Thy rope of sands,
Which petty thoughts have made, and made to thee

---

12. **pull for prime**: draw for a winning card.
  THE COLLAR 14. **bays**: a wreath of bay, or laurel, was a sign of honor or victory in classical times.

Good cable, to enforce and draw,
    And be thy law,   25
While thou didst wink and wouldst not see.
    Away! take heed;
    I will abroad.
Call in thy death's-head there; tie up thy fears.
    He that forbears   30
    To suit and serve his need,
    Deserves his load."
But as I raved and grew more fierce and wild
    At every word,
Methought I heard one calling, *Child!*   35
    And I replied, *My Lord.*

The Pulley

When God at first made man,
Having a glass of blessings standing by,
    "Let us," said he, "pour on him all we can:
Let the world's riches, which dispersèd lie,
    Contract into a span."   5

So Strength first made a way;
Then Beauty flowed; then Wisdom, Honor, Pleasure.
    When almost all was out, God made a stay,
Perceiving that alone of all his treasure
    Rest in the bottom lay.   10

    "For if I should," said he,
"Bestow this jewel also on my creature,
    He would adore my gifts instead of me,
And rest in Nature, not the God of Nature;
    So both should losers be.   15

    "Yet let him keep the rest,
But keep them with repining restlessness:
    Let him be rich and weary, that at least,
If goodness lead him not, yet weariness
    May toss him to my breast."   20

John Milton

[1608–1674]

When I Consider How My Light Is Spent

When I consider how my light is spent
　Ere half my days, in this dark world and wide,
　And that one talent which is death to hide
　Lodged with me useless, though my soul more bent
To serve therewith my Maker, and present　　　　　　　　5
　My true account, lest he returning chide;
　"Doth God exact day-labor, light denied?"
　I fondly° ask; but Patience to prevent　　　　　　　　　　*foolishly*
That murmur, soon replies, "God doth not need
　Either man's work or his own gifts; who best　　　　　　10
　Bear his mild yoke, they serve him best. His state
Is kingly. Thousands at his bidding speed
　And post o'er land and ocean without rest:
　They also serve who only stand and wait."

Sonnet XXIII

Methought I saw my late espousèd saint
　Brought to me like Alcestis from the grave,
　Whom Jove's great son to her glad husband gave,
　Rescued from death by force, though pale and faint.
Mine, as whom washed from spot of child-bed taint　　　5
　Purification in the old Law did save,
　And such as yet once more I trust to have
　Full sight of her in heaven without restraint,

SONNET XXIII (Written in 1658) 1. **late . . . saint**: i.e., the woman I lately married, now one of the blessed in heaven. Milton's first wife died in 1652. In 1656 he married Katherine Woodcock, who bore a child in 1657 and died the following year.

3. **son**: Heracles; **husband**: Admetus.

4. **death**: In Euripides' play Death is personified as a figure with whom Heracles must contend.

6. **Law**: the ceremony for the purification of women after childbirth (Lev. 12). The reference is an external comparison which is not tied up with the precise circumstances of his wife's death.

7. **once more**: In Milton's dream his wife's face is veiled (as Alcestis's would be). When he hopes "once more" to have "Full sight of her in heaven without restraint," the condensed phrasing evidently means that his present visionary sight of her will become a full reality in heaven.

Came vested all in white, pure as her mind.
   Her face was veiled, yet to my fancied sight   10
   Love, sweetness, goodness in her person shined
So clear as in no face with more delight.
   But O as to embrace me she inclined,
   I waked, she fled, and day brought back my night.

Anne Bradstreet

[1612?–1672]

Before the Birth of One of Her Children

  All things within this fading world hath end,
  Adversity doth still our joys attend;
  No ties so strong, no friends so dear and sweet,
  But with death's parting blow is sure to meet.
  The sentence past is most irrevocable,   5
  A common thing, yet oh, inevitable.
  How soon, my Dear, death may my steps attend,
  How soon't may be thy lot to lose thy friend,
  We both are ignorant, yet love bids me
  These farewell lines to recommend to thee,   10
  That when that knot's untied that made us one,
  I may seem thine, who in effect am none,
  And if I see not half my days that's due,
  What nature would, God grant to yours and you;
  The many faults that well you know I have   15
  Let be interred in my oblivious grave;
  If any worth or virtue were in me,
  Let that live freshly in thy memory
  And when thou feel'st no grief, as I no harms,
  Yet love thy dead, who long lay in thine arms.   20
  And when thy loss shall be repaid with gains
  Look to my little babes, my dear remains.
  And if thou love thyself, or loved'st me,
  These O protect from step-dame's injury.
  And if chance to thine eyes shall bring this verse,   25
  With some sad sighs honour my absent hearse;
  And kiss this paper for thy love's dear sake,
  Who with salt tears this last farewell did take.

SONNET XXIII: 9. Rev. 7.13–14.

A Letter to Her Husband, Absent upon Public Employment

My head, my heart, mine eyes, my life, nay, more,
My joy, my magazine of earthly store,
If two be one, as surely thou and I,
How stayest thou there, whilst I at Ipswich lie?
So many steps, head from the heart to sever,   5
If but a neck, soon should we be together.
I, like the Earth this season, mourn in black,
My Sun is gone so far in's zodiac,
Whom whilst I 'joyed, nor storms, nor frost I felt,
His warmth such frigid colds did cause to melt,   10
My chilled limbs now numbed lie forlorn;
Return, return, sweet Sol,° from Capricorn;°   sun/winter
In this dead time, alas, what can I more
Than view those fruits which through thy heat I bore?
Which sweet contentment yield me for a space,   15
True living pictures of their father's face.
O strange effect! now thou art southward gone,
I weary grow the tedious day so long;
But when thou northward to me shalt return,
I wish my Sun may never set, but burn   20
Within the Cancer° of my glowing breast,   summer
The welcome house of him my dearest guest.
Where ever, ever stay, and go not thence,
Till nature's sad decree shall call thee hence;
Flesh of thy flesh, bone of thy bone,   25
I here, thou there, yet both but one.

In Memory of My Dear Grand-Child Elizabeth Bradstreet, Who Deceased August, 1665, Being a Year and a Half Old

Farewell dear babe, my heart's too much content,
Farewell sweet babe, the pleasure of mine eye,
Farewell fair flower that for a space was lent,
Then ta'en away unto eternity.
Blest babe, why should I once bewail thy fate,   5

Or sigh thy days so soon were terminate,
Sith thou art settled in an everlasting state.

By nature trees do rot when they are grown,
And plums and apples thoroughly ripe do fall,
And corn and grass are in their season mown,   10
And time brings down what is both strong and tall.
But plants new set to be eradicate,
And buds new blown to have so short a date,
Is by His hand alone that guides nature and fate.

The Author to Her Book

Thou ill-formed offspring of my feeble brain,
Who after birth did'st by my side remain,
Till snatched from thence by friends, less wise than true,
Who thee abroad exposed to public view;
Made thee in rags, halting, to the press to trudge,   5
Where errors were not lessened, all may judge.
At thy return my blushing was not small,
My rambling brat (in print) should mother call;
I cast thee by as one unfit for light,
Thy visage was so irksome in my sight;   10
Yet being mine own, at length affection would
Thy blemishes amend, if so I could:
I washed thy face, but more defects I saw,
And rubbing off a spot, still made a flaw.
I stretched thy joints to make thee even feet,   15
Yet still thou run'st more hobbling than is meet;
In better dress to trim thee was my mind,
But nought save homespun cloth, in the house I find.
In this array, 'mongst vulgars may'st thou roam;
In criticks hands beware thou dost not come;   20
And take thy way where yet thou are not known.
If for thy Father asked, say thou had'st none;
And for thy Mother, she alas is poor,
Which caused her thus to send thee out of door.

THE AUTHOR TO HER BOOK: This is Bradstreet's humorous reaction to seeing her poems
in print in 1650 without her authorization or correction. It appears that she intended this to
stand last among her poems when she revised them about 1666 for a proposed second edition.
Whoever sent the volume to the printer after her death added a subsequent section of thirteen
"Posthumous Poems."

Andrew Marvell

[1621–1678]

To His Coy Mistress

Had we but world enough, and time,
This coyness, lady, were no crime.
We would sit down, and think which way
To walk, and pass our long love's day.
Thou by the Indian Ganges' side   5
Shoudst rubies find; I by the tide
Of Humber would complain. I would
Love you ten years before the flood,
And you should, if you please, refuse
Till the conversion of the Jews.   10
My vegetable love should grow
Vaster than empires and more slow;
An hundred years should go to praise
Thine eyes, and on thy forehead gaze;
Two hundred to adore each breast,   15
But thirty thousand to the rest;
An age at least to every part,
And the last age should show your heart.
For, lady, you deserve this state,
Nor would I love at lower rate.   20
   But at my back I always hear
Time's wingèd chariot hurrying near;
And yonder all before us lie
Deserts of vast eternity.
Thy beauty shall no more be found;   25
Nor, in thy marble vault, shall sound
My echoing song; then worms shall try
That long-preserved virginity,
And your quaint° honor turn to dust,   overscrupulous
And into ashes all my lust: 30
The grave's a fine and private place,

---

6. **rubies**: associated with virginity.
7. **Humber**: the river than runs through Marvell's native town, Hull.
10. **the conversion of the Jews**: supposedly to occur at the end of time.
11. **vegetable love**: a reference to the idea that vegetables have the power to grow but lack consciousness.

But none, I think, do there embrace.
   Now therefore, while the youthful hue
Sits on thy skin like morning dew
And while thy willing soul transpires°   breathes forth 35
At every pore with instant fires,
Now let us sport us while we may,
And now, like amorous birds of prey,
Rather at once our time devour
Than languish in his slow-chapped° power.   slow-jawed 40
Let us roll all our strength and all
Our sweetness up into one ball,
And tear our pleasures with rough strife
Thorough the iron gates of life:
Thus, though we cannot make our sun   45
Stand still, yet we will make him run.

The Garden

How vainly men themselves amaze°   bewilder
To win the palm, the oak, or bays,
And their incessant labors see
Crowned from some single herb, or tree,
Whose short and narrow-vergèd shade   5
Does prudently their toils upbraid;
While all flowers and all trees do close
To weave the garlands of repose!

Fair Quiet, have I found thee here,
And Innocence, thy sister dear?   10
Mistaken long, I sought you then
In busy companies of men.
Your sacred plants, if here below,
Only among the plants will grow;
Society is all but rude°   uncivilized 15
To° this delicious solitude.   compared to

No white nor red was ever seen
So am'rous as this lovely green.
Fond lovers, cruel as their flame,

THE GARDEN 2. **palm, oak, or bays**: For military, political, and literary achievement.

Cut in these trees their mistress' name: 20
Little, alas, they know, or heed
How far these beauties hers exceed!
Fair trees, wheresoe'er your barks I wound,
No name shall but your own be found.

When we have run our passion's heat,   25
Love hither makes his best retreat.
The gods, that mortal beauty chase,
Still in a tree did end their race:
Apollo hunted Daphne so,
Only that she might laurel grow;   30
And Pan did after Syrinx speed,
Not as a nymph, but for a reed.

What wondrous life is this I lead!
Ripe apples drop about my head;
The luscious clusters of the vine   35
Upon my mouth do crush their wine;
The nectarine and curious peach
Into my hands themselves do reach;
Stumbling on melons, as I pass,
Insnared with flowers, I fall on grass.   40

Meanwhile the mind, from pleasure less,
Withdraws into its happiness;
The mind, that ocean where each kind
Does straight its own resemblance find;
Yet it creates, transcending these,   45
Far other worlds and other seas,
Annihilating all that's made
To a green thought in a green shade.

Here at the fountain's sliding foot,
Or at some fruit tree's mossy root,   50
Casting the body's vest° aside,   vestment
My soul into the boughs does glide:
There, like a bird, it sits and sings,
Then whets° and combs its silver wings,   preens

32. **but for a reed**: According to ancient mythology, Apollo pursued Daphne, who, spurning him, prayed for help and was transformed by the gods into a laurel tree. Syrinx similarly fled from Pan: Calling for help, she was turned into a tuft of reeds, which Pan made into his musical instrument—the shepherd's pipe.

And, till prepared for longer flight,   55
Waves in its plumes the various light.

   Such was that happy garden-state,
While man there walked without a mate:
After a place so pure, and sweet,
What other help could yet be meet°!   fitting 60
But 'twas beyond a mortal's share
To wander solitary there:
Two paradises 'twere in one
To live in paradise alone.

   How well the skillful gardener drew   65
Of flowers and herbs this dial new,
Where, from above, the milder sun
Does through a fragrant zodiac run;
And as it works, th' industrious bee
Computes its time as well as we!   70
How could such sweet and wholesome hours
Be reckoned but with herbs and flowers?

John Dryden

[1631–1700]

To the Memory of Mr. Oldham

Farewell, too little, and too lately known,
Whom I began to think and call my own;
For sure our souls were near allied, and thine
Cast in the same poetic mold with mine.
One common note on either lyre did strike,   5
And knaves and fools we both abhorred alike.
To the same goal did both our studies drive;
The last set out the soonest did arrive.
Thus Nisus fell upon the slippery place,

TO THE MEMORY OF MR. OLDHAM: John Oldham (1653–1683), English satirical poet.
  9. Nisus: As recounted in Virgil's *Aeneid*, Nisus fell when leading a race but tripped his
nearest competitor so that his friend Euryalus could win.

While his young friend performed and won the race.   10
O early ripe! to thy abundant store
What could advancing age have added more?
It might (what nature never gives the young)
Have taught the numbers of thy native tongue.
But satire needs not those, and wit will shine   15
Through the harsh cadence of a rugged line.
A noble error, and but seldom made,
When poets are by too much force betrayed.
Thy generous fruits, though gathered ere their prime,
Still showed a quickness; and maturing time   20
But mellows what we write to the dull sweets of rhyme.
Once more, hail and farewell; farewell, thou young,
But ah too short, Marcellus of our tongue;
Thy brows with ivy, and with laurels bound;
But fate and gloomy night encompass thee around.   25

Aphra Behn

[1640–1689]

The Willing Mistress

Amyntas led me to a grove,
   Where all the trees did shade us;
The sun itself, though it had strove,
   It could not have betrayed us.
The place secured from human eyes   5
   No other fear allows
But when the winds that gently rise
   Do kiss the yielding boughs.

Down there we sat upon the moss,
   And did begin to play   10
A thousand amorous tricks, to pass
   The heat of all the day.

---

14. **numbers**: measured rhythm in verse.
  23. **Marcellus**: favorite nephew of the Roman emperor Augustus. His untimely death at age 20 is mentioned in Virgil's *Aeneid*.
  THE WILLING MISTRESS: Song from Behn's play *The Dutch Lover*.

A many kisses did he give
    And I returned the same,
Which made me willing to receive   15
    That which I dare not name.

His charming eyes no aid required
    To tell their softening tale;
On her that was already fired,
    'Twas easy to prevail.   20
He did but kiss and clasp me round,
    Whilst those his thoughts expressed:
And laid me gently on the ground;
    Ah who can guess the rest?

Anne Finch

[1661–1720]

The Introduction

Did I my lines intend for public view,
How many censures° would their faults pursue,   condemnations
Some would, because such words they do affect,
Cry they're insipid, empty, uncorrect.
And many have attained, dull and untaught,   5
The name of wit only by finding fault.
True judges might condemn their want° of wit,   lack
And all might say they're by a woman writ.
Alas! a woman that attempts the pen
Such an intruder on the rights of men,   10
Such a presumptuous creature is esteemed,
The fault can by no virtue be redeemed.
They tell us we mistake our sex and way;
Good breeding, fashion, dancing, dressing, play
Are the accomplishments we should desire;   15

---

19. **fired**: i.e., made warm with desire.

To write, or read, or think, or to enquire
Would cloud our beauty, and exhaust our time,
And interrupt the conquests of our prime;°   i.e., of life
Whilst the dull manage of a servile house
Is held by some our utmost art, and use.   20
    Sure 'twas not ever thus, nor are we told
Fables, of women that excelled of old;
To whom, by the diffusive hand of Heaven
Some share of wit and poetry was given.
On that glad day on which the Ark returned,   25
The holy pledge for which the land had mourned,
The joyful tribes attend it on the way,
The Levites do the sacred charge convey,
Whilst various instruments before it play;
Here holy virgins in the concert join,   30
The louder notes to soften and refine,
And with alternate verse complete the hymn divine.
Lo! the young poet, after God's own heart,
By Him inspired, and taught the Muses' art,
Returned from conquest, a bright chorus meets,   35
That sing his slain ten thousand in the streets.
In such loud numbers they his acts declare,
Proclaim the wonders of his early war,
That Saul upon the vast applause does frown,
And feels its mighty thunder shake the crown.   40
What, can the threatened judgment now prolong?
Half of the kingdom is already gone;
The fairest half, whose influence guides the rest,
Have David's empire o'er their hearts confessed.
    A woman here leads fainting Israel on,   45
She fights, she wins, she triumphs with a song,
Devout, majestic, for the subject fit,
And far above her arms exalts her wit,
Then to the peaceful, shady palm withdraws,
And rules the rescued nation with her laws.   50

---

   25. **Ark**: the Ark of the Covenant, a chest containing the Ten Commandments, was carried by the Hebrews during their exile. The Ark was carried into Jerusalem by the priests of the Levites amid great celebration.

   33. **young poet**: David, a young Israelite musician and warrior, who killed the giant Goliath and defeated the Philistine army. King Saul of Israel grew jealous of the "vast applause" with which his people met David's heroism.

   45. Deborah, a prophetess who led the Israelites in battle, and wrote a song to praise the Lord for avenging her people.

How are we fallen, fallen by mistaken rules?
And education's, more than nature's fools,
Debarred from all improvements of the mind,
And to be dull, expected and designed,
And if some one would soar above the rest,   55
With warmer fancy and ambition pressed,
So strong th'opposing faction still appears.
The hopes to thrive can ne'er outweigh the fears.
Be cautioned then my Muse, and still retired;°   restrained
Nor be despised, aiming to be admired;   60
Conscious of wants, still with contracted wing,
To some few friends and to thy sorrows sing;
For groves of laurel thou wert never meant;
Be dark enough thy shades, and be thou there content.

Jonathan Swift

[1667–1745]

A Satirical Elegy on the Death of a Late Famous General

His Grace! impossible! what dead!
Of old age too, and in his bed!
And could that mighty warrior fall,
And so inglorious after all!
Well, since he's gone, no matter how,   5
The last loud trump° must wake him now;   trumpet
And, trust me, as the noise grows stronger,
He'll wish to sleep a little longer.

And could he be indeed so old
As by the news-papers we're told!   10
Threescore, I think, is pretty high,

---

63. **laurel**: laurel leaves were used to crown famous poets.
    A SATIRICAL ELEGY. . .: The subject is John Churchill, first Duke of Marlborough (1650–1722), English military commander and statesman. Dismissed from office on charges of embezzlement of public money, Churchill later was reinstated to his military post. He died of apoplexy.

'Twas time in conscience he should die:
This world he cumber'd° long enough,   encumbered
He burnt his candle to a snuff,
And that's the reason some folks think,   15
He left behind *so great a stink.*

Behold his funeral appears,
Nor widows sighs, nor orphans tears,
Wont at such time each heart to pierce,
Attend the progress of his herse.   20
But what of that, his friends may say,
He had those honours in his day;
True to his profit and his pride,
He made them weep before he dy'd.

    Come hither, all ye empty things   25
Ye bubbles rais'd by breath of kings,
Who float upon the tide of state,
Come hither, and behold your fate:
Let pride be taught by this rebuke,
How very mean a thing's a D—ke;   30
From all his ill-got honours flung,
Turn'd to that dirt, from whence he sprung.

Alexander Pope

[1688–1744]

From Part II of *An Essay on Criticism*

. . . Thus Critics, of less judgment than caprice,
Curious not knowing, not exact but nice,
Form short Ideas; and offend in arts
(As most in manners) by a love to parts.   ingenious
    Some to *Conceit*° alone their taste confine,   thought, or
                                                            elaborate metaphor.
And glittering thoughts struck out at every line;   90
Pleased with a work where nothing's just or fit;
One glaring Chaos and wild heap of wit.
Poets like painters, thus, unskilled to trace
The naked nature and the living grace,
With gold and jewels cover every part,   95
And hide with ornaments their want of art.

True Wit is Nature to advantage dressed,
What oft was thought, but ne'er so well expressed;
Something, whose truth convinced at sight we find,
That gives us back the image of our mind.   100
As shades more sweetly recommend the light,
So modest plainness sets off sprightly wit.
For works may have more wit than does 'em good,
As bodies perish through excess of blood.
     Others for *Language* all their care express,   105
And value books, as women men, for Dress:
Their praise is still,—the Style is excellent:
The Sense, they humbly take upon content.
Words are like leaves; and where they most abound,
Much fruit of sense beneath is rarely found.   110
False Eloquence, like the prismatic glass,
Its gaudy colours spreads on every place;
The face of Nature we no more survey,
All glares alike, without distinction gay:
But true Expression, like th' unchanging Sun,   115
Clears, and improves whate'er it shines upon,
It gilds all objects, but it alters none.
Expression is the dress of thought, and still
Appears more decent, as more suitable;
A vile conceit in pompous words expressed,   120
Is like a clown in regal purple dressed:
For different styles with different subjects sort,
As several garbs with country, town, and court.
Some by old words to fame have made pretence,
Ancients in phrase, mere moderns in their sense;   125
Such laboured nothings, in so strange a style,
Amaze th' unlearned, and make the learnèd smile.
Unlucky, as Fungoso in the Play,
These sparks with awkward vanity display
What the fine gentleman wore yesterday;   130
And but so mimic ancient wits at best,
As apes our grandsires, in their doublets drest.
In words, as fashions, the same rule will hold;
Alike fantastic, if too new, or old:
Be not the first by whom the new are tried,   135
Nor yet the last to lay the old aside.
     But most by Numbers° judge a Poet's song;   poetic meters
And smooth or rough, with them is right or wrong:
In the bright Muse though thousand charms conspire,

---

128. Play: Ben Jonson's *Every Man Out of His Humour.*

Her Voice is all these tuneful fools admire;   140
Who haunt Parnassus but to please their ear,
Not mend their minds; as some to Church repair,
Not for the doctrine, but the music there.
These equal syllables alone require,
Though oft the ear the open vowels tire;   145
While expletives their feeble aid do join;
And ten low words oft creep in one dull line:
While they ring round the same unvaried chimes,
With sure returns of still expected rhymes;
Where'er you find "the cooling western breeze,"   150
In the next line, it "whispers through the trees:"
If crystal streams "with pleasing murmurs creep,"
The reader's threatened (not in vain) with "sleep:"
Then, at the last and only couplet, fraught
With some unmeaning thing they call a thought,   155
A needless Alexandrine ends the song,
That, like a wounded snake, drags its slow length along.
Leave such to tune their own dull rhymes, and know
What's roundly smooth, or languishingly slow;
And praise the easy vigour of a line,   160
Where Denham's strength, and Waller's sweetness join.
True ease in writing comes from art, not chance,
As those move easiest who have learned to dance.
'Tis not enough no harshness gives offence,
The sound must seem an Echo to the sense: 165
Soft is the strain when Zephyr gently blows,
And the smooth stream in smoother numbers flows;
But when loud surges lash the sounding shore,
The hoarse, rough verse should like the torrent roar:
When Ajax strives some rock's vast weight to throw,   170
The line too labours, and the words move slow;
Not so, when swift Camilla scours the plain,
Flies o'er th' unbending corn, and skims along the main.
Hear how Timotheus' varied lays surprise,
And bid alternate passions fall and rise!   175
While, at each change, the son of Libyan Jove

---

141. **Parnassus**: Mountain home of the Muses.
161. Sir John **Denham** (1615–1669) and Edmund **Waller** (1606–1687) were poets Pope admired.
166. **Zephyr**: The West Wind.
170. **Ajax**: A strong warrior in Homer's *Iliad*.
172. **Camilla**: A maiden warrior in Vergil's *Aeneid*.
174. **Timotheus**: A Greek musician.
176. **the son of Libyon Jove**: A reference to Dryden's poem in praise of music, "Alexander's Feast."

Now burns with glory, and then melts with love;
Now his fierce eyes with sparkling fury glow,
Now sighs steal out, and tears begin to flow:
Persians and Greeks like turns of nature found,   180
And the World's victor stood subdued by Sound!
The power of Music all our hearts allow,
And what Timotheus was, is DRYDEN now.
    Avoid Extremes; and shun the fault of such,
Who still are pleased too little or too much.   185
At every trifle scorn to take offence,
That always shows great pride, or little sense;
Those heads, as stomachs, are not sure the best,
Which nauseate all, and nothing can digest.
Yet let not each gay Turn thy rapture move;   190
For fools admire,° but men of sense approve: wonder at
As things seem large which we through mists descry,
Dulness is ever apt to magnify.
    Some foreign writers, some our own despise;
The Ancients only, or the Moderns prize.   195
Thus Wit, like Faith, by each man is applied
To one small sect, and all are damned beside.
Meanly they seek the blessing to confine,
And force that sun but on a part to shine,
Which not alone the southern wit sublimes,   200
But ripens spirits in cold northern climes;
Which from the first has shone on ages past,
Enlights the present, and shall warm the last;
Though each may feel increases and decays,
And see now clearer and now darker days.   205
Regard not then if Wit be old or new,
But blame the false, and value still the true.
    Some ne'er advance a Judgment of their own,
But catch the spreading notion of the Town;
They reason and conclude by precedent,   210
And own stale nonsense which they ne'er invent.
Some judge of authors' names, not works, and then
Nor praise nor blame the writings, but the men.
Of all this servile herd, the worst is he
That in proud dulness joins with Quality.   215
A constant Critic at the great man's board,
To fetch and carry nonsense for my Lord.
What woeful stuff this madrigal would be,
In some starved hackney sonneteer, or me?
But let a Lord once own the happy lines,   220
How the wit brightens! how the style refines!

Before his sacred name flies every fault,
And each exalted stanza teems with thought!
   The Vulgar thus through Imitation err;
As oft the Learned by being singular;   225
So much they scorn the crowd, that if the throng
By chance go right, they purposely go wrong:
So Schismatics the plain believers quit,
And are but damned for having too much wit.
Some praise at morning what they blame at night;   230
But always think the last opinion right.
A Muse by these is like a mistress used,
This hour she's idolized, the next abused;
While their weak heads like towns unfortified,
Twixt sense and nonsense daily change their side.   235
Ask them the cause; they're wiser still, they say;
And still tomorrow's wiser than today.
We think our fathers fools, so wise we grow;
Our wiser sons, no doubt, will think us so.
Once School divines this zealous isle o'erspread;   240
Who knew most Sentences, was deepest read;
Faith, Gospel, all, seemed made to be disputed,
And none had sense enough to be confuted:
Scotists and Thomists, now, in peace remain,
Amidst their kindred cobwebs in Duck Lane.   245
If Faith itself has different dresses worn,
What wonder modes in Wit should take their turn?
Oft, leaving what is natural and fit,
The current folly proves the ready wit;
And authors think their reputation safe,   250
Which lives as long as fools are pleased to laugh.
   Some valuing those of their own side or mind,
Still make themselves the measure of mankind:
Fondly we think we honour merit then,
When we but praise ourselves in other men.   255
Parties in Wit attend on those of State,
And public faction doubles private hate.
Pride, Malice, Folly, against Dryden rose,
In various shapes of Parsons, Critics, Beaus;
But sense survived, when merry jests were past;   260
For rising merit will buoy up at last.
Might he return, and bless once more our eyes,

---

244. **Scotists** and **Thomists**: Followers of the differing theologians Duns Scotus (1265?–1308) and Thomas Aquinas (1225?–1274).
245. **Duck Lane**: A London street known for dealers in old books.

New Blackmores and new Milbourns must arise:
Nay should great Homer lift his awful head,
Zoilus again would start up from the dead.   265
Envy will merit, as its shade, pursue;
But like a shadow, proves the substance true;
For envied Wit, like Sol° eclipsed, makes known *the Sun*
Th' opposing body's grossness, not its own.
When first that sun too powerful beams displays, 270
It draws up vapours which obscure its rays;
But even those clouds at last adorn its way,
Reflect new glories, and augment the day.
 Be thou the first true merit to befriend;
His praise is lost, who stays till all commend. 275
Short is the date, alas, of modern rhymes,
And 'tis but just to let them live betimes.
No longer now that golden age appears,
When Patriarch wits survived a thousand years:
Now length of Fame (our second life) is lost, 280
And bare threescore is all even that can boast;
Our sons their fathers' failing language see,
And such as Chaucer is, shall Dryden be.
So when the faithful pencil has designed
Some bright Idea of the master's mind, 285
Where a new world leaps out at his command,
And ready Nature waits upon his hand;
When the ripe colours soften and unite,
And sweetly melt into just shade and light;
When mellowing years their full perfection give, 290
And each bold figure just begins to live,
The treacherous colours the fair art betray,
And all the bright creation fades away!
 Unhappy Wit, like most mistaken things,
Atones not for that envy which it brings. 295
In youth alone its empty praise we boast,
But soon the short-lived vanity is lost:
Like some fair flower the early spring supplies,
That gaily blooms, but even in blooming dies.
What is this Wit, which must our cares employ? 300
The owner's wife, that other men enjoy;
Then most our trouble still when most admired,
And still the more we give, the more required;
Whose fame with pains we guard, but lose with ease,

---

263. Richard **Blackmore** (1652–1729) and Luke **Milbourn** (1649–1720) attacked Dryden.
265. **Zoilus**: critic of Homer, fourth century B.C.

Sure some to vex, but never all to please;   305
'Tis what the vicious fear, the virtuous shun,
By fools 'tis hated, and by knaves undone!
   If Wit so much from Ignorance undergo,
Ah let not Learning too commence its foe!
Of old, those met rewards who could excel,   310
And such were praised who but endeavoured well:
Though triumphs were to generals only due,
Crowns were reserved to grace the soldiers too.
Now, they who reach Parnassus' lofty crown,
Employ their pains to spurn some others down;   315
And while self-love each jealous writer rules,
Contending wits become the sport of fools:
But still the worst with most regret commend,
For each ill Author is as bad a Friend.
To what base ends, and by what abject ways,   320
Are mortals urged through sacred lust of praise!
Ah ne'er so dire a thirst of glory boast,
Nor in the Critic let the Man be lost.
Good nature and good sense must ever join;
To err is human, to forgive, divine.   325
   But if in noble minds some dregs remain
Not yet purged off, of spleen and sour disdain;
Discharge that rage on more provoking crimes,
Nor fear a dearth in these flagitious° times.   vicious
No pardon vile Obscenity should find,   330
Though wit and art conspire to move your mind;
But Dulness with Obscenity must prove
As shameful sure as Impotence in love.
In the fat age of pleasure, wealth and ease,
Sprung the rank weed, and thrived with large increase: 335
When love was all an easy Monarch's care;
Seldom at council, never in a war:
Jilts ruled the state, and statesmen farces writ;
Nay wits had pensions, and young Lords had wit:
The Fair sat panting at a Courtier's play,   340
And not a Mask went unimproved away:
The modest fan was lifted up no more,
And Virgins smiled at what they blushed before.
The following license of a Foreign reign
Did all the dregs of bold Socinus drain;   345
Then unbelieving Priests reformed the nation,
And taught more pleasant methods of salvation;

---

345. **Socinus**: Author of the Socinian heresy condemned by the Inquisition.

Where Heaven's free subjects might their rights dispute,
Lest God himself should seem too absolute:
Pulpits their sacred satire learned to spare,   350
And Vice admired to find a flatterer there!
Encouraged thus, Wit's Titans braved the skies,
And the press groaned with licensed blasphemies.
These monsters, Critics! with your darts engage,
Here point your thunder, and exhaust your rage!   355
Yet shun their fault, who, scandalously nice,
Will needs mistake an author into vice;
All seems infected that th' infected spy,
As all looks yellow to the jaundiced eye.

Thomas Gray

[1716–1771]

Elegy Written in a Country Churchyard

The curfew tolls the knell of parting day,
    The lowing herd wind slowly o'er the lea,
The plowman homeward plods his weary way,
    And leaves the world to darkness and to me.

Now fades the glimmering landscape on the sight,   5
    And all the air a solemn stillness holds,
Save where the beetle wheels his droning flight,
    And drowsy tinklings lull the distant folds;

Save that from yonder ivy-mantled tower
    The moping owl does to the moon complain   10
Of such, as wandering near her secret bower,
    Molest her ancient solitary reign.

Beneath those rugged elms, that yew tree's shade,
    Where heaves the turf in many a moldering heap,
Each in his narrow cell forever laid,   15
    The rude° forefathers of the hamlet sleep.   rustic

The breezy call of incense-breathing morn,
    The swallow twittering from the straw-built shed,

The cock's shrill clarion, or the echoing horn°,   hunter's horn
   No more shall rouse them from their lowly bed.   20

For them no more the blazing hearth shall burn,
   Or busy housewife ply her evening care;
No children run to lisp their sire's return,
   Or climb his knees the envied kiss to share.

Oft did the harvest to their sickle yield,   25
   Their furrow oft the stubborn glebe° has broke;   soil
How jocund did they drive their team afield!
   How bowed the woods beneath their sturdy stroke!

Let not Ambition mock their useful toil,
   Their homely joys, and destiny obscure;   30
Nor Grandeur hear with a disdainful smile
   The short and simple annals of the poor.

The boast of heraldry, the pomp of power,
   And all that beauty, all that wealth e'er gave,
Awaits alike the inevitable hour.   35
   The paths of glory lead but to the grave.

Nor you, ye proud, impute to these the fault,
   If Memory o'er their tomb no trophies raise,   ornately
Where through the long-drawn aisle and fretted° vault   carved
   The pealing anthem swells the note of praise.   40

Can storied urn or animated° bust   lifelike
   Back to its mansion call the fleeting breath?
Can Honor's voice provoke° the silent dust,   call forth
   Or Flattery soothe the dull cold ear of Death?

Perhaps in this neglected spot is laid   45
   Some heart once pregnant with celestial fire;
Hands that the rod of empire might have swayed,
   Or waked to ecstasy the living lyre.

But Knowledge to their eyes her ample page
   Rich with the spoils of time did ne'er unroll;   50
Chill Penury repressed their noble rage°,   ardor
   And froze the genial current of the soul.

---

41. **storied urn**: an urn giving a person's history in a descriptive epitaph.

Full many a gem of purest ray serene,
   The dark unfathomed caves of ocean bear:
Full many a flower is born to blush unseen,   55
   And waste its sweetness on the desert air.

Some village Hampden, that with dauntless breast
   The little tyrant of his fields withstood;
Some mute inglorious Milton here may rest,
   Some Cromwell guiltless of his country's blood.   60

The applause of listening senates to command,
   The threats of pain and ruin to despise,
To scatter plenty o'er a smiling land,
   And read their history in a nation's eyes,

Their lot forbade: nor circumscribed alone   65
   Their growing virtues, but their crimes confined;
Forbade to wade through slaughter to a throne,
   And shut the gates of mercy on mankind,

The struggling pangs of conscious truth to hide,
   To quench the blushes of ingenuous shame,   70
Or heap the shrine of Luxury and Pride
   With incense kindled at the Muse's flame.

Far from the madding° crowd's ignoble strife,   milling
   Their sober wishes never learned to stray;
Along the cool sequestered vale of life   75
   They kept the noiseless tenor of their way.

Yet even these bones from insult to protect
   Some frail memorial still erected nigh,
With uncouth rhymes and shapeless sculpture decked,
   Implores the passing tribute of a sigh.   80

Their name, their years, spelt by the unlettered Muse,
   The place of fame and elegy supply:
And many a holy text around she strews,
   That teach the rustic moralist to die.

For who to dumb Forgetfulness a prey,   85
   This pleasing anxious being e'er resigned,

---

57. **Hampden**: John Hampden expressed opposition to a tax levied by Charles I, one of the events leading to civil war.

Left the warm precincts of the cheerful day,
    Nor cast one longing lingering look behind?

On some fond breast the parting soul relies,
    Some pious drops the closing eye requires;   90
Even from the tomb the voice of Nature cries,
    Even in our ashes live their wonted fires.

For thee, who mindful of the unhonored dead
    Dost in these lines their artless tale relate;
If chance, by lonely contemplation led,   95
    Some kindred spirit shall inquire thy fate,

Haply some hoary-headed swain may say,
    "Oft have we seen him at the peep of dawn
Brushing with hasty steps the dews away
    To meet the sun upon the upland lawn.   100

"There at the foot of yonder nodding beech
    That wreathes its old fantastic roots so high,
His listless length at noontide would he stretch,
    And pore upon the brook that babbles by.

"Hard by yon wood, now smiling as in scorn,   105
    Muttering his wayward fancies he would rove;
Now drooping, woeful-wan, like one forlorn,
    Or crazed with care, or crossed in hopeless love.

"One morn I missed him on the customed hill,
    Along the heath and near his favorite tree;   110
Another came; nor yet beside the rill,
    Nor up the lawn, nor at the wood was he;

"The next, with dirges due, in sad array,
    Slow through the churchway path we saw him borne.
Approach and read (for thou canst read) the lay°,   poem 115
    Graved on the stone beneath yon agèd thorn."

––––––– The Epitaph –––––––

Here rests his head upon the lap of Earth
    A youth to Fortune and to Fame unknown.
Fair Science° frowned not on his humble birth,   learning
    And Melancholy marked him for her own.   120

Large was his bounty, and his soul sincere;
  Heaven did a recompense as largely send:
He gave to Misery all he had, a tear;
  He gained from Heaven ('twas all he wished) a friend.

No farther seek his merits to disclose,   125
  Or draw his frailties from their dread abode
(There they alike in trembling hope repose),
  The bosom of his Father and his God.

Christopher Smart

[1722–1771]

From *Jubilate Agno*

For I will consider my Cat Jeoffry.
For he is the servant of the Living God, duly and daily serving him.
For at the first glance of the glory of God in the East he worships in his
  way.
For is this done by wreathing his body seven times round with elegant   700
  quickness.
For then he leaps up to catch the musk, which is the blessing of God
  upon his prayer.
For he rolls upon prank to work it in.
For having done duty and received blessing he begins to consider
  himself.
For this he performs in ten degrees.
For first he looks upon his forepaws to see if they are clean.   705
For secondly he kicks up behind to clear away there.
For thirdly he works it upon stretch with the forepaws extended.
For fourthly he sharpens his paws by wood.
For fifthly he washes himself.
For sixthly he rolls upon wash.   710

JUBILATE AGNO: ''Rejoice in the Lamb''; i.e., in Christ, the Lamb of God; written while
Smart was incarcerated for insanity.

For seventhly he fleas himself, that he may not be interrupted upon
   the beat.°   i.e., daily rounds

For eighthly he rubs himself against a post.
For ninthly he looks up for his instructions.
For tenthly he goes in quest of food.
For having considered God and himself he will consider his neighbor.   715
For if he meets another cat he will kiss her in kindness.
For when he takes his prey he plays with it to give it a chance.
For one mouse in seven escapes by his dallying.
For when his day's work is done his business more properly begins.
For he keeps the Lord's watch in the night against the adversary.   720
For he counteracts the powers of darkness by his electrical skin and
   glaring eyes.
For he counteracts the Devil, who is death, by brisking about the life.
For in his morning orisons° he loves the sun and the sun loves him.   prayers
For he is of the tribe of Tiger.
For the Cherub Cat is a term of the Angel Tiger.   725
For he has the subtlety and hissing of a serpent, which in goodness he
   suppresses.
For he will not do destruction if he is well-fed, neither will he spit
   without provocation.
For he purrs in thankfulness when God tells him he's a good Cat.
For he is an instrument for the children to learn benevolence upon.
For every house is incomplete without him, and a blessing is lacking in
   the spirit.   730
For the Lord commanded Moses concerning the cats at the departure
   of the Children of Israel from Egypt.
For every family had one cat at least in the bag.
For the English Cats are the best in Europe.
For he is the cleanest in the use of his forepaws of any quadruped.
For the dexterity of his defense is an instance of the love of God to   735
   him exceedingly.
For he is the quickest to his mark of any creature.
For he is tenacious of his point.
For he is a mixture of gravity and waggery.
For he knows that God is his Saviour.
For there is nothing sweeter than his peace when at rest.   740
For there is nothing brisker than his life when in motion.
For he is of the Lord's poor, and so indeed is he called by benevolence
   perpetually—Poor Jeoffry! poor Jeoffry! the rat has bit thy throat.
For I bless the name of the Lord Jesus that Jeoffry is better.
For the divine spirit comes about his body to sustain it in complete cat.
For his tongue is exceeding pure so that it has in purity what it wants   745
   in music.
For he is docile and can learn certain things.

For he can sit up with gravity, which is patience upon approbation.
For he can fetch and carry, which is patience in employment.
For he can jump over a stick, which is patience upon proof positive.
For he can spraggle upon waggle at the word of command.   750
For he can jump from an eminence into his master's bosom.
For he can catch the cork and toss it again.
For he is hated by the hypocrite and miser.
For the former is afraid of detection.
For the latter refuses the charge.   755
For he camels his back to bear the first notion of business.
For he is good to think on, if a man would express himself neatly.
For he made a great figure in Egypt for his signal services.
For he killed the Icneumon rat, very pernicious by land.
For his ears are so acute that they sting again.   760
For from this proceeds the passing quickness of his attention.
For by stroking of him I have found out electricity.
For I perceived God's light about him both wax and fire.
For the electrical fire is the spiritual substance which God sends from
     heaven to sustain the bodies both of man and beast.
For God has blessed him in the variety of his movements.   765
For, though he cannot fly, he is an excellent clamberer.
For his motions upon the face of the earth are more than any other
     quadruped.
For he can tread to all the measures upon the music.
For he can swim for life.
For he can creep.   770

Phillis Wheatley

[ca. 1753?–1784]

On Being Brought from Africa to America

'Twas mercy brought me from my pagan land,
Taught my benighted soul to understand
That there's a God, that there's a Saviour too:
Once I redemption neither sought nor knew.

---

759. **Icneumon rat**: The ichneumon, a type of weasel.

Some view that sable race with scornful eye: 5
"Their colour is a diabolic dye."
Remember, Christians, Negroes black as Cain
May be refined and join the angelic strain.

To the Right Honourable William, Earl of Dartmouth, His Majesty's Principal Secretary of State for North America, Etc.

Hail, happy day, when, smiling like the morn,
Fair Freedom rose New England to adorn:
The northern clime beneath her genial ray,
Dartmouth, congratulates thy blissful sway:°   leadership
Elate with hope her race no longer mourns,   5
Each soul expands, each grateful bosom burns,
While in thine hand with pleasure we behold
The silken reins, and Freedom's charms unfold.
Long lost to realms beneath the northern skies
She shines supreme, while hated Faction dies: 10
Soon as appeared the goddess long desir'd,
Sick at the view, she languish'd and expir'd;
Thus from the splendors of the morning light
The owl in sadness seeks the caves of night.

No more, America, in mournful strain   15
Of wrongs, and grievance unredressed complain,
No longer shalt thou dread the iron chain
Which wanton Tyranny with lawless hand
Had made, and with it meant to enslave the land.

Should you, my lord, while you peruse my song,   20
Wonder from whence my love of Freedom sprung,

ON BEING BROUGHT FROM AFRICA TO AMERICA 7. Cain murdered his brother Abel, and for this God "marked" him so that his crime would be known. This mark was sometimes interpreted as the origin of the Negro.
   TO THE RIGHT HONORABLE WILLIAM . . .: Lord Dartmouth was appointed secretary in charge of the American colonies in 1772.

Whence flow these wishes for the common good,
By feeling hearts alone best understood,
I, young in life, by seeming cruel fate,
Was snatched from Afric's fancied happy seat: 25
What pangs excruciating must molest,
What sorrows labour in my parents' breast?
Steeled was that soul and by no misery moved
That from a father seized his babe beloved:
Such, such my case. And can I then but pray   30
Others may never feel tyrannic sway?

    For favours past, great Sir, our thanks are due,
And thee we ask thy favors to renew,
Since in thy power, as in thy will before,
To soothe the griefs which thou didst once deplore.   35
May heavenly grace the sacred sanction give
To all thy works, and thou forever live
Not only on the wings of fleeting Fame,
Though praise immortal crowns the patriot's name,
But to conduct to heaven's refulgent fane,   40
May fiery coursers° sweep the ethereal plain,   swift horses
And bear thee upwards to that blessed abode,
Where, like the prophet, thou shalt find thy God.

William Blake

[1757–1827]

The Clod & the Pebble

"Love seeketh not Itself to please,
Nor for itself hath any care;
But for another gives its ease,
And builds a Heaven in Hell's despair."

    So sang a little Clod of Clay,   5
    Trodden with the cattle's feet;

But a Pebble of the brook
Warbled out these metres meet:

"Love seeketh only Self to please,
To bind another to its delight,   10
Joys in another's loss of ease,
And builds a Hell in Heaven's despite."

The Lamb

   Little Lamb, who made thee?
   Dost thou know who made thee?
Gave thee life & bid thee feed,
By the stream & o'er the mead;
Gave thee clothing of delight,   5
Softest clothing wooly bright;
Gave thee such a tender voice,
Making all the vales rejoice!
   Little Lamb who made thee?
   Dost thou know who made thee?   10

   Little Lamb I'll tell thee,
   Little Lamb I'll tell thee!
He is calléd by thy name,
For he calls himself a Lamb:
He is meek & he is mild,   15
He became a little child:
I a child & thou a lamb,
We are calléd by his name.
   Little Lamb God bless thee.
   Little Lamb God bless thee.   20

The Tyger

Tyger! Tyger! burning bright
In the forests of the night,
What immortal hand or eye
Could frame thy fearful symmetry?

In what distant deeps or skies   5
Burnt the fire of thine eyes?
On what wings dare he aspire?
What the hand, dare seize the fire?

And what shoulder, & what art,
Could twist the sinews of thy heart?   10
And when thy heart began to beat,
What dread hand? & what dread feet?

What the hammer? what the chain?
In what furnace was thy brain?
What the anvil? what dread grasp   15
Dare its deadly terrors clasp?

When the stars threw down their spears,
And water'd heaven with their tears,
Did he smile his work to see?
Did he who made the Lamb make thee?   20

Tyger! Tyger! burning bright
In the forests of the night,
What immortal hand or eye
Dare frame thy fearful symmetry?

Ah Sun-flower

Ah, Sun-flower! weary of time,
Who countest the steps of the Sun,
Seeking after that sweet golden clime
Where the traveller's journey is done;

Where the Youth pined away with desire,   5
And the pale Virgin shrouded in snow,
Arise from their graves and aspire,
Where my Sun-flower wishes to go.

The Sick Rose

O Rose, thou art sick!
The invisible worm

That flies in the night,
In the howling storm,

Has found out thy bed   5
Of crimson joy:
And his dark secret love
Does thy life destroy.

London

I wander thro' each charter'd° street   Pre-empted or rented
Near where the charter'd Thames does flow,
And mark in every face I meet
Marks of weakness, marks of woe.

In every cry of every man,   5
In every Infant's cry of fear,
In every voice, in every ban,
The mind-forg'd manacles I hear.

How the Chimney-sweeper's cry
Every blackning Church appalls;   10
And the hapless Soldier's sigh
Runs in blood down Palace walls.

But most thro' midnight streets I hear
How the youthful Harlot's curse
Blasts the new-born Infant's tear,   15
And blights with plagues the Marriage hearse.

Robert Burns

[1759–1796]

A Red, Red Rose

O my luve's like a red, red rose,
    That's newly sprung in June;
O my luve's like the melodie
    That's sweetly played in tune.

As fair art thou, my bonnie lass,   5
    So deep in luve am I;
And I will luve thee still, my dear,
    Till a' the seas gang dry.

Till a' the seas gang dry, my dear,
    And the rocks melt wi' the sun: 10
O I will love thee still, my dear,
    While the sands o' life shall run.

And fare thee weel, my only love,
    And fare thee weel awhile!
And I will come again, my luve,   15
    Though it were ten thousand mile.

To a Mouse

ON TURNING HER UP IN HER NEST WITH THE PLOUGH, NOVEMBER, 1785

Wee, sleekit,° cow'rin, tim'rous beastie,   *sleek*
O, what a panic's in thy breastie!
Thou need na start awa sae hasty,
    Wi' bickering° brattle!°   *hurried/clatter*
I wad be laith to rin an' chase thee,   5
    Wi' murd'ring pattle!°   *paddle*

I'm truly sorry man's dominion
Has broken Nature's social union,
An' justifies that ill opinion
    Which makes thee startle   10
At me, thy poor earth-born companion,
    An' fellow-mortal!

I doubt na, whiles but thou may thieve;
What then? poor beastie, thou maun° live!   *must*
A daimen° icker° in a thrave°   *occasional/corn-ear/bundle* 15
    'S a sma' request:
I'll get a blessin wi' the lave,°   *rest*
    And never miss't!

Thy wee bit housie, too, in ruin!
Its silly° wa's the win's are stewin!   *feeble* 20

An' naething, now, to big° a new ane,   build
        O' foggage° green!   mosses
An' bleak December's winds ensuin,
        Baith snell° an' keen!   severe

Thou saw the fields laid bare and waste,   25
An' weary winter comin fast,
An' cozie here, beneath the blast,
        Thou thought to dwell,
Till crash! the cruel coulter° past   plowshare
        Out thro' thy cell.   30

That wee bit heap o' leaves an' stibble°   stubble
Has cost thee mony a weary nibble!
Now thou's turned out, for a' thy trouble,
        But° house or hald,   without
To thole° the winter's sleety dribble,   endure 35
        An' cranreuch° cauld!   hoarfrost

But, Mousie, thou art no thy lane,°   not alone
In proving foresight may be vain:
The best laid schemes o' mice an' men
        Gang° aft a-gley.°   go/awry 40
An' lea'e us nought but grief an' pain
        For promised joy.

Still thou art blest, compared wi' me!
The present only toucheth thee:
But och! I backward cast my e'e   45
        On prospects drear!
An' forward, tho' I canna see,
        I guess an' fear!

William Wordsworth

[1770–1850]

Sonnet: The World Is Too Much with Us

The world is too much with us; late and soon,
Getting and spending, we lay waste our powers:

Little we see in Nature that is ours;
We have given our hearts away, a sordid boon°!   gift
This Sea that bares her bosom to the moon;   5
The winds that will be howling at all hours,
And are up-gathered now like sleeping flowers;
For this, for everything, we are out of tune;
It moves us not.—Great God! I'd rather be
A Pagan suckled in a creed outworn;   10
So might I, standing on this pleasant lea,
Have glimpses that would make me less forlorn;
Have sight of Proteus rising from the sea;
Or hear old Triton blow his wreathèd horn.

The Solitary Reaper

Behold her, single in the field,
Yon solitary Highland Lass!
Reaping and singing by herself;
Stop here, or gently pass!
Alone she cuts and binds the grain,   5
And sings a melancholy strain;
O listen! for the Vale profound
Is overflowing with the sound.

No Nightingale did ever chaunt
More welcome notes to weary bands   10
Of travelers in some shady haunt,
Among Arabian sands;
A voice so thrilling ne'er was heard
In springtime from the Cuckoo bird,
Breaking the silence of the seas   15
Among the farthest Hebrides.

Will no one tell me what she sings?—
Perhaps the plaintive numbers flow
For old, unhappy, far-off things,
And battles long ago;   20
Or is it some more humble lay,
Familiar matter of today?

THE WORLD IS TOO MUCH WITH US 13–14. **Proteus . . . Triton:** classical sea gods.
Triton's conch-shell horn calmed the waves.

Some natural sorrow, loss, or pain,
That has been, and may be again?

Whate'er the theme, the Maiden sang   25
As if her song could have no ending;
I saw her singing at her work,
And o'er the sickle bending;—
I listened, motionless and still;
And, as I mounted up the hill,   30
The music in my heart I bore,
Long after it was heard no more.

Lines

COMPOSED A FEW MILES ABOVE TINTERN ABBEY, ON REVISITING
THE BANKS OF THE WYE DURING A TOUR. JULY 13, 1798

Five years have passed; five summers, with the length
Of five long winters! and again I hear
These waters, rolling from their mountain-springs
With a soft inland murmur.— Once again
Do I behold these steep and lofty cliffs,   5
That on a wild secluded scene impress
Thoughts of more deep seclusion; and connect
The landscape with the quiet of the sky.
The day is come when I again repose
Here, under this dark sycamore, and view   10
These plots of cottage ground, these orchard tufts,
Which at this season, with their unripe fruits,
Are clad in one green hue, and lose themselves
Mid groves and copses°. Once again I see   thickets
These hedgerows, hardly hedgerows, little lines   15
Of sportive wood run wild: these pastoral farms,
Green to the very door; and wreaths of smoke
Sent up, in silence, from among the trees!
With some uncertain notice, as might seem
Of vagrant dwellers in the houseless woods,   20
Or of some Hermit's cave, where by his fire
The Hermit sits alone.

These beauteous forms,
Through a long absence, have not been to me
As is a landscape to a blind man's eye:
But oft, in lonely rooms, and 'mid the din   25

Of towns and cities, I have owed to them,
In hours of weariness, sensations sweet,
Felt in the blood, and felt along the heart;
And passing even into my purer mind
With tranquil restoration:—feelings too   30
Of unremembered pleasure: such, perhaps,
As have no slight or trivial influence
On that best portion of a good man's life,
His little, nameless, unremembered, acts
Of kindness and of love. Nor less, I trust,   35
To them I may have owed another gift,
Of aspect more sublime; that blessed mood,
In which the burthen of the mystery,
In which the heavy and the weary weight
Of all this unintelligible world,   40
Is lightened:—that serene and blessed mood,
In which the affections gently lead us on,—
Until, the breath of this corporeal frame
And even the motion of our human blood
Almost suspended, we are laid asleep   45
In body, and become a living soul:
While with an eye made quiet by the power
Of harmony, and the deep power of joy,
We see into the life of things.

                        If this
Be but a vain belief, yet, oh! how oft—   50
In darkness and amid the many shapes
Of joyless daylight; when the fretful stir
Unprofitable, and the fever of the world,
Have hung upon the beatings of my heart—
How oft, in spirit, have I turned to thee,   55
O sylvan Wye! thou wanderer through the woods,
How often has my spirit turned to thee!

   And now, with gleams of half-extinguished thought,
With many recognitions dim and faint,
And somewhat of a sad perplexity,   60
The picture of the mind revives again:
While here I stand, not only with the sense
Of present pleasure, but with pleasing thoughts
That in this moment there is life and food
For future years. And so I dare to hope,   65
Though changed, no doubt, from what I was when first
I came among these hills; when like a roe
I bounded o'er the mountains, by the sides

Of the deep rivers, and the lonely streams,
Wherever nature led: more like a man   70
Flying from something that he dreads than one
Who sought the thing he loved. For nature then
(The coarser pleasures of my boyish days,
And their glad animal movements all gone by)
To me was all in all.—I cannot paint   75
What then I was. The sounding cataract
Haunted me like a passion: the tall rock,
The mountain, and the deep and gloomy wood,
Their colors and their forms, were then to me
An appetite; a feeling and a love,   80
That had no need of a remoter charm,
By thought supplied, nor any interest
Unborrowed from the eye.—That time is past,
And all its aching joys are now no more,
And all its dizzy raptures. Not for this   85
Faint I, nor mourn nor murmur; other gifts
Have followed; for such loss, I would believe,
Abundant recompense. For I have learned
To look on nature, not as in the hour
Of thoughtless youth; but hearing oftentimes   90
The still, sad music of humanity,
Nor harsh nor grating, though of ample power
To chasten and subdue. And I have felt
A presence that disturbs me with the joy
Of elevated thoughts; a sense sublime   95
Of something far more deeply interfused,
Whose dwelling is the light of setting suns,
And the round ocean and the living air,
And the blue sky, and in the mind of man:
A motion and a spirit, that impels   100
All thinking things, all objects of all thought,
And rolls through all things. Therefore am I still
A lover of the meadows and the woods,
And mountains; and of all that we behold
From this green earth; of all the mighty world   105
Of eye, and ear,—both what they half create,
And what perceive; well pleased to recognize
In nature and the language of the sense
The anchor of my purest thoughts, the nurse,
The guide, the guardian of my heart, and soul   110
Of all my moral being.

              Nor perchance,
If I were not thus taught, should I the more

Suffer my genial spirits° to decay: powers
For thou art with me here upon the banks
Of this fair river; thou my dearest Friend,   115
My dear, dear Friend; and in thy voice I catch
The language of my former heart, and read
My former pleasures in the shooting lights
Of thy wild eyes. Oh! yet a little while
May I behold in thee what I was once,   120
My dear, dear Sister! and this prayer I make,
Knowing that Nature never did betray
The heart that loved her; 'tis her privilege,
Through all the years of this our life, to lead
From joy to joy: for she can so inform°   give form to   125
The mind that is within us, so impress
With quietness and beauty, and so feed
With lofty thoughts, that neither evil tongues,
Rash judgments, nor the sneers of selfish men,
Nor greetings where no kindness is, nor all   130
The dreary intercourse of daily life,
Shall e'er prevail against us, or disturb
Our cheerful faith, that all which we behold
Is full of blessings. Therefore let the moon
Shine on thee in thy solitary walk;   135
And let the misty mountain winds be free
To blow against thee: and, in after years,
When these wild ecstasies shall be matured
Into a sober pleasure; when thy mind
Shall be a mansion for all lovely forms,   140
Thy memory be as a dwelling place
For all sweet sounds and harmonies; oh! then,
If solitude, or fear, or pain, or grief
Should be thy portion, with what healing thoughts
Of tender joy wilt thou remember me,   145
And these my exhortations! Nor, perchance—
If I should be where I no more can hear
Thy voice, nor catch from thy wild eyes these gleams
Of past existence—wilt thou then forget
That on the banks of this delightful stream   150
We stood together; and that I, so long
A worshiper of Nature, hither came
Unwearied in that service: rather say
With warmer love—oh! with far deeper zeal
Of holier love. Nor wilt thou then forget   155

---

115. **Friend:** Wordsworth's sister, Dorothy.

That after many wanderings, many years
Of absence, these steep woods and lofty cliffs,
And this green pastoral landscape, were to me
More dear, both for themselves and for thy sake!

Samuel Taylor Coleridge

[1772–1834]

Kubla Khan

OR A VISION IN A DREAM. A FRAGMENT

In Xanadu did Kubla Khan
A stately pleasure-dome decree:
Where Alph, the sacred river, ran
Through caverns measureless to man
   Down to a sunless sea.   5
So twice five miles of fertile ground
With walls and towers were girdled round:
And there were gardens bright with sinuous rills,
Where blossomed many an incense-bearing tree;
And here were forests ancient as the hills,   10
Enfolding sunny spots of greenery.

But oh! that deep romantic chasm which slanted
Down the green hill athwart a cedarn cover!
A savage place! as holy and enchanted
As e'er beneath a waning moon was haunted   15
By woman wailing for her demon-lover!
And from this chasm, with ceaseless turmoil seething,
As if this earth in fast thick pants were breathing,
A mighty fountain momently was forced:
Amid whose swift half-intermitted burst   20
Huge fragments vaulted like rebounding hail,
Or chaffy grain beneath the thresher's flail:
And 'mid these dancing rocks at once and ever
It flung up momently the sacred river.
Five miles meandering with a mazy motion   25

KUBLA KHAN: The poem is named after the first ruler of the Mongol dynasty in thirteenth-century China. Coleridge's topography and place names are imaginary.

Through wood and dale the sacred river ran,
Then reached the caverns measureless to man,
And sank in tumult to a lifeless ocean:
And 'mid this tumult Kubla heard from far
Ancestral voices prophesying war!   30
     The shadow of the dome of pleasure
     Floated midway on the waves;
     Where was heard the mingled measure
     From the fountain and the caves.
It was a miracle of rare device,   35
A sunny pleasure-dome with caves of ice!

     A damsel with a dulcimer
     In a vision once I saw:
     It was an Abyssinian maid,
     And on her dulcimer she played,   40
     Singing of Mount Abora.
     Could I revive within me
     Her symphony and song,
     To such a deep delight 'twould win me,
That with music loud and long,   45
I would build that dome in air,
That sunny dome! those caves of ice!
And all who heard should see them there,
And all should cry, Beware! Beware!
His flashing eyes, his floating hair!   50
Weave a circle round him thrice,
And close your eyes with holy dread,
For he on honey-dew hath fed,
And drunk the milk of Paradise.

George Gordon, Lord Byron

[1788–1824]

She Walks in Beauty

1

She walks in beauty, like the night
     Of cloudless climes and starry skies;

And all that's best of dark and bright
  Meet in her aspect and her eyes:
Thus mellowed to that tender light   5
  Which heaven to gaudy day denies.

2

One shade the more, one ray the less,
  Had half impaired the nameless grace
Which waves in every raven tress,
  Or softly lightens o'er her face;   10
Where thoughts serenely sweet express
  How pure, how dear their dwelling place.

3

And on that cheek, and o'er that brow,
  So soft, so calm, yet eloquent,
The smiles that win, the tints that glow,   15
  But tell of days in goodness spent,
A mind at peace with all below,
  A heart whose love is innocent!

Percy Bysshe Shelley

[1792–1822]

Ozymandias

I met a traveler from an antique land
Who said: Two vast and trunkless legs of stone
Stand in the desert . . . Near them, on the sand,
Half sunk, a shattered visage lies, whose frown,
And wrinkled lip, and sneer of cold command,   5
Tell that its sculptor well those passions read
Which yet survive, stamped on these lifeless things,
The hand that mocked them, and the heart that fed:
And on the pedestal these words appear:

OZYMANDIAS: Greek name for the Egyptian ruler Rameses II, who erected a huge statue in his own likeness.

"My name is Ozymandias, king of kings: 10
Look on my works, ye Mighty, and despair!''
Nothing beside remains. Round the decay
Of that colossal wreck, boundless and bare
The lone and level sands stretch far away.

Ode to the West Wind

1

O wild West Wind, thou breath of Autumn's being,
Thou, from whose unseen presence the leaves dead
Are driven, like ghosts from an enchanter fleeing,

Yellow, and black, and pale, and hectic red,
Pestilence-stricken multitudes: O thou,   5
Who chariotest to their dark wintry bed

The wingéd seeds, where they lie cold and low,
Each like a corpse within its grave, until
Thine azure sister of the Spring shall blow

Her clarion° o'er the dreaming earth, and fill   trumpet call   10
(Driving sweet buds like flocks to feed in air)
With living hues and odors plain and hill:

Wild Spirit, which art moving everywhere;
Destroyer and preserver; hear, oh, hear!

2

Thou on whose stream, mid the steep sky's commotion,   15
Loose clouds like earth's decaying leaves are shed,
Shook from the tangled boughs of Heaven and Ocean,

Angels° of rain and lightning: there are spread   messengers
On the blue surface of thine aëry surge,
Like the bright hair uplifted from the head   20
Of some fierce Maenad, even from the dim verge
Of the horizon to the zenith's height,
The locks of the approaching storm. Thou dirge

ODE TO THE WEST WIND 21. **Maenad:** frenzied female worshipper of Dionysus, god of wine and fertility.

Of the dying year, to which this closing night
Will be the dome of a vast sepulcher,   25
Vaulted with all thy congregated might

Of vapors, from whose solid atmosphere
Black rain, and fire, and hail will burst: oh, hear!

3

Thou who didst waken from his summer dreams
The blue Mediterranean, where he lay,   30
Lulled by the coil of his crystàlline streams,

Beside a pumice isle in Baiae's bay,
And saw in sleep old palaces and towers
Quivering within the wave's intenser day,

All overgrown with azure moss and flowers   35
So sweet, the sense faints picturing them! Thou
For whose path the Atlantic's level powers

Cleave themselves into chasms, while far below
The sea-blooms and the oozy woods which wear
The sapless foliage of the ocean, know   40

Thy voice, and suddenly grow gray with fear,
And tremble and despoil themselves: oh, hear!

4

If I were a dead leaf thou mightest bear;
If I were a swift cloud to fly with thee;
A wave to pant beneath thy power, and share   45

The impulse of thy strength, only less free
Than thou, O uncontrollable! If even
I were as in my boyhood, and could be

The comrade of thy wanderings over Heaven,
As then, when to outstrip thy skyey speed   50
Scarce seemed a vision; I would ne'er have striven

As thus with thee in prayer in my sore need.
Oh, lift me as a wave, a leaf, a cloud!
I fall upon the thorns of life! I bleed!

A heavy weight of hours has chained and bowed   55
One too like thee: tameless, and swift, and proud.

5

Make me thy lyre, even as the forest is:
What if my leaves are falling like its own!
The tumult of thy mighty harmonies

Will take from both a deep, autumnal tone,   60
Sweet though in sadness. Be thou, Spirit fierce,
My spirit! Be thou me, impetuous one!

Drive my dead thoughts over the universe
Like withered leaves to quicken a new birth!
And, by the incantation of this verse,   65

Scatter, as from an unextinguished hearth
Ashes and sparks, my words among mankind!
Be through my lips to unawakened earth

The trumpet of a prophecy! O Wind,
If Winter comes, can Spring be far behind?   70

John Keats

[1795–1821]

La Belle Dame sans Merci

O what can ail thee, knight-at-arms,
    Alone and palely loitering?
The sedge has withered from the lake
    And no birds sing.

O what can ail thee, knight-at-arms,   5
    So haggard, and so woebegone?
The squirrel's granary is full
    And the harvest's done.

LA BELLE DAME SANS MERCI: the beautiful lady without mercy.

I see a lily on thy brow,
    With anguish moist and fever dew,   10
And on thy cheeks a fading rose
    Fast withereth too.

"I met a lady in the meads°,   *meadows*
    Full beautiful—a faery's child,
Her hair was long, her foot was light   15
    And her eyes were wild.

"I made a garland for her head,
    And bracelets too, and fragrant zone°;   *belt*
She looked at me as she did love,
    And made sweet moan.   20

"I set her on my pacing steed
    And nothing else saw all day long,
For sidelong would she bend and sing
    A faery's song.

"She found me roots of relish sweet,   25
    And honey wild, and manna dew,
And sure in language strange she said
    'I love thee true.'

"She took me to her elfin grot
    And there she wept and sighed full sore,   30
And there I shut her wild wild eyes
    With kisses four.

"And there she lulléd me asleep,
    And there I dreamed—Ah! woe betide!
The latest dream I ever dreamt   35
    On the cold hill side.

"I saw pale kings and princes too,
    Pale warriors, death-pale were they all;
They cried, 'La Belle Dame sans Merci
    Hath thee in thrall!'   40

"I saw their starved lips in the gloam,
    With horrid warning gapéd wide,
And I awoke, and found me here
    On the cold hill's side.

"And this is why I sojourn here,   45
    Alone and palely loitering,
Though the sedge is withered from the lake,
    And no birds sing."

Ode to a Nightingale

1

My heart aches, and a drowsy numbness pains
    My sense, as though of hemlock I had drunk,
Or emptied some dull opiate to the drains°   dregs
    One minute past, and Lethe-wards had sunk:
'Tis not through envy of thy happy lot,   5
    But being too happy in thine happiness—
        That thou, light-wingèd Dryad° of the trees,   tree nymph
            In some melodious plot
Of beechen green, and shadows numberless,
    Singest of summer in full-throated ease.   10

2

O, for a draught of vintage! that hath been
    Cooled a long age in the deep-delved earth,
Tasting of Flora and the country green,
    Dance, and Provençal song, and sunburnt mirth!
O for a beaker full of the warm South,   15
    Full of the true, the blushful Hippocrene,
        With beaded bubbles winking at the brim,
            And purple-stained mouth;
That I might drink, and leave the world unseen,
    And with thee fade away into the forest dim: 20

3

Fade far away, dissolve, and quite forget
    What thou among the leaves hast never known,

ODE TO A NIGHTINGALE 2. **hemlock:** opiate; poisonous in large quantities.
4. **Lethe-wards:** towards Lethe, the river of forgetfulness.
13. **Flora:** goddess of the flowers.
14. **Provençal song:** Provence, in southern France, home of the troubadours.
16. **true . . . Hippocrene:** wine. A fountain on Mount Helicon in Greece, whose waters
reputedly stimulated poetic imagination.

The weariness, the fever, and the fret
  Here, where men sit and hear each other groan;
Where palsy shakes a few, sad, last gray hairs,   25
  Where youth grows pale, and specter-thin, and dies;
    Where but to think is to be full of sorrow
      And leaden-eyed despairs,
  Where Beauty cannot keep her lustrous eyes,
    Or new Love pine at them beyond tomorrow.   30

4

Away! away! for I will fly to thee,
  Not charioted by Bacchus and his pards,
But on the viewless° wings of Poesy,   *invisible*
  Though the dull brain perplexes and retards:
Already with thee! tender is the night,   35
  And haply° the Queen-Moon is on her throne,   *perhaps*
    Clustered around by all her starry Fays°;   *fairies*
      But here there is no light,
  Save what from heaven is with the breezes blown
    Through verdurous glooms and winding mossy ways.   40

5

I cannot see what flowers are at my feet,
  Nor what soft incense hangs upon the boughs,
But, in embalmèd° darkness, guess each sweet   *scented*
  Wherewith the seasonable month endows
The grass, the thicket, and the fruit-tree wild;   45
  White hawthorn, and the pastoral eglantine°;   *sweetbriar*
    Fast fading violets covered up in leaves;
      And mid-May's eldest child,
  The coming musk-rose, full of dewy wine,
    The murmurous haunt of flies on summer eves.   50

6

Darkling° I listen; and, for many a time   *in darkness*
  I have been half in love with easeful Death,
Called him soft names in many a musèd rhyme,
  To take into the air my quiet breath;
Now more than ever seems it rich to die,   55
  To cease upon the midnight with no pain,

---

32. Bacchus . . . pards: the god of wine and revelry and the leopards who drew his chariot.

While thou are pouring forth thy soul abroad
  In such an ecstasy!
Still wouldst thou sing, and I have ears in vain—
  To thy high requiem become a sod.   60

7

Thou wast not born for death, immortal Bird!
  No hungry generations tread thee down;
The voice I hear this passing night was heard
  In ancient days by emperor and clown:
Perhaps the self-same song that found a path   65
  Through the sad heart of Ruth, when, sick for home,
    She stood in tears amid the alien corn;
      The same that oft-times hath
Charmed magic casements, opening on the foam
  Of perilous seas, in faery lands forlorn.   70

8

Forlorn! the very word is like a bell
  To toll me back from thee to my sole self!
Adieu! the fancy cannot cheat so well
  As she is famed to do, deceiving elf.
Adieu! adieu! thy plaintive anthem fades   75
  Past the near meadows, over the still stream,
    Up the hill-side; and now 'tis buried deep
      In the next valley-glades:
Was it a vision, or a waking dream?
  Fled is that music:—Do I wake or sleep?   80

Ode on a Grecian Urn

1

Thou still unravished bride of quietness,
  Thou foster-child of silence and slow time,
Sylvan° historian, who canst thus express   woodland
  A flowery tale more sweetly than our rhyme:

66–67. **Ruth . . . corn:** A Biblical heroine who worked in the harvest fields in a foreign land.

What leaf-fringed legend haunts about thy shape   5
    Of deities or mortals, or of both,
        In Tempe or the dales of Arcady?
    What men or gods are these? What maidens loath?
What mad pursuit? What struggle to escape?
        What pipes and timbrels? What wild ecstasy?   10

2

Heard melodies are sweet, but those unheard
    Are sweeter; therefore, ye soft pipes, play on;
Not to the sensual ear, but, more endeared,
    Pipe to the spirit ditties of no tone:
Fair youth, beneath the trees, thou canst not leave   15
    Thy song, nor ever can those trees be bare;
        Bold Lover, never, never canst thou kiss,
Though winning near the goal—yet, do not grieve;
        She cannot fade, though thou hast not thy bliss,
    Forever wilt thou love, and she be fair!   20

3

Ah, happy, happy boughs! that cannot shed
    Your leaves, nor ever bid the Spring adieu;
And, happy melodist, unwearièd,
    For ever piping songs for ever new;
More happy love! more happy, happy love!   25
    For ever warm and still to be enjoyed,
        For ever panting, and for ever young;
All breathing human passion far above,
    That leaves a heart high-sorrowful and cloyed,
        A burning forehead, and a parching tongue.   30

4

Who are these coming to the sacrifice?
    To what green altar, O mysterious priest,
Lead'st thou that heifer lowing at the skies,
    And all her silken flanks with garlands dressed?
What little town by river or sea shore,   35
    Or mountain-built with peaceful citadel,
        Is emptied of this folk, this pious morn?
And, little town, thy streets for evermore

---

7. **Tempe . . . Arcady:** In Greece, beautiful rural regions.

Will silent be; and not a soul to tell
  Why thou art desolate, can e'er return.   40

5

O Attic shape! Fair attitude! with brede°   woven pattern
  Of marble men and maidens overwrought,
With forest branches and the trodden weed;
  Thou, silent form, dost tease us out of thought
As doth eternity: Cold Pastoral!   45
  When old age shall this generation waste,
    Thou shalt remain, in midst of other woe
  Than ours, a friend to man, to whom thou say'st,
"Beauty is truth, truth beauty,"—that is all
    Ye know on earth, and all ye need to know.   50

Elizabeth Barrett Browning

[*1806–1861*]

To George Sand

A RECOGNITION

True genius, but true woman! dost deny
The woman's nature with a manly scorn,
And break away the gauds° and armlets worn   ornaments
By weaker women in captivity?
Ah, vain denial! that revolted cry   5
Is sobbed in by a woman's voice forlorn,—
Thy woman's hair, my sister, all unshorn
Floats back dishevelled strength in agony,
Disproving thy man's name: and while before
The world thou burnest in a poet-fire,   10
We see thy woman-heart beat evermore
Through the large flame. Beat purer, heart, and higher,
Till God unsex thee on the heavenly shore
Where unincarnate spirits purely aspire!

TO GEORGE SAND: The pen name of Lucie Aurore Dupin Dudevant (1804–76), a French
female novelist whose writing and iconoclastic style of life were highly controversial.

Alfred, Lord Tennyson

[1809–1892]

Ulysses

It little profits that an idle king,
By this still hearth, among these barren crags,
Matched with an aged wife, I mete and dole
Unequal laws unto a savage race,
That hoard, and sleep, and feed, and know not me.   5
I cannot rest from travel; I will drink
Life to the lees. All times I have enjoyed
Greatly, have suffered greatly, both with those
That loved me, and alone; on shore, and when
Thro' scudding drifts the rainy Hyades   10
Vext the dim sea. I am become a name;
For always roaming with a hungry heart
Much have I seen and known,—cities of men
And manners°, climates, councils, governments,   customs
Myself not least, but honored of them all,—   15
And drunk delight of battle with my peers,
Far on the ringing plains of windy Troy.
I am a part of all that I have met;
Yet all experience is an arch wherethro'
Gleams that untraveled world whose margin fades   20
For ever and for ever when I move.
How dull it is to pause, to make an end,
To rust unburnished, not to shine in use!
As tho' to breathe were life! Life piled on life
Were all too little, and of one to me   25
Little remains; but every hour is saved
From that eternal silence, something more,
A bringer of new things; and vile it were
For some three suns to store and hoard myself,
And this gray spirit yearning in desire   30
To follow knowledge like a sinking star,
Beyond the utmost bound of human thought.
    This is my son, mine own Telemachus,
To whom I leave the scepter and the isle,—

ULYSSES: According to Dante (in *The Inferno*, Canto 26) Ulysses, having been away for ten years during the Trojan War, is restless upon returning to his island kingdom of Ithaca, and he persuades a band of followers to accompany him on a journey.
    10. **Hyades:** a constellation of stars whose rising with the sun forecasts rain.

Well-loved of me, discerning to fulfill   35
This labor, by slow prudence to make mild
A rugged people, and thro' soft degrees
Subdue them to the useful and the good.
Most blameless is he, centered in the sphere
Of common duties, decent° not to fail   proper   40
In offices° of tenderness, and pay   duties
Meet° adoration to my household gods,   appropriate
When I am gone. He works his work, I mine.
　　There lies the port; the vessel puffs her sail;
There gloom the dark, broad seas. My mariners,   45
Souls that have toiled, and wrought, and thought with me,—
That ever with a frolic welcome took
The thunder and the sunshine, and opposed
Free hearts, free foreheads,—you and I are old;
Old age hath yet his honor and his toil.   50
Death closes all; but something ere the end,
Some work of noble note, may yet be done,
Not unbecoming men that strove with gods.
The lights begin to twinkle from the rocks;
The long day wanes; the slow moon climbs; the deep   55
Moans round with many voices. Come, my friends,
'Tis not too late to seek a newer world.
Push off, and sitting well in order smite
The sounding furrows; for my purpose holds
To sail beyond the sunset, and the baths   60
Of all the western stars, until I die.
It may be that the gulfs will wash us down;
It may be we shall touch the Happy Isles,
And see the great Achilles, whom we knew.
Tho' much is taken, much abides; and tho'   65
We are not now that strength which in old days
Moved earth and heaven, that which we are, we are,—
One equal temper of heroic hearts,
Made weak by time and fate, but strong in will
To strive, to seek, to find, and not to yield.   70

Robert Browning

[1812–1889]

My Last Duchess

FERRARA

That's my last Duchess painted on the wall,
Looking as if she were alive. I call
That piece a wonder, now: Frà Pandolf's hands
Worked busily a day, and there she stands.
Will't please you sit and look at her? I said   5
"Frà Pandolf" by design, for never read
Strangers like you that pictured countenance,
The depth and passion of its earnest glance,
But to myself they turned (since none puts by
The curtain I have drawn for you, but I)   10
And seemed as they would ask me, if they durst,
How such a glance came there; so, not the first
Are you to turn and ask thus. Sir, 'twas not
Her husband's presence only, called that spot
Of joy into the Duchess' cheek: perhaps   15
Frà Pandolf chanced to say, "Her mantle laps
Over my lady's wrist too much," or "Paint
Must never hope to reproduce the faint
Half-flush that dies along her throat." Such stuff
Was courtesy, she thought, and cause enough   20
For calling up that spot of joy. She had
A heart—how shall I say?—too soon made glad,
Too easily impressed; she liked whate'er
She looked on, and her looks went everywhere.
Sir, 'twas all one! My favour at her breast,   25
The dropping of the daylight in the West,
The bough of cherries some officious fool
Broke in the orchard for her, the white mule
She rode with round the terrace—all and each
Would draw from her alike the approving speech,   30
Or blush, at least. She thanked men—good! but thanked
Somehow—I know not how—as if she ranked
My gift of a nine-hundred-years-old name
With anybody's gift. Who'd stoop to blame
This sort of trifling? Even had you skill   35
In speech—(which I have not)—to make your will

Quite clear to such an one, and say, "Just this
"Or that in you disgusts me; here you miss,
"Or there exceed the mark"—and if she let
Herself be lessoned so, nor plainly set   40
Her wits to yours, forsooth, and made excuse,
—E'en then would be some stooping; and I choose
Never to stoop. Oh sir, she smiled, no doubt,
Whene'er I passed her; but who passed without
Much the same smile? This grew; I gave commands;   45
Then all smiles stopped together. There she stands
As if alive. Will't please you rise? We'll meet
The company below, then. I repeat,
The Count your master's known munificence
Is ample warrant that no just pretense   50
Of mine for dowry will be disallowed;
Though his fair daughter's self, as I avowed
At starting, is my object. Nay, we'll go
Together down, sir. Notice Neptune, though,
Taming a sea-horse, thought a rarity,   55
Which Claus of Innsbruck cast in bronze for me!

Emily Brontë

[1818–1848]

Alone I sat; the summer day

Alone I sat; the summer day
Had died in smiling light away;
I saw it die, I watched it fade
From misty hill and breezeless glade:

And thoughts in my soul were gushing,   5
And my heart bowed beneath their power;
And tears within my eyes were rushing
Because I could not speak the feeling,
The solemn joy around me stealing
In that divine, untroubled hour.   10

I asked myself, "O why has heaven
Denied the precious gift to me,
The glorious gift to many given
To speak their thoughts in poetry?

"Dreams have encircled me," I said,   15
"From careless childhood's sunny time;
Visions by ardent fancy fed
Since life was in its morning prime."

But now, when I had hoped to sing,
My fingers strike a tuneless string;   20
And still the burden of the strain°   tune
Is "Strive no more; 'tis all in vain."

Riches I hold in light esteem

Riches I hold in light esteem
And Love I laugh to scorn
And lust of Fame was but a dream
That vanished with the morn—

And if I pray, the only prayer   5
That moves my lips for me
Is—"Leave the heart that now I bear
And give me liberty."

Yes, as my swift days near their goal
'Tis all that I implore—   10
Through life and death, a chainless soul
With courage to endure!

Walt Whitman

[1819–1892]

Out of the Cradle Endlessly Rocking

Out of the cradle endlessly rocking,
Out of the mocking-bird's throat, the musical shuttle,
Out of the Ninth-month midnight,
Over the sterile sands and the fields beyond, where the child leaving
   his bed wandered alone, bareheaded, barefoot,
Down from the showered halo,   5
Up from the mystic play of shadows twining and twisting as if they
   were alive,

Out from the patches of briers and blackberries,
From the memories of the bird that chanted to me,
From your memories sad brother, from the fitful risings and fallings I
    heard,
From under that yellow half-moon late-risen and swollen as if with
    tears,   10
From those beginning notes of yearning and love there in the mist,
From the thousand responses of my heart never to cease,
From the myriad thence-aroused words,
From the word stronger and more delicious than any,
From such as now they start the scene revisiting,   15
As a flock, twittering, rising, or overhead passing,
Borne hither, ere all eludes me, hurriedly,
A man, yet by these tears a little boy again,
Throwing myself on the sand, confronting the waves,
I, chanter of pains and joys, uniter of here and hereafter,   20
Taking all hints to use them, but swiftly leaping beyond them,
A reminiscence sing.

Once Paumanok,
When the lilac-scent was in the air and Fifth-month grass was
    growing,
Up this seashore in some briers,   25
Two feathered guests from Alabama, two together,
And their nest, and four light-green eggs spotted with brown,
And every day the he-bird to and fro near at hand,
And every day the she-bird crouched on her nest, silent, with bright
    eyes,
And every day I, a curious boy, never too close, never disturbing them, 30
Cautiously peering, absorbing, translating.

Shine! shine! shine!
Pour down your warmth, great sun!
While we bask, we two together.

Two together!   35
Winds blow south, or winds blow north,
Day come white, or night come black,
Home, or rivers and mountains from home,
Singing all time, minding no time,
While we two keep together.   40

Till of a sudden,
May-be killed, unknown to her mate,
One forenoon the she-bird crouched not on the nest,

Nor returned that afternoon, nor the next,
Nor ever appeared again. 45

And thenceforward all summer in the sound of the sea,
And at night under the full of the moon in calmer weather,
Over the hoarse surging of the sea,
Or flitting from brier to brier by day,
I saw, I heard at intervals the remaining one, the he-bird, 50
The solitary guest from Alabama.

Blow! blow! blow!
Blow up sea-winds along Paumanok's shore;
I wait and I wait till you blow my mate to me.

Yes, when the stars glistened, 55
All night long on the prong of a moss-scalloped stake,
Down almost amid the slapping waves,
Sat the lone singer wonderful causing tears.

He called on his mate,
He poured forth the meanings which I of all men know. 60

Yes my brother I know,
The rest might not, but I have treasured every note,
For more than once dimly down to the beach gliding,
Silent, avoiding the moonbeams, blending myself with the shadows,
Recalling now the obscure shapes, the echoes, the sounds and sights
    after their sorts, 65
The white arms out in the breakers tirelessly tossing,
I, with bare feet, a child, the wind wafting my hair,
Listened long and long.

Listened to keep, to sing, now translating the notes,
Following you my brother. 70

Soothe! soothe! soothe!
Close on its wave soothes the wave behind,
And again another behind embracing and lapping, every one close,
But my love soothes not me, not me.

Low hangs the moon, it rose late, 75
It is lagging—O I think it is heavy with love, with love.

O madly the sea pushes upon the land,
With love, with love.

O night! do I not see my love fluttering out among the breakers?
What is that little black thing I see there in the white?   80

Loud! loud! loud!
Loud I call to you, my love!

High and clear I shoot my voice over the waves,
Surely you must know who is here, is here,
You must know who I am, my love.   85

Low-hanging moon!
What is that dusky spot in your brown yellow?
O it is the shape, the shape of my mate!
O moon do not keep her from me any longer.

Land! land! O land!   90
Whichever way I turn, O I think you could give me my mate back again if you
    only would,
For I am almost sure I see her dimly whichever way I look.

O rising stars!
Perhaps the one I want so much will rise, will rise with some of you.

O throat! O trembling throat!   95
Sound clearer through the atmosphere!
Pierce the woods, the earth,
Somewhere listening to catch you must be the one I want.

Shake out carols!
Solitary here, the night's carols!   100
Carols of lonesome love! death's carols!
Carols under that lagging, yellow, waning moon!
O under that moon where she droops almost down into the sea!
O reckless despairing carols.

But soft! sink low!   105
Soft! let me just murmur,
And do you wait a moment you husky-noised sea,
For somewhere I believe I heard my mate responding to me,
So faint, I must be still, be still to listen,
But not altogether still, for then she might not come immediately to me.   110

Hither my love!
Here I am! Here!
With this just-sustained note I announce myself to you,
This gentle call is for you my love, for you.

Do not be decoyed elsewhere,
That is the whistle of the wind, it is not my voice,   115
That is the fluttering, the fluttering of the spray,
Those are the shadows of leaves.

O darkness! O in vain!
O I am very sick and sorrowful.   120

O brown halo in the sky near the moon, drooping upon the sea!
O troubled reflection in the sea!
O throat! O throbbing heart!
And I singing uselessly, uselessly all the night.

O past! O happy life! O songs of joy!   125
In the air, in the woods, over fields,
Loved! loved! loved! loved! loved!
But my mate no more, no more with me!
We two together no more.

The aria sinking.   130
All else continuing, the stars shining,
The winds blowing, the notes of the bird continuous echoing,
With angry moans the fierce old mother incessantly moaning,
On the sands of Paumanok's shore gray and rustling,
The yellow half-moon enlarged, sagging down, drooping, the face of
    the sea almost touching,   135
The boy ecstatic, with his bare feet the waves, with his hair the
    atmosphere dallying,
The love in the heart long pent, now loose, now at last tumultuously
    bursting,
The aria's meaning, the ears, the soul, swiftly depositing,
The strange tears down the cheeks coursing,
The colloquy there, the trio, each uttering,   140
The undertone, the savage old mother incessantly crying,
To the boy's soul's questions sullenly timing, some drowned secret
    hissing,
To the outsetting bard.

Demon or bird! (said the boy's soul,)
Is it indeed toward your mate you sing? or is it really to me?   145
For I, that was a child, my tongue's use sleeping, now I have heard
    you,
Now in a moment I know what I am for, I awake,

And already a thousand singers, a thousand songs, clearer, louder and
  more sorrowful than yours,
A thousand warbling echoes have started to life within me, never to
  die.

O you singer solitary, singing by yourself, projecting me,   150
O solitary me listening, never more shall I cease perpetuating you,
Never more shall I escape, never more the reverberations,
Never more the cries of unsatisfied love be absent from me,
Never again leave me to be the peaceful child I was before what there
  in the night,
By the sea under the yellow and sagging moon,   155
The messenger there aroused, the fire, the sweet hell within,
The unknown want, the destiny of me.

O give me the clue! (it lurks in the night here somewhere,)
O if I am to have so much, let me have more!

A word then, (for I will conquer it,)   160
The word final, superior to all,
Subtle, sent up—what is it?—I listen;
Are you whispering it, and have been all the time, you sea-waves?
Is that it from your liquid rims and wet sands?

Whereto answering, the sea,   165
Delaying not, hurrying not,
Whispered me through the night, and very plainly before daybreak,
Lisped to me the low and delicious word death,
And again death, death, death, death,
Hissing melodious, neither like the bird nor like my aroused child's
  heart,   170
But edging near as privately for me rustling at my feet,
Creeping thence steadily up to my ears and laving me softly all over,
Death, death, death, death, death.

Which I do not forget,
But fuse the song of my dusky demon and brother,   175
That he sang to me in the moonlight on Paumanok's gray beach,
With the thousand responsive songs at random,
My own songs awaked from that hour,
And with them the key, the word up from the waves,
The word of the sweetest song and all songs,   180
That strong and delicious word which, creeping to my feet,
(Or like some old crone rocking the cradle, swathed in sweet garments,
  bending aside,)
The sea whispered me.

Crossing Brooklyn Ferry

1

Flood-tide below me! I see you face to face!
Clouds of the west—sun there half an hour high—I see you also face
  to face.

Crowds of men and women attired in the usual costumes, how curious
  you are to me!
On the ferry-boats the hundreds and hundreds that cross, returning
  home, are more curious to me than you suppose,
And you that shall cross from shore to shore years hence are more to
  me, and more in my meditations, than you might suppose.   5

2

The impalpable sustenance of me from all things at all hours of the
  day,
The simple, compact, well-join'd scheme, myself disintegrated, every
  one disintegrated yet part of the scheme,
The similitudes of the past and those of the future,
The glories strung like beads on my smallest sights and hearings, on
  the walk in the street and the passage over the river,
The current rushing so swiftly and swimming with me far away,   10
The others that are to follow me, the ties between me and them,
The certainty of others, the life, love, sight, hearing of others.

Others will enter the gates of the ferry and cross from shore to shore,
Others will watch the run of the flood-tide,
Others will see the shipping of Manhattan north and west, and the
  heights of Brooklyn to the south and east,   15
Others will see the islands large and small;
Fifty years hence, others will see them as they cross, the sun half an
  hour high,
A hundred years hence, or ever so many hundred years hence, others
  will see them,
Will enjoy the sunset, the pouring-in of the flood-tide, the falling-back
  to the sea of the ebb-tide.

3

It avails not, time nor place—distance avails not,   20
I am with you, you men and women of a generation, or ever so many
  generations hence,
Just as you feel when you look on the river and sky, so I felt,

Just as any of you is one of a living crowd, I was one of a crowd,
Just as you are refresh'd by the gladness of the river and the bright
    flow, I was refresh'd,
Just as you stand and lean on the rail, yet hurry with the swift current,
    I stood yet was hurried, 25
Just as you look on the numberless masts of ships and the thick-
    stemm'd pipes of steamboats, I look'd.

I too many and many a time cross'd the river of old,
Watched the Twelfth-month° sea-gulls, saw them high in the air   December
    floating with motionless wings, oscillating their bodies,
Saw how the glistening yellow lit up parts of their bodies and left the
    rest in strong shadow,
Saw the slow-wheeling circles and the gradual edging toward the
    south, 30
Saw the reflection of the summer sky in the water,
Had my eyes dazzled by the shimmering track of beams,
Look'd at the fine centrifugal spokes of light round the shape of my
    head in the sunlit water,
Look'd on the haze on the hills southward and south-westward,
Look'd on the vapor as it flew in fleeces tinged with violet, 35
Look'd toward the lower bay to notice the vessels arriving,
Saw their approach, saw aboard those that were near me,
Saw the white sails of schooners and sloops, saw the ships at anchor,
The sailors at work in the rigging or out astride the spars,
The round masts, the swinging motion of the hulls, the slender
    serpentine pennants, 40
The large and small steamers in motion, the pilots in their pilot-houses,
The white wake left by the passage, the quick tremulous whirl of the
    wheels,
The flags of all nations, the falling of them at sunset,
The scallop-edged waves in the twilight, the ladled cups, the frolicsome
    crests and glistening,
The stretch afar growing dimmer and dimmer, the gray walls of the
    granite storehouses by the docks, 45
On the river the shadowy group, the big steam-tug closely flank'd on
    each side by the barges, the hay-boat, the belated lighter,
On the neighboring shore the fires from the foundry chimneys burning
    high and glaringly into the night,
Casting their flicker of black contrasted with wild red and yellow light
    over the tops of houses, and down into the clefts of streets.

4

These and all else were to me the same as they are to you,
I loved well those cities, loved well the stately and rapid river, 50

The men and women I saw were all near to me,
Others the same—others who look back on me because I look'd
   forward to them,
(The time will come, though I stop° here to to-day and to-night.)   stay

5

What is it then between us?
What is the count of the scores or hundreds of years between us?   55

Whatever it is, it avails not—distance avails not, and place avails not,
I too lived, Brooklyn of ample hills was mine,
I too walk'd the streets of Manhattan island, and bathed in the waters
   around it,
I too felt the curious abrupt questionings stir within me,
In the day among crowds of people sometimes they came upon me,   60
In my walks home late at night or as I lay in my bed they came upon
   me,
I too had been struck from the float forever held in solution,
I too had receiv'd identity by my body,
That I was I knew was of my body, and what I should be I knew I
   should be of my body.

6

It is not upon you alone the dark patches fall,   65
The dark threw its patches down upon me also,
The best I had done seem'd to me blank and suspicious,
My great thoughts as I supposed them, were they not in reality
   meager?
Nor is it you alone who know what it is to be evil,
I am he who knew what it was to be evil,   70
I too knitted the old knot of contrariety,
Blabb'd, blush'd, resented, lied, stole, grudg'd,
Had guile, anger, lust, hot wishes I dared not speak,
Was wayward, vain, greedy, shallow, sly, cowardly, malignant,
The wolf, the snake, the hog, not wanting in me,   75
The cheating look, the frivolous word, the adulterous wish, not
   wanting,
Refusals, hates, postponements, meanness, laziness, none of these
   wanting,
Was one with the rest, the days and haps of the rest,
Was call'd by my nighest name by clear loud voices of young men as
   they saw me approaching or passing,
Felt their arms on my neck as I stood, or the negligent leaning of their
   flesh against me as I sat,   80

Saw many I loved in the street or ferry-boat or public assembly, yet
    never told them a word,
Lived the same life with the rest, the same old laughing, gnawing,
    sleeping,
Play'd the part that still looks back on the actor or actress,
The same old role, the role that is what we make it, as great as we like,
Or as small as we like, or both great and small.   85

7

Closer yet I approach you,
What thought you have of me now, I had as much of you—I laid in
    my stores in advance,
I consider'd long and seriously of you before you were born.

Who was to know what should come home to me?
Who knows but I am enjoying this?   90
Who knows, for all the distance, but I am as good as looking at you
    now, for all you cannot see me?

8

Ah, what can ever be more stately and admirable to me than mast-
    hemm'd Manhattan?
River and sunset and scallop-edg'd waves of flood-tide?
The sea-gulls oscillating their bodies, the hay-boat in the twilight, and
    the belated lighter?
What gods can exceed these that clasp me by the hand, and with voices
    I love call me promptly and loudly by my nighest name as I
    approach?   95
What is more subtle than this which ties me to the woman or man that
    looks in my face?
Which fuses me into you now, and pours my meaning into you?

We understand then do we not?
What I promis'd without mentioning it, have you not accepted?
What the study could not teach—what the preaching could not
    accomplish is accomplish'd, is it not?   100

9

Flow on, river! flow with the flood-tide, and ebb with the ebb-tide!
Frolic on, crested and scallop-edg'd waves!
Gorgeous clouds of the sunset! drench with your splendor me, or the
    men and women generations after me!

Cross from shore to shore, countless crowds of passengers!
Stand up, tall masts of Mannahatta! stand up, beautiful hills of
    Brooklyn! 105
Throb, baffled and curious brain! throw out questions and answers!
Suspend here and everywhere, eternal float of solution!
Gaze, loving and thirsting eyes, in the house or street or public
    assembly!
Sound out, voices of young men! loudly and musically call me by my
    nighest name!
Live, old life! play the part that looks back on the actor or actress! 110
Play the old role, the role that is great or small according as one makes
    it!
Consider, you who peruse me, whether I may not in unknown ways be
    looking upon you;
Be firm, rail over the river, to support those who lean idly, yet haste
    with the hasting current;
Fly on, sea-birds! fly sideways, or wheel in large circles high in the air;
Receive the summer sky, you water, and faithfully hold it till all
    downcast eyes have time to take it from you! 115
Diverge, fine spokes of light, from the shape of my head, or any one's
    head, in the sunlit water!
Come on, ships from the lower bay! pass up or down, white-sail'd
    schooners, sloops, lighters!
Flaunt away, flags of all nations! be duly lower'd at sunset!
Burn high your fires, foundry chimneys! cast black shadows at
    nightfall! cast red and yellow light over the tops of the houses!
Appearances, now or henceforth, indicate what you are, 120
You necessary film, continue to envelop the soul,
About my body for me, and your body for you, be hung our divinest
    aromas,
Thrive, cities—bring your freight, bring your shows, ample and
    sufficient rivers,
Expand, being than which none else is perhaps more spiritual,
Keep your places, objects than which none else is more lasting. 125

You have waited, you always wait, you dumb, beautiful ministers,
We receive you with free sense at last, and are insatiate henceforward,
Not you any more shall be able to foil us, or withhold yourselves from
    us,
We use you, and do not cast you aside—we plant you permanently
    within us,
We fathom you not—we love you—there is perfection in you also, 130
You furnish your parts toward eternity,
Great or small, you furnish your parts toward the soul.

Matthew Arnold

[1822–1888]

Dover Beach

The sea is calm tonight.
The tide is full, the moon lies fair
Upon the straits; on the French coast the light
Gleams and is gone; the cliffs of England stand,
Glimmering and vast, out in the tranquil bay.   5
Come to the window, sweet is the night-air!
Only, from the long line of spray
Where the sea meets the moon-blanched land,
Listen! You hear the grating roar
Of pebbles which the waves draw back, and fling,   10
At their return, up the high strand,
Begin, and cease, and then again begin,
With tremulous cadence slow, and bring
The eternal note of sadness in.

Sophocles long ago   15
Heard it on the Aegean, and it brought
Into his mind the turbid ebb and flow
Of human misery; we
Find also in the sound a thought,
Hearing it by this distant northern sea.   20

The Sea of Faith
Was once, too, at the full, and round earth's shore
Lay like the folds of a bright girdle furled.
But now I only hear
Its melancholy, long, withdrawing roar,   25
Retreating, to the breath
Of the night-wind, down the vast edges drear
And naked shingles of the world.

Ah, love, let us be true
To one another! for the world, which seems   30
To lie before us like a land of dreams,
So various, so beautiful, so new,

DOVER BEACH: See Sophocles, *Antigone*, ll. 583–591.

Hath really neither joy, nor love, nor light,
Nor certitude, nor peace, nor help for pain;
And we are here as on a darkling plain   35
Swept with confused alarms of struggle and flight,
Where ignorant armies clash by night.

Emily Dickinson

[1830–1886]

A narrow Fellow in the Grass

A narrow Fellow in the Grass
Occasionally rides—
You may have met Him—did you not
His notice sudden is—

The Grass divides as with a Comb—   5
A spotted shaft is seen—
And then it closes at your feet
And opens further on—

He likes a Boggy Acre
A Floor too cool for Corn—   10
Yet when a Boy, and Barefoot—
I more than once at Noon

Have passed, I thought, a Whip lash
Unbraiding in the Sun
When stopping to secure it   15
It wrinkled, and was gone—

Several of Nature's People
I know, and they know me—
I feel for them a transport
Of cordiality—   20

But never met this Fellow
Attended, or alone
Without a tighter breathing
And Zero at the Bone—

Tell all the Truth but tell it slant

Tell all the Truth but tell it slant—
Success in Circuit lies
Too bright for our infirm Delight
The Truth's superb surprise

As Lightning to the Children eased   5
With explanation kind
The Truth must dazzle gradually
Or every man be blind—

I heard a Fly buzz—when I died

I heard a Fly buzz—when I died—
The Stillness in the Room
Was like the Stillness in the Air—
Between the Heaves of Storm—

The Eyes around—had wrung them dry—   5
And Breaths were gathering firm
For that last Onset—when the King
Be witnessed—in the Room—

I willed my Keepsakes—Signed away
What portion of me be   10
Assignable—and then it was
There interposed a Fly—

With Blue—uncertain stumbling Buzz—
Between the light—and me—
And then the Windows failed—and then   15
I could not see to see—

I never lost as much but twice

I never lost as much but twice,
And that was in the sod.

Twice have I stood a beggar
Before the door of God!

Angels—twice descending   5
Reimbursed my store—
Burglar! Banker—Father!
I am poor once more!

Success is counted sweetest

Success is counted sweetest
By those who ne'er succeed.
To comprehend a nectar
Requires sorest need.

Not one of all the purple Host   5
Who took the Flag today
Can tell the definition
So clear of Victory

As he defeated—dying—
On whose forbidden ear   10
The distant strains of triumph
Burst agonized and clear!

I taste a liquor never brewed—

I taste a liquor never brewed—
From Tankards scooped in Pearl—
Not all the Vats upon the Rhine
Yield such an Alcohol!

Inebriate of Air—am I—   5
And Debauchee of Dew—
Reeling—thro endless summer days—
From inns of Molten Blue—

When "Landlords" turn the drunken
  Bee
Out of the Foxglove's door—   10

When Butterflies—renounce their
  "drams"—
I shall but drink the more!

Till Seraphs swing their snowy Hats—
And Saints—to windows run—
To see the little Tippler   15
Leaning against the—Sun—

A Bird came down the Walk

A Bird came down the Walk—
He did not know I saw—
He bit an Angleworm in halves
And ate the fellow, raw,

And then he drank a Dew   5
From a convenient Grass—
And then hopped sidewise to the Wall
To let a Beetle pass—

He glanced with rapid eyes
That hurried all around—   10
They looked like frightened Beads, I
  thought—
He stirred his Velvet Head

Like one in danger, Cautious,
I offered him a Crumb
And he unrolled his feathers   15
And rowed him softer home—

Than Oars divide the Ocean,
Too silver for a seam—
Or Butterflies, off Banks of Noon
Leap, plashless as they swim.

There's a certain Slant of light

There's a certain Slant of light,
Winter Afternoons—

That oppresses, like the Heft
Of Cathedral Tunes—

Heavenly Hurt, it gives us—   5
We can find no scar,
But internal difference,
Where the Meanings, are—

None may teach it—Any—
'Tis the Seal Despair—   10
An imperial affliction
Sent us of the Air—

When it comes, the Landscape listens—
Shadows—hold their breath—
When it goes, 'tis like the Distance   15
On the look of Death—

The Soul selects her own Society

The Soul selects her own Society—
Then—shuts the Door—
To her divine Majority—
Present no more—

Unmoved—she notes the Chariots—
    pausing   5
At her low Gate—
Unmoved—an Emperor be kneeling
Upon her Mat—

I've known her—from an ample
    nation—
Choose One—   10
Then—close the Valves of her
    attention—
Like Stone—

Much Madness is divinest Sense

Much Madness is divinest Sense—
To a discerning Eye—

Much Sense—the starkest Madness—
'Tis the Majority
In this, as All, prevail—   5
Assent—and you are sane—
Demur—you're straightway dangerous—
And handled with a Chain—

This is my letter to the World

This is my letter to the World
That never wrote to Me—
The simple News that Nature told—
With tender Majesty

Her Message is committed   5
To Hands I cannot see—
For love of Her—Sweet—countrymen—
Judge tenderly—of Me

I never saw a Moor

I never saw a Moor—
I never saw the Sea—
Yet know I now the Heather looks
And what a Billow be.

I never spoke with God   5
Nor visited in Heaven—
Yet certain am I of the spot
As if the Checks were given—

Because I could not stop for Death

Because I could not stop for Death—
He kindly stopped for me—
The Carriage held but just Ourselves—
And Immortality.

We slowly drove—He knew no haste 5
And I had put away
My labor and my leisure too,
For His Civility—

We passed the School, where Children
   strove
At Recess—in the Ring— 10
We passed the Fields of Gazing
   Grain—
We passed the Setting Sun—

Or rather—He passed Us—
The Dews drew quivering and chill—
For only Gossamer, my Gown— 15
My Tippet—only Tulle—

We paused before a House that seemed
A swelling of the Ground—
The Roof was scarcely visible—
The Cornice—in the Ground— 20

Since then—'tis Centuries—and yet
Feels shorter than the Day
I first surmised the Horses' Heads
Were toward Eternity—

Thomas Hardy

[1840–1928]

The Darkling Thrush

I leant upon a coppice gate
   When Frost was specter-gray,
And Winter's dregs made desolate
   The weakening eye of day.
The tangled bine-stems scored the sky 5

THE DARKLING THRUSH 1. **coppice:** thicket or small woods.
5. **bine-stems:** shoots of a climbing plant or vine.

Like strings of broken lyres,
  And all mankind that haunted nigh
    Had sought their household fires.

The land's sharp features seemed to be
  The Century's corpse outleant°,   stretched out   10
His crypt the cloudy canopy,
  The wind his death-lament.
The ancient pulse of germ and birth
  Was shrunken hard and dry,
And every spirit upon earth   15
  Seemed fervorless as I.

At once a voice arose among
  The bleak twigs overhead
In a full-hearted evensong
  Of joy illimited;   20
An aged thrush, frail, gaunt, and small,
  In blast-beruffled plume,
Had chosen thus to fling his soul
  Upon the growing gloom.

So little cause for carolings   25
  Of such ecstatic sound
Was written on terrestrial things
  Afar or night around,
That I could think there trembled through
  His happy good-night air   30
Some blessed Hope, whereof he knew
  And I was unaware.

Transformations

Portion of this yew
Is a man my grandsire knew,
Bosomed here at its foot:
This branch may be his wife,
A ruddy human life   5
Now turned to a green shoot.

These grasses must be made
Of her who often prayed,
Last century, for repose;
And the fair girl long ago   10
Whom I often tried to know
May be entering this rose.

So, they are not underground,
But as nerves and veins abound
In the growths of upper air,   15
And they feel the sun and rain,
And the energy again
That made them what they were!

Gerard Manley Hopkins

[*1844–1889*]

God's Grandeur

The world is charged with the grandeur of God.
    It will flame out, like shining from shook foil;
    It gathers to a greatness, like the ooze of oil
Crushed. Why do men then now not reck his rod?
Generations have trod, have trod, have trod;   5
    And all is seared with trade; bleared, smeared with toil;
    And wears man's smudge and shares man's smell: the soil
Is bare now, nor can foot feel, being shod.

And for all this, nature is never spent;
    There lives the dearest freshness deep down things;   10
And though the last lights off the black West went
    Oh, morning, at the brown brink eastward, springs—
Because the Holy Ghost over the bent
    World broods with warm breast and with ah! bright wings.

GOD'S GRANDEUR: 2. **foil:** gold or tinsel foil.
4. **Crushed:** as when olives are crushed for their oil.

The Windhover

To Christ Our Lord

I caught this morning morning's minion°, king-   darling
   dom of daylight's dauphin°, dapple-dawn-drawn Falcon, in his   prince
     riding
Of the rolling level underneath him steady air, and striding
High there, how he rung upon the rein of a wimpling° wing   rippling
In his ecstasy! then off, off forth on swing,   5
   As a skate's heel sweeps smooth on a bow-bend: the hurl and gliding
   Rebuffed the big wind. My heart in hiding
Stirred for a bird,—the achieve of, the mastery of the thing!

Brute beauty and valour and act, oh, air, pride, plume, here
   Buckle! AND the fire that breaks from thee then, a billion
Times told lovelier, more dangerous, O my chevalier°!   knight 10

   No wonder of it: shéer plód makes plough down sillion°   furrow
Shine, and blue-bleak embers, ah my dear,
   Fall, gall themselves, and gash gold-vermilion.

Spring and Fall

To a Young Child

   Márgarét, áre you grieving
   Over Goldengrove unleaving?
   Leáves, líke the things of man, you
   With your fresh thoughts care for, can you?
   Áh! ás the heart grows older   5
   It will come to such sights colder
   By and by, nor spare a sigh
   Though worlds of wanwood leafmeal lie;
   And yet you *wíll* weep and know why.
   Now no matter, child, the name: 10
   Sórrow's spríngs áre the same.
   Nor mouth had, no nor mind, expressed

THE WINDHOVER: a kestrel, a kind of falcon.

What heart heard of, ghost guessed:
It ís the blight man was born for,
It is Margaret you mourn for.

A. E. Housman

[1859–1936]

When I Was One-and-Twenty

When I was one-and-twenty
  I heard a wise man say,
"Give crowns and pounds and guineas
  But not your heart away;
Give pearls away and rubies   5
  But keep your fancy free,"
But I was the one-and-twenty,
  No use to talk to me.

When I was one-and-twenty
  I heard him say again,   10
"The heart out of the bosom
  Was never given in vain;
'Tis paid with sighs a plenty
  And sold for endless rue."
And I am two-and-twenty,   15
  And oh, 'tis true, 'tis true.

To an Athlete Dying Young

The time you won your town the race
We chaired you through the market-place;
Man and boy stood cheering by,
And home we brought you shoulder-high.

To-day, the road all runners come,   5
Shoulder-high we bring you home,
And set you at your threshold down,
Townsman of a stiller town.

Smart lad, to slip betimes away
From fields where glory does not stay   10
And early though the laurel grows
It withers quicker than the rose.

Eyes the shady night has shut
Cannot see the record cut,
And silence sounds no worse than cheers   15
After earth has stopped the ears:

Now you will not swell the rout
Of lads that wore their honours out,
Runners whom renown outran
And the name died before the man.   20

So set, before its echoes fade,
The fleet foot on the sill of shade,
And hold to the low lintel up
The still-defended challenge-cup.

And round that early-laurelled head   25
Will flock to gaze the strengthless dead
And find unwithered on its curls
The garland briefer than a girl's.

William Butler Yeats

[1865–1939]

The Scholars

Bald heads forgetful of their sins,
Old, learned, respectable bald heads
Edit and annotate the lines
That young men, tossing on their beds,
Rhymed out in love's despair   5
To flatter beauty's ignorant ear.

All shuffle there; all cough in ink;
All wear the carpet with their shoes;
All think what other people think;

All know the man their neighbor knows. 10
Lord, what would they say
Did their Catullus walk that way?

The Magi

Now as at all times I can see in the mind's eye,
In their stiff, painted clothes, the pale unsatisfied ones
Appear and disappear in the blue depth of the sky
With all their ancient faces like rain-beaten stones,
And all their helms of silver hovering side by side, 5
And all their eyes still fixed, hoping to find once more,
Being by Calvary's turbulence unsatisfied,
The uncontrollable mystery on the bestial floor.

Easter 1916

I have met them at close of day
Coming with vivid faces
From counter or desk among gray
Eighteenth-century houses.
I have passed with a nod of the head 5
Or polite meaningless words,
Or have lingered awhile and said
Polite meaningless words,
And thought before I had done
Of a mocking tale or gibe 10
To please a companion
Around the fire at the club,
Being certain that they and I
But lived where motley is worn:
All changed, changed utterly: 15
A terrible beauty is born.

EASTER 1916: The title refers to an insurrection of Irish nationalists on Easter Monday, 1916; the four leaders mentioned were executed by the English.
  14. motley: fool's costume.

That woman's days were spent
In ignorant good will,
Her nights in argument
Until her voice grew shrill.   20
What voice more sweet than hers
When, young and beautiful,
She rode to harriers°?   hounds
This man had kept a school
And rode our wingèd horse;   25
This other his helper and friend
Was coming into his force;
He might have won fame in the end,
So sensitive his nature seemed,
So daring and sweet his thought.   30
This other man I had dreamed
A drunken, vainglorious lout.
He had done most bitter wrong
To some who are near my heart,
Yet I number him in the song;   35
He, too, has resigned his part
In the casual comedy;
He, too, has been changed in his turn,
Transformed utterly:
A terrible beauty is born.   40

Hearts with one purpose alone
Through summer and winter seem
Enchanted to a stone
To trouble the living stream.
The horse that comes from the road,   45
The rider, the birds that range
From cloud to tumbling cloud,
Minute by minute they change;
A shadow of cloud on the stream
Changes minute by minute;   50
A horse-hoof slides on the brim,
And a horse plashes within it;
The long-legged moor-hens dive,
And hens to moor-cocks call;
Minute by minute they live: 55
The stone's in the midst of all.

Too long a sacrifice
Can make a stone of the heart.
O when may it suffice?
That is Heaven's part, our part   60

To murmur name upon name,
As a mother names her child
When sleep at last has come
On limbs that had run wild.
What is it but nightfall?   65
No, no, not night but death;
Was it needless death after all?
For England may keep faith
For all that is done and said.
We know their dream; enough   70
To know they dreamed and are dead;
And what if excess of love
Bewildered them till they died?
I write it out in a verse—
MacDonagh and MacBride   75
And Connolly and Pearse
Now and in time to be,
Wherever green is worn,
Are changed, changed utterly:
A terrible beauty is born.   80

The Second Coming

Turning and turning in the widening gyre°   spiral
The falcon cannot hear the falconer;
Things fall apart; the center cannot hold;
Mere anarchy is loosed upon the world,
The blood-dimmed tide is loosed, and everywhere   5
The ceremony of innocence is drowned;
The best lack all conviction, while the worst
Are full of passionate intensity.

Surely some revelation is at hand;
Surely the Second Coming is at hand;   10
The Second Coming! Hardly are those words out
When a vast image out of *Spiritus Mundi*
Troubles my sight: somewhere in sands of the desert
A shape with lion body and the head of a man,
A gaze blank and pitiless as the sun,   15

THE SECOND COMING: The title alludes to the prophesied return of Jesus Christ and also
to the beast of the Apocalypse. See Matthew 24 and Revelation.
12. *Spiritus Mundi:* for Yeats, a common storehouse of images, a communal human
memory.

Is moving its slow thighs, while all about it
Reel shadows of the indignant desert birds.
The darkness drops again; but now I know
That twenty centuries of stony sleep
Were vexed to nightmare by a rocking cradle,   20
And what rough beast, its hour come round at last,
Slouches towards Bethlehem to be born?

The Wild Swans at Coole

The trees are in their autumn beauty,
The woodland paths are dry,
Under the October twilight the water
Mirrors a still sky;
Upon the brimming water among the stones   5
Are nine-and-fifty swans.

The nineteenth autumn has come upon me
Since I first made my count;
I saw, before I had well finished,
All suddenly mount   10
And scatter wheeling in great broken rings
Upon their clamorous wings.

I have looked upon those brilliant creatures,
And now my heart is sore.
All's changed since I, hearing at twilight,   15
The first time on this shore,
The bell-beat of their wings above my head,
Trod with a lighter tread.

Unwearied still, lover by lover,
They paddle in the cold   20
Companionable streams or climb the air;
Their hearts have not grown old;
Passion or conquest, wander where they will,
Attend upon them still.

But now they drift on the still water,   25
Mysterious, beautiful;
Among what rushes will they build,
By what lake's edge or pool

Delight men's eyes when I awake some day
To find they have flown away?   30

Leda and the Swan

A sudden blow: the great wings beating still
Above the staggering girl, her thighs caressed
By the dark webs, her nape caught in his bill,
He holds her helpless breast upon his breast.

How can those terrified vague fingers push   5
The feathered glory from her loosening thighs?
And how can body, laid in that white rush,
But feel the strange heart beating where it lies?

A shudder in the loins engenders there
The broken wall, the burning roof and tower   10
And Agamemnon dead.
                              Being so caught up,
So mastered by the brute blood of the air,
Did she put on his knowledge with his power
Before the indifferent beak could let her drop?   15

Sailing to Byzantium

I

That is no country for old men. The young
In one another's arms, birds in the trees
—Those dying generations—at their song,
The salmon-falls, the mackerel-crowded seas,
Fish, flesh, or fowl, commend all summer long   5

LEDA AND THE SWAN: Zeus, in the guise of a swan, raped Leda, Queen of Sparta. Helen,
their daughter, married Menelaus, King of Sparta, but ran off with Paris, son of Priam, King
of Troy. A ten-year siege of Troy by the Greeks ensued to bring Helen back.
   SAILING TO BYZANTIUM: Byzantium was the capital of the eastern Roman Empire and an
important center of art and architecture.

Whatever is begotten, born, and dies.
Caught in that sensual music all neglect
Monuments of unaging intellect.

II

An aged man is but a paltry thing,
A tattered coat upon a stick, unless   10
Soul clap its hands and sing, and louder sing
For every tatter in its mortal dress,
Nor is there singing school but studying
Monuments of its own magnificence;
And therefore I have sailed the seas and come   15
To the holy city of Byzantium.

III

O sages standing in God's holy fire
As in the gold mosaic of a wall,
Come from the holy fire, perne° in a gyre°,   descend/spiral
And be the singing-masters of my soul.   20
Consume my heart away; sick with desire
And fastened to a dying animal
It knows not what it is; and gather me
Into the artifice of eternity.

IV

Once out of nature I shall never take   25
My bodily form from any natural thing,
But such a form as Grecian goldsmiths make
Of hammered gold and gold enameling
To keep a drowsy Emperor awake;
Or set upon a golden bough to sing   30
To lords and ladies of Byzantium
Of what is past, or passing, or to come.

The Song of Wandering Aengus

I went out to the hazel wood,
Because a fire was in my head,
And cut and peeled a hazel wand,
And hooked a berry to a thread;

And when white moths were on the wing,   5
And moth-like stars were flickering out,
I dropped the berry in a stream
And caught a little silver trout.

When I had laid it on the floor
I went to blow the fire aflame,   10
But something rustled on the floor,
And some one called me by my name:
It had become a glimmering girl
With apple blossom in her hair
Who called me by my name and ran   15
And faded through the brightening air.

Though I am old with wandering
Through hollow lands and hilly lands,
I will find out where she has gone,
And kiss her lips and take her hands;   20
And walk among long dappled grass,
And pluck till time and times are done
The silver apples of the moon,
The golden apples of the sun.

Among School Children

I

I walk through the long schoolroom questioning;
A kind old nun in a white hood replies;
The children learn to cipher and to sing,
To study reading-books and history,
To cut and sew, be neat in everything   5
In the best modern way—the children's eyes
In momentary wonder stare upon
A sixty-year-old smiling public man.

II

I dream of a Ledaean body, bent
Above a sinking fire, a tale that she   10
Told of a harsh reproof, or trivial event
That changed some childish day to tragedy—
Told, and it seemed that our two natures blent

Into a sphere from youthful sympathy,
Or else, to alter Plato's parable,   15
Into the yolk and white of the one shell.

III

And thinking of that fit of grief or rage
I look upon one child or t'other there
And wonder if she stood so at that age—
For even daughters of the swan can share   20
Something of every paddler's heritage—
And had that colour upon cheek or hair,
And thereupon my heart is driven wild:
She stands before me as a living child.

IV

Her present image floats into the mind—   25
Did Quattrocento finger fashion it
Hollow of cheek as though it drank the wind
And took a mess of shadows for its meat?
And I though never of Ledaean kind
Had pretty plumage once—enough of that,   30
Better to smile on all that smile, and show
There is a comfortable kind of old scarecrow.

V

What youthful mother, a shape upon her lap
Honey of generation had betrayed,
And that must sleep, shriek, struggle to escape   35
As recollection or the drug decide,
Would think her son, did she but see that shape
With sixty or more winters on its head,
A compensation for the pang of his birth,
Or the uncertainty of his setting forth?   40

VI

Plato thought nature but a spume that plays
Upon a ghostly paradigm of things;
Solider Aristotle played the taws
Upon the bottom of a king of kings;
World-famous golden-thighed Pythagoras   45
Fingered upon a fiddle-stick or strings

What a star sang and careless Muses heard:
Old clothes upon old sticks to scare a bird.

VII

Both nuns and mothers worship images,
But those the candles light are not as those   50
That animate a mother's reveries,
But keep a marble or a bronze repose.
And yet they too break hearts—O Presences
That passion, piety or affection knows,
And that all heavenly glory symbolise—   55
O self-born mockers of man's enterprise;

VIII

Labour is blossoming or dancing where
The body is not bruised to pleasure soul,
Nor beauty born out of its own despair,
Nor blear-eyed wisdom out of midnight oil.   60
O chestnut-tree, great-rooted blossomer,
Are you the leaf, the blossom or the bole?
O body swayed to music, O brightening glance,
How can we know the dancer from the dance?

Amy Lowell

[1874–1925]

Patterns

I walk down the garden-paths,
And all the daffodils
Are blowing, and the bright blue squills.
I walk down the patterned garden-paths
In my stiff, brocaded gown.   5
With my powdered hair and jeweled fan,
I too am a rare
Pattern. As I wander down
The garden-paths.

My dress is richly figured,   10
And the train
Makes a pink and silver stain
On the gravel, and the thrift
Of the borders.
Just a plate of current fashion,   15
Tripping by in high-heeled, ribboned shoes.
Not a softness anywhere about me,
Only whalebone and brocade.
And I sink on a seat in the shade
Of a lime tree. For my passion   20
Wars against the stiff brocade.
The daffodils and squills
Flutter in the breeze
As they please.
And I weep;   25
For the lime-tree is in blossom
And one small flower has dropped upon my bosom.

And the plashing of waterdrops
In the marble fountain
Comes down the garden-paths.   30
The dripping never stops.
Underneath my stiffened gown
Is the softness of a woman bathing in a marble basin,
A basin in the midst of hedges grown
So thick, she cannot see her lover hiding,   35
But she guesses he is near,
And the sliding of the water
Seems the stroking of a dear
Hand upon her.
What is Summer in a fine brocaded gown!   40
I should like to see it lying in a heap upon the ground.
All the pink and silver crumpled up on the ground.
I would be the pink and silver as I ran along the paths,
And he would stumble after,
Bewildered by my laughter.   45
I should see the sun flashing from his sword-hilt and the buckles on his
    shoes.
I would choose
To lead him in a maze along the patterned paths,
A bright and laughing maze for my heavy-booted lover.
Till he caught me in the shade,   50
And the buttons of his waistcoat bruised my body as he clasped me,
Aching, melting, unafraid.
With the shadows of the leaves and the sundrops,

And the plopping of the waterdrops,
All about us in the open afternoon—   55
I am very like to swoon
With the weight of this brocade,
For the sun sifts through the shade.

Underneath the fallen blossom
In my bosom   60
Is a letter I have hid.
It was brought to me this morning by a rider from the Duke.
"Madam, we regret to inform you that Lord Hartwell
Died in action Thursday se'ennight."
As I read it in the white, morning sunlight,   65
The letters squirmed like snakes.
"Any answer, Madam," said my footman.
"No," I told him.
"See that the messenger takes some refreshment.
No, no answer."   70
And I walked into the garden,
Up and down the patterned paths,
In my stiff, correct brocade.
The blue and yellow flowers stood up proudly in the sun,
Each one.   75
I stood upright too,
Held rigid to the pattern
By the stiffness of my gown;
Up and down I walked,
Up and down: 80

In a month he would have been my husband.
In a month, here, underneath this lime,
We would have broke the pattern;
He for me, and I for him,
He as Colonel, I as Lady,   85
On this shady seat.
He had a whim
That sunlight carried blessing.
And I answered, "It shall be as you have said."
Now he is dead.   90

In Summer and in Winter I shall walk
Up and down
The patterned garden-paths.
The squills and daffodils
Will give place to pillared roses, and to asters, and to snow.   95
I shall go

Up and down
In my gown.
Gorgeously arrayed,
Boned and stayed.   100
And the softness of my body will be guarded from embrace
By each button, hook, and lace.
For the man who should loose me is dead,
Fighting with the Duke in Flanders,
In a pattern called a war.   105
Christ! What are patterns for?

Robert Frost

[1874–1963]

Mending Wall

Something there is that doesn't love a wall,
That sends the frozen-ground-swell under it,
And spills the upper boulders in the sun;
And makes gaps even two can pass abreast.
The work of hunters is another thing: 5
I have come after them and made repair
Where they have left not one stone on a stone,
But they would have the rabbit out of hiding,
To please the yelping dogs. The gaps I mean,
No one has seen them made or heard them made,   10
But at spring mending-time we find them there.
I let my neighbor know beyond the hill;
And on a day we meet to walk the line
And set the wall between us once again.
We keep the wall between us as we go.   15
To each the boulders that have fallen to each.
And some are loaves and some so nearly balls
We have to use a spell to make them balance:
'Stay where you are until our backs are turned!'
We wear our fingers rough with handling them.   20
Oh, just another kind of outdoor game,
One on a side. It comes to little more:
There where it is we do not need the wall:
He is all pine and I am apple orchard.

My apple trees will never get across 25
And eat the cones under his pines, I tell him.
He only says, 'Good fences make good neighbors.'
Spring is the mischief in me, and I wonder
If I could put a notion in his head:
'*Why* do they make good neighbors? Isn't it 30
Where there are cows? But here there are no cows.
Before I built a wall I'd ask to know
What I was walling in or walling out,
And to whom I was like to give offense.
Something there is that doesn't love a wall, 35
That wants it down.' I could say 'Elves' to him,
But it's not elves exactly, and I'd rather
He said it for himself. I see him there
Bringing a stone grasped firmly by the top
In each hand, like an old-stone savage armed. 40
He moves in darkness as it seems to me,
Not of woods only and the shade of trees.
He will not go behind his father's saying,
And he likes having thought of it so well
He says again, 'Good fences make good neighbors.' 45

Fire and Ice

Some say the world will end in fire,
Some say in ice.
From what I've tasted of desire
I hold with those who favor fire.
But if it had to perish twice, 5
I think I know enough of hate
To say that for destruction ice
Is also great
And would suffice.

After Apple-Picking

My long two-pointed ladder's sticking through a tree
Toward heaven still,
And there's a barrel that I didn't fill
Beside it, and there may be two or three
Apples I didn't pick upon some bough. 5

But I am done with apple-picking now.
Essence of winter sleep is on the night,
The scent of apples: I am drowsing off.
I cannot rub the strangeness from my sight
I got from looking through a pane of glass   10
I skimmed this morning from the drinking trough
And held against the world of hoary grass.
It melted, and I let it fall and break.
But I was well
Upon my way to sleep before it fell,   15
And I could tell
What form my dreaming was about to take.
Magnified apples appear and disappear,
Stem end and blossom end,
And every fleck of russet showing clear.   20
My instep arch not only keeps the ache,
It keeps the pressure of a ladder-round.
I feel the ladder sway as the boughs bend.
And I keep hearing from the cellar bin
The rumbling sound   25
Of load on load of apples coming in.
For I have had too much
Of apple-picking: I am overtired
Of the great harvest I myself desired.
There were ten thousand thousand fruit to touch,   30
Cherish in hand, lift down, and not let fall.
For all
That struck the earth,
No matter if not bruised or spiked with stubble,
Went surely to the cider-apple heap   35
As of no worth.
One can see what will trouble
This sleep of mine, whatever sleep it is.
Were he not gone,
The woodchuck could say whether it's like his   40
Long sleep, as I describe its coming on,
Or just some human sleep.

Desert Places

Snow falling and night falling fast, oh, fast
In a field I looked into going past,

And the ground almost covered smooth in snow,
But a few weeds and stubble showing last.

The woods around it have it—it is theirs.   5
All animals are smothered in their lairs.
I am too absent-spirited to count;
The loneliness includes me unawares.

And lonely as it is, that loneliness
Will be more lonely ere it will be less—   10
A blanker whiteness of benighted snow
With no expression, nothing to express.

They cannot scare me with their empty spaces
Between stars—on stars where no human race is.
I have it in me so much nearer home   15
To scare myself with my own desert places.

Acquainted with the Night

I have been one acquainted with the night.
I have walked out in rain—and back in rain.
I have outwalked the furthest city light.

I have looked down the saddest city lane.
I have passed by the watchman on his beat   5
And dropped my eyes, unwilling to explain.

I have stood still and stopped the sound of feet
When far away an interrupted cry
Came over houses from another street,

But not to call me back or say good-by;   10
And further still at an unearthly height
One luminary clock against the sky

Proclaimed the time was neither wrong nor right.
I have been one acquainted with the night.

Rainer Maria Rilke

[1875–1926]

The Song the Beggar Sings

Translated by Robert Bly

I go all the time from door to door,
scorched, soaked to the skin.
Then all at once I lay my right ear down
in my right hand.
Then my voice seems strange to me,   5
and I've never heard it like that!

Then I don't know exactly who is calling,
me or someone else.
I cry out about a cent or two,
the poets cry about more.   10

Finally, using both my eyes
I close my face,
and when it lies with its weight in my hand
it looks almost like rest.
That's so they won't think I have nowhere   15
to lay my head.

Portrait of My Father as a Young Man

Translated by Stephen Mitchell

In the eyes: dream. The brow as if it could feel
something far off. Around the lips, a great
freshness—seductive, though there is no smile.
Under the rows of ornamental braid
on the slim Imperial officer's uniform: 5
the saber's basket-hilt. Both hands stay
folded upon it, going nowhere, calm
and now almost invisible, as if they
were the first to grasp the distance and dissolve.
And all the rest so curtained with itself,   10

so cloudy, that I cannot understand
this figure as it fades into the background—.

Oh quickly disappearing photograph
in my more slowly disappearing hand.

Spanish Dancer

Translated by Stephen Mitchell

As on all its sides a kitchen-match darts white
flickering tongues before it bursts into flame:
with the audience around her, quickened, hot,
her dance begins to flicker in the dark room.

And all at once it is completely fire.   5

One upward glance and she ignites her hair
and, whirling faster and faster, fans her dress
into passionate flames, till it becomes a furnace
from which, like startled rattlesnakes, the long
naked arms uncoil, aroused and clicking.   10

And then: as if the fire were too tight
around her body, she takes and flings it out
haughtily, with an imperious gesture,
and watches: it lies raging on the floor,
still blazing up, and the flames refuse to die—.   15
Till, moving with total confidence and a sweet
exultant smile, she looks up finally
and stamps it out with powerful small feet.

Wallace Stevens

[1879–1955]

The Snow Man

One must have a mind of winter
To regard the frost and the boughs
Of the pine-trees crusted with snow;

And have been cold a long time
To behold the junipers shagged with ice,   5
The spruces rough in the distant glitter

Of the January sun; and not to think
Of any misery in the sound of the wind,
In the sound of a few leaves,

Which is the sound of the land   10
Full of the same wind
That is blowing in the same bare place

For the listener, who listens in the snow,
And, nothing himself, beholds
Nothing that is not there and the nothing that is.   15

Thirteen Ways of Looking at a Blackbird

1

Among twenty snowy mountains,
The only moving thing
Was the eye of the blackbird.

2

I was of three minds,
Like a tree   5
In which there are three blackbirds.

3

The blackbird whirled in the autumn winds.
It was a small part of the pantomime.

4

A man and a woman
Are one.   10
A man and a woman and a blackbird
Are one.

5

I do not know which to prefer,
The beauty of inflections
Or the beauty of innuendoes,   15
The blackbird whistling
Or just after.

6

Icicles filled the long window
With barbaric glass.
The shadow of the blackbird   20
Crossed it, to and fro.
The mood
Traced in the shadow
An indecipherable cause.

7

O thin men of Haddam,   25
Why do you imagine golden birds?
Do you not see how the blackbird
Walks around the feet
Of the women about you?

8

I know noble accents   30
And lucid, inescapable rhythms;
But I know, too,
That the blackbird is involved
In what I know.

9

When the blackbird flew out of sight,   35
It marked the edge
Of one of many circles.

10

At the sight of blackbirds
Flying in a green light,

Even the bawds of euphony   40
Would cry out sharply.

11

He rode over Connecticut
In a glass coach.
Once, a fear pierced him,
In that he mistook   45
The shadow of his equipage
For blackbirds.

12

The river is moving.
The blackbird must be flying.

13

It was evening all afternoon.   50
It was snowing
And it was going to snow.
The blackbird sat
In the cedar-limbs.

Anecdote of the Jar

I placed a jar in Tennessee,
And round it was, upon a hill.
It made the slovenly wilderness
Surround that hill.

The wilderness rose up to it,   5
And sprawled around, no longer wild.
The jar was round upon the ground
And tall and of a port in air.

It took dominion everywhere.
The jar was gray and bare.   10
It did not give of bird or bush,
Like nothing else in Tennessee.

Of Modern Poetry

The poem of the mind in the act of finding
What will suffice. It has not always had
To find: the scene was set; it repeated what
Was in the script.
               Then the theatre was changed   5
To something else. Its past was a souvenir.
It has to be living, to learn the speech of the place.
It has to face the men of the time and to meet
The women of the time. It has to think about war
And it has to find what will suffice. It has   10
To construct a new stage. It has to be on that stage
And, like an insatiable actor, slowly and
With meditation, speak words that in the ear,
In the delicatest ear of the mind, repeat,
Exactly, that which it wants to hear, at the sound   15
Of which, an invisible audience listens,
Not to the play, but to itself, expressed
In an emotion as of two people, as of two
Emotions becoming one. The actor is
A metaphysician in the dark, twanging   20
An instrument, twanging a wiry string that gives
Sounds passing through sudden rightnesses, wholly
Containing the mind, below which it cannot descend,
Beyond which it has no will to rise.
                     It must   25
Be the finding of a satisfaction, and may
Be of a man skating, a woman dancing, a woman
Combing. The poem of the act of the mind.

William Carlos Williams

[1883–1963]

The Red Wheelbarrow

so much depends
upon

a red wheel
barrow

glazed with rain
water

beside the white
chickens.

The Widow's Lament in Springtime

Sorrow is my own yard
where the new grass
flames as it has flamed
often before but not
with the cold fire   5
that closes round me this year.
Thirtyfive years
I lived with my husband.
The plumtree is white today
with masses of flowers.   10
Masses of flowers
loaded the cherry branches
and color some bushes
yellow and some red
but the grief in my heart   15
is stronger than they
for though they were my joy
formerly, today I notice them
and turned away forgetting.
Today my son told me   20
that in the meadows,
at the edge of the heavy woods
in the distance, he saw
trees of white flowers.
I feel that I would like   25
to go there
and fall into those flowers
and sink into the marsh near them.

Spring and All

By the road to the contagious hospital
under the surge of the blue

mottled clouds driven from the
northeast—a cold wind. Beyond, the
waste of broad, muddy fields   5
brown with dried weeds, standing and fallen

patches of standing water
the scattering of tall trees

All along the road the reddish
purplish, forked, upstanding, twiggy   10
stuff of bushes and small trees
with dead, brown leaves under them
leafless vines—

Lifeless in appearance, sluggish
dazed spring approaches—   15

They enter the new world naked,
cold, uncertain of all
save that they enter. All about them
the cold, familiar wind—

Now the grass, tomorrow   20
the stiff curl of wildcarrot leaf
One by one objects are defined—
It quickens: clarity, outline of leaf

But now the stark dignity of
entrance—Still, the profound change   25
has come upon them: rooted, they
grip down and begin to awaken

A Sort of a Song

Let the snake wait under
his weed
and the writing
be of words, slow and quick, sharp
to strike, quiet to wait,   5
sleepless.

—through metaphor to reconcile
the people and the stones.

Compose. (No ideas
but in things) Invent!   10
Saxifrage is my flower that splits
the rocks.

To a Poor Old Woman

munching a plum on
the street a paper bag
of them in her hand

They taste good to her
They taste good   5
to her. They taste
good to her

You can see it by
the way she gives herself
to the one half   10
sucked out in her hand

Comforted
a solace of ripe plums
seeming to fill the air
They taste good to her   15

The Young Housewife

At ten A.M. the young housewife
moves about in negligee behind
the wooden walls of her husband's house.
I pass solitary in my car.

Then again she comes to the curb   5
to call the ice-man, fish-man, and stands
shy, uncorseted, tucking in
stray ends of hair, and I compare her
to a fallen leaf.

The noiseless wheels of my car   10
rush with a crackling sound over
dried leaves as I bow and pass smiling.

Raleigh Was Right

We cannot go to the country
for the country will bring us no peace
What can the small violets tell us
that grow on furry stems in
the long grass among lance shaped leaves?   5

Though you praise us
and call to mind the poets
who sung of our loveliness
it was long ago!
long ago! when country people   10
would plough and sow with
flowering minds and pockets at ease—
if ever this were true.

Not now. Love itself a flower
with roots in a parched ground.   15
Empty pockets make empty heads.
Cure it if you can but
do not believe that we can live
today in the country
for the country will bring us no peace.   20

Landscape with the Fall of Icarus

According to Brueghel
when Icarus fell
it was spring

a farmer was ploughing
his field   5
the whole pageantry

RALEIGH WAS RIGHT: Williams's reply to Marlowe (p. 649) and Raleigh (p. 648).

of the year was
awake tingling
near

the edge of the sea   10
concerned
with itself

sweating in the sun
that melted
the wings' wax   15

unsignificantly
off the coast
there was

a splash quite unnoticed
this was   20
Icarus drowning

D. H. Lawrence

[1885–1930]

Snake

A snake came to my water-trough
On a hot, hot day, and I in pajamas for the heat,
To drink there.

In the deep, strange-scented shade of the great dark carob-tree
I came down the steps with my pitcher   5
And must wait, must stand and wait, for there he was at the trough
   before me.

He reached down from a fissure in the earth-wall in the gloom
And trailed his yellow-brown slackness soft-bellied down, over the
   edge of the stone trough
And rested his throat upon the stone bottom,
And where the water had dripped from the tap, in a small clearness,   10
He sipped with his straight mouth,

Softly drank through his straight gums, into his slack long body,
Silently.

Someone was before me at my water-trough,
And I, like a second comer, waiting.   15

He lifted his head from his drinking, as cattle do,
And looked at me vaguely, as drinking cattle do,
And flickered his two-forked tongue from his lips, and mused a
    moment,
And stooped and drank a little more,
Being earth-brown, earth-golden from the burning bowels of the earth   20
On the day of Sicilian July, with Etna smoking.

The voice of my education said to me
He must be killed,
For in Sicily the black, black snakes are innocent, the gold are
    venomous.

And voices in me said, If you were a man   25
You would take a stick and break him now, and finish him off.

But must I confess how I liked him,
How glad I was he had come like a guest in quiet, to drink at my
    water-trough
And depart peaceful, pacified, and thankless,
Into the burning bowels of this earth?   30

Was it cowardice, that I dared not kill him?
Was it perversity, that I longed to talk to him?
Was it humility, to feel so honored?
I felt so honored.

And yet those voices:
If you were not afraid, you would kill him!   35

And truly I was afraid, I was most afraid,
But even so, honored still more
That he should seek my hospitality
From out the dark door of the secret earth.

He drank enough   40
And lifted his head, dreamily, as one who has drunken,

And flickered his tongue like a forked night on the air, so black,
Seeming to lick his lips,
And looked around like a god, unseeing, into the air,
And slowly turned his head,   45
And slowly, very slowly, as if thrice adream,
Proceeded to draw his slow length curving round
And climb again the broken bank of my wall-face.

And as he put his head into that dreadful hole,
And as he slowly drew up, snake-easing his shoulders, and entered
    farther,   50
A sort of horror, a sort of protest against his withdrawing into that
    horrid black hole,
Deliberately going into the blackness, and slowly drawing himself
    after,
Overcame me now his back was turned.

I looked round, I put down my pitcher,
I picked up a clumsy log   55
And threw it at the water-trough with a clatter.

I think it did not hit him,
But suddenly that part of him that was left behind convulsed in
    undignified haste.
Writhed like lightning, and was gone
Into the black hole, the earth-lipped fissure in the wall-front,   60
At which, in the intense still noon, I stared with fascination.

And immediately I regretted it.
I thought how paltry, how vulgar, what a mean act!
I despised myself and the voices of my accursed human education.

And I thought of the albatross   65
And I wished he would come back, my snake.

For he seemed to me again like a king,
Like a king in exile, uncrowned in the underworld,
Now due to be crowned again.

And so, I missed my chance with one of the lords   70
Of life.
And I have something to expiate;
A pettiness.

Ezra Pound

[1885–1972]

In a Station of the Metro

The apparition of these faces in the crowd;
Petals on a wet, black bough.

Fan-Piece, for Her Imperial Lord

O Fan of white silk,
        clear as frost on the grass-blade,
You also are laid aside.

The River-Merchant's Wife: A Letter

While my hair was still cut straight across my forehead
I played about the front gate, pulling flowers.
You came by on bamboo stilts, playing horse,
You walked about my seat, playing with blue plums.
And we went on living in the village of Chōkan: 5
Two small people, without dislike or suspicion.

At fourteen I married My Lord you.
I never laughed, being bashful.
Lowering my head, I looked at the wall.
Called to, a thousand times, I never looked back.   10

At fifteen I stopped scowling,
I desired my dust to be mingled with yours
Forever and forever and forever.
Why should I climb the look out?

THE RIVER-MERCHANT'S WIFE: A LETTER: Pound's English version of a Chinese poem by
Rihaku (Li T'ai Po); so is the next poem, "The Jewel Stairs' Grievance."

At sixteen you departed,   15
You went into far Ku-tō-en, by the river of swirling eddies,
And you have been gone five months.
The monkeys make sorrowful noise overhead.

You dragged your feet when you went out.
By the gate now, the moss is grown, the different mosses,   20
Too deep to clear them away!
The leaves fall early this autumn, in wind.
The paired butterflies are already yellow with August
Over the grass in the West garden;
They hurt me. I grow older.   25
If you are coming down through the narrows of the river Kiang,
Please let me know before hand,
And I will come out to meet you
        As far as Chō-fū-Sa.   30

The Jewel Stairs' Grievance

    The jewelled steps are already quite white
      with dew,
    It is so late that the dew soaks my gauze
      stockings,
    And I let down the crystal curtain
    And watch the moon through the clear autumn.

Epitaphs

Fu I

    Fu I loved the high cloud and the hill,
    Alas, he died of alcohol.

THE JEWEL STAIRS' GRIEVANCE: *Pound's Note*—Jewel stairs, therefore a palace. Grievance, therefore there is something to complain of. Gauze stockings, therefore a court lady, not a servant who complains. Clear autumn, therefore he has no excuse on account of weather. Also she has come early, for the dew has not merely whitened the stairs. but has soaked her stockings. The poem is especially prized because she utters no direct reproach.

Li Po

And Li Po also died drunk.
He tried to embrace a moon
In the Yellow River.

The Garden

EN ROBE DE PARADE
—*Samain*

Like a skein of loose silk blown against a wall
She walks by the railing of a path in Ken-
  sington Gardens,
And she is dying piece-meal
  of a sort of emotional anæmia.

And round about there is a rabble
Of the filthy, sturdy, unkillable infants of the very
  poor.   5
They shall inherit the earth.

In her is the end of breeding.
Her boredom is exquisite and excessive.
She would like some one to speak to her,
And is almost afraid that I   10
  will commit that indiscretion.

H. D. (Hilda Doolittle)

[1886–1961]

Heat

O wind, rend open the heat,
  cut apart the heat,
  rend it to tatters.

THE GARDEN: Compare to Amy Lowell's "Patterns," pp. 755–758.

Fruit cannot drop
through this thick air—   5
fruit cannot fall into heat
that presses up and blunts
the points of pears
and rounds the grapes.

Cut the heat—   10
plough through it,
turning it on either side
of your path.

Marianne Moore

[1887–1972]

Poetry

I, too, dislike it: there are things that are important beyond all this
    fiddle.
    Reading it, however, with a perfect contempt for it, one discovers in
    it after all, a place for the genuine.
        Hands that can grasp, eyes
        that can dilate, hair that can rise   5
            if it must, these things are important not because a

high-sounding interpretation can be put upon them but because they
    are
    useful. When they become so derivative as to become unintelligible,
    the same thing may be said for all of us, that we
        do not admire what   10
        we cannot understand: the bat
            holding on upside down or in quest of something to

eat, elephants pushing, a wild horse taking a roll, a tireless wolf under
    a tree, the immovable critic twitching his skin like a horse that feels
        a flea, the base-
        ball fan, the statistician—   15
            nor is it valid
                to discriminate against "business documents and

school-books"; all these phenomena are important. One must make
  a distinction
    however: when dragged into prominence by half poets, the result
      is not poetry,
    nor till the poets among us can be   20
      "literalists of
      the imagination"—above
        insolence and triviality and can present

for inspection, "imaginary gardens with real toads in them," shall
  we have
  it. In the meantime, if you demand on the one hand,   25
  the raw material of poetry in
    all its rawness and
    that which is on the other hand
      genuine, you are interested in poetry.

T. S. Eliot

[1888–1965]

Journey of the Magi

'A cold coming we had of it,
Just the worst time of the year
For a journey, and such a long journey:
The ways deep and the weather sharp,
The very dead of winter.'   5
And the camels galled, sore-footed, refractory,
Lying down in the melting snow.
There were times we regretted
The summer palaces on slopes, the terraces,
And the silken girls bringing sherbet.   10
Then the camel men cursing and grumbling
And running away, and wanting their liquor and women,
And the night-fires going out, and the lack of shelters,
And the cities hostile and the towns unfriendly
And the villages dirty and charging high prices: 15
A hard time we had of it.
At the end we preferred to travel all night,
Sleeping in snatches,

With the voices singing in our ears, saying
That this was all folly.   20

Then at dawn we came down to a temperate valley,
Wet, below the snow line, smelling of vegetation;
With a running stream and a water-mill beating the darkness,
And three trees on the low sky,
And an old white horse galloped away in the meadow.   25
Then we came to a tavern with vine-leaves over the lintel,
Six hands at an open door dicing for pieces of silver,
And feet kicking the empty wine-skins.
But there was no information, and so we continued
And arrived at evening, not a moment too soon   30
Finding the place; it was (you may say) satisfactory.

All this was a long time ago, I remember,
And I would do it again, but set down
This set down
This: were we led all that way for   35
Birth or Death? There was a Birth, certainly,
We had evidence and no doubt. I had seen birth and death,
But had thought they were different; this Birth was
Hard and bitter agony for us, like Death, our death.
We returned to our places, these Kingdoms,   40
But no longer at ease here, in the old dispensation,
With an alien people clutching their gods.
I should be glad of another death.

The Love Song of J. Alfred Prufrock

S'io credessi che mia risposta fosse
A persona che mai tornasse al mondo,
Questa fiamma staria senza più scosse.
Ma per ciò che giammai di questo fondo
Non tornò vivo alcun, s'i'odo il vero,
Senza tema d'infamia ti rispondo.

THE LOVE SONG OF J. ALFRED PRUFROCK: Epigraph from Dante's *Inferno*, Canto XXVII, 61–66. The words are spoken by Guido da Montefeltro when asked to identify himself: "If I thought my answer were given to anyone who could ever return to the world, this flame would shake no more; but since none ever did return above from this depth, if what I hear is true, without fear of infamy I answer thee."

Let us go then, you and I,
When the evening is spread out against the sky
Like a patient etherized upon a table;
Let us go, through certain half-deserted streets,
The muttering retreats   5
Of restless nights in one-night cheap hotels
And sawdust restaurants with oyster-shells:
Streets that follow like a tedious argument
Of insidious intent
To lead you to an overwhelming question . . .   10
Oh, do not ask, "What is it?"
Let us go and make our visit.

In the room the women come and go
Talking of Michelangelo.

The yellow fog that rubs its back upon the window-panes,   15
The yellow smoke that rubs its muzzle on the window-panes,
Licked its tongue into the corners of the evening,
Lingered upon the pools that stand in drains,
Let fall upon its back the soot that falls from chimneys,
Slipped by the terrace, made a sudden leap,   20
And seeing that it was a soft October night,
Curled once about the house, and fell asleep.

And indeed there will be time
For the yellow smoke that slides along the street
Rubbing its back upon the window-panes;   25
There will be time, there will be time
To prepare a face to meet the faces that you meet;
There will be time to murder and create,
And time for all the works and days of hands
That lift and drop a question on your plate;   30
Time for you and time for me,
And time yet for a hundred indecisions,
And for a hundred visions and revisions,
Before the taking of a toast and tea.

In the room the women come and go   35
Talking of Michelangelo.

And indeed there will be time
To wonder, "Do I dare?" and, "Do I dare?"
Time to turn back and descend the stair,
With a bald spot in the middle of my hair—   40
(They will say: "How his hair is growing thin!")

My morning coat, my collar mounting firmly to the chin,
My necktie rich and modest, but asserted by a simple pin—
(They will say: "But how his arms and legs are thin!")
Do I dare   45
Disturb the universe?
In a minute there is time
For decisions and revisions which a minute will reverse.

For I have known them all already, known them all—
Have known the evenings, mornings, afternoons,   50
I have measured out my life with coffee spoons;
I know the voices dying with a dying fall
Beneath the music from a farther room.
  So how should I presume?

And I have known the eyes already, known them all—   55
The eyes that fix you in a formulated phrase,
And when I am formulated, sprawling on a pin,
When I am pinned and wriggling on the wall,
Then how should I begin
To spit out all the butt-ends of my days and ways?   60
  And how should I presume?

And I have known the arms already, known them all—
Arms that are braceleted and white and bare
(But in the lamplight, downed with light brown hair!)
Is it perfume from a dress   65
That makes me so digress?
Arms that lie along a table, or wrap about a shawl.
  And should I then presume?
  And how should I begin?
   ·   ·   ·   ·   ·

Shall I say, I have gone at dusk through narrow streets   70
And watched the smoke that rises from the pipes
Of lonely men in shirt-sleeves, leaning out of windows? . . .

I should have been a pair of ragged claws
Scuttling across the floors of silent seas.
   ·   ·   ·   ·   ·

And the afternoon, the evening, sleeps so peacefully!   75
Smoothed by long fingers,
Asleep . . . tired . . . or it malingers,
Stretched on the floor, here beside you and me.
Should I, after tea and cakes and ices,
Have the strength to force the moment to its crisis?   80
But though I have wept and fasted, wept and prayed,

Though I have seen my head (grown slightly bald) brought in upon a
    platter,
I am no prophet—and here's no great matter;
I have seen the moment of my greatness flicker,
And I have seen the eternal Footman hold my coat, and snicker,   85
And in short, I was afraid.

And would it have been worth it, after all,
After the cups, the marmalade, the tea,
Among the porcelain, among some talk of you and me,
Would it have been worth while,   90
To have bitten off the matter with a smile,
To have squeezed the universe into a ball
To roll it toward some overwhelming question,
To say: "I am Lazarus, come from the dead,
Come back to tell you all, I shall tell you all"—   95
If one, settling a pillow by her head,
    Should say: "That is not what I meant at all.
    That is not it, at all."

And would it have been worth it, after all,
Would it have been worth while,   100
After the sunsets and the dooryards and the sprinkled streets,
After the novels, after the teacups, after the skirts that trail along the
    floor—
And this, and so much more?—
It is impossible to say just what I mean!
But as if a magic lantern threw the nerves in patterns on a screen: 105
Would it have been worth while
If one, settling a pillow or throwing off a shawl,
And turning toward the window, should say:
    "That is not it at all,
    That is not what I meant, at all."   110
   .   .   .   .   .

No! I am not Prince Hamlet, nor was meant to be;
Am an attendant lord, one that will do
To swell a progress,° start a scene or two,   *royal journey*
Advise the prince; no doubt, an easy tool,
Deferential, glad to be of use,   115
Politic, cautious, and meticulous;

---

82. **head . . . platter:** John the Baptist was beheaded at the order of King Herod to please
his wife and daughter. See Matthew 14:1–11.
    94. **Lazarus:** Jesus raised him from the dead. See John 11:1–44.

Full of high sentence°, but a bit obtuse;   sententiousness
At times, indeed, almost ridiculous—
Almost, at times, the Fool.

I grow old . . . I grow old . . .   120
I shall wear the bottoms of my trousers rolled.

Shall I part my hair behind? Do I dare to eat a peach?
I shall wear white flannel trousers, and walk upon the beach.
I have heard the mermaids singing, each to each.

I do not think that they will sing to me.   125

I have seen them riding seaward on the waves
Combing the white hair of the waves blown back
When the wind blows the water white and black.

We have lingered in the chambers of the sea
By sea-girls wreathed with seaweed red and brown   130
Till human voices wake us, and we drown.

John Crowe Ransom

[*1888–1974*]

Bells for John Whiteside's Daughter

There was such speed in her little body,
And such lightness in her footfall,
It is no wonder her brown study°   reverie
Astonishes us all.

Her wars were bruited° in our high window.   sounded 5
We looked among orchard trees and beyond
Where she took arms against her shadow,
Or harried unto the pond

The lazy geese, like a snow cloud
Dripping their snow on the green grass,   10
Tricking and stopping, sleepy and proud,
Who cried in goose, Alas,

For the tireless heart within the little
Lady with rod that made them rise
From their noon apple-dreams and scuttle   15
Goose-fashion under the skies!

But now go the bells, and we are ready,
In one house we are sternly stopped
To say we are vexed at her brown study,
Lying so primly propped.

Anna Akhmatova

[*1889–*]

Requiem

Translated by Robin Kemball

No, not far beneath some foreign sky then,
Not with foreign wings to shelter me,—
I was with my people then, close by them
Where my luckless people chanced to be.

By Way of a Preface

In the terrible years of the Yezhovshchina, I spent seventeen months in the prison queues in Leningrad. Somehow, one day, someone "identified" me. Then a woman standing behind me, whose lips were blue with cold, and who, naturally enough, had never even heard of my name, emerged from that state of torpor common to us all and, putting her lips close to my ear (there, everyone spoke in whispers), asked me:

—And could you describe *this?*

And I answered her:

—I can.

Then something vaguely like a smile flashed across what once had been her face.

1 April 1957
Leningrad

REQUIEM: Preface. **Yezhovshchina:** roughly, "the reign of Yezhov." Yezhov was head of the Soviet secret police in the late 1930's until he himself became a victim of one of Stalin's purges.

Dedication

Mountains bow beneath that boundless sorrow,
And the mighty river stops its flow.
But those prison bolts are tried and thorough,
And beyond them, every "convict's burrow"
Tells a tale of mortal woe.   5
Someone, somewhere, feels the cool wind, bracing,
Sees the sun go nestling down to rest—
We know nothing, we, together facing
Still the sickening clank of keys, the pacing
Of the sentries with their heavy steps.   10
We'd rise, as for early Mass, each morning,
Cross the callous city, wend our way,
Meet, more lifeless than the dead, half mourning,
Watch the sun sink, the Neva mist forming,   15
But with hope still singing far away.
Sentenced . . . And at once the tears come rolling,
Cut off from the world, quite on her own,
Heart reduced to shreds, and almost falling,
Just as if some lout had sent her sprawling,
Still . . . She staggers on her way . . . Alone . . .   20
Where are now the friends of my misfortune,
Those that shared my own two years of hell?
What do the Siberian snow-winds caution,
What bodes the moon circle for their fortunes?
Theirs be this, my greeting and farewell.   25

Prelude

It was when no one smiled any longer
Save the dead, who were glad of release.
And when Leningrad dangled, incongruous,
By its prisons—a needless caprice.
And when, out of their minds with sheer suffering,   30
The long lines of the newly condemned
Heard the engines' shrill whistles go sputtering
A brief song of farewell to their friends.
Stars of death stood above us, and Russia,
In her innocence, twisted in pain   35
Under blood-spattered boots, and the shudder
Of the Black Marias in their train.

1

It was dawn when they took you. I followed,
As a widow walks after the bier.
By the icons—a candle, burnt hollow;   40
In the bed-room—the children, in tears.
Your lips—cool from the kiss of the icon,
Still to think—the cold sweat on your brow . . .
Like the wives of the Streltsy, now I come
To wail under the Kremlin's gaunt towers.   45

2

Silent flows the silent Don,
Yellow moon looks quietly on,

Cap askew, looks in the room,
Sees a shadow in the gloom.

Sees this woman, sick, at home,   50
Sees this woman, all alone,

Husband buried, then to see
Son arrested . . . Pray for me.

3

No, this is not me, this is somebody else that suffers.
I could never face that, and all that has happened: 55
Let sackcloth and ashes enshroud it,
And see all the lamps are removed . . .
          Night.

4

You, my mocking one, pet of society,
And gay sinner of Tsarskoe Selo: 60
Had you dreamt, in your sweet notoriety,
Of the future that lay in store—

---

37. **Black Marias:** black automobiles used to carry off prisoners abducted during the night
during the time of Stalin's purges.
60. **Tsarskoe Selo:** The poet spent her youth here.

How you'd stand at the Crosses, three-hundredth
In the queue, each bleak New Year,
Hug your precious parcel of comforts,   65
Melt the ice with your hot bright tears.
There the poplar, used to imprisonment,
Sways aloft. Not a sound. But think
Of the numbers rotting there, innocent . . .

5

For seventeen long months my pleas,   70
My cries have called you home.
I've begged the hangman on my knees,
My son, my dread, my own.
My mind's mixed up for good, and I'm
No longer even clear   75
Who's man, who's beast, nor how much time
Before the end draws near.
And only flowers decked with dust,
And censers ringing, footprints thrust
Somewhere-nowhere, afar.   80
And, staring me straight in the eye
And warning me that death is nigh—
One monumental star.

6

Weeks fly past in light profusion,
How to fathom what's been done: 85
How those long white nights, dear son,
Watched you in your cell's seclusion.
How once more they watch you there,
Eyes like hawks' that burn right through you,
Speak to you of death, speak to you   90
Of the lofty cross you bear.

7
Sentence

And the word in stone has fallen heavy
On my breast, which was alive till now.
Never mind—for, mark you, I was ready,
I shall get along somehow.   95

---

63. **the Crosses:** a prison in Leningrad whose buildings form a cross.

So much to be done before tomorrow:
Crush the memory till no thoughts remain,
Carve a heart in stone, immune to sorrow,
Teach myself to face life once again,—

And if not . . . The rustling heat of summer   100
Fills my window with its festive tone.
I long since foresensed that there would come a
Sunny day like this—and empty home.

8

To Death

You'll come in any case—then why not right away?
I'm waiting—life has dragged me under.   105
I've put the lamp out, left the door to show the way
When you come in your simple wonder.
For that, choose any guise you like: Burst in on me,
A shell with poison-gas container,
Or, bandit with a heavy weight, creep up on me,   110
Or poison me with typhus vapour.
Or be a fable, known *ad nauseam*
To everyone denounced in error,
So I may see the top of that blue cap, and scan
The face of the house-porter, white with terror.   115
But nothing matters now. The Yenisey° swirls by,   a river
The Pole star shines above the torrent.
And the glint of those beloved eyes
Conceals the last, the final horror.

9

So madness now has wrapped its wings   120
Round half my soul and plies me, heartless,
With draughts of fiery wine, begins
To lure me towards the vale of darkness.

And I can see that I must now
Concede the victory—as I listen,   125
The dream that dogged my fevered brow
Already seems an outside vision.

---

114. **blue cap:** refers to the uniform worn by the secret police (NKVD).

And though I go on bended knee
To plead, implore its intercession,
There's nothing I may take with me,   130
It countenances no concession:

Nor yet my son's distracted eyes—
The rock-like suffering rooted in them,
The day the storm broke from clear skies,
The hour spent visiting the prison,   135

Nor yet the kind, cool clasp of hands,
The lime-tree shadows' fitful darting,
The far light call across the land—
The soothing words exchanged on parting.

10
Crucifixion
Weep not for Me, Mother,
that I am in the grave.

I

The angels hailed that solemn hour and stately,   140
The heavens dissolved in tongues of fire. And He
Said to the Father: "Why didst Thou forsake Me!"
And to His Mother: "Weep thou not for Me . . . "

II

Magdalena sobbed, and the disciple,
He whom Jesus loved, stood petrified.   145
But there, where His Mother stood in silence,
No one durst so much as lift their eyes.

Epilogue
I

I've learned how faces droop and then grow hollow,
How fear looks out from underneath the lids,
How cheeks, carved out of suffering and of sorrow,   150
Take on the lines of rough cuneiform scripts.
How heads of curls, but lately black or ashen,

Turn suddenly to silver overnight,
Smiles fade on lips reduced to dread submission,
A hoarse dry laugh stands in for trembling fright.   155
I pray, not for myself alone, my cry
Goes up for all those with me there—for all,
In heart of winter, heat-wave of July,
Who stood beneath that blind, deep-crimson wall.

II

The hour of remembrance is with us again.   160
I see you, I hear you, I feel you as then:

There's one they scarce dragged to the window, and one
Whose days in the land of her forebears are done,

And one tossed her beautiful head back when shown
Her corner, and said: "It's like being back home!"   165

I'd like to remember each one by her name,
But they took the list, and there's no more remain.

I've worked them a funeral shroud from each word
Of pain that escaped them, and I overheard.

I'll think of them everywhere, always, each one.   170
I shall not forget them in dark days to come.

And should they once silence my mortified lips,
Let one hundred millions for whom my voice speaks—

Let *them* take my place, and remember each year
Whenever my day of remembrance draws near.   175

And should they one day, in this country, agree
To raise a memorial somewhere to me,

I'd willingly give my consent to their plan,
But on one condition, which is—that it stand,

Not down by the sea, where I entered this world   180
(I've cut the last links that once bound us of old),

Nor yet by the tree-stump in old Tsarsky Sad,
Whose shade seeks me still with disconsolate love,

But here, where they let me stand three hundred hours,
And never so much as unbolted the doors.   185

For even in death I still fear to forget
The grim Black Marias, their thundering tread,

The sickening slam of that loathsome cell-door,
The old woman's howl, like a wounded beast's roar.

And may the snow, melting, well forth clear and strong,   190
Like tears from my eye-lids, unmoving, like bronze,

And may the lone prison-dove coo from afar,
And boats travel silently down the Neva.

Claude McKay

[1890–1948]

The Tropics in New York

Bananas ripe and green, and ginger-root,
    Cocoa in pods and alligator pears,
And tangerines and mangoes and grape fruit,
    Fit for the highest prize at parish fairs,

Set in the window, bringing memories   5
    Of fruit-trees laden by low-singing rills,
And dewy dawns, and mystical blue skies
    In benediction over nun-like hills.

My eyes grew dim, and I could no more gaze;
    A wave of longing through my body swept,   10
And, hungry for the old, familiar ways,
    I turned aside and bowed my head and wept.

Archibald MacLeish

[*1892–1982*]

Ars Poetica

A poem should be palpable and mute
As a globed fruit,

Dumb
As old medallions to the thumb,

Silent as the sleeve-worn stone   5
Of casement ledges where the moss has grown—

A poem should be wordless
As the flight of birds.

A poem should be motionless in time
As the moon climbs,   10

Leaving, as the moon releases
Twig by twig the night-entangled trees,

Leaving, as the moon behind the winter leaves,
Memory by memory the mind—

A poem should be motionless in time   15
As the moon climbs.

A poem should be equal to:
Not true.

For all the history of grief
An empty doorway and a maple leaf.   20

For love
The leaning grasses and two lights above the sea—

A poem should not mean
But be.

e. e. cummings

[1894–1962]

pity this busy monster

pity this busy monster, manunkind,

not. Progress is a comfortable disease:
your victim(death and life safely beyond)

plays with the bigness of his littleness
—electrons deify one razorblade   5
into a mountainrange;lenses extend

unwish through curving wherewhen till unwish
returns on its unself.
                         A world of made
is not a world of born—pity poor flesh   10

and trees,poor stars and stones,but never this
fine specimen of hypermagical

ultraomnipotence. We doctors know

a hopeless case if—listen:there's a hell
of a good universe next door;let's go

my father moved through dooms of love

my father moved through dooms of love
through sames of am through haves of give,
singing each morning out of each night
my father moved through depths of height

this motionless forgetful where   5
turned at his glance to shining here;
that if (so timid air is firm)
under his eyes would stir and squirm

MY FATHER MOVED THROUGH DOOMS OF LOVE: cummings's father, Rev. Edward
Cummings, was a Unitarian minister in Boston.

newly as from unburied which
floats the first who,his april touch   10
drove sleeping selves to swarm their fates
woke dreamers to their ghostly roots

and should some why completely weep
my father's fingers brought her sleep:
vainly no smallest voice might cry   15
for he could feel the mountains grow.

Lifting the valleys of the sea
my father moved through griefs of joy;
praising a forehead called the moon
singing desire into begin   20

joy was his song and joy so pure
a heart of star by him could steer
and pure so now and now so yes
the wrists of twilight would rejoice

keen as midsummer's keen beyond   25
conceiving mind of sun will stand,
so strictly (over utmost him
so hugely) stood my father's dream

his flesh was flesh his blood was blood:
no hungry man but wished him food;   30
no cripple wouldn't creep one mile
uphill to only see him smile.

Scorning the pomp of must and shall
my father moved through dooms of feel;
his anger was as right as rain   35
his pity was as green as grain

septembering arms of year extend
less humbly wealth to foe and friend
than he to foolish and to wise
offered immeasurable is   40

proudly and (by octobering flame
beckoned) as earth will downward climb,
so naked for immortal work
his shoulders marched against the dark

his sorrow was as true as bread: 45
no liar looked him in the head;
if every friend became his foe
he'd laugh and build a world with snow.

My father moved through theys of we,
singing each new leaf out of each tree   50
(and every child was sure that spring
danced when she heard my father sing)

then let men kill which cannot share,
let blood and flesh be mud and mire,
scheming imagine,passion willed,   55
freedom a drug that's bought and sold

giving to steal and cruel kind,
a heart to fear,to doubt a mind,
to differ a disease of same,
conform the pinnacle of am   60

though dull were all we taste as bright,
bitter all utterly things sweet,
maggoty minus and dumb death
all we inherit,all bequeath

and nothing quite so least as truth   65
—i say though hate were why men breathe—
because my father lived his soul
love is the whole and more than all

Jean Toomer

[*1894–1967*]

Reapers

Black reapers with the sound of steel on stones
Arc sharpening scythes. I see them place the hones
In their hip-pockets as a thing that's done,
And start their silent swinging, one by one.
Black horses drive a mower through the weeds,   5
And there, a field rat, startled, squealing bleeds,

His belly close to ground. I see the blade,
Blood-stained, continue cutting weeds and shade.

Face

Hair—
silver-gray,
like streams of stars,
Brows—
recurved canoes   5
quivered by the ripples blown by pain,
Her eyes—
mist of tears
condensing on the flesh below
And her channeled muscles   10
are cluster grapes of sorrow
purple in the evening sun
nearly ripe for worms.

Federico Garcia Lorca

[1899–1936]

Rider's Song

Translated by Stephen Spender and J. L. Gili

Córdoba.
Far away and alone.

Black pony, big moon,
and olives in my saddle-bag.
Although I know the roads   5
I'll never reach Córdoba.

Through the plain, through the wind,
black pony, red moon.
Death is looking at me
from the towers of Córdoba.   10

Ay! How long the road!
Ay! My valiant pony!
Ay! That death should wait me
before I reach Córdoba.

Córdoba.   15
Far away and alone.

Sleepwalking Ballad

Translated by William Logan

Green, how I want you green.
Green wind. Green branches.
The ship out on the sea
and the horse on the mountain.
With the shade around her waist   5
she dreams on her balcony,
green flesh, her hair green,
with eyes of cold silver.
Green, how I want you green.
Under the gypsy moon,   10
all things are watching her
and she cannot see them.

Green, how I want you green.
Big hoarfrost stars
come with the fish of shadow   15
that opens the road of dawn.
The fig tree rubs its wind
with the sandpaper of its branches,
and the forest, cunning cat,
bristles its brittle fibers.   20
But who will come? And from where?
She is still on her balcony
green flesh, her hair green,
dreaming in the bitter sea.

—My friend, I want to trade   25
my horse for her house,
my saddle for her mirror,
my knife for her blanket.
My friend, I come bleeding
from the gates of Cabra.   30

—If it were possible, my boy,
I'd help you fix that trade.
But now I am not I,
nor is my house now my house.
—My friend, I want to die   35
decently in my bed.
Of iron, if that's possible,
with blankets of fine chambray.
Don't you see the wound I have
from my chest up to my throat?   40
—Your white shirt has grown
thirty dark brown roses.
Your blood oozes and flees
around the corners of your sash.
But now I am not I,   45
nor is my house now my house.
—Let me climb up, at least,
up to the high balconies;
Let me climb up! Let me,
up to the green balconies.   50
Railings of the moon
through which the water rumbles.

Now the two friends climb up,
up to the high balconies.
Leaving a trail of blood.   55
Leaving a trail of teardrops.
Tin bell vines
were trembling on the roofs.
A thousand crystal tambourines
struck at the dawn light.   60

Green, how I want you green,
green wind, green branches.
The two friends climbed up.
The stiff wind left
in their mouths, a strange taste   65
of bile, of mint, and of basil.
My friend, where is she—tell me—
where is your bitter girl?
How many times she waited for you!
How many times would she wait for you,   70
cool face, black hair,
on this green balcony!
Over the mouth of the cistern
the gypsy girl was swinging,

green flesh, her hair green,   75
with eyes of cold silver.
An icicle of moon
holds her up above the water.
The night became intimate
like a little plaza.   80
Drunken "Guardias Civiles°"   Civil Guards
were pounding on the door.
Green, how I want you green.
Green wind. Green branches.
The ship out on the sea.   85
And the horse on the mountain.

Jorge Luis Borges

[1899–1986]

The Blind Man

Translated by Alastair Reid

1

He is divested of the diverse world,
of faces, which still stay as once they were,
of the adjoining streets, now far away,
and of the concave sky, once infinite.
Of books, he keeps no more that what is left him   5
by memory, that brother of forgetting,
which keeps the formula but not the feeling
and which reflects no more than tag and name.
Traps lie in wait for me. My every step
might be a fall. I am a prisoner   10
shuffling through a time which feels like dream,
taking no note of mornings or of sunsets.
It is night. I am alone. In verse like this,
I must create my insipid universe.

2

Since I was born, in 1899,   15
beside the concave vine and the deep cistern,

frittering time, so brief in memory,
kept taking from me all my eye-shaped world.
Both days and nights would wear away the profiles
of human letters and of well-loved faces.   20
My wasted eyes would ask their useless questions
of pointless libraries and lecterns.
Blue and vermilion both are now a fog,
both useless sounds. The mirror I look into
is gray. I breathe a rose across the garden,   25
a wistful rose, my friends, out of the twilight.
Only the shades of yellow stay with me
and I can see only to look on nightmares.

Francis Ponge

[1899–   ]

The Cigarette

Translated by Cid Corman

Let us render first the atmosphere at once misty and dry, dishevelled, in which the cigarette is always set askew since continuedly creating it.

Then her person: a small torch a good deal less luminous than scented, from which are detached and drop to a rhythm to be determined a calculable number of small masses of ash.

Her passion at last: this glowing bud, desquamating in silvery scurf, which an immediate muff made of the most recent encircles.

Les Mûres/*blackberries*

Translated by Cid Corman

In the typographical bushes constituted by the poem on a way that leads neither beyond things nor to the mind/spirit, certain fruits are formed from an agglomeration of spheres that a drop of ink fills.

*

Black, pink and *kaki*-red together in the cluster, they offer rather the spectacle of an arrogant family of different ages than a very keen temptation to be plucked.

In view of the disproportion of the pips to the pulp the birds esteem them little, so very little in the end remains of them when from beak to anus they have gone through them.

*

But the poet in the course of his professional promenade takes of their seed with reason: "Just so," says he to himself, "by and large the patient efforts of a very fragile flower although defended by a forbidding entanglement of thorns succeed. Without a great many other qualities,— blackberries *(mûres)*, are perfectly ripe *(mûres)*—even as this poem comes to its perfection."

Arna Bontemps

[1902–   ]

A Black Man Talks of Reaping

I have sown beside all waters in my day.
I planted deep, within my heart the fear
That wind or fowl would take the grain away.
I planted safe against this stark, lean year.

I scattered seed enough to plant the land   5
In rows from Canada to Mexico
But for my reaping only what the hand
Can hold at once is all that I can show.

Yet what I sowed and what the orchard yields
My brother's sons are gathering stalk and root,   10
Small wonder then my children glean in fields
They have not sown, and feed on bitter fruit.

Countee Cullen

[1903–1946]

Incident

Once riding in old Baltimore,
    Heart-filled, head-filled with glee,
I saw a Baltimorean
    Keep looking straight at me.

Now I was eight and very small,   5
    And he was no whit bigger,
And so I smiled, but he poked out
    His tongue and called me, "Nigger."

I saw the whole of Baltimore
    From May until December;   10
Of all the things that happened there
    That's all that I remember.

Langston Hughes

[1903–1967]

The Negro Speaks of Rivers

I've known rivers:
I've known rivers ancient as the world and older than the flow
    of human blood in human veins.

My soul has grown deep like the rivers.

I bathed in the Euphrates when dawns were young.
I built my hut near the Congo and it lulled me to sleep.   5
I looked upon the Nile and raised the pyramids above it.
I heard the singing of the Mississippi when Abe Lincoln went
    down to New Orleans, and I've seen its muddy bosom turn
    all golden in the sunset.

I've known rivers:
Ancient, dusky rivers.

My soul has grown deep like the rivers.

Harlem

What happens to a dream deferred?

Does it dry up
like a raisin in the sun?
Or fester like a sore—
And then run?
Does it stink like rotten meat?   5
Or crust and sugar over
like a syrupy sweet?

Maybe it just sags
like a heavy load.

Or does it explode?

Theme for English B

The instructor said,

  Go home and write
  a page tonight.
  And let that page come out of you—
  Then, it will be true.   5

I wonder if it's that simple?
I am twenty-two, colored, born in Winston-Salem.
I went to school there, then Durham, then here
to this college° on the hill above Harlem.   Columbia University
I am the only colored student in my class.   10
The steps from the hill lead down into Harlem,
through a park, then I cross St. Nicholas,°   St. Nicholas Avenue
Eighth Avenue, Seventh, and I come to the Y,

the Harlem Branch Y, where I take the elevator
up to my room, sit down, and write this page: 15

It's not easy to know what is true for you or me
at twenty-two, my age. But I guess I'm what
I feel and see and hear, Harlem, I hear you:
hear you, hear me—we two—you, me, talk on this page.
(I hear New York, too.) Me—who?   20

Well, I like to eat, sleep, drink, and be in love.
I like to work, read, learn, and understand life.
I like a pipe for a Christmas present,
or records—Bessie,° bop, or Bach.   Bessie Smith
I guess being colored doesn't make me *not* like   25
the same things other folks like who are other races.
So will my page be colored that I write?

Being me, it will not be white.
But it will be
a part of you, instructor.   30
You are white—
yet a part of me, as I am a part of you.
That's American.
Sometimes perhaps you don't want to be a part of me.
Nor do I often want to be a part of you.   35
But we are, that's true!
As I learn from you,
I guess you learn from me—
although you're older—and white—
and somewhat more free.   40

This is my page for English B.

Pablo Neruda

[*1904–*   ]

The United Fruit Co.

Translated by Robert Bly

When the trumpet sounded, it was
all prepared on the earth,

and Jehovah parceled out the earth
to Coca-Cola, Inc., Anaconda,
Ford Motors, and other entities: 5
The Fruit Company, Inc.
reserved for itself the most succulent,
the central coast of my own land,
the delicate waist of America.
It rechristened its territories   10
as the "Banana Republics"
and over the sleeping dead,
over the restless heroes
who brought about the greatness,
the liberty and the flags,   15
it established the comic opera:
abolished the independencies,
presented crowns of Caesar,
unsheathed envy, attracted
the dictatorship of the flies,   20
Trujillo flies, Tacho flies,
Carias flies, Martinez flies,
Ubico flies, damp flies
of modest blood and marmalade,
drunken flies who zoom   25
over the ordinary graves,
circus flies, wise flies
well trained in tyranny.

Among the bloodthirsty flies
the Fruit Company lands its ships,   30
taking off the coffee and the fruit;
the treasure of our submerged
territories flows as though
on plates into the ships.

Meanwhile Indians are falling   35
into the sugared chasms
of the harbors, wrapped
for burial in the mist of the dawn:
a body rolls, a thing
that has no name, a fallen cipher,   40
a cluster of dead fruit
thrown down on the dump.

Ode to My Socks

Translated by Robert Bly

Maru Mori brought me
a pair
of socks
which she knitted herself
with her sheep-herder's hands,   5
two socks as soft
as rabbits.
I slipped my feet
into them
as though into   10
two
cases
knitted
with threads of
twilight   15
and goatskin.
Violent socks,
my feet were
two fish made
of wool,   20
two long sharks
seablue, shot
through
by one golden thread,
two immense blackbirds,   25
two cannons,
my feet
were honored
in this way
by   30
these
heavenly
socks.
They were   35
so handsome
for the first time
my feet seemed to me
unacceptable
like two decrepit

firemen, firemen   40
unworthy
of that woven
fire,
of those glowing
socks.   45

Nevertheless
I resisted
the sharp temptation
to save them somewhere
as schoolboys   50
keep
fireflies,
as learned men
collect
sacred texts,   55
I resisted
the mad impulse
to put them
in a golden
cage   60
and each day give them
birdseed
and pieces of pink melon.
Like explorers
in the jungle who hand   65
over the very rare
green deer
to the spit
and eat it
with remorse,   70
I stretched out
my feet
and pulled on
the magnificent
socks   75
and then my shoes.

The moral
of my ode is this:
beauty is twice
beauty   80
and what is good is doubly

good
when it is a matter of two socks
made of wool
in winter.   85

W. H. Auden

[1907–1973]

Musée des Beaux Arts

About suffering they were never wrong,
The Old Masters: how well they understood
Its human position; how it takes place
While someone else is eating or opening a window or just walking
    dully along;
How, when the aged are reverently, passionately waiting   5
For the miraculous birth, there always must be
Children who did not specially want it to happen, skating
On a pond at the edge of the wood:
They never forgot
That even the dreadful martyrdom must run its course   10
Anyhow in a corner, some untidy spot
Where the dogs go on with their doggy life and the torturer's
    horse
Scratches its innocent behind on a tree.

In Brueghel's *Icarus*, for instance: how everything turns away
Quite leisurely from the disaster; the ploughman may   15
Have heard the splash, the forsaken cry,
But for him it was not an important failure; the sun shone
As it had to on the white legs disappearing into the green
Water; and the expensive delicate ship that must have seen
Something amazing, a boy falling out of the sky,   20
Had somewhere to get to and sailed calmly on.

MUSÉE DES BEAUX ARTS: Museum of Fine Arts.
   14. Icarus: Pieter Brueghel the Elder's *Landscape with the Fall of Icarus* (c. 1558), which hangs
in the Musées Royaux des Beaux-Arts in Brussels. Compare this poem with William Carlos
Williams's "Landscape with the Fall of Icarus," pp. 771–772.

In Memory of W. B. Yeats

(D. JAN. 1939)

I

He disappeared in the dead of winter:
The brooks were frozen, the airports almost deserted,
And the snow disfigured the public statues;
The mercury sank in the mouth of the dying day.
What instruments we have agree   5
The day of his death was a dark cold day.

Far from his illness
The wolves ran on through the evergreen forests,
The peasant river was untempted by the fashionable quays;
By mourning tongues   10
The death of the poet was kept from his poems.

But for him it was his last afternoon as himself,
An afternoon of nurses and rumours;
The provinces of his body revolted,
The squares of his mind were empty,   15
Silence invaded the suburbs,
The current of his feeling failed; he became his admirers.

Now he is scattered among a hundred cities
And wholly given over to unfamiliar affections.
To find his happiness in another kind of wood   20
And be punished under a foreign code of conscience.
The words of a dead man
Are modified in the guts of the living.

But in the importance and noise of to-morrow
When the brokers are roaring like beasts on the floor of the
     Bourse,   25
And the poor have the sufferings to which they are fairly
     accustomed,
And each in the cell of himself is almost convinced of his freedom,
A few thousand will think of this day
As one thinks of a day when one did something slightly unusual.
What instruments we have agree   30
The day of his death was a dark cold day.

II

You were silly like us; your gift survived it all:
The parish of rich women, physical decay,
Yourself. Mad Ireland hurt you into poetry.
Now Ireland has her madness and her weather still,   35
For poetry makes nothing happen: it survives
In the valley of its making where executives
Would never want to tamper, flows on south
From ranches of isolation and the busy griefs,
Raw towns that we believe and die in; it survives,   40
A way of happening, a mouth.

III

Earth, receive an honoured guest:
William Yeats is laid to rest.
Let the Irish vessel lie
Emptied of its poetry.   45

In the nightmare of the dark
All the dogs of Europe bark,
And the living nations wait,
Each sequestered in its hate;

Intellectual disgrace   50
Stares from every human face,
And the seas of pity lie
Locked and frozen in each eye.

Follow, poet, follow right
To the bottom of the night,   55
With your unconstraining voice
Still persuade us to rejoice;

With the farming of a verse
Make a vineyard of the curse,
Sing of human unsuccess   60
In a rapture of distress;

In the deserts of the heart
Let the healing fountain start,
In the prison of his days
Teach the free man how to praise.

Buddhadeva Bose

[1908–   ]

Frogs

Translated from Bengali by the author

The rains have come, and frogs are full of glee.
They sing in chorus, with voices loud and lusty,
They sing in primeval joy:
There is nothing but fear today, neither hunger nor death.
Nor the wanton stones of fate.   5

Cloud-like the grasses thicken,
And in the fields the clear waters stand,
And the care-free hours of the day
Are passed in insolent singing.

In the sensual rain there is ecstasy of touch.   10
How luscious is the mud, how young, how soft!

They are neckless, though their throats are swollen;
They are an embodiment of the song's seventh pitch.

O what sleek bodies—cloud-like yellow and green!
Eyes staring upwards in glassy transparence,   15
Like the sombre stare of a mystic
Seeking God, in deep meditation.

The rain is ceased, the shadows aslant.
Hymn-like rises their singing, solemn in silent skies.

As the day pants and dies, the loud shrillness faints,   20
And the darkness is pierced with a sleep-begetting monophonic
    screech.

It is midnight. We have closed our doors and are comfortably in bed.
And the stillness is broken by a single tireless voice.

It is the final *sloka* of the mystic chanting.
The croak, croak croak of the last lonely frog.

Theodore Roethke

[1908–1963]

The Premonition

Walking this field I remember
Days of another summer.
Oh that was long ago! I kept
Close to the heels of my father,
Matching his stride with half-steps   5
Until we came to a river.
He dipped his hand in the shallow:
Water ran over and under
Hair on a narrow wrist bone;
His image kept following after,—   10
Flashed with the sun in the ripple.
But when he stood up, that face
Was lost in a maze of water.

Old Florist

That hump of a man bunching chrysanthemums
Or pinching-back asters, or planting azaleas,
Tamping and stamping dirt into pots,—
How he could flick and pick
Rotten leaves or yellowy petals,   5
Or scoop out a weed close to flourishing roots,
Or make the dust buzz with a light spray,
Or drown a bug in one spit of tobacco juice,
Or fan life into wilted sweet-peas with his hat,
Or stand all night watering roses, his feet blue in rubber boots.

I Knew a Woman

I knew a woman, lovely in her bones,
When small birds sighed, she would sigh back at them;

Ah, when she moved, she moved more ways than one:
The shapes a bright container can contain!
Of her choice virtues only gods should speak,   5
Or English poets who grew up on Greek
(I'd have them sing in chorus, cheek to cheek).

How well her wishes went! She stroked my chin,
She taught me Turn, and Counter-turn, and Stand;
She taught me Touch, that undulant white skin;   10
I nibbled meekly from her proffered hand;
She was the sickle; I, poor I, the rake,
Coming behind her for her pretty sake
(But what prodigious mowing we did make).

Love likes a gander, and adores a goose: 15
Her full lips pursed, the errant note to seize;
She played it quick, she played it light and loose;
My eyes, they dazzled at her flowing knees;
Her several parts could keep a pure repose,
Or one hip quiver with a mobile nose   20
(She moved in circles, and those circles moved).

Let seed be grass, and grass turn into hay:
I'm martyr to a motion not my own;
What's freedom for? To know eternity.
I swear she cast a shadow white as stone.   25
But who would count eternity in days?
These old bones live to learn her wanton ways:
(I measure time by how a body sways).

Dolor

I have known the inexorable sadness of pencils,
Neat in their boxes, dolor of pad and paper-weight,
All the misery of manilla folders and mucilage,
Desolation in immaculate public places,
Lonely reception room, lavatory, switchboard,   5
The unalterable pathos of basin and pitcher,
Ritual of multigraph, paper-clip, comma,
Endless duplication of lives and objects.
And I have seen dust from the walls of institutions,

Finer than flour, alive, more dangerous than silica, 10
Sift, almost invisible, through long afternoons of tedium,
Dropping a fine film on nails and delicate eyebrows,
Glazing the pale hair, the duplicate grey standard faces.

The Waking

I wake to sleep, and take my waking slow.
I feel my fate in what I cannot fear.
I learn by going where I have to go.

We think by feeling. What is there to know?
I hear my being dance from ear to ear. 5
I wake to sleep, and take my waking slow.

Of those so close beside me, which are you?
God bless the Ground! I shall walk softly there,
And learn by going where I have to go.

Light takes the Tree; but who can tell us how? 10
The lowly worm climbs up a winding stair;
I wake to sleep, and take my waking slow.

Great Nature has another thing to do
To you and me; so take the lively air,
And, lovely, learn by going where to go. 15

This shaking keeps me steady. I should know.
What falls away is always. And is near.
I wake to sleep, and take my waking slow.
I learn by going where I have to go.

The Pike

The river turns,
Leaving a place for the eye to rest,
A furred, a rocky pool,
A bottom of water.

The crabs tilt and eat, leisurely,   5
And the small fish lie, without shadow, motionless,
Or drift lazily in and out of the weeds.
The bottom-stones shimmer back their irregular striations,
And the half-sunken branch bends away from the gazer's eye.

A scene for the self to abjure!—   10
And I lean, almost into the water,
My eye always beyond the surface reflection;
I lean, and love these manifold shapes,

Until, out from a dark cove,
From beyond the end of a mossy log,   15
With one sinuous ripple, then a rush,
A thrashing-up of the whole pool,
The pike strikes.

My Papa's Waltz

The whiskey on your breath
Could make a small boy dizzy;
But I hung on like death:
Such waltzing was not easy.

We romped until the pans   5
Slid from the kitchen shelf;
My mother's countenance
Could not unfrown itself.

The hand that held my wrist
Was battered on one knuckle;   10
At every step you missed
My right ear scraped a buckle.

You beat time on my head
With a palm caked hard by dirt,
Then waltzed me off to bed   15
Still clinging to your shirt.

Elizabeth Bishop

[1911–1979]

The Fish

I caught a tremendous fish
and held him beside the boat
half out of water, with my hook
fast in a corner of his mouth.
He didn't fight.   5
He hadn't fought at all.
He hung a grunting weight,
battered and venerable
and homely. Here and there
his brown skin hung in strips   10
like ancient wallpaper,
and its pattern of darker brown
was like wallpaper:
shapes like full-blown roses
stained and lost through age.   15
He was speckled with barnacles,
fine rosettes of lime,
and infested
with tiny white sea-lice,
and underneath two or three   20
rags of green weed hung down.
While his gills were breathing in
the terrible oxygen
—the frightening gills,
fresh and crisp with blood,   25
that can cut so badly—
I thought of the coarse white flesh
packed in like feathers,
the big bones and the little bones,
the dramatic reds and blacks   30
of his shiny entrails,
and the pink swim-bladder
like a big peony.
I looked into his eyes
which were far larger than mine   35
but shallower, and yellowed,

the irises backed and packed
with tarnished tinfoil
seen through the lenses
of old scratched isinglass°.   mica   40
They shifted a little, but not
to return my stare.
—It was more like the tipping
of an object toward the light.
I admired his sullen face,   45
the mechanism of his jaw,
and then I saw
that from his lower lip
—if you could call it a lip—
grim, wet, and weaponlike,   50
hung five old pieces of fish-line,
or four and a wire leader
with the swivel still attached,
with all their five big hooks
grown firmly in his mouth.   55
A green line, frayed at the end
where he broke it, two heavier lines,
and a fine black thread
still crimped from the strain and snap
when it broke and he got away.   60
Like medals with their ribbons
frayed and wavering,
a five-haired beard of wisdom
trailing from his aching jaw.
I stared and stared   65
and victory filled up
the little rented boat,
from the pool of bilge
where oil had spread a rainbow
around the rusted engine   70
to the bailer rusted orange,
the sun-cracked thwarts,
the oarlocks on their strings,
the gunnels—until everything
was rainbow, rainbow, rainbow!   75
And I let the fish go.

Robert Hayden

(1913–1980)

Those Winter Sundays

Sundays too my father got up early
and put his clothes on in the blueblack cold,
then with cracked hands that ached
from labor in the weekday weather made
banked fires blaze. No one ever thanked him.   5

I'd wake and hear the cold splintering, breaking.
When the rooms were warm, he'd call,
and slowly I would rise and dress,
fearing the chronic angers of that house,

Speaking indifferently to him,   10
who had driven out the cold
and polished my good shoes as well.
What did I know, what did I know
of love's austere and lonely offices?

Frederick Douglass

When it is finally ours, this freedom, this liberty, this beautiful
and terrible thing, needful to man as air,
usable as earth; when it belongs at last to all,
when it is truly instinct, brain matter, diastole, systole,
reflex action; when it is finally won; when it is more   5
than the gaudy mumbo jumbo of politicians:
this man, this Douglass, this former slave, this Negro
beaten to his knees, exiled, visioning a world
where none is lonely, none hunted, alien,
this man, superb in love and logic, this man   10
shall be remembered. Oh, not with statues' rhetoric,
not with legends and poems and wreaths of bronze alone,
but with the lives grown out of his life, the lives
fleshing his dream of the beautiful, needful thing.

Runagate Runagate

I.

Runs falls rises stumbles on from darkness into darkness
and the darkness thicketed with shapes of terror
and the hunters pursuing and the hounds pursuing
and the night cold and the night long and the river
to cross and jack-muh-lanterns beckoning beckoning   5
and blackness ahead and when shall I reach that somewhere
morning and keep on going and never turn back and keep on
   going

               Runagate
                    Runagate
                        Runagate   10
Many thousands rise and go
many thousands crossing over

                         O mythic North
                    O star-shaped yonder Bible city

Some go weeping and some rejoicing   15
some in coffins and some in carriages
some in silks and some in shackles

       Rise and go or fare you well

No more auction block for me
no more driver's lash for me   20

    If you see my Pompey, 30 yrs of age,
    new breeches, plain stockings, negro shoes;
    if you see my Anna, likely young mulatto
    branded E on the right cheek, R on the left,
    catch them if you can and notify subscriber.   25
    Catch them if you can, but it won't be easy.
    They'll dart underground when you try to catch them,
    plunge into quicksand, whirlpools, mazes,
    turn into scorpions when you try to catch them.
And before I'll be a slave   30
I'll be buried in my grave

    North star and bonanza gold

RUNAGATE RUNAGATE: An interesting companion piece to this poem is Frederick Douglass' speech on pages 903–919.

I'm bound for the freedom, freedom-bound
and oh Susyanna don't you cry for me

    Runagate
           Runagate   35

              II.

Rises from their anguish and their power,

           Harriet Tubman,

           woman of earth, whipscarred,
           a summoning, a shining

           Mean to be free   40

And this was the way of it, brethren brethren,
way we journeyed from Can't to Can.
Moon so bright and no place to hide,
the cry up and the patterollers riding,
hound dogs belling in bladed air.   45
And fear starts a-murbling, Never make it,
we'll never make it. *Hush that now,*
and she's turned upon us, levelled pistol
glinting in the moonlight:
Dead folks can't jaybird-talk, she says;   50
you keep on going now or die, she says.

Wanted   Harriet Tubman   alias The General
alias Moses   Stealer of Slaves

In league with Garrison   Alcott   Emerson
Garrett   Douglass   Thoreau   John Brown   55

Armed and known to be Dangerous

Wanted   Reward   Dead or Alive

       Tell me, Ezekiel, oh tell me do you see
       mailed Jehovah coming to deliver me?

Hoot-owl calling in the ghosted air,   60
five times calling to the hants in the air.
Shadow of a face in the scary leaves,
shadow of a voice in the talking leaves:

       Come ride-a my train

Oh that train, ghost-story train   65
through swamp and savanna movering movering,
over trestles of dew, through caves of the wish,
Midnight Special on a sabre track movering movering,
first stop Mercy and the last Hallelujah.

Come ride-a my train   70

Mean mean mean to be free.

Henry Reed

[1914–   ]

Naming of Parts

Today we have naming of parts. Yesterday,
We had daily cleaning. And tomorrow morning,
We shall have what to do after firing. But today,
Today we have naming of parts. Japonica°   flowering shrub
Glistens like coral in all of the neighboring gardens,   5
    And today we have naming of parts.

This is the lower sling swivel. And this
Is the upper sling swivel, whose use you will see,
When you are given your slings. And this is the piling swivel,
Which in your case you have not got. The branches   10
Hold in the gardens their silent, eloquent gestures,
    Which in our case we have not got.

This is the safety-catch, which is always released
With an easy flick of the thumb. And please do not let me
See anyone using his finger. You can do it quite easy   15
If you have any strength in your thumb. The blossoms
Are fragile and motionless, never letting anyone see
    Any of them using their finger.

NAMING OF PARTS: Published as part of a series of three poems called "Lessons of War."

And this you see is the bolt. The purpose of this
Is to open the breech, as you see. We can slide it   20
Rapidly backwards and forwards: we call this
Easing the spring. And rapidly backwards and forwards
The early bees are assaulting and fumbling the flowers:
    They call it easing the Spring.

They call it easing the Spring: it is perfectly easy   25
If you have any strength in your thumb: like the bolt,
And the breech, and the cocking-piece, and the point of balance,
Which in our case we have not got; and the almond-blossom
Silent in all of the gardens and the bees going backwards and
    forwards,
    For today we have naming of parts.   30

John Berryman

[1914–1972]

From Homage to Mistress Bradstreet

1

The Governor your husband lived so long
moved you not, restless, waiting for him? Still,
you were a patient woman—
I seem to see you pause here still:
Sylvester, Quarles, in moments odd you pored   5
before a fire at, bright eyes on the Lord,
all the children still.
'Simon . .' Simon will listen while you read a Song.

From HOMAGE TO MISTRESS BRADSTREET: *Here and on the following pages are Berryman's notes for "Mistress Bradstreet":*
  Born 1612 Anne Dudley, married at 16 Simon Bradstreet, a Cambridge man, steward to the Countess of Warwick and protégé of her father Thomas Dudley secretary[,] to the Earl of Lincoln. Crossed in the *Arbella* [*Arabella*], 1630, under Governor Winthrop.
  Stanzas 1–4: The poem is about the woman, but this exordium is spoken by the poet, his voice modulating in stanza 4, line 8 [4.8] into hers.
  1.1 He was not Governor until after her death.
  1.5 Sylvester (the translator of Du Bartas) and Quarles, her favourite poets; unfortunately.

2

Outside the New World winters in grand dark
white air lashing high thro' the virgin stands
foxes down foxholes sigh,
surely the English heart quails, stunned.
I doubt if Simon than this blast, that sea,   5
spares from his rigour for your poetry
more. We are on each other's hands
who care. Both of our worlds unhanded us. Lie stark,

3

thy eyes look to me mild. Out of maize & air
your body's made, and moves. I summon, see,
from the centuries it.
I think you won't stay. How do we
linger, diminished, in our lovers' air,   5
implausibly visible, to whom, a year,
years, over interims; or not;
to a long stranger; or not; shimmer and disappear.

4

Jaw-ript, rot with its wisdom, rending then;
then not. When the mouth dies, who misses you?
Your master never died,
Simon ah thirty years past you—
Pockmarkt & westward staring on a haggard deck   5
it seems I find you, young. I come to check,
I come to stay with you,
and the Governor, & Father, & Simon, & the huddled men.

5

By the week we landed we were, most, used up.
Strange ships across us, after a fortnight's winds
unfavouring, frightened us;
bone-sad cold, sleet, scurvy; so were ill
many as one day we could have no sermons;   5
broils, quelled; a fatherless child unkennelled; vermin
crowding & waiting: waiting.
And the day itself he leapt ashore young Henry Winthrop

5.4,5 Many details are from quotations in Helen Campbell's biography, the Winthrop
papers, narratives, town histories.

6

(delivered from the waves; because he found
off their wigwams, sharp-eyed, a lone canoe
across a tidal river,
that water glittered fair & blue
& narrow, none of the other men could swim   5
and the plantation's prime theft up to him,
shouldered on a glad day
hard on the glorious feasting of thanksgiving) drowned.

7

How long with nothing in the ruinous heat,
clams & acorns stomaching, distinction perishing,
at which my heart rose,
with brackish water, we would sing.
When whispers knew the Governor's last bread   5
was browning in his oven, we were discourag'd.
The Lady Arbella dying—
dyings—at which my heart   rose, but I did submit.

8

That beyond the Atlantic wound our woes enlarge
is hard, hard that starvation burnishes our fear,
but I do gloss for You.
Strangers & pilgrims fare we here,
declaring we seek a City. Shall we be deceived?   5
I know whom I have trusted, & whom I have believed,
and that he is able to
keep   that I have committed to his charge.

9

Winter than summer worse, that first, like a file
on a quick, or the poison suck of a thrilled tooth;
and still we may unpack.
Wolves & storms among, uncouth
board-pieces, boxes, barrels vanish, grow   5
houses, rise. Motes that hop in sunlight slow
indoors, and I am Ruth
away: open my mouth, my eyes wet: I would smile:

8.4ff. Scriptural passages are sometimes ones she used herself, as this in her *Meditation liii.*

10

vellum I palm, and dream. Their forest dies
to greensward, privets, elms & towers, whence
a nightingale is throbbing.
Women sleep sound. I was happy once . .
(Something keeps on not happening; I shrink?)   5
These minutes all their passions & powers sink
and I am not once chance
for an unknown cry or a flicker of unknown eyes.

11

Chapped souls ours, by the day Spring's strong winds swelled,
Jack's pulpits arched, more glad. The shawl I pinned
flaps like a shooting soul
might in such weather Heaven send.
Succumbing half, in spirit, to a salmon sash   5
I prod the nerveless novel succotash—
I must be disciplined,
in arms, against that one, and our dissidents, and myself.

12

Versing, I shroud among the dynasties;
quaternion on quaternion, tireless I phrase
anything past, dead, far,
sacred, for a barbarous place.
—To please your wintry father? all this bald   5
abstract didactic rime I read appalled
harassed for your fame
mistress neither of fiery nor velvet verse, on your knees

13

hopeful & shamefast, chaste, laborious, odd,
whom the sea tore.—The damned roar with loss,
so they hug & are mean
with themselves, and I cannot be thus.
Why then do I repine, sick, bad, to long   5
after what must not be? I lie wrong
once more. For at fourteen
I found my heart more carnal and sitting loose from God,

11.8 *that one:* the Old One.
12.5–13.2 The poet interrupts.

14

vanity & the follies of youth took hold of me;
then the pox blasted, when the Lord returned.
That year for my sorry face
so-much-older Simon burned,
so Father smiled, with love. Their will be done.　　　　　5
He to me ill lingeringly, learning to shun
a bliss, a lightning blood
vouchsafed, what did seem life. I kissed his Mystery.

15

Drydust in God's eye the aquavivid skin
of Simon snoring lit with fountaining dawn
when my eyes unlid, sad.
John Cotton shines on Boston's sin—
I ám drawn, in pieties that seem　　　　　5
the weary drizzle of an unremembered dream.
Women have gone mad
at twenty-one. Ambition mines, atrocious, in.

16

Food endless, people few, all to be done.
As pippins roast, the question of the wolves
turns & turns.
Fangs of a wolf will keep, the neck
round of a child, that child brave. I remember who　　　　　5
in meeting smiled & was punisht, and I know who
whispered & was stockt.
We lead a thoughtful life. But Boston's cage we shun.

17

The winters close, Springs open, no child stirs
under my withering heart, O seasoned heart
God grudged his aid.
All things else soil like a shirt.
Simon is much away. My executive stales.　　　　　5
The town came through for the cartway by the pales,
but my patience is short,
I revolt from, I am like, these savage foresters

18

whose passionless dicker in the shade, whose glance
impassive & scant, belie their murderous cries
when quarry seems to show.
Again I must have been wrong, twice.
Unwell in a new way. Can that begin?   5
God brandishes. O love, O I love. Kin,
gather. My world is strange
and merciful, ingrown months, blessing a swelling trance.

19

So squeezed, wince you I scream? I love you & hate
off with you. Ages! *Useless.* Below my waist
he has me in Hell's vise.
Stalling. He let go. Come back: brace
me somewhere. No. No. Yes! everything down   5
hardens I press with horrible joy down
my back cracks like a wrist
shame I am voiding oh behind it is too late

20

hide me forever I work thrust I must free
now I all muscles & bones concentrate
what is living from dying?
Simon I must leave you so untidy
Monster you are killing me Be sure   5
I'll have you later Women do endure
I can *can* no longer
and it passes the wretched trap whelming and I am me

21

drencht & powerful, I did it with my body!
One proud tug greens Heaven. Marvellous,
unforbidding Majesty.
Swell, imperious bells. I fly.
Mountainous, woman not breaks and will bend: 5
sways God nearby: anguish comes to an end.
Blossomed Sarah, and I
blossom. Is that thing alive? I hear a famisht howl.

18.8 Her first child was not born until about 1633.

Dylan Thomas

[1914–1953]

A Refusal to Mourn the Death, by Fire, of a Child in London

Never until the mankind making
Bird beast and flower
Fathering and all humbling darkness
Tells with silence the last light breaking
And the still hour   5
Is come of the sea tumbling in harness

And I must enter again the round
Zion of the water bead
And the synagogue of the ear of corn
Shall I let pray the shadow of a sound   10
Or sow my salt seed
In the least valley of sackcloth to mourn

The majesty and burning of the child's death.
I shall not murder
The mankind of her going with a grave truth   15
Nor blaspheme down the stations of the breath
With any further
Elegy of innocence and youth.

Deep with the first dead lies London's daughter,
Robed in the long friends,   20
The grains beyond age, the dark veins of her mother,
Secret by the unmourning water
Of the riding Thames.
After the first death, there is no other.

Fern Hill

Now as I was young and easy under the apple boughs
About the lilting house and happy as the grass was green,

FERN HILL: A country house where the poet spent summer holidays as a boy.

The night above the dingle starry,
    Time let me hail and climb
  Golden in the heydays of his eyes,   5
And honoured among wagons I was prince of the apple towns
And once below a time I lordly had the trees and leaves
    Trail with daisies and barley
  Down the rivers of the windfall light.

And as I was green and carefree, famous among the barns   10
About the happy yard and singing as the farm was home,
    In the sun that is young once only,
      Time let me play and be
  Golden in the mercy of his means,
And green and golden I was huntsman and herdsman, the calves   15
Sang to my horn, the foxes on the hills barked clear and cold,
    And the sabbath rang slowly
  In the pebbles of the holy streams.

All the sun long it was running, it was lovely, the hay
Fields high as the house, the tunes from the chimneys, it was air   20
    And playing, lovely and watery
      And fire green as grass.
    And nightly under the simple stars
As I rode to sleep the owls were bearing the farm away,
All the moon long I heard, blessed among stables, the night-jars   25
    Flying with the ricks, and the horses
      Flashing into the dark.

And then to awake, and the farm, like a wanderer white
With the dew, come back, the cock on his shoulder: it was all
    Shining, it was Adam and maiden,   30
      The sky gathered again
    And the sun grew round that very day.
So it must have been after the birth of the simple light
In the first, spinning place, the spellbound horses walking warm
    Out of the whinnying green stable   35
      On to the fields of praise.

And honored among foxes and pheasants by the gay house
Under the new made clouds and happy as the heart was long,
    In the sun born over and over,
      I ran my heedless ways,   40
    My wishes raced through the house high hay
And nothing I cared, at my sky blue trades, that time allows
In all his tuneful turning so few and such morning songs

Before the children green and golden
　　　Follow him out of grace,　　　　　　　　　　　　45

Nothing I cared, in the lamb white days, that time would take me
Up to the swallow thronged loft by the shadow of my hand,
　　　In the moon that is always rising,
　　　　　Nor that riding to sleep
　　　I should hear him fly with the high fields　　　　50
And wake to the farm forever fled from the childless land.
Oh as I was young and easy in the mercy of his means,
　　　Time held me green and dying
　　　Though I sang in my chains like the sea.

The Force That Through the Green Fuse Drives the Flower

The force that through the green fuse drives the flower
Drives my green age; that blasts the roots of trees
Is my destroyer.
And I am dumb to tell the crooked rose
My youth is bent by the same wintry fever.　　　　　5

The force that drives the water through the rocks
Drives my red blood; that dries the mouthing streams
Turns mine to wax.
And I am dumb to mouth unto my veins
How at the mountain spring the same mouth sucks.　　　10

The hand that whirls the water in the pool
Stirs the quicksand; that ropes the blowing wind
Hauls my shroud sail.
And I am dumb to tell the hanging man
How of my clay is made the hangman's lime.　　　　15

The lips of time leech to the fountain head;
Love drips and gathers, but the fallen blood
Shall calm her sores.
And I am dumb to tell a weather's wind
How time has ticked a heaven round the stars.　　　20

And I am dumb to tell the lover's tomb
How at my sheet goes the same crooked worm.

Do Not Go Gentle into That Good Night

Do not go gentle into that good night,
Old age should burn and rave at close of day;
Rage, rage against the dying of the light.

Though wise men at their end know dark is right,
Because their words had forked no lightning they   5
Do not go gentle into that good night.

Good men, the last wave by, crying how bright
Their frail deeds might have danced in a green bay,
Rage, rage against the dying of the light.

Wild men who caught and sang the sun in flight,   10
And learn, too late, they grieved it on its way,
Do not go gentle into that good night.

Grave men, near death, who see with blinding sight
Blind eyes could blaze like meteors and be gay,
Rage, rage against the dying of the light.   15

And you, my father, there on the sad height,
Curse, bless, me now with your fierce tears, I pray.
Do not go gentle into that good night.
Rage, rage against the dying of the light.

Robert Lowell

[1917–1977]

For the Union Dead

"Relinquunt Omnia Servare Rem Publicam."

The old South Boston Aquarium stands
in a Sahara of snow now. Its broken windows are boarded.

DO NOT GO GENTLE . . .: Written during the final illness of Thomas's father.
FOR THE UNION DEAD: Epigraph: "They sacrifice everything to serve the republic."

The bronze weathervane cod has lost half its scales.
The airy tanks are dry.

Once my nose crawled like a snail on the glass;   5
my hand tingled
to burst the bubbles
drifting from the noses of the cowed, compliant fish.

My hand draws back. I often sigh still
for the dark downward and vegetating kingdom   10
of the fish and reptile. One morning last March,
I pressed against the new barbed and galvanized

fence on the Boston Common. Behind their cage,
yellow dinosaur steamshovels were grunting
as they cropped up tons of mush and grass   15
to gouge their underworld garage.

Parking spaces luxuriate like civic
sandpiles in the heart of Boston.
A girdle of orange, Puritan-pumpkin colored girders
braces the tingling Statehouse,   20

shaking over the excavations, as it faces Colonel Shaw
and his bell-cheeked Negro infantry
on St. Gaudens' shaking Civil War relief,
propped by a plank splint against the garage's earthquake.

Two months after marching through Boston,   25
half the regiment was dead;
at the dedication,
William James could almost hear the bronze Negroes breathe.

Their monument sticks like a fishbone
in the city's throat.   30
Its Colonel is as lean
as a compass-needle.

He has an angry wrenlike vigilance,
a greyhound's gentle tautness;

—————————————————————————

23. Sculptor Augustus Saint-Gaudens (1848–1907) made a bronze relief of Colonel Robert
Shaw (1837–1863), who led a black regiment during the Civil War.
28. William James (1842–1910), American psychologist and philosopher, professor at
Harvard.

he seems to wince at pleasure,   35
and suffocate for privacy.

He is out of bounds now. He rejoices in man's lovely,
peculiar power to choose life and die—
when he leads his black soldiers to death,
he cannot bend his back.   40

On a thousand small town New England greens,
the old white churches hold their air
of sparse, sincere rebellion; frayed flags
quilt the graveyards of the Grand Army of the Republic.

The stone statues of the abstract Union Soldier   45
grow slimmer and younger each year—
wasp-waisted, they doze over muskets
and muse through their sideburns . . .

Shaw's father wanted no monument
except the ditch,   50
where his son's body was thrown
and lost with his "niggers."

The ditch is nearer.
There are no statues for the last war° here;   i.e., W.W. II
on Boylston Street, a commercial photograph   55
shows Hiroshima boiling

over a Mosler Safe, the "Rock of Ages"
that survived the blast. Space is nearer.
When I crouch to my television set,
the drained faces of Negro school-children rise like balloons.   60

Colonel Shaw
is riding on his bubble,
he waits
for the blessèd break.

The Aquarium is gone. Everywhere   65
giant finned cars nose forward like fish;
a savage servility
slides by on grease.

Gwendolyn Brooks

[*1917–*   ]

the mother

Abortions will not let you forget.
You remember the children you got that you did not get,
The damp small pulps with a little or with no hair,
The singers and workers that never handled the air.
You will never neglect or beat   5
Them, or silence or buy with a sweet.
You will never wind up the sucking-thumb
Or scuttle off ghosts that come.
You will never leave them, controlling your luscious sigh,
Return for a snack of them, with gobbling mother-eye.   10
I have heard in the voices of the wind the voices of my dim killed
     children.
I have contracted. I have eased
My dim dears at the breasts they could never suck.
I have said, Sweets, if I sinned, if I seized
Your luck   15
And your lives from your unfinished reach,
If I stole your births and your names,
Your straight baby tears and your games,
Your stilted or lovely loves, your tumults, your marriages, aches, and your
     deaths,
If I poisoned the beginnings of your breaths,
Believe that even in my deliberateness I was not deliberate.   20
Though why should I whine,
Whine that the crime was other than mine?—
Since anyhow you are dead.
Or rather, or instead,
You were never made.   25
But that too, I am afraid,
Is faulty: oh, what shall I say, how is the truth to be said?
You were born, you had body, you died.
It is just that you never giggled or planned or cried.

Believe me, I loved you all.   30
Believe me, I knew you, though faintly, and I loved, I loved you
All.

We Real Cool

The Pool Players.
Seven at the Golden Shovel.

We real cool. We
Left school. We

Lurk late. We
Strike straight. We

Sing sin. We   5
Thin gin. We

Jazz June. We
Die soon.

Richard Wilbur

[1921–   ]

The Death of a Toad

A toad the power mower caught,
Chewed and clipped of a leg, with a hobbling hop has got
  To the garden verge, and sanctuaried him
  Under the cineraria leaves, in the shade
    Of the ashen heartshaped leaves, in a dim,   5
      Low, and a final glade.

The rare original heartsblood goes,
Spends on the earthen hide, in the folds and wizenings, flows
  In the gutters of the banked and staring eyes. He lies
  As still as if he would return to stone,   10
    And soundlessly attending, dies
      Toward some deep monotone,

Toward misted and ebullient seas
And cooling shores, toward lost Amphibia's emperies.°   empires
Day dwindles, drowning, and at length is gone   15
In the wide and antique eyes, which still appear
To watch, across the castrate lawn,
The haggard daylight steer.

First Snow in Alsace

The snow came down last night like moths
Burned on the moon; it fell till dawn,
Covered the town with simple cloths.

Absolute snow lies rumpled on
What shellbursts scattered and deranged,   5
Entangled railings, crevassed lawn.

As if it did not know they'd changed,
Snow smoothly clasps the roofs of homes
Fear-gutted, trustless and estranged.

The ration stacks are milky domes;   10
Across the ammunition pile
The snow has climbed in sparkling combs.

You think: beyond the town a mile
Or two, this snowfall fills the eyes
Of soldiers dead a little while.   15

Persons and persons in disguise,
Walking the new air white and fine,
Trade glances quick with shared surprise.

At children's windows, heaped, benign,
As always, winter shines the most,   20
And frost makes marvelous designs.

THE DEATH OF A TOAD 14. **Amphibia's**: the toad is an amphibian.

The night guard coming from his post,
Ten first-snows back in thought, walks slow
And warms him with a boyish boast:

He was the first to see the snow.   25

Denise Levertov

[*1923–*   ]

The Victors

In June the bush we call
alder was heavy, listless,
its leaves studded with galls,

growing wherever we didn't
want it. We cut it   5
savagely, hunted it from the pasture, chopped it

away from the edge of the wood.
In July, still everywhere, it appeared
wearing green berries.

Anyway it must go. It takes   10
the light and air and the good of the earth
from flowers and young trees.

But now in August
its berries are red. Do the birds
eat them? Swinging   15

clusters of red, the hedges are full of them.
red-currant red, a graceful
ornament or a merry smile.

What Were They Like?

1)   Did the people of Viet Nam
     use lanterns of stone?

2)   Did they hold ceremonies
      to reverence the opening of buds?

3)   Were they inclined to quiet laughter?

4)   Did they use bone and ivory,
      jade and silver, for ornament?

5)   Had they an epic poem?

6)   Did they distinguish between speech and singing?

1)   Sir, their light hearts turned to stone.
      It is not remembered whether in gardens
      stone lanterns illumined pleasant ways.

2)   Perhaps they gathered once to delight in blossom,
      but after the children were killed
      there were no more buds.

3)   Sir, laughter is bitter to the burned mouth.

4)   A dream ago, perhaps. Ornament is for joy.
      All the bones were charred.

5)   It is not remembered. Remember,
      most were peasants; their life
      was in rice and bamboo.
      When peaceful clouds were reflected in the paddies
      and the water buffalo stepped surely along terraces,
      maybe fathers told their sons old tales.
      When bombs smashed those mirrors
      there was time only to scream.

6)   There is an echo yet
      of their speech which was like a song.
      It was reported their singing resembled
      the flight of moths in moonlight.
      Who can say? It is silent now.

Maya Angelou

[*1924–*   ]

Africa

Thus she had lain
sugar cane sweet

deserts her hair
golden her feet
mountains her breasts 5
two Niles her tears
Thus she has lain
Black through the years.

Over the white seas
rime white and cold 10
brigands ungentled
icicle bold
took her young daughters
sold her strong sons
churched her with Jesus 15
bled her with guns.
Thus she has lain.

Now she is rising
remember her pain
remember the losses 20
her screams loud and vain
remember her riches
her history slain
now she is striding
although she had lain.

Nissim Ezekiel

[1924–   ]

Night of the Scorpion

I remember the night my mother
was stung by a scorpion. Ten hours
of steady rain had driven him
to crawl beneath a sack of rice.
Parting with his poison—flash 5
of diabolic tail in the dark room—

he risked the rain again.
The peasants came like swarms of flies
and buzzed the Name of God a hundred times
to paralyse the Evil One.   10
With candles and with lanterns
throwing giant scorpion shadows
on the sun-baked walls
they searched for him: he was not found.
They clicked their tongues.   15
With every movement that the scorpion made
his poison moved in Mother's blood, they said.
May he sit still, they said.
May the sins of your previous birth
be burned away tonight, they said.   20
May your suffering decrease
the misfortunes of your next birth, they said.
May the sum of evil
balanced in this unreal world
against the sum of good   25
become diminished by your pain.
May the poison purify your flesh
of desire, and your spirit of ambition,
they said, and they sat around
on the floor with my mother in the centre,   30
the peace of understanding on each face.
More candles, more lanterns, more neighbours,
more insects, and the endless rain.
My mother twisted through and through
groaning on a mat.   35
My father, sceptic, rationalist,
trying every curse and blessing,
powder, mixture, herb and hybrid.
He even poured a little paraffin
upon the bitten toe and put a match to it.   40
I watched the flame feeding on my mother.
I watched the holy man perform his rites
to tame the poison with an incantation.
After twenty hours
it lost its sting.   45

My mother only said
Thank God the scorpion picked on me
and spared my children.

Maxine W. Kumin

[1925–   ]

Making the Jam without You

for Judy

Old daughter, small traveler
asleep in a German featherbed
under the eaves in a postcard town
of turrets and towers,
I am putting a dream in your head.   5

Listen! Here it is afternoon.
The rain comes down like bullets.
I stand in the kitchen,
that harem of good smells
where we have bumped hips and   10
cracked the cupboards with our talk
while the stove top danced with pots
and it was not clear who did
the mothering. Now I am
crushing blackberries   15
to make the annual jam
in a white cocoon of steam.

Take it, my sleeper. Redo it
in any of your three
languages and nineteen years.   20
Change the geography.
Let there be a mountain,
the fat cows on it belled
like a cathedral. Let
there be someone beside you   25
as you come upon the ruins
of a schloss,° all overgrown   (*German*) castle
with a glorious thicket,
its brambles soft as wool.
Let him bring the buckets   30
crooked on his angel arms
and may the berries, vaster
than any forage in
the mild hills of New Hampshire,

drop in your pail, plum size,   35
heavy as the eyes
of an honest dog
and may you bear them
home together to a square
white unreconstructed kitchen   40
not unlike this one.

Now may your two heads
touch over the kettle,
over the blood of the berries
that drink up sugar and sun,   45
over that tar-thick boil
love cannot stir down.
More plainly than
the bric-a-brac of shelves
filling with jelly glasses,   50
more surely than
the light driving through them
trite as rubies, I see him
as pale as paraffin beside you.
I see you cutting   55
fresh baked bread to spread it
with the bright royal fur.

At this time
I lift the flap of your dream
and slip out thinner than a sliver   60
as your two mouths open
for the sweet stain of purple.

Allen Ginsberg

[1926–   ]

A Supermarket in California

What thoughts I have of you tonight, Walt Whitman, for I walked
down the sidestreets under the trees with a headache self-conscious
looking at the full moon.

In my hungry fatigue, and shopping for images, I went into the
neon fruit supermarket, dreaming of your enumerations!

What peaches and what penumbras! Whole families shopping at
night! Aisles full of husbands! Wives in the avocados, babies in the
tomatoes!—and you, Garcia Lorca, what were you doing down by the
watermelons?

I saw you, Walt Whitman, childless, lonely old grubber, poking
among the meats in the refrigerator and eyeing the grocery boys.
I heard you asking questions of each: Who killed the pork chops?
What price bananas? Are you my Angel?   5
I wandered in and out of the brilliant stacks of cans following you,
and followed in my imagination by the store detective.
We strode down the open corridors together in our solitary fancy
tasting artichokes, possessing every frozen delicacy, and never passing
the cashier.

Where are we going, Walt Whitman? The doors close in an hour.
Which way does your beard point tonight?
(I touch your book and dream of our odyssey in the supermarket and
feel absurd.)
Will we walk all night through solitary streets? The trees add shade
to shade, lights out in the houses, we'll both be lonely.   10
Will we stroll dreaming of the lost America of love past blue
automobiles in driveways, home to our silent cottage?
Ah, dear father, graybeard, lonely old courage-teacher, what
America did you have when Charon quit poling his ferry and you got
out on a smoking bank and stood watching the boat disappear on the
black waters of Lethe?

W. S. Merwin

[1927–   ]

When You Go Away

When you go away the wind clicks around to the north
The painters work all day but at sundown the paint falls
Showing the black walls
The clock goes back to striking the same hour

A SUPERMARKET IN CALIFORNIA 12. **Charon**: In Greek mythology, the ferryman who
conveys the dead to Hades (hell) over the River Styx. **Lethe** is the name of the river of
forgetfulness in Hades.

That has no place in the years
And at night wrapped in the bed of ashes
In one breath I wake
It is the time when the beards of the dead get their growth
I remember that I am falling
That I am the reason
And that my words are the garment of what I shall never be
Like the tucked sleeve of a one-armed boy

5

10

Elegy

Who would I show it to

Philip Levine

[*1928–*]

Ricky

I go into the back yard
and arrange some twigs
and a few flowers. I go alone
and speak to you as I never could
when you lived, when you
smiled back at me shyly.
Now I can talk to you as I talked
to a star when I was a boy,
expecting no answer, as I talked
to my father who had become
the wind, particles of rain
and fire, these few twigs
and flowers that have no name.

Last night they said a rosary
and my boys went, awkward
in slacks and sport shirts,
and later sitting under the hidden
stars they were attacked and beaten.
You are dead. It is 105,

5

10

15

the young and the old burn   20
in the fields, and though they cry
enough the sun hangs on
bloodying the dust above the aisles
of cotton and grape.

This morning they will say a mass   25
and then the mile-long line of cars.
Teddy and John, their faces swollen,
and four others will let you
slowly down into the fresh earth
where you go on. Scared now,   30
they will understand some of it.
Not the mass or the rosary
or the funeral, but the rage.
Not you falling through the dark,
moving underwater like a flower   35
no one could find until
it was too late and you had gone out,
your breath passing through dark water
never to return to the young man,
pigeon-breasted, who rode   40
his brother's Harley up the driveway.

Wet grass sticks to my feet, bright
marigold and daisy burst in the new day.
The bees move at the clumps
of clover, the carrots—   45
almost as tall as I—
have flowered, pale lacework.
Hard dark buds
of next year's oranges, new green
of slick leaves, yellow grass   50
tall and blowing by the fence. The grapes
are slow, climbing the arbor,
but some day there will be shade
here where the morning sun whitens
everything and punishes my eyes.   55

Your people worked
for some small piece of earth,
for a home, adding a room
a boy might want. Butchie said
you could have the Harley   60
if only you would come back,
anything that was his.

A dog barks down the block
and it is another day. I hear
the soft call of the dove,   65
screech of mockingbird and jay.
A small dog picks up the tune,
and then *tow-weet tow-weet*
of hidden birds, and two finches
darting over the low trees—   70
there is no end.

What can I say to this mound
of twigs and dry flowers, what
can I say now that I would speak
to you? Ask the wind, ask   75
the absence or the rose burned
at the edges and still blood red.
And the answer is you
falling through black water
into the stillness that fathers   80
the moon, the bees ramming into
the soft cups, the eucalyptus
swaying like grass under water.
My John told me your cousin
punched holes in the wall   85
the night you died and was afraid
to be alone. Your brother
walks staring at the earth.
I am afraid of water.

And the earth goes on   90
in blinding sunlight.
I hold your image
a moment, the long
Indian face
the brown almond eyes   95
your dark skin full
and glowing as you grew
into the hard body
of a young man.

And now it is bird screech   100
and a tree rat suddenly
parting the tall grass
by the fence, lumbering
off, and in the distance
the crashing of waves   105

against some shore
maybe only in memory.

We lived by the sea.
My boys wrote
postcards and missed you   110
and your brother. I slept
and wakened to the sea,
I remember in my dreams
water pounded the windows
and walls, it seeped   115
through everything,
and like your spirit,
like your breath,
nothing could contain it.

Anne Sexton

[1928–1975]

Snow White and the Seven Dwarfs

No matter what life you lead
the virgin is a lovely number:
cheeks as fragile as cigarette paper,
arms and legs made of Limoges,
lips like Vin Du Rhône,   5
rolling her china-blue doll eyes
open and shut.
Open to say,
Good Day Mama,
and shut for the thrust   10
of the unicorn.
She is unsoiled.
She is as white as a bonefish.

Once there was a lovely virgin
called Snow White.   15
Say she was thirteen.
Her stepmother,
a beauty in her own right,
though eaten, of course, by age,

would hear of no beauty surpassing her own.   20
Beauty is a simple passion,
but, oh my friends, in the end
you will dance the fire dance in iron shoes.
The stepmother had a mirror to which she referred—
something like the weather forecast—   25
a mirror that proclaimed
the one beauty of the land.
She would ask,
Looking glass upon the wall,
who is fairest of us all?   30
And the mirror would reply,
You are fairest of us all.
Pride pumped in her like poison.

Suddenly one day the mirror replied,
Queen, you are full fair, 'tis true,   35
but Snow White is fairer than you.
Until that moment Snow White
had been no more important
than a dust mouse under the bed.
But now the queen saw brown spots on her hand   40
and four whiskers over her lip
so she condemned Snow White
to be hacked to death.
Bring me her heart, she said to the hunter,
and I will salt it and eat it.   45
The hunter, however, let his prisoner go
and brought a boar's heart back to the castle.
The queen chewed it up like a cube steak.
Now I am fairest, she said,
lapping her slim white fingers.   50

Snow White walked in the wildwood
for weeks and weeks.
At each turn there were twenty doorways
and at each stood a hungry wolf,
his tongue lolling out like a worm.   55
The birds called out lewdly,
talking like pink parrots,
and the snakes hung down in loops,
each a noose for her sweet white neck.
On the seventh week   60
she came to the seventh mountain
and there she found the dwarf house.
It was as droll as a honeymoon cottage

and completely equipped with
seven beds, seven chairs, seven forks   65
and seven chamber pots.
Snow White ate seven chicken livers
and lay down, at last, to sleep.

The dwarfs, those little hot dogs,
walked three times around Snow White,   70
the sleeping virgin. They were wise
and wattled like small czars.
Yes. It's a good omen,
they said, and will bring us luck.
They stood on tiptoes to watch   75
Snow White wake up. She told them
about the mirror and the killer-queen
and they asked her to stay and keep house.
Beware of your stepmother,
they said.   80
Soon she will know you are here.
While we are away in the mines
during the day, you must not
open the door.

Looking glass upon the wall . . .   85
The mirror told
and so the queen dressed herself in rags
and went out like a peddler to trap Snow White.
She went across seven mountains.
She came to the dwarf house   90
and Snow White opened the door
and bought a bit of lacing.
The queen fastened it tightly
around her bodice,
as tight as an Ace bandage,   95
so tight that Snow White swooned.
She lay on the floor, a plucked daisy.
When the dwarfs came home they undid the lace
and she revived miraculously.
She was as full of life as soda pop.   100
Beware of your stepmother,
they said.
She will try once more.

Looking glass upon the wall . . .
Once more the mirror told   105
and once more the queen dressed in rags

and once more Snow White opened the door.
This time she bought a poison comb,
a curved eight-inch scorpion,
and put it in her hair and swooned again.   110
The dwarfs returned and took out the comb
and she revived miraculously.
She opened her eyes as wide as Orphan Annie.
Beware, beware, they said,
but the mirror told,   115
the queen came,
Snow White, the dumb bunny,
opened the door
and she bit into a poison apple
and fell down for the final time.   120
When the dwarfs returned
they undid her bodice,
they looked for a comb,
but it did no good.
Though they washed her with wine   125
and rubbed her with butter
it was to no avail.
She lay as still as a gold piece.

The seven dwarfs could not bring themselves
to bury her in the black ground   130
so they made a glass coffin
and set it upon the seventh mountain
so that all who passed by
could peek in upon her beauty.
A prince came one June day   135
and would not budge.
He stayed so long his hair turned green
and still he would not leave.
The dwarfs took pity upon him
and gave him the glass Snow White—   140
its doll's eyes shut forever—
to keep in his far-off castle.
As the prince's men carried the coffin
they stumbled and dropped it
and the chunk of apple flew out   145
of her throat and she woke up miraculously.

And thus Snow White became the prince's bride.
The wicked queen was invited to the wedding feast
and when she arrived there were
red-hot iron shoes,   150

in the manner of red-hot roller skates,
clamped upon her feet.
First your toes will smoke
and then your heels will turn black
and you will fry upward like a frog,   155
she was told.
And so she danced until she was dead,
a subterranean figure,
her tongue flicking in and out
like a gas jet.   160
Meanwhile Snow White held court,
rolling her china-blue doll eyes open and shut
and sometimes referring to her mirror
as women do.

Adrienne Rich

[1929–   ]

A Valediction Forbidding Mourning

My swirling wants. Your frozen lips.
The grammar turned and attacked me.
Themes, written under duress.
Emptiness of the notations.

They gave me a drug that slowed the healing of wounds.   5

I want you to see this before I leave:
the experience of repetition as death
the failure of criticism to locate the pain
the poster in the bus that said:
my bleeding is under control.   10

A red plant in a cemetery of plastic wreaths.

A last attempt: the language is a dialect called metaphor.
These images go unglossed: hair, glacier, flashlight.
When I think of a landscape I am thinking of a time.
When I talk of taking a trip I mean forever.   15
I could say: those mountains have a meaning
but further than that I could not say.

To do something very common, in my own way.

Planetarium

(THINKING OF CAROLINE HERSCHEL, 1750–1848,
ASTRONOMER, SISTER OF WILLIAM; AND OTHERS)

A woman in the shape of a monster
a monster in the shape of a woman
the skies are full of them

a woman   "in the snow
among the Clocks and instruments   5
or measuring the ground with poles"

in her 98 years to discover
8 comets

she whom the moon ruled
like us   10
levitating into the night sky
riding the polished lenses

Galaxies of women, there
doing penance for impetuousness
ribs chilled   15
in those spaces   of the mind

An eye,
          "virile, precise and absolutely certain"
          from the mad webs of Uranisborg
                              encountering the NOVA   20

every impulse of light exploding
from the core
as life flies out of us
     Tycho whispering at last
     "Let me not seem to have lived in vain"   25

What we see, we see
and seeing is changing

the light that shrivels a mountain
and leaves a man alive

---

1. Subtitle: **William Herschel**: Famous astronomer (1738–1822).
  19. **Uranisborg**: The observatory built by Tycho Brahe (1546–1601), the Danish
astronomer.

Heartbeat of the pulsar   30
heart sweating through my body

The radio impulse
pouring in from Taurus

    I am bombarded yet   I stand

I have been standing all my life in the   35
direct path of a battery of signals
the most accurately transmitted most
untranslateable language in the universe
I am a galactic cloud so deep   so invo-
luted that a light wave could take 15   40
years to travel through me   And has
taken   I am an instrument in the shape
of a woman trying to translate pulsations
into images   for the relief of the body
and the reconstruction of the mind.   45

Diving into the Wreck

First having read the book of myths,
and loaded the camera,
and checked the edge of the knife-blade,
I put on
the body-armor of black rubber   5
the absurd flippers
the grave and awkward mask.
I am having to do this
not like Cousteau with his
assiduous team   10
aboard the sun-flooded schooner
but here alone.

There is a ladder.
The ladder is always there
hanging innocently   15
close to the side of the schooner.

We know what it is for,
we who have used it.
otherwise
it is a piece of maritime floss   20
some sundry equipment.

I go down.
Rung after rung and still
the oxygen immerses me   25
the blue light
the clear atoms
of our human air.
I go down.
My flippers cripple me,
I crawl like an insect down the ladder   30
and there is no one
to tell me when the ocean
will begin.

First the air is blue and then
it is bluer and then green and then   35
black I am blacking out and yet
my mask is powerful
it pumps my blood with power
the sea is another story
the sea is not a question of power   40
I have to learn alone
to turn my body without force
in the deep element.

And now: it is easy to forget
what I came for   45
among so many who have always
lived here
swaying their crenellated fans
between the reefs
and besides   50
you breathe differently down here.

I came to explore the wreck.
The words are purposes.
The words are maps.
I came to see the damage that was done   55
and the treasures that prevail.

I stroke the beam of my lamp
slowly along the flank
of something more permanent
than fish or weed   60

the thing I came for:
the wreck and not the story of the wreck
the thing itself and not the myth
the drowned face always staring
toward the sun   65
the evidence of damage
worn by salt and sway into this threadbare beauty
the ribs of the disaster
curving their assertion
among the tentative haunters.   70

This is the place.
And I am here, the mermaid whose dark hair
streams black, the merman in his armored body.
We circle silently
about the wreck   75
we dive into the hold.
I am she: I am he

whose drowned face sleeps with open eyes
whose breasts still bear the stress
whose silver, copper, vermeil cargo lies   80
obscurely inside barrels
half-wedged and left to rot
we are the half-destroyed instruments
that once held to a course
the water-eaten log   85
the fouled compass

We are, I am, you are
by cowardice or courage
the one who find our way
back to this scene   90
carrying a knife, a camera
a book of myths
in which
our names do not appear.

Ted Hughes[1]

[*1930–*]

Wodwo

What am I? Nosing here, turning leaves over
Following a faint stain on the air to the river's edge
I enter water. What am I to split
The glassy grain of water looking upward I see the bed
Of the river above me upside down very clear   5
What am I doing here in mid-air? Why do I find
this frog so interesting as I inspect its most secret
interior and make it my own? Do these weeds
know me and name me to each other have they
seen me before, do I fit in their world? I seem   10
separate from the ground and not rooted but dropped
out of nothing casually I've no threads
fastening me to anything I can go anywhere
I seem to have been given the freedom
of this place what am I then? And picking   15
bits of bark off this rotten stump gives me
no pleasure and it's no use so why do I do it
me and doing that have coincided very queerly
But what shall I be called am I the first
have I an owner what shape am I what   20
shape am I am I huge if I go
to the end on this way past these trees and past these trees
till I get tired that's touching one wall of me
for the moment if I sit still how everything
stops to watch me I suppose I am the exact centre   25
but there's all this what is it roots
roots roots roots and here's the water
again very queer but I'll go on looking

---

[1]For additional poems by Hughes, see his essay on pages 973–978 of Chapter 7.
   WODWO: A Middle English word taken from line 721 of the anonymous poem *Sir Gawain and the Green Knight* and translated as "wild man of the woods" or "wood demon." The source, which is the epigraph for the book of which this is the title-poem, describes Gawain's difficult journey to the Green Knight's castle: "Now with serpents he wars, now with savage wolves, / Now with wild men of the woods, that watched from the rocks." (Translation by Marie Borroff.)

Sylvia Plath

[1932–1963]

Ariel

Stasis in darkness.
Then the substanceless blue
Pour of tor and distances.

God's lioness,
How one we grow,   5
Pivot of heels and knees!—The furrow

Splits and passes, sister to
The brown arc
Of the neck I cannot catch,

Nigger-eye   10
Berries cast dark
Hooks——

Black sweet blood mouthfuls,
Shadows.
Something else   15

Hauls me through air——
Thighs, hair;
Flakes from my heels.

White
Godiva, I unpeel——   20
Dead heads, dead stringencies.

And now I
Foam to wheat, a glitter of seas.
The child's cry

Melts in the wall.   25
And I
Am the arrow,

ARIEL: Ariel was the name of Plath's horse.

The dew that flies
Suicidal, at one with the drive
Into the red   30

Eye, the cauldron of morning.

Daddy

You do not do, you do not do
Any more, black shoe
In which I have lived like a foot
For thirty years, poor and white,
Barely daring to breathe or Achoo.   5

Daddy, I have had to kill you.
You died before I had time—
Marble-heavy, a bag full of God.
Ghastly statue with one grey toe
Big as a Frisco seal   10

And a head in the freakish Atlantic
Where it pours bean green over blue
In the waters off beautiful Nauset.
I used to pray to recover you.
Ach, du.   15

In the German tongue, in the Polish town
Scraped flat by the roller
Of wars, wars, wars.
But the name of the town is common.
My Polack friend   20

Says there are a dozen or two.
So I never could tell where you
Put your foot, your root,
I never could talk to you.
The tongue stuck in my jaw.   25

It stuck in a barb wire snare.
Ich, ich, ich, ich,
I could hardly speak.

I thought every German was you.
And the language obscene   30

An engine, an engine
Chuffing me off like a Jew.
A Jew to Dachau, Auschwitz, Belsen.
I began to talk like a Jew.
I think I may well be a Jew.   35

The snows of the Tyrol, the clear beer of Vienna
Are not very pure or true.
With my gypsy ancestress and my weird luck
And my Taroc pack and my Taroc pack
I may be a bit of a Jew.   ⋅ 40

I have always been scared of *you*,
With your Luftwaffe, your gobbledygoo.
And your neat mustache
And your Aryan eye, bright blue.
Panzer-man, panzer-man, O You—   45

Not God but a swastika
So black no sky could squeak through.
Every woman adores a Fascist,
The boot in the face, the brute
Brute heart of a brute like you.   50

You stand at the blackboard, daddy,
In the picture I have of you,
A cleft in your chin instead of your foot
But no less a devil for that, no not
Any less the black man who   55

Bit my pretty red heart in two.
I was ten when they buried you.
At twenty I tried to die
And get back, back, back to you.
I thought even the bones would do.   60

But they pulled me out of the sack,
And they stuck me together with glue.
And then I knew what to do.
I made a model of you,
A man in black with a Meinkampf look   65

And a love of the rack and the screw.
And I said I do, I do.
So daddy, I'm finally through.
The black telephone's off at the root,
The voices just can't worm through.   70

If I've killed one man, I've killed two—
The vampire who said he was you
And drank my blood for a year,
Seven years, if you want to know.
Daddy, you can lie back now.   75

There's a stake in your fat black heart
And the villagers never liked you.
They are dancing and stamping on you.
They always *knew* it was you.
Daddy, daddy, you bastard, I'm through.   80

Tulips

The tulips are too excitable, it is winter here.
Look how white everything is, how quiet, how snowed-in.
I am learning peacefulness, lying by myself quietly
As the light lies on these white walls, this bed, these hands.
I am nobody; I have nothing to do with explosions.   5
I have given my name and my day-clothes up to the nurses
And my history to the anaesthetist and my body to the surgeons.

They have propped my head between the pillow and the sheet-cuff
Like an eye between two white lids that will not shut.
Stupid pupil, it has to take everything in.   10
The nurses pass and pass, they are no trouble,
They pass the way gulls pass inland in their white caps,
Doing things with their hands, one just the same as another,
So it is impossible to tell how many there are.

My body is a pebble to them, they tend it as water   15
Tends to the pebbles it must run over, smoothing them gently.
They bring me numbness in their bright needles, they bring me sleep.
Now I have lost myself I am sick of baggage—
My patent leather overnight case like a black pillbox,
My husband and child smiling out of the family photo;   20
Their smiles catch onto my skin, little smiling hooks.

I have let things slip, a thirty-year-old cargo boat
Stubbornly hanging on to my name and address.
They have swabbed me clear of my loving associations.
Scared and bare on the green plastic-pillowed trolley   25
I watched my tea-set, my bureaus of linen, my books
Sink out of sight, and the water went over my head.
I am a nun now, I have never been so pure.

I didn't want any flowers, I only wanted
To lie with my hands turned up and be utterly empty.   30
How free it is, you have no idea how free—
The peacefulness is so big it dazes you,
And it asks nothing, a name tag, a few trinkets.
It is what the dead close on, finally; I imagine them
Shutting their mouths on it, like a Communion tablet.   35

The tulips are too red in the first place, they hurt me.
Even through the gift paper I could hear them breathe
Lightly, through their white swaddlings, like an awful baby.
Their redness talks to my wound, it corresponds.
They are subtle: they seem to float, though they weigh me down,   40
Upsetting me with their sudden tongues and their color,
A dozen red lead sinkers round my neck.

Nobody watched me before, now I am watched.
The tulips turn to me, and the window behind me
Where once a day the light slowly widens and slowly thins,   45
And I see myself, flat, ridiculous, a cut-paper shadow
Between the eye of the sun and the eyes of the tulips,
And I have no face, I have wanted to efface myself.
The vivid tulips eat my oxygen.

Before they came the air was calm enough,   50
Coming and going, breath by breath, without any fuss.
Then the tulips filled it up like a loud noise.
Now the air snags and eddies round them the way a river
Snags and eddies round a sunken rust-red engine.
They concentrate my attention, that was happy   55
Playing and resting without committing itself.

The walls, also, seem to be warming themselves.
The tulips should be behind bars like dangerous animals;
They are opening like the mouth of some great African cat,
And I am aware of my heart: it opens and closes   60
Its bowl of red blooms out of sheer love of me.
The water I taste is warm and salt, like the sea,
And comes from a country far away as health.

Michael S. Harper

[*1938–*   ]

Reuben, Reuben

I reached from pain
to music great enough
to bring me back,
swollenhead, madness,
lovefruit, a pickle of hate   5
so sour my mouth twicked
up and would not sing;
there's nothing in the beat
to hold it in
melody and turn human skin;   10
a brown berry gone
to rot just two days on
     the branch;
we've lost a son,
the music, jazz, comes in.

Seamus Heaney

[*1939–*   ]

Digging

Between my finger and my thumb
The squat pen rests; snug as a gun.

Under my window, a clean rasping sound
When the spade sinks into gravelly ground:
My father, digging. I look down   5

Till his straining rump among the flowerbeds
Bends low, comes up twenty years away

REUBEN, REUBEN: On the death of the poet's two-day-old son.

Stooping in rhythm through potato drills
Where he was digging.

The coarse boot nestled on the lug, the shaft   10
Against the inside knee was levered firmly.
He rooted out tall tops, buried the bright edge deep
To scatter new potatoes that we picked
Loving their cool hardness in our hands.

By God, the old man could handle a spade.   15
Just like his old man.

My grandfather cut more turf in a day
Than any other man on Toner's bog.
Once I carried him milk in a bottle
Corked sloppily with paper. He straightened up   20
To drink it, then fell to right away

Nicking and slicing neatly, heaving sods
Over his shoulder, going down and down
For the good turf. Digging.

The cold smell of potato mould, the squelch and slap   25
Of soggy peat, the curt cuts of an edge
Through living roots awaken in my head.
But I've no spade to follow men like them.

Between my finger and my thumb
The squat pen rests.
I'll dig with it.

Death of a Naturalist

All year the flax-dam festered in the heart
Of the townland; green and heavy headed
Flax had rotted there, weighted down by huge sods.
Daily it sweltered in the punishing sun.
Bubbles gargled delicately, bluebottles   5
Wove a strong gauze of sound around the smell.
There were dragon-flies, spotted butterflies,
But best of all was the warm thick slobber
Of frogspawn that grew like clotted water
In the shade of the banks. Here, every spring   10

I would fill jampotfuls of the jellied
Specks to range on window-sills at home,
On shelves at school, and wait and watch until
The fattening dots burst into nimble-
Swimming tadpoles. Miss Walls would tell us how   15
The daddy frog was called a bullfrog
And how he croaked and how the mammy frog
Laid hundreds of little eggs and this was
Frogspawn. You could tell the weather by frogs too
For they were yellow in the sun and brown   20
In rain.

Then one hot day when fields were rank
With cowdung in the grass the angry frogs
Invaded the flax-dam; I ducked through hedges
To a coarse croaking that I had not heard
Before. The air was thick with a bass chorus.   25
Right down the dam gross-bellied frogs were cocked
On sods; their loose necks pulsed like sails. Some hopped:
The slap and plop were obscene threats. Some sat
Poised like mud grenades, their blunt heads farting.
I sickened, turned, and ran. The great slime kings   30
Were gathered there for vengeance and I knew
That if I dipped my hand the spawn would clutch it.

Margaret Atwood

[1939–   ]

This Is a Photograph of Me

It was taken some time ago.
At first it seems to be
a smeared
print: blurred lines and gray flecks
blended with the paper;   5

then, as you scan
it, you see in the left-hand corner
a thing that is like a branch: part of a tree
(balsam or spruce) emerging
and, to the right, halfway up   10

what ought to be a gentle
slope, a small frame house.

In the background there is a lake,
and beyond that, some low hills.

(The photograph was taken   15
the day after I drowned.

I am in the lake, in the center
of the picture, just under the surface.

It is difficult to say where
precisely, or to say   20
how large or small I am:

the effect of water
on light is a distortion

but if you look long enough,
eventually   25
you will be able to see me.)

Andrei Codrescu

[1946–   ]

Alberta

When Alberta swims the whole night in the creek behind
the house where I sit counting the rooms, I want to
send owls in the branches above her with the results
of my count. 13 rooms, Alberta, 13 rooms! Or maybe
a thousand! But what owls, indeed what beasts, can last   5
the impact of her smooth, wet body leaving a trail of
warm dark men in the phosphorescent water . . . Two fishes
mate in the depression between her breasts! Waiting
their turn, all the other creatures in the creek are
emanating a light that messes up my count. How many   10
rooms did I say? Then she speaks from my faucet when
I drink and the glass of water in my hand shimmers with
an invisible lust. At the end of all these rooms, at
the end, indeed, of all rooms, there is Alberta swimming
on and her strokes inside my bloodcells culminate in   15
light, in small blue explosions.

Love Poems and Spring Poems and Dream Poems and War Poems

Translated from the Anishinabe by Gerald Vizenor

—— Love Poem, I ——

i am thinking
. . . nia

i am thinking
. . . nia

i have found my lover
. . . nia

i think it is so

—— Love Poem, II ——

the sound of a loon
i thought

it was my lover
paddling

—— Love Poem, III ——

i have been waiting
a long time around the drum
for my lover
to come over
where i am sitting

——— Spring Poem, I ———

as my eyes
look across the prairie
i feel the summer
in the spring

——— Dream Poem, I ———

the clear sky
loves to hear me sing

——— Dream Poem, II ———

with a large bird
above me
i am walking
in the sky

——— War Poem, I ———

moving forward and back
from the woodland to the prairie
dakota women
weeping
as they gather
their wounded men
the sound of their weeping
comes back to us

——— War Poem, II ———

all around the sky
flying
the loons
are singing

———— **War Poem, III** ————

brave warriors
where have you gone
ho kwi ho ho

———— **Snow, the Last** ————

by Joseph Concha

Snow comes last
for it quiets down everything.

———— **Grandfather and I** ————

by Joseph Concha

Grandfather and I
talk
Grandfather sings
I dance
Grandfather teaches   5

I learn
Grandfather dies
I cry

I wait
patiently   10
to see Grandfather
in the world of darkness

I miss
my
Grandfather   15

Patient waiting
is weighted

by loneliness
I cry and cry and cry
When
will I see him?

20

War God's Horse Song I

Navajo Song by Tall Kia ahni. Interpreted by Louis Watchman

I am the Turquoise Woman's son.
On top of Belted Mountain
beautiful horses—slim like a weasel!
My horse with a hoof like a striped agate,
with his fetlock like a fine eagle plume: 5
my horse whose legs are like quick lightning
whose body is an eagle-plumed arrow:
my horse whose tail is like a trailing black cloud.
The Little Holy Wind blows thru his hair.
My horse with a mane made of short rainbows.   10
My horse with ears made of round corn.
My horse with eyes made of big stars.
My horse with a head made of mixed waters.
My horse with teeth made of white shell.
The long rainbow is in his mouth for a bridle   15
     & with it I guide him.
When my horse neighs, different-colored horses follow.
When my horse neighs, different-colored sheep follow.
     I am wealthy because of him.

    Before me peaceful
    Behind me peaceful
    Under me peaceful   20
    Over me peaceful—
    Peaceful voice when he neighs.
I am everlasting & peaceful.
I stand for my horse.

Leslie Marmon Silko

[1948–   ]

From Storyteller

INDIAN SONG: SURVIVAL

We went north
      to escape winter
climbing pale cliffs
        we paused   to sleep at the river.

Cold water   river cold from the north   5
I sink my body in the shallow
        sink into sand and cold river water.

You sleep in the branches of
        pale river willows above me.
I smell you in the silver leaves, mountain lion man   10
        green willows aren't sweet enough to hide you.

I have slept with the river   and
        he is warmer than any man.
At sunrise
      I heard ice on the cattails.   15

Mountain lion, with dark yellow eyes
        you nibble moonflowers
        while we wait.
I don't ask why do you come
        on this desperation journey north.   20

I am hunted for my feathers
I hide in spider's web
        hanging   in a thin gray tree
           above the river.
In the night   I hear music   25
        song of branches   dry leaves scraping the moon.

Green spotted frogs sing to the river
               and I know he is waiting.
Mountain lion shows me the way
          path of mountain wind   30
          climbing higher
             up
               up to Cloudy Mountain.

It is only a matter of time, Indian
               you can't sleep with the river forever.   35
Smell winter and know.

I swallow black mountain dirt
        while you catch hummingbirds
          trap them with wildflowers
            pollen and petals   40
              fallen from the Milky Way.

You lie beside me in the sunlight
        warmth around us and
        you ask me if I still smell winter.
Mountain forest wind travels east and I answer: 45
          taste me,
             I am the wind
          touch me,
             I am the lean gray deer
          running on the edge of the rainbow.   50

   *   *   *

The Laguna people
always begin their stories
with "humma-hah":
that means "long ago."
And the ones who are listening   55
say "aaaa-eh"

This story took place
somewhere around Acoma
where there was a lake,
a lake with pebbles along the edges.   60
It was a beautiful lake
and so a little girl and her sister
went there one day.
The older girl never liked to take care of her sister
but this day   65

she seemed to be anxious to take care of her sister.
So she put the little sister
on her back
That was the traditional way
of carrying babies, you know,   70
strapped on their back—

And so they went off to this lake
and this lake had shells around it
and butterflies and beautiful flowers—
they called it Shell Lake   75
shells and other pretty pebbles
where she amused her little sister
all day long.
And finally
toward evening   80
they came home to their village home.
And all was quiet in the village
there seemed to be no one stirring around or left,
and then
when they got to their house   85
which was a two-story house
traditional home of the Keres
she called *"Deeni!* Upstairs!"
because the entrance was generally from the top.

No one answered   90
until an old man came out
decrepit and he says
"You poor children—
nobody is here.
All our people have gone to Maúhuatl."   95
That was the name
of the high place
where they all went that day
to escape the flood that was coming.
He says   100
"Today the earth is going to be
filled with water.
And everyone has gone
To Maúhuatl
that high mesa land   105
to escape drowning.
Your mother is not here.
She left early in the day
to go with the rest of the people.
Only the old people   110

who cannot travel
are left.
And if you and your little sister
follow the rest
you can tell by their foot tracks.   115
But be sure and walk fast—
make haste
because the flood may be coming up
before you reach the mesa.''

So she said they would.   120
She started off with her little sister on her back and
pretty soon they began to cry
and what they cried
is a song that is sung.
Their crying became this little song.   125
It goes like this:
      Little sister go to sleep, go to sleep.
      I suppose our mother didn't think much
      of us
      so she left us behind. Go to sleep. Go to sleep.   130
      By luck we might catch up to the crowd. Go to sleep.
      We might catch up to our mother who has gone
      ahead to Maúhuatl. Go to sleep.

That is how the song goes.
And so the little girl kept walking   135
faster and faster.
By that time
the water was coming up to her ankles.
She was wading along
and as they went along   140
her little sister on her back
began to cry again.
She sang
      Go to sleep little sister, go to sleep.
      I suppose our mother didn't think much of us   145
      Or she wouldn't have left us behind.
By that time
the water had come up her legs
almost to her knees
and finally they reached the bottom   150
of Maúhuatl which was a mesa.
And there was a trail up there
and finally the older girl
walked up the mesa steps—

stone formations like steps.   155
They got to the top
before the flood really reached the top
and they looked around and
saw the people—
all the people up there   160
who had gone before.
They looked around
but they didn't see anything
of their mother.
They sat down,   165
the older girl did.
She saw the rest of them sitting around
holding their babies
and holding their little ones on their laps
so she thought she would sit down too   170
and hold her sister on her lap.
Which she did.
She sat there for a little while
and then they all turned into stone.

The story ends there.   175
Some of the stories
Aunt Susie told
have this kind of ending.
There are no explanations.

Deer Song

Storm winds carry snow
to the mountain stream
clotted white in silence,
pale blue streak under ice
to the sea.   5

The ice shatters into glassy
bone splinters that tear deep into
soft parts of the hoof.
Swimming away from the wolves
before dawn   10
    choking back salt water
    the streaming red froth tide.

It is necessary.
Reflections that blind
from a thousand feet of   15
gray schist
          snow-covered in dying winter sunlight.
The pain is numbed by the freezing,
          the depths of the night sky,
          the distance beyond pale stars.   20

Do not think that I do not love you
if I scream
          while I die.
Antler and thin black hoof
smashed against dark rock—   25
          the struggle is the ritual
shining teeth tangled in
          sinew and flesh.

You see,
          I will go with you,
Because you call softly   30
because you are my brother
          and my sister

Because the mountain is
our mother.
I will go with you   35
because you love me
while I die.

READING/WRITING

These writing suggestions may take any form you wish, from notebook
entry to formal essay. The point of such exercises, as always, is
experimentation, a way of helping you read as well as write about
literature. Some of your responses to these writing invitations may be cast
as prose, some as verse, depending on your own inclination to try your
hand at some of the techniques exhibited in the selections of this chapter.
This is not to say that verse is the same thing as poetry: as we've pointed
out earlier in this chapter, verse is a technical term for lines that attend to
meter and occasionally to rhyme; poetry, good poetry, comes from the gut.

1. Wallace Stevens's "Thirteen Ways of Looking at a Blackbird" suggests
   a writing exercise in which you give multiple views of an object: say, a
   pencil, a bar of soap, a candy bar . . . or snow, as the following student
   has done.

Thirteen Ways to Describe Snow

As children, we were in awe of our first encounter with snow. "Is it friendly?" we wondered as we ran outside to embrace it. We stood with our arms outstretched until they were covered with millions of the delicate crystals. We sprinted home, eager to inspect the crystals more closely. We slowly opened our arms, only to find them filled with tiny droplets of cold water! This was not the white treasure we had anticipated. In our young minds, treasures were supposed to last forever and ever. They were to be hidden away and shared only with our closest friends.

The ballerina is kneeling. Her arms curve gracefully above her head. The tiara in her hair sparkles under the many lights. She is still. I can scarcely see her breathing. Suddenly, the music begins. The ballerina leaps and twirls across the stage. She and the music have become one. Her body is as light as a snowflake. The music carries her like the gentlest breeze.

I hug my puppy tight as we both peer out of the frosted windowpane. This is the first snowfall that we have shared together. My puppy sniffs at the cold glass. His warm breath causes beads of water to form. He is intrigued by the fluffy whiteness outside. I open the window and quickly scoop some snow into my hand. My puppy yelps in surprise as I sprinkle some onto his furry paw. He has not yet learned to associate snow with cold.

It smells like winter. The air is dry and biting. My nose predicts that snow is near. Sure enough, heavy flakes begin to fall from an endless sky.

The trees are lightly dusted with white powder. The peaks of the houses resemble white hills. The only movement I see is a curl of gray smoke rising from one of the chimneys. It is spiralling toward the sky. Silence reigns. I ache with the beauty of the scene.

I go out into the storm, armed with my father's big, black umbrella. I snarl menacingly. Unfortunately, the storm refuses to acknowledge my presence. I am buffeted by the wind. Its immense power is overwhelming. My snarl quickly turns into a helpless whimper. The storm is merciless. It deliberately mangles my father's big, black umbrella. I crawl back inside, defeated.

I smile as I watch the first hesitant flakes fall upon the thirsty earth. Soon the dark ground will be covered with a winter coat of white.

The snowman has two pieces of coal for eyes, a carrot for a nose and a button for a mouth. He surveys his kingdom of whiteness. He is solemn as he stands guard, holding a broom in his hands, which are made of twigs. The sun is shining, causing the kingdom to glisten brightly. His eyes begin to droop; his nose starts to run. He cries as he watches the whiteness gradually disappear.

We mold the powdery snow into bricks which are then used to build our fortress. We make balls of snow to be used as ammunition. We build the four walls higher and higher. My mother yells from the kitchen, "The cookies are ready!" We all scramble to get out, only to find that we forgot to leave a space for the door.

It's snowing. We run outside and stand still, gaping at the transformation. The dark drabness of winter is gone. We end up covered from head to toe with snow. We are the Snow People.

The falling snow quiets the city. Only the sound of shovels scraping against the concrete can be heard. It is a soothing sound. Hearing it calms me.

How am I going to cross the street? The sidewalk is surrounded by a mixture of water and brown slush. My experienced eye estimates it to be at least nine inches deep. Now I know what it is like to be stranded on a remote island. Everyone else is taking a few steps back and surveying the area, trying to find the shallowest part. They concluded that there was no alternative but to try to the shallowest part. They conclude that there is no alternative but to try to leap across. They don't make it. They wade through the lumpy mush, cursing under their breath. I look down at my less than athletic legs. They appear to be shorter and stumpier than usual. I take a deep breath. I am leaping through the air. My body feels so incredibly light! I honestly think that I'm going to make it! I land with a big splash; I do not make it. I join the others in wading through the mush, cursing under my breath.

I look outside and see the streets are covered with a smooth whiteness that is marred only by a set of footprints. I look further down the street and see a man walking slowly, lost in his own thoughts. Time stands still.

Nancy Dong

2. Using Ted Hughes's suggestions for "capturing animals" (found in his essay in Chapter 7, page 973), create a living creature of your own—in prose or poetry. Get inside the animal's skin, inside its spirit, perhaps by writing in the first person.

   The following student writer, whose work we have already seen in the Auto/Biography chapter, recasts some of what we have learned from his autobiographical narrative in this description of a pet. Here is how the author explores the theme of expatriation through the medium of another literary form—an imaginative projection of his feelings onto another living creature:

Fish

The moon looks extremely bright and round outside the window. The sky is clear and the land is covered with cold moonlight. It is so quiet, quiet at this midnight. My thoughts are flying as I sit in my living room.

My eyes move unconsciously from the window to the fishbowl in the corner of the room. I enjoy watching the fish when I am tired or sad. The fish seem to understand me. They keep silent, too.

Melissa, the only goldfish in the bowl, pays no attention to my stare. As usual she is vigilantly drifting in water. By fortune she came here: my friend gave her to me as a little gift. She is beautiful, two inches long, blood red, with two big eyes like two red pearls on her head, a maple-leaf tail which seems to be made of translucent silk, and a big stomach.

Up, right, down, left, she moves carefully, alone. She must not only protect herself from the attack of the sharks, the invaders—I have two of them—but must also keep away from the black and white angelfish, which always distastefully plays the role of lover. The catfish hides under the stone and watches her sinisterly. These are the professional slayers.

The golden fish swims carefully and helplessly. Suddenly I feel sorrow for her. I took her away from her parents and placed her in this dangerous and complex society. I think I have made a mistake. It is hard for her to live this lonely life. Her future is unclear. Today is a Chinese festival of family reunion. I think she and her parents must be missing one another.

Wanyang Ju

3. Here's a comic alternative to the previous writing exercise: Write a tribute to your cat, dog, goldfish, or favorite avocado plant, in which you list the qualities of the subject in the mock-heroic style of that wonderfully strange experimental poem by Christopher Smart about his beloved cat Jeoffrey (pages 692–694).

   Or write an ironic tribute to a loved one, as Shakespeare celebrates his mistress in the sonnet, "My Mistress' Eyes Are Nothing Like the Sun." Or write a "Satirical Elegy" for someone you do *not* admire, in the manner of Swift's poem on page 680.

4. Rilke writes about a photograph of his father (page 762); Atwood, about a photo of herself (page 865). Pick one of these poems and discuss the methods by which the author makes you 'see' the photograph in question. When you have finished your analysis of the poet's technique, you might want to flip through your own family album and select a photo to serve as the topic of a descriptive and meditative paragraph or essay.

5. Update a fairy tale you remember from your childhood, in the same ironic spirit as Anne Sexton retells the story of Snow White (pages 848–852). Perhaps relate the story to your own experience, as Sexton does; in any case, you should observe a comic disjuncture between the fairy-tale format and the contemporary tone and details of your narration. Again, this assignment may take whatever form you're comfortable with, whether verse or prose.

6. Compare Anne Sexton's version of the story with the tale of "Little Snow White" reprinted in the Short Fiction chapter. What elements appear in both versions? What elements does Sexton add or omit? How do these changes affect the meaning of the fairy tale as rendered by the poet?

7. In this collection of poems are several dramatic monologues and mask lyrics—the ruminations of a single speaker talking to himself or herself or addressing a silent listener. Tennyson's "Ulysses," Browning's "My Last Duchess," Amy Lowell's "Patterns," and Ted

Hughes's "Wodwo" are examples. Choose one of these monologues and write a brief character sketch of the speaker, in which you explain what you can infer about the character on the basis of his or her speech.

8. Ezra Pound's poem "The Garden" suggests a related assignment, for it works almost as a counterpoint to Lowell's "Patterns" in that it describes the woman who walks through the garden in Lowell's poem, but this time from an *onlooker's* point of view. In the same vein, you might recast one of the monologues listed in question 7 above from another character's perspective. In the case of the Marvell poem, for example, you might compose the mistress's reply to the speaker's argument in "To His Coy Mistress." Alternatively, you might decide to take a fictional or historical character you've read about in one of the other chapters in this anthology and write a dramatic monologue for him or her.

9. Discuss point of view in one of the poems mentioned above. What is the author's relationship to the speaker of the poem? You might analyze, for instance, the ironic stance Browning takes toward the speaker in "My Last Duchess." How does the poet indicate his distance from the speaker?

10. After reading Rilke's "Spanish Dancer" on page 763, look ahead to the photograph entitled "Flamenco Dancer" in the Ken Haas selection in Chapter 7. The photograph presents the dancer poised, frozen in time and space, whereas the poem seems all movement and action. In a short essay, analyze Rilke's poem, paying special attention to the diction, imagery, sounds, and metrics that combine to create the impression of an intense and dramatic dance.

11. *Carpe diem,* a Latin phrase meaning "seize the day," is a familiar poetic theme. In a *carpe diem* poem, the speaker exhorts a silent listener to make the most of the moment, to live for today because yesterday is gone and tomorrow may never come. This theme is especially common in sixteenth- and seventeenth-century English love poems, in which the speaker entreats his mistress to yield to desire while both lovers have their youth and beauty.

    Compare the development of the *carpe diem* theme in two of these English poems: Jonson's "Come, My Celia," Marvell's "To His Coy Mistress," and Donne's "The Flea," or compare the rendering of the theme in one of the versions of the Persian lyric (on page 644) to its treatment in one of these English poems.

12. On page 677 you'll find a poem by Aphra Behn, a woman writer of the seventeenth century. The poem we've reprinted here, "The Willing Mistress," is in some ways an answer to the seductive *carpe diem* poems written by the male poets listed above. How does Behn answer them?

Compare one of these poems to Behn's: What differences do they reveal?

13. A number of poems in this chapter are tributes to other writers—"His Prayer to Ben Jonson" by Robert Herrick, "To the Memory of Mr. Oldham" by John Dryden, "In Memory of W. B. Yeats" by W. H. Auden, "Frederick Douglass" by Robert Hayden, and "A Supermarket in California" by Allen Ginsberg. Choose one of these poems (or compare two of these poems) and analyze the ways in which the poet pays tribute or acknowledges his artistic debt to the subject through the medium of verse.

14. Alexander Pope's "Essay on Criticism," excerpted here, is a poetic essay, written in heroic couplets. Write an essay on the essay-like qualities of this poem, in which you begin by outlining the arguments Pope presents. Then consider the question of why Pope made his argument in poetry rather than in prose.

15. Among the authors whose poems are especially well-represented in this chapter are Anne Bradstreet, Emily Dickinson, Theodore Roethke, and William Carlos Williams. The lives of these poets, as well as their works, suggest a number of interesting research projects. Choose one of the poets whose work you'd like to know more about, and look up what you can find about him or her in the library: consult biographies, collections of letters, notebooks, diaries, and scholarly essays by critics. For a brief essay, you might want to focus on a particular poem or pair of poems. What can you discover about a given poem or set of poems by reading further into the life of the artist?

16. Select two poems that have the same form (two sonnets, for example) or theme and compare them to discover how two different authors handle the same structure or subject matter. You have dozens of options for this kind of comparison/contrast essay—here are just a few:

 a. Two elegies—death laments—by, for example, Jonson, Dryden, Bradstreet, Harper, Levine, Wilbur, Merwin, or Roethke. Here you will want to focus on the ways each artist finds to deal with the death of a loved one. In the introduction to this chapter, for instance, we looked at how Anne Bradstreet wrote about the loss of her house and her possessions; how, in her elegy on page 671, does she struggle with the far deeper loss of her young granddaughter? Does she reconcile herself to God's will, as in the poem on the burning of her house?

 b. Two poems on love or death by Dickinson, or two poems by Roethke, Williams, or Cummings on either of these subjects.

c. Two poems on the same subject. Possibilities include: nature versus artifice (by Jonson and Herrick); war (by Reed and Levertov); fathers (by Roethke and Hayden); freedom and slavery (by Wheatley, Langston Hughes, and Hayden); snakes (by Lawrence and Dickinson); birds (Dickinson's "A Bird Came Down the Walk" and Frost's "Dust of Snow"); reapers (by Wordsworth, Bontemps, and Toomer); blindness (by Milton and Borges); Brueghel's painting of Icarus (by Williams and Auden); fish (by Roethke, Bishop, and Ted Hughes [the latter is on pages 973–978 of Chapter 7]); "Frogs" by Bose, "The Death of a Toad" by Wilbur, "Death of a Naturalist" by Heaney, and so on.

d. Poems that reply to each other, like Raleigh's reply to Marlowe and Williams's comment on Raleigh, or Rich's poem that adapts the title of Donne's "A Valediction: Forbidding Mourning"; you might also compare two translations of the same poem by the Persian poet Sa'dī.

In your essay, it is your task to show how each poet has made the subject his or her own. The points of comparison are up to you. Among other elements we've discussed in the introduction to this chapter, appropriate matters for your consideration might include the attitude each poet takes toward the subject matter—the poem's mood and tone; the line lengths, sound patterns, rhythms, word order, and diction of the poem, the way imagery is used; the relationship between the poet and the speaker of the poem, and so on.

Of course, in this or any other writing exercise we've suggested here, you may prefer to forego comparison and instead analyze *one* poem in detail, according to the elements mentioned above.

CHAPTER
7
Essays

An essay is the result of a mind in motion, an idea pursued. We compose essays to test a thesis, to collect our thoughts on a given subject, to try ideas on for size. This is the meaning of the French word *essai*—a trial, an attempt, an experiment—by which Michel de Montaigne christened the literary genre he virtually invented in 1580, when he published his first volume of *Essais*. Montaigne spent the last twenty years of his life exploring his reactions to different subjects and situations: "I have put all my efforts into forming my life," he said; "That is my trade and my work." In a sense, Montaigne "formed" his life by thinking it out on paper, by living as a curious and astute observer. Through close examination of the external world, he was able to traverse, mentally and verbally, the pathways of the inner self.

Taken together, Montaigne's essays present an unusual self-portrait by showing how the author responded to subjects and situations. His is an autobiography of ideas, an arresting drama of a thinker who spent his life coming to terms with himself. In so combining the speculative and personal elements in his writing, Montaigne brought the modern essay into being. In his preface to *Essais*, Montaigne explains his purpose in writing this book:

To the Reader

This, reader, is an honest book. It warns you at the outset that my sole purpose in writing it has been a private and domestic one. I have had no thought of serving you or of my own fame; such a plan would be beyond my powers. I have intended it solely for the pleasure of my relatives and friends so that, when they have lost me—which they soon must—they may recover some features of my character and disposition, and thus keep the memory they have of me more completely and vividly alive.

Had it been my purpose to seek the world's favour, I should have put on finer clothes, and have presented myself in a studied attitude. But I want to appear in my simple, natural, and everyday dress, without strain or artifice; for it is myself that I portray. My imperfections may be read to the life, and my natural form will be here in so far as respect for the public allows. Had my lot been cast among those peoples who are said still to live under the kindly liberty of nature's primal laws, I should, I assure you, most gladly have painted myself complete and in all my nakedness.

So, reader, I am myself the substance of my book, and there is no reason why you should waste your leisure on so frivolous and unrewarding a subject.

Farewell then, from Montaigne,
this first day of March, 1580.

Montaigne took as his motto this question: "What do I know?" The loose organization of his mental excursions suggests the thought process itself as Montaigne considers some aspect of human nature; reacts to an idea, an object, or an incident; investigates why we behave as we do and how we should behave. Whether they are reflections on cannibals, cruelty, or the custom of wearing clothes, Montaigne's essays appear to be triggered by his desire to get to the heart of the matter, to find out what he really believes.

Writers over the years have continued to adapt this versatile form of inquiry to their own purposes. Alexander Pope, the eighteenth-century British poet, composed a number of essays in verse, including one of his best-known poems, *An Essay on Criticism.* In the section of the *Essay on Criticism* excerpted in Chapter 6, Pope presents his rules for writing poetry. Like the essayist working in prose, Pope draws on examples and illustrations to support the ideas he advances. By the same token, as you may have already noticed, several of the selections placed elsewhere in this book could have been included in this chapter. To cite just a few examples from Chapter 3 alone: Sherwood Anderson's "Unforgotten," M. F. K. Fisher's "P Is for Peas," and Natalie Zemon Davis's "The Honor of Bertrande de Rols" are all narrative *essays* as well as biographies or autobiographies. You can probably point to selections in other chapters that might appear in this chapter as well.

Today, essays appear not only in print, but via the airwaves and in photographic images. News programs on radio and television commonly feature editorials which express the speaker's point of view on issues great and trivial, from discussions about the perils of nuclear war to reviews of Broadway plays to diatribes about jars that don't open. Documentary films on endangered species, rock musicians, modern architecture, and almost any other topic you can think of are really "cinematic essays": The director, like the essay writer, investigates a subject, discovers what he or she wants to say about that subject, and then selects the film clips that best convey his or her attitudes and conclusions.

To take another example of the range of media open to the essayist: If you turn to the first selection in this chapter, you will find a series of four photographs of human subjects. These pictures are part of a more extensive "photo essay" on Americans and Europeans living in Hong Kong that the photographer, Ken Haas, calls *The Expatriates.* The theme of expatriation, of leaving one's homeland to live in another country, serves as this artist's primary concern—the issue that connects the portraits. Having grouped his subjects according to this shared characteristic, the photographer looks for specific details that will enable viewers to understand something about the nature of being an exile. Like any other essay, *The Expatriates* invites the audience to look at a subject more closely, to take some time to reflect on a topic.

This series of photographs works through the interaction of different kinds of visual details, much as a written essay draws on facts, stories, examples, statistics—those "proofs" that make a work concrete and convincing—to develop a central idea. In exposition, evidence is assembled to illustrate a thesis for the purpose of exposing or revealing something about a subject. Looking at the first photo in the group, for example, you might immediately think of Spain—the flamenco dancer's traditional dress and shawl, her classic pose and expression. Notice, though, that the dancer is performing not on a stage, but alone in a room. One item in particular seems incongruous: the small tape recorder with its 'canned' music. The dancer has tried to re-create the experience of home, but lacking a gypsy guitarist, must improvise.

As you enter the world of these photographs, pay careful attention to elements that might disclose something about the life of each expatriate. Like the theme of a short story or a poem, the theme of each portrait is constructed not only in obvious ways, such as through expression or posture, but also through more subtle signs: the relationships between light and shadow, the textures, the scale and size of objects, the point of view from which the objects are seen, and the overall composition—how the image is framed within the 'four walls' of the photo. In the case of the photos reprinted here, the photo essayist manipulates these elements to convey a central impression of each subject and to encourage viewers to imagine what it might be like to live in exile.

Take a few minutes now to examine one of these photographs. Based on the details of this portrait, what can you infer about the subject? About the nature of being an expatriate? To some degree, interpretations will vary as each viewer draws his or her own conclusions about the subject, much as the photographer has done.

As you read the essays in this chapter, you will notice differences not only in medium, but in purpose and form. Some essays, like those of Montaigne, are speculative exercises that explore concepts or feelings. Essays that rely chiefly on narrative, as you might surmise, tell stories, most often autobiographical, to animate abstract ideas. In one such essay reprinted in this chapter, George Orwell dramatizes his hatred of colonialism with the story of a haunting personal experience—the shooting of an elephant in Burma. Expository essays may also include some narrative, but as we will see in the discussion that follows, they commonly draw on a number of strategies, such as analysis and analogy, to inform, explain, and persuade. And, although the line between exposition and argument is blurred, some essays are unmistakably contentious. Argument is more emphatic and insistent than exposition:

its primary purpose is to convince, to lead the reader to perceive the subject precisely as the writer does.

But it is essential to recognize that these four broad types of essays usually overlap. Narrative essays often advance arguments; speculative essays explain as they explore; and arguments inform as well as persuade. In "The Death of the Moth," for instance, Virginia Woolf blends narrative with speculation as she contemplates mortality. Similarly, Alice Walker's "In Search of Our Mothers' Gardens" combines narrative and exposition with speculation to convince readers of the ways in which generations of black women have fed the creative spirit and shown themselves to be artists.

—— WAYS OF THINKING/WAYS OF WRITING ——

In the essays ahead, you will find a great range of topics and treatments: In addition to the photographic essay, we've chosen, among other examples, a psychological study of a well-known fairy tale, a chapter from a book on the sociological significance of different styles of clothing, a medical paper by a nineteenth-century physician, a newspaper article about the role of folklore in the late 1980s, and an impassioned anti-slavery speech delivered before an audience in 1852.

Whether an essay explores, explains, or argues a subject, authors have a number of strategies to help them organize and develop their thoughts. Each of these strategies offers a distinct way of viewing a topic and discovering ideas. As you read an essay, ask yourself how its strategies relate to the purpose and content of the piece. How do these structures influence your perception of the text? What can you as a writer learn from observing other minds at work?

Let's look first at the way a contemporary scientist puzzles out, in an essay, a phenomenon of nature he has been contemplating. In "The Panda's Thumb" (pages 985–990), Stephen Jay Gould tries to answer a question he asked himself after observing the giant panda's dexterity in stripping the leaves from its favorite food plant, bamboo: "Was the panda's 'thumb' a separately evolved sixth finger?" Gould begins by *classifying*—that is, by assigning the panda's strange sixth digit to a class of bone and describing its essential characteristics:

> The panda's thumb is not, anatomically, a finger at all. It is constructed from a bone called the radial sesamoid, normally a small component of the wrist. In pandas, the radial sesamoid is greatly enlarged and elongated until it almost equals the metapodial bones of the true digits in length. The radial sesamoid underlies a pad on the panda's forepaw; the five digits form the framework of another pad, the palmar. A shallow furrow separates the two pads and serves as a channelway for bamboo stalks.

So, not a thumb at all, the contraption on the panda's paw is actually an enlarged wristbone that enables the animal to prepare the bamboo shoots for eating. To determine if the anatomy of similar animals offers a clue to the origin of this odd skeletal arrangement, Gould goes on to contrast the panda's musculature and bone structure with that of its closest relative, the ordinary bear. Unlike other members of the order *Carnivora*, composed of predominantly flesh-eating mammals such as dogs, cats, and weasels, bears have a slightly enlarged radial sesamoid, which becomes markedly enlarged in the panda. So distinguishing characteristics, such as a sixth digit and a decided preference for bamboo, allow us to subdivide larger classifications and to see how an animal is both similar to and different from other members of its order.

But Gould's purpose in this informative and entertaining piece is not confined to the panda or its thumb. Instead, he uses this illustration of natural adaptation as the foundation for the twofold thesis he wants to prove: (1) Darwin's genius in recognizing that "odd arrangements and funny solutions are the proof of evolution" and (2) Gould's own conviction that evolution works not in gradual stages, but in sudden leaps. The panda's strange appendage, Gould theorizes, "probably reflects a simple kind of genetic change," perhaps a single mutation that caused the growth of the radial sesamoid and resulted in "a somewhat clumsy, but quite workable, solution" to the business of stripping bamboo. Note that Gould's use of classification not only provides the foundation for his thesis but also gives the reader an impression of 'objectivity' (though no writing is ever entirely objective), a tone that makes his conclusions about scientific matters seem all the more persuasive for its authority.

Authors of *narrative* essays, on the other hand, are often more concerned with eliciting the reader's subjective response. With this goal in mind, writers exercise their powers of description—the selection of specific words, images, and figures of speech to create vivid sensory impressions of a person, a place, an object, an event. Descriptive details help the reader see and experience something from the writer's point of view. Here, for example, is George Orwell's graphic account of the animal's death in "Shooting an Elephant," a combination of narrative and description etched with painfully sharp detail:

> When I pulled the trigger I did not hear the bang or feel the kick—
> one never does when a shot goes home—but I heard the devilish roar
> of glee that went up from the crowd. In that instant, in too short a time,
> one would have thought, even for the bullet to get there, a mysterious,
> terrible change had come over the elephant. He neither stirred nor fell,
> but every line of his body had altered. He looked suddenly stricken,
> shrunken, immensely old, as though the frightful impact of the bullet
> had paralysed him without knocking him down. At last, after what
> seemed a long time—it might have been five seconds, I dare say—he

sagged flabbily to his knees. His mouth slobbered. An enormous senility seemed to have settled upon him. One could have imagined him thousands of years old. I fired again into the same spot. At the second shot he did not collapse but climbed with desperate slowness to his feet and stood weakly upright, with legs sagging and head drooping. I fired a third time. That was the shot that did for him. You could see the agony of it jolt his whole body and knock the last remnant of strength from his legs. But in falling he seemed for a moment to rise, for as his hind legs collapsed beneath him he seemed to tower upward like a huge rock toppling, his trunk reaching skywards like a tree. He trumpeted, for the first and only time. And then down he came, his belly towards me, with a crash that seemed to shake the ground even where I lay.

Early on in the essay, Orwell calls his shooting of the elephant "a tiny event in itself." Here is how one student responded to Orwell's account:

After reading this essay, I couldn't get the picture of the elephant's death out of my mind. It haunted me and I kept wishing that this story were fiction so I could say to myself, "This didn't really happen." I felt as if Orwell were torturing me with all of those details. I was sure he was torturing himself.

Michael Dionysiou

As this reader suggests, Orwell's description of the beast's slow death—which continues for another two paragraphs—suggests something other than "a tiny event" and provides a punishing climax to his experiences as a colonial policeman in British-controlled Burma before World War II. Take a few minutes to reread the passage and examine your own reactions to this event. What details strike you? How are your feelings influenced by these details? How does the narrative build to a climax? Do you agree that Orwell is "torturing" the reader, along with himself? Why would he do so?

In addition to structuring an entire essay, narration, like description, may quicken one or more of its parts. Interesting or humorous anecdotes can engage the reader at the outset, clarify a concept, support a point, animate an explanation, or supply an apt conclusion. In "The Panda's Thumb," for example, the author's recollection of his childhood fondness for toy pandas and his account of a visit to the Washington zoo leads comfortably into the discussion that follows. Similarly, in his essay "Of Liars," Montaigne intersperses his ruminations on the nature of liars with illustrations of why lying requires a keen memory. By way of proof, he offers several historical—and humorous—anecdotes of politicians who were ultimately entrapped by their own clumsy and contradictory lies.

We've seen how Gould uses classification to solve a scientific problem, how Orwell draws on descriptive details to arouse subjective responses, and how Montaigne uses anecdotes as ballast for his assertions. Another method for shaping exposition is *causal analysis*, in which an author examines the causes or effects of a particular phenomenon. Here, in other words, a writer addresses the *whys* and *hows* of things, as in the newspaper article (on pages 992–995) entitled "Folklore Mirrors Life's Key Themes," which summarizes why and how contemporary Americans generate popular beliefs.

In a lengthier causal analysis that appears in this section, a chapter from a book entitled *The Language of Clothes*, Alison Lurie explains why we wear what we wear. What unifying idea does the title of her book suggest? How might clothing function as a sign system? What different messages—social, economic, and so on—might be communicated by various styles of dress? Let's examine the ways in which Lurie attempts to answer these questions.

In "Male and Female," the chapter we've excerpted, Lurie approaches her subject historically, beginning with the age-old assumption that sexual modesty is the reason for wearing clothes. She soon calls this assumption into question with historical examples of rather immodest dress, and thus paves the way for her thesis, framed as a statement of cause and effect:

> Whether it was the first cause or not, from the earliest times one important function of clothing has been to promote erotic activity: to attract men and women to one another, thus ensuring the survival of the species. If maximum fertility is to be achieved, we must select members of the opposite sex rather than our own to make love to. One basic purpose of costume, therefore, is to distinguish men from women.

How does the author support her thesis? In the ensuing discussion, Lurie shows how fashion mirrors the ideals and attitudes of an era. From the fourteenth to the eighteenth centuries, for example, European women wore brightly colored gowns made of rich, soft materials that called attention to the breasts and stomach. These costumes suggested strength, health, and energy, and flattered pregnant women. But in the early 1800s, women were "redefined as something between children and angels: weak, timid, innocent creatures of sensitive nerves and easily alarmed modesty," and accordingly their attire changed. In fact, as Lurie points out, the costumes of certain periods were actually the *cause* of what were deemed the distinctly "feminine" attributes of delicacy and weakness. The thin-soled slippers and short-sleeved, low-necked dresses worn by the women in the early nineteenth century ensured the "charming ill-health" of their wearers. In other words, Lurie explains how the attitudes of an era create the fashions of the day, and how fashion, in turn, reinforces those attitudes. By citing numerous examples of this phenomenon, Lurie brings to light certain trends or patterns the reader might not have otherwise discerned. Her progress through the history of fashion works cumulatively, with each example adding further weight to her thesis. Still, you may find reasons to question her analysis. Can you think, for instance, of specific styles of dress that do not support Lurie's assumptions?

In our discussion so far, we have concentrated on the primary strategies the authors of these essays have used to develop their central ideas, though each essay contains other means of development as well. Remember that writers are unlikely to set out to compose a "speculative" essay or a "narrative" essay. Instead, they pursue a series of ideas and let these ideas determine the course and shape of their essays. To understand this process better, we'll examine the configuration of another essay reprinted in this chapter. In "Capturing Animals," British poet Ted Hughes compares his childhood enthusiasm for drawing and hunting animals to his adult penchant for capturing animals in poetry. Take a few minutes to read the Hughes poem "Wodwo," which you'll find on page 857 of Chapter 6. Then ask yourself: Why might a poet turn to prose, to the essay, to explain his passion for capturing animals in verse?

In his essay, Hughes begins with a narrative of his early years. He might have focused on any number of events from his youth—his reading, his schoolwork, and so on—but in this piece he concentrates on his fascination with animals. He traces his progress from collecting toy animals to drawing his own pictures of creatures he found in a photo book. These animals, he writes, "looked even better in my drawings and were mine. I can remember the excitement with which I used to sit staring at my drawings, and it is a similar thing I feel nowadays with my poems." Next came scrambling about the hillsides, retrieving the magpies and owls and weasels and rats his older brother had shot, and finally hunting and fishing on his own. At fifteen, though, the author's attitude toward animals changed. He accused himself of disturbing their lives, and at about the same time, began to write poetry. Even so, it was years before he wrote his first "animal poem" and longer still before he realized that writing poems about animals was an extension of his childhood passion.

The connection between these two activities leads Hughes to an analogy, a device through which he can illustrate a difficult or abstract concept by comparing it to something familiar. By comparing the act of capturing animals to the act of writing poems, Hughes helps the reader not only to understand his transformation from hunter to poet, but also to envision a complex and elusive creative process in terms of an ordinary physical activity:

> The special kind of excitement, the slightly mesmerized and quite involuntary concentration with which you make out the stirrings of a new poem in your mind, then the outline, the mass and color and clean final form of it, the unique living reality of it in the midst of general lifelessness, all that is too familiar to mistake. This is hunting and the poem is a new species of creature, a new specimen of the life outside your own.

Hughes carries his analogy one step further by showing how the words and rhythms and images of a poem are like the living parts and spirit of an animal, explaining that "if any of the parts are dead . . . if any of the words, or images or rhythms do not jump to life as you read them . . . then the creature is going to be maimed and the spirit sickly."

Finally, Hughes tells us how he does what he does. That is, he describes and analyzes the process of writing a poem, and warns of pitfalls along the way, such as thinking laboriously instead of imagining what you are writing about, or obsessing over punctuation. At last we're ready for a few examples of the poet's own "prize catches," including the first animal poem he wrote, "The Thought Fox." Hughes explains *why* this fox, *his* fox, is "very real," and shows how another poem called "Pike" allowed him to capture a whole pond—including monsters he "never even hooked." As you can see, Hughes the essayist has used every expository technique at his disposal to help us understand Hughes the poet.

"OUT OF THE ARGUMENT WITH OTHERS, RHETORIC"

All essays contain elements of persuasion, attempts to convince readers of something. Gould's treatment of the panda's "thumb" shows that each of Darwin's books was part of the grand and coherent scheme of the naturalist's work; Lurie's analysis of clothing persuades us that there is more to jeans and T-shirts than meets the eye. You'll probably walk away from "Male and Female" thinking differently about the "meaning" of what you wear, just as "Folklore Mirrors Life's Themes" may affect your response to the next contemporary "myth" that comes your way. But whereas some essays are subtly persuasive, others are overtly so. Authors of argument essays set out to effect change, to confront an opponent, to convince others to agree and to act accordingly. It is all the more important, then, for writers of arguments to present their claims explicitly and logically, to back them up with whatever support—facts, examples, analogies, anecdotes, statistics, expert testimony, and so on—they can marshal.

Logical reasoning uses three chief methods for organizing evidence. We've seen that essays may be structured partly or primarily by analogy. Another approach is the inductive structure, which proceeds from a series of specific observations to a generalization, much as Darwin's observations of the "odd arrangements and funny solutions" of different life forms eventually led to his theories of evolution. As you'll observe in "The Boston Photographs," a magazine article reprinted in this chapter, an inductive structure can help to convey an impression of objectivity. In this essay, Nora Ephron discusses the controversial publication, in 1975, of photographs that show a woman and a child falling from a burning building. Beginning with a quotation from the photographer, Ephron goes on to describe the photographs, and then examines the angry debate that followed their appearance in newspapers all over the country. Finally, in the last few paragraphs, Ephron responds to a number of arguments justifying the publication of these photographs and presents her own markedly different position.

Far more common than inductive structure, though, is deductive ordering, which moves from the proposition—the general premise or thesis—to the specific examples that support this proposition. Take one of the essays that appears in this chapter, a paper called "Emotional Prodigality" written by a prominent physician for a medical conference in 1879. Here the author, Charles Fayette Taylor, claims that emotions are "the most exhausting of all mental attributes. It is the emotion . . . which tires and exhausts the frame." Like most writers, Taylor naturally reflects the ideas of his era, and he enlists a popular belief to support his premise. He asserts that women are more emotional than men—thus treating a widespread assumption of his time as if it were a fact—and then deduces that women are therefore more subject to physical ailments caused by strong emotion. Taylor argues that the educated woman is especially prone to nervous disorders, for she is "excitable, and in every way more dominated by her emotions than the savage woman is. Or, if the contrast is not so extreme as this, she certainly does lack the equipoise which is the characteristic of highly-educated men. . . . " He continues:

> For patience, for reliability, for real judgment in carrying out directions, for self-control, give me the little woman who has not been "educated" too much, and whose only ambition is to be a good wife and mother. She can be trusted to keep cool under trying circumstances; she does not have the backache; she does not tear herself to pieces with imaginary troubles nor insist on taking only emotional views of every incident of trouble. Her reason has not been put under the dominant influence of unmixed feeling, intensified by the process through which she obtained what is called her education. Hence her head is cool and her judgment clear. Such women are capable of being the mothers of men.

You may notice that Taylor, like Gould, uses classification to construct his argument. We've observed that this strategy commonly provides readers with a sense of the author's objectivity. Note, however, that it is essential to examine the assumption on which a classification is based. As a reader, how do you react to this paragraph? Does Taylor's assumption seem intellectually sound? Why or why not? Examine the language of this excerpt. Does the writer appeal primarily to emotion or to logic? What image of women is created by the passage? What words and phrases reveal Taylor's attitude toward educated women?

Taylor goes on to contend that the educated woman is not only a danger to herself but to her children. The mother's "emotional prodigality" causes her children—especially her daughters—to become overstimulated, draining their energy and making them susceptible to illness. In support of his claims, Taylor cites cases of youngsters who, exposed to intellectual female relatives, exhibit such maladies as ill-proportioned bodies and curvature of the spine.

This argument may strike many readers in the 1980s as absurd: You might accuse Taylor of stereotyping women or of failing to consider other causes of emotional unrest in educated women and point to other reasons why some children have large heads, weak muscles, indigestion, or imperfect teeth. And you may not find all of his evidence convincing:

> But what are the facts regarding modern and, especially, American civilized children? I speak still more especially of girls, because they are affected more by elements which disturb the natural order of things than boys are, . . . Excitable, with wide-open eyes and ears for every sight and sound which can excite feeling, rapid and intense in mental activity, with thin limbs, narrow chest, and ungainly back, we meet these twelve-year-old products of civilization going to school with an average of thirteen books under their feeble arms, for I have found by actual count that thirteen is the average number of studies which they "take" nowadays. Do they study them? Undoubtedly, for the sake of being at the head of the class, or of not being at the foot, or to recite them or to *say* they study them, etc. But you will find almost invariably some emotional motive connected with the education of girls, as now conducted, in the majority of instances. Now, what is the girl's chance for perfect development under such adverse conditions as those which I have briefly pointed out? The chance is poor indeed, and the result is deplorable. With the mind thus forced to an unnatural activity, the emotions strained up to the highest tension, at such an important period, what chance has the body to attain a perfect growth or the various functions to be properly developed? Hence we see that generation after generation becomes smaller and smaller, until nature ceases to reproduce its own, and new blood has to be brought in to keep the race from dying out. Take a walk on the avenue of a Sunday afternoon and witness the large proprotion of diminutive men and women which we shall meet. Then tell me if I have overdrawn the picture.

Stop for a few moments to consider this question: What, specifically, do you find amiss in Taylor's argument? If we can see what makes an argument invalid, we can begin to discern what constitutes a strong argument in the first place.

Whatever reservations you may have about "Emotional Prodigality," remember that you come to it armed with more than a century of medical progress and, most likely, a different persepective from that of the author. Most of Taylor's contemporaries probably nodded in agreement because they shared his assumptions that women were delicate, excitable beings whose primary and sanctifying purpose was motherhood.

In fact, the success or failure of an argument often hinges on the shared assumptions of author and audience. An author today would be hard pressed to convince American readers that education is harmful to men or women. Indeed, that education is beneficial is one of *our* shared assumptions in the twentieth century, one that most arguments on current issues in education will tacitly exploit. A major problem with Taylor's argument, then, is that it rests on a hypothesis that has been discarded.

If "Emotional Prodigality" seems dated and flawed, another argument, composed twenty-seven years before Taylor's, remains powerfully alive. In a speech delivered in Rochester, New York, on July 5, 1852, "What to the Slave Is the Fourth of July?", Frederick Douglass, a former slave, presented his audience with a vigorous indictment of slavery in the United States, exhorting his fellow citizens to recognize that the Constitution, "the fundamental law" and "the charter of our liberties," contains principles and purposes "entirely hostile to the existence of slavery." In the course of this dramatic and celebrated address, Douglass incorporates many of the same expository methods we've seen at work in other essays. What methods of development—narration, description, and so on—does Douglass use to make the following excerpt come alive for his listeners? Does the fact that this originally was a spoken rather than written argument seem to have affected the way the passage has been developed?

Behold the practical operation of this internal slave-trade, the American slave-trade, sustained by American politics and American religion. Here you will see men and women reared like swine for the market. You know what is a swine-drover? I will show you a man-drover. They inhabit all our Southern States. They perambulate the country, and crowd the highways of the nation, with droves of human stock. You will see one of these human flesh-jobbers, armed with pistol, whip and bowie-knife, driving a company of a hundred men, women, and children, from the Potomac to the slave market at New Orleans. These wretched people are to be sold singly, or in lots, to suit purchasers. They are food for the cotton-field, and the deadly sugar-mill. Mark the sad procession, as it moves wearily along, and the inhuman wretch who drives them. Hear his savage yells and his blood-chilling oaths, as he hurries on his affrighted captives! There, see the old man, with locks thinned and gray. Cast one glance, if you please, upon that young mother, whose shoulders are bare to the scorching sun, her briny tears falling on the brow of the babe in her arms. See, too, that girl of thirteen, weeping, *yes!* weeping, as she thinks of the mother from whom she has been torn! The drove moves tardily. Heat and sorrow have nearly consumed their strength; suddenly you hear a quick snap, like the discharge of a rifle; the fetters clank, and the chain rattles simul-

Flamenco Dancer

Connoisseur

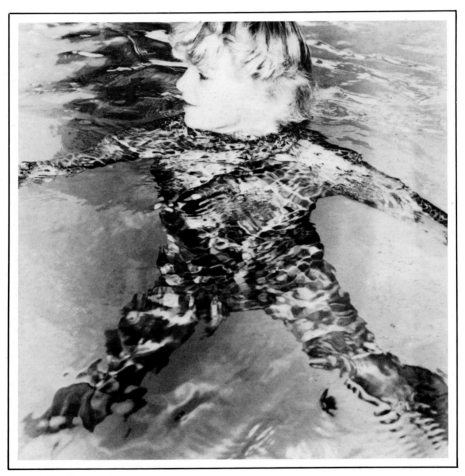

Trainer of Whales and Dolphins

Two Journalists and their Memories

taneously; your ears are saluted with a scream, that seems to have torn its way to the centre of your soul! The crack you heard, was the sound of the slave-whip; the scream you heard, was from the woman you saw with the babe. Her speed had faltered under the weight of her child and her chains! that gash on her shoulder tells her to move on. Follow this drove to New Orleans. Attend the auction; see men examined like horses; see the forms of women rudely and brutally exposed to the shocking gaze of American slave-buyers. See this drove sold and separated forever; and never forget the deep, sad sobs that arose from that scattered multitude. Tell me citizens, WHERE, under the sun, you can witness a spectacle more fiendish and shocking. Yet this is but a glance at the American slave-trade, as it exists, at this moment, in the ruling part of the United States.

Besides the modes of development you've observed in the preceding excerpt, Douglass draws on several other resources. As you read Douglass's speech, reprinted on pages 903–919, notice how and when the author uses rhetorical questions—questions that do not require answers. Think about the effect of the material he quotes—from the Bible, from Shakespeare and other well-known literary sources, from the testimony of historical figures and contemporary political leaders. Above all, attend to the ways Douglass refutes, or disproves, the arguments of his opponents, as in this exposure of the illogic of statutes concerning slaves:

> . . . Must I undertake to prove that the slave is a man? The point is conceded already. . . . The slaveholders themselves acknowledge it in the enactment of laws for their government. They acknowledge it when they punish disobedience on the part of the slave. There are seventy-two crimes in the State of Virginia, which, if committed by a black man, (no matter how ignorant he be), subject him to the punishment of death; while only two of the same crimes will subject a white man to the like punishment. What is this but the acknowledgement that the slave is a moral, intellectual, and responsible being? The manhood of the slave is conceded. It is admitted in the fact that Southern statute books are covered with enactments forbidding . . . the teaching of the slave to read or to write. When you can point to any such laws, in reference to the beasts of the field, then I may consent to argue the manhood of the slave.

But Douglass does not rest his case on reason alone. Among his most effective appeals are those to the emotions of his audience. Emotionally charged arguments can, of course, go awry, as we have seen in Charles Fayette Taylor's essay. But they can also lend moral force and commitment to an argument. To see how Douglass appeals to our hearts and consciences, return to the passage beginning on page 894 and pick out any jarring figures of speech and emotionally charged words and phrases that arouse pity and moral indignation. What images assault your senses? How do the rhythms and repetitions of Douglass's prose add to the power of his appeal?

Our response to this speech is also influenced by our sense of the man who delivers it, as this student observes in her notebook:

> Reading this speech made me angry and very, very sad. I was listening to a man who had suffered terribly and witnessed unthinkable cruelty. And even after learning about the awful experiences of his life, I couldn't imagine that Douglass would treat another human being the way others had treated his people. He is not seeking revenge, but pleading for justice.
>
> *Amy Kornbluth*

In fact, the success of any essay depends partly on the presented character of the speaker. As you read the essays reprinted here, for example, you may sense that Orwell is a decent man, that Walker is a woman with compassion and insight, that Gould is a clear and objective thinker who would not mislead his readers or carry a hypothesis further than he thought it should go. We respond, then, to more than reason alone.

As the examples we've looked at suggest, the voices you will hear in the essays ahead are as varied as their subjects and structures. Yet all share a spirit of inquiry, a question posed, an answer offered. "I do not understand; I pause; I examine" read the inscription in Montaigne's library. As readers, as writers, we too ask questions about what we do not understand; we pause; we examine. In so doing, we capture the essence of reading and writing, of discovering what we do believe, do know.

Ken Haas (1948–)

A native New Yorker, Ken Haas has earned an international reputation for both his commercial photography and his fine art images. After graduating from Queens College, Haas completed a master's degree in film at New York University, but quickly settled on the timeless qualities of the still photograph as his means of expression.

Haas has traveled widely; he lived for two years in Asia, where the experience of living in a foreign culture—and the myths one creates to romanticize that culture—provided the inspiration for his photo essay, *The Expatriates.* Four of the photos from this collection appear following page 894. Haas has recently completed a series of photographs called *Scenes from the Great Operas,* an exploration of narrative possibilities in photography. Like some of the other selections in this anthology, Haas's photographs address the nature and process of storytelling, in life as well as art.

Questions for Photographs from *The Expatriates*

1.   Look carefully at the various objects that surround the flamenco dancer. What do these objects add to your sense of this expatriate?

2.   "Connoisseur" is composed of intriguing shapes: To see the special geometry of this photograph, try viewing it from a few feet away. How many birds do you see in the picture? What can you infer about this man?

3.   Describe what you *see* in the portrait entitled "Trainer of Whales and Dolphins." What is your impression of the subject? How do the details, textures, and surfaces of the photograph help to convey this impression?

4.   What is the mood of "Two Journalists and Their Memories"? What elements contribute to this mood? And what do you make of the glass of wine that faces you?

Michel de Montaigne (1533–1592)

Born in Perigord, France, Michel de Montaigne was the son of a wealthy Catholic landowner and a woman of Spanish-Jewish descent. His father, intent upon the boy's education, allowed him to speak and hear only Latin until he was six years old. After seven years of schooling at the College de Guyenne in Bordeaux, Montaigne studied law and, from 1554 to 1570, was a magistrate in the Bordeaux Parlement.

At the age of thirty-eight, Montaigne retired and devoted himself to his writing. After publishing the first two volumes of *Essais* in 1580, he returned to public office and served as mayor of Bordeaux for five years. He spent the remaining years of his life working on his third book of *Essais*. Plagued for decades by poor health, Montaigne became increasingly infirm; yet the final additions to the *Essais* confirm that his mind had lost none of its vigor.

Of Liars

There is no man who has less business talking about memory. For I recognize almost no trace of it in me, and I do not think there is another one in the world so monstrously deficient. All my other faculties are low and common; but in this one I think I am singular and very rare, and thereby worthy of gaining a name and reputation.

Besides the natural inconvenience that I suffer by this—for certainly, in view of its necessity, Plato is right to call memory a great and powerful goddess—if in my part of the country they want to say that a man has no sense, they say he has no memory. And when I complain of the defectiveness of mine, they argue with me and do not believe me, as if I were accusing myself of witlessness. They see no distinction between memory and understanding. This makes me look a lot worse than I am.

But they do me wrong. For rather the opposite is seen by experience: that excellent memories are prone to be joined to feeble judgments. They do me wrong also in this, I who know how to do nothing so well as be a friend: that by the very words they use to denounce my malady they also make me look ungrateful. They blame my feelings for my want of memory, and of a natural lack they make a lack of conscience. "He has forgotten," they say, "this request or that promise. He does not remember his friends. He did not remember to say, or do, or be silent about such and such a thing, for my sake." Certainly I may easily forget; but careless about the charge with which my friend has entrusted me, that I am not. Let them be content with my infirmity, without making it into a sort of malice, and a malice so alien to my nature.

I have some consolation. First, because it is an evil that has shown me the way to correct a worse evil which would easily have developed in me—to wit, ambition; for lack of memory is intolerable in anyone who is involved in public negotiations. Because, as several similar examples of nature's processes demonstrate, nature has tended to strengthen other faculties in me in proportion as my memory has grown weaker; and I might easily rest my mind and judgment and let them grow languid following on others' traces, as everyone does, without exercising their own strength, if other men's discoveries and opinions were always present to me by virtue of my memory. My speech is the briefer for it. For the magazine of memory is apt to be better furnished with matter than that of invention. (If my memory had stood me in good stead, I would have deafened all my friends with babble; for topics arouse the faculty, such as it is, that I have of handling and treating them, warming up my arguments and leading them on.) This is a pity.[1] I see it confirmed by the example of some of my close friends: to the extent that memory supplies them with the thing as present and entire, they push their narrative so far back and load it with such pointless circumstances, that if the story is good they smother its goodness; if it is not, you are left cursing either the felicity of their memory or the infelicity of their judgment. And it is a difficult thing to close a train of speech and cut it short once you are under way. There is nothing in which the strength of a horse is better recognized than in making a full sharp stop. Even among people who speak to the point I see some who want to break off their run and cannot. While they are looking for the point at which to halt their steps, they go on fiddle-faddling and dragging along like men fainting from weakness. Old men especially are dangerous, whose memory of things past remains, but who have lost the memory of their repetitions. I have seen some very amusing stories become very boring in the mouth of one nobleman, everyone present having been sated with them a hundred times.

My second consolation is that I remember injuries received less, as that ancient said; I should need a prompter, like Darius, who, so as not to forget the harm he had received from the Athenians, had a page come every time he sat down to table and sing three times in his ear: "Sire, remember the Athenians." And the places and books that I revisit always smile at me with a fresh newness.

It is not unreasonably said that anyone who does not feel sufficiently strong in memory should not meddle with lying. I know very well that the grammarians make this distinction between telling a lie and lying: that telling a lie means saying something false but which we have taken for true; and that lying—as defined in Latin, from which our French is taken—implies going against our conscience, and thus applies only to those who say

---

[1] I.e., that we remember more readily than we think.

what is contrary to what they know: those of whom I am speaking. Now liars either invent everything out of whole cloth, or else disguise and alter something fundamentally true. When they disguise and change a story, if you put them back onto it often enough they find it hard not to get tangled up. For since the thing as it is has become lodged first in the memory and has imprinted itself there by way of consciousness and knowledge, it is difficult for it not to present itself to the imagination, dislodging the falsehood, which cannot have so firm and secure a foothold. Likewise, the circumstances that were learned first, slipping into the mind every moment, tend to weaken the memory of the false or corrupted parts that have been added. In what liars invent completely, inasmuch as there is no contrary impression which clashes with the falsehood, they seem to have the less reason to fear making a mistake. Nevertheless even this, since it is an empty thing without a grip, is prone to escape any but a very strong memory.

I have often seen the proof of this, and amusingly, at the expense of those who make a profession of fashioning their words only to suit the affairs they are negotiating and to please the great to whom they are speaking. For these circumstances, to which they are willing to enslave their honor and their conscience, being subject to many changes, their words must vary accordingly. Whence it happens that they describe the same thing as now gray, now yellow; to one man one way, to another another. And if by chance these men compare notes on such contrary reports, what becomes of this fine art? Let alone the fact that so often they imprudently entangle themselves; for what memory could suffice them to remember all the many different shapes into which they have cast the same subject? I have seen many in my time envy someone's reputation for this fine sort of prudence, who do not see that if the reputation is there, the effect cannot be.

In truth lying is an accursed vice. We are men, and hold together, only by our word. If we recognized the horror and the gravity of lying, we would persecute it with fire more justly than other crimes. I find that people ordinarily fool around chastising harmless faults in children very inappropriately, and torment them for thoughtless actions that leave neither imprint nor consequences. Only lying, and a little below it obstinacy, seem to me to be the actions whose birth and progress one should combat insistently. They grow with the child. And once the tongue has been put on this wrong track, it cannot be called back without amazing difficulty. Whence it happens that we see otherwise honest men subject to this vice and enslaved by it. I have a fine lad of a tailor whom I have never heard speak a single truth, not even one that is right there ready to serve his advantage.

If falsehood, like truth, had only one face, we would be in better shape. For we would take as certain the opposite of what the liar said. But the reverse of truth has a hundred thousand shapes and a limitless field. The Pythagoreans make out the good to be certain and finite, evil infinite and uncertain. A thousand paths miss the target, one goes to it.

Truly I am not sure that I could bring myself to ward off even an evident and extreme danger by a shameless and solemn lie. An ancient Church

Father [Saint Augustine] says that we are better off in the company of a dog we know than in that of a man whose language we do not know. *So that to man a foreigner is not like a man* [Pliny]. And how much less sociable is false speech than silence.

King Francis I boasted that he had trapped by this means[2] Francesco Taverna, ambassador of Francesco Sforza, duke of Milan, a man very famous for skill in talking. This man had been dispatched to present his master's excuses to His Majesty about a matter of great consequence, which was this. The king, in order to maintain some intelligence service in Italy, from which he had lately been driven out, and especially in the duchy of Milan, had decided to keep one of his own gentlemen near the duke, an ambassador in effect but in appearance a private person, who pretended to be there for his personal affairs; inasmuch as the duke, who had grown increasingly dependent on the Emperor (especially at the time, when he was negotiating a marriage with his niece, daughter of the king of Denmark, now dowager of Lorraine), could not openly deal or confer with us without great damage to himself. For this commission a Milanese gentleman named Merveille, equerry to the king, was found suitable. Dispatched with secret credentials and instructions as ambassador, and with other letters of recommendation to the duke regarding his personal affairs for mask and show, this man stayed so long with the duke that some inkling of it came to the Emperor, who, so we think, brought about what followed after: which was that on the pretext of some murder, the duke goes and has his head cut off one fine night, with his trial completed in two days. Sir Francesco, having come ready with a long counterfeit account of this affair—for the king had addressed himself, to demand satisfaction, to all the princes of Christendom and to the duke himself—was heard during the morning's business. After he had established as the basis of his case, and prepared to that end, several plausible explanations of the fact—that his master had never taken our man for anything but a private gentleman and subject of his own, who had come to do business at Milan and had never lived there in any other guise; denying even having known that he was in the service of the king's household or known to him, so far was he from taking him for an ambassador—the king in his turn, pressing him with various objections and questions and attacking him from all sides, finally cornered him on the matter of the execution performed by night, and as it were by stealth. To which the poor man, embarrassed, answered, to play the honest man, that out of respect for His Majesty, the duke would have been very reluctant to have such an execution performed by day. Anyone may imagine how he was picked up for having contradicted himself so clumsily, and that before such a nose as that of King Francis.

Pope Julius II sent an ambassador to the king of England to incite him against the French king. When the ambassador had had his audience, and the king of England had dwelt in his reply on the difficulties he found in

---

[2] I.e., by providing every chance for the liar to contradict himself.

making the preparations that would be needed to combat so powerful a king, and stated some of the reasons for those difficulties, the ambassador inappropriately replied that he for his part had also considered them and indeed had mentioned them to the Pope. From this speech, so far removed from his mission, which was to urge him headlong into war, the king of England got the first inkling of what he later actually found out, that this ambassador in his private intent leaned toward the side of France. And when the man's master had been informed of this, the man's goods were confiscated and he barely avoided losing his life.

Questions for "Of Liars"

1.   Montaigne's essay was written more than four hundred years ago, yet it strikes many readers as curiously modern. How can you account for its contemporary sound?

2.   Why does Montaigne begin his essay by talking about memory? What distinction does he make between memory and understanding? What consolations does he draw from his lack of memory?

3.   According to Montaigne, what are the pitfalls of lying? What other objections does he raise to lying?

4.   What experiences have you had with lies and liars? How do these experiences prompt you to agree or disagree with Montaigne's assertions?

5.   How would you describe the author's tone in this essay? Cite examples from the text that best illustrate this tone.

Frederick Douglass (1817–1895)

The son of Harriet Bailey, a black slave, and an unknown white father, Frederick Douglass learned to read and write (privileges forbidden to slaves) while in the service of the kindly wife of a slaveholder in Baltimore, Maryland. He twice attempted to escape from slavery, succeeding in 1838, and adopted the surname of Douglass (from the hero of Sir Walter Scott's poem, *The Lady of the Lake*).

Douglass worked as a day laborer in Massachusetts, where he was asked to become an agent for the Massachusetts Anti-Slavery Society after making an impressive impromptu speech. In 1845 he published his autobiography, *Narrative of the Life of Frederick Douglass,* a compelling and beautifully written account of his life in bondage to white masters, which soon became an American classic, and which he expanded in two subsequent revisions. In danger of being captured as a fugitive slave, he fled to England and Ireland and remained abroad until 1847, when British friends purchased his freedom.

In addition to establishing *North Star,* an abolitionist newspaper, and editing it for seventeen years, Douglass organized regiments of black soldiers to fight for the Union during the Civil War, and continued to campaign for the civil rights of his people. During Reconstruction, he worked for the government in a number of capacities, including marshal of the District of Columbia and minister to Haiti.

What to the Slave Is the Fourth of July?: An Address Delivered in Rochester, New York, on 5 July 1852

Mr. President, Friends and Fellow Citizens: He who could address this audience without a quailing sensation, has stronger nerves than I have. I do not remember ever to have appeared as a speaker before any assembly more shrinkingly, nor with greater distrust of my ability, than I do this day. A feeling has crept over me, quite unfavorable to the exercise of my limited powers of speech. The task before me is one which requires much previous thought and study for its proper performance. I know that apologies of this sort are generally considered flat and unmeaning. I trust, however, that mine will not be so considered. Should I seem at ease, my appearance would much misrepresent me. The little experience I have had in addressing public meetings, in country school houses, avails me nothing on the present occasion.

The papers and placards say, that I am to deliver a 4th [of] July oration. This certainly sounds large, and out of the common way, for me. It is true that I have often had the privilege to speak in this beautiful Hall, and to address many who now honor me with their presence. But neither their familiar faces, nor the perfect gage I think I have of Corinthian Hall, seems to free me from embarrassment.

The fact is, ladies and gentlemen, the distance between this platform and the slave plantation, from which I escaped, is considerable—and the difficulties to be overcome in getting from the latter to the former, are by no means slight. That I am here to-day is, to me, a matter of astonishment as well as of gratitude. You will not, therefore, be surprised, if in what I have to say, I evince no elaborate preparation, nor grace my speech with any high sounding exordium. With little experience and with less learning, I have been able to throw my thoughts hastily and imperfectly together; and trusting to your patient and generous indulgence, I will proceed to lay them before you.

This, for the purpose of this celebration, is the 4th of July. It is the birthday of your National Independence, and of your political freedom. This, to you, is what the Passover was to the emancipated people of God. It carries your minds back to the day, and to the act of your great deliverance; and to the signs, and to the wonders, associated with that act, and that day. This celebration also marks the beginning of another year of your national life; and reminds you that the Republic of America is now 76 years old. I am glad, fellow-citizens, that your nation is so young. Seventy-six years, though a good old age for a man, is but a mere speck in the life of a nation. Three score years and ten is the allotted time for individual men;[1] but nations number their years by thousands. According to this fact, you are, even now, only in the beginning of your national career, still lingering in the period of childhood. I repeat, I am glad this is so. There is hope in the thought, and hope is much needed, under the dark clouds which lower above the horizon. The eye of the reformer is met with angry flashes, portending disastrous times; but his heart may well beat lighter at the thought that America is young, and that she is still in the impressible stage of her existence. May he not hope that high lessons of wisdom, of justice and of truth, will yet give direction to her destiny? Were the nation older, the patriot's heart might be sadder, and the reformer's brow heavier. Its future might be shrouded in gloom, and the hope of its prophets go out in sorrow. There is consolation in the thought that America is young. Great streams are not easily turned from channels, worn deep in the course of ages. They may sometimes rise in quiet and stately majesty, and inundate the land, refreshing and fertilizing the earth with their mysterious properties. They may also rise in wrath and fury, and bear away, on their angry waves, the accumulated wealth of years of toil and hardship. They, however, gradually flow back to the same old channel, and

---

[1]Psalms 90 : 10.

flow on as serenely as ever. But, while the river may not be turned aside, it may dry up, and leave nothing behind but the withered branch, and the unsightly rock, to howl in the abyss-sweeping wind, the sad tale of departed glory. As with rivers so with nations.

Fellow-citizens, I shall not presume to dwell at length on the associations that cluster about this day. The simple story of it is that, 76 years ago, the people of this country were British subjects. The style and title of your "sovereign people" (in which you now glory) was not then born. You were under the British Crown. Your fathers esteemed the English Government as the home government; and England as the fatherland. This home government, you know, although a considerable distance from your home, did, in the exercise of its parental prerogatives, impose upon its colonial children, such restraints, burdens and limitations, as in its mature judgement, it deemed wise, right and proper.

But, your fathers, who had not adopted the fashionable idea of this day, of the infallibility of government, and the absolute character of its acts, presumed to differ from the home government in respect to the wisdom and the justice of some of those burdens and restraints. They went so far in their excitement as to pronounce the measures of government unjust, unreasonable, and oppressive, and altogether such as ought not to be quietly submitted to. I scarcely need say, fellow-citizens, that my opinion of those measures fully accords with that of your fathers. Such a declaration of agreement on my part would not be worth much to anybody. It would, certainly, prove nothing, as to what part I might have taken, had I lived during the great controversy of 1776. To say *now* that America was right, and England wrong, is exceedingly easy. Everybody can say it; the dastard, not less than the noble brave, can flippantly discant on the tyranny of England towards the American Colonies. It is fashionable to do so; but there was a time when to pronounce against England, and in favor of the cause of the colonies, tried men's souls.[2] They who did so were accounted in their day, plotters of mischief, agitators and rebels, dangerous men. To side with the right, against the wrong, with the weak against the strong, and with the oppressed against the oppressor! *here* lies the merit, and the one which, of all others, seems unfashionable in our day. The cause of liberty may be stabbed by the men who glory in the deeds of your fathers. But, to proceed.

Feeling themselves harshly and unjustly treated by the home government, your fathers, like men of honesty, and men of spirit, earnestly sought redress. They petitioned and remonstrated; they did so in a decorous, respectful, and loyal manner. Their conduct was wholly unexceptionable. This, however, did not answer the purpose. They saw themselves treated with sovereign indifference, coldness and scorn. Yet they persevered. They were not the men to look back.

---

[2]Douglass paraphrases the opening line of Thomas Paine's first *Crisis* paper, 23 December 1776.

As the sheet anchor takes a firmer hold, when the ship is tossed by the storm, so did the cause of your fathers grow stronger, as it breasted the chilling blasts of kingly displeasure. The greatest and best of British statesmen admitted its justice, and the loftiest eloquence of the British Senate came to its support. But, with that blindness which seems to be the unvarying characteristic of tyrants, since Pharoah and his hosts were drowned in the Red Sea, the British Government persisted in the exactions complained of.

The madness of this course, we believe, is admitted now, even by England; but we fear the lesson is wholly lost on our present rulers.

Oppression makes a wise man mad. Your fathers were wise men, and if they did not go mad, they became restive under this treatment. They felt themselves the victims of grievous wrongs, wholly incurable in their colonial capacity. With brave men there is always a remedy for oppression. Just here, the idea of a total separation of the colonies from the crown was born! It was a startling idea, much more so, than we, at this distance of time, regard it. The timid and the prudent (as has been intimated) of that day, were, of course, shocked and alarmed by it.

Such people lived then, had lived before, and will, probably, ever have a place on this planet; and their course, in respect to any great change, (no matter how great the good to be attained, or the wrong to be redressed by it), may be calculated with as much precision as can be the course of the stars. They hate all changes, but silver, gold and copper change! Of this sort of change they are always strongly in favor.

These people were called tories in the days of your fathers; and the appellation, probably, conveyed the same idea that is meant by a more modern, though a somewhat less euphonious term, which we often find in our papers, applied to some of our old politicians.[3]

Their opposition to the then dangerous thought was earnest and powerful; but, amid all their terror and affrighted vociferations against it, the alarming and revolutionary idea moved on, and the country with it.

On the 2d of July, 1776, the old Continental Congress, to the dismay of the lovers of ease, and the worshippers of property, clothed that dreadful idea with all the authority of national sanction. They did so in the form of a resolution; and as we seldom hit upon resolutions, drawn up in our day, whose transparency is at all equal to this, it may refresh your minds and help my story if I read it.

> "Resolved, That these united colonies *are*, and of right, ought to be free and Independent States; that they are absolved from all allegiance to the British Crown; and that all political connection between them and the State of Great Britain *is*, and ought to be, dissolved."

---

[3]Douglass probably refers to the term "Hunker," which was applied to conservative Democrats in New York state politics in the late 1840s.

Citizens, your fathers made good that resolution. They succeeded; and to-day you reap the fruits of their success. The freedom gained is yours; and you, therefore, may properly celebrate this anniversary. The 4th of July is the first great fact in your nation's history—the very ring-bolt in the chain of your yet undeveloped destiny.

Pride and patriotism, not less than gratitude, prompt you to celebrate and to hold it in perpetual remembrance. I have said that the Declaration of Independence is the RING-BOLT to the chain of your nation's destiny; so, indeed, I regard it. The principles contained in that instrument are saving principles. Stand by those principles, be true to them on all occasions, in all places, against all foes, and at whatever cost.

From the round top of your ship of state, dark and threatening clouds may be seen. Heavy billows, like mountains in the distance, disclose to the lee-ward huge forms of flinty rocks! That *bolt* drawn, that *chain* broken, and all is lost. *Cling to this day—cling to it,* and to its principles, with the grasp of a storm-tossed mariner to a spar at midnight.

The coming into being of a nation, in any circumstances, is an interesting event. But, besides general considerations, there were peculiar circumstances which make the advent of this republic an event of special attractiveness.

The whole scene, as I look back to it, was simple, dignified and sublime.

The population of the country, at the time, stood at the insignificant number of three millions. The country was poor in the munitions of war. The population was weak and scattered, and the country a wilderness unsubdued. There were then no means of concert and combination, such as exist now. Neither steam nor lightning had then been reduced to order and discipline. From the Potomac to the Delaware was a journey of many days. Under these, and innumerable other disadvantages, your fathers declared for liberty and independence and triumphed.

Fellow Citizens, I am not wanting in respect for the fathers of this republic. The signers of the Declaration of Independence were brave men. They were great men too—great enough to give fame to a great age. It does not often happen to a nation to raise, at one time, such a number of truly great men. The point from which I am compelled to view them is not, certainly, the most favorable; and yet I cannot contemplate their great deeds with less than admiration. They were statesmen, patriots and heroes, and for the good they did, and the principles they contended for, I will unite with you to honor their memory.

They loved their country better than their own private interests; and, though this is not the highest form of human excellence, all will concede that it is a rare virture, and that when it is exhibited, it ought to command respect. He who will, intelligently, lay down his life for his country, is a man whom it is not in human nature to despise. Your fathers staked their lives, their fortunes, and their sacred honor, on the cause of their country. In their admiration of liberty, they lost sight of all other interests.

They were peace men; but they preferred revolution to peaceful submission to bondage. They were quiet men; but they did not shrink from agitating against oppression. They showed forbearance; but that they knew its limits. They believed in order; but not in the order of tyranny. With them, nothing was *"settled"* that was not right. With them, justice, liberty and humanity were *"final"*; not slavery and oppression. You may well cherish the memory of such men. They were great in their day and generation. Their solid manhood stands out the more as we contrast it with these degenerate times.

How circumspect, exact and proportionate were all their movements! How unlike the politicians of an hour! Their statesmanship looked beyond the passing moment, and stretched away in strength into the distant future. They seized upon eternal principles, and set a glorious example in their defence. Mark them! . . .

The Present

My business, if I have any here to-day, is with the present. The accepted time with God and his cause is the ever-living now.

> "Trust no future, however pleasant,
>   Let the dead past bury its dead;
> Act, act in the living present,
>   Heart within, and God overhead."[4]

We have to do with the past only as we can make it useful to the present and to the future. To all inspiring motives, to noble deeds which can be gained from the past, we are welcome. But now is the time, the important time. Your fathers have lived, died, and have done their work, and have done much of it well. You live and must die, and you must do your work. You have no right to enjoy a child's share in the labor of your fathers, unless your children are to be blest by your labors. You have no right to wear out and waste the hard-earned fame of your fathers to cover your indolence. Sydney Smith[5] tells us that men seldom eulogize the wisdom and virtues of their fathers, but to excuse some folly or wickedness of their own. This truth is not a doubtful one. There are illustrations of it near and remote, ancient and modern. It was fashionable, hundreds of years ago, for the children of Jacob to boast, we have "Abraham to our father," when they had long lost Abraham's faith and spirit.[6] That people contented themselves under the shadow

---

[4]The stanza quoted is from Henry Wadsworth Longfellow's "A Psalm of Life." *Poems,* 22.

[5]Anglican minister Sydney Smith (1771–1845) was a master satirical essayist and lecturer. A highly partisan Whig, his barbed wit was employed to great effect in the causes of Catholic emancipation and parliamentary reform.

[6]Douglass appears to allude to a passage from Luke 3 : 8: "Bring forth therefore fruits worthy of repentance, and begin not to say within yourselves, We have Abraham *our* father: for I say unto you, That God is able of these stones to raise up children unto Abraham."

of Abraham's great name, while they repudiated the deeds which made his name great. Need I remind you that a similar thing is being done all over this country to-day? Need I tell you that the Jews are not the only people who built the tombs of the prophets, and garnished the sepulchres of the righteous? Washington could not die till he had broken the chains of his slaves.[7] Yet his monument is built up by the price of human blood, and the traders in the bodies and souls of men, shout—"We have Washington to *our father.*" Alas! that it should be so; yet so it is.

> "The evil that men do, lives after them,
> The good is oft' interred with their bones."[8]

Fellow-citizens, pardon me, allow me to ask, why am I called upon to speak here to-day? What have I, or those I represent, to do with your national independence? Are the great principles of political freedom and of natural justice, embodied in that Declaration of Independence, extended to us? and am I, therefore, called upon to bring our humble offering to the national altar, and to confess the benefits and express devout gratitude for the blessings resulting from your independence to us?

Would to God, both for your sakes and ours, that an affirmative answer could be truthfully returned to these questions! Then would my task be light, and my burden easy and delightful. For *who* is there so cold, that a nation's sympathy could not warm him? Who so obdurate and dead to the claims of gratitude, that would not thankfully acknowledge such priceless benefits? Who so stolid and selfish, that would not give his voice to swell the halle-lujahs of a nation's jubilee, when the chains of servitude had been torn from his limbs? I am not that man. In a case like that, the dumb might eloquently speak, and the "lame man leap as an hart."

But, such is not the state of the case. I say it with a sad sense of the dis-parity between us. I am not included within the pale of this glorious anni-versary! Your high independence only reveals the immeasurable distance between us. The blessings in which you, this day, rejoice, are not enjoyed in common. The rich inheritance of justice, liberty, prosperity and indepen-dence, bequeathed by your fathers, is shared by you, not by me. The sunlight that brought life and healing to you, has brought stripes and death to me. This Fourth [of] July is *yours*, not *mine. You* may rejoice, *I* must mourn. To drag a man in fetters into the grand illuminated temple of liberty, and call upon him to join you in joyous anthems, were inhuman mockery and sac-rilegious irony. Do you mean, citizens, to mock me, by asking me to speak to-day? If so, there is a parallel to your conduct. And let me warn you that it is dangerous to copy the example of a nation whose crimes, towering up

[7]At the time of his death, George Washington owned or held claim to over three hundred slaves. His will provided that "upon the decease of my wife it is my . . . desire that all slaves whom I hold in my own right shall receive their freedom."
[8]*Julius Caesar*, act 3, sc. 2, line 76.

to heaven, were thrown down by the breath of the Almighty, burying that nation in irrecoverable ruin! I can to-day take up the plaintive lament of a peeled and woe-smitten people!

"By the rivers of Babylon, there we sat down. Yea! we wept when we remembered Zion. We hanged our harps upon the willows in the midst thereof. For there, they that carried us away captive, required of us a song; and they who wasted us required of us mirth, saying, Sing us one of the songs of Zion. How can we sing the Lord's song in a strange land? If I forget thee, O Jerusalem, let my right hand forget her cunning. If I do not remember thee, let my tongue cleave to the roof of my mouth."[9]

Fellow-citizens; above your national, tumultous joy, I hear the mournful wail of millions! whose chains, heavy and grievous yesterday, are, to-day, rendered more intolerable by the jubilee shouts that reach them. If I do forget, if I do not faithfully remember those bleeding children of sorrow this day, "may my right hand forget her cunning, and may my tongue cleave to the roof of my mouth!" To forget them, to pass lightly over their wrongs, and to chime in with the popular theme, would be treason most scandalous and shocking, and would make me a reproach before God and the world. My subject, then fellow-citizens, is AMERICAN SLAVERY. I shall see, this day, and its popular characteristics, from the slave's point of view. Standing, there, identified with the American bondman, making his wrongs mine, I do not hesitate to declare, with all my soul, that the character and conduct of this nation never looked blacker to me than on this 4th of July! Whether we turn to the declarations of the past, or to the professions of the present, the conduct of the nation seems equally hideous and revolting. America is false to the past, false to the present, and solemnly binds herself to be false to the future. Standing with God and the crushed and bleeding slave on this occasion, I will, in the name of humanity which is outraged, in the name of liberty which is fettered, in the name of the constitution and the Bible, which are disregarded and trampled upon, dare to call in question and to denounce, with all the emphasis I can command, everything that serves to perpetuate slavery—the great sin and shame of America! "I will not equivocate; I will not excuse;"[10] I will use the severest language I can command; and yet not one word shall escape me that any man, whose judgment is not blinded by prejudice, or who is not at heart a slaveholder, shall not confess to be right and just.

But I fancy I hear some one of my audience say, it is just in this circumstance that you and your brother abolitionists fail to make a favorable impression on the public mind. Would you argue more, and denounce less, would you persuade more, and rebuke less, your cause would be much more likely to succeed. But, I submit, where all is plain there is nothing to be

---

[9]Psalms 137 : 1–6.
[10]Douglass quotes from the first issue of the *Liberator,* in which William Lloyd Garrison promised, "I am in earnest—I will not equivocate—I will not excuse—I will not retreat a single inch—and *I will be heard.*"

argued. What point in the anti-slavery creed would you have me argue? On what branch of the subject do the people of this country need light? Must I undertake to prove that the slave is a man? That point is conceded already. Nobody doubts it. The slaveholders themselves acknowledge it in the enactment of laws for their government. They acknowledge it when they punish disobedience on the part of the slave. There are seventy-two crimes in the State of Virginia, which, if committed by a black man, (no matter how ignorant he be), subject him to the punishment of death; while only two of the same crimes will subject a white man to the like punishment. What is this but the acknowledgement that the slave is a moral, intellectual and responsible being? The manhood of the slave is conceded. It is admitted in the fact that Southern statute books are covered with enactments forbidding, under severe fines and penalties, the teaching of the slave to read or to write. When you can point to any such laws, in reference to the beasts of the field, then I may consent to argue the manhood of the slave. When the dogs in your streets, when the fowls of the air, when the cattle on your hills, when the fish of the sea, and the reptiles that crawl, shall be unable to distinguish the slave from a brute, *then* will I argue with you that the slave is a man!

For the present, it is enough to affirm the equal manhood of the negro race. Is it not astonishing that, while we are ploughing, planting and reaping, using all kinds of mechanical tools, erecting houses, constructing bridges, building ships, working in metals of brass, iron, copper, silver and gold; that, while we are reading, writing and cyphering, acting as clerks, merchants and secretaries, having among us lawyers, doctors, ministers, poets, authors, editors, orators and teachers; that, while we are engaged in all manner of enterprises common to other men, digging gold in California, capturing the whale in the Pacific, feeding sheep and cattle on the hill-side, living, moving, acting, thinking, planning, living in families as husbands, wives and children, and, above all, confessing and worshipping the Christian's God, and looking hopefully for life and immortality beyond the grave, we are called upon to prove that we are men!

Would you have me argue that man is entitled to liberty? that he is the rightful owner of his own body? You have already declared it. Must I argue the wrongfulness of slavery? Is that a question for Republicans? Is it to be settled by the rules of logic and argumentation, as a matter beset with great difficulty, involving a doubtful application of the principle of justice, hard to be understood? How should I look to-day, in the presence of Americans, dividing, and subdividing a discourse, to show that men have a natural right to freedom? speaking of it relatively, and positively, negatively, and affirmatively. To do so, would be to make myself ridiculous, and to offer an insult to your understanding. There is not a man beneath the canopy of heaven, that does not know that slavery is wrong *for him*.

What, am I to argue that it is wrong to make men brutes, to rob them of their liberty, to work them without wages, to keep them ignorant of their relations to their fellow men, to beat them with sticks, to flay their flesh with the lash, to load their limbs with irons, to hunt them with dogs, to sell them at auction, to sunder their families, to knock out their teeth, to burn their flesh, to starve them into obedience and submission to their masters? Must I argue that a system thus marked with blood, and stained with pollution, is *wrong?* No! I will not. I have better employments for my time and strength, than such arguments would imply.

What, then, remains to be argued? Is is that slavery is not divine; that God did not establish it; that our doctors of divinity are mistaken? There is blasphemy in the thought. That which is inhuman, cannot be divine! *Who* can reason on such a proposition? They that can, may; I cannot. The time for such argument is past.

At a time like this, scorching irony, not convincing argument, is needed. O! had I the ability, and could I reach the nation's ear, I would, to-day, pour out a fiery stream of biting ridicule, blasting reproach, withering sarcasm, and stern rebuke. For it is not light that is needed, but fire; it is not the gentle shower, but thunder. We need the storm, the whirlwind, and the earthquake. The feeling of the nation must be quickened; the conscience of the nation must be roused; the propriety of the nation must be startled; the hypocrisy of the nation must be exposed; and its crimes against God and man must be proclaimed and denounced.

What, to the American slave, is your 4th of July? I answer: a day that reveals to him, more than all other days in the year, the gross injustice and cruelty to which he is the constant victim. To him, your celebration is a sham; your boasted liberty, an unholy license; your national greatness, swelling vanity; your sounds of rejoicing are empty and heartless; your denunciations of tyrants, brass fronted impudence; your shouts of liberty and equality, hollow mockery; your prayers and hymns, your sermons and thanksgivings, with all your religious parade, and solemnity, are, to him, mere bombast, fraud, deception, impiety, and hypocrisy—a thin veil to cover up crimes which would disgrace a nation of savages. There is not a nation on the earth guilty of practices, more shocking and bloody, than are the people of these United States, at this very hour.

Go where you may, search where you will, roam through all the monarchies and despotisms of the old world, travel through South America, search out every abuse, and when you have found the last, lay your facts by the side of the everyday practices of this nation, and you will say with me, that, for revolting barbarity and shameless hypocrisy, America reigns without a rival.

——— **The Internal Slave Trade** ———

Take the American slave-trade, which, we are told by the papers, is especially prosperous just now. Ex-Senator Benton [11] tells us that the price of men was

---

[11]Thomas Hart Benton (1782–1858) served as a U.S. senator from Missouri from 1821 to 1851.

never higher than now. He mentions the fact to show that slavery is in no danger. This trade is one of the peculiarities of American institutions. It is carried on in all the large towns and cities in one-half of this confederacy; and millions are pocketed every year, by dealers in this horrid traffic. In several states, this trade is a chief source of wealth. It is called (in contradistinction to the foreign slave-trade) *"the internal slave-trade."* It is, probably, called so, too, in order to divert from it the horror with which the foreign slave-trade is contemplated. That trade has long since been denounced by this government, as piracy. It has been denounced with burning words, from the high places of the nation, as an execrable traffic. To arrest it, to put an end to it, this nation keeps a squadron, at immense cost, on the coast of Africa. Everywhere, in this country, it is safe to speak of this foreign slave-trade, as a most inhuman traffic, opposed alike to the laws of God and of man. The duty to extirpate and destroy it, is admitted even by our DOCTORS OF DIVINITY. In order to put an end to it, some of these last have consented that their colored brethren (nominally free) should leave this country, and establish themselves on the western coast of Africa! It is, however, a notable fact that, while so much execration is poured out by Americans upon those engaged in the foreign slave-trade, the men engaged in the slave-trade between the states pass without condemnation, and their business is deemed honorable.

Behold the practical operation of this internal slave-trade, the American slave-trade, sustained by American politics and American religion. Here you will see men and women reared like swine for the market. You know what is a swine-drover? I will show you a man-drover. They inhabit all our Southern States. They perambulate the country, and crowd the highways of the nation, with droves of human stock. You will see one of these human flesh-jobbers, armed with pistol, whip and bowie-knife, driving a company of a hundred men, women, and children, from the Potomac to the slave market at New Orleans. These wretched people are to be sold singly, or in lots, to suit purchasers. They are food for the cotton-field, and the deadly sugar-mill. Mark the sad procession, as it moves wearily along, and the inhuman wretch who drives them. Hear his savage yells and his blood-chilling oaths, as he hurries on his affrighted captives! There, see the old man, with locks thinned and gray. Cast one glance, if you please, upon that young mother whose shoulders are bare to the scorching sun, her briny tears falling on the brow of the babe in her arms. See, too, that girl of thirteen, weeping, *yes!* weeping, as she thinks of the mother from whom she has been torn! The drove moves tardily. Heat and sorrow have nearly consumed their strength; suddenly you hear a quick snap, like the discharge of a rifle; the fetters clank, and the chain rattles simultaneously; your ears are saluted with a scream, that seems to have torn its way to the centre of your soul! The crack you heard, was the sound of the slave-whip; the scream you heard, was from the woman you saw with the babe. Her speed had faltered under the weight of her child and her chains! that gash on her shoulder tells her to move on. Follow this drove to New Orleans. Attend the auction; see men examined like horses; see the forms of women rudely and brutally exposed to the shocking gaze of American slave-buyers. See this drove sold and separated forever; and never forget the deep, sad sobs that arose from that scattered multitude. Tell me citizens, WHERE, under the sun, you can witness a spectacle more fiendish and shocking. Yet this is but a glance at the American slave-trade, as it exists, at this moment, in the ruling part of the United States.

I was born amid such sights and scenes. To me the American slave-trade is a terrible reality. When a child, my soul was often pierced with a sense of its horrors. I lived on Philpot Street, Fell's Point, Baltimore, and have watched from the wharves, the slave ships in the Basin, anchored from the shore, with their cargoes of human flesh, waiting for favorable winds to waft them down the Chesapeake. There was, at that time, a grand slave mart kept at the head of Pratt Street, by Austin Woldfolk.[12] His agents were sent into every town and county in Maryland, announcing their arrival, through the papers, and on flaming _"hand bills,"_ headed CASH FOR NEGROES. These men were generally well dressed men, and very captivating in their manners. Ever ready to drink, to treat, and to gamble. The fate of many a slave has depended upon the turn of a single card; and many a child has been snatched from the arms of its mother by bargains arranged in a state of brutal drunkenness.

The flesh-mongers gather up their victims by dozens, and drive them, chained, to the general depot at Baltimore. When a sufficient number have been collected here, a ship is chartered, for the purpose of conveying the forlorn crew to Mobile, or to New Orleans. From the slave prison to the ship, they are usually driven in the darkness of night; for since the anti-slavery agitation, a certain caution is observed.

In the deep still darkness of midnight, I have been often aroused by the dead heavy footsteps, and the piteous cries of the chained gangs that passed our door. The anguish of my boyish heart was intense; and I was often consoled, when speaking to my mistress in the morning, to hear her say that the custom was very wicked; that she hated to hear the rattle of the chains, and the heart-rending cries. I was glad to find one who sympathised with me in my horror.

Fellow-citizens, this murderous traffic is, to-day, in active operation in this boasted republic. In the solitude of my spirit, I see clouds of dust raised on the highways of the South; I see the bleeding footsteps; I hear the doleful wail of fettered humanity, on the way to the slave-markets, where the victims are to be sold like _horses, sheep,_ and _swine,_ knocked off to the highest bidder. There I see the tenderest ties ruthlessly broken, to gratify the lust, caprice and rapacity of the buyers and sellers of men. My soul sickens at the sight.

> "Is this the land your Fathers loved,
> The freedom which they toiled to win?

---

[12]Actually Austin Woolfolk of Augusta, Georgia, who came to Baltimore in 1819 and became the best-known slave trader in the area in the 1820s and early 1830s.

Is this the earth whereon they moved?
Are these the graves they slumber in?"[13]

But a still more inhuman, disgraceful, and scandalous state of things remains to be presented.

By an act of the American Congress, not yet two years old, slavery has been nationalized in its most horrible and revolting form. By that act, Mason & Dixon's line has been obliterated; New York has become as Virginia; and the power to hold, hunt, and sell men, women, and children as slaves remains no longer a mere state institution, but is now an institution of the whole United States. The power is co-extensive with the star-spangled banner and American Christianity. Where these go, may also go the merciless slave-hunter. Where these are, man is not sacred. He is a bird for the sportsman's gun. By that most foul and fiendish of all human decrees, the liberty and person of every man are put in peril. Your broad republican domain is hunting ground for *men. Not* for thieves and robbers, enemies of society, merely, but for men guilty of no crime. Your lawmakers have commanded all good citizens to engage in this hellish sport. Your President, your Secretary of State, your *lords, nobles,* and ecclesiastics, enforce, as a duty you owe to your free and glorious country, and to your God, that you do this accursed thing. Not fewer than forty Americans have, within the past two years, been hunted down and, without a moment's warning, hurried away in chains, and consigned to slavery and excruciating torture. Some of these have had wives and children, dependent on them for bread; but of this, no account was made. The right of the hunter to his prey stands superior to the right of marriage, and to all rights in this republic, the rights of God included! For black men there are neither law, justice, humanity, nor religion. The Fugitive Slave *Law* makes MERCY TO THEM, A CRIME; and bribes the judge who tries them. An American JUDGE GETS TEN DOLLARS FOR EVERY VICTIM HE CONSIGNS to slavery, and five, when he fails to do so. The oath of any two villains is sufficient, under this hell-black enactment, to send the most pious and exemplary black man into the remorseless jaws of slavery! His own testimony is nothing. He can bring no witnesses for himself. The minister of American justice is bound by the law to hear but *one* side; and *that* side, is the side of the oppressor.[14] Let this damning fact be perpetually told. Let it be thundered around the world, that, in tyrant-killing, king-hating, people-loving, democratic, Christian America, the seats of justice are filled with judges, who hold their offices

[13]Douglass slightly alters the first four lines of John Greenleaf Whittier's "Stanzas for the Times." Whittier, *Poetical Works,* 3 : 35.

[14]Although the 1850 Fugitive Slave Law did not specify the number of witnesses needed to establish that an individual was a fugitive slave, it did provide that "in no trial or hearing . . . shall the testimony of such alleged fugitive be admitted in evidence." No provision was made for the alleged fugitive to bring forth witnesses who might dispute the claims of the court transcript or warrant, but the commissioner or judge did have to be convinced that the person brought before him was indeed the escaped slave described in the transcript.

under an open and palpable *bribe,* and are bound, in deciding in the case of a man's liberty, *to hear only his accusers!*

In glaring violation of justice, in shameless disregard of the forms of administering law, in cunning arrangement to entrap the defenceless, and in diabolical intent, this Fugitive Slave Law stands alone in the annals of tyrannical legislation. I doubt if there be another nation on the globe, having the brass and the baseness to put such a law on the statute-book. If any man in this assembly thinks differently from me in this matter, and feels able to disprove my statements, I will gladly confront him at any suitable time and place he may select. . . .

——— The Constitution ———

Fellow-citizens! there is no matter in respect to which, the people of the North have allowed themselves to be so ruinously imposed upon, as that of the pro-slavery character of the Constitution. In *that* instrument I hold there is neither warrant, license, nor sanction of the hateful thing; but, interpreted as it *ought* to be interpreted, the Constitution is a GLORIOUS LIBERTY DOCUMENT. Read its preamble, consider its purposes. Is slavery among them? Is it at the gateway? or is it in the temple? It is neither. While I do not intend to argue this question on the present occasion, let me ask, if it be not somewhat singular that, if the Constitution were intended to be, by its framers and adopters, a slave-holding instrument, why neither *slavery, slaveholding,* nor *slave* can anywhere be found in it. What would be thought of an instrument, drawn up, *legally* drawn up, for the purpose of entitling the city of Rochester to a track of land, in which no mention of land was made? Now, there are certain rules of interpretation, for the proper understanding of all legal instruments. These rules are well established. They are plain, common-sense rules, such as you and I, and all of us, can understand and apply, without having passed years in the study of law. I scout the idea that the question of the constitutionality or unconstitutionality of slavery is not a question for the people. I hold that every American citizen has a right to form an opinion of the constitution, and to propagate that opinion, and to use all honorable means to make his opinion the prevailing one. Without this right, the liberty of an American citizen would be as insecure as that of a Frenchman. Ex-Vice-President Dallas tells us that the constitution is an object to which no American mind can be too attentive, and no American heart too devoted. He further says, the constitution, in its words, is plain and intelligible, and is meant for the home-bred, unsophisticated understandings of our fellow-citizens. Senator Berrien[15] tells us that the Constitution is the fundamental law, that

---

[15]Georgia senator John MacPherson Berrien (1781–1856), known as the "American Cicero" because of his magnificent oratory, was also regarded as one of the ablest constitutional lawyers in the U.S. Senate during the 1840s. In 1849 Berrien's *Address to the People of the United States* pleaded for compromise on the slavery question. He later voted in favor of the Fugitive Slave Law and opposed the abolition of the slave trade in the District of Columbia and the admission of California as a free state.

which controls all others. The charter of our liberties, which every citizen has a personal interest in understanding thoroughly. The testimony of Senator Breese,[16] Lewis Cass, and many others that might be named, who are everywhere esteemed as sound lawyers, so regard the constitution. I take it, therefore, that it is not presumption in a private citizen to form an opinion of that instrument.

Now, take the constitution according to its plain reading, and I defy the presentation of a single pro-slavery clause in it. On the other hand it will be found to contain principles and purposes, entirely hostile to the existence of slavery.

I have detained my audience entirely too long already. At some future period I will gladly avail myself of an opportunity to give this subject a full and fair discussion.

Allow me to say, in conclusion, notwithstanding the dark picture I have this day presented of the state of the nation, I do not despair of this country. There are forces in operation, which must inevitably work the downfall of slavery. *"The arm of the Lord is not shortened,"*[17] and the doom of slavery is certain. I, therefore, leave off where I began, with *hope*. While drawing encouragement from the Declaration of Independence, the great principle it contains, and the genius of American Institutions, my spirit is also cheered by the obvious tendencies of the age. Nations do not now stand in the same relation to each other that they did ages ago. No nation can now shut itself up from the surrounding world, and trot around in the same old path of its fathers without interference. The time *was* when such could be done. Long established customs of hurtful character could formerly fence themselves in, and do their evil work with social impunity. Knowledge was then confined and enjoyed by the privileged few, and the multitude walked on in mental darkness. But a change has now come over the affairs of mankind. Walled cities and empires have become unfashionable. The arm of commerce has borne away the gates of the strong city. Intelligence is penetrating the darkest corners of the globe. It makes its pathway over and under the sea, as well as on the earth. Wind, steam, and lightning are its chartered agents. Oceans no longer divide, but link nations together. From Boston to London is now a holiday excursion. Space is comparatively annihilated. Thoughts expressed on one side of the Atlantic are distinctly heard on the other.

The far off and almost fabulous Pacific rolls in grandeur at our feet. The Celestial Empire, the mystery of ages, is being solved. The fiat of the Almighty, *"Let there be Light,"*[18] has not yet spent its force. No abuse, no outrage whether in taste, sport or avarice, can now hide itself from the all-per-

---

[16]Sidney Breese (1800–78), Democrat from Illinois, served in the U.S. Senate for only one term (1843–49) and generally supported the positions of his fellow midwestern senator, Lewis Cass, of Michigan, on such issues as the constitutionality of slavery, popular sovereignty, and limited congressional authority over slavery.

[17]Douglass paraphrases Isa. 59 : 1: "Behold, the Lord's hand is not shortened, that it cannot save, neither His ear heavy, that it cannot hear."

[18]Genesis 1 : 3.

vading light. The iron shoe, and crippled foot of China must be seen, in contrast with nature. *Africa must rise and put on her yet unwoven garment. "Ethiopia shall stretch out her hand unto God."*[19] In the fervent aspirations of William Lloyd Garrison, I say, and let every heart join in saying it:

> God speed the year of jubilee
>   The wide world o'er!
> When from their galling chains set free,
> Th' oppress'd shall vilely bend the knee,
> And wear the yoke of tyranny
>   Like brutes no more.
> That year will come, and freedom's reign,
> To man his plundered rights again
>   Restore.
>
> God speed the day when human blood
>   Shall cease to flow!
> In every clime be understood,
> The claims of human brotherhood,
> And each return for evil, good,
>   Not blow for blow;
> That day will come all feuds to end,
> And change into a faithful friend
>   Each foe.
>
> God speed the hour, the glorious hour,
>   When none on earth
> Shall exercise a lordly power,
> Nor in a tyrant's presence cower;
> But all to manhood's stature tower,
>   By equal birth!
> THAT HOUR WILL COME, to each, to all,
> And from his prison-house, the thrall
>   Go forth.
>
> Until that year, day, hour, arrive,
> With head, and heart, and hand I'll strive,
> To break the rod, and rend the gyve,
> The spoiler of his prey deprive—
>   So witness Heaven!

---

[19]An allusion to Psalms 68 : 31: "Princes shall come out of Egypt; Ethiopia shall soon stretch out her hands unto God."

And never from my chosen post,
Whate'er the peril or the cost,
Be driven.[20]

Questions for "What to the Slave Is the Fourth of July?"

1.   The title of this speech poses a question: What is Douglass's answer?

2.   The first part of this speech recalls the American Revolution. Why do you think Douglass tells the story of the nation's fight for freedom to an audience who surely knew it well? In the introduction to this chapter, we discuss *shared assumptions*—those attitudes or beliefs common to a group of people—which writers of arguments often exploit. What is the assumption in this part of Douglass's speech that is shared by Douglass and his audience? How does he then manipulate this assumption for his own purposes?

3.   In what other ways does Douglass shape his argument according to the assumptions of those he believes will be listening?

4.   On pages 894–895, we cite examples from this speech to illustrate rhetorical techniques that play on a reader's emotions. What other strong appeals to emotion can you point to in this oration?

5.   Do you find this speech convincing? How do your own beliefs affect your reaction?

---

[20]William Lloyd Garrison, "The Triumph of Freedom," in *Liberator,* 10 January 1845.

Charles Fayette Taylor (1827–1889)

Charles Fayette Taylor grew up in Vermont and studied medicine at the University of Vermont. An orthopedic surgeon with a strong interest in nervous disorders and the diseases of women, Taylor agreed with other leading specialists of the day that an overactive nervous system consumed large amounts of energy at the expense of other bodily functions, which then became "depressed."

From 1866 to 1867, Taylor treated Alice James (whose diary is excerpted in Chapter 2 of this anthology) and for a few months she seemed much improved. Shortly thereafter, however, she suffered her first nervous breakdown, at the age of twenty.

Taylor invented braces and other orthopedic devices to treat bone and joint lesions and discovered a cure for Pott's disease, an infection of the spinal vertebrae. He is the author of *Theory and Practice of the Movement Cure* (1861), *Mechanical Treatment of Angular Curvature of the Spine or Pott's Disease of the Spine* (1863), and *Mechanical Treatment of Diseases of the Hip* (1873).

Emotional Prodigality

(Read Before the New York Odontological Society, March 18, 1879)

. . . I have determined to present some views in regard to the deleterious effects upon the bodily development and health of civilized communities of early and excessive mental activity, and to show, as I think I can, that to this cause we must look for a far larger amount of injury to special organs as well as to the frame as a whole, than we have been accustomed to do. . . .

In the first place, the mind, as a whole, may be said to be made up of several distinct parts or attributes. Some of these attributes may be active while others are at rest, and they all have very different and very independent and distinct relations to, and influence over, the bodily functions. For instance, one of the most common errors is the supposition that thinking, as distinguished from other mental activities, is the source of injury when one's health suffers from excessive mental strain, . . . In fact, it is unquestionably true that an active well-trained *thinking* capacity imparts positive strength to the bodily powers, increasing both health and longevity. It isn't the *thinking* which breaks people down, but it is an excess—often an unnecessary excess—of other mental activities which works the bodily injury; and by "other mental activities" I would especially include the *emotions* as the most exhausting of all mental attributes. It is the emotion which so often accompanies thought which tires and exhausts the frame when it is supposed to be the thinking which does the injury.

A well-known professor of theology, who had several times broken down from mental overwork, once told me that he had noticed that while recovering, after a period of rest, he would arrive at a point at which he could go on with his purely intellectual work with perfect ease and facility when he could not listen to a sermon, the emotions being then brought into play, without being completely overcome and physically prostrated by it. And what is true in the case of this theological professor is true with us all,—we are not likely to be injured by purely intellectual work. It is only when the emotions are excited that the excessive drain on the bodily powers begins, to any injurious degree. This statement is confirmed by the well-known fact that cool and well-regulated dispositions are those which, as a rule, last the longest; men of even temperaments, or those who have disciplined themselves to habits of uniformity and equanimity, are those who do the largest amount of intellectual work, and do it with the greatest ease. But excitable temperaments, those who easily become aroused and who find it difficult or impossible to subjugate their emotions, are the persons who can do the least intellectual labor, and who suffer the most bodily harm from mental activity, when in excess. The fact is, what and how much we do is of much less concern than the way we do it. The calm and placid man can go on forever, like the smoothly-flowing river, with his intellectual labors, while the emotional person is exhausted by his emotions even before he begins to think. We see this difference well enough in men; we see the different amounts of mental as well as bodily labor which they can do, varying according to the nervous waste going on through their emotional activities, rather than measured by actual thinking. But the contrast becomes stronger when we observe the mental operations of women. Characterized as a sex with less manifestation of independent thinking, whether from a feebler endowment of reasoning powers, or whether because the intellect is so habitually subordinated to simple feeling, it is not necessary to discuss. But it is certain that the women of civilized communities are more emotional than are those of less favored regions, or else my observation has been at fault. While education in men makes them self-controlling, steady, deliberate, calculating, thinking out every problem, the intellectual being the preponderating force, the so-called "higher education" for women seems to produce the contrary effect on them. I am willing to admit and believe that it is not the fact of being educated which produces contrary effects in men and women, but the different ways in which men and women are educated. Still, it holds true that while men are calmed, women are excited by the education they receive. The emotions in savage men are the ruling forces, while they are subordinated to the intellect in the educated man. But the woman who has been put through the process deemed necessary to acquire the "higher education" is nervous, excitable, and in every way more dominated by her emotions than the sava3e woman is. Or, if the contrast is not so extreme as this, she certainly does lack that equipoise which is the characteristic of highly-educated men. In my capacity of surgeon I have frequent occasion to observe how different classes of women act under corresponding circumstances. My experience is such that I do not want a so-called highly-educated woman to take care of a case of hip-joint disease, for instance. For patience, for reliability, for real judgment in carrying out directions, for self-control, give me the little woman who has not been "educated" too much, and whose only ambition is to be a good wife and mother. She can be trusted to keep cool under trying circumstances; she does not have the backache; she does not tear herself to pieces with imaginary troubles nor insist on taking only emotional views of every incident of life. Her reason has not been put under the dominant influence of unmixed feeling, intensified by the process through which she obtained what is called her education. Hence her head is cool and her judgment clear. Such women are capable of being the mothers of men. But modern communities have too few of the even tempered, such as I have just described. Civilization is not an unmixed good, it carries penalties as well as compensations in its train.

It should not be lost sight of that women are emotional as a class of human beings, and there are many things incident to civilization which tend to increase to extraordinary proportions the emotional characteristics which pertain to them by virtue of their sex. The aesthetic form of emotion is so ready to be made prominent, and is so pleasing in its legitimate expressions, that some form of emotional exercise very easily becomes the principal feature of female education, so that the first we know, unless, happily, we are continually on the watch, the girl whom we send to school is increasing the intensity of her feelings much faster than she increases her stock of knowledge. I am not, at this time, discussing how this can be changed. I only desire to call attention to facts which must be familiar to every one. Thus tendencies endowed by nature, which would only harmonize her being to her position and destiny under favoring conditions, become exaggerated by inheritance and intensified by the education of the schools and the atmosphere of society, till the woman of our modern civilization becomes the bundle of nerves which she is, almost incapable of reasoning under the tyranny of paramount emotion, and some of them wholly incapable of becoming the mothers of rightly organized children. So the children are born many of them with big heads and little bodies and almost no digestion at all, but whether born feeble or vigorous they are ushered into an atmosphere of an intensely emotional character. Whatever may be the stimuli to intellectual activity, there are ten or a hundredfold more agencies which act on the emotions alone. It is to the fact that children are brought up in a hot-bed of emotional excitements to which I wish to call your attention. It is sufficiently deleterious to incite mental activity prematurely; but to prematurely and unduly excite emotional manifestations is tenfold more hurtful. It is just here that there seems to be the densest ignorance. Children are made to minister to adult morbid craving for emotional excitation by having their own emotions brought prematurely and excessively into action, just as if their powers of endurance were unlimited in this direction. People, and especially the female portion of society, do not stop to reflect that all the fondling which children (American children, I more especially mean) receive is not for the children's, but for their own sakes. Children are literally made to become little actors; but their fond relatives are not content with an hour or two a day, which is considered sufficient for adult actors, but they are kept going from morning until night. In my large practice among children I am certain that scores are literally killed by the excessive amount of emotional excitement which they are forced to endure. And much of it is, when we properly analyze it, from a purely selfish source. All this hugging and kissing and talking to them is to excite responses of the same emotional nature in the child for the pleasure and gratification of the parents and friends. There is really no thought that it is for the child's good. . . . It does not better the matter that people are not generally aware that it is their own and not always the child's pleasure which they seek in the excessive fondling which I am deprecating. Because they do not recognize the purely selfish character of the motive which makes children act day by day for the pleasure of the family is the reason that it is done; and it is the reason also, I may say, that I think it my duty to raise a warning voice against the pernicious practice, at some risk of denunciation, I am very certain. For it is a delicate thing to trench on the private ground of personal feeling and dispute with a mother how much and in what way she may love her child. But I hold that there is not a relation in life which may not be criticised in the right spirit, nor is there one which ought to be left to blind instinct or unreasoning impulse. Even maternal love may be a purely animal feeling, and when exercised without reason it may become an engine of cruelty and even death. Many such cases I have seen; one illustration will suffice for all. A mother brings her little child to me for a disease which is curable if immediately attended to, but fatal if appropriate treatment is delayed. I explain it all to her complete understanding. She sees that it may be cured, for she sees others like it which have been cured. She also understands that the chances are against its recovery, because she meets others in sorry straits who have neglected or delayed. But she will not leave it. There are those who can remain,—an aunt, an older sister, a faithful nurse. All to no purpose. The mother has, perhaps, a younger child at home, and cannot herself remain, and so the sick one must go home to die, or, what is far worse, to endure years of agonizing suffering, and then to live a short, decrepit life, with all bright hopes blotted out forever. This is what unreasoning animal affection may do, and what it is continually doing, to my certain knowledge. Another child, a beautiful girl, lives in its grandfather's family. Of parents and grandparents, of uncles, aunts, cousins and friends there are seventeen. It is the only grandchild, and the household draws a certain large portion of its daily emotional pleasures from this babe. It continually passes from lap to lap and from lip to lip, not allowed ever to go without returning some pretty prattle for the urging and caressing which she receives from morning until night. What wonder is it that evening finds her tired, peevish, excitable, and wholly exhausted? And when disease attacks her it finds weak resistance in a frame already enfeebled, at the tender age of four, by an overwrought brain. In this case I could manage the mother, with whom I came in personal contact. But she found it impossible to make the other members of the family let the child alone, and she was actually obliged, under my advice, to imprison herself in a room with locked doors to keep her sickly child from continuing to be the plaything of the family.

Now, what is the result of the system of child-management which keeps the young mind in continual excited tension?

There is a law of human force which proclaims that for every atom used in one direction there is an equivalent atom wanting in some other direction. How can there be a well-developed body in a child whose brain is kept excited and in whom a waste of force is going on far beyond the means of supply, except by drawing it from other directions? Thus the brain is supplied, in part, at the expense of the body; that is, the body is starved to support the brain, excited by the mind into unnatural and premature activity. And the worst of it is that there are no proper compensations. On the contrary, a condition of preternatural emotional preponderance is established as the inveterate habit of life. Hence the so-called "nervous" invalids, which exist in all civilized communities and are especially abundant in this country: persons who are frightened at any sudden noise, and whom the sight of a mouse throws into a cold perspiration. No matter how sensible they may be in calmer moments, their reason is dethroned and subordinated by the superior influence of easily excited emotions. Such are the persons whose flabby muscles and nerveless frames are only surpassed as a phenomenal fact by the amount of pain they can bear and still exist. Such persons are the products of civilization,—of that civilization which does not seek for and find the cause of its abortive products and endeavor to so arrange the checks and balances supplied by intelligence that the race shall not deteriorate through preventable causes. For the causes are largely preventable, and preventive means are daily used among those who are better informed on the subject. But there should be greater precautions used against the overaction of the brains of children, and it should be better comprehended that the overaction comes, for the most part, from the direction of the emotions. My professional life is spent, for the most part, in attending to children, and I have ample opportunities to see the evil effect on the bodily development of overwrought emotions. Feebleness, asymmetry, excitability, premature arrest of growth, are some of them. So that populations of cities, which come under the influence of more things which tend to excite emotion, become less and less in size until, it is said, that cities would cease to be if it were not for the constant influx of persons who were reared in the country, and so escape some of the body-dwarfing influences to which the children of large centers are so much subjected. . . .

I may say that at least two-thirds of all lateral distortions of the spinal column are directly traceable to mental overaction, mainly, if not entirely, of an emotional origin. There can be no doubt that this is the fact, because not less than three-fifths of those of them who consult me in the earlier stages recover without any other treatment than a careful abstaining from whatever excites undue emotions in the subject of the distortion.

One little incident occurred a number of years ago, which may serve to fix the moral in your minds if I should relate it. Being in Wilmington, Delaware, at the time, I was consulted by a lady concerning her daughter, who had begun to give evidence of curvature of the spine. She was a good-sized child of about twelve, and I sought in vain, for some time, to find a cause for the weakness of the muscles which allowed the bending of her spinal column. Her lessons did not seem to be too much for her, her exercise was regular and sufficient, her food was proper, and altogether, she seemed to be well managed. Still, there was an expression of fatigue in her face, and, though her rapid growth was exhausting her somewhat, as is always the case, that alone did not seem sufficient to cause the spinal muscles to give way and the spinal column to bend out of its proper direction. So I inquired particularly in regard to any outside influences which might tend to excite the child's emotions; but such inquiries were met by prompt denials. The mother was an unusually intelligent woman and seemed to comprehend the subject better than most. Two days afterwards, this mother returned to say that perhaps she had found the source of the child's loss of power,—for she was often nerveless and languid. She said that this girl was an especial favorite of her husband's mother, and that it was her custom to pay her grandmother a visit twice every week; she added that, now that her attention had been called to the subject by my inquiries, she remembered that her daughter invariably came home from those visits tired, nervous, easy to cry, and she was always glad to get her off to bed as soon as possible, and even the next morning there were often traces of the nervous excitement which she showed more especially the night before. Her grandmother, the lady said, was a very intellectual woman, and the child looked forward to her bi-weekly visits with great anticipations, but if I thought they had anything to do with the curvature she would stop them at once. I replied that I had no doubt but that they had, and they were accordingly put an end to. In other respects no change was made in her course of life. Three months later I was in the neighborhood, when the child was brought to me, this time perfectly straight. Ceasing to visit her grandmother had cured a curvature of the spine: cured it by preventing the bi-weekly exhaustion through excessive emotional excitation; thus muscular tone was restored. As before remarked, growth, especially rapid growth, is an exhausting process, and it is of the greatest moment that the process of natural growth should not be interfered with by unusual demands made on the nervous forces at the same time. Indeed, I think there is even more danger to the health in excessive mental strain during the period of rapid growth at the age of puberty than in childhood even. This is especially true in regard to girls. Their growth is generally more rapid than it is in the other sex. They pass through a stage of physical development in one or two years which boys require five or six to perfect. There is a correspondingly greater danger of overtaxing girls at this age. If we add to the

natural bodily growth the development of the sexual functions, the important changes which take place in advancing from girlhood into womanhood,
all accomplished within a short period of time, and each one a special tax on
the vital powers, we can better comprehend how the human female is subjected to great and special causes of nervous exhaustion of a perfectly normal
character at this period of her life. . . .

But what are the facts regarding modern and, especially, American civilized children? I speak still more especially of girls, because they are affected
more by elements which disturb the natural order of things than boys are,
though boys do not escape unharmed, by any means. Cunningly devised
means for exciting feeling only, begun at the cradle, are continued through
child-life up to the very verge of womanhood. The aesthetic alone, or almost
alone, seems to be the sole idea of female mental existence. Thus they arrive
at twelve or fourteen and on the threshold of the most important period of
existence, utterly unfitted for passing through it. Excitable, with wide-open
eyes and ears for every sight and sound which can excite feeling, rapid and
intense in mental activity, with thin limbs, narrow chest, and ungainly back,
we meet these twelve-year-old products of civilization going to school with
an average of thirteen books under their feeble arms, for I have found by
actual count that thirteen is the average number of studies which they
"take" nowadays. Do they study them? Undoubtedly, for the sake of being
at the head of the class, or of not being at the foot, or to recite them or to
say they study them, etc. But you will find almost invariably some emotional
motive connected with the education of girls, as now conducted, in the
majority of instances. Now, what is the girl's chance for perfect development
under such adverse conditions as those which I have briefly pointed out? The
chance is poor indeed, and the result is deplorable. With the mind thus
forced to an unnatural activity, the emotions strained up to the highest tension, at such an important period, what chance has the body to attain a perfect growth or the various functions to be properly developed? Hence we see
that generation after generation becomes smaller and smaller, until nature
ceases to reproduce its own, and new blood has to be brought in to keep the
race from dying out. Take a walk on the avenue of a Sunday afternoon and
witness the large proportion of diminutive men and women which we shall
meet. Then tell me if I have overdrawn the picture.

Now, whatever premature and excessive mental activity does in dwarfing
the bodily growth and in enfeebling the functions in general, it effects, perhaps, even more the impairment of different organs and the curtailing of
their special functions. There are very few well-formed bodies among our
young women. The impression which an examination of the person gives is
that they have been starved. And starved they literally are. The major part
of the nourishment, which they could digest and assimilate, has gone to keep
up the constant, excessive expenditure through the brain and nervous system, leaving an inadequate supply for the bodily growth and development.
There is always a limit to human endurance at every period of life. Even with
adults, the man who thinks much must be content to work less. He cannot

do both in equal measure at the same time. Or if he works severely with his muscles he must be satisfied with less rapidity in his mental operations. The body is equally starved, whether, like the Australian bushman, from insufficiency of food, or like the Laplander, whose food is converted into fuel to keep up the animal heat; or like overworked children in some factory centers, whose bodies are dwarfed because all the food they eat is used to support their labor, and they have no vital remainder whereby growth may be effected; or as in the case of the overwrought brains of our "civilized" children, which absorb an undue share of the vital forces, and thus the body is left to starve. Hence ill shapes and distortions. Hence want of symmetry as to the trunk, and disproportion in the extremities. Hence weak muscles and indigestion. Hence teeth imperfect in development, dentine soft, enamel defective and easily penetrated. Hence decay.

One who is not accustomed to examine the persons of large numbers of people can have no idea of the varying characters of bodily deficiencies and imperfections which he will meet without attracting the notice of the ordinary observer. I have a patient now with one leg two inches longer than the other; and a difference of one inch in the lengths of the lower extremities is a relatively common occurrence. So of every portion of the body. It is seldom even tolerably perfect among the higher classes. And I have no doubt that the cause of these imperfections lies more in the diversion of the nutrition which should feed the bodily growth, from its proper direction, in consequence of emotional excitation, than any other cause which acts on the members of civilized communities. But, of course, there are exceptions to this rule as there are to every other; that is, there seem to be exceptions, but they are of such a character as to prove the rule. We see persons with poor apologies for bodies, but with excellent teeth; while we also see persons with sound, strong bodies with defective teeth. When the nutritive supply is inadequate, accident determines which particular organ shall suffer most and which shall be comparatively well nourished. When any organ *may* suffer it is pretty certain that some one eventually *will* suffer. . . .

I am aware that it has been proposed to correct imperfect bodily development by various expedients, all more or less directly concerning the nutrition, either as medicaments, containing, in larger proportion or in more easily assimilable form than is to be found in ordinary food, some of the elements supposed to be in diminished amounts in the systems of delicate persons; or by a diet of substances containing the desired elements in greater abundance than exists in the ordinary food of the people. And there can be no doubt that something can be done in either direction which will have a good tendency and be calculated to ameliorate some of the worst results of the deteriorating effects of mental exhaustion. But, after all, such proposals must be considered as proceeding from very superficial examination into the causes of bodily imperfection in civilized communities. The Chinese attain a good stature and have perfectly formed teeth on a diet of rice, and the Esquimaux have sound teeth on a diet of blubber. I do not pretend to say that either rice, blubber, or any other diet so imperfect as either must be will produce as good specimens of man, under the same or corresponding circumstances, as a food which contains the assimilable substances in better proportions. But my object is to show that there is something back of the food in the condition of the system which makes it possible for perfect men to be developed under such unfavorable conditions, or for so poor specimens to be so common in civilized communities, with all the advantages which the latter have over the barbarous in selecting food. These indisputable facts cannot be reconciled except by supposing that the greatest factor of all in modifying bodily development lies in that which most distinguishes the civilized from the savage,—the mind. It is here that we must look for most of the modifying influences on the bodily powers, and it is here where our remedies must be applied if we would see an average of bodily perfection in civilized society. . . .

Questions for "Emotional Prodigality"

1. What does Taylor mean by the term "emotional prodigality"?

2. What types of evidence do you expect in a scientific article? What kinds of evidence might Taylor have included to make this argument more convincing?

3. Which of Taylor's arguments strike you as implausible, and why?

4. Although this argument may strike contemporary readers as full of holes, there is some truth to Taylor's contentions: Many upper-class Victorian women did, in fact, suffer from nervous disorders. Does Alison Lurie's discussion of nineteenth-century ideas about women (pp. 960–972) shed any light on this phenomenon? Does Alice James's diary (pp. 47–51)? What reasons can you offer to explain the emotional instability of these women?

5. How might "The Yellow Wallpaper" (included in the short fiction chapter of this anthology) be seen as a response to certain medical theories of the day exemplified by Taylor's article?

Virginia Woolf (1882–1941)

The daughter of Sir Leslie Stephen, a major force in the intellectual life of London in his day, Virginia Woolf was educated at home, where she read voraciously in her father's extensive library. Her mother died when Woolf was thirteen, and she experienced her first bout with emotional illness soon after. The voices of insanity returned in 1913, a year after her marriage to Leonard Woolf; she was to suffer from frail health and periods of depression for the rest of her life. In March of 1941, threatened by another mental breakdown, Woolf drowned herself in the River Ouse, across the fields from her home in Rodmell, Sussex. A farewell letter to her husband explained that she was hearing voices, that this time she would not recover, that she could not go on and ruin his life.

Despite her fragility, Virginia Woolf wrote prolifically and was at the center of a circle of intellectuals called the Bloomsbury Group, which included many of the leading thinkers and artists of the time. She and Leonard Woolf founded the Hogarth Press, which published some of the most brilliant writers of the era, including T. S. Eliot and E. M. Forster.

Woolf's remarkable *oeuvre* included two biographies; several volumes of letters, diary entries, short stories, literary criticism, and essays; and a succession of novels that extended the parameters of modern fiction: *The Voyage Out* (1915), *Night and Day* (1919), *Jacob's Room* (1922), *Mrs. Dalloway* (1925), *To the Lighthouse* (1927), *Orlando* (1928), *The Waves* (1931), *The Years* (1937), and *Between the Acts* (1941).

The Death of the Moth

Moths that fly by day are not properly to be called moths; they do not excite that pleasant sense of dark autumn nights and ivy-blossom which the commonest yellow-underwing asleep in the shadow of the curtain never fails to rouse in us. They are hybrid creatures, neither gay like butterflies nor sombre like their own species. Nevertheless the present specimen, with his narrow hay-coloured wings, fringed with a tassel of the same colour, seemed to be content with life. It was a pleasant morning, mid-September, mild, benignant, yet with a keener breath than that of the summer months. The plough was already scoring the field opposite the window, and where the share had been, the earth was pressed flat and gleamed with moisture. Such vigour came rolling in from the fields and the down beyond that it was difficult to keep the eyes strictly turned upon the book. The rooks too were keeping one of their annual festivities; soaring round the tree tops until it looked as if a vast net with thousands of black knots in it had been cast up into the air; which, after a few moments, sank slowly down upon the trees until every twig seemed to have a knot at the end of it. Then, suddenly, the net would be thrown into the air again in a wider circle this time, with the utmost clamour and vociferation, as though to be thrown into the air and settle slowly down upon the tree tops were a tremendously exciting experience.

The same energy which inspired the rooks, the ploughmen, the horses, and even, it seemed, the lean bare-backed downs, sent the moth fluttering from side to side of his square of the window-pane. One could not help watching him. One was, indeed, conscious of a queer feeling of pity for him. The possibilities of pleasure seemed that morning so enormous and so various that to have only a moth's part in life, and a day moth's at that, appeared a hard fate, and his zest in enjoying his meagre opportunities to the full, pathetic. He flew vigorously to one corner of his compartment, and, after waiting there a second, flew across to the other. What remained for him but to fly to a third corner and then to a fourth? That was all he could do, in spite of the size of the downs, the width of the sky, the far-off smoke of houses, and the romantic voice, now and then, of a steamer out at sea. What he could do he did. Watching him, it seemed as if a fibre, very thin but pure, of the enormous energy of the world had been thrust into his frail and diminutive body. As often as he crossed the pane, I could fancy that a thread of vital light became visible. He was little or nothing but life.

Yet, because he was so small, and so simple a form of the energy that was rolling in at the open window and driving its way through so many narrow and intricate corridors in my own brain and in those of other human beings, there was something marvellous as well as pathetic about him. It was as if someone had taken a tiny bead of pure life and decking it as lightly as possible with down and feathers, had set it dancing and zigzagging to show us the true nature of life. Thus displayed one could not get over the strangeness of it. One is apt to forget all about life, seeing it humped and bossed and garnished and cumbered so that it has to move with the greatest circumspection and dignity. Again, the thought of all that life might have been had he been born in any other shape caused one to view his simple activities with a kind of pity.

After a time, tired by his dancing apparently, he settled on the window ledge in the sun, and, the queer spectacle being at an end, I forgot about him. Then, looking up, my eye was caught by him. He was trying to resume his dancing, but seemed either so stiff or so awkward that he could only flutter to the bottom of the window-pane; and when he tried to fly across it he failed. Being intent on other matters I watched these futile attempts for a time without thinking, unconsciously waiting for him to resume his flight, as one waits for a machine, that has stopped momentarily, to start again without considering the reason of its failure. After perhaps a seventh attempt he slipped from the wooden ledge and fell, fluttering his wings, on to his back on the window sill. The helplessness of his attitude roused me. It flashed upon me that he was in difficulties; he could no longer raise himself; his legs struggled vainly. But, as I stretched out a pencil, meaning to help him to right himself, it came over me that the failure and awkwardness were the approach of death. I laid the pencil down again.

The legs agitated themselves once more. I looked as if for the enemy against which he struggled. I looked out of doors. What had happened there? Presumably it was midday, and work in the fields had stopped. Stillness and quiet had replaced the previous animation. The birds had taken themselves off to feed in the brooks. The horses stood still. Yet the power was there all the same, massed outside indifferent, impersonal, not attending to anything in particular. Somehow it was opposed to the little hay-coloured moth. It was useless to try to do anything. One could only watch the extraordinary efforts made by those tiny legs against an oncoming doom which could, had it chosen, have submerged an entire city, not merely a city, but masses of human beings; nothing, I knew, had any chance against death. Nevertheless after a pause of exhaustion the legs fluttered again. It was superb this last protest, and so frantic that he succeeded at last in righting himself. One's sympathies, of course, were all on the side of life. Also, when there was nobody to care or to know, this gigantic effort on the part of an insignificant little moth, against a power of such magnitude, to retain what no one else valued or desired to keep, moved one strangely. Again, somehow, one saw life, a pure bead. I lifted the pencil again, useless though I knew it to be. But even as I did so, the unmistakable tokens of death showed themselves. The body relaxed, and instantly grew stiff. The struggle was over. The insignificant little creature now knew death. As I looked at the dead moth, this minute wayside triumph of so great a force over so mean an antagonist filled me with wonder. Just as life had been strange a few minutes before, so death was now as strange. The moth having righted himself now lay most decently and uncomplainingly composed. O yes, he seemed to say, death is stronger than I am.

Questions for "The Death of the Moth"

1.   What resemblances between the moth and other life forms does this essay suggest?

2.   How does Woolf refer to herself in the first three paragraphs? In the final two? How does this change in the dominant pronoun correspond to the tone and content of the final paragraphs?

3.   This essay consists of only five paragraphs. What is the focus of each paragraph? What modes of reasoning does Woolf employ?

4.   How would you describe the style of this essay? How does Woolf's use of figurative language contribute to the effect of this piece?

5.   Which details and ideas are repeated? What is the effect of these repetitions?

6.   What is the theme of this essay? Why do you think Woolf chose to use the death of a moth rather than the death of a higher life form as the foundation for her discussion?

Bruno Bettelheim (1903–   )

Bruno Bettelheim was born in Vienna, Austria. After undergoing psychoanalysis as an adolescent, he went on to receive his doctorate in psychology from the University of Vienna and to begin a distinguished career as a psychologist. Shortly afterward, he was arrested by the Nazis and placed in concentration camps at Dachau and Buchenwald from 1938 to 1939. While imprisoned, Bettelheim carefully observed the behavior of the other captives. After emigrating to the United States in 1939, he used these observations as the basis for an article that would attract international attention, "Individual and Mass Behavior in Extreme Situations."

Although Bettelheim's numerous essays and books embrace a variety of concerns, his primary interest is his work with children. His experiences with emotionally disturbed youngsters at the Sonia Shankman Orthogenic School at the University of Chicago have inspired four books: *Love Is Not Enough* (1950), *Truants from Life* (1955), *The Empty Fortress* (1967), and *A Home for the Heart* (1974). His latest work, *A Good Enough Parent* (1987), is a book on child-rearing. The following selection comes from *The Uses of Enchantment: The Meaning and Importance of Fairy Tales* (1976).

"Snow White"

"Snow White" is one of the best-known fairy tales. It has been told for centuries in various forms in all European countries and languages; from there it was disseminated to the other continents. More often than not the story's title is simply the name "Snow White," although there are many variations.[1] "Snow White and the Seven Dwarfs," the name by which the tale is now widely known, is a bowdlerization which unfortunately emphasizes the dwarfs, who, failing to develop into mature humanity, are permanently arrested on a pre-oedipal level (dwarfs have no parents, nor do they marry or have children) and are but foils to set off the important developments taking place in Snow White.

Some versions of "Snow White" begin: "A count and a countess drove by three mounds of white snow which made the count say, 'I wish I had a girl

---

[1]For example, one Italian version is called *"La Ragazza di Latte e Sangue"* ("The Girl of Milk and Blood"), which finds its explanation in the fact that in many Italian renderings the three drops of blood which the queen sheds do not fall on snow, which is very rare in most parts of Italy, but instead on milk, white marble, or even white cheese.

as white as this snow.' A short while later they came to three holes full of red blood, at which he said, 'I wish I had a girl with cheeks as red as this blood.' Finally three black ravens flew by, at which moment he desired a girl 'with hair as black as these ravens.' As they drove on, they encountered a girl as white as snow, as red as blood, and with hair as black as the raven; and she was Snow White. The count immediately made her sit in the coach and loved her, but the countess did not like it and thought only about how she could get rid of her. Finally she dropped her glove and ordered Snow White to look for it; in the meantime the coachman had to drive on with great speed.''

A parallel version differs only in the detail that the couple drive through a forest and Snow White is asked to descend to gather a bunch of beautiful roses which grow there. As she does so, the queen orders the coachman to drive on, and Snow White is deserted.

In these renderings of the story, the count and countess or king and queen are thinly disguised parents, and the girl so admired by a father figure and found by chance is a surrogate daughter. The oedipal desires of a father and daughter, and how these arouse the mother's jealousy which makes her wish to get rid of the daughter, are much more clearly stated here than in more common versions. The now widely accepted form of "Snow White" leaves the oedipal entanglements to our imagination rather than forcing them on our conscious mind.[2]

Whether openly stated or only hinted at, oedipal difficulties and how the individual solves them are central to the way his personality and human relations unfold. By camouflaging the oedipal predicaments, or by only subtly intimating the entanglements, fairy stories permit us to draw our own conclusions when the time is propitious for our gaining a better understanding of these problems. Fairy stories teach by indirection. In the versions just mentioned, Snow White is not the count's and countess' child, deeply desired and loved though she is by the count, and jealous though the countess is of her. In the well-known story of Snow White, the jealous older female is not her mother but her stepmother, and the person for whose love the two are in competition is not mentioned. So the oedipal problems—source of the story's conflict—are left to our imagination.

---

[2]Some elements of one of the earliest versions of the "Snow White" motif found in Basile's "The Young Slave" make it clear that the heroine's persecution is due to a (step)mother's jealousy, the cause of which is not just the young girl's beauty, but rather the real or imagined love of the (step)mother's husband for the girl. The girl, whose name is Lisa, dies temporarily from a comb that gets stuck in her hair. Like Snow White, she is buried in a casket of crystal in which she continues to grow as the coffin grows with her. After she has spent seven years in the coffin, her uncle goes away. This uncle, who is her foster father really, is the only father she has ever had, since her mother was magically impregnated by the leaf of a rose which she had swallowed. His wife, insanely jealous because of what she views as her husband's love for Lisa, shakes her out of the coffin; the comb drops out of her hair, and she awakes. The jealous (step)mother turns her into a slave; hence the story's title. At the end, the uncle finds out that the young slave girl is Lisa. He restores her and drives away his wife, who, out of jealousy for his love for Lisa, has nearly destroyed her.

While, physiologically speaking, the parents create the child, it is the arrival of the child which causes these two people to become parents. Thus, it is the child who creates the parental problems, and with these come his own. Fairy tales usually begin when the child's life in some manner has reached an impasse. In "Hansel and Gretel" the children's presence creates hardships for the parents, and because of this, life turns problematic for the children. In "Snow White" it is not any external difficulty such as poverty, but the relations between her and her parents which create the problematic situation.

As soon as the position of the child within the family becomes a problem to him or to his parents, the process of the child's struggle to escape the triadic existence has begun. With it, he enters the often desperately lonely course to find himself—a struggle in which others serve mainly as foils who facilitate or impede this process. In some fairy tales the hero has to search, travel, and suffer through years of a lonely existence before he is ready to find, rescue, and join one other person in a relation which gives permanent meaning to both their lives. In "Snow White" it is the years Snow White spends with the dwarfs which stand for her time of troubles, of working through problems, her period of growth.

Few fairy tales help the hearer to distinguish between the main phases of childhood development as neatly as does "Snow White." The earliest, entirely dependent pre-oedipal years are hardly mentioned, as is true of most fairy tales. The story deals essentially with the oedipal conflicts between mother and daughter; with childhood; and finally with adolescence, placing major emphasis on what constitutes a good childhood, and what is needed to grow out of it.

The Brothers Grimm's story of "Snow White" begins: "Once upon a time, in the middle of winter when the snow flakes fell like feathers from the sky, a queen sat at a window which had a frame of black ebony. And as she was sewing while looking at the snow, she pricked her finger with the needle and three drops of blood fell on the snow. The red looked so beautiful on the white snow that she thought to herself, 'I wish I had a child as white as snow, as red as the blood, and with hair as black as the wood of the window frame.' Soon after she got a little daughter who was as white as snow, as red as blood, and had hair as black as ebony, and she was therefore called Snow White. And when the child had been born, the queen died. After a year had passed, the king took himself another wife. . . . "

The story begins with Snow White's mother pricking her finger so that three drops of blood fall upon the snow. Here the problems the story sets out to solve are intimated: sexual innocence, whiteness, is contrasted with sexual desire, symbolized by the red blood. Fairy tales prepare the child to accept what is otherwise a most upsetting event: sexual bleeding, as in menstruation and later in intercourse when the hymen is broken. Listening to the first few sentences of "Snow White," the child learns that a small amount of bleeding—three drops of blood (three being the number most closely associated in the unconscious with sex)—is a precondition for conception, because only after this bleeding is the child born. Here, then, (sexual) bleeding is closely connected with a "happy" event; without detailed explanations the child learns that without bleeding no child—not even he—could have been born.

Although we are told that her mother died when she was born, during her first years nothing bad happens to Snow White, despite the fact that her mother is replaced by a stepmother. The latter turns into the "typical" fairy-tale stepmother only *after* Snow White reaches the age of seven and starts to mature. Then the stepmother begins to feel threatened by Snow White and becomes jealous. The stepmother's narcissism is demonstrated by her seeking reassurance about her beauty from the magic mirror long before Snow White's beauty eclipses hers.

The queen's consulting the mirror about her worth—i.e., beauty—repeats the ancient theme of Narcissus, who loved only himself, so much that he became swallowed up by his self-love. It is the narcissistic parent who feels most threatened by his child's growing up, because that means the parent must be aging. As long as the child is totally dependent, he remains, as it were, *part* of the parent; he does not threaten the parent's narcissism. But when the child begins to mature and reaches for independence, then he is experienced as a menace by such a parent, as happens to the queen in "Snow White."

Narcissism is very much part of the young child's make-up. The child must gradually learn to transcend this dangerous form of self-involvement. The story of Snow White warns of the evil consequences of narcissism for both parent and child. Snow White's narcissism nearly undoes her as she gives in twice to the disguised queen's enticements to make her look more beautiful, while the queen is destroyed by her own narcissism.

As long as she remained home, Snow White did nothing; we hear nothing about her life before her expulsion. We are told nothing about her relation to her father, although it is reasonable to assume that it is competition for him which sets (step)mother against daughter.

The fairy tale views the world and what happens in it not objectively, but from the perspective of the hero, who is always a person in development. Since the hearer identifies with Snow White, he sees all events through her eyes, and not through those of the queen. To the girl child, her love for her father is the most natural thing in the world, and so is his love for her. She cannot conceive of this being a problem—short of his not loving her enough, in preference to everybody else. Much as the child wants the father to love her more than her mother, she cannot accept that this may create jealousy of her in the mother. But on a preconscious level, the child knows quite well how jealous she is of the attention one parent pays to the other, when the child feels she should get that attention. Since the child wants to be loved by both parents—a fact which is well known, but in discussion of the oedipal situation is frequently neglected because of the nature of the problem—it is much too threatening for the child to imagine that love for him by one parent may create jealousy in the other. When this jealousy— as is true for the queen in "Snow White"—cannot be overlooked, then some other reason must be found to explain it, as in the story it is ascribed to the child's beauty.

In the normal course of events, the relations of parents to each other are not threatened by the love of one or both parents for their child. Unless the marital relations are quite bad, or a parent is very narcissistic, jealousy of a child favored by one parent remains small and well controlled by the other parent.

Matters are quite different for the child. First, he cannot find solace for the pangs of jealousy in a good relation such as that his parents have with each other. Second, all children are jealous, if not of their parents, then of the privileges the parents enjoy as adults. When the tender, loving care of the parent of the same sex is not strong enough to build up ever more important positive ties in the naturally jealous oedipal child, and with it set the process of identification working against this jealousy, then the latter dominates the child's emotional life. Since a narcissistic (step)mother is an unsuitable figure to relate to or identify with, Snow White, if she were a real child, could not help being intensely jealous of her mother and all her advantages and powers.

If a child cannot permit himself to feel his jealousy of a parent (this is very threatening to his security), he projects his feelings onto this parent. Then "I am jealous of all the advantages and prerogatives of Mother" turns into the wishful thought: "Mother is jealous of me." The feeling of inferiority is defensively turned into a feeling of superiority.

The prepubertal or adolescent child may say to himself, "I do not compete with my parents, I am already better than they are; it's they who are competing with me." Unfortunately, there are also parents who try to convince their adolescent children that they are superior to them—which the parents may well be in some respects, but for the sake of their children's ability to become secure, they ought to keep this fact to themselves. Worse, there are parents who maintain that they are in all ways as good as their adolescent child: the father who attempts to keep up with the youthful strength and sexual prowess of his son; the mother who tries in looks, dress, and behavior to be as youthfully attractive as her daughter. The ancient history of stories such as "Snow White" suggests that this is an age-old phenomenon. But competition between a parent and his child makes life unbearable for parent and child. Under such conditions the child wants to free himself and be rid of the parent, who forces him either to compete or to buckle under. The wish to be rid of the parent arouses great guilt, justified though it may be when the situation is viewed objectively. So in a reversal which eliminates the guilt feeling, this wish, too, is projected onto the parent. Thus, in fairy tales there are parents who try to rid themselves of their child, as happens in "Snow White."

In "Snow White," as in "Little Red Riding Hood," a male who can be viewed as an unconscious representation of the father appears—the hunter who is ordered to kill Snow White, but instead saves her life. Who else but a father substitute would seem to acquiesce to the stepmother's dominance and nevertheless, for the child's sake, dare to go against the queen's will? This is what the oedipal and adolescent girl wishes to believe about her father: that even though he does as the mother bids him, he would side with his daughter if he were free to, tricking the mother as he did so.

Why are rescuing male figures so often cast in the role of hunters in fairy tales? While hunting may have been a typically masculine occupation when fairy stories came into being, this is much too easy an explanation. At that time princes and princesses were as rare as they are today, and fairy tales simply abound with them. But when and where these stories originated, hunting was an aristocratic privilege, which supplies a good reason to see the hunter as an exalted figure like a father.

Actually, hunters appear frequently in fairy tales because they lend themselves so well to projections. Every child at some time wishes that he were a prince or a princess—and at times, in his unconscious, the child believes he is one, only temporarily degraded by circumstances. There are so many kings and queens in fairy tales because their rank signifies absolute power, such as the parent seems to hold over his child. So the fairy-tale royalty represent projections of the child's imagination, as does the hunter.

The ready acceptance of the hunter figure as a suitable image of a strong and protective father figure—as opposed to the many ineffectual fathers such as the one in "Hansel and Gretel"—must relate to associations which attach themselves to this figure. In the unconscious the hunter is seen as the symbol of protection. In this connection we must consider the animal phobias of which no child is entirely free. In his dreams and daydreams the child is threatened and pursued by angry animals, creations of his fear and guilt. Only the parent-hunter, so he feels, can scare these threatening animals away, keep them permanently from the child's door. Hence the hunter of fairy tales is not a figure who kills friendly creatures, but one who dominates, controls, and subdues wild, ferocious beasts. On a deeper level, he represents the subjugation of the animal, asocial, violent tendencies in man. Since he seeks out, tracks down, and defeats what are viewed as lower aspects of man—the wolf—the hunter is an eminently protective figure who can and does save us from the dangers of our violent emotions and those of others.

In "Snow White" the pubertal girl's oedipal struggle is not repressed, but acted out around the mother as competitor. In Snow White's story the father-huntsman fails to take a strong and definite stand. He neither does his duty to the queen, nor meets his moral obligation to Snow White to make her safe and secure. He does not kill her outright, but he deserts her in the forest, expecting her to be killed by wild animals. The hunter tries to placate both the mother by seemingly executing her order, and the girl, by merely not killing her. Lasting hatred and jealousy of the mother are the consequence of the father's ambivalence, which in "Snow White" are projected onto the evil queen, who therefore continues to reappear in Snow White's life.

A weak father is as little use to Snow White as he was to Hansel and Gretel. The frequent appearance of such figures in fairy tales suggests that wife-dominated husbands are not exactly new to this world. More to the point, it is such fathers who either create unmanageable difficulties in the child or fail to help him solve them. This is another example of the important messages fairy tales contain for parents.

Why is the mother outright rejecting in these fairy tales while the father is often only ineffectual and weak? The reason the (step)mother is depicted as evil and the father as weak has to do with what the child expects of his parents. In the typical nuclear family setting, it is the father's duty to protect the child against the dangers of the outside world, and also those that originate in the child's own asocial tendencies. The mother is to provide nurturing care and the general satisfaction of immediate bodily needs required for the child's survival. Therefore, if the mother fails the child in fairy tales, the child's very life is in jeopardy, as happens in "Hansel and Gretel" when the mother insists that the children must be gotten rid of. If the father out of weakness is negligent in meeting his obligations, then the child's life as such is not so directly endangered, although a child deprived of the father's protection must shift for himself as best he can. So Snow White must fend for herself when she is abandoned by the hunter in the forest.

Only loving care combined with responsible behavior on the part of both parents permits the child to integrate his oedipal conflicts. If he is deprived of either by one or both parents, the child will not be able to identify with them. If a girl cannot form a positive identification with her mother, not only does she get stuck in oedipal conflicts but regression sets in, as it always does when the child fails to attain the next higher stage of development for which she is chronologically ready.

The queen, who is fixated to a primitive narcissism and arrested on the oral incorporative stage, is a person who cannot positively relate, nor can anybody identify with her. The queen orders the hunter not only to kill Snow White, but to return with her lungs and liver as evidence. When the hunter brings the queen the lungs and liver of an animal to prove he has executed her command, "The cook had to cook them in salt, and the bad woman ate them and thought she had eaten Snow White's lungs and liver." In primitive thought and custom, one acquires the powers or characteristics of what one eats. The queen, jealous of Snow White's beauty, wanted to incorporate Snow White's attractiveness, as symbolized by her internal organs.

This is not the first story of a mother's jealousy of her daughter's budding sexuality, nor is it all that rare that a daughter in her mind accuses her mother of such jealousy. The magic mirror seems to speak with the voice of a daughter rather than that of a mother. As the small girl thinks her mother is the most beautiful person in the world, this is what the mirror initially tells the queen. But as the older girl thinks she is much more beautiful than her mother, this is what the mirror says later. A mother may be dismayed when looking into the mirror; she compares herself to her daugher and thinks to herself: "My daughter is more beautiful than I am." But the mirror says: "She is a thousand times more beautiful"—a statement much more akin to an adolescent's exaggeration which he makes to enlarge his advantages and silence his inner voice of doubt.

The pubertal child is ambivalent in his wish to be much better than his parent of the same sex because the child fears that if this were actually so, the parent, still much more powerful, would take terrible revenge. It is the child who fears destruction because of his imagined or real superiority, not the parent who wishes to destroy. The parent may suffer pangs of jealousy if he, in his turn, has not succeeded in identifying with his child in a very positive way, because only then can he take vicarious pleasure in his child's accomplishments. It is essential that the parent identify strongly with his child of the same sex for the child's identification with him to prove successful.

Whenever the oedipal conflicts are revived in the pubertal child, he finds life with his family unbearable because of his violently ambivalent feelings. To escape his inner turmoil, he dreams of being the child of different and better parents with whom he would have none of these psychological difficulties. Some children even go beyond such fantasizing and actually run away in search of this ideal home. Fairy tales, however, implicitly teach the child that it exists only in an imaginary country, and that when found, it often turns out to be far from satisfying. This is true for Hansel and Gretel and also for Snow White. While Snow White's experience with a home away from home is less scary than Hansel's and Gretel's, it does not work out too well either. The dwarfs are unable to protect her, and her mother continues to have power over her which Snow White cannot help giving her—as symbolized by Snow White's permitting the queen (in her various disguises) entry into the house, despite the dwarfs' warnings to beware of the queen's tricks and not let anybody in.

One cannot free oneself from the impact of one's parents and one's feelings about them by running away from home—although that seems the easiest way out. One succeeds in gaining independence only by working through one's inner conflicts, which children usually try to project onto their parents. At first every child wishes that it would be possible to evade the difficult work of integration, which, as Snow White's story also shows, is fraught with great dangers. For a time it seems feasible to escape this task. Snow White lives a peaceful existence for a while, and under the guidance of the dwarfs she grows from a child helpless to deal with the difficulties of the world into a girl who learns to work well, and to enjoy it. This is what the dwarfs request of her for living with them: she can remain with them and lack nothing if "you will take care of our household, cook, make the beds, wash, sew and knit, and will keep everything clean and in good order." Snow White becomes a good housekeeper, as is true of many a young girl who, with mother away, takes good care of her father, the house, and even her siblings.

Even before she meets the dwarfs, Snow White shows that she can control her oral cravings, great as they are. Once in the dwarfs' house, though very hungry, she eats just a little from each of the seven plates, and drinks just a drop from each of the seven glasses, so as to rob none of them too much. (How different from Hansel and Gretel, the orally fixated children, who disrespectfully and voraciously eat up the gingerbread house!)

After having satisfied her hunger, Snow White tries out all seven beds, but one is too long, another too short, until finally she falls asleep in the seventh bed. Snow White knows that these are all some other persons' beds, and that each bed's owner will want to sleep in his bed despite Snow White's lying in it. Her exploration of every bed suggests she is dimly aware of this risk, and she tries to settle into one where no such risk is involved. And she is right. The dwarfs on coming home are very much taken with her beauty, but the seventh dwarf, in whose bed she is sleeping, does not claim it but instead "slept with his companions, one hour with each, until the night had passed."

Given the popular view of Snow White's innocence, the notion that she may have subconsciously risked being in bed with a man seems outrageous. But Snow White shows, by permitting herself to be tempted three times by the queen in disguise, that, like most humans—and, most of all, adolescents—she is quite easily tempted. However, Snow White's inability to resist temptation makes her all the more human and attractive, without the hearer of the story becoming consciously aware of this. On the other hand, her behavior in restraining herself in eating and drinking, her resisting sleeping in a bed that is not just right for her shows that she also has learned to control to some degree her id impulses and to subject them to superego requirements. We find that her ego too has matured, since now she works hard and well, and shares with others.

Dwarfs—these diminutive men—have different connotations in various fairy tales. Like the fairies themselves, they can be good or bad; in "Snow White" they are of the helpful variety. The first thing we learn about them is that they have returned home from working as miners in the mountains. Like all dwarfs, even the unpleasant ones, they are hard-working and clever at their trade. Work is the essence of their lives; they know nothing of leisure or recreation. Although the dwarfs are immediately impressed by Snow White's beauty and moved by her tale of misfortune, they make it clear right away that the price of living with them is engaging in conscientious work. The seven dwarfs suggest the seven days of the week—days filled with work. It is this working world Snow White has to make her own if she is to grow up well; this aspect of her sojourn with the dwarfs is easily understood.

Other historical meanings of dwarfs may serve to explain them further. European fairy tales and legends were often residuals of pre-Christian religious themes which became unacceptable because Christianity would not brook pagan tendencies in open form. In a fashion, Snow White's perfect beauty seems distantly derived from the sun; her name suggests the whiteness and purity of strong light. According to the ancients, seven planets circle the sun, hence the seven dwarfs. Dwarfs or gnomes, in Teutonic lore, are workers of the earth, extracting metals, of which only seven were commonly known in past times—another reason why these miners are seven in number. And each of these seven metals was related to one of the planets in ancient natural philosophy (gold to the sun, silver to the moon, etc.).

These connotations are not readily available to the modern child. But the dwarfs evoke other unconscious associations. There are no female dwarfs. While all fairies are female, wizards are their male counterparts, and there are both sorcerers and sorceresses, or witches. So dwarfs are eminently male, but males who are stunted in their development. These "little men" with their stunted bodies and their mining occupation—they skillfully penetrate into dark holes—all suggest phallic connotations. They are certainly not men in any sexual sense—their way of life, their interest in material goods to the exclusion of love, suggest a pre-oedipal existence.[3]

At first sight it may seem strange to identify a figure that symbolizes a phallic existence as also representing childhood before puberty, a period during which all forms of sexuality are relatively dormant. But the dwarfs are free of inner conflicts, and have no desire to move beyond their phallic existence to intimate relations. They are satisfied with an identical round of activities; their life is a never-changing circle of work in the womb of the earth, as the planets circle endlessly in a never-changing path in the sky. This lack of change or of any desire for it is what makes their existence parallel that of the prepubertal child. And this is why the dwarfs do not understand or sympathize with the inner pressures which make it impossible for Snow White to resist the queen's temptations. Conflicts are what make us dissatisfied with our present way of life and induce us to find other solutions; if we were free of conflicts, we would never run the risks involved in moving on to a different and, we hope, higher form of living.

The peaceful pre-adolescent period Snow White has while living with the dwarfs before the queen again disturbs her gives her the strength to move into adolescence. Thus she enters once more a time of troubles—now no longer as a child who must passively suffer what Mother inflicts on her, but as a person who must take part in and responsibility for what happens to her.

Snow White and the queen's relations are symbolic of some severe diffi-

---

[3]Giving each dwarf a separate name and a distinctive personality—in the fairy tale they are all identical—as in the Walt Disney film, seriously interferes with the unconscious understanding that they symbolize an immature pre-individual form of existence which Snow White must transcend. Such ill-considered additions to fairy tales, which seemingly increase the human interest, actually are apt to destroy it because they make it difficult to grasp the story's deeper meaning correctly. The poet understands the meaning of fairy-tale figures better than a film maker and those who follow his lead in retelling the story. Anne Sexton's poetic rendering of "Snow White" suggests their phallic nature, since she refers to them as "the dwarfs, those little hot dogs."

culties which may occur between mother and daughter. But they are also projections onto separate figures of tendencies which are incompatible within one person. Often these inner contradictions originate in a child's relationships with his parents. Thus, the fairy-tale projection of one side of an inner conflict onto a parental figure also represents a historical truth: this is where it originated. This is suggested by what happens to Snow White when her quiet and uneventful life with the dwarfs is interrupted.

Nearly destroyed by the early pubertal conflict and competition with her stepmother, Snow White tries to escape back into a conflict-free latency period, where sex remains dormant and hence adolescent turmoils can be avoided. But neither time nor human development remains static, and returning to a latency existence to escape the troubles of adolescence cannot succeed. As Snow White becomes an adolescent, she begins to experience the sexual desires which were repressed and dormant during latency. With this the stepmother, who represents the consciously denied elements in Snow White's inner conflict, reappears on the scene, and shatters Snow White's inner peace.

The readiness with which Snow White repeatedly permits herself to be tempted by the stepmother, despite the warnings of the dwarfs, suggests how close the stepmother's temptations are to Snow White's inner desires. The dwarf's admonition to let nobody enter the house—or, symbolically, Snow White's inner being—is to no avail. (The dwarfs have an easy time preaching against adolescent dangers because, being fixated to the phallic stage of development, they are not subjected to them.) The ups and downs of adolescent conflicts are symbolized by Snow White's twice being tempted, endangered, and rescued by returning to her previous latency existence. Snow White's third experience with temptation finally ends her efforts to return to immaturity when encountering adolescent difficulties.

While we are not told how long Snow White lived with the dwarfs before her stepmother reappeared in her life, it is the attraction of stay-laces which induces Snow White to let the queen, disguised as a peddler woman, enter the dwarfs' dwelling. This makes it clear that Snow White is by now a well-developed adolescent girl and, in line with the fashion of times past, in need of, and interested in, laces. The stepmother laces Snow White so tightly that she falls down as if she were dead.[4]

Now, if the queen's purpose was to kill Snow White, she could easily have done so at this moment. But if the queen's goal was to prevent her daughter from surpassing her, reducing her to immobility is sufficient for a time. The queen, then, stands for a parent who temporarily succeeds in maintaining his dominance by arresting his child's development. On another level the

---

[4]Depending on the custom of time or place, it is not stay-laces but another piece of clothing which tempts Snow-White—in some versions it is a shirt or a cloak which the queen wraps so tightly around Snow White that she collapses.

meaning of this episode is to suggest Snow White's conflicts about her adolescent desire to be well laced because it makes her sexually attractive. Her collapsing unconscious symbolizes that she became overwhelmed by the conflict between her sexual desires and her anxiety about them. Since it is Snow White's own vanity which seduces her into letting herself be laced, she and the vain stepmother have much in common. It seems that Snow White's adolescent conflicts and desires are her undoing. But the fairy tale knows better, and it continues to teach the child a more significant lesson: without having experienced and mastered those dangers which come with growing up, Snow White would never be united with her prince.

On their return from work, the good dwarfs find Snow White unconscious and unlace her. She comes to life again; she retreats temporarily into latency. The dwarfs warn her once more, and more seriously, against the tricks of the evil queen—that is, against the temptations of sex. But Snow White's desires are too strong. When the queen, disguised as an old woman, offers to fix Snow White's hair—"Now I will comb you properly for once"—Snow White is again seduced and lets her do it. Snow White's conscious intentions are overwhelmed by her desire to have a beautiful coiffure, and her unconscious wish is to be sexually attractive. Once more this wish is "poisonous" to Snow White in her early, immature adolescent state, and she again loses consciousness. Again the dwarfs rescue her. The third time Snow White gives in to temptation, she eats of the fateful apple which the queen, dressed up as a peasant woman, hands to her. The dwarfs can no longer help her then, because regression from adolescence to a latency existence has ceased to be a solution for Snow White.

In many myths as well as fairy tales, the apple stands for love and sex, in both its benevolent and its dangerous aspect. An apple given to Aphrodite, the goddess of love, showing she was preferred to chaste goddesses, led to the Trojan War. It was the Biblical apple with which man was seduced to forswear his innocence in order to gain knowledge and sexuality. While it was Eve who was tempted by male masculinity, as represented by the snake, not even the snake could do it all by itself—it needed the apple, which in religious iconography also symbolizes the mother's breast. On our mother's breast we were all first attracted to form a relation, and find satisfaction in it. In "Snow White" mother and daughter share the apple. That which is symbolized by the apple in "Snow White" is something mother and daughter have in common which runs even deeper than their jealousy of each other—their mature sexual desires.

To overcome Snow White's suspicion of her, the queen cuts the apple in half, eating the white part herself, while Snow White accepts the red, "poisonous" half. Repeatedly we have been told of Snow White's double nature: she was as white as snow and as red as blood—that is, her being has both its asexual and its erotic aspect. Eating the red (erotic) part of the apple is the end of Snow White's "innocence." The dwarfs, the companions of her latency existence, can no longer bring her back to life; Snow White has made her choice, which is as necessary as it is fateful. The redness of the apple evokes sexual associations like the three drops of blood which led to Snow White's birth, and also menstruation, the event which marks the beginning of sexual maturity.

As she eats of the red part of the apple, the child in Snow White dies and is buried in a transparent coffin made of glass. There she rests for a long time, visited not only by the dwarfs but also by three birds: first an owl, then a raven, and last a dove. The owl symbolizes wisdom; the raven—as in the Teutonic god Woden's raven—probably mature consciousness; and the dove stands traditionally for love. These birds suggest that Snow White's deathlike sleep in the coffin is a period of gestation which is her final period of preparing for maturity.[5]

Snow White's story teaches that just because one has reached physical maturity, one is by no means intellectually and emotionally ready for adulthood, as represented by marriage. Considerable growth and time are needed before the new, more mature personality is formed and the old conflicts are integrated. Only then is one ready for a partner of the other sex, and the intimate relation with him which is needed for the achievement of mature adulthood. Snow White's partner is the prince, who "carries her off" in her coffin—which causes her to cough up or spit out the poisonous apple and come to life, ready for marriage. Her tragedy began with oral incorporative desires: the queen's wish to eat Snow White's internal organs. Snow White's spitting out of the suffocating apple—the bad object she had incorporated—marks her final freedom from primitive orality, which stands for all her immature fixations.

Like Snow White, each child in his development must repeat the history of man, real or imagined. We are all expelled eventually from the original paradise of infancy, where all our wishes seemed to be fulfilled without any effort on our part. Learning about good and evil—gaining knowledge—seems to split our personality in two: the red chaos of unbridled emotions, the id; and the white purity of our conscience, the superego. As we grow up, we vacillate between being overcome by the turmoil of the first and the rigidity of the second (the tight lacing, and the immobility enforced by the coffin). Adulthood can be reached only when these inner contradictions are resolved and a new awakening of the mature ego is achieved, in which red and white coexist harmoniously.

But before the "happy" life can begin, the evil and destructive aspects of our personality must be brought under our control. The witch is punished for her cannibalistic desires in "Hansel and Gretel" by being burned in the

---

[5]This period of inertness may further explain Snow White's name, which stresses only one of the three colors that account for her beauty. White frequently symbolizes purity, innocence, the spiritual. But by emphasizing the connection with snow, inertness is also symbolized. When snow covers the earth, all life seems to stop, as Snow White's life seems to have stopped while she is lying in her coffin. Then her eating of the red apple was premature; she had overreached herself. Experiencing sexuality too soon, the story warns, can lead to nothing good. But when it is followed by a prolonged period of inertia, then the girl can recuperate fully from her premature and hence destructive experiences with sexuality.

oven. In "Snow White" the vain, jealous, and destructive queen is forced to put on red-hot shoes, in which she must dance until she dies. Untrammeled sexual jealousy, which tries to ruin others, destroys itself—as symbolized not only by the fiery red shoes but by death from dancing in them. Symbolically, the story tells that uncontrolled passion must be restrained or it will become one's undoing. Only the death of the jealous queen (the elimination of all outer and inner turbulence) can make for a happy world.

Many fairy-tale heroes, at a crucial point in their development, fall into deep sleep or are reborn. Each reawakening or rebirth symbolizes the reaching of a higher stage of maturity and understanding. It is one of the fairy tale's ways to stimulate the wish for higher meaning in life: deeper consciousness, more self-knowledge, and greater maturity. The long period of inactivity before reawakening makes the hearer realize—without consciously verbalizing it—that this rebirth requires a time of rest and concentration in both sexes.

Change signifies the need to give up something one had enjoyed up to then, such as Snow White's existence before the queen became jealous, or her easy life with the dwarfs—difficult and painful growing-up experiences which cannot be avoided. These stories also convince the hearer that he need not be afraid of relinquishing his childish position of depending on others, since after the dangerous hardships of the transitional period, he will emerge on a higher and better plane, to enter upon a richer and happier existence. Those who are reluctant to risk such a transformation, such as the two older brothers in "The Three Feathers," never gain the kingdom. Those who got stuck in the pre-oedipal stage of development, such as the dwarfs, will never know the happiness of love and marriage. And those parents who, like the queen, act out parental oedipal jealousies nearly destroy their child and certainly destroy themselves.

Questions for "Snow White"

1.　Bettelheim wrote *The Uses of Enchantment,* from which this essay is taken, partly in response to the argument, propounded in the late 1960s, that fairy tales are bad for children. Based on your reading of "Little Snow-white," included in Chapter 4 of this book, why might some adults feel that fairy tales are unsuitable for children? And how might Bettelheim answer such objections?

2.　Did you find this argument convincing? Why or why not? What assumptions does Bettelheim make about his audience? What sort of reader is most likely to accept his ideas? To reject them?

3.　Describe Bettelheim's attitude toward his subject. How does the tone of this essay influence your reaction to the ideas he advances?

4.   Can you offer an interpretation of "Snow White"—or of one aspect of the story—that differs from Bettelheim's?

5.   In a feminist interpretation of "Snow White" (an interpretation that departs from Bettelheim's), Sandra Gilbert and Susan Gubar argue that the Queen "is a plotter, a plot-maker, a schemer, a witch, an artist, a woman of almost infinite creative energy, witty, wily, and self-absorbed as all artists traditionally are." In what ways is the Queen "an artist"?

6.   Gilbert and Gubar describe Snow White as the Queen's opposite, a "sort of angel" who is "sweet, ignorant, passive" and becomes "a house-keeping angel" in the dwarfs' tiny house. What is Betteleheim's view of her "housekeeping" role? What indications of Snow White's passivity do you see in this tale? Is there any point at which Snow White becomes assertive?

7.   In Chapter 6 we include Anne Sexton's poem "Snow White and the Seven Dwarfs." Compare the portraits of the Queen and Snow White in the poem to those in the Grimms' tale. How are they similar or different? Can you apply Gilbert and Gubar's comments to the poem as well as the story? In what ways is Sexton's poem a response to the traditional ideas about women that we find in the Grimms' tale of "Little Snow-white"?

George Orwell (1903–1950)

Eric Blair, who later adopted the pen name George Orwell, was born in India to British parents. He attended Eton, a prestigious English boarding school, on a scholarship, and later returned to the Far East as a member of England's Imperial Police. He resigned after five years, because he objected to colonial rule and because he wanted to write. For eight years he lived in poverty, the circumstances of which he describes vividly in his first book, *Down and Out in Paris and London* (1933). Among the memoirs and novels that followed are *Burmese Days* (1935), *Keep the Aspidistra Flying* (1938), and *Home to Catalonia* (1939).

For most of his life, Orwell earned his living by publishing articles and reviews in English newspapers and journals. His volumes of essays include *The Road to Wigan Pier* (1937), *Dickens, Dali, and Others* (1946), and *Shooting an Elephant* (1950).

Many of Orwell's writings are based on his own experiences, and all of his books are concerned with the social and political conditions of his time, especially the issue of human freedom. His final and best-known books are the political fable *Animal Farm* (1945), and the anti-utopian novel *1984* (1948). Nevertheless, Orwell was essentially an essayist, and it has been observed that even his novels are actually extended essays.

After decades of poor health, complicated by the years of poverty and by a wound he received while fighting in the Spanish Civil War, Orwell died of tuberculosis at the age of forty-seven.

Shooting an Elephant

In Moulmein, in Lower Burma, I was hated by large numbers of people—the only time in my life that I have been important enough for this to happen to me. I was sub-divisional police officer of the town, and in an aimless, petty kind of way anti-European feeling was very bitter. No one had the guts to raise a riot, but if a European woman went through the bazaars alone somebody would probably spit betel juice over her dress. As a police officer I was an obvious target and was baited whenever it seemed safe to do so. When a nimble Burman tripped me up on the football field and the referee (another Burman) looked the other way, the crowd yelled with hideous laughter. This happened more than once. In the end the sneering yellow faces of young men that met me everywhere, the insults hooted after me when I was at a safe distance, got badly on my nerves. The young Buddhist priests were the worst of all. There were several thousands of them in the town and none of them seemed to have anything to do except stand on street corners and jeer at Europeans.

All this was perplexing and upsetting. For at that time I had already made up my mind that imperialism was an evil thing and the sooner I chucked up my job and got out of it the better. Theoretically—and secretly, of course—I was all for the Burmese and all against their oppressors, the British. As for the job I was doing, I hated it more bitterly than I can perhaps make clear. In a job like that you see the dirty work of Empire at close quarters. The wretched prisoners huddling in the stinking cages of the lock-ups, the grey, cowed faces of the long-term convicts, the scarred buttocks of the men who had been flogged with bamboos—all these oppressed me with an intolerable sense of guilt. But I could get nothing into perspective. I was young and ill-educated and I had had to think out my problems in the utter silence that is imposed on every Englishman in the East. I did not even know that the British Empire is dying, still less did I know that it is a great deal better than the younger empires that are going to supplant it. All I knew was that I was stuck between my hatred of the empire I served and my rage against the evil-spirited little beasts who tried to make my job impossible. With one part of my mind I thought of the British Raj as an unbreakable tyranny, as something clamped down, in *saecula saeculorum,* upon the will of prostrate peoples; with another part I thought that the greatest joy in the world would be to drive a bayonet into a Buddhist priest's guts. Feelings like these are the normal by-products of imperialism; ask any Anglo-Indian official, if you can catch him off duty.

One day something happened which in a roundabout way was enlightening. It was a tiny incident in itself, but it gave me a better glimpse than I had had before of the real nature of imperialism—the real motives for which despotic governments act. Early one morning the sub-inspector at a police station the other end of town rang me up on the phone and said that an elephant was ravaging the bazaar. Would I please come and do something about it? I did not know what I could do, but I wanted to see what was happening and I got on to a pony and started out. I took my rifle, an old .44 Winchester and much too small to kill an elephant, but I thought the noise might be useful *in terrorem.* Various Burmans stopped me on the way and told me about the elephant's doings. It was not, of course, a wild elephant, but a tame one which had gone "must." It had been chained up, as tame elephants always are when their attack of "must" is due, but on the previous night it had broken its chain and escaped. Its mahout, the only person who could manage it when it was in that state, had set out in pursuit, but had taken the wrong direction and was now twelve hours' journey away, and in the morning the elephant had suddenly reappeared in the town. The Burmese population had no weapons and were quite helpless against it. It had already destroyed somebody's bamboo hut, killed a cow and raided some fruit-stalls and devoured the stock; also it had met the municipal rubbish van and, when the driver jumped out and took to his heels, had turned the van over and inflicted violences upon it.

The Burmese sub-inspector and some Indian constables were waiting for me in the quarter where the elephant had been seen. It was a very poor quarter, a labyrinth of squalid bamboo huts, thatched with palmleaf, winding all over a steep hillside. I remember that it was a cloudy, stuffy morning at the beginning of the rains. We began questioning the people as to where the elephant had gone and, as usual, failed to get any definite information. That is invariably the case in the East; a story always sounds clear enough at a distance, but the nearer you get to the scene of events the vaguer it becomes. Some of the people said that the elephant had gone in one direction, some said that he had gone in another, some professed not even to have heard of any elephant. I had almost made up my mind that the whole story was a pack of lies, when we heard yells a little distance away. There was a loud, scandalized cry of "Go away, child! Go away this instant!" and an old woman with a switch in her hand came round the corner of a hut, violently shooing away a crowd of naked children. Some more women followed, clicking their tongues and exclaiming; evidently there was something that the children ought not to have seen. I rounded the hut and saw a man's dead body sprawling in the mud. He was an Indian, a black Dravidian coolie, almost naked, and he could not have been dead many minutes. The people said that the elephant had come suddenly upon him round the corner of the hut, caught him with its trunk, put its foot on his back and ground him into the earth. This was the rainy season and the ground was soft, and his face had scored a trench a foot deep and a couple of yards long. He was lying on his belly with arms crucified and head sharply twisted to one side. His face was coated with mud, the eyes wide open, the teeth bared and grinning with an expression of unendurable agony. (Never tell me, by the way, that the dead look peaceful. Most of the corpses I have seen looked devilish.) The friction of the great beast's foot had stripped the skin from his back as neatly as one skins a rabbit. As soon as I saw the dead man I sent an orderly to a friend's house nearby to borrow an elephant rifle. I had already sent back the pony, not wanting it to go mad with fright and throw me if it smelt the elephant.

The orderly came back in a few minutes with a rifle and five cartridges, and meanwhile some Burmans had arrived and told us that the elephant was in the paddy fields below, only a few hundred yards away. As I started forward practically the whole population of the quarter flocked out of the houses and followed me. They had seen the rifle and were all shouting excitedly that I was going to shoot the elephant. They had not shown much interest in the elephant when he was merely ravaging their homes, but it was different now that he was going to be shot. It was a bit of fun to them, as it would be to an English crowd; besides they wanted the meat. It made me vaguely uneasy. I had no intention of shooting the elephant—I had merely sent for the rifle to defend myself if necessary—and it is always unnerving to have a crowd following you. I marched down the hill looking and feeling a fool, with the rifle over my shoulder and an ever-growing army of people jostling at my heels. At the bottom, when you got away from the huts, there was a metalled road and beyond that a miry waste of paddy fields a thousand yards across, not yet ploughed but soggy from the first rains and dotted with coarse grass. The elephant was standing eight yards from the road, his left side towards us. He took not the slightest notice of the crowd's approach. He was tearing up bunches of grass, beating them against his knees to clean them and stuffing them into his mouth.

I had halted on the road. As soon as I saw the elephant I knew with perfect certainty that I ought not to shoot him. It is a serious matter to shoot a working elephant—it is comparable to destroying a huge and costly piece of machinery—and obviously one ought not to do it if it can possibly be avoided. And at that distance, peacefully eating, the elephant looked no more dangerous than a cow. I thought then and I think now that his attack of "must" was already passing off; in which case he would merely wander harmlessly about until the mahout came back and caught him. Moreover, I did not in the least want to shoot him. I decided that I would watch him for a little while to make sure that he did not turn savage again, and then go home.

But at that moment, I glanced round at the crowd that had followed me. It was an immense crowd, two thousand at the least and growing every minute. It blocked the road for a long distance on either side. I looked at the sea of yellow faces above the garish clothes—faces all happy and excited over this bit of fun, all certain that the elephant was going to be shot. They were watching me as they would watch a conjuror about to perform a trick. They did not like me, but with the magical rifle in my hands I was momentarily worth watching. And suddenly I realized that I should have to shoot the elephant after all. The people expected it of me and I had got to do it; I could feel their two thousand wills pressing me forward, irresistibly. And it was at this moment, as I stood there with the rifle in my hands, that I first grasped the hollowness, the futility of the white man's dominion in the East. Here was I, the white man with his gun, standing in front of the unarmed native crowd—seemingly the leading actor of the piece; but in reality I was only an absurd puppet pushed to and fro by the will of those yellow faces behind. I perceived in this moment that when the white man turns tyrant it is his own freedom that he destroys. He becomes a sort of hollow, posing dummy, the conventionalized figure of a sahib. For it is the condition of his rule that he shall spend his life in trying to impress the "natives," and so in every crisis he has got to do what the "natives" expect of him. He wears a mask, and his face grows to fit it. I had got to shoot the elephant. I had committed myself to doing it when I sent for the rifle. A sahib has got to act like a sahib; he has got to appear resolute, to know his own mind and do definite things. To come all that way, rifle in hand, with two thousand people marching at my heels, and then to trail feebly away, having done nothing—no, that was impossible. The crowd would laugh at me. And my whole life, every white man's life in the East, was one long struggle not to be laughed at.

But I did not want to shoot the elephant. I watched him beating his bunch of grass against his knees, with that preoccupied grandmotherly air that elephants have. It seemed to me that it would be murder to shoot him. At that age I was not squeamish about killing animals, but I had never shot an elephant and never wanted to. (Somehow it always seems worse to kill a *large* animal.) Besides, there was the beast's owner to be considered. Alive, the elephant was worth at least a hundred pounds; dead, he would only be worth the value of his tusks, five pounds, possibly. But I had got to act quickly. I turned to some experienced-looking Burmans who had been there when we arrived, and asked them how the elephant had been behaving. They all said the same thing: he took no notice of you if you left him alone, but he might charge if you went too close to him.

It was perfectly clear to me what I ought to do. I ought to walk up to within, say, twenty-five yards of the elephant and test his behavior. If he charged, I could shoot; if he took no notice of me, it would be safe to leave him until the mahout came back. But also I knew that I was going to do no such thing. I was a poor shot with a rifle and the ground was soft mud into which one would sink at every step. If the elephant charged and I missed him, I should have about as much chance as a toad under a steam-roller. But even then I was not thinking particularly of my own skin, only of the watchful yellow faces behind. For at that moment, with the crowd watching me, I was not afraid in the ordinary sense, as I would have been if I had been alone. A white man mustn't be frightened in front of "natives"; and so, in general, he isn't frightened. The sole thought in my mind was that if anything went wrong those two thousand Burmans would see me pursued, caught, trampled on and reduced to a grinning corpse like that Indian up the hill. And if that happened it was quite probable that some of them would laugh. That would never do. There was only one alternative. I shoved the cartridges into the magazine and lay down on the road to get a better aim.

The crowd grew very still, and a deep, low, happy sigh, as of people who see the theatre curtain go up at last, breathed from innumerable throats. They were going to have their bit of fun after all. The rifle was a beautiful German thing with cross-hair sights. I did not then know that in shooting an elephant one would shoot to cut an imaginary bar running from ear-hole to ear-hole. I ought, therefore, as the elephant was sideways on, to have aimed straight at his ear-hole; actually I aimed several inches in front of this, thinking the brain would be further forward.

When I pulled the trigger I did not hear the bang or feel the kick—one never does when a shot goes home—but I heard the devilish roar of glee that went up from the crowd. In that instant, in too short a time, one would have thought, even for the bullet to get there, a mysterious, terrible change came over the elephant. He neither stirred nor fell, but every line of his body had altered. He looked suddenly stricken, shrunken, immensely old, as though the frightful impact of the bullet had paralysed him without knocking him down. At last, after what seemed a long time—it might have been five seconds, I dare say—he sagged flabbily to his knees. His mouth slobbered. An enormous senility seemed to have settled upon him. One could have imagined him thousands of years old. I fired again into the same spot.

At the second shot he did not collapse but climbed with desperate slowness to his feet and stood weakly upright, with legs sagging and head drooping. I fired a third time. That was the shot that did for him. You could see the agony of it jolt his whole body and knock the last remnant of strength from his legs. But in falling he seemed for a moment to rise, for as his hind legs collapsed beneath him he seemed to tower upward like a huge rock toppling, his trunk reaching skywards like a tree. He trumpeted, for the first and only time. And then down he came, his belly towards me, with a crash that seemed to shake the ground even where I lay.

I got up. The Burmans were already racing past me across the mud. It was obvious that the elephant would never rise again, but he was not dead. He was breathing very rhythmically with long rattling gasps, his great mound of a side painfully rising and falling. His mouth was wide open. I could see far down into caverns of pale pink throat. I waited a long time for him to die, but his breathing did not weaken. Finally I fired my two remaining shots into the spot where I thought his heart must be. The thick blood welled out of him like red velvet, but still he did not die. His body did not even jerk when the shots hit him, the tortured breathing continued without a pause. He was dying, very slowly and in great agony, but in some world remote from me where not even a bullet could damage him further. I felt I had got to put an end to that dreadful noise. It seemed dreadful to see the great beast lying there, powerless to move and yet powerless to die, and not even to be able to finish him. I sent back for my small rifle and poured shot after shot into his heart and down his throat. They seemed to make no impression. The tortured gasps continued as steadily as the ticking of a clock.

In the end I could not stand it any longer and went away. I heard later that it took him half an hour to die. Burmans were bringing dahs and baskets even before I left, and I was told they had stripped his body almost to the bones by afternoon.

Afterwards, of course, there were endless discussions about the shooting of the elephant. The owner was furious, but he was only an Indian and could do nothing. Besides, legally I had done the right thing, for a mad elephant has to be killed, like a mad dog, if its owner fails to control it. Among the Europeans opinion was divided. The older men said I was right, the younger men said it was a damn shame to shoot an elephant for killing a coolie, because the elephant was worth more than any damn Coringhee coolie. And afterwards I was very glad that the coolie had been killed; it put me legally in the right and it gave me sufficient pretext for shooting the elephant. I often wondered whether any of the others grasped that I had done it solely to avoid looking a fool.

Questions for "Shooting an Elephant"

1.   Why does Orwell shoot the elephant? How does this incident teach him to despise imperialism?

2.   Orwell twice interrupts the flow of his narrative. Locate these interruptions and consider the purpose they serve. What is the tone of these comments?

3.   Orwell makes a number of comments about the Burmese that, at first glance, seem racist. Cite a few examples and explain the part they play in this essay. Are these remarks countered by other things Orwell says?

4.   What has Orwell gained and lost by his actions?

Flannery O'Connor (1925–1964)

A brief biography of this writer appears on page 244 in Chapter 4, where you will find O'Connor's story "A Good Man Is Hard to Find." The following selection is taken from *Mystery and Manners,* a collection of essays, lectures, and critical articles selected and edited by Sally and Robert Fitzgerald after the author's death. This selection is O'Connor's explication of "A Good Man Is Hard to Find." It is best read as a companion piece to that story, but it illuminates as well the author's ideas about the nature of short fiction.

A Reasonable Use of the Unreasonable

Last fall[1] I received a letter from a student who said she would be "graciously appreciative" if I would tell her "just what enlightenment" I expected her to get from each of my stories. I suspect she had a paper to write. I wrote her back to forget about the enlightenment and just try to enjoy them. I knew that was the most unsatisfactory answer I could have given because, of course, she didn't want to enjoy them, she just wanted to figure them out.

In most English classes the short story has become a kind of literary specimen to be dissected. Every time a story of mine appears in a Freshman anthology, I have a vision of it, with its little organs laid open, like a frog in a bottle.

I realize that a certain amount of this what-is-the-significance has to go on, but I think something has gone wrong in the process when, for so many students, the story becomes simply a problem to be solved, something which you evaporate to get Instant Enlightenment.

A story really isn't any good unless it successfully resists paraphrase, unless it hangs on and expands in the mind. Properly, you analyze to enjoy, but it's equally true that to analyze with any discrimination, you have to have enjoyed already, and I think that the best reason to hear a story read is that it should stimulate that primary enjoyment.

I don't have any pretensions to being an Aeschylus or Sophocles[2] and providing you in this story with a cathartic experience out of your mythic back-

---

[1]I.e., in 1962. These remarks were made by Flannery O'Connor at Hollins College, Virginia, to introduce a reading of her story, "A Good Man Is Hard to Find," on October 14, 1963.
[2]Aeschylus (525–456 B.C.) and Sophocles (496?–406 B.C.): Greek dramatists. O'Connor refers in this paragraph to the elements of tragedy set down by Aristotle in his *Poetics*; for a discussion of these elements, see the introduction to Chapter 5 in this anthology.

ground, though this story I'm going to read certainly calls up a good deal of the South's mythic background, and it should elicit from you a degree of pity and terror, even though its way of being serious is a comic one. I do think, though, that like the Greeks[3] you should know what is going to happen in this story so that any element of suspense in it will be transferred from its surface to its interior.

I would be most happy if you had already read it, happier still if you knew it well, but since experience has taught me to keep my expectations along these lines modest, I'll tell you that this is the story of a family of six which, on its way driving to Florida, gets wiped out by an escaped convict who calls himself the Misfit. The family is made up of the Grandmother and her son, Bailey, and his children, John Wesley and June Star and the baby, and there is also the cat and the children's mother. The cat is named Pitty Sing, and the Grandmother is taking him with them, hidden in a basket.

Now I think it behooves me to try to establish with you the basis on which reason operates in this story. Much of my fiction takes its character from a reasonable use of the unreasonable, though the reasonableness of my use of it may not always be apparent. The assumptions that underlie this use of it, however, are those of the central Christian mysteries. These are assumptions to which a large part of the modern audience takes exception. About this I can only say that there are perhaps other ways than my own in which this story could be read, but none other by which it could have been written. Belief, in my own case anyway, is the engine that makes perception operate.

The heroine of this story, the Grandmother, is in the most significant position life offers the Christian. She is facing death. And to all appearances she, like the rest of us, is not too well prepared for it. She would like to see the event postponed. Indefinitely.

I've talked to a number of teachers who use this story in class and who tell their students that the Grandmother is evil, that in fact, she's a witch, even down to the cat. One of these teachers told me that his students, and particularly his Southern students, resisted this interpretation with a certain bemused vigor, and he didn't understand why. I had to tell him that they resisted it because they all had grandmothers or great-aunts just like her at home, and they knew, from personal experience, that the old lady lacked comprehension but that she had a good heart. The Southerner is usually tolerant of those weaknesses that proceed from innocence, and he knows that a taste for self-preservation can be readily combined with the missionary spirit.

This same teacher was telling his students that morally the Misfit was several cuts above the Grandmother. He had a really sentimental attachment to

---

[3]The audiences in ancient Greece were thoroughly familiar with the plots of the dramas composed by Greek playwrights.

the Misfit. But then a prophet gone wrong is almost always more interesting than your grandmother, and you have to let people take their pleasures where they find them.

It is true that the old lady is a hypocritical old soul; her wits are no match for the Misfit's, nor is her capacity for grace equal to his; yet I think the unprejudiced reader will feel that the Grandmother has a special kind of triumph in this story which instinctively we do not allow to someone altogether bad.

I often ask myself what makes a story work, and what makes it hold up as a story, and I have decided that it is probably some action, some gesture of a character that is unlike any other in the story, one which indicates where the real heart of the story lies. This would have to be an action or a gesture which was both totally right and totally unexpected; it would have to be one that was both in character and beyond character; it would have to suggest both the world and eternity. The action or gesture I'm talking about would have to be on the anagogical level, that is, the level which has to do with the Divine life and our participation in it. It would be a gesture that transcended any neat allegory that might have been intended or any pat moral categories a reader could make. It would be a gesture which somehow made contact with mystery.

There is a point in this story where such a gesture occurs. The Grandmother is at last alone, facing the Misfit. Her head clears for an instant and she realizes, even in her limited way, that she is responsible for the man before her and joined to him by ties of kinship which have their roots deep in the mystery she has been merely prattling about so far. And at this point, she does the right thing, she makes the right gesture.

I find that students are often puzzled by what she says and does here, but I think myself that if I took out this gesture and what she says with it, I would have no story. What was left would not be worth your attention. Our age not only does not have a very sharp eye for the almost imperceptible intrusions of grace, it no longer has much feeling for the nature of the violences which precede and follow them. The devil's greatest wile, Baudelaire[4] has said, is to convince us that he does not exist.

I suppose the reasons for the use of so much violence in modern fiction will differ with each writer who uses it, but in my own stories I have found that violence is strangely capable of returning my characters to reality and preparing them to accept their moment of grace. Their heads are so hard that almost nothing else will do the work. This idea, that reality is something to which we must be returned at considerable cost, is one which is seldom understood by the casual reader, but it is one which is implicit in the Christian view of the world.

---

[4]Charles Baudelaire (1821–1867): French poet and critic.

I don't want to equate the Misfit with the devil. I prefer to think that, however unlikely this may seem, the old lady's gesture, like the mustard-seed, will grow to be a great crow-filled tree in the Misfit's heart, and will be enough of a pain to him there to turn him into the prophet he was meant to become. But that's another story.

This story has been called grotesque, but I prefer to call it literal. A good story is literal in the same sense that a child's drawing is literal. When a child draws, he doesn't intend to distort but to set down exactly what he sees, and as his gaze is direct, he sees the lines that create motion. Now the lines of motion that interest the writer are usually invisible. They are lines of spiritual motion. And in this story you should be on the lookout for such things as the action of grace in the Grandmother's soul, and not for the dead bodies.

We hear many complaints about the prevalence of violence in modern fiction, and it is always assumed that this violence is a bad thing and meant to be an end in itself. With the serious writer, violence is never an end in itself. It is the extreme situation that best reveals what we are essentially, and I believe these are times when writers are more interested in what we are essentially than in the tenor of our daily lives. Violence is a force which can be used for good or evil, and among other things taken by it is the kingdom of heaven. But regardless of what can be taken by it, the man in the violent situation reveals those qualities least dispensable in his personality, those qualities which are all he will have to take into eternity with him; and since the characters in this story are all on the verge of eternity, it is appropriate to think of what they take with them. In any case, I hope that if you consider these points in connection with the story, you will come to see it as something more than an account of a family murdered on the way to Florida.

Questions for "A Reasonable Use of the Unreasonable"

(To be read in conjunction with "A Good Man Is Hard to Find")

1. Do you agree with O'Connor's assessment of the grandmother's character in "A Good Man Is Hard to Find"? Discuss O'Connor's observation that the grandmother's "wits are no match for the Misfit's, nor is her capacity for grace equal to his."

2. In this essay, O'Connor writes that much of her fiction "takes its character from a reasonable use of the unreasonable." What does she mean by this comment? How does "a reasonable use of the unreasonable" help to describe "A Good Man Is Hard to Find"?

3. In a letter to a friend, O'Connor made the following remarks:

> I don't think any genuine novelist is interested in writing about a world of people who are strictly determined. Even if he writes about characters who are mostly unfree, it is the sudden free action, the open possibility, which he knows

is the only thing capable of illuminating the picture and giving it life. So that while predictable, predetermined actions have a comic interest for me, it is the free act, the acceptance of grace particularly, that I always have my eye on as the thing which will make the story work.

How can you apply these ideas to "A Good Man Is Hard to Find"? What are the "predictable, predetermined actions" in this story? How are they comic? What is the "free act"? How does this act "make the story work"?

4.   How does O'Connor's analysis influence your interpretation of "A Good Man Is Hard to Find"? Does she point out elements of the story you missed in the first reading?

Alison Lurie (1929–   )

A native of Chicago, Alison Lurie is a graduate of Radcliffe College and a professor of English at Cornell University. Lurie has published a number of novels, including *Love and Friendship* (1962), *Imaginary Friends* (1967), *Real People* (1969), *The War Between the Tates* (1974), *Only Children* (1979), and *Foreign Affairs* (1984), as well as several books for children.

Best known for her satiric novels, Lurie has a keen eye for the evasions and self-deceptions that characterize so many upper-middle-class lives in America. In her extended essay *The Language of Clothes* (1981), from which the following chapter is taken, Lurie takes a penetrating look at the clothes we wear and what we "say" when we wear them.

Male and Female

A visitor from Mars contemplating a man in a frock coat and top hat and a woman in a crinoline might well have supposed that they belonged to different species.

—James Laver, *The Concise History of Costume and Fashion*

In the past sexual modesty was often proposed as the purpose of dress. The Bible tells us that this was the original reason for wearing clothes: Adam and Eve, once they realized that they were naked, "sewed fig leaves together, and made themselves aprons." Historically, however, shame seems to have played very little part in the development of costume. In ancient Egypt, Crete and Greece the naked body was not considered immodest; slaves and athletes habitually went without clothing, while people of high rank wore garments that were cut and draped so as to show a good deal when in motion.

Some modern writers believe that the deliberate concealment of certain parts of the body originated not as a way of discouraging sexual interest, but as a clever device for arousing it. According to this view, clothes are the physical equivalent of remarks like "I've got a secret"; they are a tease, a come-on. It is certainly true that parts of the human form considered sexually arousing are often covered in such a way as to exaggerate and draw attention to them. People done up in shiny colored wrappings and bows affect us just as a birthday present does: we're curious, turned on; we want to undo the package.

The naked unadorned body, by contrast, is not intrinsically very exciting, especially en masse. Ingres' *Le Bain turc (The Turkish Bath)*, in which twenty plump nudes are crammed into a circular frame that repeats their generous curves, can seem—as Kenneth Clark says—"almost suffocating." Without the large figure in the foreground, he adds, "the whole composition might have made us feel slightly seasick." Too much nakedness in real life can have the same effect. Many visitors to nudist camps report that the sight of all that uncovered flesh brings fatigue and a sense of being slightly unwell. Later, after one gets used to it as the ancients were, it seems merely banal. Even in isolation an unadorned human body is often less exciting than a clothed one, and the most stimulating costumes of all are those which simultaneously conceal and reveal, like a suggestively wrapped gift hinting at delights beneath.

Whether it was the first cause or not, from the earliest times one important function of clothing has been to promote erotic activity: to attract men and women to one another, thus ensuring the survival of the species. If maximum fertility is to be achieved, we must select members of the opposite sex rather than our own to make love to. One basic purpose of costume, therefore, is to distinguish men from women. In some periods this separation is absolute: what is properly worn by a man cannot be worn by a woman, and vice versa. As might be expected, at such times the birth rate is usually high. In other periods, such as our own, many items of clothing are sexually interchangeable, and the birth rate is lower. Even today, however, most garments are recognizably male or female—as anyone who has sorted rummage for a charity sale will recall.

Pink Kittens and Blue Spaceships

Sex-typing in dress begins a birth with the assignment of pale-pink layettes, toys, bedding and furniture to girl babies, and pale-blue ones to boy babies. Pink, in this culture, is associated with sentiment; blue with service. The implication is that the little girl's future concern will be the life of the affections; the boy's, earning a living. As they grow older, light blue becomes a popular color for girls' clothes—after all, women must work as well as weep—but pink is rare on boys: the emotional life is never quite manly.

In early childhood girls' and boys' clothes are often identical in cut and fabric, as if in recognition of the fact that their bodies are much alike. But the T-shirts, pull-on slacks and zip jackets intended for boys are usually made in darker colors (especially forest green, navy, red and brown) and printed with designs involving sports, transportation and cute wild animals. Girls' clothes are made in paler colors (especially pink, yellow and green) and decorated with flowers and cute domestic animals. The suggestion is that the boy will play vigorously and travel over long distances; the girl will stay home and nurture plants and small mammals. Alternatively, these designs may symbolize their wearers: the boy is a cuddly bear or a smiling tiger, the girl a flower or a kitten. There is also a tendency for boys' clothes to be fullest at the shoulders and girls' at the hips, anticipating their adult figures. Boys' and men's garments also emphasize the shoulders with horizontal stripes, epaulets or yokes of contrasting color. Girls' and women's garments emphasize the hips and rear through the strategic placement of gathers and trimmings.

——— Rectangular Men and Rounded Women ———

Even for children dress-up clothing tends to be sex-typed in shape as well as in color and decoration. By adolescence most of what we wear incorporates traditional male or female indicators: among them, for men, the garment that fastens to the right and the classic jacket, shirt and tie; for women the garment that fastens to the left, ruffles and bows, high-heeled shoes and the skirt in all its forms.

Male clothing has always been designed to suggest physical and/or social dominance. Traditionally, the qualities that make a man attractive are size and muscular strength. In the past this preference was practical: most men were farmers, hunters or warriors, and the woman who attached herself to a big, strong man had a better chance of survival. Men's garments therefore tended to enlarge the body through the use of strong colors and bulky materials, and to emphasize angularity with rectangular shapes and sharp points. They suggested or called attention to well-developed leg, shoulder and arm muscles by means of tight hose, trousers and jackets; and they increased the width of shoulders and chest with padding.

The modern sack suit, on the other hand, though often dark and always rectangular in cut, suppresses or conceals all the features that are supposed to constitute male beauty: broad shoulders, slim waist and hips, flat stomach and well-muscled legs. But . . . for a man who lacks these attributes the sack suit is flattering. If it is well cut it can hide a sunken chest or a small pot. And whether a man is athletically built or not, it diverts attention from his physical qualifications and focuses attention on his economic and social status. The sack suit is a middle-class indicator, and in a world in which class membership is a safer guarantee of prosperity than pure brawn, an expensive version may have considerable erotic charm, especially for women who are looking for husbands rather than lovers.

Female costume, during most of modern European history, was designed to suggest successful maternity. It emphasized rounded contours and rich, soft materials, and tended to center interest on the breasts and stomach. Energy, strength and health were regarded as attractive, and they were expressed through bright, glowing colors and full-cut gowns with strong, sweeping curves that often accommodated and flattered the pregnant woman. Such clothes can be seen in many paintings of the Renaissance and Baroque period, and (in a somewhat more refined form) in those of the Rococo.

——— Romantic Frailty ———

In the early nineteenth century, however, a new feminine ideal appeared. Women were redefined as something between children and angels: weak, timid, innocent creatures of sensitive nerves and easily alarmed modesty who could only be truly safe and happy under the protection of some man. Physical slightness and fragility were admired, and what was now called "rude health" was considered coarse and lower-class. To be pale and delicate, to blush and faint readily and lie about on sofas was ladylike; strength and vigor were the characteristics of vulgar, red-cheeked, thick-waisted servants and factory girls. The more useless and helpless a woman looked, the higher her presumed social status, and the more elegant and beautiful she was perceived as being.

Early nineteenth-century fashions were designed to give a look of fragile immaturity. They emphasized weakness of both structure and substance through the use of pale colors and delicate, easily damaged materials. More ominously, these clothes ensured the charming ill-health of their wearers by putting them into thin-soled slippers and short-sleeved, low-necked dresses of semitransparent muslin. When worn in the drafty ballrooms and along the icy, muddy lanes of a British or North American winter, such clothes were almost a guarantee of the feverish colds and sore throats that are so common in the novels of Jane Austen and the Brontës; looking at portraits of the period, it seems no surprise that consumption was the most dreaded disease of the time.

——— Fashionable Debility: The Corset ———

By the 1830s, female fashions offered somewhat more protection from the climate, but they continued to suggest—and to promote—physical frailty. Early-Victorian costume not only made women *look* weak and helpless, it made them weak and helpless. The main agent of this debility, as many writers have pointed out, was the corset, which at the time was thought of not as a mere fashion but as a medical necessity. Ladies' "frames," it was believed, were extremely delicate; their muscles could not hold them up without assistance. Like many such beliefs, this one was self-fulfilling. Well-brought-up little girls, from the best motives, were laced into juvenile versions of the corset as early as three or four. Gradually, but relentlessly, their stays were lengthened, stiffened and tightened. By the time they reached late adolescence they were wearing cages of heavy canvas reinforced with whalebone or steel, and their back muscles had often atrophied to the point where they could not sit or stand for long unsupported. The corset also deformed the internal organs and made it impossible to draw a deep breath. As a result the fashionably dressed lady blushed and fainted easily, suffered from lack of appetite and from digestive complaints, and felt weak and exhausted after any strenuous exertion. When she took off her corset her back soon began to ache; and sometimes she still could not breathe properly because her ribs had been permanently compressed inward.

Over this debilitating foundation garment the Victorian woman wore several layers of shifts and chemises, three or more petticoats, a hoop skirt or crinoline and a long dress that might contain twenty yards of heavy wool or silk and was often also boned in the bodice and trimmed with additional fabric, ribbon and beads. When she left the house she added a heavy woolen shawl and a large bonnet or hat decorated with feathers, flowers, ribbons and veiling. Altogether she might carry from ten to thirty pounds of clothing; a contemporary writer, feeling this to be a bit of a burden, suggested seven pounds as the minimum for a respectable woman. Yet even with all this weight on her back the Victorian lady was not protected from the climate, since fashion (especially evening fashion) often demanded that her neck, shoulders and chest be exposed.

In this costume it was difficult to move about or walk vigorously, and almost impossible to run. But then, ladies did not "walk," since in polite discourse they had no legs—rather they "glided" or "swept" across the floor like carpet sweepers—and they certainly did not run. In an emergency the proper thing to do was to faint, relying on the protection of the nearest gentleman.

Even more important than the medical justification of the corset was its social justification. Women were considered the frailer sex not only physically but morally: their minds and their wills as well as their backs were weak. A lady might be pure and innocent, of course, but this purity and innocence could be preserved only by constant vigilance. Therefore she must not attend a university or follow a profession; she must not travel without a chaperone; she must not visit a man's rooms; and she must not see any play or read any book that might inflame her imagination—even Shakespeare was dangerous except in the expurgated version of Thomas Bowdler. Even thus guarded, the early-Victorian woman was in constant danger of becoming the victim of man's lust and her own weakness. She needed to be at once supported and confined, in a many-layered, heavily reinforced costume that would make undressing a difficult and lengthy process.

Although she was so heavily armored against a frontal assault, the mid-Victorian woman was often readily accessible in another direction, since she had no underpants in the modern sense. She might if she chose wear what were called "drawers"—loose, wide-legged undershorts made in two separate sections, joined only at the waist and otherwise completely open—but these conferred status rather than protection. Though this left the Victorian lady embarrassingly exposed in case of accident, closed underpants were considered immodest because they imitated male garments. Victorian feminists later drew attention to this contradiction: Dr. Mary Walker, for instance, remarked that "If men were really what they profess to be they would not compel women to dress so that the facilities for vice would always be so easy."

These extremes of inconvenience and discomfort, it should be noted, were suffered mainly by ladies, especially those who were well-to-do, since it is a universal rule that when clothes are uncomfortable, high-status clothes will be more uncomfortable. Working woman (except when they were on holiday) wore looser and simpler clothes and much looser corsets, and they carried far less weight of cloth.

——— The Lady as a Luxury Item ———

Why did the early-Victorian woman put up with early-Victorian fashions? Partly, no doubt, because they were admired by men and described everywhere as beautiful, elegant and charming. But also, certainly, because she believed the current propaganda: she thought of the clothes that imprisoned and deformed her as medically necessary and morally respectable. Tight lacing was associated in the popular mind with virtue: a well-dressed woman whose stays were loose, however rich her costume, was probably a loose woman. A girl of relatively modest means, however, if her shoes and gloves were tight enough, her dress properly fragile and her corset laced so that she could scarcely breathe, might hope to be admired. She might even, if lucky, become the petted and indulged and confined wife of a man of means.

In a patriarchal society a helpless, foolish, pretty woman is the ultimate object of Conspicuous Consumption. Rich men chose to purchase and maintain such a woman as a sign of their own economic and sexual power. What she looks like physically is not important; she may be a plump odalisque, a proper Victorian lady, or a twentieth-century Dumb Blonde of the Petty Girl type (now a vanishing species). For maximum status gain, however, such a woman must be of no practical use. She must be unable to type, cook, clean, care for children, manage an estate or keep track of your investments—all these things must be done by paid employees. Ideally, the clothes this woman wears will identify her as a luxury item. The Dumb Blonde is supposed to be in bouncy good health and to have a Florida tan, but her tight satin sheath, spike heels and long, brittle, varnished nails—like the Victorian lady's corset and crinoline—make her prestigious uselessness obvious.

The costumes of the Victorian lady and the expense-account blonde are examples of the principle still in force, that clothes which make a woman's life difficult and handicap her in competition with men are always felt to be sexually attractive. This is true not only of tight, figure-revealing garments, but also of heavy, clumsy fashions such as platform shoes and the trailing skirt. As Thorstein Veblen pointed out over a hundred years ago, "The substantial reason for our tenacious attachment to the skirt is just this: it is expensive and it hampers the wearer at every turn and incapacitates her for all useful exertion." The woman who chooses to wear such clothes announces to everyone that she is willing to be handicapped in life in relation to men; men reward her for this by finding both her and her clothes attractive.

Aesthetic and Reform Dress

In a highly patriarchal period such as the mid-nineteenth century, as James Laver has noted, the costumes of men and women tend to be clearly differentiated, and anyone who adopts the dress of the opposite sex in public is likely to be considered shocking or even disgusting. Mrs. Amelia Bloomer's campaign for the divided skirt in the 1850s was greeted with ridicule and social ostracism. Though she gave her name to a garment, she failed utterly. Thirty years later, when the first partially successful reforms in female clothing appeared, they were not imitations of masculine styles: instead they merely attempted to moderate the most inconvenient and painful aspects of feminine fashion.

The Aesthetic and Reform Dress of the 1880s followed contemporary styles, though dresses were cut looser and had fuller sleeves. To us these clothes look very Victorian; at the time, however, they were considered revolutionary and thought to resemble medieval or Renaissance costume. The Dress Reform Movement was also concerned with what women wore beneath their dresses. A few radicals advised the abandonment of the corset; most, however, merely thought it should be reshaped to provide the "necessary" support without too rigid a constriction of the waist. The introduction of "health underwear" of wool (Jaeger) or cotton (Aertex) gave women more protection from the climate (and from sudden assault). Only a minority, however, adopted reformed dress, and they were mostly middle-class intellectuals, socialists and bohemians—the same sort of people who now go on antinuclear demonstrations, eat health foods and write poetry.

The Superficially Liberated Woman

The more conventional late-Victorian and Edwardian woman, though she was no longer supposed to be childish and frail, was far from liberated by modern standards. Though her appearance was queenly, like most queens of recent years her freedom was hedged round with duties and restrictions. She was often called "divine"—and, as is the custom with goddesses, stood on a pedestal, which is an inconvenient place to stand if you want to do anything other than be worshipped. If you move at all, you are in danger of falling off—of becoming, in the popular phrase of the time, a "fallen woman."

The first wave of feminism, as historians of costume have pointed out, did not liberate most women from the bulky and elaborate clothes of the period. Indeed in many ways the female fashions of the time were more oppressive than those of midcentury. The corset had previously ended at or just below the waist, accommodating the many pregnancies of the early-Victorian woman. Now advances in medical science had decreased infant mortality, and it was no longer necessary or fashionable to have many children. The late-Victorian corset lengthened to midthigh, severely restricting locomotion. Gradually it began to push the chest forward and the hips back, creating the S-bend figure with its low-slung monobosom and protruding monorump. Over the corset were worn a corset cover, a camisole, several petticoats, and dresses with trailing skirts and trains. All these garments were richly trimmed with lace, ruffles, tucks, ribbons and embroidery; they were in constant danger of being rumpled or soiled, often giving a literal meaning to the current euphemism "soiled dove."

The ordinary woman who held a job or emancipated opinions might wear, instead of a lace-trimmed gown, a more plainly cut wool or linen suit (the "tailor-made") with a shirtwaist, tie and straw boater that imitated those of men. But this imitation was superficial. Beneath her clothes her corset was as uncomfortable and confining as ever, and when she lifted her heavy floor-length skirt she showed a froth of delicate petticoats and lacy stockings. The message of this costume was clear: the masculine efficiency or intellectual force were only external; underneath she was still a member of the frailer sex. To wear such clothes, however, did not necessarily mean acceptance of the status quo. Some feminists wore them deliberately in order to confuse or disarm their opponents: indeed, several of the leaders of the Emancipation Movement were famous for their stylishness. This stratagem was also used during the second wave of women's liberation, by Gloria Steinem among others.

The Modern Girl

In the early twentieth century substantial gains in dress reform were achieved. Slowly, women began to liberate themselves from the duty of acting as walking advertisements of their own helplessness and their male relatives' wealth. (The struggle was an uphill one, however, and it is by no means over.) There was also a gradual relaxation of the corset and a rise in the skirt, which cleared the ground by 1905, and by 1912 was above the ankle. Once women could breathe a little more easily and had no trains to trip over they were better able to take part in sports. Some, though to our eyes still absurdly handicapped, joined in professional competition. By the end of World War I women's clothes had become relatively unconfining, but they were still sex-typed, and by no means as comfortable as those of men. Various counterrevolutionary efforts were made—notably, the introduction of the hobble skirt in 1910—but these were generally unsuccessful. As in all transitional periods, however, they provided a useful guide to the political and social views of the women who wore them.

The clothes of the 1920s were thought at the time to represent an extreme of freedom for women, and certainly they were a relief to anyone old enough to have worn the styles of twenty years earlier. For one thing, they drastically reduced the time spent in washing, ironing and mending, and also in simply getting dressed and undressed. The woman who bobbed her waist-length hair, for instance, saved several hours a week that had previously been employed in brushing it out, washing and drying it, braiding it at night and putting it up in a pompadour over pads of wire mesh and false hair every morning.

Twenties' dresses often had little-boy collars or ties, but these were no more than piquant additions to a recognizably feminine costume; they declared that their wearer was charmingly boyish, but not that she was a boy. The fulminations of contemporary critics against mannish women and womanish men seem exaggerated today. In photographs of the twenties men and women do look alike; but this is because they both look more like children, and the difference between the sexes is less pronounced in childhood. Even in her Buster Brown or Peter Pan collar the flapper of the 1920s (like the Gibson Girl of a generation earlier in her mannish shirt and tie) is only male from the waist up. Below it, her skirt, silk stockings and pumps proclaim that basically she is a female.

Wearing the Pants

Reform of the bottom half of women's costume got seriously underway in the 1890s, when the introduction of the bicycle was followed by the introduction of the divided skirt for female bicyclists. Though at first it was called unfeminine and even shocking, the divided skirt was in fact voluminously modest. Eventually it was generally accepted—possibly because no one could mistake it for masculine dress.

Real trousers took much longer to become standard female wear. It was not until the 1920s that women and girls began to wear slacks and even shorts for sports and lounging. The new style was greeted with disapproval and ridicule. Women were told that they looked very ugly in trousers, and that wanting to wear The Pants—in our culture, for centuries, the symbolic badge of male authority—was unnatural and sexually unattractive. Nevertheless the fashion spread, and by the mid-1930s a woman could go on a picnic, play tennis or dig in the garden in clothes that did not handicap her. This freedom, however, was limited to the private and informal side of life. Wearing slacks to the office or to a party was out of the question, and any female who appeared on a formal occasion in a trouser suit was assumed to be a bohemian eccentric and probably a lesbian. Most schools and colleges insisted on skirts for classes and in the library until the 1960s; and even today this custom occasionally survives. At the Frick Collection Library in New York women may not be admitted unless they are wearing skirts; a particularly ancient and unattractive skirt is kept at the desk for the use of readers ignorant of this rule.

The woman who wore slacks or shorts before 1960, too, was only outwardly liberated. Underneath her clothes she was more pinched and squeezed and trussed-up than she had been in the twenties. Her bra hauled her breasts up toward the shoulders and forced them into the currently fashionable shape, often with the help of wires or deceptive padding. The straps of this bra usually cut into the flesh, leaving sore red lines on her shoulders and around her body to match the sore red lines left lower down by her tight elastic girdle. Even slim women wore girdles, since the fashionable figure had almost no hips or derrière, and a bouncy rear end was thought vulgar. There was also no other decent way to hold up the obligatory stockings: unless your skirt was very full, any garter belt would show an embarrassing outline beneath it.

—— To Freedom and Partway Back ——

The fifties and early sixties were the years of the baby boom, togetherness and the feminine mystique; and, as usually happens in patriarchal periods, female and male clothes were sharply distinguished. The New Look Woman and the Man in the Gray Flannel Suit were almost as distinct in silhouette as their grandparents. Nevertheless it was in this period that trousers for women began to edge their way into respectability. At first they took rather peculiar and unbecoming forms. The popular "toreador" or "Capri" pants, for instance, came in odd, glaring colors and ended a tight, awkward six inches above the ankle as if they had shrunk in the wash. They were often worn under maternity or mock-maternity smocks, producing a costume that resembled that of a medieval page. It was accompanied by shoes as narrow and sharply pointed—and no doubt as uncomfortable—as those fashionable in the fourteenth and fifteenth centuries. This outfit was appropriate, since the harassed, untrained middle-class mother of the baby-boom years— unlike her own parents—had no servants, and was reduced to waiting hand and foot on her husband and too many children.

In the late 1960s trousers for women finally became elegant as well as respectable, and underwear vanished or mutated into harmless forms. Even before the second wave of women's liberation got underway, the long struggle for comfort and freedom in female dress seemed to have been won at last. The introduction of panty hose freed women from the ugly and often painful rubber and metal and plastic hardwear they had been using to hold up their stockings. It was again permissible to have curves below the waist as well as above; and millions of girdles went into the trash can, where they were soon joined by millions of padded and wired bras. During the 1970s pants suits and slacks were worn to work, to parties, to the theater, in elegant restaurants and on international planes, by women of all ages. They were usually accompanied by comfortable low-heeled shoes or boots. Fashion editors asserted, and women believed, that the bad old days were over forever.

In the last few years, however, there have been ominous signs of retrenchment, and a counterrevolutionary movement seems to be gaining force. If one is pessimistic it is possible to see the sixties and seventies as merely a period of temporary victory. Indeed, the entire history of female fashion from 1910 to the present can be viewed as a series of more or less successful campaigns to force, flatter or bribe women back into uncomfortable and awkward styles, not only for purposes of Vicarious Ostentation and security of sexual ownership, but also and increasingly in order to handicap them in professional competition with men. The hobble shirt, the girdle, the top-heavy hats of the teens and the forties, the embarrassingly short dresses of the twenties and the sixties, all have aided this war effort. Today its most effective strategic devices are fashionable footwear and the demand for slimness.

The Shoe as a Strategic Weapon

Attempts to limit female mobility by hampering locomotion are ancient and almost universal. The foot-binding of upper-class Chinese girls and the Nigerian custom of loading women's legs with pounds of heavy brass wire are extreme examples, but all over the world similar stratagems have been employed to make sure that once you have caught a women she cannot run away, and even if she stays around she cannot keep up with you. What seems odd is that all these devices have been perceived as beautiful, not only by men but by women. The lotus foot, which seems to us a deformity, was passionately admired in China for centuries, and today most people in Western society see nothing ugly in the severely compressed toes produced by modern footwear. The high-heeled, narrow-toed shoes that for most of this century have been an essential part of woman's costume are considered sexually attractive, partly because they make the legs look longer—an extended leg is the biological sign of sexual availability in several animal species—and because they produce what anthropologists call a "courtship strut." They also make standing for any length of time painful, walking exhausting and running impossible. The halting, tiptoe gait they produce is thought provocative—perhaps because it guarantees that no woman wearing them can outrun a man who is chasing her. Worst of all, if they are worn continually from adolescence on, they deform the muscles of the feet and legs so that it becomes even more painful and difficult to walk in flat soles.

Literally as well as figuratively modern women's shoes are what keeps Samantha from running as fast as Sammy. As anyone who has worn them can testify, it is hard to concentrate on your job when your feet are killing you—especially if you are faint with hunger because you had only half a grapefruit and coffee for breakfast so as to stay a glamorous ten pounds below your natural healthy weight. For a while in the sixties and seventies it was not necessary to be handicapped in this way unless you chose to be. During the last few years, however, women have begun wearing tight high-heeled shoes again, even with pants; and the most fashionable styles are those that, like clogs and ankle-strap sandals, give least support to the feet and make walking most difficult.

Counterrevolution and Ambiguity

There have been other signs recently that all is not well with the independent woman. One is the gradual demotion of the pants suit for both daytime and evening wear. By now it has become a low-status indicator, especially when made of polyester, and is seldom seen in middle-class circumstances. It has been replaced by the "skirted suit" recommended as the proper costume for white-collar success, which must of course be worn with panty hose and heels. Another ominous sign is the narrowing of the skirt to the point where ordinary gestures like sitting on a low sofa or stepping over a puddle become difficult.

Prudence Glynn, a former fashion editor of the London *Times,* was one of the first to point out the internal contradictions of much post-feminist fashion. The platform shoes and clogs that became popular during the seventies, for instance, are usually made on a wide last which does not compress the foot; however, they produce a clumping, awkward gait and are not only hard to manage but dangerous, often leading to serious injury. As Prudence Glynn puts it, "By their height they cater to an instinct in women to be taller and thus of more consequence vis-à-vis men. By their construction, which makes walking extremely difficult, they cater to an instinct to remain vulnerable."

Another popular style of the time, known as the Annie Hall Look after the clothes worn by Diane Keaton in the film of the same name, was ambiguous in a more complex way. Essentially it involved the wearing of actual men's clothing: elegant three-piece suits, vests, shirts, ties and hats in pale colors— beige, off-white, tan and gray—often with a twenties look. Everything was worn very large and loose—collars open, shirts ballooning out, sleeves and trouser legs rolled up. These clothes were accompanied by huge handbags and kooky, childish costume jewelry: ceramic and wood and painted-tin ice cream cones and rainbows and Mickey Mice.

The wearing of men's clothes can mean many different things. In the thirties, sophisticated actresses such as Marlene Dietrich in top hat and tails and elegantly cut suits projected sophistication, power and a dangerous eroticism. The slacks and sweaters of the war period, and the jeans and pants outfits of the sixties and early seventies, were serious gestures toward sexual equality.

The Annie Hall style is a double message. It announces that its wearer is a good sport, a pal: not mysteriously and delicately female, but an easy-going, ready-for-anything tomboy type, almost like one of the guys. She will not demand to be protected from the rain or make a fuss about having to stand up at a football game. She probably enjoys active sports and is good at them (though not annoyingly, competitively good). Besides, you can see from her Snoopy pin that she has a sense of humor and is just a kid at heart.

At the same time, however, these clothes convey an ironic antifeminist message. Because they are worn several sizes too large, they suggest a child dressed up in her daddy's or older brother's things for fun, and imply "I'm only playing; I'm not really big enough to wear a man's pants, or do a man's job." This is a look of helpless cuteness, not one of authority; it invites the man to take charge, even when he is as incompetent himself as the characters played by Woody Allen.

Questions for "Male and Female"

1.   To support and develop her premise that one important function of clothing is to promote erotic activity, Lurie draws on analogy, comparison/ contrast, expert testimony, and so on. Take a few minutes to skim "Male and Female" for specific examples of the different rhetorical methods the author employs.

2.   Do you find her evidence convincing? Why or why not? What additional examples can you offer in support of her premise? Can you think of examples of fashion that would seem to refute this idea?

3.   Use Lurie's analysis to discuss current trends in children's, men's, or women's fashions. What "messages" do these fashions send?

Ted Hughes (1930–   )

Born in Yorkshire, England, and educated at Cambridge University, Ted Hughes was married for several years to the American poet Sylvia Plath, who committed suicide in 1963. Hughes's first volume of verse, *The Hawk in the Rain,* appeared in 1957, followed by numerous collections of poems, several plays, children's books, and essays on poetry.

Hughes has been called one of the most powerful poets writing in English today. Critic Marjorie Perloff observes that "for Hughes, the violence of nature . . . seems to be the essential and universal human condition. His poems are characterized by stark presentation, stark definition. . . ." In the selection that follows, a chapter from *Poetry Is* (1970), Hughes explains how animals and nature imagery came to dominate his poetry.

Capturing Animals

There are all sorts of ways of capturing animals and birds and fish. I spent most of my time, up to the age of fifteen or so, trying out many of these ways and when my enthusiasm began to wane, as it did gradually, I started to write poems.

You might not think that these two interests, capturing animals and writing poems, have much in common. But the more I think back the more sure I am that with me the two interests have been one interest. My pursuit of mice at threshing time when I was a boy, snatching them from under the sheaves as the sheaves were lifted away out of the stack and popping them into my pocket till I had thirty or forty crawling around in the lining of my coat, that and my present pursuit of poems seem to me to be different stages of the same fever. In a way, I suppose, I think of poems as a sort of animal. They have their own life, like animals, by which I mean that they seem quite separate from any person, even from their author, and nothing can be added to them or taken away without maiming and perhaps even killing them. And they have a certain wisdom. They know something special . . . something perhaps which we are very curious to learn. Maybe my concern has been to capture not animals particularly and not poems, but simply things which have a vivid life of their own, outside mine. However all that may be, my interest in animals began when I began. My memory goes back pretty clearly to my third year, and by then I had so many of the toy lead animals you could buy in shops that they went right round our flat-topped fireplace fender, nose to tail, with some over.

I had a gift for modeling and drawing, so when I discovered plasticine my zoo became infinite, and when an aunt bought me a thick green-backed animal book for my fourth birthday I began to draw the glossy photographs. The animals looked good in the photographs, but they looked even better in my drawings and were mine. I can remember very vividly the excitement with which I used to sit staring at my drawings, and it is a similar thing I feel nowadays with poems.

My zoo was not entirely an indoors affair. At that time we lived in a valley in the Pennines in West Yorkshire. My brother, who probably had more to do with this passion of mine than anyone else, was a good bit older than I was, and his one interest in life was creeping about on the hillsides with a rifle. He took me along as a retriever and I had to scramble into all kinds of places collecting magpies and owls and rabbits and weasels and rats and curlews that he shot. He could not shoot enough for me. At the same time I used to be fishing daily in the canal, with the long-handled wire-rimmed curtain mesh sort of net.

All that was only the beginning. When I was about eight, we moved to an industrial town in South Yorkshire. Our cat went upstairs and moped in my bedroom for a week, it hated the place so much, and my brother for the same reason left home and became a gamekeeper. But in many ways that move of ours was the best thing that ever happened to me. I soon discovered a farm in the nearby country that supplied all my needs, and soon later, a private estate, with woods and lakes.

My friends were town boys, sons of colliers and railwaymen, and with them I led one life, but all the time I was leading this other life on my own in the country. I never mixed the two lives up, except once or twice disastrously. I still have some diaries that I kept in those years: they record nothing but my catches.

Finally, as I have said, at about fifteen my life grew more complicated and my attitude to animals changed. I accused myself of disturbing their lives. I began to look at them, you see, from their own point of view.

And about the same time I began to write poems. Not animal poems. It was years before I wrote what you could call an animal poem and several more years before it occurred to me that my writing poems might be partly a continuation of my earlier pursuit. Now I have no doubt. The special kind of excitement, the slightly mesmerized and quite involuntary concentration with which you make out the stirrings of a new poem in your mind, then the outline, the mass and color and clean final form of it, the unique living reality of it in the midst of the general lifelessness, all that is too familiar to mistake. This is hunting and the poem is a new species of creature, a new specimen of the life outside your own.

I have now told you very briefly what I believe to be the origins and growth of my interest in writing poetry. I have simplified everything a great deal, but on the whole that is the story. Some of it may seem a bit obscure to you. How can a poem, for instance, about a walk in the rain, be like an animal? Well, perhaps it cannot look much like a giraffe or an emu or an octopus, or anything you might find in a menagerie. It is better to call it an assembly of living parts moved by a single spirit. The living parts are the words, the images, the rhythms. The spirit is the life which inhabits them when they all work together. It is impossible to say which comes first, parts or spirit. But if any of the parts are dead . . . if any of the words, or images or rhythms do not jump to life as you read them . . . then the creature is going to be maimed and the spirit sickly. So, as a poet, you have to make sure that all those parts over which you have control, the words and rhythms and images, are alive. That is where the difficulties begin. Yet the rules, to begin with, are very simple. Words that live are those which we hear, like "click" or "chuckle," or which we see, like "freckled" or "veined," or which we taste, like "vinegar" or "sugar," or touch, like "prickle" or "oily," or smell, like "tar" or "onion." Words which belong directly to one of the five senses. Or words which act and seem to use their muscles, like "flick" or "balance."

But immediately things become more difficult. "Click" not only gives you a sound, it gives you the notion of a sharp movement . . . such as your tongue makes in saying "click." It also gives you the feel of something light and brittle, like a snapping twig. Heavy things do not click, nor do soft bendable ones. In the same way, tar not only smells strongly. It is sticky to touch, with a particular thick and choking stickiness. Also it moves, when it is soft, like a black snake, and has a beautiful black gloss. So it is with most words. They belong to several of the senses at once, as if each one had eyes, ears and tongue, or ears and fingers and a body to move with. It is this little goblin in a word which is its life and its poetry, and it is this goblin which the poet has to have under control.

Well, you will say, this is hopeless. How do you control all that. When the words are pouring out how can you be sure that you do not have one of these side meanings of the word "feathers" getting all stuck up with one of the side meanings of the word "treacle," a few words later. In bad poetry this is exactly what happens, the words kill each other. Luckily, you do not have to bother about it so long as you do one thing.

That one thing is, imagine what you are writing about. See it and live it. Do not think it up laboriously as if you were working out mental arithmetic. Just look at it, touch it, smell it, listen to it, turn yourself into it. When you do this the words look after themselves, like magic. If you do this you do not have to bother about commas or full-stops or that sort of thing. You do not look at the words either. You keep your eyes, your ears, your nose, your taste, your touch, your whole being on the thing you are turning into words. The minute you flinch, and take your mind off this thing, and begin to look at the words and worry about them . . . then your worry goes into them and they set about killing each other. So you keep going as long as you can, then look back and see what you have written. After a bit of practice, and after telling yourself a few times that you do not care how other people have written about this thing, this is the way you find it; and after telling yourself you are going to use any old word that comes into your head so long as it seems right at the moment of writing it down, you will surprise yourself. You will read back through what you have written and you will get a shock. You will have captured a spirit, a creature.

After all that, I ought to give you some examples and show you some of my own more recently acquired specimens.

An animal I never succeeded in keeping alive is the fox. I was always frustrated: twice by a farmer, who killed cubs I had caught before I could get to them, and once by a poultry keeper who freed my cub while his dog waited. Years after those events I was sitting up late one snowy night in dreary lodgings in London. I had written nothing for a year or so but that night I got the idea I might write something and I wrote in a few minutes the following poem: the first "animal" poem I ever wrote. Here it is—*The Thought-Fox.*

> I imagine this midnight moment's forest:
> Something else is alive
> Beside the clock's loneliness
> And this blank page where my fingers move,
>
> Through the window I see no star:
> Something more near
> Though deeper within darkness
> Is entering the loneliness:
>
> Cold, delicately as the dark snow,
> A fox's nose touches twig, leaf;
> Two eyes serve a movement, that now
> And again now, and now, and now
>
> Sets neat prints into the snow
> Between trees, and warily a lame
> Shadow lags by stump and in hollow
> Of a body that is bold to come
>
> Across clearings, an eye,
> A widening deepening greenness,
> Brilliantly, concentratedly,
> Coming about its own business
>
> Till, with a sudden sharp hot stink of fox
> It enters the dark hole of the head.
> The window is starless still; the clock ticks,
> The page is printed.

This poem does not have anything you could easily call a meaning. It is about a fox, obviously enough, but a fox that is both a fox and not a fox. What sort of a fox is it that can step right into my head where presumably it still sits . . . smiling to itself when the dogs bark. It is both a fox and a spirit. It is a real fox; as I read the poem I see it move, I see it setting its prints, I see its shadow going over the irregular surface of the snow. The words show me all this, bringing it nearer and nearer. It is very real to me. The words have made a body for it and given it somewhere to walk.

If, at the time of writing this poem, I had found livelier words, words that could give me much more vividly its movements, the twitch and craning of its ears, the slight tremor of its hanging tongue and its breath making little clouds, its teeth bared in the cold, the snow-crumbs dropping from its pads as it lifts each one in turn, if I could have got the words for all this, the fox would probably be even more real and alive to me now, than it is as I read the poem. Still, it is there as it is. If I had not caught the real fox there in the words I would never have saved the poem. I would have thrown it into the wastepaper basket as I have thrown so many other hunts that did not get what I was after. As it is, every time I read the poem the fox comes up again out of the darkness and steps into my head. And I suppose that long after I am gone, as long as a copy of the poem exists, every time anyone reads it the fox will get up somewhere out in the darkness and come walking towards them.

So, you see, in some ways my fox is better than an ordinary fox. It will live for ever, it will never suffer from hunger or hounds. I have it with me wherever I go. And I made it. And all through imagining it clearly enough and finding the living words.

Here, in this next poem, is one of my prize catches. I used to be a very keen angler for pike, as I still am when I get the chance, and I did most of my early fishing in a quite small lake, really a large pond. This pond went down to a great depth in one place. Sometimes, on hot days, we would see something like a railway sleeper lying near the surface, and there certainly were huge pike in that pond. I suppose they are even bigger by now. Recently I felt like doing some pike fishing, but in circumstances where there was no chance of it, and over the days, as I remembered the extreme pleasures of that sport, bits of the following poem began to arrive. As you will see, by looking at the place in my memory very hard and very carefully and by using the words that grew naturally out of the pictures and feelings, I captured not just a pike, I captured the whole pond, including the monsters I never even hooked. Here is the poem which I called *Pike.*

> Pike, three inches long, perfect
> Pike in all parts, green tigering the gold.
> Killers from the egg: the malevolent aged grin.
> They dance on the surface among the flies.
>
> Or move, stunned by their own grandeur,
> Over a bed of emerald, silhouette
> Of submarine delicacy and horror.
> A hundred feet long in their world.

In ponds, under the heat-struck lily pads—
Gloom of their stillness:
Logged on last year's black leaves, watching upwards.
Or hung in an amber cavern of weeds.

The jaws' hooked clamp and fangs
Not to be changed at this date;
A life subdued to its instrument;
The gills kneading quietly, and the pectorals.

Three we kept behind glass,
Jungled in weed: three inches, four,
And four and a half: fed fry to them—
Suddenly there were two. Finally one

With a sag belly and the grin it was born with.
And indeed they spare nobody.
Two, six pounds each, over two feet long,
High and dry and dead in the willow-herb—

One jammed past its gills down the other's gullet:
The outside eye stared: as a vice locks—
The same iron in this eye
Though its film shrank in death.

A pond I fished, fifty yards across,
Whose lilies and muscular tench
Had outlasted every visible stone
Of the monastery that planted them—

Stilled legendary depth:
It was as deep as England. It held
Pike too immense to stir, so immense and old
That past nightfall I dared not cast

But silently cast and fished
With the hair frozen on my head
For what might move, for what eye might move.
The still splashes on the dark pond,

Owls hushing the floating woods
Frail on my ear against the dream
Darkness beneath night's darkness had freed,
That rose slowly towards me, watching.

Questions for "Capturing Animals"

1. Why does Hughes feel that his fox is "better than an ordinary fox"?

2. Based on what you've learned about poetry, both from Ted Hughes and from what you've read in Chapter 6, discuss the interaction of sounds, images, and meaning in "The Thought Fox" and "Pike."

Nora Ephron (1941–   )

A native New Yorker, Nora Ephron was educated at Wellesley College. She has worked as a reporter, a freelance writer, a columnist, and an editor for a variety of publications, including the *New York Post, Esquire, Cosmopolitan,* and *New York* magazine. Known for her witty, biting, and often autobiographical prose, Ephron is the author of *Wallflower at the Orgy* (1970); *Crazy Salad: Some Things about Women* (1975); *Scribble, Scribble: Notes on the Media* (1979), a collection of essays; and *Heartburn* (1983), a novel. She is also the co-author of the screenplay for the movie *Silkwood* (1983). In the essay below, Ephron discusses a series of controversial photographs that appeared in the newspapers in the fall of 1975.

The Boston Photographs

"I made all kinds of pictures because I thought it would be a good rescue shot over the ladder . . . never dreamed it would be anything else. . . . I kept having to move around because of the light set. The sky was bright and they were in deep shadow. I was making pictures with a motor drive and he, the fire fighter, was reaching up and, I don't know, everything started falling. I followed the girl down taking pictures. . . . I made three or four frames. I realized what was going on and I completely turned around, because I didn't want to see her hit."

You probably saw the photographs. In most newspapers, there were three of them. The first showed some people on a fire escape—a fireman, a woman and a child. The fireman had a nice strong jaw and looked very brave. The woman was holding the child. Smoke was pouring from the building behind them. A rescue ladder was approaching, just a few feet away, and the fireman had one arm around the woman and one arm reaching out toward the ladder. The second picture showed the fire escape slipping off the building. The child had fallen on the escape and seemed about to slide off the edge. The woman was grasping desperately at the legs of the fireman, who had managed to grab the ladder. The third picture showed the woman and child in midair, falling to the ground. Their arms and legs were outstretched, horribly distended. A potted plant was falling too. The caption said that the woman, Diana Bryant, nineteen, died in the fall. The child landed on the woman's body and lived.

The pictures were taken by Stanley Forman, thirty, of the *Boston Herald American*. He used a motor-driven Nikon F set at 1/250, f 5.6–8. Because of the motor, the camera can click off three frames a second. More than four hundred newspapers in the United States alone carried the photographs; the tear sheets from overseas are still coming in. The *New York Times* ran them on the first page of its second section; a paper in south Georgia gave them nineteen columns; the *Chicago Tribune,* the *Washington Post* and the *Washington Star* filled almost half their front pages, the *Star* under a somewhat redundant headline that read: SENSATIONAL PHOTOS OF RESCUE ATTEMPT THAT FAILED.

The photographs are indeed sensational. They are pictures of death in action, of that split second when luck runs out, and it is impossible to look at them without feeling their extraordinary impact and remembering, in an almost subconscious way, the morbid fantasy of falling, falling off a building, falling to one's death. Beyond that, the pictures are classics, old-fashioned but perfect examples of photojournalism at its most spectacular. They're throwbacks, really, fire pictures, 1930s tabloid shots; at the same time they're technically superb and thoroughly modern—the sequence could not have been taken at all until the development of the motor-driven camera some sixteen years ago.

Most newspaper editors anticipate some reader reaction to photographs like Forman's; even so, the response around the country was enormous, and almost all of it was negative. I have read hundreds of the letters that were printed in letters-to-the-editor sections, and they repeat the same points. "Invading the privacy of death." "Cheap sensationalism." "I thought I was reading the *National Enquirer.*" "Assigning the agony of a human being in terror of imminent death to the status of a side-show act." "A tawdry way to sell newspapers." The *Seattle Times* received sixty letters and calls; its managing editor even got a couple of them at home. A reader wrote the *Philadelphia Inquirer:* "*Jaws* and *Towering Inferno* are playing downtown; don't take business away from people who pay good money to advertise in your own paper." Another reader wrote the *Chicago Sun-Times:* "I shall try to hide my disappointment that Miss Bryant wasn't wearing a skirt when she fell to her death. You could have had some award-winning photographs of her underpants as her skirt billowed over her head, you voyeurs." Several newspaper editors wrote columns defending the pictures: Thomas Keevil of the *Costa Mesa* (California) *Daily Pilot* printed a ballot for readers to vote on whether they would have printed the pictures; Marshall L. Stone of Maine's *Bangor Daily News,* which refused to print the famous assassination picture of the Vietcong prisoner in Saigon, claimed that the Boston pictures showed the dangers of fire escapes and raised questions about slumlords. (The burning building was a five-story brick apartment house on Marlborough Street in the Back Bay section of Boston.)

For the last five years, the *Washington Post* has employed various journalists as ombudsmen, whose job is to monitor the paper on behalf of the public. The *Post's* current ombudsman is Charles Seib, former managing editor of the *Washington Star;* the day the Boston photographs appeared, the paper received over seventy calls in protest. As Seib later wrote in a column about the pictures, it was "the largest reaction to a published item that I have experienced in eight months as the *Post's* ombudsman. . . .

"In the *Post's* newsroom, on the other hand, I found no doubts, no second thoughts . . . the question was not whether they should be printed but how they should be displayed. When I talked to editors . . . they used words like 'interesting' and 'riveting' and 'gripping' to describe them. The pictures told something about life in the ghetto, they said (although the neighborhood where the tragedy occurred is not a ghetto, I am told). They dramatized the need to check on the safety of fire escapes. They dramatically conveyed something that had happened, and that is the business we're in. They were news. . . .

"Was publication of that [third] picture a bow to the same taste for the morbidly sensational that makes gold mines of disaster movies? Most papers will not print the picture of a dead body except in the most unusual circumstances. Does the fact that the final picture was taken a millisecond before the young woman died make a difference? Most papers will not print a picture of a bare female breast. Is that a more inappropriate subject for display than the picture of a human being's last agonized instant of life?" Seib offered no answers to the questions he raised, but he went on to say that although as an editor he would probably have run the pictures, as a reader he was revolted by them.

In conclusion, Seib wrote: "Any editor who decided to print those pictures without giving at least a moment's thought to what purpose they served and what their effect was likely to be on the reader should ask another question: Have I become so preoccupied with manufacturing a product according to professional traditions and standards that I have forgotten about the consumer, the reader?"

It should be clear that the phone calls and letters and Seib's own reaction were occasioned by one factor alone: the death of the woman. Obviously, had she survived the fall, no one would have protested; the pictures would have had a completely different impact. Equally obviously, had the child died as well—or instead—Seib would undoubtedly have received ten times the phone calls he did. In each case, the pictures would have been exactly the same—only the captions, and thus the responses, would have been different.

But the questions Seib raises are worth discussing—though not exactly for the reasons he mentions. For it may be that the real lesson of the Boston photographs is not the danger that editors will be forgetful of reader reaction, but that they will continue to censor pictures of death precisely because of that reaction. The protests Seib fielded were really a variation on an old theme—and we saw plenty of it during the Nixon-Agnew years—the "Why doesn't the press print the good news?" argument. In this case, of course, the objections were all dressed up and cleverly disguised as righteous indignation about the privacy of death. This is a form of puritanism that is often justifiable; just as often it is merely puritanical.

Seib takes it for granted that the widespread though fairly recent newspaper policy against printing pictures of dead bodies is a sound one; I don't know that it makes any sense at all. I recognize that printing pictures of

Stanley J. Forman, Pulitzer Prize, 1976. (*The photographs were not originally published with the Ephron essay.*)

corpses raises all sorts of problems about taste and titillation and sensationalism; the fact is, however, that people die. Death happens to be one of life's main events. And it is irresponsible—and more than that, inaccurate—for newspapers to fail to show it, or to show it only when an astonishing set of photos comes in over the Associated Press wire. Most papers covering fatal automobile accidents will print pictures of mangled cars. But the significance of fatal automobile accidents is not that a great deal of steel is twisted but that people die. Why not show it? That's what accidents are about. Throughout the Vietnam war, editors were reluctant to print atrocity pictures. Why *not* print them? That's what that war was about. Murder victims are almost never photographed; they are granted their privacy. But their relatives are relentlessly pictured on their way in and out of hospitals and morgues and funerals.

I'm not advocating that newspapers print these things in order to teach their readers a lesson. The *Post* editors justified their printing of the Boston pictures with several arguments in that direction; every one of them is irrelevant. The pictures don't show anything about slum life; the incident could have happened anywhere, and it did. It is extremely unlikely that anyone who saw them rushed out and had his fire escape strengthened. And the pictures were not news—at least they were not national news. It is not news in Washington, or New York, or Los Angeles that a woman was killed in a Boston fire. The only newsworthy thing about the pictures is that they were taken. They deserve to be printed because they are great pictures, breathtaking pictures of something that happened. That they disturb readers is exactly as it should be: that's why photojournalism is often more powerful than written journalism.

Questions for "The Boston Photographs"

1. Ephron begins her essay with a direct quotation. What purpose does this strategy serve?

2. Look carefully at Ephron's description of the photographs in the fourth paragraph: How does she indicate her opinion of these pictures?

3. Discuss the various arguments for and against the publication of the Boston photographs. How does Ephron refute these arguments? How is her argument different from the others? What is her thesis statement? How does she build up to this thesis?

4. Would you have published these pictures? Why or why not?

Stephen Jay Gould (1941–   )

Stephen Jay Gould was born in New York City, received his Ph.D. from Columbia University, and trained as a paleontologist in the study of fossils. Gould is a professor of geology at Harvard University and the award-winning author of numerous books on natural history. His ability to explain difficult scientific theories in a style that is lucid, entertaining, and informative has made him one of our most popular science writers.

Several of Gould's books are collections of essays originally written for a monthly column in *Natural History* magazine. In *The Panda's Thumb* (1983), the title article of which is reprinted here, Gould states his goals in writing these essays: "I said to myself in the beginning that I would depart from a long tradition of popular writing in natural history. I would not tell fascinating tales of nature for their own sake. I would tie any particular story to a general principle of evolutionary theory."

Among Gould's books are *Ever Since Darwin* (1977), *Ontogeny and Phylogeny* (1977), *A View of Life* (1981), *The Mismeasure of Man* (1981), *Hen's Teeth and Horse's Toes* (1983), and *An Urchin in the Storm* (1987).

The Panda's Thumb

Few heroes lower their sights in the prime of their lives; triumph leads inexorably on, often to destruction. Alexander wept because he had no new worlds to conquer; Napoleon, overextended, sealed his doom in the depth of a Russian winter. But Charles Darwin did not follow the *Origin of Species* (1859) with a general defense of natural selection or with its evident extension to human evolution (he waited until 1871 to publish *The Descent of Man*). Instead, he wrote his most obscure work, a book entitled: *On the Various Contrivances by Which British and Foreign Orchids Are Fertilized by Insects* (1862).

Darwin's many excursions into the minutiae of natural history—he wrote a taxonomy of barnacles, a book on climbing plants, and a treatise on the formation of vegetable mold by earthworms—won him an undeserved reputation as an old-fashioned, somewhat doddering describer of curious plants and animals, a man who had one lucky insight at the right time. A rash of Darwinian scholarship has laid this myth firmly to rest during the past twenty years. Before then, one prominent scholar spoke for many ill-informed colleagues when he judged Darwin as a "poor joiner of ideas . . . a man who does not belong with the great thinkers."

In fact, each of Darwin's books played its part in the grand and coherent scheme of his life's work—demonstrating the fact of evolution and defending natural selection as its primary mechanism. Darwin did not study orchids solely for their own sake. Michael Ghiselin, a California biologist who finally took the trouble to read all of Darwin's books (see his *Triumph of the Darwinian Method*), has correctly identified the treatise on orchids as an important episode in Darwin's campaign for evolution.

Darwin begins his orchid book with an important evolutionary premise: continued self-fertilization is a poor strategy for long-term survival, since offspring carry only the genes of their single parent, and populations do not maintain enough variation for evolutionary flexibility in the face of environmental change. Thus, plants bearing flowers with both male and female parts usually evolve mechanisms to ensure cross-pollination. Orchids have formed an alliance with insects. They have evolved an astonishing variety of "contrivances" to attract insects, guarantee that sticky pollen adheres to their visitor, and ensure that the attached pollen comes in contact with female parts of the next orchid visited by the insect.

Darwin's book is a compendium of these contrivances, the botanical equivalent of a bestiary. And, like the medieval bestiaries, it is designed to instruct. The message is paradoxical but profound. Orchids manufacture their intricate devices from the common components of ordinary flowers, parts usually fitted for very different functions. If God had designed a beautiful machine to reflect his wisdom and power, surely he would not have used a collection of parts generally fashioned for other purposes. Orchids were not made by an ideal engineer; they are jury-rigged from a limited set of available components. Thus, they must have evolved from ordinary flowers.

Thus, the paradox, and the common theme of this trilogy of essays: Our textbooks like to illustrate evolution with examples of optimal design—nearly perfect mimicry of a dead leaf by a butterfly or of a poisonous species by a palatable relative. But ideal design is a lousy argument for evolution, for it mimics the postulated action of an omnipotent creator. Odd arrangements and funny solutions are the proof of evolution—paths that a sensible God would never tread but that a natural process, constrained by history, follows perforce. No one understood this better than Darwin. Ernst Mayr has shown how Darwin, in defending evolution, consistently turned to organic parts and geographic distributions that make the least sense. Which brings me to the giant panda and its "thumb."

Giant pandas are peculiar bears, members of the order Carnivora. Conventional bears are the most omnivorous representatives of their order, but pandas have restricted this catholicity of taste in the other direction—they belie the name of their order by subsisting almost entirely on bamboo. They live in dense forests of bamboo at high elevations in the mountains of western China. There they sit, largely unthreatened by predators, munching bamboo ten to twelve hours each day.

As a childhood fan of Andy Panda, and former owner of a stuffed toy won by some fluke when all the milk bottles actually tumbled at the county fair, I was delighted when the first fruits of our thaw with China went beyond ping pong to the shipment of two pandas to the Washington zoo. I went and watched in appropriate awe. They yawned, stretched, and ambled a bit, but they spent nearly all their time feeding on their beloved bamboo. They sat upright and manipulated the stalks with their forepaws, shedding the leaves and consuming only the shoots.

I was amazed by their dexterity and wondered how the scion of a stock adapted for running could use its hands so adroitly. They held the stalks of bamboo in their paws and stripped off the leaves by passing the stalks between an apparently flexible thumb and the remaining fingers. This puzzled me. I had learned that a dexterous, opposable thumb stood among the hallmarks of human success. We had maintained, even exaggerated, this important flexibility of our primate forebears, while most mammals had sacrificed it in specializing their digits. Carnivores run, stab, and scratch. My cat may manipulate me psychologically, but he'll never type or play the piano.

So I counted the panda's other digits and received an even greater surprise: there were five, not four. Was the "thumb" a separately evolved sixth finger? Fortunately, the giant panda has its bible, a monograph by D. Dwight Davis, late curator of vertebrate anatomy at Chicago's Field Museum of Natural History. It is probably the greatest work of modern evolutionary comparative anatomy, and it contains more than anyone would ever want to know about pandas. Davis had the answer, of course.

The panda's "thumb" is not, anatomically, a finger at all. It is constructed from a bone called the radial sesamoid, normally a small component of the wrist. In pandas, the radial sesamoid is greatly enlarged and elongated until it almost equals the metapodial bones of the true digits in length. The radial sesamoid underlies a pad on the panda's forepaw; the five digits form the framework of another pad, the palmar. A shallow furrow separates the two pads and serves as a channelway for bamboo stalks.

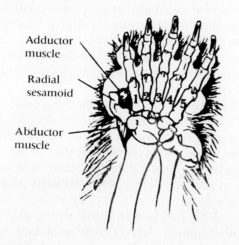

Adductor
muscle

Radial
sesamoid

Abductor
muscle

D. L. CRAMER

The panda's thumb comes equipped not only with a bone to give it strength but also with muscles to sustain its agility. These muscles, like the radial sesamoid bone itself, did not arise *de novo*. Like the parts of Darwin's orchids, they are familiar bits of anatomy remodeled for a new function. The abductor of the radial sesamoid (the muscle that pulls it away from the true digits) bears the formidable name *abductor pollicis longus* ("the long abductor of the thumb"—*pollicis* is the genitive of *pollex*, Latin for "thumb"). Its name is a giveaway. In other carnivores, this muscle attaches to the first digit, or true thumb. Two shorter muscles run between the radial sesamoid and the pollex. They pull the sesamoid "thumb" towards the true digits.

Does the anatomy of other carnivores give us any clue to the origin of this odd arrangement in pandas? Davis points out that ordinary bears and raccoons, the closest relatives of giant pandas, far surpass all other carnivores in using their forelegs for manipulating objects in feeding. Pardon the backward metaphor, but pandas, thanks to their ancestry, began with a leg up for evolving greater dexterity in feeding. Moreover, ordinary bears already have a slightly enlarged radial sesamoid.

In most carnivores, the same muscles that move the radial sesamoid in pandas attach exclusively to the base of the pollex, or true thumb. But in ordinary bears, the long abductor muscle ends in two tendons: one inserts into the base of the thumb as in most carnivores, but the other attaches to the radial sesamoid. The two shorter muscles also attach, in part, to the radial sesamoid in bears. "Thus," Davis concludes, "the musculature for operating this remarkable new mechanism—functionally a new digit—required no intrinsic change from conditions already present in the panda's closest relatives, the bears. Furthermore, it appears that the whole sequence of events in the musculature follows automatically from simple hypertrophy of the sesamoid bone."

The sesamoid thumb of pandas is a complex structure formed by marked enlargement of a bone and an extensive rearrangement of musculature. Yet Davis argues that the entire apparatus arose as a mechanical response to growth of the radial sesamoid itself. Muscles shifted because the enlarged bone blocked them short of their original sites. Moreover, Davis postulates that the enlarged radial sesamoid may have been fashioned by a simple genetic change, perhaps a single mutation affecting the timing and rate of growth.

In a panda's foot, the counterpart of the radial sesamoid, called the tibial sesamoid, is also enlarged, although not so much as the radial sesamoid. Yet the tibial sesamoid supports no new digit, and its increased size confers no advantage, so far as we know. Davis argues that the coordinated increase of both bones, in response to natural selection upon one alone, probably reflects a simple kind of genetic change. Repeated parts of the body are not fashioned by the action of individual genes—there is no gene "for" your thumb, another for your big toe, or a third for your pinky. Repeated parts are coordinated in development; selection for a change in one element causes a corresponding modification in others. It may be genetically more complex to enlarge a thumb and *not* to modify a big toe, than to increase both together. (In the first case, a general coordination must be broken, the thumb favored separately, and correlated increase of related structures suppressed. In the second, a single gene may increase the rate of growth in a field regulating the development of corresponding digits.)

The panda's thumb provides an elegant zoological counterpart to Darwin's orchids. An engineer's best solution is debarred by history. The panda's true thumb is committed to another role, too specialized for a different function to become an opposable, manipulating digit. So the panda must use parts on hand and settle for an enlarged wrist bone and a somewhat clumsy, but quite workable, solution. The sesamoid thumb wins no prize in an engineer's derby. It is, to use Michael Ghiselin's phrase, a contraption, not a lovely contrivance. But it does its job and excites our imagination all the more because it builds on such improbable foundations.

Darwin's orchid book is filled with similar illustrations. The marsh Epipactus, for example, uses its labellum—an enlarged petal—as a trap. The labellum is divided into two parts. One, near the flower's base, forms a large cup filled with nectar—the object of an insect's visit. The other, near the flower's edge, forms a sort of landing stage. An insect alighting on this runway depresses it and thus gains entrance to the nectar cup beyond. It enters the cup, but the runway is so elastic that it instantly springs up, trapping the insect within the nectar cup. The insect must then back out through the only available exit—a path that forces it to brush against the pollen masses. A remarkable machine but all developed from a conventional petal, a part readily available in an orchid's ancestor.

Darwin then shows how the same labellum in other orchids evolves into a series of ingenious devices to ensure cross-fertilization. It may develop a complex fold that forces an insect to detour its proboscis around and past the

Marsh, Epipactis, lower sepals removed

a. Runway of labellum depressed after insect lands

D. L. CRAMER

b. Runway of labellum raised after insect crawls into cup
below

D. L. CRAMER

pollen masses in order to reach nectar. It may contain deep channels or guiding ridges that lead insects both to nectar and pollen. The channels sometimes form a tunnel, producing a tubular flower. All these adaptations have been built from a part that began as a conventional petal in some ancestral form. Yet nature can do so much with so little that it displays, in Darwin's words, "a prodigality of resources for gaining the very same end, namely, the fertilization of one flower by pollen from another plant."

Darwin's metaphor for organic form reflects his sense of wonder that evolution can fashion such a world of diversity and adequate design with such limited raw material:

> Although an organ may not have been originally formed for some special purpose, if it now serves for this end we are justified in saying that it is specially contrived for it. On the same principle, if a man were to make a machine for some special purpose, but were to use old wheels, springs, and pulleys, only slightly altered, the whole machine, with all its parts, might be said to be specially contrived for that purpose. Thus throughout nature almost every part of each living being has probably served, in a slightly modified condition, for diverse purposes, and has acted in the living machinery of many ancient and distinct specific forms.

We may not be flattered by the metaphor of refurbished wheels and pulleys, but consider how well we work. Nature is, in biologist François Jacob's words, an excellent tinkerer, not a divine artificer. And who shall sit in judgment between these exemplary skills?

Questions for "The Panda's Thumb"

1. What strategies does Gould employ to demonstrate that Darwin did not study orchids solely for their own sake?

2. In what ways does the panda's thumb provide "an elegant zoological counterpart to Darwin's orchids"?

3. Gould's columns and books on natural history have been remarkably popular with scientists and lay readers alike. His ability to explain difficult concepts is surely one reason for his success. Describe the style and tone of "The Panda's Thumb": What other characteristics of Gould's writing may also contribute to his success?

Sandra Blakeslee (1943–   )

Born in Flushing, New York, and raised in the metropolitan area, Sandra Blakeslee was graduated from the University of California at Berkeley with a degree in political science. While a member of the Peace Corps, Blakeslee lived on the island of Borneo with a tribe of headhunters and spent a year and a half in Cameroon, West Africa, where both of her children were born. Over the years, notes Blakeslee, "I have been exposed to folklore on four continents."

For twenty years, Blakeslee has been a regular contributor to the science department of *The New York Times*, for which she wrote the following article in 1986. She now lives in California and is currently co-authoring a book, tentatively entitled *Second Chances*, which explores the long-range effects of divorce on children.

Folklore Mirrors Life's Key Themes

Most people find contemporary superstitions and popular beliefs quaint, and sometimes amusing. In Illinois, for example, driving around the house in low gear is said to cure a family member's illness. In North Carolina, if the first bird seen on New Year's morning is flying high there will be good health during the year. But to professional folklorists, these beliefs are no less than a window into the psyche and a revelation of national character.

"Folklore is not a matter of running down little wart cures," said Alan Dundes, who teaches the subject at the University of California, Berkeley. "It is a serious subject that deals with the essence of life."

So powerful are the insights gained through the examination of folklore that scholars at the University of California at Los Angeles are compiling an encyclopedia of American superstitions and popular beliefs. Nearly one million entries, written on note cards, are being categorized and cross-referenced.

"Folk beliefs and superstitions are found among people all over the world and apparently have always been a part of man's intellectual and spiritual legacy, if not to say his residual thought and mental baggage," said Dr. Wayland Hand, professor emeritus of folklore and Germanic languages at U.C.L.A. "Even with the advance of learning and the rise of education in most cultures, these ancient mental heirlooms persist and even flourish. The encyclopedia project thus documents an important aspect of human thought and activity."

Although scholars distinguish among ballads, legends, myths, jokes, superstitions and popular beliefs, these folklore genres overlap and are studied as symbolic manifestations of certain central themes—birth, death and life.

As such, scholars say, folklore in its many forms provides a socially acceptable way for people to deal openly with anxiety, risk, danger—frightening things that are not within their control. It involves the subjects people worry about, which in the United States today might include politics, racism, religion and sex.

According to Roger Abrahams, a professor of folklore at the University of Pennsylvania, folklore deals with central truths, such as the distinction between clean and dirty, pure and impure. "People are protecting themselves as a group and as individuals from malevolent forces," he explained. "In some societies it is witches. For Americans, it is germs." As evidence of this, he noted that a third of the shelf space in most American supermarkets is devoted to products that deal with "excrescences of the body."

Such truths, folklorists say, are immutable; only the details change. Indeed, a quarter of the American popular beliefs being assembled at U.C.L.A. were traced to considerably older, European roots.

"I did not expect to find so much of the old stuff turn up in modern collections," Dr. Hand said. "It's like finding new wine in old bottles." Among the vintages, he noted that entering the door with the right foot first, a practice followed by many modern-day Californians, was popular among Germans in the 1700's. Similarly, hundreds of years ago, one would walk, instead of drive, around the house to cure the illness of a relative, he said.

Contemporary events have also become the nuclei of folklore, Dr. Abrahams said. "We have a need to ratify one another's existence by having things to talk about that are of a risky or thrilling sort." Thus, after the hijacking of Trans World Airlines Flight 847 after takeoff from Athens, innumerable people claimed to know someone who was supposed to have been on the next flight out of the airport or who had just missed boarding Flight 847 itself. "This is the equivalent of sitting around a campfire and making a circle against the night," Dr. Abrahams said. "It's ancient stuff in modern guise."

To the experts, then, America today is awash in folklore. Headlines and news stories about killer bees, tainted cheese, poisoned watermelons, cancer, nuclear war, robots, computers and street crime—all generate folklore. Office photocopying machines circulate it in the form of cartoons and jokes that are shared by office workers. Shaggy dog stories are modern folk legends.

Changing patters of ethnicity, religion, occupation, class and even migration have produced new genres of folklore in the United States—urban folklore, for example. These are expressed as "urban legends," stories about kidnappings from shopping malls, alligators in the sewers, pets that are put into microwave ovens to dry and end up exploding, or grandmothers who die in the back seat of the family car while the family is on vacation.

There is also now a kind of corporate folklore—none of it true, most of it reflecting our lack of trust in corporations: tales of Devil worship at the Procter & Gamble Company and a tale, currently making the rounds in Detroit, of poisonous snake eggs found in the sleeves of clothes manufactured in Taiwan. "In terms of detail, these are purely American phenomena, but the attitudes they draw on are as medieval as you can get," said Dr. Abrahams, referring to the belief in Satan and the fear of competition—military and economic—from other countries and city states.

Medicine has become the subject of many new entries to American folklore, in part because modern medicine is rife with uncertainty. "So there is a lot of counteractive medicine around," said Frances Tally, an archivist of the U.C.L.A. collection. In short, what modern medicine cannot cure, modern folklore can: for cystitis, there is a peeled onion in the sock and for high blood pressure a dose of garlic. Experts point out that, as in the case of garlic, which has been found useful in treating hypertension, many of these folk remedies contain a kernel of truth.

According to Dr. Tally, American folklore does not exhibit significant regional differences. In Pennsylvania, children are told that babies are found under rocks in the forest, while in Arizona the story is that babies are found under desert stones, Dr. Tally said. The differences in detail are born largely of geography and the types of animals, plants and weather characteristic of an area.

The basic stories, however, are the same. "I am firmly convinced that people all over the world think alike," Dr. Tally said. "And they have been thinking the same things for thousands of years."

In contrast to the almost structureless folk tale, many superstitions follow the formula: if A then B with an optional C, Dr. Dundes said. For example: If you break a mirror, then you will have seven years' bad luck, unless you throw the broken pieces into a moving stream. Or, if you spill salt, then you will have bad luck, unless you throw some over your left shoulder.

The meaning of these superstitions has often been lost to the conscious mind, Dr. Dundes said. "But," he added, "behavior doesn't exist without meaning. People would not practice customs unless they meant something to the psyche."

Thus an American bride still throws her bouquet because she is considered deflowered. Whoever catches the bouquet is supposedly endowed with sympathetic magic and will be the next bride.

Many societies share the same superstitions. The evil eye, for one, is found in Indo-European and Semitic cultures. Where people believe in the evil eye, Dr. Dundes said, one never says a child is pretty for fear that it will get sick, nor does one talk about a job application in case such talk jinxes the chances of employment. People who come from evil-eye cultures will never praise the cooking or hospitality enjoyed at the home of a son-in-law or daughter-in-law—again, fearing that praise will bring misfortune.

"The strength of such beliefs is that people can live and die by them," Dr. Dundes said. "People are scared to death of violating their belief structure." He noted, for example, that in the United States, doctors and family members often wonder whether to tell terminally ill people that they are going to die.

"Or would the telling somehow dictate that death, as an expression of the evil eye?" Dr. Dundes said.

The way in which a superstition is contrived, experts say, reveals a culture's fundamental traits. Fatalistic societies, such as those in Asia and the Middle East, do not have the "optional C" escape clause in their superstitions, Dr. Dundes said. If A happens, B follows and there is no way out. Such societies, he said, tend to be oriented to the past and use divination techniques to find out why things happened. Meanwhile, folklore in agrarian societies, such as medieval Europe, tends to deal with harvest and calendar cycles.

In American folklore, stories that idealize strangers, such as tales of the Lone Ranger, reflect our fixation with the unknown—the frontier. (The current manifestation of this is a spate of movies on extraterrestrial themes.) For another, our concern with signs and portents of what is to come—including our obsession with polling and survey research—reflects an orientation toward the future. Finally, our reinterpretation of such things as Halloween, which in Europe honors the dead but in the United States celebrates childhood, points to a national adoration of youth.

Americans are also anxious about the forces of nature and science's ability to control those forces. That is why Bigfoot, UFO's, astrology and supernatural phenomena will never die in this country, scholars say. "It doesn't matter that Bigfoot doesn't exist," Dr. Dundes said. "Its role in our culture is to outsmart science. People need to believe in it."

In a sense, then, Dr. Abrahams said, American folklore highlights not the American dream but the "American dread." "We have a need to tell one another how dangerous modern life has gotten," he said. "And we need to seek out things that are threatening to us. We worry most that we won't be where something is happening."

Questions for "Folklore Mirrors Life's Key Themes"

1.   Does this article, written for a newspaper, differ in style or tone from some of the other essays in this chapter? How?

2.   What is the author's thesis, and what types of evidence does the author use to support this thesis?

3.   What contemporary legends, like stories of alligators living in sewers, have you heard lately? What modern superstitions and beliefs can you add to the examples in this article? How might you explain them?

Alice Walker (1944–   )

Born in Eatonton, Georgia, Alice Walker was one of eight children. When she was eight years old, one of her brothers accidentally shot her in the face with a BB gun, leaving her blind in one eye. Walker received her B.A. from Sarah Lawrence College and has taught literature and Afro-American studies at Wellesley College, the University of Massachusetts, the University of California at Berkeley, and Brandeis University.

Winner of the Pulitzer Prize and the American Book Award for *The Color Purple* (1982), Walker has published three volumes of poetry, a book on the poet Langston Hughes, and several works of fiction, including *In Love Trouble* (1967), *The Third Life of Grange Copeland* (1970), *You Can't Keep a Good Woman Down* (1971), and *Meridian* (1976). Walker's central characters are almost invariably black women, and themes of racism and sexism dominate her work; yet her writing manages to transcend the boundaries of culture, class, and gender. The following essay, first published in 1974, is included in *In Search of Our Mothers' Gardens* (1983), a collection of prose that explores the traditions of black women and the issues of feminism.

In Search of Our Mothers' Gardens

I described her own nature and temperament. Told how they needed a larger life for their expression. . . . I pointed out that in lieu of proper channels, her emotions had overflowed into paths that dissipated them. I talked, beautifully I thought, about an art that would be born, an art that would open the way for women the likes of her. I asked her to hope, and build up an inner life against the coming of that day. . . . I sang, with a strange quiver in my voice, a promise song.

—Jean Toomer, "Avey,"
CANE

The poet speaking to a prostitute who falls asleep while he's talking—

When the poet Jean Toomer walked through the South in the early twenties, he discovered a curious thing: black women whose spirituality was so intense, so deep, so *unconscious*, that they were themselves unaware of the richness they held. They stumbled blindly through their lives: creatures so abused and mutilated in body, so dimmed and confused by pain, that they considered themselves unworthy even of hope. In the selfless abstractions their bodies became to the men who used them, they became more than "sexual objects," more even than mere women: they became "Saints." Instead of being perceived as whole persons, their bodies became shrines: what was thought to be their minds became temples suitable for worship. These crazy Saints stared out at the world, wildly, like lunatics—or quietly, like suicides; and the "God" that was in their gaze was as mute as a great stone.

Who were these Saints? These crazy, loony, pitiful women?

Some of them, without a doubt, were our mothers and grandmothers.

In the still heat of the post-Reconstruction South, this is how they seemed to Jean Toomer: exquisite butterflies trapped in an evil honey, toiling away their lives in an era, a century, that did not acknowledge them, except as "the *mule* of the world." They dreamed dreams that no one knew—not even themselves, in any coherent fashion—and saw visions no one could understand. They wandered or sat about the countryside crooning lullabies to ghosts, and drawing the mother of Christ in charcoal on courthouse walls.

They forced their minds to desert their bodies and their striving spirits sought to rise, like frail whirlwinds from the hard red clay. And when those frail whirlwinds fell, in scattered particles, upon the ground, no one mourned. Instead, men lit candles to celebrate the emptiness that remained, as people do who enter a beautiful but vacant space to resurrect a God.

Our mothers and grandmothers, some of them: moving to music not yet written. And they waited.

They waited for a day when the unknown thing that was in them would be made known; but guessed, somehow in their darkness, that on the day of their revelation they would be long dead. Therefore to Toomer they walked, and even ran, in slow motion. For they were going nowhere immediate, and the future was not yet within their grasp. And men took our mothers and grandmothers, "but got no pleasure from it." So complex was their passion and their calm.

To Toomer, they lay vacant and fallow as autumn fields, with harvest time never in sight: and he saw them enter loveless marriages, without joy; and become prostitutes, without resistance; and become mothers of children, without fulfillment.

For these grandmothers and mothers of ours were not Saints, but Artists; driven to a numb and bleeding madness by the springs of creativity in them for which there was no release. They were Creators, who lived lives of spiritual waste, because they were so rich in spirituality—which is the basis of Art—that the strain of enduring their unused and unwanted talent drove them insane. Throwing away this spirituality was their pathetic attempt to lighten the soul to a weight their work-worn, sexually abused bodies could bear.

What did it mean for a black woman to be an artist in our grandmothers' time? In our great-grandmothers' day? It is a question with an answer cruel enough to stop the blood.

Did you have a genius of a great-great-grandmother who died under some ignorant and depraved white overseer's lash? Or was she required to bake biscuits for a lazy backwater tramp, when she cried out in her soul to paint watercolors of sunsets, or the rain falling on the green and peaceful pasture-lands? Or was her body broken and forced to bear children (who were more often than not sold away from her)—eight, ten, fifteen, twenty children—when her one joy was the thought of modeling heroic figures of rebellion, in stone or clay?

How was the creativity of the black woman kept alive, year after year and century after century, when for most of the years black people have been in America, it was a punishable crime for a black person to read or write? And the freedom to paint, to sculpt, to expand the mind with action did not exist. Consider, if you can bear to imagine it, what might have been the result if singing, too, had been forbidden by law. Listen to the voices of Bessie Smith, Billie Holiday, Nina Simone, Roberta Flack, and Aretha Franklin, among others, and imagine those voices muzzled for life. Then you may begin to comprehend the lives of our "crazy," "Sainted" mothers and grandmothers. The agony of the lives of women who might have been Poets, Novelists, Essayists, and Short-Story Writers (over a period of centuries), who died with their real gifts stifled within them.

And, if this were the end of the story, we would have cause to cry out in my paraphrase of Okot p'Bitek's[1] great poem:

> O, my clanswomen
> Let us all cry together!
> Come,
> Let us mourn the death of our mother,
> The death of a Queen
> The ash that was produced
> By a great fire!
> O, this homestead is utterly dead
> Close the gates
> With *lacari* thorns,
> For our mother
> The creator of the Stool is lost!
> And all the young women
> Have perished in the wilderness!

But this is not the end of the story, for all the young women—our mothers and grandmothers, *ourselves*—have not perished in the wilderness. And if we ask ourselves why, and search for and find the answer, we will know beyond all efforts to erase it from our minds, just exactly who, and of what, we black American women are.

One example, perhaps the most pathetic, most misunderstood one, can

---

[1]Okot p'Bitek (1931–   ): Ugandan writer and poet.

provide a backdrop for our mothers' work: Phillis Wheatley, a slave in the 1700s.

Virginia Woolf, in her book *A Room of One's Own,* wrote that in order for a woman to write fiction she must have two things, certainly: a room of her own (with key and lock) and enough money to support herself.

What then are we to make of Phillis Wheatley, a slave, who owned not even herself? This sickly, frail black girl who required a servant of her own at times—her health was so precarious—and who, had she been white, would have been easily considered the intellectual superior of all the women and most of the men in the society of her day.

Virginia Woolf wrote further, speaking of course not of our Phillis, that "any woman born with a great gift in the sixteenth century [insert "eighteenth century," insert "black woman," insert "born or made a slave"] would certainly have gone crazed, shot herself, or ended her days in some lonely cottage outside the village, half witch, half wizard [insert "Saint"], feared and mocked at. For it needs little skill and psychology to be sure that a highly gifted girl who had tried to use her gift for poetry would have been so thwarted and hindered by contrary instincts [add "chains, guns, the lash, the ownership of one's body by someone else, submission to an alien religion"], that she must have lost her health and sanity to a certainty."

The key words, as they relate to Phillis, are "contrary instincts." For when we read the poetry of Phillis Wheatley—as when we read the novels of Nella Larsen or the oddly false-sounding autobiography of that freest of all black women writers, Zora Hurston—evidence of "contrary instincts" is everywhere. Her loyalties were completely divided, as was, without question, her mind.

But how could this be otherwise? Captured at seven, a slave of wealthy, doting whites who instilled in her the "savagery" of the Africa they "rescued" her from . . . one wonders if she was even able to remember her homeland as she had known it, or as it really was.

Yet, because she did try to use her gift for poetry in a world that made her a slave, she was "so thwarted and hindered by . . . contrary instincts, that she . . . lost her health. . . ." In the last years of her brief life, burdened not only with the need to express her gift but also with a penniless, friendless "freedom" and several small children for whom she was forced to do strenuous work to feed, she lost her health, certainly. Suffering from malnutrition and neglect and who knows what mental agonies, Phillis Wheatley died.

So torn by "contrary instincts" was black, kidnapped, enslaved Phillis that her description of "the Goddess"—as she poetically called the Liberty she did not have—is ironically, cruelly humorous. And, in fact, has held Phillis up to ridicule for more than a century. It is usually read prior to hanging Phillis's memory as that of a fool. She wrote:

> The Goddess comes, she moves divinely fair,
> Olive and laurel binds her *golden* hair.

> Wherever shines this native of the skies,
> Unnumber'd charms and recent graces rise. [My italics]

It is obvious that Phillis, the slave, combed the "Goddess's" hair every morning; prior, perhaps, to bringing in the milk, or fixing her mistress's lunch. She took her imagery from the one thing she saw elevated above all others.

With the benefit of hindsight we ask, "How could she?"

But at last, Phillis, we understand. No more snickering when your stiff, struggling, ambivalent lines are forced on us. We know now that you were not an idiot or a traitor; only a sickly little black girl, snatched from your home and country and made a slave; a woman who still struggled to sing the song that was your gift, although in a land of barbarians who praised you for your bewildered tongue. It is not so much what you sang, as that you kept alive, in so many of our ancestors, *the notion of song*.

Black women are called, in the folklore that so aptly identifies one's status in society, "the *mule* of the world," because we have been handed the burdens that everyone else—*everyone* else—refused to carry. We have also been called "Matriarchs," "Superwomen," and "Mean and Evil Bitches." Not to mention "Castraters" and "Sapphire's Mama." When we have pleaded for understanding, our character has been distorted; when we have asked for simple caring, we have been handed empty inspirational appellations, then stuck in the farthest corner. When we have asked for love, we have been given children. In short, even our plainer gifts, our labors of fidelity and love, have been knocked down our throats. To be an artist and a black woman, even today, lowers our status in many respects, rather than raises it: and yet, artists we will be.

Therefore we must fearlessly pull out of ourselves and look at and identify with our lives the living creativity some of our great-grandmothers were not allowed to know. I stress *some* of them because it is well known that the majority of our great-grandmothers knew, even without "knowing" it, the reality of their spirituality, even if they didn't recognize it beyond what happened in the singing at church—and they never had any intention of giving it up.

How they did it—those millions of black women who were not Phillis Wheatley, or Lucy Terry[2] or Frances Harper[3] or Zora Hurston or Nella Larsen or Bessie Smith; or Elizabeth Catlett,[4] or Katherine Dunham,[5] either—brings me to the title of this essay, "In Search of Our Mothers' Gardens," which is

---

[2]Lucy Terry (1730–1821): A slave who was one of the first black poets in America.
[3]Frances Harper (1825–1911): A poet and Abolitionist.
[4]Elizabeth Catlett (1919–   ): A painter and sculptor.
[5]Katherine Dunham (1910–   ): An anthropologist and a leading exponent of primitive dance in the U.S. Known as the "Mother of Afro-American Dance."

a personal account that is yet shared, in its theme and its meaning, by all of us. I found, while thinking about the far-reaching world of the creative black woman, that often the truest answer to a question that really matters can be found very close.

In the late 1920s my mother ran away from home to marry my father. Marriage, if not running away, was expected of seventeen-year-old girls. By the time she was twenty, she had two children and was pregnant with a third. Five children later, I was born. And this is how I came to know my mother: she seemed a large, soft, loving-eyed woman who was rarely impatient in our home. Her quick, violent temper was on view only a few times a year, when she battled with the white landlord who had the misfortune to suggest to her that her children did not need to go to school.

She made all the clothes we wore, even my brothers' overalls. She made all the towels and sheets we used. She spent the summers canning vegetables and fruits. She spent the winter evenings making quilts enough to cover all our beds.

During the "working" day, she labored beside—not behind—my father in the fields. Her day began before sunup, and did not end until late at night. There was never a moment for her to sit down, undisturbed, to unravel her own private thoughts; never a time free from interruption—by work or the noisy inquiries of her many children. And yet, it is to my mother—and all our mothers who were not famous—that I went in search of the secret of what has fed that muzzled and often mutilated, but vibrant, creative spirit that the black woman has inherited, and that pops out in wild and unlikely places to this day.

But when, you will ask, did my overworked mother have time to know or care about feeding the creative spirit?

The answer is so simple that many of us have spent years discovering it. We have constantly looked high, when we should have looked high—and low.

For example: in the Smithsonian Institution in Washington, D.C., there hangs a quilt unlike any other in the world. In fanciful, inspired, and yet simple and identifiable figures, it portrays the story of the Crucifixion. It is considered rare, beyond price. Though it follows no known pattern of quilt-making, and though it is made of bits and pieces of worthless rags, it is obviously the work of a person of powerful imagination and deep spiritual feeling. Below this quilt I saw a note that says it was made by "an anonymous Black woman in Alabama, a hundred years ago."

If we could locate this "anonymous" black woman from Alabama, she would turn out to be one of our grandmothers—an artist who left her mark in the only materials she could afford, and in the only medium her position in society allowed her to use.

As Virginia Woolf wrote further, in *A Room of One's Own:*

Yet genius of a sort must have existed among women as it must have existed among the working class. [Change this to "slaves" and "the wives and daughters of sharecroppers."] Now and again an Emily Brontë or a Robert Burns [change this to "a Zora Hurston or a Richard Wright"] blazes out and proves its presence. But certainly it never got itself on to paper. When, however, one reads of a witch being ducked, of a woman possessed by devils [or "Sainthood"], of a wise woman selling herbs [our root workers], or even a very remarkable man who had a mother, then I think we are on the track of a lost novelist, a suppressed poet, of some mute and inglorious Jane Austen. . . . Indeed, I would venture to guess that Anon, who wrote so many poems without signing them, was often a woman. . . .

And so our mothers and grandmothers have, more often than not anonymously, handed on the creative spark, the seed of the flower they themselves never hoped to see: or like a sealed letter they could not plainly read.

And so it is, certainly, with my own mother. Unlike "Ma" Rainey's songs, which retained their creator's name even while blasting forth from Bessie Smith's mouth, no song or poem will bear my mother's name. Yet so many of the stories that I write, that we all write, are my mother's stories. Only recently did I fully realize this: that through years of listening to my mother's stories of her life, I have absorbed not only the stories themselves, but something of the manner in which she spoke, something of the urgency that involves the knowledge that her stories—like her life—must be recorded. It is probably for this reason that so much of what I have written is about characters whose counterparts in real life are so much older than I am.

But the telling of these stories, which came from my mother's lips as naturally as breathing, was not the only way my mother showed herself as an artist. For stories, too, were subject to being distracted, to dying without conclusion. Dinners must be started, and cotton must be gathered before the big rains. The artist that was and is my mother showed itself to me only after many years. This is what I finally noticed:

Like Mem, a character in *The Third Life of Grange Copeland,*[6] my mother adorned with flowers whatever shabby house we were forced to live in. And not just your typical straggly country stand of zinnias, either. She planted ambitious gardens—and still does—with over fifty different varieties of plants that bloom profusely from early March until late November. Before she left home for the fields, she watered her flowers, chopped up the grass, and laid out new beds. When she returned from the fields she might divide clumps of bulbs, dig a cold pit, uproot and replant roses, or prune branches from her taller bushes or trees—until night came and it was too dark to see.

Whatever she planted grew as if by magic, and her fame as a grower of flowers spread over three counties. Because of her creativity with her flowers, even my memories of poverty are seen through a screen of blooms—sunflowers, petunias, roses, dahlias, forsythia, spirea, delphiniums, verbena . . . and on and on.

---

[6]*The Third Life of Grange Copeland:* a novel by Alice Walker.

And I remember people coming to my mother's yard to be given cuttings from her flowers; I hear again the praise showered on her because whatever rocky soil she landed on, she turned into a garden. A garden so brilliant with colors, so original in its design, so magnificent with life and creativity, that to this day people drive by our house in Georgia—perfect strangers and imperfect strangers—and ask to stand or walk among my mother's art.

I notice that it is only when my mother is working in her flowers that she is radiant, almost to the point of being invisible—except as Creator: hand and eye. She is involved in work her soul must have. Ordering the universe in the image of her personal conception of Beauty.

Her face, as she prepares the Art that is her gift, is a legacy of respect she leaves to me, for all that illuminates and cherishes life. She has handed down respect for the possibilities—and the will to grasp them.

For her, so hindered and intruded upon in so many ways, being an artist has still been a daily part of her life. This ability to hold on, even in very simple ways, is work black women have done for a very long time.

This poem is not enough, but it is something, for the woman who literally covered the holes in our walls with sunflowers:

> They were women then
> My mama's generation
> Husky of voice—Stout of
> Step
> With fists as well as
> Hands
> How they battered down
> Doors
> And ironed
> Starched white
> Shirts
> How they led
> Armies
> Headragged Generals
> Across mined
> Fields
> Booby-trapped
> Kitchens
> To discover books
> Desks
> A place for us
> How they knew what we
> *Must* know
> Without knowing a page
> Of it
> Themselves.

Guided by my heritage of a love of beauty and a respect for strength—in search of my mother's garden, I found my own.

And perhaps in Africa over two hundred years ago, there was just such a mother; perhaps she painted vivid and daring decorations in oranges and yellows and greens on the walls of her hut; perhaps she sang—in a voice like Roberta Flack's—*sweetly* over the compounds of her village; perhaps she wove the most stunning mats or told the most ingenious stories of all the village storytellers. Perhaps she was herself a poet—though only her daughter's name is signed to the poems that we know.

Perhaps Phillis Wheatley's mother was also an artist.

Perhaps in more than Phillis Wheatley's biological life is her mother's signature made clear.

Questions for "In Search of Our Mothers' Gardens"

1.   Walker prefaces her essay with a quotation from Jean Toomer: How does she use this quotation to launch her essay?

2.   What is the main idea of this essay? What strategies does Walker employ to organize and develop her argument? For example, how does Walker use the example of Phillis Wheatley—and the excerpt from one of her poems—to develop her thesis?

3.   Discuss the significance of the title. What are "our mothers' gardens"? And why is it important that we find them?

4.   What does Walker mean when she says, "Guided by my heritage of a love of beauty and a respect for strength—in search of my mother's garden, I found my own"?

5.   What assumptions does Walker seem to make about her readers?

6.   What is your impression of the character of this speaker? How do the style and tone of this essay affect your response to Walker's argument?

READING/WRITING

The selections in this chapter suggest the wide range of possibilities open to the essayist. You may wish to choose from the following suggestions for essay topics, or to adapt any of these assignments to your own interests and needs.

1. In the spirit of Montaigne, write a speculative and anecdotal essay that addresses a human vice, virtue, practice, or folly. You may want to conduct your own examination "of liars," or to glean inspiration from

this sampling of titles from *Essais:* "On the Power of the Imagination," "Of the Inconvenience of Greatness," "Of the Art of Conversation," "Of Vanity," "Of Solitude," "Of Sorrow," "Of Fear," "Of Friendship," "On the Education of Children," "On Idleness." Whatever your topic, take your cue from Montaigne by meandering along the pathways of your thoughts, discovering what you believe and what you know about this particular aspect of human nature.

2. Like George Orwell, we've all undergone experiences that have affected us deeply and changed our way of thinking or acting. In a narrative essay, tell the story of a personal experience, an event that taught you something or caused you to perceive an abstract idea, such as tyranny or racism, in a concrete and vivid way.

3. The chapter from *The Language of Clothes* reprinted in this section is called "Male and Female," yet Lurie devotes most of her attention to the matter of *women's* clothing, especially over the past two centuries. Using a similar approach, consider in an essay what styles of dress men have favored over the years (you will probably want to research this topic, concentrating on a specific era). What attitudes and assumptions do these particular male fashions reflect?

4. In response to "Male and Female," a number of our students chose to develop topics that Lurie touches on, from shoes and jewelry to hairstyles and current college fashions. A few analyzed the "ideal" masculine or feminine stereotypes of the late 1980s, while others chose to interpret different sign systems, such as the "language" of cars, cuisines, and perfume advertisments. Feel free to borrow from their ideas—or to explore a sign system of your own choice. Whatever your topic, consider both the symbolic significance of the item and the beliefs or attitudes that have made it popular with a particular group of people.

5. "Folklore Mirrors Life's Key Themes" is a newspaper article that summarizes recent research in contemporary superstitions and popular beliefs. Often, as is the case in this article, a brief overview of a topic provides a wealth of ideas for more detailed essays. For example, one of our students wrote about a superstition that has played a major role in her family's life, the belief that pinning red ribbons to one's clothing wards off the "evil eye." Another student recalled childhood chants, sayings such as "Step on a crack; Break your mother's back," that had once terrified him, and decided to analyze the meaning of typical children's superstitions.

You may wish to research a single superstition, ancient or modern, to find its origins, its variants, and its symbolic dimensions. Or you may want to analyze the superstitions shared by a particular culture or subculture. Other possibilities include the reasons for the customs associated with significant events in our lives, such as weddings and funerals. Alternatively, you may consider the ways in which our concerns, fears, and hostilities are expressed in the jokes now making the rounds, the types of movies attracting large audiences this year, current hits in the rock music world, and so on.

In the following essay, written in response to this assignment, one student analyzes his own superstitious behavior. Like Flannery O'Connor's essay, this selection could be entitled "A Reasonable Use of the Unreasonable."

Superstitions and Sports

There were times during the 1986 football season when I felt a bit sorry for New York Giants head coach, Bill Parcells. Parcells, who won 17 of 19 games including the Super Bowl that season, was the focus of a bizarre sports ritual. Near the end of each imminent Giant victory, veteran defensive lineman Harry Carson would ceremoniously dump an enormous cooler of sticky orange Gatorade over the head of Coach Parcells. Carson naively believed that the Gatorade shower brought the Giants good luck. So did I.

Why? Because I'm not an ordinary sports fan. I'm what you might call a "metafan." A metafan does more than root for a team, more than hope for victory. Metafans have spiritual, metaphysical obligations to their teams. Not only do they want their teams to win, they want to be part of the reason why.

How did I become initiated into this mysterious cult? Mainly through trial and error. Honestly, I didn't know the difference between a baseball and a bass guitar until I was eight years old. I saw my first Yankee game on television in 1973, and by the age of ten I had enough rudimentary knowledge of the major sports—baseball, football, hockey, and basketball— to have reached the first level. I was now a fan.

You may wonder when I made the leap from fan to metafan. Since the Yankees were the first team I ever rooted for, I should explain how I came to devise the rituals that brought New York two World Series championships in the late 1970s.

The Yankees of the late 1960s and early 1970s, as many New York fans remember, were a team in decline and despair. Casey Stengel, one of baseball's greatest managers and raconteurs, had retired after many championship seasons. Mickey Mantle's legs, weakened by injuries and a rare bone disease, reduced the once loping centerfielder to an immobile first baseman, and Roger Maris would never again come close to hitting 61 home runs in a season. The irresponsible antics of Joe Pepitone had made Yankee fans long for another Joe, Joe Dimaggio, whose Hall of Fame talent and affable manner made him a living symbol of past Yankee pride and achievement. After many bitter losing seasons, pride and achievement were two words missing from the Yankees' vocabulary.

The lexicographer responsible for correcting these omissions was a multi-millionaire shipbuilder from Tampa named George Steinbrenner III. He purchased the Yankees in 1973 (coincidentally, the same year I became a Yankee fan) from CBS for $10 million and immediately began to build his team into contenders once more. Steinbrenner shopped the free agent market with an open wallet, eager to purchase proven superstars who could bolster the Yankee lineup. With a few trades and some new blood, the Yankees were back in the running for the American League's Eastern Division title by 1975.

But money alone cannot make a winning ballclub: luck must also play a part. Luck is where the metafan becomes important, and where I reenter this story. As the Yankees began to win more often, my commitment to victory transported me into a rarefied realm of fan frenzy. I realized that it was now my duty to protect the Yankees from such misfortunes as a dropped fly ball and pave the way to victory. So one night in July of 1975, after another Yankee loss in what had become a prolonged losing streak, I decided to act. A metafan was about to be born.

I quickly kissed my pillow three times and then whispered, "Hooray for the Yankees," three times. My head bobbed up and down in the reenactment of a Jewish prayer ritual known as "dovening." If baseball is America's secular religion, the metafan is its high priest, mediating between the hopes of ordinary fans and the powers of divine intervention.

Even after the Yankees had become world champions, I knew that my work was far from done. I had chosen my calling and there could be no rest until every New York team had won a championship. Kissing a pillow was now a ritual suited only to Little League sports. I had to escalate my powers because six other New York teams—the Mets, Giants, Jets, Islanders, Rangers, and Knicks—sorely needed my help. Hence, by the time I was 15, I had the most elaborate ritual ever devised by a sports fan, metafan that is, living in Bayside, Queens. At exactly 10:30 every night, I would touch each arm of a swivel chair three times (three, of course, being a magic number) with the tips of both index fingers. Next I would run to my bedroom and straighten out all the objects on my desk, placing them in a carefully predetermined order, and touch each item twice. Clearly, my ministrations worked—the Islanders won four consecutive Stanley Cups.

Of course, I know I had nothing to do with the success of the Yankees or the Islanders. I just wanted to think that I did. I wanted these teams to win so badly that I was willing to try anything. So, during the course of each baseball or hockey game, I suspended my customary belief in cause and effect: I was omnipotent, and crossing my legs at the right time could change the course of a game.

This irrational behavior was wedded to two logical fallacies at the root of all superstitions: the fallacy of composition and the *post hoc* fallacy. The fallacy of composition is the belief that what works in one case works in all cases. Because I thought my rituals had helped the Yankees to win, I assumed that similar rites would bring victory to the Islanders.

The *post hoc* fallacy, named after the Latin phrase meaning "after this, therefore because of this," is the source of most superstitions. One example of the power of this fallacy is the age-old belief in omens. In ancient times if someone saw a comet across the sky, and a king died the next year, it was deduced that a comet was an omen forecasting the death of a king. My superstitious behavior worked on a similar principle. If I was sitting in a particular position, say, crossing my legs, while watching a ballgame, and the Yankees won, I would sit in that position for the next game, hoping for the same results. If they lost, I'd find a new position, and keep moving until they won again.

I was still confusing cause and effect: a team wins or loses for a number of reasons, including talent, skill, playing conditions, and luck. Since I didn't have the athletic ability to be on the field with my team, I counted on my rituals to improve the luck factor, which could produce a timely base hit or a fumble by the opposition that would wrench certain victory from the jaws of defeat.

I know better now, and the rituals are largely gone. But I still can't shake the habit of sitting in a fixed position in front of the television during a crucial game. As luck would have it, the Mets were involved in several cliffhangers during this year's playoffs. It was the sixth game of the World Series that raised my superstitions—and my anxiety—to an all-time high.

The Mets were trailing the Red Sox by two runs in the bottom of the tenth inning. Two quick outs and two strikes later, the Mets were one strike from defeat. On the verge of metafan failure, I could barely watch, hunched forward on the couch with my elbows on my knees, the palm of my right hand pressing against my forehead. Then the Mets began their comeback, the crowd cheering wildly, yet I displayed all the emotion of a corpse. I would not let myself enjoy the comeback. I could not afford to move a single muscle. What if the Mets should stumble because I had been careless?

I freed myself from psychological *rigor mortis* only after the winning run was safely across home plate. Leaping into the air, I celebrated our victory, and paid silent homage to my powers. Was my superstitious folly worth all the torment it had caused me? It must have been. After all, the Mets are world champions.

Robert Magnus

6. Select a famous speech, perhaps one by Winston Churchill, Martin Luther King, Jr., John F. Kennedy, or any cultural hero you admire, and analyze its appeals both to reason and emotion.

7. Choose a current issue you feel strongly about—such as nuclear power plants, drunk drivers, drug dealers, or the right to choose your own death—and compose a speech that is both intellectually and emotionally convincing.

8. Do some research on a plant, insect, or animal that intrigues you and write an essay that not only describes and classifies this form, but also attends to its distinguishing characteristics. Like Stephen Jay Gould in "The Panda's Thumb," you'll also want to give your reader some sense of what originally piqued your interest in this plant or animal.

9. Take one of your childhood pursuits, like Ted Hughes's passion for capturing animals, and connect it to something you pursue now—a hobby, a talent, your major in college, or the like. You might follow Hughes's approach by moving from narrative—the story of your childhood activity—on to analogy, process description, and causal analysis. One of our students, for example, spent much of his time as a child building things out of wood, and compared that process to a current pastime, writing short stories. Another student discovered

similarities between his lifelong love of reading all kinds of books and the college major he now pursues, the study of film, which involves "a different kind of reading."

10. Write an essay agreeing with or refuting Dr. C. Fayette Taylor's argument about the "emotional prodigality" of educated Victorian women. To help you reach your own conclusions as to why so many upper-class women suffered from nervous disorders in the nineteenth century, do some research into the Victorian era. You may want to find out how girls were reared, what kinds of educations they received, and what behavior or interests were expected of the women of the day. Your reading will probably lead you to reasons very different from Dr. Taylor's, but you may also find that his descriptions of these "bundles of nerves" are not simply one man's distorted view. In fact, Taylor's ideas do contain a measure of common sense, and you may be able to make use of some of them. In your essay, though, be sure to avoid the shortcomings of Taylor's argument, such as stereotyping and failing to consider more than one cause for a given effect.

11. In response to "The Boston Photographs," a number of our students wrote essays about the influence of the media on our individual and collective lives. (In fact, Ephron's essay appears in a collection of essays, *Scribble, Scribble,* which is subtitled *Notes on the Media.*) One student investigated charges that extensive press coverage of certain crimes, such as airplane hijackings and cyanide-laced pills placed in bottles of pain relievers, leads to a rash of similar, or "copy-cat," crimes. Another student compared the ways in which three very different newspapers reported a particularly vicious murder. Other topics included the role of television in political campaigns and an analysis of the values reflected in an especially popular—and violent— weekly television series. Choose one such topic and develop your own thesis about the way our lives are affected by radio, TV, films, or periodicals.

12. Taking your cue from Bettelheim's interpretation of "Little Snow-white," write a detailed analysis that explores the latent content and psychological meaning of a fairy tale—or of any children's story—that interests you.

13. In "A Reasonable Use of the Unreasonable," Flannery O'Connor discusses the use of violence in modern fiction. Choose a story, a film, or a play in which a violent situation is not an end in itself but essential to our understanding of character and theme, as in "A Good Man Is Hard to Find." In an essay, analyze the ways in which this violence reveals character and meaning. Alternatively, you may wish to examine a work in which you believe the violence is gratuitous and explain why the violence in this case contributes nothing to our understanding of character or theme.

14. In "A Reasonable Use of the Unreasonable," O'Connor also talks about what makes a story work: "some action, some gesture of a character that is unlike any other in the story. . . . an action or a gesture which was both totally right and totally unexpected." For an essay that considers how such a gesture "indicates where the real heart of the story lies," choose one of the stories included in Chapter 4, and analyze the ways in which a single action, like that of the grandmother in "A Good Man Is Hard to Find," is central to the meaning and effect of the work.

15. Like Virginia Woolf in "The Death of the Moth," you may have experienced a time when observing a seemingly insignificant event led you to reflect upon a significant human question. Use your reaction to this experience to structure a contemplative, philosophical essay that reflects your perception of one of life's mysteries. Following Woolf, you may wish to use metaphors and other figures of speech to convey your impressions of this particular event and its abstract implications.

16. After reading Walker's essay, we may be inspired to go "In Search of Our Mothers' Gardens," to discover what historical facts and cultural restrictions may have stifled a person's creativity and development, to learn what activity served as this person's "garden." Choose a relative—parent, grandparent, great-grandparent—and consider the forces that prevented this relative from achieving his or her potential. What became this person's "art"?

Appendix: Writing about Literature

BREAKING THE BLANK PAGE

If you have tried any of the exercises in this anthology, even if you responded only by freewriting on a scrap of paper, you have already written about literature. In Chapter 1, we discuss the reciprocal relationship between reading and writing: the ways in which these two activities comment on and illuminate one another. Reading invites active participation in the construction of a literary work and its meaning, while writing about a text, whether in the form of notebook responses or formal essays, enriches our understanding of a work and our appreciation of its artistry. As the students whose work we quote throughout this book demonstrate, writing about literature encourages us to attend carefully to what is stated and what is implied.

In preparation for an essay about a literary topic, it may be useful to reread the introduction in this anthology to the particular genre you are treating—biography, short story, drama, poetry, essay. For as the title of this book suggests, each genre has its own form, and each text in that genre will reflect certain characteristics of this form. Similarly, each genre has some of its own techniques and terminology. In fiction, for example, we speak of plot, character, setting, point of view, and so on. To these elements, drama adds components such as stage directions and extended dialogue, while poetry often relies more heavily on figurative language and the rhythm and sound created by meter and rhyme scheme. Rereading the introduction to a chapter will reacquaint you with the special features of the genre and refresh your critical vocabulary. At the same time, reviewing the introduction with a specific work in mind may help to focus your thinking and sharpen your powers of analysis.

Whether the topic for an essay comes from your instructor, the Reading/Writing sections of this book, or your own choosing, your notebook is apt to provide several ideas worth pursuing. What did you think after your first reading of the text? After subsequent readings? What questions remain in your mind? How were your thoughts about the text influenced by class discussion? And what do you think now?

Try listing each of your main ideas about your topic on the top of a separate sheet of paper. Now consider *why* you think what you think and jot down those details you recall from the reading selection that support each of your ideas. Then return to the text, rereading with care. What additional support can you find for each of your main ideas? What new ideas come to mind? Annotate the text as you read and reread, making notes in the margin and underlining words or phrases that provide clues to the topic at hand. Repeating this process over several days will refine your thinking, help you to develop and support your ideas more clearly, and provide a foundation for the essay to come.

APPROACHES TO WRITING
ABOUT LITERATURE

As you may gather from many of the assignments suggested in the Reading/ Writing sections of this book, the types of papers most often called for in literature courses are explication, analysis, and comparison/contrast. Of course, most essays about literature draw on a combination of these critical strategies, even though one may be dominant. Regardless of approach, however, the soundness of your interpretation depends on details, examples, and quotations from the text.

Explication is a detailed explanation of a passage of prose or poetry. Because explication involves a line-by-line study of a text, it is usually confined to a short poem or a representative passage from a longer work. Through a close examination of the language of the selection—the connotations of words, style, tone, irony, images and figures of speech, allusions, symbols, rhythm, sounds, and so forth—writers of explication interpret layers of meaning as they explore the ways in which a work achieves its effect. You might, for example, explicate the opening scene of a play or the first page of a short story to demonstrate how it establishes tone or mood and anticipates what is to come, or you might treat a short lyric poem in its entirety. Whatever the case, remember that your task is not merely to summarize the selection, but to remark specifically on the effects and meanings created by the author's use of language, to discuss how a text conveys ideas and impressions.

Analysis most often focuses on a single element in a work, such as plot, character, or point of view, and relates that element to the central effect or meaning of the text. Analysis breaks a subject down into its components to investigate the relationship among its parts. You might analyze the importance of setting or the use of images in prose or poetry and show how this aspect of the text contributes to its overall effect, or consider the function of a minor character in a story or a play. Whatever the element, your purpose is to demonstrate its relevance to the larger concerns of the work as a whole.

Comparison/contrast explores the similarities and differences between two aspects of a single work or between kindred elements in different works. You might compare or contrast two characters in a story or a play, the protagonists in two different works, or the ways in which two poems treat the same subject. If you select your own topic, make sure you have chosen aspects of a work or works that can be meaningfully compared or contrasted. Choose texts that share a significant characteristic, such as subject, style, situation, authorship, or notable use of a particular device, like irony or point of view. Because your purpose is to reach a clearer understanding of the texts you are treating, not merely to produce a set of similarities or differences, your thesis should state exactly what is to be gained from examining these two elements together.

To structure a comparison/contrast essay, writers generally use one of two basic patterns: the block method, in which you discuss all the qualities of A, and then discuss—in roughly the same order—all the qualities of B; or the alternating method, in which each paragraph contains a point-by-point comparison or contrast of A and B.

PREPARING THE FIRST DRAFT

Your first draft is rather like an initial rehearsal for a performance: You will be feeling your way through the material, and you can expect to hesitate and stumble. If you plan ahead and allow ample time for writing and rewriting, it will be easier to relax and pursue your ideas in a thoughtful, unhurried manner. To organize your ideas and the evidence that supports them, it may be helpful to draw up a tentative outline and to arrange your notes accordingly. As you write, leave wide margins and plenty of space between lines so that you have room to make corrections and additions later on.

In your first draft, concentrate on the body of the paper—introductions and conclusions will come more quickly when you have a stronger sense of your thesis. Think of this first draft as an opportunity to discover what you have to say, and be receptive to new ideas that occur along the way. Instead of worrying about mechanics like spelling and punctuation, direct your energies to exploring your thoughts on paper. Chances are your essay will undergo many changes before it's ready for submission, and fixating on errors at this stage will only interrupt the flow of your ideas.

SUPPORTING YOUR IDEAS

Like any piece of expository writing, an essay about literature requires support for each of the ideas it advances. Unless you are preparing a research paper, in which you consult secondary sources (books and articles on your topic that will supplement your own ideas), support lies in the text itself. Your job, of course, is to select the textual evidence—descriptions, details of action, images, symbols, uses of language, dialogue, structure—that best illustrates each of your points. If you make use of the observations about good readers in Chapter 1 of this book and follow the suggestions on the preceding pages, you will have marshaled much of your evidence before you begin your first draft.

Quoting the text is often a convincing way to illustrate and support your ideas. To use quotations correctly and effectively, observe the guidelines below.

1. If you are quoting no more than four typed lines of prose or three lines of poetry, the quotation should be clearly introduced, set off by quotation marks, and integrated into your prose:

   "The Magic Barrel" is the story of a rabbinical student who comes to realize, as Malamud puts it, "that he did not love God so well as he might, because he had not loved man."

   Use a slash to indicate a division between lines of poetry:

   In "My Papa's Waltz," the poet recalls how a small boy "hung on like death:/ Such waltzing was not easy."

2. Longer quotations—more than four lines of prose or poetry—are set off from the body of your text. Separate the passage by skipping an extra line above and below, and indent ten spaces from the left margin (or slightly less for long lines of poetry). Since the indentation signals a quote, do not add quotation marks, but do copy exactly any quotation marks that appear in the passage. Most often, the passage is introduced with a colon:

   In "Capturing Animals," Ted Hughes's tone is sincere and inviting, as he encourages us to try our hands at poetry:

   > That one thing is, imagine what you are writing about. See it and live it. Do not think it up laboriously, as if you were working out mental arithmetic. Just look at it, touch it, smell it, listen to it, turn yourself into it. When you do this, the words look after themselves, like magic.

   If the extracted passage opens with a phrase that completes your own sentence, use no punctuation:

   About Iago, Othello believes

   > This fellow's of exceeding honesty,
   > And knows all qualities, with a learned spirit
   > Of human dealings.

3. Use brackets to add explanatory words to a quotation or to change the grammatical form of a quotation so that it agrees with your sentence:

   Othello says, "Iago knows/That she [Desdemona] with Cassio hath the act of shame/A thousand times committed."

4. If you omit words from within a sentence, use ellipses (. . .) to indicate the omission:

> In his speech, Frederick Douglass observes that the manhood of the slave "is admitted in the fact that the Southern statute books are covered with enactments forbidding . . . the teaching of the slave to read or write."

If you drop words from the end of a sentence, use ellipses and a period:

> Dr. C. Fayette Taylor asserts that the educated woman "certainly does lack the equipoise which is the characteristic of highly educated men. . . . "

Use a line of spaced periods to signal the omission of a line or more of poetry or more than one paragraph of prose.

5. As these examples indicate, commas and periods belong inside quotation marks unless a parenthetical reference to a source follows the quotation. (See pages 1017–1020 for guidelines on documentation.) However, punctuation marks other than commas and periods go outside the quotation marks unless they appear in the quoted material:

> What does Leo mean when he says, "I came to God not because I loved Him, but because I did not"?

REVISING AND EDITING

Upon completing each draft of your paper, wait a day or so before you attempt revision. You'll be a more objective critic if there is some distance between you and your prose. After a weekend of writing, problems with content, structure, and mechanics will be more apparent on Tuesday morning than late on Sunday night. Another useful strategy is to read your essay aloud: You may hear such infelicities as cumbersome phrases, missing transitions, vague or wordy sentences, and choppy prose more readily than you see them. Most important, you'll want to review your argument rigorously. Is it clearly presented, logically developed, adequately supported?

When the body of your essay seems in order, turn your attention to the introduction, which will create a reader's first impression of your essay. The opening paragraph should identify the author and title of the work to be discussed, introduce your topic in a way that would arouse *your* interest if you were reading this essay for the first time, and, in most cases, present a clear thesis statement that prepares the reader for the material to follow. Finally, consider your conclusion, which should emphasize the significance of what you've discussed. Avoid introducing new ideas or new evidence in the final paragraph, and be sure that your essay does not just stop, but rather leaves the reader with a sense of completion, of "wrapping up."

To aid you in the revision process, we offer the following list of questions to ask yourself during and after the composing process.

Guidelines for Revision

1. Does the opening paragraph identify the title and author of the work to be examined? Does it introduce the topic in an interesting manner? Does the thesis statement clearly indicate what the paper will discuss?

2. Do most paragraphs have a clear topic sentence? Is each topic sentence adequately supported by relevant evidence from the text? Are there other details, examples, or quotations from the work that would develop this idea more fully? Is each paragraph related to the thesis statement? (To see how one writer attended to these matters, look at the first page of Nedeva Kain's revised essay on page 1025.)

3. Are there transitions linking ideas, evidence, and paragraphs, so that the reader can follow the flow of your thoughts and reasoning? To take one example, look at the first three or four paragraphs of the essay reprinted on pages 1024–1026.

4. Is the essay logically organized? Does the progression of ideas and evidence flow smoothly? To see how a writer orders material, you may find it helpful to outline the student essay we mention above. What reasons can you give for the way this writer has arranged the material in the body of her paper?

5. Are your tone and diction appropriate throughout, or do you sometimes slip into slang (such as using *kid* instead of *child* or *guy* instead of *man*)?

6. Are there sentences that seem wordy, vague, awkward, or ungrammatical? Are there any unnecessary shifts in verb tense? Have you correctly used the *present tense* to summarize events or the plot of a story?

7. Is there any unnecessary plot summary? On the other hand, have you left out some information the reader might need to follow your logic?

8. Does the concluding paragraph emphasize the significance of the thesis and provide a sense of closure?

9. Does the title reflect the nature and focus of the essay?

10. Finally, have you proofread your paper—more than once—with care and concentration?

DOCUMENTING OUTSIDE SOURCES

Another way to develop your thinking and support your ideas about a literary text is to research what other critics have said about this work. If you elect to include the contributions of others in your essay, you must give credit by documenting your sources. This rule applies to direct quotations, paraphrases (passages recast in your own words), ideas, or obscure facts you might have borrowed from another source.

Giving proper credit to the ideas and efforts of others is not only ethical but also helpful to readers, who may wish to look more closely at the works you have cited. Most often, literary essays follow the MLA (Modern Language Association of America) guidelines for documentation. Although these guidelines have recently been revised, the earlier form may also be used. We have illustrated both forms here. For a comprehensive guide to the new MLA style, see the *MLA Handbook for Writers of Research Papers*, second edition, by Joseph Gibaldi and Walter S. Achtert.

New MLA Style

Whenever you refer to a specific section of an outside source, give the author and page number or numbers in parentheses. (You must, of course, provide a bibliography at the end of your paper, so that your reader can locate the source to which each page number refers. Bibliographic form is illustrated on pages 1018–1019.) If you have included the author's name in your reference to the work, only the page numbers need follow:

> As one writer observes, "Violence is a force which can be used for good or evil" (O'Connor 113).

> According to Flannery O'Connor, "Violence is a force which can be used for good or evil" (113).

Add the title of a work if your paper refers to two or more selections by the same author:

> According to Flannery O'Connor, "Violence is a force which can be used for good or evil" ("A Reasonable Use of the Unreasonable" 113).

Other types of citations common in literature papers include the following:

A work in an anthology:

> Frederick Douglass's "What to the Slave Is the Fourth of July?" is a searing indictment of slavery in the United States (Costello and Tucker 903–918).

(Editors' names and page numbers are placed in parentheses.)

A classic verse play or poem:

Othello calls himself "one that loved not wisely, but too well" (V.i.340).

(Act, scene, and line numbers replace page numbers. Arabic numbers may also be used for act and scene: (5.1.340).)

In Part 2 of the *Essay on Criticism,* Pope observes that "most by Numbers judge a Poet's song:/And smooth or rough, with them is right or wrong" (138–39).

(Line numbers replace page numbers.)

Preparing a Bibliography

Sources are arranged alphabetically, according to the author's surname. Types of entries common to literature papers appear below.

A book by one author:

Bloom, Harold. *Yeats.* New York: Oxford, 1970.

(The author's name is followed by the book title, the city where the book was published, the publisher, and the date of publication.)

An article in a book:

Chase, Richard. "Walt Whitman as American Spokesman." *Whitman: A Collection of Critical Essays.* Ed. Roy Harvey Pearce. Englewood Cliffs, NJ: Prentice-Hall, 1962. 155–163.

(The author's name and the title of the article are followed by the book in which it was published, the editor's name, the publication information, and the pages on which the article appears. All lines after the first are indented 5 spaces.)

An article in a journal:

Proffit, Edward. "Allusion in Adrienne Rich's 'A Valediction Forbidding Mourning.'" *Concerning Poetry* 15 (Spring 1982): 21–24.

(The article appeared in issue 15 of the journal *Concerning Poetry.*)

A selection from an anthology:

Hughes, Ted. "Wodwo." *Forms of Literature: A Writer's Collection.*" Eds. Jacqueline Costello and Amy Tucker. New York: Random House, 1989. 733.

If you are using more than one selection from an anthology, cite the anthology itself. The selections can then be given without repeating the anthology title and publication information.

Costello, Jacqueline and Amy Tucker, eds. *Forms of Literature: A Writer's Collection.* New York: Random House, 1989.

Hughes, Ted. "Wodwo." Costello and Tucker. 733.

A translation:

Kafka, Franz. *The Penal Colony.* Trans. Willa and Edwin Muir. New York: Schocken Books, 1961.

(The translators' names follow the title of the book.)

A particular edition; a multivolume work:

Abrams, M. H. et al., eds. *The Norton Anthology of English Literature.* 4th ed. 2 vols. New York: Norton, 1979.

(*Et al.* is Latin for "and others": This term indicates that there are more than three authors or editors. The particular edition and the number of volumes follow the book title.)

Alternate MLA Style

This mode of documentation pairs consecutively ordered note numbers placed in the text with end notes or footnotes. Note numbers are raised slightly above the last word of the quotation or information to which they refer. They appear *after* all punctuation, except a dash:

According to Flannery O'Connor, "Violence is a force which can be used for good or evil."[1]

If you make several references to the same text in your paper, you may use parenthetical citations after the first note and eliminate unnecessary notes:

O'Connor believes that "the man in the violent situation reveals those qualities least dispensable in his personality" (958).

Each of the note numbers in your text refers the reader to a footnote or an endnote. Footnotes appear at the bottom of the page on which the reference occurs. Skip four lines between the last line of the text and the first line of the footnote. Endnotes are placed together on a separate page that follows the final page of your essay.

Here is how some of the sources listed above would appear in endnote form. Make careful note of the way each reference is punctuated according to a precise formula (explained in detail in the *MLA Handbook*). Notice too that specific page references appear not in parentheses in the text, but in the notes themselves.

[1]Flannery O'Connor, "A Reasonable Use of the Unreasonable," in *Mystery and Manners,* eds. Sally and Robert Fitzgerald (New York: Farrar, Straus, & Giroux, 1961) 113.

[2]Harold Bloom, *Yeats* (New York: Oxford, 1970) 123–24.

[3]Richard Chase, "Walt Whitman as American Spokesman," in *Whitman: A Collection of Critical Essays,* ed. Roy Harvey Pearce (Englewood Cliffs, NJ: Prentice-Hall, 1962) 155–163.

[4]Edward Proffit, "Allusion in Adrienne Rich's 'A Valediction Forbidding Mourning,'" *Concerning Poetry* 15 (Spring 1982): 21–24.

[5]Franz Kafka, *The Penal Colony,* trans. Willa and Edwin Muir (New York: Schocken Books, 1961) 73.

[6]M. H. Abrams et al., eds., *The Norton Anthology of English Literature,* 4th ed., 2 vols. (New York: Norton, 1979) 2:437.

[7]Bloom, 74.

Notice that the final note refers to a work already cited. In this case, it is usually sufficient to list only the author's last name and the appropriate page number. If you are referring to more than one work by the same author, replace the author's name with the title of the work in subsequent references.

THE EVOLUTION OF AN ESSAY

Approaches to composing an essay vary considerably, but it can be beneficial to observe the procedures another writer has followed. Here, for example, one of our students, Nedeva Kain, describes the evolution of her essay on the character of the grandmother in Flannery O'Connor's "A Good Man Is Hard to Find":

The essay was due after spring break, which gave me plenty of time to think about my topic. I had already decided to write about the grandmother, so I started by jotting down key adjectives that captured her traits, and beneath each adjective I listed whatever she says or does in the story that creates this impression. I looked at what I had written in my notebook after my first and second readings of the story, read the story again, and added more examples and another adjective to my outline. Two days later, I returned to my outline. I changed two adjectives, crossed out some examples and added others. The next day I wrote my first draft and put it away without even looking at it. Meanwhile, I read the story again, but waited two days to begin my second draft. By the end of the week, I was ready for the final version. I worked on rough spots in the body of my essay, evaluated each topic sentence, and tried to make sure that I had sufficient support for each idea and that the content of my paper flowed smoothly. After spending some time improving the introduction and conclusion, I checked spelling, grammar, and punctuation. I proofread twice more, at two different times, and found a few errors. Overall, though, I was confident that this was my best work so far. The process had taken a week, but was worth the effort.

To illustrate the steps that Nedeva followed in this process, we've reprinted excerpts from various stages of her essay, drawn from her notebook and successive drafts. First, you'll see her getting started with a preliminary outline:

> Thesis
>
> Character of grandma appears to be bad - nothing but a dope but in the end realize that she is not totally evil, although stupid - we don't regard her as evil b/c see a noble gesture in the end - where we see she really is noble;
>
> grandmother appears to be evil, stupid but we don't react to her like think we may dislike her but not totally b/c in the end she was noble
>
> immature: ① sneaks a cat in car - like a child sneaks things.
>
> "legs crossed under her like a childs" ② called cat "Pitty Sing" - instead of Pretty thing - as if in baby language.
>
> ③ tells lie - but doesn't admit to it when realizes she is wrong.
>
> ④ has a big mouth - talks alot b/c needs the attention children do - do things, say things just to get attention.
>
> Selfish: ① brings cat - doesn't care how manipulator anyone else feels
>
> ② manipulates to get what she wants - to go to Tennessee - 1st ⨍ talks about can't go b/c of Misfit
>
> ③ tells a lie so she can get to the house - yet when realizes she is wrong doesn't tell anyone.
>
> silly, foolish: ① wears flower so if die will graciousness know she's a lady. not dressed to kill but dressed to be killed.
>
> ② thinks cat will asphyxiate himself.
>
> know it all: ① knows what it means to be a lady.
>
> yet ...
>
> deep down inside; is a women, soft - hearted, christian women - she is a woman who tries to make the right gesture - as O'connor comments say - at time of

> evil see true self - time here of her
> death - see true self - she's reaching
> out - does something noble.
>
> p. 110
> p. 111
> p. 112
> ✳ p. 113

Now look at a few paragraphs from Nedeva's first draft. You may not be able to decipher some of her additions and deletions, but you can see a mind at work:

— 1 —

① ¶ The various members of the Bailey family in Flannery O'comor's <u>a good man is Hard to Find</u>, are nicely individualized. But the story is focused on the grandmother, who is set apart from the others. She appears to be a self-righteous know-it-all who causes terrible things to happen to her family. The reader wants to hate the grandmother and call her evil but is unable to do so because of one noble gesture that she makes. The gesture allows the reader to remember the grandmother as gracious rather than as evil.

~~As the story opens, Mr. Bailey is about to take his wife, children and their grandmother on a vacation to Florida. The grandmother pleads~~

② ¶ The readers first impression of the grandmother is that of a selfish, manipulating women. As the story opens, Mr. Bailey is about to take his wife, children and their grandmother on a vacation to Florida. The grandmother wants to go to Tennessee instead to visit some relatives. ~~In order to try and get her way she manipulates her son into~~ She tries to manipulate her son into going to Tennessee by explaining that it is unsafe to go to Florida because a criminal called the "Misfit" is on the loose.

ఞ
_____

-2-

Like many children the grandmother has a constant need for attention. The Best way to get attention is by telling ~~and, as a result, she talks about~~. When the ~~whole~~ family is in the car the grandmother talks about everything under the sun - she talks about the weather, the speed limit, the patrol men, the scenery and the old days. ¶

As the trip continues, suddenly the grandmother ~~out of a sudden~~ remembers a nice old mansion from the days of her youth. The old lady, in a successful effort to arouse the interest of the family, craftily embellishes her description by adding a secret panel, where the family silver was said to be hidden. This too reveals the women's childness. She tells a ~~lie~~ in order to get what she wants never really realizing whether it is morally correct. What further emphasizes this is that when she finally ~~does~~ realizes she has made a mistake and the mansion was never there ~~but rather~~ in a diff. state, she does not admit to her mistake. She tries to ignore it like many children do when they make mistakes.

Nedeva decided to type her next draft, a portion of which appears below:

. . . The story opens with Bailey about to take his family on a vacation to Florida. The grandmother wants to go to Tennessee instead to visit some "connections." She tries to manipulate her son into going to Tennessee by claiming it is unsafe to go to Florida because a criminal called "The Misfit" is on the loose. She says "I wouldn't take my children, in any direction with a criminal like that aloose in it." Unfortunately, her plan does not work and Bailey and his family prepare to go to Florida.

As the family piles into the car, the grandmother hides a basket in the car with "Pitty Sing," the cat, in it. Bailey makes it very clear that he does not want the cat along, but she brings the cat anyway.

An additional dimension of the grandmother's character is that of immaturity. She is "the first one in the car, ready to go" when the family starts out on their trip. Like a child who is looking forward to a trip, she is the first one aboard. The old woman's constant need for attention also suggests her immaturity. As the family drives to Florida, the grandmother talks about everything under the sun. She discusses the weather, the speed limit, the patrolmen, the scenery, and the old days.

As the trip continues, the grandmother suddenly remembers an old mansion from the days of her youth. In a successful effort to arouse the interest of the family, she craftily embellishes her description by adding a secret panel, where the family silver is said to be hidden. The grandmother lies like a child in order to get what she wants, to visit the old house. She even adds that it would be very educational for the children just to get her way. When she realizes that she has made a mistake and the mansion is not in Georgia but in Tennessee, she does not admit her mistake. She ignores it (like many children do) and hopes it will be forgotten.

The grandmother is a foolish woman. She doesn't intend to leave the cat alone because she thinks "he will miss her too much," and she is afraid that he might brush up against one of the gas burners and accidentally asphyxiate himself. The chances of that happening are very small. The grandmother writes down the mileage on the car because she thinks it will be interesting to say how many miles they have been when they get back from their trip. The old lady is dressed in a navy blue dress with a "purple spray of cloth violets containing a sachet pinned at her neckline." The narrator says, "In case of an accident, anyone seeing her dead on the highway would know at once that she was a lady." If she is not precisely dressed to kill, she is dressed to be killed.

When she returned to her essay, Nedeva realized that some fine tuning was in order. She tightened a number of sentences, eliminated extraneous material, replaced vague words with more specific ones, reorganized some of her material, focused her paragraphs with topic sentences, and improved her introduction and conclusion. As you read the final version of her essay, reprinted below, you may wish to refer to the guidelines for revision on page 1026 to see how Nedeva applied what she had learned about the process of reading, writing, and revision.

Discovering a Good Woman in "A Good Man Is Hard to Find"

According to Flannery O'Connor, "It is the extreme situation that best reveals what we are essentially" ("A Reasonable Use of the Unreasonable" 958). In "A Good Man Is Hard to Find," O'Connor shows what happens when an unremarkable character is confronted with an "extreme situation." The central figure in this ironic story about an ill-fated family vacation is a grandmother, a rather selfish, hypocritical, and foolish old lady who seems an unlikely hero. However, when she is faced with a mass murder and her own imminent death, the grandmother responds with an extraordinary gesture that reveals her essential goodness and nobility.

Initially, however, the grandmother appears selfish and hypocritical. As the story opens, her son Bailey is about to take the family on a vacation to Florida, but the grandmother wants to visit some "connections" in Tennessee. Determined to have her own way, she tells her son that it is unsafe to go to Florida because a criminal called "The Misfit" has escaped. She declares, "I wouldn't take my children in any direction with a criminal like that aloose in it. I couldn't answer to my conscience if I did" ("A Good Man Is Hard to Find" 244). Then she argues that the children have already been to Florida and should see different parts of the world. Next, she sneaks her cat in the car against Bailey's wishes, and later lies when she wants him to detour so that she can see a plantation she once visited as a young lady. Knowing that Bailey will not want to lose time looking at an old house, she craftily embellishes her description, saying the house has a secret panel behind which the family silver is said to be hidden. She then insists that seeing the house would be educational for the children, who immediately begin screaming to go, so that Bailey is forced to relent. Shortly after, she has "a horrible thought," suddenly recalling that the house is in another state, but chooses not to mention her mistake.

Much of the story's humor results from the grandmother's antics. Like a child, she is "the first one in the car, ready to go" ("A Good Man Is Hard to Find" 245) when the family starts out on their trip. She sneaks her cat along because she fears he might brush up against the gas burners and asphyxiate himself. She writes down the mileage on the car as they leave because she thinks it will be interesting to say how many miles they have gone when they return. She demands constant attention, talking about everything under the sun: the weather, the speed limit, the patrolmen, the scenery, the old days.

The grandmother's pretensions are comical as well. For example, the children's mother wears slacks and has her hair tied up in a kerchief for the long car trip, but the grandmother is elaborately attired. She wears white gloves, a navy blue sailor hat, and a navy blue dress with a white organdy collar and cuffs trimmed with lace. At her neckline she has pinned "a purple spray of cloth violets containing a sachet," so that "In case of an accident, anyone seeing her dead on the highway would know at once that she was a lady" ("A Good Man Is Hard to Find" 245).

Ironically, the grandmother *is* dressed to be killed. Through a series of minor misdeeds and ironic coincidences, she unwittingly leads the family to its death. First, she hides the cat in the car because he might asphyxiate himself if left behind, and then she lies about the house with the secret panel. Upon realizing that the house is in another state, she accidentally upsets the valise with the cat in it. The cat springs onto Bailey's shoulder, causing Bailey to lose control and the car to flip over and land in a gulch. When the Misfit appears on the scene, the grandmother seals the family's fate by shrieking, "You're the Misfit!" ("A Good Man Is Hard to Find" 252).

And yet, despite her flaws and the terrible consequences of her misdeeds, the grandmother is not a villain. In fact, she is the only character in the story who reaches out to others. For example, she worries about the cat and tries to entertain the children with stories and games. She stops them from throwing garbage out the car window and tries to teach them good manners. She offers to hold the baby, takes him in her lap, talks to him, makes funny faces, and bounces him about. In contrast, none of the other characters shows concern for anyone.

Indeed, as O'Connor points out, "It is true that the old lady is a hypocritical old soul . . . yet I think the unprejudiced reader will feel that the grandmother has a special kind of triumph in this story which instinctively we do not allow to someone altogether bad" ("A Reasonable Use of the Unreasonable" 957). The grandmother's special triumph comes as she faces "the extreme situation." Her family has been murdered and she is alone, facing the Misfit and her own death. She babbles on, trying to delay the inevitable. Suddenly, in an extraordinary gesture, she reaches out to the man before her, saying "Why you're one of my babies. You're one of my own children!" ("A Good Man Is Hard to Find" 256). Here the grandmother recognizes her kinship with and responsibility for another human being, and her noble, heroic action shows that she is something more than a foolish old lady.

As O'Connor observes, "Violence is a force which can be used for good or evil" and "the man in the violent situation reveals those qualities least dispensable in his personality, those qualities which are all he will have to take into eternity with him" ("A Reasonable Use of the Unreasonable" 958). At the end of "A Good Man Is Hard to Find," we see that along with her foibles, the grandmother enters eternity with an essential goodness disclosed in a violent moment of truth.

ACKNOWLEDGMENTS

CHAPTER 1

Bernardino de Sahagun– *Florentine Codex,* Book XI, trans. Charles E. Dibble and Arthur J. O. Anderson, School of American Research and the University of Utah; copyright 1963 University of Utah.

Theodore Roethke– "Elegy for Jane" copyright 1950 by Theodore Roethke from *The Collected Poems of Theodore Roethke.* Reprinted by permission of Doubleday & Company.

V. I. Pudovkin– from *Film Technique and Film Acting,* translated into English by Ivor Montagu (Vision Press, 1958), pp.168–169.

Ernest Hemingway– "Cat in the Rain" from *In Our Time.* Copyright 1925 Charles Scribner's Sons; copyright renewed 1953 Ernest Hemingway. Reprinted with the permission of Charles Scribner's Sons, a division of Macmillan, Inc.

CHAPTER 2

Sei Shonagon– from *The Pillow Book of Sei Shonagon.* © Ivan Morris 1967. Reprinted from *The Pillow Book of Sei Shonagon* translated and edited by Ivan Morris (1967) by permission of Oxford University Press.

Samuel Pepys– from "The Diary of Samuel Pepys," in *The Illustrated Pepys,* edited by Robert Latham, University of California Press. © 1983 The Masters and Fellows of Cambridge University.

Charles Darwin– from "Journal of Researches" in *The Book of Darwin* by George Gaylord Simpson. Copyright © 1983 by George Gaylord Simpson. Reprinted by permission of Washington Square Press, a division of Simon & Schuster, Inc.

Alice James– from *The Diary of Alice James.* Reprinted by permission of Dodd, Mead & Company, Inc. from *The Diary of Alice James,* edited by Leon Edel. Copyright © 1964 by Leon Edel.

Sigmund Freud– from *The Interpretation of Dreams by Sigmund Freud.* Translated from the German and edited by James Strachey. Published by Basic Books, Inc. by arrangement with George Allen & Unwin Ltd. and The Hogarth Press, Ltd. Reprinted by permission of Basic Books, Inc., Publishers.

Franz Kafka– from *The Diaries of Franz Kafka/1910–1913* trans. by Joseph Kresh, edited by Max Brod. Copyright © 1948, renewed © 1976 by Schocken Books Inc. From *The Diaries of Franz Kafka 1914–1923* edited by Max Brod, trans. by Martin Greenberg with the Co-operation of Hannah Arendt. Copyright © 1949, © renewed 1977 by Schocken Books Inc.

Martha Graham– from "The Bronzeless Net," "The Center of a Hurricane," and "The Voyage" from *The Notebooks of Martha Graham,* copyright © by Martha Graham. Reprinted by permission of Harcourt Brace Jovanovich, Inc.

Joan Didion– "Los Angeles Notebook" from *Slouching Towards Bethlehem.* Copyright © 1967, 1968 by Joan Didion. Reprinted by permission of Farrar, Straus and Giroux, Inc.

CHAPTER 3

Charles Darwin– "May 31st, 1876: Recollections of the Development of My Mind and Character" from *The Autobiography of Charles Darwin,* copyright © 1958 by Nora Barlow. Reprinted by permission of Harcourt Brace Jovanovich, Inc. and A. D. Peters & Co., Ltd.

Vincent Van Gogh– from *The Complete Letters of Vincent Van Gogh.* By permission of Little, Brown and Company in conjunction with The New York Graphic Society. All rights reserved.

Sherwood Anderson– "Unforgotten" from *Sherwood Anderson's Memoirs: A Critical Edition.* Reprinted by permission of Harold Ober Associates Incorporated. Copyright 1942 by Eleanor Anderson. Copyright renewed 1969 by Eleanor Copenhaver Anderson.

M. F. K. Fisher– "P Is for Peas" from *An Alphabet for Gourmets.* Reprinted with permission of Macmillan Publishing Company from *The Art of Eating* by M. F. K. Fisher. Copyright 1949, and renewed 1977, by M. F. K. Fisher.

Maxine Hong Kingston– "No Name Woman" from *The Woman Warrior: Memoirs of a Childhood Among Ghosts,* by Maxine Hong Kingston. Copyright © 1975, 1976 by Maxine Hong Kingston. Reprinted by permission of Alfred A. Knopf, Inc.

Theresa A. Finegan– "An Interview with Patrick McMahon, an Irish Immigrant." Reprinted by permission of Theresa A. Finegan.

Natalie Zemon Davis– "The Honor of Bertrand de Rols." Reprinted by permission of the publishers from *The Return of Martin Guerre,* by Natalie Zemon Davis. Cambridge, Mass.: Harvard University Press, Copyright © 1983 by The President and Fellows of Harvard College.

CHAPTER 4

Delaware Indians– "Creation Song" adapted from *American Indian Literature: An Anthology,* Edited and with an Introduction by Alan R. Velie. Copyright © 1979 by the University of Oklahoma Press.

Luke– 11–31 is taken from the *New American Bible,* copyright © 1970, by the Confraternity of Christian Doctrine, Washington, D.C., and used by permission of copyright owner. All rights reserved.

Buddhist parable– "The Lost Son" from *The Buddhist Tradition: In India, China and Japan,* Edited by Theodore de Bary. Copyright © 1969 by Theodore de Bary. Reprinted by permission of Random House, Inc.

Ekai– "Joshu Washes the Bowl" from *The Gateless Gate* in *Zen Flesh and Zen Bones* by Paul Reps, the Charles E. Tuttle Co., Inc., of Tokyo, Japan.

The Brothers Grimm– "Little Snow-White" from *The Complete Grimm's Fairy Tales,* by Jakob Ludwig Grimm and Karl Wilhelm Grimm, translated by Margaret Hunt and James Stern. Copyright 1944 by Pantheon Books, Inc. and renewed 1972 by Random House, Inc. Reprinted by permission of Pantheon Books, a Division of Random House, Inc.

Italo Calvino– "Catherine the Wise" from *Italian Folktales* by Italo Calvino, copyright © 1956 by Giulio Einaudi editore, s.p.a.; English translation copyright © 1980 by Harcourt Brace Jovanovich, Inc. Reprinted by permission of Harcourt Brace Jovanovich, Inc.

Anton Chekhov– "Heartache" from *The Portable Chekhov*, edited and translated by Avrahm Yarmolinsky. Copyright 1947, © 1968 by The Viking Press, Inc. Copyright renewed © 1975 by Avrahm Yarmolinsky. Reprinted by permission of Viking Penguin Inc.

Charlotte Perkins Gilman– "The Yellow Wallpaper" and "Why I Wrote" from *The Charlotte Perkins Gilman Reader*, by Charlotte Perkins Gilman, edited by Ann J. Lane. Pantheon Books, a Division of Random House, Inc.

James Joyce– "Araby" from *Dubliners* by James Joyce. Copyright 1916 by B. W. Huebsch. Definitive text copyright © 1967 by the Estate of James Joyce. Reprinted by permission of Viking Penguin Inc.

Franz Kafka– "The Metamorphosis." Reprinted by permission of Schocken Books Inc. from *The Penal Colony* by Franz Kafka, trans. Willa and Edwin Muir. Copyright © 1948, 1976 by Schocken Books, Inc.

Ryunsuke Akutagawa– "In a Grove" from *Rashomon and Other Stories* by Ryunsuke Akutagawa, the Charles E. Tuttle Co., Inc., of Tokyo, Japan.

Flannery O'Connor– "A Good Man Is Hard to Find" from *A Good Man is Hard to Find and Other Stories* by Flannery O'Connor, copyright 1953 by Flannery O'Connor; renewed 1981 by Mrs. Regina O'Connor. Reprinted by permission of Harcourt Brace Jovanovich, Inc.

Bernard Malamud– "The Magic Barrel" from *The Magic Barrel* by Bernard Malamud. Copyright © 1954, 1958 by Bernard Malamud. Copyright renewed © 1982 by Bernard Malamud. Reprinted by permission of Farrar, Straus and Giroux, Inc.

Tillie Olsen– "I Stand Here Ironing" excerpted from the book *Tell Me A Riddle* by Tillie Olsen. Copyright © 1956, 1957, 1960, 1961 by Tillie Olsen. Reprinted by permission of Delacorte Press/Seymour Lawrence.

Donald Barthelme– "The Glass Mountain." © 1970 by Donald Barthelme. Reprinted by permission of International Creative Management.

Gabriel García Márquez– "A Very Old Man with Enormous Wings" from *Leaf Storm and Other Stories* by Gabriel García Márquez, Translated by Gregory Rabassa (Originally appeared in *New American Review*). Copyright © 1971 by Gabriel García Márquez. Reprinted by permission of Harper & Row, Publishers, Inc.

James Alan McPherson– "Why I Like Country Music" from *Elbow Room* by James Alan McPherson. First appeared in *The Harvard Advocate*. By permission of Little, Brown and Company, in association with The Atlantic Monthly Press.

Grace Paley– "A Conversation with My Father" from *Enormous Changes at the Last Minute* by Grace Paley. Copyright © 1972, 1974 by Grace Paley. Reprinted by permission of Farrar, Straus and Giroux, Inc.

Ursula Le Guin– "The Ones Who Walk Away from Omelas," from *The Wind's Twelve Quarters*. Copyright © 1973, 1975 by Ursula K. Le Guin: reprinted by permission of the author and the author's agent, Virginia Kidd.

Angela Carter– "The Snow Child" from *The Bloody Chamber and Other Adult Tales* by Angela Carter. Copyright © 1979 by Angela Carter. Reprinted by permission of Harper & Row, Publishers, Inc.

Jamaica Kincaid– "The Circling Hand" from *Annie John* by Jamaica Kincaid. Copyright © 1983, 1984, 1985 by Jamaica Kincaid. Originally appeared in *The New Yorker*. Reprinted by permission of Farrar, Straus and Giroux, Inc.

CHAPTER 5

William Shakespeare– from *The Tragedy of Othello* by William Shakespeare, edited by Alvin Kernan. Copyright © 1963 by Alvin Kernan. Reprinted by arrangement with NAL Penguin Inc., New York, NY.

Henrik Ibsen– *A Doll House* from *Henrik Ibsen: Four Major Plays,* translated by Rolf Fjelde. Copyright © 1965 by Rolf Fjelde. Reprinted by arrangement with NAL Penguin Inc., New York, NY.

Tina Howe– *Painting Churches* from *Three Plays: Museum, The Art of Dining, and Painting Churches* by Tina Howe. Reprinted by permission of Avon Books from *Three Plays* by Tina Howe. Copyright © 1984 by Tina Howe.

Akira Kurosawa– *Rashomon.* Reprinted by permission of Grove Press, Inc. *Rashomon* copyright © 1950 by Akira Kurosawa and Daiei Motion Picture Co. *Rashomon* with English subtitles copyright © 1952 by RKO Pictures, Inc. English screenplay © 1969 by Grove Press, Inc. Photos appear courtesy of Janus Films.

CHAPTER 6

James Joyce– "Alone" from *Collected Poems* by James Joyce. Copyright 1918 by B. W. Huebsch. Copyright 1927, 1936 by James Joyce. Copyright renewed 1946 by Nora Joyce. Reprinted by permission of Viking Penguin, Inc.

Anne Bradstreet– "Upon the Burning of Our House" from *The Works of Anne Bradstreet* edited by Jeannine Hensley. Reprinted by permission of Harvard University Press. © 1967 by The President and Fellows of Harvard College.

Francis Ponge– "The Oyster" translated by Beth Archer in *The Voice of Things* published by McGraw-Hill, Inc., 1972, and "The Oyster" translated by Cid Corman in *Things* published by Grossman Publishing Co., 1971. Published originally in French by Editions Gallimard, Paris.

Seamus Heaney– "Oysters" from *Field Work* by Seamus Heaney. Copyright © 1976, 1979 by Seamus Heaney. Reprinted by permission of Farrar, Straus and Giroux, Inc. and Faber and Faber Ltd.

W. S. Merwin– "The Last One" from *The Lice.* Copyright © 1967 W. S. Merwin. Reprinted with the permission of Atheneum Publishers, a division of Macmillan, Inc. First appeared in *Poetry* Magazine.

E. E. Cummings– "somewhere i have never travelled, gladly beyond" is reprinted from ViVa, poems by E. E. Cummings, edited by George James Firmage, by permission of Liveright Publishing Corporation. Copyright 1931, 1959 by E. E. Cummings. Copyright © 1979, 1973 by The Trustees for the E. E. Cummings Trust. Copyright © 1979, 1973 by George James Firmage.

Robert Frost– "The Secret Sits." Copyright 1942 by Robert Frost. Copyright © 1969 by Holt, Rinehart and Winston, Inc. Copyright © 1970 by Lesley Frost Ballantine. Reprinted from *The Poetry of Robert Frost* edited by Edward Connery Lathem, by permission of Henry Holt and Company, Inc.

William Carlos Williams– "The Dance" from *Collected Later Poems.* Copyright 1944, 1948 by William Carlos Williams.

William Carlos Williams– "The Wedding Dance in the Open Air" from *Pictures from Brueghel.* Copyright © 1960, 1962 by William Carlos Williams.

Richard Wilbur– "Digging for China" from *Things of This World,* copyright © 1956, 1984 by Richard Wilbur. Reprinted by permission of Harcourt Brace Jovanovich, Inc.

Sappho– "Seizure." Reprinted by permission of Schocken Books Inc. from *Greek Lyric Poetry* translated by Willis Barnstone. Copyright © 1962, 1967 by Willis Barnstone.

Li Ch'ing Chao– "Autumn Evening Beside the Lake" and "Alone in the Night" from Kenneth Rexroth, *One Hundred Poems from the Chinese.* Copyright © 1971 by Kenneth Rexroth. All rights reserved. Reprinted by permission of New Directions Publishing Corporation.

Sa'di of Shirāz– Translation of a classical Persian lyric by Sa'dī of Shirāz, from *Translations of Eastern Poetry and Prose,* by R. A. Nicholson. Copyright Cambridge University Press. Reprinted with permission.

Footnotes and glosses that accompany– "One day I wrote her name upon the strand" by Edmund Spencer; "The Nymph's Reply to the Shepherd" by Sir Walter Raleigh; "The Passionate Shepherd to His Love" by Christopher Marlow; "When in disgrace with fortune and men's eyes," "Not marble, nor the gilded monuments," "Let me not to the marriage of true minds," "The expense of spirit in a waste of shame," and "My mistress' eyes are nothing like the sun" by William Shakespeare; "Adieu! Farewell, Earth's Bliss!" by Thomas Nashe; "Song," "Hymn to God My God, in My Sickness," "A Valediction: Forbidding Mourning," "The Flea," and "Batter my heart, three-personed God" by John Donne; "On My First Daughter," "On My First Son," "Still to be neat, still to be dressed," and "Come, my Celia" by Ben Jonson; "When I consider how my light is spent" and "Sonnet XXIII" by John Milton are from *Literature: Reading Fiction, Poetry, Drama and the Essay* by Robert DiYanni, copyright Random House, Inc.

Anne Bradstreet– "Before the Birth of One of Her Children," "A Letter to Her Husband, Absent upon Public Employment," "In Memory of My Dear Grand-Child Elizabeth Bradstreet, Who Deceased August, 1665, Being a Year and a Half Old," and "The Author to Her Book." Reprinted by permission of Harvard University Press. © 1967 by The President and Fellows of Harvard College.

Footnotes and glosses that accompany– "To His Coy Mistress" by Andrew Marvell are from *Literature: Reading Fiction, Poetry, Drama and the Essay* by Robert DiYanni, copyright Random House, Inc.

Footnotes for Part II– of "An Essay on Criticism by Alexander Pope" appeared in *To Read Literature: Fiction, Poetry, and Drama* edited by Donald Hall. Copyright 1981 by Holt, Rinehart and Winston. Reprinted by permission of Holt, Rinehart and Winston, Inc.

Footnotes and glosses that accompany– "Elegy Written in a Country Churchyard" by Thomas Gray; "The World Is Too Much with Us," "The Solitary Reaper," and "Lines" by William Wordsworth; "Kubla Khan" by Samuel Taylor Coleridge; "Ozymandias," and "Ode to the West Wind" by Percy Bysshe Shelley; "La Belle Dame sans Merci," "Ode to a Nightingale," and "Ode on a Grecian Urn" by John Keats; "Ulysses," by Alfred, Lord Tennyson; and "Dover Beach" by Matthew Arnold are from *Literature: Reading Fiction, Poetry, Drama and the Essay* by Robert DiYanni, copyright Random House, Inc.

Emily Dickinson– Poems #984, 1129, 465, 67, 214, 328, 258, 303, 435, 1052, and 712. Reprinted by permission of the publishers and the Trustees of Amherst College from *The Poems of Emily Dickinson,* edited by Thomas H. Johnson, Cambridge, Mass.: The Belknap Press of Harvard University Press, Copyright 1951, © 1955, 1979, 1983 by The President and Fellows of Harvard College.

Thomas Hardy– "The Darkling Thrush" and "Transformations" from *The Complete Poems of Thomas Hardy* edited by James Gibson (New York: Macmillan, 1978). (This collection is published outside the U.S. by Macmillan (London) Ltd., 1976.)

A. E. Housman– "When I Was One-and-Twenty" and " To an Athlete Dying Young." Copyright 1939, 1940, © 1965 by Holt, Rinehart and Winston. Copyright © 1967, 1968 by Robert E. Symons. Reprinted from *The Collected Poems of A. E. Housman,* by permission of Henry Holt and Company, Inc.

William Butler Yeats– "The Scholars" and "The Wild Swans at Coole." Reprinted with permission of Macmillan Publishing Company from *Collected Poems* by W. B. Yeats. Copyright 1919 by Macmillan Publishing Company, renewed 1947 by Bertha Georgie Yeats. Reprinted by permission of A. P. Watt Ltd. on behalf of Michael B. Yeats and Macmillan London Ltd.

William Butler Yeats– "Easter 1916" and "The Second Coming." Reprinted with permission of Macmillan Publishing Company from *Collected Poems* by W. B. Yeats. Copyright 1924 by Macmillan Publishing Company, renewed 1952 by Bertha Georgie Yeats. Reprinted by permission of A. P. Watt Ltd. on behalf of Michael B. Yeats and Macmillan London Ltd.

William Butler Yeats– "Leda and the Swan," "Sailing to Byzantium," and "Among School Children." Reprinted with permission of Macmillan Publishing Company from *Collected Poems* by W. B. Yeats. Copyright 1928 by Macmillan Publishing Company, renewed 1956 by Georgie Yeats. Reprinted by permission of A. P. Watt Ltd. on behalf of Michael B. Yeats and Macmillan London Ltd.

William Butler Yeats– "The Magi." Reprinted with permission of Macmillan Publishing Company from *Collected Poems* by W. B. Yeats. Copyright 1916 by Macmillan Publishing Company, renewed 1944 by Bertha Georgie Yeats. Reprinted by permission of A. P. Watt Ltd. on behalf of Michael B. Yeats and Macmillan London Ltd.

Amy Lowell– "Patterns" from *The Complete Poetical Works of Amy Lowell.* Copyright © 1955 by Houghton Mifflin Company. Copyright © 1983 renewed by Houghton Mifflin Company, Brinton P. Roberts, Esquire and G. D'Andelot Belin, Esquire. Reprinted by permission of Houghton Mifflin Company.

Robert Frost– "Mending Wall," "Fire and Ice," "After Apple-Picking," and "Desert Places" from *The Poetry of Robert Frost* edited by Edward Connery Lathem. Copyright © 1969 by Holt, Rinehart and Winston, Inc. Copyright © 1962 by Robert Frost. Copyright © 1975 by Lesley Frost Ballantine. Reprinted by permission of Henry Holt and Company, Inc.

Rainer Maria Rilke– "The Song the Beggar Sings" from *Selected Poems of Rainer Maria Rilke* translated from the German by Robert Bly. Copyright © 1981 by Robert Bly. Reprinted by permission of Harper & Row, Publishers, Inc.

Rainer Maria Rilke– "Portrait of My Father as a Young Man" and "Spanish Dancer" from *The Selected Poetry of Rainer Maria Rilke* edited and translated by Stephen Mitchell. Copyright © 1982 by Stephen Mitchell. Reprinted by permission of Random House, Inc.

Wallace Stevens– "The Snow Man" and "Thirteen Ways of Looking at a Blackbird." Copyright 1923 and renewed 1951 by Wallace Stevens. "Anecdote of the Jar" and "Of Modern Poetry," copyright 1942 by Wallace Stevens and Renewed 1970 by Holly Stevens. Reprinted from *The Collected Poems of Wallace Stevens* by permission of Alfred A. Knopf, Inc.

William Carlos Williams– "The Red Wheelbarrow," "The Widow's Lament in Springtime," "Spring and All," "To a Poor Old Woman," and "The Young Housewife" from *Collected Poems Volume I: 1909–1939.* Copyright 1938 by New Directions Publishing Corporation.

William Carlos Williams– "A Sort of Song," "Raleigh Was Right," and "The Dance" from *Collected Later Poems.* Copyright 1944, 1948 by William Carlos Williams.

William Carlos Williams– "Landscape with the Fall of Icarus" from *Pictures from Brueghel.* Copyright © 1960, 1962 by William Carlos Williams.

D. H. Lawrence– "Snake" from *The Complete Poems of D. H. Lawrence* by D. H. Lawrence, collected and edited with an introduction and notes by Vivian de Sola Pinto and Warren Roberts. Copyright © 1964, 1971 by Angelo Ravagli and C. M. Weekley, Executors of the Estate of Frieda Lawrence Ravagli. Reprinted by permission of Viking Penguin Inc.

Ezra Pound– "In a Station of the Metro," "Fan-Piece for Her Imperial Lord," "The River Merchant's Wife: A Letter," "The Jewel Stair's Grievance," "Epitaph," and "The Garden" from *Personae.* Copyright 1926 by Ezra Pound.

H. D. (Hilda Doolittle)– "Heat" from *Selected Poems.* Copyright © 1957 by Norman Holmes Pearson.

Marianne Moore– "Poetry." Reprinted with permission of Macmillan Publishing Company from *Collected Poems* by Marianne Moore. Copyright 1935 by Marianne Moore, renewed 1963 by Marianne Moore and T. S. Eliot.

T. S. Eliot– "Journey of the Magi" and "The Love Song of J. Alfred Prufrock" from *Collected Poems 1909–1962* by T. S. Eliot, copyright 1936 by Harcourt Brace Jovanovich, Inc.; copyright © 1963, 1964 by T. S. Eliot. Reprinted by permission of the publisher and Faber and Faber Ltd.

John Crowe Ransom– "Bells for John Whiteside's Daughter." Copyright 1924 by Alfred A. Knopf, Inc. and renewed 1952 by John Crowe Ransom. Reprinted from *Selected Poems, Third Edition, Revised and Enlarged* by John Crowe Ransom, by permission of Alfred A. Knopf, Inc.

Anna Akhmatova– "Requiem" from *Selected Poems,* edited by Walter Arndt, and translated by Robin Kemball.

Claude McKay– "The Tropics in New York." Copyright 1981 and reprinted with permission of Twayne Publishers, a division of G. K. Hall & Co., Boston.

Archibald MacLeish– "Ars Poetica" from *New and Collected Poems 1917–1976* by Archibald MacLeish. Copyright © 1976 by Archibald MacLeish. Reprinted by permission of Houghton Mifflin Company.

E. E. Cummings– "pity this busy monster manunkind," copyright 1944 by E. E. Cummings; renewed 1972 by Nancy T. Andrews. Reprinted from *Complete Poems 1913–1962* by E. E. Cummings by permission of Harcourt Brace Jovanovich, Inc.

E. E. Cummings– "my father moved through dooms of love," copyright 1940 by E. E. Cummings; renewed 1972 by Nancy T. Andrews. Reprinted from *Complete Poems 1913–1962* by E. E. Cummings by permission of Harcourt Brace Jovanovich, Inc.

Jean Toomer– "Reapers" and "Face." "Reapers" and "Face" are reprinted from *Cane* by Jean Toomer, by permission of Liveright Publishing Corporation. Copyright 1923 by Boni & Liveright. Copyright renewed 1951 by Jean Toomer.

Federico Garcia Lorca– "Romance Sonambulo" ("Sleepwalking Ballad"), from *Obras Completas.* Copyright © Heredos de Federico Garcia Lorca. Used with permission. All rights reserved. English translation by William Logan. Copyright © William Logan. Used with permission. All rights reserved.

Federico Garcia Lorca– "Rider's Song" from *Selected Poems.* Copyright 1952 by New Directions Publishing Corporation. Translated by Stephen Spender and J. L. Gili.

Jorge Luis Borges– "The Blind Man" from *The Gold of the Tigers: Selected Later Poems* by Jorge Luis Borges, translated by Alastair Reid. English translation copyright © 1976, 1977 by Alastair Reid. Reprinted by permission of the publisher, E. P. Dutton, a division of NAL Penguin Inc.

Francis Ponge– "The Cigarette" and "Les Mûres/Blackberries" translated by Cid Corman in *Things* published by Grossman Publishing Co., 1971. Published originally in French by Editions Gallimard, Paris.

Arna Bontemps– "A Black Man Talks of Reaping." Reprinted by permission of Harold Ober Associates Incorporated. Copyright © 1963 by Arna Bontemps.

Countee Cullen– "Incident" from *On These I Stand: An Anthology of the Best Poems of Countee Cullen.* Copyright 1925 by Harper & Row, Publishers, Inc.; renewed 1953 by Ida M. Cullen. Reprinted by permission of Harper & Row, Publishers, Inc.

Langston Hughes– "The Negro Speaks of Rivers," copyright 1926 by Alfred A. Knopf, Inc. and renewed 1954 by Langston Hughes. Reprinted from *Selected Poems of Langston Hughes,* by permission of Alfred A. Knopf, Inc.

Langston Hughes– "Harlem," copyright 1951 by Langston Hughes. Reprinted from *Selected Poems of Langston Hughes,* by permission of Alfred A. Knopf, Inc.

Langston Hughes– "Theme for English B" from *Montage of a Dream Deferred.* Reprinted by permission of Harold Ober Associates Incorporated. Copyright 1951 by Langston Hughes. Copyright renewed 1979 by George Houston Bass.

Pablo Neruda– "The United Fruit Co." and "Ode to My Socks" from *Neruda and Vallejo: Selected Poems,* translated by Robert Bly. Copyright © 1970 by Robert Bly, reprinted with his permission.

W. H. Auden– "Musée des Beaux Arts" and "In Memory of W. B. Yeats." Copyright 1940 and renewed 1968 by W. H. Auden. Reprinted from *W. H. Auden: Collected Poems* edited by Edward Mendelson, by permission of Random House, Inc. and from *Collected Poems* by permission of Faber and Faber Ltd.

Buddhadeva Bose– "Frogs" from *Poems from India,* edited by Thomas Crowell.

Theodore Roethke– "The Premonition," "I Knew a Woman," and "The Waking" copyright 1941, 1954 and 1953 respectively by Theodore Roethke, "Old Florist" copyright 1946 by Harper & Brothers, "Dolor" copyright 1943 by Modern Poetry Association, "My Papa's Waltz" copyright 1942 by Hearst Magazines, Inc. and "The Pike" copyright © 1963 by Beatrice Roethke as Administratrix of the Estate of Theodore Roethke. All poems from *The Collected Poems of Theodore Roethke.* Reprinted by permission of Doubleday Publishing Group.

Elizabeth Bishop– "The Fish" from *The Complete Poems* by Elizabeth Bishop. Copyright © 1940, copyright renewed 1968 by Elizabeth Bishop. Reprinted by permission of Farrar, Straus and Giroux, Inc.

Robert Hayden– "Those Winter Sundays," "Frederick Douglass," and "Runagate Runagate." Reprinted from *Angle of Ascent, New and Selected Poems,* by Robert Hayden, by permission of Liveright Publishing Corporation. Copyright © 1975, 1972, 1970, 1966 by Robert Hayden.

Henry Reed– "Naming of Parts" from *A Map of Verona.* Reprinted by permission of Jonathan Cape Ltd.

John Berryman– from *Homage to Mistress Bradstreet* by John Berryman. Copyright © 1956 by John Berryman. Copyright renewed © 1984 by Kate Berryman. Reprinted by permission of Farrar, Straus and Giroux, Inc.

Dylan Thomas– "A Refusal to Mourn the Death, by Fire . . . ," "Fern Hill," "The Force That Through . . . ," and "Do not go gentle into that good night" from *The Poems of Dylan Thomas.* Copyright 1939 by New Directions Publishing Corporation, 1945 by the Trustees for the Copyrights of Dylan Thomas, 1952 by Dylan Thomas.

Robert Lowell– "For the Union Dead" from *For the Union Dead* by Robert Lowell. Copyright © 1960 by Robert Lowell. Reprinted by permission of Farrar, Straus and Giroux, Inc.

Gwendolyn Brooks– "The Mother," and "We Real Cool." Reprinted with permission of Gwendolyn Brooks (The David Company).

Richard Wilbur– "The Death of a Toad" from *Ceremony and Other Poems,* copyright 1950, 1978 by Richard Wilbur. Reprinted by permission of Harcourt Brace Jovanovich, Inc.

Richard Wilbur– "First Snow in Alsace" from *The Beautiful Changes and Other Poems,* copyright 1947, 1975 by Richard Wilbur. Reprinted by permission of Harcourt Brace Jovanovich, Inc.

Denise Levertov– "The Victors" and "What Were They Like?" from *Poems 1960–1967.* Copyright © 1964 by Denise Levertov Goodman. Reprinted by permission of New Directions Publishing Corporation.

Maya Angelou– "Africa" from *Oh Pray My Wings Are Gonna Fit Me Well*, by Maya Angelou. Copyright © 1975 by Maya Angelou. Reprinted by permission of Random House, Inc.

Nissim Ezekiel– "Night of the Scorpion" from *Latter-Day Psalms*. Reprinted by permission of Oxford University Press.

Maxine Kumin– "Making the Jam without You" from *Our Ground Time Will Be Brief* by Maxine Kumin. Copyright © 1979 by Maxine Kumin. All rights reserved. Reprinted by permission of Viking Penguin, Inc.

Allen Ginsberg– "A Supermarket in California" from *Collected Poems: 1947-1980* by Allen Ginsberg. Copyright © 1955 by Allen Ginsberg. Reprinted by permission of Harper & Row, Publishers, Inc.

W. S. Merwin– "When You Go Away" from *The Lice*. Copyright © 1967 W. S. Merwin. Reprinted with the permission of Atheneum Publishers, a division of Macmillan, Inc.

Philip Levine– "Ricky" from *Seven Years from Somewhere*. Copyright © 1979 Philip Levine. Reprinted with the permission of Atheneum Publishers, a division of Macmillan, Inc.

Anne Sexton– "Snow White and the Seven Dwarfs" from *Transformations* by Anne Sexton. Copyright © 1971 by Anne Sexton. Reprinted by permission of Houghton Mifflin Company.

Adrienne Rich– "A Valediction Forbidding Mourning," "Planetarium," and "Diving into the Wreck." Reprinted from *The Fact of a Doorframe, Poems Selected and New, 1950–1984*, by Adrienne Rich, by permission of W. W. Norton & Company, Inc. Copyright © 1984 by Adrienne Rich. Copyright © 1975, 1978 by W. W. Norton & Company, Inc. Copyright © 1981 by Adrienne Rich.

Ted Hughes– "Wodwo" from *New Selected Poems* by Ted Hughes. Copyright © 1962 by Ted Hughes. Reprinted by permission of Harper & Row, Publishers, Inc. and Faber and Faber Ltd.

Sylvia Plath– "Ariel," copyright © 1965 by The Estate of Sylvia Plath; "Daddy," copyright © 1963 by Ted Hughes; "Tulips," copyright © 1962 by Ted Hughes from *The Collected Poems of Sylvia Plath* edited by Ted Hughes. Reprinted by permission of Harper & Row, Publishers, Inc. and Olwyn Hughes, London.

Michael S. Harper– "Reuben, Reuben," published by the University of Illinois Press.

Seamus Heaney– "Digging" and "Death of a Naturalist" from *Poems 1965–1975* by Seamus Heaney. Copyright © 1966, 1969, 1972, 1975, 1980 by Seamus Heaney. Reprinted by permission of Farrar, Straus and Giroux, Inc. and Faber and Faber Ltd.

Margaret Atwood– "This Is a Photograph of Me" from *The Circle Game*, © 1966 Margaret Atwood (Toronto: House of Anansi Press). Reprinted by permission.

Modern American Indian Poems– "Love Poem I," "Love Poem II," "Love Poem III," "Spring Poem I," "Dream Poem I," "Dream Poem II," "War Poem I," "War Poem II," "War Poem III" from *Love Poems and Spring Poems and Dream Poems and War Poems*, translated by Gerald Vizenor. © Gerald Vizenor.

Andrew Codrescu– "Alberta" from *The History of the Growth of Heaven*, Persea Books.

Joseph Concha– "Snow, the Last" and "Grandfather and I," © 1969, Joseph L. Concha.

Tall Kia ahni– "War God's Horse Song I" from *The Navaho Indians* by Dane & Mary Roberts Coolidge. Copyright 1930 by Dane Coolidge and Mary Roberts Coolidge.

Leslie Marmon Silko– "Indian Song: Survival" and "Deer Song" from *Storyteller*. Copyright © 1981 by Leslie Marmon Silko. Reprinted from *Storyteller* by Leslie Marmon Silko, published by Seaver Books, New York, New York 1981.

CHAPTER 7

Michel de Montaigne– "Of Liars." Reprinted from *The Complete Essays of Montaigne,* translated by Donald M. Frame, with the permission of the publisher, Stanford University Press. © 1958 by The Board of Trustees of the Leland Stanford Junior University.

Frederick Douglass– "What to the Slave Is the Fourth of July?" from *The Frederick Douglass Papers,* Series 1, Vol. 2 edited by John W. Blassingame. Published by Yale University Press.

Virginia Woolf– "The Death of the Moth" from *The Death of the Moth and Other Essays* by Virginia Woolf, copyright 1942 by Harcourt Brace Jovanovich, Inc.; renewed 1970 by Marjorie T. Parsons, Executrix. Reprinted by permission of the Publisher, the estate of Virginia Woolf and The Hogarth Press.

Bruno Bettelheim– "Snow White" from *The Uses of Enchantment: The Meaning and Importance of Fairy Tales* by Bruno Bettelheim. Copyright © 1975, 1976 by Bruno Bettelheim. Reprinted by permission of Alfred A. Knopf, Inc.

George Orwell– "Shooting an Elephant" from *Shooting an Elephant and Other Essays* by George Orwell, copyright 1950 by Sonia Brownell Orwell; renewed 1978 by Sonia Pitt-Rivers. Reprinted by permission of Harcourt Brace Jovanovich, Inc., The Estate of the Late Sonia Brownell Orwell and Secker and Warburg Limited.

Flannery O'Connor– "A Reasonable Use of the Unreasonable" from *Mystery and Manners* by Flannery O'Connor. Copyright © 1957, 1961, 1963, 1964, 1966, 1967, 1969 by Flannery O'Connor. Reprinted by permission of Farrar, Straus and Giroux, Inc.

Alison Lurie– "Male and Female" from *The Language of Clothes* by Alison Lurie. Copyright © 1981 by Alison Lurie. Reprinted by permission of Random House, Inc.

Ted Hughes– "Capturing Animals" from *Poetry Is* by Ted Hughes. Copyright © 1967 by Ted Hughes. Reprinted by permission of Doubleday Publishing Group and from *Poetry in the Making* by permission of Faber and Faber Ltd.

Nora Ephron– "The Boston Photographs" from *Scribble, Scribble: Notes on the Media* by Nora Ephron. Copyright © 1975, 1976, 1977, 1978 by Nora Ephron. Reprinted by permission of Alfred A. Knopf, Inc.

Stephen Jay Gould– "The Panda's Thumb." Reprinted from *The Panda's Thumb, More Reflections in Natural History,* by Stephen Jay Gould, by permission of W. W. Norton & Company, Inc. Copyright © 1980 by Stephen Jay Gould.

Sandra Blakeslee– "Folklore Mirrors Life's Key Themes." Copyright © 1985 by The New York Times Company. Reprinted by permission.

Alice Walker– "In Search of Our Mothers' Gardens" from *In Search of Our Mothers' Gardens,* copyright © 1974 by Alice Walker. Reprinted by permission of Harcourt Brace Jovanovich, Inc.

AUTHOR AND TITLE INDEX

"Acquainted with the Night" (Frost), 761

"Adieu, Farewell, Earth's Bliss" (Nashe), 654–55

Aesop: "Wolf and the Mastiff, The," 133, 154

"Africa" (Angelou), 839–40

"After the Apple Picking" (Frost), 759–60

Akhmatova, Anna
"Requiem," 785–92

Akutagawa, Ryunosuke, 236
"In a Grove," 141, 144, 236–42

"Alberta" (Codrescu), 870

"Alone" (Joyce), 612–13, 633–34

"Alone in the Night" (Li), 643–44

"Alone I Sat; the Summer Day" (Brontë), 722

Alphabet for Gourmets, An (Fisher), 103–6, 884

American Indian poems, modern, 866–70

"Among School Children" (Yeats), 753–55

Anderson, Sherwood, 95
"Discovery of a Father" ("Unforgotten"), 75–78, 95–102, 884

"Anecdote of the Jar" (Stevens), 766

Angelou, Maya: "Africa," 839–40

"Araby" (Joyce), 144, 146–47, 149, 194–99, 612

"Ariel" (Plath), 858–59

Aristotle, 340–41
Poetics, 341

Arnold, Matthew
"Dover Beach," 734–35

"Ars Poetica" (MacLeish), 793

Atwood, Margaret: "This Is a Photograph of Me," 865–66

Auden, W. H., 23, 103, 620
"In Memory of W. B. Yeats," 810–11
"Museé des Beaux Arts," 809

"Author to Her Book, The" (Bradstreet), 672

Barthelme, Donald, 279
"Glass Mountain, The," 139, 279–83

Barthes, Roland, 75, 76

"Batter My Heart, Three-Personed God" (Donne), 662

"Because I Could Not Stop for Death" (Dickinson), 740–41

Beckett, Samuel: *Endgame,* 338

"Before the Birth of One of Her Children" (Bradstreet), 670

Behn, Alpha: "Willing Mistress, The," 677–78

"Bells for John Whiteside's Daughter" (Ransom), 784–85

Berryman, John: "Homage to Mistress Bradstreet," 823–28

Bettelheim, Bruno, 933
"Snow White," 933–46

"Between Walls" (Williams), 613–14

"Bird Came Down the Walk, A" (Dickinson), 738

Bishop, Elizabeth: "Fish, The," 817–18

"Black Man Talks of Reaping, A" (Bontemps), 802

Blake, William
"Ah Sun-flower," 698
"Clod and the Pebble, The," 696–97
"Lamb, The," 697
"London," 699
"Sick Rose, The," 698–99
"Tyger, The," 697–98

Blakeslee, Sandra: "Folklore Mirrors Life's Key Themes," 889, 891, 992–95

"Blind Man, The" (Borges), 800–801

Bontemps, Arna: "Black Man Talks of Reaping, A," 802

Book of One's Own, A (Mallon), 25–26

Borges, Jorge Luis: "Blind Man, The," 800–801

Bose, Buddhadeva: "Frogs," 812

"Boston Photographs, The" (Ephron), 892, 980–84

Bradstreet, Anne
  "Author to Her Book, The," 672
  "Before the Birth of One of Her Children," 670
  "Here Follows Some Verses upon the Burning of Our House," 617, 624–28
  "In Memory of My Dear Grand-Child . . . ,"671–72
  "Letter to Her Husband, A . . . ,"671
Brontë, Emily
  "Alone I Sat; the Summer Day," 722
  "Riches I Hold in Light Esteem," 722–23
Brooks, Gwendolyn
  "mother, the," 835–36
  "We Real Cool," 836
Browne, E. G., 644
Browning, Elizabeth Barrett
  "To George Sand," 718
Browning, Robert: "My Last Duchess," 621n, 721–22
Brueghel, Peter, the Elder, 636
  Wedding Dance, The (painting), 638
Burns, Robert
  "Red, Red Rose, A," 699–700
  "Mouse, To a," 700–701
Byrd, William, 26–27
Byron, Lord Gordon, George
  "She Walks in Beauty," 708–709

Calvino, Italo, 167
  "Catherine the Wise," 134, 141, 143, 146, 167–72
  Italian Folktales, 326
Campbell, Joseph, 132
"Canonization, The" (Donne), 657–58
"Capturing Animals" (Hughes), 22, 890–91, 973–78
Carter, Angela, 314
  "Snow Child, The," 134, 314–15
"Catherine the Wise" (Calvino), 134, 141, 143, 146, 167–72
"Cat in the Rain" (Hemingway), 11–21, 135, 136–37, 143–44, 145, 149
Cheever, John, 75, 76
Cheever, Susan, 78
Chekhov, Anton, 173
  "Heartache," 135–36, 139–40, 143, 173–77
Chopin, Kate
  "Emancipation: A Fable," 135, 158
  "Story of an Hour, The," 338
"Cigarette, The" (Ponge), 801
"Circling Hand, The" (Kincaid), 140–41, 316–25

"Clod and the Pebble, The" (Blake), 696–97
Codrescu, Andrei: "Alberta," 870
Coleridge, Samuel Taylor
  "Kubla Khan," 707–708
"Collar, The" (Herbert), 667–68
"Come, My Celia" (Jonson), 664
Concha, Joseph
  "Grandfather and I," 868–69
  "Snow, the Last," 868
"Conversation with My Father, A" (Paley), 138, 140, 303–7
"Crossing Brooklyn Ferry" (Whitman), 729–33
Cullen, Countee: "Incident," 803
cummings, e. e.: "somewhere i have never travelled," 617, 630–31, 633
  "my father moved through dooms of love," 794–96
  "pity this busy monster," 794

"Daddy" (Plath), 859–61
"Dance, The" (Williams), 636–39
"Darkling Thrush" (Hardy), 741–42
Darwin, Charles, 887, 892
  autobiography of, 77, 80–84
  Journal of Researches, 43–46
  notebooks of, 28, 43
Davis, Natalie Zemon, 121
  "Honor of Bertrande de Rols, The," 121–25, 884
  Return of Martin Guerre, The, 5–7, 22, 79, 121–25
Davis, Rebecca Harding: *Life in the Iron Mills*, 272
"Death, Be Not Proud" (Donne), 661
"Death of the Moth, The" (Woolf), 886, 929–31
"Death of a Naturalist" (Heaney), 864–65
"Death of a Toad, The" (Wilbur), 836–37
"Deer Song" (Silko), 875–76
"Defense of Poetry" (Shelley), 617
"Delight in Disorder" (Herrick), 665
"Demon Lover, The," 645–47
"Desert Places" (Frost), 760–61
Dickinson, Emily, 614
  "Because I Could Not Stop for Death," 740–41
  "Bird Came Down the Walk, A," 738
  "I Heard a Fly Buzz—When I Died," 736
  "I Never Lost as Much but Twice," 736
  "I Never Saw a Moor," 740
  "I Taste a Liquor Never Brewed—," 737–38
  "Much Madness is Divinest Sense," 739–40
  "Narrow Fellow in the Grass, A," 735

"Soul Selects Her Own Society, The," 739
"Success Is Counted Sweetest," 737
"Tell All the Truth but Tell It Slant," 736
"There's a Certain Slant of Light," 738–39
"This Is My Letter to the World," 740
Didion, Joan: "Los Angeles Notebook," 29, 66–70
"Digging" (Heaney), 863–64
"Digging for China" (Wilbur), 640–42
"Discovery of a Father" ("Unforgotten") (Anderson), 75–76, 95–102, 884
"Diving into the Wreck" (Rich), 854–56
Doll House, A (Ibsen), 335–40, 345, 348, 454–513
"Dolor" (Roethke), 814–15
Donne, John
 "Batter My Heart, Three-Personed God," 662
 "Canonization, The," 657–58
 "Death, Be Not Proud," 661
 "Flea, The," 660–61
 "Hymn to God My God, in My Sickness," 658–59
 "Song," 656
 "Valediction, A: Forbidden Mourning," 659–60
"Do Not Go Gentle into That Good Night" (Thomas), 832
Douglass, Frederick, 902
 "What to the Slave Is the Fourth of July?" 894–96, 903–19
"Dover Beach" (Arnold), 734–35
"Dream Poem" I, II (American Indian), 867
Dryden, John: "To the Memory of Mr. Oldham," 676–77
Dubliners (Joyce), 194
Dupont, Kevin, 29
Duras, Marguerite, 4

"Easter 1916" (Yeats), 747–49
"Easter Wings" (Herbert), 666
Ekai: "Joshu Washes the Bowl," 157
"Elegy" (Merwin), 845
"Elegy for Jane" (Roethke), 8–9
"Elegy Written in a Country Churchyard" (Gray), 688–92
Eliot, George: *Letters and Journals,* 51
Eliot, T. S.: "Love Song of J. Alfred Prufrock, The," 621n, 780–84
 "Journey of the Magi," 799–80
"Emancipation: A Fable" (Chopin), 135, 158
"Emotional Prodigality" (Taylor), 892–94, 920–28
Endgame (Beckett), 338

Ephron, Nora, 965
 "Boston Photographs, The," 892, 980–84
"Epitaphs" (Pound), 776–77
Essais (Montaigne), 883–84
"Essay on Criticism, An" (Pope), 681–88, 884
Expatriates, The (Haas), 884–85, 897ff.
"Expense of Spirit in a Waste of Shame, Th'" (Shakespeare), 653
Ezekiel, Nissim: "Night of the Scorpion," 840–41

"Face" (Toomer), 797
"Fan-Piece, for Her Imperial Lord" (Pound), 775
"Fern Hill" (Thomas), 829–31
Finch, Anne: "Introduction, The," 678–80
Finegan, Theresa: "Interview with Patrick McMahon, an Irish Immigrant," 79, 117–20
"Fire and Ice" (Frost), 759–60
"First Snow in Alsace" (Wilbur), 837–38
"Fish, The" (Bishop), 817–18
Fisher, M. F. K., 77, 103
 "P Is for Peas," 103–6, 884
"Flea, The" (Donne), 660–61
"Folklore Mirrors Life's Key Themes" (Blakeslee), 889, 891, 992–95
"Force That through the Green Fuse Drives the Flower, The" (Thomas), 831
"For the Union Dead" (Lowell), 832–34
"Frederick Douglass" (Hayden), 819
Freud, Sigmund, 75, 76, 624
 Interpretation of Dreams, The, 52–55
 journal of, 28, 52
"Frogs" (Bose), 812
Frost, Robert, 619
 "After Apple Picking," 759–60
 "Acquainted with the Night," 761
 "Desert Places," 760–61
 "Fire and Ice," 759–60
 "Mending Wall," 632–33, 758–59
 "Secret Sits, The," 633

García Márquez, Gabriel, 284
 "Very Old Man with Enormous Wings, A," 137–38, 149, 284–89
"Garden, The" (Marvell), 674–76
"Garden, The" (Pound), 777
Gass, William, 2–3, 7
Gilman, Charlotte Perkins
 "Why I Wrote 'The Yellow Wallpaper,'" 192–93
 "Yellow Wallpaper, The," 144, 179–91

Ginsberg, Allen: "Supermarket in California, A," 843–44
"Glass Mountain, The" (Barthelme), 139, 279–83
"God's Grandeur" (Hopkins), 743
"Good Man Is Hard to Find, A" (O'Connor), 137, 143, 144, 146, 149, 244–57, 944
Gould, Stephen Jay, 896, 985
  "Panda's Thumb, The," 886–89, 891, 985–990
Graham, Martha, 29, 62–65
"Grandfather and I" (Concha), 868–69
Gray, Thomas: "Elegy Written in a Country Churchyard," 688–92
Grimm, Jacob and Wilhelm, 160
  "Little Snow-White," 134, 136, 141, 160–66

Haas, Ken, 897
  Expatriates, The, 884–85, 897
Hardy, Thomas
  "Darkling Thrush, The," 741–42
  "Transformations," 742–43
"Harlem" (Hughes), 804
Harper, Michael S.: "Reuben, Reuben," 863
Hayden, Robert
  "Frederick Douglass," 819
  "Those Winter Sundays," 819
  "Runagate Runagate," 820–22
H.D.
  "Heat," 777–78
Heaney, Seamus
  "Death of a Naturalist," 864–65
  "Digging," 863–64
  "Oysters," 620–23
"Heartache" (Chekhov), 135–36, 139–40, 143, 173–77
"Heat" (H.D.), 777–78
Hemingway, Ernest: "Cat in the Rain," 11–21, 135, 136–37, 143–44, 145, 149
Herbert, George
  "Collar, The," 667–68
  "Easter Wings," 666
  "Jordan (I)," 666–67
  "Pulley, The," 668
"Here Follows Some Verses upon the Burning of Our House" (Bradstreet), 617, 624–28
Herrick, Robert
  "Delight in Disorder," 665
  "His Prayer to Ben Jonson," 665
  "Upon Julia's Clothes," 664
"His Prayer to Ben Jonson" (Herrick), 665
"Homage to Mistress Bradstreet" (Berryman), 823–28

"Honor of Bertrande de Rols, The" (Davis), 121–25, 884
Hopkins, Gerard Manley
  "God's Grandeur," 743
  "Spring and Fall," 744–45
  "Windhover, The," 744
Housman, A. E.
  "To an Athlete Dying Young," 745–46
  "When I Was One-and-Twenty," 745
Howe, Tina, 514
  Museum, 346–47
  Painting Churches, 346, 514–62
Hughes, Langston
  "Harlem," 804
  "Negro Speaks of Rivers, The," 803–4
  "Theme for English B," 804–5
Hughes, Ted, 973
  "Capturing Animals," 22, 890–91, 973–78
  "Wodwo," 857
"Hymn to God My God, in My Sickness" (Donne), 658–59

Ibsen, Henrik, 454
  Doll House, A, 335–40, 345, 348, 454–513
"I Heard a Fly Buzz—When I Died" (Dickinson), 738
"I Knew a Woman" (Roethke), 813–14
"In a Grove" (Akutagawa), 141, 144, 236–42
"In a Station of the Metro" (Pound), 775
"Incident" (Cullen), 803
"Indian Song: Survival" (Silko), 871–75
"I Never Lost as Much but Twice" (Dickinson), 736
"I Never Saw a Moor" (Dickinson), 740
"In Memory of My Dear Grand-Child . . . " (Bradstreet), 671–72
"In Memory of W. B. Yeats" (Auden), 810–11
"In Search of Our Mothers' Gardens" (Walker), 886, 996–1004
Interpretation of Dreams, The (Freud), 52–55
"Interview with Patrick McMahon, an Irish Immigrant" (Finegan), 79, 117–20
"Introduction, The" (Finch), 678–80
"I Stand Here Ironing" (Olsen), 137, 141, 144, 145, 149, 272–78
Italian Folktales (Calvino), 326
"I Taste a Liquor Never Brewed—" (Dickinson), 737–38

James, Alice, 27–28, 47–51, 924
James, Henry, 28, 47

James, William, 28, 47
  "Moral Philosopher and the Moral Life, The," 313
"Jewel Stairs' Grievance" (Pound), 776
Jonson, Ben
  "Come, My Celia," 664
  "On My First Daughter," 662
  "On My First Son," 663
  "Still to Be Neat, Still to Be Dressed," 663
"Jordan (I)" (Herbert), 666–67
"Joshu Washes the Bowl" (Ekai), 157
Journal of Researches (Darwin), 43–46
"Journey of the Magi" (Eliot), 799–80
Joyce, James, 194
  "Alone," 612–13, 633–34
  "Araby," 144, 146–47, 149, 194–99, 612
  Dubliners, 194
Jubilate Agno (Smart), 692–94

Kafka, Franz
  Diaries of, 24, 27, 28–29, 57–60
  "Metamorphosis, The," 57, 137, 149, 200–234
  Travel Diaries, 57–60
Keats, John
  "La Belle Dame sans Merci," 712–14
  "Ode on a Grecian Urn," 716–18
  "Ode to a Nightingale," 714–16
Kincaid, Jamaica, 316
  "Circling Hand, The," 140–41, 316–25
Kingston, Maxine Hong
  "No Name Woman," 107–16
  Woman Warrior, The, 77–78, 107
"Kubla Khan" (Coleridge), 707–708
Kuleshov, Lev, 351
Kumin, Maxine W.: "Making the Jam without You," 842–43
Kurosawa, Akira, 564
  Rashomon, 7, 236, 348–50, 352, 564–607
  Something Like a Biography, 22

"La Belle Dame sans Merci" (Keats), 712–14
"Lamb, The" (Blake), 697
"Landscape with the Fall of Icarus" (Williams), 771–72
Language of Clothes, The (Lurie), 889–90, 985–97
"Last One, The" (Merwin), 628–31
Lawrence, D. H.
  "Snake," 772–74
"Leda and the Swan" (Yeats), 751

Le Guin, Ursula, 308
  "Ones Who Walk Away from Omelas, The," 137, 138–39, 144, 147–48, 308–13
"Let Me Not to the Marriage of True Minds" (Shakespeare), 652–53
Letters and Journals (Eliot), 51
"Letter to Her Husband, A . . . " (Bradstreet), 671
Levertov, Denise
  "Victors, The," 838
  "What Were They Like?" 838–39
Levine, Philip: "Rickey," 845–48
"Liars, Of" (Montaigne), 898–902
Li Ch'ing Chao, 619
  "Alone in the Night," 643–44
Life in the Iron Mills (Davis), 272
"Lines" (Wordsworth), 703–707
"Little Snow-White" (Grimm), 134, 136, 141, 160–66
"London" (Blake), 699
Lorca, Federico Garcia
  "Rider's Song," 797–98
  "Sleepwalking Ballad," 798–99
"Los Angeles Notebook" (Didion), 29, 66–70
"Lost Son, The" (parable), 155–57
"Love Poem" I–III (American Indian), 866–67
"Love Song of J. Alfred Prufrock, The" (Eliot), 621n
Lowell, Amy
  "Patterns," 755–58
Lowell, Robert: "For the Union Dead," 832–34
Lurie, Alison, 960
  Language of Clothes, The, 889–90, 960
  "Male and Female," 960–972

McKay, Claude
  "Tropics in New York, The," 792
McPherson, James Alan, 290
  "Why I Like Country Music," 146, 290–302
MacLeish, Archibald
  "Ars Poetica," 793
"Magic Barrel, The" (Malamud), 133, 137, 141–43, 145, 258–71
Magnus, Robert: "Superstitions and Sports," 1010–12
Mahon, Susan: "Psychology of Creation Myths, The," 327–28
"Making the Jam without You" (Kumin), 842–43

Malamud, Bernard, 258
  "Magic Barrel, The," 133, 137, 141–43, 145, 258–71
"Male and Female" (Lurie), 891, 960–72
Mallon, Thomas: *Book of One's Own, A,* 25–26
Marlowe, Christopher: "Passionate Shepherd to His Love, The," 649–50
Marvell, Andrew
  "Garden, The," 674–76
  "To His Coy Mistress," 673–74
"Mending Wall" (Frost), 632–33
Merwin, W. S.
  "Elegy," 845
  "Last One, The," 628–30
  "When You Go Away," 844–45
"Metamorphosis, The" (Kafka), 57, 137, 149, 200–234
Milton, John
  Sonnet XXIII, 669–70
  "When I Consider How My Light Is Spent," 669
MLA Handbook for Writers of Research Papers (Gibaldi/Achtert), 1021
"Modern Poetry, Of" (Stevens), 767
Montaigne, Michel de, 896, 898
  Essais, 883–84, 898
  "Of Liars," 898–902
Moore, Marianne
  "Poetry," 778–79
"Moral Philosopher and the Moral Life, The" (James), 313
"mother, the" (Brooks), 835–36
"Mouse, To a" (Burns), 700–701
"Much Madness is Divinest Sense" (Dickinson), 739–40
"Mûres, Les/*blackberries*" (Ponge), 801–2
"Musée des Beaux Arts" (Auden), 809
Museum (Howe), 346–47
"my father moved through dooms of love" (cummings), 794–96
"My Last Duchess" (Browning), 621n
"My Mistress' Eyes Are Nothing Like the Sun" (Shakespeare), 653
"My Papa's Waltz" (Roethke), 617, 635–36, 816

Nabokov, Vladimir, 4–5, 7
"Naming of Parts" (Reed), 822–23
"Narrow Fellow in the Grass, A" (Dickinson), 735
Nashe, Thomas: "Adieu, Farewell, Earth's Bliss," 654–55

"Negro Speaks of Rivers, The" (Hughes), 803–4
Neruda, Pablo, 619
  "Ode to My Socks," 807–9
  "United Fruit Co., The," 805–7
Nicholson, R. A., 644–45
"Night of the Scorpion" (Ezekiel), 840–41
"No Name Woman" (Kingston), 107–16
"Not Marble, nor the Gilded Monuments" (Shakespeare), 652
"Nymph's Reply to the Shepherd, The" (Raleigh), 648–49

O'Connor, Flannery, 244, 955
  "Good Man Is Hard to Find, A," 137, 143, 144, 146, 149, 244–57, 955
  "Reasonable Use of the Unreasonable, A," 955–58
"Ode on a Grecian Urn" (Keats), 712–14
"Ode to a Nightingale" (Keats), 714–16
"Ode to My Socks" (Neruda), 807–9
"Ode to the West Wind" (Shelley), 617
"Old Florist" (Roethke), 813
Olsen, Tillie, 272
  "I Stand Here Ironing," 137, 141, 144, 145, 149, 272–78
"On Being Brought from Africa to America" (Wheatley), 694–95
"One Day I Wrote Her Name upon the Strand" (Spenser), 648
"Ones Who Walk Away from Omelas, The" (Le Guin), 137, 138–39, 144, 147–48, 308–13
"On My First Daughter" (Jonson), 662
"On My First Son" (Jonson), 663
"On the Power of the Imagination" (Montaigne), 889
Orwell, George, 885, 896, 948
  "Shooting an Elephant," 887–88, 948–53
Othello (Shakespeare), 341–45, 353–452
"Out of the Cradle Endlessly Rocking" (Whitman), 723–28
"Oyster, The" (Ponge), 618–20, 623
"Oysters" (Heaney), 620–23
"Ozymandias" (Shelley), 709–10

Painting Churches (Howe), 346, 514–62
Paley, Grace, 303
  "Conversation with My Father, A," 138, 140, 303–7

"Panda's Thumb, The" (Gould), 886–89, 891, 985–990

"Passionate Shepherd to His Love, The" (Marlowe), 649–50

"Patterns" (Lowell, A.), 755–58

Pepys, Samuel, 25, 28, 35–41

Perloff, Marjorie, 949

"Pike, The" (Roethke), 815–16

Pillow Book, The (Shonagon), 24–26, 30–34

"P Is for Peas" (Fisher), 103–6, 884

"pity this busy monster" (cummings), 794

"Planetarium" (Rich), 853–54

Plath, Sylvia, 949
  "Ariel," 858–59
  "Daddy," 859–61
  "Tulips," 861–62

Poetics (Aristotle), 341

"Poetry" (Moore), 778–79

Ponge, Francis, 617–19
  "Cigarette, The," 801
  "Mûres, Les/*blackberries*," 801–2
  "Oyster, The," 618–20, 623
  Soap, 22–23
  "Voice of Things, The," 23

Pope, Alexander: "Essay on Criticism, An," 681–88, 884

"Portrait of My Father as a Young Man" (Rilke), 762–63

Pound, Ezra, 613
  "Epitaphs," 776–77
  "Fan-Piece, for Her Imperial Lord," 775
  "Garden, The," 777
  "In a Station of the Metro," 775
  "Jewel Stairs' Grievance," 776
  "River-Merchant's Wife: A Letter," 775–76

"Premonition, The" (Roethke), 813

Prodigal Son, parable of, 154–55

"Psychology of Creation Myths, The" (Mahon), 327–28

Pudovkin, V. I., 351

"Pulley, The" (Herbert), 668

Raleigh, Sir Walter: "Nymph's Reply to the Shepherd, The," 648–49

"Raleigh Was Right" (Williams), 771

Ransom, John Crowe
  "Bells for John Whiteside's Daughter," 784–85

Rashomon (Kurosawa), 7, 236, 348–50, 352

"Reapers" (Toomer), 796–97

"Reasonable Use of the Unreasonable, A" (O'Connor), 944–47

"Red, Red Rose, A" (Burns), 699–700

"Red Wheelbarrow, The" (Williams), 767–68

Reed, Henry: "Naming of Parts," 822–23

"Refusal to Mourn the Death, by Fire, of a Child in London, A" (Thomas), 829

"Requiem," (Ahkmatova), 785–92

Return of Martin Guerre, The (Davis), 5–7, 22, 79, 121–25

"Reuben, Reuben" (Harper), 863

Rexroth, Kenneth, 619, 643–44

Rich, Adrienne
  "Diving into the Wreck," 854–56
  "Planetarium," 853–54
  "Valediction Forbidding Mourning, A," 852

"Riches I Hold in Light Esteem," (Brontë), 722–23

"Ricky" (Levine), 845–48

"Rider's Song" (Lorca), 797–98

Rilke, Rainer Maria, 619
  "Portrait of My Father as a Young Man," 762–63
  "Song the Beggar Sings, The," 762
  "Spanish Dancer," 763

"River-Merchant's Wife: A Letter" (Pound), 775–76

Roethke, Theodore
  "Dolor," 814–15
  "Elegy for Jane," 8–9
  "I Knew a Woman," 813–14
  "My Papa's Waltz," 617, 635–36, 816
  "Old Florist," 813
  "Pike, The," 815–16
  "Premonition, The," 813
  "Waking, The," 815

"Runagate Runagate" (Hayden), 820–22

Sa'dī of Shīrāz, 644–45

"Sailing to Byzantium" (Yeats), 751–52

Sappho: "Seizure," 642–43

"Satirical Elegy on the Death of a Late Famous General, A" (Swift), 680–81

"Scholars, The" (Yeats), 746–47

"Second Coming, The" (Yeats), 746–47

"Secret Sits, The" (Frost), 633

"Seizure" (Sappho), 642–43

Sexton, Anne: "Snow White and the Seven Dwarfs," 848–52

Shakespeare, William, 353
  "Expense of Spirit in a Waste of Shame, Th'," 653
  "Let Me Not to the Marriage of True Minds," 652–53

Shakespeare, William (*cont.*)
   "My Mistress' Eyes Are Nothing Like the Sun," 653
   "Not Marble, nor the Gilded Monuments," 652
   Othello, 341–45, 353–452
   "Since brass, nor stone, nor earth, nor boundless sea," 651
   "That Time of Year Thou May'st in Me Behold," 623–24, 634–35
   Twelfth Night, 654
   "When I have seen by time's fell hand defaced," 651
   "When in Disgrace with Fortune and Men's Eyes," 651–52
   "When to the sessions of sweet silent thought," 650
Shelley, Percy Bysshe: "Defense of Poetry," 617
   "Ode to the West Wind," 710–12
   "Ozymandias," 709–10
"She Walks in Beauty" (Byron), 708–709
Shikibu, Lady Murasaki, 30
Shonagon, Sei: *Pillow Book, The.* 24–26, 30–34
"Shooting an Elephant" (Orwell), 887–88, 948–53
"Sick Rose, The" (Blake), 698–99
Silko, Leslie Marmon
   "Deer Song," 875–76
   "Indian Song: Survival," 871–75
"Since brass, nor stone, nor earth, nor boundless sea" (Shakespeare), 651
"Sleepwalking Ballad" (Lorca), 798–99
Smart, Christopher: *Jubilate Agno,* 692–94
"Snake" (Lawrence), 772–74
"Snow Child, The" (Carter), 134, 314–15
"Snow Man, The" (Stevens), 763–64
"Snow, the Last" (Concha), 868
"Snow White" (Bettelheim), 933–46
"Snow White and the Seven Dwarfs" (Sexton), 848–52
"Solitary Reaper, The" (Wordsworth), 702–703
Something Like a Biography (Kurosawa), 22
"somewhere i have never travelled" (cummings), 617, 630–31, 633
"Song" (Donne), 656
"Song of Wandering Aengus, The" (Yeats), 752–53
"Song the Begger Sings, The" (Rilke), 762
"Sort of Song, A" (Williams), 769–70
"Spanish Dancer" (Rilke), 763
"Spring and All" (Williams), 768–69
Sonnet XXIII (Milton), 669–70

"Soul Selects Her Own Society, The" (Dickinson), 739
Spenser, Edmund: "One Day I Wrote Her Name upon the Strand," 648
"Spring and Fall" (Hopkins), 744–45
"Spring Poem, I" (American Indian), 867
Stevens, Wallace
   "Anecdote of the Jar," 766
   "Modern Poetry, Of," 767
   "Snow Man, The," 763–64
   "Thirteen Ways of Looking at a Blackbird," 764–66
"Still to Be Neat, Still to Be Dressed" (Jonson), 663
"Story of an Hour, The" (Chopin), 338
"Success Is Counted Sweetest" (Dickinson), 737
"Supermarket in California, A" (Ginsberg), 843–44
"Superstitions and Sports" (Magnus), 1010–12
Swift, Jonathan: "Satirical Elegy on the Death of a Late Famous General, A," 680–81

Taylor, Charles Fayette, 920
   "Emotional Prodigality," 892–94, 920–28
"Tell All the Truth but Tell It Slant" (Dickinson), 736
Tennyson, Alfred, Lord: "Ulysses," 621n, 719–20
"That Time of Year Thou May'st in Me Behold" (Shakespeare), 623–24, 634–35
"Theme for English B" (Hughes), 804–5
"There's a Certain Slant of Light" (Dickinson), 738–39
"They Flee from Me" (Wyatt), 647
"Thirteen Ways of Looking at a Blackbird" (Stevens), 764–66
"This Is a Photograph of Me" (Atwood), 865–66
"This Is My Letter to the World" (Dickinson), 740
Thomas, Dylan
   "Do Not Go Gentle into that Good Night," 832
   "Fern Hill," 829–31
   "Force That through the Green Fuse Drives the Flower, The," 831
   "Refusal to Mourn the Death, by Fire, of a Child in London, A," 829
"Those Winter Sundays" (Hayden), 819
"To an Athlete Dying Young" (Housman), 745–46

"To a Poor Old Woman" (Williams), 770
"To George Sand" (Browning, E.), 718
"To His Coy Mistress" (Marvell), 673–74
"To the Memory of Mr. Oldham" (Dryden), 676–77
"To the Right Honourable William, Earl of Dartmouth . . . " (Wheatley), 695–96
Toomer, Jean
  "Face," 797
  "Reapers," 796–97
"Transformations" (Hardy), 742–43
Travel Diaries (Kafka), 57–60
"Tropics in New York, The" (McKay), 792
"Tulips" (Plath), 861–62
Twelfth Night (Shakespeare), 654
"Tyger, The" (Blake), 697–98

"Ulysses" (Tennyson), 621n
"Unforgotten" ("Discovery of a Father") (Anderson), 75–78, 95–102, 884
"United Fruit Co., The" (Neruda), 805–7
"Upon Julia's Clothes" (Herrick), 664
Uses of Enchantment, The (Bettelheim), 134

"Valediction, A: Forbidden Mourning" (Donne), 659–60
"Valediction Forbidding Mourning, A" (Rich), 852
Valéry, Paul, 634
Van Gogh, Vincent, 22, 86
  letters of, 76, 77, 86–93
"Very Old Man with Enormous Wings, A" (García Márquez), 137–38, 149, 284–89
"Victors, The" (Levertov), 838

"Waking, The" (Roethke), 815
Walam Olum, 133, 150–54
Walker, Alice, 896, 996
  "In Search of Our Mothers' Gardens," 886, 996–1004
"War God's Horse Song I" (American Indian), 869–70
"War Poem" I–III (American Indian), 868
Wedding Dance, The (Brueghel), 636, 638
"Wedding Dance in the Open Air, The" (Williams), 636–39
"We Real Cool" (Brooks), 836
"What to the Slave Is the Fourth of July?" (Douglass), 894–96, 903–19
"What Were They Like?" (Levertov), 838–39

Wheatley, Philis
  "On Being Brought from Africa to America," 694–95
  "To the Right Honourable William, Earl of Dartmouth . . . ," 695–96
"When I Consider How My Light Is Spent" (Milton), 669
"When I have seen by time's fell hand defaced" (Shakespeare), 651
"When in Disgrace with Fortune and Men's Eyes" (Shakespeare), 651–52
"When I was One-and-Twenty" (Housman), 745
"When to the sessions of sweet silent thought" (Shakespeare), 650
"When You Go Away" (Merwin), 844–45
Whitman, Walt, 613
  "Crossing Brooklyn Ferry," 729–33
  "Out of the Cradle Endlessly Rocking," 723–28
"Why I Like Country Music" (McPherson), 146, 290–302
"Why I Wrote 'The Yellow Wallpaper'" (Gilman), 192–93
"Widow's Lament in Springtime, The" (Williams), 768
Wilbur, Richard
  "Death of a Toad, The," 836–37
  "Digging for China," 640–42
  "First Snow in Alsace," 837–38
"Wild Swans at Coole, The" (Yeats), 750–51
Williams, William Carlos
  "Between Walls," 613–14
  "Dance, The," 636–39
  "Landscape with the Fall of Icarus," 771–72
  "Raleigh Was Right," 771
  "Red Wheelbarrow, The," 767–68
  "Sort of Song, A," 769–70
  "Spring and All," 768–69
  "To a Poor Old Woman," 770
  "Wedding Dance in the Open Air, The," 636–39
  "Widow's Lament in Springtime, The," 768
  "Young Housewife, The," 770
"Willing Mistress, The" (Behn), 677–78
"Windhover, The" (Hopkins), 744
"Wodwo" (Hughes), 857
"Wolf and the Mastiff, The" (Aesop), 135, 154
Woman Warrior, The (Kingston), 77, 107
Woolf, Virginia, 4, 11, 23, 933
  "Death of the Moth, The," 886, 929–31

Wordsworth, William
  "Lines," 703–707
  "Solitary Reaper, The," 702–703
  "World is Too Much with Us, The," 701–702
Wyatt, Thomas: "They Flee from Me," 647

Yeats, William Butler, 614
  "Among School Children," 753–55

"Easter 1916," 747–49
"Leda and the Swan," 751
"Sailing to Byzantium," 751–52
"Scholars, The," 746–47
"Second Coming, The," 749–50
"Song of Wandering Aengus, The," 752–53
"Wild Swans at Coole, The," 750–51
"Yellow Wallpaper, The" (Gilman), 144, 179–91
"Young Housewife, The" (Williams), 770

SUBJECT INDEX

Alliteration, 147, 633
Allusions, 138
Analysis, 1016
Anapest, 635
Artistic sense, 11
Autobiography, 75–79
Aztec word definitions, 614–16

Bibliography, 1022–23
Biography, 77–79

Cadence, 2–4
Caesurae, 638
Change, 149
Character, 142
Cinema. *See* Film
Climax, 140
Comedy, 345–47
Comparison/contrast, 1016–17
Complications, 140
Conflict, 140–41
Connotations vs. denotations, 627
Consonance, 634
Counter-images, 623

Dactyl, 635, 636
Dénouement. *See* Resolution
Diaries, 24–29. *See also* Journals
Diction, 145
Drama. *See* Theater
Dramatic irony, 144
Dramatic monologue, 621n

End rhymes, 633
End-stopped vs. enjambed lines, 636
English (Shakespearean) sonnet, 634
Essays, 883–96
Explication, 1016
Exposition, 140

Fables, 133, 136
Fairy tales. *See* Folktales
Fiction, 134–35
    vs. drama, 335–40
    early forms of, 132–34
    elements of, 139–49
    modern short, 134–39
Figures of speech, 622
Film, 347–52
    vs. theater, 347–48
    vocabulary of, 349–50
Film editing, 348
Film sequence, 349
First-person narrator, 144
Fixed (closed) form, 636
Folklore, 132
Folktales, 133–34, 136
Form. *See* Structure
Free (open) form, 636

Haiku, 350

Imagery, 145–46, 620–24
Imagination, 5–7
Irony, 144
Italian (Petrarchan) sonnet, 634

Limited omniscience, 143
Lyric poem, 633

Mask lyric, 621n
Memory, 5, 7
Metafiction, 138–39
Metaphors, 622, 624
Meter, 613
Montage. *See* Film editing
Mood, 147
Movies. *See* Film
Multiple narrators, 144

Myths, 132–33, 136–38
  creation, 327–28

Narrative poem, 633
Narrator, 142–44
Notebooks
  reader's, 11–22
  writer's, 24–29
  See also Diaries; Journals

Objective narrator, 143–44
Omniscient narrator, 143
Onomatopoeia, 638

Parables, 133
Persona, 142–43
Petrarchan sonnet, 634
Plot, 137, 140–41
Poetry, 612–42
  images in, 620–24
  lyric vs. narrative, 633
  and meter and rhyme, 613
  music of, 633–39
  symbols in, 624–33
  and word choice and translation, 617–20
Point of view, 136, 143, 144, 621n
Protagonist, 136

Reader's notebook, 11–22
Reading, 1–23
  and artistic sense, 11
  and cadence, 2–4
  and imagination, 5–7
  and memory, 5, 7
  with pen or pencil, 9–11
  recursive vs. speed, 2–3
  and rereading, 7
  vs. viewing, 334–35, 341–42, 346–47
  and word meanings, 9
Realism, 135–37
  departures from, 137–39

Resolution, 140
Rhyme, 613, 633, 636

Setting, 139–40, 149
Shakespearean sonnet, 634
Short fiction, 132–49
  early forms of, 132–34
  modern, 134–39
  realistic, 135–37
Similes, 622
Slant rhymes, 636
Sonnet, 634
Stories. *See* Short fiction
Structure, 141
Style, 144–47
Subject vs. theme, 148
Summary vs. scene, 136
Symbols, 137, 624–33
Synesthesia, 630
Syntax, 145

Theater, 334–47
  vs. fiction, 335–40
  vs. film, 347–48
Theme, 148–49
Third-person narrator, 143
Tone, 146–48
Tragedy, 340–45
Tragicomedy, 345
Translation, 618–20

Verbal irony, 144
Verse vs. prose, 613
Voice, 146–48

Writing about literature, 1015–30
  approaches to, 1016–17
  and documenting sources, 1021–24
  and first draft, 1017
  and revising and editing, 1019–20
  and supporting ideas, 1017–19

ABOUT THE AUTHORS

Jacqueline Costello is Director of the Writing Skills Workshop at Queens College of the City University of New York. She received her B.A. from William Paterson College and her Ph.D. in English literature from New York University. She has taught ESL, composition, and English literature at William Paterson College, LaGuardia Community College, New York University, and Lingnan College in Hong Kong.

Amy Tucker is Director of the ESL Composition Program in the English department of Queens College. She received her B.A. from Barnard College and her Ph.D. in American literature from New York University. Her teaching interests and publications range from American literature and art to linguistics and composition theory. Her forthcoming book on ESL theory, also to be published by Random House, is entitled *Decoding ESL: Non-Native Students in the American College Classroom.*

Professors Costello and Tucker are the authors of *The Random House Writing Course for ESL Students.*